Index of Model Periodicals 1971 through 1975

by

PAUL CARDWELL, Jr.

The Scarecrow Press, Inc.
Metuchen, N.J. 1977

Library of Congress Cataloging in Publication Data

Cardwell, Paul.
 Index of model periodicals, 1971 through 1975.

  1. Models and modelmaking--Periodicals--Indexes.
 I. Title.
 TT154.C34   016.745'28   77-1737
 ISBN 0-8108-1027-1

Copyright © 1977 by Paul Cardwell, Jr.

Manufactured in the United States of America

BRIEF TABLE OF CONTENTS

Contents of the Index	v
Introduction	1
Magazines Indexed	4
Gaps in Coverage	9
Note on Terminology	10
Note on Arrangement	12
A Personal Note	15
Acknowledgments and Thanks	18
Abbreviations	20
Magazines	20
Dates	20
Organizations	20
General	21

THE INDEX [fuller contents begin page v]

I.	Static Scale	27
II.	Operating Scale	175
III.	Color Patterns	208
IV.	Non-Scale Models	349
V.	Articles	387
VI.	Reviews	568

CONTENTS OF THE INDEX*

I. STATIC SCALE

AIRCRAFT

Scale Drawings
    Before World War I   27
    World War I (by countries)   27
    Between World Wars (by countries)   29
    World War II (by countries)   35
    Post World War II (civil, military by countries)   43
    Experimental Configurations   54
    Aircraft Distinctions   54
    Aircraft Accessories   55
Scratch-Building Plans   55
Kit Conversions   56
    World War I   56
    Between World Wars (civil & military)   57
    World War II (by countries)   58
    Post World War II (helicopters, airplanes by countries)   59
Superdetailing (by periods)   67
Kit Construction (by periods)   68
Kit Corrections (by periods)   69

ARMOR

Scale Drawings
    APCs & ICVs   71
    ARVs & Funnies   72
    Armored Cars (by countries)   72
    Artillery   74
    Edged Weapons   75
    Half Tracks   75
    Self-Propelled Artillery (by countries)   76

---

*See Brief Table of Contents, preceding, for front matter.

Contents of Index   vi

(I. Static Scale, cont.)

Small Arms	78
Softskins (by countries)	79
Tanks (by countries)	82
Armor Distinctions	86
Armor Accessories	86
Scratch-Building Plans (by types)	87
Kit Conversions	89
APCs & ICVs	89
ARVs & Funnies	89
Armored Cars	90
Artillery	90
Half Tracks	90
Self-Propelled Artillery (by countries)	91
Softskins (by countries)	93
Tanks (by countries)	95
Superdetailing (by countries)	97
Kit Construction	97
Kit Corrections	100

AUTOMOBILES

Scale Drawings	
Cars (by types)	100
Circus Wagons	102
Trucks	102
Other Civil Vehicles	103
Scratch-Building Plans (by types)	103
Conversions (by types)	103
Superdetailing (by types)	104
Kit Construction (by types)	105

FIGURES

Armies	106
General Studies of Cultures	107
Heraldry (Military)	107
Badges & Insignia	107
Flags & Other Military Colors	108
Uniforms	110
Ancient	110
Medieval & Renaissance	110
1600-1790	111
Napoleonic (by countries)	112
1820-1914	116
World War I to 1939	118
World War II	118

Contents of Index

Post World War II	119
separate listings	119
Uniform Accessories	133
Scratch-Building Plans	133
Figures	133
Accessories	133
Conversions (by periods)	134
Superdetailing	136
Kit Construction	136
Kit Corrections	141

RAILROAD (non-operating)

Conversion	141
Superdetailing	141

MISSILES & SPACE VEHICLES

Scale Drawings	141
Superdetailing	141

SHIPS

Scale Drawings	
Unpowered	142
Waterline (by type)	142
Full Hull (by type)	143
separate listings	146
Surface Effect Vehicles	152
Ship Accessories & Details	152
Scratch-Building Plans	153
Conversions	153
Superdetailing	154
Kit Construction	154
Kit Corrections	155

STRUCTURES

Scale Drawings	
Bridges	155
Buildings (by type)	156
Docks	162
Railroad Structures Other Than Buildings (by type)	163
Scratch-Building Plans	167
Bridges	167
Buildings (by type)	167
Railroad Structures Other Than Buildings (by type)	168

Contents of Index viii

(I. Static Scale, cont.)

Conversions	169
Superdetailing	170
Kit Construction	170

MISCELLANEOUS STATIC SCALE

Scale Drawings (by type)	170
Diorama (by period)	171
Conversions	173
Kit Construction	174

II. OPERATING SCALE

AIRCRAFT

Free Flight (by type)	175
Control Line	177
Radio Control (by category)	177
Carrier Event (by class)	179
Semi-Scale	180
Free Flight (by type)	180
Tether	180
Control Line (by engine class)	180
Radio Control (by category)	181

BOATS

Free Running	184
Radio Control (by engine type)	184
Improving Kits	185
Converting Static Scale to Operating	185

CARS

Radio Control	186
Improving Ready-to-Run	186

RAILROAD ROLLING STOCK

Scale Drawings	186
Complete Trains	186
Cars	186
Freight (by type)	186
Non-Revenue	190
Non-Scale	191

Contents of Index

```
        Passenger (by type)              191
        Locomotives                      194
            Diesel                       194
            Electric                     196
            Steam (by type)              196
            Miscellaneous Power Forms    199
        Rail Motor Cars                  199
        Traction                         200
        Rolling Stock Accessories        201
    Scratch-Building Plans               201
    Conversions                          201
        General                          201
        Cars                             201
            Freight                      202
            Non-Revenue                  202
            Passenger                    203
        Locomotives                      203
        Traction                         205
    Superdetailing                       205
    Kit Construction                     206
    Kit Corrections                      206
    Track--Scale Drawings                206

ROCKETS--NAR Scale                       207
```

III. COLOR PATTERNS

AIRCRAFT

```
General
    Colors                               208
    Markings                             209
    separate listings                    210
World War I (by countries)               212
Between World Wars (by countries)        219
World War II (by countries)              233
Post World War II (by countries)         271
```

ARMOR

```
General
    Colors                               333
    Heraldry                             334
APCs & ICVs                              334
Armored Cars                             335
Artillery                                335
```

Contents of Index x

(III. Color Patterns, cont.)

Half Tracks	335
Self-Propelled Artillery	336
Softskins	337
Tanks (general & by countries)	337
AUTOMOBILES (by type)	345
FIGURES	346
MISSILES	346
RAILROAD	347
SHIPS (by type)	347
SPACE VEHICLES	348
SIGNS	348

IV. NON-SCALE MODELS

AIRCRAFT

Free Flight	
Gliders (by type)	349
Rubber (by type)	352
Rocket (by type)	355
Electric	356
Gas (by engine class, then type)	356
Old Timer	359
Other than Airplanes (by type)	359
Kit Construction	360
Tether	360
Control Line	360
Combat (by type)	360
Exhibition	361
Speed (by type)	361
Stunt (by type)	363
Trainer/Sport (by enging size)	365
Autogyro	366
Radio Control	367
Category I (by enging size)	367
Category II (by engine size)	368
Category III (by engine size & aircraft type)	372
Combat	377
Pylon Racers (by event type)	377
Improving Ready-to-Fly	379

Kit Modification	380
Kit Construction	381
BOATS	**382**
Free Running	382
Power (by engine type)	382
Sail (by class)	382
Tether (by type)	383
Radio Control (by engine type)	384
Kit Construction	385
CARS--Radio Control (by type)	**385**
ROCKET (by type)	**386**

V. ARTICLES

CONSTRUCTION

Materials (by type)	387
Aircraft--Operating	390
General	390
General Techniques	390
Strengthening	391
Flying Scale	391
Helicopter	393
Repair	393
Components	393
Fuselage	393
Landing Gears	394
Power Mounting	395
Wing & Stab	395
Armor--Operating	396
Boats--Operating	396
General	396
Repair	397
Sails	397
Railroad--Operating	397
Layouts	397
Lighting	399
Operating Scenery/Accessories	399
Rolling Stock	399
Construction	399
Kit Improvement	400
Signaling Equipment	401
Track	401

(V. Articles, cont.)

Traction	402
Turntables	402
Yard Equipment	403
Miscellaneous	403
Static Scale	403
General	403
Aircraft	404
Armor	405
Ancient & Medieval Weaponry	405
Automobiles	405
Bridges	406
Diorama	406
Figures	406
Scenery	407
Backgrounds	407
Terrain	408
Vegetation	408
Water	409
Miscellaneous	409
Ship	409
Structures	410
Wargames Models	411

CONTROL

Aircraft	412
Free Flight	412
Control Line	412
Radio Control	413
Boats	414
Free Running	414
Vane Control	414
Radio Control	414
Radio Control Equipment	415
General	415
Construction	415
Parts	416
Railroad	417
Accessories (Electrical)	417
Circuitry	417
Control Circuitry	419
Detectors	420
Lighting Control	420
Ramps	420
Signals	421

Switch Machines 421
Throttles & Walkaround Controls 421

DESIGN

Aircraft 422
  Aerodynamics 422
    All Control Systems 422
    Free Flight 422
    Control Line 423
    Radio Control 423
    Airfoils 424
    Performance 425
  Components 425
    Fuselage 425
    Landing Gear 425
    Power Systems 426
    Wing & Stab 426
  Control Systems 426
    Free Flight 426
    Control Line 427
    Radio Control 427
  Non-Standard Types 428
    Autogyros 428
    Flying Scale 428
    Helicopter 428
  Kitting 429
Boats 429
Railroad 430
  Layout (general, then by size) 430
  Other 436
Scenery 436
Structures 436
Drafting Techniques 437

ENGINES & PROPS

Electric Motors 437
  General 437
  Construction 438
  Tuning & Souping 438
Internal Combustion 438
  General 438
  Design 439
  Construction 439
  Conversion 439
  Cooling 439

Contents of Index   xiv

(V. Articles, cont.)

Exhaust	440
Fuel System	440
Ignition	441
Noise	441
Troubleshooting	442
Tuning & Souping	442
Rubber	442
Steam	442
Fuel	443
Propellers	443
Rubber	443
Gas	444
Boat	444

FINISH

Color Chips	444
Color Mix	446
Aircraft (by countries)	446
Armor	448
Figures	449
Ships	449
Covering	449
Details	450
Paint	450
General	450
Airbrushes	452
Weathering	452
Miscellaneous Finishing	452

HISTORY--AIRCRAFT

General	453
Air Bases	453
Air Battles & Campaigns	454
Air Forces	455
Nations	455
Organization Charts	457
Unit Histories	457
Air Races & Air Shows	458
Aircraft--Individual	459
Pre World War I	459
World War I	459
Between World Wars	460
Civil	460
Military	461

Contents of Index

World War II	462
Civil	462
Military (by countries)	462
Post World War II (by countries, civil & military)	466
Helicopters	474
separate listings	474
Prototype Flight Characteristics	477
Surviving Examples	478
Airlines	478
Airports	481
Biography	482
Directories	482
Downed Aircraft, Survival, Escape, Rescue	482
Flying Full-Size Aircraft	483
Manufacturing	483
Photographic Studies (not accompanied by plans)	484
Private Aviation	484
Research & Development	485
Tactics	485
Training	486
Use in Movie Making	486
Weapons	486

HISTORY--ARMOR

Category Surveys	486
General	486
APCs, ICVs, ARVs & Funnies	487
Armored Cars	488
Artillery	489
Half Tracks	489
Small Arms	489
Softskins	489
Tanks	490
Accessories & Details	490
Individual Types	490
APCs & ICVs	490
ARVs & Funnies	491
Armored Cars	491
Artillery	492
Half Tracks	492
Self-Propelled Artillery	493
Small Arms	493
Softskins	494
Tanks	495
Photographic Studies (not accompanied by plans)	496
Sketches (not accompanied by plans)	496
Specifications	497

Contents of Index xvi

(V. Articles, cont.)

APCs, ICVs, ARVs & Funnies	497
Armored Cars	497
Artillery	497
Self-Propelled Artillery	498
Small Arms	498
Softskins	498
Tanks	498

HISTORY--ARMY

Arms Manufacturers	499
Army Histories	499
Battles & Campaigns	501
Pre World War II	501
World War II	502
Post World War II	503
Biography	503
Equipment (other than arms & vehicles)	503
Fortifications	504
Movies	504
Organization Charts	504
Larger than Regiment	504
Regiment or Lower (by countries)	505
Tactics	506
Unit Histories	507

HISTORY--AUTOMOBILES

General	508
Racers	508
Formula 1	508
Grand Prix	508
Other	509
Trucks	509

HISTORY--MISSILES

HISTORY--MODELING

General	510
Biographies	510
Plant Tours	511
Record Attempts	512
Use in Movies	513

Contents of Index

HISTORY--MUSEUMS

General	513
Aviation	513
Maritime	515
Military	515
Railroad	516

HISTORY--POLITICAL

HISTORY--RAILROAD

Accidents & Disasters	516
Incline Railways	516
Equipment (other than rolling stock)	516
Equipment Manufacturers	517
Operations	517
General	517
Military	518
Regional	519
Rail Lines	519
Rolling Stock	521
Traction & Rapid Transit	522

HISTORY--SHIPS

General	523
Civil	523
Naval	523
Individual	524
Civil	524
Naval (by countries)	525
Miscellaneous	528
Movies	528
Naval Incidents, Non-Combat	528
Operations	528
Photographic Studies (not accompanied by plans)	528
Sea Battles	528

HISTORY--SPACE VEHICLES

HISTORY--MISCELLANEOUS

INTRODUCTIONS

Aircraft	529
General	529
Free Flight	529

Contents of Index   xviii

(V. Articles, cont.)

Control Line	530
Radio Control	530
Flying Scale	532
Boats	532
Cars	532
Radio Control	532
Railroad	533
Rockets	534
Static Scale	534
Miscellaneous	535

OPERATING TECHNIQUES

Aircraft	535
Free Flight	535
Tether	536
Control Line	536
Radio Control	536
Boats	537
Cars	538
Railroad	538
Layout Operation	538
Maintenance	539
Troubleshooting	539
Safety	539
Weather	540

STANDARDS & TECHNICAL INFORMATION

TEST EQUIPMENT

Aircraft	543
Boats	544
Electronic	544
Meteorological	545
Railroad	545

TOOLS

Accessories	545
Battery Chargers	545
Field Boxes	546
Glider Launching Equipment	547
Model Display & Storage	548
Modelborne Accessories	548

Railroad	549
Starters	549
Stooges	549
Winders	549
Cameras	550
Charts & Nomographs	550
Drafting Tools	550
Glossaries	550
Hand Tools	551
Commercial	551
Jigs	551
Make Your Own	552
Power Tools	553
Commercial	553
Make Your Own	553
Workbenches	554
Workshops	554
Miscellaneous	555

WARGAMING

Construction	555
Playing	555
separate listings	556

MISCELLANEOUS

Club Organization & Operation	559
Collecting	559
Contests	560
Boat	560
Flying	560
Static Scale	560
Humor	560
Model Building Classes	562
Model Facilities	562
Modeling in Education	562
Non-Models	563
Photography	563
Public Relations	564
Research	564
Rules	565
Discussion	565
Official	566
Unofficial	566
Miscellaneous	567

Contents of Index xx

VI. REVIEWS

BOOK REVIEWS

Aircraft	568
Air Battles (by periods)	568
Air Forces (by countries)	570
Air Shows & Races	573
Airlines	573
Biographies	574
Color Patterns	576
Companies	578
Development	579
Directories	580
Engines	581
General Aircraft (by periods)	582
Identification	586
Individual Aircraft	587
Comparisons	587
Publication Surveys & Collections	588
By Periods	588
Lighter Than Air	596
Military Operations	596
Pioneering Aircraft, Records, & Epics	597
Private Flying	599
Regional Aviation	599
Training	600
Unit Histories	600
Miscellaneous	602
Armor	602
General	602
APCs & ICVs	604
ARVs & Funnies	604
Armored Cars	605
Artillery	605
Edged Weapons	606
Half Tracks	606
Self-Propelled Artillery	607
Small Arms	607
Softskins	609
Tanks (general, then by countries)	610
Color Patterns & Markings	613
Army	614
Biography	614
Covert Operations	614
Fortifications	614
Heraldry	615

xxi   Contents of Index

Land Battles & Wars (general, then by periods) 616
Strategy & Tactics 620
Uniforms (general, then by periods) 620
Units (general, then by periods) 625
   Miscellaneous 629
Astronomy 630
Automobiles 630
   General 630
   Horse-Drawn 630
   Individual 631
   Traction 631
Missiles & Space Vehicles 631
Models 632
   General 632
   Aircraft 632
   Boats 633
   Railroads 633
   Static Scale 634
      General 634
      Aircraft 635
      Armor 635
      Automobiles 635
      Figures 636
      Ships 636
      Structures 637
   Tools & Materials 637
Museums 637
Politics 638
Railroad 638
   General 638
   Biographies 640
   Logging 640
   Memorabilia & Literature 641
   Rail Fans & Rail Travel 641
   Rail Lines 642
      General 642
      By Countries 642
      Regional 647
      Traction 648
   Rolling Stock 651
      Cars 651
      Locomotives (by type) 652
      Manufacturers 656
      Traction & Rail Cars 657
   Miscellaneous 657
Research Aids 658
Ships 658

Contents of Index xxii

(VI. Reviews, cont.)

Naval Battles & Wars	658
Navies	659
Ships	659
Civil	659
Naval (general, then by countries)	660
Structures	663
Wargames	664
Battles	664
Playing	665
Miscellaneous	666

ENGINE REVIEWS

Electric Motors	667
Internal Combustion (by class)	668
Jets	670

KIT REVIEWS (1)--Static Scale

Subject Reviews	670
Aircraft	671
Range Reviews	671
World War I (Allies & Central)	671
Between World Wars (by countries)	673
World War II (by countries)	676
Post World War II (by countries)	686
Helicopters	694
Accessories	695
Armor	695
Range Reviews	695
APCs, ICVs, ARVs & Funnies	696
Armored Cars	696
Artillery	697
Half Tracks	697
Self-Propelled Artillery (by countries)	698
Small Arms	699
Softskins (by countries)	700
Tanks (by countries)	701
Accessories	705
Automobiles	705
Animal-Powered	705
Motorcycles	705
Passenger Cars	707
Racing Cars	708
Ready-Assembled	708
Tractors	709

xxiii   Contents of Index

Trucks & Trailers	709
Engines	709
Figures	710
Subject Reviews	710
Range Reviews (by scales)	710
Figures (by scales)	712
Accessories	716
Missiles & Space Vehicles	716
Railroad (non-operating)	717
Ships	717
Range Reviews	717
Powered	717
Civil	717
Naval (by countries)	718
Sail	721
Unpowered Vessels & Research Devices	721
Fittings	721
Structures	722
Range Reviews	722
Bridges	722
Building Parts (exterior, interior)	722
Buildings	723
Sets	723
Commercial	724
House	724
Industries	725
Railroad Stations	726
Roundhouses, Sheds, etc.	726
Shanty & Signal	727
Other	727
Non-Buildings	728
Docks	728
Water Tanks	728
Yard Structures	728
Miscellaneous	729

KIT REVIEWS (2)--Operating Scale

Aircraft	730
Surveys	730
Free Flight	730
Control Line	730
Radio Control	731
ARF	731
Gliders	731
Helicopters	732
Pylon Racers	732

Contents of Index xxiv

(VI. Reviews, cont.)

Scale & Semi-Scale	733
Sport	734
Stunt	734
Trainer	735
Armor	736
Automobile	736
Boats	736
Power	736
Sail	737
Railroad	737
Range Reviews	737
Complete Trains	737
European Rolling Stock	737
Freight Cars (by type)	738
Non-Revenue & Special	742
Passenger (by type)	742
Locomotives	744
NMRA separate listing	744
Diesel (by scale)	746
Electric	747
Steam (by scale)	748
Traction	749
Rail Cars	750
Parts (by type)	750
Control Systems	752
Signals	753
Track	754
Turntables	755

REVIEWS OF OTHER PRODUCTS

Adhesives	755
Covering	755
Finish	755
Scenery Materials	756
Tools	757
Airbrushes & Accessories	757
Aircraft Flight Equipment	757
Cleaners (ultrasonic)	758
Hand Tools	758
Jigs	759
Power Tools	759
Test Equipment	759
Radio Control	760
Complete	760

Contents of Index

Control Components 761
Kits 761
Servos 761
Wargames 762
Miscellaneous 763

PARODIES 764

INTRODUCTION

The Magazines

This is what I hope will be the first index of a series. The magazines covered in this first volume were taken largely from my own library, and the libraries of a few friends, and therefore there are a few gaps (see page 9). I have written to the relevant magazines I have located (some 91 as of this writing) about exchanging a complimentary subscription for guaranteed inclusion in future volumes and some have been kind enough to accept this cooperative arrangement. While I so far have contacted only English language ones, I would be glad to include any in any language.

The requirements for inclusion of a magazine are simple: (a) it must be available, through either subscription or membership in an open organization, to any modeler with the requisite fee; (b) it must include in every issue scale drawings, color schemes, technique articles, or product reviews of direct use to modelers; and (c) it must strive for accuracy in its coverage. (This last point, as far as I have found, excludes only a certain California firm with heavy newsstand sales that is noted for its multiplicity of titles and its habit of stealing material from individuals and other publications, as well as its total unreliability for accuracy.) Reputable magazines are welcome and will be included in future volumes. Publishers desiring to insure inclusion in the next volume should provide copies back to January 1976. Please write the author c/o Scarecrow Press, 52 Liberty St., Metuchen, N.J., 08840. Given the above three requirements, any periodical is eligible, no matter how small its subscription list. Magazines not provided by their publishers will also be included to the limit of my budget for subscription prices.

Kinds of Information Not Indexed

Because of their limited usefulness and because this

Introduction 2

Index must be kept to a manageable size, the following items or categories in the magazines covered are not indexed:

(1) House organ material. The internal workings of organizations are of major concern to those in the organizations, but to few others.

(2) Coverage of contests, exhibitions, military exercises, rallies, etc. Coverage of most major modeling events is generally published three or four months after the event, while prototype activities are covered (if at all) one to two years after.

(3) Notice of new products not in the nature of a review. There are too many for their lasting value. IPMS-UK has an excellent directory, "Scale Plastic Kits of the World" published by MAP, for this area of modeling and it is hoped that other organizations would do analogous directories for flying models, metal figures, etc.

(4) Reviews of magazines. Because of the time-lag between the publication of the review and the publication of the next volume of this index, these will be too outdated to be of value since magazines change over the years far more than other products.

(5) Decal reviews. They are often updated because of reviewer criticism and few of them have been more than an elaborate notice of new products since they generally go into details of the contents, rather than accuracy, quality of register, adhesion, thickness, etc.

(6) Editorials. Editorials should speak to a matter of immediate concern and therefore will become dated by the time-lag. If not, they will be considered an article regardless of label and indexed accordingly.

(7) Regular columns which cover or touch on a number of items, or articles or pages of miscellaneous tips and hints on a wide variety of subjects. Occasionally some items will have enough significance to be extracted, but generally the brevity of the piece works against it.

(8) Plans which do not include enough material for an expert modeler to build a model. The borderline here is in flying models which take up about two or three column inches. If the airfoil and the basic structure are included, they are

indexed with the notation "sp" (small plan); if not, they are omitted.

(9) Book reviews of items of fiction. There is enough of a problem in classifying material for reference without trying to pigeon-hole novels as well. While interesting escape, they are seldom of direct value to the modeler.

(10) Letters to the editor unless offering corrections or additions to previously published articles or other generally useful information. The criterion here is: if it were in the main text of the publication, would it be considered an article or filler?

(11) Requests for information unless accompanied by an answer of sufficient scope to have otherwise warranted indexing.

(12) Photographs. There are two problems here. First, the problem of identifying accurately the large number of uncaptioned photos in model magazines. Second, that of space (and thus cost); an index of photos would be about the same size as this index. Anyone capable of the task is welcome to it. Photo-essays of at least one full page, covering one specific subject, are indexed and photos accompanying scale drawings are noted in the drawing reference.

(13) Ads. With the rare exception of those containing material which would otherwise warrant indexing.

(14) Reviews of die-cast cars and similar items directed at the collector rather than modeler.

(15) Wargame rules reviews. Although the wargames themselves and background books directed primarily at wargamers are covered, the problem of space again precludes coverage of items not directed at modelers.

MAGAZINES INDEXED

Data given here are as of February 1976 and are subject to change both in content and in price of subscription and/or membership.

AFV G2. Baron Publishing, Box 820, La Puente CA 91747. Nominally monthly, but appears at one to four month intervals. Cost is $1 per issue or $10 per year (foreign subscriptions, $11) and includes twelve issues (thus the subscription period is actually for more than a year). Coverage is of all types of military land vehicles (including amphibians) both prototype and model, and military unit organization and history.

Aeromodeller. Model and Allied Publications, Box 35, Bridge Street, Hemel Hempstead, Herts., England HP1 1EE. Monthly. Cost is 30p (or $1.50) per issue or £5.00 (or $15) per year. Coverage is basically flying models, both competition and sport, with some scale documentation and kit and book reviews. Full size plans are included as inserts about once a year.

Air Enthusiast/Air International. Box 16, Bromley, Kent, England BR2 7RB. Monthly. Cost is $1.25 (U.S. and Canada), 90 cents (Australia), and 75 cents (New Zealand and South Africa) per issue or £4.50 (or $15) per year. Coverage is basically prototype aircraft but there is a model column including color schemes and kit and book reviews with some technique articles.

Airfix Magazine. Surridge Dawson, 136/142 New Kent Road, London SE 1. Monthly. Cost £5.10 or $12 per year. Coverage is all types of static scale models, largely (but not entirely) based on Airfix kits. There is some cover-

4

age of prototype subjects and kits, books, wargames, and other products are reviewed.

American Aircraft Modeler. Out of print after March 1975.

Armies & Weapons. 2 Gartenstrasse, 6300 Zug, Switzerland. Bi-monthly. 75p (or $2.50) per issue, £3.75 (or $12.50) per year. Coverage is principally contemporary military equipment and organization, but articles appear consistently on military history (generally 18th century or later) and modelers will particularly benefit from the scale drawings of equipment, colored sketches of uniforms, and book reviews.

Aviation News. 2 Sheepfold Lane, Amersham, Bucks., England. Fortnightly. Cost is 95 cents each or $30 per year. Coverage is aviation history with scale drawings and color schemes for one aircraft type per issue as well as kit and book reviews and some technique articles.

Flying Models. Carstens Publications, Box 700, Newton NJ 07860. Monthly. Cost is 75 cents per issue or $7 per year, $13 per two years, $15 per three years U.S. and Canada, foreign $1 per year extra. Coverage is mainly flying models, but a boat department gives coverage to RC craft, both sail and power, including articles on working scale boats. Kit reviews cover both aircraft and boat model kits, model parts and equipment are also reviewed.

Fusilier. Baron Publishing, Box 293, La Puente CA 91747. Nominally quarterly, but "occasionally" would better describe it. Cost is $1.25 per issue or $4.50 per year (or per four issues). Foreign prices are $1.50 and $5.50. Coverage is both military history and military figure modeling with kit reviews constituting a substantial part.

IPMS Magazine. International Plastic Modellers' Society--U.K. Bi-monthly. This publication will have changed with the January 1976 issue to one of house-organ material plus kit reviews. UK static scale modelers will benefit from IPMS membership, but those in other countries would do better

IPMS Quarterly. International Plastic Modeler's Society--
U.S.A. Box 163, Ben Franklin Station, Washington DC
20044. Quarterly. Cost of membership is $8.50 per
year and also includes their house-organ bi-monthly, Update. The Quarterly is strictly static scale articles, plans, and color patterns, mostly aircraft, considerable armor, occasional ships in its coverage. Kit reviews are in Update, as are some technique articles.

Military Modelling. Model and Allied Publications, Box 35, Bridge Street, Hemel Hempstead, Herts., England HP1 1EE. Monthly. Cost is 35p (or $1.75) per issue or £5.75 (or $18) per year. Coverage is static scale military vehicles and figures, with kit & book reviews.

Model Airplane News. White Plains Plaza, One No. Broadway, White Plains NY 10601. Monthly. Cost is $1.25 per issue or $10 per year, $18 for two years, Canada $11.75 per year, other countries $12.25 per year in U.S. funds. Coverage is flying models with kit and product reviews.

Model Boats. Model and Allied Publications, Box 35, Bridge Street, Hemel Hempstead, Herts., England HP1 1EE. Monthly. Cost is 30p (or $1.50) per issue or £5 (or $15) per year. Coverage is on both operating and static scale boat and ship models and includes reviews of equipment and occasionally kits. Full-size plans are occasionally included as inserts.

Model Railroader. Kalmback Publishing, 1027 N. 7th St., Milwaukee WI 53233. Monthly. Cost is 75¢ per issue or $9 per year, $17 for two years, $24 for three years, $1 per year extra outside the Americas. Coverage is all phases of model railroading, but almost entirely indoor electrically-powered layouts. Reviews cover kits, equipment, and books.

Modelworld. Out of print after February 1974.

Magazines Indexed

NMRA Bulletin. National Model Railroad Association, 4602 4th St. N.W., Canton OH 44708. Monthly. Cost is $1 per issue or $10 per year. About half of the content is NMRA house-organ material, the remainder general articles on model railroading and plans; reviews cover books and performance of locomotives.

Narrow Gauge and Short Line Gazette. Box 1046, Felton CA 95018. Bi-monthly. Cost is $1.25 per issue or $6.50 per year ($15.50 first class postage). Coverage is all phases of narrow-gauge model railroad construction and a study of prototype narrow-gauge and short-line railroads. Kits and books are reviewed. This publication grew out of two previous ones: Finelines and Slim Gauge News.

PAM [Plastic Aircraft Modeller] News. 22 Slayleigh Ave., Sheffield, S. Yorks., England S10 3 RB. Quarterly. Cost is 30p (or $1) per issue or £1.60 (or $4) per year. Coverage is static scale aircraft with kit, product, and book reviews and occasional articles on prototype aircraft.

RC Sportsman. Box 11247, Reno NV 89510. Monthly. Cost is 75 cents per issue or $8 per year, $14 for two years, $20 for three years, outside U.S. and Canada $10 per year. Coverage is radio controlled aircraft, boat, and car models. The format will have changed from magazine to tabloid newspaper with the January 1976 issue and a full-size model plan will be bound into each issue of the new format. There are also kit and book reviews.

Radio Control Modeler. 120 W. Sierra Madre Blvd., Sierra Madre CA 91024. Monthly. Cost is $1.50 per issue or $16.50 per year or $32 for two years, $2.50 extra per year foreign. Coverage is on all aspects of RC flying with some articles on boats and cars. Kits and products are reviewed.

Railroad Model Craftsman. Carstens Publications, Box 700, Newton NJ 07860. Monthly. Cost is 75 cents per issue or $9 per year, $17 for two years, $21 for three years, $1 per year extra foreign. Coverage is on all aspects of model railroading although live steam is rarely covered. Kits, products, and (usually) books are reviewed.

Magazines Indexed

Random Thoughts. International Plastic Modellers' Society--Canada. Box 626, Sta B, Ottawa, Ont. K1P 5P7, Canada. Monthly. Cost is $5 (Canadian) per year or $5.75 foreign (i.e., U.S.). Coverage is static scale, mostly aircraft, usually armor, occasionally figures, and rarely ships. Kit and occasional decal or book reviews are included.

Replica in Scale. 4014 Belle Grove, San Antonio TX 78230. Quarterly. Cost is $2 per issue or $7 ($11 foreign airmail) per year. Coverage is all areas of static scale including kit, decal, and book reviews and a feature is one aircraft type per issue including markings of all U.S. units ever to fly it.

Scale Models. Model and Allied Publications, Box 35, Bridge Street, Hemel Hempstead, Herts., England HP1 1EE. Monthly. Cost is 35p (or $1.75) per issue or £6 (or $18) per year. Coverage is static scale aircraft, ships, and civil vehicles, including kit, decal, and book reviews.

Sword & Lance. 38 Coniscliffe Road, Darlington, Co. Durham, England. Bi-monthly. Cost is £2.60 (or $6 by sea, $12 by air)--cost overseas is the same as UK if paid in pounds. Coverage is military miniatures and wargaming with major coverage of military history. Kits, books and wargames are reviewed.

World War 2 Journal (formerly World War Enthusiast). 218 Beech Street, Bennington, VT 05201. Bi-monthly. Cost is $1.50 ($1.80 foreign) per issue, or $8 ($9.80 foreign) per year, or $15 ($18.60 foreign) for two years. Coverage is mainly historical documentation, with some scale drawings and color patterns for modelers. Kit, book, and wargame reviews are regular features.

    All of these publications have something to offer the modeler--as the remainder of this book will show. If you find one or more which meet your own needs consistently, get a subscription. And when you do, please mention this index. Several magazines have been generous enough to contribute subscriptions to help in compiling this work, and others might if they knew they would get something for their

Magazines Indexed

trouble. Let them know the index helped and they will help make the next edition even more useful.

Gaps in Coverage

The gaps in coverage (i. e., individual issues not available to the compiler even after much effort to locate them) listed below were reduced to the small number they are mainly because of the generous work of those listed in the Acknowledgments.

<u>AFV G2</u>: Jan. 1971 (vol. 3, no. 10)

<u>Armies & Weapons</u>: nos. 1, 15, and 18 (only the posters were not covered in the latter two)

<u>Aviation News</u>: 26 May 1972 (vol. 1, no. 1), 25 June 1972 (vol. 1, no. 3), 21 July 1972 (vol. 1, no. 5), 1 Sept. 1972 (vol. 1, no. 8), 15 Sept. 1972 (vol. 1, no. 9), 5 Jan. 1973 (vol. 1, no. 17), 4 Jan. 1974 (vol. 2, no. 16)

<u>PAM News</u>: April 1973 (no. 1), July 1973 (no. 2)

<u>Sword & Lance</u>: Aug. 1975 (no. 9)

<u>World War Enthusiast</u>: July 1974 (vol. 1, no. 4)

Some of the material appearing in these "missing" magazines is indexed herein. This is because their presence has been indicated elsewhere, such as their having been part of serialized articles or having been listed in an annual index by the publisher. Typically, material of this type that is indexed herein is missing page numbers, but it was felt that incomplete citation was preferable to exclusion altogether.

The user should note that any corrections, additions, and discussions arising from items published in the period covered by this index, but appearing in issues after 1975, will be included in the planned next volume of this work. There are a few 1976 references of this kind in the present work but they have not been included on a systematic basis.

A NOTE ON TERMINOLOGY

Modeling, like most specialized fields, has its own language ("universe of discourse," to be technical) that does not quite coincide with normal English. Terminology in this index is that of modeling and therefore a few words of explanation are needed for the non-modeler to be able to use it easily.

Category terms are far more inclusive in modeling. "Automobiles" includes all civilian land vehicles not using rails--passenger cars, trucks, off-the-road vehicles, farm machinery, and even animal-drawn vehicles (which are hardly "auto" at all). Likewise "armor" includes all military land vehicles whether they have armor or are merely military versions of what, under other ownership, would be considered "automobile."

Since the various fields of modeling, like their prototype subjects, have developed independently of one another, there are some terms whose definition depends on the category using them. "Traction" is a good example of this. In automobiles, it is tractors, particularly steam tractors of the late nineteenth century. In railroading, traction includes street cars, interurbans, and similar trolley-contact electric rail vehicles.

Different fields will have different terms for the same thing too. Static scale calls a model that is made from one or more kits of a different subject "conversions" while model railroaders call it "kitbashing." "Prototype" does not necessarily mean the first-produced of a type, but the full-scale subject of a scale model. However, in scale drawings and color schemes, the use of the word prototype is in its more conventional definition--that of a first or experimental variant.

Because models are often three-dimensional historical documents (either of a past artifact or a research device for future ones), "history" includes articles on prototype subjects as well as articles more normally included in the definition of history. For the same reason of historicity and because organizational systems rarely translate from one culture to another, many terms are usually employed in their original language in serious modeling circles. Thus the use of a term such as the French escadrille is not an affectation, but an acknowledgment that it does not really mean the same as "squadron." In fact, there are differences among "squadrons" in the Canadian, British, and United States' air forces.

A NOTE ON ARRANGEMENT

A standard indexing format is followed in this volume (with exceptions which will make far more sense to a modeler than to a librarian).* The format may look strange at first, but it is easy to learn and will quickly become automatic.

The identifying code looks something like this: RT Jl 75 8/7:80-81. The first item is the letter code for the magazine (in this case Random Thoughts). The next is the date, July 1975. The "fraction" is the volume and number--i.e., volume 8, number 7. If there is no "fraction," the magazine does not use volumes, just numbers. After the colon comes the page number (in the above case, pages 80 and 81). If this number had a + after it, the item would be continued on a non-consecutive page.

Generally there is only one magazine reference for each listing. If the first volume, number, and date reference is followed by another one, without the magazine code, it is part of a serial article. If the magazine code is used again, it means that the same reference was reprinted in the later magazine. The only exception to this is in reviews (book, engine, kit, or other products) and airfoils, where all references to this one item will be included in the same listing. The reason this was not done with other kinds of listings is the difficulty in accurately determining whether two items are absolutely the same or only similar.

---

*There are too many anonymous writings or works identified only by a trademark on a drawing to justify the librarian's familiar main arrangement by author's names. Besides, there are only a few writers well enough known by name for this additional labor and space to yield a valuable reference point. Sorry authors, I know how it is; some of my stuff is indexed in here and you will never know which.

Arrangement

Because of the multiplicity of terms in use and/or in the interests of logic, there are a few occasions when alphabetical order is not followed. Three notable examples are in the model airplane control systems, in engine type and size, and in static scale. In the first, the order is from least to greatest amount of control: thus free flight is followed by tethered, that by control line, and finally radio control. Radio control, in turn, goes from one controlled surface (category I) to two, to three, to all surfaces plus controlled accessories. Engine size goes from glider to rubber to electric to steam to internal combustion. The latter from the smallest to the largest piston classes and finally the noisiest of all, jet. Static scale is arranged in order of difficulty to a modeler, i.e., with only the drawings, with a scratch-building plan, conversions, superdetailing, kit construction articles, and finally kit corrections (although as modelers know all too well, sometimes these last approach conversion in difficulty).

Order in color references is: name of subject, unit or owner, place, date, operator. In case of two locations, the first is the home base and the second is where the pattern was recorded.

Serialized articles follow chronological order, but column features are alphabetized.

Division of scale drawings and historical articles by period follows chronological order and may be further divided by country. These are somewhat arbitrary in that normally a subject is classified in the period in which it was best known. Country is assigned on the basis of manufacture in the case of scale drawings, but on the basis of national markings or registration regardless of ownership in the case of color patterns. Thus the Condor Legion is found under Between World Wars, Spain, Nationalist, even though the unit was entirely German in manpower, organization, and equipment.

Classification as to world wars or non-wartime is made on the basis of when a given country entered the war. Thus there is a significant number of U.S. aircraft in Between World Wars long after September 1939. Likewise, Finland is divided between the Winter War (1939-40), considered between wars, and the Continuation War when, because of co-belligerent status with Germany, it is in World War II. With neutrals, August 1914 to November 1918 and September 1939 to August 1945 will determine the periods.

Arrangement   14

With the exception of wargame reviews, products are listed alphabetically by manufacturers rather than subject.

When all else fails, try the Table of Contents or ask a modeler.

Cross-Referencing

When a conversion article is accompanied by scale drawings, each will be indexed in the appropriate category, as will historical background in a construction article and color patterns on a scale drawing. However, there are some categories that would require whole sections to be repeated. In the interests of keeping down the size of this index, while preserving its full usefulness, these categories are listed below:

Kit reviews have their own listing. However, there is considerable commentary of a kit review nature in items listed under kit construction, kit correction, and superdetailing.

Historical background articles are often indexed separately, even when accompanying scale drawings. However, many of these drawings, particularly in railroading, have only a paragraph of historical material, and therefore have not been cross-referenced.

The largest bit of cross-referencing material is the entry "see separate listing." Unless another location is given, these will be found at the end of that particular classification, in alphabetical order.

In the interest of ease in locating, items buried within other articles are indexed only on the page on which they appear, even if it is in the middle of an article. Since scale drawings are sometimes included in fairly long historical articles, the page numbers for scale drawings refer only to the pages of the drawings, even though the entry may also refer to "pph" (prototype photographs) which appear on other pages within the article. This is a bit of a bother, but less so than looking through a 10- or 15-page article for one page of three-views or an interior sketch. Likewise layouts refer only to the page of the track diagram even if they are within another article.

A PERSONAL NOTE

Complaints and prejudices of the compiler concerning model magazines:

Model magazines have not been indexed in traditional library publications and it shows in the magazines themselves. There are many items essential to the indexer which are missing from many model magazines. In fact, I have found one otherwise excellent publication which not only does not have page numbers, but no volume number or date! I am still trying to find out how they refer to back issues themselves.

Several publications have changed the method of volume numeration during the period of this index. This is usually merely a matter of slight confusion, but one changed systems so that there are about ten pairs of issues sharing the same volume and number, although of a different date.

A large number omit page numbers for several pages in succession. This makes identifying pages difficult since under U.S. laws advertisements and inserts must be numbered, while other countries only number the regularly printed parts. Some include the covers in numbered pages and others don't.

The identification of books under review is also troublesome. The magazines come from three different countries and the books they are reviewing are often published in two or three countries at once, but the reviewer only gets the one from his country, and only it is cited. A library or bookstore ought to be of help in determining if a given book is available in one's own country. Copyright dates seem to be known to only three of the periodicals indexed--a real problem for books which are in several editions. Some magazine reviews even omit the publisher's name, which is a major difficulty for your local bookstore if you want to order a copy.

Personal Note

There is one problem I am not sure can be solved. There are many items of technique or equipment buried in articles on other subjects: painting tips in a construction plan, launching techniques in a contest report, operating accessories in a track layout plan, etc. I have tried to catch these in magazines from my own collection, but may have let some slip by when indexing borrowed copies. I can only apologize for any such slips.

There are several other problems which not only affect persons undertaking the task of indexing, but also the modelers for whom the periodicals are published in the first place. Therefore I would like to use this forum to complain and hope the editors will take note.

Scale drawings seldom have interior details, even though the interior is readily visible from the outside. They also often omit cross-sections. I realize that these are more difficult features to document since they can rarely be scaled off of photographs. Yet these essential references are missing from drawings which have been measured from museum specimens and accompanied by interior photographs which prove the researcher had permission to enter these areas and thus could have measured them too.

Color pattern documentation will give excellent detail, exact official shade, and even stencils, but give no historical context for the subject. As long as scale models attempt to be three-dimensional historical documents, the sources for this documentation should treat the historical nature of the subject seriously.

Non-scale model plans suffer from a similar fault in that flying models will have no information as to what size engine is required. Any flying modeler knows what a profound effect comes from a slight change in engine size, so this is essential to build the model; yet I have read entire construction articles vainly looking for this information. Since I have classified these plans partly by engine size, I had to rely on my experience, so don't go by this index when building these models or you may have a plane too mushy or too hot to do well.

There are even omissions as obvious as a kit review which neglects to give the scale. If the scale is not given on the box or can't even be determined by the reviewer, this is a valid part of the review and should be mentioned. Even

Personal Note

recourse to "Scale Plastic Kits of the World" is of little help in some of these cases since the company has issued the kit in more than one scale and there is then no way to know which scale is being reviewed.

There is a similar problem with railroad scales in that some magazines have started giving scale ratios rather than gauges. This is a particular problem in the 0 gauge area where the nominal scale (1/48) and the gauge ($1\frac{1}{4}$") do not coincide. This discrepancy has led to three forms of 0 gauge: (a) leave it alone with the track too wide; (b) enlarge the scale and retain the gauge, otherwise called O_{17} (from the scale of 17/64":1') or 1/43 scale; or (c) retain the $\frac{1}{4}$":1' scale and reduce the gauge, called Q gauge in the old days. While the use of 1/43 clearly implies O_{17}, 1/48 does not distinguish between true O and Q gauges. In the case of Q-Car products, this is assumed, but theirs is a traction firm so the conventional railroad products are still ambiguous. Why not go back to the three old terms and keep things clear?

This is the first of what I hope will be a long series of these indexes. Therefore I welcome any suggestions for improvement. Because complaints are always more vocal than praise, I would like especially to know what you like as well as dislike. That way I won't think a feature is unnecessary and eliminate it when it is serving a valuable function.

ACKNOWLEDGMENTS AND THANKS

As mentioned earlier, most of the material for this first volume of the index came from my own library. However there are some notable exceptions. Those who have loaned me their magazines for sometimes long periods for indexing deserve not only the free copy of the finished work for their trouble, but also a little public recognition. Thanks to:

Euan Callendar, for vast portions of Model Railroader and Railroad Model Craftsman as well as for helping track down some dozen or more of the almost one hundred model magazines published in English--all while being active in the National Model Railroad Association and wargaming and being president of IPMS-Vancouver.

Henry Uytengsu, for covering my sizeable gaps in Aviation News, Aircraft International, PAM News, and IPMS-Magazine, while being an honor student at the University of British Columbia and president of IPMS-Richmond.

Norman Kirk, for the entire load of NMRA Bulletin even though we had just met. He is an active model railroader and his sons are active in IPMS-Vancouver.

The Messrs. Edgar Seay, Sr. and Jr., for filling gaps in Airfix Magazine and Aeromodeller as well as for the use of a back room in MAL Hobbies in Irving, Texas, in which to index them.

Geoff Pincott, of the Vancouver Public Library, for technical help from the librarian's side of the problem. He is also a railroad modeler.

Tony Souza, for being the catalyst that got the project from "one of these days" to "current" status and with regrets that schedule conflicts prevented him from a more active collaboration.

18

Mark Johnson, for *Sword & Lance* issues even though he had deadlines with his own wargamer magazine.

And to the publishers of *RC Sportsman*, *Narrow Gauge and Short Line Gazette*, and *World War Enthusiast / World War 2 Journal*, for not only agreeing to provide material for the next edition, but also providing back issues so that they might be included in this one as well.

To all of these who worked beyond the call of duty, my heartfelt thanks.

ABBREVIATIONS

MAGAZINES (see pp. 4-8)

A&W	Armies & Weapons	MW	Modelworld
AE	Aircraft Enthusiast	NMRA	NMRA Bulletin
Aero	Aeromodeller	NSG	Narrow Gauge and Short Line Gazette
AFV	AFV G2		
Afx	Airfix Magazine	PAM	PAM [Plastic Aircraft Modeller] News
AI	Aircraft International	RC	Radio Control Modeler
AM	American Modeler, American Aircraft Modeler, Aircraft Modeler	RCS	RC [Radio Control] Sportsman
		RiS	Replica in Scale
AN	Aviation News	RMC	Railroad Model Craftsman
FM	Flying Models		
Fus	Fusilier	RT	Random Thoughts
IM	IPMS Magazine	S&L	Sword & Lance
MAN	Model Airplane News	Sc	Scale Models
MB	Model Boats	WWE	World War Enthusiast
MM	Military Modelling	WW2J	World War 2 Journal
MR	Model Railroader		

DATES

Months: Ja, F, Mr, Ap, My, Je, Jl, Ag, S, O, N, D

Seasons: W, Sp, Su, Au

ORGANIZATIONS

AMA   Academy of Model Aeronautics; U.S. flying modelers

Abbreviations

- **FAI** Fédération Aeronautique Internationale; international body for all aerospace competition including models; thus, by extension, a model designed for competition under FAI rules
- **IPMS** International Plastic Modeler's Society; world-wide static scale model group
- **NMRA** National Model Railroad Association; English-speaking world railroad modelers
- **NRHA** National Railroad Historical Society; U.S. railroad and traction historians

---

- **½A** piston engine, displacement up to .05 cubic inches
- **I, II, III** one, two or three flight axes controlled; RC competition categories
- **3v, 4v, 2½v, etc.** number of views shown in drawings; ½v is detail drawing of a side or variant not shown on any full view
- **A** piston engine, displacement from .051 to .20 cubic inches
- **acc** accessories shown on drawings of a type not listed under other categories
- **add** additional information
- **AEW** airborne electronics warfare; electronics surveillance aircraft
- **APC** armored personnel carrier
- **ARF** almost ready to fly; assembly takes only a couple of hours
- **arm** armament details shown on drawings
- **ARV** armored recovery vehicle
- **ASM** air to surface missile
- **ASR** air sea rescue
- **ASW** anti-submarine warfare
- **B** piston engine, displacement from .20 to .3 cubic inches
- **C** piston engine, displacement from .3 to .65 cubic inches
- **CAR** coupled aileron and rudder (smoother control but less stunting possible) on Category II

Abbreviations

cd   covering details shown on drawings (where the seams are, possibly rivet lines, lacing, and similar fasteners)

CdH   coupe d'hiver class; rubber-powered free flight

CL   control line

CLT   center-line thrust; a twin (usually engined aircraft configuration in which both engines are mounted on the aircraft's center-line, one with a tractor propeller, the other with a pusher.

CO_2 piston engine powered by compressed gas, usually carbon dioxide

col   colors of the finish shown on drawings

comp   compiled by

conv   conversion; the subject was modified from another type, generally a one-off specimen; in kit reviews, this abbreviation refers to a kit containing the parts needed to convert another kit to a different subject or variant

cor   correction

cpph   color prototype photographs included with drawings

D   piston engine, displacement over .65 cubic inches

dep   depicted (followed by year); when appearance is different from that of the date built--typically for ships

det   details of parts such as retracting mechanism, winches, lifeboats, etc., shown on drawings

dim   dimensions shown on drawings

disc   discussion (generally between corrector and author, but occasionally a real round table)

DT   dethermalizer--device for limiting flight time of FF model

e   electric motor powered

e&a   Category II using elevator and aileron rather than the more conventional elevator and rudder

ed   edited by

eng   engine details shown on drawings

FAW   fighter, all-weather; primarily a British term, but U.S. has used F(AW)

FF   free flight

Abbreviations

- fp   floor plan shown on drawings
- ICV   infantry combat vehicle (sometimes "ISV," infantry support vehicle); an APC with offensive armament so it can also function as a light tank
- incl   including
- int   interior details shown on drawings; in buildings, means furniture too
- IP   instrument panel, dashboard, etc., shown on drawings
- ISV   <u>see</u> ICV
- mat   material list included in article
- mod   modified; may be either field or factory modification, but generally several were produced
- nameless   no name of model is given, but designer's name is included (when it is given) for distinguishing
- ng   narrow gauge
- nom   nominal scale; refers to stated scale on package where different from actual scale. Any use of this designation comes from kit reviews (not all reviewers check for scale accuracy, so this is often on the basis of only one review)
- oc   open cockpit
- org   originally
- pat   pattern of finish shown on drawings
- phan   phantom drawing
- pos   possibly
- posed   propaganda photo(s) are basic pattern documentation --generally non-standard pattern
- pph   prototype photograph(s) included with drawings
- present   in use at the time the pattern was printed
- prob   probably
- pt   part
- r   rubber power
- RC   radio control; when referring to engines, a piston engine with throttle control
- rLG   retracting landing gear

Abbreviations

ROG   rise-off-ground; capable of taking off in a prototype manner (as opposed to vertically or hand-launched)

ROW   rise-off-water; either flying boat or float plane

RTF   ready to fly; no construction required, just assembly of normally disassembled (for transport or storage) model

s2v, s3v, etc.   split two, three, etc. views; top and bottom views shown in half, sharing a common centerline

SAM   surface-to-air missile

sec   cross-sections included on drawings

sil   silhouette   in engine reviews, the full-size outline, generally side view and mounting hole spacing; in organization charts, a graphic portrayal of the equipment used by the unit

site   area surrounding a structure shown on drawings

sk   sketch

sl   scale-like; looks like a scale or semi-scale model but no prototype

sp   small plans; two to four column inches, useful to expert scratch-builders only

specs   specifications, statistics

SSM   surface-to-surface missile

standard   official color pattern rather than that of a particular example

std   standard gauge

sten   stencils, decals, placards, etc. details included in drawings

STOL   short-length take-off and landing

struc   structural details (which are under the covering) shown on drawings

tcol   color scheme in text but not on drawings

tpat   color pattern in text but not on drawings

trans   translated by

vac   vacuum-formed (as opposed to injected) plastic kit

var   variant(s)

vss   very semi-scale; non-scale planform with scoops, paint design, and other non-essential features suggesting a prototype

VTOL   vertical take-off and landing (because of redundancy, not applied to helicopters)

wd   wiring diagram, component scheme, or printed circuit board pattern included in article

wl   waterline; mainly for ships, but occasionally for amphibious vehicles

The Index

I. STATIC SCALE

AIRCRAFT

SCALE DRAWINGS

Before World War I

Blackburn Monoplane: 3v, sec, cd, pat, col, pph; 1912 British:
    Sc F 74 5/60:104
nameless Chanute biplane hang glider: 3v, cd, pat, col, spec; 1896
    U.S.: FM F 75 78/2:12
Voisin Bird of Passage: 3v, cd, eng, pph; 1909 French biplane:
    Sc N 72 3/11:598-600

World War I

(Austro-Hungary)

Hansa-Brandenburg D.1: 3v, sec, struc, cd, pat, col, pph; 1914
    fighter: Sc Ag 74 5/59:418-419

(France)

Morane Saulnier type L Parasol: 3v, sec, struc, cd, pat, tcol,
    pph; monoplane fighter: Sc N 75 6/74:560
Morane Saulnier type N Bullet: 3v, sec, cd, pat, col, pph; mono-
    plane fighter: Sc N 72 3/11:593-594
Nieuport 17: $5\frac{1}{2}$v, sec, cd, pat, col, pph; 1916 fighter: AN 6 Jl
    73 2/4:8-9
Nieuport 28C-1: 5v, sec, cd, pat, col, pph; 1917 fighter: AN 21
    F 75 3/19:8-9
SPAD A.2: 3v, sec, cd, pat, col, det, var; 1915 mid-prop fighter:
    RT F 74 7/2:22

27

I. Static Scale 28

(Germany)

Albatros D. II: 3v, sec, struc, cd, pat; 1916 fighter: Sc Ap 73 4/4: 259-260
Albatros D. V & D. Va: 5v, sec, cd, pat, col, pph; 1917 fighter: Sc S 72 3/9:490-491
Brandenburg C. 1 Phönix series 29: 5v, sec, struc, cd, pat, col, pph, 7 var; 1915 recon: AN 20 S 74 3/8:8-9
Etrich Taube: 3v, sec, cd, tpat, tcol, pph; 1913 observation: Sc S 74 5/60:474-476
Fokker D. VII: $4\frac{1}{2}$v, sec, cd, pat, col; 1917 fighter: RCS S 75 1/5: (40-41)
Fokker D. VII: 4v, sec, struc, cd, pat, col, pph: Sc F 74 5/2:85
Fokker D. VIII: 5v, sec, struc, cd, pat, col, pph; 1918 monoplane fighter: AM Ag 74 78/8:34-35
Fokker D. VIII: 5v, sec, struc, cd, pat, col, sten, pph: AN 13 O 72 1/11:8-9
Fokker E. V/D. VIII: 2v, sec, struc, cd, pat, det: MAN N 73 87/5: 50-51; 1v, sec, struc: Ja 74 88/1:54-55
Gotha G. O & G. V: 3v, cd, int, det, pph; 1915 heavy bomber: IM N 73 10/11-12:4-7; cor Ja 74 10/13-14:insert
Hannover Cl. IIIa: 3v, sec, struc, cd, pph; two-seat fighter: Sc Mr 73 4/3:177-178
Hansa Brandenburg W-29 (HM. I): 6v, sec, struc, cd, pat, col; float scout: MAN Jl 72 84/1:46-47
LFD Roland D. II: $4\frac{1}{2}$v, sec, cd, pat, col, pph; fighter: Aero Mr 73 38/446:159-151
LVG C. VI: $7\frac{1}{2}\frac{1}{2}\frac{1}{2}$v, sec, struc, cd, pat, col, int, eng, det, pph; 1918 recon: Sc Ja 73 4/1:35+
Pfalz D. III: 3v, dim, det, pph; fighter: IM S 73 10/9:2-6+
Pfalz D. VIII: $5\frac{1}{2}\frac{1}{2}$v, sec, cd, pat, col, pph; 1918 fighter: AM Jl 73 77/1:42-43
Pfalz Dr. 1: $3\frac{1}{2}$v, sec, cd, pat, col; 1917 triplane fighter: MAN D 74 98/6:58
Rumpler C. IV: $4\frac{1}{2}$v, sec, struc, cd, pat, col, int, pph; 1917 observation: Sc F 75 6/65:74-75
Zepplin P Type: $3\frac{1}{2}\frac{1}{2}$v, cd, pat, tcol, pph; L10-L19 airships, 1915: Sc N 75 6/74:558-559

(U. K.)

Airco DH 2: $4\frac{1}{2}\frac{1}{2}$v, sec, struc, pat, col, det, pph; 1915 scout: Sc Je 72 3/6:320-324
Avro 504K: $4\frac{1}{2}\frac{1}{2}$v, sec, struc, cd, pph: 1914 trainer: AM Jl 71/73/1:30-31
Avro 504K: 5v, sec, struc, cd, pat, col, pph: AN 27 D 74 3/15:8-9
Avro 504K: 5v, sec, struc, cd, pat, col, pph: Sc My 75 6/68:217
BE2e: s4v, struc, cd, pat, col, acc; 1916 recon/bomber: RC Ag 71 8/8:32-33
BE12e: s3v, struc, cd, pat, col, acc; 1916 single-seat BE2e: RC Ag 71 8/8:32-33
Bristol F. 2B Mk. I: 5v, sec, cd, pat, col, pph; 1916 two-seat

fighter/recon: AN 12 O 73 2/11:7-9
Bristol F. 2B Mk II; trainer; dual control; Sunbeam Arab engine variants: 1v, cd, each; AN 12 O 73 2/11:7-9
De Havilland DH 4: 4v, sec, cd, pat, col, pph; 1916 light bomber: AN 16 My 75 3/25:8-9
De Havilland DH 9: IP, pph; recon/bomber: Sc My 74 5/56:281
DH 9: s4v, sec, struc, cd, pat, tcol: SC O 75 6/72:485
FE 8: 3v, sec, cd, tpat, tcol; observation: Afx Je 72 13/10:566-568
Handley Page 0-400: phan, pph; 1918 heavy bomber: AE Ag 73 5/2:76-77
Sopwith Camel: 4v, sec, phan, struc, cd, pat, col, IP, det, pph; 1917 fighter: Sc My 74 5/56:267-269
Sopwith Pup: 3v, sec, struc, cd, pat, col, pph; 1916 fighter: Sc Je 75 6/69:273
Sopwith Snipe: phan, pph; 1916 fighter: AE Ap 74 6/4:192-193
Sopwith Triplane: 5v, sec, cd, pat, col, pph; 1916 fighter: AN 8 D 72 1/15:8-9
Sopwith Triplane: 3v, sec, struc, phan, cd, pat, col, pph: Sc Mr 74 5/54:143+

(U. S.)

Packard-Lepere LUSAC-11: $4\frac{1}{2}$v, sec, cd, pat, col, pph; 1918 two-plane fighter: AM S 74 74/9:24
Pigeon-Fraser Pursuit (Albree Scout): 5v, sec, struc, cd, pat, col, det, sk; 1917 scout: MAN S 74 89/3:54-56

Between World Wars

(Czechoslovakia Military)

Avia B. 534: IP; 1937 biplane fighter: IM Ag 71 8/8:2
Avia B. 534-I: phan, pph: AI Jl 74 7/1:28-29
Avia B. 534-IV: s3v, phan, cd, pat, col, pph: AI Jl 74 7/1:30-32
Letov Š-328: 4v, sec, cd, pph; 1934 biplane fighter: IM Ja 73 10/1:5
Letov Š-328: s4v, sec, cd, pat: Sc D 73 4/12:846

(Denmark Military)

Hawker Dankok (LB II): $4\frac{1}{2}\frac{1}{2}$v, cd, pat, col, det, eng; 1926 license-built variant on Gloster Woodcock: MAN Je 72 84/6:15-16

(France Military)

Caudron Renault CR 714: 5v, sec, struc, cd, pat, col, int, det,

I. Static Scale 30

pph; 1939 fighter: Aero Je 71 36/425:314-317
Mureaux ANF 117: 1v, struc, cd, pat, col, det; 1935 recon/bomber: IM S 73 10/9:15

(Germany Civil)

Bücker Bü 131B Jungmann: $4\frac{1}{2}\frac{1}{2}\frac{1}{2}\frac{1}{2}\frac{1}{2}$v, sec, cd, pat, col, pph; 1934 trainer: Aero F 74 39/457:89-91
Dornier DO-X: 3v, sec, cd, pat, col, pph; 1926 12-engined flying boat: Aero F 71 36/421:84-87
Focke Wulf Fw 200 Condor: phan, pph; 1936 four-engined airliner: AE Ja 73 4/1:24-25
Heinkel He 64C: $3\frac{1}{2}\frac{1}{2}$v, sec, cd, pat, col, pph; 1931 competition tourer: MAN Ap 75 90/4:32
Heinkel He 70G Blitz: phan: AI F 75 8/2:78-79
Junkers Ju 52: $4\frac{1}{2}$v sec, cd, pat, col, pph; 1932 tri-motor airliner: AM My 73 76/5:74-75
Ju 52/3m: phan, pph: AI Ag 74 7/2:78-79
Junkers Ju 86B-0; V-4; Z-7: 1v, cd, each; twin-engine airliner: AN 18 Ag 72 1/7:8-9
Ju 86C-1: phan, pph: AE Ja 72 2/1:28-29

(Germany Military)

Focke Wulf Fw 44J Steiglitz: s3v, sec, cd, pat, col; 1932 trainer: RCS Je 75 1/2:(40-41)
Focke Wulf Fw 56A-1 Stösser: 4v, sec, cd, pat, col, pph: AN 2 F 72 1/19:8-9
Heinkel He 45C: 3v, cd, pat, col; biplane dive bomber/recon: MW Ap 73 1/8:408
Heinkel He 51: 4v, cd; biplane dive bomber: WWE N 74 1/6:180-181
He 51A-1; B-1; B-2; C-1: 10v, sec, cd, pat, col: MAN My 73 86/5:66-67
He 51A-1; B-1: 4v, sec, cd, pat, col, sk: Sc O 71 2/10:551-553
He 51B-1; B-2: $6\frac{1}{2}$v, sec, pph: AM D 72 76/6:34-35
He 51B-1 production: 5v, cd, pat, col, pph: MW Je 73 1/10:519
He 51B-2: 4v, cd, pat, col, pph: MW Jl 73 1/11:575
Heinkel He 59A; C-2; D-1: 1v, cd, each; 1930 twin float biplane patrol: AN 24 N 72 1/14:8-9
He 59B-2: $4\frac{1}{2}$v, sec, cd, pat, col, pph: AN 24 N 72 1/14:8-9
Henschel Hs 123A-1: 4v, struc, cd, pat, col, pph; 1937 biplane dive bomber: MW Mr 73 1/7:348-349
Junkers Ju 86D-1; E-2: 4v, sec, cd, pat, col, pph; 1936 bomber: AN 18 Ag 72 1/7:8-9
Ju 86G-1: 1v, cd: AN 18 Ag 72 1/7:8-9
Messerschmitt Bf 109B-2: phan: 1937 fighter: AE N 71 1/7:8-9
Messerschmitt Bf 163: 7v, sec, cd, pat; 1937 variable-incidence STOL observation: Sc Ap 71 2/4:175-177

Aircraft

(Italy Civil)

Savoia Marchetti S-55X: 4v, sec, cd, pat, col, sk, pph; 1933 twin hull CLT flying boat: Sc O 73 4/10:679

(Italy Military)

Fiat CR 32: 5v, cd, pat, col, pph; 1933 biplane fighter: AN 18 Ja 74 2/17:8-9

(Netherlands Civil)

Fokker F. 22: phan, pph; four-engine airliner: AE N 71 1/6:294-295

(Netherlands Military)

De Schelde S. 21: phan, pph; pusher, pod & boom fighter design: AE F 74 6/2:75
Fokker D. XIII: 5v, sec, struc, cd, pat, col, pph; 1923 sesquiplane fighter: AM Ja 75 75/1:58-59
Fokker D. XXI: s3v, cd, pat, col, phan, pph; 1937 fighter: AE Ag 71 1/3:155-157
Fokker D. XXIII: phan, pph; 1939 CLT fighter: AE F 74 6/2:72-73
Fokker G. 1: phan; pusher pod-and-boom fighter: AI N 74 7/5:240-241

(Poland Civil)

Lublin R-XVI b: $3\frac{1}{2}$v, sec, struc, cd, pat, col, pph; 1932 ambulance/light transport: Aero Mr 75 40/470:151-153

(Poland Military)

PZL P-23A & B Karas: $4\frac{1}{2}$v, sec, cd, pat, col, IP, det, pph; 1935 recon/bomber: Aero O 72 37/441:574-577
P-23B: 4v, cd, pat, col: IM N 73 10/11-12:22-23
P-23B: longitudinal sec: Q Ja 75 10/3:94

(USSR Military)

Polikarpov I-16: 5v, sec, struc, cd, pat, col; 1933 fighter: AM Je 74 78/7:60+
Polikarpov I-16 type 24: 4v, cd, pat, col; 1936 fighter: AE Mr 72 2/3:156
Polikarpov Po-2: int: 1928 utility biplane: RC Je 73 10/6:24

I. Static Scale 32

(U.K. Civil)

De Havilland DH 71 Tiger Moth: 5v, sec, struc, cd, pat, col, det, pph; 1927 King's Cup racer: Aero My 74 38/460:245-248
De Havilland DH 82 Tiger Moth: s4v, sec, struc, cd, pat, tcol, floats; 1932 trainer: Sc D 73 4/12:815-817
De Havilland DH 85 Leopard Moth: 3v, sec, struc, cd, pat, pph; 1933 cabin monoplane: Aero Jl 73 38/450:378-380
De Havilland DH 87A & B Hornet Moth: 6v, sec, cd, pat, col, pph; 1934 cabin biplane: Aero O 71 36/429:563-566
De Havilland DH 88 Comet: 5v, sec, struc, cd, pat, col, det, int, pph; 1933 distance racer: Aero D 72 37/443:705-707
De Havilland DH 91 Albatross: phan, pph: 1935 four-engine airliner: AE My 73 4/5:236-237
De Havilland Fox Moth: 3v, sec, cd, pat, col; open cockpit, cabin biplane: Afx N 71 13/3:216-217
De Havilland Humming Bird prototype: 4v, cd, pat, col, pph; 1923 ultra-light: Afx My 73 14/9:482
De Havilland Moth Major: 3v, cd, pat, col: 1934 biplane Afx F 72 13/6:329

(U.K. Military)

Armstrong Whitworth Siskin IIIA: 3v, sec, struc, cd, pat, col; 1923 fighter: Sc My 71 2/5:228-230
Avro 504N: 5v, sec, cd, pat, col; 1922 trainer: AN 27 D 74 3/15:9
Blackburn Cubaroo: 3v, sec, cd, pat, col; 1924 torpedo bomber: Afx F 74 15/6:353
Blackburn Shark: 3v, dim; torpedo bomber: Sc My 71 2/5:253
Bristol Bulldog TM: 3v, sec, cd, pat, col; two-seat trainer var: Afx D 73 15/4:218-219
Bristol Bulldog IIA: phan, pph; biplane fighter: AE Ja 73 4/1:32-33
Bristol F.2B Mk I; Hispano-Suiza engine; recon: 1v, cd, each; recon: AN 12 O 73 2/11:8-9
F.2B Mk IV: 5v, sec, cd, pat, col; 1928 recon: AN 12 O 73 2/11:8-9
Bristol 138A: 3v, sec, cd, pat, col, pph; 1935 high-altitude research: Afx N 74 16/3:178-179
De Havilland DH 82 Tiger Moth: 5v, struc, sec, cd, pph; 1931 trainer: AM Ap 72 74/4:30-31
DH 82a: struc, int, Canadian canopy: MAN D 75 91/6:58-59
De Havilland Genet Moth: s3v, cd, pat, col; utility biplane: RT My 73 6/5:50
Fairey Seafox: 4v, sec, struc, cd, pat, col, pph; 1939 biplane scout: Sc S 75 6/72:446-449
Fairey III Mk III: 3v, sec, cd, pat, col, pph; biplane scout: AN 9 N 73 2/13:8-10
Fairey III Mk IVC; IIIM; IIIF: 1v, cd, each: AN 9 N 73 2/13:8-9
Gloster Gamecock Mk I & II: $4\frac{11}{22}$v, sec, struc, cd, pph; 1925-27 fighter: Sc Je 74 5/57:306
Gloster Gladiator: 5v, sec, cd, pat, col, pph; 1937 biplane fighter:

Sc Ag 73 4/8:553

Gladiator I: s3v, cd, pat, phan, pph; AE Mr 73 4/3:128-129+

Gloster Gorcock: 3v, sec, struc, cd, pat; biplane fighter: Sc D 74 5/63:661

Handley Page Heyford Mk IA: 4v, sec, cd, pat, col, pph; 1933 bomber: AN 31 Ag 73 2/8:7-9

Handley Page Heyford Mk II prototype; Mk III: 1v, cd, each: AN 31 Ag 73 2/8:7-9

Hawker Hart: s4v, sec, struc, cd, pat, det; 1931 two-seat fighter; Sc Ap 73 4/4:249-251

Hawker Tomtit: 3v, sec, cd, tpat, tcol, IP, pph; 1928 trainer: Sc Ja 74 5/1:17

Saro London II: 6v, sec, cd, pat, col, pph; flying boat: AN 9 Ag 74 3/5:8-9

Supermarine Southampton: cockpit, IP, wing struc, pph; 1925 flying boat: Sc S 75 6/72:437-440

Vickers Vernon I: 4v, cd, pat, col; Vimy transport mod: AN 17 O 75 4/10:8-10

Vernon II: 4v, cd, pat, col, pph: AN 17 O 75 4/10:8-10

Vickers Vimy: 5v, sec, cd, pat, col, pph; 1919 bomber: AN 17 O 75 4/10:8-10

(U.S. Civil airliners)

Boeing 314 Clipper: 3v, dim, sec; flying boat: FM F 71 407:41

Lockheed 12A: phan, pph; 1933 twelve-passenger: AE My 72 2/5: 264-265

(U.S. Civil lightplanes & executive aircraft)

Beech Staggerwing: 4v, sec, cd, pat, col; cabin biplane: RCS Jl 75 1/3:(40-41)

Cessna Airmaster: $4\frac{1}{2}\frac{1}{2}$v, sec, cd, pph; 1935 high wing monoplane: AM My 74 78/5:64+

Airmaster: 3v, sec, cd, pat: RCS O 75 1/6:49

Curtiss Robin: $6\frac{1}{2}$v, sec, struc, cd, pat, col, int, IP, eng (Challenger & OX-5); three-place lightplane: RC Ja 73 10/1:64-65

Fairchild 71: 3v, cd, tpat, tcol, pph; 1934 bush plane: PAM O 75 11:188-189

Gere Sport: 3v, sec, struc, cd; 1933 homebuilt biplane: AM My 71 72/5:33

Lockheed Sirius: 4v, cd, pat, IP, pph: executive: AM Ap 73 76/4:22

Sirius "Tingmissartoq": 4v, sec, cd, pat, col; Lindberg's: RCS Ap 75 1/1:(40-41)

Lockheed 5C Vega: 4v, sec, cd, pat, col: executive & light airliner: RCS N 75 1/7:(36-37)

Loughead S-1: s3v, cd, pat, col, int, IP, pph: 1920 one-off biplane, first Lockheed: AM O 72 75/4:42-43

Northrop Gamma: $5\frac{1}{2}\frac{1}{2}$v, sec, cd, pph: 1932 research & transcontinental record holder: AM Mr 71 72/3:30-31

I. Static Scale 34

Rose Parrakeet A-1: 3v, sec, cd; 1936 sport biplane: AM Ap 72 74/4:38-39
Rouffaer Model R-6: 3v, sec, struc, cd, tpat, tcol, pph; 1936 one-off (intended homebuilt kit): AM O 74 74/10:37
Spartan 7W Executive: s$2\frac{1}{2}$v, sec, int, cd, pat, col; lightplane: RT S 75 8/9:104-105
Travel Air 2000: 3v, sec, cd, pph; two-place utility biplane: Sc Jl 73 4/7:478-479+
Waco CTO Taperwing: 4v, sec, cd, pat, col; 1929 sport biplane (mod for aerobatics post WW-II): MAN Ag 75 91/2:26-27; int, pph: S 75 91/3:16

(U. S. Civil racers)

Art Chester Special/Jeep: $3\frac{1}{2}\frac{1}{2}\frac{1}{2}$v, sec, cd, pat, col, IP; 1933-1938 Thompson: RC Ap 73 10/4:60-61
Bellanca 28-70: 5v, sec, cd, pat, col, pph; 1935-36 distance racer: AM Ag 72 75/2:42-43
Brown B-2 "Miss Los Angeles": $3\frac{1}{2}$v, sec, struc, cd, pat, col; 1934-39 Thompson: RC N 72 9/11:60-61
Curtiss Hawk AE-3: s3v, sec, struc, cd, pat, col, pph; 1930 parasol: AM O 71 73/4:30-31
Curtiss R3C-1 & 2: 4v, sec, cd, pat, col, pph; 1925 Pulitzer & Schneider: AM Je 77/1:54-55
Dayton-Wright Bauman RB-1: 5v, sec, cd, pat; 1920 variable-camber: AM Jl 71 73/1:52
Folkerts Speed King: 5v, sec, cd, pat, col, pph; 1937 Thompson: AM F 73 76/2:42-43
Gee Bee Model Z SuperSportster: s3v, sec, cd, pat, col; 1931 Thompson: RCS Ag 75 1/4:(40-41)
Howard DGA-6 "Mr. Mulligan": $4\frac{1}{2}$v, sec, cd, pat, col, 1935-36 Thompson & Bendix: RC Jl 73 10/7:60-61
Knight Twister: 3v, dim, cd, pat, col, pph; 1928 biplane: AM Ap 74 78/4:48
Laird-Turner LTR-14 "Pesco Special": 3v, sec, cd, pat, col, IP; 1938 Thompson: MAN O 73 78/4:48
Laird-Turner LTR-14: $3\frac{1}{2}$v, sec, cd, pat, col; 1938-39 Thompson: RC Je 73 10/6:60-61
Schoenfeldt Firecracker: $4\frac{1}{2}$v, sec, cd, pat, col; 1937 Thompson, 1939 mod: RC D 72 9/12:60-61
Travel Air 5000 "Woolaroc": 4v, sec, cd, pat, col; 1927 Dole: Aero Ap 72 37/435:221-224+
Wedell-Williams NR-61Y: 4v, sec, cd, pat, col, pph; 1932: AM Ja 71 92/1:21-23

(U. S. Military)

Boeing P-12B: s3v, sec, cd, pat, col; 1928 biplane fighter: RCS O 75 1/6: (38+)
Boeing P-26A Peashooter: 4v, sec, cd, pat, col, IP, det, pph; 1935 fighter: Sc N 74 5/62:588-590

Aircraft

Brewster F2A-1 Buffalo: 3v, cd, pat, col, pph; 1938 fighter: Afx Mr 74 16/7:403-405
F2A-1: 5v, cd, IP, pph: MW O 73 2/2:69+; 2v, pat, col: D 73 2/4:180-181
Brewster 339 Buffalo: 3v, cd, pat, col, pph; export version: Afx Jl 75 16/11:640
Brewster 339: int pph: Q Su 75 10/4:174
Chance Vought SB2U Vindicator: 3v, sec, cd, pat, col; 1937 dive bomber: MAN D 74 24/287:70
Curtiss Hawk 75: $4\frac{1}{2}$v, cd; 1938 fighter, export P-36; Sc N 72 3/11: 602-603
Hawk 75A-2: phan, pph: AE N 71 1/6:308-309
Hawk 75A-3: s3v, cd, pat, col, pph: AE D 71 1/7:376
Curtiss Hawk III: phan, pph; 1934 dive bomber: AE O 72 3/4:196-197
Curtiss P-36A Hawk: 3v, cd, pat; 1938 fighter: Sc D 71 2/12: 660-661
Grumman F3F-1: s5v, sec, cd, pat, col, det, pph; 1935 biplane fighter: AM D 71 73/6:24-25
Martin YB-12A: 3v, cd, pat, col, pph, var; 1933 bomber: Q O 74 10/2:66-67
Ryan ST-A: $3\frac{1}{2}$v, sec, cd, pat, col; 1932 trainer: RC F 73 10/2: 60-61
Seversky P-35A: s$3\frac{1}{2}$v, cd, pat, col; 1940 fighter: Q Jl 73 7/3:96
Thomas-Morse S4C Scout: 3v, sec, cd, pat, pph; 1920 scout: Sc Jl 73 4/7:482-483
Vultee V-11-GB: phan; 1935 dive bomber: AE Jl 72 3/1:40-41
Vultee V-12-C: phan; 1939 dive bomber: AE Jl 72 3/1:39

(Yugoslavia Military)

Ikarus IK-2: 3v, sec, cd, pat, col; 1937 fighter: Q Au 75 11/1:2

World War II

(Australia)

Commonwealth Boomerang: phan, pph; 1942 fighter: AE F 72 2/2: 94-95
Commonwealth CA-15: 4v, sec, struc, cd, pat, col; 1945 fighter prototype: MAN F 74 88/2:56-57; 5v, cd, int, var: Mr 74 88/3:51-52
Commonwealth Wirraway: $3\frac{1}{2}$v, sec, cd, pat, col, pph; 1944 strike: Aero Ja 73 38/444:41
Wirraway: 4v, cd, pat, col: RiS Ag 72 1/1:29

I. Static Scale 36

(France)

Morane Saulnier MS 406: phan, pph; 1938 fighter: AE S 73 5/3: 134-135

(Finland)

VL Pyörremyrsky: 3v, cd, phan, pph; 1944 fighter: AE O 71 1/5: 274-275

(Germany bombers)

Arado Ar 234B Blitz: s4v, sec, cd, int, arm, det, pph; 1944 jet: Aero Mr 72 37/434:149-153
Ar 234: cockpit, phan, pph: AE F 73 4/2:74+
Ar 234B-2: 4v, sec, cd, pat, col, pph: AM Je 72 75/6:24-25
Dornier Do 17E-1; P-1; Z-2: 5v each, sec, cd, pat, col, pph; 1937 light bomber: AN 9 Je 72 1/2:8-9
Dornier Do 217K-1: s3v, cd, pat, phan, cockpit; light bomber: AI My 75 8/5:234-236+
Focke Wulf Fw 200C-3 Condor: s3v, cd, pat, cockpit, phan, pph; bomber conv of airliner: AE S 74 7/3:145-147
Heinkel He 111H-2: 5v, sec, cd, pat, col, sk, pph; medium bomber: Sc S 71 2/9:478-481
He 111H-3: phan, cockpit, pph: AE N 73 5/5:233-235
Heinkel He 177 Greif: cockpit: medium bomber: Sc Je 74 5/57: 326
He 177A-3/R2: all gun position sk: RT Je 72 5/6:64-66
He 177A-5: phan, cockpit: AI Ap 75 8/4:180-183
Heinkel He 277B-5/R2: 3v, cd; four-engine: RT S 74 7/9:102-103
Junkers Ju 87B: IP, sk; dive bomber: PAM Ap 74 5:74
Ju 87B: 4v, sec, cd, pat, col: RCS D 75 1/8:(40-41)
Ju 87D-3: s3v, cd, pat, col, pph; D-1: phan: AI Jl 74 7/1:20-22
Junkers Ju 88A-4: 5v, sec, cd, pat, col; medium bomber: AN 3 Ag 73 2/6:8-9
Ju 88G: s3v, cd, pat, phan, pph: AI D 75 9/6:285-287
Ju 88H-1; P v1; A-14; P-1; A-15; A-17; B-0; S-1; A-4/Bf 109F Mistel S1: 1v, cd, each: AN 3 Ag 73 2/6:8-9
Junkers Ju 188A-2: 3v, cd, pat; 1942 medium bomber: Afx F 72 13/6:322+
Ju 188E-1: $3\frac{1}{2}\frac{1}{2}\frac{1}{2}$v, sec, cd, pat, col, det, pph: Sc Je 75 6/69: 284-287+
Junkers Ju 287 V-1: 2v, pph; four-engine jet: AM Je 72 75/6:44

(Germany fighters)

Bachem Ba 349A Natter: phan; rocket interseptor: AE S 71 1/4: 206-207
Ba 349A: 2v, cd, sk, launch tower: Q Ap 71 6/2:18-19
Dornier Do 217N-2: phan; night fighter: AI S 75 9/3:130-131

Aircraft

Dornier Do 335A-0 Pfeil: 4v, sec, cd; 1943 CLT fighter: PAM Mr 75 9:143
Do 335A-10; A: 1v, cd, each: PAM Mr 75 9:143
Do 335B-2P: s3v, cd, pat, phan, pph: AE Ja 73 4/1:18-21
Do 335B-4: 4v, sec, cd: PAM Mr 75 9:143
Do 335 V-1; V-3; V-13; A-0; A-12; A-5; B: 6v, sec, cd, pat, col, int, det, phan, pph: Sc Jl 76 6/70:350-357; cor A-10, A-11; Ap 76 7/79:(179); cor Jl 76 7/82:330
Focke Wulf Fw 190: IP, exhausts, LG doors, gun muzzles, step: IM Jl 71 8/7:16
Fw 190A-3: cockpit: IM My 71 8/5:16
Fw 190A-8/R1: struc, phan, cockpit, det: RT Ap 73 6/4:35+
Fw 190B: s3v, cd: WWE S 74 1/5:129
Fw 190B-0 Kanguruh: s3v, cd: WWE N 74 1/6:169
Fw 190F-8: s3v, cd: WWE S 74 1/5:129
Fw 190V-1: 3v, cd: WWE N 74 1/6:169
Heinkel He 162 Volksjäger: s3v, cd, pat, phan, pph; 1944 jet: AE Je 72 2/6:297-299
He 162A-2: 5v, sec, cd, pat, col; 1945 var: AN 29 Mr 74 2/22:8-9
Heinkel He 219 Uhu: s3v, cd, pat, phan, cockpit; night fighter: AI Jl 75 9/1:24+
He 219A-2; A-0: s3v, sec, cd, pat, col, cockpit, int, det, pph: RT D 71 4/12:138-143
He 219A-5/R1; B-2; A-0; A5/R4: 1v, cd, each: AN 23 Ag 74 3/6:8-9
He 219A-7/R4: 5v, sec, cd, pat, col, pph: AN 23 Ag 74 3/6:8-9
Messerschmitt Bf 109E: cockpit: IM F 71 8/2:8-9
Bf 109E: cockpit, LG det: Sc F 72 3/2:110-111+
Bf 109G-14/U4: phan, pph: AE Je 73 4/6:302
Bf 109K: s2v, sec, cockpit: Q Ap 71 6/2:8
Messerschmitt Bf 110C-4: cockpit; 1939 twin-engine fighter: PAM O 73 3:42
Bf 110G-4b/R3: phan, IP: AE O 73 5/4:178-181
Bf 110G4/R: night fighter details: RT S 71 4/9:102
Messerschmitt Me 163 Komet: phan; rocket fighter: Sc Mr 74 5/54:154-155
Me 163B-1a: s3v, cd, pat, phan, pph: AE S 72 3/3:132-133+
Messerschmitt Me 262 Schwalbe: s3v, cd, pat, cockpit, phan, pph; 1944 twin jet fighter: AE N 72 3/5:243-246
Me 262: V-1; V-2; A1V1; B-2a: 1v, cd, each; A2a/U2; A1/U1: $\frac{1}{2}$v, cd, each: IM Mr 73 10/3:16
Me 262A-1a/U1: s3v, cd; WW2J 2/4:12
Me 262B-1a: s3v, cd: WW2J 2/4:12

(Germany other aircraft)

Arado Ar 96B-5: 5v, sec, cd, pat, col, pph; 1938 trainer: AN 13 Ap 73 1/25:8-9
Fiesler Aerodyamische Versuchsanstalt AF 2: 3v, cd, pat, col; boundery layer experiments: MW F 73 1/6:293
Fieseler Fi 156C Storch: 5v, cd, pat, col, det, pph; 1935 STOL

I. Static Scale 38

light-plane: MW Ja 73 1/5:234-239
Fi 156C: 3v, cd, pat, col, pph: Afx Ja 75 16/5:291
Focke Wulf Fw 189A: crew compartments sk; 1938 twin-boom observation: IM My 73 1/6:293
Fw 189A-1: 3v, cd, pat, col, pph: MW Ag 73 1/12:631-632; int, det: N 73 2/3:123-128
Fw 189A-2: cockpit, phan, pph: AI O 74 7/4:184-185+
Junkers Ju 53/3m g4e (MS): $3\frac{1}{2}$v, cd, pat, col, pph; minesweeping var of tri-motor airliner: AN 3 O 75 4/9:8-9
Ju 53/3m g7r: phan; military transport var: AI O 75 9/4:182-183

(Italy)

Caproni 311A: phan; recon/bomber: AE Jl 71 1/2:100-101
Fiat G. 50 Freccia: 3v, cd, pat, col, pph; 1938 fighter: Afx Mr 74 15/7:403-405
Fiat G. 55/I Centauro: s3v, cd, pat, col, phan, pph; 1942 fighter: AE My 74 6/5:234+
Maachi C. 202 Folgore: 4v, sec, cd, pat, IP, pph: 1941 fighter: Aero Je 72 13/10:334-336
Maachi C. 202/III: s3v, cd, pat, col, phan, pph: AE Ja 72 2/1: 18-23
Maachi C. 202/IX: s2v, cd, pat, col: RT Jl 72 5/7:73
Maachi C. 205 Veltro: s3v, cd, pat, col, det; 1944 fighter: RT D 72 5/12:138
Reggiane Re. 2001 Falco II: 6v, sec, cd, pat, col, pph; 1940 fighter: AN 11 Jl 75 4/3:13
Savioa Marchetti SM 79 Sr I: crew stations, LG & door det; tri-motor transport: RT N 74 7/11:124-125
Savioa Marchetti SM 82 Marsupiale: 3v, sec, struc, cd, pat, col, pph: twin engine transport: AN 13 Je 75 4/1:8-9

(Japan)

Aichi E13A1 Jake: cockpit; float recon; RT O 72 5/10:117
Kawanishi E15K1 Shiun Norm: s3v, cd, pat, col; 1943 float fighter: RT My 73 6/5:53
Kawanishi N1K1-J Shinden-Kai George: s3v, cd, pat, col, phan, pph; 1942 fighter: AE Ap 73 4/4:180+
Kawasaki Ki-45 Toryu Nick: IP, cockpit, LG det, arm, pph; 1942 twin-engine fighter: IM Ag 73 10/8:14-15
Ki-45-Kai: 2v, gunbay det: Q O 73 8/4:211
Ki-45-Kai-Hei: phan: AE N 73 5/5:228-229
Kawasaki Ki-61-I-Kai-hei Hien Tony: phan: 1942 fighter: AI Ag 75 9/2:80-81
Ki-61-IIA: 5v, sec, cd, pat, col, pph: AN 1 F 74 2/18:8-9
Ki-61-II-Kai: s3v, cd, pat, tcol: Q O 73 8/4:213
Ki-61-III; I: 1v, cd, each: AN 1 F 74 2/18:8-9
Mitsubishi J2M3 Raiden Jack: s3v, cd, pat, col, phan, pph; 1943 fighter: AE Jl 1/2:69-71
Nakajima B5N2 Kate: s2v, cd, pat, col, int, antennae; carrier tor-

Aircraft

    pedo bomber: RT Ja 72 5/1:1+
Nakajima Ki-44 Shoki Tojo: cockpit; fighter: RT N 72 5/11:131
Ki-44-II Otsu: s3v, cd, pat, col, phan, pph: 1942 var: AE Jl 72 3/1:22-24
Ohka: 4v, cd, pat, col, int, phan; manned bomb: RiS Su 73 1/4: 136-137

(Sweden)

FFVS J-22: 5v, cd, pat, col; 1944 fighter: IM My 74 10/(16):9-10

(USSR)

Anatov A-7: 3v, sec, struc, cd, int, IP; troop glider: RT Ap 74 7/4:44
BI: s3v, cd, pat, col, phan, pph; 1943 rocket fighter: AE D 73 5/6:285-286
Ilyushin Il-2: 4v, int, det, pph; 1939 ground-support: Sc Ap 74 5/55:193+
Ilyushin Il-10: 4v, sec, cd; 1944 ground-support: RT F 72 5/2: 20
Il-10: 1v, int: RT O 73 6/10:111
Il-10: IP, arm, det: Sc My 72 3/5:260-261
Lavochkin La-5FN: 5v, sec, cd, pat, col; 1943 fighter: Aero Ap 71 36/423:190-193
Lavochkin La-7 & 7UTI: 5v, sec, cd, pat, col, pph; 1944 fighter & trainer: Aero Ap 71 36/423:190-193
Lisunov Li-2: 6v, sec, cd, pat, col, pph; armed, license-built DC-3: AN 12 D 75 4/14:8-9
MiG 3: s3v, cd, pat, col, phan, pph; 1940 fighter: AE O 71 1/5: 251-257
Sukhoi Su-5 prototype: s3v, sec, cd, pat, tcol; 1944 prop & jet fighter: WW2J S 75 2/5-6:30
Su-5: s3v, sec, int, IP, cd, pat, tcol: WW2J S 75 2/5-6:31
Yak-1: s3v, cd, pat, phan; 1942 fighter: AI Je 75 8/6:300-301+
Yak-3: s3v, cd, phan; 1943 fighter: AI N 75 9/5:233-235
Yak-9 U; P; D; DD; T; M: 10v, sec, cd, pat, col, pph; 1942 fighter: Aero D 71 36/431:696-699
Yak-9P: phan: AI N 75 9/5:236-237

(U.K. bombers)

Armstrong Whitworth AW 41 Albermarle: 2v, IP, cockpit: 1938 light bomber: PAM O 73 3:34
Avro Lincoln: nose, nacelles, int sk; 1944 four engine heavy bomber: Q O 73 8/4:247
Lincoln B. 2: 5v, sec, cd, pat, col, pph: AN 28 Je 74 3/2:8-10
Bristol Beaufighter TF Mk X: s3v, cd, pat, cockpit; 1944 torpedo bomber: AE Mr 74 6/3:128+
Beaufighter Mk X: 1v, cd, torpedo installation: AN 13 Ap 73 1/24: 8-10

I. Static Scale

Bristol Bombay: $4\frac{1}{2}$v, sec, cd, pat, col, pph; 1939 light bomber: AN 23 N 73 2/14:8-9
Fairey Albacore: 6v, sec, cd, pat, col, pph; biplane torpedo bomber: AN 22 Ag 75 4/6:8-9
Albacore: 3v, cd, pat, col, pph: MW S 72 1/1:22-23
Fairey Barracuda: phan; 1942 carrier bomber: Sc D 72 3/12:657
Barracuda Mk II: 5v, sec, cd, pat, col, pph; 1942 ASW var: AN 4 Ja 74 2/16:8-9
Barracuda Mk III; V: 1v, cd, each: AN 4 Ja 74 2/16:8-9
Handley Page Hampden TB Mk I: s3v, cd, pat, pph; torpedo bomber var: AE S 71 1/4:199
Short Stirling B.1: s3v, sec, cd, pat, col, pph; 1940 four-engine heavy: AN 19 Ja 73 1/18:8-9
Stirling Mk I: cockpit: IM Ag 73 10/8:17
Vickers Wellington Mk Ic: $4\frac{1}{2}$v, sec, cd, pat, col, pph; 1938 medium bomber: AN 4 Ag 72 1/6:8-9
Wellington Mk X; XIV; XVIII; II: 1v, cd, each: AN 4 Ag 72 1/6:8-9

(U.K. fighters)

Bristol Beaufighter Mk IF: phan, pph; 1940 twin-engine fighter: AE Ja 74 6/1:28-29
Beaufighter Mk IF: s3v, sec, cd, pat, col, phan, int, pph: Sc My 74 5/60:260-261+
Beaufighter Mk II; VIC: 1v, cd, each; AN 13 Ap 73 1/24:8-10
Beaufighter Mk VI: $4\frac{1}{2}$v, cd, pat, col, pph: AN 14 Ap 73 1/24:8/10
Beaufighter TF Mk X: s3v, cd, pat, cockpit; 1944 torpedo fighter-bomber var: AE Mr 74 6/3:128+
Boulton Paul Defiant IA: 5v, sec, cd, pat, col, pph; 1937 turret fighter: AN 10 My 74 2/25:8-10
Defiant II NF; IA NF; I: 1v, cd, each: AN 10 My 74 2/25:8-10
Fairey Firefly F.Mk I: s3v, cd, pat, phan, pph; 1943 carrier fighter: AE Mr 72 2/3:142-144
Hawker Hurricane FH.40 slipwing: 4v, cd, pat; ferry variant biplane: AM Ja 75 75/1:73
Hawker Sea Hurricane Mk X: 5v, cd, pat, col; 1942 Canadian Car & Foundry built var: RT O 72 5/10:114
Hawker Tempest Mk I-VI: $8\frac{1}{2}\frac{1}{2}\frac{1}{2}\frac{1}{2}\frac{1}{2}\frac{1}{2}$v, sec, struc, cd, pat, col, sten, int, acc, det, phan, pph; 1942 single-engine heavy fighters: Sc F 73 4/2:93-100
Hawker Typhoon: $2\frac{1}{2}$v, struc, eng, arm, pph; 1941 single-engine heavy: Sc F 74 5/2:81
Typhoon prototype: 1v, cd, pat, col: Sc N 75 6/74:544
Typhoon Mk Ia: 1v, cd, pat, col: Sc N 75 6/74:544
Typhoon F.Mk IB: phan: AE Ag 72 3/2:94-95
Typhoon Mk IB: 6v, sec, struc, cd, pat, col, int, arm, det, pph: Sc N 75 6/74:543-545
Supermarine Seafire Mk XV: 5v, sec, cd, pat, col; 1944 carrier var of Spitfire: RT Jl 74 7/7:80
Supermarine Spitfire: 2v, cd; float experiment: RT Ja 71 4/1:8

Aircraft

Supermarine Spitfire I: 4v, sec, cd, pat, col, int, pph: Sc Ap 71 2/4:190-191
Spitfire II: 3v, dim, sec, cd; FM Ap 71 409:67
Westland Whirlwind: 2v, cd, pat; 1940 twin-engine fighter: MW Ja 73 1/5:256
Whirlwind I: 3v, cd, pat, col, int, phan, pph: AE Jl 73 3/1:37-38
Whirlwind I: $5\frac{1}{2}\frac{1}{2}$v, sec, cd, pat: Sc Ja 72 3/1:38-39

(U.K. other aircraft)

Airspeed Horsa: phan, pph; troop & vehicle glider: AE Ap 72 2/4:214-215
Airspeed Oxford I: 5v, cd, pat, col, pph; 1937 utility: AN 13 D 74 3/14:8-9
Oxford I late production; I twin-tail; I Gipsy Queen IV engine; III; V: 1v, cd, each: AN 13 D 74 3/14:8-9
Oxford I ambulance: 1v, cd, pat, col: AN 13 D 74 3/14:8-9
Armstrong Whitworth AW 27 Ensign: phan, pph: 1941 four-engine transport: AE F 72 2/2:80-81
Avro Anson C.19: 5v, sec, cd, pat, col, pph; 1944 light transport: AN 26 O 73 2/12:8-9
Anson T.20; T.21; T.22: 1v, cd, each; trainer var: AN 26 O 73 2/12:8-9
Anson T.20: cockpit: Sc Jl 74 5/58:385
Bristol Bombay: $4\frac{1}{2}$v, sec, cd, pat, col, pph; 1939 transport: AN 23 N 73 2/14:8-9
Coldiz Cock: 3v, struc, pph; 1944 two-place escape glider: Sc Ap 74 5/55:208
Fairey Battle Target Tug & Trainer: 4v, sec, cd, pat, col, pph, var: Sc Ja 71 2/1:36
Short Stirling C.V: s3v, sec, cd, pat, col, pph; 1945 transport mod: AN 19 Ja 73 1/18:8-9
Westland Lysander I & III: 4v, sec, cd, pat, col, pph; 1938 observation: AN 27 Je 75 4/2:8-9
Lysander Mk I, II, III, IIIa: 6v, sec, struc, cd, pat, col, det, phan, pph: Sc F 74 5/2:111-113
Lysander Mk III special duties: 1v, cd, pat, col: AN 27 Je 75 4/2:8-9
Lysander P.12: 3v, sec, cd, pat, col; tandem-wing experiment: AN 27 Je 75 4/2:8-9
Lysander TT Mk III (target tug); Mk II; Mk I (glider tug): 1v, cd each: AN 27 Je 75 4/2:8-9

(U.S. bombers)

Boeing B-17C Flying Fortress: phan; four-engine bomber: AI D 74 7/6:282-283
B-17E; F; G: sk: Sc D 75 6/75:602-603
Consolidated Liberator I: s3v, cd, pat, pph; four-engine bomber: AE F 72 2/2:90

I. Static Scale   42

Douglas A-20 Havoc/Boston: 3v, sec, cd, pat, int, det: 1942 intruder/bomber PAM Jl 73 6:84-85
A-20G Havoc: 2v, sec, cd, pat, col: AN 30 My 75 3/26:8-9
Boston: phan, pph: AE D 71 1/7:382-383
Boston III: 4v, sec, cd, pat, col: AN 30 My 75 3/26:8-9
Havoc II: 2v, sec, cd: AN 30 My 75 3/26:8-9
Douglas SBD-3 & 5 Dauntless: 5v, sec, cd, pat, col, det, bomb; carrier dive bomber: Sc My 71 2/5:242-243
Douglas TBD 1 Devastator: 4v, cd, pat, pph; carrier torpedo bomber: WWE My 74 1/3:72-73
Grumman TBM-3E; 3E; 3W; Avenger 4: 4v each, sec, cd, pat, col, pph; 1942 carrier torpedo bomber: AN 27 O 72 1/12:8-9
Martin B-26 Marauder: sk of all crew positions; 1941 medium bomber: PAM Ja 74 9:147+
B-26A & B; Marauder I & II: $s7\frac{1}{2}\frac{1}{2}\frac{1}{2}v$, sec, cd, pat, col, det, pph: Sc My 73 4/5:330+
North American B-25 Mitchell: sk of all crew positions, arm, det; 1941 medium bomber: Q Ja 73 8/1:6-7

(U. S. fighters)

Bell P-39 Airacobra I: phan: 1940 strike AE Ag 71 1/3:140-141
Airacobra: 4v, sec, cd, pat, col, pph: AM S 73 77/3:26-27
Chance Vought F4U-1A Corsair II: 4v, sec, cd, pat, col, det, pph; carrier fighter: Afx S 71 13/1:14-15; cockpit pph: D 71 13/4: 189
F4U: $3\frac{1}{2}v$, sec, cd, pat: MAN Je 72 84/6:52
F4U-1A: 4v, int, det: Q Ja 71 6/21-27; cor Ap 71 6/2:3
F4U-1 & 1D: canopies: Sc F 71 2/2:98
Curtiss P-40A Kittyhawk: 3v, sec, cd; 1939: AN 6 S 74 3/7:8-9
P-40C: 5v, cd, pat, col: AN 6 S 74 3/7:8-9
P-40D Kittyhawk I; E Kittyhawk IA; F Kittyhawk II (Warhawk); K Kittyhawk II; N Kittyhawk: 1v, cd, each: AN 6 S 74 3/7:8-9
P-40E Kittyhawk I: phan, pph: AI Ag 74 7/2:98-9
Grumman XF4F-3; Martlet II; Eastern FM-2 Wildcat VI; Martlet I; XF4F-3: 1v, cd, each; 1939-1942 carrier fighters: AN 7 F 75 3/18:8-9
Eastern FM-1 Wildcat IV & V (Grumman F4F): 6v, sec, cd, pat, col, pph; 1944 var: AN 7 F 75 3/18:8-9
Grumman F6F-3; F6F-3N; F6F-5; F6F-5N Hellcat: 5v, cd, pat, col, int, det: Q Au 75 11/1:26-37
Lockheed P-38L Lightning: 4v, sec, cd, pph; 1939 twin-engine fighter: 4v, sec, cd, pph: AM Ap 71 72/4:30-31
North American P-51 B & C Mustang: $6\frac{1}{2}\frac{1}{2}v$, sec, cd, pph; 1942: AM Mr 72 74/3:34-35
P-51B; C; D: 6v, sec, cd, pat, col, det, pph: Sc Mr 72 3/3: 140-142
Northrop P-61 Black Widow: s3v, cd, pat, col, pph; 1942 night fighter: AE Je 71 1/1:47
P-61: int sk: Q O 74 10/2:52-53
Republic P-43 Lancer: 3v, sec, cd, pat, col, arm; 1938: MAN Mr 71 82/3:70-71

Aircraft

Republic P-47B; D-21-RE; D-22-RE; D-25 Thunderbolt: $5\frac{11}{22}$v, sec, cd, pat, col, det, acc, arm, int, pph; 1942: Sc Ag 71 2/8: 418-420
P-47D-21-RE: 4v, sec, cd, pat, col, pph: AM S 72 75/3:36-37
P-47D: 2v, cd, arm: MW Ag 73 1/12:637

(U. S. other aircraft)

Chance Vought OS2U Kingfisher: 7v, sec, cd, pat, col; 1937 scout: RT D 74 7/12:136-137
OS2U-1; 2; 3: $9\frac{111}{222}$v, sec, cd, pat, col: MAN Mr 72 84/3:14-15
OS2U-3; Kingfisher I: 3v, sec, cd, pat, col, float & beaching gear, pph: Afx Ap 72 13/8:424
OS2U-3: 5v, sec, cd, arm, det, pph: AM N 71 73/5:18-19
Consolidated PBY Canso: antennae; patrol flying boat: RT D 74 7/12:143; antennae & pph: Ja 75 8/1:4
PBY-1: $\frac{11}{22}$v, cd; XP3Y-1: 1v, cd, XPBY-1: $\frac{1}{2}$v, cd; PB2Y-1: $\frac{1}{2}$v, cd; PBY-4: $\frac{1}{2}$v, cd; PB2B-2: 1v, cd, pat, col; Catalina VIA: $\frac{1}{2}$v, cd: AN 1 N 74 3/11:89
PBY-3: 1v, cd, pat, col: AN 1 N 74 3/11:8-9
PBY-5A Catalina III: 3v, sec, cd, pat, col, pph; 1941 amphibious var: AN 1 N 74 3/11:8-9
Curtiss SC-1 Seahawk: 3v, cd, pat, col, pph; 1944 scout: AM N 74 74/11:84
Douglas C-54 Skymaster: s4v, cd, pat, col, pph; 1942 transport: AN 18 Ap 75 3/23:7-9
Douglas C-54M Skymaster: $\frac{1}{2}$v, cd: AN 18 Ap 75 3/23:7-9
Fleet 60 Fort: 3v, cd, pat, col: 1940 trainer: RT D 75 8/12: 143
North American T-6 Texan: s3v, sec, cd, pat, col, det; 1940 trainer: RC N 72 9/11:41
Northrop F-15 Reporter: 3v, cd, pat, col, int; photo-recon var of P-61B: Q O 72 7/4:144-147
Northrop OQ-2A: 3v, sec, struc, pph; 1941 radio-controlled target drone: AM Mr 71 72/3:20-21
Ryan ST (PT-21; PT-22): 4v, sec, cd, det, pph; 1934 primary trainer: AM Ag 71 73/2:34-35

Post World War II

(Civil airliners)

Airbus A300B: phan; multi-national jumbo jet: AE Ag 72 3/2:68-69
Airbus A300B-2: phan, pph, cpph: AI S 74 7/3:130-131
Anatov AN-22: 4v, sec, cd, pat, col; Russian four-turbo-prop; Sc Mr 71 2/2:139
Britten-Norman Islander: phan; British light feeder: AE O 71 1/5: 242

I. Static Scale

BN-2A Islander: 4v, sec, cd, det, pph: Sc Jl 72 3/7:386-387
Britten-Norman Trislander: phan; three-engine mod of Islander: AI S 74 7/3:112-113
Trislander: phan: AI Jl 75 9/1:44-45
Canadair CL-86: phan; Canadian VTOL experiment: AE Ja 72 2/1:16
Canadair CL-246: phan; Canadian VTOL experiment: AE Ja 72 2/1:14-15
Dassault/Breguet Mercure: phan, pph; French short-haul jet: AE Mr 72 2/3:122-123
De Havilland Canada DHC-6 Twin Otter: phan: light airliner: AI F 75 8/2:96-97
De Havilland Canada DHC-7 Dash Seven: phan: four-engine STOL feeder: AE D 3/6:284-285
Embraer EMB-110 Bandeirante: phan, pph, cpph; Brazilian light airliner: AE Je 74 6/6:286-287
Fokker F28 Fellowship Mk 5000: phan, pph; Dutch feeder: AE F 73 6/2:66-67
Hawker Siddeley HS 121 Trident 3B: phan; British four-jet; AE Jl 71 1/2:88-89
Hawker Siddeley HS 146: phan; British four-jet; AE S 74 7/3:114-115
Lockheed L-1011 TriStar: phan, pph, cpph; U.S. jumbo: AE Jl 73 5/1:18-19
McDonnell Douglas DC-9-30: 3v, cd, pat, col, pph; 1966 twin-jet: AN 12 Jl 74 3/3:8-9
McDonnell Douglas DC-10 series 30 CF: phan, pph, cpph: U.S. tri-jet jumbo: AE D 73 5/6:274-275
Republic XR-12 Rainbow: 3v, cd, pat, pph: 1947 experiment: AM N 71 73/5:46
Short Skyvan Series 3: $3\frac{1}{2}$v, cd, pat, col; British light freighter: RT Ap 71 4/4:46
Sikorsky S-61N: $3\frac{1}{2}$v, int, pat, col, pph: helicopter feeder: Afx S 71 13/1:26+
VFW-614: phan; German twin-jet short-haul: AE D 71 1/7:370-371

(Civil executive)

GAF Nomad 22: phan, pph: Australian: AE Je 73 4/6:284-285
Hawker Siddeley HS 125 series 600: phan, pph: British: AE N 72 3/5:234-235
Mitsubishi MU-2J: phan, pph: Japanese: AE N 73 5/5:220-221

(Civil homebuilt)

Acro-Sport: 3v, cd, pph; biplane: Sc Jl 73 4/7:472
Bede BD-5: 4v, cd, pph; kitted ultra-light: FM My 73 76/5:33
Bede BD-5J: 3v, dim, pph; 1973 jet version of BD-5: Sc O 73 4/10:688
Bowers Fly-Baby I-B: $3\frac{1}{2}$v, sec, struc, cd, int, pph; biplane var of Fly Baby: Aero D 75 40/479:1048

Aircraft

Fly-Baby I-B: 3v, sec, struc, cd, pat, pph: AM O 73 77/4:77
Druine Turbulent D-31: 3v, sec, cd, pat, cpph; 1953 French: RC Ag 75 12/8:47
Durand Mark V Biplane: 3v, specs: RCS Jl 75 1/3:13
El Chuparosa: 3v, sec, cd, pat, col, int, pph: 1959 biplane: Aero Jl 72 37/437:392-394
Hiperbipe: 3v, cd; 1973 biplane stunt: FM N 74 77/11:28
Icarus: 3v, dim, cd, pph; hang glider: Sc Je 73 4/6:412
Lloyd Liberty Sport Model A: 5v, sec, cd, pat, col, IP; biplane: MAN Ag 71 83/2:29
Miller JM-2: $4\frac{1}{2}$v, sec, cd, pat, col, int, sk; 1973 ducted-prop pusher: MAN O 75 91/4:67
JM-2: 3v, cd: RC F 75 8/2:46
Osprey 1: 3v, pph; flying boat: AM Jl 73 77/1:37
Pazmany PL-1: 4v, sec, cd, pat, col, Taiwan trainer version: AM F 74 78/2:50-51
Robin DR. 253 Regent: phan, pph; Jodel var: AE My 72 2/5:244-245
Thorp T-18 Tiger: 3v, sec, struc, cd, pph; 1964 sport: Aero F 72 37/433:83
Volmer VJ-23 Swing Wing: 3v, struc, cd, tpat, tcol: 1973 hang glider: RC O 74 11/10:23
Swing Wing: 3v, cd, pph: Sc Je 73 4/6:413

(Civil lightplanes)

Acrostar: 3v, sec, cd, pat, pph; aerobatic: AM Ag 71 73/2:26-28+
Ajep-Wittman Tailwind: $3\frac{1}{2}$v, sec, cd, pat, col, int, pph; Aero N 72 37/442:633-636
BN 3: s3v, sec, cd, IP: British high-wing four-place: PAM O 73 3:40
Brouček W-01: 4v, sec, struc, cd, pat, IP, pph; 1970 Czech sport: Aero My 71 36/424:242-244
Cessna 150 Akrobat: s3v, sec, cd, pat; U.S. high-wing: PAM O 73 3:41
De Havilland Canada DHC-2 Beaver: IP; 1947 bush-plane: Q O 73 8/4:222
Beaver: 4v, cd, pat, col, int, det, pph: RiS W 74 2/2:45-48
Edelweiss Siren C-30 prototype: 4v, sec, cd, pat, col, IP, phan; sailplane: MAN Ag 75 91/2:56-57
Falconer Teal: 3v, cd; amphibian: FM Mr 73 78/3:24
Fournier RF-5: 4v, sec, cd, pat, col, int, pph; 1966 powered sailplane: Aero Je 73 38/449:308-311
Hardy Dragonfly: 3v, sec, cd; man-powered: Aero My 75 40/472:294
IAI Arava 201: phan, pph, cpph; Israeli STOL utility: AE F 74 6/2:60-61
Mooney Mite M-18C 55: 3v, cd, pat, pph; 1951 single-place: AM Mr 75 75/3:54
Morane Saulnier MS 880 Rallye Club: s3v, sec, cd, pat, tcol, pph: PAM Ja 74 4:59-60

I. Static Scale

Piper Cherokee Arrow: s4v, sec, cd, pph: Sc D 75 6/75:614-615
Piper Cherokee 140: s4v, sec, cd, pph; Sc D 75 6/75:614-615
Piper Cherokee Six: s4v, sec, cd, pph: Sc D 75 6/75:614-615
Piper Pawnee Brave: 3v, cd, pph; agricultural spray plane: Sc Ja 73 4/1:20
Pitts S-2A: $4\frac{1}{2}$v, sec, cd, pat, col, int, pph; aerobatic biplane: Aero S 74 39/464:(192-195)
Pitts S-2A: 3v, cd: AM D 73 78/6:28
Pitts S-2A: $2\frac{1}{2}$v, sec, cd: MAN My 74 88/5:72; Je 74 88/6:34
Rollason D-62B Condor: 4v, sec, cd, pat, col, IP, sk, pph: Afx Je 72 13/10:539-540
Ryan STA Super 200 Special: 6v, sec, cd, pat, col, int, IP; aerobatic conv of trainer: MAN S 71 83/3:26
S-4 Kania 3: 3v, sec, struc, cd, pat, col, IP, pph; 1957 parasol glider tug: Aero S 71 36/428:504-506
Scottish Aviation Bulldog: 3v, cd, pat, col, phan, pph, cpph: 1973; AE Ag 73 5/2:62-65
Stephens Akro: 3v, cd, pat, pph; 1971 aerobatic: AM Ag 73 77/2: 41-42
Akro: 3v, cd, pat: AM Mr 75 75/3:44
Thruxton Jackaroo: 5v, sec, struc, cd, pat, col, pph; 1957 Tiger Moth four-place conv: Sc Ap 75 6/67:188
Windecker Eagle: 3v, cd: FM F 73 76/2:32
Yak 18PB & PS: 6v, sec, cd, pat, col, pph; Russian aerobatic: Aero Mr 71 36/422:139-143
Zlin 22: 3v, sec, cd, pat, IP; aerobatic: PAM O 73 3:38

(Civil racing)

Anderson Special: 3v; Goodyear: Aero Mr 71 36/422:149
Cassutt Model 2: 3v, sec, cd, pat, col, IP; 1959 Goodyear: RC My 73 10/5:60-61
Ginny: 3v; Goodyear: Aero F 71 36/421:95
Johnson Special: 3v; Goodyear: Aero F 71 36/421:97
Lil Rebel: 3v; Goodyear: Aero Mr 71 36/422:149
Lil Spook: 3v; Goodyear: Aero Mr 71 36/422:151
Little Mike: 3v, cd, pat; Goodyear: MAN Ja 71 82/1:38
Long LA-1: $4\frac{1}{2}$v, sec, cd, pat, col; 1949 Goodyear (P-Shooter & Midget Mustang): RC O 72 9/10:60-61
Mace R-2 Shark: 4v, sec, struc, cd, pat, col, IP, pph; 1969 Goodyear; Aero N 71 36/430:636-638
Miller Little Gem: 3v; 1951 & 1954 Goodyear: Aero F 71 36/421: 96
Little Gem: 5v, sec, cd, pat, col: RC Mr 73 10/3:58-59
Mirage: 3v; Goodyear: Aero Mr 71 36/422:150
OR-65-2 Owl: 5v, sec, cd, pat, col, IP, pph; 1969 Goodyear: Aero Ja 72 37/432:46-47
Owl: 3v, cd, pat, col, IP, pph: AM Ap 71 72/4:23-24
Rivets: 4v, sec, cd, pat, col, pph; 1964 Goodyear: AM F 72 74/2:24-25
Rollason Beta: $8\frac{1}{2}\frac{1}{2}\frac{1}{2}$v, sec, struc, cd, pat, col, IP, int, pph: 1964 Formula 1: Aero Jl 71 36/426:264-368

Aircraft

Wittman V: 3v, sec, cd, pat, tcol, pph; 1970 Formula V: AM F 74 78/2:54
Zipper: 3v; Goodyear: Aero F 71 36/421:95

(Civil other types)

Canadair CL-215: phan; fire bomber: AI O 75 9/4:164-165

(Military helicopter)

Bell CUH-1H Huey: IP, int: RT O 74 6/10:115
UH-1H: cockpit, seat det, sten, antenna: Q Ap 71 6/2:27
Bell Kiowa/Jet Ranger: 3v, dim, IP, int, arm: RT Ap 74 7/4:41-42
Boeing Vertol YUH-61A: phan: AI Ag 75 9/2:70-71
Sikorski SH-3D Sea King: phan, pph: AE N 72 3/5:226-227
Sikorski YUH-60A: phan: AI Ag 75 9/2:72-73
Westland Commando: phan: AE S 74 7/3:122-123
Westland Lynx: phan: AE Je 72 2/6:288-289
Westland Scout: 4v, sec, cd, pat, col, pph; 1961 army: AN 8 Je 2/2:8-9
Westland Wasp: 4v, sec, cd, pat, col, pph; 1960 navy: AN 8 Je 73 2/2:8-9
Westland Wessex HC. 2: 5v, sec, cd, pat, col, pph: AN 21 Mr 75 3/21:8-9
Wessex HU. 5; HCC. 4; HAS. 3; HAS. 1; Sikorsky S-58T: 1v, cd, each: AN 21 Mr 75 3/21:8-9

[Post World War II Military by country listings begin here]

(Brazil) (prop)

Neiva T-25 Universal: phan, IP, pph: AI My 75 8/5:230-231

(Canada) (jet)

Avro CF-100: IP (both cockpits), seat det: RT Ap 75 8/4:4
Avro CF-105 Arrow: $3\frac{1}{2}$v, cd, pat, col, det: RT Ap 73 6/4:44
Canadair CL-13 Sabre F.Mk 4: s3v, cd, pat, phan, pph: AE Ap 72 2/4:198-201

(Canada) (prop)

Canadian Post War Lancs in Detail: pilot, navigator, radio operator, bomb aimer, flight engineer, camera, sonobuoy operator positions; Avro Lancaster: RT N 75 8/11:126-129

I. Static Scale

(Czechoslovakia) (jet)

Aero L 39: phan: AI Je 75 8/6:284

(France) (jet)

Dassault-Breguet/Dornier Alpha Jet: phan: AI Je 75 8/6:281-282
Dassault Mirage: cockpit, arm, acc, pph: IM D 72 9/12:10-13
Mirage F-1: phan: AE Ap 72 2/4:276-277
Mirage F1C: phan: AI Je 75 8/6:286-287
Mystère IVA: 3v, sec, cd, pat, col: Afx O 72 14/2:86-89
Sepecat Jaguar: phan, cockpit, pph: AE Je 74 6/6:280-283
Jaguar GR Mk I: 3v, cd, pat, phan, pph: AE S 72 3/3:122-125

(Germany) (jet)

Dassault-Breguet/Dornier Alpha Jet: phan: AI Je 75 8/6:281-282
Panavia MRCA: 3v, cd: Afx Jl 73 14/11:592-953
MRCA: 3v, cd, pat, col, pph: AI S 74 7/3:118-119
MRCA: phan: AI Mr 75 8/3:120-121
Panavia 200 MRCA: 2v, cd, pat: AN 18 O 74 3/10:6

(India) (jet)

HAL HJT-16 Kiran: phan: AI F 75 8/2:72-73; AI Je 75 8/6:274-277

(Italy) (jet)

Aermacchi MG. 326: 4v (1 & 2 seat), sec, cd, pat, col, pph: 1966/1957 trainer: AN 16 F 73 1/20:8-10
Aermacchi MB 326K: phan: AI Je 8/6:276-277
Panavia MRCA: see Germany - jet

(Japan) (jet)

Kawasaki C-1: phan; STOL jet transport: AI Jl 75 9/1:8-9
Mitsubishi T-2: phan; trainer: AI Ap 75 8/4:174-175
XT-2: 5v, sec, cd: PAM Ap 75 9:155

(Spain) (prop)

CASA 212 Aviocar: phan, pph; 1972 transport: AE Ap 73 4/4:166-167

Aircraft

(Sweden) (jet)

SAAB J-21R: s2v, cd; jet var of J-21 twin-boom fighter: IM O 73 10/10:10
SAAB J-29 Tunnen: 4v, sec, cd, pat, col, pph; 1951 fighter: AN 11 My 73 1/26:8-9
SAAB J-35A; B; D; XD; E; SK-35C; TF-35: 1v, cd, each: AN 26 Jl 74 3/4:8-10
J-35F Draken: 5v, sec, cd, pat, col, pph; 1960 fighter: AN 26 Jl 74 3/4:8-10
SAAB AJ-37 Viggen: phan, pph; 1964 canard double delta: AE Je 73 4/6:270-271
AJ-37: 6v, sec, cd, pat, col, pph: AN 31 O 75 4/11:8-9
J-37: 5v, sec, cd, pat, col, acc, pph: AM Ja 74 78/1:66-67
J-37: int, LG det: RT O 71 4/10:119
SH-37: 1v, cd: AN 31 O 75 4/11:9
Sk-37: 1v, cd; trainer: AN 31 O 75 4/11:8
SF-37 prototype: 1v, cd, pat, col: AN 31 O 75 4/11:9

(Sweden) (prop)

SAAB J-21A-2: 5v, sec, cd, pat, col, pph; 1946 pusher boom-tail fighter: AM F 71 72/2:30-31
SAAB-MFI 17: 3v, cd, pph: 1972 trainer/light attack lightplane: Sc F 73 4/2:112
SAAB-Scania/SAAB-MFI 17: 3v, cd, pat, sk, pph: AM D 74 74/12:35
SAAB-Scania Supporter: 3v, cd, IP, phan: AI Ja 75 8/1:24-27

(USSR) (jet)

Ilyushin Il-28: s3v, cd, pat, phan, pph; 1948 light bomber: AE D 71 1/7:353
MiG-15bis: phan: AE D 72 3/6:304-305
MiG-15bis: 5v, sec, cd, pat, col, pph: AN 14 S 73 2/9:8-9
Mig-15bis R; 15 UTI; 15 UTI w/A1 radar: 1v each: AN 14 S 73 2/9:8-9
MiG-17 PFU: phan, pph: AE D 72 3/6:306-307
MiG-19PM: 3v, cd, pat, col; 1955 fighter: AN 18 O 74 3/10:8-9
MiG-19S: 5v, sec, cd, pat, col: AN 18 O 74 3/10:8-9
MiG-21FL: s3v, cd, pat, pph: AE Jl 73 5/1:14
MiG-21MF Fishbed J: 5v, cd, pat, pph; 1959 fighter: AE Ag 71 1/3:124
MiG-21MF: 5v, cd, pat, col, arm: Afx D 75 17/4:224-225
Yak-15: phan: AI N 74 7/5:236-237
Yak-23: phan, pph; 1948 fighter: AE My 73 4/5:232-233

(USSR) (prop)

Tupalov Tu-20 Bear: 3v, cd, pph: AE O 71 1/5:266

I. Static Scale 50

(U.K.) (jet)

Alpha Jet: phan, pph: AI O 74 7/4:170-171
BAC Strikemaster: phan, pph; 1968 light attack: AE Mr 73 4/3: 118-119
Strikemaster: Phan: AI Je 75 8/6:270-272
Strikemaster Mk 80: 5v, sec, cd, pat, col, pph: AN 26 Ap 74 2/24:8-9
BAC TSR-2: 4v, sec, cd, pat, col; 1965 bomber experiment: AN 30 Mr 73 1/23:8-9
Dassault-Breguet-BAC Sepecat Jaguar: $9\frac{1}{2}\frac{1}{2}\frac{1}{2}$v, sec, cd, pat, col, pph: Aero Ja 71 36/420:26-32
Jaguar: 4v, sec, cd, pat: AM Ja 72 37/432:22-23
Jaguar Types A, B, E, M, S: 9v, sec, cd, pat, col, pph: Sc Je 73 4/6:402-405
De Havilland Vampire NF.10: 5v, cd, pat, col: MW D 72 1/4: 186-187
English Electric Canberra B.Mk 8: $3\frac{1}{2}$v, sec, cd, pat, col, LG det, sten: Sc Ja 74 5/1:31; add Je 74 5/57:327
English Electric Lightning F.3; F.6: 5v, cd, pat, col, pph; 1964, 1967 fighter: MW O 73 2/2:84-85
Lightning F.6: $6\frac{1}{2}$v, sec, cd, pat, col, arm, pph: Sc F 71 2/2: 84-87
Gloster Javelin FAW 7: 5v, sec, cd, pat, col, pph; 1958 delta fighter: AN 1 Mr 74 2/20:7-9
Javelin FAW 8; FAW 9; FAW 1; FAW 4; FAW 5; T 3: 1v each: AN 1 Mr 74 2/20:7-9
Gloster Meteor NF.11: 5v, sec, cd, pat, col, pph; 1950 night fighter: AN 25 My 73 2/1:8-9
Meteor NF.14; NF.12: 1v each: AN 25 My 73 2/1:8-9
Hawker Hunter Mk V: s3v, sec, cd, pat, col, sten, pph: Sc Ap 74 5/55:201
Hawker Siddeley Harrier: phan, pph: AE My 72 2/5:236-237
Harrier GR Mk I: 5v, sec, cd, pph: AM Je 71 72/6:24-25
Harrier GR Mk I & T 2: 7v, sec, cd, pat, col, int, arm, det, pph: Sc F 71 2/2:84-87
Harrier GR Mk 3: phan: AI D 74 7/6:266-267
Harrier T. Mk 2: sten, pat, col: Afx Jl 71 12/11:579-580
Hawker Siddeley Hawk: s3v, sec, cd, pat, col, pph; 1974 trainer: Afx D 74 16/4:229
Hawk: phan, pph: AE My 73 4/5:226-227
Hawk: longitudinal sec: AN 6 S 74 3/7:13
Hawk T. Mk. 1: phan: AE S 74 7/3:116-117
Hawk T. Mk 1: phan: AI Je 75 8/6:280-281
Hawker Siddeley Nimrod MR Mk I: phan, pph, cpph; 1964 patrol mod of De Havilland Comet 4 airliner: AE D 73 5/6:262-263
Nimrod MR 1: 3v, sec, cd, pat, col, pph: AN 10 Ja 75 3/16:8-9
Hawker Siddeley Sea Vixen FAW.1: 5v, sec, cd, pat, col, pph; 1957 carrier fighter: AN 28 S 73 2/10:7-9
Sea Vixen FAW.2: 4v, sec, cd, pat, col, pph; 1962: AN 28 S 73 2/10:7-9
Panavia MRCA: see Germany, jet

Aircraft

(U. K.) (prop)

Blackburn Firebrand PA, Mk IV: s3v, cd, pat, col, pph; 1945 carrier fighter: Afx My 72 13/9:494-495
Fairey Firefly: 4v, cd, pat, col, pph: 1948 var of 1941 carrier bomber: AM N 73 77/5:74-75
Firefly V: 5v, sec, cd, pat, col, pph: AM N 73 77/5:74-75
Fairey Gannet AEW.3: 6v, sec, cd, pat, col, pph: AN 8 Ag 75 4/5:8-9
Gannet AS 1 & 4: 6v, sec, cd, pat, col, pph: AN 8 Ag 75 4/5:8-9
Handley Page Hastings C.Mk 1: 4v, cd, pat, col, pph: AN 5 S 75 4/7:7-9
Hawker Sea Fury X & XI: IP, cockpit: RT Ap 74 7/4:47
Sea Fury T.Mk 20: cockpit sk: PAM Ja 75 8:133
Hunting Percival Provost Mk I: 5v, sec, cd, pat, col, pph, armed & trainer var: AN 15 N 74 3/12:8-9
Vickers Valetta C.1: 4v, sec, cd, pat, col, pph; 1947 transport: AN 24 Ja 75 3/17:8-10
Vickers Varsity T.1: 4v, sec, cd, pat, col, pph; 1951 crew trainer: AN 24 Ja 75 3/17:8-10
Westland Wyvern T.Mk.3: s3v, sec, cd, pat, col, pph; 1950 prototype: AN 7 Jl 72 1/4:8

(U. S.) (jet)

(Boeing)
E-3A: phan: AI Ja 75 8/1:20-21
T-63A: phan, pph, cpph; navigation trainer mod of 737 airliner: AE S 73 5/3:112-113

(Cessna)
A-37B Dragonfly: phan; light attack: AI My 75 8/5:218-219
A-37B: 5v, cd, pat, col, int, pph: RiS Mr 75 3/1:40-43
T-37 Tweety Bird: IP, seat det, sten: Q Ja 72 7/1:16-19
T-37: 4v, cd, pat, col: RT Ap 71 4/4:43
T-37B: 5v, cd, pat, col, IP: RiS Mr 75 3/1:34-36

(Chance Vought, LTV)
A-7D Corsair II: 5v, sec, cd, pat, col, pph: AN 12 Ap 74 2/23:8-9
A-7E: 5v, sec, cd, arm, pph: AM Ja 71 72/1:46-47
F8U-3 Crusader: 2v, sec, cockpit: IM N 71 8/11:8-9+
RF-8G Crusader: 6v, sec, cd, pat, col, pph: AN 26 D 75 4/15:8-9
YA-7H Corsair II[2]: $3\frac{11}{22}$v, cd, pat, col, cockpit, pph: Q O 74 10/2:56-58

(Fairchild-Republic)
A-10: phan, pph, cpph: AE My 74 6/5:220-221

I. Static Scale

(General Dynamics, Convair)
B-58 Hustler: 4v, cd, pat, col, int: Q Ja 73 8/1:26-29
F-102 Delta Dagger: s3v, cd, pat, col, sten, LG det, int: RiS N 72 1/2:53-55
F-106 Delta Dart: int, LG det: IM Ja 71 8/1:8-9
F-106: s3v, phan, cd, pat, col, int, det, pph: RiS Su 73 1/4: 122-125+
F-111D: phan: AI Mr 75 8/3:118-119
F-111E: 4v, sec, cd, LG det, crew escape module, pph: Sc Je 71 2/6:298-299
YF-16: phan, pph, cpph: AI Ag 74 7/2:62-63

(Grumman)
F10F-1 Jaguar: phan: AI Mr 75 8/3:130-131
F-14 Tomcat: phan, pph: AE Je 73 2/6:274-275
F-14: phan, pph, cpph: AE Ja 74 6/1:12-13
F-14: 9v, sec, cd, pat, col, arm: MAN Ap 74 88/4:72-73
F-14: s2v, sec, cd, pat, col, det: Q Jl 72 7/3:89-92
F-14A: phan: AI Mr 75 8/3:118-119
F-14A: 5v, sec, cd, pat, col, pph: Sc S 73 4/9:620-623
XF10F Jaguar: cockpit: AI Mr 75 8/3:142

(Lockheed)
S-3A Viking: phan, pph, cpph; 1973 ASW: AI Jl 74 7/1:8-9
U-2A; 2C; 2CT: int & LG pph: Q O 73 8/4:72-73
U-2C: 3v, pat, col, pph: AM Jl 72 75/1:33

(McDonnell Douglas)
A-4M Skyhawk: phan: AE D 71 1/7:361
F2H-3 Banshee: 1v, cd: AN 15 Mr 74 2/21:8-10
F2H-3: s3v, sec, cd, pat, col, seat, LG det, canopy, IP, det, pph: RT O 73 6/10:112-114
F2H-4: 5v, sec, cd, pat, col, pph: AN 15 Mr 74 2/21:8-9
F4D-1 Skyray: 5v, sec, cd, pat, col, pph: AN 4 Ap 75 3/22:8-9
F-4K & M Phantom: $5\frac{1}{2}$v, sec, struc, cd, pat, col, pph: Sc Jl 71 2/7:358-360
F-15 Eagle: phan, pph, cpph: AE Mr 74 6/3:120-121
F-15: 5v, sec, cd, pat, tcol, IP, seat det, LG det, arm: Q Ja 74 9/1:8-11
F-15: 4v, sec, cd, pph: Sc F 75 6/65:66-67
F-101B Voodoo: 5v, cd, pat, col, int, arm: RiS Au 73 2/1:15+
YC-15: phan: AI D 75 9/6:278-280

(North American Rockwell)
B-1: phan: AE Jl 72 3/1:12-13
B-1 prototype: phan: AI F 75 8/2:60-61
B-1A: phan: AI Mr 75 8/3:122-123
F-86 Sabre: s3v, cd, pat, col, cockpit, seat det, phan, pph: RiS Sp 74 2/3-4:98-99
F-100 Super Sabre: cockpit & seat det: IM Ap 71 8/4:16
F-100C: s2v, cd, pat, col, pph: RiS Jl 75 3/2:70; add Ja 76 3/3: 162
F-100D: s4v, cd, pat, col, phan, IP, seat det, pph: RiS Jl 75

3/2:68-71; add Ja 76 3/3:162
F-107: 2½v, sec, cd, pat, col: Q Ja 73 8/1:42-43
FJ-1 Fury: 4v, sec, cd, pat, col; carrier var of F-86 Sabre: AN 14 N 75 4/12:7-9
FJ-2 Fury: 4v, sec, cd, pat, col: AN 14 N 75 4/12:7-9
FJ-3 Fury: 4v, sec, cd, pat, col: AN 14 N 75 4/12:7-9
FJ-4B Fury: 4v, sec, cd, pat, col: AN 14 N 75 4/12:7-9
RA-5C Vigilante: s3v, cd, pat, phan: AI N 75 9/5:218-219+
T-2C Buckeye: phan, pph, cpph: AE O 73 5/4:164-165
T-2C: phan: AI Je 75 8/6:272-273
T-39 Sabreliner: 5v, sec, cd, pat, col, pph: AN 7 D 73 2/15:8-9
XFV-12A: phan, pph: AE F 74 6/2:66-67

(Northrop)
A-9A: phan, pph: AE Ja 73 4/1:10-11
F-5E Tiger II: phan, pph: AE O 72 3/4:188-189
F-5E Tiger II: phan, pph: AE Je 73 4/6:278-279
P-530: phan: AE Ag 72 3/2:12-13
P-530: phan: AE Je 73 4/6:280-281
YF-17: phan, pph: AE Mr 74 6/3:106-107

(U. S.) (prop)

Cavalier X-22 Mustang 3: s3v, cd: IM Ja 74 10/13-14:33
Cessna O-1 Bird Dog: col, int: Q Ap 74 9/2:52-55
O-1E: 6v, sec, cd, pat, col, int: MAN F 71 82/2:18-20; Mr 71 82/3:49
Chance Vought XF5U-1 Skipper: phan, pph: AE Je 73 4/6:290-291
Convair B-36: all interior positions sk: Q Ja 74 9/1:23; LG, bomb rack & hoist det sk: Su 75 10/4:(144)
Grumman F8F Bearcat: 3v, sec, struc, cd, pat, col, det: 1945 carrier fighter: PAM O 74 7:108-110
F8F-1: 5v, sec, cd, pat, col, pph: AN 10 N 72 1/13:9
Grumman HU-16A Albatross: 2v, cd, pph; 1947 amphibian: AN 29 N 74 3/13:8-10
HU-16A: 3v, cockpit, navigation compartment: RT S 73 6/9:99
HU-16B/D: 3v, sec, cd, pat, col, pph: AN 29 N 74 3/13:8-10
HU-16B (ASW): 1v, cd, pat, col: AN 29 N 74 3/13:8-10
HU-16B: 3v, cockpit & 3 var of cabin sk, JATO det, pph: RiS Sp 73 1/3:77-78+
Grumman OV-1 Mohawk: bay int; 1961 observation: Q O 73 8/4: 204-206
OV-1A: 5v, sec, cd, pat, col, pph: AN 15 F 74 2/19:8-9
OV-1B; 1D: 1v, each: AN 15 F 74 2/19:8-9
Grumman S-2A (S2-F1) Tracker; E-1B (WF-2) Tracer; C-1A (TF-1) Trader: 1v each: AN 22 D 72 1/16:8-10
S-2E: 5v, sec, cd, pat, col, pph; 1951 ASW: AN 22 D 72 1/16:8-10
Hughes D-2: 4v; plywood light bomber experiment: MAN F 72 84/2:86
Hughes XF-11: $5\frac{1}{2}\frac{1}{2}\frac{1}{2}$v, sec, cd, pat, col, int; 1945 photo-recon: MAN F 72 84/2:84-89

I. Static Scale 54

Lockheed C-130H Hercules: phan: AI N 74 7/5:228-229
Lockheed Orion: s3v, cd, pat, phan: AI S 75 9/3:121-123
North American AJ-1 Savage: 4v, sec, cd, pat, col: 1948 carrier bomber: AN 25 Jl 75 4/4:8-9
AJ-2 Savage: 3v, sec, cd, pat, col, pph; 1949 carrier bomber: AN 25 Jl 75 4/4:8-9
North American OV-10: Bronco 5v, cd, pat, col, int, arm, det: RiS Ag 72 1/1:6-11
OV-10A: 4v, cd, pat; 1968 light attack: Q O 74 10/2:80-81
OV-10A: int: Q Ja 75 10/3:115
North American T-28D Trojan: 4v, sec, cd, pat, col, pph; trainer: AN 19 S 75 4/8:8-9
North American YAT-28E: 5v, sec, cd, pat, col, pph; 1964 light attack var of T-28: MAN Ja 75 90/1:56-58
North American YOV-10A: 4v, cd, floats, arm; early OV-10 var: Q O 74 10/2:78-79

Experimental Configurations

Critical Crusader: 2v, sec, cd, pat, col, pph; 1971 NASA Critical Wing experiment: Q Ja 75 10/3:123-131
HL-10: 3v, cd, pat, tcol; NASA lifting-body experiment: Afx S 72 14/1:20
M2-F2: 3v, cd, pat, tcol; NASA lifting-body experiment: Afx S 72 14/1:21
Rolls-Royce Flying Bedstead: 3v, cd, tpat, tcol, pph; 1953 jet VTOL testbed: Afx Mr 75 16/7:419

Aircraft Distinctions

Avia B.534: I, II, III, IV: IM N/D 73 10/11-12:19
Avro Lancaster: Canadian Post-World War II Mks: 10 S, P, R, N, AR, DC: RT N 75 8/1:126
BAC Canberra: 20 var: Afx O 73 15/2:90-99
Boeing B-17E, F, G: Sc D 75 6/75:604-605
Chance Vought F4U Corsair: MAN Je 72 84/6:52
Commonwealth CA-15 prototypes: MAN Mr 74 88/3:52
De Havilland Mosquito: Afx N 73 15/3:172
Mosquito: RT My 71 4/5:58
Douglas Dauntless 3, 4, 5 in New Zealand Service: IM S 74 10/(18):4
The Early Cats: Consolidated PBY-1 through -4: Q W 75 11/2:75+
Fiesler Storch: MW Ja 73 1/5:233-235; F 73 1/6:294-295
Focke Wulf Fw 189: MW Ag 73 1/12:634-635
Grumman F4F-3 Wildcat: four production batches: Q Jl 74 10/1: 41
Hawker Sea Hurricane: PAM O 75 11:183

Heinkel He 70 Blitz: AI F 75 Je 75 8/6:302
Junkers Ju 88 Night Fighters: 12 var: Afx My 74 15/9:516-525
Junkers Ju 188: Sc Je 75 6/69:289
Kawasaki Ki. 60-Ki. 61-II-kai-ko Hein: AI Ag 75 9/2:79
Lisunov Li-2: license-built Russian DC-3: AN 12 D 75 4/14:11
Lockheed C-130 Hercules: AI D 74 7/6:276-277
Lockheed Orion: AI S 75 9/3:143
Lockheed P-2 Neptune: Q Jl 74 10/1:25
Lockheed U-2: A, C, CG: Q O 73 8/4:215
Messerschmitt Bf 110B, C, D: MW O 72 1/2:70-71; D, E, F, G:
    N 72 1/3:121-122; D 72 1/4:178
MiG-21: AE Ag 71 1/3:122
MiG-21: AE My 74 6/5:228-229
North American F-86 Sabre: RiS Mr 75 3/1:24
North American Mustangs & Their Kinks: kink in leading edge root
    on D vs. A,B,C: IM Mr 75 11/2:14
Sepecat Jaguar: AE S 72 3/3:123
Supermarine Spitfire/Seafire var: Afx Ag 74 15/12:70-706
Yak 1 through 7V/DM-4C: AI Je 75 8/6:302
Yak 3: AI N 75 9/5:233
Yak 9: AI N 75 9/5:240

Aircraft Accessories

American Aircraft Bombs: 1v each: Afx D 71 13/4:194-195
Bachem Natter Launching Tower: Q Ap 71 6/2:18-19
Balloon Cable Fender for He 111H: Afx Ag 75 16/12:704-705
Bits & Pieces for the Me 109: accessories & modifications: MW
    My 73 1/9:473-475
Edo Floats: for lightplanes: 3v, cd; Sc D 73 4/12:815 (for 1/72);
    848 (for 1/48)
Luftwaffe Bombs: 1v each: Afx D 71 13/4:194-195
Mauser Mg 151/20; Mg 151/15: 6v, sec, cd; Sc S 75 6/72:451
112 lb HE Mk V bomb: 1v, cd, pat, col; U.K. WW-I: IM Ja 75
    11/1:6
230 lb HE bomb: 1v, cd, pat, col; U.K. WW-I: IM Ja 75 11/1:6

SCRATCH-BUILDING PLANS

Airco DH2: 1915 scout: Sc Je 72 3/6:325-327
Antonov AN-22: foam & styrene sheet: Sc Mr 71 2/3:133-137
Armstrong Whitworth Siskin: 1923 biplane fighter: Sc My 71 2/5:
    231-236
Blackburn Monoplane: 1910: Sc F 74 5/2:98-104; Ap 74 5/55:214-
    216
HL-10: NASA Lifting Body: Afx S 72 14/1:18-22
Handley Page 0.400 Night Bomber: PAM O 73 3:35-36

I. Static Scale   56

Hawker Siddeley HS 1182 Hawk: Afx D 74 16/4:226-232
LVG C. VI: 1/24 two-seat WW-I fighter: Sc Ja 73 4/1:32-36; F 73 4/2:120-122
M2-F2: NASA Lifting Body: Afx S 72 14/1:19-22
Morane Saulnier N: 1914 monoplane fighter 1/48: Sc N 72 3/11: 590-595
North American F-107A: Q Ja 73 8/1:42-43
Panavia MRCA: Afx Jl 73 14/11:592-594+
Rolls Royce Flying Bedstead: 1953 jet VTOL test: Afx Mr 75 16/7:416-420
Zeppelin LZ 38: rigid airship bomber: Sc N 75 6/74:554-558

KIT CONVERSIONS

World War I

Albatros D. II: from Revell D. III: Sc Ap 73 4/4:259-260
Albatros W. 4 floatplane: from Albatros D. III: Q Ap 72 7/2:50-51
Curtiss Canuck: from Aurora or Lindberg Jenny: Rt Mr 71 4/3: 29
De Havilland DH 9a: from DH 4: RT O 72 5/10:118
DH 9: from Airfix DH 4: Sc O 75 6/72:487-488
FE 8: from Airfix Avro 504K & DH 4: Afx Je 72 13/10:566-568
Fokker D. VI: from Airfix Fokker Dr. 1 & Revell D. VII: Afx Jl 72 13/11:612-613
Fokker D. VIII: from Airfix Chipmunk wing & scratch fuselage: Afx Ja 71 12/5:242-243
Fokker D. VIII: from Dr. 1 and scratch: RT D 72 5/12:136
Handriot HD 1: from Airfix Sopwith Camel: Afx Jl 71 12/11:572-573
Morane L Parasol: from Revell Fokker E. III: Sc N 75 6/7:558-561
Pfalz D. IIIA: from several kits: Sc My 72 3/5:278-280
Rumpler C. IV: from two Airfix Hannovers & sheet plastic: Sc F 75 6/65:74-75
SPAD A. 2: from Airfix Fokker Dr. 1, SPAD 7 & Avro 504K: RT F 74 7/2:22-23
Siemens-Schuckert D. I: from Revell Nieuport 17 & Morane N: Sc Ja 73 4/1:22+
Sopwith C115 Trainer: from Airfix Sopwith Pup: Sc Je 75 6/69: 274
Sopwith 1½ Strutter: from Airfix Avro 504K: Afx Ap 72 13/8:462
Sopwith Pup carrier fighter: from Airfix Sopwith Pup: Sc Je 75 6/69:276
Sopwith Pup nightfighter: from Airfix Sopwith Pup: Sc Je 75 6/69: 275
Vickers Vimy Mk IV: from Frog trans-Atlantic Vimy: IM Ja 75 11/1:4-7

Aircraft

Between World Wars

(Civil)

Cierva Avro Autogyro prototype: from Avro 504K: RT N 71 4/11: 130
Cierva C-6C: from Avro 504K: RT N 71 4/11:130; add F 72 5/2: 14
Cierva C-6D; 1926 wingless var: from Avro 504K: RT N 71 4/11: 130
Cierva C-8R large wing var: from Avro 504K: RT N 71 4/11:130
De Havilland DH 4b: from DH 4: RT O 72 5/10:118
De Havilland DH 53 Hummingbird prototype: from Airfix Tiger Moth or Frog Gipsy Moth: Afx My 73 14/9:481-482
De Havilland Fox Moth: from Airfix Tiger Moth: Afx N 71 13/3: 126-127
De Havilland Gennet Moth: from Frog Gipsy Moth: PAM O 75 11: 195
Gennet Moth: from Frog Tipsy Moth: RT My 73 6/5:50
De Havilland Moth "Jason": from Frog Gipsy Moth: PAM O 75 11: 195
Moth; on floats: from Frog Gipsy Moth & Airfix Auster Antarctic: PAM O 75 11:195
De Havilland Moth Major: from Airfix Tiger Moth & Frog Gipsy Moth: Afx F 72 13/6:327-315+

(Military)

Avia B.534 series 1, 2, 3: from KP B.534 series 4: MW Je 73 1/10:532-535+
Avro 504R in Estonian service: from 504K: Q Jl 72 7/3:98; cor Jl 73 8/3:174
Avro 552 Viper: from Avro 504K & SE 5: RT Je 73 6/6:62-63
Brewster B-239; Finnish var: from Revell F2A-1 Buffalo: IM N 72 9/11:4
Brewster F2A-2: from Airfix F2A-1: Sc F 73 4/2:125-127+
Bristol Bulldog TM; 2 seat trainer: from Airfix Bulldog: Afx D 73 15/4:218-219
Consolidated PBY-1, 2, 3, 4: from PBY-5A: RT D 72 5/12:142
Curtiss P-36A: from Monogram P-40 & scratch cowl: Sc D 71 2/12:660-662
Fairey Battle, Belgian var: from Airfix Battle: RT O 71 4/10:113
Fokker D-21 in Finnish service: from D-21: Sc Jl 71 2/7:349
Gloster Gladiator I & II in Finnish service: from Airfix Gladiator: Afx Je 73 14/10:537-542
Gladiator II: from Gladiator I: Q Ap 72 7/2:48
Hawker B-4 (Swedish Hart): from Airfix Hawker Hart/Demon: IM Ap 73 10/2:14-16
Hawker Hart: from Hawker Demon: Sc S 74 5/60:492-493; cor N 74 5/62:616
Hawker Nimrod: from Airfix Hawker Fury: Afx My 71 12/9:458-459+

I. Static Scale   58

Nimrod: from Impact Fury: IM My 73 10/5:5-8
Hawker Osprey: from Airfix Hawker Hart/Demon: IM Ap 73 10/4: 12-14
Northrop B-5 (Swedish A-17): from Airfix Dauntless: IM F 73 10/2:8-11
PZL P. 24: from Revell PZL P. 11: IM Ag 72 9/8:12-13
PZL P. 24: from Revell PZL P. 11: RT Ja 72 5/1:8
Seversky P. 25: from Italaerei Reggiane Re 2000: Q Jl 73 7/3:94-95

World War II

(Australia)

Commonwealth Wirraway: from Airfix Boomerang & Harvard: MW N 72 1/3:146-147
Wirraway: from Airfix Harvard: RiS Ag 72 1/1:28-29

(Canada)

De Havilland DH 82C Tiger Moth; RCAF ski & canopy var: from Airfix Tiger Moth: RT My 72 5/5:59

(Germany bombers)

Focke Wulf Fw 190A-5/U14 torpedo bomber: from Hasegawa 1/32 Fw 190: Q Ap 72 7/2:82-83
Fw 190F-8/U14 torpedo bomber: from Hasegawa 1/32 Fw 190: Q Ap 72 7/2:82-83; cor Jl 73 7/3:87
Heinkel He 111H-8 balloon fender: from Airfix He 111: Afx Ag 75 16/12:701-707
He 111H-8 fender var: from Frog He 111H-3: PAM Ja 74 4:49
Junkers Ju 87B-1: from Heller Ju 87B-2: PAM Ap 74 5:74
Ju 87D/G: all var from Matchbox Ju 87D/G: PAM O 75 11:192
Junkers Ju 88A-5: from Airfix Ju 88A-4: PAM O 73 3:39
Junkers Ju-287 jet bomber: from He 177, B-47, two Ar 234, & conv kit: AM Je 72 74/6:42-44
Messerschmitt Bf 109G-2/R1; dive bomber: from Airfix Bf 109F/G: Afx N 72 14/3:146-148
Messerschmitt Me 262A-2a/U2 bomber nose: IM Mr 73 10/3:16
Mistel: from Frog Bf 109F & Revell Ju 88; from Matchbox Fw 190A & Ju 88G-1; & from Matchbox Fw 190A & Revell Ju 88 or matchbox Ju 188: PAM Ja 75 8:126-127

Aircraft

(Germany fighters)

(Jet)
Messerschmitt Me 262A1 V8 (50mm cannon); A-1/U1; C-1a; B-2a; from Me 262: IM Mr 73 10/3:16

(Multi-Engine)
Junkers Ju 88 G-1 night fighter: from Revell Ju-88D: RiS Sp 73 1/3:91-93
Ju 88 night fighter variants C-1 (V7); C-2; C-4; C-5; C-6; C-7b; G-1; G-6b; G-7a; G-7b; G-7c; H-1; R-1: from Airfix Ju 88: Afx My 74 15/9:516-522+
Junkers Ju 188A-2: from Airfix Ju-88 & Airmodel conv kit: Afx F 72 13/6:321-322
Messerschmitt Bf 109Z; siamese-twin: from two Airfix Bf 109Gs: Afx Jl 72 13/11:610-611
Messerschmitt Bf 110B: from Airfix Me 110: MW O 72 2/2:69-70
Bf 110C-4: from Monogram 110E: PAM O 73 3:42
Bf 110D-1/R1; D-3; F-1: from Airfix Me 110: MW N 72 1/3:121-122
Bf 110G-4b/R3; G-4c/R4; G-4a; G-4/U5; G-4/U6: from Airfix Me 110: MW D 72 1/4:175-179

(Single Engine)
Focke Wulf Fw 190A-3: from Airfix, Revell, Frog Fw-190: Sc D 71 2/12:650-652
Fw 190F-8: from Frog Fw 190: Sc D 71 2/12:652-655
Focke Wulf Ta 152 series: from Frog or Airfix Fw 190: Afx Mr 71 12/7:348-350
Ta 152H: from Fw 190: Sc Je 71 2/6:314-321
Messerschmitt Bf 109E/Trop: from Airfix 1/24 Bf 109E: Sc F 72 3/2:108
Bf 109E-4b/Trop: from Revell Bf 109E: PAM O 73 3:33
Bf 109F/Trop: from Frog Bf 109F: IM Ag 71 8/8:3-6
Bf 109G-6/U4-N: from Airfix Bf 109F/G: Afx N 72 14/3:146-148
Bf 109G-10 or G-14/U-4: from Airfix Bf 109G: IM Ag 71 8/8:3-6
Bf 109G-14: from Airfix Bf 109F/G: Afx N 72 14/3:146-148
Bf 109H-0: from Airfix Bf 109G: Afx D 72 14/4:198-200
Bf 109K-2 or K-4: from Airfix Bf 109G: IM Ag 71 8/8:3-6
Messerschmitt Me 262 V1: prop-powered prototype of jet fighter: IM Mr 73 10/3:16

(Germany observation, trainer)

Fiesler Storch; Finnish var: from Airfix Storch: Afx Ja 75 16/5:290
Focke Wulf Fw 190A-8/U1; two-seat trainer: from Airfix Fw 190D: Afx N 73 15/3:142-144
Henschel 129; several var: from Airfix & Lindberg parts: MW S 72 1/1:11-17
Messerschmitt Bf 109G-12 tandem trainer: from Airfix Bf 109F/G: Afx N 72 14/3:146-147

I. Static Scale

(Italy)

Macchi MC 205 Veltro: from Frog MC 202: RT D 72 5/12:138 or
 IM Ap 73 10/8:15-16

(Japan)

Kawanishi E7K2 Alf radial: from Hasegawa E7K1 inline: RT O 71
 4/10:118
Kawasaki Ki-61-Ib: from Revell Ki-61-I Kai: RT Mr 73 6/3:26
Ki-61-II: from Revell Ki-61 I Kai: RT Mr 73 6/3:26
Ki-61-II Kai: from Nichimo Ki-61-II: Q O 73 8/4:212
Mitsubishi G4M2e/Ohka Betty mod 24J: from Hasegawa & Lindberg
 Betty: Q Ap 74 9/2:84-85
Mitsubishi Ki-15-II: from Mania Ki-15: RT N 73 6/11:127
Mitsubishi Ki-67-I kai; kamakazi: from LS Ki-109 Peggy: Q Ap 74
 9/2:82
Mitsui L2D3 Tabby: from Airfix C-47: RT S 73 6/9:105
Nakajima B5N1 Kate: from Nichimo B4N2 1/48: RT Jl 72 5/7:82
Nakajima Ki 97A: from Mania Nakajima Ki 27 Nate: 1/72: IM Jl
 8/7:6-7
Yokosuka MXY7 training glider: from Hasegawa Ohka: RT N 73
 6/11:127

(Spain)

Hispano Ha-1112 MIL Buchon: from Airfix Bf 109G: IM N 73 10/11-
 12:33
CASA 2111: from Airfix He 111: Afx Ag 72 13/12:659-660

(Sweden)

FFVS J-22: from Frog Fw 190 & P-40: RT Mr 71 4/4:33
J-22: from several kits: RT N 71 4/10:131
SAAB J-21: from several Airfix kits: IM O 73 10/10:6-9+

(USSR)

Ilyushin Il-2M-82 FN: from Airfix Il-2 & Fw 190: IM Ap 72 9/4:
 11
Yak 1: from Airfix Yak 9: Afx Je 72 13/10:556-558
Yak 3: from Airfix Yak 9: Afx Je 72 13/10:556-558

(U. K. bombers)

Avro Lancaster B.1 Special; tallboy bomber: from Airfix Lancaster
 B1: Afx Ja 73 14/5:262-266; F 73 14/6:312-314
Lancaster Dambuster: from Airfix Lancaster: Afx Ag 73 14/12:
 660-667

Aircraft

Avro Lincoln: from Frog Shackleton & Airfix Lancaster: Afx Ja 72 13/5:267-272+
Lincoln: from Lancaster: AM Ap 72 74/4:36-37
Lincoln: from Frog Shackleton & Airfix Lancaster: Q O 73 8/4: 243-245
Fairey Albacore: from two Airfix Swordfish & scrap: MW S 72 1/1:21-24
Vickers Wellington T. Mk X: from Airfix Wellington Mk II: Sc N 74 5/62:592-595

(U.K. fighters)

Bristol Beaufighter Thimblenose: from Matchbox Beaufighter TF X: PAM Jl 74 6:91
Bristol Blemheim IF (A1 Mk. III radar) night fighter: from Frog Blenheim I: PAM Ja 74 4:51
Boulton Paul Defiant Mk. II: from Airfix Defiant I: IM Ja 74 10/13-14:16-18
De Havilland Mosquito NF XIII: from Airfix Mosquito: Afx Ap 73 14/8:434
Mosquito NF XV: from Airfix Mosquito: Afx Ap 73 14/8:435-437
Hawker Hurricane Mk I trop: from Airfix Hurricane: Afx O 72 14/2:76-77
Hawker Sea Hurricane: from Airfix Hurricane: Afx O 72 14/2:76-77
Sea Hurricane: from Frog, Airfix, or Matchbox Hurricane Mk. II: PAM O 75 11:184-186
Hawker Tornado: from Revell 1/144 Hurricane & Typhoon: Sc D 74 5/63:642-643
Supermarine Spitfire float: from Airfix Spitfire & Frog Shark: Afx Ja 72 13/5:273+
Spitfire float: from Spitfire & Shark floats: RT Ja 71 4/1:9-10
Spitfire LF Mk Vb: from Matchbox Spitfire IX: PAM Ja 74 4:52
Spitfire VII: from Airfix Spitfire IX: Afx Ag 71 12/12:626-628
Spitfire VIII: from Airfix Spitfire IX: Afx Ag 71 12/12:626-628
Spitfire XII: from Frog Spitfire XIV: IM N 73 10/11-12:20-21
Spitfire FR XIVe: from Frog Spitfire XIV: IM N 73 10/11-12:20-21
Spitfire 24: from Frog Spitfire XIV: Sc Je 74 5/57:318-321

(U.K. other aircraft)

Avro Anson Mk I: from Airfix Anson: Afx Ap 71 12/8:415-418
Anson T. Mk. I: from Ansom Mk I: Afx Mr 71 12/7:359-361+
Anson II: from Anson I: Q Ap 72 7/2:49
Anson T. Mk 20: from Airfix Anson: Afx F 71 12/6:305-307
De Havilland Mosquito PR XVI: from Airfix Mosquito: Afx Mr 73 14/7:380-382
De Havilland Queen Bee: RC target: from Tiger Moth: IM Mr 73 10/3:2-3
Hawker Hurricane Mk I PR: from Airfix Hurricane: Afx O 72 14/2:76-77

I. Static Scale   62

Hurricane PR IIC: from Airfix Hurricane: Afx O 72 14/2:76-77
Hurricane T IIC: from Airfix Hurricane: Afx O 72 14/2:76-77
Short Stirling IV; parachute transport & glider tug: from Airfix Stirling II IM N 74 10/19:4-6
Westland Lysander I, Finnish var: from Lysander I: Afx Ja 75 16/5:290
Lysander III(S): from Frog Lysander: IM N 75 11/6:6

(U. S.)

Chance Vought Chesapeake: from Airfix Dauntless & Rareplanes SB2U-1 Vindicator: Afx Jl 71 12/11:581-588
Consolidated PBN-1 Nomad: from PBY-5A: RT D 72 5/12:142
Consolidated PBY-6A Catalina VI: from PBY-5A: RT D 72 5/12:152
Curtiss P-40 variants F, K. L, N: from P-40B or E: Afx D 73 15/4:214-215
P-40M & N: from Airfix or Revell P-40E: Q O 71 6/4:35-36
Douglas Boston III: from Airfix Boston: MW Mr 73 1/7:381
Douglas Havoc: from Airfix Boston: MW Mr 73 1/7:380-381
Havoc Turbinlite: from Frog A-20, working light: PAM Jl 74 6:86
Grumman Hellcat: from Matchbox. Frog. & Airfix kits: Q Au 75 11/1:28-30
Grumman Martlet I, II, III, IV, V: from Revell F4F-4: Q Ap 72 7/2:53
Lockheed F-5; photo-recon P-38: from Frog P-38J/L: RiS W 74 2/2:69-70
Lockheed Lightning I: from Airfix P-38F: Afx Ja 74 15/5:295-300
Lightning Swordfish research aircraft: from P-38G or H: RT Ag 74 7/8:94-95
P-38M Lightning: from Airfix P-38F: Afx Ja 74 15/5:295-300
North American A-27, armed T-6: from Airfix Harvard: AM Jl 71 73/1:18-19
North American P-51A Mustang: from Monogram 1/48 P-51B: MW Ja 74 2/5:264-265
P-51A: from Frog P-51 & Monogram P-51B: RiS W 74 2/2:60-61; cor Sp 74 2/3-4:124
P-51D: from Monogram & Airfix kits: RT Mr 72 5/3:34; cor My 72 5/5:50-51
North American T-6G Harvard: from T-6: Afx Je 71 12/10:525-532
Republic P-47B Thunderbolt: from Revell P-47D: Sc Ag 71 2/8:422-423
Col. Kearby's Thunderbolt: from Airfix & Frog P-47s: AM My 71 72/5:22-23+

Aircraft

Post World War II

(Helicopters)

Sikorsky H-34: from Frog Westland Wessex: RT F 71 4/2:16
Sikorsky HH-3F, USCG: from Revell 1/72 HH-3E Jolly Green Giant: Sc Je 74 5/57:314-315+
Sikorsky S-61N airliner: from Airfix Sea King: Afx S 71 13/1:25-32

(Canada civil)

De Havilland Canada DHC-1 Chipmunk: from Airfix U.K.-built Chipmunk: IM Mr 74 10/(15):6
DHC-1 Chipmunk, ag plane conv: from Airfix Chipmunk: Afx O 71 13/2:81
De Havilland Canada DHC-2 Beaver: from Airfix British military Beaver: RiS W 74 2/2:47-50
DHC-2 Mk 3 Turbo Beaver: from Airfix Beaver: IM O 72 9/10: 10-11+; RT D 73 6/12:138

(Canada military)

Canadair CL-13 Sabre Mk.6: from Hasegawa 1/32 F-86-F Sabre: RT D 75 8/12:140-141
Canadair CL-52: from Frog B-47: Sc F 72 3/2:87-89

(France military)

Dassault Mirage 3E; 3R; 5; 3B; 3D; 3BE; Milan: from Airfix Mirage 3C: IM D 72 9/12:2-6+
Dassault Mystère IVA: from Airfix Super Mystère: Afx O 72 14/2: 85-89

(Sweden military)

SAAB J-21R: from several Airfix kits: IM O 73 10/10:6-10
SAAB Sk 35C Draken trainer: from Airfix Draken: RT S 73 6/9: 96-97

(USSR military)

Antonov 12: from Soviet State Antonov 10: Afx Ja 72 13/5:276-279
MiG-17A; D/E; Limm-5, 6 (Polish-built): from Hasegawa 1/72 MiG 17: IM Jl 74 10/(11):10
MiG-21F (Fishbed C); 21PRM (Fishbed E); 21PRM (Fishbed F); 21

I. Static Scale 64

   MF (Fishbed J): from Airfix Fishbed D: RT N 72 5/11:124-127
MiG-21MF (Fishbed J): from Airfix MiG 21 Fishbed C: Afx D 75 17/4:223-227
MiG-21MF; PFMA: from Matchbox MiG-21: AI N 74 9/5:249-250
MiG-21MF (Fishbed J): from Frog MiG-21F: Sc F 74 5/2:90-94
MiG-21PF (Fishbed D): from Airfix MiG-21F: Sc F 74 5/2:90-94
Making a Mongol; MiG 21 trainer: from Airfix & Airmodel kits: Afx Ja 71 12/5:252-253
Yak-15: from Airfix Yak 9: Afx Je 72 13/10:556-558

(U.K. civil)

Beagle Pup: from Airfix Beagle 206 Bassett & Cessna O-2: Afx F 71 12/6:298-299
Bristol 170: from Airfix Bristol Super Freighter: RT N 72 5/11:130
Britten Norman Trislander: from Two Airfix Islanders: MW O 72 1/2:84-86
De Havilland Sea Tiger: from Airfix Tiger Moth: Sc D 73 4/12:812-817
De Havilland Tiger Moth "Deacon," air show mod: from Airfix Tiger Moth: IM Mr 73 10/3:2-3
Tiger Moth spray plane: from Airfix Tiger Moth: Afx O 71 13/2:81
Gloster Javelin Mk 8: from Frog Mk 9: IM Jl 75 11/4:16
Handley Page Jetstream Prototypes: 3 var from Airfix Jetstream: Afx Ag 72 13/12:667-669
Jetstream Mk 1: from Airfix Jetstream: IM Jl 72 9/7:6-8
Jetstream Mk 2: from Airfix Jetstream: IM Jl 72 9/7:6-8
Rollason Condor: from Airfix DHC Chipmunk: Afx Je 72 13/10:538-540
Thruxton Jackaroo: from Airfix Tiger Moth: Sc Ap 75 6/67:190-193
Westland Aerospatiale Gazelle: from Airfix military var: RT Mr 75 8/3:33

(U.K. military)

(jet)
Avro Vulcan B. Mk. 2: from Lindberg Mk. 1: Sc Ag 75 6/71:393-396
BAC Canberra; all 20 var: from any Canberra: Afx O 73 15/2:90-96
Canberra T4; T22; T17; T11: from Airfix Canberra B. 6: Afx Ap 75 16/8:475-479
De Havilland Vampire III; FB 5; I; NF 10; Mk 30 (Australian): from Vampire: RT Ja 72 5/1:70
Vampire NF 10: from Frog Vampire FB 5 & Airmodel NF 10/TT11 conv kit: MW D 72 1/4:185-187
English Electric Lightning F3: from Airfix Lightning F1: MW O

Aircraft

73 2/2:83+
Lightning trainer: from Airfix Lightning: Afx Jl 75 16/11:648-650
Folland Gnat fighter: from trainer Gnat: Afx My 71 12/9:485-488
Gloster Meteor 8; NF 11; TT 20; T7: from Frog Meteor 4 or Airfix Meteor 3: Sc D 72 3/12:644-651
Hawker Hurricane Trainer: from Hurricane & Frog Sea Fury or Tempest V canopy: RT Ag 74 7/8:95
Hawker Hunter T7: from Airfix Hunter F6 & Airframe conv kit: Afx Mr 72 13/7:382-387
Hawker Siddeley Harrier T2: from Airfix Harrier: Afx Ap 71 12/8:412-413+
Harrier T2: from Airfix Harrier: Sc N 73 2/3:756-75
Harrier twin-seat trainer: from Airfix Harrier & Air Conversion parts: Afx Mr 73 14/7:361
Hawker Siddeley Kestral FGA Mk.1: from Airfix P1127: MW Ap 73 1/8:437
Hawker Siddeley Nimrod: from Airfix Comet IV: 1/144: Sc Ag 72 3/8:432-435+
Hawker Siddeley P1040; P1052: from Airfix Seahawk: PAM Ap 75 9:151-153
Hawker Siddeley P1109: from Airfix Seahawk: PAM Jl 75 10:170-173
Hawker Siddeley P1127 prototype: from Airfix P1127: MW Ap 73 1/8:437
Hawker Siddeley Sea Harrier: from Airfix 1/32 Harrier: Afx O 75 17/2:95-99
Hunting Percival Jet Provost T3: from Airfix SL T3: PAM O 74 7:113-114

(prop)
Blackburn Firebrand: from Airfix Skyraider & other parts: Afx D 71 13/4:203-209
Britten Norman Defender: from Airfix Islander: Afx D 72 13/4: 205-207
Defender: from Airfix Islander: Afx Ag 75 16/12:17-19
Defender: from Airfix Islander: PAM Jl 74 6:88-89
De Havilland Sea Hornet: from Frog 1/72 Hornet: MW F 74 2/6: 291
Fairey Firefly AS Mk 7: from Airfix Mk 5: Afx My 73 14/9:490-494
Firefly T.Mk 5: from Airfix Mk 5: Afx My 73 14/9:490-494
Fairey Gannet AEW 3: from Frog Gannet AS1 & Airmodel conv kit: AN 27 Ap 73 1/25:14-15

(U.S. civil)

Bell Airacobra, Thompson Trophy winner: from Revell or Airfix P-39: Sc Mr 75 6/66:126-129
Boeing 707, BEA cargo var: from Airfix 707: Afx F 75 16/6:362-364
Chance Vought FG-1D (Goodyear-built) Corsair, 1946 Bendix Trophy racer: from Airfix Corsair: Sc Ja 75 6/64:38-39

I. Static Scale 66

Douglas B-26B: German civil conv: from A-26 Invader: IM Ap 73 10/4:9
Douglas Super DC-3: from DC-3: RT S 73 6/9:104

(U. S. military)

(jet)
High & Mighty: B-52/X-15 combination: MW S 73 2/1:21-25+
Boeing T-43A: from Aurora 737 airliner: RT N 74 7/11:131
Cessna T-37: from Hasegawa A-37A Dragonfly: RT Ap 71 4/4:42; cor Ja 72 5/1:2
Chance Vought F8C; F8E; TF8A; F8ERN; RF8G: from F8 Crusader: IM N 71 8/11:4-16
Lockheed P-80 Shooting Star: from Hasegawa T-33: MW Ja 73 1/5: 260-261; cor My 73 1/9:495
P-80: from T-33: RiS N 72 1/2:42; cor Sp 73 1/3:94
E4J; E4B Phantoms: from Airfix Phantom: Afx S 74 16/1:32-33
McDonnell F2H-3 Banshee: from Hawk F2H-2: RT O 73 6/10:116
McDonnell Douglas F4B USMC var: from Revell USN version: Sc O 71 2/10:529-531
F-4E Phantom; RAAF standards: from Hasegawa 1/72 or Fujimi 1/50: IM N 73 10/11-12:28-29
McDonnell Douglas F-101B Voodoo: from Frog/Hasegawa & Airmodel kits: MW Mr 73 1/7:363-366
F-101B: from Hasegawa RF-101C: RiS Au 73 2/1:15-19
RF-4E Phantom: from Airfix Phantom & Airframe conv kit: Afx S 75 16/1:33-34; add F 76 17/6:365
North American F-86A-5; F-25; H-5; E-10 Sabres: from Hasegawa F-86F-40: RiS Sp 74 2/3-4:95
North American FJ-3 Fury: from Hasegawa 1/72 Sabre: IM Mr 74 10/(15):10-11
XFJ-2 Fury prototype: from Hasegawa 1/32 Sabre: Q Ja 74 9/1: 20-21
Northrop T-38A, Thunderbirds: from Hasegawa T-38B: RT O 74 7/10:112; cor My 75 8/5:50

(prop)
Grumman C-2a Greyhound: from E-2A, fully scratch fuselage, 2v, sec: Q Ja 73 8/1:36-38
Grumman HU-16A Albatross: from Monogram HU-16B: RT Ag 73 6/8:86-87
Grumman TBM-3W2; TBM-3; TBM-3S: Canadian, French, & U.S. var: from Airfix TBM: Afx My 75 16/9:529-535
McDonnell Douglas AEW 1 Skyraider: from Airfix Skyraider: Afx N 75 17/3:158+
North American OV-10A; OV-10B; OV-10B(Z); OV-10C; YOV-10A: from Hasegawa, Airfix, & Revell OV-10: Q O 74 10/2:76-77
North American P-51D RCAF standards: from P-51B: RT Mr 72 5/3:34-35; My 72 5/5:50

Aircraft

SUPERDETAILING

World War I

Airfix Avro 504K: Sc My 75 6/68:218-221
Airfix Sopwith Pup: Sc Je 75 6/69:272-273
Hawk Nieuport 17: IM N 71 8/11:2-3; D 71 8/12:1
Revell Fokker Dr.1: 1/72: Sc Ap 73 4/4:262-263
Revell SPAD XIII: MM Mr 73 3/3:142

Between World Wars

Airfix Brewster Buffalo: MW D 73 2/4:179
Airfix Gladiator: Afx My 72 15/9:498-500
Airfix Henschel Hs 123: MW Mr 73 1/7:347-350
Heller ANF Mureaux 117: IM S 73 10/9:14-16
Matchbox Prattle's Gladiator: PAM Ap 74 5:65
Revell Brewster 239, Finnish: IM N 72 9/11:4-5

World War II

Airfix Avro Anson I: Q Ja 71 6/1:13
Airfix Fiesler Storch: MW Ja 73 1/5:234-235
Airfix Focke Wulf Fw 189: MW Ag 73 1/12:630+
Airfix Grumman F6F Hellcat: MW F 74 2/6:321
Airfix Messerschmitt Bf 109: 1/24, working stick: RT Je 73 6/6: 63-64
Airfix Messerschmitt Bf 110:   Afx Ag 71 12/12:636-637+
Airfix Bf 110: landing gear bay: MW N 72 1/3:175-178
Airfix Supermarine Spitfire Mk IA: 1/24: Sc Ap 71 2/4:186-193
Airfix Spitfire: 1/24: electrical mod: IM My 71 8/5:10
Airfix Westland Whirlwind: MW Ja 73 1/5:254-256
Frog F6F Hellcat: MW F 74 2/6:321
Hasegawa Me 262: 1/32: IM Ag 73 10/8:4-9
Monogram P-51D Mustang: 1/32: MW Jl 73 1/11:576-579
Airfix & Lindberg Henschel 129: MW S 72 1/1:11-14
unnamed kit Focke Wulf Ta 152H: RT Ag 71 4/8:630+

Post World War II

Airfix De Havilland Canada Chipmunk: IM Ja 74 10/13-14:2-5
Airfix Fairey Firefly: Sc My 73 4/5:362-365
Airfix Hawker Siddeley Harrier: 1/24: Sc Ja 75 6/64:28-29
Airfix Hawker Siddeley Seahawk: PAM Ap 75 5:65
Airfix McDonnell Douglas Phantom: Afx S 74 16/1:28-34
Airfix F-4B Phantom: Sc S 71 2/9:462-465
Airfix Scottish Aviation Bulldog: IM Jl 75 11/4:4
Aurora Avro CF-105 Arrow: RT Ap 73 6/4:44
Frog Handley Page HPR Dart Herald series 200: RT D 73 6/12:146

I. Static Scale 68

Frog Hawker Buccaneer: MW D 72 1/4:199-200
Hasegawa F-100D: RiS Jl 75 3/2:66-67
Lindberg YF-100: RiS Jl 75 3/2:67
Matchbox Strikemaster: IM Je 73 10/6:2+
Monogram HU-16 Albatross: RiS Sp 73 1/3:80-84
Monogram T-28: Q Ja 73 8/1:8-9
unnamed kit McDonnell Douglas F-4E Phantom, RAAF standards: IM N 73 10/11-12:28-29
unnamed kit T-38 Talon, Thunderbirds standards: RT Ja 75 8/1:2

KIT CONSTRUCTION

Before World War II

Airfix Bristol Bulldog: MW O 72 1/2:79-81
Airfix Hanover Cl. IIIa: Sc Mr 73 4/3:176-179
Airfix Roland C. II: Sc Je 74 5/57:304-305; cor Jl 74 5/58:370
Airframe Etrich Taube: Sc S 74 5/60:474-476
Delta Savoia Marchetti S-55X: Sc O 73 4/10:674-679
Frog Gloster Gladiator: Sc Ag 73 4/8:546-553
Hasegawa Boeing P-12E, 1/32: Sc Ag 71 2/8:434-436+
Hasegawa P-12E: Sc D 71 2/12:658-659+
Hasegawa Boeing P-26A Peashooter: Sc N 74 5/62:586-591
Hasegawa Curtiss BF2C-1, 1/32: Sc Ag 71 2/8:434-439; cor S 71 2/9:461
Rareplanes Sopwith Snipe: Sc Ag 73 4/8:534-539
Revell Fokker D. VII, 1/72: Sc F 74 5/2:86-88
Revell SE 5a, 1/72: Sc Ja 74 5/1:33-37
Revell Sopwith Camel, 1/72: Sc My 74 5/56:266-270
Revell Sopwith Triplane 1/72: Sc Mr 74 5/54:142-144
Revell SPAD XIII: 1/28: MW O 73 4/10:92-94
Skybird Siskin: Sc D 75 6/75:610-611
Sutcliffe Supermarine Southampton Mk II: Sc S 75 6/72:437-440
Sutcliffe/Frog Vickers Vernon: Vickers Vimy conv kits: Sc D 75 6/75:606-609

World War II

Airfix De Havilland Mosquito, 1/72: Sc Ja 73 4/1:12-15
Airfix Hawker Hurricane, 1/24: Sc D 73 4/12:822-831
Airfix Hurricane, 1/24: Sc Ja 74 5/1:23-28
Airfix Messerschmitt Bf 109E, 1/24: Sc F 72 3/2:104-114
Airfix P-51D Mustang, 1/24: Sc F 73 4/2:104-106
Airfix Spitfire Mk Ia, 1/24: Sc Ap 71 2/4:186-193
Frog Focke Wulf Ta 152H, 1/72: Sc Je 71 2/6:313-317
Hasegawa Messerschmitt Be 163B Komet, 1/32: Sc Mr 74 5/54: 154-156
KP Ilyushin Il-10: Sc My 72 3/5:260-261
Matchbox Westland Lysander: Sc F 74 5/2:110-114

Monogram P-47D-25-RE, 1/48:   MW Ag 73 4/8:635-637
Nichimo (originally Monogram) Douglass SBD-4 Dauntless, 1/72:
    Sc My 71 2/5:240-244
Rareplanes Fairey Fulmar: Sc Jl 75 6/70:340-341
Revell Bristol Beaufighter, 1/32:   Sc My 74 5/56:256-259
Revell Mosquito Mk IV, 1/32:   Sc S 72 3/9:482-485
Revell Hawker Hurricane, 1/32:   Sc My 71 2/5:248-251
Revell Hawker Typhoon, 1/32:   Sc F 74 5/2:78-83
Revell Kawasaki Ki 45 Toryu Nick, 1/72:   Sc 72 3/10:533-534+
Revell Kawasaki Ki 64 Hein Tony, 1/32:   Sc O 72 3/10:528-533
Revell Lockheed P-38J Lightning, 1/32:   Sc Jl 71 2/7:368-372
Revell Messerschmitt Me 110G, 1/32:   IM Jl 74 10/(17):16
Revell Mitsubishi J2M3 Jack, 1/32:   Sc Je 71 2/6:290-292
Revell North American P-51D Mustang III, 1/32:   Sc Ap 72 3/4:
    198-199
Revell Republic P-47D Thunderbolt, 1/32:   Sc Ag 71 2/8:417-423
Tamiya Lancaster B.1, 1/48:   Sc Ag 75 6/71:386-392
Airfix/Rareplanes North American P-51H, 1/72:   Afx Je 75 16/10:
    585-586+

Post World War II

Airfix De Havilland Canada DHC-2 Beaver, 1/72:   RiS W 74 2/2:
    47-50
Airfix Hawker Hunter: Sc Ap 73 4/4:200-202
Airfix Hawker Siddeley Harrier, 1/24:   Sc Ja 75 6/64:26-29
Hasegawa Convair F-102 Delta Dagger: Sc Je 73 4/6:408-411+
Hasegawa North American F-86F Sabre: 1/32:   Sc Jl 73 4/7:496-
    499
Matchbox Folland Gnat as 9-plane Red Arrows aerobatic team: Sc
    O 74 5/61:538-543; D 74 5/63:673
Monogram Grumman F-14, 1/72:   Q Jl 73 7/3:88-92
Nitto Boeing 747:   Sc My 73 4/5:344-345+
Nichimo Fuji FA-200, 1/20:   Sc Je 73 4/6:398-400
Rareplanes Constellation: Sc Je 75 6/69:282-283
Revell Harrier, 1/32:   Sc N 73 4/11:751-761
Monogram F-14, 1/72:   Sc S 73 4/9:614-619
Frog/Airmodel Fairey Gannet AEW.3:   AN27 Ap 73 1/25:14-15

KIT CORRECTIONS

Pre World War II

Ruch PZL P.23 Karas: Q Ja 75 10/3:92-93

World War II

Airfix Aichi Val: RT My 74 7/5-6:60

I. Static Scale 70

Airfix Bell P-39: IM Ja 72 9/1:6-8
Airfix Curtiss SB2C Helldiver: IM Mr 75 11/2:6-9
Airfix Fiat G. 50: RiS W 74 2/2:67-68
Airfix Ilyushin Il-2 Shturmovick: RiS N 72 5/11:62-65
Airfix Messerschmitt Bf 109G: IM Ag 71 8/8:4-5
Airfix Messerschmitt Me 110: MW O 72 1/2:69
Airfix Westland Lysander: Afx Mr 75 16/7:443
Airfix Westland Whirlwind: Sc Ja 72 3/1:36-40
Airfix Yak 9: RT Ag 71 4/8:91
Aosima Kawanishi Norm: RT My 73 6/5:52+
Aosima Nakajima C6N1 Myrt: RiS Sp 74 2/3-4:118-120
Frog Mosquito Mk IV/VI: Q Jl 71 6/3:24-25
Frog Focke Wulf Ta 152H: RT Ag 71 4/8:94
Frog Heinkel He 111: AN 13 O 72 1/11:18
Frog Ju 87D Stuka: RiS Au 73 2/1:27-29
Frog Messerschmitt Bf 109F: IM Ag 71 8/8:3-5
Frog Bf 110G: MW D 72 1/4:177-178
Frog Spitfire VIII-IX: Sc Ja 75 6/64:20-21; Jl 75 6/7:334
Frog Spitfire Mk.14: Q O 71 6/4:27
Hasegawa F6F Hellcat, 1/32: Q Au 75 11/1:29-31
Hawk P-47D: Sc Ag 71 2/8:412-413
Italaerei Fiat G.55: RiS W 74 2/2:67-68
Matchbox Bristol Beaufighter TFX: PAM Jl 74 6:91
Matchbox Curtiss SB2C Helldiver: IM Mr 75 11/2:6-9
Matchbox Focke Wulf Fw 190: PAM Ja 74 4:55-56
Matchbox Hellcat: Q Au 75 11/1:28
Nitto K5Y Willow: RT F 74 7/2:20-21
Otaki K5Y Willow: RT F 74 7/2:20-21
Revell Bell P-39: IM Ja 72 9/1:6-8
Revell F4F-4 Wildcat FM 2 Martlet: RT Ag 71 4/8:89
Revell Hawker Typhoon, 1/32, prop & spinner: Sc Mr 74 5/54:141
Revell Kawasaki Ki 61 Hein Tony, 1/32: RT Mr 73 6/3:26-28
Revell Ki 61, 1/72: RiS Su 73 1/4:112
Revell Republic P-47D: Sc Ag 71 2/8:417-423

Post World War II

Airfix BAC-111: RT Ap 75 8/4:40
Airfix Boeing 747, 1/144: Q Ap 72 7/2:81
Airfix Douglas AC-47 Gunship: AN 17 Ag 73 2/7:14
Airfix Hunting Proctor Jet Provost T3: PAM O 74 7:113-114
Airfix Ilyushin Il-28: IM Ja 74 10/13-14:25
Airfix Lockheed F-104 Starfighter, 1/72: Afx Je 74 15/10:582
Airfix MiG 21PF Fishbed D: RT N 72 5/11:124
Airfix McDonnell Douglas F-4B Phantom: Sc S 71 2/9:462-465
Artiplast Lockheed F-104 Starfighter, 1/50: Afx Je 74 15/10:578+
Frog Gloster Javelin Mk 9: IM Jl 75 11/4:16
Frog Hawker Sea Fury: RT S 72 5/9:103
Frog Hawker Siddeley Buccaneer S.2: MW N 72 1/3:156; D 72 1/4: 199-200
Frog/Hasegawa Lockheed F-104 Starfighter, 1/72: Afx Je 74 15/10:582-583

Frog Sepecat Jaguar A2/T2: 1/72: PAM Jl 74 6:90
Hasegawa MiG-17: PAM Jl 74 6:96
Hawk Lockheed F-104 Starfighter, 1/48: Afx Je 74 15/10:578+
Matchbox Jaguar S, 1/72: PAM Jl 74 6:90
Monogram Grumman F-14 Tomcat: Q Jl 72 7/3:88-92
Monogram North American T-28D: Q Ja 73 8/1:8-9
Tamiya Lockheed F-104 Starfighter, 1/100: Afx Je 74 15/10:583
Hasegawa & KP MiG-17 with scrap bin parts: RT Ag 75 8/8:89

ARMOR

SCALE DRAWINGS

APCs & ICVs

AMX-10: 3v, cd, pph; 1973 French: A&W S 73 7:34
AMX-10P: 3v, dim cd, pph; 1969 French ICV: MM D 74 4/12:763
APC 302: 2v, cd, pph; MM N 71 1/11:583
BMP-76: 3v, cd, pph; 1967 Russian ICV: A&W My 74 11:24
BTR-60: 3v, cd, pph, cpph: Russian: A&W Ja 75 15:26
FV 432: 4v, cd, tpat, tcol, pph: British: Afx My 74 15/9:512
FV 432: 3v, cd, pph; A&W N 72 2:36
Fiat 6614 CM: 4v, dim, cd, pph, cpph; Italian APC: A&W Mr 75 16:41-42
Fowler B5 Armoured Traction Engine & Road Train: 4v, sec, cd: British, Boer War: Afx Mr 71 12/7:367
Humber FV 1611 "Pig": 4v, cd, pat, tcol, pph; British APC: Afx Ap 74 15/8:460-461
LVTP-7: 2v, dim, cd, pph; U.S. amphibious APC: A&W N 74 14:21
Lancia: 4v, cd, pph; 1922-30 RAF: MM Ap 72 2/4:201
M-113: 3v, dim, cd, pph, cpph; U.S. APC: A&W Ja 74 9:36
M-113: 4v, cd, tpat, tcol, pph: MM N 74 4/11:692-693
M-113: 5v, cd, pat, col: RiS Jl 75 3/2:99
M-113A1: 4v, cd, pat, col: AFV Mr 74 4/10:18
M-113A1: 3v, dim, crew positions: A&W Mr 75 16:25
M-577A1: 3v, cd, M-113 var: AFV Mr 74 4/10:19
Marder: 4v, cd; 1969 German ICV: AFV Ja 72 3/5:16-17
Marder: 4v, cd, pph, cpph: A&W N 73 8:33
Marder: 4v, cd, pat, pph; 1971 ICV: MM D 72 2/12:667
Mowag Tornado: 4v, cd, pph, cpph; 1962 Swiss ICV: A&W My 74 11:34
Ram Kangaroo: 4v, cd, pph; 1944 Canadian APC: MM Mr 72 2/3:127
Ram Kangaroo: int, pph: RT Ag 75 8/8:92-94
Rheinstahl UR 416: 4v, sec, cd, pph: A&W S 73 7:22-23
Saracen FV-603: 4v, dim, cd, cphan; 1952 British APC: A&W S

I. Static Scale

74 13:poster
Saracen Mk 2 (FV-603): 4v, dim, cd, pph, cpph: A&W S 75 19:41
Saracen FV 603C: 4v, cd, pat, col, pph; Belfast var: RT Ag 74 7/8:90; add S 74 7/9:98
Saracen: 4v, cd, pph: MM Ap 71 1/4:197
Schutzenpanzer Steyr Daimler-Puch Saurer 4K 4FA: 3v, cd, pph, 2 var; 1958 Austrian ICV: A&W Ja 73 3:20
Universal Carrier: 3v, cd, tpat, tcol; British APC: S&L Ag 74 3:21

ARVs & Funnies

Armoured Recovery Vehicle 82: 2v, cd, pph; Swedish: MM N 71 1/11:582
Bergepanther: 2v, det; German WW-II ARV: MM N 73 3/11:767-768
Bridgelayer 941: 2v, cd, pph; Swedish: MM N 71 1/11:583
Catepillar D.8 Armored Bulldozer: 4v, cd, pat, tcol: MM S 72 2/5:463
Centaur Dozer: 4v, cd, pat, col,. pph; British WW-II tank-dozer: MM O 72 2/6:524
Light Dragon Mk III: 4v, cd, pph; British prime mover: Afx Jl 73 13/11:598
Sherman ARV Mk II: 4v, cd, pph, det: MM Je 73 3/6:356
Sherman BARV Sea Lion: 4v, cd, pph; beach recovery vehicle: MM Je 73 3/6:355

Armored Cars

(Belgium)

FN 4 RM/62 FAB: 4v, dim, cd, pph; 1965 90mm gun & mortar or 60mm gun & machine gun: A&W Mr 73 4:19

(France)

AMX-10RC: 2v, dim, cd, 1973: MM D 74 4/12:763
Panhard AML with H 60-12 turret: 4v, dim: MM Ja 72 2/1:32
Panhard AML with S 530 turret: 3v, dim, pph; 1969: MM Ja 72 2/1:31

(Germany)

Rheinstahl UR 416: 4v, sec, cd, pph; 90mm recoiless rifle: A&W S 73 7:22-23

Armor

SdKfz 222: 4v, cd: Afx Jl 72 13/11:624+
SdKfz 222: 4v, cd, pph: WW2J S 2/5-6:35
SdKfz 234/1: 4v, cd: AFV D 74 5/1:18-19
SdKfz 234/1: 4v, cd, det, pph: IM My 71 8/5:11-15
SdKfz 234/2: 4v, cd: AFV D 74 5/1:18-19
SdKfz 234/2: 4v, cd, det, pph: IM My 71 8/5:11-15
SdKfz 234/3: 4v, cd, det: IM F 72 9/2:12+
SdKfz 234/4: 4v, cd, det: IM F 72 9/2:12+

(Italy)

Autoblinda AB40: 4v, cd: Afx Je 72 13/10:560
Autoblinda AB41: 4v, cd; 1941: AFV F 71 2/11:28-29
Fiat 6616: 4v, dim, cd, pph, cpph: A&W Mr 75 16:41-42
Fiat 6616A: struc: A&W My 75 17:poster

(Poland)

Kubus: 4v, sk; 1944 improvised: RT Ag 71 4/8:92

(Sweden)

Mod. 31 Light Armored Car: 2v, cd: AFV My 73 4/4:17

(USSR)

BA-10: 5v, cd; 6-wheel: AFV Ja 74 4/9:18-19
BA-64: 3v, cd: AFV Je 73 4/5:15

(U.K.)

AC Armoured Car: 4v, cd, pph; 1915: MM Ja 75 5/1:42-43
AEC Armoured Command Vehicle HP 6x6 Mk I: 3v, dim, pph; 1941
    command post: IM Ag 73 10/8:12-13+
AEC Mk I: 4v, cd; 1942: MM Je 72 2/6:291
AEC Mk III: 5v, cd, pat, col, det: MM Jl 75 5/7:401
Alvis-Straussler type A: MM My 72 2/5:239
Armadillo: 3v, cd, pat, col; 1940 mobile pill box on armored truck:
    MM O 72 2/10:522
Beaverbug: 4v, cd, pph: MM Jl 72 2/7:354
Bedford OXA: 4v, cd, pat, tcol, pph; 30 cwt truck modified into
    anti-tank rifle armored car: MM Ap 73 3/4:241
Daimler Fox CVR (W): 3v, cd, pph; 1970: Afx Mr 75 16/7:408
GKN Sankey Internal Security Vehicle AT-104: 3v, cd, pph: AFV
    S 75 5/6:29-31
Humber LRC Mk IIIA: 4v, cd: MM Ag 72 2/8:412
Humber Mk III: 3v, cd, tpat, tcol: MM Ja 73 3/1:28-29
Leyland Beaver Eel: 5v, cd, pat, col; 1940 armored truck: IM

I. Static Scale 74

O 72 9/10:2-3
Marmon-Herrington "Breda Car" Mk II: 4v, cd, pat, col, pph; 1941: MM Je 75 5/6:351
Marmon-Herrington Mk III: 4v, sec, cd, tpat, tcol: Afx My 72 13/9:505
Rolls Royce: 4v, cd, pph; 1921 RAF: MM Mr 72 2/3:145
Saladin FV 601: 4v, dim, cd, cphan; 1958: A&W My 74 11:poster
Saladin Mk 2 (FV 601C): 4v, dim, cd, pph, cpph: A&W My 75 17:41
Saladin: 4v, cd, pph: MM Ap 71 1/4:195
Shortland AOC: 4v, cd, pph; on Landrover chassis: MM Ag 73 3/8:529

(U. S.)

Cadillac-Gage Commando V-100: 3v, cd, pph; 1964: A&W Ja 73 3:24
M-8 Grayhound: 4v, cd, pph; 1942 6-wheel: MW Ag 73 3/8:629
M-20 Armored Utility Vehicle: 5v, cd; turretless Grayhound: AFV Ja 75 5/2:20-21
M3A1 Scout Car: 4v, cd, pph: AFV Ap 75 5/4:22-23

Artillery

Allied Ammunition 1939-1945: see separate listing
Bofors 40mm LAA Gun: 3v, cd: Afx Jl 75 16/11:662
Bofors 40/70: 3v, dim, cd, pph, cpph; original & autoloading var: A&W S 74 13:33-34
Carriage Mountain RML 2.5 Inch, Mk II: 2v, cd; 1878 "screw gun," animal-packed: MW S 73 2/1:41
Carronade: 3v; Tower of London: MM My 71 1/5:259
Congor: 4v, cd, pph; mine-clearing rocket in gutted carrier: MM My 72 2/5:225
Congreve Rocket Launcher: 2v, cd, tpat, tcol; 1814: MM Mr 73 2/3:163
Creusot 75mm gun: 3v, limber: 1892 Boer fieldpiece: MM N 72 2/11:582
8" Mk 5 Howitzer: 3v, cd, det, pph; 1916 siege piece: MM Je 74 5/1:335
18 pdr Mk 1 Field Gun: 1v, pph: MW Je 73 1/10:536
15cm Schwere Feldhaubitze 18: 3v, cd, tpat, tcol; 1934 howitzer: MW Ja 74 2/5:243
Flakvierling 38: 2v, dim, pph: WWE Mr 75 2/2:50
Hazemeyer Gun: 3v, cd; radar-directed twin 40mm Bobors: MM Ap 73 3/4:236-238
K5E Railway Gun: 4v, sec, cd, tpat, tcol, pph; German WW-II: IM Jl 75 11/4:8-12
Krupp 42cm Howitzer: 4v, cd, tpat, tcol, pph; 1911 "Big Bertha": MM My 75 5/5:271

Armor

Lancia DA 90/53: 4v, cd, tpat, tcol, pph; Italian general purpose gun: MM D 73 2/2:827-828+
Luftgeschütz 40: 2v; German paratroop recoiless gun: Afx F 72 13/6:306-307
Madsen 51mm Mortar: 3v, dim, pph; Danish anti-tank mortar: Fus W 74 1/2:26-27
Oerlikon 20mm on Mk IIA mounting: 2v, cd: MM Ag 74 4/8:465
Oerlikon 20mm on Mk 4 mounting: 2v, dim: MW Ap 73 1/8:423
Oerlikon 20mm Mk 5 twin mounting: 2v, cd: MM Ja 75 5/1:36
PAK 3.7cm; 45mm model 37; 45mm model 42: 4v, cd, pph: Q Au 75 11/1:21
PAK 38: $2\frac{1}{2}$v, cd, det, pph; 50mm anti-tank gun: Afx Ja 73 14/5:257
PAK 40: 2v, det; 7.5cm anti-tank gun: IM F 72 9/2:16
Panzerbüsche 41: 2v, cd; Afx D 71 13/4:193+
7.2" Howitzer: 4v, cd; modified 8" howitzer: MM Mr 73 3/3:154-156
7.7cm Feld-Kanone 96 n/A: 2v, cd, pat, col, sk, pph, site; WW-I German: MW Ja 73 1/5:263-264
17 pdr Anti-Tank Gun: 6v, cd, tpat, tcol, pph: Afx Ap 72 13/8:420-422
6" 26 cwt Howitzer Mk I: 1v, controls, det, pph; 1915 British field piece: Fus Sp 75 2/1:25-29
12 pdr cannon: 3v, sec, cd, det, limber; 1800-1860 field cannon: MM Ap 72 2/4:187; My 72 2/5:246-247
2 pdr Anti-Tank Gun: 5v, cd, pat, col, det, pph; portee-mounted anti-tank gun: MW O 73 2/2:88+
Vickers Machine Gun in Mk V power turret mounting: 3v: MM N 74 4/11:681

(Allied Ammunition 1939-1945) [all RT]

1v, cd, pat, tcol:

37mm: Canister M2; Shell HE M63; Shot AO M74; Shot APD M51; Packing case; Bore brush: S 75 8/9:101
2 pdr (40mm) British: AP Mk 1; Shot QF AP Mk III; Shot, Practice, Flathead QF Mk II; Cartridge QF Blank; Container, Ammunition Mk I: N 75 8/11:124

Edged Weapons

Luftwaffe Edged Weapons: 1934 & 1938 daggers; Officer's sword: WWE Mr 74 1/2:43

Half-Tracks

Feuerleitpanzer auf Zugkeraftwagen 8t: 2v; V-2 mobile firing center:

I. Static Scale

MM Jl 73 3/7:447
Leichter Zugkraftwagen SdKfz 11 Ausf H: 4v, dim, cd: 3 ton prime mover: Q Ap 73 8/2:78
M3: 4v, cd, pph; 1940s Finnish mod of U.S. White: AFV Je 75 5/5:22-23
M3 75mm Gun Motor Carriage: 4v, cd, pph; 1941 tank destroyer: AFV O 72 3/11:18-19
M9A1: 4v, cd, IP, det: IM My 72 9/5:8-9
NSU SdKfz 2 Kleines Kettenkrad: 4v, cd; 1941 motorcycle half-track: AFV N 71 3/3:25
SdKfz 251 Ausf A/B: 5v, cd, pat, int, arm (37mm PAK); 1939; Afx Ag 74 15/12:688+
SdKfz 251 Ausf A & B: 5v, cd, int, det: Q Jl 72 7/3:108; O 72 7/4:131-133; Ja 73 8/1:16-21
SdKfz 251 Ausf C: 5v, cd, int, det: Q Jl 72 7/3:109; O 72 7/4: 131-133; Ja 73 8/1:16-21
SdKfz 251 Ausf D: 5v, cd, int, det: Q Jl 72 7/3:110; O 72 7/4: 131-133; Ja 73 8/1:16-21
Souma MCL Artillery Tractor: 3v, cd, tpat, tcol; 1933 French truck; MW Ja 74 2/5:249

Self-Propelled Artillery

(France)

AMX-13T: 4v, pph; 155m howitzer: MM O 71 1/10:529

(Germany)

Bison (SdKfz 138/1): 3v, cd, pph; 1940 150mm on 38(t) chassis: Afx Ap 73 14/8:422
Bison Ausf H: 4v; 1942; AFV F 73 4/2:18-19
Bison Ausf H: 4v, pph: MM Ap 71 1/4:205; MM F 74 4/2:89
Bison Ausf M: 4v, cd: AFV Je 73 4/6:18-19
FlakPanzer 38(t) mit 2cm Flak 38: 3v, cd: AFV Mr 72 3/7:8
Grille 8/8 Sfl: 3v, cd; 1944 three-off experiment: AFV Mr 72 3/7:16-17
Hummel: 4v, cd, tpat, tcol; 105mm howitzer on PzKw III/IV chassis: Afx N 71 13/3:151
Hummel (mis-labeled Wasp, cor Mr 71 1/3:132): 4v, pph: MM F 71 1/2:85
Hummel: 4v, sec, cd, det: MM S 73 3/9:611
Jagdpanzer IV, L/48: 4v, cd, det; 1943: Q Jl 71 6/3:36-40
Jagdpanzer IV/70: 4v, cd, det, pph; 1944: Q Jl 71 6/3:36-40
Jagdpanzer 38(t) Hetzer: sec, pph; IM S 73 10/9:9-11+
Jagdpanzer 38(t) Hetzer: 5v, cd, pph; MW F 73 1/6:306-307
Jagdpanzer Kanone JPZ 4-5 (Widder): 4v, cd, pph; 1965: A&W Mr 74 10:24
JPZ 4-5: 4v, sec, cd, pph: MM Je 73 3/6:373

Karl 041:   4v, pph; 600mm mortar: MM My 71 1/5:247
Lorraine Schlepper: 4v, sec, cd, eng, pph; 1941 150mm on French chassis: MM Ap 71 1/4:205
Marder II: 3v, cd, pat, col; 75mm anti-tank gun on Panzer II chassis: RiS Ag 72 1/1:19
Marder III (SdKfz 138):   3v, cd, pph; 1942 75mm anti-tank gun on Czech chassis 38(t): AFV O 71 3/2:5
Marder III: 4v, cd: Afx Ap 73 14/8:421
Marder III: 3v, cd, tpat, tcol: MM S 74 4/9:531
Marder III Ausf M: 5v, cd, pat, col, sk: RT Ap 72 5/4:37
Panzer IV/70 (SdKfz 162/1):   2v, cd, pph; MM O 72 2/10:519
Panzer IV/70 (Zwischenlüsung):   4v, cd: MM S 72 2/9:460
Panzer Draisine: 3v, cd; 1941 railway "tank": AFV N 73 4/8:18-19
Panzerjäger K Steyr-Daimler-Puch Saurer 4KH6FA FL-12:   3v, cd, pph; 1958; A&W Ja 73 3:21
Panzerjäger Nashorn: 3v, cd, tpat, tcol: IM Mr 75 11/2:12
Panzerjäger Ib mit 4.7cm PAK(t):   3v, cd; 1939: AFV S 71 3/1:21
Panzerjäger Ib mit 4.7cm PAK(t):   4v, cd, pph: AFV F 75 5/3:25
Panzerjäger 38(t):   5v, cd, tpat, tcol, pph: IM My 74 10/(16):16
7.5cm PAK 40/3 auf Selbatfahrlafette 38:   4v, sec, cd; 1943 anti-tank: AFV D 72 3/12:18-19
Stug III: 2v, cd, pat; disguised as U.S.: Q O 74 10/2:60
Stug III L24:   4v, pph; 150mm on SIG PzKw II chassis: MM Mr 71 1/3:133
Stug III L48:   4v, pph; 1940 75mm: MM Mr 71 1/3:131
Stug IV (L/48):   4v, cd; 75mm: MM S 72 2/9:458
Sturmpanzer IV Brummbar: 4v, cd, col, pph; 1944: MM Je 72 2/6:301
Sturmpanzer IV Brummbar: 2v, cd, pph: MM O 72 2/10:519
Sturmpanzer VI: 4v, cd: MW D 72 1/4:182
Sturmtiger: 4v, pph; 150mm bomb thrower: MM My 71 1/5:245
Sturmtiger: 4v, cd, ammo: MM Je 73 3/6:384-385

(Italy)

Semovente M42:   4v, pph; 1942 75mm or 105mm howitzer: MM Je 71 1/6:298

(Japan)

Ha-To: 2v, cd, pat, col, det: type 4 300mm heavy mortar carrier, 1944: Q O 73 8/4:219
Ha-To: 2v, cd, pph: WWE N 74 1/6:173

(Sweden)

Bofors VK-155 L/50:   4v, dim, cd, pph; 1950 155mm gun: A&W N 73 8:26
Ikv 103:   4v, cd, pat, col, exploded sk; 105mm: RT My 72 5/5:56

I. Static Scale

SAV m/43: 4v, cd, pat, col, sk 2 var; 1943, on 38(t) chassis: RT Ag 73 6/8:92-93

(USSR)

ASU-85: 4v, cd, pat, col; Q Jl 73 8/3:171
JS/D 400mm Rocket Launcher: 5v, cd; 1957: MM N 71 1/11:565
SU-76M: 5v, cd; 1942 76.2mm: AFV Jl 72 3/9:16-17
SU-100: $3\frac{1}{2}$v, cd, pph: IM Je 72 9/6:4-6
SU-152: 4v, cd, tpat, tcol; 1943: Afx Ag 73 4/12:668
SU-152: 3v, cd: Q Jl 74 10/1:8

(U.K.)

Abbot: 4v, pph; 105mm howitzer: MM S 71 1/9:474
Bishop: 6v, cd, pph; 25 pdr on Valentine chassis: MM Jl 71 8/7: 370
Bishop: 4v, cd: MM Jl 74 4/7:382-383
Gun Carrier Mk I: 4v, cd, pph; 6" howitzer on Mk IV tank chassis, WW-I: MM F 71 1/2:83
Sexton: 4v, cd, pph; 25 pdr on Ram chassis: MM Jl 71 8/7:371
Sexton: 3v, cd, int, acc: RT My 73 6/5:57

(U.S.)

M-10 Tank Destroyer: 4v, cd, col; 75mm in turret on Sherman chassis: IM My 72 9/5:5-6
M-36 Tank Destroyer: 3v, cd; 1944: AFV Mr 71 2/12:4-7
M-43: 4v, cd, pat, pph: 105/155mm howitzer on M 40 motor carriage: MM Ag 71 1/8:423
M-52: 5v, pph; 105mm howitzer: MM S 71 1/9:475
M-53: 4v, pph; 155mm gun: MM O 71 1/10:529
M-107: 3v, cd, pph, cpph; 1958 175/60mm howitzer: A&W Ja 75 3:32
M-110: 3v, cd, pph; 1963 203/25mm howitzer: A&W Ja 73 3:32
M-110: 4v, pph: MM O 71 1/10:530

Small Arms

Beretta BM 59 FAL: $2\frac{1}{2}$v, sec, cd, pph; Italian assult rifle: A&W S 74 13:22
Boys Anti-Tank Rifle: 2v, cd; 1937 .55 cal rifle: Fus Au 73 1/1: 24-25
Colt CMG-2: phan, pph: A&W Jl 73 6:21
Degtyarev Machine Guns: 3v, cd, pph; 1929 & 1944 Russian: MM O 74 4/7:600-601
FN FAL: 2v, sec, cd, pph; 1953 Belgian automatic rifle: A&W

My 73 11:20
Fallschirmjäger Gewehr 42: 2v, pph; light sub-machinegun: MM Je 74 4/6:330-331+
Heckler & Koch G-3 Automatic & 7.62mm NATO & 9mm P.B. Derivatives: phan, var: A&W Mr 73 4:poster
Lewis Gun: 2v, cd, pph: MM O 74 4/7:607
MAS 49/56: 2v, sec, cd, pph; 1956 French army rifle: A&W N 72 8:19
Maschinengewehr 34: 2v, ammo case, pph; MM Jl 74 4/7:396-397+
Maschinengewehr 345: 2v, ammo case: MM Jl 74 4/7:398-399
Mauser MG 151/20 & 151/15: 6v, sec, cd, pat; German 20mm & 15mm aircraft cannon: Sc S 75 6/72:451
SIG Mg 710-3: 1v, phan, pph: A&W Mr 74 10:20-21
Vickers .5 inch machinegun: 1v, cd: MM N 74 4/8:684
XM 175 Grenade Launcher: 4v, dim, pph; U.S.: Fus Sp 74 1/3:8

Softskins

(Canada)

Chevrolet CGT Field Artillery Tractor: 4v, cd; 1940 prime mover: AFV S 75 5/6:22-23
Chevrolet C60L 3-ton 4x4 Petrol: 3v, cd, tpat, tcol: MM D 75 5/12:737
Chevrolet 30 cwt GS truck: 7v, cd, pat, col; Sc Ap 71 2/4:198
Chevrolet or Ford CMP: 4v, sec, cd, tpat, tcol, int, acc; 1941 3 ton truck/portee: MW Ja 74 2/5:257-258
Ford 3 ton 4x4 Portee: 4v, cd: Afx F 71 12/6:300

(Germany)

Adler 60/61 truck $1\frac{1}{2}$T 4x2: 3v, cd, tpat, tcol: MM N 74 4/11:691
BMW R75 Side Car: 1v, sec, cd: Sc F 73 4/2:109
Faun R600 D565 Schwerer Lastkraftwagen: 4v, cd, tpat, tcol, pph; 6x4 transport: Afx D 73 15/4:238-240
Henschel Dreiachs Kraftwagen Type 33D1: 4v, cd, pph; 1934 6x4 truck: Sc Jl 73 4/7:489
Horch Kfz. 70: 4v, sec, struc, cd, pat, tcol; heavy passenger car: Q O 71 6/4:37-40
Kübelwagen: 4v, (3 var 1v each), cd, det, pph; 1939 utility: Sc Ag 71 2/8:403+
Open SdKfz IV (Maultier): 4v; half-track truck: MM S 72 2/9:479
Sanitatskraftwagen Kfz 31: $4\frac{1}{2}$v, cd, pat, tcol, pph; ambulance: MW F 74 4/2:329
Sd Ah 115: 2v, cd, pph; tank transport trailer: Afx Ja 74 15/5:294
Steyr 640: 4v, cd, pat, col; 6-wheel communications van: Q O 72 7/4:158

I. Static Scale

Two Wheel Fuel Trailer: 3v, cd, pat, col, det: IM Jl 71 8/7:14-15
Vidal (V-2 trailer): 2v: MM Jl 73 3/7:446-447
Wehrmacht Omnibus Command Post: 5v, cd, tpat, tcol, int: MM Ag 75 5/8:496-498

(Italy)

Fiat 6602 (CP/62, CP/70) 4x4 Tactical Vehicle: 4v, dim, cd: A&W Mr 75 16:28
Fiat 6605 FM 6x6 Artillery Tractor: 4v, dim, cd: A&W Mr 75 16:28
Fiat 6605 N(TM/69) 6x6 Artillery Tractor: 4v, dim, cd: A&W Mr 75 16:29
Fiat 6607 (CP/62 & CP/70 6x6) 6x6 Tactical Vehicle: 4v, dim, cd: A&W Mr 75 16:29
Fiat 6615 AM Light Tactical Supply Vehicle: 4v, dim, cd: A&W Mr 75 16:28
Fiat 6640 4x4 Amphibious Vehicle: 4v, dim, cd: A&W Mr 75 16:28
Lancia 6 RO: 4v, cd, tpat, tcol, int, pph; truck: MM N 73 3/11: 767-768

(Japan)

Kurogane Type 85 4x4 Scout Car "Black Medal": 4v, cd, pph; 1935 "jeep": MM Ap 75 5/4:230-231

(USSR)

GAZ 67A: 4v, cd, pph: MM Jl 72 2/7:364

(U.K.)

AEC 9854 Refueller Mk.2: 3v, cd, tpat, tcol: MM D 75 5/12:737
AEC 0854 6x6 Heavy Artillery Tractor, Prototype, Armoured: 3v, cd, tpat, tcol: MM D 75 5/12:737
Albion CX23N 10-ton 6x4 GS: 2v, cd, tpat, tcol: MM O 75 5/10:593
Albion 350 Gallon Refueller: 5v, cd, det; 1937: IM Mr 71 8/3:12-16
Alvis Stalwart: 3v, cd, tpat, tcol, pph; 1966 6-wheel truck: Afx N 73 15/3:170
Stalwart FV 622 & 623: 5v, phan, pph: MM Je 71 1/6:316-317
Austin K2 Ambulance: 2v, cd, pat, tcol: RT N 73 6/11:129
Austin K3 3-ton 4x2 GS: 3v, cd, tpat, tcol: MM Ag 75 5/8:485
Austin K5 3-ton 4x4 GS: 3v, cd, tpat, tcol: MM D 75 5/12:735+; cor F 76 6/2:86
Austin K6 Breakdown Gantry & $7\frac{1}{2}$ ton Recovery Trailer: $7\frac{1}{2}$v, cd, pat, tcol, pph: MM My 73 3/5:289-290

Austin K6 3-ton 6x4 GS: 3v, cd, tpat, tcol: MM Ag 75 5/8:485
Bedford OX: 3v, cd, pph; trailer tractor: Afx F 72 13/6:318-320
Bedford OY 3-ton 4x2 Laboratory: 3v, cd, tpat, tcol: MM O 75 5/10:593
Bedford OXD: 30 cwt 4x2 GS: 4v, cd, pat, tcol; 1939: MM Ap 73 3/4:241; My 73 3/5:291
Bedford OXD: 3v, cd, tpat, tcol: MM O 75 5/10:593
Bedford OYC 800 Gallon Petrol Tanker: 4v, cd, pat, tcol; 1943: MM Ap 73 3/4:241; My 73 3/5:291
Bedford OYD: 3-ton 4x2 GS: 4v, cd, pat, tcol: MM Ap 73 3/4:241; My 73 3/5:291
Bedford QL Army Fire Service Tender with Dennis Trailer Pump: 4v, cd, pat, col, bed int: MM F 73 3/2:93-94
Bedford QLD 3-ton 4x4, general service lorry: 2v, cd, pat, col: MM Ag 71 1/8:404
Bedford QLT 3-ton 4x4 troop carrier: 2v, cd, pat, col: MM Ag 71 1/8:404
Bedford QLR 3-ton 4x4 wireless van: 4v, cd, pat, col, pph: MM Ag 71 1/8:404
Bedford RAF 15 cwt van: 4v, cd, van int: 1942 instrument repair van: IM Je 73 10/6:8-9
Coles Mk VI Crane: pph: Afx Je 72 13/10:547-548
Coles Mk VII Crane: 2v, cd, for AEC or Thornycraft trucks: Afx F 72 13/6:307
Commer Q2 15 cwt: 5v, cd, pat, col: Sc F 71 2/2:77
Crossley IGL8 3-ton 6x4 Derrick: 3v, cd, tpat, tcol: MM Ag 75 5/8:485
Humber Staff Car: 3v, sk: Sc F 73 4/2:129-130
Humber Utility Vehicle: 4v, cd, pat, tcol, pph: IM Ja 74 10/13-14:9
Leyland Retriever 3-ton 6x4 wireless lorry: 4v, cd, pat, col; 1940: MM Ap 74 4/4:194
Mobile VHF D/F Unit: 5v, cd, pat, col, int: mobile direction finder van: MM Ag 71 1/8:394-395
Morris-Commercial CS 11/30 4x2 Ambulance: 3v, cd, tpat, tcol: MM Ag 75 5/8:485
Pink Panther: 4v, cd, pph; SAS Land Rover: MM Ja 73 3/1:39-41
SAS Jeep: 4v, pph: MM Ag 72 2/8:413-414+
Scammell Pioneer: 4v, cd, pat, tcol, pph; 1936 6x4 truck & prime mover: MM Mr 73 3/3:154-155
Tasker Queen Mary: 4v, cd, det; fighter aircraft transport semi-trailer: Afx F 72 13/6:318-320
Terrapin Mk I: 6v, pph; amphibious truck: MM Jl 71 1/7:257
Thornycroft Amazon: 4v, cd, pph; mobile crane: Afx Ja 72 13/5:257-258
Thornycroft Amazon WF8/NR6/Coles Mk. VII series 7: 2v, cd, tpat, tcol: MM O 75 5/10:593

(U. S.)

Flextrac Nodwell Dynatrac: 4v, cd, pph; tracked cargo: MM Ag 72 2/8:231-232

I. Static Scale

Ford "T" 1914-1918: 4v, cd, pph, regular & machinegun var: Afx
 Ap 71 12/8:421-422
M-548 tracked cargo carrier: 3v, cd, pph: AFV My 73 4/4:15
Mack Tank Transporter: 4v, cd, det, var, tpat, tcol: Afx N 72
 14/3:131
Truck, Utility, ¼-ton 4x4, M-151A: 3v, cd, pph; 1954 Jeep: AFV
 Ja 75 4/9:16-18
XM-761: 5v (1/48), 3v (1/76), cd, pph; 1968 $2\frac{1}{2}$ to 5 ton truck
 prototype: MM O 72 2/10:538-541

Tanks

(Canada)

Ram I: 3v, sec, int; 1941: RT Je 75 8/6:66-67
Skink: 2v, dim, cd, pph: quad 20mm AA on Firefly chassis: RT
 F 75 8/2:18

(Czechoslovakia)

Lt Vz 35: 4v, cd, pat, col, pph; 1937 Skoda: MW D 73 3/12:189
TL Vz 38: 4v, cd; 1938 light tank (basis of German 38(t) var):
 AFV N 71 3/3:7
38(t): suspension det: RT Ag 73 6/8:93

(Finland)

T26E Panssarivaunut: 4v, sec, cd, pat, col, 3 var; 1941 mod of
 Russian light tank: Q Ja 75 10/3:102

(France)

Char B1: 3v, cd, pph: heavy: AFV F 72 3/6:16-17

(Germany)

Aufklarungspanzer 38(t): 3v, cd: Afx Ap 73 14/8:423
Leopard: 3v, dim, cd, pph; 1965: MM F 72 2/2:89
Leopard I A2: 4v, cd; AFV S 74 4/12:18-19
MBT-70 Kpz 70: 3v, dim, cd, pph: A&W S 74 13:43
Maus: 3v, cd; 1944 ultra-heavy: AFV Mr 71 2/12:14-17
Maus: $4\frac{1}{2}\frac{1}{2}$v, cd, tpat, tcol: IM S 74 10/(18):12-14
Maus: 4v, cd, det: RT Ja 71 4/1:6
Panther: 3v, mods, cd, pat, pph; disguised as U.S. M-10: Q O
 74 10/2:60+
Panzerbefehlwagen Ib: 5v, cd, pph; 1935 command tank: AFV F

75 5/3:21
Panzerjäger auf PzKw I Ausf B mit 4.7cm PAK (t): 3v, cd: AFV S 71 3/1:21
PzKpfw Ib: 5v, cd, pph; 1935 light tank: AFV F 75 5/3:20
PzKpfw I Ausf A: 2v, cd, 1935 light tank: IM Mr 73 10/3:12
PzKpfw III Ausf M: 4v, cd: Afx Ja 71 12/5:259
PzKpfw III Ausf N: 3v, cd: Afx Ja 71 12/5:259
PzKpfw IV Ausf D: 4v, cd, pph: Afx O 71 13/2:73
PzKpfw IV Ausf E: 4v, det: Q Ap 71 6/2:32
PzKpfw IV Ausf Fl: 4v, det: Q Ap 71 6/2:33
PzKpfw IV Ausf J: 4v, pph: Afx O 71 13/2:73
PzKpfw VI Tiger I: 5v, cd, pat, col, det: RT Ja 72 5/1:5
PzKpfw VI Tiger I: phan: WWE Mr 74 1/2:38
PzKpfw VI Tiger I Ausf E: 7v, cd, pat, col: MM Ja 1/1:36-37
PzKpfw VI Tiger I Ausf E: 4v, cd: WWE Ja 74 1/1:8
SdKfz 302, 303 Goliath: 3v, sec, cd, tpat, tcol, pph; gas & electric var, robot explosive tank: IM Mr 74 10/(15):2
SdKfz 304 Springer: 4v, sec, cd, tpat, tcol, RC explosive tank: IM Mr 74 10/(15):3-4
Tiger II: 4v, cd: Q Su 75 10/4:143
VK 4501(P):   4v, cd, tpat, tcol; 1941 heavy tank prototype: IM S 74 10/(18):15-16

(Japan)

Chi-Ha Type 97: $3\frac{1}{2}$v, cd: RiS Mr 75 3/1:26
K-3:   2v, cd; remote control tank: WWE S 74 1/5:132
Ka-Mi type 2:   4v, cd; 1942 amphibious var of type 95 light tank: AFV My 72 3/8:16-17
Ka-Mi type 2:   4v, cd, sk, pph: WWE Ja 75 2/1:18-19
Kyu-Go type 95:   5v, cd; 1935 light tank: AFV Mr 73 4/3:18-19
STB-1 type 74:   4v, cd, pph, cpph; 1974:   A&W N 75 20:61
STB-3 type 74:   4v, cd, pph, cpph: 1974:   A&W N 75 20:61
Shinhoto Chi-Ha type 97: $2\frac{1}{2}\frac{1}{2}$v, cd, pph: RiS Mr 75 3/1:26

(Italy)

C.V. 33:   4v, cd; 1933 tankette: RiS Su 73 1/4:117
Carro Armato L6/40:   2v, cd: MM Ap 73 3/4:23

(Sweden)

Light Tank 91:   3v, dim, cd, pph; 1970:   MM N 71 1/11:583
Tank S: 4v, dim, cd, pph; turretless tank: AFV F 71 2/11:13-16

(Switzerland)

PZ-61:   3v, cd, pph, cpph; 1961:   A&W Mr 73 4:38

I. Static Scale

(USSR)

BT-42: 4v, cd, pat, col, pph: Q Ja 75 10/3:105-106
KB-1: 3v, cd; 1940: Q Ap 74 9/2:77
KB-1: 3v, cd; 1942 heavy tank: Q Ap 74 9/2:76-77
KB-85: 4v, cd, pat, col; 1942 heavy tank: Q Jl 74 10/1:8
KV 1A: 4v, cd, tcol; 1939: IM S 72 9/9:11
JS-I: 4v, cd, tpat, tcol: RT F 71 4/2:21
JS-II: 3v, cd, tpat, tcol: RT F 71 4/2:21
JS-III Pika: 4v, cd; 1945 heavy tank: Q Jl 74 10/1:9
PT-76: 4v, cd, pph: AFV Jl 74 4/11:18-19
PT-76: 3v, cd, pph: A&W N 72 2:25
PT-76: 4v, cd, pat, col; 1955 amphibious recon: Q Jl 73 8/3:170
T-26, model 1937: 4v, cd, tpat, tcol, pph: MW N 73 3/11:143
T-28: 3v, cd, turret var; 1939 (var 1940), three-turret tank: Q Ap 74 9/2:72
T-34/76A1 "short gun": 4v, cd; 1940: Q Ap 72 7/2:74
T-34/76A2 "long gun": 4v, cd; 1941: Q Ap 72 7/2:74
T-34/76A3 "flat back": 3v, cd; 1941: Q Ap 72 7/2:74
T-34/76A4: turret 2v (otherwise same as A2); 1941: Q Ap 72 7/2:74
T-34/76B1, rolled plate: 2v, cd; 1941: Q Ap 72 7/2:75
T-34/76B2, cast hull: 2v, cd; 1941: Q Ap 72 7/2:75
T-34/76B3, cast-weld: 4v, cd; 1941: Q Ap 72 7/2:75
T-34/76C1: 4v, cd; 1942: Q Ap 72 7/2:76
T-34/76C2: turret 2v, cd (otherwise same as C1); 1942: Q Ap 72 7/2:76
T-34/76C2 "flat front": 1v, cd; 1942: Q Ap 72 7/2:76
T-34/76C3 "flat front": 1v, cd; 1942: Q Ap 72 7/2:76
T-34/85A: 4v, cd; 1943: Q Ap 72 7/2:77
T-34/85B1: 3v, cd; 1943: Q Ap 72 7/2:77
T-34/85B2: turret 1v, cd (otherwise same as B1); 1945: Q Ap 72 7/2:77
T-35: 4v, cd; 1935 five-turret tank: AFV My 73 4/4:19-22
T-35: 3v, cd: Q Ap 74 9/2:72
T-43: 1v + 1v turret (basically same as C1); 1943: Q Ap 72 7/2:76
T-54/55: 2v, cd, each; phan, cphan; Egyptian use: A&W Jl 73 6:poster
T-60A: 4v, cd, tpat, tcol, det, pph: IM N 73 10/11-12:17-18

(U.K.)

A13 Mk Cruiser Tank Mk III: 4v, cd: MM Jl 75 5/7:425
Carrier, Tracked, Towing (Loyd): 4v, cd, tpat, tcol, pph: MM Jl 73 3/7:451
Churchill AVRE with Bullshorn Plough & Porpoise: $4\frac{1}{2}$v, cd, pat, col; 1944 minesweeper: MM D 72 2/12:649
Churchill AVRE Fascine: 4v, cd, pph: MM My 71 1/5:234-236
Churchill AVRE with Folding SBG Assault Bridge: 1v, cd, unfolding det: MM O 71 1/10:518
Churchill AVRE with Log Carpet: 4v, cd, det; 1944: MM Ap 72

2/4:191
Churchill AVRE with SBG Assault Bridge Trailer: 3v, cd: MM O 71 1/10:520
Churchill Ark Mk. I: 4v, cd, pat, col; 1943 bridge/fascine: MM Je 72 2/6:279
Churchill Carpet Layer Type C: 4v, cd: MM Je 71 1/6:293
Churchill Crocodile Flamethrower: $4\frac{1}{2}$v, cd, det, pph: MM N 71 1/11:573
Churchill Crocodile Fuel Trailer: 4v, cd: IM D 71 8/12:233
Churchill Pusher & Skid Bailey Bridge: 3v (bridge), 4v (tank), cd, det; 1945: MM Jl 72 2/7:366-367
Centurion I: 4v, cd; 1945 prototype: RT O 72 5/10:113
Cruiser Mk 1: 4v, cd, pph: Afx Je 75 16/10:590-592; col, det, pph: Jl 75 16/11:636
Cruiser Mk IVa: 4v, cd, pph: Afx Ap 75 16/8:468-469; sec, pat, col: My 75 16/9:538
Crusader AA Tank: turret 4v, cd: Afx Ap 72 13/8:444
Crusader III AA Mk II: 3v, cd; 1943: AFV D 71 3/4:21
Light Tank Mk VIB: 5v, cd, tpat, tcol; 1936 tankette: Afx Ag 75 16/12:692
Mk VI: 5v, cd: AFV F 71 2/11:22-23; pat, col: F 71 2/11:4-5
Matilda Mk I: 5v, cd, tpat, tcol, pph; 1938: Afx S 75 17/1:28-29
Matilda Mk II: 4v, cd: MM O 73 3/10:667
Medium Mk A Whippet: $4\frac{1}{2}$v, cd, pat, col, pph: MM My 73 3/5: 305
Whippet: $4\frac{1}{2}$v, cd, pat, col: RT F 71 4/2:13
Medium MK D: 4v, var, track det; 1919: MM Mr 71 1/3:140-141
Scorpion: 3v, dim, cd, pph: Afx N 71 13/3:147
Scorpion: 3v, cd, pph: Afx D 74 16/4:247
Sherman Firefly: 4v, cd, tpat, tcol; 1944: MM S 73 3/9:585
Firefly VC: sk, int: AFV Ja 75 5/2:12-15+
Tank, Cruiser, A27M Cromwell Mk IV: 4v, cd: MM Ja 74 4/1:47
Vickers Falcon: 3v, cd, pph, cpph; 1970 AA tank: A&W My 73 5: 32

(U.S.)

Buffalo Carpet-Layer: 4v, cd, pat, col, pph: MM Ag 71 1/8:411
Buffalo Mk II: armoured, unarmored & 17 pdr anti-tank variants: 4v, sec, det: MM S 71 1/9:269+
Buffalo Mk IV: 3v & wl, arm var: MM Ag 71 1/8:413
Duplex Drive Sherman: 5v, cd, amphibious mod of Sherman: Afx D 75 17/4:210
Sherman DD: 4v, det, pph: MM N 72 2/11:605
Grant CDL: 4v, cd, pph; searchlight mod, 1944: MM F 72 2/3:73
Grant CDL: 1v, 3v turret, cd: RT D 71 4/12:5
M3A1 Stuart: 4v, cd: MM Mr 73 3/3:141
M3A1 Lee: 4v, cd; 1941 medium tank: AFV S 72 3/10:16-17
M5A1 Stuart: 4v, cd: Afx Jl 71 12/11:578
M6A1: 4v, cd, pat, pph; 1941 heavy tank experiment: AFV Ja 73 4/1:18-19
M-18 GMC Hellcat: 4v, cd: Afx F 71 12/6:302

I. Static Scale

M-24 Chaffee: 5v, cd: AFV O 71 3/2:18-19; N 71 3/3:18-19
M-48: longitudinal sec: A&W N 72 2:33
Sherman Crab Mine Clearer: 4v, cd, det, pph: MM D 71 1/12: 635
Sherman M32 Tank Recovery: 3v; MM S 71 1/9:465

Armor Distinctions

KV-1 Differences: Q Ap 74 9/2:74-75
M2 & M3 Half Tracks: AFV N 73 4/8:17
M-113: all var: A&W Ja 74 9:32-34
Panther Ausf D2; A; G: MM D 75 5/12:727-728
Quad Distinctions: British Morris C8; U.S. Chevrolet; Canadian Ford: RT Jl 75 8/7:83
Rolls Royce Armoured Cars: AFV Ja 75 5/2:8-9
Scorpion Family: tank, APC, & other var: Afx D 74 16/4:246-247
SdKfz 251/series: MM Jl 73 3/7:471-473
Soviet Light Tanks: T-26B; T-37; T-40; T-60; T-70: AFV S 73 4/7:7
Soviet Self-Propelled Guns: SU 122s; 85s, 100: AFV Je 73 4/5:30
T-34 Russian Tanks: Q Ap 72 7/2:73
Trucks: Long Range Desert Group types: MM Ap 73 3/1:204
U.S. WW-II half-tracks: IM My 72 9/5:9
White Half Track: RT Mr 75 8/3:34

Armor Accessories

AFV Aerial Bases: radio antenna attachments: RT N 74 7/11:123
British Ammunition Boxes: MW Mr 73 1/7:357
British 4 Gallon Fuel Can: MW Mr 73 1/7:357
British 2 Gallon Fuel Can: MQ Mr 73 1/7:357
Churchill Crocodile Fuel Trailer: IM D 71 8/12:2-3
Crocodile Trailer: MM N 71 1/11:573
Desert Tyres: Western Desert tread design: MM Ag 75 5/8:469; cor O 75 5/10:600
Drums: 55 gallon in 1/35: plastic card: RT F 72 5/2:23
Fire Extinguishers: Carbon Tetrachloride & Methyl Bromide types: RT Mr 7/3:35
German Military Semaphore Signals, 1939-1945: visual tank communication equipment: MW Ja 73 1/5:253
Gutted Carrier: Bren carrier chassis as trailer: MM Ja 72 2/1: 36-37
Ostkette: extension track for higher flotation of tanks; 1944 German: AFV F 73 4/2:15
SBG Assault Bridge: trailer & carried versions for Churchill tanks: MM O 71 8/10:518

SdKfz 251/3 Radio Antenna Configuration for German Half-Tracks:
  IM O 71 8/10:11

SCRATCH-BUILDING PLANS

(Armored Personnel Carriers)

Fowler B5 Armoured Traction Engine, Boer War: Afx Mr 71 12/7:
  366-368
Universal Carrier: S&L (O 74) 4:19-21

(Armored Cars)

AEC Armoured Command Vehicle HP 6x6 Mk I: IM Ag 73 10/8:
  12-13+
Autoblinda AB 40:   Afx Je 72 13/10:560-561
FV 432: British APC: Afx My 74 15/9:512-515
Humber FV 1611 "Pig":   Afx Ap 74 15/8:460-461
Humber 4x4 Light Recce Car Mk III: MM Ja 73 3/1:28-29
Marmon-Herrington MK II: Afx My 72 13/9:504-505
SdKfz 222:   Afx Jl 72 13/11:624+

(Artillery)

Big Bertha: MM My 75 4/5:270-272
Bofors 40mm: MW Ap 73 1/8:73
Bofors 40mm LAA Gun: Afx Jl 75 16/11:661-663
Bofors 40mm Single mount: ship's AA gun: MB N 72 21/251:460-
  461
Congreve rocket launcher: MM Mr 73 3/3:163
8" Mk 5 Howitzer: MM Je 74 4/6:334-336
15cm Schwere Feldhaubitze 18: 1943 German howitzer: MW Ja 74
  2/5:251-243+
4" Naval Gun with Shield: MB Ja 73 23/256:27
German 8cm Mortar: AFV Mr 73 4/3:8-9
German 105mm Field Gun: pressed steel & spoked wheel var: MM
  D 72 2/12:640-642
K5E Railway Gun: German WW-II: IM Jl 75 11/4:8-12
Luftgeschütz 40: paratroop recoiless rifle: Afx F 72 13/6:306-307
Oerlikon 20mm: MB D 72 21/252:522
PAK 38: 2v, sk: Afx N 72 14/3:139
PAK 38 50mm anti-tank gun: Afx Ja 73 14/5:254-257
7M85 German 75mm anti-tank gun: Afx Mr 73 14/7:371-372
17 pdr Anti-Tank Gun: Afx Ap 72 13/8:420-422
6 pdr: American Civil War Field Piece: MM Ja 74 4/1:40-41+;
  Limber: Ap 74 4/4:208-209
2 prd Anti-Tank Gun: MW O 73 2/2:87-90

I. Static Scale

(Half Tracks)

NSU Kettenkrad: Afx Mr 72 13/7:374-375
Opel SdKfz IV Maultier: MM S 72 2/9:478-481
Souma MCL: 1933 French truck/prime mover: MW Ja 74 2/5:249

(Self-Propelled Artillery)

Bishop: British 25 pdr: MM Jl 74 4/7:382-383
L40 Da 47/42 Semovente: MM F 75 5/2:108-109
SAV m/43: Swedish 25 pdr or 105mm gun on 38(t) chassis: RT Ag 73 6/8:92

(Small Arms)

Gardner Five-Barrelled Machine Gun: 3v, det: Afx N 72 14/3: 156-159

(Softskins)

Alvis Stalwart: Afx N 73 15/3:170-172
BV 202 Snowcat: MM Mr 71 1/3:153-155
Berna C2 Lorry: WW-I: Afx Je 71 12/10:523-524
CMP 3-ton truck: early & late cab var: Afx F 75 15/6:355
CMP 3-ton truck: portee for 2 pdr anti-tank gun; 1941: MW Ja 74 2/5:256-259+
Faun R600: German tank transporter: Afx D 73 15/4:238-240
Ford 3 ton 4x4 Portee: Afx F 71 12/6:300-301
Horch Kfz 70: German heavy passenger car: Q O 71 6/4:37-40
Leyland RAF Type Lorry: WW-I: Afx Je 71 12/10:523-524
Mack Tank Transporter: Afx N 72 14/3:130-132
Sanitatskraftwagen Kfz 31: German ambulance: MW F 74 2/6:328-329
Sd Ah 115 tank trailer: Afx Ja 74 15/5:294
6 pdr Portee: Afx F 75 15/6:359
Tasker's Queen Mary Semi-Trailer: Afx F 72 13/6:318-320
Terrapin Mk I: amphibious truck: MM Jl 71 1/7:358-359
Thornycroft Amazon: mobile crane: Afx Ja 72 13/5:257-258
2 pdr Portee: Afx F 75 15/6:359
Two Wheeled Fuel Trailer: German armored forces: IM Jl 71 8/7:14-15
Vidal: V-2 transport trailer: MM Jl 73 3/7:448
Vulcan Lorry: WW-I: Afx Je 71 12/10:522-524

(Tanks)

A13 Mk 1 Cruiser Tank Mk III: MM Jl 75 5/7:424-426
C.V. 33: Italian tankette: RiS Su 73 1/4:116-119
Carro Armato L6/40: 1940 Italian light tank: MM Ap 73 3/4:228-230

Cruiser Tank Mk I: Afx Je 75 16/10:590-594; Jl 75 16/11:634-636+
Cruiser Mk IVa: Afx Ap 75 16/8:465-469; My 75 16/9:536-540
Light Tank Mk VI: AFV F 71 2/11:22-23
Light Tank Mk VIB: Afx Ag 75 16/12:688-692+
M3A1 Light Tank Stuart: MM Mr 73 3/3:140-141
Matilda Mk I: Afx S 75 17/1:25-26+
Medium Tank Mk. A Whippet: British WW-I: MM My 73 3/5:304-305+
PzKpfw I Ausf A: 2v, cd; 1935 German tank: IM Mr 73 10/5:12-14
Sherman Firefly: MM S 73 3/9:584-586+
Skoda Lt Vz 35: Czech light tank: MW D 73 2/4:188-191+
T-60A: Russian light tank: IM N 73 10/11-12:16-18

KIT CONVERSIONS

APCs & ICVs

APC Kangaroo: from Airfix Lee/Grant: MM Jl 71 1/7:365+
Light Dragon Mk III: from Airfix Bren Carrier: Afx Jl 73 14/11: 598-60
Loyd Carrier: from Airfix Bren Carrier: MM Jl 73 3/7:450-451
M-113: from several kits: MM Ja 72 2/1:34-35
Ram Kangaroo: from Airfix Sherman: MM Mr 72 2/3:127

ARVs & Funnies

Bergpanther Recovery: from Tamiya Panther A: MM N 73 2/11:742-743+
Centaur Dozer: from Airfix Crusader: MM O 72 2/10:523-524
Centurion ARV: from Tamiya Centurion: MM Jl 72 2/7:358-361
Churchill ARK Mk I: from Airfix Churchill: MM Je 72 3/6:280-281
Crusader Gun Tractor: from Airfix Crusader: Afx Mr 72 13/7: 370-376+
Gutted Carrier: from Airfix Bren Carrier: MM Ja 72 2/1:37; My 72 3/5:225
Leopard ARV: from Airfix Leopard: Afx Je 72 13/10:544-545+
Leopard Trainer Tank: from Airfix Leopard: Afx Jl 72 13/11:617
Matilda Workshop Crane: from Airfix Matilda: Afx S 73 15/1:18+
PzKpfw III Recovery Vehicle: from Airfix Panzer III: Afx Mr 74 15/7:414
Sherman ARV Mk II: from Airfix Sherman: MM Je 73 3/6:367
Sherman BARV Sea Lion: from Airfix Sherman: MM Je 73 3/6:367
Skid Bailey Bridge Pusher: from Airfix Churchill: MM Jl 72 2/7: 265-267
Wespe Munitionsträger: from Bandai 1/48 Wespe: MW D 73 2/4: 202-203

I. Static Scale 90

Armored Cars

Ardennes Jeep: 82nd Airborne armor conversion of Jeep, 1944-45: MW Mr 73 1/7:362
Armadillo: from Minitank 6x6: MM O 72 2/10:521-522
Austin Armoured Car: 3v, cd, tpat, tcol: from Airfix Dennis Fire Engine: Afx S 71 13/1:18-20
BA 64: from Tamiya GAZ: MM D 73 3/12:814-815
Fox: from Airfix Scorpion: Afx Mr 75 16/7:407-410
Humberette Light Reconnaissance Car: from Airfix Humber Staff Car: Afx F 73 14/6:314+
Leyland Beaver Eel: from Airfix Emergency Kit's K6: IM O 72 9/10:2-3
Pkw K1 (Type 82) Kübelwagen: 1941 armored var: AFV O 72 3/11: 9
SdKfz 234/1; /2: from Airfix 234/4: IM My 71 8/5:11-15
SdKfz 234/3: from Airfix 234/4: IM F 72 9/2:12-17

Artillery

Conger: minefield clearing device from Airfix Bren carrier: MM My 72 2/5:226
Congreve Rocket Car: from Hinchliffe 20mm British Artillery Limber: MM Mr 73 3/3:162-163; Ap 73 3/4:216
Soviet 45 mm model 37 AT Gun: from Tamiya 3.7cm PAK: Q Au 75 11/1:19-22
Soviet 45mm model 42 AT Gun: from Tamiya 3.7 cm PAK: Q Au 75 11/1:19-22
18-25 pdr: WW-I British gun from Airfix 25 pdr & scratch limber: Afx My 73 14/9:476-478
57mm Anti-tank Gun: U.S. version of British 6 pdr; from Tamiya 6 pdr: Q Jl 74 10/1:16-17
17 pdr Mk II: from Airfix 17 pdr & 25 pdr: Afx D 73 15/4:224
75mm Howitzer & Light Field Cart: German WW-II horse-drawn; from Airfix Civil War Artillery: Afx Ja 71 12/5:262
6 pdr U.S. Civil War Cannon: from Timpo toy cannon: MM Ja 74 4/1:40-41+
10.5cm L FM(18)M gun: from Bandai 1/48 Wespe: MW D 73 2/4: 202-203

Half-Tracks

Feuerleitpanzeraufzugkraftwagen 8t: V-2 command vehicle: from Airfix SdKfz 7: MM Jl 73 3/7:448
Flakvierling on SdKfz 7: from Tamiya SdKfz 7 & Monogram Wirbelwind: IM Jl 73 10/7:9-11
Hanomag with rockets: from Fujimi SdKfz 251/1 Ausf B: Afx Ja 75 16/5:302-303
M-2: from Airfix M3A1: IM My 72 9/5:9
M2A1: from Airfix M3A1: IM My 72 9/5:9
M3: from Airfix M3A1: IM My 72 9/5:9

Armor

M4 Mortar Carrier: from Airfix 1/76 or Monogram 1/35 M3: MW Ap 73 1/8:429-431
M5: from Airfix M3A1: IM My 72 9/5:9
M5A1: from Airfix M3A1: IM My 72 9/5:9
M9A1: from Airfix M3A1: IM My 72 9/5:9
Maultier Panzerwerfer: rocket launcher conv of Bandai Maultier: MM Ag 73 3/8:522-524
SdKfz 7/1 2cm Flak: from Airfix SdKfz 7: Afx Jl 72 13/11:598-599
SdKfz 251/1 Ausf C: from Nitto Hanomag SdKfz 251/1 Ausf B: AFV N 71 3/3:14-16
SdKfz 251/7 Engineer Vehicle: from Nitto SdKfz 251 Hanomag: AFV My 72 3/8:12-13+
SdKfz 251/9: from Tamiya SdKfz 251: IM S 75 11/5:6
SdKfz 251/22: from Tamiya SdKfz 251: IM S 75 11/5:7
U. S. Anti-Aircraft Halftrack: from Monogram M3 & H&R Bofors: RiS N 72 1/2:50-51; add Sp 73 1/3:94

Self-Propelled Artillery

(Germany)

Bison SdKfz 138/1: from Fujimi 38(t): Afx My 73 14/8:421-422
Bison Ausf H: from Italaerei Marder III: MM F 74 4/2:88-89
Bison: late var: from Fujimi 38(t): Afx My 73 14/9:484-485
Elefant (early type): from Fujimi 1/76: Q Ja 74 9/1:5
Flakpanzer IV Wirbelwind: from Airfix Panzer IV: IM Mr 73 10/3:10-12
Flakpanzer mit Flak 30 or 38 L/55: from Fujimi 38(t): Afx My 73 14/9:485-486
Hetzer: from Fujimi 38(t): Afx My 73 14/9:486-487
Hetzer: from Airfix Assault Gun (StuG III) & Panther: IM Ja 72 9/1:12-13
Hummel (Geschuetzen III/IV): from Airfix PzKpfw IV: Afx N 71 13/3:150-151
Jagdpanzer IV: from Airfix PzKpfw IV: Afx S 71 13/1:22-23
Jagdpanzer IV, L/48: from Monogram StuG IV Ausf G: Q Jl 71 6/3:37-38
Jagdpanzer IV/70: from Monogram StuG IV Ausf G: Q Jl 71 6/3:37-39
Jagdtiger: from Airfix Panther & Tiger: Afx My 71 12/9:464-465
Leopard AA Tank: scratch turret for Airfix Leopard: Afx My 72 13/9:490-491
Marder II: from Tamiya PzKpfw II: AFV Jl 72 3/9:12-13
Marder II: from Tamiya Panzer II & gun from Italaerei Marder III: MM My 74 4/5:265-267
Marder II: from Tamiya Panzer II: RiS Ag 72 1/1:18-23
Marder III: from Fijimi 38(t): Afx Ap 73 14/8:420-421
Marder III: from Italaerei Marder III: MM S 74 4/9:528-531
Marder III Ausf M: from Fujimi 38(t): Afx My 73 14/9:484-485
Mobelwagen: from Airfix Panzer III/IV: MM O 74 4/10:602-604

I. Static Scale

Mobelwagen: 3.7cm Flak 43 on PzKpfw IV: from Airfix PzKpfw IV: Afx D 72 14/4:192
Mobelwagen: 2cm Flak 38 on PzKpfw IV: from Airfix PzKpfw IV: Afx D 72 14/4:193
150mm GwII (15cm) sIG 33 howitzer: from Tamiya Pzkpfw II F/G: AFV S 72 3/10:10-11
Ostwind: 3.7cm Flak 43 on PzKpfw IV: from Airfix PzKpfw IV: Afx D 72 14/4:193
Panzer IV/70 SdKfz 162/1: from Airfix Panzer IV: MM O 72 2/10:518-520
Panzer IV/70 (Zwischenlüsung): from Airfix Panzer IV: MM S 72 2/9:460
Panzerjäger Nashorn: from ESCI 1/72 Hummel: IM Mr 75 11/2:12
Panzerjäger 38(t): from Italaerei Marder III: IM My 74 10/(16): 15-16
Panzerjäger Ib mit 4.7cm PAK(t): from Tamiya Panzer II: AFV F 75 5/3:14-16+
Sturmgeschuetz IV: from Airfix PzKpfw IV & StuG III: Afx Ja 72 13/5:250-251
Sturmgeschütz IV: from Airfix StuG III & Panzer IV: MM S 72 2/9:458-459
Sturmpanzer IV Brummbär: last production var: from Monogram Brummbär, StuG IV: IM N 74 10/19:12-13
Brummbär: from Monogram PzKpfw IV: MM Je 72 2/6:299-302
Brummbär: from Airfix Panzer IV: MM O 72 2/10:518-520
Sturmpanzer VI: from Tiger: MW D 72 1/4:182-183
Sturmtiger: from Tamiya PzKpfw VI Tiger I Ausf E: AFV D 72 3/12:8-9
Sturmtiger: from Airfix Tiger: IM O 71 8/10:14-15
Sturmtiger: from Tamiya Tiger I: MM Je 73 3/6:381-386
Wespe 10.5cm: from Tamiya PzKpfw II: AFV Jl 72 3/9:12-13
Wespe 10.5cm: from Tamiya Panzer II: MW My 73 1/9:465-467+
Wirbelwind: 2cm Flak 38 on PzKpfw IV: from Airfix PzKpfw IV: Afx D 72 14/4:193

(Sweden)

Ikv 103: from StuG III: RT My 72 5/5:56

(USSR)

JSU 152: from Airfix Josef Stalin III: IM Ag 71 8/8:11-13+
KV-2: from Tamiya 1/35 KV-1: MM Ja 71 1/1:22-24
SU 76: from Airfix StuG III: Afx Mr 73 14/7:360
SU 76i: from Airfix StuG III: Afx D 71 13/4:192
SU 85: from Airfix T-34: IM Jl 72 9/7:12-13
SU 100: from Airfix T-34: IM Je 72 9/6:4-6
SU 152: from Fujimi KV2 & Airfix JS III: Afx Ag 73 14/12:668-670

Armor

(U.K.)

Bishop: from Airfix Valentine & 25 pdr & limber: Afx N 75 17/3: 154

(U.S.)

M7 Priest: from Airfix Grant: Afx N 75 17/3:153
Priest: from Airfix Lee/Grant: MM Jl 71 1/7:364-366
M10 Tank Destroyer: from Airfix 1/76 Sherman: IM My 72 9/5:5+

Softskins

(Canada)

Chevrolet C60 L 3-ton 4x4 Petrol Tanker: from Airfix Bedford QL: MM D 75 5/12:735-736
Chevrolet 30 cwt truck: from Airfix Bedford QL: Sc Ap 71 2/4: 199-201

(Germany)

15cm Panzerwerfer 42 Maultier: from Airfix Bren Carriers: Afx Je 73 14/10:551-552
SdKfz 305: bed box for Opel Blitz: MM Mr 75 5/3:234-236
Wehrmacht Omnibus Command Post: from Italaerei Opel Blitz: MM Ag 75 5/8:495-498
Zundapp KA 600 Combination: from Tamiya 1/35 Zundapp motorcycle & side-car: MW Ag 73 1/12:655-657

(U.K.)

AEC 0854 6x6 Refueller Mk 2: from Airfix AEC refueler: MM D 75 5/12:736-737+
AEC 0854 6x6 Heavy Artillery Tractor, prototype, armoured: from AEC refueler: MM D 75 5/12:737+
Albion CX23N 10-ton 6x4 GS: from Airfix recovery set: MM O 75 5/10:591-593+
Albion 350 Gallon Refueller: from Airfix RAF crash set: IM Mr 71 8/3:12-13
Austin K3 4x2 3-ton GS (MVD 7): from Airfix Austin K6 or K2: MM Ag 75 5/8:484; cor O 75 5/10:600
Austin K5 3-ton 4x4 GS; from Austin Bedford QL: MM D 76 5/12: 735+; cor F 76 6/2:86
Austin K6 Aircrew Coach: from Austin K6 (Airfix emergency set):

IM Jl 71 8/7:12-13
Austin K5 Breakdown Gantry: from Airfix Austin K6: MM My 73 3/5:290-291
Austin K6 6x4 3-ton GS (MVD 15): from Airfix Austin K6 fire tender: MM Ag 75 5/8:483-484; cor O 75 5/10:600
Bedford OY 3-ton 4x2 Laboratory: from Airfix recovery set: MM O 75 5/10:591-593+
Bedford OXA; OXD; OYC; OYD: from Airfix Austin K6: MM Ap 73 3/4:241-242
Bedford OXD 30 cwt GS: from Airfix recovery set: MM O 75 5/10:591-593+
Bedford QL Fire Tender & Trailer Pump: from Airfix Bedford QL aircraft refueler: MM F 73 3/2:94-95
Bedford QL 3-ton 4x4 GS: from Airfix Matador: MM D 75 5/12:734+
Bedford QLD; QLR; QLT: from Airfix WL refueler: MM Ag 71 1/8:406
Bedford QLT Troop Carrier: from Airfix refueling set: Afx My 71 12/9:475
Coles Mobile Crane Mk VII series 7 on AEC Chassis: from Airfix refueling set: Afx Ja 72 13/5:256-257
Commer Q2 15 cwt truck: RAF airfield utility truck from Airfix K2 ambulance: Sc F 71 2/2:76-78+
Crane 90 ton Trailer & Wimpy Tractor: from Airfix Scammell tank transporter: Afx Ag 71 12/12:638-645
Crossley 6x4 Derrick (MVD 9): from Airfix Austin K6: MM Ag 75 5/8:489+; cor O 75 5/10:600
Humber Utility Vehicle: from Airfix Humber Snipe ("Monty's Humber"): IM Ja 74 10/13-14:8-12+
Morris-Commercial CS11/30 4x2 Ambulance: from Airfix Austin K2 ambulance: MM Ag 75 5/8:484
SAS Land Rover Pink Panther: from Britain's die-cast long wheelbase Land Rover: MM N 72 2/11:608-609
Scammell Pioneer: from Airfix Scammell tank retriever: MM Mr 73 3/3:156
Thornycroft Amazon WF8/NR6; Coles Mk.VII series 7: from Airfix recovery set: MM O 75 5/10:591-593+
Troop Carrier of WW-I: from Airfix B type bus: Afx Ja 72 13/5:264

(U. S.)

Ambulance 1914-1918: from Revell 1912 Packard: MW S 72 1/1:18-19
American Civil War Observation Balloon: from Airfix Wagon Train: Afx F 73 14/6:304
FWD Truck of 1914-1918: from Airfix fire engine: MW Jl 73 1/11:602-603
Military Model T: 1914-1918 machine gun carrier: from Airfix Ford Model T: Afx Ap 71 12/8:420-422
Personnel Carrier Jeep: stretched; from Tamiya 1/35 Jeep: IM Jl 73 10/7:15

Rocket Firing Jeep: IM Ja 71 8/1:4-6

Tanks

(Canada)

Canadian Valentine: from Fujimi 1/76 Valentine: RT N 73 6/11: 131

(Germany)

Aufklärungspanzer 38(t): from Fujimi 38(t): Afx Ap 73 14/8:422- 423
Henschel turret for Bandai King Tiger: scratch turret: AFV Ap 75 5/4:28-31
Kugelblitz: one-off AA tank: from Airfix PzKpfw IV: Afx Jl 72 13/11:604-605
Mighty Maus: from Aurora Tiger, Tamiya King Tiger & Jagdpanther: IM S 74 10/(18):12-14
Panther D: from Airfix Panther A: MM Ag 71 1/8:390-391
Panther G: from Airfix Panther A: MM Ag 71 1/8:390-391
The Tank That Never Was: Panther II: from Airfix Panther & Tiger: MW N 72 2/3:126-127
Porshe King Tiger: from Fujimi King Tiger: MM Ja 73 3/1:49-50
PzKpfw II Ausf A; B; C: from Tamiya PzKpfw II Ausf F/G: IM Je 73 10/6:15-16
PzKpfw III: from Airfix StuG III: IM F 72 9/2:2-3
PzKpfw III Ausf E: from Tamiya PzKpfw III M/N: AFV Ja 73 4/1:10-11+; F 73 4/2:20-21
PzKpfw III Ausf F: from Tamiya PzKpfw III M/N: AFV Ja 73 4/1: 10-11+; F 73 4/2:20-21
PzKpfw III Ausf G: from Tamiya PzKpfw III M/N: AFV Ja 73 4/1: 10-11+; F 73 4/2:20-21
PzKpfw III Ausf G: from Tamiya PzKpfw III M/N: MW D 72 1/4: 188-190
PzKpfw III Ausf M: from Airfix StuG III: Afx Ja 71 12/5:258-259+
PzKpfw IV var: from Monogram PzKpfw IV: AFV S 71 3/1:26+
PzKpfw IV var: cupola conv: from Monogram PzKpfw IV: AFV O 71 3/2:28
PzKpfw IV Ausf D & J: from Airfix PzKpfw IV Ausf F: Afx O 71 13/2:72-74
PzKpfw IV Ausf F1 & F2: from Airfix PzKpfw IV: IM Je 71 8/6: 14
PzKpfw IV Ausf E; F1; G: from Monogram PzKpfw IV: Q Ap 71 6/2:30-35
PzKpfw IV Ausf F2: from Monogram PzKpfw IV Ausf I: MM D 71 1/12:620+
PzKpfw IV Ausf G: from Monogram PzKpfw IV Ausf G: IM Ja 75 11/1:2-3

I. Static Scale

PzKpfw IV Aûsf H: from Monogram PzKpfw IV Ausf I: MM D 71 1/12:617-618
PzKpfw IV Ausf J: from Monogram PzKpfw IV Ausf I: MM D 71 1/12:617-618
PzKpfw IV, late mods: RT Ap 73 6/4:45
PzKpfw VI Tiger I Ausf H: from Airfix Tiger: MM Ja 71 1/1: 34-37
SdKfz 302; 303 Goliath: from Airfix StuG III: IM Mr 74 1/(15):4
SdKfz 304 Springer: from two Nitto Kettenkrad: IM Mr 74 10/(15):4
The Tiger That Wasn't: VK 4501(P): from Fujimi Elefant: IM S 74 10/(18):26+

(Israel)

Isherman: from Airfix Sherman: Afx Ap 71 12/8:404
Panturion: from Centurion: Q O 74 10/2:72

(Japan)

Chi-Ha type 97: from Aurora Shinhoto Chi-Ha: Q Su 75 10/4:159-162
Shi-Ki type 97 command tank: from Chi-Ha: Q Su 75 10/4:159-162

(USSR)

KB-85: from Fujimi KV-1 or KV-2: Sc S 74 5/60:479
KV-1 mod 40: from Fujimi KV-1: Q Ap 74 9/2:74
KV-1 mod 41: from Fujimi KV-1: Q Ap 74 9/2:75+
KV-1 mod 41 var: from Fujimi KV-1: Q Ap 74 9/2:78
KV-1 mod 42: from Fujimi KV-1: Q Ap 74 9/2:78
KV-1 mod 43 Skorotsnoi: from Fujimi KV-1: Q Ap 74 9/2:78
KV-1A: from Airfix JS III: IM S 72 9/9:10-12
KV-1B: from Fujimi KV-1A: MM Ja 73 3/1:22-24
KV-2: from Tamiya KV-1: MM Ja 73 3/1:22-24
KV-2 mod 40: from Fujimi KV-2: Q Ap 74 9/2:75
KV-2A & B: from Fujimi KV-1: IM Ap 73 10/4:2-4
T-34/76: from Tamiya 1/25 T-34/85: MW O 72 1/2:64-65
T-34/76A & B: from Airfix T-34: Q Ap 72 7/2:73
T-34/76C & /85: from Airfix T-34: Q Ap 72 7/2:73

(U. K.)

Bullshorn Plough & Porpose: from Airfix Churchill: MM D 72 2/12:650
Churchill AVRE Assault Bridge: MM O 71 1/10:521
Churchill AVRE: fascine; from Airfix Churchill: MM My 71 1/5: 234-236
Churchill AVRE: log carpet; from Airfic Churchill: MM Ap 72 2/4: 190+

Churchill Carpet Layer Type C: from Airfix Churchill: MM Je 71 1/6:292-295
Churchill Crocodile: with scratch trailer; from Airfix Churchill: MM N 71 1/11:572-574
Cromwell: from Nichimo 1/35 Charioteer: MW Je 73 1/10:542-543
Crusader AA Tank: from Airfix Crusader: Afx Ap 72 13/8:444-445
Little Willie: 1915 first tank: from Airfix Mk 1 tank: MW Ja 74 2/5:262-263+
Matilda Baron flail: from Airfix Matilda: Afx Ja 74 16/5:289-290+
Matilda Frog: flamethrowing var; from Matilda: MW O 73 2/2:80-81
Submarine Chieftain: deep-wading gear added to Airfix Chieftain: Afx S 72 14/1:12-13

(U. S.)

Buffalo Carpet Layer: from Airfix Mk IV Buffalo: MM Ag 71 1/8: 412+
Buffalo Mk II: from Airfix Mk IV Buffalo: MM S 71 1/9:470
Duplex Drive Sherman: from Airfix Sherman: Afx D 75 17/4:208+
Duplex Drive Sherman: from Airfix Sherman: MM N 72 2/11:607-608
Grant CDL: from Monogram Grant: IM N 74 10/19:14-15
Grant CDL: from Airfix Lee/Grant: MM F 72 2/2:74
Grant CDL: from Airfix Grant: RT D 71 4/12:138
LVT-3 Bushmaster: from Airfix Buffalo: IM Je 71 1/6:14-16
M-4 Sherman: from Revell E8: RiS W 74 2/2:64-66; cor Sp 74 2/3-4:124
M3 Stuart I: from Tamiya Stuart: Q Au 75 11/1:40-41
M5A1 Stuart: from Minitanks M4 Cargo Carrier & Airfix Lee/Grant: Afx Jl 71 12/11:578-579
M-10A1: from Tamiya M-36: MM F 73 3/2:74-75
M-18 Hellcat: from Airfix Leopard: Afx F 71 12/6:301-302+
M-32 Sherman Tank Recovery: from Sherman: MM S 71 1/9:464-465
T-34 Calliope: from Airfix Sherman: Afx Mr 71 12/7:369
M-551 Sheridan, Viet Nam variant: from Tamiya Sheridan: RiS Sp 73 1/3:56-89
Sherman Crab: flail; from Airfix Sherman: MM D 71 1/12:636-637
Sherman in Detail: applique armor: AFV F 71 2/11:11
Unstated (in index): from Fujimi M4 Sherman: WWE Jl 74 1/4:108-?

SUPERDETAILING

(Canada)

Clarks Chevrolet 30 cwt 1/76 LRDG truck: MM F 73 3/2:99-101

I. Static Scale 98

(Germany)

AHM Minitank Jagdtiger Z-171: AFV D 72 3/12:26-27
Airfix Panther A: MM Ag 71 1/8:390-391
Airfix SdKfz 234/4: IM F 72 9/2:12-16
Airfix SdKfz 251: 1/32: Afx Ag 74 15/12:686-691
Bandai Elefant: AFV D 74 5/1:29+
Bandai Hummel: MM Ag 73 3/8:506-509; S 73 3/9:610-612; D 73 3/12:806
Bandai Panther G: 1/24: MM Ja 73 3/1:18-19
Bandai SdKfz 251/1 Ausf B: MM Jl 73 3/7:453
Bandai Wespe: MM Jl 73 3/7:452-453
Fujimi Hetzer: IM S 73 10/9:7-9+
Fujimi King Tiger: IM Ja 73 10/1:6-10
L&S P.38 pistol: MM Ja 74 4/1:48-50
Midori SdKfz 222: MM My 73 3/5:272-274+
Midori SdKfz 232: MM My 73 3/5:272-274+
Midori SdKfz 250: MM My 73 3/5:272-274+
Monogram German Gasoline Cans: 1/32: Afv Mr 72 3/1:25
Nitto SdKfz 251: Q Jl 72 7/3:107
Tamiya BMW R.75: IM My 73 10/5:12-13
Tamiya 88mm Gun: MM F 73 3/2:105-107
Tamiya NSU Kettenkrad: AFV Mr 74 4/10:10-12
Tamiya PzKpfw III: AFV Ja 72 3/5:10-11+
Tamiya SdKfz 7, canvas top: AFV My 73 4/4:36
Tamiya Tiger I; working hatch: AFV F 72 3/6:19
Tamiya Tiger I; two Wittman var: Q Jl 73 8/3:148-149
Tamiya Tiger I: RT Mr 71 4/3:31
Tamiya Tiger I: RT Ja 72 5/1:5
Almark, Armour Accessories, Tamiya MG 34: MW Ag 73 3/8:646-647

(Japan)

Airfix Chi-Ha: Q Su 75 10/4:162
Fujimi Chi-Ha: Q Su 75 10/4:162

(USSR)

Airfix T-34/76B3 or T-34/85B1: Q Ap 72 7/2:73

(U.K.)

Airfix Austin Ambulance: Afx Ag 71 12/12:649+
Airfix Cromwell 1/33 (nom 1/32) toy: MM Ja 74 4/1:46-47
Airfix Humber Snipe: Afx Je 74 15/10:572-573+
Humber Snipe: MM Ja 73 3/1:25
Humber Snipe: Sc F 73 4/2:129-130
Airfix Recovery Set: MM Jl 73 3/7:443
Airfix Scorpion: IM My 75 11/3:8-9

Armor

Fujimi's Valentine: IM Jl 74 10/(17):15
Hinchliffe 10 pdr Amstrong Muzzle Loading Rifle: MM N 73 3/11: 738
Nichimo Charioteer Tank Destroyer: IM Ag 72 9/8:14-16
Tamiya Daimler Scout Cars: MW F 73 1/6:298-299
Belfast Saracens: RT Ag 74 7/8:91-92
British Vehicles in Belfast: mods to std British vehicles: RT Mr 72 5/3:31

(U. S.)

Airfix M3A1 halftrack: IM My 72 2/5:7-9
Bandai M. 60A1 Main Battle Tank: MM Ja 73 3/1:27-28
Hasegawa M24 Chaffee: Q O 74 10/2:49
Nichimo M109 Howitzer: Q Au 75 11/1:45-50
Tamiya Jeep: MM F 73 3/2:102-104
Tamiya M8 armored car: MW Ag 73 1/12:628-629
American Half Tracks: MW D 72 1/4:202-203
M4A3 Sherman: MW O 72 1/2:76-77

KIT CONSTRUCTION

Airfix Panzer IV & Argyle vac Brummbär: Afx My 72 14/9:493-494
Bandai Panther G: 1/24: MM Ja 73 10/1:18-19
ESCI BMW R. 75: 1/9: Sc S 72 3/9:478-480+; O 72 3/10:538-540
ESCI Harley-Davidson WLA-45: 1/9: MM O 73 3/10:686-687
WLA-45: Sc S 73 4/9:634-641
ESCI Zundapp KS-750: 1/9: MM My 74 4/5:254-257+
Historex Gun Team & Limber: MM Ap 72 2/4:193-195; My 72 2/5: 244-245; Je 72 2/6:304-305
Italaerei Marder III: MM F 74 4/2:89-90
Monogram M3 Grant: MM O 74 4/10:596-598
Monogram PzKpfw IV Ausf I: MM D 71 1/12:616-622; Ja 72 2/1:13
Monogram Sturmgeschutz IV L/48: MM O 73 3/10:658-660
Nichimo Panzer IV: 1/30: MM S 71 1/9:453-455; N 71 1/11:630-607
Nichimo Panzer IV Ausf H: 1/30: Sc N 71 2/11:603-607
Nichimo Sherman: 1/35: MM Ja 75 5/1:46-47
Nitto Kettenkraftrad: MM Ap 74 4/4:206-207
Old Guard M3 Stuart: 1/35 metal casting: MM O 73 3/10:673-675
Tamiya BMW R. 75: Sc F 73 4/2:107-109
Tamiya Centurion: 1/25: MM Je 74 4/6:337-339
Tamiya Daimler "Dingo" Mk II: MM Ap 73 3/4:231-233
Tamiya GAZ: MM D 73 3/12:812-814
Tamiya Grant M3: MM O 74 4/10:596-598
Tamiya Jagdpanther: 1/25: MM D 72 2/12:676-677
Tamiya Kettenkraftrad: MM Ap 74 4/4:206-207
Tamiya Kübelwagen: Sc Ag 71 2/8:407
Tamiya M-113: MM N 74 4/11:692-694

I. Static Scale 100

Tamiya Matilda Mk II: AFV N 73 4/8:4-6+
Matilda Mk II: MM O 73 3/10:666-667+
Matilda Mk II: Sc O 73 4/10:682-686
Tamiya Quad & 25 pdr: MM F 75 5/2:104-105
Tamiya SAS Jeep: Sc O 74 4/10:596-598
Tamiya SdKfz 222:   MM S 75 5/9:531
Tamiya SdKfz 251:   MM Jl 73 3/7:456-457+
Tamiya Stuart: MM F 75 5/2:103
Tamiya StuG III: Sc S 75 6/72:496-499
Tamiya T-34/76:   MM Ag 75 5/8:474-475

KIT CORRECTIONS

Airfix Tiger: MM Ja 71 1/1:34-37
Aurora Type 97 Shinhoto Chi-Ha: Q Ap 74 9/2:59-60
Aurora Type 97:   RiS Mr 75 3/1:25-26
Bandai Hummel: 1/30: MM S 73 3/9:610-612
Fujimi Tiger: Q Su 75 10/4:142-143
Tamiya Royal Tiger: turret corrections: Q Su 75 10/4:142
Tamiya 25 pdr: MM Jl 75 5/7:413

AUTOMOBILES

SCALE DRAWINGS

Cars

(Formula One Racers)

AVS DN3 Shadow: 4v, sec, cd, pat, tcol, pph; 1973:   Sc F 75 6/65:83
B.R.M. P.180:   6v, sec, cd, pat, col, pph; 1970:   Sc F 73 4/2:134-135+
Brabham BT 42:   4v, sec, cd, pat, col, pph; 1973:   Sc My 74 5/56:252-254
Eifelland March 721:   4v, sec, cd, pat, col; 1972:   Sc Ap 73 4/4:283-284
John Player Special: 4v, sec, cd, pat, col; 1972:   Sc Ap 73 4/4:283-284
Lola F.1 T370:   4v, sec, cd, pat, tcol, pph; 1974:   Sc Ja 75 6/64:13
March 711:   4v, cd, pat, col, phan, pph, det: Sc Je 71 2/6:310-312

March 721 Ford: 4v, sec, cd, pat, col; 1972: Sc Ap 73 4/4:283-284
March 721G: 4v, sec, cd, pat, tcol, pph; 1971: Sc My 73 4/5: 359-360
March 721X: 4v, sec, cd, pat, tcol, pph; 1972: Sc My 73 4/5:361
McLaren M-20: 4v, sec, cd, pat, col, pph; 1972: Sc Je 73 4/6: 428-429
McLaren M-23: 4v, sec, cd, pat, tcol, pph: Sc Jl 73 4/7:503-505
T.S. 7: 4v, sec, cd, pat, col, phan, pph: Sc Ja 71 2/1:22-24
Tecno F.1: 4v, cd, pph; 1973: Sc Ja 74 5/1:41-42
Texaco-Marlboro McLaren M23: 5v, sec, cd, pat, tcol; drivers' helmet pat, col; 1974: Sc Mr 75 6/66:131-132

(Grand Prix Racers)

Alfa-Romeo T33TT: 4v, sec, cd, pat, tcol, var 1v; 1972: Sc Ja 73 4/1:58-61
Alfa-Romeo T33/12: 4v, sec, cd, pat, tcol, pph; 1974: Sc Je 75 6/7:302-303
BMW CSL: 4v, sec, cd, pat, tcol, pph; 1973: Sc D 73 4/12:841
C-Type Jaguar: 5v, sec, cd, pat, tcol, pph; 1953 Le Mans: Sc Ag 73 4/8:557
Ferrari 312 B3: 4v, sec, cd, pat, col, pph; 1972: Sc N 73 4/11: 766-768
Ferrari 312 B3: 5v, sec, cd, pat, tcol, pph; helmet tcol; 1975: Sc My 75 6/68:241+
Gulf Mirage Long Tail: 4v, sec, cd, pat, tcol, pph; 1973: Sc Ag 73 4/8:559
JPS 9: 4v, sec, cd, pat, tcol, pph; 1974: Sc D 74 5/63:647
Matra Simca 670: 4v, sec, cd, pat, pph, cpph; 1974: Sc Ap 75 6/67:170
Porsche Carrera: 4v, sec, cd, pat, col; 1973: Sc O 73 4/10:703
Porche 917/30: 4v, sec, cd, pat, pph; 1974 Can-Am: Sc O 74 5/61:545-547
Surtees TS 16: 4v, cd, pat, tcol, pph; 1974 & 1975: Sc S 75 6/72:453+
Tyrrell 007: 4v, sec, cd, pat, tcol, pph; 1974-1975 var: Sc Jl 75 6/70:343-344

(Other Racers)

Auto-Union A type: 4v, cd, pph; 1934: Sc D 71 2/12:646-647
Auto-Union B type: 4v, cd, pph; 1935: Sc D 71 2/12:646-647
Auto-Union C type: 5v, sec, cd, pat; 1937: Sc D 71 2/12:648-649
Chevrolet Camaro: 4v, sec, cd, pat, tcol; 1972 Touring Group Two: Sc Jl 74 5/58:387-388
Jabford 1172: 4v, sec, cd, col, pph; light sports car: Sc Jl 71 2/7:364
Lancia Stratos: 4v, sec, cd, pat, tcol, pph; 1973 road racer: Sc Ag 75 5/59:399
Lola T-330: 4v, sec, cd, pat, col, pph; Formula 500: Sc S 73

I. Static Scale 102

    4/9:628-631
McLaren M.16 Indianapolis: 4v, cd, pat, pph; Indy racer: Sc S 71 2/9:482-484
Proteus Bluebird: 4v, sec, cd, pat, tcol, pph; 1969 turbine absolute racer: Sc Je 74 5/57:330-331
Renault Alpine A364:   4v, sec, cd, pat, tcol; 1971 Formula 3: Sc Mr 73 4/3:173-175
Tatra Racing Car: 4v, sec, cd, pat: Sc Mr 73 4/5:206
Trojan T101:   4v, sec, cd, pat, tcol; 1973 Formula 5000: Sc Mr 74 5/54:163-164

(Other Than Racers)

Jaguar SS 100:   4v, cd, col, pph; 1937: Sc N 71 2/11:601-602
MG Midget series TD: 4v, struc, cd, pat, col, det, pph; 1952 sports car: Sc Jl 72 3/7:372-375; Ag 72 3/8:430-431+; S 72 3/9:486-488; O 72 3/10:547-551
Morgan Sports: 4v, cd; 1929: Sc My 72 3/5:277

Circus Wagons

Baggage Wagon; William Bros: $4\frac{1}{2}$v, dim, cd, pat: NMRA S 73 39/1:9
Cage Wagon; Williams Bros: $3\frac{1}{2}$v, dim, cd, pat: NMRA S 73 39/1:10
Giraffe Wagon; Williams Bros: $3\frac{1}{2}$v, dim, cd, pat: NMRA S 73 39/1:12
Pie Wagon; Williams Bros: 4v, fp, dim, cd, pat, det: NMRA S 73 39/1:10
Ticket Wagon; Barnes & Sells Floto: 3v, cd: NMRA S 73 39/1:12
Ticket Wagon; Williams Bros: $3\frac{1}{2}$v, dim, cd, pat: NMRA S 73 39/1:13

Trucks

American La France Ladder Chief: 2v, cd, tpat, tcol: Sc Ja 72 3/1:32
Bulldog Mack; Ringling Bros: 3v, cd; 1949: NMRA S 73 39/1:10
Dennis Motor Fire Engine: 2v, pph; 1914 ladder truck: Sc D 73 4/12:836
Dodge L700 with 14' Stake Bed: 2v, cd, det: Sc D 72 3/12:667-669
Ford T Hucks Starter: 4v, cd, tpat, tcol, pph: Afx F 73 14/6:302
Fort WT 9000 6x4 Truck with 707 series Gas Turbine Engine: 4v, cd, pat; 1970 tractor: Sc My 74 5/56:275
Land Rover Crash Truck: 4v, cd, tpat, tcol, int; 1972 (dep 1974) dry chemical fire truck: RT Jl 75 8/7:78-79
Matador Breakdown Lorry: 3v, cd, tpat, tcol; auto wrecker from WW-II truck: Sc My 75 6/68:223

Matador 4x4 Logging Lorry: 4v, det, cd, tpat, tcol, pph: Sc Je 75 6/60:296
Matador 6x6 Crane Lorry Conv: 4v, cd, tpat, tcol, det, pph: Sc Jl 75 6/70:335
Pyrene Pathfinder: 4v, cd, pph; 1973 airport crash truck: Sc Ja 74 5/1:21

Other Civil Vehicles

Farm Cart: $4\frac{1}{2}\frac{1}{2}$v, cd, det, pph: British one-horse: Sc Jl 74 5/58:383-384
New Huber: 2v, cd, det, sk; 1903 steam tractor: Sc N 75 6/74:562-565
Ski-Doo Alpine & Invader: 3v, cd, pat, col; 1970 snowmobile: Sc Je 72 3/6:340
Ski-Doo Nordic: 3v, cd, pat, col; 1970 snowmobile: Sc Je 72 3/6:340

SCRATCH-BUILDING PLANS

(Animal-Drawn)

Farm Cart: British 2-wheel 1-horse, dumping utility cart: Sc Jl 74 5/58:382-384; add S 74 5/60:480

(Cars)

MG Midget TD: 1952 sports car, working steering: Sc Jl 72 3/7:372-375; Ag 72 3/8:430-431+; S 72 3/9:486-488; O 72 3/10:547-551
Morgan Sports: 1929 three-wheel sports car: Sc My 72 3/5:275+

(Traction)

New Huber: 1903 British: Sc N 75 6/74:562-565

CONVERSIONS

(Cars)

Austin Mini Stock Car: from Airfix Mini: Afx Ja 72 13/5:274-275
Clubman Special: from Airfix Triumph TR 4 & scratch vac body: Afx S 72 14/1:26-27
Ford Hot Rod: from Airfix Model T Ford: Afx Ap 72 13/8:454-455

I. Static Scale

Ford 1915 Landau: from Airfix 1911 Rolls Royce & Pyro Ford
   Couplet: RT F 72 5/2:19
Jaguar: open engine racer: from Airfix E-Type: Afx O 71 13/2:
   67+
Lineside Lime Spreader: from Airfix Matador: Afx S 72 14/1:30-31
Matador Breakdown Lorry: from Airfix Matador: Sc My 75 6/68:
   222-224
Matador 4x4 Logging Lorry: from Airfix Matador: Sc Je 75 6/69:
   295-297
Matador 6x6 Crane Lorry: from Airfix Matador: Sc Jl 75 6/70:334-
   336
Street Rod: freelance; from Ford T Runabout, Ford 3 litre GT,
   Jaguar 420G: IM Jl 73 10/:2-3+
Volkswagen Beetle Baja Chopper: from Afx VW 1200: Afx Ag 72
   13/12:673-674
Volkswagen dune buggy: from Airfix VW: Afx Ap 71 12/8:408-409

(Trucks)

Dodge/Fargo 14' stake-side truck on L 70 frame: from IMC Dodge/
   Fargo L 700 tractor: Sc D 72 3/12:666-669
Ford T Hucks Starter: from Airfix Ford T: Afx F 73 14/6:302-303
Ford T One-Ton: from Pyro Pie Wagon: Sc O 71 2/10:535-537
Ford T Truck: from Airfix 1/32; 1912: Sc Mr 71 2/3:141-143
Quad Hopper Loader: agricultural aircraft loader; from Airfix
   Quad: Afx O 71 13/2:82
Renault Commercial Van, 1906: from Pyro Towne Car: Sc Ag 71
   2/8:429-431
Vans for Piggyback Fans: 1/48 scale trailers from AMT 1/43
   trailers: MR D 75 42/12:102-105

SUPERDETAILING

(Cars)

Airfix Bentley: 1930 $4\frac{1}{2}$ litre, 1/12: IM N 73 10/11-12:12-14
Bentley: Sc O 75 6/72:500-501; cor D 75 6/75:595; disc Ap 76 7/79:
   187
Gakken Jaguar SS-100: 1/16: Sc Mr 75 6/33:122-125
Tamiya Tyrrell Ford: IM Mr 75 11/2:13-14

(Motorcycles)

Tamiya Honda 750: Sc Ap 71 2/4:194-197

Automobiles

(Trucks)

AMT Kenworth Long Nose & Trailer: Sc S 74 5/60:488-491

KIT CONSTRUCTION

(Cars)

Albatros Stutz 1914 Roadster: 1/18 cardstock: Sc N 72 3/11:582-583
Finecast Jaguar SS 10: 1/24 metal: Sc N 71 2/11:596-597+
Gakken MG Midget series TC: Sc Mr 73 4/3:202-205
Gakken Mercedes-Benz 540K: Sc Jl 75 6/70:326-328
Protar Ferrari 312-b2: 1/9: Sc Ap 73 3/4:278-281
Revell Mr. Revell: IM Ja 75 11/1:14
Tamiya Datsun 240ZG: 1/12: Sc Je 74 5/57:311-314
Tamiya Ferrari 312B: 1/2: Sc Ja 3/1:18-21+
Tamiya John Player Special: 1/12: Sc Ap 74 5/55:204-205
Tamiya McLaren M23: 1/12: Sc Mr 75 6/66:134-135
Tamiya Tyrrell Ford Formula One: 1/12: Sc Ag 73 4/8:566-569

(Motorcycles)

Protar Greaves 360 Challenger: 1/9: Sc Mr 71 2/3:144-145+
Tamiya BMW R. 75/5: 1/6: Sc Mr 73 4/3:185-189
Tamiya Honda 750cc: 1/6: Sc Ap 71 2/4:194-197+

(Trucks)

AMT American La France Ladder Chief: 1/25: ScJa 72 3/1:33-35
AMT Ford C. 600 City Delivery Truck: 1/25: Sc Ja 74 5/1:44-45
Bandai Dennis Motor Fire Engine: 1/16: Sc D 73 4/12:834-839
IMC Dodge/Fargo L 70 & flatbed trailer: 1/25: Sc D 72 3/12:666-669

(Other Civil Vehicles)

Phoenix Brougham: 1/32 carriage: Sc N 74 5/62:596-597

I. Static Scale

FIGURES

ARMIES

[Organization, History, Uniforms, Weapons, Modeling (scratch & conv) plans]

Afrika Korps: see separate listing
The Eighth Army in the Desert: see separate listing
Fallshirmjäger: see separate listing

Afrika Korps [all Afx]

Introduction, Organization: My 72 13/9:486-487
Engineers: Je 72 13/10:562-563
Artillery: Jl 72 13/11:598-599
Reconnaissance Units: Ag 72 13/12:665-666
Panzer Troops: S 72 14/1:24-25
Headquarters Units: O 72 14/2:72-73
Panzerjäger Forces: N 72 14/3:138-139
Luftwaffe Ground Troops: D 72 14/4:200-201

The Eighth Army in the Desert [all Afx]

Background, Organization: Jl 73 14/11:589-591
Headquarters troops: Ag 73 14/12:657-659
Infantry: S 73 15/1:44-47
Armoured formations: O 73 15/2:87-88
Artillery: D 73 15/3:220-223
Reconnaissance Units: Ja 74 15/4:302-304
Lines of Communication: F 74 15/5:339+
Engineer & Ordinance Units: Mr 74 15/6:390-392
Formation organization: Ap 74 15/7:468+

Fallschirmjäger [all Afx]

Uniforms, Equipment, Organization: S 71 13/1:21+; O 71 13/2:95+
Uniforms & Personal Equipment: N 71 13/3:154-151
Uniforms 1943-1945, Weapons: D 71 13/4:193
Small Arms & Infantry Weapons 1944-1945: F 72 13/6:306-307
Additional Weapons: Mr 72 13/7:374-375

GENERAL STUDIES OF CULTURES

Apache: MM D 74 4/12:342-345; cor My 75 5/5:299; Je 5/6:336
Eaters of Men: Zulu 1897: MM My 74 4/5:262-264; Je 74 4/6:322-324
Johnnie Reb of 1861: MM Ja 75 5/1:25-27; cor Mr 75 5/3:154-155; Je 75 5/6:336
Plains Indians: MM Je 75 5/6:342-345; Jl 75 5/7:410-412; Ag 75 5/8:480-481; S 75 5/9:548-549; O 75 5/10:617
U. S. Cavalry in the Indian Wars: MM O 74 4/10:613-617; N 74 4/11:672+; cor F 75 5/2:89

HERALDRY (MILITARY)

Badges & Insignia

Bundeswehr Unit Sleeve Insignia: Fus W 74 1/2:10-11
Condor Legion: rank insignia: MW Ag 73 1/12:638-639
Dutch NSB Insignia: Dutch SS unit, German army, WW-II: Fus Sp 74 1/3:25
Formation Badges of the Korean War: Belgium; Columbia; Ethiopia; 1st Commonwealth Div; 27th Infantry Brigade: MW O 73 2/2: 92-93
French Army Airborne Berets & Insignia: Fus Au 73 1/1:38; W 74 1/2:7+
German Ski-Jäger Insignia: Fus Au 73 1/1:15
Guatemalan Airborne Insignia: Fus Su 74 1/4:6-8
Luftwaffe Embroidered Badges: Fus Sp 74 1/3:23
Medieval Heraldry: see separate listing
Nazi Mothers Cross: WW2J S 2/5-6:38
Polish WW-II Shoulder Rank Badges & U. S. Equivalents: Q Ja 74 9/1:16
Regimental Cap Badges of the British Army: Royal Fusiliers 1685-1968: Fus Au 73 1/1:10-11
Russian Naval Officer Insignia of Rank: MM Je 73 3/6:364
U. S. Airborne Forces Cap Insignia: Fus Su 74 1/4:18-19
U. S. Army Distinctive Unit Insignia: Fus Su 74 1/4:9-13
U. S. Army Special Forces Beret Insignia: Fus W 74 1/2:12-15
Wehrmacht Breast Eagles: all embroidered types: WW2J S 2/5-6: 38

Medieval Heraldry [all MM]

Origins of Heraldry: N 71 1/11:560-561
The Shield: D 71 1/12:624-625
Honourable & Sub-Ordinate Charges: Ja 72 2/1:24-25
Shield Charges: F 72 2/2:82-83

I. Static Scale

Head, Body, & Horse Furnishings: Mr 72 2/3:138-139
Variants: Ap 72 2/4:188-189
Flags: My 72 2/5:242-243

Flags & Other Military Colors

British Army Colours: details for 54mm figures: MM My 71 1/5: 260-262
British Infantry Colours at Waterloo: see separate listing
Condor Legion: Commander in Chief, Chief of Staff: MW Ag 73 1/12:638
French Forces in the U.S. War of Independence: Agenois; Armagnac; Auxerrois; Bourbonnais; Champàgne; Dillon; Foix; Gatinois; Hainault; Marine Sayonne; Royal Deux Points; Saintonge; Soissonnais; Touraine; Walsh: MW My 73 1/9:472; Irish Walsh; Royal Deux Points: Jl 73 1/10:571
German Regiments in the U.S. War of Independence: Anspach Bayreuth; Brunswick: Prinz Frederick, Rhetz, Riedessel, Specht; Hesse Cassel: Dittfurth, Donop, Lieb du Corps, Lossberg, Mirbach, Prinz Carl; Hesse Hanau: MW F 73 1/6:314
Infantry Uniforms & Standards of Frederick the Great: see separate listing
Musketeers, 1 & 2 Btn, Danish, 1813: S&L (Je 75) 8:19
Nassau Grenadiers: 1810 standard: MM N 75 5/11:673
Russian Napoleonic Colours at Borodino: 1797, 1800, 1803 patterns: Arakcheev; Astrakhan; Ekaterinoslav; Fanagoria; Kiev; Leib Grenadiers; Malorossia; Moscow; Pavlov; St. Petersburg; Siberia; Taurida: MM S 75 5/9:554
3rd Infantry Rgt of Jutland, 1813 Danish: S&L (Je 75) 8:19
10th Rgt of Foot: Regimental Colour, King's Colour: MW N 72 1/3:142
Uniforms & Colours of the British Army: see separate listing

British Infantry Colors at Waterloo [all MM]

1st Foot Guards (later Grenadier), 2nd & 3rd Btn: Je 71 1/6:289
2nd or Coldstream Guards, 2nd Btn: Je 71 1/6:289
3rd Foot Guards (later Scots), 2nd Btn: Jl 71 1/7:340
4th Foot, The King's Own Regiment, 1st Btn: Jl 71 1/7:341
14th Foot, the Buckinghamshire Regiment, 3rd Btn: Jl 71 1/7:341
23rd Foot, The Royal Welsh Fusiliers, 1st Btn: Ag 71 1/8:400
27th Foot, the Inniskilling Regiment, 1st Btn: Ag 71 1/8:400
28th Foot, The North Gloucestershire Regiment, 1st Btn: Ag 71 1/8:400-401
30th Foot, the Cambridgeshire Regiment, 2nd Btn: Ag 71 1/8:401
32nd Foot, the Cornwall Regiment, 1st Btn: Ag 71 1/8:401
33rd Foot, 1st Yorks (West Riding) Regiment, 2nd Btn: S 71 1/9: 448
40th Foot, the 2nd Somerset Regiment, 1st Btn: Ag 71 1/8:400

42nd Foot, The Royal Highland Regiment, 1st Btn: S 71 1/9:448
44th Foot, the East Essex Regiment, 2nd Btn: S 71 1/9:448
51st Foot, 2nd Yorks (West Riding) Regiment: S 71 1/9:448-449
52nd Foot, the Oxfordshire Regiment, 1st Btn: S 71 1/9:448-449
69th Foot, the South Lincolnshire Regiment, 2nd Btn: S 71 1/9:449
71st Foot, the Glasgow Highland Light Infantry, 1st Btn: S 71 1/9: 449
79th Foot, the Cameron Highlanders, 1st Btn: O 71 1/10:512
92nd Foot, the Gordon Highlanders, 1st Btn: O 71 1/10:512

Infantry Uniforms & Standards of Frederick the Great

A&W Ja 73 3:poster
 1st Winterfield Rgt: Rgt Colors, Type 1
 22nd Prinz Moritz von Anhalt-Dessau: Rgt colors, Type 2
 12th Fink Rgt: Btn colors, Type 3
 32nd Tresckow Rgt: Btn colors, Type 4
 18th Prinz von Preussen Rgt: Rgt colors, Type 5
 15th Guards Rgt: Rgt colors, Type 6
 34th Prinz Ferdinand von Presudden Rgt: Btn colors, Type 7
 40th Kreitzen Rgt: Rgt colors, Type 8

Uniforms & Colors of the British Army [all MM]

The King's Own Regiment of Foot, 1745: Colonel's & Lieutenant-Colonel's Colours, drum crest: D 71 1/12:631
Royal Regiment of Fusiliers, 1685: Colonel's & Lieutenant-Colonel's Colours: Ja 72 2/1:19
1st Btn, Royal Welch Fusiliers, 1899: Regimental Colours, Queen's Colour: F 72 2/2:76-77
6th Dragoon Guards (Carabiniers), 1912: Regimental Standard: Mr 72 2/3:136-137
1st Btn, Royal Inniskilling Fusiliers, 1968: Regimental Colours, Queen's Colour: Ap 72 2/4:178-179
Life Guards, 1935: Regimental Standard, Union or Squadron Standard: My 72 2/5:241
First Regiment of Foot Guards: Colonel, Lt. Colonel, Major, Captain's Colours: Je 72 2/6:295
Drum Horse of the 19th Hussars: Drum Banners: Jl 72 2/7:344-345
1st Btn, 60th (Royal American) Rgt, 1800: King's Colour, Regimental Colour: Ap 73 3/4:207
Royal Marines, 1972: Queen's Colour, Regimental Colour, drum badge: Je 73 3/6:358-359
1st & 2nd Life Guards, 1816: Sovereign's Standard, Union Badge Guidon, Officer's Dress Sabretache: Jl 73 3/7:434-435
Northumberland Fusiliers, 1913: King's Colour, Regimental Colour, Drummer's Colour: S 73 3/9:606-607
Drum Horse of the 11th Hussars, 1903-1904: Drum Banner, Shabraque Badge: O 73 3/10:662-663

I. Static Scale 110

Regiment of Foot Guards, 1815: Major's Colour, 8th Coy Colour, Drum Badge: N 73 3/11:740-741
Royal Horse Artillery, 1896: Dress & Undress Sabretache: D 73 3/12:809
92nd (Gordon Highlanders) Rgt of Foot, 1807: King's Colour, Regimental Colour: Ja 74 4/1:26-27
15th/19th King's Royal Hussars, 1961: Regimental Guidon: Ap 74 4/4:190-191
85th (Bucks Volunteers) or King's Light Infantry Rgt, 1826: King's Colour, Regimental Colour: My 74 4/5:250-251
14th King's Light Dragoons, 1832: King's Guidon, Squadron Guidon: Je 74 4/6:318-319

UNIFORMS

Ancient

Byzantine: senior & junior officer, infantry, standard bearer: MM Mr 73 3/3:153
Egyptain Heavy Infantry, 1288 BC: MM O 75 5/10:607; cor Ja 76 6/1:17
Egyptain War Chariot & Crew, 1288 BC: MM O 75 5/10:607
Greek Hoplite: MM Jl 74 4/7:387
Greek Hoplites: 5 var: MM D 75 5/12:742-743; cor F 76 6/2:110
Helmets & Headdresses Through the Ages: Ancident: S&L Jl 74 2:22-23; Ag 74 3:22-23; cor (O 74) 4:(3)
Macedonian Phalangite: Alexanderian: MM N 73 3/11:753
Median Cavalry: Alexanderian: MM N 73 3/11:753
Normans: MM Ap 75 5/4:212-213
Nubian Auxiliary Archer, 1288 BC: MM O 75 5/10:607
Persian Bowman: MM Jl 74 4/7:387
Persian Infantryman: Alexanderian: MM N 73 3/11:753
Persian Infantryman: MM Jl 74 4/7:387
Persian Light Cavalry: MM Jl 74 4/7:387
Roman Legionary, winter marching gear: MM N 75 5/11:674
Roman Standard Bearer: IM O 72 9/10:13
Sherden Mercenary, 1288 BC: MM O 75 5/10:607
Vikings: 3 var: MM Ja 74 4/1:38-39+

Medieval & Renaissance

English Archer: Crecy: S&L (Ap 75) 7:18
English Infantry of the 15th Century: 3 var: MM Je 74 4/6:342-344
Helmets & Headdresses Through the Ages: Days of Chivalry: S&L (D 74) 5:16-17; (F 75) 6:12-13
Janizaries: 4 var from various periods: MM N 73 3/11:754
Knights c.1250-1330: 3 var: MM Je 75 5/6:358
Knights: Crecy, new & old style armor: S&L (Ap 75) 7:21
Landsknechts: Appenzel; Basel; Bern; Schaffausen; Schwitz; Solothurn;

Uri: MM Ap 72 2/4:196-198
Landsknechts: 2 var: MM D 73 3/12:811
Landsknechts: uniforms & weapons: MM Ap 75 5/4:224
Polish Winged Hussars: Colonel: S&L (D 74) 5:8
Renaissance Warfare: see separate listing
Uniforms of the Swiss Guard: 1506: MM Ag 73 3/8:531

1600-1790

Anspach-Bayreuth: Officer, Jäger Btn, 1781: MM S 75 5/9:547
Army of the Ancien Regime: see separate listing
Austrian Dragoons: seven years war: MM D 75 5/12:729
Austro-Hungarian Infantry: see separate listing
Black Watch (42nd): private, campaign dress, 1776: MM S 75 5/9:532
The British Army 1685-1700: see separate listing
British Army Uniforms: see separate listing
British Officer: seven years war: S&L (O 75) 10:5
The Dress of Marlborough's Armies: Marlborough (3 var); Eugene; Marshal Tallard; Horse Officer; Life Guard; First Foot Guards Officer; Musketeer; Grenadier; Foot Soldier; Dutch Pioneer: N 71 1/11:568-569
11th Dragoon, Light Squadron, 1757: S&L (O 75) 10:6
Facing Colours in War of Spanish Succession: MM Ag 75 5/8:472
1st Georgia: rifleman, 1777: MM S 75 5/9:547; cor Ja 76 6/1:17
Fraser's Highlanders (71st): private, full dress, 1776: MM S 75 5/9:533
Gatineau Rgt: Grenadier, Siege of Yorktown, 1780: MM S 75 5/9:546
Hesse-Cassel Infantry, Rgt Erbprinz: officer, 1780: MM S 75 5/9:547
Infantry Uniforms & Standards of Frederick the Great: see separate listing
Iroquois Warrior: British, American Revolution: MM S 75 5/9:547
Ladies in Uniform: "Military Fashions" of late 18th century England, 3 var: MM Ag 75 5/8:478+
Light Company, von Riedesel Rgt, Brunswick, 1776: MM S 75 5/9:547
Louis XV French Uniforms: see separate listing
Marlborough's coachman, foot runner, equerry, ADC: MM S 73 3/8:603-604
Military Album: see separate listing
New Model Army: Col. Kirk's Rgt of Foot, 1686, Musketeer, Grenadier; Wentworth's Rgt of Foot Guards, 1661, Musketeer: MW S 73 2/1:17+
Once Upon a Time There was a Simple Bonnet: see separate listing
Polish Winged Hussar 17th Century: MM Mr 75 5/3:165
Quebec Militia, 1776: Officer: MM S 75 5/9:547
Regiment Bourbonnaise, 1786: standard bearer: RT Ap 74 7/4:45
Rogers Rangers: winter, ranger, officer: MM D 74 4/12:766-767
2nd Canadian Rgt (Congress's Own): 1776 & 1779 var: RT F 75 8/2:21

I. Static Scale   112

2nd Rhode Island Rgt, 1779: officer: MM S 75 5/9:546
2nd Rgt Musketeer, Prussia, Frederick the Great: A&W Ja 73 3:61
7th Dragoons 1769: officer: MM N 75 5/11:672
62nd Rgt of Foot, 1777: private: MM S 75 5/9:535
Swiss Guard, 1792 French Service: guard, grenadier officer, drummer: MM Je 75 5/6:356-357
37th Rgt of Foot, 1776: grenadier: MM S 75 5/9:546
12th Rgt Drummer, Prussia, Frederick the Great: A&W Ja 73 3:61
20th Rgt of Foot, 1759: Grenadier: S&L (O 75) 10:6
Uniforms & Colours of the British Army: see separate listing
War of Independence: see separate listing

Napoleonic

(Austro-Hungary)

Austrian Chevauleger: all units: MM N 75 5/11:673
Austrian Hussar, 1796-1806: A&W Mr 73 4:65
Austrian Mounted Jäger & Light Dragoon, 1800: A&W Mr 73 4:61
Austro-Hungarian Generals: 5 var: MM My 75 5/5:289
Campaign in Friuli: see separate listing
42nd Infantry Rgt, 1792: fusilier: S&L (D 75) 11:12
Saxe Coburg Saalfeld, 1815: lancer: S&L (D 75) 11:12

(Argentina)

8th Infantry Btn, 1816: headgear only: A&W S 74 13:65

(Belgium)

Belgian Infantryman, 1815: center coy: IM Jl 73 10/7:8
Dutch/Belgian Carabinier: 3 var: MM Mr 75 5/3:165

(Bavaria)

Bavarian Foot Artillery, 1812-1814: gunner (3 var), 1st Lieutenant: MM Ja 74 4/1:30-31
Bavarian Horse Artillery, 1812-1815: gunner, 1st Lieutenant: MM Ja 74 4/1:30-31

(Brunswick)

Black Brunswicker Infantryman, 1809: S&L (O 75) 10:24

(Denmark)

Corporal, Rifle Coy, 1813: S&L (Je 75) 8:19
Den Kongelige Livgarde til Hest (Royal Danish Horseguard): 1808 parade, rank emblems: S&L (Ap 75) 7:14-15
Kongens Livjaeger Corps (King's Lifecorps of Riflemen): Officer 1801; Officer 1807; Rifleman 1804; S&L (D 75) 11:67
Officer 1813: S&L (Je 75) 8:19
Rifleman, summer, 1813: S&L (Je 75) 8:19

(France)

Campaign in Friuli: see separate listing
Cannonniers Garde-Cotes: 1807 gunner, 1810 gunner & officer: MW Ja 74 2/5:266-267
Cavalry School at St. Germain, 1810 & 1811 var: MW Je 73 1/10: 528-529+
Chasseurs à Pied de la Garde, 1813: MW Ja 74 2/5:260-261
Drummer, French Line Artillery, 1807: MM O 73 3/10:665
Drummer, Garde d'Honneur de Lyon, 1804-1814: MM O 73 3/10:665
1815: see separate listing in figure conversions
French Carabiniers, 1812: officers, rank, trumpeter: MM Ag 75 5/8:473
French Horse Artillery of the Line: corporal, gunner, captain: MM Ag 75 5/8:466-467
Grenadier, French Infantrie de Ligne, 1811: MM N 75 5/11:675
Legion Irlandaise, 1805: MM Jl 75 5/7:429
Line Chasseurs à Cheval accessories: MM My 75 5/5:281
Mamelukes: MM Jl 75 5/7:428
NCO, French Line Infantry, 1815: sword knots: MM S 75 5/9:555
Napoleonic Cavalry: hussar, horse grenadiers of the guard, carabiniers: MM Ag 75 5/8:473
Officers of Chasseurs à Cheval of the Line at Waterloo: MM S 75 5/9:555
Once Upon a Time There Was a Simple Bonnet: see separate listing
1 Coy, Mousquetaires de la Garde du Roi, 1815: MM D 75 5/12: 728
Regiment de Prusse, 1806: MM N 75 5/11:672-673
Soldier of the Month: see separate listing
Standard Bearer, 12th Demi-Brigade, 6 (Armagnac) Rgt, 1794: RT My 74 7/5-6:62
Tenue de Route: 2 Rgt Chevau-Legers-Lanciers, 3 Rgt Trompeter: MM Je 75 5/6:356
13th Hussars (Bacciochi), c. 1813: MM N 75 5/11:666
Thus Fought Napoleon: see separate listing
Trooper, Chevau-Legers Polonaise de la Garde: 1810-1812: MM Je 75 5/6:357
Vélites des Chasseurs à Cheval, 1806: MM Jl 75 5/7:428
Vélites de Grenadiers à Cheval, 1806: MM Jl 75 5/7:429-429

I. Static Scale 114

(Hannover)

Militia, 1814: 2 var: S&L (O 75) 10:20-21

(Hesse-Darmstadt)

Hesse-Darmstadt Infantry, 1806-1812: Leib Garde Rgt, Officer; Leib Rgt, Fusilier; Rgt Gross-und-Erbprinz, Fusilier; Rgt Gross-und-Erbprinz, Grenadier (2 var); Rgt Gross-und-Erbprinz, Officer; Rgt Gross-und-Erbprinz, Voltigeur: MW O 73 2/2:76-77+

(Italy)

Campaign in Friuli: see separate listing
Royal Italian Guard Dragoon: MW D 72 1/4:197

(Netherlands)

Dutch/Belgian Carabinier: 3 var: MM Mr 75 5/3:165
Dutch Infantry, 1806-1810: Grenadier, Drum Major, Voltigeur Officer: MM Je 75 5/6:338-339; cor S 75 5/9:526; add N 75 5/11: 677
Dutch Infantry, 1815: NCO, flank coy: IM Jl 73 10/7:8

(Poland)

Dutchy of Warsaw, 16th Pulk Ulanow, 1797-1814: officer, trumpeter: MM Jl 75 5/7:429
Napoleonic Uniforms: Polish Foot Artillery, c.1810: gunner, mounted officer, sergeant: MM N 75 5/11:670
Polish Infantry Uniforms of the Napoleonic Wars: see separate listing

(Portugal)

Portuguese Army after 1811: line, grenadier, & Caçaderes: MM Ag 75 5/8:473

(Prussia)

1815: see separate listing in figure conversions
Fusilier, campaign dress, Waterloo: S&L (F 75) 6:10
Fusilier Officer, 2nd (1st Pommeranian) Rgt, infantry: S&L (Je 75) 8:23
Landwehr Officer, 1815: MM O 75 5/10:596
Leib-Grenadier-Garde Officer, 1798: headgear only: A&W W 74 13:65

Musketeer, parade & campaign dress, Waterloo campaign: S&L (F 75) 6:11
Musketeer, 7th (2nd West Prussian) Rgt, infantry: S&L (Je 75) 8:22
Prussian Artillery, 1815: MM D 75 5/12:729
Prussian Dragoons: 1st King's; 2nd West Prussian; 3rd Lithuanian; 4th West Prussian; 5th Brandenburg (Prinz Wilhelm); 6th Neumark; 7th Rhein; 8th Magdeburg: MM O 74 4/10:590
Prussian Dragoons 1815: trooper & bugler: MM Jl 75 5/7:402-403; add S 75 5/9:525; N 75 5/11:676
Prussian Grenadiers: 1st East Prussian; 2nd East Prussian; Pommeranian; Leib-Grenadier; Silesian: MM D 74 4/12:760
Prussian Horse & Foot c.1806: gunner, NCO, Officer: MM D 75 5/12:722-723
Prussian Kürassiers, 1814: Graf Wrangel (East Prussian) 3: MM D 75 5/12:730; cor F 76 6/2:110
Prussian Kürassiers, 1815: MM D 75 5/12:729
Prussian Officers, Cavalry, Couriers, Foot Jagers: 7 var: MM My 75 5/5:281
Prussian Ulans: 1st West Prussian; 2nd Silesian; Brandenburg; trumpets: MM O 74 4/10:590
31st Rgt, infantry, private: S&L (Ap 75) 7:12
25th Rgt, infantry, private: S&L (Ap 75) 7:10

(Russia)

Baschkir: 1811-1812 Russian Mongolian troops: MM Ap 75 5/4:223
Cossacks: 9 var: MM My 75 5/5:289
Grenadier Rgt "Pavlovski," Russian Imperial Guard, 1813-1815: MM Ap 75 5/4:223
Jelissawetgrad Rgt, flanker, late 1812: S&L Ag 74 3:8
Once Upon a Time There was a Simple Bonnet: see separate listing
Russian Cuirassier, Little Russia Rgt, 1812: MM D 74 4/12:740

(Saxony)

Saxon Army 1810-1812: line infantry, grenadiers, Jäger, Schützen: MM D 75 5/12:729; add F 76 6/2:111

(Spain)

Catalonian Guerrilla, Peninsular War: MM Mr 75 5/3:164
Dragoon, 7 (Numancia) Rgt, 1808: RT Mr 75 8/3:26
Once Upon a Time There Was a Simple Bonnet: see separate listing
Spanish Dragoons, Almansa Rgt, 1808: saddle furniture: MM Je 75 5/6:357; add & cor S 75 5/9:554

(Sweden)

Leibgrenadiercorps, 1807: headgear only: A&W S 74 13:65

I. Static Scale 116

(U. K.)

British Army Uniforms: see separate listing
British Dragoons, Trumpeter: MM Ag 75 5/8:472-473
British Foot Artillery (Royal Artillery), 1810: officer, sergeant, gunner: MM O 75 5/10:614-615
Chasseurs Britannique, 1801: MM N 75 5/11:672
Chasseurs Britannique: officer, chasseur, light infantry officer: S&L (D 74) 5:14-15; add (Ap 75) 7:23
Coldstream Guards, Light Company, 2nd btn, 1815: MM Jl 74 4/7: 410
Congreve Rocket Artillery Trooper, 1814: MM Ap 73 3/4:216-217
1815: see separate listing in figure conversions
57th Foot: Corporal, Battalion Coy, 1811: MM N 75 5/11:675
42nd Highlanders: private, Battalion Coy, 1811: MM N 75 5/11:675
43rd Light Infantry, 1812: private: Afx S 75 17/1:45
King's German Legion: Officer of Sharpshooters, parade, 1812-1816; Private, Line Infantry, 1803-1808: S&L (O 75) 10:23
King's Own Regiment of Foot, c. 1800-1815: Officer; Pioneer: MM O 75 5/10:596-597
Lieutenant General William Carr Beresford, 1811: MM N 75 5/11: 675
Military Album: see separate listing
95th Rifles, 1810: rifleman; bugler: MM N 74 4/11:670-671+; cor Mr 75 5/3:155
95th Rifle Brigade: MM Jl 75 5/7:428
Once Upon a Time There Was a Simple Bonnet: see separate listing
Royal African Corps, 1808: Officer & Other Ranks: MW D 73 2/4:185
Royal Horse Artillery, 1811: Troop Officer: MM N 75 5/11:675
Royal Horse Guards (The Blues) 1819: MM N 75 5/11:672
Royal Westminster Volunteers, 1798: Private, Btn Coy; Private, Grenadier Coy; Private, Light Coy: MM F 75 5/2:90-91
Staindrop Gentlemen & Yeomanry: cavalry home defense: S&L Ag 74 3:20; add (O 74) 4:15
Ces Terribles Bearskin Cap Fittings: var of Scots Grey bearskin cord lines: S&L Ag 74 3:7; add (O 74) 4:14
Uniforms & Colors of the British Army: see separate listing

(Westphalia)

Westphalian Tambour Major, 1810: 4th Westphalian Line Rgt: MM D 75 5/12:730

1820-1914

Afgan Amir (chieftain), 1879-1880: MW S 73 2/1:31
Austro-Hungarian Infantry: see separate listing
Battle of Montebello: see separate listing
Black Watch, 42nd Highlanders, Tel-el-Kibir, Egypt, 1882: S&L Jl 74 2:24

Figures

Cacciatori delle Alpi, 1859: see separate listing
Collector's Choice: see separate listing
Crow Scout, U. S. Army, 1870: MM N 74 4/11:672
8th Hussars, 1854-1855, Crimea War: Officer, Ranks, Bugler: MM Ap 75 5/4:223
11th Hussars in Crimea: Officer, Trumpeter: MM O 74 4/10:622-623; cor Mr 75 5/3:154
4th Light Dragoons, 1882: Officer: MM Ap 75 5/4:224
French Infantry, 1900-1914: 3 var: MW F 74 2/6:297-299
Guards Camel Rgt, River War, 1884-1889: trooper: S&L (D 74) 5:4
Highland Light Infantry, Tel-el-Kebir, Egypt, 1882: S&L Jl 74 2:24
Imperial Yeomanry of the Boer War: Sharpshooters trooper, full dress, 1901; Officer, Roughriders, 1912; Officer, Surrey Yeomanry, 1907; Imperial Yeomanry Scouts, 1901 (2 var): MM Ap 74 4/4:201+; disc Jl 74 4/7:408
Indian Scout, U. S. Army, full dress, 1895: MM N 74 4/11:672
Johnny Reb: see separate listing
Life Guards, 1882: Corporal of Horse: MW F 74 2/6:297-299
Line Infantryman, light marching order, British, 1879: MM Jl 74 4/7:390
Military Album: see separate listing
Military Bands of the Indian Army: see separate listing
Mountain Artillery, 2nd Afgan War 1879-1880: officer, sergeant, gunner: MW S 73 2/1:26-27+
Native Horse, Zulu War, 1879: Trooper: MM Jl 74 4/7:389
Naval Brigade Officer, Zulu War, 1879: 2 var: MM Ag 74 4/8: 458-459
91st Highlanders: Sergeant; Private, light marching order, 1879: MM Jl 74 4/7:391; Officer: Ag 74 4/8:467
Once Upon a Time There Was a Simple Bonnet: see separate listing
Prussian Garde Jäger, 1870: Jäger & Officer: MM My 75 5/5: 274-275
Royal Berkshire Yeomanry Cavalry: Officer, Trooper signaler: MM F 75 5/2:100-101
Russian Life Guard Dragoon Rgt, 1896-1914: MM S 75 5/9:555
Russo-Turkish War 1853: Russian Marksman; Infantry Officer; Turkish Soldier: A&W My 73 5/61:64-65
Scots Guards, 1882: Private: MW F 74 2/6:300
Skinner's Horse: British Officer; Indian Trooper: MM O 75 5/10: 603-604; add Ja 76 6/1:18
Soldier of the Month: see separate listing
Spanish American War Infantry, U. S.: RiS Au 73 2/1:30-31; cor W 74 2/2:70
Standartenträger of the Gardes du Corps, 1900: heavy cavalry rgt, German: MW My 73 1/9:485
3/60th Rifles, Zulu War, 1879: Other Ranks, light marching order: MM Ag 74 4/8:458
23rd Rgt of Bombay Native Infantry (123rd Outram rifles): S&L (O 75) 10:16
2/21st Royal Scots Fusiliers: Officer, campaign dress, Zulu War 1879: MM Ag 74 4/8:458
U. S. Cavalry in Indian Wars: Officer (3 var), cavalry, trumpeter,

I. Static Scale 118

    sergeant: MM O 74 4/10:616-617
Uniforms & Colors of the British Army: see separate listing
Union Light Artillery: MM S 75 5/9:554-555
Union Uniforms of the Civil War: see separate listing

World War I to 1939

Air Service: U.S. 1925 winter flying suits, 2 var: RiS Mr 75 3/1:30
Austro-Hungarian Army, 1914-1918: see separate listing
Bolivian Army, Chaco War, 1932-1935: MM O 75 5/10:597
Condor Legion: Legionär, Oberst: MW Ag 73 1/12:638-639
French Army, 1914-1918: see separate listing
French Infantry, 1914: 3 var: MM Ag 74 4/8:474-475
German Cavalry & Artillery, 1914-1918: see separate listing
German Infantry Uniforms, 1914-18: see separate listing
Military Bands of the Indian Army: see separate listing
Once Upon a Time There Was a Simple Bonnet: see separate listing
Uniforms & Colors of the British Army: see separate listing
Uniforms of the Third Reich: see separate listing
Wimmera Rgt, 19th Light Horse (Armoured Car) Rgt, 1936: Australian: AFV Ja 74 4/9:29+

World War II

Afrika Korps: see scparate listing
British Army Battledress: MW Ja 74 2/5:251-252
Elefant SPA crew uniform: MM Ag 75 5/8:469
15th Uhlans, Polish Army, 1939: Trooper: MW Ja 74 2/5:241
56th Fighter Group, Europe, U.S.A.A.F.: pilot: RiS Ag 72 1/1:17
Finnish Army: MM Ap 75 5/4:227
German Navy: see separate listing
German U-Boat: Oberbootsmannaat (CPO); Lt. zur See (Sub-Lt.); Oberleutnant zS (Lt.) 2 var: MW Ja 74 2/5:247-248
Goering Parade Uniform: MM Ag 75 5/8:472
Once Upon a Time There Was a Simple Bonnet: see separate listing
Red Army Man of 1941: 2 var: S&L (F 75) 6:4-5
SS Officer, 1944: RT Ag 72 5/8:94
SS Stormpostmann: bicycle & sidecar mail delivery: MM D 74 4/12:765; cor Ap 75 5/4:211
2nd Corps, 2 Brygada Pancerny, Polish Army, Italy, 1944: Porucznik (Lt.): Q Ja 74 9/1:16
Service Uniforms of the Italian Army: see separate listing
Soldier of the Month: see separate listing
U.S. Army Helmet Markings: 30 var: MM Je 72 2/6:287
Uniforms & Colors of the British Army: see separate listing
Uniforms of the Luftwaffe: see separate listing
Uniforms of the SS: see separate listing
Waffen SS: Unterscharführer; 4 headgear var: RT Je 75 8/6:68
Wehrmacht Heer: Panzerschütze; 4 headgear var: RT Je 75 8/6:68

Post World War II

Anti-G Cutaway Garments: 1960 & 1966 var, USAF: RiS Jl 75 3/2:100
British Household Divisions: see separate listing
Devonshire & Dorset Rgt: present dress uniform: MW F 74 2/6: 314-315
11th Hussars, 1962: Sergeant, battledress, #1 dress (ceremonial), #2 dress (walking out): MM Ag 75 5/8:486-487
Flying Uniform: USAF A/P22S-2 high-altitude flying suit: RiS Su 73 1/4:135
Modern Italian Army Uniforms: all units, 68 var: A&W N 73 8: poster
Once Upon a Time There Was a Simple Bonnet: see separate listing
Swiss Guards: Halberdier in undress with rifle; Halberdier, full dress; Sergeant, full dress; Officer, full dress: MM Ag 73 3/8:531
U.S. Army Infantry: radioman & rifleman, c. 1969, Vietnam: RiS Jl 75 3/2:92
Uniforms & Colors of the British Army: see separate listing

Separate Listings

Afrika Korps

A&W N 72 2:poster
General
Panzertruppen Lieutenant, Summer 1942
Corporal
Lance Corporal, Summer 1941
Infantry Sergeant, Winter Uniform

Army of the Ancien Regime [all A&W]

French Cavalry, 1745, Dragoon: Mr 74 10:60
French Infantry, 1740, Rgt Royal Comtois: Mr 74 10:60
French Colonial Infantry, 1754, Rgt de Lally: Mr 74 10:61
French Infantry, 1757, Rgt de Vaisseaux: Mr 74 10:61
French Infantryman, 18th Century: Mr 74 10:64
Prussian Cuirassier, 1757: Mr 74 10:64
Austrian Infantry, 1760: Mr 74 10:65
English Infantry, 1745: Mr 74 10:65
Maison du Roi, 1760, Light Cavalry: My 74 11:64
Royal Italian Rgt, Infantry, 1757: My 74 11:64
Artois Rgt, 1757, Infantry: My 74 11:65
Guiyenne Rgt, Infantry, 1760: My 74 11:65

I. Static Scale   120

                    *Austro-Hungarian Infantry 1708-1866

A&W S 73 7:<u>poster</u>--
1708 Eberhard Friedrich Graf Neipperg Foot Rgt, Musketeer
1713 Heinrich Tobias Freiheer von Hasslingen Foot Rgt, Musketeer
1757 August Voncolln-Teutschmeister Infantry Rgt, Musketeer
1750 Anhalt-Zerbst Principality Infantry Rgt, Grenadier
1776 Franz Moriz Graf Lacy 22nd Infantry Rgt, Fusilier
1790 Carl Graf Clerfayt 9th Infantry Rgt, Fusilier
1806 Anton Freiherr von Zach 15th Infantry Rgt, Fusilier
1809 Carl Eugen Graf Erbach 42nd Infantry Rft, Grenadier
1813 Wenzel Graf Kaunitz-Rietberg 20th Infantry Rgt, Drummer
1813 Erzherzor Ludwig Joseph 8th Infantry Rgt, Sergeant-Major
1848 Anton Graf Kinsky 47th Infantry Rgt, Private
1848 Franz Gyulai Graf von Maros-Nemethy und Nadaska 33rd
    Hungarian Infantry Rgt, Private
1859 Ludwig III Grossherzog von Hessen 14th Infantry Rgt, Lieu-
    tenant
1859 Gustav Wilhelm Prinz Hohenlohe-Langenburg 17th Infantry Rgt,
    Private
1866 Leopold II, Konig der Belgier 27th Infantry Rgt, Private
1866 Wilhelm, Herzog von Wurttemberg 73rd Infantry Rgt, Captain

                    Austro-Hungarian Army 1914-1918

A&W N 75 20:<u>poster</u>--
Infantry, parade order, 1914
Infantry Officer, 1914: 2 var
Infantry, 1914
Tyrolean Kaiser Jäger Officer, 1914
Kaiserschützen, 1914
Hungarian Infantry, 1914
Bosnian Infantry, 1914
Uhlan, 1914
Hussar, 1914
Dragoon, 1914
General 1915
Cavalry 1916
Infantry High-Ranking Officer 1916
Bosnian Infantry 1917
Combat Order 1918

                    Battle of Montebello, 1859

A&W Ja 74 2/5:60-61, 64-65--
Aosta Light Cavalry
Sardinian Infantry Officer
Army Train
Montebello Light Cavalry
Austrian Infantry
Austrian Infantry Officer

French Infantry Officer
Sardinian Infantry
  Bgd Granatieri
  Bgd Savoia E Pinerolo
  Bgd Piemonte E Aosta
  Bgd Cuneo
  Bgd Regina E Savona
  Bgd Casale E Acqui
Sardinian Light Cavalry
  Aosta
  Novaro
  Saluzzo
  Monferrato
  Alessandria
Sardinian Line Cavalry
  Nizza
  Genova
  Novara
  Piemonte Reale
Other Sardinian Units
  State Maggiore
  Bersaglieri
  Genio
  Carabinieri
  Artiglieria
  Guide

The British Army 1685-1700

MW D 73 2/4:209-212--
  Grenadier, 4th Rgt of Foot, 1680-1690
  Pikeman, Rgt of Foot
  Officer, Rgt of Foot
  Musketeer
  Sergeant, Musketeer Coy, Rgt of Foot, 1700-1792
  Musketeer, Rgt of Foot, 1700
  Hautboist
  Drummer, Rgt of Foot

British Army Uniforms [all Afx]

Officer, Musketeer, 1660; Musketeer, 1672; Pikeman, 1682; Musketeer, Grenadier, 1685-1700: Ap 74 15/8:456-458
1st Rgt of Foot Guards, 1685: 2 Officers, Sergeant, Pikeman, Musketeer: My 74 15/9:506-507
2nd Coldstream Rgt, HM Foot Guards, 1685: Je 74 15/10:586-588
3rd Rgt, HM Scots Foot Guards, 1685: Jl 74 15/11:626-628
Artillery Train, pre-1716: carter, 2 gunners, field officer, matross: Jl 74 15/11:626-628
Grey Dragoons: Officer, 1692; Dragoon 1684; Dragoon 1687: Ag 74 15/12:695-696

I. Static Scale   122

First Troop of Horse Guards, 1685: Officer & Trooper; Trooper of
   Horse Guards; Horse Grenadier; horse furniture: S 74 16/1:
   36-38
Coldstream Guards, 1703-1704: Grenadier; Private, Junior Officer,
   Sergeant: O 74 16/2:78-80
Marlborough's Grenadiers: N 74 16/3:180-181
Marlburian Ensigns: D 74 16/4:248-250
Foot Guards, 1742: Officer, Center Coy Private; Grenadier; Center
   Coy Corporal: Ja 75 16/5:315-317
15th Foot, 1750: Btn Coy Private; Sergeant; Private in marching
   order; Grenadier; Btn Coy Officer: Mr 75 16/7:435-436
1st Royal Dragoons, 1742: Ap 75 16/8:490-492; Je 75 16/10:606-
   607
20th Foot, 1749: Btn Coy Officer; Grenadier; Btn Coy Private:
   My 75 16/9:524-525
Royal Artillery, 1742-1748: Jl 75 16/11:650-652
Royal Dragoons, 1767: Ag 75 16/12:714-716
Royal American Rgt of Foot: Officer; Private: S 75 17/1:34-36
First Light Cavalry, 1746: Cumberland Dragoons corporal & trooper, 1746; 11th Dragoons Light Troop trooper, 1756: O 75 17/2:
   92-94
Rgt of Marines: Captain, Private, 1685-1690; Sergeant 1684: N 75
   17/3:166-167+
15th (The King's) Light Dragoons, c. 1778: Captain: D 75 17/4:
   221-222

Cacciatori delle Alpi

A&W Jl 74 12:60-65--
   Cacciatori delle Alpi: Soldier, Officer
   Guide
   Genoese Carabiniere: 2 var
   Cacciatori degli Appennini: Officer
   Evolution of Cacciatori degli Appenini Officer Badges: 1860, 1871,
   1879, 1902, 1919, 1923, 1934, 1943, 1970

Campaign in Friuli

A&W Jl 73 6:60-61, 64-65--
   Italian
      Guards Infantry Rgt, Carabinieri
      Guards Cacciatori Rgt, Fusiliers
      Guards Veliti Rgt, Grenadiers
      1st Light Rgt, Officer
      2nd Light Rgt, Grenadiers
      4th Light Rgt, Light Infantry
      7th Line Rgt, Light Infantry
      3rd Line Rgt, Grenadiers
      1st Line Rgt, Officer
   French
      Line

Hussars
Chasseurs
Dragoons
Austrian
  General
  Dragoons
  Light Cavalry
  Infantry

A&W S 73 7:60-66--
  Cisalpine Republic 1787
    Infantry Grenadier
    Infantry Rifleman
    Infantry Officer
    Infantry Carabiniere
  Italian Republic 1803
    Infantry Grenadier
    Infantry Rifleman
    Infantry Officer
    Infantry Carabiniere
  Kingdom of Italy
    Napoleon Dragoon Rgt, 1812
    Foot Artillery, 1812
    Dalmation Grenadier Rgt, 1812
    2nd Rgt of the Line, Fusiliers, 1812
    3rd Light Cavalry Rgt, Selected Coy, 1812
    1st Light Cavalry Rgt, 1812
    Light Cavalry Btn of the Istria Grenadiers, 1812
    Sapper of the 1st Light Cavalry Rgt, 1804-1805
    Sapper of the 1st Light Cavalry Rgt, 1812
    Bugler of the 2nd Rgt of Hussars, 1804-1805

Collector's Choice [all MM]

Royal Fusiliers, 1881-1914: Officer, Other Ranks, Drummer (2 var each): S 72 1/1:37+
Rifle Regiments, 1881-1914: London Rifle Bgd, 1900: sergeant, other ranks: O 72 1/2:90
Royal Artillery, 1900: 3rd Middlesex Artillery Volunteers Field Battery: N 72 1/3:148
Royal Horse Artillery, 1880-1914: Honourable Artillery Coy Gun Battery: D 72 1/4:204
Artists' Rifle, 1900: Ja 73 1/5:259
Royal Engineers, 1900: F 73 1/6:304
26th (Cyclist) Rifle Volunteers, 1900: Private: Mr 73 1/7:376
Scottish Infantry, 1900: Lance Corporal, Glasgow Highlanders; Private, 1st Lanark Rifles; Piper, 1st Sutherland Rifle Volunteers; Royal Scots Fusiliers, Home Service marching order, 1885; Field Officer, Cameron Highlanders, 1897; Sergeant, Gordon Highlanders, marching order, 1885: My 74 1/9:468
Royal Navy, 1890: Seaman (3 var); Officer (2 var); Marine, active service dress: Je 73 1/10:541

I. Static Scale

4th Hussars, 1895: Troopers: Jl 73 1/11:597

German Cavalry & Artillery, 1914-1918

A&W Mr 75 16:poster--
 Uhlans, 1914
 Bavarian Uhlans, 1914
 Cuirassiers, 1914
 Hussar, 1914
 Artillery, 1914
 Dragoons, 1915
 Field Artillery, 1915
 Foot Artillery, 1915
 Anti-Aircraft Artillery, 1915
 Cavalry, 1916
 Hussars, 1916
 Uhlans, 1916
 Mounted Rifles, 1917
 Artillery Officer, 1917
 Cavalry NCO, 1918
 Cavalry Assault Section, 1918

German Infantry Uniforms 1914-1918

A&W N 74 14:poster--
 Officer, 1914
 Rifleman, 1914
 Officer, 1914: fatigues
 Grenadier Officer, 1914
 Bavarian Chasseur, 1914
 Bavarian Rifleman, 1914
 Chasseur Officer, 1914
 Saxony Chasseur, 1914
 Officer, 1915
 Rifleman, 1915
 Chasseur, 1915
 General, 1916
 Rifleman, 1916
 Bavarian Chasseur, 1917
 Officer, 1918
 Rifleman, 1918

German Navy 1914-1918 [all WWE]

Commissioned, Warrant, & 1st Class Petty Officers Uniforms: My 74 1/3:79
Shoulder & Sleve Insignia, Commissioned Officers: Jl 74 1/4:112
Petty Officers, 2nd & 3rd Class, & Seamen: S 74 1/5:159
Rating Insignia, Service Badges, Corps Insignia: N 74 1/6:193
Field Gray Uniform: Shoulder insignia, rating insignia, corps in-

signia; Ja 75 2/1:35
Field Gray Uniform: Officers & Men of Naval Artillery: Ja 75 2/1:36

French Army 1914-1918

A&W S 75 19:poster--
  Colonial Infantry, 1914
  African Chasseur, 1914
  Algerian Marksman, 1914
  Senegalese Marksman, 1914
  Spahis, 1914
  General, 1915
  Infantry Officer, 1915
  Alpine Chasseur, 1915
  Cuirassier, 1915
  Infantry, 1916
  Moroccan Marksman, 1917
  Dragoon, 1917
  Mountain Artillery, 1918
  African Chasseur, 1918
  Foreign Legion, 1918
  General, 1918

Infantry Uniforms & Standards of Frederick the Great

A&W Ja 73 3:poster--
  Sapper, 22nd Rgt
  Fusilier, 47th Rgt
  Officer, 18th Rgt
  Field Officer, 12th Rgt
  Grenadier, 5th Rgt
  Jaeger
  Musketeer, 18th Rgt
  Grenadier, 15th Rgt, 1st Btn-Guards
  Grenadier Warrant Officer, 6th Rgt-Guards
  Musketeer, 15th Rgt, 1st Btn-Guards
  Officer, 15th Rgt, 1st Btn-Guards
  Ensign Warrant Officer, 1st Rgt
  Warrant Officer, Musketeers, 26th Rgt

Johnny Reb

MM Ja 75 5/1:25-27--
  Private, 5th Battery, Virginia Artillery
  Captain, Rough & Ready Guards, 14th North Carolina Rgt: cor Je 5/6:336
  Corporal, 7th Louisiana Volunteers: cor Mr 75 5/3:154; rebuttal Je 75 5/6:336
  1st Lieutenant, Infantry

I. Static Scale

Lieutenant Colonel of Cavalry
Corporal of Cavalry
Private, 2nd Rgt of Missouri State Guard
Artilleryman
General Officer: Ja 75 5/1:27
Text & Detail sk cor: Mr 75 5/3:154-155

Louis XV French Uniforms

A&W Mr 74 10:poster--
1745 Fusiliers de la Morlière
1756 Garde-Française
Maison du Roi, Garde de la porte
1750 Fusilier au Régt de Provence, Grenadier de France
1720-80 Garde de la Prévoté de l'hôtel du Roi
1762 Dragon, Régt de Saxe
1725 Régt Colonel Général
1730 Mainson du Roi: Garde du corps, compagnie d'Harcourt
Gendarme de la garde
1725 Sous-brigadier des Mousquetaires, 1re Compagnie

Military Album [all MM]

Royal Dragoons, 1895: Sergeant, Lieutenant (mounted), Kettledrummer (mounted): S 72 1/1:20
Royal Fusiliers, 1812-1815: Private, Sergeant, Officer (2 var), Field Officer: O 72 1/2:78
Royal Scots Greys, 1815: Officer, Trooper: N 72 1/3:145
24 Rgt of Foot (2nd Warwickshire), 1879: Officer (2 var); Private: D 72 1/4:184
1st King's Dragoon Guards, 1799: Officer, full dress & regular; Trooper: Ja 73 1/5:242
The Queen's Bays, 1900: Musician; Lieutenant; Trooper; Trumpeter: F 73 1/6:300
17th Lancers, 1904: Officer; Regimental Sergeant Major; Trooper: Mr 73 1/7:356
First Foot Guards, 1742: Officer; Fifer; Drummer; Private Btn Coy; Sergeant: Ap 73 1/8:412
Army Service Corps, 1913: Officer (full & walking out dress); Sergeant: Je 73 1/10:544
17th Leicestershire Rgt, 1830: Officer & Sergeant of Grenadier Coy; Drum Major & Bandsman (serpent); Officer of Btn or Center Coy: Jl 73 1/11:580
10th Light Dragoons, 1792: Officer, Trumpeter, Sergeant (2 var): Ag 73 1/12:658
Royal Welch Fusiliers, 1900-1904: Lieutenant, 1904; Field Officer, 1900, full dress: N 73 2/3:152-153

Military Bands of the Indian Army, 1860-1937

A&W J1 74 12:poster--
 Bugler, band, 3rd Sikh Rgt, 1860, service uniform
 Sergeant Bugler, band, 1st Sikh Rgt (Punjab Frontier Force), 1880, service uniform
 Drum Major, band, 7th Bombay Infantry, 1888, service & dress uniform
 Drummer, band, 7th Bombay Infantry, 1888, field uniform
 Piper, band, 1st Btn, 4th Gurkha Rifles, 1895, service uniform
 Pipe Major, band, 42nd Deoli Rgt, 1909, service & dress uniform
 Bandsman (bass drum), band, 42nd Deoli Rgt, 1909, service & dress uniform
 Drum Major, pipes & drums, 45th Battray's Sikhs, 1910, service & dress uniform
 Piper, band, 6th Gurkha Rifles, 1920, service uniform
 Drummer, band, Bombay Sappers & Miners, 1937, dress uniform

"Once Upon a Time There Was a Simple Bonnet"

A&W S 73 13:60-65--[headgear only]
 Piedmontese Dragoons, 1690
 France: Carignan-Salières Rgt, 1665
 France: General of the First Empire
 U.K.: Honourable Artillery Coy, 1803
 France: 4th Hussars, 1804
 Portugal: Officer of the Cazadores, 1832
 France: Voltigeur de la Garde (Second Empire)
 Belgium: Officer of the 1st Guides Rgt, 1940
 Holland: Mounted Artillery, 1972
 U.K.: Officer of the Queens Own Royal Irish Hussars, 1972
 Italy: Bersaglieri, 1972
 Italy: President's Carabineer Guards, 1972
 Russia: Line Infantry, 1711
 France: 14th Cuirassiers, 1814
 U.K.: 17th/21st Lancers, 1965
 Germany: Gebirgsjäger, 1940
 Denmark: Grenadier, 1709
 Brandenburg Electorate: Grenadier Guard, 1700
 Prussia: Alt. Dohna Rgt, 1709
 France: NCO, Grenadier Guards, early 18th Century
 France: Bombardier, 1733
 U.K.: 5th Rgt of Foot, 1750
 U.K.: Horse Grenadier Guards, 1751
 Russia: Bombardier of Catherine II
 United Provinces: von Friesheim Rgt, 1701
 Russia: Line Infantry, 1740
 Hesse-Darmstadt: Leib-Grenadier-Garde, 1788
 Prussia: 51st Infantry Btn, 1780
 Russia: Officer, Grenadier Guards, 1763
 Hesse-Darmstadt: Sapper, Leibregiment, 1788
 Russia: Rgt of Major-General Count Kamensky, 1799

I. Static Scale   128

Prussia: Kaiser Alexander Garde Grenadier, 1st Rgt, 1914
Spain: Walloon Royal Guard, 1703
France: Mounted Grenadier of the Maison du Roi, 1735
Spain: Walloon Royal Guard, 1760
Sweden: Halsing Rgt, 1748
Prussia: Dragoon of the von Kleist Freicorps, 1760
U.K.: 73rd Highlanders, 1777
Electorate of Saxony: Leib-Grenadier-Garde, 1784
Austria: Grenadier, 1812
France: Foot Grenadier of the Imperial Guard, 1804
Spain: Regiment of Guadalajara, 1808
U.K.: Life Guards, 1822
Belgium: Gendarmerie, 1832
Denmark: Drummer, Den Kongelige Livgard, 1972
U.K.: Scots Guards, 1972
U.K.: Royal Scots Dragoon Guards, 1972
Kenya: Drummer, Kenya African Rifles, 1966
France: Line Infantry, 1832
The Two Sicilies: 3rd Swiss Rgt, 1854
U.S.A.: 1st Div, 11th Corps, Federal Army, 1865
Belgium: Carabineer, 1914
France: Dragoon of Louis XV
France: Cuirassier, 1810
U.K.: Life Guards, 1814
Sardinia: Dragoon, 1840
U.K.: 21st Light Dragoons (Royal Foresters), 1760
U.S.A.: Light Infantry, 1776
Austria: Infantry officer, 1792
Prussia: Officer of the Leib-Grenadier-Garde, 1798
Sweden: Leibgrenadiercorps, 1807
U.K.: 27th Rgt of Foot (Inniskilling), 1814
Argentina: 8th Infantry Btn, 1816
Russia: Mounted Grenadier, 1850

Polish Infantry of the Napoleonic Wars

MW F 74 2/6:294-296--
  4th Infantry Rgt
    Lieutenant of Centre Coy
    Drummer
    Fusilier Sergeant
    Grenadier
    Voltigeur
  7th Infantry Rgt
    Grenadier NCO, 1810
    Eagle
    Voltigeur, 1811-1812
    Captain, 1811
    Regimental Pioneer, 1812
    Fusilier, 1812
  9th Infantry Regiment
    Drummer, 1808

Grenadier Officer, 1810-1812
Grenadier, 1810-1812
Fusilier Officer, 1810-1812
Voltigeur, 1810-1812
Fusilier, 1812

Renaissance Warfare [all Afx]

Introduction: Je 73 14/10:532-534
Infantry Weapons & Organization: Jl 73 14/11:608-611
Infantry Missile Weapons: Longbow, Composite Bow, Crossbow, Arquebus, Musket: Ag 73 14/12:652-654
Artillery: Types, Organization, Effectiveness: S 73 15/1:48-51
Cavalry: Heavy & Light Cavalry, Eastern Cavalry, Weapons, Organization: O 73 15/2:100-103
Henry VIII's Army: 4 foot, 14 flags: N 73 15/3:156-159
Irish Army of the 16th Century: 4 foot: D 73 15/4:227-229
The Universal Soldier (Lansknecht): 12 foot, 2 flags: Ja 74 15/5: 280-285
The Swiss: 8 foot, 21 flags: F 74 15/6:357-360+
Turks: Spahis: 2 mounted: Mr 74 15/7:398-402
Turks: Janissaries & Others: 6 foot, 1 mounted, 8 flags, 6 shields: Ap 74 15/8:448-452
Scots: 5 foot, 1 horse, 2 flags: My 74 15/9:530-534
Polish: 7 foot, 2 mounted, 9 flags: Je 74 15/10:560-561+
Spanish Infantry: 15 foot: Jl 74 15/11:641-645
Spanish Ginetes to Caballos Corazas: 5 foot, 4 mounted, 1 horse, 15 flags: Ag 74 15/12:710-712+
French: 6 foot, 2 mounted, 12 flags: S 74 16/1:17-21
The Imperialists (Holy Roman Empire): 12 foot, 6 mounted, 12 flags: O 74 16/2:88-94
Persians & Other Easterners: 11 foot, 6 mounted, 4 flags: N 74 16/3:166-170
Dutch: 4 foot, 2 mounted, 10 flags: D 74 16/4:233-238
Swedish: 10 foot: Ja 75 16/5:298-302; 5 foot, 9 flags: F 75 16/6:372-375
Muscovites: 7 foot, 5 mounted: Mr 75 16/7:425+; 5 foot, 3 mounted, 21 flags: Ap 75 16/8:483-487
The English Civil War: 4 foot, 2 mounted, 25 flags: My 75 16/9: 544-548

Service Uniforms of the Italian Army [all Fus]

Enlisted Tunics & Insignia: Au 73 1/1:12-14
Officer Tunics & Insignia: W 74 1/2:28-29+
Regimental Collar Badges: Sp 74 1/3:12-13
Headwear & Insignia: Sp 75 2/1:21-23+

I. Static Scale 130

Soldier of the Month [all MW]

color drawings, pph, conversion ideas

Waffen SS Panzer-Grenadier: SS Sturmann, 23 Friewilligen Pz-Div-Nederland, 1943; SS Unterscharführer, 1942; SS-Mann, 3 SS-Pz-Div Totenkopf; SS-Sturmann, early camouflage: S 73 2/1:37-40
Foot Guards Rgt: Field Officer, review order, 1930; undress frock coat: O 73 2/2:96-97+
2nd Westphalian Hussar Rgt 11: Standardtenträger, 1913; service dress: N 73 2/3:149-150
Soviet Officers, 1943: Greatcoat; Tunic: D 73 2/4:206-207
Chasseurs à Pied de la Garde, 1813: campaign dress: Ja 74 2/5: 260-261
German Officer, 1941: Hauptmann of Artillery, 1936, service dress; General Officer; 3 headgear var: F 74 2/6:316-317

Thus Fought Napoleon

A&W N 73 8:60-65--
Selected Gendarmerie of the Guard, 1805
Foot Cacciatori of the Guard, 1805
Volteggiatori of the Guard, 1811
Grenadiers of the Guard, 1806
Engineering Sappers of the Guard, 1810
Marines of the Guard, 1806
Light Cavalry Lancers of the Guard, 2nd Rgt, 1811
Dragoons of the Guard, 1806
Light Infantry, 1809
Line Infantry, 1809
Foot Artillery, 1810
Artillery of the Guard, 1810
Horse Cacciatori, 1808
Hussars, 16th Rgt, 1810
Carabinieri, 1811
Cuirassiers, 9th Rgt, 1812

Uniforms & Colors of the British Army [all MM]

The King's Own Regiment of Foot, 1745: Ensign, Private, Drummer: D 71 1/12:631
Royal Regiment of Fusiliers, 1685: Lieutenant, Grenadier, Drummer: Ja 72 2/1:19
1st Btn, Royal Welch Fusiliers, 1899: Lieutenant, Drum Major, Goat Major: F 72 2/2:76-77
6th Dragoon Guards (Carabiniers), 1912: Lieutenant; Troop Sergeant Major, full dress; Trumpeter, undress: Mr 72 2/3:136-137
1st Btn, Royal Inniskilling Fusiliers, 1968: Drum Major, ceremonial; Regimental Piper, full dress; Officer, #1 (ceremonial); Officer, working dress: Ap 72 2/4:178-179
Life Guards, 1935: Trumpeter, Barrack Guard Order; Trooper, Bar-

rack Guard Order; Corporal, Full Dress, Mounted Guard: My
   72 2/5:240-241
1st Rgt Foot Guards, 1790: Ensign, Btn Coy; Sergeant, Btn Coy;
   Grenadier Private; Drummer: Je 72 2/6:294-295
Drum Horse, 19th Hussar: Jl 72 2/7:344-345
1st Btn, 60th (Royal American) Rgt, 1800: Officer, Btn Coy; Officer, Light Coy; Sergeant, Grenadier Coy; Private, Light Coy:
   Ap 73 3/4:206-207
5th & 6th Btns, 60th (Royal American) Rgt, 1800: Private, 6th Btn;
   Private, 5th Btn; Officer, 5th Btn: My 73 3/5:282-283
Royal Marines, 1972: Officer, #1 Dress; Drum Major; Marine Com-
   mando; Corporal Bugler: Je 73 3/6:358-359
1st & 2nd Life Guards, 1816: Trumpeter; Coronet; Trooper: Jl 73
   3/7:434-435
Northumberland Fusiliers, 1913: Sergeant, Officer, Drummer,
   Drum Major: S 73 3/9:606-607
Drum Horse of the 11th Hussars, 1903-1904: O 73 3/10:662-663
Regiment of Foot Guards, 1815: Private, Grenadier & Light Coys;
   Captain, Btn Coy; Private, Btn Coy; Drummer, Btn Coy: N
   73 3/11:740-741
Royal Horse Artillery, 1896: Captain, Trumpeter, Sergeant, Bombardier: D 73 3/12:808-809
92nd (Gordon Highlanders) Rgt of Foot, 1807: Officer, Grenadier
   Coy; Drummer; Private, Light Coy; Sergeant, Btn Coy: Ja 74
   4/1:26-27
15th/19th King's Royal Hussars, 1961: Officer, shirt sleeve order;
   Officer, #1 dress; Trooper; Sergeant: Ap 74 4/4:190-191
85th (Bucks Volunteers) of the King's Light Infantry Rgt, 1826:
   Officer, Sergeant, Private: My 74 4/5:250-251
14th King's Light Dragoons, 1932: Officer, mounted review order;
   Sergeant; Private: Je 74 4/6:318-319

Uniforms of the Luftwaffe [all MM]

Panzer Obergefreiter, tank crew, 1944: Je 73 3/6:380
Panzer Stabsfeldwebel, self-propelled gun crew, 1943: Je 73 3/6:
   380
Mess Dress: MM Jl 73 3/7:455
Unteroffizer, parachute troops (before Luftwaffe), 1938: Ag 73 3/
   8:510-511
Unterfeldwebel, Luftwaffe Fallshirmjaeger, 1942: Ag 73 3/8:511
Flight Coverall: O 73 3/10:678
Fighter Pilot's Uniform: O 73 3/10:678
Standardbearer: My 74 4/5:270-271
Hats, Caps, & Helmets: Ap 74 4/4:204-205+
Flight Tunics & Walking Out Dress: S 74 4/9:546-547

Uniforms of the SS [all MM]

First SS Uniform, 1923: O 74 4/10:618-621
Second Pattern Brown Shirt: N 74 4/11:666-669

I. Static Scale

Black Service Tunic: N 74 4/11:666-669
SS-VT: officer & enlisted uniforms: D 74 4/12:742-745
SS Brigade Ehrhardt: Ja 75 5/1:32-34
Coats & Cloaks: 5 var: F 75 5/2:98-99+
Liebstandarte Adolf Hitler standard bearer: My 75 5/5:286-288
Mess Dress & Formal Evening Attire: 4 var: Je 75 5/6:340-341
SS Heimwehr Danzig Standard Bearer: Jl 75 5/7:414-415

Uniforms of the Third Reich [all MW]

German Police, 1938: S 72 1/1:40+
Reich Labour Corps: Standard Bearer: O 72 1/2:87
5th Cavalry, 1935: Hauptmann, walking out order: N 72 1/3:128
Gebeitsführer of Hitler Junge, 1933: D 72 1/4:201
Mountain Troops: Spiess (sergeant major), 1943: Ja 73 1/5:262
Kreigsmarine Petty Officer, torpedo section, Sept 1939: F 73 1/6: 317
Reichsleiter, walking out dress: F 73 1/6:317+
SA (Sturmabteilung) Obertruppführer (sergeant), 1943: Mr 73 1/7: 373
Luftwaffe Service Uniform for Enlisted Ranks, 1939: Ap 73 1/8:429
Waffen SS Tank Crew Camouflaged Coverall, 1943: My 73 1/9:488
Panzer Uniform: 1943: My 73 1/9:488
Werkscharführer of NSDAP: Je 73 1/10:524
National Socialist Studenten Bund: Je 73 1/10:534
Hitler Youth Ski Outfit, 1933: Jl 73 1/11:600
Hitler Youth, 1944: Jl 73 1/11:600+
Luftwaffe Service Uniform for Officer Ranks: Ag 73 1/12:655
Reichsluftschutzbund Standard Bearer, 1938: S 73 2/1:20
German Police Standard Bearer, 1938: S 73 2/1:20
Kreigsmarine Leading Seaman, 1940: O 73 2/2:73-74
Feldwebel of the Marine Artillery, 1939: O 73 2/2:73-74
Luftwaffe Flieger-Oberingenieur, 1939: N 73 2/3:132
NSFK Rottenführer, 1937: D 73 2/4:204-205

Uniforms of the Civil War

A&W N 72 2:60-65--
  Cavalry
    Trooper
    Officer: 2 var
  Infantry
    Private
    Officer

War of Independence [all MW]

British Infantry: Sergeant; Officer; 10th Foot, Light Coy; Drummer; Private, Centre Coy; 40th Foot; list of all units with colors of lace & facing: N 72 1/3:138-142

German Infantry: Fusilier, Grenadier, Officer, Pioneer, Mounted Jaeger, Musketeer, Foot Jaeger, Jaeger Officer; list of all units with all uniform colors: Ja 73 1/5:244-245+
Other German Units: Colours, model conversions: F 73 1/6:314-315+
French: Fusilier Corporal, Drummer du Cap, Grenadier, Officer, 2nd Lieutenant, Lauzun's Legion; list of all units with uniform colors: My 73 1/9:469-472; colours & model conversions: Jl 73 1/11:571-572

Uniform Accessories

British Decorations for Valor: see separate listing
Condor Legion: MW Ag 73 1/12:638-639
German Army Field Equipment: see separate listing
German Wehrmacht Helmet Netting: Fus W 74 1/2:18-19
Medals & Decorations of Our "Unsung Heroes": WW-II medals for merchant mariners: WWE N 74 1/5:188-189
U.S. Army Helmet Markings: MM Je 72 2/6:287

British Decorations for Valor [all Fus]

Army: Au 73 1/1:26-27
RAF: W 74 1/2:8-9
Royal Navy: Su 74 1/4:32-33+

German Army Field Equipment [all MM]

Y Straps, Packs, Mess Kit, Gas Mask: Mr 74 4/3:136-139
Waterbottles, Cups, Entrenching Tools, Bayonets, Map Cases, Ammo Boxes: My 74 4/5:268-270
Small Arms, Spotting & Phone Equipment: Ag 74 4/8:485-486

SCRATCH

Figures

15th Century Knight: 133mm, wood: MM D 73 3/12:824-826
Fisherman: MB My 71 21/245:206

Accessories

British Army Packs, 1939-1945: MW Ja 74 2/5:252
British Greatcoat, WW-II: MW Ja 74 2/5:269
British Military Pack, WW-II: MW Mr 73 1/7:359

I. Static Scale

CONVERSIONS

(No Particular Period)

Equus caballos/assinus: mule from Airfix Hussar horse: RT Jl 75 8/7:77

(Ancient)

Byzantine Senior Officer, Junior Officer, Infantry, Standard Bearer: from Airfix 54mm figures: MM Mr 73 3/3:153; add Jl 73 3/7: 445
Hun Raider: from Airfix Hussar: MM Jl 75 5/7:422-423
Sassanid Persian Clibanarii (heavy cavalry): from metal horse & fuzzy-wuzzy": MM My 71 1/5:237-238
Samite Gladiator: from Airfix Highlander: MM Ag 73 3/8:537

(Medieval & Renaissance)

John, 2nd Earl of Beaumont: from Historex figure, Airfix horse; in jousting armor: MM O 72 2/10:525-526
Knight of Charlemagne: from Airfix Coldstream Guardsman: MM S 73 3/7:616
Renaissance Warfare: converting Airfix 20mm to Renaissance armies: Afx N 75 17/3:149-153; D 75 17/4:218-220
Spanish 16th Century Soldiers: from Airfix plastic or from lead figures: Afx Ag 74 15/12:715
13th Century Samurai: from Airfix 19th Hussar: MM N 73 3/11: 755-756

(1600-1790)

Black Watch, 1740: from Airfix 42nd Highlander: MM S 73 3/9: 619
Civil War Officer: from Airfix Guardsman: MW Ap 73 1/8:432
Long John Silver: from Airfix American Soldier: Grenadier: Afx My 75 16/9:526-528
Musketeer of 1608: from Airfix Coldstream Guardsman: MW S 72 2/1:48
Oliver: from Airfix 7" Oliver Cromwell figure: change of pose: Afx Ag 72 13/12:670+
Robinson Crusoe: from Airfix Grenadier, Coldstream Guard, & toy dog: Afx My 75 16/9:526-528
Standard Bearer, Rgt Bourbonnais, 1786: from Historex Standard Bearer, Hussar Officer, Infantry of the Line: RT Ap 74 7/4: 45
Von Barner's Brunswick Jäger: American Revolution mercenary from Airfix 1775 U.S. Infantryman: Afx O 75 17/2:100-101

Figures

(Napoleonic)

British Infantryman: from Airfix 42nd Highlander & Imperial Guardsman: Afx S 75 17/1:45-46
Caçadore, 4th Portuguese Caçadore Btn, 1810: from Airfix 95th Rifle, Coldstream Guard: Afx Mr 75 16/7:421-422
Cannonniers Garde-Côtes: from Historex line infantry: MW Ja 74 2/5:266-267
Chasseurs à pied de la Garde, 1813: from Airfix Imperial Guard Grenadiers: MW Ja 74 2/5:260
Coldstream Guards Musician, drill order, 1815: from Airfix Guardsman: Afx F 74 15/6:355
David's Napoleon at Mount St. Bernard: from Historex parts: MM Ja 73 3/1:47-48
1815: see separate listing
82nd Foot Private, 1808: from Airfix Coldstream Guards, 42 Highlander, & Rifleman: Afx Jl 75 16/11:658-660
Major, 50th Foot: from Airfix Rifleman: Afx Ag 75 16/12:710-711
45th Foot, Sergeant, 1810: from Airfix Coldstream Guard: Afx Jl 75 16/11:658-660
French Infantryman Retreating from Moscow, 1812: from toy U.S. soldier & Airfix Imperial Guardsman equipment: S&L (Je 75) 9:10-11
French Lieutenant: from Airfix Rifleman & Imperial Guard Grenadier: Afx Je 75 16/10:602-603
Grenadier, 1st Rgt, Garde de Paris, 1812: from Airfix Foot Grenadier of Imperial Guard: Afx F 75 16/6:360-361
Guards Cavalry Corps Trooper, 1799: from Airfix Hussar, Scots Grey, & Polish Lancer: MM Ja 75 5/1:22-23
Legion Irlandaise Drummer Boy: from Britains farm boy: S&L (D 74) 5:6-7
Mameluke, 1812: from Airfix WW-II German grenade thrower: S&L (Ap 75) 7:8-9
Napoleon's Camel Corps: from Historex: MM My 71 1/5:263+
95th Rifle Officer: from Airfix 10th Hussar: Afx Ap 75 16/8:460-461
Officer of the Horse Gunners, 1815: from Elastolin Roman Centurion: MM F 72 2/2:80-81
Polish Lancer: from Airfix Polish Lancer & 10th Hussar horse: S&L Jl 74 2:4
Regiment d'Isembourg, 1808: grenadier, fusilier/chasseur, & sappeur: from Historex tirailleur & chasseur: MW Ag 73 1/12:651+
Regiment d'Isembourg, 1808: Voltigeur, Officer, Horn, Drum Major, Musician, Drummer, Chef de Musique: from Historex parts: MW N 73 2/3:137-138+
Royal Italian Guard: Officers & Men, 1805-1815: from Historex Imperial Guard Dragoon: MW D 72 1/4:197
Sapper at Rest: Historex Imperial Guard Sapper, posing: MW N 72 1/3:135
2nd Dutch Lancer: from Airfix Polish Lancer & 10th Hussar horse: S&L Jl 74 2:5
7th Royal Fusiliers, 1805-1815: from Airfix Guardsman: Afx F

I. Static Scale 136

74 15/6:355-356
Spanish Dragoon, Almansa Rgt, 1808: from Historex parts: MM S 73 3/9:582-583
Spanish Line Grenadier of 1813: from Airfix Rifleman & Coldstream Guards: Afx My 75 16/9:520-521
Tartare Lithuanian Lancer: from Airfix 10th Hussar & Polish Lancer horse: S&L Jl 74 2:5
Trumpeter of the Royal Italian Guard, 1805-1815: from Historex Empress Dragoons: MW O 72 1/2:68
Trumpeter of 3rd Rgt of Dragoons, 1816: from Historex Dragoon: MW S 72 1/1:46-47
23rd or Royal Welch Fusiliers, 1805: from Airfix Guardsman: Afx F 74 15/6:355-356
U. S. Infantry, 1813-1814: from Airfix Rifleman & Coldstream Guards: Afx N 75 17/3:140-142
Virginia Dragoon, 1811: from Historex carabinier: RiS Su 73 1/4: 115

(1815) [all Afx]

Anglo-Dutch Infantry: Ja 71 12/5:240-241+
Anglo-Dutch Cavalry: F 71 12/6:318-319; Mr 71 12/7:347
French Cavalry: Ap 71 12/8:402-403+
French Infantry: My 71 12/9:456-457
Prussians: Je 71 12/10:541-542
Prussian Cavalry: Jl 71 12/11:571+
French Artillery: Ag 71 12/12:632

(1820-1914)

Afgan War 10th Hussar: from Britains Military Rider: Afx Ap 73 14/8:446+
British Soldier, Indian Mutiny, 1857: from Britains American Civil War Figures: Afx Je 72 13/10:565+
British Soldier, Zulu War 1879: from Britains ACW & Rose head: Afx Je 72 13/10:566-568
Cavalry School at St. Germain: from Historex: MW Je 73 1/10: 528-529+
Charge of the Light Brigade: see separate listing
Cheering Zulu: from Hinchliffe throwing Zulu: MM Jl 75 5/7:421
Crimean War Casualty: Russian cavalry in Gibb painting: from Airfix 10th Hussar: MW D 72 1/4:191+
5th Royal Irish Lancers, 1899-1902: Bugler; from Historex: MM Je 71 1/6:286-287
French Infantry, 1900-1914: from Airfix French Infantry & French Foreign Legion: MW F 74 1/6:299
French Foreign Legion Voltigeur, 1832: from Series 77 Legionnaire: MM S 74 4/9:536-537
Fuzzy-Wuzzy Swordsman: from Britains Red Indian Brave: Afx Ag 72 13/12:650-651+
Gordon Relief Expedition Camel Rider: from Timpo camel & His-

torex or Airfix rider: Afx D 73 15/4:211-212
Heliograph Team, British Colonial Wars: from Almark Japanese Infantry: Afx N 71 13/3:152-153; D 71 13/4:198-199
Home Service Soldier, 1880-1900: from Almark American Infantryman: Afx My 72 13/7:388
King's Troop Royal Horse Artillery: from Airfix Civil War Artillery: Afx My 71 12/9:468-469
Lord Cardigan in Miniature: from Airfix Guardsman & Hussar: MW Ja 73 1/5:246+
Mexican Cavalry Sergeant, 1836: Rose or Historex Chevau-leger major: RiS Sp 73 1/3:90
Mexican 11th Infantry, 1847: from Airfix French Line Infantryman & 95th Rifleman: Afx D 75 17/4:231-232+
Officer, Mounted, Egyptian War of 1882: from Britains Mountie, Historex horse, Rose head; color var for Life Guards & 27th Cavalry (Indian): Afx Ag 71 12/12:630-631
Post Office Rifles Private, 1898: from Historex: MM Ap 71 1/4: 200-202
Return from Balaclava: see separate listing
Royal Hungarian Lifeguards: from Airfix Hussar: MW Jl 73 1/11: 570+
Royal Navy Gardner Gun Team of 1880s: from Britains American Civil War Gun Crew, ACW officer, U.S. Infantryman with submachinegun, & U.S. Infantryman kneeling: Afx O 72 14/2:96-100; scratch Gardner Gun: N 72 14/3:156-159
Royal Scot Greys: Captain in dismounted review order: from Airfix 1/12 Life Guards & Coldstream Guards: Afx D 71 13/4: 190-191
Royal Scot Greys Trumpeter: from Airfix 1/12 Life Guards & Coldstream Guards: Afx D 71 13/4:190-191
Running British Soldier: from Hinchliffe Zulu War standing figure: MM Jl 75 5/7:420
Running Zulu: from Hinchliffe walking Zulu: MM Jl 75 5/7:420
Skinner's Horse: from Airfix George Washington & Historex parts: MM O 75 5/10:602-604
Soudan Campaign Rifle Unit: from Airfix Japanese Infantry & Rose heads: Afx Ap 71 12/8:406-407
3rd Croatian Rgt of Infantry: Grenadier, Voltigeur, Fusilier: from Historex French Imperial Guard Dragoon: MW Ja 73 1/5:232+ ; Drummer, Sapeur, Officer: from Historex Tirailleur Chasseurs: MW F 73 1/6:328-329
3rd Hussar Private in Walking-Out Dress, late 19th Century: from Airfix Coldstream Guard: Afx My 73 14/9:478+
U.S. Western Plains Infantry: from Airfix French Grenadier; 2 poses: MM S 74 4/9:536-537
Wounded Soldier & assisting comrade: from Hinchliffe Zulu War standing & walking figures: MM Jl 75 5/7:421
Wounded Soldier & Zulu coupe de grace: from Hinchliffe Zulu War standing soldier & cheering Zulu: MM Jl 75 5/7:421
Yemen Runner: Chinese runner; from Historex Chasseur & Airfix Hussar: MM Mr 74 4/3:144-145
Zouave Tambour: from Historex fusilier drummer: MM N 75 5/11:659

I. Static Scale   138

Zulu uThulwana Rgt: from Britains Red Indian Brave: Afx Ag 72
  13/12:650-651+

(Charge of the Light Brigade) [all Afx]

Three More Lancers: F 73 14/6:327+
Captain Louis Edward Nolan: Mr 73 14/7:377-379
Captain G. Lockwood: Ap 73 14/8:438-439
Captain H. F. B. Maxse: My 73 14/9:488-490
Lieutenant G. Wombewell: Je 73 14/10:540-542
Captain William Morris: Jl 73 14/11:611-614
Captain J. A. Oldham: Ag 73 15/1:38-40
13th Dragoon Trooper: S 73 15/1:38-40
Entangled Dragoon: O 73 15/2:104+
Dismounted 11th Hussar: N 73 15/3:153-154
Wounded Horse: D 73 15/4:323+

(Return from Balaclava) [all Afx]

Leading foot figure: O 74 15/2:98-101
Trooper & wounded horse: N 74 15/3:152+
Wounded trooper & friend: D 74 15/4:243-245
Blinded trooper: Ja 75 15/5:286-288
Sitting trooper & horse: F 75 15/6:376-380
Mounted trooper carrying wounded comrad: Mr 75 15/7:430-434
Wounded lancer lying on ground: Je 75 16/10:574-576

(World War I)

Army Nursing Sister: from Sanderson nude: Afx Je 71 12/10:520-
  521+
Army Nursing Sister: from Rose Greek Dancing Girl: Afx Jl 73
  14/11:614-615
British Dragoon of World War I: from Airfix Scots Grey man &
  10th Hussar horse: S&L Ag 74 3:4-5
British Infantry, Flanders, 1914-1915: from Historex: MM My 71
  1/5:263-265
British Staff Officer: from Airfix 54mm spectator: Afx Ap 72 13/
  4:453
First World War British Lewis Gun team: from Almark Japanese
  Infantry: Afx Mr 73 14/7:392-394
First World War German Hussar: from Airfix Hussar: Afx Ja 73
  14/5:248-249
Life Guards Officer: from Historex parts: Afx Je 71 12/10:521+
World War One German Dragoon: from Airfix 10th Hussar: S&L
  (O 74) 4:26-27
World War One Highlander, 1916-1918: from Airfix 42nd Highlander:
  MM S 74 4/9:619

Figures

(World War II)

Afrika Korps Infantry Gefreiter: MW Je 73 1/10:530-531
Afrika Korps Infantry Lieutenant: from Schwimmwagen figures: RT Ap 71 4/4:42
British Army Battledress: see separate listing
British Dingo & Officer's Conference: from Airfix Racing figures: Afx Ja 71 12/5:260-261
British WW-II Vehicle Crewman: 3 var; from Airfix & Tamiya figures: Afx O 73 15/2:80-81
Desert Patrol, 1939-1945: Arab Legionaire & camel from Airfix 10th Hussar & Elastolin camel: MM Ap 73 3/4:80-81
Eighth Army in the Desert: see separate listing
German MG Group: NCO, gunner, loader: from Almark German & American figures: Afx S 71 13/1:18-20
German MG 34 Team in Action: from Almerk German & U.S. Soldiers: Afx D 72 14/4:216-219
Jeep Recoilless Rifle Team: Bandai Jeep & Almerk US Infantry: Afx Jl 71 12/11:574-575
MG 42 Team: from Armour Accessories Components: Afx Jl 74 15/11:656-657; Ag 74 15/12:708+
PAK 38 Detachment in Action: from Almark Panzer Grenadier: Afx Ja 73 14/5:275-276
Polish Lancer, 1939: from Airfix Hussar: MW Ja 74 2/5:755-756
Resistance Forces in Miniature: 25mm from Airfix civilians; 54mm from Airfix Afrika Korps: Afx D 73 15/4:226
2 pdr Anti-Tank Gun Crew: from Airfix 20mm 8th Army: Afx D 74 16/4:221
Vickers Machine Gun Crew: from Airfix 20mm 8th Army: Afx D 74 16/4:220

(British Battle Dress)

MW Ja 74 2/5:253-255--[from Almark 20mm British figures]
 Mortar Team
 Mine Detecting Team (probing)
 Vickers Machinegun Team
 Riflemen (advancing & firing)
 Officer with Pistol
 Rifleman (kneeling & firing)
 NCO with Sten Gun

(Eighth Army in the Desert)

Afx S 74 16/1:45-47--
 Boys Anti-Tank Rifle
 2" Mortar
 Rifle to Bren Gun
 Tommy Gun & Bren Gun superdetailing
 Reposing

I. Static Scale   140

(Post World War II)

Aladdin Miniature: David Bowie from Historex & Airfix Coldstream Guardsman: MW S 72 1/1:48
Argyle & Sutherland Highlander: from Airfix 42nd Highlander: MM S 73 3/9:618
Foot Guards Officer: from Rose Fusilier Officer: MW O 73 2/2: 97+
Glostershire Rgt: UN duty in Cyprus: from Historex parts: MM O 71 1/10:510-511
Historex Hippy: from Historex Musician: Sc Ap 72 3/4:218-219
King's Royal Rifle Corps: from Airfix 54mm Coldstream Guards: Afx Jl 72 13/11:615-616
Modelling a Regimental Band: from Britains figures: MM Mr 74 4/3:146-147
Modern British Army Figures: from Airfix WW-I German: Afx Ja 73 14/5:246
Scots Guard Adjutant: from Britains Medical Officer: MW O 73 2/2: 97
Swiss Guards Drummer: from Airfix 54mm Coldstream Guards: Afx Je 72 13/10:559+
Thunderbird Aerobatic Team Pilot: from Historex Old Guard: Fus Sp 75 2/1:32-34+

SUPERDETAILING

Airfix Spitfire 1/24 Pilot: reposed: IM O 71 8/10:12-13
Commando Forces: from Airfix Commando set: Afx Je 73 14/10: 556
German 5cm Light Mortar: from Almark 54mm plastic & metal figures: MW Mr 73 1/7:420-421
Almark Wehrmacht Officer: MW F 74 2/6:316
Jackboot Waffen SS Walking MG 34 Gunner: MW S 73 2/1:39-40
Olive South Africa 1900: MW O 73 2/2:97
Women's Royal Naval Service Rating: reposed & detailed Valda WRNS: Afx Jl 73 14/11:615
Ama-Zulu: superdetailing Zulu figures: MM Je 74 4/6:324-326

KIT CONSTRUCTION

[see also Soldier of the Month under Uniforms, Scale Drawings]

Airfix Coldstream Guardsman: MM Ja 72 2/1:16-18
Airfix 42nd Highlander: MM D 72 2/12:652
Airfix Polish Lancer: MM F 74 4/2:92-95
Airfix Scots Grey colour detail: MM F 73 3/2:87; disc Mr 73 3/3: 166; Ap 73 3/4:205; My 73 3/5:279

Airfix 10th Hussar: MM Ja 72 2/1:16-18
Airfix 10th Hussar: Sc F 72 3/2:81-83
Historex Gun Team & Limber: MM Ap 72 2/4:193-195; My 72 2/5: 244-245; Je 72 2/6:304-305
Historex Mamelukes: MM O 73 3/10:684-685
Historex Scots Grey: MM My 72 2/5:230-231; Ja 73 3/1:21
Old Guard Samurai General: MM S 73 3/9:594-597
Phoenix Young Winston: MM F 73 3/2:86
Series 77 French Dromadaires: MM Ja 74 4/1:28-29
Series 77 Turkish Camel Trooper: MM Ja 74 4/1:28-29

KIT CORRECTIONS

Airfix Coldstream Guardsman: Afx Je 72 13/10:552
Airfix 10th Hussar: Afx Je 72 13/10:552

RAILROAD

CONVERSION

GWR "King" Locomotive: from Airfix Harrow: Afx Jl 72 13/11: 618-620

SUPERDETAILING

Airfix Schools-Class Locomotive: IM N 73 10/11-12:30-31

MISSILES & SPACE VEHICLES

SCALE DRAWINGS

Fiesler FZG-76 V-1 buzz bomb: 3v, cd, tpat, tcol, pph: AN 18 Ag 72 1/7:5; cor 24 N 72 1/14:13
V-1: 4v, sec, cd: Fus Sp 74 1/3:28-29

SUPERDETAILING

Airfix SAM-2: Afx Jl 74 15/11:665-666
Airfix LEM: The Eagle Has Landed: MW N 72 1/3:130-134+

I. Static Scale

Revell V-2: MM Je 73 3/6:448
Apollo 11 LEM: One Small Step for Man: MW Ap 73 1/8:413-416

SHIPS

SCALE DRAWINGS

Unpowered

Floating Pile Driver: $2\frac{1}{2}$v, dim, sec, cd, det, barge-mounted: NMRA F 73 38/6:47

Waterline

(Sail)

Hispaniola ex Ryelands: 4v, sec, cd, pph: movie ship from 3-mast schooner: MB D 75 25/299:648-649

(Paddle)

SS Minto: 3v, fp, cd, pph; 1898 stern wheel: NMRA S 74 40/1: 48-50
Pearl: $1\frac{1}{2}$v, cd; 1851 Great Lakes: NMRA Ag 73 38/12:9

(Propeller)

(Civil)
Douglas: $1\frac{1}{2}$v, cd, pat; 1879 Great Lakes steamer: NMRA Ag 73 38/12:9
SS Franconia: 3v, cd, pat, col: MB F 71 21/242:78-79
MV Karen Bay: 4v, cd, sk; free-lance rail ferry: MR My 75 42/5:42
MS Manchester Challenge: 3v, cd, pat, col; 1968 containership: MB Ja 71 21/241:35
MS Seaman: 3v, cd, pat, col; 1967 ocean tug: MB Ja 71 21/241:35
Simplified Mercantile Ships: 3v, cd, pat, col, 1/100: see separate listing
Smiths Dock Whalecatcher: 1v, cd, basis for WW-II corvette hull: MM S 3/9:600

(Naval)
HMS Alacrity: 2v, cd, det; sloop: Afx D 71 13/4:212
Algerine minesweeper: 2v, det: Afx Ag 72 13/12:664

Ships

Ashigara: 2v, cd; 1929 Japanese heavy cruiser: WWE S 74 1/5:140
Assault Landing Craft: 1v, templates, pph: 1939 Thornycroft: MW S 72 1/1:25-27
HMS Black Swan: 2v, cd, det; sloop: Afx D 71 13/4:212
USS Buckley: 2v, cd; dep at time of transfer to RN: MW Ap 73 1/8:422
USS Buckley: 2v, pph; 1945 destroyer escort: MW O 73 2/2:79+
Caio Duilio: 2v, cd, pph; 1940 Italian battleship: MW S 73 2/1:14
HMS Fal: 2v, cd, pph; 1943 River-class frigate: MB O 74 24/285: 426-427
Fighting Fleets in Miniature: 2v, cd, 1/1200: see separate listing
Flower Class Corvettes: see separate listing
Hosho: 2v, cd, pat, specs; 1922 Japanese aircraft carrier: WWE Mr 74 1/2:40-41
HMS Kent: 2v, cd, pph: WWE Mr 75 2/2:56-57
Leander: 2v, cd, pat, col, pph: IM S 75 11/5:8-11
HMS Lion: 2v, cd, tpat, tcol, pph: 1912 battleship: Sc Ja 75 6/64:17
Lutzow (ex-Deutschland): 3v, cd, det, pph; 1/600: Sc Ap 72 3/4: 210-211
Minesweepers: British WW-II: see separate listing
Moskva: 3v, cd; Afx Mr 71 12/7:374
HMS Newcastle: 2v, cd; MB Je 72 22/258:249
HMS Pelican: 2v, cd, det, pph; sloop: Afx D 71 13/4:212-213
Royal Navy DE: 2 var, USN lend-lease: MW Ap 73 1/8:424
USS San Francisco: 2v, cd, pph, specs: WWE My 74 1/3:68-69
Scheer: 3v, cd, det, pph: 1/600: Sc Ap 72 3/4:210-211; cor Jl 3/7:371
Sverdlov: 2v, cd, det, pph: Afx Mr 71 12/7:374
HMS Tracker, Ruler: 2v, sec, cd, tpat, tcol, pph; escort carrier: IM N 75 11/6:11-13

Full Hull

(Civil)

(Sail or Oar)
Canal Narrow Boat: typical horse-drawn English barge: 2v, sec, cd, pph: MB Jl 73 40/7:276-277
East Coast Gun Punt: 3v, det, cd; waterfowler's boat: MB N 75 25/298:576-577; add Ap 76 26/303:205; cor to Ja add: Jl 76 26/306:401-402
SS Great Britain: 2v, sec, cd, pat, col, det; 1843 5-mast steam & sail liner: Sc D 71 2/12:656-657
Simon & Jude: 2v, sec, cd; 1662 British catamaran: MB Mr 73 40/3:117-118
Vollenhovense Bol: 3v, sec, cd, pat, col, rig; 1970s Dutch yacht: MB Je 75 42/6:276-277

I. Static Scale

(Paddle)
Scale Model Ships: 2v, sec, cd, pat, col: see separate listing
PS Shanklin: 2v, cd, tpat, tcol, pph; 1924 excursion steamer: MB O 75 25/297:528-529

(Propeller)
Anonity: 3v, sec, cd, pat, col, pph; coastal tanker with negligible freeboard: MB F 72 22/254:65+
Canal Narrow Boats: 2v, sec, cd, pph; typical self-propelled barge: MB Jl 73 23/271:276-277
Cruiser: 2v, sec, cd, pat, col, det, pph: MB O 71 21/250:402
Delta 28: 3v, sec, cd, pat, 2 var: Sc S 71 2/9:493
Gelderland: 4v, sec, cd, tpat, tcol, pph; 1921 Dutch ocean tug: MB Ag 74 24/284:374
SS Hector: 3v, sec, cd, pat, col, pph: Blue Funnel cargo liner: MB Je 72 22/258:232-234
Hermes: 2v, cd; 1920s fisherman: MB Jl 75 25/294:331; 2v, sec, det, net: Ag 75 25/295:391
Knight of St. Patrick: 4v, sec, tpat, tcol; 1886 sea-going tug: MB Jl 74 24/282:268-272
Lady L: $1\tfrac{11}{22}$v, cd, pat, coal; coal puffer: MB S 75 25/296:476-477
Metinda III: 3v, sec, cd, pat, col, pph; salvage tug: MB N 74 24/286:486-487
Nandhimitra: 3v, sec, cd, pat, col; 1966 Sri Lanka tug: MB Mr 75 25/290:126
Northwestern Miller: 3v, sec, cd, pat, col; 1915 British freighter: MB Ag 71 21/248:316-317
Ocean Reward: 3v, sec, cd, pat, tcol; 1914 steel drifter: MB D 75 25/299:646
Portia: 2v, sec, cd, pat, col; diesel-electric trawler: MB S 71 21/249:354-355
MV Pundua: 2v, sec, cd; 1945 freighter: MB Je 74 24/281:218-219
St. Elmo: 2v, cd; 1941 side trawler: MB S 75 25/296:457; 4v, sec, cd, pat; col, net: O 75 25/297:540
Scale Model Ships: 2v, sec, cd, pat, col: see separate listing
Seefalke: 3v, sec, cd, tpat, tcol, pph; 1924 German ocean tug: MB S 74 24/284:374
SS Shengking: 3v, sec, cd, pat, col, pph; 1931 passenger-cargo: MB N 74 24/286:268-272

(Naval)

(Sail or Oar)
Cinq Ports Ship, c. 1250: 2v, cd, pat, tcol: RT D 75 8/12:136+
Period Ships: 2v, sec: see separate listing
Stationary Floating Battery, 1794: 3v, sec, cd, pat; British: Sc Ap 71 2/4:185
nameless: 3v, sec, int, no rig; 1800 Dutch ship of the line: MB F 72 22/253:74

(Power--U.K.)
Albion: 3v, sec, cd, det, pph; 1954 commando carrier: MM O 71 1/10:523-525
BPB Type 2: 2v, sec, cd, pat, int, pph; 63' ASR launch: MB Jl 75 25/294:341-344+
Blake: 3v, sec, cd, det, pph; 1961 destroyer to command helicopter carrier: MM D 71 1/12:645-646
Bluebell: 2v, sec, cd, pat, tcol, det: MM O 71 1/10:408-409
British Power Boat 64' HSL: 2v, sec, cd, pat, tcol, pph; 1936 high speed launch: MB O 75 25/297:521-524
Caesar: 2v, sec, cd, tpat, tcol, pph: MM Jl 72 2/7:348-352
Canada: 2v, sec, cd: MB Jl 72 22/259:287
Chester: 2v, sec, cd, det: MB F 72 22/254:66-67
Devastation: 2v, sec, cd, tpat, tcol, pph; 1891 battleship: MB My 71 21/245:200-201
Flower Class Corvettes: see separate listing
Glasgow: 2v, sec, det, pph; 1909 Town Class cruiser: MB Ap 74 24/279:126-127
Grey Goose: 2v, cd, pat, pph; steam gunboat: MM D 74 4/12:755-757; int, pph: Ja 75 5/1:35-36
Hants & Dorset 68' ASR launch: $2\frac{1}{2}$v, sec, cd, pat, col, pph: MB S 75 25/296:461-465
Lady Shirley: 4v, cd, pat, tcol, det; 1941 armed trawler: MB D 71 21/252:495-496
MTB 53: 2v, sec, int, cd, pph; 1939: MM O 74 4/10:606-607
MTB 379-395 (Vosper 73'): 2v, int, cd; 1944: MM N 74 4/11:681+
MTB 347-362 (Vosper 70'6"): 2v, cd, chartroom, pph, 1943: MM N 74 4/11:682-683
MTB 538: 2v, cd; 1943 one-off experiment: MM Ag 74 4/8:466-457; S 74 4/9:535
Marine Modelling: 2 or 3v, sec, cd, pat, col, det, some pph, 1/600: see separate listing
Rattlesnake: 2v, sec, cd, pat, tcol, 2 var; 1943 Algerine minesweeper: MB Ap 72 22/256:162-163
Rattlesnake: 2v, sec, cd, pph: MM Je 73 3/6:368-370
Thornycroft 67' HSL: 3v, sec, cd, pat, tcol; 1942 ASR launch: MB Ag 75 25/295:401-404+
Vindictive: 2v, pph; 1918 carrier (designed as cruiser): MB My 74 24/280:170-171+

(Power--Other Countries)
Aurora: 2v, sec, cd, sk, pph; 1902 Russian cruiser: MM N 71 1/11:576-582
USS Garcia: 2v, cd, det: destroyer: Q Ap 73 8/2:94-95
Jeanne D'Arc: 3v, sec, cd, pat, col, det, pph; Super Frelon helicopter: 3v, cd, pat, col: MM S 71 1/9:456-460
Marine Modelling: 2 or 3v, sec, cd, pat, col, det, some pph, 1/600: see separate listing
USS Monitor: 3v, sec, cd, det, flag: Q Ap 71 6/2:15-17
Moskva: $3\frac{1}{2}$v, sec, cd, pat, col, sk, pph; hormone helicopter: 3v, cd: MM Jl 71 1/7:350-352
KD Perdana: 4v, sec, cd, pat, 1972 Malasian patrol boat: MB Ja 75 25/288:22-23

I. Static Scale 146

Perkasa: 3v, cd, pat, tcol, int; Malaysian patrol boat: Sc N 71 2/11:613-615
Potemkin: 2v, sec, cd, pat, col, pph; 1903 Russian battleship: MM My 73 3/5:308-309
Scharnhorst: 4v, cd, pat, col, pph: Sc N 75 6/74:550-551
Schlesien: 2v, sec, cd, pph; 1906 Deutschland-class battleship: MM Ja 71 1/1:39-40
Steam Cutter, USN 30': lines only; 1915: MB Ag 72 22/260:335
Steam Cutter, USN 40': 1v, sec, cd, int, det; 1900: MB Ag 72 22/260:334-335; rig: S 72 22/261:388
Type IX U-Boat: 2v, sec, cd, tpat, tcol, pph: Sc D 74 5/12:656-657

Separate Listings

Fighting Fleets in Miniature [all MB]

(Austro-Hungary)
Helgoland: 1914 cruiser: Ag 71 21/248:322-323
Tatra: 1917 destroyer: Ag 71 21/248:322-323
Viribus Unitis: 1912 battleship: F 73 23/266:70-71

(Brazil)
Minas Gerais: 1919 (also dep 1939) battleship: F 72 22/254:72-73

(Canada)
Oakville: 1941 corvette: Ag 75 25/295:407

(France)
Jean de Vienne: 1936 cruiser: Mr 74 24/278:82-84
Lamotte-Picquet: 1926 (dep 1941) cruiser: D 75 25/299:665
Le Terrible: 1936 destroyer: Mr 74 24/278:82-84

(Germany)
Admiral Scheer & Admiral Graf Spee: 1939 pocket battleship: Ja 75 25/288:31-32
Deutschland 1933/Lutzow 1945: pocket battleship: Ja 75 25/288:31-32
Gneisenau: 1938 battle cruiser: S 71 21/249:368-369
SMS Königsberg: 1907 cruiser: O 74 24/285:434
Lebrecht Maass: 1937 destroyer: Mr 71 21/243:112-114
Mainz: 1909 cruiser: Mr 73 23/267: 114-115
Prinz Eugen: 1938 heavy cruiser: Mr 71 21/243:112-114
Schleswig-Holstein: 1908 battleship, 1930 training ship: Ap 74 24/279:132-133
Stettin: 1907 cruiser: Mr 73 23/267:114-115
Tirpetz: 1941 battleship: S 73 23/273:378-379+
SMS Von der Tan: 1910 battle-cruiser: Mr 72 22/255:116-117
U-39: 1938 submarine: Jl 75 25/294:347
U-94: type VIIc submarine: Ag 75 25/295:407

Ships

U-118: 1941 minelaying submarine: S 75 25/296:467+
U-460: 1941, type XIV submarine: O 75 25/297:531
U-2540: 1945, type XXI submarine: N 75 25/298:587
Z-17: 1938 destroyer: S 72 22/261:384-385+
Z-25: 1939 destroyer: S 72 22/261:384-385
Z-35: 1941 destroyer: S 72 22/261:384-385+

(Italy)
Attilio Regolo: 1942 cruiser: Ja 74 24/277:30-31
Conte di Cavour: 1915 battleship (dep 1915 & 1925): Ag 74 24/283:328-329
Conte di Cavour: 1938 battleship: S 74 24/284:378-379
Curatone: 1924 destroyer: Ja 72 22/253:24-25
Dante Alighieri: 1913 battleship: Jl 73 23/271:290-291
Eritrea: 1935 colonial sloop: Jl 71 21/247:282-283
Guiseppe Garibaldi: 1901 armored cruiser: Jl 72 22/259:292-293
Guiseppe Miraglia: 1927 seaplane carrier: Jl 71 21/247:282-283
Leone: 1924 destroyer: Ja 72 22/253:24-25
Luigi Cadorna: 1933 cruiser: Ja 71 21/241:24-25+
Pisa: 1909 armored cruiser: Jl 72 22/259:292-293
Pola: 1932 cruiser: Ja 73 23/265:24-26
San Marco: 1956 destroyer, converted from Attilio Regolo: Ja 74 24/277:30-31
Trento: 1933 cruiser: Ja 71 21/241:24-25+
Turbine: 1927 destroyer: Ja 72 22/253:24-25
Zara: 1931 cruiser: Ja 73 23/265:24-26

(Japan)
Aoba: 1927 heavy cruiser: N 71 21/251:454-455
Hatsushimo: 1934 destroyer: My 73 23/269:202-203
Hiei: 1914 battleship: My 71 21/245:204-205
Hiryu: 1939 carrier: N 73 23/275:470-472
Kako: 1926 heavy cruiser: N 71 21/251:454-455
Kumano: 1937 (dep 1940) battleship: N 72 22/263:472-473
Nagato: 1920 battleship: Ap 75 25/291:182-183+; (dep 1944): My 75 25/292:238-240
Oi: 1921 (dep 1937) cruiser: Je 74 24/281:220-221
Yamagumo: 1938 destroyer: My 73 23/269:202-203
Yamashiro: 1917 battleship: My 72 22/257:202-203
Yubari: 1923 (dep 1927) cruiser: Je 74 24/281:220-221

(Thailand)
Ayuthia: 1938 (dep 1941) "pocket heavy cruiser": D 75 25/299:665

(USSR, Russia)
Aurora: 1903 cruiser: Ag 73 23/272:334-335
Chervonaya Ukraina: 1927 cruiser: Ag 73 23/272:334-335
Knyaz Souvorov: 1905 battleship: Ag 72 22/260:338-339+
Marat: 1939 battleship; rebuilt from Petropavlovsk: F 71 21/242:68-69
Petropavlovsk: 1919 battleship: F 71 21/242:68-69

I. Static Scale 148

(U. K.)
Ajax: 1935 (dep 1939) cruiser: F 75 25/289:82-83+
Ambuscade: 1924 destroyer: Ap 72 22/256:258-159+
Arethusa: 1914 destroyer: My 74 24/280:175-177
Arethusa: 1936 destroyer: My 74 24/280:175-177
Ark Royal: 1937 carrier: Ap 71 21/244:156-157+
Aubretia: 1940 corvette: Jl 75 25/294:347
Bicester: 1942 destroyer escort: S 75 25/296:466-467+
Bleasdale: 1942 destroyer escort: N 75 25/298:587
Brecon: 1942 escort destroyer: N 75 25/298:587
Broadway: 1920 destroyer: Ag 75 25/295:407
Chatham: 1912 cruiser: D 74 24/287:535
Cumberland: 1928 (dep 1939) cruiser: Mr 75 25/290:136-137
Eglinton: 1940 destroyer escort: S 75 25/296:466-467+
Egret: 1938 sloop: Jl 75 25/294:347
Exeter: 1931 (dep 1939) cruiser: F 75 25/289:82-83+
Goliath: 1900 battleship: N 74 24/286:482-483
Good Hope: 1902 armored cruiser: O 71 21/250:410-411+
Helmsdale: 1943 frigate: Ag 75 25/295:407
Hesprus: 1939 destroyer: N 75 25/298:586
Intrepid: 1937 destroyer: Ap 72 22/256:158-159+
Iron Duke: 1916 battleship: O 72 22/262:428-430
Javelin: 1939 destroyer: Ap 72 22/256:158-159+
Lock: 1944 frigate: N 75 25/298:586
Marmion: 1915 destroyer: O 73 23/274:426-427
Natal: 1907 armored cruiser: O 71 21/250:410-411+
Oakville: 1941 corvette: Ag 75 25/295:407
Rodney: 1927 battleship: Ap 73 23/268:154-155
Severn: 1914 monitor: D 74 24/287:534-535
Strathcoe: 1919 (dep 1939) trawler: Jl 75 25/294:347
Trojan: 1918 destroyer: O 73 23/274:426-427
Versatile: 1918 (dep 1943) long range escort: Ag 75 25/295:407
Vivien: 1918 (dep 1939) anti-aircraft escort: Jl 75 25/294:347
Weymouth: 1911 cruiser: N 74 24/286:482-483
Whimbrel: 1943 sloop: S 75 25/296:467+
Wivern: 1919 destroyer: O 73 23/274:426-427

(U. S.)
Alabama: 1942 battleship: Je 71 21/246:234-235
Arizona: 1916 battleship: D 72 22/264:526-527
Arkansas: 1912 (dep 1942) battleship: Jl 74 24/282:274-275
Baltimore: 1943 heavy cruiser: Je 72 22/258:244-245
Benham: 1938 destroyer: O 75 25/297:531
Bogue: 1941 escort carrier: O 75 25/297:530
Borie: 1920 destroyer: O 75 15/197:531
Buckley: 1943 destroyer escort: O 75 25/297:531
Dixie: no date, destroyer tender: D 71 21/252:506-507+
Essex: 1942 carrier: Je 73 23/270:244-246
Porter: 1937 destroyer: D 73 23/276:528-530
Salt Lake City: 1929 heavy cruiser: D 73 23/276:528-530
Terror: 1942 mine layer: D 71 21/252:506-507+
Wyoming: 1912 battleship: Je 75 25/294:290-291

Flower Class Corvette [all MM]

Begonia: 2v, cd, pat; S 73 3/9:598-599
Buttercup: 2v, cd, pat: N 73 3/11:748-749+
Gardenia: 1v, cd: O 73 3/10:672
Genista: 2v, cd; O 73 3/10:670-671
Kingfisher class: 1v, cd: 1935-1939: S 73 3/9:601
Lotus: 1v, cd; 1942: N 73 3/11:747
Saxifrage: 1v, cd; 1918: S 73 3/9:601
Willowherb: 1v, cd; 1943: N 73 3/11:747; $\frac{1}{2}$v, det, sk, pph: D 73 3/12:816-818
Wisteria: 2v, cd; 1916: S 73 3/9:600
DNC 30/B39: 1v, cd; March 1940: O 73 3/10:672
DNC 30/B39A: 1v, cd; March 1942: O 73 3/10:672
DNC 30/B303: 1v, cd; June 1942: O 73 3/10:672

Marine Modelling [all Sc]

RRS Bransfield: British research vessel: Je 72 3/6:329-331
HMS Bristol: 1972 guided missile destroyer: Ja 74 5/1:18-19
Chapaev: Russian cruiser: N 74 5/11:610-611
Coleraine: British fire-fighting tug, late 1960s: O 74 5/10:538-539
Duquesne: 1969 French Sufferen-class guided missile leader: Jl 74 5/7:368-369
Dzershinski: Russian Sverdlov-class cruiser: S 74 5/9:494-495
Grisha: Russian corvette: Je 74 5/6:309
Kanin: Russian guided missile destroyer: O 73 4/10:697
Kaskin: Russian destroyer: Ja 72 3/1:42-43
Kildin: Russian destroyer: F 72 3/2:92-93
Kirov: 1938 (dep 1973) Russian cruiser: N 73 4/11:746-747
Komar: Russian torpedo boat: My 72 3/5:262-263
Kotlin: Russian destroyer: Mr 72 3/3:149-151
Kotlin: with helicopter: S 73 4/9:606-607
Kotlin SAM II: guided missile destroyer: D 73 4/12:821
USS Knox: 1969 destroyer: O 75 6/10:498-499
Kresta II: Russian missile cruiser: Ja 73 4/1:40-41
Krivak: Russian destroyer escort: Ag 72 3/8:442-443
Kronstadt: Russian patrol vessel: D 72 3/12:653
Krupny: 1958 Russian destroyer: Ag 71 2/8:432-433
Leningrad: 1935 Russian destroyer: My 74 5/5:272
Lloydsman: British salvage tug: F 73 4/2:110-111
Mikkel Mols: 1960 Danish ferry: My 71 2/5:238-239
Nanunchka: Russian surface missile corvette: Je 74 5/6:309
Osa: Russian missile patrol boat: Jl 72 3/7:382
Petya II: Russian escort vessel: Jl 73 4/7:510
Plejad: 1960 Swedish torpedo boat: N 72 3/11:606-607
Riga: Russian destroyer escort: Mr 73 4/3:196
HMS Sheffield: guided missile destroyer: F 75 6/2:78-79
Skory: Russian destroyer: Ag 73 4/8:554-555
Song of Norway: Norwegian cruise liner: Ap 72 3/4:220-222
Storoshevoi: 1936 Russian destroyer: Ap 74 5/4:213
Sverdlov: 1956 Russian cruiser: F 74 5/2:105-107

I. Static Scale 150

Tallin: Russian destroyer, 1952: Je 73 4/6:432
Taskhent: 1937 Russian destroyer: Mr 74 5/3:161

Minesweepers [all MM]

[1/384 scale and of U.K. unless otherwise noted]

Aberdare: 1v, cd; 1943: Ag 72 2/8:411
Albury: 1v, cd; 1942: Ag 72 2/8:410
Algerine: $1\frac{11}{22}$v, cd; 1/384 (1v) & 1/256 ($\frac{11}{22}$v); May 1942: N 72 2/11:589-591
Alresford: 1v, cd; 1/1200; 1942: Ag 72 2/8:409
Asheldam: 1v, cd; 1954: Ja 73 3/1:33
HMAS Bendigo: 1v, cd; 1941: 1v, cd: Ja 73 3/1:34
Blackpool: 1v, cd; 1942: O 72 2/10:530
Bramble: 1v, cd; 1945: S 72 2/9:471
Bridlington: 1v, cd; 1943: O 72 2/10:532
Caraquet: 1v, cd; Aug 1943: O 72 2/10:530
Catherine: 1v, cd: Ja 73 3/1:34
Coniston: 1v, cd; 1954: Ja 73 3/1:35
Courier: $2\frac{1}{2}$v, cd: D 72 2/12:656
Early Type BYMS: 1v, cd: Ja 73 3/1:35
Fantome: 1v, cd; Dec 1942: N 72 2/11:591
Fly: 1v, cd; 1949: D 72 2/12:656
Harrier: 2v, cd, sec; 1934: S 72 2/9:470+
Harrier: 1v, cd; July 1942: S 72 2/9:471
Hazard: 1v, cd; 1/1200 June 1942: S 72 2/9:473
Heythrop: 2v, cd; 1917: Ag 72 2/8:410
Lotus: 1v, cd; 1942: Ja 73 3/1:33
MMS 291 (Small type): 1v, cd: Ja 73 3/1:34
MMS 1017 (Large type): 1v, cd: Ja 73 3/1:33
Mariner: $\frac{11}{22}$v, cd; 1956-1958: D 72 2/12:658
Mistley: 1v, cd; 1918: Ag 72 2/8:410
Niger (M/S HQ ship): 1v, cd; 1945: N 72 2/11:590
Pangbourne: 1v, cd; 1942: Ag 72 2/8:410
Parrsborough: 1v, cd, 1/1200 full hull making sweep: O 72 2/10:532
Polruan: 2v, cd; May 1941: O 72 2/10:530
Recruit: 1v, cd; Jan 1944: N 72 2/11:590
Seaham: 1v, cd; 1944: O 72 2/10:531
Speedy: 1v, cd; 1945: S 72 2/9:470
Star of Orkney (requisitioned trawler): 1v, cd: Ja 73 3/1:35
Stormoway (fitted as fleet tug): 1v, cd; April 1945: O 72 2/10:531
Vallay: 1v, cd; 1945: Ja 73 3/1:34
4" Gun Shield & flare projector: 4v, cd; 1/150: D 72 2/12:657

Period Ships [all MB]

American Man-of-war Brig: 1812: N 72 22/263:476-477
Billyboy of 1880: sail barge: F 73 23/266:76-77

HMS Captain: sail & steam turret ship, 1870: Je 71 21/246:240-241
Cat of 1770: merchant ship: Ap 73 23/268:152-153
French Frigate of 1794: D 72 22/264:534-535
Spanish Three Decker, 1797: Ag 73 23/272:332-333
nameless: 1814 British mortar ship (several converted to exploration ships): Jl 71 21/247:284-285

Scale Model Ships [all MB]

Introduction: N 71 21/251:450-451
PS Albion: 1893 Bristol Channel paddle steamer: My 73 23/269: 198-201
Armora: 1911 three-island steamer: Ag 73 23/272:328-331
Bilsdale: 1900 pleasure paddle steamer: D 72 22/264:508-511
SS Brighton: 1903 cross-channel steamer: My 72 22/257:197-200
Channel Queen: 1912 well-deck steamer: Ap 72 22/256:149-151
Chieftain: 1899 paddle tug: Jl 73 23/271:286-289
Cluthas: 19th century Clyde ferry: Ja 73 23/265:14-17
Cumbrae: 1869 packet: D 71 21/252:490-492
Dutchess of Kent: 1897 paddle steamer: Ja 72 22/253:21-23+
Flying Duck: 1956 tug: D 73 23/276:523-527
SS Grangemouth: East Coast (U.K.) passenger/cargo steamer: N 72 22/263:274-277
H.S. Type Tug: WW-I Admiralty tug: Ag 72 22/260:323-325+
Hotspur: 1897 twin-screw dock tug: F 73 23/266:66-69+
Inchcolm: 1909 Clyde puffer: Ja 74 24/77:14-17
SS Juno: 1898 Clyde paddle steamer: Je 72 22/258:241-244
SS Kyle Rhea: 1912 single-hatch coaster: Mr 73 23/267:110-113
Marmion: 1906 paddle steamer: O 73 23/276:422-425+
Mona: 1903 Tyne ferry: Je 73 23/270:241-243
Moygannon: raised quarterdeck coaster: O 72 22/262:418-421
New Fawn: 1923 island passenger cargo: F 72 22/254:78-80
St. Clair: 1937 northern isles steamer: Ap 73 23/268:156-159
Saint Class Salvage Tug: 1919 Admiralty tug: Mr 72 22/255:109-111
T.I.D. Class Tug: WW-II Admiralty tug: S 72 22/261:372-375
Thames Penny Steamer: 19th century passenger paddle steamers: Jl 72 22/259:274-277
Totnes Castle: 1923 River Dart paddle steamer: N 73 23/275:473-475
TSS Victoria: 1907 Isle of Man steamer: S 73 23/273:373-376

Simplified Mercantile Ships [all MB]

SS Albertville: 1928 Belgian passenger liner: Ag 72 22/260:344
SS Arundel Castle: 1921 British passenger/cargo: D 72 22/264: 532-533
RHMS Britannia (ex Monterey): 1932 (dep 1970) British cruise liner: Je 74 24/281:230-231
MS Columbialand: 1968 Swedish bulk carrier: Ag 73 23/272:338-339

I. Static Scale 152

MS Cunard Adventurer: 1972 British cruise ships: D 73 23/276: 538-539
MS Eagle: 1971 British passenger & car ferry: Jl 74 24/282-283
MS France Maru: 1967 Japanese cargo liner: Jl 73 23/271:293
SS Isle of Jersey: 1930 British Channel Islands passenger: Ap 73 23/268:166-167
SS Isle of Thanet: 1925 British cross-channel steamer: S 72 22/261:392
MS Lion: 1967 British vehicle & passenger ferry: Ja 74 24/277:35
MS Munster: 1968 Irish Irish Sea ferry: Mr 74 24/278:91
MS Nihon: 1972 Swedish container ship: Mr 73 23/267:118-119
SS Orcades: 1937 British passenger/cargo liner: N 72 22/263:468-469
MS Ophir: 1928 Dutch passenger/cargo liner: O 72 22/262:431
SS President Roosevelt: 1922 U.S. passenger/cargo liner (built as hospital/troopship): Ja 73 23/265:32-33
Prince Baudouin: 1934 Belgian cross-channel passenger: F 73 23/266:65
Tor Mercia: 1970 British vehicle ferry: N 73 23/275:469
SS Uganda: 1952 German school & cruise ship: My 73 23/269:206-207
MS Vortigern: 1969 British train & car ferry: O 73 23/274:431
MS Zambéze: 1971 French container cargo liner: Je 73 23/270: 252-253

Surface Effect Vehicles

RFB (Lippisch) X 113 Am Aerofoil Boat: 6v, cd, pt, tcol, pph; 1971 German experiment: MB S 73 23/273:488-490+

Ship Accessories & Details

British Warship Detail: see separate listing
Functional Ventilators: MB My 75 25/242:243
Lowering the Funnel: Tyne tug stack folding variants: MB F 71 21/242:74
Model Fishing Gear: on-board equipment: MB Ap 71 21/244:142-145

British Warship Detail [all MB; started Mr 69]

Watertight Doors & Hatches: Ja 71 21/241:32-34
4" twin HA/LA guns: F 71 21/242:76-77+
Davits: Ap 71 21/244:166-167
Sailing Launch, 42': My 71 21/245:208-209
Motor Launch, 36': My 71 21/245:208-209

Ships

SCRATCH-BUILDING PLANS

SS Amarapoora: wood (plans in MB D 70 20/240:522): Sc Ja 71 2/1:33-35
Ancient Warships: 2v, det: see separate listing
Assault Landing Craft: MW S 72 1/1:25-27
Cinq Ports Ship, c. 1250: plastic sheet: RT D 75 8/12:136-138+
Launch Out: freelance trawler: MB Ap 72 22/256:146-148; My 72 22/257:204-205; Je 72 22/258:253-254; Jl 72 22/259:288-289
HMS Lion: plastic card: Sc Ja 75 6/64:16-19

Ancient Warships [all Afx]

Goliath: Philistine, 1200 BC: D 72 14/4:194+
Greek Pentere Agammemnon: Mr 73 14/7:366-370
Greek Trireme Achilles: F 73 14/6:318-321
Phoenician Bireme Melkart: Ja 73 14/5:258-261
Rameses: 1200 BC Egyptain: N 72 14/3:134-136
Roman Bireme Romulus: Ap 73 14/8:430-433

CONVERSIONS

USS Antietam: from Hasegawa Hancock: Q Au 75 11/1:18
Algerine Class Minesweeper: from Airfix HMS Hotspur: Afx Ag 72 13/12:661+
Algerine Fleet Escort, 1942: from Ensign HMS Marvel 1/1200 metal: MW N 73 2/3:151-152
Andrea Doria (battleship): from Mini-Ship Littorio: MW S 73 2/1: 14-16
USS Bennington: from Hasegawa Essex: Q Au 75 11/1:18
USS Bon Homme Richard: from Hasegawa Essex: Q Au 75 11/1:18
USS Boxer: from Hasegawa Hancock: Q Au 75 11/1:18
USS Bunker Hill: from Hasegawa Essex: Q Au 75 11/1:18
Canadian Thermopylae: 1892-1896 barque-rig from Revell Thermopylae: RT Jl 75 8/7:80-81
Carrack Mataro: 13-14th century naval vessel: from Heller Mataro carack: MW Je 73 1/10:540+
HMS Defender: from Airfix Hotspur: Q Jl 74 10/1:15
Destroyer Escorts of the US Navy: Buckley class from Revell HMS Bligh: MW O 73 2/2:78-79
USS Franklin: from Hasegawa Essex: Q Au 75 11/1:13
USS Garcia: from Monogram USS Brooke: Q Ap 73 8/2:94-95
USS Gato: from Revell USS Growler: Q O 73 8/4:223-225
USS Hornet: from Hasegawa Essex: Q Au 75 11/1:13
USS Intrepid: from Hasegawa Essex: Q Au 75 11/1:13
Lebrecht Maass class destroyer in 1/1200: from Ensign Narvik class (metal): MW O 73 2/2:100-101
USS Lexington: from Hasegawa Essex: Q Au 75 11/1:13

I. Static Scale 154

Myoko: 1929 Japanese cruiser (dep 1929, 1936, 1941, 1944): from
    Hasegawa 1/700: RT S 73 6/9:100-101
USS Randolph: from Hasegawa Hancock: Q Au 75 11/1:13
USS Ranger modelled in 1/1200 scale: from Mini-Ships Hornet:
    MW Ag 73 1/12:640-643
USS Shangri-La, from Hasegawa Hancock: Q Au 75 11/1:18
USS Ticonderoga: from Hasegawa Hancock: Q Au 75 11/1:13
HMS Tracker: from Revell USS Montrose: IM N 75 11/6:11-13
Tribal Class Destroyer: from Revell Ark Royal Escort: MW S 73
    2/1:12+
USS Wasp: from Hasegawa Essex: Q Au 75 11/1:18
Yamato in 1/1200 scale: Mini-Ship to 1945 var: MW F 74 2/6:
    311
USS Yorktown: from Hasegawa Essex: Q Au 75 11/1:12-13

SUPERDETAILING

Airfix HMS Amazon: Afx O 75 17/2:109-112
Amazon: IM Mr 75 11/2:3-5
Airfix HMS Hood: 1/1200 & 1/600: Afx O 74 16/2:82-84+
Hood: IM My 74 10/(16):4-8; Jl 74 10/(17):4-6
Airfix Hunt Class Destroyers: Afx Ja 71 12/5:244-246; F 71 12/6:
    292-295
Airfix Royal Sovereign: Afx F 72 13/6:332-333
Almark USS Missouri: 1/1200: MW Jl 73 1/1:582-583
Hasegawa USS Essex & Hancock: Q Au 75 11/1:7-9
Revell HMS Bligh: MW Ap 73 1/8:422-425+
Revell USS Growler: Q O 73 8/4:223-225
Revell Prinz Eugen: 1/720: MW N 73 2/3:130-131+
Tamiya Perkasa: updating: IM Ja 72 9/1:3
Wilhelmshaven Hamburg: 1/250 cardstock destroyer: Sc O 71 2/
    10:540-541; N 71 2/11:620-621

KIT CONSTRUCTION

Airfix Vosper 1943 (third series) MTB: 1/72: IM S 72 9/9:3-10
Almark Hornet: 1/1200: Tokyo raid configuration: MW Je 73 1/
    10:516-517
Aoshima Yamashiro: Sc O 73 4/10:692-696
Hasegawa Akagi: Sc Ag 74 5/9:426-427
Ingenia le Protecteur: cardstock ship of the line: Sc S 72 3/9:
    500-501
Nichimo U-Boat: Sc D 74 5/12:659-661
Revell HMS Ark Royal: 1/720 wl: MW Ag 73 1/12:652-653
Revell Cutty Sark: Sc Ag 75 6/8:382-385
Revell Mayflower: IM Je 71 8/6:5-6
Revell U-47: Sc Jl 75 6/7:324-325

Tamiya Perkasa: 1/72: SS.12 missile launchers: IM Ja 72 9/1:4
Tamiya Scharnhorst: Sc N 75 6/74:550-553
Tamiya Vosper Fast Patrol Boat: 1/72: Sc N 71 2/11:613-616

KIT CORRECTION

Aoshima Yakikaze: MW D 73 2/4:192-193
Hasegawa Myoko: RT S 73 6/9:100-101

STRUCTURES

SCALE DRAWINGS

Bridges

B&O Short Girder Bridge: 2v, sec, pph: MR Je 71 38/6:39
B&OCT Bascule Bridge: 4v, dim, cd, det, pph: MR D 73 40/12: 58-60
Canadian Forces Roads, Bridges, & Camouflage Practice: RT Jl 75 8/7:77
Charley Creek Bridge: 3v; log railroad bridge: NMRA N 73 39/3: 50
Chicago, Aurora & Elgin Wood Trestle: 2v, dim, sec, cd, pph: RMC N 75 44/6:37
D&RG Narrow Gauge Pile Trestle: 3v, dim, mat: NMRA O 75 41/2:39
D&RGW Ballasted Deck Pile Trestle: 3v, dim, sec, struc: NMRA D 75 41/4:45
D&RGW Framed Bents for Standard Trestle Bridges: 1v, dim: NMRA D 74 40/4:17
D&RGW Pile Bents for Standard Trestle Bridges: 2v, dim: NMRA F 75 40/6:35
GM Concrete Trestle: 1v, dim, sec: NMRA Je 75 50/10:61
Illinois Central Bridge 434-1: 1v, det: NMRA D 72 38/4:7-8
John Allen Memorial Bridge: 2v, cd, mat: MR N 73 40/11:62-67
Military Bridges: see separate listing
Pennsylvania RR Underpass, Creston PA: 2v, dim, cd, pph: NMRA Ap 75 40/8:58
Simple Truss Bridge: 3v, dim, pph: MR O 75 42/10:48
Timber Culvert: 2v, det, pph: NMRA D 72 38/4:44-45
Timber Trestle for Albion Lumber Co.: 3v, det: NMRA Ag 71 36:13:22+
Truss Bridge: N: 3v: MR F 71 38/2:55

I. Static Scale   156

(Military Bridges) [all MW]

Basic Bailey Bridge: S 72 1/1:30-33+
Bailey Pontoon Bridge: O 72 1/2:91-94
Small Box Girder Bridge: N 72 1/3:149-151
Pontoon Bridge Equipment Mk III: WW-I: D 72 1/4:205-209
Folding Boat Equipment Mk II: WW-II: Ja 73 1/5:247-249
Classification of Bridges: WW-II Allied systems: F 73 1/6:303
Folding Boat Equipment Mk III: WW-II: Mr 73 1/7:367-370
Inglis Bridging Equipment: 1916 & later: My 73 1/9:479-483
Inglis Mk II & III: Jl 73 1/11:574-587
Unit Construction Railway Bridge: N 73 2/3:133-136+
UCRB Equipment: Unit Construction Railroad Bridge: MW F 74
   2/6:304-306

Buildings

(Interlocking Signal Towers)

Great Northern Standard Interlocking Cabin: 2v, dim, cd, pat; 1906:
   NMRA D 73 39/4:40
John Street Tower: 4v, dim, cd, tpat, tcol, pph: RMC Ap 72 40/
   11:28-29
Kerney Junction Tower: 2v, fp, cd, det, pph, site: NMRA Jl 75
   40/11:56-58
Mt. Royal Tower: $2\frac{1}{2}$v, dim, cd: RMC Jl 73 42/2:46-47
Tower at Tuckahoe Junction: 4v, fp, dim, cd, pph: RMC Ja 75
   43/8:59-61

(Industries)

Bishop Creek No. 2 Hydro Plant: 2v, fp, dim, cd: MR Jl 75 42/7:
   52-53
Bishop Creek No. 2 Transformer House: 2v, dim, cd: MR Jl 75
   42/7:51-52
Build Your Own Gold Mine: headframe: 4v, dim, cd, det, site,
   const: MR Ja 75 42/1:46-51; 4v, dim, cd, const: F 75 42/2:
   72-77
Bulk Material Shipment: Starch Bulk Storage Silo: 3v, dim, cd,
   pph: NMRA Ja 74 39/5:56-57
Bunn's Feed & Seed Plant: 3v, dim, cd, mat: MR Ag 73 40/8:34-
   37
Carolina Foundry: 4v, fp, dim, cd, mat: MR Ja 72 39/1:44-47
Chair & Desk Factory: 5v, dim, cd: MR D 72 39/12:65-71
Coal Loading Facilities: pph of various prototype concepts: NMRA
   Ag 71 36/13:12-13
Coal Yard: 2v, cd, det, pph; "grain elevator" style: RMC D 75
   44/7:42-43
Coal Yard Scale & Office Building: 4v, dim, sec, cd, tpat, tcol,
   pph: RMC N 72 41/6:58-60

Structures

Compressed Gas Factory: 2v, dim, cd, pph: MR Mr 71 38/3:42-47
Cornwall Coalyard: 4v, fp, dim, cd, pph, site: MR Ag 71 38/8: 41-43
East Tipton Substation: 4v, dim, sec, cd, pph: MR Jl 75 42/7: 50-52
Factory: dim, struc, site, mat: MR F 74 41/2:60-65
Idaho Grain Elevator: 5v, fp, sec, cd, det, pph: NMRA D 71 37/4:6-10
Jones Chemical: 5v, dim, cd, mat: MR Mr 74 41/3:42-45
Laceyville Milk Station: 4v, dim, cd, tpat, tcol: RMC S 71 40/4: 20-22
Log Warehouse: 3v, dim, cd, sk: NSG N 75 1/5:30-31
Malt Tower Beside a Harbor: 5v, dim, cd, det, pph: MR Jl 73 40/7:56-61
Mill office: 5v, dim, cd, pph: MR Mr 75 42/3:42-45
Missouri Pacific RR Power House, Wichita KA: 4v, fp, dim, sec, cd: NMRA S 71 37/1:8-10
Moore's Modern Mill: 3v, dim, cd, det; feed mill: RMC Je 72 41/1:42-45
Mr. Pottle's Potworks: 4v, dim, cd: MR S 75 42/9:62-65
Nickels Milling & Feed Plant: 4v, dim, cd, site, pph, mat: MR Je 72 39/6:38-42
North Abington Coal Shed: 1v, fp, dim, sec, struc, cd, pph: MR Jl 74 41/7:41-44
Nostalgic Warehouse: 3v, fp, cd, const: RMC My 72 40/12:39-42
Oak Lake Grain Elevator: 4v, dim, cd, pph: MR Ag 74 41/8:54-57
Peters Sausage: 3v, fp, dim, cd, site, pph, const: MR Ap 74 41/4:60-65
Pingrove Machine Shop: 4v, fp, dim, cd, cpph, site: MR Mr 72 39/3:62-66
RMC Paper Company: 3v, dim, cd, mat: RMC Ap 74 42/11:40-44
Redlands Steam Plant: 2v, fp, dim, sec, cd, pph: MR Jl 75 42/7: 51-53
Ridley's Mill: 5v, cd; overshoot waterwheel grist mill: RMC N 71 40/6:31-35
Riford's Ice Company: 2v, dim, sec, cd: RMC Je 73 42/1:37-39
Rube's Rhubarb Plant: 4v, dim, cd, processing plant taking rhubarb stalks: RMC Jl 74 43/2:26-31
Small Grain Elevator: 4v, dim, cd, pph: MR S 72 39/9:46-47
Southern California Edison Substation & Local Business Office: 4v, fp, dim, sec, cd: MR Jl 75 42/7:50-51
Standard Oil Bulk Plant, Lindsay CA: 3 buildings, tank, pph: NMRA Mr 71 36/7:23-26
Supply Building: 4v, fp, dim, pph: NMRA F 73 38/6:27-30
Waukesha Feed Mill: 4v, cd, pph: RMC Ap 73 41/11:34-37
Wayside Warehouse: 5v, dim, cd, struc: MR Je 74 41/6:30-33

(Roundhouses & Engine Sheds)

Backwoods Engine House: 3v, fp, dim, const: RMC Jl 72 41/2: 44-48

I. Static Scale 158

D&RGW Chama NM Narrow Gauge Roundhouse: 2v, dim, struc, cd, pph, site: NMRA Je 73 38/10:35-37
East Broad Top Narrow Gauge Engine House: 1v, dim, sec, pph: NMRA S 75 51/1:56-57
Enginehouse: 3v, dim, sec, cd: MR Mr 73 40/12:52
Four Bay Roundhouse: 3v, fp, dim, cd: MR D 73 40/12:52
ICRR Dyersburg IN Roundhouse: 3v, fp, dim, sec, cd, pph: NMRA Ja 75 40/5:35-40
Rock Island Frame Engine Houses, 1914: 3v, fp, dim, cd: NMRA S 73 39/1:31-34
20 Stall Roundhouse: fp, dim, sec, struc, site: NMRA N 72 38/3:31
2 Stall Wood Car Barn: 2v, fp, dim, det: NMRA O 75 41/2:18-19

(Section Houses, Handcar Sheds, Tool Houses)

C&NW Supply Shed: 4v, cd, mat, const: RMC My 71 39/12:25-27
Erie Section House: 3v, dim, cd, tpat, tcol, pph; large (5 bays): RMC O 71 40/5:44-45
Grand Trunk Standard Tool House: 2v, fp, dim, cd; two cars: RMC F 74 42/9:51
Grand Trunk Standard Tool House: 2v, fp, dim, cd; one car: RMC F 74 42/9:51
Santa Fe Tool House, Capistrano CA: 4v, cd: NMRA F 72 37/6:40
Section Hand Car & Tool House: 2v, dim, sec, cd: NMRA Jl 75 40/11:46
Section Houses: 2v, dim, sec, cd, 3 var: NMRA Jl 72 37/11:50-51
Section Tool Box: 3v, dim, cd: NMRA Jl 75 40/1:46
Section Tool House: 3v, dim, sec, struc, det: NMRA S 71 37/1:31
Section Tool House: 2v exterior, 5v int, sec, det, mat: NMRA O 73 39/2:40
Tool & Handcar Shed: 4v, dim, cd: MR D 71 38/12:56-59

(Shanties)

Brick Shanty: 3v, fp, dim, cd, tpat, tcol, pph: RMC N 71 40/6:45
EL's Anderson Street Tower: 4v, dim, cd, pat, tcol, pph; watchman's shanty for manual crossing gates: RMC F 75 43/9:58-59
Tunnel Watch Shanties: 3v, fp, dim, cd, pph: NMRA N 72 38/3:34
Watchman's Shanty: 2v, fp, dim, sec, cd: NMRA F 72 37/6:11

(Railroad Stations--combination)

Airy Hall Halt: 4v, fp, dim, cd, pph; flagstop: MR Ja 71 38/1:64-65

Branchline Station: 3v, dim, cd, cpph, const: RMC Ag 72 41/3: 30-34
Brick Depot, Lloyd FL: 4v, fp, dim, cd, pph: NMRA Ag 72 37/13:16-20
Build a Spacious Station in No Space at All: Lehigh Valley, Easton PA: 4v, dim, sec, cd, pph, site: NMRA F 74 39/7:30-35
Canadian National's Weston Depot: $2\frac{1}{2}$v, fp, sec, cd: RMC O 72 41/5:28-29
Chama NM Depot: 2v, fp, dim, cd, pph; passenger, freight, & station agent's house: NMRA Je 73 38/10:31-34
Chicago Rock Island & Pacific Standard Depot #16: 2v, fp, dim, cd, pph: NMRA Jl 73 38/11:28-29
Colorado & Southern RY Depot (Between Pueblo & Walsenberg CO, 1911): 4v, fp, dim, sec, cd; passenger, freight & station agent's house: NMRA F 71 36/6:24-26
Combination Depot: 4v, fp, dim, cd, pph, site: NMRA Mr 73 38/7:42-44
Covered Depot for the Carrabasset: 3v, dim, cd, pph, mat, const: RMC F 75 43/9:31-39
Depot at Wagon Wheel Gap (D&RG): 4v, fp, sec, cd, pph: NMRA Je 71 36/10:22-26
Depot for the Town of Spartan: 3v, fp, dim, cd, const: RMC N 73 42/6:60-64
Front Royal Station: 4v, fp, dim, cd, pat, site: MR O 71 38/10:43-45
Kansas City & Emporia Depot, Lebo KA: 2v, fp, dim, sec, cd: NMRA My 74 39/10:34-35
Kansas City Southern Station, Watts OK: 4v, fp, dim, sec, cd, pph: NMRA O 73 39/2:29-34
Local Arrival & Departure Board: O, S, HO, N patterns: NMRA Jl 74 39/12:19
MKT Standard Small Station: 3v, fp, dim, sec, cd: NMRA S 72 38/1:24-25
MKT Station, Katy TX: 4v, fp, dim, cd, pph: NMRA O 74 40/2:31-34
Mayo FL Station: 4v, fp, dim, cd, pph; NMRA Ag 73 38/27-31
Missouri Pacific Frame Combination Station: 1v, fp, dim, cd: NMRA Ap 72 37/8:24-25
Missouri Pacific Railroad Station, Chidester, AR: 4v, fp, dim, cd, pph: NMRA Je 72 37/10:7-10
Morgans Bluff Depot: 4v, dim, cd, pph (Carol Stream on C&NW), const: RMC Ag 71 40/3:17
Mount Hope Station: 4v, fp, dim, cd, pph: MR N 75 42/11:58-63
Otis Station: 3v, dim, cd, pph: MR O 74 41/10:62-63
Peace Dale Station: 4v, fp, dim, cd, pph: MR S 74 41/9:42
Quinnimont: 3v, dim, cd, pph, cpph: RMC S 73 42/4:34-35; cor N 73 42/6:80
Railroad Structure of the Steam Diesel Era: L&N Crestwood KY: 2v, fp, dim, cd, pph: NMRA O 73 39/2:53-56
Reader Railroad Depot, Reader AR: 4v, fp, dim, cd, pph: NMRA N 71 37/3:14-16
Rowley Station: 4v, fp, dim, sec, cd, pph, const: MR Ja 74 41/1:50-56

I. Static Scale

Santa Fe Station, Buna TX: 3v, fp, dim, cd, pph: NMRA N 74 40/3:31-34
Silver Springs Depot: 4v, fp, dim, cd, pph: RMC Jl 74 43/2:49-51
Southern Railway Station, Fisherville KY: 2v, fp, dim, cd, pph: NMRA O 75 41/2:42-45
Station: N, small: MR Ap 71 38/4:34-35
A Three Towered Station: 2v, fp, dim, cd, mat, const; for rail crossing: MR N 74 41/11:68-74
Wakefield Station: 3v, dim, cd: MR S 74 41/9:42

(Railroad Stations--freight)

Bottled Gas Dock: pph: RMC D 74 43/7:64
C&NW Depot, Palatine IL, 1947: 2v, dim, cd, pph: NMRA O 71 37/2:22
CMR&P Freight House: 4v, cd, const: RMC D 71 40/7:24-29
Cotton Belt Unloading Ramp: 2v, dim: NMRA Mr 72 37/11:55
Division Point Freight House: 2v, fp, dim, sec, cd, pat: NMRA D 72 38/4:47
Mineral City Depot: 4v, dim, cd, tpat, tcol, pph: RMC Ag 75 44/3:30-33
Roanoke Freight Station: 4v, fp, cd, mat: MR Jl 71 38/7:52-57
Rock Springs Freight Station: 2v, fp, cd, tpat, tcol: MR Mr 73 40/3:70
Team Track Dock & Shed: 2v, fp, dim, det, light: NMRA O 71 37/2:8-9
Tennessee & Northern Station, Reform AL: 4v, fp, dim, cd, pph: NMRA Mr 74 39/8:50-53
Useful Freight Platform: 4v, fp, cd, mat: MR F 73 40/2:43-45

(Railroad Stations--passenger)

Bank Becomes Interurban Station: 3v, dim, cd, sk; mod of bank (F 74 39/7:34) into city interurban terminal: NMRA N 75 41/3:30-32
C&NW Depot, Palatine IL: 4v, fp, dim, cd, pph, site; 1947: NMRA O 71 37/2:23-27
Contemporary Suburban Depot: 2v, dim, pph; small windbreak waiting stand: NMRA Jl 75 40/11:53-54
Depot at Peace Dale: 4v, cd, pph: RMC Ag 73 42/3:27-29
Duplex Station at Linden: 4v, fp, dim, cd, pat, pph: MR Je 75 42/6:38-41
Edgebrook Commuter Shelter: 4v, fp, struc, sec, cd, pat, tcol, pph: MR N 71 38/22:42-43
Lackawana Plaza, Patterson NJ mountainside station: 3v, dim, sec, cd, pph: NMRA Je 74 39/11:23-25
MKT Station, Brookshire TX: 4v, dim, cd, pat, col; one-room: NMRA F 73 38/6:24-27
Medium Sized Station: 2v, fp, sec, cd: NMRA Je 73 38/10:41
Passenger Shelter: 2v, dim, cd, int: NMRA Je 72 37/10:12

Point of Rocks Depot: 2½v, fp, dim, struc, cd, pph: RMC Ja 74 42/8:29-33
St. Louis & San Francisco Station, Bolivar MO: 4v, fp, dim, cd, pph, 1914: NMRA Ja 74 39/5:44-47
Rock Island Passenger Pagoda: 2v, dim, cd, int, mat; booth shelter: NMRA D 72 38/4:31
Small Station: 1v, fp, dim, cd: NMRA S 71 37/1:43
Suburban Flagstop Station: 5v, fp, dim, site: NMRA Jl 71 36/11: 16-17
T&NO Orange TX & GH&SA Seguin TX Brick Passenger Depot: 4v, fp, dim, cd, pph, site: NMRA Ja 73 38/5:10-14
Train Order Station: 4v, dim, cd, pph: MR F 75 42/2:47-50
Up-Town Station: 4v, fp, dim, sec, cd: NMRA Jl 73 38/11:44-45
Yosemite Valley RR, Bagby CA: 4v, cd, pph: NMRA D 74 40/4:8
Yosemite Valley RR, Incline CA: 2v, cd: NMRA D 74 40/4:9
Yosemite Valley RR, Merced CA: 1v, cd, pph: NMRA D 74 40/4: 14

(Railroad Scales)

Illinois Central Scale House: 4v, cd, pph, const: RMC Mr 72 40/ 10:24-26
Scale House: dim, site, sk: NMRA N 75 41/3:26

(Rest Rooms)

Chicago, Rock Island & Pacific Ry Standard Privy: 2v, cd: NMRA Je 72 37/10:47
Kansas City Southern Outhouse: 3v, fp, dim, sec, cd: NMRA O 73 39/2:35-36
Logging Loo: 2v, cd, int; rail-truck mounted: NMRA Mr 74 39/ 8:59
Prestigious Privies of the Cumberland: 2v, fp, dim, sec, struc, cd: NMRA O 75 41/2:51
The Woodsline: 2v, fp, dim, sec, cd; 2-hole: NMRA S 75 41/1: 53

(Yard Offices & Repair Shops)

IC Roundhouse Foreman's Office: 3v, fp, dim, struc, cd: NMRA F 75 40/6:18-19
MP Freight Car Repair Shed, Kansas City, MO: 2v, dim, cd; 2 mods 2v, dim, cd, each: NMRA F 72 37/6:23-26
Machine Shop: 4v, fp, dim, cd: MR D 73 40/12:50-51
Missouri Pacific Proposed Loco Shop, East Bottoms, Kansas City, MO: 3v, fp, dim, sec: NMRA N 38/3:7
Office Shelter & Shop Building, Dyersburg: 1v, fp, dim, sec: NMRA F 75 40/6:18-19
Quinnimont: 3v, dim, cd, pph, cpph; yard office, ex-station: RMC S 73 42/4:34-35; cor N 73 42/6:80

I. Static Scale 162

Ramshackle Yard Office: from old passenger car & shanty: 1v, pph: MR N 72 39/11:57-59
Small Yardmaster's Office: 3v, fp, dim, cd: NMRA My 71 36/9: 12-13

(Other Than Industrial or Railroad)

Building Front Short Cut: 1v, pat, tcol, pph; store: RMC Ja 75 43/8:45
Cal's Lumberyard: 4v, dim, cd, mat: MR Ap 73 40/4:62-66
Old Sacramento's Railroad Museum: 4v, fp, dim, cd, site, sk: NMRA N 75 41/3:18-21
Crooksville Bank Block: 2v, fp, dim, cd, pph: MR O 72 39/10: 68-69
Crosby's Bandstand: 2v, dim, cd, mat; park bandstand: RMC N 72 41/6:32-35
Fabry Cyclery: 4v, dim, cd, pph; bicycle shop: MR S 73 40/9: 40-41
Farmhouse: 4v, fp, pph, const: RMC D 72 41/7:34-39; const: Ja 73 41/8:42-45
Fox Hill School: 3v, cd, pph: NMRA Mr 71 36/7:28-29
Grandma Byrdee's House: fp, dim, sk; free-lance 1900 house: NMRA N 74 40/3:38-39
Hotel for Trainmen at McGehee AR: 2v, fp, cd: NMRA N 72 38/3:38-41
The Light at Thatcher's Inlet: 2v, dim, cd, const; small lighthouse: RMC S 73 42/4:36-37
Long Island Potato Storage House: 1v, dim, sk: NMRA Ag 74 39/ 13:17
1900 Brick Store: 3v, fp, dim, cd, pat: NMRA Mr 72 37/7:35
Perkins Produce Project: 1v, dim, cd, const; store: MR D 74 41/12:54-60
Second National Bank: 1v, sec, cd, pph: MR My 74 41/5:34-36
Section Dwelling House: 2v, fp, dim: NMRA N 73 39/3:37
Standard Section House for Foreman: 2v, fp: NC&StL Ry: NMRA Je 71 36/10:33
Station Drugs: 2v, fp, cd, const: MB My 71 38/5:36-42
A Whole Town in One Building: 4v, fp, cd, pph; Valentown Hall, 1879 shopping center: RMC Mr 75 43/10:42-45

Docks

River Ferry Dock: rolling ramp type: 2v, dim, sec, cd: RMC Ja 71 39/8:52-53

Structures

Railroad Structures Other Than Buildings

(Bumping Posts)

Bumping Post: 2v, dim; wooden: NMRA Ag 71 36/13:37
Concrete Bumping Blocks: 2v, dim, pph: RMC Je 72 41/1:40-41

(Crossing Gates)

Crossing Gate: 2v, cd, pat, site: NMRA Mr 71 36/7:33

(Icing Docks)

Bananas in Kentucky: ice loader: 2v, dim in N & HO scales, site, pph: NMRA N 73 39/3:30-35
Chicago, Rock Island & Pacific Station Ice House: 3v, fp, sec, det: NMRA S 72 38/1:41

(Locomotive Fuel Facilities)

Coal Storage Bunker: $2\frac{1}{2}\frac{1}{2}\frac{1}{2}$v, cd, pph, mat: RMC Ja 72 40/8:22-25; const: F 72 40/9:28-32
DT&I Concrete Coal Dock: 2v, cd, pph, const: RMC Ja 71 39/8:21-25
Norwood & St. Lawrence Coaling Dock: 2v, fp, dim, cd, det, pph: NMRA Mr 74 39/8:31-34
100-Ton Steel Coaling Station: 3v, dim, sec, cd: MR D 75 42/12:76-77
Reinforced Concrete Coaling Tower: 3v, sec, cd: NMRA My 72 37/9:26
Simple Scenic Structures: coaling stage: Afx Ja 71 12/5:247
Timber Coal Tower: 2v, dim, sec, cd, int: NMRA O 71 37/2:44
25-Ton Coaling Station: 4v, dim, cd, pat, pph: MR My 75 42/5:64-65
Wood for Your Woodburners: wood rack: MR Je 73 40/6:69
Yosemite Valley RR Oil Tank, Merced: prob conv from water tank: NMRA D 74 40/4:15

(Locomotive Sand Houses)

Illinois Central Wet Sand Bin & Sand Drying House: 2v, fp, dim, struc, cd, pph: NMRA F 75 40/16:16-17
Rock Island Sand Plant: 3v, fp, dim, sec, cd: NMRA Ap 73 38/8:10-13
Ross White Diesel Sanding Station: 3v, dim, cd, pph: NMRA F 74 39/7:51-54

I. Static Scale

(Locomotive Water Tanks)

CP Enclosed Water Tank: 3v, dim, cd: MR S 72 39/9:37
CP Square Water Tank: 2v, dim, cd, pph, const: MR Ja 73 40/1: 73-78
Chesapeake & Ohio Water Column: 2v, dim, cd, pat, col, pph: RMC Je 75 44/1:42-43
Great Northern Railway Standard 50,000 Gallon Water Tank: 2v, cd: NMRA Je 73 38/10:48-49
Poage Water Column Style H Automatic: 2v, pph, site: NMRA D 74 40/4:33-35
Rectangular Water Tank: 2v, dim, cd, struc, pph: MR O 73 40/10:38-39
76,000 Gallon Wooden Water Tank: 2v, dim, cd: NMRA D 73 39/4:51
Simple Scenic Structures: water tower: Afx Ja 71 12/5:247
Simple Water Tower: 2v, det, pph: Afx Je 72 13/10:550-551
16x18 Water Tank, Illinois Central: 2v, dim, cd: NMRA F 75 40/6:21
Track Water Tanks: for loading water on the move: NMRA N 72 38/3:13
Yosemite Valley RR Water Tank, Bagby CA: 2v, cd: NMRA D 74 40/4:12

(Mail Cranes)

Metal Mail Cranes: 3 var: 2v, cd, each: NMRA Ag 71 26/13:6-8
Wooden Mail Cranes: 4 var: 2v, dim, cd, each: NMRA Je 71 26/10:10-12

(Railroad Cattle Equipment)

Cattle Loading Pen: 2v, dim, cd, site: MR Mr 74 41/3:77
Cattle Ramp: 2v, dim, cd, pph: RMC Je 73 42/1:28-29
D&RGW Standard Stockyards: 2v, dim, cd, det: NMRA Ag 75 40/12:31
Wing & Apron Fences: 2v, det; cattle guards: NMRA D 72 38/4:18

(Railroad Communications)

D&RGW Standard Telephone Booth: 3v, sec, struc, cd, int, mat: NMRA Je 75 40/10:61
Line Poles: turn of the century traction & modern concrete power or telegraph poles: NMRA Ap 71 36/8:29
More ACI: automatic car identification scanner: 2v, site: NMRA F 75 40/6:45
Railroad Structures of the Steam Diesel Era: mail pick-up stand: 3v, dim, cd; flag: 1v, dim, cd, pat; telephone box: 1v, dim, cd; message box: sk, dim: NMRA O 73 39/2:56

Trackside Telephone Box: 2v, dim, cd, pph: MR Je 73 40/6:69

(Railroad Signaling Equipment)

Automatic Flashing Crossing Signal: 3v, wd, fiberoptics: NMRA Ap 73 38/8:36-37+
Banjo Signals: 2v, dim, sec, mountings: NMRA Je 72 37/10:32-33
Cantilever Signal Bridge: 3v, dim, cd, pph, mat: NMRA Ap 73 38/8:44-45
D&RGW Tell Tale: 2v, dim, det: NMRA Ag 74 39/13:30
A Few Easy Lights for Your Layout: dwarf signals: NMRA N 71 37/3:35
New Light on an Old Signal: photocell train-actuated signal: NMRA Ag 74 39/15:37
SP Searchlight Signal: 2v, dim, cd, pph: RMC D 75 44/7:73
Semaphore Signals: 3v, dim, det: NMRA D 73 38/4:10-11
Signals by the Peck: target & block types: 2v, dim, det, each: NMRA Ag 72 37/13:58-59
Tell-Tale: 1v, dim: NMRA Je 71 36/10:16
Three Color Signals with One Lamp: 2v, cd, wd: MR D 74 41/12:78
Wig-Wag Signal with a Bell: mechanism: NMRA Jl 72 37/11:12

(Railroad Signs)

Along the Right of Way: D&RGW: tunnel, curve, highway, flange, derail, bridge, tresspass: 2v each; section, mile: 3v each; junction, station, crossing markers, depot, highway, limit, slow, stop, block signals, boundary: 1v each; dim, cd, pat, col, each: NMRA D 73 39/4:56-58
CB&Q Speed Restriction Signs: 2v, dim, cd, pat, tcol, 2 var: RMC Mr 71 38/10:41-44
Highway Crossing Signal: 1v, dim, cd, pat: NMRA Ag 75 40/12:52
Railroad Signs: property, speed, crossing, elevation: 1v, dim, cd, pat, each: NMRA Je 71 36/10:21
Railroad Signs: whistle, ring, stop, dump ashes, section sign, yard limit, mile post: 1v, dim, cd, pat, each: NMRA D 73 39/4:54; Ag 75 40/12:62
Roadway Signs: mile board, section post; Southern Pacific: NMRA Ag 75 40/12:61
Southern Pacific Common Standard Signs: derail, curve warning, city limit, yard limit, one mile board: 1v, dim, cd, pat, each: NMRA N 72 38/3:37
Southern Pacific Common Standard Signs: property, county, bridge & culvert numbers: NMRA Jl 74 39/12:37
Standard Highway Crossing Sign, D&RGW: 2v, dim, cd, pat, col, det: NMRA D 73 39/4:59

I. Static Scale   166

(Railroad Snow Protection)

Portable Snow Fence: 2v, dim: NMRA Ja 71 36/5:39
Snow Shed Details: 2 var: 1v, dim, each: NMRA Jl 72 37/11:55
Snow Sheds: 2v, dim: NMRA O 71 37/2:27
Snow Sheds on the Canadian Pacific Railway: 8 var: 1v, dim, det, each: NMRA N 71 37/3:21-22

(Railroad Steam & Air Lines)

Overhead Steam Lines: NMRA Ag 74 39/13-41
Yark Air Connection: RMC Ag 74 43/2:29

(Railroad Tools)

Simple Coal Loader: stiff-leg derrick: 1v, dim: NMRA Ja 74 39/5:43
Craneway: 2v, dim, cd, pph; light gantry with electric hoist: NMRA My 75 40/9:29
Dead Engine Hauler: 3v, cd: MR F 73 40/2:49
Light Duty Jib Crane: 1v, sec: NMRA My 75 40/9:29
Rip Track Crane: 3v, dim, cd, struc: MR Ag 71 38/8:32-33
Stand: 2v, dim, sk: for supporting cars after removing trucks: NMRA My 75 40/9:29
Steam Servicing Rack: yard tool rack: NMRA O 75 41/2:52
Track Tools: sledge, maul, ballast hammer, grub-hoe, rail tongs, pick, track walker's hammer, wrench, chisel, claw bar, lining bar, tampping bar, pinch bar: NMRA Jl 72 37/11:37

(Turntables)

Bethlehem Twin-Span turntable: 2v, dim, sec, cd, pph: MR F 73 40/2:48-51
Deck Girder Turntable: 2v, det: NMRA Ag 71 36/13:29
IC RR Standard 100' Turntable, 1918: 2v, dim, sec, pph: NMRA Ja 75 40/5:33-34
Manually Operated Turntable Gallows: 3v, cd, det, const: RMC Ja 74 42/8:37-41
90' Turntable: 2v, dim, sec, cd: MR Mr 72 39/3:41-47
Ontario Northland 90' Turntable: 2v, sec, cd: RMC D 71 40/7:30
Standard No. 3 Wooden Turntable: 2v, dim, cd: NMRA D 71 37/4:16-17
Turntable: 3v, dim: MR D 73 40/12:52

Structures

SCRATCH-BUILDING PLANS

Bridges

Bridging the Gap: doorway drop-down girder bridge: 2v, struc, det, wd, mat: RMC D 75 44/7:47+

Buildings

(Railroad Stations)

Branchline Station: RMC Ag 72 41/3:30-34
CMR&P Freight House: RMC D 71 40/7:24-29
Covered Depot for the Carrabasset: RMC F 75 43/9:31-39
Depot for the Town of Spartan: RMC N 73 42/6:60-64
Morgans Bluff Depot: Carol Stream on C&NW: RMC Ag 71 40/3: 17
Narrow Gauge Station: Afx Je 71 12/10:518-519+
Rock Island Passenger Pagoda: booth shelter: NMRA D 72 38/4: 31
Rowley Station: MR Ja 74 41/1:50-56
A Three Towered Station: for rail crossover: MR N 74 41/11: 68-74
Useful Freight Platform: MR F 73 40/2:43-45
Victorian Depot: large: RMC F 73 41/9:42-46; cor O 74 43/5:72-73

(Miscellaneous Railroad Buildings)

Backwoods Engine House: RMC Jl 72 41/2:44-48
Engine Shed for Narrow Gauge: Afx Ap 71 12/8:423+
Engine Depot: Afx Jl 71 12/11:576-577
Illinois Central Scale House: RMC Mr 72 40/10:24-26
Mt. Royal Tower: RMC Jl 73 42/2:45-48
Section Tool House: NMRA O 73 39/2:40
Tool & Section Car House: RMC F 74 42/9:48-50
Yard Office--Supply Shed: RMC S 72 41/4:32-36

(Buildings Other Than Railroad)

Buildings for Wargamers: see immediately below
Bunn's Feed & Seed Plant: MR Ag 73 40/8:34-37
Cal's Lumberyard: MR Ap 73 40/4:62-66
Carolina Foundry: MR Ja 72 39/1:44-47
Crosby's Bandstand: park bandstand: RMC N 72 41/6:32-35
Factory: MR F 74 41/2:60-65
Farmhouse: RMC D 72 41/7:34-39; Ja 73 41/8:42-45
Fish Processing Plant: for narrow triangular site: RMC Ag 74

I. Static Scale   168

    43/2:26-28
Freelanced Material Bins: coal, gravel, ballast, etc: RMC O 73
    42/5:35-37
Gold Mine: MR Ja 75 42/1:46-51; F 75 42/2:72-77
Jones Chemical: MR Mr 74 41/3:42-45
Knocked About a Bit: ruined house: Afx My 71 12/9:482-483
The Light at Thatcher's Inlet: small lighthouse: RMC S 73 42/4:
    36-37
Nichols Milling & Feed Plant: MR Je 72 39/6:38-42
Period Gas Pump: gravity feed: RMC O 73 42/5:38-39
Perkin's Produce Project: store: MR D 74 41/12:54-60
Peters Sausage: MR Ap 74 41/4:60-65
RMC Paper Company: RMC Ap 74 42/11:40-44
Station Drugs: MR My 71 38/5:36-42

                (Buildings for Wargamers) [all Afx]

Wargame Cottage: Jl 73 14/11:602-605
Russian Front Houses: Ag 73 14/12:670-671
French & Belgian Houses: S 73 15/1:27-28+
Russian Church: O 73 15/2:110-112
Peninsular War Buildings: N 73 167-168
American Civil War Buildings: D 73 15/4:215-216

    Railroad Structures Other Than Buildings

                (Signaling Equipment)

Automatic Flashing Crossing Signal: fiberoptics: NMRA Ap 73 38/
    8:36-37+
Banjo Signals: NMRA Je 72 37/10:32-33
Cantilever Signal Bridge: NMRA Ap 73 38/8:44-45
A Few Easy Lights for Your Layout: dwarf signals: NMRA N 71
    37/3:35
LED Searchlight Signal: RMC D 75 44/7:70-73
New Light on an Old Signal: photoelectric detector operated:
    NMRA Ag 74 39/15:37
Semaphore Signals: NMRA D 73 38/4:10-11
Signals by the Peck: target & block types: NMRA Ag 72 37/13:58-
    59
Three Color Signals with One Lamp: MR D 74 41/12:78
Wig-Wag Signal with a Bell: NMRA Jl 72 37/11:12

                (Yard Equipment)

CP Square Water Tank: MR Ja 73 40/1:73-78
Coal Storage Bunker: RMC Ja 72 40/8:22-25; F 72 40/9:28-32
DT&I Concrete Coal Dock: RMC Ja 71 39/8:21-25

From Boiler to Sand Tower: pph; from old steam boiler: RMC Ja 75 43/8:44
Manually-Operated Turntable Gallows: RMC Ja 74 42/8:37-41
Modern Sanding Tower: pph: RMC O 75 44/5:39
100-Ton Steel Coaling Station: MR D 75 42/12:72-77
Scratchbuild a Sandhouse: 3 var: RMC F 71 39/9:42-44

CONVERSIONS

Alfabett Printing Company: from 2 AHM Ramsey Journal Buildings: RMC O 75 44/5:58
Barn, Stables, & Farmhouse: from Airfix Waterloo Farmhouse: Afx N 72 14/3:148-149+
Buildings for Wargamers: see separate listing
Coal Storage Facility: from plastic gondola: RMC S 73 42/4:29
Creamery: from Casket Company, Sandhouse, & scribed stock: RMC Je 74 43/1:28
Diesel Fuel Facility: from single dome tank car: RMC Ap 75 43/11:52-53
Enlarged Freight House: from AHM/Revell Freight House: RMC Ja 73 41/8:23
Expanding the Airfix Sherwood Castle: Afx D 71 13/4:188-189; Ja 72 13/5:252-253; F 72 13/6:312-314; Mr 72 13/7:366-367+
Freight Warehouse: from 3 Bachmann Freight Houses: RMC Je 75 44/1:37-39
Half-a-Box Workshop: from cut-down boxcar; work shelter: RMC Mr 74 42/10:50
Interurban Freight House: from 2 Grusom Casket Factory: NMRA F 73 38/6:23-26
Kitbashing a Skewed Deck Truss Bridge: from Vollmer truss bridge: NMRA Ja 71 36/5:24-25
Little Signal Box: from Airfix Signal Box (signal tower): Afx F 71 12/6:296-297
Medieval Church: from Airfix Roman Fort: Afx S 72 14/1:40-41
Medieval Walled Town: from Airfix Roman Fort: Afx Je 72 13/10:554-55; Jl 72 13/11:594-595; Ag 72 13/12:656+
Modifying Switchstands: from Grandt: RMC Ap 74 42/11:49
Panther Turret Pillbox: from Panther tank: Afx Ja 73 14/5:252-253
Quinnimont--with a Difference: yard office from AHM Ma's Place & Signal Tower: RMC Mr 74 42/10:45-47
Rock Bunker: from hopper car: RMC O 74 43/5:48
Ruins: adapting for use in dioramas: Afx F 72 13/6:316-317
A Simple Guardroom, Stable & Stores: from Britains stable: MM Ja 72 2/1:23+
Tender Water Tank: from Tyco tender, Grandt spout, & scratch bents: RMC Ap 74 42/11:26-27
Utility Building: from boxcar, pph of several types: RMC Mr 75 43/10:56
Wilbur's Waterstop: from AHM water tank, Atlas interlocking

I. Static Scale

tower, etc.: RMC My 73 43/12:26-27
Yard Office-Storehouse: from baggage/mail car & boxcar: RMC
  Ja 74 42/8:53

Buildings for Wargamers [all Afx]

WW-II Barrack Hut, Hay Barn, General Store, Workshop: from Airfix Service Station: Ja 73 14/5:266-267
Ivy House: from Airfix Country Inn: F 73 14/6:308-310
Three Houses: from Airfix Country Inn: Mr 73 14/7:383
Southern Court House, Small Southern Farmhouse European Lodge or Southern Utility House: Ap 73 14/8:449-450
Twentieth Century Factory, Riding School, Town Cross: from Airfix Engine Shed: My 73 14/9:496-497
WW-II Vickarage, 17th Century timbered house: from Airfix detached house: Je 73 14/10:552-553

SUPERDETAILING

Airfix Battle of Waterloo Farm House: Afx O 72 14/2:74-75
Planked Station Platform: paving on ground rather than elevated:
  RMC Ja 73 41/8:60
Signal Base from Ties: RMC My 74 42/12:28

KIT CONSTRUCTION

Modakit Nissen Hut: 1/72: IM F 71 8/2:5-6
St. George Chapel Windsor Castle: Sc S 75 6/72:435
Schreiber Burg Dreienfels: 1/160 cardstock castle: MW My 73
  1/9:460-461
Schreiber Falkenstein Castle: 1/1200 cardstock: Sc F 72 3/2:36

MISCELLANEOUS STATIC SCALE

SCALE DRAWINGS

(Airfield Equipment)

Airfield Equipment, British, WW-II: see separate listing
Fire Fighting Operations in the USA: fire retardant tanks & filling

Miscellaneous

equipment: sk, dim, pat, col: IM Jl 75 11/4:20
Pundit Airfield Beacon: 4v, cd, pat, tcol: IM F 71 8/2:12-13

(Airfield Equipment)

Sc Ap 75 6/67:195-197--
  Accumulator Trolley: 3v, cd
  CO_2 Extinguisher Trolley: 2v, cd, tpat, tcol
  Engine Shelter Tent, Type N: 3v, struc, cd
  Fire Extinguisher: 2-bottle CO_2: 2v, cd, pat, col
  Ground Supply (battery cart): 3v, cd, tpat, tcol
  Hand Fire Extinguisher: 2v, cd, tpat, tcol
  Hydraulic Tripod Jack: 2v, cd, tpat, tcol
  Ladder, 6-step folding: 2v, cd
  Levelling Pole, 12' (for trammelling, photographs, etc.): 2v, cd, tpat, tcol
  Maintenance Platform, 4-Foot: 3v, cd, tpat, tcol
  No Smoking Sign: 2v, cd, tpat, tcol
  Picket Block: 2v, cd, tpat, tcol
  Pneumatic Servicing Trolley: 3v, cd
  Runway Controllers Caravan: 2v, cd, pat, tcol
  Trail Support Trestle: 3v, cd, tpat, tcol
  Typhoon Engine Heater Cover: 2v, cd, pat
  Water (Glycol) Can, $1\frac{1}{2}$ Gallon: 3v, cd, tpat, tcol
  Wheel Chock: 3v, cd, tpat, tcol

(Miscellaneous Equipment)

Baggage Wagons: 4v, dim, cd, pph: RMC O 71 40/5:43
Conversation Piece - Prototypical: paving machine for concrete railroad roadbeds: NMRA O 73 39/2:49-52
Portable Conveyor-Loader: 2v, dim, cd, pph: farm equipment: NMRA Ja 75 40/5:24-25
Power Poles: 1v, dim, each of 5 var: MR Jl 75 42/7:48
Power Transmission Tower: 2v, dim, sec, cd, pph: MR Jl 75 42/7:46
Rocky's Gravel Pit: Power Shovel: 2v, pph; small open-pit type: NMRA O 72 38/2:34-36
A Wagon for the Baggage: 4v, dim, cd, tpat, tcol, const: RMC Ag 73 42/3:24-26
Wind Machine: 1v, dim, cd; to keep frost from citrus groves: NMRA D 74 40/4:51

DIORAMAS

(Before 1790)

The Final Feast: Cavalier inn: MM F 74 4/2:90-91; Mr 74 4/3: 128-130

I. Static Scale

John Paul Jones: Bon Homme Richard quarterdeck: MM My 75 5/3:295-297
Modelling Hadrians Wall: mile castle section from Airfix Roman fort & legionaries: Afx Mr 71 12/7:352-353+
Pressed into Service: press gang in tavern: MM Ag 74 4/8:478-479
Revenge Fights Again: Afx Je 75 16/10:576+
Viking Longship: ocean raider, beached, battle forming: MW Mr 73 1/7:346+

(Napoleonic)

Another Ruddy Hole: bivouac scene from Airfix French Imperial & Coldstream Guardsmen: S&L (O 75) 10:8-10
The Charge of the Greys: cavalry charge: MM N 72 2/11:600-602
Clobbering of the Cobbler: press gang: S&L (O 74) 4:6-8
Death of a Lancer: French Light Horse: MM Je 73 3/6:360-361+
Here We Must Die: last stand of the Old Guard: MM Je 74 4/6:340-341+
The King, Mr. President: incident in 28th (1st Glosters) Rgt history: MM Ap 73 3/4:234-235
Morning at Le Poulet: MM Jl 73 3/7:430-431
Retreat from Moscow: MM Ap 73 3/4:214-215
So I Decided to Convert This Airfix Model...: French Guardsmen off-duty, from Britains farm hands, Airfix French & Coldstream Guards, scratch building: S&L Je 74 1:56
Soirée de l'Empereur: MM Ag 75 5/8:470-471
Teamwork: Gun team: MM Ap 72 2/4:193-195; My 72 2/5:244-245; Je 2/6:304-305
Voltigeur Guard Room: MW F 74 2/6:430-431
Waterloo Colour Party: Coldstream Guard, 1815: MW N 72 1/3:129

(1820-1914)

Apache: MM D 74 4/12:750-751; cor My 75 5/5:299; Je 75 5/6:336
The Birds Have Flown: abandoned outpost in Soudan Wars: Afx Ja 74 15/5:309-310
The Charmer: British India troops & snake charmer: S&L (F 75) 6:8-9
Lonesome Death: Wild West: Fus Sp 75 2/1:36-38
Pelham's Battery: Confederate artillery: MM O 75 5/10:598-599; Ja 76 6/1:17-18; cor F 76 6/2:111; add Mr 76 6/3:156
Saving His Bunkie: Indian Wars Cavalry: MM D 75 5/12:738-739
Tsandhlwana: Zulu War battle: MM Je 75 5/6:354-355+; Jl 75 5/7:418-421
2.5" Screw Gun: boulder emplacement: MW S 72 2/1:40-42

(World War I)

HMS Furious: decorated base for Sopwith Pup carrier var: Sc Je

Miscellaneous

75 6/6:277
The Rittmeister Is Missing: Manfred von Richtofen wreckage: MM Ag 73 3/8:512-513+
Saturday Night at the Beer Hall: German troops: Fus Su 74 1/4: 48-51
To the Victor: German soldier with trophy: Fus Sp 74 1/3:44-45
WVR & Motor Transport Driver: British women: Afx S 73 15/1: 30-31
Western Front, 1914-1915: Royal Fusiliers: MW F 73 1/6:320-322
With Care to Petrograd: 1916 tank loading onto flat car: MW S 72 1/1:34-36

(World War II)

British Officers & Dog: Afx Mr 71 12/7:354-355
Capture of the General: capture of O'Connor & Neame: MW Jl 73 1/11:581+
Cyrenaica, Spring 1941: carrier & light tank: MW Mr 73 1/7:357-359
Felixtowe, 1944: MTB base: MW Mr 73 1/7:374-375
Field Service: German tank repair: MM Ag 73 3/8:532-533+
German Mountain Trooper with Mule: Afx Mr 74 15/7:407-408
Invasion Beachhead: MW N 72 1/3:144+
Japanese Mortar Team: Afx F 71 2/6:308+
Panzerbüschse Rifle Team: MW Je 73 1/10:550-551
Route Napoleon: German units near Moscow: MM N 74 4/11:690-691
Route to Cassino: MW Ag 73 1/12:648-650+
Set a Dingo to Catch a Pig: armored car crew stalking dinner: Afx Je 73 14/10:558-559
Tamiya Jeep: hedgerow action: MM F 73 3/2:102-104
Tram Stop 14, Leningrad: German armor: MW D 73 2/4:186-187+
Withdrawal to Prepared Positions: German: MM Ja 75 5/1:28-30

(Post World War II)

Algeria...1960: street scene in war for independence: MM F 73 3/2:96-98
Harrier Hideaway: camouflaged VTOL jet revetment: MW F 74 2/6:292-293
Six Day War Diorama: MM Je 71 1/6:290-291
Thatcher's Inlet: small port & railroad town: RMC F 72 40/9:36-42; Mr 72 40/10:38-42; Ap 72 40/11:30-34; My 72 40/12:24-28
With the Tanks in Korea, 1952: MW O 73 2/2:98-99+

CONVERSIONS

Do It Wright: Wright J-6 from Williams J-5 engine: RC Ag 75

I. Static Scale 174

12/8:77-79+
Easy-to-Make Conveyor: bulk loading equipment: from AHM Honest
   John rocket launcher: RMC F 73 41/9:37

KIT CONSTRUCTION

Entex Ford Turbine Engine: Sc My 74 5/5:276-277
Williams Wright J5 Whirlwind: 1/6: Sc Ag 72 3/8:428-429

II. OPERATING SCALE

AIRCRAFT

FREE FLIGHT

(Indoor Competition)

Bucker Jungmeister: inline & radial variants: FM F 71 407:22-27
Chance Vought Kingfisher: FM Ap 72 409:23-26
North American BC-1: Canadian var of AT-6: FM Ap 71 409:38-40

(Peanut Scale)

Avia B-534-IV: 1935 biplane fighter: AM My 73 76/5:70
Avro 511 Arrowscout: 1914 scout: FM F 75 78/2:34-37
Avro 534C Racing Baby: Aero My 75 40/472:277-280
B. A. T. Baboon: 1918 trainer: Aero O 75 40/477:915-918
Bristol Scout: all balsa; British WW-I biplane: FM D 71 417:36-39
Buhl Bullpup Peanut: MAN Ap 75 90/4:22-24+
Cessna Airmaster: FM O 73 76/10:26-30
Davis DA-2A: lightplane: MAN D 72 85/6:36-39
Handley Page Type 39: all balsa; 1929 Air Safety Contest finalist: Aero Ap 73 14/8:207-208
Lacy M-10: homebuilt lightplane: AM F 75 75/2:55-57
P'Nut Luton Minor: MAN Ag 74 89/2:17-19+
Peanut Hawker Fury: FM D 74 77/12:28-32
Poullin J. P. 30: all balsa; French single seat lightplane: AM Je 71 72/6:47-48

(Outdoor Rubber)

Airspeed Envoy: sp; twin rubber, light transport: Sc Jl 71 2/7:342
Akromaster: aerobatic monoplane: Aero Ag 72 37/439:450+

II. Operating Scale

American Eagle: 1929 oc biplane: FM Jl 75 78/7:28-32
Avia B-534-IV: sp; 1935 Czech biplane fighter: AM Mr 73 72/3: 70
Avro Arrow Scout: FM F 75 78/2:34-37
Barling NB-3: 1928 lightplane: FM Jl 74 77/36-39
Bücker Jungmeister: inline & radial enging var: FM F 71 407:22-27
Curtiss Robin OX-5: AM Mr 73 76/3:66-68
De Havilland Puss Moth: Aero D 73 38/455:703-704
Puss Moth: FM Je 74 77/6:38-42
Douglas O-38: observation biplane: Aero Ag 71 36/427:445-447
Focke Wulf Fw 47D: 1930s parasol oc observation: MAN Je 72 84/6:11-13+
Focke Wulf Fw 190D: FM My 73 76/5:25-29
Focke Wulf Ta 152: polystyrene foam construction, geared rubber: AM O 73 77/5:65-69+
Fornier RF-5: foam construction, geared rubber: Aero Jl 75 40/474:735-738
Found FBA-2: FM Mr 74 77/5:44-48
Gloster Gladiator: Aero Jl 71 26/426:372-376
Luscombe Phantom I: 1934 lightplane: FM O 75 78/10:19-23
Miles M9 Kestrel: sp, geared rubber, trainer: Sc Jl 71 2/7:343
Monocoupe 90AL: MAN Jl 74 89/1:12-14+
Nord NC 853S: 1947 lightplane: AM My 73 76/5:76-77+
Pilatus Porter: STOL; ROW & ROG var: AM Mr 72 74/3:14-17
Pilatus Turbo-Porter: STOL; ROW & ROG var: AM Mr 72 74/3:14-17
Rearwin M-6000 Speedster: MAN S 72 85/3:18-20+
S-4 Kania 3: Aero Ap 75 40/471:202-205
Sperry Messenger: 1920 army laison: RM My 71 410:44-47
Spinks Akromaster: aerobatic: MAN Je 71 82/6:11-13+
Standard Model J: 1916 trainer: FM O 74 77/10:19-23
Waco S-220: 1969 lightplane: FM N 71 416:34-37
Waco Taperwing: FM My 75 78/5:44-50
Waco 10: FM My 75 78/5:44-50
Westland Lysander: Aero F 73 38/445:93-94

(CO_2)

ABC Robin: 1920s ultra-light: MAN O 74 89/4:11-13+
Osprey 1: ROW; homebuilt flying boat: AM Jl 73 77/1:36-38+
Pilatus Porter: ROW & ROG var: AM Mr 72 74/3:14-17
Pilatus Turbo Porter: ROW & ROG var: AM Mr 72 74/3:14-17
REP Type B: 1910 monoplane, pph: MAN S 73 87/3:17-19+

(Gas)

BE 12b: $\frac{1}{2}$A/A; 1916 scout: Aero Mr 73 38/446:134-136
Barling NB-3: .02; 1928 lightplane: FM Jl 74 77/7:36-39
Bücker Jungmann: $\frac{1}{2}$A; 1934 trainer: FM O 74 77/10:19-23
De Havilland DH9A: $\frac{1}{2}$A; WW-I bomber: Aero Ja 75 38/456:18-21
De Havilland DH 82a Tiger Moth: $\frac{1}{2}$A/A trainer: Aero Mr 72 37/

Aircraft

434:134-136+
Douglas Mailplane: A: AM Ag 71 73/2:14-17+
Etrich Taube: .02; 1913 bird-shape scout: FM N 75 78/11:19-23
L. 9: .02 rigid airship of uncompleted prototype, British: MM D 71 1/12:640-644
Longster: $\frac{1}{2}$A/A; 1933 ultralight: AM N 71 73/5:14-15+
Miles M. 5 Sparrowhawk: $\frac{1}{2}$A; 1935 King's Cup Racer: Aero Ja 71 36/420:16-17
PZL Wilga 35: $\frac{1}{2}$A; Polish glider tug: Aero Ja 73 38/444:16-17
Pietenpol Air Camper: $\frac{1}{2}$A; homebuilt: MAN O 73 87/4:11-13+
Ryan SC: $\frac{1}{2}$A; 1930s low wing monoplane: AM Ag 72 75/2:45-47+
Sopwith Camel: $\frac{1}{2}$A/A; Aero D 71 36/431:688-689
Sopwith Pup: A; WW-I fighter: AM Je 71 72/6:42-44+
Standard Model J: .02; 1916 trainer: FM O 74 77/10:19-23
Thomas-Morse S4C Scout: $\frac{1}{2}$A/A; U.S. WW-I fighter-trainer: Aero My 71 36/424:262-263

CONTROL LINE

Akromaster: B; aerobatic monoplane: MAN Jl 72 85/1:12-14+
Beagle Basset: twin A; British executive: Aero Ja 72 37/432:16-17
Boulton Paul Defiant: C; turret fighter: MAN Ag 73 87/2:17-19+
F4U-4E Corsair: C: FM Jl 71 412:26-29
Fairchild 22 C-7-F: B/C; 1930s parasol oc trainer: MAN O 72 85/4:17-19+
Keith Rider R-5 Jackrabbit: C; 1930s racer: MAN Je 72 84/6:17-19
Kittiwake: B/C; British glider-tug: MAN My 73 86/5:11-13+
Miss Champion: C; Turner Pesco Special: MAN O 73 87/4:17-19+
Nesmith Cougar: C; homebuilt: AM Ap 71 72/4:25-27+
Penguin: C; 1932 non-flying ground trainer: AM Ja 72 74/1:26-29
Ryan STA Super 200 Special: C; aerobatic conversion of trainer: MAN S 71 83/3:26-31+
Spezio Sport Tuholer: C; oc lightplane: AM S 73 77/3:28-31
Spitfire Mk IIA: C, flaps, rLG, int: AM D 72 75/6:22-26+

RADIO CONTROL

(Category I)

Barling NB-3: .02; 1928 lightplane: FM Jl 74 77/7:36-39
De Havilland DH 82A Tiger Moth: $\frac{1}{2}$A: Aero Mr 72 37/434:134-136+
Luton Minor: A/B; ultralight homebuilt: AM Ja 71 72/1:48-49
P Type Zepplin: twin $\frac{1}{2}$A; WW-I airship: MM D 71 1/12:640-644
Sopwith Pup: A; WW-I fighter: AM Je 71 72/6:42-44
Standard Model J: .02; 1916 trainer: FM O 74 77/10:19-23

II. Operating Scale 178

(Category II)

Aeronca C3: B; lightplane: RC Ja 74 11/1:18-25+
De Havilland DH 82A Tiger Moth: ½A/A: Aero Mr 72 37/434:134-136+
Lincoln Sport: .02; 1926 homebuilt: FM Je 75 78/5:45-48
Luton Minor: A/B; ultralight homebuilt: AM Ja 71 72/1:48-49
Sopwith Pup: A; WW-I fighter: AM Je 71 72/6:42-44

(Category III)

(no or single engine, no accessories)
Aeronca LB: C/D: RCS N 75 1/7:38-42+
Ansaldo SVA-5: C; 1917 Italian scout/bomber: RC F 71 8/2:26-29+
BE2e: C; 1915 bomber: RC Ag 71 4/8:24-35+
Baby Ace: C; 1955 Mechanix Illustrated homebuilt: RC D 74 11/12: 23-28+
CSS-11: C; 1948 Polish aerobatic: MAN S 75 91/3:30-33+
Cessna Agwagon: C; crop duster: RC Jl 71 8/7:26-29
Cessna Airmaster C-38: B: RCS O 75 1/6:46-51+
Curtiss Hawk P-6E: C; biplane fighter: MAN Ap 72 84/4:28-31+
Curtiss Robin: C: FM N 74 77/11:34-39
De Havilland DH2: C; WW-I pusher fighter: RC S 74 11/9:24-31
De Havilland DH 82A Tiger Moth: A: Aero Mr 72 37/434:134-136+
Druine Turbulent: C: MAN N 71 83/5:40-42+
Turbulent D-31 Libelle: C: RC Ag 75 12/8:40-47+
EAA Acro-Sport: C; biplane stunt, homebuilt: AM N 74 74/11:20-26
Fairey Junior: C; British oc ultralight: RC Ja 73 10/1:18-22+
Hanriot HD-1: C; Belgian WW-I fighter: RC Je 72 9/6:24-31
der Jäger: C; homebuilt biplane: RC S 72 9/9:18-27+
Lepere LUSAC-11: D; 1918 2-place fighter: AM S 74 78/9:19+
Little Toot: C; aerobatic biplane: MAN Ag 75 91/2:30-33+
Lloyd's Liberty Sport Model A: C; 1966 aerobatic biplane, 2-seat: MAN Ag 71 83/2:26-29+
Lockheed Sirius: C; 1929 2-seat monoplane: AM Ap 73 76/4:21+
Pfalz D. IIIa: C; German WW-I fighter: FM Je 71 411:25-31
Pitts Special: C; aerobatic biplane: RC My 73 10/5:26-32+
Ryan Mailplane M-1: C; MAN O 75 91/4:10-13
Senior Aero Sport: D; aerobatic biplane: AM Mr 75 75/3:18-22+
Sopwith Pup: C: FM D 75 78/12:36-41
Velie Monocoupe: B; 1929 cabin lightplane: RC Ja 73 10/1:26-28+
Volmer VJ 23 Swingwing: g; hang glider: RC O 74 11/10:18-23

(no or single engine, accessories)
Focke Wulf Fw 190D-9: C, rLG; fighter: MAN D 71 83/6:26-29+
Fletcher FU-24: C, flap, brakes, duster dump; Australian crop duster: AM S 71 73/3:20-24+
Heinkel 64C: B, flap; 1931 Europa Rundflug: MAN Ap 75 90/4:30-33+
Ibex: g, flaps: RC S Jl 75 1/3:19-23+
Loughhead S-1: C, folding wings; 1920, first Lockheed: AM O

72 75/4:40-48
Mitchell-Procter Kittiwake: B/C, flap; 1967 British homebuilt: MAN My 73 86/5:11-13+
Mooney Executive: C, rLG, flaps: RCS D 75 1/8:46-51
Pazmany PL-1: C, flap; Taiwan-built trainer version of U.S. homebuilt: AM F 74 78/2:43-45+
Piper Cherokee Arrow 200: C, rLG, flaps; lightplane: RM Ja 74 77/1:21-25
Polikarpov PO-2: C, controls connected to stick & pedals; 1928 Russian utility biplane: RC Je 73 10/6:18-25+
Ryan STA Super 200 Special: C, flap; aerobatic conv of STA trainer: MAN S 71 83/3:26-31+
T-6F: C, flap; armed version of Texan/Harvard trainer: RC N 72 9/11:40-47+
Victa Airtourer 115: C, flap; Australian lightplane: RC D 72 9/12:30-35+
Windecker Eagle: C, flap, rLG: FM F 73 76/2:30-37
Yak-3: C, flap, rLG; 1943 Russian fighter: MAN O 72 85/4:26-29

(multi-engine)
B-17G Flying Fortress: quad B, flap, rLG, bomb bay, bomb drop: FM Ja 73 76/1:30-37
Britten-Norman BN-2A Islander: twin B/C; light airliner: MAN S 73 87/3:27-30+
Cessna 310G: twin C, rLG, executive: MAN Mr 74 88/3:26+
Douglas DC-3: twin C, flaps, rLG; transport/airliner: MAN Je 71 82/6:30-33+
Douglas Dolphin: twin B; amphibian: RC D 71 8/12:16-23
Ju 52: C nose, twin $\frac{1}{2}$A wing, flaps; German tri-motor transport: RC Ja 72 9/1:18-29+

CARRIER EVENT

(Class I)

Douglas Devastator: C; AM Jl 72 75/1:26-28+
North American Bronco: twin B, no hook needed: AM O 72 75/4:27-31+

(Class II)

Blackburn Firebrand: C: Aero My 73 28/448:248-249
FR-1 Fireball: C; prop & jet fighter: MAN S 71 83/3:11-13+
Grumman Guardian: C; MAN Mr 74 88/3:17-19+
Westland Wyvern: C: MAN My 71 82/5:11-13+

II. Operating Scale   180

                    (Trainers & Profile)

Carrier Pigeon: A; profile: MAN Ag 74 89/2:11-13+
Condor: C; profile: MAN D 75 91/6:16-18+
Mo-Bipe: C; profile free lance biplane with variable rudder: AM Ja 73 76/1:42-44+
Mo-Ho: C; profile: MAN F 73 76/2:11-13+
Skyhawk: C; profile delta: AM Ap 73 76/4:28-30+

SEMI-SCALE

    Free Flight

                    (rubber)

Fairey Barracuda: AM D 73 77/6:32-35+

                    (CO_2)

Osprey: flying boat: AM Jl 73 77/1:36-38+

                    (Gas)

Bristol Scout: $\frac{1}{2}$A; British WW-I fighter: Aero D 75 40/479:1039-1040
English Electric Lightning: $\frac{1}{2}$A ducted fan; jet fighter: Aero F 72 37/433:76-79
Fairey Barracuda: $\frac{1}{2}$A; British WW-II torpedo bomber: Aero Mr 71 36/422:126-127
Nieuport 11: .02/.049; French WW-I fighter: Aero D 72 37/443:482-483

    Tether

Fw 190: conv of Guillow rubber free flight to electric: Aero Ap 71 36/423:188

    Control Line

                    (gliders)

Waco CG-15: for towing behind control line C-46: AM My 71 72/5:34-35+

                    ($\frac{1}{2}$A)

Pazmany PL-4: homebuilt: MAN Ag 75 91/2:11-13

Aircraft

Volksplane: homebuilt: MAN Jl 74 89/1:17-19

(A)

Curtiss SB2C-1: sp; dive bomber: AM Jl 71 73/1:26+
Vickers Wellesley: foam wing; 1930s long-range bomber: AM Je 74 78/6:46-48+

(B)

Sopwith Camel: WW-I fighter: MAN N 75 91/5:10-12+

(Twin B)

C-46 Commando: transport, glider tug: AM My 71 72/5:34-35+

(C)

Akromaster: AM N 74 74/11:29-34
Avro Vulcan: MAN Jl 74 89/1:26+
Shoestring: Goodyear racer: FM S 71 414:39-41
Skyraider: carrier bomber: FM Mr 72 420:24-28
Stephens Akro: aerobatic monoplane: AM Mr 75 75/3:42-45+
Yak 9: Russian fighter: MAN Mr 73 86/3:17-19+

(Twin C)

Meteor F. Mk. 8: ducted fan: AM Ja 74 78/1:68-73+

Radio Control

(Category I)

Fairey Barracuda: $\frac{1}{2}$A; British torpedo bomber: Aero Mr 71 36/422:126-127
Fournier RF5D: .02; powered sailplane: RC Ap 72 9/4:44-47+
Gypsy: g; V-tail sailplane: RC O 72 9/10:33-35+
Hamilcar: g; troop glider: MAN S 72 85/3:26-29+
Mitsubishi Zero: A; Japanese fighter: Aero S 73 38/452:482-483
Supermarine Sparrow: .02; 1926 ultralight: RC N 74 11/11:24-27+
Tiger Moth: .02; oc trainer: RC Mr 75 12/3:32-36

(Category II)

Arrowbile: C; roadable flying wing: RC D 71 8/12:24-34
Avro Vulcan: C; delta bomber: MAN Jl 74 89/1:26-30
BD-5: $\frac{1}{2}$A/A, foam wing, homebuilt: MAN S 75 91/3:44-45+
Bowlus-Nelson Bumble Bee: $\frac{1}{2}$A; powered sailplane: RCS D 75 1/8:22-25

II. Operating Scale

Bonzo: ½A, Goodyear racer: RC Ag 71 8/8:16-19+
Cassutt: ½A; Goodyear racer: RC Ag 71 8/8:16-19+
DH-6: A; WW-I bomber: RC S 75 12/9:56-59+
EAA Headwind: A; homebuilt: FM Ap 75 78/4:18-22
Flexi-Flier: g; Rogallo hang glider: AM Ap 74 78/4:21-24+
Fornier RF 4: e/A; powered glider: RC My 74 11/5:40-45
Hamilcar: g; troop glider: MAN S 72 85/3:26-29
Little Lightning: ½A (in nose only): from Guillow P-38 kit: AM Ja 75 75/1:62-64
Mister Funster: B; homebuilt: MAN Jl 74 89/1:47-49
1911 Avro Biplane: B/C: FM Jl 71 412:18-23
Partenavia P-68 Victor: twin e (Astro 05); executive: RC N 75 12/11:24-30+
Pietenpol: B/C; Air Camper homebuilt: RC S 75 12/9:24-37
Puffin: A; Queen Monoplane, 1911 mail plane: RC Ja 75 12/1:31-35+
Slingsby Skylark 4: g; thermal sailplane: RC Mr 73 10/3:19-23+
Sopwith Triplane: A; WW-I fighter: RC Ja 72 9/1:30-33+
Taube: B/C; 1910 German bird-shape: MAN Ja 71 82/1:29-32+

(Category III--Twin e)

Partenavia P-68 Victor: (Astra 05); executive: RC N 75 12/11:24-30+

(½A)

1920 Dayton-Wright Racer: FM Je 74 77/6:28-34

(A)

Cassutt Special: Goodyear racer: RC Je 71 8/6:22-23+
Lake Buccaneer: flying boat, pusher pylon: RM D 71 4/17:19-23
Supermarine S-5: ROW Schneider Cup racer: RC F 74 11/2:36-42+

(Twin A)

Britten Norman Islander: light airliner: RC F 74 11/2:18-22

(B)

Buhl Pup: lightplane: RC Ap 74 11/4:18-21
Culver V: 1946 lightplane: FM Ap 74 77/4:19-22
Piper Vagabond: lightplane: RC Jl 72 9/7:18-23
Schweizer 1-30: lightplane: FM Ag 71 413:33-35
Spectra: flying boat, nacelle on fin: AM Ag 73 77/2:38-39+
Supermarine S-5: ROW; Schneider Cup racer: RC F 74 11/2:36-42+
Tiger Moth: trainer: FM N 71 416:47-49

Aircraft

Wildcat: WW-II fighter: FM S 72 75/9:22-26

(Twin B)

Grumman XF5F-1 Skyrocket: flap, rLG; twin engine carrier fighter: FM O 75 78/10:38-44

(C, no accessories)

AT-6/SNJ: trainer: RC S 71 8/9:22-29
Acro-Star: homebuilt biplane: RC Ap 73 10/4:31-44+
Aeronca LB: lightplane: RCS N 75 1/7:38-42+
Aeronca Model L: lightplane: FM O 74 77/10:36-40
Baby Ace: homebuilt: MAN N 75 91/5:30-33
Berliner-Joyce P-16/PB-1: 2-place biplane fighter-bomber: RC D 74 11/12:43-53+
Bf 109F: fighter: RC Mr 75 12/3:18-25+
Bristol M1B: WW-I monoplane fighter: FM Mr 74 77/3:28-31
Buhl Pup: homebuilt: FM O 73 76/10:21-25
Culver Cadet: lightplane: RC Mr 71 8/3:18-21+
Curtiss Robin: lightplane: FM N 74 77/11:34-39
Douglas A-4D-5 Skyhawk: spinner for radome: FM S 73 76/9:22-25
F6F-3 Hellcat: fighter: FM F 74 77/2:36-40
Focke Wulf Ta 152H: fighter: RC Ap 72 9/4:28-35
Hiperbipe: homebuilt aerobatic biplane: FM N 74 77/11:26-30
Great Lakes Trainer: radial & inline cowls: MAN Ag 74 89/2:26+
Me-109: fighter: RC Ja 73 10/1:30-37+
Mustang: modified P-51 racer: RC Ap 72 9/4:20-27
Nesmith Cougar I: homebuilt: FM F 72 419:33-37
1910 Henri Farman: FM My 74 77/5:34-39
Pazmany PL-1: homebuilt: AM F 74 78/2:43-45+
Pete: Howard racer: MAN Jl 83/1:26-29+
Pitts S-1A: aerobatic biplane: MAN Ap 74 88/4:28-31+
Spectra: flying boat, nacelle on fin: AM Ag 73 77/2:38-39+
Spectra: RC Jl 71 8/7:32-42+
Stearman PT-17; trainer biplane: FM N 73 76/11:21-24
Stephen's Akro: aerobatic monoplane: MAN D 75 91/6:30-33+
Tipsy Nipper Mk 2: lightplane: RC D 73 10/12:30-35+
Tony: fighter: RC Ja 73 10/1:30-37+
Tremendous Taube: WW-I scout: FM Ja 74 77/1:36-40
Waterman Arrowbile: roadable: RC D 71 8/12:24-34
Wildcat: fighter: FM S 72 75/9:22-26
Yak-9: fighter: FM Ag 75 78/8:19-23

(C, with accessories)

Beech Staggerwing: rLG, flaps; cabin biplane: RC D 75 12/12:24-31
Blohm und Voss BV 141B: rLG; asymetrical observation: MAN Je 72 84/6:26-29+

II. Operating Scale   184

Bonanza: flap; V-tail lightplane: AM Jl 71 73/1:20-23
Curtiss SB2C-1 Helldiver: flaps; dive bomber: RC My 75 12/5:
   32-37
Debonair: flap; standard-tail Bonanza: AM Jl 71 73/1:20-23
Falconar Teal: flap, rLG; homebuilt amphibian: FM Mr 73 76/3:
   20-24
Focke Wulf Fw 190D-9: rLG: FM Jl 75 78/7:36-41
Fw 190D-9 or Ta 152C: rLG: RC My 75 12/5:48-54+
Heinkel He 100: rLG, flap; fighter: RC Ag 74 11/8:18-23
Ju 87D-5 Stuka: flap: RC Ap 72 9/4:36-42
Mooney M-18: rLG; lightplane: FM My 74 77/5:25-29
SAAB J-21: rLG; Swedish boom-tail fighter: AM Ag 74 78/8:43-46+
Stuka: flap: FM Ja 75 78/1:36-39
Vultee Vanguard: rLG; 1930s fighter: FM Ag 73 76/8:21-25

(C multi-engine)

Grumman SA-16B Albatross: twin, flap: MAN Ap 73 86/4:27-30+
Henschel Hs 129B: twin; anti-tank: MAN Ap 71 82/4:30-33+
Tin Goose: C, twin $\frac{1}{2}$A; Ford trimotor 5-AT: RC O 74 11/10:24-31+

(D)

Aeronca LB: lightplane: RCS N 75 1/7:38-42+
Citabria Pro: parasol-wing aerobatic: FM D 74 77/12:33-39
Hanriot HD 1: WW-I fighter: FM Ag 74 77/8:24-27
Tremendous Taube: WW-I observation: FM Ja 74 77/1:36-40

BOATS

FREE-RUNNING--Electric

Arthur: Norwegian trawler of WW-II underground: MB Mr 71 21/
   243:102-104+
Sunda: early steam yacht, freelance: MB D 71 21/252:500-503+;
   Ja 72 22/253:32
Turbinia: 1894 first turbine ship: MB Ja 72 22/253:16-17

RADIO CONTROL

(Electric)

Cruiser: 1904 tug: MB O 71 21/250:401-404+

HMS Dreadnought: 1906 battleship: MB Ap 75 25/291:178-179+
Electric powered Pedalo: pedal-powered catamaran with two doll crew: MB Ap 71 21/248:319-321+
Glen-L Sport Fisherman: cabin cruiser: FM Jl 74 77/7:59-62
USS John F. Kennedy: aircraft carrier, working anchor: RCS S 75 1/5:52-54; O 75 1/6:53-56+
MFV Launch-Out: trawler: MB Ap 72 22/256:146-148; My 72 22/257:204-205; Je 72 22/258:253-254; Jl 72 22/259:288-289
Nandhimitra: 1966 Sri Lanka tug: MB Mr 75 25/290:125-127
A Radio Controlled What?: duck decoy: RC My 74 11/5:52-53
Vickers Vedette: MB D 75 25/299:633-635 + insert

(Steam)

Wide-A-Wake: steam launch: MB F 72 22/254:56-59; Mr 72 22/255; Ap 72 22/256:160-161

(Gas)

Century Sea Maid: D; inboard runabout: MAN My 71 82/5:41-43+; cor Jl 71 83/1:58
Claymore: D: inboard, training launch, pph: MB Ap 74 24/279:121-123; My 74 24/280:164-165+
Portia: C; inboard, trawler: MB S 71 21/249:364-365

IMPROVING KITS

Rigging the Cigarette to Win: RC scale to competition hydroplane: FM Ja 75 78/1:59-61
Schuco-Hegi Submarine: strengthening, improving trim & sealing: FM F 75 78/2:63

CONVERTING STATIC SCALE TO OPERATING

Making a Twin Screw Vosper MTB: Airfix 1/72: Afx O 72 14/2:84-85
Motorizing the Iron Duke: Afx Ja 71 12/3:250
Motorizing the Vosper MTB: Airfix 1/72: Afx S 71 14/1:16-18
Simple Plastic Kit Conversions: Mabuchi submerged motor conversions: MB Ja 73 23/265:30
Tamiya Vosper FPB Perkasa: RC: Sc Jl 72 3/7:297-299

CARS

RADIO CONTROL

RC Trailer Truck: GM series 450 tractor & fuel trailer: RCS Je 75 1/2:28-32+

IMPROVING READY-TO-RUN

Cox RC Ski-Do: converting free-running toy to RC: MAN Ja 75 90/1:41-43
Hopping up Heath's Spectre R/C Car: FM Ap 71 409:41
Nostalgia in Yellow: RC for Monogram 1932 Ford Coupe 1/8 scale: RC Je 75 12/6:56-59+

RAILROAD ROLLING STOCK

SCALE DRAWINGS

Complete Trains

Pioneer Zephyr: 2v, fp, dim, cd, pat; all three units: RMC F 71 39/9:27-29; 1v each Twin Cities, Flying Yankee, & Mark Twain locos; 1v, fp, dim, pph; Pioneer Zephyr Car 500 (replaced original B unit): MR 71 38/10:20-25

Cars--Freight

(Boxcars)

Boxcars Aplenty: variations in outside-braced cars: NMRA Mr 74 39/8:42-43
Bulletin Car: free lance private revenue car, printed sides in O, S, HO, N: NMRA D 72 38/4:24-28
CNJ wood-sheathed boxcar: 2v, dim, cd, pat: MR F 72 39/2:62
Canadian National 70-ton boxcar: $2\frac{1}{2}$v, dim, cd, pat, tcol: MR Ap 74 41/4:55
Central of Georgia ventilated boxcar: 2v, dim, cd, pat: MR F 72 39/2:62

Central Pacific Coast box car: s3v, dim, cd, pat; n3: NMRA My 74 39/10:14
Colorado Midland boxcar: 2v, dim, cd, pat: MR Ag 72 39/8:47
Denver & Rio Grande box car: 3v, dim, cd, pat, pph; NSG My 75 1/2:15-16
Denver & Rio Grande four-wheel box car: 2v, cd, pat: NSG My 75 1/2:17
East Broad Top Box Car: s3v, cd, pat; n3: NMRA Ja 73 38/5:28
1890 Brake Rigging: 3v: NMRA Jl 75 40/11:55
First Automobile Box Car: 1v, fp, cd; 1906: NMRA Je 74 38/11:15
Florida East Coast ventilated boxcar: 2v, dim, sec, cd, pat, tcol, pph: MR D 75 42/12:59
NYC&HR box car: printed cardboard sides & ends, O, S, HO, TT, N, Z: NMRA D 74 40:4:32-32b
PRR X23 boxcar: s3v, fp, cd: MR Ap 71 38/4:36; cor Jl 71 38/7:14
Santa Fe wood-side steel-end boxcar: 3v, cd, pat, tcol, const: RMC Je 73 42/1:40-42
Sumpter Valley boxcar: 3v, cd, pat; n3: NMRA Ap 74 39/9:47
Vert-A-Pac: 3v, dim, sec, cd, pat, pph: MR O 71 38/10:51-55

(Cabooses)

B&O I-5b wagon top caboose: 2v, dim, cd, pat, pph: RMC S 74 43/4:56
Boxcar or Caboose: PRR X23 boxcar conv to caboose: 2v, dim, cd, struc, pph: MR Ap 71 38/4:37-41
CNR wood caboose: 3v, fp, dim, sec, cd, pat, pph, cpph, const: RMC F 72 40/9:28-32
CS&CCD caboose: 2v, fp, dim, cd, pat: MR S 72 39/9:36
Canadian Pacific four-wheel wood caboose: 3v, fp, dim, cd, tpat, tcol, pph: MR N 75 42/11:85
Chesapeake & Ohio wood-sheathed caboose: 2v, dim, cd, pat, col, pph: MR D 72 39/12:80-81
Columbus & Greenville caboose: 2v, fp, dim, cd, pat: MR Je 72 39/6:57
D&H caboose: 2v, dim, cd, det, pph: MR My 72 39/5:40-41
D&RGW long caboose: 2v, dim, pph: NSG N 75 1/5:25
DL&W four-wheel caboose: 2v, dim, cd: RMC O 73 42/5:32
DT&I modern caboose: 3v, fp, dim, sec, pat, tcol, pph incl int: MR Je 74 41/6:38-41
EBT steel frame caboose: 2v, fp, dim, cd, pph; n3: RMC My 74 42/12:35
East Broad Top caboose: 3v, dim, cd, pat, int: NMRA Ja 73 38/5:28
Erie bay window caboose: 2v, dim, cd, pph: RMC D 72 41/7:40-41
Illinois Central outside-braced caboose: 2v, fp, sec, cd, pph: MR My 73 40/5:46-47
Illinois Central wood caboose: 2v, fp, dim, cd, pat, pph: MR Jl 71 38/7:60-61

II. Operating Scale 188

L&N class NE caboose: 2v, dim, cd, pat, pph: RMC Ag 75 44/3: 49
NKP 451-500 series bay window caboose: 3v, fp, dim, cd, pph, cpph: RMC S 73 42/4:50-52
New York, Ontario & Western four-wheel caboose: $2\frac{1}{2}$v, dim, cd, pat: MR Ja 74 41/1:69
Newfoundland narrow gauge caboose: 3v, fp, dim, sec, cd, pph; n$3\frac{1}{2}$:RMC Mr 74 42/10:48-49
Ontario Northland caboose: 2v, dim, cd, pat, tcol, pph: RMC My 72 40/12:29
Santa Fe 500 series caboose: 3v, cd, pph: NMRA F 72 37/6:36
Sumpter Valley Railway caboose: 2v, cd: NMRA F 71 36/6:21
Vagao caboose: 2v, fp, dim, sec, cd, pph; nm Brazilian streamline: NMRA Ap 74 39/9:40-41
Union Pacific steel caboose: 2v, fp, dim, sec, cd, pph: RMC Ja 74 42/8:44-45
WP 426-260 series caboose: 2v, dim, cd, tcol, pph: RMC Jl 73 42/2:29
WP wood bay-window caboose: 2v, dim, cd, pph, cpph: RMC D 73 42/7:34

(Flat Cars)

Aroostock Valley flatcar: $2\frac{1}{2}$v, dim, cd, pat, pph: MR My 75 42/5:57
Disconnect logging trucks: 3v, dim, cd, det: MR Je 71 38/6:56-59
1890 Brake Rigging: 3v: NMRA Jl 75 40/11:55
IC flatcar for heavy loads: 3v, dim, sec, cd, pph; 1953: MR Mr 73 40/3:49
Kodak well car: $3\frac{1}{2}$v, dim, cd, pat: MR Ja 72 39/1:65
Oregon Lumber Co. log car: 3v, cd, pat; n3: NMRA F 73 38/6:11
Sandy River flatcar: 3v, cd; n2: RMC Jl 71 40/2:25
Westside Lumber flat: s4v, cd: NMRA S 72 38/1:14

(Gondola)

Bangor & Aroostock Railroad pulpwood car: 2v, dim, cd; side-dumping gondola: NMRA Ag 73 38/12:42-43
CP 105-ton rotary dump gondola: 2v, dim, sec, cd, pph: MR O 71 38/10:40
Coal Car: s3v, dim, cd; 1890 40,000 lb gondola: NMRA Mr 71 36/7:37
Colorado Midland gondola: $2\frac{1}{2}$v, dim, cd, pat: MR Ag 72 39/8:47
Dilapidated dump car: 2v, cd, pph; side-dumping gondola: NMRA N 75 41/3:61-62

Railroad

(Hoppers)

ATSF unit train hopper: $2\frac{1}{2}$v, sec, cd, pat, col, pph, const: RMC Mr 72 40/10:44-47
CN 60-ton iron ore hopper: 4v, dim, cd, pph: RMC D 71 40/7: 50-51
East Broad Top 35-ton triple hopper: 2v, dim, cd, pat, pph: RMC F 74 42/9:55
East Broad Top triple hopper: 2v, dim, cd, pat; n3: NMRA Ja 73 38/5:29
Erie 50-ton covered hopper car: s4v, dim, sec, cd, pat, det, pph: MR Ag 75 42/8:64-65
Erie Lackawanna 50-ton twin hopper ACF 1949: 2v, cd, pat, pph: RMC Je 71 40/1:25
Lehigh Valley "King Coal" hopper car of the 1890s: s4v, dim, cd; RMC Mr 74 42/10:54-55
Pullman-Standard 125-ton covered hopper car: 3v, dim, cd, pph: MR F 74 41/2:59
Q&TL rock car: s3v, dim, sec, cd, tpat, tcol, pph: NSG Mr 75 1/1:9-10
St. Paul Road hopper ore car: s4v, dim, sec, cd, pph: MR Jl 73 40/7:44-45
Santa Fe refrigerated hopper: 2v, dim, cd, pat, det, pph: NMRA N 72 38/3:18-19
Wood frame hopper car: s4v, struc, cd, pat; n3: NMRA Ap 72 37/8:12

(Mine & Ore Cars)

C&NW composite ore car of 1905: s4v, dim, sec, cd, pph: MR Jl 73 40/7:44-45
Colorado Central covered ore car: 2v, cd, pat, pph: NSG Mr 75 1/1:31-32
ON/CN side discharge ore car: 2v, dim, cd, pat, tcol, pph: RMC N 72 41/6:51
Ore car: s4v, dim, cd: NMRA Jl 73 38/11:59
Union Pacific 100-ton ore car: 4v, cd, pat, col, pph: NMRA Je 72 37/10:24-25

(Special Purpose Cars)

Schnabel Car WECX-102: 2v, dim, sec, cd, pph; 44-wheel girder-load generator transport: NMRA Ag 72 37/13:30-33

(Stock Cars)

D&RGW On3 stock cars: 2v, cd: NMRA O 74 40/2:48-50
Narrow Gauge Stock Cars: 3v, dim, struc, cd; n3: NMRA Mr 71 36/7:40
Pennsylvania open-top stock car: 3v, dim, const: RMC My 73 41/12:27

II. Operating Scale 190

RG&W 30' Stockcar: 4v, dim, sec, cd, pat, col; n3: MR N 72 39/11:54-56
Stock Car: s4v, sec, cd; 1890: NMRA S 74 40/1:47
Sumpter Valley Railroad stockcar: s2v, cd: NMRA O 74 40/2:48-50

(Reefers)

Heinz Baked Beans: billboard reefer printed cardboard sides in O, S, HO, TT, Z: NMRA D 73 39/4:30-32b
Illinois Central 38' refrigerator car: 4v, dim, struc, cd: NMRA D 72 38/4:22
Liberty Bond Reefer: printed cardboard sides & ends in O, S, HO, N, Z: NMRA D 75 41/4:32-33
Peerbolte Onion Sets reefer: printed sides in HO: MR Ag 71 38/8:35

Cars--Non-Revenue

American Hoist & Derrick ditchers: $2\frac{1}{2}$v each SN & RGS, 4v chassis, 2v machinery, 4v boom, 4v pile driver; dim, sec, det, pph: NSG Jl 75 1/3:23-29
Baker White Pine Lumber Co. camp car: 2v, dim, sec, struc; 1890: NMRA Ap 75 40/8:32-33
Buffalo, Lockport & Rochester motor flat car: 3v, dim, sec, cd; snow-plow: NMRA F 73 38/6:18
CN commissary car or bunk car: 3v, dim, cd, pph: RMC Ja 73 41/8:33
CNR section car: 3v, dim, cd, tpat, tcol, pph: RMC Ap 72 40/11:43
CP/SP rotary No. 2 snowplow: 3v, dim, sec, cd, pph: RMC F 75 43/9:46-47
Compact Economy Model Flanger: 2v, cd, pat: NMRA N 73 39/3:38-39
DL&W four-wheel caboose oil sprayer: 3v, dim, cd: RMC O 73 42/5:32
Feather River Pine Mills caboose (workshop): 2v, dim, struc, cd, pph: NSG N 75 1/5:19
Goodyear Logging Co. camp car: 4v, dim, cd, pph: NMRA S 75 41/1:8
Missouri Pacific pile driving car: 2v, dim, sec, struc; 1890: NMRA Ap 75 40/8:32-33
N&W inspection car: $2\frac{1}{2}$v, fp, dim, cd, pph: RMC Ag 72 41/3:26-27
NC&SL work car: 3v, dim, struc, cd, pph: NMRA D 73 39/4:33
Ohio Locomotive Crane Co. 8-wheel 20-ton crane: 3v, cd, det: NMRA S 73 39/1:44-45
Pennsylvania Railroad paycar: 4v, fp, dim, cd, pat: MR Mr 74 41/3:46-47

Railroad

Rio Grande pile driver OB: 1v, cd, pat, pph; n3: NMRA My 72 37/9:38
Scale Test Car: 2v, cd, tpat, tcol; RMC Ja 72 40/8:26-27
Steeplecab snowplow: 5v, dim, cd, pat, tcol, pph: MR Ja 74 41/1:43
T&YR derrick trailer: 2v, dim, cd, pph; unpowered wheeled utility derrick for traction yard: RMC Ja 73 41/8:61
Wedge Snowplow from MP: s4v, dim, cd, pat, col, pph: MR D 72 39/12:60

Cars--Non-Scale

Continuous Track Cleaning: NMRA S 72 38/1:21
Do Not Hump: booby-trapped boxcar to test care in yardwork: NMRA Ja 75 40/5:55
Dynamometer Car: NMRA S 71 37/1:7
Four Purpose Flat Car: traction clearance & load tester: NMRA Je 71 36/10:38
Idler Car for Dual Gauge Kadees: for interchanging std & ng rolling stock in dual gauge yards: RMC N 75 44/6:71-72
Not Another Track Cleaner Car: NMRA Ag 75 40/12:30-31
Transit Damage: mercury switch impact recorder: wd, damage pph: NMRA Jl 74 39/12:32-34

Cars--Passenger

[see also NMRA Tech Info, Pass Cars, in Stand's & Tech Info]

(Business & Private Cars)

Algoma Central business car Agawa: 3v, fp, dim, cd, pat, pph, cpph: RMC F 71 39/9:38-40
Great Northern business car A22: 3v, fp, dim, cd, pat, pph: RMC Mr 72 40/10:28-29
Illinois Central private car: 2v, dim, cd, pat: RMC My 71 39/12:34-35
Josephina: 3v, dim, cd, pat, const; director's car: RMC N 74 43/6:46-51
Modern Business Car: CN car 91: 3v, fp, dim, cd, pat, pph: MR Je 73 40/6:48-50
PRR business car Chesapeake: 4v, fp, dim, sec, cd, pat, pph: MR O 71 38/10:56-60

(Chair Cars)

ATSF/Auto Train big dome series 506-513 Budd 1954: $2\frac{1}{2}$v, fp, dim,

II. Operating Scale

cd, pph, cpph: RMC Ap 74 42/11:45-47
Auto Train: 2v, fp, dim, cd, pph, cpph: MR D 74 41/12:46-47
Auto Train car interiors: Dome Coach: fp both levels, 2 var: MR Ja 75 42/11:32-33
Boston & Albany Standard passenger car: 4v, dim, struc, cd; 1892: NMRA Jl 73 38/1:32-33
Colorado Midland chair car: 2v, 3 fp var, dim, sec, cd, pat, tcol: MR N 74 41/11:62-63
Detroit & Mackinac car 100: $3\frac{1}{2}$v, fp, dim, cd, pat, tcol, pph: MR Ja 73 40/1:40-41
East Broad Top coach #6: dim, int, pph; n3: NMRA S 73 39/1:30
Milwaukee 1890 coach: 3v, fp, dim, cd, det, pph: MR F 71 38/2: 60-61
Milwaukee Road "Super Dome" series 50-59 P-S, 1952: 2v, fp, dim, cd, pat, pph: RMC S 71 40/4:38-39
Missouri Pacific Imperial coach-dormitory: 2v, fp, dim: MR Je 75 42/6:49
New York Central & Hudson 54' coach, 1892: 2v, dim, sec, struc, cd, int, det: NMRA N 71 37/3:35
Northern Pacific series 586-587 coach, P-S 1954: $2\frac{1}{2}$v, fp, dim, cd, pat, pph: RMC Ja 72 40/8:44-45
Surry, Sussex & Southampton Ry passenger train coach: 2v, dim, sec, cd, int; n3: NMRA Mr 72 37/7:24-25

(Diners)

California Zephyr 48 seat diner: 2v, fp, dim, cd, pph: RMC N 73 42/6:34-35
Great Northern Imperial diner: 2v, fp, dim: MR Je '75 42/6:49
Milwaukee 1890 dining car: 3v, fp, dim, cd, pat: MR Je 71 38/6: 44
PRR class D78c dining car: $2\frac{1}{2}$v, fp, dim, sec, cd, pat: MR N 74 41/11:64-65
Rio Grande Imperial lunch-counter lounge: 2v, fp, dim: MR Je 75 42/6:49
Union Pacific dome diner: 3v, dim, cd, int: NMRA Mr 71 36/7: 42
Union Pacific dome-diners 8000-8009 ACF 1955: 3v, fp, dim, cd, pat, pph: RMC Ja 71 39/8:26-27
Union Pacific Imperial lunch-counter diner: 2v, fp, dim: MR Je 75 42/6:49

(Front-End Cars)

AT&SF baggage-dormitory transition cars series 3477-3479: $2\frac{1}{2}$v, fp, dim, cd, pat, pph: RMC Jl 73 42/2:34-35
CNW baggage-smoker combine: 3v, fp, dim, sec, cd, pat: MR Ag 71 38/8:48
PRR combine: 3v, fp, dim, sec, cd, pph: MR N 73 40/11:56-58
Rio Grande baggage-dormitory-coach: 2v, fp, dim: MR Je 75 42/6: 49

Southern Pacific mail-baggage series 5005-5010 Budd 1950: 2v, fp, dim, cd, pat: RMC O 71 40/5:38-39

WP/CB&Q/D&RGW baggage car, Budd 1948-1949: 2v, fp, dim, cd, pph: RMC Ja 73 41/8:52-53

White Pass & Yukon baggage & express cars 201-203: 2v, dim, cd, pph: RMC Ap 75 43/11:43

White Pass & Yukon combination smokers 214 & 216: 2v, fp, dim, cd, pph: RMC Ap 75 43/11:42-43

(Lounge & Observation Cars)

CB&Q/D&GRW/WP dome observation, Budd: 3v, fp, dim, cd, pph: RMC D 72 41/7:46-47

CP sight-seeing observation car: 2v, fp, dim, cd, pat, col, pph: MR N 71 38/11:56-57

CRI&P 2 double bedroom, 1 drawing room, buffet, observation lounge, P-S 1947-1948: $3\frac{1}{2}$v, fp, dim, cd, ($\frac{1}{2}$v, fp, dim, cd, var), pph: RMC Ag 74 43/2:34-35

California Zephyr vista dome-dormitory-buffet lounge: 2v, fp, dim, cd, pph: RMC Je 73 42/1:34-35

Milwaukee Road 1890 parlor car: 2v, fp, dim, cd, pat, pph: MR Je 71 38/6:44-45

Milwaukee Road lounge-observation 186-189, 1948: $3\frac{11}{22}$v, fp, dim, cd, pat, pph, cpph: RMC N 71 40/6:40-41

Milwaukee Road tap-lounge car, 1947: 3v, fp, dim, cd, pph: RMC Jl 71 40/2:40-41

Pennsylvania parlor cars series 7130-7145, Budd: $2\frac{1}{2}$v, fp, dim, cd, pat, pph: RMC F 73 41/9:54-55

Reader Railroad parlor lounge car Rambler: 3v, dim, int, pph: NMRA Je 72 37/10:36-37

Sacramento Northern "Moraga": 3v, fp, dim, sec, cd, det, pph; rail motor car converted to observation: NMRA Ja 75 40/5: 18-20

Union Pacific dome-lounge 9000-9014 ACF 1955: 4v, fp, dim, cd, pat, pph: RMC Je 71 40/1:32-33

White Pass & Yukon car 200 "Lake Fraser" observation: 2v, fp, dim, cd: RMC Ap 75 43/11:42

(Sleeping Cars)

CZ 6 double bedroom, 5 compartment Pullman, Budd 1952: 2v, fp, dim, cd, pph: RMC Jl 74 43/2:38-39

CZ 10 roomette, 6 double bedroom sleeper, Budd: 2v, fp, dim, cd, pph: RMC Jl 75 44/2:40-41

CZ 16 section sleeper, Budd: 2v, fp, dim, cd, pph: RMC Jl 75 44/2:40-41

Heavyweight Pullmans, 4158 & 4172, 1948-1950: 3v, fp, dim, cd, pat, pph: RMC Je 72 41/1:38-39

Milwaukee Road/Canadian National sleepers P-S 1948: $2\frac{1}{2}$v, fp, dim, cd, pat, pph: RMC Ap 72 40/11:44-45

II. Operating Scale

Milwaukee Road 1890 Lake Pepin Pullman: 1v, fp, dim, cd, pat: MR F 71 38/2:63
Milwaukee Road 1890 Palace sleeping car: 2v, fp, dim, cd, pat, pph: MR Je 71 38/6:45
Milwaukee Road 1890 Pullman Palace: 2v, fp, dim, sec, cd, pat: MR F 71 38/2:62
Milwaukee Road sleeper: 3v, fp, dim, sec, cd, pat, pph: MR Jl 72 39/7:44-45
Milwaukee Road Skytop sleeper-observation, Creek series, P-S 1948: $3\frac{1}{2}\frac{1}{2}$v, fp, dim, cd, pat, cpph: RMC N 71 40/6:38-39+
Northern Pacific/Southern Pacific sleeper 4140C/D, P-S 1950: $2\frac{1}{2}$v, fp, dim, tpat, tcol, pph: RMC Jl 72 41/2:38-39
Pullman-Standard 14 bedroom: 4v, fp, dim, cd, pat: RMC Ap 71 39/11:40-41
Pullman-Standard 16 section: 4v, fp, dim, cd, pat: RMC Ap 71 39/11:40-41
Pullman-Standard 10 section, 1 drawing room, 2 compartments: 3v, fp, dim, cd, pat: RMC Ap 71 39/11:38-39
Pullman-Standard 10 section, 2 drawing room: 3v, fp, dim, cd, pat: RMC Ap 71 39/11:38-39
Southern Pacific Sunset Limited sleeper 9000-9029: 4v, fp, dim, pat, pph: RMC N 72 41/6:52-53
UP Sleeper "Twin Peaks": 2v, fp, dim, sec, cd, pat, pph: MR Je 75 42/6:50-51

Cars--Special

Combo Car: 2v, dim, cd, pat: NMRA S 73 39/1:7
Elephant Car: 2v, cd, pat: NMRA S 73 39/1:7
Machinegun Car: 3v, dim; WW-I: NMRA Mr 71 37/7:19
Panzer Draisine: 3v, cd; O & HO 1941 German railway "tank": AFV N 73 4/8:18-19
Warren Flat No. 55: sec, det, pph; circus flatcar: NMRA S 73 39/1:8

Locomotives--Diesel

Alco 1500 hp "Black Maria" A&B units, 1945: 3v (A), 2v (B), dim, cd, pph: RMC Je 75 44/1:32
Alco 2000 hp DL 103b, 1939: 4v, dim, cd, pph: RMC Ag 75 44/3:41
Alco GE DL 109: 3v, dim, cd, pph: MR Ap 71 38/4:51-55
Baldwin Road Switcher AS 616: 2v, dim, cd: MR Jl 75 42/7:40-41
Baldwin Sharknose RF16: 2v, dim, cd, each of A & B: RMC My 72 40/12:43
CN Oil Electric Locomotive: 5v, fp, dim, sec, cd, pat, pph: MR Ag 74 41/8:44+

EMD E6: $2\frac{1}{2}$v, dim, cd, each A & B: RMC Ja 75 43/8:43
EMD 1750/1800 hp FL9, 1946-1950: 3v, dim, cd, pph: RMC O 72 41/4:29
EMD 2000 hp E7 A unit, 1945: 4v ($\frac{1}{2}$v var), dim, cd, pph, cpph: RMC Ja 72 40/8:36-39; B unit, 1945-1959: 3v, dim, cd, pph: Mr 72 40/10:43
EMD 2300 hp SD 39, 1968-1970: 4v, dim, cd, pph: RMC N 72 41/6:37
EMD 2300 hp SDL39, 1969: 4v, dim, cd, pph: RMC Jl 72 41/2:29-31
EMD 3000 hp GO40P 1968: 4v, dim, cd, pph: RMC Ag 72 41/4:29
EMD 3000 hp SD40T-2, 1974: 4v, dim, cd, pph, cpph: RMC My 75 43/12:33
EMD 3000 hp SDP40F, 1973, Amtrak 5000-539: $4\frac{1}{2}$v, dim, cd, pph, cpph: RMC O 73 42/5:48-50
EMD 3600 hp F45: 4v, dim, cd, pph: RMC S 73 42/4:30
EMD 3600 hp SD45-2, 1972: 4v, dim, cd, pph: RMC My 73 41/12:45
EMD 3600 hp SD45T-2, 1972: 4v, dim, cd, pph: RMC My 73 41/12:42-43
EMD 4200 hp SD45X, 1970: 4v, dim, cd, pph: RMC My 73 41/12:41
EMD FP45: 4v, dim, cd, pph: MR F 72 39/2:47-50
EMD SD 30: 4v, dim, cd, gap in SD series, never built: RMC S 72 41/4:29
Electro-Motive E2 Passenger Locomotive: 3v, dim, cd, pat, pph: MR S 73 40/9:43-47
Electro-Motive F 45: 4v, dim, cd, pph, cpph: MR D 75 42/12:70-71
Electro-Motive FT: 4v, dim, cd, pat, col, pph: MR Ap 75 42/4:48-51
Erie Lackawanna SD45-2: 1v, cd, pph: RMC My 73 41/12:44
FM Erie-Builts: 3v, dim, cd, pph, cpph, 5var 1v each: RMC O 75 44/5:60-64+
GE 44-ton switcher: 3v, dim, cd, pph: MR Ap 73 40/4:50-51
GE 45-ton 3000 HP switcher: 3v, dim, cd, pph: NMRA Ap 74 39/3:22-23
GE 5000 hp U50C, 1969: 4v, dim, cd, pph: RMC Jl 75 44/2:38
GE's New Floating Bolster Truck FB-2: s2v, dim, cd, pph; U-boat truck: RMC Ap 74 42/11:37
GE's 23-ton Two-Footers: 3v, dim, cd, pph; n2: RMC N 74 43/6:44-45
GM 1000 hp switching locomotive SW 1001: 5v, dim, sec, cd, int: NMRA O 72 38/2:23-25
GM 1500 hp switching locomotive SW 1500: 5v, dim, sec, cd, int, pph: NMRA N 72 38/3:23-25
General Electric 2250 hp U23B, 1968: 5v, dim, cd, pph: RMC Ap 74 42/11:34-36
General Electric 80-ton diesel: 2v, dim, sec, cd, switcher: NMRA Ja 72 37/5:43
General Electric 1200/1800/2000 hp ABBA Test Set 1954: 2v, dim, cd, pph, cpph, each: RMC F 75 43/9:40-41
General Electric 2250 hp U23B, 1968: 5v, dim, cd, pph: RMC N

II. Operating Scale

73 42/6:51-53
General Electric U25B: 3v, dim, sec, cd, pph: MR S 71 38/9:44-47
High Lead Yarder: 2v, cd, pph: NMRA Mr 73 38/7:26-31
Inside Story on CB/Q 9900: 2v, dim, cd, pat: prototype Burlington Zephyr: RMC Jl 71 40/2:42-43
Montreal Locomotive Works 2000 hp M420: 4v, dim, cd, pph, cpph: RMC D 74 43/7:58
Norfolk & Western SD 45: 3v, dim, cd, pph: MR O 75 42/10:73
1000 hp switching locomotive: 5v, int, dim, cd, pph: NMRA Ja 71 36/5:24-25
Paducah 1850 hp GP 10 8113 1969 rebuild: 4v, dim, cd, pph, cpph: RMC D 74 43/7:58
SP EMD SD45T-2: 4v (truck 2v), dim, cd, pph: MR Jl 72 39/7:60-62
Santa Fe 1500 hp CF7, Cleburne Shops, 1970: 4v, dim, cd, pat, pph: RMC Mr 71 38/10:36-39
South Shore Line Steeplecab Locomotive: 2v, dim, sec, cd, pat, pph: MR Ap 74 41/4:48+
South Shore R2: $2\frac{1}{2}$v, dim, cd, pat, pph: MR Ag 71 38/8:44-47
Sumpter Valley Railway Narrow Gauge Diesel: 2v, cd, pat, 1937: NMRA Mr 72 37/7:13
Zeitler Gas-Hydraulic Loco: 2v, fp, dim, cd, pat: NMRA N 75 41/3:66

Locomotives--Electric

DD1: s4v, fp, sec, cd, pat, pph; 1909 third-rail: MR Mr 71 38/3:48-50
GG1: 5v, dim, sec, cd, pat, det, pph, cpph: RMC D 75 44/7:55-61
General Electric 6000 hp E60c, 1972: 3v, dim, cd, pph: RMC Ap 73 41/11:28-29
Milwaukee's Boxcab Electrics: EF & EP series: 4v, dim, cd, pph: RMC Ja 71 39/8:28-32
NYC class T3a Electric Locomotive: 2v, dim, cd, pat, pph: MR O 72 39/10:47-50
New Haven Electric Locomotive: 2v, dim, cd, pph: NMRA Mr 71 36/7:12-13

Locomotives--Steam

(Geared)

Baker White Pine Lumber Climax: 2v, cd, pat: NMRA O 75 41/2:48
Oregon Lumber Shay No. 102: 3v, cd; n3: NMRA Jl 74 38/12:35
Shay class 150-3: 4v, dim, sec, cd, pat, pph; largest Shay built:

MR My 71 38/5:43-46
Silver City, Pinos Altos & Mogollon RR Shay: 6v, dim, sec, int, pph; n2: MR My 71 38/5:56-59
13-ton 2-cylinder Shay: 3v, cd; n3: NMRA F 71 36/6:7

(Rod)

(0-4-0)
B&O dockside switcher: s3½v, dim, cd, pat, pph; 1926 var of 1912: NMRA O 75 41/2:56
B&O saddle tank loco: 3v, dim, cd, pat, pph; 1912 switcher: NMRA O 75 41/2:54
B&O "York" 1831: 2v, dim, cd, pph: RMC S 71 40/4:37
Brooks Locomotive Works class 8 ET: 3v, cd, pph, spec; n2½: NSG Mr 75 1/1:24
Diamond Rock saddle tank: 4v, dim, sec, cd, pat: MR O 71 38/10:42
Klondike Mines No. 4: 3v, cd, pph: NSG S 75 1/4:26-27
PRR A5: 4v, dim, sec, cd, pat, pph: MR O 73 40/10:46-49
PRR A5s: 4v, dim, sec, cd: MR Ja 74 41/1:75
Reading: 4v, dim, sec, cd, pat, pph, each of 2 var: MR Jl 74 41/7:56-59

(0-4-2)
Forney: s3v, sec, cd; n2: NMRA Mr 72 37/7:32-33

(0-4-4T)
Mason Double Truck: s4½v, sec, cd, det; 1883: NMRA Ja 72 37/5:7-10

(4-4-0)
Canadian National eight wheel: 2v, dim, cd; 1888: NMRA Ag 72 37/13:57

(2-6-2)
Pacific Great Eastern Prairie: 2v, dim, cd, pat; 1908: NMRA F 74 39/7:40
Six-Coupled Double-End Switcher: 3½v, dim, sec, cd, pat, pph: MR S 72 39/9:34-35

(2-6-6T)
Mason Bogie: 3v, cd; 1880: NMRA Ja 72 37/5:6; s5v, dim, cd, pph: Ja 72 37/5:12

(4-6-0)
Grand Trunk Pacific: 2v, dim, cd: NMRA F 75 40/6:61
Southern Railway's class F-1: 4v, dim, cd, pat, tcol, pph: MR N 75 42/11:64-67

(4-6-2)
DSH popet-valve Pacific: 3v, dim, sec, cd, pat, tcol, pph: MR F 75 42/2:52-55

II. Operating Scale   198

(4-6-4)
Toronto, Hamilton & Buffalo Hudson: $1\frac{1}{2}$v, dim, cd: NMRA Ag 71 36/13:38-39

(4-6-4T)
Grand Trunk/Canadian National Suburban type: s4v, dim, cd; 1914: NMRA Ja 71 36/5:23

(0-8-0)
Canadian Pacific switcher: s2v, dim, cd, pat, col; 1930: NMRA N 71 37/3:44

(2-8-0)
Baldwin 1879: s2v, dim; New Zealand: NSG S 75 1/4:24
Baldwin 1885-6: s2v, dim; New Zealand: NSG S 75 1/4:24
DSP&P Consolidation: 2v, dim, cd, pat, pph: NSG My 75 1/2:24-25
Intercolonial Railway (CN) Consolidation: 2v, dim, cd: NMRA O 71 37/2:35
M&PA: 3v, dim, sec, cd, pph: MR My 72 39/5:56-57
Missouri Pacific: 4v, dim, sec, cd, pph: MR O 74 41/10:48-53
PRR H6sb Consolidation: 4v, dim, sec, cd, pph: MR Ja 74 41/1: 76-77
Reading Camelback: 3v, dim, sec, cd, pat: MR Je 72 39/6:56
WM: 4v, dim, sec, cd, pph: MR N 72 39/11:49-53

(2-8-2)
D&RG K-27: 4v, dim, sec, cd, pat, pph; n3: MR Mr 73 40/3:58-60
D&RG/RGS K-27: 5v, dim, sec, cd, pat, pph; n3: MR Je 73 40/6:38-47
East Broad Top Mikados 14 & 15: 2v (tender 4v), dim, cd, pat, pph, cpph: RMC N 75 44/6:54-5
Liberation Mikado: 2v, dim, sec, cd, pph: MR Jl 73 40/7:56-61
White Pass & Yukon Mikado: 2v, dim, sec, cd, pat, col; n3: NMRA Ap 72 37/8:36
White Pass & Yukon: 4v, dim, sec, pat, pph; n3: MR Je 74 41/6:50-53

(4-8-2)
NYO&W Y-class Alco 1922-1923: 3v, dim, sec, cd, pat, pph: RMC Ap 72 40/11:41
Norfolk & Western: 4v, dim, sec, cd, pph: MR N 74 41/11:59-61
Wabash: 4v, dim, sec, cd, pph: MR Jl 71 38/7:47-51

(4-8-4)
Canadian National/Grand Trunk Western northern: 2v, dim, cd, pat, col: NMRA My 71 36/9:43
DL&W Q-1: s3v, dim, sec, pph: RMC F 74 42/9:42-43
E1: 1v, dim, cd: MR My 74 41/5:54
GS Classes & Daylights: 3v, dim, sec, cd, pat, col, pph; streamliner: MR Ap 72 39/4:42-51

Railroad

SP No. 4449 class GS: 2v, dim, cd, pph; tender 3v, dim, cd, pph: NMRA Jl 75 40/11:32-33

(0-10-0)
St. Clair Tunnel: 3v, dim, sec, cd, pat, pph: MR Ag 73 40/8: 46-47

(2-10-2)
Canadian National Santa Fe Type: s2v, cd, pat: NMRA Je 73 38/10:46

(4-6-6-4)
Northern Pacific Z-8: 2v, dim, sec, cd, pph: MR My 74 41/5:55

(2-8-8-0)
B&O EL-3a: 3v, sec, pat, col; RMC Ag 74 43/3:38-39
EL-3a: 3v, dim, sec, cd, pat, pph: RMC S 74 43/4:42-43

(2-8-8-2)
Duluth, Missabe & Iron Range: 3v, dim, sec, cd, pph: MR Jl 75 42/7:54-57

(2-8-8-4)
B&O E1: 3v, sec, cd; tender 4v, cd: NMRA S 73 39/1:22

(Locomotive Stack Detail)
Union Pacific, 1867-1892: NMRA Je 73 38/10:50-51

(turbine)

C&O Steam Turbine Locomotives: 2v, dim, cd, pat, pph: MR F 71 38/2:48-50

Locomotives--Miscellaneous Power Forms

Diablo Incline: platform: 2v, dim, struc; car: 2v; counterbalance car: 1v: NMRA Mr 73 38/7:13-14
Mount Lowe Incline: 3v, dim, cd, pph; NMRA Ap 71 36:8:6-8
Yosemite Sugar Pine Lumber Co. Incline Railway: 1v, site, block car: NMRA O 71 37/2:37

Rail Motor Cars

Bowen Motors Railway Corp: 2v, fp, dim, cd; motor car & trailer: NMRA Je 75 40/12:43
California Western's Skunk M-300: 3v, dim, cd, pat, col, pph:

II. Operating Scale

RMC Ag 71 40/3

Illinois Central Electric Highliner: 3v, cd, pat, col, int: NMRA Ja 72 37/5:24-25

McKeen Wasn't the Only One: GE Gas-Electric: 2v, fp, dim, cd: NMRA Ap 74 39/9:51

Missouri Pacific RR A-65 motor car: 4v, dim, cd; O gandy-dancer chariot: NMRA Ag 75 40/12:43

Sandy River & Rangely Lakes #4: 3v, dim, On2 railbus: NMRA Mr 74 39/8:20

Southern Pacific Combination Baggage-Passenger motor cars: $4\frac{1}{2}$v, dim, sec, cd: NMRA Mr 73 38/7:32-33

WI&M "The Potlacher": 5v, fp, dim, cd, pat, pph: MR S 75 42/9:47

Traction

Brill E-1; E-1$\frac{1}{2}$; E-2; E-3 traction trucks: 3v, dim, cd, each: MR N 71 38/11:77

Brill No. 27G Truck: 3v, dim, sec, cd: MR Jl 71 38/7:37

Cincinnati Car Co. single end: 3v, dim, sec, struc, framing: NMRA Ag 74 39/13:7-11

Denver & Interurban M-151-156: 1v, fp, dim, cd, pph: NMRA D 75 41/4:11

Denver & Interurban M-157-158: 1v, fp, dim, cd, pph: NMRA D 75 41/4:11

GN 99300: 3v, cd, pph; 1938 interurban work car: NMRA Ja 71 36/5:38-39

IC Bilevel MU Cars: $3\frac{11}{22}$v, fp, dim, cd, pat, pph: MR Mr 72 39/3:48-49

Indianapolis 100 series streetcars: 3v, fp, dim, cd, pat, tcol, pph: MR F 71 38/2:44-45

Lackawanna & Wyoming Valley's 401-403: 2v, dim, cd, pph: RMC S 72 41/4:44-45

MCB Traction Trucks: 3v, dim, cd, pph: MR My 71 38/5:61-63

Napa Valley Route: 3v, cd, int, pantograph interurban: NMRA Je 72 37/10:42

New York City Transit Snow Plow: 3v, cd: NMRA N 71 37/3:48

North Shore Electroliners: 2v, fp, dim, sec, pph; 4-unit interurban: MR My 74 41/5:43-49

North Shore Line dining car: 4v, fp, dim, sec, det, cd, pat, tcol: MR Mr 75 42/3:53-56

Oshawa Railway: 3v, dim, cd, pat; traction work unit: NMRA Mr 75 40/7:18

Pacific Electric Blimp Combos: $5\frac{1}{2}$v, dim, cd, pph; interurban combo: NMRA My 71 36/9:23-25

Pacific Electric 1000 class car: $4\frac{1}{2}$v, fp, dim, cd, pat, col, det, pph, var: MR Ap 71 38/4:56-68

Toronto class F four-wheel streetcar: 2v, fp, dim, cd, pat, tcol, pph: MR Je 72 38/6:48-49

Toronto's PCCs: 3v, fp, dim, cd, each of two int var; pph, cpph: RMC My 72 40/12:46-47

Utility Cars of Philadelphia: 4v, dim, cd, pat, pph: NMRA F 73 38/6:16-17
United Railways of Oregon interurban No. 7: 3v, fp, dim, cd, pat: RMC O 72 41/5:35

Rolling Stock Accessories

Loco Cranes: 1v, cd, pph: for 0-4-0 industrial switchers: RMC Mr 71 38/10:26-27

SCRATCH-BUILDING PLANS

Building a Locomotive from Wood & Card: M&PA 2-8-0: MR My 72 39/5:48-55
CP Sight Seeing Observation Car: MR N 71 38/11:56-61
D&RGW Ditchers OW & OX: NSG Jl 75 1/3:32-34 (scale drawings 23-29)
Dilapidated Dump Car: NMRA N 75 41/3:61-62
Disconnect Logging Trucks: MR Je 71 38/6:56-59; cor Ag 71 38/8:9-10+
Dome Car: MR O 72 39/10:58-62
Feather River Pine Mills caboose: mat; workshop: NSG N 75 1/5: 16-19
Flanger Car: MR O 74 30/10:65-70
Freelanced Narrow Gauge Flatcar: HOn3: RMC Je 72 41/1:34-35
Freelanced Three Footers: 3v, cd, pat, mat; HOn3 four-wheel boxcars: RMC N 72 41/6:28-29
Josephina: director's car: RMC N 74 43/6:46-51; D 74 43/7:50-53
Multi-Purpose MoW Car: RMC Ja 73 41/8:30-34
Pennsylvania Open-Top Stock Car: RMC My 73 41/12:24-28
Q&TL Rock Car: mat; working dump: NSG Mr 75 1/1:5-10
Riveted Steel Covered Hopper: mat: MR Ag 75 42/8:58-63
SR&RL No. 10: freelanced reconstruction of ng private car: NSG My 75 1/2:20-23
Sandy River 2' Gauge Flatcar: mat: RMC Jl 71 40/2:25
Ventilated Boxcar: MR F 72 39/2:62-64

CONVERSIONS

General

Converting Kadee N Scale Couplers for HOn3: NMRA Ag 72 37/13: 38-39+
Toy Trains to Hi-Rail: converting tinplate: NMRA Ja 75 40/5:10-15

II. Operating Scale

Cars--Freight

Bad Order Piggy Back: train wreck cars transported to repairs: RMC Ja 74 42/8:46

Baggage Cars into Logging Cars: from Athearn 72' baggage car, Weyerhaeuser ex Northern Pacific: MR D 72 39/12:72-73

Beer Can Tank Car: from Athearn 62' chemical tank car: RMC D 71 40/7:39-41

Boxcar or Caboose: caboose from PRR X23 boxcar: MR Ap 71 38/4:37-41

Caboose from a Picture: transfer caboose from two Athearn work cabooses: MR F 75 42/2:56-58

De-Peaking Offset-Side Hopper Ends: modifying to standard end: RMC Ag 75 44/3:38-39

Dome Observation Car: from AHM observation car & Vista-dome coach: MR Jl 73 40/7:62-65

Double Plug-Door Boxcar External-Braced Grain Carrier: from PRR 50' box car: NMRA S 71 37/1:15

Heavy-Duty Depressed-Center Flatcar: from 2 Athearn heavy-duty flatcars: MR Ap 75 42/4:38-39

High Iron: Santa Fe 500 series Caboose: from Athearn cabooses & box car: NMRA F 72 37/6:37-38

High Side Pulpwood: from 2 40' gondolas; pph: MR My 73 40/5:58-59

Incline Tank Car: from Model Die Casting 24' old time tank car: MR O 75 42/10:64-65

Modern Steel Stockcar: from plastic boxcar: MR F 73 40/2:46-47

Modernize the Freight Cars: MR D 71 38/12:91-93

105-ton Goldola: from 2 Athearn quad hoppers: MR O 74 41/10:70-72

PC N9E Transfer Caboose: from Athearn box car: RMC Je 74 43/1:43-46

Panelled-Side Hopper Car: from Athearn ribbed-side hopper: MR D 74 41/12:76-77

Pellet Extensions for Ore Cars: RMC Jl 75 44/2:30-31

Twin Dome Tank Car: from Athearn three-dome tank car: NMRA O 71 37/2:18

Veneer Car Conversion: from 40' or 50' steel boxcar: MR S 73 40/9:52-53

Cars--Non-Revenue

Big Hook: from Athearn HO crane: MR D 75 42/12:60-61

Boom Tender Car: pph, sk: RMC S 74 43/4:33

Boreas Zephyr: from Jordan Model T; inspection car: NSG My 75 1/2:36-38

Crane on a Flat Car: Atlas O flat car & Corgi boom crane with clam bucket, pph; NYC: RMC S 74 43/4:32

Ice Breaker Car: open hopper modified to clear tunnel icicles:

Railroad

RMC D 73 42/7:56-57
Office on a Flatcar: from 50' flat car & container; pph, CN: RMC S 74 43/4:30
Railroad Maintenance Trucks: from Mini-Lindy cement mixer; HO: RMC N 75 44-6:44
Snowplow: from Athearn work caboose frame; pph: RMC S 74 43/4:32
Stretching Athearn's Work Caboose: MR Jl 72 39/7:42-43
Utility Work Car: from Ultrich truss-rod flat car & Athearn work caboose; pph: RMC S 74 43/4:30
Weed-Spraying Unit: 00, European couplers; from flatcar & Airfix Landrover: Afx N 71 13/3:131+
Wheel & Hoist Car: from LaBelle outside-braced boxcar: RMC S 73 42/4:38-39

Cars--Passenger

Great Domes: Great Northern full-length dome cars from Bachmann Auto-Train cars: MR S 75 42/9:48-51
Imperial 4-4-2: 4 double bedroom, 4 compartment, 2 drawing room: from AHM streamline coach: MR Je 75 42/6:47-49
LaBelle Coach to Combine: RMC Jl 72 41/2:36-37
Modernized Passenger Cars: from Athearn coach: MR F 74 41/2:40-43
More Model Cars of the Nineties: coach, Pullman (2 var; from LaBelle HO-4 vestibule day coach or O-57 coach): MR F 71 38/2:64-66; dining car, parlor car, sleeping car; from same: Je 71 38/6:48-49
Office Car: from AHM 10 roomette/6 double bedroom sleeper: MR Je 73 40/6:51-55
Office Car: from 2 AHM duplex room sleepers: MR Je 73 40/6:51-55
Office Car: from Con-Cor streamline diner: MR Je 73 40/6:51-55

Locomotives--Diesel

Baldwin AS 616: from 2 Athearn S12s: MR Jl 75 42/7:40-42
Chop-Nose BN Geep in N Scale: from Rapido GP7: RMC Ap 71 39/11:26-27
EMD FT: one A unit & one B unit from 3 AHM A units: MR Ap 75 42/4:44-47
EMD-izing a Katy FA1: from Alco FA: RMC N 73 42/6:36-37
EMD SD 39 Conversion: from Alco EMD SD 40: RMC Jl 73 42/2:38-40
EMD 3600 hp F45: from AHM FP 45: RMC S 73 42/4:30-31
E6: from Atlas N Scale EMD E8: RMC Ja 75 43/8:42-43

II. Operating Scale

FP7: from Athearn & Hobbytown F7: MR Ap 72 39/4:40+
GM&O FA: from Train-Miniature FA1: RMC Ag 73 42/3:46-49
GP 30: from GP 35: MR Ja 75 42/1:66-67
Heavy Power for the Carrabasset: $HOn2\frac{1}{2}$ from Minitrix N Fairbanks-Morse H12-44; mat: RMC N 74 43/6:39-43
High Hood for SD/GPs: from Athearn SD45, GP35 shell: RMC F 71 39/9:45
Paducah's Geeps: GP 8 & GP 10: from Athearn GP 7s, Hustler, GP 35 & details: RMC Mr 75 43/10:46-50
SD 40 or GP 40: from Athearn GO35 & SDP40: RMC Ja 71 39/8:28-32
Slug Unit: from 2 Athearn GP35s: MR Ag 75 42/8:66-67

Locomotives--Electric

Box-Cab electric: from Diesel: NMRA O 71 37/2:28-29

Locomotives--Steam

ATSF 2-10-4: from Pacific Fast Mail 2-10-2: RMC F 73 41/9:47-49
Branchline Loco: from Tyco 4-6-0: RMC Je 71 40/1:26-29
Casey Jones 4-4-0: from 4-6-0 Ten Wheeler: MR My 75 42/5:44-48
Converting to a Wootten Firebox: Atlas B&O N 0-4-0 to Reading var: MR Jl 74 41/7:60-61
H6sb: from Red Ball B6sb 2-8-0: MR Ja 74 41/1:72-77
Narrow Gauge Lokie: from Minitrain Baldwin: Afx My 71 12/9:462-463
PRR A5s 0-4-0 switcher: from Altoona Works Photoengravings & parts from H6sb: MR Ja 74 41/1:74-75
PRR H10 Consolidation: from Atlas IHB 0-8-0 & many other parts: MR D 75 42/12:50-53
PRR Mikado in N Scale: from Atlas chassis & Minitrix PRR K-4s Boiler: RMC Mr 74 42/10:30-32
Pennsy E3sd 4-4-2: from Bowser or Gem E6: MR Ag 74 41/8:43
Q1 4-6-4-4: from Westiside Q2 4-4-6-4: MR Mr 73 40/3:34-35
Rotary Snowplow: from Nickel Plate Leslie: MR Ja 73 40/1:68-69
Santa Fe 3450 class Hudson: from ATSF Berkshire boiler & Hudson or Pacific frame: RMC Jl 72 41/2:41
Simple Narrow Gauge Locomotive; 0-6-0 00n3: from Triang TT Jitney: Afx D 71 13/4:214-215
2-8-0: from Atlas 0-8-0: MR Ap 72 39/4:41

Traction

Denver & Interurban M-159: from Model Die Casting Pullman
    Palace sleeper: NMRA D 75 41/4:13-15
Yakima Trolley: from Tyco trolley: NMRA Mr 75 40/7:15

SUPERDETAILING

Another Type of Caboose Marker: emblems for crews to find their
    caboose in a yard; pph: RMC D 74 43/7:62-63
Back Shopping a Southern Pacific Atlantic: NMRA Jl 71 36/11:20
Catching Mail on the Fly: hook unit for car, mail crane: NMRA
    Jl 75 40/11:38-39
Detailing a Four Wheel Bobber: mat: RMC My 75 43/12:47-51;
    Je 75 44/1:44-46; Jl 75 44/2:53-55
Diesels Needn't Be Dull: working fans & scale engine detailing:
    MR N 75 42/11:83-84
An Easy Way to fine-Flange Wheels: flexible bolster for better
    tracking: MR Ag 75 42/8:68-69
Equalizers for Steam Locomotives: MR S 72 39/9:62-67
Illuminate Those Marker Lights from the Side: NMRA D 74 40/4:
    49
Install Working Headlights: for locomotives: MR Jl 73 40/7:66
The Last Straw: soda straws for pipe loads: NMRA Jl 75 40/11:
    28-29
Marker Lights for Those Tail-End Cars: wd: NMRA Ja 74 39/5:16
Modeling an Early Trailing Truck: New Haven I-2 Pacific from
    later period loco: MR N 73 40/11:80-85
Modeling Norfolk & Western's SD 45s: mat, U.S. Hobbies O gauge:
    MR O 75 52/10:70-72
Modifying the IHB 0-8-0 Rivarossi O gauge: MR S 71 38/9:35-41
N&W Bell Bracket for high hood diesels: RMC D 71 40/7:54-55
Operating Valve Gear for the 0-6-0 Roundhouse Switcher: NMRA
    F 75 40/11:38-39
Pneumatic Pole Bases: NMRA Ja 71 36/5:35
The Rebirth of 2174: mat, 2-8-8-2: RMC Jl 72 41/2:42-43
Self-Acting Trolley Retriever: working: NMRA S 72 38/1:34-35
Simple Locomotive Detailing: basic superdetailing: NMRA Je 74
    39/11:43-44
Southern Pacific's SD-45s: What're Those Lights & Symbols?:
    NMRA Jl 72 37/11:20
A Spruced-Up Heisler: Westside On3; superdetailing & sound: MR
    F 73 40/2:66-73
Steam Engine Brake Rigging: MR Ag 71 38/8:61-65
Tenders First: MR S 73 40/9:48-51
Top Performance & Sound from a Shay: MR N 73 40/11:46-49
Transporting Wheel Sets: car loads: NMRA Jl 71 36/11:21
Try Updating Freight Cars: cushion underframes: MR N 73 40/11:
    78-79

II. Operating Scale   206

Updating the Atlas Plug-Door Boxcar: MR Mr 73 40/3:52
Wheel Car: 1v, pph; car loads: RMC S 74 43/4:31
Wood Pilots: NMRA My 72 37/9:33
Working Stephenson Valve Gear: MR Ja 75 42/1:68-69

KIT CONSTRUCTION

Building a Durango Press Westside Snowplow: NSG Jl 75 1/3:8-9
Construction Notes on the Kemtron Shay: NSG 1/5:40-43

KIT CORRECTIONS

Chopping a Growler Down to Size: AHM GE Switcher: NMRA N 72 38/3:30

TRACK--SCALE DRAWING

switch stands

Anatomy of a Stub Switch: full detail sk, 2v, dim on tieplates & spikes: NMRA S 75 41/1:35-40
C&NW Ry Rigid Switch Stand: 4v, dim, cd: NMRA F 71 36/6
D&RGW Ground Throw Switch Stand: 1 or 2v, dim, for each part: NMRA O 75 41/2:60
D&RGW Standard Switch Stand #4 Low Star: 2v, dim, det: NMRA Jl 74 39/12:40
D&RGW Standard Switch Stand #6 High Star: 2v, dim, det: NMRA Je 74 39/11:44
D&RGW Switch Stand: 3v, dim, cd, det, mat: NMRA N 75 41/3:29
D&RGW Switch Stand; Parallel Ground Throw: 1 or 2v & dim for each part: NMRA S 75 41/1:47
Switch Stand, Extra High: 3v, cd: NMRA My 72 37/9:43
Switch Stand; low & high: 2v, dim, each: NMRA My 74 39/10:43

others

Brant Two-Foot Gauge Switch: 1v, pph: RMC S 71 40/4:29
Ferry Apron: 2v, dim, det, mat: rail ferry dock: MR Ag 72 39/8:32-36

ROCKETS

NAR SCALE

Natter: rocket interceptor, wings fall off on launch: AM Ja 71 72/ 1:50+

III. COLOR PATTERNS

AIRCRAFT

GENERAL

Colors

Aircraft Camouflage & Markings of the Netherlands East Indies: Q Su 75 10/4:166-169
Aircraft of the Fleet Air Arm: present official color schemes: Sc S 73 4/9:608-611
Army Aviation Colours: British AOP, helicopters, & funnies: Sc D 72 3/12:660-665
Basic Colours: RNAS, RFC, RAF; WW-I: IM N 71 8/11:3
Bombing Colours: see separate listing
A Brief Description of Markings & Camouflage Schemes--Battle of Britain Period: RAF & Luftwaffe: PAM Jl 75 10:166
Colors: Fed. 595 numbers for USAAF, USN, RAF, RN, Luftwaffe colors: RC Ja 73 10/1:6+
Colour Schemes for the Invader: Afx Mr 72 13/7:376-379+
Combat Colours: present RAF color schemes: Sc Jl 73 4/7:473-474
Fighting Colours 1914-1937: see separate listing
French Air Force, 1938-40: Q W 75 11/2:59-68
German Lozenge Camouflage: "Knowlton" pattern: Q Ja 71 6/1:28
Irish Air Corps: general colors for all aircraft, 1922 to present: Q Jl 73 8/3:141-143
Luftwaffe Standards in Camouflage & Markings, 1939-1945: Sc F 72 3/2:74-80; Mr 72 3/3:155-157; Ag 72 3/8:436-441
The New Luftwaffe's Markings, 1954-75: Q W 75 11/2:87-90
Night Fighter Finishes: RAF WW-II: IM F 71 8/2:14-15
Non-Standard Luftwaffe Schemes: Sc Mr 72 3/3:155-157
Russian Aircraft Colours, WW-II: IM Ag 72 9/8:11-12
USN camouflage & national insignia, 1940-1944 patterns: Q Su 75 10/4:151

Markings

A-4 Squadron Allocations 1959-1974: tall codes, bases, variants:

Aircraft

RiS Mr 75 3/1:9
Beginner's Guide to NATO Aircraft Stencils: Afx Jl 72 13/11:660
British Military Aircraft Serial Numbers, 1912: MW S 73 2/1:18-19
British Transport Aircraft Code Markings: 1945-46; Berlin Air Lift; 1947-57: AN 14 N 75 4/12:4-6
CF-100 Squadron Markings 1954-56: Canadian: RT Ap 75 8/4:41
Current USAF Tail Codes: AN 16 F 73 1/20:6-7
Fleet Air Arm Codes in WW-II: AN 1 F 74 2/18:4-6
Fleet Air Arm Codes, 1945-55: AN 27 D 74 3/15:4-6+
French Escadrille Markings, 1914-1918: Sc O 72 3/10:541-546
German Aircraft Insignia: RC My 71 8/5:83-85
German Aircraft Markings 1919-1939: civil registration & national insignia: Sc F 71 2/2:79-83
German National Markings, 1914-1918: see separate listing
Hawker Hurricane Mk 1: sten: AN 7 Jl 72 1/4:9
International Service Markings: national insignia: AE F 74 6/2:86-87; Mr 74 6/3:144; My 74 6/5:255; Je 74 6/6:303; cor Je 74 6/6:313
Japanese Bomb Markings: IM Jl 74 10/(17):10
Lancaster Formation Markings: RAF, WW-II: AN 16 F 73 1/20:11
Luftwaffe Marking & Code Systems: WW-II ID codes: IM Mr 72 9/3:6-7
Luftwaffe Serial System: post WW-II: AN 10 Ja 75 3/16:10
National Markings of the German Army Air Service & Naval Air Service, 1914-1918: IM N 72 9/11:12-16
RAF Roundels: WW-I & WW-II: RC S 71 8/9:6+
RFC/RAF Squadron Markings: see separate listing
Rhodesian Insignia & Flashes: 1945-54; 1954-64; 1964-: RT Je 75 8/6:69
Royal Hungarian Air Force National Markings: 1938-May 1945, incl stab: RT S 74 7/9:99-100
Russian National Insignia: RT D 74 7/12:134
Stork Escadrille Emblem: Sc O 72 3/10:546; cor N 72 3/11:604
Soviet National Markings: Sc Ja 71 2/1:41
Squadron Codes, RAF 1939-1956: see separate listing
Swedish Markings: proportions for national insignia: RT Jl 72 5/7:77
T-37: sten: Q Ja 74 7/1:16-18
They Went to War on a Name: USAAF 8th AF nose art: AN 24 Ja 75 3/17:6-7
UK Civil Propeller & Tail Rotor Patterns: for ground safety: AN 18 Ja 74 2/17:3
US Coast Guard Marking & Serial Numbers: AN 1 N 74 3/11:11-12
US Navy & Marine Corps Aircraft Nose Numbers: RiS Au 73 2/1:4-14
U.S. Red Stripe Insignia: AM Je 71 72/6:39
Victory Markings of the Luftwaffe Fighter Aces: var: WW2J S 75 2/5-6:16-19
What Are All Those Funny Letters & Numbers?: USN codes: AN 15 Mr 74 2/21:4-5
WW-I German Cross Changes: effect of overpainting: Sc Ap 73

III. Color Patterns

4/4:264

Separate Listings

Army Colors 1914-1937 [all Afx]

Prime Role of the Air Arm: D 74 16/4:223-224
First Artillery Observation Aircraft: Ja 75 16/5:304-307
Little Ack & Big Ack: FK 3 & FK 8:   F 75 16/5:304-307
Close Support: Mr 75 16/7:422-423
Adapting the Bristol Fighter: Ap 75 16/8:461-462+
Armstrong Whitworth Atlas: My 75 16/9:541-543
Wapiti: Maid of All Work: Je 75 16/10:594-596
Audax--the Hart with a Hook: Jl 75 16/11:652-654
Adapting for Army Co-op: Ag 75 16/12:712+
Hawker Hector: Last of the Biplanes: S 75 17/1:22+
Introducing the Lysander: O 75 17/2:104-109
No. 22 Group Goes to War: Lysanders: N 75 17/3:146+
Lysander in Action: D 75 17/4:211-212+
[series continues]

Bombing Colors [all Afx]

started Mr 69
Phoney War: Ja 71 12/5:254-256
The Fight in Earnest: F 71 12/6:314-316
Battle of France: Mr 71 12/7:362-365
Short Stirling: Ap 71 12/8:424-427
Avro Manchester: My 71 12/9:476-481
The Early Halifax: Je 71 12/10:536-540
On the Offensive: Jl 71 12/11:594-597+
The 1942 Scene: Ag 71 12/12:650-653+
Prelude to the Great Offensive: S 71 13/1:34-39
The Middle East: O 71 13/2:87-91
Japan Enters the War: D 71 13/4:200-202+
The Bomber Offensive: Ja 72 13/5:259-263+
Prelude to Overlord: F 72 13/6:392-395+
Finale in the Middle East: Mr 72 13/7:392-395+
Victory in the East: Ap 72 13/8:448-451

Fighting Colors 1914-1937 [all Afx]

Scouts of the Royal Flying Corps: Jl 72 13/11:606-609
Scouts of the Royal Naval Air Service: Ag 72 13/12:679-681
Early Pusher Fighters: Vickers Gunbus & DH2:   S 72 14/1:35-37+
Camouflage Introduced: O 72 14/2:94-96
The Factory Fees (FE series):   N 72 14/3:152-155
French Fighters in British Service: D 72 14/4:213-216
Mid-War Sopwiths: $1\frac{1}{2}$ Strutter, Pup, & Triplane: Ja 73 14/5:269+

Aircraft

Fighters with Reservations: DH-5 & Bristol Monoplane: F 73 14/6:322-323
Sopwith's Classic & Supreme--Camel & Snipe: Mr 73 14/7:374-377
SEs by the Squadron: Ap 73 14/8:440-442
the Bristol Fighter: My 73 14/9:502+
End of War Fighters: Je 73 14/10:554-555
The Colourful Twenties: Jl 73 14/11:606-607
Greve & Gamecock: Ag 73 14/12:672+
Colour Controversy & the Woodcock: S 73 15/1:32-34
Siskin: O 73 15/2:82+
Bristol Bulldog: N 73 15/3:160+
Putting on the Gauntlet: D 73 15/4:235-237
Guide to the Gladiator: Ja 74 15/5:305-306+
World's Most Beautiful Biplane - Hawker Fury: F 74 15/6:346-348
Two Seat Fighter Revival - Hawker Demon: Mr 74 15/7:393-394+
End of an Era--and its effect: Ap 74 15/8:462-463

German National Markings 1914-1918 [all Afx]

Army Aircraft, 1914--mid 1916: My 74 15/9:502-504
Army Aircraft, July 1916--March 1918: Je 74 15/10:569-570
Army Aircraft, March 1918--November 1918: Jl 74 15/11:649-650+
Naval Aircraft, August 1914--November 1918: Ag 74 15/12:692+
German Army Serial Numbers: S 74 16/1:22+
Naval Serial Numbers: O 74 16/2:108-112

RFC/RAF Squadron Markings [all MM]

3: Camels: Ja 71 1/1:22
65: Camels: Ja 71 1/1:23
73: Camels: Ja 71 1/1:22
148 Aero (American Sqn attached to RAF): Camels: F 71 1/2:80
28: Camels: F 71 1/2:81
80: Camels: F 71 1/2:81
18: DH 4: Mr 71 1/3:135
50: BE2c, SE5a, Camels: Mr 71 1/3:135
62: Bristol Fighters: Ap 71 1/4:190
84: SE5a: Ap 71 1/4:191
19: BE 12, SPAD 7, SPAD 13, Sopwith Dolphin: Je 71 1/6:302-303; Ag 71 1/8:415
112: Sopwith Pup, Camel: Je 71 1/6:303
87: Dolphin: O 71 1/10:508-509
94: SE5a: D 71 1/12:660+
100: FE 2B, HP 0/400: Mr 72 2/3:135
139: Bristol Fighters: Jl 72 2/7:343

Squadron Codes, RAF, 1939-1956 [all Afx]

Introduction: Mr 73 14/7:364-366
A-AH: Ap 73 14/8:150-151

III. Color Patterns 212

AI-9A: My 73 14/9:498+
B-BQ: Je 73 14/10:544-546
BQ-9B: Jl 73 14/11:600-602
C-CZ: Ag 73 14/12:656
C2-DS: S 73 15/1:41-42+
DT-DX: O 73 15/2:78
DX-9D: N 73 15/3:173-174
Code changes during war: AA-DR: D 73 15/4:242-243; add Ja 74 15/5:318
EA-EL: Ja 74 15/5:286+
EM-EQ: F 74 15/6:344
EX-FO: Mr 74 15/7:412-413
FO-F4: My 74 15/9:528+
F5-GP: Je 74 15/10:590-592
CQ-G4: Jl 74 15/11:628+
G5-9G: Ag 74 15/12:709
HA-HR: S 74 16/1:41-42+ ; cor O 75 17/2:124
HR-H3: O 74 16/2:95
H4-9H: N 74 16/3:184
IA-IO: D 74 16/4:251
IO-I3: Ja 75 16/5:317
I4-7I: F 75 16/6:376
8I-JE: Mr 75 16/7:429
JE-JT: Ap 75 16/8:492-493
JU-OJ: My 75 16/9:522+
KA-KK: Je 75 16/10:601
KK-KQ: Jl 75 16/11:646
KR-KZ: Ag 75 16/12:723
K2-LE: S 75 17/1:21
LF-LJ: O 75 17/2:117
LJ-LU: N 75 17/3:172
LV-9L: D 75 17/4:237
[series continues]

World War I

(Australian)

Bristol Fighter: 1 Sqn, Middle East: Afx My 73 14/9:504
RE 8: 96 (Asl) Sqn, RFC/3 Sqn AFC, Sept 1917: Afx Ja 75 16/5: 305

(Austro-Hungary)

Albatros D. III: Flik 41J, Prosecco, Dec 1917, Brumowski: Q Au 75 11/1:38
Albatros D. III: Flik 41J, Prosecco, Dec 1917, Linke-Crawford: Q Au 75 11/1:38
Albatros D. III: Flik 42J, Motta di Livensa, late 1917, Gräser:

Q Au 75 11/1:38
Albatros D. III: OU Fliegertruppe, Istrian Sesana, March 1918, Brumowski: IM Jl 71 8/7:2-4
Hansa-Brandenburg D. 1:   Flik 41, 1917, Bromowski: Sc Ag 74 5/59:419

(Belgium)

Bleriot Monoplane: c.1915: Q Ap 73 8/2:76
Bristol F. 2B: Q Ap 73 8/2:77
Fokker D. VII: 9 (Thistle) Esc, late in war: Q Ap 73 8/2:77
Nieuport 17: 1 Esc Comette: AN 6 73 2/4:9
Nieuport 17C: 1 Esc Comete, Thieffry: Q Ap 73 8/2:77
RE 8: 6 Esc, July 1917-May 1918: Q Ap 73 8/2:76
RE 8: 180hp re-engine, late 1917, Simonet: Q Ap 73 8/2:76
SPAD VII: 5 Esc Comete, Ciseler: Q Ap 73 8/2:77

(Canada)

Canadian Aeroplanes 504K: unit unstated, 1918: AN 27 D 74 3/15:8
Curtiss Canuck: Aerial Fighting Sqn 1, RFC Beamsville, Ont: RT Mr 71 43/30
Canuck: 81 Training Sqn, Deseronto, Ont, 1917: RT S 71 4/9:104
Canuck: 84 Training Sqn: RT S 71 4/9:104
Canuck: 85 Sqn, Camp Borden, 1918: RT Mr 71 4/3:30
Canuck: 88 Training Sqn, Camp Taleafarro, TX, winter 1917: RT S 71 4/9:104
Canuck: "Lundys Lane" presentation, July 1918: RT Mr 71 4/3:29
Canuck: "Montreal" presentation: RT Mr 71 4/3:30
Canuck: "Winnipeg" presentation, 1st official airmail, Toronto-Ottawa, 1918; RT Mr 71 4/3:29

(France)

Albatros D. II: captured: Q O 72 7/4:152
Albatros D. III: captured April 1917: Q O 72 7/4:152
Albatros D. V: Q O 72 7/4:155
Nieuport 11: Esc Americaine, McConnell: IM Mr 73 10/3:9
Nieuport 11: Esc N. 3, Guynemer: IM S 72 9/9:12; cor O 72 9/10:1
Nieuport 17: American Aviation School, Isseudon: AN 6 Jl 73 2/4:9
Nieuport 17: N. 3, Guynemer: AN 6 Jl 73 2/4:9
Nieuport 17: Esc N. 3, Guynemer: IM Mr 73 10/3:9
Nieuport 17: Nungesser: AN 6 Jl 73 2/4:9
Nieuport 17: 1916, Santa Maria: IM Ag 72 9/8:6
Nieuport 17: unit unknown: IM Ag 72 9/8:6
Nieuport 17c: SPA 3, 1916, Brocard: Sc O 72 3/10:543
SPAD VII: SPA 3, 1917, Guynemer: Sc O 72 3/10:542
SPAD VII: SPA 3, 1917, Heurtaux: Sc O 72 3/10:543
SPAD XIII: standard five-color camouflage: Sc O 72 3/10:545

III. Color Patterns 214

SPAD XIII: SPA 73, 1918, Duellin: Sc O 72 3/10:543
SPAD XIII: SPA 77, GC 16, summer 1918, Boyau: Sc N 74 5/62: 603
SPAD XIII: SPA 112, GC 16, Dec 1917: Sc N 74 5/52:603
SPAD XIII: SPA 150, GC 16, Dec 1917: Sc N 74 5/62:603
SPAD XIII: SPA 158, GC 16, May 1918: Sc N 74 5/62:603
SPAD XIII: Esc SPA 159: IM Mr 73 10/3:9

(Germany)

Albatros C. III: IM Jl 72 9/7:14
Albatros: Jasta 5, 14 var: Sc N 71 2/11:586-591
Albatros D. III: Goering: IM O 71 8/10:4
Albatros D. III: Jasta II, Schäefer: IM My 72 9/5:16
Albatros D. III: Jasta 11, Allmenroder: IM D 71 8/12:3
Albatros D. V with D. III rudder: prob prototype: IM Je 72 9/6:8
Albatros D. V: factory finish: IM Je 72 9/6:9
Albatros D. V: Mueller: IM Je 72 9/6:9
Albatros D. V: L. von Richthofen: IM O 71 8/10:5
Albatros D. V: Jasta 4, 1917, Clausnitzer: AI O 75 9/4:199
Albatros D. V: Jasta 5: 2 var: AI O 75 9/4:199
Albatros D. V: Jasta 5, Rumey: AI O 75 9/4:199
Albatros D. V: Jastaführer, Jasta 5, Bäumer & Lehmann: AI O 75 9/4:199
Albatros D. V: Jastaführer, Jasta 5, Flasher: AI O 75 9/4:198
Albatros D. V: Jasta 15, Dingel: AI O 75 9/4:198
Albatros D. V: Jasta 26, Loerzer: IM Mr 73 10/3:7
Albatros D. Va: Jasta 4, Wusthoff: Q O 71 6/4:15
Albatros D. Va: Jasta 5, 1917-18, von Hipple: Q O 71 6/4:14; cor Ja 72 7/1:3
Albatros D. Va: Jasta 5, spring 1918, von Hipple: AI O 75 9/4: 199
Brandenburg C.1 series 26: 1st version prototype: AN 20 S 74 3/8:8
Brandenburg C.1 series 29: AN 20 S 74 3/8:8
Brandenburg C.1 series 369: AN 20 S 74 3/8:8
Brandenburg C.1 series 369; late version: AN 20 S 74 3/8:8
Brandenburg C.1 series 429: AN 20 S 74 3/8:8
DFW C. V (Aviatik-built): Ft. Abt. 187, late 1917: Sc Mr 71 2/3: 146
Fokker D. VII: RCS S 75 1/5:(40-41)
Fokker D. VII: JG 1, Goering: IM O 71 8/10:4
Fokker D. VII: Jasta 7, 1918, Degelow: Sc My 74 5/56:250
Fokker D. VII: Jasta 10, May 1918, Friederich: RT Ap 75 8/4:45
Fokker D. VII: Jasta 11, L. von Richtofen: IM Mr 73 10/3:7
Fokker D. VII: Jasta 18, Hazebrouck, June 1918, Schultz: IM Ja 73 10/1:13
Fokker D. VIII: factory finish: MAN Ja 74 88/1:54
Fokker D. VIII: Jasta 6: AM Ag 74 78/8:34-35
Fokker D. VIIIg: Goebel Goe engine: AN 13 O 72 1/11:9
Fokker Dr.1: M. von Richthofen: IM Mr 73 10/3:7
Fokker Dr.1: Stapenhorst: IM O 71 8/10:5

Aircraft

Fokker Dr.1:   Jasta 6, Kirschstein: IM Mr 75 11/2:20
Fokker Dr.1:   Jasta 7, Jacobs: Q Ap 71 6/2:5
Fokker E.V: AN 13 O 72 1/11:9
Fokker E.V: factory finish: AN 13 O 72 1/11:9
Fokker E.V: Jasta 1, 1918, Liebig: AN 13 O 72 1/11:9
Fokker E.V: Jasta 6, Benes: AN 13 O 72 1/11:9
Fokker V26:   1st prototype of D.VIII, 1918: MAN Ja 74 88/1:54
Hansa-Brandenburg W-29 (HM1): MAN Jl 72 88/1:47
Nieuport 17:   1916, ex Santa Maria in capture markings: IM Ag 72 9/8:6
Pfalz D.III: Bonneuil, Feb 1918, Hageler: IM My 72 9/5:14
Pfalz D.III: Jasta 7, 1918, Degelow: Sc My 74 5/56:250
Pfalz D.III: Jasta 10, 1917, Voss: IM S 72 9/9:13
Pfalz D.III: Marine feld Jasta 2, Undiener: IM Ja 72 9/1:15-17

(Italy)

Macchi-Nieuport: unit unstated: AN 6 Jl 73 2/4:9

(Netherlands)

Avro 504A: 1915: Q O 73 8/4:236
Bristol F2B: Q O 73 8/4:237
Halberstadt Cl.II: prob 1917: Q O 73 8/4:237
Hannover Cl.IIIA: Axel, April 1918: Q O 73 8/4:237
Pfalz D.III: 1918: Q O 73 8/4:236
SE5a: Brielle, Jan 1918: Q O 73 8/4:237
Sopwith Pup: 1917: Q O 73 8/4:236

(Rumania)

Nieuport 11:   3FS, Cioara, attached to 1 Rumanian Army, Sept 1917: AE Je 71 1/1:28

(Russia)

Nieuport 10C1: RT Jl 71 4/7:79
Nieuport 17:   RT Jl 71 4/7:79
SPAD A.2:   1915; RT F 74 7/2:22

(Turkey)

Halberstadt D.V: 1918: AE Jl 71 4/7:84
Nieuport 17:   Ottoman Fleigerabteilung 6: RT Jl 71 4/7:79

III. Color Patterns 216

(U. K. captured aircraft)

Albatros D. I: School of Aerial Fighting, Ayr, Scotland, April 1918, ex-Jasta Boelke, Buttner: Q O 72 7/4:151
Albatros D. II: Abbeville, May 1917, ex-Lemke: Q O 72 7/4:151
Albatros D. III: Q O 72 7/4:152
Albatros D. III: ex-Jasta 11, downed by Simon, May 1917: Q O 72 7/4:154
Albatros D. III: Palestine, 1918: Q O 72 7/4:155
Albatros D. V: ex-Jasta 4, Clausnitzer, 2 var: Q O 72 7/4:153
Albatros D. V: ex-Jasta 24, Wackwitz, downed by Bentune, Dec 1917: Q O 72 7/4:154
Pfalz D. III: ex-Hegeler, in capture markings: IM My 72 9/4:14

(U. K. bombers)

De Havilland DH 10 Mk III: std: AN 14 Je 74 3/1:8-9

(U. K. observation)

FK 8: 2 Sqn, Aug 1917: Afx F 75 16/6:371
FK 8: 8 Sqn, Aug-Sept 1917: Afx F 75 16/6:371
FK 8: 10 Sqn, July 1917: Afx F 75 16/6:371
FK 8: 35 Sqn, France, Aug 1917: Afx F 75 16/6:371
FK 8: 82 Sqn, France, Nov 1917: Afx F 75 16/6:371
RE 8: 4 Sqn, Jan 1918: Afx Ja 75 16/5:306
RE 8: 4 Sqn, co-op with Port Army, Jan-March 1918: Afx Ja 75 16/5:306
RE 8: 5 Sqn, aut 1917: Afx Ja 75 16/5:306
RE 8: 6 Sqn, aut 1917: Afx Ja 75 16/5:306
RE 8: 7 Sqn, aut 1917: Afx Ja 75 16/5:306
RE 8: 9 Sqn, aut 1917: Afx Ja 75 16/5:306
RE 8: 12 Sqn, aut 1917: Afx Ja 75 18/5:306
RE 8: 13 Sqn, aut 1917: Afx Ja 75 16/5:306
RE 8: 15 Sqn, aut 1917: Afx Ja 75 16/5:306
RE 8: 16 Sqn, aut 1917: Afx Ja 75 16/5:306
RE 8: 21 Sqn, spring 1917: Afx Ja 75 16/5:306
RE 8: 34 Sqn, spring 1917: Afx Ja 75 16/5:306
RE 8: 42 Sqn, April 1917, Italy: Afx Ja 75 16/5:305
RE 8: 52 Sqn, France, Aug 1917: Afx Ja 75 16/5:305
RE 8: 53 Sqn, Jan 1916: Afx Ja 75 16/5:305
RE 8: 59 Sqn, Aug 1917: Afx Ja 75 16/5:305

(U. K. fighters--Sopwith)

F. 1 Camel: factory finish: IM Ap 72 9/4:3
F. 1 Camel: Italy, Barker: IM D 71 8/12:5-6
F. 1 Camel: 4 Sqn: IM Ap 72 9/4:4
F. 1 Camel: 28 Sqn, Barker: IM Mr 73 10/3:5
F. 1 Camel: 43 Sqn, Woollet: IM D 71 8/12:4-5

Aircraft

F.1 Camel: 44 Sqn, March 1918, Adam: IM Jl 74 10/(17):7
F.1 Camel: 44 Home Defence Sqn: RT D 71 4/12:144
F.1 Camel: 45 Sqn, Italian Front: IM O 71 8/10:5+
F.1 Camel: 45 Sqn, A Flight: IM Ap 72 9/4:4
F.1 Camel: 65 Sqn, now in RAF Museum: AE Ap 74 6/4:198
F.1 Camel: 201 Sqn: IM Ap 72 9/4:15
2F.1 Camel: RNAS std: IM Jl 72 9/7:14
2F.1 Camel: 18 Sqn, France, Aug 1917, Colishaw: IM Jl 71 8/7: 9; cor S 71 8/9:9
2F.1 Camel: 18 Sqn, Aug 1917, Colishaw: Q Jl 71 6/3:18
Dolphin: 87 Sqn, April 1918: Afx Je 73 14/10:555
1½ Strutter: 43 Sqn: Afx Ja 73 14/5:273
Pup: RT D 71 4/12:144
Pup: 46 Sqn: Afx Ja 73 14/5:273
Pup: 46 Sqn, France, May-Nov 1917: IM Jl 71 8/7:8
TF2 Salamander: RFC std: Afx Mr 75 16/7:424
Snipe: 208 Sqn, 1918: AE S 71 1/4:193
Triplane: 1 (Naval) Sqn: Afx Ja 73 14/5:273
Triplane: 1 (Naval) Sqn, Sept 1917, Wilford: AN 8 D 72 1/15:9
Triplane: 1 (Naval) Sqn, Oct 1917: AN 8 D 1/15:9
Triplane: 8 (Naval) Sqn: AN 8 D 72 1/15:9
Triplane: 8 (Naval) Sqn, 2 var: RT S 73 6/9:102
Triplane: 8 (Naval) Sqn, Mont St. Eloi, July 1917: AN 8 D 72 1/15:9
Triplane: 8 (Naval) Sqn, Vert Galant, Jenner-Parsons: AN 8 D 72 1/15:9
Triplane: 10 (Naval) Sqn, Collishaw: IM D 71 8/12:4
Triplane: 10 (Naval) Sqn, 1917: AN 8 D 72 1/15:9
Triplane: 10 (Naval) Sqn, July 1917, Kent: AN 8 D 72 1/15:9

(U.K. fighters--other)

Avro 504K: fighter mod, 77 Sqn, Penston, Scotland: RT D 71 4/12:144
Bristol F.2B: 22 Sqn, Aug 1917--March 1918: Afx My 73 14/9:504
Bristol F.2B: 22 Sqn, April 1918: AN 12 O 73 2/11:9
Bristol F.2B: 139 Sqn, Italy: IM My 72 9/7:14
Bristol F.2B Mk II: std: AN 12 O 73 2/11:9
Bristol F.2B Sunbeam Arab engine: AN 12 O 73 2/11:9
Bristol Scout C: on delivery, RNAS, Oct 1915: Afx Ag 72 13/12:681
Bristol Scout C: RNAS, April 1916: Afx Ag 72 13/12:681
Bristol Scout C: RNAS training unit, Sept 1916: Afx Ag 72 13/12:681
De Havilland DH 2: first production batch: Sc Je 72 3/6:320
DH 2: 24 Sqn, July 1916: Sc Je 72 3/6:323
DH 2: 29 Sqn, Sept 1916: Sc Je 72 3/6:323
DH 4: 2 (Naval) Sqn: AN 16 My 75 3/25:9
DH 4: 18 Sqn: AN 16 My 75 3/25:9
Martinsyde S1: factory finish, spring 1915: Afx Jl 72 13/11:607
Nieuport: rocket-carrying, Navarre: IM Jl 71 8/7:17

III. Color Patterns 218

Nieuport 17: 1 Sqn, April 1917, Wood: IM Ja 72 9/1:11
Nieuport 17: 29 Sqn, 1917: IM Ag 72 9/8:6
Nieuport 17: 40 Sqn: AN 6 Jl 73 2/4:9
Nieuport 17: 40 Sqn, Bishop: AN 6 Jl 73 2/4:9
Nieuport 17: 56 Sqn, Ball: IM D 71 8/12:5
Nieuport 17C: 60 Sqn, Bishop: IM O 71 8/10:4-5
Nieuport 23: 29 Sqn, June 1917: Afx D 72 14/4:214
SE 4: 1st British field camouflage, 1914: Afx Jl 72 13/11:609
SE 5A: factory finish: IM Ja 72 9/1:11-12
SE 5A: prototype, now in RAF Museum: AE Ap 74 6/4:198
SE 5A: 74 Sqn, Mannock: IM O 71 8/10:4
SE 5A: 74 Sqn, late 1918: Afx Ap 73 14/8:441
SE 5A: 85 Sqn, Springs: IM Mr 73 10/3:5
SPAD S. VII: 19 Sqn, March 1917: Afx D 72 14/4:214

(U. K. trainers)

Avro 504J: A Flight, Gosport School of Special Flying: AN 27 D 74 3/15:8-9
Avro 504J: 8 Training Sqn, Pflaum: AN 27 D 74 3/15:8
Avro 504K: AN 27 D 74 3/15:8-9
Avro 504K: 5 Training Sqn, Michenhampton: AN 27 D 74 3/15:9
Avro 504K: 8 Training Sqn, Leighterton, 1918: AN 27 D 74 3/15: 8-9
Bristol F. 2B dual control: AN 12 O 73 2/11:9
Hewlett & Blondeau 504K: 7 Training Sqn, 1918: AN 27 D 74 3/15: 8-9
Saunders 504K: AN 27 D 74 3/15:8-9
Sopwith Pup: East Anglia/Dover training instructor, McCudden: IM Mr 73 10/3:5

(U. S.)

Curtiss Canuck: 1918: RT Mr 71 4/3:30
Nieuport 28C-1: 1 PG: AN 21 F 75 3/19:9
Nieuport 28C-1: 27 PS: AN 21 F 75 3/19:9
Nieuport 28C-1: 94 PS, 4 var: AN 21 F 75 3/19:9
Nieuport 28C-1: 95 PS, 4 var: AN 21 F 75 3/19:9
Packard-Lepere LUSAC 11: test unit unstated: AM S 74 78/9:24
SE5a: B Flight, 25 Sqn, Landis: Q Jl 74 10/1:10
SE5a: B Flight, 25 Sqn, Watts: Q Jl 74 10/1:10
SPAD XII: 13 Sqn, France, Biddle: Q Ap 74 9/2:68
SPAD XIII: 27 Sqn, France, Hartney: Q Ap 74 9/2:67
SPAD XIII: 28 Sqn, France, Jones: Q Ap 74 9/2:66
SPAD XIII: 91 Sqn, France, Cook: Q Ap 74 9/2:65
SPAD XIII: 93 Sqn, France, D'Olive: Q Ap 74 9/2:64
SPAD XIII: 213 Sqn, France, Hambleton: Q Ap 74 9/2:69

Between World Wars

(Argentine Military)

Curtiss Hawk III: Gr de Caza, I Rgt Aerea: AE O 72 3/4:205
Fairey IIIF Mk IIIM: navy unit unstated, 1928: AN 9 N 73 2/13:9
Martin 139WAA: 1 Bomb Rgt, 1938: AI Ag 74 7/2:92
Martin 139WAN: Q O 74 10/2:68

(Austria Military)

Fiat CR. 32bis: AN 18 Ja 74 2/17:9
Focke-Wulf Fw 56 Stösser: 1938: AN 2 F 73 1/19:9

(Australia Military)

Airco DH 9A: 1920: AE Mr 74 6/3:140
Hawker Demon: late 1930s: AE Mr 74 6/3:140
RE 8: 3 Sqn: IM Ja 72 9/1:10
SE5a: 1920s: AE Mr 74 6/3:140
Westland Wapiti: 1930s: AE Mr 74 6/3:140

(Belgium Military)

Bristol F. 2B: c.1923: Q Ap 73 8/2:77
Bristol F. 2B: presentation from Handley Page Ltd to King Albert, May 1920: Q Ap 73 8/2:77
Fairey Battle: 3 Air Rgt, Evere, 1940: RT O 71 4/10:112+
Fokker D. VII: Q Ap 73 8/2:77

(Canada Civil)

Avro 504K: Winnipeg to LaPas, 1918: RT N 73 6/11:130
De Havilland DH-4: G-CYCW, High River, Alta: RT Ap 74 7/4:43
De Havilland DH-9A: G-CYAJ, first trans-Canada air mail, 1920: RT O 72 5/10:118
De Havilland DH 60 Cirrus Moth (float): Ontario Provincial Air Service, 1928: RT O 74 7/10:118
De Havilland DH 87A Hornet Moth: Consolidated Mining & Smelting: Aero O 71 36/429:564-565
DH 87B Hornet Moth: Consolidated Mining & Smelting: Aero O 71 36/429:564-565

(Canada Military)

Armstrong Whitworth Siskin: RCAF aerobatic team, early 1930s: Q Su 75 10/4:136

III. Color Patterns 220

Avro 504K: June 1920, prob Camp Borden: RT Je 73 6/6:62
Avro 552A Viper: High River, Alta, March 1925, forestry patrol:
 RT Je 73 6/6:62; cor S 76 9/9:110
Blackburn Shark II: as delivered to Rockcliffe, Nov 1936: RT D
 74 7/12:133
Shark II: 6(TB) Sqn, June 1939: RT D 74 7/12:133
Shark II: 7(GP) Sqn, winter 1937-38: RT D 74 7/12:133
Bristol F. 2B: G-registration: RT Ap 72 5/4:47
De Havilland Genet Moth: Feb 1928--Jan 1932: RT My 73 6/5:50
SE5a: pre-RCAF: RT Ja 72 5/1:5

(Chile Military)

Fairey IIIF Mk IVC: navy, 1927: AN 9 N 73 2/13:9-10

(China Military)

Curtiss Hawk II/III (export BF2C-1): 1936-40: Q O 72 7/4:134
Curtiss Hawk III: 1938: AE N 72 3/5:205
Fiat CR. 32: 1938: AN 18 Ja 74 2/17:8-9
Martin 139-WC: Q O 74 10/2:68
Polikarpov I-16 type 10: Hankow, 1939: AE Mr 72 2/3:153
SB-2: northern Shansi, 1937-38: AE Ja 74 6/1:34

(Czechoslovakia Civil)

Avia B 534/IV: Czech Air Police: AE D 73 5/6:290
Avia B 534/IV: Czech Air Police: IM Ag 71 8/8:2

(Czechoslovakia Military)

Avia B 71/SB-2: 3 var: Q Ja 72 7/1:34-35
B 71: 71 Sqn, 6 Air Rgt, Praha, 1938: AE Ja 74 6/1:35
B 71: 72 Sqn, 1 Peruta, 6 Air Rgt, Praha, early 1938: AE Ja
 74 6/1:35
Avia B 534/IV: 1 Air Rgt, 32 Staffel: IM Ag 71 8/8:2
Nieuport 17: 1920: AN 6 Jl 73 2/4:9

(Denmark Military)

Avro 504K: c.1923: AN 27 D 74 3/15:9
Avro 504K: naval: AN 27 D 74 3/15:9
Bristol Type 105D Bulldog: 1 Esk, 1932: AE F 73 4/2:93
Hansa Brandenburg W-29 (Copenhagen Naval Dockyard-built): MAN
 Jl 72 88/1:46
Hawker Danerod (license Nimrod): IM My 73 10/5:7

Aircraft

(Estonia Military)

Airco DH. 9: 1923: IM O 73 10/10:15
Avro 504K: Q Jl 72 7/3:99
Avro 504R: 1928: Q Jl 72 7/3:99; cor Jl 73 8/3:174
Sopwith 2F. 1 Camel: 1919: Q Ja 72 7/1:36-37

(Finland Military)

Brewster B-239: 4 Flt, LeLv 24: MW D 73 2/4:182
Fokker D. XXI: Osato L, LeLv 24, Dec 1939-March 1940, Luukkanen; 2 var: Q Jl 74 10/1:12
Fokker D. XXI: 3/LeLv 24, spring - Dec 1939, Luukkanen: Q Jl 74 10/1:12
Gloster Gladiator I: F 19, early 1940: Afx Je 73 14/10:548
Gladiator I: Swedish Flygflottilj 19, Northern Finland, Jan-Feb 1940: AE Ja 73 4/1:41
Hawker B-4 Hart: IM F 73 10/2:15
Hart: LeR 18 (Swedish Volunteer Unit F. 19), Northern Finland, Jan-March 1940: RT Ag 73 6/8:83

(France Military)

ANF 113: GCN II/41: IM S 73 10/9:15
ANF 114: CN: IM S 73 10/9:15
ANF 115: G. A. O. I/520: IM S 73 10/9:15
ANF 115: G. A. O. I/551: IM S 73 10/9:15
ANF 115: S/L Petit: IM S 73 10/9:15
Breguet Bre 691: Brussels Aero Meet, July 1939: Q W 75 11/2:61
Caudron Renault CR 714: first production, Guyancourt, June 1939: Aero Je 71 36/425:316-317
Potez 540: Ecole de l'Air (Salon): IM Je 73 10/6:13
Potez 540: I/32, Dijon, 1937: IM Je 73 10/6:13
Potez 540: I/51, Tours, 1937: IM Je 73 10/6:13
Potez 540: I/55, Lyon, 1937: IM Je 73 10/6:13
Potez 540: I/63: IM Je 73 10/6:13
Potez 540: II/52, Nancy, 1938: IM Je 73 10/6:13
Potez 540 modified: GT II/15: IM Je 73 10/6:13

(Germany Civil)

Arado Ar 96 V2: AN 27 Ap 73 1/25:8
Ar 96 V3: AN 27 Ap 73 1/25:8-9
Fiesler Fi 156 V4: test bed: MW F 73 1/6:295
Fi 156A-0: pre-production with short slats, 1937: MW F 73 1/6:295
Focke Wulf Fw 56 Stösser: 3 var: AN 2 F 73 1/19:8-9
Stösser: company demonstrator: AN 2 F 73 1/19:9
Fokker D. VIII: air shows, Udet: MAN Ja 74 88/1:54
Heinkel 51A-1: early 1935; 2 var: IM Ag 71 8/8:16
Heinkel He 70G-1 Blitz: Lufthansa, 1935-37: AI F 75 8/2:90

III. Color Patterns 222

Junkers Ju 52: Lufthansa, 1932: AM My 73 76/5:74-75
Junkers Ju 86 V-4: Lufthansa, 1935: AN 18 Ag 72 1/7:10
Ju 86B: unstated airline: AN 18 Ag 72 1/7:10
Junkers Ju 88 V-1: prototype, 1936: AN 3 Ag 73 2/6:7

(Germany Military)

Dornier Do 17E-1: AN 9 Je 72 1/2:10
Do 17E-1: III/KG 155 (Alpen Geschwader), Air Exercises, 1937: AN 9 Je 72 1/2:10
Arado Ar 96 V6: production prototype for Ar 96A: AN 27 Ap 73 1/25:8
Fiesler Fi 156C-1 Storch: early production type with experimental wing tips: MW F 73 1/6:295
Focke Wulf Fw 56 Stösser: 2nd prototype: AN 2 F 73 1/19:9
Focke Wulf Fw 189 V-1: Aut 1938: MW Ag 73 1/12:633
Fw 189 V-1b: Bremen, spring 1939: MW S 73 2/1:34
Fw 189 V-3: Sept 1938, testing: MW Ag 73 1/12:633
Fw 189 V-4: chemical spray trials: MW Ag 73 1/12:633
Fokker D. VIII: Doberitz, 1919: AN 13 O 72 1/11:9
Fokker D. XIII: Lipezk Russia training base, 1932-33, Kroll: AM Ja 75 75/1:58
Heinkel HE 51A (prototype): summer 1933: MW Je 73 1/10:520
He 51A-04: fourth pre-production, early summer 1934: MW Je 73 1/10:520
He 51A-1: 1/JG, Döberitz, 1935: MW Je 73 1/10:520
He 51A-1: 1 Staffel Fliegergruppe Damm (II JG 132 Richthofen), Juterborg-Dam, summer 1935: MW Je 73 1/10:521
He 51A-1: 1/StG 165, Kitzigen, 1936-37: MW Je 73 1/10:520
He 51A-1: 3/JG 233, Wien-Aspern, Aug 1938: AE N 73 5/5:240-241
He 51B: ex 9th prototype, upgraded as trainer, 1938: MW Je 73 1/10:521
He 51B-1: 1 KuJSt/136, aut 1938, Ubben: MW Je 73 1/10:520
He 51B-1: Küstenjagdgruppe 136, 1936, float: MAN My 73 86/5:66
He 51B-1: Küstenjagdgruppe 136, Kiel-Hottenau: MW Jl 73 1/11:575
He 51B-1: Staffelführer 1/St. G 165, Kitzingen, 1936-37: RT Mr 71 4/3:25
He 51B-1: 2/JG 132 Richthofen; MW Jl 73 1/11:574
He 51B-1: 2/JG 132 Richthofen, Döberitz, 1937: AE N 73 5/5:240-241
He 51B-1: 2/JG 132 Richthofen, 1937: MAN My 73 86/5:67
He 51B-1: 2/JG 132 Richthofen, Döberitz, 1937: RT Mr 71 4/3:28
Heinkel He 59a: 2nd prototype (& only one with wheel LG): AN 24 N 72 1/14:10
Heinkel He 70G-2 Blitz: Aufklärungsgruppe (F)/123, 1 Staffel, Grossenheim, 1936: AI F 75 6/2:90
Henschel Hs 123A: 7/STG 165 Immelmann, Fürstenfeldbruck, Oct 1937: AE S 72 3/3:152
Hs 123A-1: 2/StG 165 Immelmann, military manoeuvers, 1937:

MW Mr 73 1/7:351
Junkers Ju 86 V5: 3rd bomber prototype, Aug 1935: AN 18 Ag 72 1/7:10
Junkers Ju 86D-1: unit unknown, LuftkreisKommando 4, Munster, 1938: AN 18 Ag 72 1/7:10
Junkers Ju 86G-1: factory finish, 1938: AN 18 Ag 72 1/7:10
Messerschmitt Bf 109B-1: Luftwaffe Schule, Berlin, late 1938: AE Mr 74 6/3:137
Bf 109B-1: 6/JG 132 Richthofen, Döbertiz, 1937: AE N 73 5/5: 240-241
Messerschmitt Bf 110B-0: prototype: MW O 72 1/2:70

(Guatemala Military)

Boeing P-26A: RT S 71 4/9:107

(Hungary Military)

Brandenburg C.1 series 269: Red Air Arm, 1918: AN 7 F 75 3/18: 8-9
Fiat CR 32: 1/1 Sqn, 1/I FG, Börgönd, Veszprém, summer 1939: AI D 74 7/6:296
Heinkel He 170A: 2 Sqn, 1 Önálló Távolfelderitö Osztály (Independent Long Range Recon Gp), Kecskemet, spring, 1939: AI F 75 8/2:91

(Ireland Civil)

Bellanca 28-70 Irish Swoop: 1936 racing season: AM Ag 72 75/2: 42-43

(Ireland Military)

Bristol F.2B: July 1922: Q Jl 73 8/3:144
Gloster SS.37 Gladiator: March 1938: Q Jl 73 8/3:144
Westland Lysander: July 1939: Q Jl 73 8/3:144

(Italy Civil)

Savio Marchetti SM 79C I-5: Istres-Damascus-Paris race, 1937, Biseo: AI D 75 9/6:300

(Italy Military)

Fiat CR 32: pre-1938 std: AN 18 Ja 74 2/17:9
Fiat CR 32: 85 Sqd, 17 Gr, 3 St, Bresso, Milan, late 1935: AI D 74 7/6:296

III. Color Patterns

Fiat CR 32: 155 Sqd, 3 Gr, 6 St "Diavoli Rossi," Campoformido, Udine, early 1936: AI D 74 7/6:297
Fiat CR 32: 360 Sqd, 52 St, Pontedera, Pisa, mid 1939: AI D 74 7/6:296

(Japan Military)

Fiat BR. 20: 1 Chu, 12 Hikosentai: AE My 73 4/5:249
Kawanishi Type 97-1 "Alf" floatplane: Yokosuka NAS: IM Ag 71 8/8:14
Mitsubishi Ki. 15-I: 1 Chu, 14 Hikosen: AE My 73 4/5:249
Mitsubishi Ki. 21-I-Otsu: 2 Chu, 60 Hikosen: AE My 73 4/5:249
Mitsubishi Ki. 30: 2 Chu, 10 Hikosen: AE My 73 4/5:249
Nakajimi Ki. 27 otsu: CO, 1 Chu, 1 Hikosen, Inoue: AE My 73 4/5:249

(Netherlands Military)

Fokker D. VIII: AN 13 O 72 1/11:9
Fokker G. 1: prototype: AI N 74 7/5:242
G. 1: 4 JaVA, Bergen, before Oct 1939: AI N 74 7/5:242
G. 1: re-engined prototype: AI N 74 7/5:242
Martin 139WH1: NEIAF: Q O 74 10/2:68
Martin 139WH2: NEIAF: Q O 74 10/2:68
Martin 139WH2: 1938: AI Ag 74 7/2:92
Martin 139WH2: 1941: NEIAF: AI Ag 74 7/2:92-93

(New Zealand Military)

Bristol F. 2B: 1927: AN 12 O 73 2/11:9

(Poland Civil)

Lublin R XVIb: first prototype, ambulance: Aero Mr 75 40/470: 153

(Poland Military)

Albatros D-III: Kosciuszko Sqn, Lwów, 1919, Fauntleroy: Q W 75 11/2:85
Albatros D-III: Kosciuszko Sqn, Lwów, 1919, Rorison: Q W 75 11/2:85
Albatros D-III: Kosciuszko Sqn, Polonne field, summer 1920, Clark: Q W 75 11/2:85
Ansaldo SVA-1: Kosciuszko Sqn, Senkowski: Q W 75 11/2:85
Ansaldo SVA-1: Kosciuszko Sqn, Rorison: Q W 75 11/2:85
PZL P. 11c: unit unknown, Sept 1939: AE S 73 5/3:138-139
P. 11c: CO, 113 Sqn, IV Dyon, 1 Air Rgt, Warsaw-Okecie: AE S

73 5/3:138-139
P.11c: 121 Sqn, III Dyon, 2 Air Rgt, Krakow, 1938:   AE S 73 5/3:138-139
PZL P.23 Karas: Training Sqn, 1 Air Rgt: Q Ja 75 10/3:95
P.23B: unit unknown: Q Ja 75 10/3:95
P.23B: 11 Line Sqn, 1 Air Rgt: Q Ja 75 10/3:95
P.23B: 12 Line Sqn, 1 Air Rgt: Q Ja 75 10/3:95
P.23B: 42 Line Sqn, 1 Air Rgt: Q Ja 75 10/3:95
P.23B: 42 Line Sqn, 4 Air Rgt, Tourun, 1938:   Q Ja 75 10/3:94

(Portugal Military)

Avro 504K: AN 27 D 74 3/15:8-9

(Rumania Military)

Armstrong Siddeley Siskin: std export scheme: Afx O 73 15/2:86
Liore et Olivier LeO 10:   NBS, Air Combat Flot, Pipera-București, 1929:   AE Je 71 1/1:28-29
PZL P.11b: Fighter Flot, Pipera-București, 1935:   AE Je 71 1/1:28
P.11b: Fighter Flot, Pipera-București, 1935-36:   AE S 73 5/3:138-139
P.11f: 1937-1938:   AE S 73 5/3:138-139
Savoia-Marchetti SM 55:   Naval Flot, Constanza, 1934:   AE Je 71 1/1:29

(Spain, Nationalist Military)

Arado Ar 68E: Grupo 9, La Cernia, Oct 1938:   MW Ap 73 1/8:409
Dornier Do 17E-1:   Kampfgruppe 88, Condor Legion, 1937-38:   MW Ap 73 1/8:409
Fiat CR 32:   Gruppo unknown, 2 var: Q Ja 74 9/1:44
Fiat CR 32:   Aviacion del Tercio, early civil war: Q Ja 74 9/1:44
Fiat CR 32:   Spanish Morocco, Aug 1946:   Q Ja 74 9/1:44
Fiat CR 32:   101 Sqd, 10 Gr Auto Ca "Baleri," late 1936:   AI D 74 7/6:296
Fiat CR 32:   24 Sqd, 16 Gr Ca "La Cucaracha," 1936:   AI D 74 7/6:297
Fiat CR 32:   6 Gruppo "Gambi di Ferro":   Q Ja 74 9/1:47
Fiat CR 32:   10 Gr "Balaeri":   AN 18 Ja 74 2/17:9
Fiat CR 32:   10 Gr "Balaeri":   Q Ja 74 9/1:45
Fiat CR 32:   pos 10 Gr "Balaeri":   Q Ja 74 9/1:44
Fiat CR 32:   10 Gr "Balaeri," aut 1938:   AN 18 Ja 74 2/17:9
Fiat CR 32:   10 Gr "Balaeri," aut 1938:   Q Ja 74 9/1:47
Fiat CR 32:   10 Gr "Balaeri," Majorca: Q Ja 74 9/1:44
Fiat CR 32:   16 Gruppo "Cucaracha":   Q Ja 74 9/1:47
Fiat CR 32:   23 Gr "Asso di Bastoni":   Q Ja 74 9/1:45
Fiat CR 32:   23 Gruppo, 2 var: Q Ja 74 9/1:45
Fiat CR 32:   CO, 23 Gruppo: Q Ja 74 9/1:45

III. Color Patterns

Fiat CR 32: Sqd Auto Caccia e Mitragliamento: Q Ja 74 9/1:47
Fiat CR 32: Sqd "Fracce": Q Ja 74 9/1:47
Fiat CR 32-1: Palma di Majorca, sum 1938: AN 18 Ja 74 2/17:9
Fiat G. 50: 1 Gr Sperimentale, Escalona, SW of Madrid, March 1939: AE Je 74 6/6:306
Fiesler Fi 156A Storch with pre-production exhausts: El Burgo, 1937: MW F 73 1/6:296
Heinkel He 45C: He 45 Kette, Condor Legion, Leon, Nov 1937: MW Ap 73 1/8:407
He 45C: He 45 Kette, Condor Legion, Torrelavega, Sept 1937: MW Ap 73 1/8:408
Heinkel He 51A-1: 3/JG 233: AE N 73 5/5:241
He 51B: Condor Legion, Nov 1936, Trautloft: MW Ap 73 1/8:409
He 51B: 1 Staffel, Jagdgruppe 88, Legion Condor, aut 1937: MW My 73 1/9:465
He 51B-1: Grupo de Cadena 1-G-2, 1937: MW Jl 73 1/11:574
He 51B-1: 1/Jagdgruppe 88, Leon, summer 1937: RT Mr 71 4/3:28
He 51B-2: AS/88, Condor Legion, 1936-37: MW Ap 73 1/8:409
He 51B-1: 2/JG 88, Legion Condor, spring 1937: AE N 73 5/5:241
He 51C-1: JG 88, Condor Legion, 1937: MAN My 73 86/5:67
He 51C-1: 4/JG 88, Legion Condor, late summer 1938: AE N 73 5/5:240-241
He 51C-1: 4/JG 88, Condor Legion, 1938-39: MW Jl 73 1/11:574
Heinkel He 59B-2: See-Aufklärungstaffel AS/88, 1936: AN 24 N 72 1/14:10
Heinkel He 70: Aufklärungstaffel 88, Condor Legion, early 1937: MW My 73 1/9:464
He 70F-2: Gr 7-G-14, Battle of Brunete, summer 1937: AI F 75 8/2:91
He 70F-2: Gr 7-G-14, under Brig del Aire 1, Teruel operations, winter 1937-38: AI F 75 8/2:91
Heinkel He 111B: K/88, Condor Legion, Special Versuchsbomberstaffel, 1937: MW Ap 73 1/8:407
He 111B-1: K/88, Condor Legion: MW My 73 1/9:464
He 111B-1: K/88, Condor Legion, late 1937: MW My 73 1/9:464
Henschel Hs 123: Condor Legion, Leon: May 1939: RT Ja 71 4/1:76
Hs 123A: Condor Legion, Leon: MW My 73 1/9:464
Hs 123A: Grupo 24, Tablada, 1939: RT Ja 71 4/1:76
Hs 123A-1: Grupo 24, Tablada, spring 1939: MW Mr 73 1/7:351
Henschel Hs 126: A/88, Condor Legion, late 1938: MW Ap 73 1/8:407
Junkers Ju 52: K/88 Condor Legion, early 1937: MW Ap 73 1/8:407
Junkers Ju 87A-1: Jolanthe Kette, Condor Legion, late 1937: MW My 73 1/9:464
Messerschmitt Bf 108: Condor Legion courier aircraft: MW My 73 1/9:464
Messerschmitt Bf 109B: 2/JG/88, Condor Legion, June 1937: MW Ap 73 1/8:407
Bf 109D: JG/88, Legion Condor, 1937: WW2J S 75 2/5-6:18

Bf 109D-1: Gr 6-G-6, Logroño, April 1939: AE Mr 74 6/1:137
Bf 109E-1: 2/JG 88, Condor Legion, near end of war: MW Ap 73 1/8:409
Savio Marchetti SM 79/AR. 126: 52 Sqn, 27 Gr, Palma, Majorca, May 1938: AI D 75 9/6:300

(Spain, Republican Military)

Bristol Bulldog II: International group in support of Basque forces, 1936-37: AE F 73 4/2:93
Bristol F. 2B: 1924: AN 12 O 73 2/11:9
Polikarpov I-16 type 10: Gruppo 21, 1938: AE Mr 72 2/3:153
SB-2: Gr de Bomb 24, early 1939: AE Ja 74 6/1:34

(Sweden Military)

Avro 504K: navy, winter 1919: RT F 73 6/6:59
Bristol Bulldog IIA: F1, 1935: AE F 73 6/2:93
Focke Wulf Sk 12 (Fw 44J Stieglitz): 1937-40: RCS Je 75 1/2: (40-41)
Hawker Hart B-4: 4 var: IM F 73 10/2:15
Junkers B-3 (Ju 86K): F1 bomber wing, 1938: RT My 73 6/5:56; RT Jl 74 7/7:72
Northrop B-5 (A-17): prototype, in US prior to shipment: IM F 73 10/2:10
Seversky EP-106: F8: Q Jl 72 7/3:96

(Turkey Military)

Bristol Blenheim I: Bomb Btn, 3 Rgt, Ismir, 1939: AE Jl 71 1/2: 84
Breguet XIX. 7: recon-bomber unit, 1935: AE Jl 71 1/2:84-85
Curtiss Hawk 81A-3 (Tomahawk IIB): Eskişehir, 1942: AE Jl 71 1/2:85
Curtiss Hawk II: FB, 3 Rgt, Izmir, 1940: AE Jl 71 1/2:84-85
Martin 139WT: 1937: AI Ag 74 7/2:92-93
PZL P. 24C: Yeşilköy, 1940: AE Jl 71 1/2:84-85
SPAD XIII: Graeco-Turkish War, 1922: AE Jl 71 1/2:84-85
Vultee V-11-GB: 2 Rgt, Diyarbakir, 1939: AE Jl 71 1/2:84-85
Westland Lysander II: Yeşilköy, 1940: AE Jl 71 1/2:85

(USSR Civil)

PBY-1: Russian Biological Expedition, 1937: RT D 72 5/12:142

(U. K. Civil)

Cierva C-6D Avro 575: Berlin, 1926, Udet: RT N 71 4/11:130

III. Color Patterns 228

Cierva C-8R Avro 587: 1927: RT N 71 4/11:130
De Havilland DH 4A: India, 1920s: AN 16 My 75 3/25:9
De Havilland DH Fox Moth: Hillman Airways, 1932: Afx N 71 13/3:127
De Havilland DH 71 Tiger Moth: 1927 King's Cup Race, Barnard: Aero My 74 39/460:246-247
DH 71 Tiger Moth: 1927 King's Cup Race, Broad: Aero My 74 39/460:246-247
Fokker Super Universal: Canada barren lands flight, 1928, Dickens: RT Ja 74 7/1:5

(U.K. Military Bombers)

Blackburn Cubaroo: prototype: Afx F 74 15/6:353
Blackburn Shark: pre-1938 std: IM Jl 73 10/7:4-5
Blackburn Skua: pre-1938 std: IM Jl 73 10/7:4-5
Bristol Blenheim I: 90 Sqn, Bichester, Oxon, winter 1938-39: AE Ap 74 6/4:202
Blenheim I: 108 Sqn, Bassingbourn, Cambs, summer 1938: AE Ap 74 6/4:202
Blenheim I: 114 Sqn, Wyton, Hunts, summer 1937: AE Ap 74 6/4:202
De Havilland DH 10 Mk III: 97 Sqn, Juhu, India, 1929, mail flights, Bombay-Karachi: AN 14 Je 74 3/1:9
DH 10 Mk III: 216 Sqn, 2 var: AN 14 Je 74 3/1:8-9
DH 10 Mk III: 216 Sqn, Kantara, Egypt, 1921, 2 var: AN 14 Je 3/1:8-9
Fairey Albacore: 2nd prototype, trials, summer 1939: AN 22 Ag 75 4/6:9
Fairey Swordfish I: 820 Sqn, HMS Ark Royal, 1939: AE N 72 3/5:256
Swordfish I: 822 Sqn, HMS Courageous, 1939: AE N 72 3/5:254
Swordfish I: 823 Sqn, HMS Glorious, 1936: AE N 72 3/5:254
Handley Page Heyford Mk IA: 10(b) Sqn: AN 31 Ag 73 2/8:7
Heyford Mk II: prototype: AN 31 Ag 73 2/8:7
Heyford Mk II: 7(b) Sqn: AN 31 Ag 73 2/8:7
Vickers Vimy: prototype: AN 17 O 75 4/10:10
Vimy IV: 7 Sqn: AN 17 O 75 4/10:10
Vimy (Westland-built): AN 17 O 75 4/10:10
Vickers Wellington Mk I: 38 Sqn, late 1938: AN 4 Ag 73 1/6:10

(U.K. Military Fighters)

(multi-place)
Bristol F.2B Mk IV: AN 12 O 73 2/11:9
Bristol Fighter: 2 Sqn, U.K., 1927: Afx Ap 75 16/8:462
Bristol Fighter: 12 Sqn, B Flt, Germany, 1919: Afx Ap 75 16/8:462
Bristol Fighter: 31 Sqn, India, 1928: Afx Ap 75 16/8:462
Bristol Fighter: 208 Sqn, Egypt, 1927: Afx Ap 75 16/8:462
Fairey Battle I: 106 Sqn, Abingdon, Oxon, Aug 1938: AE Ag 72 3/2:88

Aircraft

Gloster Grebe II two-seat: 56 Sqn: Afx Ag 73 14/12:672
Hawker Demon: 23 Sqn, 1933: Afx Mr 74 15/7:393
Demon: 29 Sqn, 1935: Afx Mr 74 15/7:394
Demon: 41 Sqn, Sept, 1934, 2 var: Afx Mr 74 15/7:394
Demon: 601 Sqn, 1937: Afx Mr 74 15/7:394
Hawker Hart: 57 Sqn, now in RAF Museum: AE Ap 74 6/4:198

(single-seat)
Armstrong Whitworth Siskin IIA: 1 Sqn, 1927: Q Su 75 10/4:136
Siskin III: 111 Sqn, 1924-1927: Afx O 73 15/2:84
Siskin IIIA: 1 Sqn, 1927-1931: Afx O 73 15/2:84
Siskin IIIA: 29 Sqn, 1928-1931: Afx O 73 15/2:84
Siskin IIIA: 43 Sqn, 1928-31: Afx O 73 15/2:84
Siskin IIIA: 43 Sqn, 1929: AE S 71 1/4:193
Siskin IIIA: 56 Sqn, 1927-32: Afx O 73 15/3:84
Siskin IIIA: 111 Sqn, 1929: Q Su 75 10/4:136
Bristol Bulldog II: 17 Sqn, 1930: Afx N 73 15/3:162
Bulldog II: 32 Sqn, 1932: Afx N 73 15/3:162
Bulldog IIA: 3 Sqn, 1930: Afx N 73 15/3:162
Bulldog IIA: 3 Sqn, 1934: AE S 71 1/4:193
Bulldog IIA: 17 Sqn, Upavon, 1934: AE F 73 4/2:93
Bulldog IIA: 23 Sqn, July 1931 - Sept 1932, 2 var: MW O 72 1/2:80
Gloster Gamecock I: 23 Sqn: Afx Ag 73 14/12:676
Gamecock I: 23 Sqn, 1929: AE S 71 1/4:193
Gamecock I: 43 Sqn: Afx Ag 73 14/12:676
Gloster Gauntlet I: 19 Sqn, 1935: Afx D 73 15/4:236
Gauntlet II: 111 Sqn, 1937: Afx D 73 15/4:236
Gauntlet II: 151 Sqn, 1937: Afx D 73 15/4:236
Gloster Gladiator: 3 Sqn, 1937: Afx Ja 74 15/5:308
Gladiator: 72 Sqn, 1938: Sc Ag 73 4/8:553
Gladiator: 73 Sqn: Afx My 72 13/9:498
Gladiator: 73 Sqn, 1937: Afx Ja 74 15/5:308
Gladiator: 87 Sqn, Debden, 1938; now in RAF Museum: AE Ap 74 6/4:198
Gladiator: 94 Sqn: Afx My 72 13/9:498-499
Gladiator II: 25 Sqn, 1939: AE S 71 1/4:193
Gloster Grebe II: 19 Sqn: Afx Ag 73 14/12:674
Grebe II: 25 Sqn: Afx Ag 73 14/12:674
Grebe II: 29 Sqn: Afx Ag 73 14/12:674
Grebe II: 32 Sqn: Afx Ag 73 14/12:672
Hawker Fury I: CO, 1 Sqn, 1935: Afx F 74 15/6:347
Fury I: 1 Sqn, 1935: AE S 71 1/4:193
Fury I: CO, 43 Sqn, 1933: Afx F 74 15/6:347
Fury II: 25 Sqn, 1935: Afx F 74 15/6:347
Hawker Nimrod I: Flt CO, 800 Sqn, HMS Courageous: IM My 73 10/5:6
Nimrod I: 800 Sqn, HMS Courageous: IM My 73 10/5:6
Nimrod I: 802 Sqn, HMS Glorious: Afx My 71 12/9:459
Nimrod I: 802 Sqn, HMS Glorious: IM My 73 10/5:7
Nimrod I: Flt CO, 408 Flt (later 802 Sqn), HMS Glorious: IM My 73 10/5:6
Nimrod II: 800 Sqn, HMS Courageous: IM My 73 10/5:7

III. Color Patterns 230

Hawker Woodcock II: 3 Sqn, 1925: Afx S 73 15/1:33
Woodcock II: 17 Sqn, 1926: Afx S 73 15/1:33

(U. K. Military Trainers)

Airspeed Oxford I: 3 FTS, South Cerney, c. 1938: AN 13 D 74 3/14:8-9
Armstrong Whitworth Atlas: Oxford UAS, 1929: AN 28 N 75 4/15:7
Armstrong Whitworth Hart Trainer: now in RAF Museum: AE Ap 74 6/4:198
Avro 504K: mod, RAE Farnborough, 1922: AN 27 D 74 3/15:8-9
Avro 504L: prototype, floats: AN 27 D 74 3/15:8-9
Avro 504N: c. 1930: AN 27 D 74 3/15:9
Avro 504N: Cambridge UAS, 1926: AN 28 N 75 4/13:7
Avro 504N: Oxford UAS, 1926: AN 28 N 75 4/13:7
Avro Tutor: Cambridge UAS: AN 28 N 75 4/13:8
Tutor: Oxford UAS: AN 28 N 75 4/13:8
Bristol Bulldog TM: RAF College, Cranwell: Afx D 73 15/4:218-219
Bristol F. 3B Trainer: Oxford UAS, 1930: AN 12 O 73 2/11:9
Bristol Fighter: Cambridge UAS, 1929: AN 28 N 75 4/13:7
Bristol Fighter: Oxford UAS, 1929: AN 28 N 75 4/13:7
Hawker Demon (T): 29 Sqn, 1937: Afx Mr 74 15/7:394
Demon (T): 29 Sqn, 1937: Afx Mr 74 15/7:394
Hawker Hart: London UAS: AN 28 N 75 4/13:8
De Havilland Gennet Moth: Central Flying School aerobatic team: PAM O 75 11:195
Vickers Vimy: pos Henlow parachute trainer: AN 17 O 75 4/10:10

(U. K. Military Other Aircraft)

Armstrong Whitworth Atlas: 16 Sqn, 1930: Afx My 75 16/9:543
Avro Anson Mk I: 48 Sqn, RAF Manston, 1938: Afx Ap 71 12/8:416-417
Cierva C-6C Avro 675: 1926: RT N 71 4/11:130; add F 72 5/2:14
Consolidated Model 28 Catalina (PBY-4): July 1939: Q W 75 11/2:79
De Havilland DH. 4: communications unit, immediately post-war: AN 16 My 75 3/25:8
Fairey III Mk III: Mediterranean Fleet Catapult Sqn, 1936: AN 9 N 73 2/13:9
Fairey IIIF: HMS Norfolk, 1932-34: AN 9 N 73 2/13:9
Fairey IIIF Mk IVM: 207 Sqn, Eastchurch: AN 9 N 73 2/13:10
Hawker Audax: 4 Sqn: Afx Jl 75 16/11:653
Audax: 16 Sqn: Afx Jl 75 16/11:653
Hawker Osprey: Mediterranean cruiser unstated: IM Ap 73 10/4:13
Osprey Mk I: cruiser unstated: IM Ap 73 10/4:14
Osprey Mk I: 803 Sqn, HMS Eagle: IM Ap 73 10/4:14
Heinkel He 70G-1 Blitz: Kestrel engine testbed, 1937-1939: AI F

75 8/2:90
Saro London: 2 var: AN 9 Ag 74 3/5:8-9
Vickers Vernon I: AN 17 O 75 4/10:10
Vernon II: AN 17 O 75 4/10:10

(U. S. Civil)

Art Chester Special (Jeep): 1935 racing season, Chester: RC Ap 73 10/4:60-61
Beech Staggerwing: factory finish: RCS Jl 75 1/3:(40-41)
Bellanca 28-70 Dorothy (ex-Irish Swoop): 1936 trans Atlantic record, Mollison: AM Ag 72 75/2:42-43
Brown B-2 "Miss Los Angeles": 1934 Thompson, Minor: RC N 72 9/11:60-61
Curtiss P1B: supposedly German in movie "Wings," 1938: Sc Jl 73 4/7:477
Curtiss Robin: "St. Louis Robin," endurance record plane: RC Ja 73 10/1:60-61
De Havilland DH. 4: U. S. Mail Services: AN 16 My 75 3/25:8
DH 4B: U. S. Mail Services: RT O 72 5/10:118
Fokker D. VII: Hispano-Suizs engine, movie "Men With Wings," 1938: Sc Jl 73 4/7:477
Fokker F7b/3M: "Josephine Ford," Byrd Arctic Expedition, North Pole flight, May 1926, Bennett: RT Ja 74 7/1:5
Folkers Speed King SK-3 Jupiter: 1937 Thompson, Kling: AM F 73 76/2:42-43
Gee Bee Model Z SuperSportster: 1931 racing season: RCS Ag 75 1/4:(40-41)
Grumman JRF-5 amphibian: USCG, 1939-1941: Q Ap 72 7/2:72
Howard DGA-6 Mr. Mulligan: Thompson & Bendix Races, 1935-1936, Howard: RC Jl 73 6/7:60-61
Keith Rider R-4: Schoenfieldt Firecracker, 1938 Greve race, Le Vier: RC D 72 9/12:60-61
Laird-Turner LTR-4 Pesco Special: Thompson Trophy, 1938-1939, Turner: RC Je 73 6/6:60-61
Lockheed 5C Vega: Winnie Mae, 1933 round the world solo, Post: RCS N 75 1/7:(36-37)
Lockheed Sirius: Tingmissartoq, 1931, Lindbergh: RCS Ap 75 1/1:(40-41)
Nieuport 28C-1: movie "The Lost Squadron," 1934: Sc Jl 73 4/7: 477
Thomas Morse MB-3A (Boeing-built): supposedly a SPAD in movie "Wings," 1926: Sc Jl 73 4/7:476
Thomas Morse S4C Scout: mod to resemble Sopwith, movie "Hell's Angels," 1928-29: Sc Jl 73 4/7:476
Travel-Air 2000: Hispano-Suiza engine; Wichita Fokker in movie "Men With Wings," 1938: Sc Jl 73 4/7:477
Wedell-Williams Glimore Red Lion: 1932 Bendix race, Turner: AM Ja 71 72/1:21-23

III. Color Patterns

(U. S. Military Bombers)

Chance Vought SB2U Vindicator: 4 Sec, USS Lexington, 1937-1941:
   MAN D 74 89/6:70
SB2U-1: VB-3, USS Saratoga, early 1938: Afx Jl 71 12/11:582
Curtiss BFC-2: VB-3, 1937: Q Ja 74 9/1:33
BFC-2: VB-6: Q Ja 74 9/1:33
Curtiss SBC-3: VF-6 supernumery, USS Enterprise, c. 1937: Q
   Ja 74 9/1:30
SBC-3: USS Yorktown: Q Jl 72 7/3:120
SBC-3: CO, USS Yorktown Carrier Air Group: Q Ja 74 9/1:30
SBC-4: Air Group CO, USS Enterprise: Q Jl 72 7/3:121
Curtiss BF2C-1: VB-5, USS Ranger, 1935: AE O 72 3/4:205
BF2C-1: CO, VB-5B, USS Ranger, late 1934 to mid-1935, Barner:
   IM My 71 8/5:4-5
Curtiss XSBC-1: prototype: Q Jl 72 7/3:120
Curtiss XSB2C-1: Dec 1940, Child: Q Jl 72 7/3:121
Martin B-10B: 28 BS, Camp Nichols, Luzon, Philippines, 1937-41:
   AI Ag 74 7/2:92
Martin B-12A: Hamilton Field CA, c. 1935: AI Ag 74 7/2:92-93
Martin T4M-1: VT-2, USS Saratoga: Q Ja 74 9/1:30
T4M-1: VT-95, c. 1929: Q Ja 74 9/1:30

(U. S. Military Fighters)

Boeing F4B-2: VF-5, USS Lexington, 1932: Q Ja 74 9/1:30
Boeing P-12B: 95 AS: RCS O 75 1/6:(38+)
P-12E: 27 PS, 1 PG, Selfridge Field, Detroit, early 1930s aero-
   batic team, 4 var: Q Ja 74 9/1:71; IM S 74 10/(18):16
Boeing P-26A Peashooter: 34 PS "Thunderbirds": Sc N 74 5/63:
   589
Brewster F2A-1: second production model: MW D 73 2/4:182
F2A-2: VF-2: MW D 73 2/4:182
F2A-2: VF-2: Q Ja 74 9/1:41; cor O 74 10/2:47
Chance Vought XF4U-1: prototype, May 1940, Bullard: Afx N 71
   13/3:133
Curtiss F8C-4: VF-18, USS Saratoga: Q Ja 74 9/1:30
Curtiss F11C-2: VB-2, before 1937: Q Ja 74 9/1:33
Curtiss P-40B: 33 PS, Reykjavik, Aug 1941: AN 6 S 74 3/7:10
Curtiss P-40C: 57 PG, Mitchell Field, NY, 1941: AE My 72 2/5:
   257
P-40C: 77 PS, 20 PG, Hamilton Field CA, 1941: AE My 72 2/5:
   257
P-40E: 79 PS, 20 PG, Hamilton Field CA, 1941: AE My 72 2/5:
   257
De Havilland DH. 4: AN 16 My 75 3/25:9
De Havilland DH. 4: 11 Sqn: AN 16 My 75 3/25:9
Grumman F3F-1: Marine VF-4M: Q Ja 74 9/1:33
F3F-2: Marine VMF-2, July 1937: Q Ja 74 9/1:33
Grumman F4F-3: 1941: Q Ja 74 9/1:41
F4F-3: VF-41, USS Ranger: Q Ja 74 9/1:41
F4F-3A: AN 7 F 75 3/18:9

Aircraft

SE 5e: 1922: RT F 75 8/2:23
Seversky P-35A: 17 PS, Nichols Field, Philippines, summer 1941,
    Wagner: Q Jl 72 7/3:96

(U. S. Military Scout & Patrol Aircraft)

Chance Vought OS2U-2 Kingfisher: std, 1941: Afx Ap 72 13/8:426
OS2U-2: Cape May: Afx Ap 72 13/8:426
OS2U-2: CO, 4 Naval Dist, Inshore Patrol Sqn (VS-5D4), Cape May,
    NJ: RT D 74 7/12:138
OS2U-2: USS North Carolina, spring 1941: RT D 74 7/12:138
Chance Vought O2U-1: VO-35, USS Raleigh, 1927: Q Ja 74 9/1:32
Chance Vought SBU Corsair: USN Flag Unit, first delivery, 1934:
    Q O 72 7/4:148
SBU: Scouting 41, USS Ranger, July 1937: Q O 72 7/4:148
Chance Vought XOS2U-1: prototype Kingfisher: Afx Ap 72 13/8:
    416
Consolidated PBY-1: VP-6: Q W 75 11/2:76-77
PBY-2: BP-10: Q W 75 11/2:79
PBY-4: PatWing Ten, VP-21: Q W 75 11/2:79
Consolidated PBY-4: 1936: AN 1 N 74 3/11:8
PBY-5: VP-52: Q Ja 74 9/1:36
Consolidated P2Y-2: Q Ja 74 9/1:36
Curtiss SOC-1: VCS 9, USS St. Louis, 1940: Q Su 75 10/4:150
SOC-1: VS-95, USS Salt Lake City: Q Ja 74 9/1:32
SOC-3: VO-4, USS Colorado: Q Ja 74 9/1:32

(U. S. Military Other Aircraft)

Cessna AT-17A Bobcat: RT O 75 8/10:119
De Havilland DH-4 Amb-1: Navy ambulance: RT O 72 5/10:118
Fokker D. VII: USMC, 1919: RT S 71 4/9:97
Fokker D. VIII: McCook Field, 1920-21: AN 13 O 72 1/11:9
Ryan ST-A: USAAF std, 1941: RC F 73 10/2:60-61

(Yugoslavia Military)

Ikarus IK-2: 34 Grupa, 1941: Q Au 75 11/1:2

World War II

(Australia)

Airspeed Auster Mk VI: RT Ja 72 5/1:10
Avro Lincoln Mk 30: School of Air Navigation, Sale: Q O 73 8/4:
    246
Lincoln Mk 30: 6 Sqn, Amberly, Queensland: Q O 73 8/4:246

III. Color Patterns

Brewster B-439 Buffalo: MW D 73 2/4:181
Bristol Beaufighter TF Mk X: 455 Sqn, U.K., late 1944: AE Ja 74 6/1:31
Beaufighter 21: May 1944: AE Mr 74 6/3:141
Bristol Beaufort: 100 Sqn, 1944: AE Mr 74 6/3:141
Bristol Bombay: 1 Air Ambulance Unit, with RAF 216 Sqn, Middle East: AN 23 N 73 2/14:8
Commonwealth Whirraway: Dec 1942: AE Mr 74 6/3:140
Whirraway: CO, Central Gunnery School, Cressy, Vic, 1945: MW N 72 1/3:147
Whirraway CA-9: 5 Sqn, Bouganville, early 1945: RiS Ag 72 1/1:29
Commonwealth CA-12 Boomerang: 2 OTU, Mildura NSW, 1943: AE F 72 2/2:97
CA-12: 2nd production aircraft: AE F 72 2/2:97
Commonwealth CA-13 Boomerang: 4 Sqn, New Guinea, late 1943: AE F 72 2/2:97
CA-13: 4 Sqn, New Guinea, early 1944: AE F 72 2/2:97
CA-13: 5 Sqn, Bougainville, 1944: AE F 72 2/2:97
Consolidated PBY-5A: 8 Communications Flight: IM F 72 9/2:8-9
PBY-5A: 113 Air Rescue Flight: IM F 72 9/2:8-9
Curtiss Kittyhawk IA (P-40E-18E): 75 Sqn, Milne Bay, 1942, Watson: Q O 71 6/4:34
Kittyhawk III: 76 Sqn, Momote, 1944, O'Meara: Q O 71 6/4:34
Kittyhawk III: 86 Sqn, Merauke, 1944, Maguire: Q O 71 6/4:34
Kittyhawk IV (P-40N-1CU): 75 Sqn, Vivigni Strip, Goodenough Is, Dec 1943, Williams: Q O 71 6/4:34
Kittyhawk IV: 80 Sqn, 1944: AE Mr 74 6/3:141
Kittyhawk IV (P-40N-35): 80 Sqn, Moratai, 1945, Cargill: Q O 71 6/4:35
De Havilland Mosquito FB VI: 1(b) Sqn, Labuan, July 1945, 3 var: AN 20 Jl 73 2/5:5
Mosquito FB 40: 1st Australian-built Mosquito, 1943: AN 20 Jl 73 2/5:5
Mosquito FB 40: 3rd Australian-built Mosquito: AN 20 Jl 73 2/5:5
Douglas Boston III: 22 Sqn: AE D 71 1/7:381
Fairey Battle: 1 BGS, Evans Head, 2 var: Sc Ja 71 2/1:38
Battle: 1 BGS, Evans Head: Sc Ja 71 2/1:40
Battle: 1 BGS, Evans Head, 1941: Sc Ja 71 2/1:40
Battle: 1 OTU, Bairnsdale, 1942: Sc Ja 71 2/1:40
Battle: 2 OTU, Mildura, Vic: Sc Ja 71 2/1:38
Lockheed F-4 Lightning: 1 Photo Recon Unit, Darwin, 1944: AI Je 75 8/6:295
Noorduyn Norseman: RT D 72 5/12:140
North American B-25J: 2 Sqn, NW Asl, spring 1945: AI S 74 7/3:141
Supermarine Spitfire VIII: Burma 1944-45: Sc Ja 75 6/64:21

(Belgium)

Fairey Battle I: 5 Esc, Gr III, 3 Rgt, Evène-Bruxelles, May 1940:

AE Ag 72 3/2:88
Gloster Gladiator I: 1 Esc "La Comète," 2 Rgt, Diest-Schaffen, May 1940: AE Ja 73 4/1:41

(Brazil)

Republic P-47D-25-RE: 1 Gr de Caça, Tarquinia, Italy, Nov 1944: AI Mr 75 8/3:149
Vultee Vengeance Mk II: IM Ag 73 10/8:3

(Bulgaria)

Arado Ar 196A-3: 161 Esk, Varna, spring 1943: AE Ag 73 5/2: 96
Avia B 534 IV: II Rgt, 1941-42: AE D 73 5/6:290-291
Dewoitine D. 520: 3 Sqn, 6 F Orliak, Bojourishté, Feb 1944: AI My 75 8/5:245
Fiesler Storch Fi 156C-3: courier: MW F 73 1/6:297
Junkers Ju 87D-5: against partizans in Bulgaria, summer 1944: AE My 74 6/5:254
Letov Š 328: 161 Esk, Balchic, 1941-42: AE D 73 5/6:287
Messerschmitt Bf 109G-6: 6 Fighter Rgt, Wrasdebna, April 1944: AE D 71 1/7:384
SB-2 (Czech-built): V Orliak, Plovdiv, early 1941: AE Ja 74 6/1: 35

(Canada Bombers)

Avro Lancaster Mk II: 408 (Goose) Sqn: RT S 74 7/9:97
Lancaster Mk II: 408 (Goose) Sqn, Linton-on-Ouse, Yorks, 1943-44, Mill: RT S 74 7/9:97
Bristol Bollingbroke B. IV: 8 (BR) Sqn, Sea Island, B, C., 1942, 4 var: RT F 72 5/2:16
Consolidated Liberator B III: 111 OTU, Nassau, Bahamas, 1943: RT Mr 74 7/3:28
Liberator B. VI: 5 OTU, Abbotsford, B. C., March 1945: RT Mr 74 7/3:29
Liberator B. VI: 5 OTU, Abbotsford, B. C., April 1945: RT Mr 74 7/3:29
Liberator B. VI: 5 OTU, Boundery Bay, B. C., early 1945: RT Mr 74 7/3:29
Liberator GR. V: 111 OTU, Nassau, Bahamas, 1943, 5 var: RT Mr 74 7/3:28
Liberator GR. VIII: 111 OTU, 1945: RT Mr 74 7/3:28
De Havilland Mosquito B. Mk VII: Q Ja 75 10/3:100
Fairey Barracuda Mk III: HMS Nabob, 1944: RT Je 73 7/6:67
Fairey Swordfish Mk II: Naval Air Gunnery School, Yarmouth N. S., 1944: RT Mr 72 5/3:28
Swordfish Mk II: Naval Air Gunnery School, Yarmouth N. S., 1944, 2 var: RT Mr 72 5/3:29; RT Jl 74 7/7:73

III. Color Patterns

Swordfish Mk IV: Naval Air Gunnery School, Yarmouth N. S., 1944: RT Mr 72 5/3:25
Swordfish Mk IV: Naval Air Gunnery School, Yarmouth N. S., 1944, 2 var: RT Mr 72 5/3:28
Swordfish Mk IV: Naval Air Gunnery School, Yarmouth N. S., 1944: RT Mr 72 5/3:30
Swordfish Mk IV: Naval Air Gunnery School, Yarmouth N. S., 1944: RT Mr 72 5/3:29; RT Jl 74 7/7:73
Swordfish Mk IV: 1 Naval Air Gunnery School: 1944: AE N 72 3/5:256
Lockheed Hudson Mk III: Feb 1941 crash (killed insulin-discoverer Fred Banting): RT Je 72 5/6:61
Lockheed Ventura II: ski trials: RT My 71 4/5:52; RT Jl 74 7/7:74
Ventura GR.V: Patricia Bay, Aug 1943: RT My 71 4/5:53
Ventura GR.V: 8(BR) Sqn, Patricia Bay, B.C., June 1944: RT My 71 4/5:54
Ventura GR.V: 34 OTU, Pennfield Ridge, N.B., Aug 1943: RT My 71 4/5:52; RT Jl 74 7/7:74
Ventura GR.V: 115(BR) Sqn, Tofino, May 1944: RT My 71 4/5:54
Ventura GR.V: 145(BR) Sqn, Torbay, Nfld, Aug 1943: RT My 71 4/5:52; RT Jl 74 7/7:74
Vickers Wellington X: 429 (Bison) Sqn, RCAF, Eastmoor, Yorks, April 1943: RT S 75 8/9:108
Westland Wapiti: RCAF Trenton, Ont, Aug 1940: RT F 71 4/2:18
Wapiti: 10 BR Sqn, Halifax N.S., Nov 1939: RT F 71 4/2:18

(Canada Fighters)

Curtiss Kittyhawk: 14(F) Sqn, Alaska, 1942-43, entire sqn: RT S 71 4/9:100
Kittyhawk: 133(F) Sqn, Western Air Command, spring 1945: RT Ap 71 4/4:37
Kittyhawk I: 118(F) Sqn, Annette Island, Alaska, Oct 1942, 2 var: RT Ag 72 5/8:88
Curtiss P-40: 111 (Thunderbird) FS: RT Je 71 4/6:67
P-40: 111 (Thunderbird) Sqn, June 1943: RT Je 71 4/6:67
P-40: 111 (Thunderbird) Sqn, Anchorage, Alaska, Sept 1942: RT Je 71 4/6:66
P-40: 111 (Thunderbird) Sqn, Whitehorse, Yukon, in transit to Alaska: RT Je 71 4/6:66
P-40K: Kodiak, January 1943, Gooding: RT Je 71 4/6:67
Curtiss Tomahawk IIA: 403 Sqn, Baginton, April 1941: AE My 72 2/5:259
Hawker Sea Hurricane Mk X: 126(F) Sqn: RT O 72 5/10:114
Supermarine Spitfire Vb: 401 "Ram" Sqn, Redhill Surrey, July 1943: RT My 72 5/5:49
Spitfire FR IX: 414 (Sarnia Imperials) Sqn, Europe, Feb 1945: RT N 73 6/11:121
Spitfire Mk IX: 416 (City of Oshawa) Sqn, May 1944, northeast France, Lundberg: RT Jl 73 6/7:71; cor Mr 74 7/3:26

Aircraft

(Canada Other Aircraft)

Airspeed Auster Mk VI: RT Ja 72 5/1:10
Airspeed Hotspur II: training glider, Oct 1942-Nov 1945: RT Mr 73 6/3:23
Avro Anson Mk I: 7 Air Observer School, Portage La Prairie, 1941: RT Ag 74 7/8:88
Anson II: 18 Service Flying Training School, Gimli, Aug 1943: Sc F 75 6/65:86
Anson Mk V: 7 Air Observer School, Portage La Prairie, 1945: RT Ag 74 7/8:88
Blackburn Shark II: target tug of 122 Sqn, Patricia Bay, B.C., Dec 1941: RT N 71 4/11:121
Cessna Crane I (Bobcat): 2TC: RT O 75 8/10:119
Crane I: 147(BR) Sqn: RT O 75 8/10:118
Crane IA: CFS: RT O 75 8/10:119
Crane IA: 2 TC: RT O 75 8/10:117
Consolidated Canso (Catalina): std camouflage for coastal aircraft, May 1943: RT D 74 7/12:141
Canso: 1943 std: RT D 74 7/12:141
Canso: Torbay, Nfld, March 1944: RT D 74 7/12:142
Canso: 162 Sqn, Camp Maple Leaf near Reykjavik, Iceland, Oct 1944, 2 var: RT D 74 7/12:142
Consolidated PB2B-2 Catalina V: RT D 72 5/12:142
Fairey Battle T: 3 Bombing & Gunnery School, MacDonald, 1943: AE Ag 72 3/2:88
Battle T: 8 Service Flying Training School, Moncton, mid-1943: AE Ag 72 3/2:88
Fleet 60 Fort: last one made: RT D 75 8/12:143
North American Harvard Mk 2: 1 Training Command, Trenton, Ont, early 1941: RT O 72 5/10:109
Spartan 7W Executive: RCAF Malton, late 1943, early 1944: RT S 75 8/9:104

(China)

Curtiss Hawk 81A-3: 1 PS, AVG, Magwe, Burma, 1942: AE My 72 2/5:257
Hawk 81A-3: 2 PS, AVG, Toungoo, Burma, 1942, Geselbracht: AE My 72 2/5:257
Hawk 81A-3: 3 PS, AVG, Mingaladon, Burma, Jan 1942, Older: AE My 72 2/5:257
Hawk 85A-5: Kunming, 1942: AE N 71 1/6:313
Hawk III: 1940: AE O 72 3/4:205
Kawasaki Ki-61-Ib: AN 1 F 74 2/18:9
Lockheed F-5E Lightning: summer 1945: AI Je 75 8/6:294

(Croatian Co-Belligerent)

Messerschmitt Bf 109G-10/U4: kroatJagdstaffel, Eichwalde, Nov 1944: AE D 71 1/7:384

III. Color Patterns

(Finland)

Brewster B-239 Buffalo: std camouflage, incl sten: Q O 72 7/4: 160-161
B-239: MW D 73 2/4:180
B-239: LeLv 24, Luukkanen: Afx Mr 74 15/7:404-405
B-239: 1/LeLv 24, 1941: Q O 73 8/4:214
B-239: 1/LLv 24: Luukkanen: Q O 72 7/4:162
B-239: 1/LLv 24, Selänpää airfield, July 1941, Sarvanto: IM N 72 9/11:10-11
B-239: 1/LLv 24, June-Nov 1942, Luukkanen; Nov 1942-May 1943, Wind; 3/LLv 24, May 1943-May 1944, Wind: IM N 72 9/11: 8-9
B-239: 2/LLv 24, Nissinen: Q O 72 7/4:162
B-239: 3/LeLv 24, 1941: Q O 73 8/4:214
B-239: 3/LLv 24, Katajainen: Q O 72 7/4:163
B-239: 3/LLv 24, Sept 1943, Wind: Q O 72 7/4:163
B-239: 3/LLv 24, Juutilainen: Q O 72 7/4:162
B-239: 3/LLv 24, Karhunen: Q O 72 7/4:162
B-239: 3/LLv 24, Eastern Karelia, June 1942, Juutilainen: IM N 72 9/11:8-9
B-239: 4/LeLv 24, 1941: Q O 73 8/4:214
B-239: 4/LLv 24: Magnusson (CO of LLv 24): Q O 72 7/4:163
B-239: 4/LLv 24, Karelian Isthmus, aut 1941, Sovelius: IM N 72 9/11:10-11
B-239: Osato L, April 1940 - June 1942, Luukkanen: Q Jl 74 10/1:12
B-239: CO, recon sqn, LeLv 30, June-Oct 1942, Luukkanen: Q Jl 74 10/1:13
Bristol Bulldog IVA: TLeLv 35, spring 1942: AE F 73 4/2:93
Curtiss Hawk 75A: 1/HLeLv 32, June 1944: RT Jl 73 6/7:78
Hawk 75A: 3/HLeLv 32, June 1944: RT Jl 73 6/7:77
Hawk 75A: 1/LeLv 32, summer 1943, Koskinen: RT Jl 73 6/7:77
Hawk 75A: 1/LeLv 32, Nurmoila, summer 1942: RT Jl 73 6/7:77
Hawk 75A: 1/LeLv 32, Nurmoila, summer 1942, Erkinheimo: RT Jl 73 6/7:78
Hawk 75A: 2/LeLv 32, Nurmoila, summer 1942: RT Jl 73 6/7:77
Hawk 75A: 2/LeLv 32, Nurmoila, July 1942: RT Jl 73 6/7:78
Hawk 75A: 3/LeLv 32, Aug 1941: RT Jl 73 6/7:77
Hawk 75A: 3/LeLv 32, aut 1943: RT Jl 73 6/7:78
Hawk 75A: 3/LeLv 32, Nurmoila, summer 1942, Karhila: RT Jl 73 6/7:77
Hawk 75A-3: HLeLv 32, Nurmoila, winter 1942-43: AE N 71 1/6: 313
Dornier Do 17Z-2: PLeLv 46, 1943: AN 9 Je 1/2:10
Fiat G. 50, FA-17: LeLv 16 (Lentorykmentii 3), Ilmavoimat, summer 1942: AE Je 74 6/6:306
Fiat G. 50: 1/LeLv 26, summer 1943: Afx Mr 74 15/7:405
Fiat G. 50: 2/LeLv 26, autumn 1941: Afx Mr 74 15/7:405
Fiat G. 50: 2/LeLv 26, autumn 1941: Afx Mr 74 15/7:405
Fiesler Fi 156C Storch: AF HQ, 1942: Afx Ja 75 16/5:291
Gloster Gladiator I: 1/LeLv 16, summer 1942: Afx Je 73 14/10: 548

Aircraft

Hawker Hurricane I: HLeLv 26, Malmi, 1942-43: Q Ja 72 7/1:33
Junkers Ju 88A-4: PLeLv 43, 1943: AN 3 Ag 73 2/6:7
Messerschmitt Bf 109G-2: CO, HLeLv 34, March 1943 - March 1944, Luukkanen: Q Jl 74 10/1:13
Bf 109G-2: 1/HLeLv 34, Ilmavoimat, Halmi-Helsinki, summer 1943: AE Je 73 4/6:301
Bf 109G-6: HLeLv 34, April-June 1944, Luukkanen: Q Jl 74 10/1:13
Mörkö Moraani (MSv-637): HLeLv 28, Luonetjärvi, autumn 1944: AE O 73 5/4:187
Westland Lysander I: 2/LeLv 16, summer 1942: Afx Ja 75 16/5:294

(France, Free French)

Amiot 143: GB I/34: Q W 75 11/2:68
Amiot 143: GM II/35: Q W 75 11/2:68
Bell P-39N: GC II/6 "Travail," 3 Esc, FAFL, 1943: AE Ag 71 1/3:136
Bloch 152: 3 Esc, II/1, Etampes, May 1940: AE F 74 6/2:90
Bloch 152: 3 Esc, II/8, Marignane, early 1941: AE F 74 6/2:90
Bloch MB 152: 3 Esc, GC II/8: Q W 75 11/2:63
Bloch 152: 4 Esc, II/1, Laon, May 1940: AE F 74 6/2:90
Bloch 152: 6 Esc, III/9, Sept 1940: AE F 74 6/2:91
Bloch MB 152: CG II/9: Q W 75 11/2:63
Bloch MB 152: CG III/10: Q W 75 11/2:63
Breguet Bre 693: 4 Sec, GBA II/54, Roye, May 1940: AE My 73 4/5:252
Breguet Bre 693 AB 2: 2 Esc, GBA I/51, 1940: Q W 75 11/2:64
Curtiss Hawk 75A-1: 1 Esc, GC II/5, winter 1939-40: AE N 71 1/6:316
Curtiss Hawk 75A-1: 2 Esc, GC II/5, 1939: Q W 75 11/2:61
Hawk 75A-1: Feb 1940: Q W 75 11/2:61
Hawk 75A-3: 1 Esc, GC I/5, Casablanca, Morocco, summer 1941: AE N 71 1/6:316
Hawk 75A-3: 1 Esc, GC 1/5: Q W 75 11/2:63
Hawk 75A-3: 1 Esc, GC II/4: Q W 75 11/2:63
Hawk 75A-3: 2 Esc, GC I/4, Casablanca, Morocco, spring 1941: AE N 71 1/6:316
Dewoitine D. 520: SNCASE, Toulouse, June 1940: AI My 75 8/5:244
D. 520: GC Doret, Toulouse-Blagnac, Sept 1944: AI My 75 8/5:245
D. 520: GC I/3, Cannes-Mandelieu, April-May 1940: AI My 75 8/5:245
D. 520: 3 Esc, GC II/7, Gabés, Tunisia, autumn 1942: AI My 75 8/5:245
D. 520C: GC I/3, May 1940: Q W 75 11/2:63
Douglas DB-7: 1 Esc, GM II/19: Q W 75 11/2:68
Junkers Ju 88 A: I/3 "Aunis" Gr de Bomb, FFI, winter 1944-45, attack on Bordeaux: RT Je 73 6/6:68

III. Color Patterns

Liore-et-Olivier LeO 451: GB II/31: Q W 75 11/2:64
LeO 451: GB II/31: Q W 75 11/2:68
Martin 167: GB I/39, Syria, 1940: Q W 76 11/2:68
Lockheed F-5G Lightning: Gr de Recon II/33, Colmar, spring 1945: AI Je 75 8/6:294
Martin Maryland VIP transport: North Africa, 1942, Jannequin: RT F 75 8/2:22
Messerschmitt Bf 109E: Orleans-Bricy, Dec. 1939: PAM O 75 11:187
Morane Saulnier MS 406: factory finish, Puteaux: Q W 75 11/2:60
MS 406: factory finish SNCAO/Bouguenais, 2 var: Q W 75 11/2:60
MS 406: CO, GC II/3: Q W 75 11/2:61
MS 406: GC III/1: Q W 75 11/2:61
MS 406C: 3 Esc, GC II/2: Q W 75 11/2:60
MS 406C1: 1 Esc, I/2, Nimes, July 1940: AE O 73 5/4:187
Morane-Saulnier MS 500 (ex-Fi 156C-7 Storch): GR 3/33 "Perigord," Forces Française de l'Atlantique, Nov 1944-May 1945: MW F 73 1/6:296
North American Mitchell III: 342 (Lorraine) Sqn, Gilze Rijen, Netherlands, April 1945: AI S 74 7/3:137
Potez 631: ECN I/13, late May, 1940: Q W 75 11/2:64
Potez 631: GC II/7, late 1939: Q W 75 11/2:61
Vought V-156: AB3, Aeronavale: Q W 75 11/2:64
Vultee Vengeance: Fort Leote, North Africa, 1943: IM Ap 73 10/8:3

(France, Vichy)

Bloch 152: 2 Esc, II/1, Bron, 1942: AE F 74 6/2:91
Bloch 152: 4 Esc, II/8, Marignane, June 1942: AE F 74 6/2:91
Breguet Bre 693: 2 Esc, GBA I/51, Lézignan, 1942: AE My 73 4/5:252
Curtiss Hawk 75A-3: CO, GC I/4, Dakar, Senegal, 1941, Stehlin: AE N 71 1/6:316
Hawk 75A-3: 2 Esc, GC II/4, Dakar, Senegal, summer 1942: AE N 71 1/6:316
Dewoitine D. 520: 5 Esc, GC III/6, Rayak, Syria, June 1941: AI My 75 8/5:245
D. 520: 6 Esc, GC III/6, Rayak, Syria, June 1941: AI My 75 8/5:244
Morane Saulnier MS 406C1: Sec D'Entrainement, Toulouse, 1941: AE O 73 5/4:187

(Germany Bombers)

Arado Ar 234B-2 Blitz: CO, KG 76, Achmer, May 1945, Kowalewski: Aero Mr 73 37/434:150
Ar 234B-2: 9 Staffel III/KG 76, Segelsdorf, Feb 1945: Aero Mr 72 37/434/151

Aircraft

Dornier Do 17F-1: unit unknown: AN 9 Je 72 1/2:10
Do 17P: 4/II, FernAufklärungsgruppe 121, prob Polish invasion with Lehr Div: Q Ja 73 8/1:25
Do 17P-2: factory finish: AN 9 Je 72 1/2:10
Do 17Z-1: 1 Staffel, I/KG 53, Lille, Sept 1940: PAM Jl 75 10: 167
Do 17Z-2: Stab/KG 3: AN 9 Je 1/2:10
Do 17Z-2: 2 Croatian Volunteer Formation, 15/KG 53: AN 9 Je 72 1/2:10
Focke Wulf Fw 190A-4/U3: 10 (Jabo)/JG 54, early 1943: PAM O 75 11:191
Fw 190A-5/U3: 1 Staffel, 1/SKG 10, Dreux, late 1943: PAM O 75 11:191
Heinkel He 111H: KG 26, Firth of Forth raid, Oct 1939: RT Ja 74 7/1:4
He 111H-2: III/KG 53, Battle of Britain, summer 1940: Sc S 71 2/9:278-279
He 111H-3: 2 Staffel, I/KG 53, Lille, Sept 1940: PAM Jl 75 10: 167
He 111H-6: 2/KG 26, Ottana, Sardinia, Aug 1943: AE N 73 5/5: 237
He 111H-8: Afx Ag 75 16/12:707
He 111H-8: downed in England, autumn 1940: Afx Ag 75 16/12: 706
He 111H-8: Geschwader Boelcke: Afx Ag 75 16/12:703
He 111H-22 & Fi 103; V-1 bomb launcher: KG 53, 1944-45: IM Ag 71 9/8:8-9
He 111P-2: KG 55, Dreux, Chartres & Villacoublay, autumn 1940: AE N 73 5/5:237
Henschell Hs 123A-1: Schlachtgruppe unknown, Russian front, 1942-43: MW Mr 73 1/7:352
Hs 123A-1: Luftdienstkommando 67, Rerik/Mecklberg area, 1940-1041: MW Mr 73 1/7:352
Hs 123A-1: G 1, Russian front, 1941: MW Mr 73 1/7:352
Hs 123A-1: II(Schlacht)/LG2, 1st ground support in WW-II, Alt-Rosenberg, Sept 1939: MW Mr 73 1/7:351
Hs 123A-1: II/SG 2, eastern front, 1944, 1944: MW Mr 73 1/7: 353
Hs 123A-1: II/SG 2, Menapace: MW Mr 73 1/7:353
Hs 123A-1: prob II/SG 2, Russian front, 1944: MW Mr 73 1/7: 352
Junkers Ju 86E-2: Neubrachenbury, 1940: AN 18 Ag 72 1/7:10
Junkers Ju 87B: RCS D 75 1/8:(40-41)
Ju 87B-1: 9 Staffel II/G 1, Pas-de-Calais, Sept 1940, Blumers & Koch: PAM Jl 75 10:165
Ju 87D-1: III/StG 3, eastern front, spring 1942: AE My 74 6/5: 254
Ju 87D-1/trop: 8/StG 3, Libya, mid 1942: AE My 74 6/5:254
Ju 87D-3: II/2 "Immelmann," Stalingrad area, autumn-winter 1942: AI Jl 74 7/1:322
Junkers Ju 88A-1: Stab I/KG 30: AN 3 Ag 73 2/6:7
Ju 88A-1: 2 Staffel, I/KG 77, Laon, Aug 1940: PAM Jl 75 10:167
Ju 88A-4: II/KG 30, Gilze-Rijen, Sept, 1940: IM Mr 72 9/3:8

III. Color Patterns

Ju 88A-4: IV/10 KG 1, Russia, 1944: AN 3 Ag 73 2/6:7
Ju 88A-4/trop: KLG.1, Libya, 1942: AN 3 Ag 73 2/6:7
Junkers Ju 188A-1: 6/KG 200: Sc Je 75 6/69:284-285
Ju 188E-1: Erprobungstaffel KG 6: Sc Je 75 6/69:284-285
Messerschmitt Bf 109 F-4/B: 10 (Jabo), JG 2, Beaumont-le-Roger, early 1942: PAM O 75 11:191
Bf 109F-4/B: St. Kap. 10 (Jabo)/JG 2, Beaumont, France, March 1942, Liesendahl: RT Ja 71 4/1:1
Mistel I: Bf 109F/Ju 88A-4, Einsats Staffel, N/KG 101, spring 1944: PAM Ja 75 8:128
Mistel II: Fw 190A-6/Ju 88G-1, II/KG 200, early 1945: PAM Ja 75 8:128
Mistel S3A: Fw 190A-6/Ju-88A5, PAM Ja 75 8:129

(Germany Captured Aircraft)

Avia B 534 IV: 3/JG 71, Eutingen, Nov 1939: AE D 73 5/6:291
Bloch 152: AE F 74 6/2:91
Bloch 152: ex II/8 Vichy: AE F 74 6/2:91
Boeing B-17F: KG 200: Q Ja 72 7/1:31
Consolidated B-24G: Q Ja 72 7/1:30
B-24H: KG 200, Berphaffenhfen, Germany: Q Ja 72 7/1:30
Dewoitine D.520: JG 105, Chartres, May 1944: AI My 75 8/5:245
Fokker G1: AI N 74 7/5:243
Fokker G1: Flugzeugführerschule (B) 8, Wiener Neustadt: AI N 74 7/5:243
Lockheed P-38E: Sonderkommando Rosarius, 1943-44: AI Je 75 8/6:295
North American NAA-64 (AT-6): Q Ja 72 7/1:31
Republic P-47D: Q Ja 7/1:31
P-47D: Sond. Aufkl. St. 103, Orly, spring 1944: AI Mr 75 8/3:149
P-47D: 2/Vers. Verb. Ob. d. L (Long Range Recce Test Unit), Hustedt, Sept 1944: AI Mr 75 8/3:148
Short Stirling Mk I: (ex 7 Sqn, RAF) Erprobungsselle, Rechlin, Sept 1942: IM O 73 10/10:4-5
Stirling I: Gilze Rijen, mid 1942: AN 19 Ja 72 1/19:9
Vickers Wellington MK IA: (ex 331 Sqn, RAF) late 1940: AN 4 Ag 72 1/6:10

(Germany Fighters)

(Multi-Engine)
Dornier Do 335 V1 Pfeil: 1st prototype: Sc Jl 75 6/70:353
Do 335 V3: 3rd prototype: Sc Jl 75 6/70:353
Do 335 V3: 1 Staffle/Versuchsverband Ob.d.L.: Sc Jl 75 6/70:349
Do 335 V13: prototype for B-1 series: Sc Jl 75 6/70:354
Do 335A-0: 2nd production: Sc Jl 75 6/70:355
Heinkel He 219 Uhu: 1/NJG 1: AN 23 Ag 74 3/6:8
He 219 V4: ejection seat trials, Rechlin, 1943-44: AN 23 Ag 74 3/6:8

Aircraft

He 219A-0: Streib: AN 23 Ag 74 3/6:8
He 219A-2: 1/NJG 1, Knokke/Sylt, spring 1945: RT D 71 4/12: 140
He 219A-7/R4: 1/NJG 1: AN 23 Ag 74 3/6:8
Henschel Hs 129B-1: 8/Sch. G. 2, Tunis-Aounnia, Feb 1943: MW S 72 1/1:16
Hs 129B-1/R2: 4(Pz)/Sch. G. 1, eastern front, winter 1942-43: MW S 72 1/1:15
Hs 129B-1/R4: 4/Sch. G. 2, Tripoli, Jan 1943: MW S 72 1/1:16
Hs 129B-2/R2: Staffel kapt 10(Pz)/SG 9, Russian front, 1944, Ruffer: MW S 72 1/1:15
Hs 129B-2/R2: 4/Sch. G. 1, eastern front, summer 1943: MW S 72 1/1:15
Hs 129B-2/R2: 8/Sch. G. 1, Russia, early 1943: MW S 72 1/1:15
Hs 129B-3/Wa: Gruppe Stab IV(Pz)/SG 9, Russia, 1944-45: MW S 72 1/1:16
Junkers Ju 88C-6c: 4/NJG I/II Gruppe, Defence of Reich, 1944: IM Mr 72 9/3:10
Junkers Ju 88G-7a: NJG 3: RT D 71 4/12:143; cor Ja 72 5/1:2
Messerschmitt Bf 109Z: Afx Jl 72 13/11:611
Messerschmitt Bf 110: 1/ZG 52, May-June 1940: MW O 72 2/2:72
Bf 110B-1: 30mm cannon test bed: MW O 72 2/2:72
Bf 110B-3: Erganzungs (Replacement) Staffle, autumn 1940: MW O 72 2/2:72
Bf 110C: 1/NJG 1, Western Desert, 1941-42: MW D 72 2/4:179
Bf 110C: 1/ZG 52, May-June 1940: MW O 72 2/2:75
Bf 110C: 1/ZG 79, Russian front, autumn 1941, Specht: MW N 72 2/3:123
Bf 110C-1: 1/ZG 76, Polish campaign, 1939, Reinecke: MW O 72 2/2:75
Bf 110C-3: 3/ZG 26 "Horst Wessel," Lenham, Kent, Sept 1940: MW O 72 2/2:73
Bf 110C-4: 6 Staffel II/ZG 76, Abbeville, Sept 1940, Piduhn & Conde: PAM Jl 75 10:165
Bf 110C-4/B: 2/Erg.G 210, attack on Bristol Aircraft, Sept 1940, Rossinger: MW O 72 2/2:73
Bf 110C-4/B: 8/ZG 26, Oct 1940: MW O 72 2/2:73
Bf 110C-5: 3/(F)/22, Dno, Russia, Feb 1942, Fischer: MW N 72 2/3:123
Bf 110D: NJG 6, Kitzingen, Jan 1944, Weinmann: RT N 73 6/11:124
Bf 110D: NJG 6, Otopeni, April 1944, Weinmann: RT F 74 7/2:17
Bf 110D: NJG 6, Zilistea, April 1944, Weinmann: RT N 73 6/11:124
Bf 110D: NJG 6, Zilistea, April 1944, Weinmann: RT F 74 7/2:17
Bf 110D: II/SKG 210, Russia, Oct 1941, Tonne, rudder only: WW2J S 75 2/5-6:18
Bf 110D-0: 1/ZG 76, April-May 1940: MW O 72 2/2:72
Bf 110D-1/R1: 3/ZG 76, Aalbord, Denmark, Aug 1940: MW O 72 2/2:72
Bf 110D-3: 7/III/ZG 26, Mediterranean patrols, 1941: MW N 72

III. Color Patterns

2/3:123
Bf 110E: Staff I/Schlachtgeschwader I, Russia, 1941-42: MW N 72 2/3:123
Bf 110E-1: 1/SKG 210, Seschtinskaya, Russian front, Sept 1941, Schenck: MW O 72 2/2:75
Bf 110E-1: 9/ZG 26, Daba, North Africa: MW N 72 2/3:123
Bf 110F-1: 3/SKG 210, Russia, summer 1943: MW N 72 2/3:124
Bf 110G: Kitzingen, Dec 1944, Weinmann: RT S 74 7/9:104
Bf 110G: RJG 6, Gerolshofen, Feb 1945, Weinmann: RT My 75 8/5:56
Bf 110G-2: 5/ZG 1, Italy, summer 1943: MW N 72 2/3:124
Bf 110G-2: 7/NJG 1, German, day operations, summer 1943: MW D 72 2/4:179
Bf 110G-2/R3: Waffenwanne 151Z: 9/ZG 26, day interceptor, Germany, summer 1943: MW N 72 2/3:124
Bf 110G-3: Kunstenstaffle Krim, coastal recon & anti-shipping, Crimea, Aug 1943: MW N 72 2/3:124
Bf 110G-4: NJG 4, 1945, Schaufer: MW D 72 2/4:180
Bf 110G-4a: Russian front, with 8/NJG 1 codes, but not that unit: MW D 72 2/4:179
Bf 110G-4b/R3: 5/NJG 6, interned Switzerland, April 1944, Johnen: MW D 72 2/4:180
Bf 110G-4b/R3: Gruppenkommandeur III/NJG 1, Loan-Athies, March 1944, Drewes: MW D 72 2/4:179
Bf 110G-4c/R3: 7/NJG 1, late in war: MW D 72 2/4:180
Bf 110G-4d/R3: Einsatz Kommando NJG 101, late in war: MW D 72 2/4:181
Bf 110G-4d/R3: 1/NJG 4: MW D 72 2/4:180
Bf 110G-4d/R3: 2/NJG 5: MW D 72 2/4:181
Bf 110G-4d/R3: II/NJG 7, Gruppe Adjutant: MW D 72 2/4:180

(single-engine)
Focke Wulf Fw 190A: Staffelkaptain, 9/JG2 "Richthofen," France, July 1943, Wurmheller, rudder only: WW2J S 75 2/5-6:18
Fw 190A-4: I/JG 1, Arnheim, 1942: Q W 75 11/2:54
Fw 190A-8: Stab/JG 2: AI Ja 75 8/1:38
Fw 190A-8: I/JG 6: AI Ja 75 8/1:38
Fw 190A-8: I/JG 1: AI Ja 75 8/1:38
Fw 190A-8: 1/JG 11, Darmstadt, spring 1945: RT F 72 5/2:13
Fw 190A-8: II/JG 4: AI Ja 75 8/1:38
Fw 190A-8: III/JG 11: AI Ja 75 8/1:38
Fw 190D-9: II/JG 26: AI Ja 75 8/1:39
Fw 190D-9: III/JG 2: AI Ja 75 8/1:38
Fw 190D-9: III/JG 54: AI Ja 75 8/1:39
Fw 190F: unit unknown, Russian front, Klassen: RT My 75 8/5:52
Fw 190F-8: SG 4: AI Ja 75 8/1:39
Focke Wulf Ta 152 v20: B-5/R11 prototype: Afx Mr 71 12/7:350
Ta 152C-0/R11: Afx Mr 71 12/7:350
Ta 152H-1: exhibited at Farnborough, Oct 1945: Afx Mr 71 12/7:350
Ta 152H: 2 Staffel I/JG 301, spring 1945: Afx Mr 71 12/7:350
Henschell Hs 123: (S)LG 2, Polish campaign, Sept 1030: RT Jl 71

4/7:76
Hs 123A: A/B 71, Prosanitz, Moravia, sum 1941: AE S 72 3/3: 152
Hs 123A: 5(Schlact)/LG 2, St. Trond, Belgium, May 1940: AE S 72 3/3:152
Messerschmitt Bf 109D-1: A/B 123 (kroat), Agram Zagreb, March 1942: AE Mr 74 6/3:137
Bf 109D-1: JFS I, Werneuchen, 1940: AE Mr 74 6/3:137
Bf 109D-1: I/JGr 102, Bernburg, 1939: AE Mr 74 6/3:137
Bf 109D-1: 10(N)JG 26, Jerver, autumn 1939: AE Mr 74 6/3:137
Bf 109E: Staff Flight II/JG 77, 1942-43: IM Ja 71 8/1:7
Bf 109E: 11/JG 54, Woerth, France, Nov 1939: PAM O 75 11: 187
Bf 109E-1: CO, 3/JG 2, July-Aug 1940, Wick: Q W 75 11/2:82
Bf 109E-3: unit unstated, Wick: RT O 72 5/10:116
Bf 109E-3: Wick, prob fake: Q W 75 11/2:82
Bf 109E-3: JG 2 "Richthofen," Aug-Nov 1940, 5 var, Wick: Q Jl 72 7/3:93; cor O 72 7/4:127
Bf 109E-3: 2 Staffel I/JG 52, Coquelles, Aug 1940, Zaunbrecher: PAM Jl 75 10:165
Bf 109E-4: Gruppenkommandeur, I/JG 2, Sept 1940, Wick: Q W 75 11/2:82
Bf 109E-4: Gruppenkommandeur, I/JG 2, Oct, 1940, Wick: Q W 75 11/2:82
Bf 109E-4: Geschwader Kommodore, JG 2, Nov 1940, Wick: Q W 75 11/2:82
Bf 109E-4/B: 4 II(s)/JG 3, Mörschel: Afx N 72 14/3:146
Bf 109E-4/trop: I/JG 27, North Africa, July 1941, Franzisket: Q Ap 71 6/2:12
Bf 109E-4b/Trop: Stab /II Schlechtgeschwader 2, Libya, 1941: PAM O 73 3:33
Bf 109F: 4/JG 54: Q Ap 71 6/2:10
Bf 109F: Staffelkapitan, 7/JG 58 "Grunherz," Russia, May 1942, Osterman; rudder only: WW2J S 75 2/5-6:18
Bf 109F-2/trop: I/JG 27, North Africa, late 1941, Neumann: Q Ap 71 6/2:12
Bf 109F-2/trop: I/JG 27, North Africa, Dec 1941, Espenlaub: Q Ap 71 6/2:13
Bf 109F-2/trop: 3 JG 27, North Africa, Feb 1942, Holmuth: Q Ap 71 6/2:13
Bf 109F-4/trop: II/JG 27, North Africa, May 1942, Düllberg: Q Ap 71 6/2:14
Bf 109F-4/trop: 7 JG 27, North Africa, May 1942, Sinner: Q Ap 71 6/2:14
Bf 109G-2: II/JG 54 "Grünherz," Siverskaya, Russia, autumn 1942: AE Je 63 4/6:301
Bf 109G-2/trop: II/JG 52 "Mölders," Casa Zeppera, Sardinia, summer 1943: AE Je 73 4/6:301
Bf 109G-5: I/JG 52, Leipzig, Rumania, summer 1944: AE D 71 1/7:384
Bf 109G-6: IV/JG 5, Petsamo, Russia, winter 1943-44: AE Je 73 4/6:301
Bf 109G-6/R2: 9 Staffle, III/JG 3 "Udet," Bad Worishoften, spring

III. Color Patterns 246

1944: PAM Jl 74 6:82
Bf 109G-6/R6/trop: 7 Staffle, III/JG 27, Fels a/Wagram, Vienna, Aug 1944: PAM Jl 74 6:82
Bf 109G-6U4: 9/JG 3: Q Ap 71 6/2:10
Bf 109G-10: I/JG 3: AI Ja 75 8/1:38
Bf 109G-14: II/NJG 11, Müller: Afx N 72 14/3:146
Bf 109G-14: III/JG 27: AI Ja 75 8/1:39
Bf 109G-14/U4: 4/JG unknown: Q Ap 71 6/2:10
Bf 109G-U4/N: 6/JG 300: Afx N 72 14/3:146
Bf 109K: II/JG 77, northern Germany: Q Ap 71 6/2:8-9
Bf 109K-2 (or 4): Q Ap 71 6/2:11
Bf 109K-4: I/JG 27: AI Ja 75 8/1:38
Bf 109K-4: II/JG 77: AI Ja 75 8/1:39

(Reaction-Power)
Heinkel He 162: II/JG 1, Leck, 1945: AN 29 Mr 74 2/22:8-9
He 162 V1: Dec 1944, Peter: AN 29 Mr 74 2/22:8-9
He 162A-2: Junkers-built: AN 29 Mr 74 2/22:9
He 162A-2: I/JG 1W: AN 29 Mr 74 2/22:8-9
He 162A-2: III/JG 1 Demuth, or Stab/JG 1, Hatchl: AN 29 Mr 74 2/22:8-9
Messerschmitt Me 163B-0: Q Ja 71 6/1:7
Me 163B-1: Q Jl 71 6/1:7
Me 163B-1: Q Ja 71 6/1:8
Me 163B-1a: Q Ja 71 6/1:7
Me 163B-1a: Erprobungskommando 16, 1944-1945: Q Ja 71 6/1:7
Me 163B-1a: JG 400, 1945: Q Ja 71 6/1:7
Me 163B-1a: 2/JG 400, 1945: Q Ja 71 6/1:7
Me 163Ba-1 (V 35): test unit: Q Ja 71 6/1:7
Me 163Ba-1: 1/JG 400, 1945: Q Ja 71 6/1:7
Messerschmitt Me 262A-1a: pos JG 44: Q W 75 11/2:54
Me 262B-1a/U1 Schwalbe: 10 Staffel, NJG 11, Magedburg, April 1945: AI Ap 75 8/4:196-197

(Germany Observation & Rescue)

Aerodynamische Versuchsanstalt AF 2: boundary layer experiment Storch mod, Gottingen: MW F 73 1/6:295
Arado Ar 196A-3: 1/Bordfliegergruppe 196, Loften Islands, Norway, Feb 1944: AE Ag 73 5/2:96
Ar 196A-3: 2/SAGr 125, Aegean, 1942: AE Ag 73 5/2:96
Fiesler Fi 156A Storch: 5 Staffel, 11 Gruppe, FernAufklärungs-gruppe 120, Germany, 1941: Q Ja 73 8/1:24
Fi 156C-1: Geschwaderstab, Lehrgeschwader 2, 1939: MW Ja 73 1/5:237
Fi 156C-3: courier for 1. Gruppe/JG 54, Russia 1942-43: MW Ja 73 1/5:237
Fi 156C-3: Heeresaufklärungsgruppe 41, France, May 1940: MW Ja 73 1/5:237
Fi 156C-3: Geschwaderstab, Luftlandegeschwader 1, Russian front, 1943: MW Ja 73 1/5:237
Fi 156C-3: Kurierstaffel Ob d. L, Don Sector, Aug 1942: AI Ap

75 8&3:200
Fi 156C-3/Trop: 2 (H)/14, Afrika Korps, March-May 1941: AI Ap 75 8/4:200
Fi 156C-5/Trop: Afrika Korps: MW Ja 73 1/5:238
Fi 156C-5/Trop: 1. Wustennotstaffle, North Africa, desert rescue sqn: MW Ja 73 1/5:237
Fi 156C-7: Panserfaust carrier, prob. PanzerAufklärungsschwarme, Luftflotten-Kommando 6, spring 1945: MW F 73 1/6:297
Fi 156D-0: Mediterranean, 1941: MW Ja 73 1/5:238
Fi 156D-1: ambulance flight unknown, Russia, with Luftflotte 4: MW Ja 73 1/5:239
Fi 156D-1: Tunisia, early 1943: MW Ja 73 1/5:238
Fi 156E-0: tracked landing gear experiment: MW F 73 1/6:295
Focke Wulf Fw 189 V1b: after modifications, Bremen, 1939: MW S 73 2/1:34
Fw 189 V6: prototype for C series, early 1940: MW S 73 2/1:34
Fw 189A: Stab I/NJG 100; Greifswald, Feb 1945: AI O 74 7/4:189
Fw 189A-1: factory finish, March 1941: MW Ag 73 1/12:633
Fw 189A-1: factory for tropical operation, Oct 1941: MW Ag 73 1/12:634
Fw 189A-1: unit unknown, Russian front, 1941-42: MW N 73 2/3:129
Fw 189A-1: General Kesselring private transport, Russian front: MW N 73 2/3:127
Fw 189A-1: NAGr I, Dnepropetrovsk, Ukraine, March 1943: AE Ap 73 4/4:193
Fw 189A-1: 1(H)/13: Russian front, summer 1942: MW N 73 2/3:127
Fw 189A-1: 1(H)/32, Kemi, Central Finland, June 1942: AE Ap 73 4/4:193
Fw 189A-1: 1(H)/32, Petsamo, Northern Finland, Dec 1942: AI O 74 7/4:189
Fw 189A-1: 5(H)/12, Eastern front, 1941: MW Ag 73 1/12:634
Fw 189A-1: 5(H)/12, Poltava, Ukraine, summer 1942: AI O 74 7/4:189
Fw 189A-1: Nachtkette/NAGr 15, VIII Fliegerkorps, Naglowitz, southern Poland, Oct 1944: AI O 74 7/4:189
Fw 189A-2: 1(H)/31, Rostov area, Jan 1943: AI O 74 7/4:189
Fw 189A-2: 1(H)/32, Finland, 1942: MW Ag 73 1/12:634
Fw 189A-2: 1(H)/32, White Sea area, 1942: MW N 73 2/3:129
Fw 189A-2: 2(H)/31, Russia, prob winter 1942: MW Ag 73 1/12:634
Fw 189A-2: NAG 3, 1942: MW Ag 73 1/12:633
Fw 189B-1: delivery, late 1939: MW S 73 2/1:34
Fw 189F-1: Kunstenstaffel Krim, Russian front, 1942: MW N 73 2/3:127
Heinkel He 59B-2: factory finish: AN 24 N 72 1/14:10
He 59C-2: ASR with civil registration, North Sea, 1940: AN 24 N 72 1/14:10
He 59D-1: Seenostaffel unknown, ASR operations, early WW-II: AN 24 N 72 1/14:10
Heinkel He 70E-1 Blitz: A/B 116, Göppingen, winter 1940-41: AI

III. Color Patterns

F 75 8./2:90
Henschel Hs 126A-1:   2(H)/14, North Africa, July 1941:   AI F 75 8/2:87
Hs 126A-1:   2(H)/31 Pz, Greece, April 1941:   AI F 75 8/2:87
Hs 126B-1:   2/NAGr 12, Graz, April 1945:   AI F 75 8/2:87
Hs 126B-1:   3(H)/21, Don Front, Jan 1943:   AI F 75 8/2:87

(Germany Other Aircraft)

Arado Ar 96B-1:   unit unknown: AN 27 Ap 73 1/25:8-9
Ar 96B-1:   FFS A/B 23, Kaufbeuren, 1943:   AN 27 Ap 73 1/25:8-9
Ar 96B-5:   school unknown, 1943:   AN 27 Ap 73 1/25:8-9
Avia B-71:   prob Fliegerzielgeschwader 1, target tug, 1940-41: AE Ja 74 6/1:35
Avia B 534/IV: Jagdschulgeschwader 71:   IM Ag 71 8/8:2
DFS 230B: troop glider of unknown unit: Q Ja 73 8/1:25
DFS 230B: unit unknown, Comiso, Italy, 1942:   Q Ja 73 8/1:25
Fiat CR. 42:   I/NSGr 7, Banya-Luka, Croatia, May 1944:   AE Jl 73 5/1:44
Fiesler Fi 156C-3:   glider tug, Bavaria, 1945:   MW F 73 1/6:296
Fiesler Fi 156U: ASW evaluation prototype, Erprobungsstelle Rechlin, 1940:   MW F 73 1/6:296
Focke Wulf Fw 56 Stösser: flying school unknown, Borkheide, 1940: AN 2 F 73 1/19:9
Fw 56:   Flugzeugführerschule A/B 112, Langenlebam: AN 2 F 73 1/19:9
Fw 56:   Jagdfliegerschule 101, Zerbst, 1943:   AN 2 F 73 1/19:9
Heinkel He 51B trainer: unstated Jagdfliegerschule, winter 1941: RT Mr 71 4/3:28
He 51B: A/B 71, Prosnitz (Prostějov), 1942:   AE N 73 2/3:240-241
He 51B: A/B 123, Agram (Zagreb), spring 1942:   AE N 73 2/3: 240-241
He 51B-1:   1941-42, 2 var: MW Jl 73 1/11:574
Heinkel He 59N: navigation trainer, after 1940:   AN 2 F 73 1/19:9
Henschel Hs 123:   8/SG 1, Russia, 1942:   RT Jl 71 4/7:76
Hs 123A: II/SG 1, Novotscharkask, southern Russia, 1941-42:   Q O 72 7/4:128
Hs 123A: 4/SchG 1, eastern front, winter 1942-43:   AE S 72 3/3: 152
Junkers Ju 52/3m g4e (MS):   1 Minensuchgruppe: AN 3 O 75 4/9: 8-9
Letov Š 328:   A/B Schule, Olomouc-Holice, spring 1940:   AE D 73 5/6:287
Messerschmitt Bf 109G-2/R1:   500 kg bomb carrying experiment (one-off):   Afx N 72 14/3:146
Bf 109G-12 tandem trainer: prototype: Afx N 72 14/3:146

(Greece)

Fairey Battle I: 33 Mira Vomvardismou, Oct 1940:   AE Ag 72 3/2: 88

Aircraft

(Hungary)

Arado Ar 96B-1: 1940: AN 27 Ap 73 1/25:8
Avia B 534 IV: civil registration, Ferihegy, 1940-42: AE D 73 5/6:291
Fiat CR. 32: before autumn 1942: AN 18 Ja 74 2/17:8-9
Focke Wulf Fw 189A-2: 3/1 Short-range Recon Sqn, with Luftflotte 4, Zamocz, east Poland, March 1944: AI O 74 7/4:189
Héja I (Reggiane Re 2000): 1/1 Szazad, Onálló Vadász Osztály (Ind FG), Air Bgd, 2 Hungarian Army, Russia, summer 1942: AI Ag 75 9/2:93
Héja I: 1/1 Szazad, Vadász Ezred (Rgt), Szolnok, summer 1941: AI Ag 75 9/2:93
Héja II (MAVG-built): training & home defense, Ferihegy, spring 1943: AI Ag 75 9/2:93
Junkers Ju 87D-3: 102/1 Dive Bomber Sqn: AE My 74 6/5:254
Mavag Hejja: 5 FS, 101/I FG, 1945, Partos: RT S 74 7/9:101
Messerschmitt Bf 109E-4: Csoka: Q Ap 71 6/2:6
Bf 109G-6: 102 Ind, FG, summer 1944: AE D 71 1/7:381
Bf 109G-14: 4 Air Command, East Special Section: Q Ap 71 6/2:6

(Ireland)

Hawker Hurricane Mk I: 1941: Q Jl 73 8/3:145
Miles M. 19 Master Mk II: March 1943: Q Jl 73 8/3:145

(Italy, Republica Sociale Italiana Bombers)

Cant Z1007: 211 Sqd, 50 Gr, 16 St BT: Q Ja 74 7/1:4
Z1007bis: 60 Sqd, 33 Gr, 11 St BT: Q Ja 74 7/1:4
Z1007bis: 211 Sqd, 50 Gr, 16 St: IM Ap 73 10/4:7
Z1007bis: 211 Sqd, 50 Gr, 16 St, Vincenza: IM Ap 73 10/4:7
Z1007bis: 230 Sqd, 50 Gr, 16 St BT: Q Ja 74 7/1:4
Z1007bis: 260 Sqd, 106 Gr, 47 St, Grottaglie, 1941: IM Ap 73 10/4:7
Z1007bis series V: 215 Sqd, 50 Gr, 16 St, Manduria, 1942, Bruscantini: IM Ap 73 10/4:6
Fiat BR 20: prob 4 Sqd, 11 Gr, 13 St: RT O 74 7/10:116
BR 10: 65 Sqd, 31 Gr, 18 St: RT O 74 7/10:116
Savoia Marchetti SM-79: 1 Gr AS: Q Ja 75 10/3:122
SM-79: 50 Sqd, 38 Gr, 32 St: RT O 74 7/10:116
SM-79: 283 Sqd, 130 Gr Auto: RT O 74 7/10:116
SM-79/AR. 128: Gr Aerosiluranti "Buscaglia," Northern Italy, 1944 (RSI): AI D 75 9/6:301
SM-79/P. XI: 193 Sqd, 87 Gr, Sicily, 1941: AI D 75 9/6:301
SM-79/P. XI: 257 Sqd, 108 Gr, Sicily, early 1941: AI D 75 9/6:301
SM-79/P. XI: 283 Sqd, 130 Gr Auto, Mediterranean, 1942: AI D 75 9/6:301
Savoia Marchetti SM-81: 1 Gr AT: Q Ja 75 10/3:122

III. Color Patterns 250

(Italy, Republica Sociale Italiana Fighters)

Breguet Bre 693: 1943: AE My 73 4/5:252
Dewoitine D. 520: 164 Sqd, 161 Gr Auto Ca, Reggio Calabria, Italy, May 1943: AI My 75 8/5:244
D. 520: Reggio, Sept 1943: RT My 73 1/6:296
Fiat CR 32: 160 Sqd, 12 Gr, Tobruk, Oct 1940: AI D 74 7/6:296
Fiat CR 42: 95 Sqd, 18 Gr CT, 56 St, Eechloo, Belgium, Nov 1940, Salvadori: AE Jl 73 5/1:44
Fiat G. 50bis: 20 Gr, 51 St. Ursel, Belgium, Oct 1940 - April 1941: AE Je 74 6/6:306
Fiat G. 55: factory finish: Q Ja 75 10/3:122
Fiat G. 55: prob Montefusco Sqd: Q Ja 75 10/3:122
Fiat G. 55: 4 Sqd, Cascina Vaga, April 1944 (RSI): Q Ja 75 10/3:120
Fiat G. 55: 4 Sqd (RSI): Q Ja 75 10/3:120
Fiat G. 55: 5 Sqd, 2 Gr, 3 var: Q Ja 75 10/3:121
Fiat G. 55: 6 Sqd, 2 GCT: Q Ja 75 10/3:121
Fiat G. 55/I: 5 Sqd "Nicola Magaldi," 2 Gr CT, spring 1944: AE My 74 6/5:234
Macchi MC. 200: 86 Sqd, 7 Gr, 54 St, Palermo, early 1942: AI O 74 7/4:196
MC. 200: 356 Sqd, 21 Gr, Soviet front, late summer 1942: AI O 74 7/4:196
MC. 200: 371 Sqd, 22 Gr, Ciampino, June 1940: AI O 74 7/4:196
MC. 200: 373 Sqd, 153 Gr, Cirenaica, 1941: AI O 74 7/4:196
Macchi MC. 202 Folgore: 73 Sqd, 9 Gr, 4 St, "F Baracca": AE Ja 72 2/1:20
MC. 202: 369 Sqd, 22 Gr Auto: AE Ja 72 2/1:20
MC. 202 I: 168 Sqd, 54 St: AE Ja 72 2/1:20
MC. 202 III: 151 Sqd, 51 St: AE Ja 72 2/1:20
MC. 202 III: 378 Sqd, 155 Gr, 51 St: AE Ja 72 2/1:20
MC. 202 IX: 96 Sqd, 4 St, Catania, Sicily, Aug 1943: RT Jl 72 5/7:73
Macchi MC. 205 Veltro: RSI: RT D 72 5/12:138; IM Ap 73 10/4:15
MC. 205V: 1 Sqd, 2 var, (RSI): Q Ja 75 10/3:118
MC. 205V: 1 Gr CT, (RSI): Q Ja 10/3:118
MC. 205V: 3 Sqd, 1 GrCT, (RSI): Q Ja 75 10/3:119
MC. 205V: ex 85 Sqd, (RSI): Q Ja 75 10/3:118
Messerschmitt Bf 109G-6: 1 Sqd, 1 Gr (RSI): Q Ja 75 10/3:118
Bf 109G-6: 3 Sqd "Diavoli," 2 Gr CT, Villafranca, Verona, Oct 1944: AE D 71 1/7:384
Bf 109G-6: 4 Sqd, 2 Gr, 2 var, (RSI): Q Ja 75 10/3:118
Bf 109G-10: 2 Sqd, 1 Gr CT, (RSI): Q Ja 75 10/3:119
Reggiane Re 2000 I: evaluation, Guidonia, early 1941: AI Ag 75 9/2:92
Re 2000 III: 1 Sqd, Sarzana, 1942: AI Ag 75 9/2:92
Re 2000 GA III: 377 Sqd Auto, Palermo-Boccadiflaco, March 1942: AI Ag 75 9/2:93
Reggiane Re 2001 Falco II: prototype, 1940: AN 11 Jl 75 4/3:13
Re 2001: 150 Sqd, 2 Gr, Pantelleria, 1942: AN 11 Jl 75 4/3:13
Re 2001: 362 Sqd, 22 Gr, Sardinia, 1942: AN 11 Jl 75 4/3:13

Aircraft

(Italy, Republica Sociale Italiana Other Aircraft)

Fiat G. 50bis: Scuola Caccia III Periodo, summer 1942: AE Je 74 6/6:306
Fiesler Fi 156C-1 Storch: late 1942: MW F 73 1/6:296
Fi 156C-5: Commando Aeronautica Albania, Tirana, March 1941: AI Ap 75 8/4:200
Savoia Marchetti SM 82 Marsupiale: 604a Sqd Trans, North Africa, 1942: AN 13 Je 75 4/1:8-9

(Italy Co-Belligerent)

Bell P-39N: 4 St, Yugoslavia, 1944: AE Ag 71 1/3:136
Reggiane Re. 2001 Falco II: 82 Sqd, 21 Gr: AN 11 Jl 75 4/3:13

(Japan Bombers)

Aichi Type 99 D3A1 "Val": IJNS Akagi, April 1941: RT My 74 7/5-6:54
D3A1: IJNS Akagi, Pearl Harbor: RT My 74 7/5-6:54
D3A1: IJNS Hiryu, Midway: RT My 74 7/5-6:55
D3A1: IJNS Hiryu, Pearl Harbor: RT My 74 7/5-6:55
D3A1: IJNS Junyo, May 1942, 2 var: RT My 74 7/5-6:55
D3A1: IJNS Junyo, Solomons, April 1943: RT My 74 7/5-6:56
D3A1: IJNS Kaga: RT My 74 7/5-6:54
D3A1: IJNS Shokaku, Coral Sea: RT My 74 7/5-6:56
D3A1: IJNS Shokaku, Marianas, June 1944: RT My 74 7/5-6:56
D3A1: IJNS Shokaku, Pearl Harbor: RT My 74 7/5-6:56
D3A1: IJNS Soryu, 2 var: RT My 74 7/5-6:54-55
D3A1: IJNS Zuikaku, Battle of Coral Sea: RT My 74 7/5-6:53
D3A1: IJNS Zuikaku, Battle of Santa Cruz, Oct 1942: RT My 74 7/5-6:53
D3A1: IJNS Zuikaku, Leyte Gulf, Oct 1944: RT My 74 7/5-6:54
D3A1: IJNS Zuikaku, Pearl Harbor: RT My 74 7/5-6:53
D3A1: IJNS Zuikaku, Pearl Harbor, Iwutsuki: RT My 74 7/5-6:53
D3A1: IJNS Zuikaku, Pearl Harbor, Takahashi: RT My 74 7/5-6:53
D3A1: 2 Ko, Philippines, Nov 1942: RT My 74 7/5-6:57
D3A1: 14 Ko, Sept 1941: RT My 74 7/5-6:57
D3A1: 31 Ko, Philippines, Nov 1942: RT My 74 7/5-6:57
D3A1: 33 Ko, Aug 1942: RT My 74 7/5-6:57
D3A1: 35 Ko, Feb 1942: RT My 74 7/5-6:57
D3A1: 40 Ko: RT My 74 7/5-6:58
D3A1: 40 Ko, Sept 1944: RT My 74 7/5-6:58
D3A1: 552 Ko: RT My 74 7/5-6:58
D3A1: Yokosuka Ko, operational test & evaluation: RT My 74 7/5-6:59
D3A2: 35 Ko: RT My 74 7/5-6:57
D3A2: 322 Ko, Philippines, March 1944: RT My 74 7/5-6:58
D3A2: 553 Ko, Philippines, April 1944: RT My 74 7/5-6:58
D3A2: 582 Ko: RT My 74 7/5-6:59
D3A2: 582 Ko, New Guinea, June 1943: RT My 74 7/5-6:59

III. Color Patterns 252

D3A2: 761 Ko, Philippines, July 1944: RT My 74 7/5-6:59
D3A2: 1001 Ko, July 1943: RT My 74 7/5-6:59
D3A2: Nagoya Ko: RT My 74 7/5-6:60
D3A2: Yatabe Ko: RT My 74 7/5-6:60
D3A2: Yokosuko Ko, 1943: RT My 74 7/5-6:60
Mitsubishi G4M1 "Betty": Ie-Shima, Aug 1945, Surrender: Q Ap 74 9/2:79
G4M1: Kanoya Ko, Formosa, 1941: Q Ap 74 9/2:79
G4M2-E Model 24J & Okha: Q Ap 74 9/2:84
Mitsubishi Ki. 15-II: RT N 73 6/11:127
Ki. 67-I-Kai Hiryu "Peggy": 7 Sen kamakazi, 2 var: Q Ap 74 9/2:83
Nakajima B5N2 "Kate": 931 AC, Saipan, June 1944: RT Ja 72 5/1:1
B5N2: Usa Kotutai, 1941: RT Jl 72 5/7:82

(Japan Fighters)

(Multi-Engine)
Kawasaki Ki. 45 Kai-Hei Toryu "Nick": Shinten unit, 53 Sen, Matsudo, Chiba Pref, Aug 1945: AE Mr 73 4/3:148
Ki. 45 Kai-Hei: 4 Sen, 1 Chu, Kasiwa, Chiba Fref. spring 1943: AE Mr 73 4/3:148
Ki. 45 Kai-Hei: 13 Sen, 2 Chu, Rabaul, summer 1943: AE Mr 73 4/3:148
Ki. 45 Kai-Hei: 21 Sen, HQ Chu, Palembang, Sumatra, May 1945: AE Mr 73 4/3:148
Ki. 45 Kai-Hei: 27 Sen, 2 Chu, Philippines, Nov 1944: AE Mr 73 4/3:148
Ki. 45 Kai-Hei: 53 Sen, 1 Chu CP, Matsudo, Chiba Pref, winter 1944-45: AE Mr 73 4/3:148
Ki. 45 Kai-Hei: 53 Sen, 3 Chu, Matsudo, Tokyo, winter 1944-45: AE Mr 73 4/3:148
Ki. 45 Kai-Hei: 10 Air Div, 53 Sen, 3 Chu, Shinten kamakazi unit: Q O 73 8/4:211
Ki. 45 Kai-Ko: CO: 4 Sen, 2 Chu, Q O 73 8/4:211
Ki. 45 Kai-Otsu: 5 Sen, 3 Chu, 1943: Q O 73 8/4:211

(Single Engine)
Brewster 339 Buffalo: 2 var: Afx Jl 75 16/11:638
Kawanishi N1K2-J Shiden-Kai "George": 301 Sen, 343 Naval AC, Matsuyama, Shikoku, spring 1945, Kanno: AE Ap 73 4/4:18
Kawasaki Ki. 61-I Hein "Tony": 3 var: AN 1 F 74 2/18:9
Ki. 61-I: Akeno Fighter Training School, 2 var: AN 1 F 74 2/18:9
Ki. 61 Kai: 56 Sen: Q O 73 8/4:213
Ki. 61-I-Kai: 1 Chu, 244 Sen, Tokyo District, 1944-45: AI N 74 7/5:247
Ki. 61-I-Kai: 3 Chu, 19 Sen, Okinawa, 1944-45: AI N 74 7/5:247
Ki. 61-I-Kai: 23 (Ind) Chu, Yontan, Okinawa, April 1945: AI N 74 7/5:247
Ki. 61-I-Kai-Hai: 1 Chu, 55 Sen: AI N 74 7/5:247
Ki. 61-I-Otsu: 3 Chu, 59 Sen, Ashiya, Japan, Aug 1945: AI N 74 7/5:247

Aircraft

Ki. 61-Ib: 224 Sen: AN 1 F 74 2/18:9
Ki. 61-I-Kai-hei: HQ Chu, 244 Sen, Chofu Afld, Japan, 1945:   AI N 74 7/5:246-247
Ki. 61-Ib: 244 Sen, Chofu, Nov 1944, Kobayashi: RT My 73 6/3:29
Ki. 61-I-Kai C: 244 Sen, Chofu, Kobayashi, 3 var; RT Mr 73 6/3: 29
Ki. 61-I-Kai C: 244 Sen, Chofu, Kobayashi's last aircraft: RT My 73 6/3:29
Ki. 61-IIA: 59 Sen, 1 Chu, Okinawa, 1945:   AN 1 F 74 2/18:9
Ki. 61-IIA: CO, 59 Sen, 2 Chu, Okinawa, 1944-45:   Q Ap 73 8/2: 79
Mitsubishi A6M2 Zero-Sen " Zeke":   6 AC, Rabaul, New Britain, Nov 1942:   AE O 71 1/5:271
A6M2:   12 Combined AC, Hankow Region, winter 1940-41:   AE O 71 1/5:271
A6M2:   251 AC, Formosa, Nov 1942:   AE O 71 1/5:271
A6M2:   402 Sen, 341 AC, Clark Field, Philippines, winter 1944: AE O 71 1/5:271
A6M2:   Genzan AC (Training), Wonsan, North Korea, winter 1944: AE O 71 1/5:271
A6M2:   IJNS Hiryu, Pearl Harbor, Dec 1941:   AE O 71 1/5:271
A6M2c: 303 Chu, 203 AC, Kagoshima NAS, June 1945:   Q Ap 71 6/2:2
J2M3 Raiden model 21:   302 Kokutai, home defence, autumn 1944: AE Jl 71 1/2:68-69
Nakajima Ki. 27 Otsu "Nate":   CO, 1 Chu, 2 Sho, 1 Sen, Shimodate, 1943:   RT Mr 75 8/3:30
Ki. 27 Otsu: 1 Chu, 1 Sen, Hong Kong, Feb 1942:   RT Mr 75 8/3: 30
Nakajima Ki 43 I-Hei Hayabusa "Oscar":   CO, 1 Chu, 1 Sen: RT Mr 75 8/3:31
Ki. 43 I-Ko: 1 Chu, 3 Sho, 3 a/c, 1 Sen, Burma, summer 1942: RT Mr 75 8/3:31
Ki. 43 I-Ko: 3 Chu, 2 Sho, 1 a/c: 1 Sen, Burma, summer 1942: RT My 75 8/3:31
Ki. 43 I-Ko: 3 Chu, 2 Sho, 3 a/c, 1 Sen, Burma, summer 1942: RT Mr 75 8/3:31
Ki. 43 II-Kai: 1 Chu, 1 Sen, Philippines, Oct 1944:   RT Mr 75 8/3: 30
Ki. 43 II-Otsu: 1 Chu, 2 Sho, 1 Sen, Shimodate, 1943:   RT Mr 75 8/3:30
Ki. 43 IIb: 59 Sen, 2 Chu, Dagua Afld, New Guinea, Feb 1944:   Q Ap 72 7/2:58
Ki. 43 IIb: 77 Sen, 3 Chu, Dagua, Feb 1944:   Q Ap 72 7/2:58
Ki. 43 II-Otsu: 1 Chu, 1 Sho, 1 Sen, Home Defence, 1943-45:   RT Mr 75 8/3:30
Ki. 43 II-Otsu: 1 Chu, 1 Sen, New Guinea, June 1943:   RT Mr 75 8/3:30
Ki. 43 II-Ko: 3 Chu, 1 Sen, Rabaul, late 1943:   RT Mr 75 8/3:31
Nakajima Ki. 44 Shoki "Tojo":   3 Ho, 47 Chu, Malaya, Jan 1942, Kuroe: AE Jl 72 3/1:19
Ki. 44:   85 Sen, HQ Chu, Canton, China, 1944:   Q Ap 71 6/2:2
Ki. 44-I-Hei: Instructors' Chu, Akeno AT Div, 1944:   AE Jl 72 3/1: 19

III. Color Patterns

Ki. 44-II-Otsu: 23 Sen, Japan, 1944: AE Jl 72 3/1:19
Ki. 44-II-Otsu: 85 Sen, Canton, summer 1944, Saito: AE Jl 72 3/1:19
Ki. 44-II-Otsu: 87 Sen, 2 Chu, Japan I Eastern Defence Sector, early 1945, Inayama: AE Jl 72 3/1:19
Ki. 44-II-Otsu: Seinten Air Superiority Unit, 47 Sen, Nerimasu Afld, Tokyo, summer 1944: AE Jl 72 3/1:19
Nakajima Ki. 84 Hayate "Frank": 184 Shimbu Tai (kamakazi), Japan, 1945: Q Jl 74 10/1:36
Ki. 84-Ko: 1 Chu, 1 Sen, Philippines, Oct 1944: RT Mr 75 8/3:31
Ki. 84-Ko: 3 Chu, 1 Sen, Philippines, Oct 1944: RT Mr 75 8/3:31

(Japan Reconnaissance)

Aichi M6A1 Seiran (no Allied name): Q O 71 6/4:6
Kawanishi E7K "Alf": pos cruiser Atago: RT D 74 7/12:140
E7K1: 2 var: RT O 71 4/10:118
E7K1: Kure Ko: RT D 74 4/12:140
E7K1: cruiser Mikuma: RT D 74 7/12:140
E7K2: Chinkai Ko: RT D 74 7/12:140
E7K2: Kirishima NAS, 1942: IM Ag 71 8/8:14
Kawanishi E15K1 Shiun "Norm": cruiser Oyoda, 1944: RT My 73 7/5:52
E15K1: 902 Ko, Palau, 1943: RT My 73 6/5:53
Mitsubishi Ki 15-II "Babs": RT N 73 6/11:127
Mitsubishi Ki. 46 III "Dinah": 2 Sen, Philippines, 1944: RT N 75 8/11:124

(Japan Other Types)

Boeing B-17E: Q Ja 72 7/1:31
Grumman F6F-5 Hellcat: Q Jl 73 8/3:166
Mitsui L2D3 "Tabby" (license-built DC-3): navy: RT S 73 6/9:106
Yokosuka MXY7 training glider: Aug 1945: RT N 73 6/11:127

(Manchuko Co-Belligerent)

Nakajima Ki. 43-II-Ko: Mukden, 1944: AI Jl 75 9/1:39

(Netherlands, Netherlands East Indies)

Brewster B-239: 4 var: MW D 73 2/4:180
Brewster 339D: NEIAF, 3 var: Q Su 75 10/4:172
Curtiss Hawk 75A-7: std camouflage, NEIAF: Q Su 75 10/4:168
Hawk 75 A-7: delivery scheme, NEIAF: Q Su 75 10/4:168
Hawk 75A-7: 1 Vliegtuigafdeling, KNIL Luchtvaartafdeling, Madioen, Dec 1941, Boxman: AE N 71 1/6:313
Curtiss Wright CW-21B: NEIAF: Q Su 75 10/4:170
Consolidated 28-5MNE (PBY-5): NEIAF: Q Su 75 10/4:170
Fokker D. XXI: 2 Jachtvliegtuigafdeling, Schiphol, spring 1940: AE

Ag 71 1/3:155
Fokker G1: 4 JaVA, Schiphol, May 1940, 2 var: AI N 74 7/5:242
Fokker G1: Jachtvliegschool, Texel, May 1940: AI N 74 7/5:243
Martin 139WH-2: NEIAF: Q Su 75 10/4:170
North American B-25J: 18 Sqn, NEIAF, Batchelor Field, Darwin, Australia, autumn 1944: AI S 74 7/3:137
Ryan STM: NEIAF, 2 var: Q Su 75 10/4:170

(New Zealand)

Chance Vought F4U-1A Corsair: China, 1945 (pos Canton), 2 var: Q Ja 73 8/1:50
F4U-1A: 22 Sqn: Q Ja 71 6/1:26
Corsair II (F4U-1): Bouganville, 1944: Q Jl 73 8/3:140
Corsair II: 4 OTU, Ardmore, N.Z.: Afx S 71 13/1:13
Douglas Dauntless SBD-5: 25 Sqn, Piva, Bougainville, 1944, Forsberg: IM S 74 10/(18):5
SBD-5: 25 Sqn, Piva, Bougainville, 1944, Hayman: IM S 74 10/(18):5
SBD-5: 25 Sqn, Piva, Bougainville, 1944, Johnson: IM S 74 10/(18):5
Lockheed Hudson III: 2 Sqn: AE Jl 72 3/1:44
North American Harvard: 4 var: Afx S 73 15/1:25-26
Supermarine Spitfire Mk XIVc: China 1945: Q Ja 73 8/1:50

(Norway)

Curtiss Hawk 75A: Island Airport, Lake Ontario, 1941: AE N 71 1/6:313
Hawk 75A-8: 1940: RT O 71 4/10:117
Gloster Gladiator III: Fornebo, Oslo, April 1940: AE Ja 73 4/1:41

(Philippines)

Boeing P-26A Peashooter: Dec 1941: WWE Ja 74 1/1:17
Boeing Stearman PT-17A Kaydet: RT My 74 7/5-6:49; S 74 7/9:108

(Portugal)

Gloster Gladiator II: Esq de Caça, 2 Base Aérea, Ota, 1940: AE Ja 73 4/1:41
Lockheed P-38F Lightning: Esq OK, Ota (BA 2), July 1943: AI Je 75 8/6:295

III. Color Patterns

(Rumania)

Arado Ar 196A-3: Esc 102, Flotila de hidroavaiatie, Odessa, late 1943: AE Ag 73 5/2:90
Bristol Blenheim I: 3 BF, Russian front, 1942: AE Je 71 1/1:28-29
Consolidated B-24D: Brasov: Q Ja 72 7/1:30
Heinkel He 111H-3: 5 Gp, Zaporzh'ye area, Ukraine, early 1943: AE Je 71 1/1:29
He 111H-3: Grupul 5, Corpul 1, Aerian, Zaporosh'ye area, Ukrain, early 1943: AE N 73 5/5:237
Heinkel He 112B-1: Bessarabia, Sept 1941: AE Je 71 1/1:28-29
IAR 39: army co-op, autumn 1945: AE Je 71 1/1:28-29
IAR 81c: 2 FG, summer 1945: AE Je 71 1/1:28
Junkers Ju 87D-3: Dive Bomber Gp 6, 1 AC, Russia, summer 1943: AE My 74 6/5:254
Messerschmitt Bf 109G-4/R6: Mariupol, Ukraine, 1943: AE Je 73 4/6:301
PZL P.23 Karas: 3 BF, Focşani, June 1941: AE Je 71 1/1:29
Potez 633B: 2 BF, Râmnicu Sărat, June 1941: AE Je 71 1/1:28
Savoia-Marchetti SM 79-JR (IAR-built): 3 AC, 1943: AE Je 71 1/1:28

(Slovak Co-Belligerent)

Avia B.534: IM Ag 71 8/8:2
B.534 IV: Zitomir-Kiev, Ukraine, 1941: AI Jl 74 7/1:290-291
B.534 IV: prob 13 Sqn, Zitomir-Kiev, Ukraine, 1941-42: AE D 73 5/6:287
Focke Wulf Fw 189A-1: 1942: MW N 73 2/3:127
Heinkel He 111H-3: transport & training, Trenčin, spring 1943: AE N 73 5/5:237; cor Ap 74 6/4:205
Letov Š 328: 1 recon Sqn, Pieštany, mid-1943: AE D 5/6:287
Messerschmitt Bf 109G-6: 14 Slovakian FS, Crimea, spring 1943: AE D 71 1/7:384

(Slovak Insurgent)

Avia B.534 IV: Tri Duby, Zvolen, Sept 1944: AE D 73 5/6:291
Letov Š 328: Tri Duby, Zvolen, Sept 1944: AE D 73 5/6:287

(South Africa)

Douglas Boston IIIA: 24 Sqn, 1943: AE D 71 1/7:381
Douglas C-47A-1-DK: 5 Wing, 1945: Afx Ap 72 13/8:436
Fairey Battle I: 15 Sqn, Algato, East Africa, July 1941: AE Ag 72 3/6:88
Martin B-26: 21 Sqn, Italy, 1944-45: PAM Ap 75 9:148-149
North American Harvard: CFS, 1943: Afx N 71 13/3:140
Harvard: 42 AS, 1944-45: Afx N 71 13/3:140

(Spain)

Fiat G. 50: Ejército del Aire, March 1940:   AE Je 74 6/6:306
SB/M-100:   Gru 24, with Gru 20W, 1939-40:   AE Ja 74 6/1:34

(Sweden)

FFVS J-22A: 1 Div, F 9, Gothenburg: RT Mr 71 4/3:32; RT My 74 10/(16):9
J-22A: 3 Div, F 9:   RT Mr 71 4/3:33
J-22B: F 3:   RT Mr 71 4/3:33; IM My 74 10/(16):9
J-22B: 3 Div, F 3, 1945:   RT Ap 72 5/4:44
J-22B: 3 Div, F 9, early 1944:   RT Ap 72 5/4:44
J-22B: 1 Div, F 13, late 1944:   RT Ap 72 5/4:44
Northrop B-5 (A-17):   F 4, Ostersund, 1940:   IM F 73 10/2:10
B-5:   F 4, Ostersund, 1944:   IM F 73 10/2:10
B-5:   F 6, Karlsborg: IM F 73 10/2:10
B-5 with ski: F 4, Ostersund, 1944:   IM F 73 10/2:10
Reggiane J-20 (RE 2000):   1 Div, F 10, early 1945:   AI Ag 75 9/2:92
J-20:   3 Div, F 10, Angelholm, 1943:   AI Ag 75 9/2:92

(Switzerland)

Messerschmitt Bf 109"D" (C with B engine):   RT Ap 73 6/4:41
Bf 109E-1:   RT Ap 73 6/4:41
Bf 109G: RT Ap 73 6/4:41
Bf 109G-6:   Fliegerkompagnie 7, autumn 1944:   AE D 71 1/7:384
Morane Saulnier (license-built) D. 3801 (MS 406):   Fk 21, 1944-45:   AE O 73 5/4:187
North American P-51B-10NA: interned: IM Ja 71 8/1:15

(Royal Thai Co-Belligerent)

Curtiss Hawk III: 1942-45:   AE O 72 3/4:205

(Turkey)

Bristol Beaufighter TF Mk X: 1944:   AN 14 Ap 73 1/24:10
Focke Wulf Fw 190A-3:   3 Coy, 5 AR, Bursa, 1944:   AE Jl 71 1/2:84-85

(USSR)

Bell P-39:   VV, 1943, Chlopov: Q Jl 71 6/3:7
P-39Q: unit unknown, Guljajev: RT Ap 74 7/4:37
P-39Q: Southern Sector, 1943-44, Pokryshkin: AE Ag 71 1/3:136
P-39Q-15-BE: downed in Finland, now at Tampere Museum: Q

III. Color Patterns 258

Л 71 6/3:6
Bereznyak-Isaev BI: rocket experiment: AE D 73 5/6:286
Curtiss P-49N: Valkjärvi, Finland, Dec 1943: IM S 73 10/9:17
Curtiss Tomahawk IIB: Northern sector, early 1942: AE My 72 2/5:259
Ilyushin Il-2M-82 FN: radial engine experiment, 1943: IM Ap 72 8/4:10-11
Ilyushin Il-10: IM Ap 72 8/4:12
Il-10: RT O 73 6/10:110
Il-10: 200 Div, Ost, Germany: IM Ap 72 8/4:12
Il-10U: dual control: RT O 73 6/10:110
LaGG La-5FN: Poland, 1944, Popkov: Aero Ap 71 37/435:191
Lisunov Li-2: std camouflage: AN 12 D 75 4/14:9
Messerschmitt Bf 110C-(5?): unit unknown, apparently used in action: MW N 72 1/3:124
MiG-3: unit unknown, summer 1942, 2 var: AE O 71 1/5:254
MiG-3: Leningrad region, Sept 1942: AE O 71 1/5:254
MiG-3: recon, central sector, spring 1942: AE O 71 1/5:254
MiG-3: 12 IAP, Moscow Army Region, winter 1942-43: AE O 71 1/5:254
MiG-3: 34 IAP, winter 1941-42: AE O 71 1/5:257
MiG-3: 34 IAF, Vnukova (Western sector), winter, 1941-42: AE O 71 1/5:254
Polikarpov I-16 type 24: Central sector, summer 1941: AE Mr 72 2/3:153
I-16 type 24: Odessa, autumn-winter 1941: AE Mr 72 2/3:153
I-16 type 24: V-MF Rgt, Murmask, 1941-42: AE Mr 72 2/3:153
Polikarpov I-153 Chaika: Russia, 1941: Q O 71 6/4:19
I-153: Russia, Feb 1941: Q O 71 6/4:18
SM/M-100A: Aug 1941: AE Ja 74 6/1:34
Yak 1: Lily Litvyak: IM Ap 71 8/4:10
Yak 3: Normandie-Niémen: Q Ja 72 7/1:10
Yak 3: Normandie-Niémen, 1945: IM Ap 71 8/4:11
Yak 3: prob Normandie-Niémen, 1944-45: IM Ap 71 8/4:11
Yak 3: Normandie Niémen, Delfino: AI N 75 9/5:233
Yak 3: Normandie-Niémen, 1945, Iribarne: IM Ap 71 8/4:11
Yak 3: Normandie-Niémen, Sauvage: Q Ja 72 7/1:10
Yak 7a: Finland, 1943: IM Ap 71 8/4:10
Yak 9: Normandie-Niémen, April 1944, Toula: Q Ja 72 7/1:10
Yak 9D: 1943: IM Ap 71 8/4:10
Yak 9D: Guards Fighter Rgt, 1943: Aero D 71 36/431:699
Yak 9D: Guards Fighter Rgt, Sevastopol, May 1944: AI N 74 9/5:238
Yak 9D: Little Theatre presentation, 1943: IM Ap 71 8/4:10
Yak 9D: Normandie-Niémen, Sauvage: Q Ja 72 7/1:10
Yak 9D: 1 (Rouen) Sqn, Normandie-Niémen: Q Ja 72 7/1:10
Yak 9D: Polish 1 Fighter Rgt, "Warszawa," 1944-45: IM Ap 71 8/4:10
Yak 9U: Poznan, Poland, Feb 1945: AI N 75 9/5:239
Yak 9U: Guards Fighter Rgt, aut 1944: Aero D 71 36/341:697

Aircraft

(U.K. Bombers)

(Single-Engine)
Fairey Albacore I: Coastal Command, 1944:   AN 22 Ag 75 4/6:9
Albacore I: 820 Sqn, Operation Torch, Sept 1942:   AN 22 Ag 75 4/6:9
Albacore II: 826 Sqn, mid 1940:   AN 22 Ag 75 4/6:9
Fairey Barracuda Mk II: 715 Sqn, RNAS Yovilton/St. Merryn, 1943-44:   AN 4 Ja 74 2/16:9
Fairey Swordfish: std: Sc Mr 74 5/54:146-152
Swordfish I: Catapult Flight, HMS Malaya, 1940:   AE N 72 3/5:256
Swordfish I: 821 Sqn, HMS Ark Royal, 1940:   AE N 72 3/5:256
Swordfish I: 824 Sqn, HMS Eagle, 1940:   AE N 72 3/5:254
Swordfish II: 1 Naval Air Gunnery School, Yarmouth, N.S., 1943:   AE N 72 3/5:254
Swordfish II: 811 Sqn, HMS Biter, 1944:   AE N 72 3/5:254
Swordfish III: 119 Sqn, Coastal Command, 1945:   AE N 72 3/5:256
Vultee Vengeance: std RAF: IM Je 71 8/6:8
Vengeance I: 82 Sqn, March 1943:   Afx D 71 13/4:201
Vengeance I: 82 Sqn, India, 1942, 2 var: IM Je 71 8/6:8
Vengeance II: Bombing Development Unit, Feltwell, Aug 1943:   Afx D 71 13/4:201
Vengeance II: 45 Sqn, India, 1943:   IM Je 71 8/6:8

(Twin-Engine)
Armstrong Whitworth Whitley V: 77 Sqn, Nov 1940:   Afx Mr 71 12/7:365
Avro Manchester: 106 Sqn, March 1942:   Afx My 71 12/9:477
Manchester: 207 Sqn, Dec 1940:   Afx My 71 12/9:479
Manchester: 207 Sqn, April 1941:   Afx My 71 12/9:479
Bristol Beaufighter TF Mk X: Sc My 74 5/56:265
Beaufighter X: 236 Sqn, 1944:   AN 13 Ap 73 1/24:10
Beaufighter X: 254 Coastal Command, 1944:   AN 13 Ap 73 1/24:10
Bristol Blenheim I: 60 Sqn, Lahore, India, winter 1940-41:   AE Ap 74 6/4:202
Blenheim I: 113 Sqn, Greece (prob Larisa), March-April 1941:   AE Ap 74 6/4:202
Blenheim IF: 54 OTU, summer 1941:   AE Ap 74 6/4:230
Blenheim IV: 14 Sqn, North Africa, Dec 1941:   Afx O 71 13/2:89
Blenheim IV: 60 Sqn, Burma, 1942:   Afx D 71 13/4:201
Blenheim IV: 82 Sqn, May 1940:   Afx F 71 12/6:315
Blenheim IV: 107 Sqn, Jan 1940:   Afx Ja 71 12/5:255
Blenheim IV: 139 Sqn, Oct 1939:   Afx Ja 71 12/5:155
Blenheim V: Fayid, 1942:   Afx Mr 72 13/7:395
Blenheim V: Foggia, late 1943:   Afx Mr 72 13/7:395
Bristol Bombay: North Africa, summer 1940:   Afx O 71 13/2:89
De Havilland Mosquito: 105 Sqn, March 1944:   Afx F 72 13/6:335
Mosquito: 692 Sqn, 1944, 2 var: Afx F 72 13/6:335
Mosquito IV: May 1942, Hatfield: Afx S 71 13/1:32
Mosquito B.Mk IV: 105(b) Sqn, Oct 1942, Lang: Q Jl 71 6/3:23; RT Ag 73 6/8:90
Mosquito IX: 105 Sqn, autumn 1944:   Afx F 72 13/6:335
Mosquito XVI: 571 Sqn, June 1944:   Afx F 72 13/6:335
Mosquito XXV: 162 Sqn, Bourn, March 1945:   Afx F 72 13/6:335

III. Color Patterns 260

Douglas A-20G (Boston): 18 Sqn, 47 BG, 236 Wing, Marcienise,
  Italy, May-July 1944: Q Ja 72 7/1:28
Boston III: 18 Sqn, 47 BG, 236 Wing, Desert AF, 1943, McCurdy:
  Q Ja 72 7/1:28
Boston III: 107 Sqn, 1942: AE D 71 1/7:381
Boston III: 107 Sqn, late 1942: Afx S 71 13/1:39
Boston IIIA: 88 (Hong Kong) Sqn, 1944: AE D 71 1/7:381
Boston IIIA: 107 Sqn, April 1943: AN 30 My 75 3/26:9
Boston IV: 18 Sqn, 47 BG, 236 Wing, Desert AF, 1944-45, Samain:
  Q Ja 72 7/1:28
Douglas Havoc I (BD-7a Intruder): 23 Sqn, 1941: MW Mr 73 1/7:
  378
Havoc I: 23 Sqn, 1941: MW Mr 73 1/7:381
Havoc I: 23 Sqn, May 1942: MW Mr 73 1/7:380
Havoc I: 23 Sqn, Ford, c.1941: AN 30 My 75 3/26:9
Douglas A-26C-25-DL Invader: 1st delivered to RAF: Afx Mr 72
  13/7:377
Handley Page Hampden: 420 Sqn, Feb 1942: Afx Jl 71 12/11:597
Lockheed Hudson V: 48 Sqn, Coastal Command, 1941: AE Jl 72
  3/1:44
Hudson VI: Coastal Command: AE Jl 72 3/1:44
Lockheed Ventura II: July 1942: RT My 71 4/7:53
Martin Marauder I: Desert Air Force: Sc My 73 4/5:330
North American B-25D-20-NA Mitchell II: 320 Sqn, 139 Wing, Nov
  1944: IM S 71 8/9:4
Mitchell II: 226 Sqn, Gilze Rijen, Netherlands, June 1944: AI S
  74 7/3:146
Mitchell II: 320 (Neth) Sqn, 2 Gp, Bomber Command, Dunsfold,
  Surrey, April 1944: AI S 74 7/3:136
Mitchell III (B-25J): 180 Sqn, 139 Wing, Feb 1945, Cox: IM S 71
  8/9:5
Vickers Wellington IA: 115 Sqn, Dec 1939: Afx Ja 71 12/5:255
Wellington IC: Mildenhall, Sept 1941: Afx Jl 71 12/11:597
Wellington IC: 99 Sqn, Newmarket Heath, late 1940: Afx Mr 71 12/
  7:365
Wellington IC: 115 Sqn, May 1940: Afx F 71 12/6:315
Wellington IC: 149 Sqn, July 1940: Afx Mr 71 12/7:365
Wellington IC: 149 Sqn, Aug 1940: Afx Mr 71 12/7:365
Wellington II: 214 Sqn, mid 1941: AN 4 Ag 72 1/6:10
Wellington III: Bourn, March 1942: Afx Jl 71 12/11:597
Wellington III: 419 Sqn, spring 1942: AN 4 Ag 72 1/6:10
Wellington V: prototype: AN 4 Ag 72 1/6:10
Wellington VIA: AN 4 Ag 72 1/6:10
Wellington X: 420 Sqn: Afx Mr 72 13/7:395

(Four-Engine)
Avro Lancaster: std: Sc Ag 75 6/71:404-406
Lancaster: 44 Sqn, 1942: Afx Ag 71 12/12:651
Lancaster: 207 Sqn, June 1942: Afx S 71 13/1:39
Lancaster: 428 Sqn, Middleton: Afx My 72 13/9:509
Lancaster: 429 Sqn, Leeming: Afx My 72 13/9:509
Lancaster: 431 Sqn, Croft: Afx My 72 13/9:509
Lancaster: 434 Sqn, Croft: Afx My 72 13/9:509

Aircraft

Lancaster I: 15 Sqn, Mildenhall, 1945: Sc Ag 75 6/71:405
Lancaster I: 44 (Rhodesia) Sqn, Waddington, Jan 1942: Sc Ag 75 6/71:405
Lancaster I: 44 (Rhodesia) Sqn, Waddington, May 1942: Sc Ag 75 6/71:405
Lancaster I: 467 Sqn, now in RAF Museum: AE Ap 74 6/4:199
Lancaster B.I Special: 617 Sqn, Feb 1945: Afx F 73 14/6:313
Lancaster B.I Special: 617 Sqn, March 1945: Afx F 73 14/6:313
Lancaster III: 97 Sqn, Coningsby, 1944-45: Sc Ag 75 6/71:405
Lancaster X: 419 Sqn, Middleton St. George: Afx My 72 13/9:509
Lancaster X with radome: 419 Sqn, Middleton St. George: Afx My 72 13/9:509
Avro Lincoln: 3rd prototype: AN 28 Je 74 3/2:10
Lincoln I: 138 Sqn: AN 28 Je 74 3/2:10
Lincoln II: 214 Sqn: AN 28 Je 74 3/2:10
Consolidated Liberator: Far East: Afx Ap 72 13/8:449
Liberator I: Ferry Command, spring 1941: RT Ja 71 4/1:7
Liberator GR III: 160 Sqn, Sigirya, Ceylon, 2 var: RT Ja 72 5/1:6
Liberator VI: 99 Sqn, Far East: Afx Ap 72 13/7:377
Liberator VIII: Far East: Afx Ap 72 13/8:449
Handley Page Halifax: October 1941: Afx Je 71 12/10:537
Halifax: January 1942: Afx Je 71 12/10:537
Halifax: AFDU trials, Duxford, March 1941: Afx Je 71 12/10:537
Halifax II: Middleton St. George, winter 1943-44, 5 var: Afx Ja 72 13/5:260
Halifax V: Middleton St. George, mining duties, April 1944: Afx Ja 72 13/5:260
Short Stirling: 7 Sqn, Oakington, Feb 1941: Afx Ap 71 12/8:425
Stirling: 15 Sqn, summer 1941: Afx Ap 71 12/8:425
Stirling: 15 Sqn, Wyton, March 1942: Afx Ap 72 12/8:425
Stirling I: 7 Sqn, Oakington, spring 1941: AN 19 Ja 73 1/18:10
Stirling I: 7 Sqn, Oakington, Cambs, Nov 1941, 2 var: RT Ja 74 7/1:6
Stirling I: 15 Sqn, Feb 1942: Afx Ag 71 12/12:651
Stirling I: 15 Sqn, Alconbury, spring 1942: AN 19 Ja 73 1/18:10

(U.K. Captured Aircraft)

Focke Wulf Fw 189A-1: Farnborough, Sept 1945: MW N 73 2/3:127
Focke Wulf Fw 190A-3: 1426 Flt, EA Evaluation Unit: Q Jl 73 8/3:167; cor Ja 74 9/1:3
Fw 190A-8: 41 Sqn, Germany, 1945: RT Je 73 6/6:68
Messerschmitt Bf 109E: Boscombe Down, May 1940, Hilly-Brown: PAM O 7511:187
Bf 109E-4: 1426 Flt, EA Evaluation Unit: Q Jl 73 8/3:167; cor Ja 74 9/1:3
Bf 109G-5: 1426 Flt, EA Evaluation Unit: Q Jl 73 8/3:167; cor Ja 74 9/1:3

III. Color Patterns 262

(U.K. Fighters)

(Carrier-Based)
Chance Vought Corsair I: 1835 Sqn: Afx S 71 13/1:13
Corsair II: 1834 Sqn, HMS Victorious: Afx S 71 13/1:14-15
Corsair II: 1836 Sqn, HMS Victorious, East Indies, Jan 1945: Afx S 71 13/1:23
Corsair IV: HMS Vengeance, 1945: Afx S 71 13/1:13
Grumman Hellcat I (F6F-3): std camouflage: Q Jl 73 8/3:164-165
Hellcat I: MW F 74 2/6:320
Hellcat I: 800 Sqn, HMS Emperor, Aegean Sea, Sept 1944: IM My 72 9/5:12
Hellcat I: 800 Sqn, HMS Emperor, Mediterranean, summer 1944: AI S 75 9/3:148
Hellcat II: 800 Sqn, HMS Emperor, Indian Ocean, July-Aug 1945: IM My 72 9/5:12; IM Je 72 9/6:11
Hellcat II: South East Asia, 2 var: MW F 74 2/6:320
Grumman Martlet I: 1940: Q Ap 72 7/2:54
Martlet I: Western Desert, 1941: AN 7 F 75 3/18:9
Martlet I: 804 Sqn, March 1941: AN 7 F 75 3/18:9
Martlet I: 805 Sqn, El Gamil, Africa, July 1942: RT Ag 71 4/8:85
Martlet II: Le Senia AB, Oran, Dec 1942: Q Ap 72 7/2:54
Martlet III: 805 Sqn, Western Desert, Aug 1941: Q Ap 72 7/5:55
Martlet V: June 1944: Q Ap 72 7/2:55
Grumman FM-2 Wildcat VI: HMS Indomitable, 1944: AN 7 F 3/18:9
Hawker Sea Hurricane Mk Ia: Lee-on-Solent, 1941: PAM O 75 11:185
Sea Hurricane Mk IIc: 835 Sqn, HMS Nairana, 1942: PAM O 75 11:185
Sea Hurricane Mk XII (Canadian Car & Foundry-built): Operation Torch, Nov 1942: PAM O 75 11:185
Supermarine Seafire Mk IIc: 885 Sqn, HMS Formidable, Gibraltar area, Jan 1943, Parker: IM S 75 11/5:15
Seafire FR III: 880 Sqn, Pacific, July 1945, Crossley: IM S 75 11/5:15
Seafire L III: 887 Sqn, Aug 1945, Pacific: AM S 75 11/5:15

(Multi-Engine)
Bristol Beaufighter: RAF std: Sc Jl 74 5/58:360-367
Beaufighter I: thimble-nose radar prototype: AN 13 Ap 73 1/24:10
Beaufighter I: 604 Sqn, spring 1941: AE O 71 1/5:251
Beaufighter IC: 252 Sqn, Edcu, mid-1942: AE Ja 74 6/1:31
Beaufighter IF: 25 Sqn, late summer 1940, prob North Weald: AE Ja 74 6/1:31
Beaufighter IF: 604 (County of Middlesex) Sqn, 2 var: Sc My 74 5/56:264
Beaufighter IIF: 225 Sqn, Coltishal, Sept 1941: Sc My 74 5/56:264
Beaufighter VI: 272 Sqn, Malta, 1942: AN 13 Ap 73 1/24:10
Beaufighter VIF: 600 (City of London) Sqn: AN 13 Ap 73 1/24:10
Bristol Blenheim IF: 25(F) Sqn, North Weald, Essex, early 1940: AE Ap 74 6/4:96

Aircraft

De Havilland Mosquito NF XIII: 409 Sqn, France, Nov 1944: RT
    My 71 4/5:58
Mosquito NF Mk 30: 85 Sqn: Afx Ap 73 14/8:436-437
Westland Whirlwind: 137 Sqn, late 1942: MW Ja 73 1/5:255
Whirlwind: 263 Sqn, summer 1940: MW Ja 73 1/5:255
Whirlwind: 263 Sqn, winter 1941-42: AE O 71 1/5:251
Whirlwind: 263 Sqn, Exeter, Jan 1941: AE Jl 73 5/1:37

(Single-Engine, Land-Based)
Bell Aracobra I: 601 Sqn, Oct 1941: AE Ag 71 1/3:136
Boulton Paul Defiant Mk I: 141 Sqn, Hawkins, July 1940, Donald:
    PAM Jl 75 10:165
Defiant I: 264 Sqn: AN 10 My 74 2/25:10
Defiant I NF: 151 Sqn, Wittering, 1941-42: AN 10 My 74 2/25:10
Defiant I NF: 410 Sqn: AN 10 My 74 2/25:10
Curtiss Kittyhawk IA: 112 Sqn: AN 6 S 74 3/7:10
Curtiss Tomahawk IB: 400 (Canada) Sqn, Odiham, spring 1942: AI
    Ag 74 7/2:96
Tomahawk IIA (Hawk 81A-2): 1941: AE My 72 2/5:259
Tomahawk IIA: 2 (Army Co-op) Sqn, Sawbridgeworth, Herts, summer 1941: AI Ag 74 7/2:96
Tomahawk IIA: 26 Sqn: AN 6 S 74 3/7:10
Tomahawk IIA: 349 (Belgium) Sqn, Feb 1943: AE My 72 2/5:259
Tomahawk IIB: 112 Sqn, Sidi Haneish, Oct 1941: AE My 72 2/5:259
Tomahawk IIB: 112 Sqn, Sidi Haneish, autumn 1941: AI Ag 74 7/2:96
Tomahawk IIB: 250 Sqn, Egypt, 1941: AE My 72 2/5:259
Tomahawk IIB: 414 (Canada) Sqn, Croydon, autumn 1941: AI Ag
    74 7/2:96
Fairey Battle I: 12 Sqn, France, 1940: Afx F 71 12/6:315
Gloster Gladiator II: 615 Sqn, Vitry-en-Artois, Northern France,
    May 1940: AE Ja 73 4/1:41
Gloster Sea Gladiator: Malta: Afx My 72 13/9:498-499
Hawker Hurricane: std: Sc Ja 74 5/1:23-26
Hurricane: now in RAF Museum: AE Ap 74 6/4:199
Hurricane I: 73 Sqn, France, winter 1939-40: AE O 71 1/2:251
Hurricane I: 85 Sqn, Battle of Britain, Townsend: Q Ja 73 8/1:48
Hurricane I: 501 Sqn, Battle of Britain, Lacey: Q Ja 73 8/1:47
Hurricane I: 501 Sqn, Battle of Britain, Lee: Q Ja 73 8/1:48
Hurricane I: 501 Sqn, Gravesend, Sept 1940, Lacey: PAM Jl 75
    10:165
Hurricane IIA: 30 Sqn, Ratamalana Afld, Ceylon, spring 1942: RT
    Je 71 4/6:61
Hurricane IIC: 1 Sqn, Maclachlan: Q Ja 74 5/1:29; add Jl 73 8/3:174
Hawker Tempest V series 2: 3 Sqn, 122 Wing, May 1945, Closterman: Sc F 75 6/65:94-95
Hawker Typhoon: prototype: Sc N 75 6/7:544
Typhoon IA: early production; Sc N 75 6/7:544
Typhoon IB: now in RAF Museum: AE Ap 74 6/4:199
Typhoon IB: Nov 1941, Beamont: Sc N 75 6/7:544

III. Color Patterns

Typhoon IB: 181 Sqn, 1945: Sc N 75 6/75:543
Typhoon IB: 198 Sqn, summer 1944: AE O 71 1/5:251
Typhoon IB: 198 Sqn, Normandy, Aug 1944: Sc N 75 6/74:543
Lockheed Lightning I: evaluations, RAF Boscombe Down, spring 1942: AI Je 75 8/6:294
North American Mustang III: 19 Sqn, Ford, summer 1944: AI Ja 75 8/1:42
Mustang IIIB: 316 (Polish) Sqn, Coltishall, June 1944: AI Ja 75 8/1:42
Republic P-47D-25 Thunderbolt II: 81 Sqn, South East Asia: Sc Ag 72 2/8:419
P-47D-30-RA Thunderbolt II: 79 Sqn, Wangjing, Burma, Nov 1944: AI Mr 75 8/3:148
Supermarine Spitfire Mk I: 65 Sqn, Henley, Aug 1940, Allen: PAM Jl 75 10:165
Spitfire I: 603 (Edinburg) Sqn, Aug 1940, Carbury: Q Ag 71 2/8: 419
Spitfire I: 609 Sqn, late 1939: Q Jl 71 6/3:2
Spitfire IA: 72 Sqn, 1939, now in RAF Museum: AE Ap 74 6/4: 199
Spitfire II: 41 Sqn, autumn 1940: AE O 71 1/5:251
Spitfire II: 91 Sqn, Feb 1941, McKay: Q Jl 71 6/3:2
Spitfire Vb: 65 Sqn, Louchy, 1 var: Q Ap 73 8/2:106; cor Jl 73 8/3:106
Spitfire HF VII: 131 Sqn: Afx Ag 71 12/12:627
Spitfire FH VIII: Gerbini, Sicily: Afx Ag 71 12/12:628
Spitfire IXc: 310 Sqn: Q Ap 73 8/2:106
Spitfire IX F: 238 Sqn, Corsica, June 1944: IM N 75 11/6:2
Spitfire F XIVc: 350 (Belgium) Sqn, Aug 1944: Q O 71 6/4:24

(U.K. Other Aircraft)

Airspeed Auster IV: RT Ja 72 5/1:10
Airspeed Oxford I: 14 SFTS Cranfield, c.1940: AN 13 D 74 3/14:9
Oxford I: 24 Sqn, late 1942, ambulance conversion: AN 13 D 74 3/14:9
Avro Anson II: 16 SFTS, Hagersville, Ont, April 1943: Q Ap 72: 49
Bristol Bombay: last production, 216 Sqn, Sept 1942: AN 23 N 73 2/14:8
Boulton Paul Defiant TT.1: 286 Sqn, Exeter, 1943-45: AN 10 May 74 2/25:10
Chance Vought OS2U-3 Kingfisher I: 1943: Afx Ap 72 13/8:424
Kingfisher I: April 1942: RT D 74 7/12:137
Kingfisher I: 107 Sqn, RAF, 1942: Afx Ap 72 13/8:426
Consolidated PB2B-2 Catalina; 1945: AN 1 N 74 3/11:8
De Havilland Queen Bee: IM Mr 73 10/3:2-3
De Havilland Tiger Moth: std camouflage for University Air Squadrons: AN 28 N 75 4/13:8-9
Fairey Battle T: Sept 1941: AE Ag 72 3/2:88
Gloster Gladiator II: 1402 Weather Flight, Aldergrove & Ballyhalvert, N. Ireland, Aug 1944-Jan 1945: Q Ap 72 7/2:48

Lockheed Hudson III: ASR mod, Stirgate, 1942: AE Jl 72 3/1:44
Martin PBM-3D Mariner: 524 Sqn, Coastal Command, Oban, late 1943: AN 17 Ag 73 2/7:7
Short Stirling I: 1657 Heavy Conversion Unit, March 1943: RT Ja 74 7/1:6
Stirling IV: glider tug, 1944: RT Ja 74 7/1:7
Stirling IV: glider tug, June 1944: RT Ja 74 7/1:7
Stirling IV: 299 Sqn, Shepherds Grove, 1944, glider tug: AN 19 Ja 72 1/18:10
Stirling IV: 570 Sqn, Sept 1945, transport & glider tug: IM N 74 10/19:7
Vought Sikorsky Chesapeake I: 811 Sqn, Lee-on-Solent, 1941, target tug: Afx Jl 71 12/11:587
Westland Lysander: 13 Sqn, Aug 1940: Afx D 75 17/4:214
Lysander: 13 Sqn, France, early 1940: Afx D 75 17/4:214
Lysander: 16 Sqn, Cambridge, Aug 1940: Afx D 75 17/4:215
Lysander: 225 Sqn, 1940, now in RAF Museum: AE Ap 74 6/4:199
Lysander: 225 Sqn, Aug 1940: Afx D 75 17/4:215
Lysander I: 239 Sqn, c. 1941: AN 27 Je 75 4/2:9
Lysander III: unstated special duties sqn: AN 27 Je 75 4/2:9
Lysander II: 161 Sqn, June 1944, Newhouse: RT My 75 8/3:25
Lysander II(S): 357 Sqn, C Flight, Drigh Rd, July 1945, Hallet: IM N 11/6:7
Westland P. 12: tandem-wing Lysander experiment: AN 27 Je 75 4/2:9

(U. S. Bombers)

(Single-Engine)
Curtiss SB2C-3 Helldiver: CVG-20, USS Enterprise, Oct 1944: Q Jl 72 7/3:121
SB2C-4E: VB-89, USS Antietam, 1945: Q Ap 73 8/2:109
Douglas SBD-3 Dauntless: VS-2, USS Lexington, Battle of the Coral Sea, May 1942, Leppla: Sc My 71 2/5:242-243
Grumman TBF Avenger: 89 AG, USS Antietam, 1945, 2 var: Q Ap 73 8/2:108
TBM-3E Avenger: VT 89, USS Antietam, 1945: Q Ap 73 8/2:109
Vultee A-35 Vengeance: std: IM Je 71 8/6:9
A-35: 446 heavy BG, Suffolk, 1945: IM Je 71 8/6:8
A-35B: IM Ag 73 10/8:3
A-35B: Halesworth, England, Feb 1945: IM Ag 73 10/8:3
Vengeance II: prior to delivery to U. K.: IM Ag 7310/8:3

(Twin-Engine)
Douglas A-20G-20-Do Havoc: 9 AF, England, 1943: AN 30 My 75 3/26:9
Douglas A-26 Invader: Okinawa, 1945: Q Ja 73 8/1:50
A-26B-25-DL: 552 BS, 286 BG, 9 AF; Afx Mr 72 13/7:377
XA-26: prototype, 1942, Howard: Afx Mr 72 13/7:377
Lockheed Hudson III/A-29: AE Jl 72 3/1:44
Lockheed PV-1 Ventura: Tofino, B.C., April 1944: RT My 71 4/5:53

III. Color Patterns

Martin B-26B Marauder: 552 BS, 386 BG, 9 AF, Great Dunmow, England & Beaumont-sur-Boise, France, 1944-45: IM D 71 8/12:9
B-26B: 669 BS, 416 BG, 9 AF, Westhersfield, England & Melun, France, 1944-45: IM D 71 8/12:8
B-26B-4: Sc My 73 4/5:330
B-26B-50: 558 BS, 387 BG: Sc My 73 4/5:330
B-26B-55: 454 BS, 328 BG: Sc My 73 4/5:330
B-26C: IM D 71 8/12:9
North American B-25A Mitchell: 34 BS, 17 BG, McCord Field, Tacoma, late 1941: AI S 74 7/3:136
B-25C: nose art, 12 BG, North Africa, 4 var: Q Ja 73 8/1:4-5
B-25C: 83 Sqn, 12 BG, North Africa, Aug 1942-early 1943: Q Ja 73 8/1:4
B-25C: 434 BS, 12 BG, North Africa, Aug 1942: Q Ja 73 8/1:5
B-25C-15: 488 BS, 340 BG, 9 AF, Sfax, Tunisia, April 1943: AI S 74 7/3:136
B-25C-20: 81 BS, 12 BG, 12 AF, Gerbini, Sicily, Aug 1943: AI S 74 7/3:137
B-25J-32: 499 BS, 345 BG, Ie Shima, July 1945: AI S 74 7/3:137

(Four-Engine)
Boeing B-17E Flying Fortress: 97 BG: Q Ap 73 8/2:98
B-17G: 8 AF, summer 1943 "Sir Baboon McGoon": Q Ja 71 7/1:8
B-17G: 487 BG, 3 Div, Lavenham, England, Schrader: Q Ap 73 8/2:98
B-17G: 500 BS, 398 BG, North Hampstead, England, Feb-May 1944, Wintersteen: Q Jl 71 6/3:26
B.17G: 534 BS, 381 BG, Ridgewell, England, late 1944-45, Marelius: Q Jl 71 6/3:27
Consolidated B-24D Liberator: 514 BS, 376 BG, 19 AF, Soluch, Libya, 1943, "Lady Be Good," pph, det: Q Ja 72 7/1:15
B-24H: 417 BG, 8 AF, 1944: Q O 71 6/4:2
B-24H-DT: 781 BS, 465 BG, 55 BW, 15 AF, Q Ap 73 8/2:101
B-24J: 5 AF, Philippines, 1945: Q Ap 73 8/2:100
B-24J: 459 BF, 15 AF, 1944-45: Q O 71 6/4:2
B-24J: 67 BS, 44 BG, 8 AF: Q Ap 73 8/2:98

(U. S. Fighters)

(Carrier-Based)
Chance Vought F4U-1: VF-17, New Goergia: WW2J My 75 2/3:95
F4U-1: VMF-123, Russell Island, Soloman Islands: WW2J My 2/3:95
F4U-1: VMF-124, Walsh: WW2J My 75 2/3:95
F4U-1: VMF 213, Hanson: Afx N 71 13/3:133
F4U-1: VMF-214, Turtle Bay airstrip, Espiritu Santo, Sept 1943: WW2J My 75 2/3:95
F4U-1A bubble top: VF-12: Q Ja 71 6/1:27
F4U-1A: VF-17: Q Ja 71 6/1:27
F4U-1A: VMF 111: Afx N 71 13/3:133
F4U-1A: VMF-111: Q Ja 71 6/1:27

Aircraft

F4U-1A: VMF-214, Boyington: WW2J My 75 2/3:98
F4U-1A: VMF-214, Dec 1943, Carl: WW2J My 75 2/3:98
F4U-1D: USS Franklin, 1945: WW2J My 75 2/3:98
F4U-1D: VF-84, USS Bunker Hill, Feb 1945: WW2J My 75 2/3:98
F4U-1D: VMF-111 "Devil Dogs," 4 Marine Air Wing: WW2J My 75 2/3:96-97
F4U-1D: VMF 215, Hanson: WW2J My 75 2/3:98
F4U-2: USS Enterprise: WW2J My 75 2/3:95
F4U-2: VMF(N)-532, USS Windham Bay: WW2J My 75 2/3:95
F4U-4: VBF 89, USS Antietam, 1945: Q Ap 73 8/2:109
Goodyear FG-1D Corsair: 2 Marine Air Division: Afx N 71 13/3:133
FG-1D: VMF-312, Kadena airfield, Okinawa, April 1945: WW2J My 75 2/3:98
Grumman F4F-3 Wildcat: VMF-224, Galer: Q Ja 74 9/1:41
FM-1 Wildcat IV: USS Hancock, 1943: AN 7 F 75 3/18:9
FM-2 Wildcat: USS Kitkun Bay, 1944: AN 7 F 75 3/18:18
Grumman Martlet IV: Operation Torch, Nov 1942: Q Ap 72 7/2:55
Grumman F6F Hellcat: std camouflage: Q Jl 73 8/3:156
F6F-3: std camouflage for NAS, Operational Training aircraft, March 1943: Q Jl 73 8/3:157
F6F-3: VF-6, USS Intrepid, Feb 1944, Vraciu: Q Au 75 11/1:36
F6F-3: VF-16, USS Lexington, Marianas Turkey Shoot, Vraciu: Q Au 75 11/1:36
F6F-3: VF-27, USS Princeton, summer 1944: Q Au 75 11/1:36
F6F-3: VF-27, USS Princeton, mid 1944: AI S 75 9/3:148
F6F-5: std camouflage: Q Jl 73 8/3:156
F6F-5: VF-24, USS Santee, July 1945: Q Au 75 11/1:37
F6F-5: VF-27, Battle of Leyete Gulf, Brown: Q Au 75 11/1:37
F6F-5: VF-83, USS Essex, March-July 1945: Q Au 75 11/1:37
F6F-5: VF-89, 89 AG, CV 36 (USS Antietam), 1945: Q Ap 73 8/2:109
F6F-6: VF-12, USS Randolph, early 1945

(Multi-Engine)
Bristol Beaufighter Mk VIF: 416 NFS, Corsica, 1943-44: AE Ja 74 6/1:31
Lockheed P-38 (C, E, F, or G unknown): April 1943, Yamamoto shooting: Q Ja 72 7/1:39
P-38: unit unknown, Homer: Q Jl 72 7/3:119
P-38: 8 FG, 5 AF, Southwest Pacific, Robbins: Q Jl 72 7/3:96
P-38: 35 FS, Ie Shima, Aug 1945: RiS W 74 2/2:62
P-38: 36 FS, Ie Shima, Aug 1945: RiS W 74 2/2:62
P-38: 80 FS, Ie Shima, Aug 1945: RiS W 74 2/2:62
P-38F: 14 FG, Algeria: Afx Ja 74 15/5:298
P-38F-5A: 9 Photo Sqn, 7 BG: Afx Ja 74 15/5:298
P-38J: 338 FS, 55 FG, 8 AF, Nuthampstead, spring 1944: AI Je 75 8/6:295
P-38J: 401 FS, 270 FG, 9 AF, Florennes, Belgium, Nov 1944: AI Je 75 8/6:294
P-38J: 432 FS, 475 FG, 5 AF, New Guinea, winter 1943: AI Je 75 8/6:295
P-38J "Droop Snoot": 485 FS, 370 FG, 9 AF; Afx Ja 74 15/5:298

III. Color Patterns

P-38J-5: 79 FS, 20 FG, 8 AF, Kingscliffe, spring 1944: AI Je 75 8/6:294
P-38J-15-LO: 55 FS, 20 FG, 8 AF: Afx Ja 74 15/5:298

(Single-Engine, Land-Based)
Bell P-39L Airacobra: 93 FS, 81 FG, Tunisia, 1943: AE Ag 71 1/3:136
P-39Q: 362 FS, Hayward, CA, summer 1943: Q Ja 72 8/1:27
Brewster B339 Buffalo: 5 AF: MW D 73 2/4:181
B439 Buffalo: 1944: MW D 73 2/4:181
F2F-3 Buffalo: NAS Pensacola: MW D 73 2/4:182
Curtiss P-40E Tomahawk: 49 PG, Australia, 1942, Preddy: Q Ja 72 7/1:2
P-40E: 11 PS, Umnak, 1942: RT Je 71 4/6:68
P-40F Warhawk: Italian front, 1943: AN 6 S 74 3/7:10
P-40N-20: 80 FG, Assam, India, 1944, Smith: RiS N 72 1/2:67
P-400: 67 FS, 35 FG, New Caledonia, 1942: AE Ag 71 1/3:136
Fiat C.200: 79 FG; AI O 74 7/4:196
North American P-51B Mustang: 318 FS, 325 FG, 15 AF, Italy, late 1944: AI Ja 75 8/1:42
P-51B: 334 FS, 4 FG, 8 AF, April 1944, Beeson: WW2J Jl 75 2/4:27
P-51B: 334 FS, 4 FG, 65 FW, 8 AF, April 1944, Beeson: Q O 72 7/4:126
P-51B: 336 FS, 4 FG, 8 AF, Debden, 1944: AI Ja 75 8/1:42
P-51B: 352 FG, 1944: Q O 72 7/4:150; cor Ja 73 8/1:3
P-51B: 354 FS, 355 FG, Brown: Q Ap 72 7/2:52
P-51B: 364 FS, 357 FG, 8 AF, Leiston, spring 1944: AI Ja 75 8/1:42
P-51B: 370 FS, 359 FG, late 1944--early 1945: Q Ap 72 7/2:42
P-51B: 374 FS, 361 FG, Hopkins: Q Ap 72 7/2:52
P-51B: 374 FS, 361 FG, 8 AF, Bottisham, June 1944: AI Ja 75 8/1:42
P-51B: 505 FS, 339 FG, 66 FW, 8 AF, March 1944: Q O 72 7/4:150
P-51B-1-NA: 336 FS, Europe, 1944, Glover: Q O 71 6/4:8
P-51B-1-NA: 336 FS, April 1944, Glover: Sc Mr 72 3/3:140
P-51B-5-NA: 4 FG, Europe, 1944, Blakeslee: Q O 71 6/4:8
P-51B-5-NA: 334 FS, Europe, 1944, Hively: Q O 71 6/4:9
P-51B-5-NA: 334 FS, Europe, 1944, Megura: Q O 71 6/4:9
P-51B-5-NA: 336 FS, Europe, 1944, Godfrey: Q O 71 6/4:8; cor Jl 72 7/3:113
P-51B-10-NA: 334 FS, Europe, 1944, Clark: Q O 71 6/4:9
P-51B-10-NA: 354 FS, 355 FG, 65 FW, 8 AF, Steeple Morden, Cambridge, April 1944, Brown: Q Jl 73 8/3:152-153
P-51C?: 362 FS, 357 FG, Leiston, East Anglia, 1944, Perry: Q Ja 72 7/1:27
P-51D: 1 FS, 2 Air Commando Group, Burma, 1945, 2 var: Q Jl 71 6/3:14-15
P-51D: 2 FS, 2 ACG, Burma, 1945, 2 var: Q Jl 71 6/3:14-15
P-51D: 39 FS, 314 FGB, 5 AF, Luzon, 1945: Q O 71 6/4:30
P-51D: 39 FS, 314 FBG, 5 AF, Luzon, 1945: Q Ap 73 8/2:80-81
P-51D: 40 FS, 314 FBG, 5 AF, Luzon, 1945: Q Ap 73 8/2:81

Aircraft

P-51D: 41 FS, 314 FBG, 5 AF, Luzon, 1945: Q Ap 73 8/2:81
P-51D: 52 FG, 15 AF: Q Ja 72 7/1:29
P-51D: 55 FS, 20 FG: Afx Ap 74 15/8:455
P-51D: 118 TRS, 23 FG, 14 AF: IM O 71 8/10:16
P-51D: 118 TAC Recon Sqn, 14 AF, Luzon, 1945, McComas: Q Ap 73 8/2:80; cor Jl 73 8/3:139
P-51D: 334 FS, 4 FG, June 1944, Sobanski: Q Jl 72 7/3:113
P-51D: 350 FS, 356 FG, 8 AF, 1945, Hockmeyer: Q O 72 7/4:150
P-51D: 354 FS, 355 FG, Brown: Q Ap 72 7/2:52
P-51D: 369 FS, 359 FG, 1945, Burtner: Q Ap 72 7/2:42
P-51D: 370 FS, 359 FG, 1945, Wetmore: Q Ap 72 7/2:42
P-52D: 383 FS, 364 FG, 8 AF: Afx Ap 74 15/8:455
P-51D: 383 FS, 364 FG, 67 FW, 8 AF, Field: Q Ap 73 8/2:81
P-51D: 384 FS, 364 FG, 8 AF, Lowell: Q Ap 73 8/2:107; add Jl 73 8/3:139
P-51D: 385 FS, McCubbin: Q Ap 73 8/2:107
P-51D: 435 FS, 479 FG, 8 AF: Afx Je 73 14/10:539
P-51D-5-NA: 334 FS, 4 FG, Oct 1944, Lang: Q Ja 72 7/1:7
P-51D-5-NA: 336 FS, 4 FG, Sept 1944, Emerson: Q Ja 72 7/1:6; cor Jl 72 7/3:113
P-51D-5-NA: 336 FS, 4 FG, June 1944, Goodson: Q Ja 72 7/1:6; cor Jl 72 7/3:113
P-51D-5-NA: 343 FS, 55 FG, Afx Ap 74 15/8:455
P-51D-5-NA: 375 FS, 361 FG, D-Day: Sc Mr 72 3/3:140
P-51D-10-NA: 335 FS, 4 FG, March 1945, O'Donnel: Q Ja 72 7/1:6; cor Jl 72 7/3:113
P-51D-10-NA: 376 FS, 361 FG, 8 AF: Afx Je 73 14/10:538
P-51D-10-NA: 487 FS, 352 FG, 8 AF: Afx Je 73 14/10:538
P-51D-10-NA: 487 FS, 352 FG, 8 AF, 1944-45, Meyer: Q O 72 7/4:150
P-51D-15-NA: 334 FS, 4 FG, Dec 1944, Montgomery: Q Ja 72 7/1:7
P-51D-15-NA: 368 FS, 359 FG, 8 AF: Afx Je 73 14/10:538
P-51D-20-NA: 82 FS, 78 FG: Afx Ap 74 15/8:455
P-51D-20-NA: 336 FS, 4 FG, June 1945, Stewart: Afx Ap 74 15/8:455
P-51D-25-NA: 334 FS, 4 FG, April 1945, Norley: Q Ja 72 7/1:7; cor Jl 72 7/3:113
P-51D-25-NA: 354 FS, 355 FG, 8 AF, Kinnard: Afx Je 73 14/10:536
P-51D-25-NA: 360 FS, 356 FG: Afx Ap 74 15/8:455
P-51D-30-NA: 352 FS, 353 FG, 8 AF: Afx Je 73 14/10:538
P-51D-30-NA: 362 FS, 357 FG, 8 AF: Afx Je 73 14/10:539
P-51H: 62 FS: Afx Je 75 16/10:37
P-51K: 29 FS, 314 FBG, 5 AF: Q O 71 6/4:30
Republic P-36C Lancer: std, early 1942: AE N 71 1/6:313
Republic P-47: 10,000th built, Italy, 1943: RT S 72 5/9:97
P-47C: 334 FS, 4 FG, 8 AF, autumn 1943, Beeson: WW2J Jl 75 2/4:27
P-47C: 334 FS, 4 FG, 65 FW, 8 AF, autumn 1943, Beeson: Q O 72 7/4:127
P-47D: 86 FS, 79 FG, Fano, Italy, Feb 1945: AI Mr 75 8/3:149

III. Color Patterns

P-47D-12: 368 FS, 359 FG, early 1944: Q Ap 72 7/2:42
P-47D-20-RA: 19 FS, 318 FG, Saipan, July 1944: AI Mr 75 8/3:149
P-47D-21-RE: 61 FS, 56 FG, May 1944, Johnson: AM S 72 75/3: 36-37
P-47D-21-RE: 62 FS, 56 FG, Johnson: Sc Ag 71 2/8:418
P-47D-22-RE: 82 FS, 78 FG: Sc Ag 71 2/8:419
P-47D-23-RE: 80 FG, Assam, India, 1944, Smith: RiS N 72 1/2: 67
P-47D-25-RE: 352 FS, 353 FG, Raydon, Suffolk, July 1944: AI Mr 75 8/3:148
P-47D-30-RA: 365 FS, 358 FG, 1 TAF(P), Base Y-79, Mannheim, April 1945, Volkmer: Q Jl 72 7/3:123
P-47D-30-RA: 366 FS, 358 FG, Toul, France, winter 1944: AI Mr 75 8/3:148
P-47D-30-RA: 512 FS, 406 FG, Nordholz, summer 1945: AI Mr 75 8/3:149
P-47M-RE: 63 FS, 56 FG, Boxted, U.K., 1945, Keeler: RiS Ag 72 1/1:25
P-47M-1-RE: 63 FS, 56 FG, Boxted, Essex, spring 1945: AI Mr 75 8/3:149
P-47N: 5 AF, Luzon: Q O 71 6/4:31
P-47N: 5 AF, Luzon, 1945: Q O 71 6/4:31
P-47N-2-RE: 463 FS, 507 FG, Ie Shima, 1945: RiS N 72 1/2:49
Seversky P-35A: 34 PS, Del Carmen Field, Philippines, D 1941, Marrett: Q Jl 72 7/3:96

(U. S. Observation & Reconnaissance)

Chance Vought OS2U Kingfisher: Aleutians: RT D 74 7/12:137
OS2U: USS West Virginia, Pearl Harbor, Dec 1941: RT D 74 7/12:137
OS2U: VS-46, 1944: RT D 74 7/12:137
Consolidated PBY-3 Catalina: Corpus Christi, 1942: Q W 75 11/2:79
PBY-5A: Atlantic Air Fleet, 1942: IM F 72 9/2:8
PBY-5A: VSB 63, Dunkeswell, Devon, 1945: IM F 72 9/2:7
PBY-5A: VSB 63, Gibralter, Feb 1944, Mad Cat: IM F 72 9/2: 5-6
PBY-6A: 1945: AN 1 N 74 3/11:8
Curtiss SOC Seagull: USS Charger, May 1942: Q Su 75 10/4:150
SOC-1: USS Charger, Feb 1945: Q Su 75 10/4:152
SOC-1: VCS 7, Aug 1943: Q Su 75 10/4:152
SOC-2: VCS 7, USS Tuscaloosa, off Newfoundland, May 1943: Q Su 75 10/4:152
SOC-3: Operation Torch, Nov 1942: Q Su 75 10/4:152
SOC-3: USS Salt Lake City, invasion of Kiska, Aug 1943: Q Su 75 10/4:152
SOC-3A: USS Long Island, May 1942: Q Su 75 10/4:150
De Havilland F-8 Mosquito: prototype: Q Ja 75 10/3:100
F-8: Dec 1944: Q Ja 75 10/3:101
F-8: 802 Recon Gp: Q Ja 75 10/3:101
Martin B-26B: 10 Tac Recon Sqn, 69 Recon Gp: IM D 71 8/12:8

Aircraft

B-26B: 10 Tac Recon Sqn, 69 Recon Gp, Nancy, France, 1945: IM D 71 8/12:9
Stinson L-5B Vigilant: 155 LS, 2 ACG: Q Jl 71 6/3:14

(U.S. Other Aircraft)

Avro (Canada) AT-20 (Anson II): RT N 71 4/11:126
Bell TP-39: RT Jl 71 4/7:82
TP-39D-1: Q Ja 74 9/1:7
Curtiss TP-40E Warhawk trainer: RT Jl 71 4/7:82
Focke Wulf Fw 190A-8: 325 FG, North Africa: RT Je 73 6/6:68
Lockheed P-38J Lightning: "Yippee," 5,000th production aircraft, promotional tour: Sc F 75 6/65:88-89
Lightning Swordfish: P-38 mod for research: RT Ag 74 7/8:94
Nordyun C-64 Norseman: 1945: RT N 71 4/11:126
UC-64 Norseman: 1 Air Commando Group, Burma, 1944: RT D 72 5/12:140
North American B-25J: 5 AF, VIP transport: Q O 71 6/4:31
North American TP-51B Mustang trainer: RT Jl 71 4/7:82
Piper L-4B Grasshopper: D-Day stripes: RCS Je 75 1/2:54

(Yugoslavia)

Messerschmitt Bf 109E-3: 6 Ftr Rgt, 1940: AE S 71 1/4:211

Post World War II

(Abu-Dhabi Military)

Britten-Norman Defender: Afx D 72 14/4:206-207
Westland-Aérospatiale Puma: Afx Ap 73 14/8:428

(Afghanistan Civil)

Boeing 727: Ariana: IM Mr 71 8/3:6-7

(Algeria Military)

Ilyushin Il-28: IM Ja 74 10/13-14:27

(Argentina Military)

Aermacchi MB.326GB: AN 16 F 73 1/20:10
Avro Lincoln: AN 28 Je 74 3/2:10
Dassault Mirage 3EA: IM D 72 9/12:9

III. Color Patterns

Lockheed P-2E Neptune: 2 Gr de Patrulla, NAS Norfolk, Aug 1972: Q Jl 74 10/1:26
McDonnell Douglas A-4B Skyhawk: IV Gr Caza-Bombardeo, Villa Reynolds, 1970: AE F 72 2/2:100

(Australia Civil)

De Havilland Canada DHC 1 Chipmunk: IM Ap 72 9/4:16; cor S 72 9/9:16
Chipmunk: Royal Victorian Aero Club, 1969: IM Ap 72 9/4:16; cor S 72 9/9:16
Hawker Sea Fury Mk 11: ex RAN, Fawcett Aviation, Bankstown, 1969: RT Ja 73 6/1-2:20
McDonnell Douglas DC-9-30: Ansett Airlines: AN 12 Jl 74 3/3:9

(Australia Military)

Aermacchi MB.326H: AN 16 F 73 1/20:10
Avro Lincoln Mk 30: 1 Sqn, Tengah, Singapore: Q O 73 8/4:246
Lincoln Mk 31: 10 Sqn, Townsville, Queensland: Q O 73 8/4:246
Lincoln Mk 32: 10 Sqn: AN 28 Je 74 3/2:10
Bell 206B-1 Ranger: Army, 1972: RT O 74 7/10:113
CAC Sabre: 76 Sqn, "The Panthers" aerobatic team: AE Mr 74 6/3:141
Chance Vought Kingfisher: Australian National Antarctic Research Expedition, 1948: IM My 72 9/5:11; cor S 72 9/9:16
Dassault Mirage IIIO: calibration tests, Avalon Afld: AE Mr 74 6/3:141
De Havilland Mosquito FB 40: 1(B) Sqn, Amberley, May 1948: AN 20 Jl 73 2/5:5
Mosquito FB 40: 2 ADT&F Flight, Clark Field, Philippines, March 1946: AN 20 Jl 73 2/5:5
De Havilland Canada DHC-2 Beaver: Australian National Antarctic Research Expedition, 1964: Sc My 72 3/5:268
De Havilland Canada DHC-4 Caribou: Tan Son Nhut, Vietnam, 1970: Q Jl 73 8/3:154
Fairey Firefly T 5: navy: Afx My 73 14/9:493
GAF Canberra B.20: 2 Sqn, Vietnam, 1967-71: AE Mr 74 6/3:141
General Dynamics F-111C: June 1973: AE Mr 74 6/3:141
Gloster Meteor Mk.8: 77 Sqn, Kimpo, Korea, 1951: RT S 74 7/9:107
Meteor Mk.8: 77 Sqn, Kimpo, Korea, early 1960s: Q Ap 73 8/2:91
Hawker Sea Fury: Kimpo, 1951: RT S 74 7/9:107
Sea Fury Mk 11: RNAS Nowra, NSW, 1963, 2 var: RT Ja 73 6/2-3:19
Lockheed P-2E Neptune: 11 Sqn, NAS Sangley Point, May 1966: Q Jl 74 10/1:27
SP-2H Neptune: 11 Sqn, Richmond (Asl.), Jan 1967: Q Jl 74 10/1:27
Martin PBM-3S Mariner: AN 17 Ag 73 2/7:7

McDonnell Douglas A-4 Skyhawk: navy: AE F 72 2/2:100
Vultee Vengeance: 21 Sqn, in spurious German markings for movie
 "Tobruk": IM Ag 73 10/8:2

(Austria Military)

SAAB J-29F: 1 Jagdbomber Staffel: AN 11 My 73 1/26:9
Short Skyvan 3M: 1974: PAM Ja 75 8:125

(Bahrain Military)

Westland Scout: Police: AN 8 Je 73 2/2:9

(Belgium Civil)

North American Harvard AT-6: IM Ja 74 10/13-14:15
Harvard AT-6F: IM Ja 74 10/13-14:14
Short Stirling MK V: AN 19 Ja 72 1/18:10

(Belgium Military)

Avro (Canada) CF-100 Canuck: 349 Esc: RT Je 75 8/6:64
CF-100: 350 Esc: RT Je 75 8/6:64
Dassault Mirage 5 BA: 2 Sqn, 2 Wing: AN 7 Mr 75 3/20:8
Mirage 5 BR: IM D 72 9/12:7-8
Douglas C-37 Dakota: 20 Sqn, 15 Wing: AN 7 Mr 75 3/20:9
Lockheed F-104 Starfighter: 349 Sqn: AN 7 Mr 75 3/20:9
Supermarine Spitfire F XIV: 2 Sqn, 2 Wing, 2 var: Q O 71 6/4: 25
Spitfire FR XIV: 1 Sqn, 2 Wing, 1 var: Q O 71 6/4:25
Spitfire FR XIVe: Ecole de Chasse, Coxyde: Q O 71 6/4:25

(Brazil Civil)

Boeing 737: Wasp: IM Mr 71 6/3:8-9
Convair CV-990: Varig: Q Jl 71 6/3:32

(Brazil Military)

Aermacchi MB.326B: AN 16 F 73 1/20:10
Cessna T-37C Tweet: RiS Mr 75 3/1:45
Douglas B-26B: 6 Gr: Q Jl 71 6/3:10
Douglas C-47: 1 Grp de Transport, Galeao AFB, Rio de Janeiro:
 Q Ap 72 7/2:67
Grumman HU-16A Albatross: 1974: RT O 74 7/10:120
Albatross: 2a/10 GAV, São Paulo, 2 var: RT F 74 7/2:18
Lockheed P-2E Neptune: 7 Gr: Q Jl 74 10/1:26

III. Color Patterns 274

Lockheed TF-33A: FAB, 3 var: Q Jl 72 7/3:101

(Burma Military)

Hunting Percival Provost Mk I: AN 15 N 74 3/12:8-9

(Cambodia Military)

MiG-17P: 1971: AE D 72 3/6:312

(Canada Civil)

Avro York: airline unstated: RT My 75 8/5:59
Beechcraft K.35 Bonanza: C.V. Antenna, Winnipeg: RT Ja 75 8/1:10
Boeing 727: CP Air: RT D 73 6/12:141
Boeing 727: Pacific Western: RT D 73 6/12:140
Boeing 727: Wardair: RT D 73 6/12:140
Boeing 737: CP Air: RT D 73 6/12:136
Boeing 737: Eastern Provincial: RT D 73 6/12:137
Boeing 737: Nordair: RT D 73 6/12:137
Boeing 737: Pacific Western: RT D 6/12:136
Boeing 737: Transair: RT D 73 6/12:136
Bristol 31 Freighter: Pacific Western: RT N 72 5/11:130
Bristol 170 Freighter: Norcanair, 1974: RT S 74 8/9:100
Convair CV-990: Nordair, leased later to Modern Air Transport (U.S.): Q Jl 71 6/3:30
De Havilland Canada DHC 2 Beaver: BC Air Lines, Ocean Falls, 1964-65: RT O 74 7/10:118
Beaver: Bradley Air Services, Ltd, Carp, Ont: Sc My 72 3/5:272
Beaver: CF-OMI: Sc My 72 3/5:271
Beaver: Eastern Provincial Airways: IM O 72 9/10:6
Beaver: Hudson's Bay Co.: Sc My 72 3/5:270
Beaver: Laurentian Air Services: RT D 73 6/12:133+
Beaver: Ontario Provincial Air Service, 1974: RT O 74 7/10:118
Beaver: RCMP, old pattern: Sc My 72 3/5:272
Beaver: RCMP, new pattern: Sc My 72 3/5:270
Beaver: Wardair, winter (ski) rig: Sc My 72 3/5:269
Beaver: West Coast Air Services: Sc My 72 3/5:268
De Havilland Canada DHC 2 Mk 3 Turbo-Beaver: factory demonstration: IM O 72 9/10:10
Turbo-Beaver: Government of Manitoba Air Service: RT D 73 6/12:138
Turbo-Beaver: Ilford Airways: RT D 73 6/12:138
Turbo-Beaver: Ilford Riverton Airways: RT D 73 6/12:139
Turbo-Beaver: Newfoundland & Labrador Forest Service: RT D 73 6/12:138
Turbo-Beaver: RCMP: RT D 73 6/12:139
Dornier Do 28 Skyservant: Field Aviation, Calgary: RT Ja 75 8/1:10

Aircraft

Douglas A-26 Invader: Conair Aviation, Ltd. Abbotsford, fire fighter, pph: RT Jl 72 5/7:78
Douglas DC-3: "Arctic 7," Field Aviation, Buttonville, 1971: RT My 72 5/5:55
DC-3: BC Forest Products, Vancouver Airport, 1973: RT My 74 7/5:66
DC-3: CP Air, Vancouver, 1974: RT S 74 7/5:106
DC-3: CF-RXY, Calgary: RT S 73 6/9:104
DC-3: Duplate of Canada, executive aircraft, 1974: RT Mr 75 8/3:28
DC-3: Eldorado Aviation, 1958: RT Ja 74 7/1:8
DC-3: Gateway Aviation: RT Ap 74 7/4:46
DC-3: Gateway Aviation, 1973: RT Ap 74 7/4:46
DC-3: Harrison Airways, 1973, Vancouver Airport: RT Mr 75 8/3:28
DC-3: Harrison Air Lines, transition livery from CP Air, 1975: RT Jl 75 8/7:82
DC-3: Harrison Air Lines "Tweedsmuir," 1975 (ex-CP Air): RT Jl 75 8/7:82
DC-3: Mobil Oil Canada, 1973: RT Ja 74 7/1:8
DC-3: Northcoast Air Services, Vancouver fog dispersal mod: RT Mr 74 7/3:34
DC-3: Norcanair, 1972: RT D 72 5/2:137
DC-3: Northern Thunderbird Airlines, 1975: RT My 75 8/5:55
DC-3: Transair, 1970: RT D 72 5/12:137
DC-3: Trans-Provincial, Terrace, B.C., 1973: RT Mr 75 8/3:28
Grumman Avenger: Skyway Air Services, Abbotsford, B.C., 1966: RT My 73 6/12:146
Grumman CS2F1 Tracker: Ontario Provincial Air Service fire bomber, 1974: RT O 74 7/10:118
Handley Page HPR7 Dart Herald series 200: Eastern Provincial Airways: RT D 73 6/12:146
Hawker Sea Fury: CF-CHB: RT S 72 5/9:100-103
Martin Mars: fire bomber, 2 var: RT Ag 71 4/8:88
McDonnell Douglas DC-9-10: Air Canada: AN 12 Jl 74 3/3:8-9
Piper Cherokee Arrow: 927 Airlines, Winnipeg: RT Ja 75 8/1:10
Short Skyvan series 3: Selkirk Air Services "Irish Rover": RT Ap 71 4/4:40-41

(Canada Military--Helicopter)

Bell CH-118 Iroquois: RT O 74 7/10:119
Bell CH-135 Twin Huey: RT O 74 7/10:119
CH-135: 1974: RT Mr 74 7/5:64
CH-135: 450 Sqn: RT O 74 7/10:114
Bell COH-58A Kiowa: std: RT N 73 6/11:128
Kiowa: 4 var: RT Ap 74 7/4:40
Kiowa: 205 Sqn: RT Ag 72 5/8:92
Kiowa: 427 Sqn: RT O 74 7/10:114
Bell CUH-1H Huey: 1970: RT N 74 7/11:126
Huey: 1972: RT N 74 7/11:126

III. Color Patterns

Huey: 1973, 2 var: RT N 74 7/11:126
Huey: Base Rescue Flight, Cold Lake, 1974: RT O 74 7/10:114
Huey: Base Rescue Flight, CFB Moose Jaw: RT Mr 74 7/3:25
Boeing-Vertol CH 113 Labrador: 103 Sqn, Summerside, Dec 1968: RT F 71 4/2:17
Sikorsky CHSS-2 Sea King: navy: RT Jl 71 4/7:73
Westland H-34 (Wessex): Cold Lake, June 1969: RT F 71 4/2:16

(Canada Military--Propeller)

Avro Shackleton Mk 2: Maritime Proving & Evaluation Unit: RT Ap 71 4/4:47
Beechcraft T-34 Mentor: 4 Flying Training School, Penhold, Alta, mid 1950s: RT Ag 74 7/8:85
Bristol 170: prob 1967: RT N 72 5/11:129
Bristol 170 Mk 31M: 1951: RT N 72 5/11:130
Canadair CL-84-1: Tripartite V/STOL trials: AE N 73 5/5:244
Cessna L-19 Bird Dog: Army, late 1950s: RT N 74 7/11:121
Consolidated RY-3 (Liberator CL): icing research, 9(T) Group, RCAF Rockcliffe, 1946: RT Jl 71 4/7:78
De Havilland Canada DHC-1 Chipmunk: IM Mr 74 10/(15):7
De Havilland Canada CC-108 Caribou: 115 ATU: Q Jl 73 8/3:155
Douglas DC-3/C-47 Dakota: mid 1950s: RT Je 73 6/6:66
Dakota: 429 Sqn, present: RT N 73 6/11:128
Grumman CS2-F Tracker: VS 880, HMCS Bonaventure: Q W 75 11/2:73
Grumman CSR-110 Albatross: Air Transport Command: RiS Sp 73 1/3:86
CSR-110: 442 Transport & Rescue Sqn: RiS Sp 73 1/3:86
Grumman TBM-3S Avenger: navy: Afx My 75 16/9:534
Avenger 4: AN 27 O 72 1/12:10
Hawker Sea Fury: RCN std: RT Ja 73 6/1-2:10-11
Sea Fury FB 10: W. E. Flight, RCAF Station Edmonton, late 1947-- early 1948: RT Ja 73 6/1-2:5
Sea Fury FB 11: 803 Sqn, HMCS Magnificent/Shearwater, 1948-49: RT Ja 73 6/1-2:1
Sea Fury FB 11: 803 Sqn, RCN Shearwater, c.1949-50, Rice: RT Ja 73 6/1-2:6-7
Sea Fury FB 11: 803 Sqn, RCN, c.1950-52 2 var: RT Ja 73 6/1-2:8-9
Sea Fury FB 11: 883 Sqn, HMCS Magnificent/Shearwater, 1949-51: RT Ja 73 6/1-2:1
Sea Fury FB 11: Commander?, HMCS Shearwater, c.1954-55: RT Ja 73 6/1-2:12
Sea Fury FB 11: Air Group Commander?, RNAS Eglinton & HMCS Shearwater, 1948: RT Ja 74 6/1-2:7
Sea Fury FB 11: Air Group Commander?, HMCS Shearwater, 1948: RT Ja 73 6/1-2:8
Sea Fury FB 11: VS 870 Sqn, CJATC Rivers, summer 1955: RT Ja 73 6/1-1:12
Sea Fury FB 11: VS 870 Sqn, HMCS Shearwater, 1953: RT Ja 73 6/1-2:10-11

Aircraft

Sea Fury FB 11: storage, Devert N. S., 1955-56: RT Ja 73 6/1-2: 1
Sea Fury FB 11: RCAF Winter Experimental Establishment, RCAF Edmonton, Feb 1950: RT Ja 73 6/1-2:10-11
Lockheed C-130 Hercules: 435 Sqn, Trenton, Oct 1968, to Biafra: RT Jl 74 7/7:77
Lockheed P2B-7 Neptune: 2 MOTU, Summerside PEI, May 1963, after visit to Jacksonville NAS: RT N 71 4/11:127
Lockheed P3A Orion: Operational Test & Evaluation Force: RT Ap 71 4/4:45
Lockheed Vega Ventura Target Tug: Sea Island, Vancouver, 1946: RT My 71 4/5:49
North American Harvard: Goldilocks, Harvard Aerobatic Team, Moose Jaw, 1964: RT S 72 5/8:104
Harvard: RCAF training, Alberta, 1964, Smith: PAM Jl 75 10: 168-169
Harvard II: 442 (aux) Sqn, Vancouver, 1948: RT O 71 4/10:116
Harvard IV: static display, Penhold Alta: RT F 74 7/2:23; cor Ap 74 7/4:45
Harvard IV: 400 Sqn, Downsview, Toronto: Afx Je 71 12/10:526
North American P-51 Mustang: Central Air Command Composite Flight, Trenton: RT Ap 75 8/4:46
P-51: Experimental & Proving Establishment, Uplands: RT Ap 75 8/4:46
P-51: No. 1 Flying Training School, Centralia: RT Ap 75 8/4:46
P-51: 402 "City of Winnipeg" Sqn: RT Ap 75 8/4:47
P-51: 424 "City of Hamilton" Sqn: RT Ap 75 8/4:46
P-51: 443 "City of New Westminster" Sqn: RT Ap 75 8/4:47; cor Jl 75 8/7:74
P-51D: 402 "City of Winnipeg" Sqn, before 1960: RT Mr 72 5/3: 34
P-51D/K: Comox, before 1960: RT S 74 7/9:107
Supermarine Seafire XV: RT Jl 74 7/7:80
Seafire XV: 803 Sqn, autumn 1946: RT My 73 6/5:54
Seafire XV: 803 Sqn, 1947: RT My 73 6/5:54

(Canada Military--Jet Fighter)

Avro CF-100 Canuck: 433 Sqn, North Bay, Mid 1950s: RT F 74 7/2:13
CF-100 Mk 4: 409 Sqn, Comox, B.C., 1954: RT Ap 75 8/4:44
CF-100 Mk 4: 419 Sqn, North Bay, Ont, 1954: RT Ap 75 8/4:43
CF-100 Mk 4: 423 Sqn, St. Hubert, PQ, 1954: RT Ap 75 8/4:42
CF-100 Mk 4: 425 Sqn, St. Hubert, PQ, 1954: RT Ap 75 8/4:44
CF-100 Mk 4: 428 Sqn, Uplands, 1955, RT Ap 75 8/4:42
CF-100 Mk 4: 432 Sqn, Bagotville, PQ, 1954: RT Ap 75 8/4:44
CF-100 Mk 4: 433 Sqn, North Bay, Ont, 1955: RT Ap 75 8/4:42
CF-100 Mk 4: 440 Sqn, Bagotville, PQ, 1954: RT Ap 75 8/4:42
CF-100 Mk 4: 445 Sqn, Uplands, 1954: RT Ap 75 8/4:42
Avro CF-105 Arrow: test aircraft: RT Ap 73 6/4:44
Canadair CF-5 Freedom Fighter: 433 Sqn, after 1973: RT N 73 6/11:128

III. Color Patterns

CF-5D: AE Je 72 2/6:324
Canadair CF-104 Starfighter: first Canadian assembly (components Lockheed-built), testbed: RT Ja 75 8/1:11
CF-104: 1 Can Air Gp, Baden Spellingen, Jan 1972: RT Je 72 5/6:69
CF-104: 4 ATAF, 11 AFCENT Tac Weapons Meet, CAB Baden-Soellingen, May--June 1974: RT N 74 7/11:128
CF-104: 417 Sqn: RT N 73 6/11:128
CF-104: 439 Sqn, 1 AG: AN 7 Mr 75 3/20:37
CF-104: 439 (Sabre Toothed Tiger) Sqn, 1 Wing, Lahr, 1969 Tiger Meet, Woodbridge, England, Aug 1969: RT Jl 74 7/7:75-76; Sc F 75 6/65:86
CF-104D: 441 TFS, 1 CAG, May 1974: RT N 74 7/11:128
Canadair Sabre Mk. 2: 434 Sqn, 3 Wing, Zweibrucken, Germany: RT Ja 74 7/1:1
Sabre Mk. 4: Central Exp & Prov Estab/Air Armament Evaluation Detach, Cold Lake, 1959: RT O 74 7/10:109
Sabre Mk. 4: 422 "Tomahawk" Sqn, RCAF Uplands, Ottawa, Aug 1953: RT D 72 5/12:133
Sabre Mk. 5: 1(F) OTU, Chatham, N. B., 1958: RT Jl 74 7/7:83
Sabre Mk. 5: 413 Sqn, Frescati (Metz), Operation Carte Blanche, 1955: RT Jl 74 7/7:83
Sabre Mk. 5: 416 Sqn, Frescati (Metz), Operation Carte Blanche, 1955: RT Jl: 7/7:83
Sabre Mk. 5: 416 Sqn, Gros Tinquin, 1955-56: RT Jl 74 7/7:83
Sabre Mk. 6: 422 Sqn, Baden-Soligen, 1957-58: RT Jl 74 7/7:83
Sabre Mk. 6: 427 Sqn, Zwie-Brucken, 1960: RT Jl 74 7/7:83
Sabre Mk. 6: 439 Sqn, Marville, France, 1957: AE Ap 72 2/4:204
De Havilland Vampire I: 442 (Aux) Sqn, Victoria, 1949: RT Jl 74 7/7:78-79
Vampire III: std, RCAF: RT Je 72 5/6:68
Vampire III: 401 Sqn (Aux) Sqn, Montreal/St. Hubert, 1956: RT Je 72 5/6:68; RT Jl 72 5/7:74
Vampire III: 410 Sqn, Uplands, 1949: RT Je 72 5/6:68
Vampire III: 438 Sqn (Aux) Sqn, St. Hubert, c. 1955: RT Je 72 5/6:68
Gloster Meteor F. Mk 4: Avro Orenda afterburner testbed: RT Jl 72 5/7:76
Meteor T. 7: 421 Sqn, 2 Wint, RAF Odiham, England, Jan-Nov 1951: RT Jl 72 5/7:76
Lockheed T-33AN: 1 CAB Baden Sollingen, Feb 1974: IM S 75 11/5:21
McDonnell CF-101 Voodoo: 409 Sqn, Moose Jaw: RT Ag 72 5/8:91
CF-101: 417 Sqn, Moose Jaw: RT Ag 72 5/8:91
CF-101B: 1961: RT My 72 5/5:53
CF-101B: 409 Sqn, 1963-68: RT My 72 5/5:53
CF-101B: 409 Sqn, July 1970: MW Mr 73 1/7:364-365
CF-101B: 409 Sqn, Comox, B.C., 1971: RiS Au 73 2/1:26
CF-101B: 409 Sqn, Bagotville, 1968: RT My 72 5/5:54
CF-101B: 416 Sqn, 1970: RT My 72 5/5:54
CF-101B: 416 Sqn, Chatham, Ont: RiS Au 73 2/1:26
CF-101B: 425 Sqn, 1967: RT My 72 5/5:53

CF-101B: 425 Sqn, Bagotville, Que, 1972: RiS Au 73 2/1:26
McDonnell F2H-3 Banshee: Navy, May 1958, 2 var: RT O 73 6/10:115
F2H-3: Navy, Aug 1962: RT O 73 6/10:115
F2H-3: VF-830, 1958: AN 15 Mr 74 2/21:8

(Canada Other Aircraft)

Canadair CL-41 Tutor: Red Knights aerobatic team, 1969: RT Ag 71 4/8:90
Canadair T-33 Silver Star: RT N 73 6/11:128
T-33: Cold Lake: RT Ja 75 8/1:7
T-33: Moose Jaw, 1965: RT My 72 5/5:58
T-33: Moose Jaw, 1967: RT My 72 5/5:58
T-33: Moose Jaw, 1969: RT My 72 5/5:58
T-33: 3 Flying Instructors School, Portage La Prairie, Man, 2 var: RT My 74 7/5-6:63
T-33: 402 (City of Winnipeg) Aux Sqn, mid-1950s: RT F 74 7/2:19
T-33: 409 (Nighthawk) Sqn, CFB Comox, 1973: RT F 74 7/2:19; cor Ap 74 7/4:45
T-33: 410 (Cougar) Sqn: RT Ja 75 8/1:7
T-33: 410 (Cougar) Sqn: CFB Bagotville, Aug 1973: RT F 75 8/2:17
T-33: 414 Sqn, CAF Black Knight aerobatic team, 2 var: RT O 72 5/10:112
T-33: 429 (Buffalo) Sqn: RT Ja 75 8/1:7
T-33: 429 (Bison) Sqn, CFB Winnipeg, Aug 1973: RT F 75 8/2:17
T-33: Snowbirds aerobatic team support aircraft: RT O 73 6/10:126
T-33 Mk 3: Chatham, target tug?, 1964-65: RT Jl 74 7/7:82
T-33 Mk 3: 1 OTU, Chatham, 1957: RT Jl 74 7/7:82
T-33A-N Mk 3: 2 Adv Flying School, 1956: RT Jl 74 7/7:82
T-33 Mk 3: 2 AFS, Portage la Prairie, Man, 1960: RT D 72 5/12:143
T-33 Mk 3: 3 Adv, Flying School, Gimli, 1957: RT Jl 74 7/7:82
T-33 Mk 3: 32 Sqn, HMCS Shearwater, 1961: RT Jl 74 7/7:82
T-33A-N: 408 Sqn, CAB Rivers, Man, late 1960: RT N 73 6/11:126
T-33A-N: 418 (City of Edmonton) Aux Sqn, mid 1950: RT N 73 6/11:126
T-33 Target Tug: unit unknown, Whidbey Island NAS open house 1974: RT Jl 75 8/7:73
Dassault Falcon 20, CC117: Airborne Sensing Unit, Cold Lake, April 1972: RT N 72 5/11:128
Falcon: 412 Sqn: RT My 75 8/3:35

(Chile Military)

Douglas B-26C: Q Jl 71 6/3:11

III. Color Patterns 280

(China, People's Republic of, Military)

MiG-15: 2 var: IM F 71 8/2:16
MiG-15bis: Korean war: AN 14 S 73 2/9:8-9
MiG-17F: 1958, 2 var: RT Ag 75 8/8:90
MiG-19SF: AE Ja 72 2/1:33

(China, Taiwan, Military)

North American F-100A-10-NA Super Sabre: RiS Jl 75 3/2:90
F-100A-20-NA: 2 var: RiS Jl 75 3/2:90
F-100F-15-NA: Ri S Jl 75 3/2:90
Pazmay PL-1: prototype homebuilt-design trainer: AM F 74 78/2: 50-51

(Colombia Military)

Canadair CL-13B Sabre Mk 6: Esc de Caza, Palanguero, 1957: AE Ap 72 2/4:204
Cessna T-37C: Palanguero AB, 1970: RiS Mr 75 3/1:45
Douglas B-26C: Q Jl 71 6/3:11

(Cuba Military)

MiG-19P: AN 18 O 74 3/10:8

(Czechoslovakia Civil)

Brouček W-01: one-off lightplane design, April 1970, Werner: Aero My 71 36/423:242
Lisunov Li-2P: Ceskoslovenska Letecka Spolechost (CLS): AN 12 D 75 4/14:9

(Czechoslovakia Military)

Avia B-33 (Ilyushin Il-10): 2 var: IM Ap 72 9/4:12-13
B-33 trainer: IM Ap 72 9/4:13
Avia C.2B-1 (Arado Ar 96B), 1949: AN 27 My 73 1/25:9
Avia L-29 Delfin: Q Ja 72 7/1:22
Ilyushin Il-10: RT O 73 6/10:110
Il-10: dual control: RT O 73 6/10:110
MiG 15 (S.102): AN 14 S 73 2/9:8-9
MiG 15bis: aerobatic unit: AN 14 S 73 2/9:8
MiG 17F: RT Ag 75 8/8:88
MiG 17PF: 3 var: RT Ag 75 8/8:88
MiG 18S: AN 18 O 74 3/10:8-9
MiG-21MF: AI N 75 9/5:248
MiG-21MF (Fishbed J): RT N 72 5/11:122

MiG-21R: AI N 75 9/5:248
S-90 (Focke Wulf Fw 190): Q Ja 72 7/1:2
Supermarine Spitfire IX clipped wing: Central Flying School, Hradec
 Kralov, 1946: AN 2 Mr 73 1/21:8-9
Spitfire LF IXe: Ruzyné Airport, Aug 1945: Q Ap 73 8/2:106

(Denmark Civil)

Convair CV-990: Internord (charter line), ex American Airlines:
 Q Jl 71 6/3:30

(Denmark Military)

De Havilland Canada DHC-1 Chipmunk: Vaerlose AB, 1972: IM Mr
 74 10/(15):7
Douglas C-47 Dakota: 721 Esk: AN 7 Mr 75 3/20:9
Douglas C-54: 721 Esk: AN 7 Mr 75 3/20:8-9
North American F-100D Super Sabre: 727 Esk: AN 7 Mr 75 3/20: 8
F-100D-5-NA: 727 Esk: RiS Jl 75 3/2:90
F-100D-15-NA: 1973: RiS Jl 75 3/2:90
F-100D-40-NH: 730 Esk: RiS Jl 75 3/2:90
SAAB J-35XD Draken: 725 Esk: AN 26 Jl 74 3/4:8-9
Draken: 729 Esk: AN 7 Mr 75 3/20:9
Sikorsky S-61B: 722 Esk: AN 7 Mr 75 3/20:8-9
Supermarine Spitfire PR Mk. XI: 722 PR Sqn, 1954: AN 2 Mr 73
 1/21:9

(Dominican Republic Military)

Bristol Beaufighter TF Mk X: 1945: AE Ja 74 6/1:31

(Egypt Military)

Aero L-29 Delfin: Q Ja 7/1:23
Delfin: std camouflage: RT Jl 71 4/7:77
Ilyushin Il-28: IM Ja 74 10/13-14:27
MiG 17F, 1957: RT Ag 75 8/8:90
MiG 17F, 1959: RT Ag 75 8/8:91
MiG 17F, 1967: RT Ag 76 8/8:91; cor My 76 9/5:61-62
MiG21 Fishbed C: IM Ja 74 10/13-14:29
MiG 21 Fishbed D: IM Ja 74 10/13-14:28
MiG 21 MF: Yom Kippur War: AE My 74 6/5:250
MiG 21 PF: AE Je 73 4/6:304
MiG 21 RF: AI N 75 9/5:248
Mil Mi-8: Yom Kippur War: AE My 74 6/5:250
Sukhoi Su-7: std: RT Jl 71 4/7:77
Sukhoi Su-7BM: Yom Kippur War: AE My 74 6/5:250

III. Color Patterns 282

(Ethiopia Military)

Fairey Firefly T. Mk 2: Afx My 73 14/9:493

(Finland Civil)

McDonnell-Douglas DC-9-10: Finnair: AN 12 Jl 74 3/3:8-9

(Finland Military)

Brewster B. 239: AF HQ, 1947: Q O 73 8/4:214
Curtiss Hawk 75A: HLeLv 11, Kauhava, summer, 1946: RT Jl 73 6/7:77
Hawk 75A-1: HävLv 13: Q O 73 8/4:214
De Havilland Canada DHC 2 Beaver: Q O 73 8/4:221
Douglas C-47A-80-DL: Q Ja 73 8/1:46
Folland Gnat Mk I: HaLv 21, 1959: Afx My 71 12/9:486
Ilyushin Il-28 target tug: IM Ja 74 10/13-14:27
Junkers Ju 88A-4: PLeLv 43, 1948: AN 3 Ag 73 2/6:7
Messerschmitt Bf 109G-5/U2: night flight, HLeLv 31, Ilmavoinat, Utti, 1948: AE Je 73 4/6:301
MiG 15 UTI: AN 14 S 73 2/9:8
MiG 15 UTI Midget: HävLv 31, 1963: Q Jl 72 7/3:122
SAAB 35BS Draken: AN 26 Jl 74 3/4:10

(France Civil)

Beech 99A: Air Champagne Ardenne: AN 2 My 75 3/24:9
Boeing 707-328: Air France: AN 2 My 75 3/24:8-9
Boeing 727-214: Air Charter International: AN 2 My 75 3/24:8
Caravelle III: Air Inter: AN 2 My 75 3/24:8
Convair CV-990: Air France, later leased to Modern Air (U. S.): Q Jl 71 6/3:32
Dassault Mystère 20: Air France: AN 2 My 75 3/24:9
De Havilland Canada Twin Otter: Air Alpes: AN 2 My 75 3/24:8
Fokker F. 27 Friendship 200: Touraine Air Transport: AN 2 My 75 3/24:9
Lear-Jet 24: Euralair: AN 2 My 75 3/24:9
McDonnell-Douglas DC-10-30: UTA: AN 2 My 75 3/24:8-9
North American AT-6C: Air France: IM Ja 74 10/13-14:15
Sud SA-341: prototype on trials, French Police: IM S 75 11/5:16
Vickers V952 Vanguard: Europe Aero Service: AN 2 My 75 3/24:9

(France Military)

BAC/Breguet Jaguar A-04: strike prototype: AE Jl 71 1/2:92
Jaguar E: Esc 1/7 "Province," St. Dizier: PAM Ap 74 5:69-96
Jaguar E-02: trainer prototype: AE Jl 71 1/2:92
Jaguar M-05: naval prototype: AE Jl 71 1/2:92

Chance Vought F4U-7 Corsair: 14 F, Arromanches, Suez 1956:
  Afx N 71 13/3:134
Dassault Mirage Milan: IM D 72 9/12:8
Mirage 3BE: IM D 72 9/12:5
Mirage 3C: IM D 72 9/12:7
Mirage 3E: IM D 72 9/12:3
Dassault Mystère IVA: 2 Esc de Chasse: Afx O 72 14/2:89
Dassault Super Mystère B2: 1 Esn, 12 Esc "Cambrésis," Cambrai,
  1968: AI Jl 74 7/1:42-43
Super Mystère B2: Esn 2/12 "Cornouailles": AI Jl 74 7/1:42-43
Super Mystère B2: SPA 162, 1972 Tiger Meet at Cambrai: AI Jl
  74 7/1:43
Douglas B-26B Invader: GB 1/19 "Gascogne," Tourane, Indo-China,
  Dec 1953: IM D 71 8/12:10
B-26B: GB 11/23 "Guyene," 1959: IM D 71 8/12:10
B-26B: GB 11/91 "Guyene," 1959: IM D 71 8/12:10
B-26C: GB 1/25 "Tunisie," Algeria, 1952: IM D 71 8/12:10
B-26Z: CEAM, 1961: IM O 71 8/12:10
Grumman F6F-5 Hellcat: Esc 1F, Arromanches, Mediterranean,
  Nov 1953: AI S 75 9/3:148
Grumman F8F(FN) Bearcat: Flotille 12F: IM N 71 8/11:7
F8F-1: GC 11/21 "Auvergne," Tan Son Nhut, Indochina, 1954:
  AN 25 Je 72 1/13:10
F8F-1: GC II/21, Tan Son Nhut, Indochina, 1953-54: AE F 73
  4/2:96
Grumman TBM-3S Avenger: Flot 9F, La Fayette, Suez operation:
  AN 27 O 72 1/12:10
TBM-3W: Flot 4F, Karoubia: Afx My 75 16/9:534
TBM-3W: Flot 4F, Karoubla: AN 27 O 72 7/1:43
Heinkel He 162: Mont de Marsan, 1948: AN 29 Mr 74 2/22:9
Lockheed SP-2H Neptune: navy: Q Jl 74 10/1:28
Messerschmitt Me 262A-1a: WW2J Jl 75 2/4:12
Morane Saulnier MS 501 Criquet (Fi 156C): Flot 28 F, 1949-50:
  AI Ap 75 8/4:200
Nakajima Ki. 43-II-Kai: GC I/7, Phnom-Penh, Indo-China, Dec
  1945: AI Jl 75 9/1:39
North American F-100-10-NA: 11 Esc, 1972: RiS Jl 75 3/2:91;
  cor & add Ja 76 3/3:162
F-100-15-NA: 11 Esc, 1966: RiS Jl 75 3/2:91
F-100D-1-NA: 3 Esc: RiS Jl 75 3/2:91
North American T-6 Texan: 03/004, Armée de l'Air, Algeria,
  1957: RT Je 72 5/6:72
North American T-28S-1 Fennec: COIN operations in Algeria: AN
  19 S 75 4/8:9

(Germany, East, Military)

MiG-15: Bandarenko: IM O 71 8/10:6
MiG-21 Fishbed F: IM Ja 74 10/13-14:28
MiG-21MF: AI N 75 9/5:248

III. Color Patterns 284

(Germany, West, Civil)

BAC One-Eleven: Germanair: AN 2 My 75 3/24:9
Beech 65-C90 King Air: Lufthansa: AN 2 My 75 3/24:9
Boeing 737: Lufthansa: IM Mr 71 8/3:8-9
Boeing 737-130: Lufthansa: AN 2 My 75 3/24:8
Boeing 747,230B: Condor: AN 2 My 75 3/24:8-9
Douglas B-26B civil conv: Helsinki Airport, July 1972: IM Ap 73 8/4:9
Hawker Sea Fury TT20: 2 var: IM My 72 9/5:2-4
North American AT-6F: IM Ja 74 10/13-14:14
Sud SA-341: Bavarian State Police: IM S 75 21/5:16
Yakovlev Yak-40FG: General Air: AN 2 My 75 3/24:9

(Germany, West, Military)

Boeing 707-320C: VIP Flight, Bonn: AN 7 Mr 75 3/20:8
Breguet Atlantic: MGF-3: AN 7 Mr 75 3/20:8
Canadair CL-13B Sabre Mk 6: JG 71 "Richthofen," Wittmandhafen, 1963: AE Ap 72 2/4:204
CL-13B Sabre Mk 6: JG 72: Q E 75 11/2:89
Dornier Do-28: Marineflieger: Q W 75 11/2:89
Fairey Gannet T.Mk. 5: navy: AN 8 Ag 75 4/5:7
Fiat G.91R: LKG-43: AN 7 Mr 75 3/20:8
Fiat G.91R-3: LeKG 43, 1961: AN 1 Mr 74 2/20:5
Grumman HU-16D (UF-2) Albatross: RiS Sp 73 1/3:86
HU-16D: navy, 2 var: RT My 74 7/5-6:65; cor Jl 74 7/7:71
Lockheed F-104F Starfighter 2-seat trainer: Combat Training School 10, Jever: AN 19 Ja 73 1/18:5
F-104G: 2/Marinefliegergeschwader 1: AN 19 Ja 73 1/18:5
F-104G: JaBo 33, Buchel, early 1960s: AN 19 Ja 73 1/18:5
F-104G: JaBo G 34: Q W 75 11/2:89
F-104G: JaBo 36, Rhein-Hopsten: AN 19 Ja 73 1/18:5
RF-104G: AKG 51 "Immelmann": AN 19 Ja 73 1/18:5
Lockheed T-33A: LeKG 44: Q E 75 11/2:89
McDonnell Douglas F-4F Phantom: JG 74: AN 7 Mr 75 3/20:8
RF-4E Phantom: std camouflage: Q O 72 7/4:139
RF-4E: Aufklärungsgeschwader 51 "Immelmann": AE S 71 1/4: 200
North American T-6 Harvard IV: Kaufbeuren Fliegerhorst TSLw 1: Afx Je 71 12/10:526
Harvard: Flugzeugfuhrerschule A, Landsberg: Q W 75 11/2:89
Panavia MRCA: test colors: AI S 74 7/3:121
Piaggio P.149: Bremgarten: AN 7 Mr 75 3/20:9
Republic F-84 Thunderstreak: immediately after delivery: RT Ag 75 8/8:91
F-84F: JaBo G 32: Q W 75 11/2:89
Sikorsky CH-53G: AN 7 Mr 75 3/20:8
Sikorsky S-58: MGF-5: AN 7 Mr 75 3/20:9
Transall C.160: LTG-61: AN 7 Mr 75 3/20:8
Westland Sea King Mk. 41: navy: Afx F 73 14/6:316

(Ghana Military)

Aermacchi MB. 326F: AN 16 F 73 1/20:10
Britten-Norman Islander: PAM Jl 74 6:88-89
De Havilland Canada DHC 1 Chipmunk: 1961: IM Mr 74 10/(15):7
De Havilland Canada DHC 2 Beaver: IM O 72 9/10:10

(Greece Military)

Cessna T-37C: RiS Mr 75 3/1:45
Grumman HU-16B AWS: AN 29 N 74 3/13:10
Lockheed F-104 Starfighter: 335 Sqn: AN 7 Mr 75 3/20:8-9
Northrop F-5A-40: 341 Sqn, 111 Wing, Achialos: AE Je 72 2/6: 324
Republic F-84F Thunderstreak: 345 Sqn; AN 7 Mr 75 3/20:8

(Honduras Military)

Lockheed P-38L-5: Tocontin AB, 1948: AI Je 75 8/6:295

(Hong Kong Military)

Britten-Norman Islander: Afx D 72 14/4:206

(Hungary Military)

Ilyushin Il-10: Tapoloa, 1956: IM Ap 72 9/4:13

(India Military)

Armstrong Whitworth Sea Hawk Mk FGA 4: 330 "White Tigers," Navy: AN 16 Mr 73 1/22:8-9
Sea Hawk Mk 6: navy: Q Su 75 10/4:145
BAC Canberra B. Mk. 66: AE Ap 72 2/4:181
Canberra B. Mk. 66: AN 16 Mr 73 1/22:8
Breguet Alize: 310 "White Cobras," Navy: AN 16 Mr 73 1/22:9
Consolidated B-24J-90-CF: 6 Sqn, March 1969: Q Ap 73 8/2:99
Dassault Mystère IVA: AE Ap 72 2/4:181
De Havilland Canada DHC-4 Caribou: AN 16 Mr 73 1/22:8-9; cor 11 My 73 1/26:15
HAL Gnat Mk 1: AE Ap 72 2/4:181
Gnat Mk. 1: AN 16 Mr 73 1/22:8
Gnat Mk. 1: Q Su 75 10/4:148
HAL HF-24 Marut Mk 1: AE Ap 72 2/4:181
Marut Mk 1: AN 16 Mr 73 1/22:9
HAL HT-2 trainer: AN 16 Mr 73 1/22:8
HJT-16 Kiran jet trainer: Navy: AN 16 Mr 73 1/22:9
Hawker Hunter F. Mk. 45: AE Ap 72 2/4:181

III. Color Patterns

Hunter F. Mk. 56: AN 16 Mr 73 1/22:8
Lockheed L-1049 Constellation: RAF Northolt: AN 16 Mr 73 1/22:
  8-9; cor AN 11 My 73 1/26:15
MiG-21: Q Su 75 10/4:147
MiG-21 Fishbed E: India-Pakistan War, 1972: IM Ja 74 10/13-14:
  29
MiG-21 FL (PF): AE Je 73 4/6:304
MiG-21 FL (PL): Red Archer aerobatic team: AE Je 73 4/6:304
MiG-21PFM: AE Ap 72 2/4:181
MiG-21PFM: AN 16 Mr 73 1/22:9
Sukhoi Su-7: AE Ap 72 2/4:181
Su-7: unit markings deleted, Indo-Pakistan war: AN 16 Mr 73 1/
  22:9
Westland Sea King: Q Su 75 10/4:145
Sea King Mk. 42: 330 Sqn, Navy: AN 16 Mr 73 1/22:8-9

(Indonesia Civil)

Convair CV-990: Garuda (Indonesian Airways): Q Jl 71 6/2:32

(Indonesia Military)

Fairey Gannet AS. Mk. 4: AN 8 Ag 75 4/5:7
Grumman HU-16A Albatross: RT Ag 73 6/8:88
MiG-15UTI: AN 14 S 73 2/9:8
MiG-17F: Djarkarta, early 1960s: RT Ag 75 8/8:91; cor My 76
  9/5:61-62
MiG-17F: 11 Sqn, 1965: AE D 72 3/6:312
MiG-19S: AN 18 O 74 3/10:8

(Iran Military)

Fokker F-27 series 400M Friendship: Farnborough, Sept 1972: IM
  Jl 73 10/7:14
Hawker Hurricane trainer: RT Ag 74 7/8:94
McDonnell Douglas F-4D Phantom: 306 FS: AE S 71 1/4:200
Northrop F-5A-25 Talon: 302 FS, Mehrabad: AE Je 72 2/6:324

(Iraq Military)

Aero L-29 Delfin: Q Ja 72 7/1:23
Hunting Percival Provost Mk I: AN 15 N 74 3/12:8-9
MiG-19S: AN 18 O 74 3/10:8

(Ireland Military)

Avro 652 Anson C Mk 19: April 1946: Q Jl 73 8/3:146
De Havilland DH 104 Dove 8: 1971: Q Jl 73 8/3:147

De Havilland DH 115 Vampire T. Mk 55: July 1950: Q Jl 73 8/3: 147
De Havilland Canada DHC-1 Chipmunk T. Mk 22: 1965: Q Jl 73 8/3:147
Hunting Percival Provost I: last Provost built: AN 15 N 74 3/12: 8-9
Provost T. Mk. 51: March 1954: Q Jl 73 8/3:146
Miles M. 14A Magister: 1946: Q Jl 73 8/3:145
Sud Aviation SE-3160 Alouette III: 1964: Q Jl 73 8/3:147
Supermarine 358 Seafire LF Mk 3: 1947: Q Jl 73 8/3:146
Supermarine 361 Spitfire T. Mk. 9 (two-seat): June 1951: Q Jl 73 8/3:146

(Israel Civil)

Boeing 747: El Al: Q Ap 72 7/2:80

(Israel Military)

Augusta Bell AB 205: Yom Kippur War: AE My 74 6/5:251
Dassault Mirage IIICJ: IM S 75 11/5:20
Mirage IIICJ: Yom Kippur War: AE My 74 6/5:251
Dassault Mystère IVA: 2 var: Afx O 72 14/2:89
Dassault Super Mystère B2: AE Jl 74 7/1:42-43
Super Mystère B2: Yom Kippur War: AE My 74 6/5:251
Super Mystère B2: October 1973: AI Jl 74 7/1:42-43
De Havilland Mosquito B. 9: Q Ap 74 9/2:91
Mosquito FB VI: 3 var: Q Ap 74 9/2:90-91
Mosquito NF 30: Q Ap 74 9/2:90-91
Mosquito T. 3: 2 var: Q Ap 74 9/2:91
McDonnell Douglas A-4E Skyhawk: AE F 72 2/2:100
A-4E: Yom Kippur War: AE My 74 6/5:251
McDonnell Douglas F-4E Phantom: AE S 71 1/4:200
F-4E: Yom Kippur War: AE My 74 6/5:251
MiG 21 Fishbed C: IM Ja 74 10/13-14:29
Supermarine Spitfire IXe: 1946: AN 2 Mr 73 1/21:9

(Italy Civil)

Aermacchi MB. 326: Alitalia trainer: AN 16 F 73 1/20:9
McDonnell Douglas DC-9-30 cargo: Alitalia: AN 12 Jl 74 3/3:9
DC-9-32: Alitalia: AN 2 My 75 3/24:9
Westland-Aerospatiale Puma SA 33P: Afx Ap 73 14/8:426

(Italy Military)

Aermacchi MB. 326: AN 16 F 73 1/20:9
Curtiss S2C Helldiver: Corpus Christi NAS, TX, 1951: RT F 75 8/2:22

III. Color Patterns 288

S2C-5 Target tug: Crottaglie: RT F 75 8/2:22
Agusta-Bell AB. 204: 2 Gr, Navy: AN 7 Mr 75 3/20:8
Fiat G. 91 PAN: Frecce Tricolori, 1962 aerobatic team: AN 1 Mr 74 2/20:5
G. 91R: 5 St: AN 7 Mr 75 3/20:8
G. 91T: Adv Jet Training School, SVBAA: AN 7 Mr 75 3/20:9
G. 91T Scuola Volo Basico Avanzato su Aviogetto, Amendola, near Foggia, 1964: AN 1 Mr 74 2/20:5
Grumman HU-16A Albatross: 84 Gr, 15 St, early 1960s: RT S 73 6/9:98
HU-16A: 84 Gr, 15 St, present: RT S 73 6/9:98
HU-16A: 84 Gr, 15 St: AN 7 Mr 75 3/20:8-9
Lockheed F-104G Starfighter: 9 Gr, 4 St. Caccia, 1970: Q Jl 71 6/3:16
F-104G: 10 Gr, 9 St. Ca, 1970: Q Jl 71 6/3:16
F-104G: 102 Gr, 5 St. Ca Bomb, 1970: Q Jl 71 6/3:16
F-104Gr: 6 St Ca Bomb, 1970: Q Jl 71 6/3:16
Lockheed P-38L Lightning: 4 St., Capodichino, 1946: AI Je 75 8/6:194
Lockheed T-33A: 3 Serobrigata: AN 7 Mr 75 3/20:9
Messerschmitt Me 262B-1a: WW2J Jl 75 2/4:12; cor British Ja 76 3/1:36
North American F-86E(M) Sabre Mk. 4: 4 Aerobrigata, Pratica di Mare, 1955: AE Ap 72 2/4:204
Piaggio P. 166: Adv multi-engine training school, SVBAP: AN 7 Mr 75 3/20:8

(Japan Civil)

Boeing 727: JAL: IM Mr 71 8/3:4-5

(Japan Military)

Grumman HU-16 Albatross: RiS Sp 73 1/3:86
UF-2 (HU-16D): Omura Kokutai, 1973: RT D 74 7/12:134
Grumman S-2A Tracker: 11 Sqn, 3 AG, Tokushima, 1957: AN 22 D 72 1/16:10
S-2F Tracker: 14 Sqn, 14 Air Group, Shimousa NAS: Q W 75 11/2:72
Grumman TBM-3S Avenger: AN 27 O 72 1/12:10
TBM-3W: Afx My 75 16/9:534
TBM-3W: 1954: AN 27 O 72 1/12:10
Lockheed P-2H Neptune: 51 Experimental Sqn, Osaka: Q Jl 74 10/1:30
P-2J (Kawasaki-built): Iruma AB, Oct 1968: Q Jl 74 10/1:30

(Kenya Military)

BAC Strikemaster: AN 26 Ap 74 2/14:9
Strikemaster Mk 87: AE O 73 5/4:65

Aircraft

De Havilland Canada DHC-1 Chipmunk: 1967: IM Mr 74 10/(15):7
Scottish Aviation Bulldog 103: AE Ag 73 5/2:65

(Korea, North, Military)

Ilyushin Il-10: IM Ap 72 9/4:13
Il-10: RT O 73 6/10:110
Ilyushin Il-28: IM Ja 74 10/13-14:27
MiG-21 Fishbed F: IM Ja 74 10/13-14:27
Polikarpov PO-2: harassment aircraft, over Kimpo Afld, early 1950s: Q Ap 73 8/2:88

(Korea, South, Military)

Cessna O-1 Bird Dog: Chu Lai, Vietnam, 1966: Q Ap 74 9/2:58
Grumman S2F-1 Tracker: Q W 75 11/2:72
Lockheed AT-33A: Osan AB, March 1971: IM Ja 73 10/1:16
North American T-6F: navy float conv, Aug 1951: RT D 74 7/12: 139

(Kuwait Military)

BAC Strikemaster: AN 26 Ap 74 2/24:9
Strikemaster Mk 83: AE O 73 5/4:194

(Lebanon Civil)

Convair CV-990: Lebanese International airlines, destroyed Dec 1968 in Israeli raid on Beruit airport: Q Jl 71 6/3:33

(Lebanon Military)

De Havilland Canada DHC-1 Chipmunk: 1961: IM Mr 74 10/(15):7
Savio Marchetti SM 79/P.XI: 1956: AI D 75 9/6:301

(Malaysia Military)

CAC Sabre 32: 11 Sqn: AE Ag 71 1/3:148
Canadair CL-41 C Tabuan (Tutor): 9 Sqn, Kuantan: AE Ag 71 1/3: 148
De Havilland Canada DHC-4 Caribou: 5 Sqn: AE Ag 71 1/3:148
Handley Page Herald 401: 4 Sqn: AE Ag 71 1/3:148
Hunting Percival Provost 51: Flying Training School, Alor Star: AE Ag 71 1/3:148
Scottish Aviation Bulldog 102: AE Ag 73 5/2:65
Sikorsky S-61A-4 Nuri: 10 Sqn, Kuantan: AE Ag 71 1/3:148
Sud Alouette III: 3 Sqn, Kuala Lumpur: AE Ag 71 1/3:148

III. Color Patterns   290

(Mexico Civil)

Northrop F-15 Reporter: Cia Mexicana Aerofoto, Mexico City, 1957:
    PAM Jl 75 10:160

(Mexico Military)

Douglas B-26: VIP transport mod: Q Jl 71 6/3:10
Lockheed T-33: IM S 75 11/5:21

(Muscat & Oman Military)

BAC 167 Strikemaster: IM Je 73 10/6:3
Britten-Norman BN2A-21 Defender: Afx Ag 75 16/12:718
Hunting Percival Provost I: AN 15 N 74 3/12:9

(Netherlands Civil)

McDonnell Douglas DC-9-30: KLM: AN 23 Jl 74 3/3:9
DC-9-30: Martinair: AN 23 Jl 74 3/3:9
North American AT-6: IM Ja 74 10/13-14:15
T-6: RT O 74 7/10:113
AT-16: IM Ja 74 10/13-14:14

(Netherlands Military)

Breguet Atlantic: 321 Sqn: AN 7 Mr 75 3/20:9
Grumman S-2A (S2F-1) Tracker: 2 Sqn, navy, Valkenburg: AN 22
    D 72 1/16:10
S2F-1: 4 Sqn, HMS Karel Doorman: Q W 75 11/2:69-71
S2N: 1 Sqn, Valkenburg NAS: Q W 75 11/2:69
Grumman TBM-3S Avenger: navy: AN 27 O 72 1/12:10
TBM-3W: 1953-54: AN 27 O 72 1/12:10
TBM-3W: Karel Doorman: Afx My 75 16/9:534
Hawker Hunter T7: Afx Mr 72 13/7:385
Lockheed F-104 Starfighter: ex West German, 1963: Afx Je 74
    16/10:579
F-104: 312 Sqn, 1974: Afx Je 74 16/10:579
F-104: 322/323 Sqn, 1968: Afx Je 74 16/10:579
F-104G: 322 Sqn, Leeuwarden, 1967: Afx Je 74 16/10:580
F-104G: 322/323 Sqn, Leeuwarden: Afx Je 74 16/10:580
RF-104G: 306 Sqn, 1974: Afx Je 74 16/10:579
TF-104G: std camouflage: Afx Je 74 16/10:580
TF-104G: "The Dutch Masters," Twenthe: Afx Je 74 16/10:580
Lockheed P-2 Neptune: 320 Neptune: 320 Sqn: AN 7 Mr 75 3/20:
    9
SP-2H Neptune: 320 Sqn, NAS Norfolk VA, May 1965: Q Jl 74
    10/1:28
Lockheed T-33A: AN 7 Mr 75 3/20:9

Martin PBM-5A Mariner: AN 17 Ag 73 2/7:7
North American Harvard II: Afx Je 71 12/10:526
Northrop NF-5B Talon: NF-5 Conversion School, Twenthe: AE Je 72 2/6:324
Supermarine Spitfire Mk IX trainer: 1950: AN 2 Mr 73 1/21:8-9
Westland AH-12A Wasp: naval: AN 8 Je 73 1/21:8-9

(New Zealand Military)

BAC Strikemaster: IM Je 73 10/6:3
Strikemaster Mk 88: AE O 73 5/4:194
Goodyear FG-1D Corsair IV: 14 Sqn, Iwakuni, Japan, 1946-48: Q Jl 73 8/3:140
Corsair IV: 14 Sqn, HMS Glory, Japan, March 1946: Q Ja 73 8/1:50; cor Jl 73 8/3:140
McDonnell Douglas A-4K Skyhawk: 75 Sqn: AE F 72 2/2:100
Westland Wasp: HMNZS Waikata: AN 8 Je 73 2/2:8

(Nicaragua Military)

Douglas B-26B: Q Jl 71 6/3:10

(Nigeria Military)

Ilushin Il-28: IM Ja 74 10/13-14:27

(Norway Military)

Lockheed P-3 Orion: Skv 333: AN 7 Mr 75 3/20:8
North American AT-16: IM Ja 74 10/13-14:14
North American Sabre F-86F-30-NA: 332 Skv: Q O 74 10/1:42-43
Northrop CF-5A: 332 Skv: RT Mr 74 7/3:33
F-5: 332 Skv: AN 7 Mr 75 3/20:8
F-5A: 334 Skv: RT D 75 8/12:142
Westland Sea King Mk 45: Afx F 73 14/6:316
Sea King: Air Sea Rescue Service: AN 7 Mr 75 3/20:8

(Pakistan Military)

Bristol 31: 1962: RT N 72 5/11:130
Canadair CL-13B Sabre Mk 6: 17 Sqn, Maruipur, 1968: AE Ap 72 2/4:204
Dassault Mirage III EP: Q Su 75 10/4:149
Mirage 3 RP: IM D 72 9/12:9
Martin B-57C Canberra: Q Su 75 10/4:147
MiG-15 UTI: AN 14 S 73 2/9:8
MiG-15 UTI: Q Jl 72 7/3:122
MiG-19SF: AE Ja 72 2/1:33

III. Color Patterns 292

MiG-19 (Chinese-built): Q Su 75 10/4:148
Shenyang F-6 (Chinese-built MiG-19): AN 18 O 74 3/10:8-9
North American F-86 Sabre; 2 var: Q Su 75 10/4:146
F-6: Sarghoda: RT N 74 7/11:129
F-6: Sargodha, Punjab: AN 18 O 74 3/10:8

(Peru Civil)

Boeing 727: Faucett: IM Mr 71 8/3:4-5
Convair CV-990: Aerolineas Peruanas (APSA): Q Jl 71 6/3:32

(Peru Military)

Curtiss Hawk 75: Military Aviation School, 1955: RT Ag 72 5/8: 90
Dassault Mirage 5P: IM D 72 9/12:8
Douglas B-26C: Q Jl 71 6/3:11
Grumman J2F Duck: 1965: RT Ag 72 5/8:90

(Philippines Military)

De Havilland Canada L-20 Beaver: Nichols AFB, 1973: RT Jl 75 8/7:76
Northrop F-5A: Clark Field, Pampanga: RT Jl 75 8/7:76

(Poland Civil)

CSS-11: MAN S 75 91/3:32
Lisunov Li-1P: Polskie Linie Lotnicze (LOT): AN 12 D 75 4/14:9
S. 4 Kania 3: Szybowcowy Zaklad Doswiadczaly (Experimental Glider Establishment); Bielsko-Biala, Poland: Aero S 71 36/238:505
TS-8 bies: Poznan Fair, July 1956: Aero Ja 75 40/468:30-31

(Poland Military)

Ilyushin Il-10: Air Museum, Krakow: IM Ap 72 9/4:13
Limm-5M (Polish-built MiG-17): IM Jl 74 10/(17);13
Limm-6: IM Jl 74 10/(17):12
MiG-15bis: AN 14 S 73 2/9:8
MiG-15bisR: AN 14 S 73 2/9:8
MiG-17F: 1971-72: AE D 72 3/6:312
MiG-10PM: AE Ja 72 2/1:33

(Portugal Military)

Aérospatiale SA 316 Allouette III: Portuguese Guinea, 1971: AE F 72 2/2:62

Bristol Beaufighter X: 8 Esq, Portella de Sacavem, 1945: AE Ja 74 6/1:31
Dornier Do 27: Nambuangongo, Angola, 1968: AE F 72 2/2:62
Fiat G. 91/R4: Gr Operaccional RA 12, Bissau, Portuguese Guinea, 1967: AE F 72 2/2:62
Lockheed P2V-5 Neptune: Northolt, Feb 1968: Q Jl 74 10/1:29
Lockheed PV-2 Harpoon: BA 9, Luanda, Angola, 1962: AE F 72 2/2:62
Lockheed T-33A: Fighter Pilots School B. 2: AN 7 Mr 75 3/20:8-9
Nord 2501D Noratlas: Esq de Transportes, 1968: AE F 72 2/2:62
Noratlas: AB-1: AN 7 Mr 75 3/20:9
North American T-6G Texan: BAI Sintra, 1950: AE F 72 2/2:62

(Rhodesia Military)

Douglas DC-3: 1952: RT Je 75 8/6:70
DC-3: 1954-62: RT Je 75 8/6:70
DC-3: No. 3 Transport Sqn, 1969: RT Je 75 8/6:70
Hunting Percival Provost I: AN 15 N 74 3/12:9

(Rumania Military)

MiG 15bis: AN 14 S 73 2/9:8
MiG 21F: Intercept Rgt, 1967: AE Je 71 1/1:29

(Saudi Arabia Military)

BAC 167 Strikemaster: 2 var: AN 26 Ap 74 2/24:9
Strikemaster: 2 var: IM Je 73 10/6:3
Strikemaster Mk. 80: AE O 73 5/4:194

(Singapore Military)

BAC 167 Strikemaster: IM Je 73 10/6:3
Strikemaster: 2 var: AN 26 Ap 74 2/24:9
Strikemaster Mk 84: 1972: RT F 75 8/2:16
Hawker Hunter F. 74B: 1973: RT F 75 8/2:16
Short Skyvan 3M: Air Defence Command, Rescue, 1973: PAM Ja 75 8:125

(South Africa Civil)

Boeing 727: South African Airways: IM Mr 71 8/5:4-5

(South Africa Military)

Aeromacchi MB. 326M: AN 16 F 73 1/20:10

III. Color Patterns   294

De Havilland Vampire FB. 6:   2 Sqn, 1954: MW Je 73 1/10:521
Vampire FM. 9:   AFS, 1965: MW Je 1/10:527
Vampire FM. 9:   AOS, Langejaanweg, 1959: MW Je 73 1/10:527
Vampire T. 55:   AFS, late 1950s: MW Je 73 1/10:527
Vampire T. 55:   AFS, 1965: MW Je 73 1/10:527
Douglas C-47A-15-DK: 60 Sqn, 1948: Afx Ap 72 13/8:436
C-47B: 28 Sqn, 1954:   Afx Ap 72 13/8:436
C-47B: 28 Sqn, 1962:   Afx Ap 72 13/8:441
C-47B: 28 Sqn, after 1962:   Afx Ap 72 13/8:441
C-47B: 44 Sqn, 1962:   Afx Ap 72 13/8:441
Hawker Siddeley Buccaneer S. 50:   24 Sqn, Waterkloof AFB, 1966: MW D 72 1/4:198
North American Harvard: 1961:   Afx N 71 13/3:145
Harvard: 1 Sqn, late 1940s: Afx N 71 13/3:140
Harvard: 5 Sqn, 1954:   Afx N 71 13/3:145
Harvard: CFS, 2 var: Afx N 71 13/3:145
Harvard: CFS, 1947:   Afx N 71 13/3:145
Harvard: Old Type A, 2A target tug, & Type B std patterns: Afx O 71 13/2:77
Westland Aérospatiale Puma: Afx Ap 73 14/8:426
Westland Wasp: navy: AN 8 Je 73 2/2:9

(South Arabia [Yemen] Military)

BAC 167 Strikemaster: IM Je 73 10/6:3

(Spain Civil)

Convair CV-990:   Spantex (Iberia charter company) with Iberia name: Q Jl 71 6/3:33

(Spain Military)

CASA 211-A: Ala 94, late 1950s: AE N 73 5/5:237
Grumman HU-16A Albatross: RT Ag 73 6/8:89
Hu-16B: AN 29 N 74 3/13:10
Heinkel He 70F-2:   personal transport General Ejército del Aire, Esc 101:   AI F 75 8/2:90

(Sudan Military)

BAC 167 Strikemaster: IM Je 73 10/6:3
Hunting Percival Provost I: AN 15 N 74 3/12:9

(Sweden Civil)

Boeing 727:   Transair: IM Mr 71 8/3:4-5
Boeing 747:   SAS: Q Ap 72 7/2:80

Convair CV-990: SAS: Q Jl 71 6/3:30
North American AT-6A: IM Ja 74 10/13-14:15

(Sweden Military)

De Havilland Mosquito J 30: in delivery, 1948: IM F 73 10/2:12-13
J 30: F 1, night fighter wing, Vasteras, 1948: IM F 73 10/2:12-13
Junkers 86K B3: F 17, transport, 1950s: RT My 73 6/5:56
T 3: F 17 Torpedo Wing, 2 Div, 1946: RT Jl 74 7/7:72; RT My 73 6/5:56
North American Harvard Sk 16A: 4 9, Säve, Jan 1967, Bjuggeren: IM F 73 10/2:4
SAAB A-29B Tunnan: F 7, 3 Sqn, Satenas: AN 11 My 73 1/26:9
J-29B: F 3, 3 Sqn, Malmslatt: AN 11 My 73 1/26:9
J-29B: F 8, 3 Sqn, Barkaby: AN 11 My 73 1/26:9
J-29B: F 10, Angelholm: AN 11 My 73 1/26:9
J-29C: F 11, Nykoping: AN 11 My 73 1/26:9
SAAB J 35B Draken: F 13, Norrkoping (Bravalla): AN 26 Jl 74 3/4:10
J 35B: F 16, 1968 War Games: RT Je 72 5/6:67
J 35D: early std: AN 26 Jl 74 3/4:8-9
J 35D: F 3, 1968 War Games: RT Je 72 5/6:67
J 35E: F 11: RT Je 72 5/6:67
J 35F: F 10, Angelholm (Barkara): AN 26 Jl 74 3/4:10
J 35F: F 13: RT Je 72 5/6:67
S 35C: F 16, Uppsala: AN 26 Jl 74 3/4:8-9
S 35E: F 21, Lulea (Kallax): AN 26 Jl 74 3/4:10
Sk 35C: trainer: RT S 73 6/9:96-97
SAAB 37: second prototype: AN 31 O 75 4/11:9
AJ 37: std camouflage: AN 31 O 75 4/11:8-9
SF 37: prototype: AN 31 O 75 4/11:9
Scottish Aviation Bulldog 101: F 5, Ljungbyhed: AE Ag 73 5/2: 64-65

(Switzerland Civil)

Convair CV-990: Balair (Swissair charter affiliate): Q Jl 71 6/3:30
CV-990: Swissair: Q Jl 71 6/3:30

(Switzerland Military)

Dassault Mirage III: Esc de Chasse et d'Oversavation 10, White Sands NM, 1964: RT O 71 4/10:109
Mirage 3RS: IM D 72 9/12:9
North American P-51D: c. 1952: IM My 71 8/5:17

III. Color Patterns   296

(Syria Military)

MiG 17F: Betzer, Israle, 1970: AE D 72 3/6:312
MiG 17F: Yom Kippur War: AE My 74 6/5:250
MiG 17F Fresco C: 1970: IM Jl 74 10/(17):11
MiG 19SF: AE Ja 72 2/1:33
MiG 21PF: AE Je 73 4/6:304
MiG 21PF: Yom Kippur War: AE My 74 6/5:250
MiG 21PFM (Fishbed E): RT N 72 5/11:122

(Thailand Civil)

Convair CV-990: Thai Airways International, leased from SAS: Q Jl 71 6/3:32

(Thailand Military)

Cessna T-37C: RiS Mr 75 3/1:45
Grumman F8F-1 Bearcat: 2 FBW: AN 10 N 72 1/13:10
F8F-1: 23 Sqn, 2 FBW, 1954: AE F 73 4/2:96
Martin 139W-1: Q O 74 10/2:68
North American OV-10c: Q O 74 10/2:83-84
North American T-28D: 22 Sqn, Udorn, Thailand: AN 19 S 75 4/8:9
Supermarine Spitfire 14: Trat, 1957: Q Ap 73 8/2:79

(Trinidad & Tobago Civil)

Boeing 727: British West Indian Airways: IM Mr 71 8/3:4-5

(Tunisia Military)

Aermacchi MB.326B: AN 16 F 73 1/20:9

(Turkey Military)

Cessna T-37C Tweet: Cigli AB, 1964: RiS Mr 75 3/1:45
Convair F-102A: 141 Sqn: AN 7 Mr 75 3/20:8-9
Douglas B-26B: target tug & hack: Afx Mr 72 13/7:379
North American F-100 Super Sabre: 111 Sqn: AN 7 Mr 75 3/20:8
F-100D: 111 Sqn, Eskişehir, Aug 1974: PAM Jl 75 10:174-175
F-100D-15: 1 TAF, Bandirma, 1969: AE Jl 71 1/2:85
F-100D-15-NA: 113 Sqn: RiS Jl 75 3/2:91
F-100D-25-NA: 111 Sqn, 1971: RiS Jl 75 3/2:91
F-100F-15-NA: 1962: RiS Jl 75 3/2:91
Northrop F-5B Talon: 1 TAF: AE Je 72 2/6:324
Republic F-84FQ Thunderstreak: 1 TAF, Eskişehir, 1970: AE Jl 71 1/2:84

Republic F-84G-16 Thunderjet: 3 TAF, Diyarbakir, 1954: AE Jl 71 1/2:84

(Uganda Civil)

Westland Scout: police: AN 8 Je 73 2/2:8

(Uganda Military)

Aero L-29 Delfin: Q Ja 72 7/1:23
MiG 21 Fishbed C: IM Ja 74 10/13-14:29

(USSR Civil)

Antonov An 22: Aeroflot: Sc Mr 71 2/3:135
Ilyushin Il-20 (civil Il-28): Aeroflot mail: IM Ja 74 10/13-14:27
Lisunov Li-2P: Aeroflot: AN 12 D 75 4/14:9

(USSR Military)

Aero L-29 Delfin: Q Ja 72 7/1:23
Ilyushin Il-28: over Czechoslovakia, Aug 1968: IM F 71 8/2:16
Il-28: Czechoslovakian invasion, 1968: IM Ja 74 10/13-14:27
MiG 15: prototype: AN 14 S 73 2/9:8-9
MiG 15bis: aerobatic team: AN 14 S 73 2/9:8-9
MiG 17: Aerobatic team, Cottbus, DDR, 1957: RT Ag 75 8/8:90
MiG 17 Fresco A: IM Jl 74 10/(17):13
MiG 17 Fresco A: V-VS aerobatic team: IM Jl 74 10/(17):14
MiG 19PM: AN 18 O 74 3/10:8
MiG 21 Fishbed E: Uppsala, Sweden, Oct 1967: IM Ja 74 10/13-14:28
MiG 21 Fishbed F: IM Ja 74 10/13-14:28
MiG 21 Fishbed F: Czechoslovakian invasion, 1968: IM Ja 74 10/13-14:27
MiG 21 Fishbed F: USSR aerobatic team: IM Ja 74 10/13-14:28
MiG 21 MF: 3 var: PAM Ja 75 8:134-135
MiG 21 MF: Rissala, Aug 1974: PAM Ja 75 8:134
MiG 21 MF: Fighter Rgt, Kiev Military district: AI N 75 9/5:248
MiG 21 PF: AE Je 73 4/6:304
MiG 21 PF: Fishbed: Q Ja 71 6/1:29
Yak 18 PM: Russian Aerobatic Team, World Championships, Hullavington, July 1970: Aero Mr 71 36/422:142-143
Yak 18 PS: Russian Aerobatic Team, World Championships, Hullavington, July 1970: Aero Mr 71 36/422:142-143

(U.K. Civil)

Ajep-Wittman Tailwind: 1972 King's Cup Race: Aero N 72 37/442:

III. Color Patterns

634-635
Avro Anson: Air Service Training, Hamble: Afx Ag 72 13/12:655
Anson: Hunting Aerosurveys: Afx Ag 72 13/12:655
Anson: Kemp's Aerial Surveys, Southampton: Afx Ag 72 13/12:655
Anson: Railway Air Services: Afx Ag 72 13/12:655
Britten Norman Islander: factory finish: PAM Jl 74 6:88-89
Islander: Loganair: PAM Jl 74 6/88-89
Britten Norman Trislander: Aurgny Air Service: MW O 72 1/2:86
Boeing 707 Cargo: BEA: Afx F 75 16/6:362-363
Boeing 747: British Airways, 1973: AN 3 Ag 73 2/6:1
Cessna 337A: King Aviation Skycabs: Afx My 71 12/9:467
Cessna 337B: By-Air: Afx My 71 12/9:467
Cessna 337D: Westair Flying Services: Afx My 71 12/9:467
Cessna F. 337D: first French-built Cessna 337 registered in U.K.: Afx My 71 12/9:467
De Havilland DH 82a Tiger Moth: "The Deacon," airshows, present: IM Mr 73 10/3:2-3
Tiger Moth spray plane: Farm Aviation: Afx O 71 13/2:81
De Havilland Canada DHC-1 Chipmunk Ag Plane: Farm Aviation: Afx O 71 13/2:81
Gloster Gladiator I/II hybrid: Shuttleworth Collection: Sc Ag 73 4/8:553
Gloster Meteor IV: factory demonstrator, 1946: PAM Ap 74 5:72
Meteor 4: 1946: RT N 73 6/11:130
Handley Page Jetstream: 1st prototype: Afx Ag 72 13/12:669
Jetstream: 2nd prototype: Afx Ag 72 13/12:669
Jetstream: 8th production aircraft: Afx Ag 72 13/12:669
Jetstream I: factory demonstrator: IM Jl 72 9/7:(9)
Jetstream I: British Steel Corp: IM Jl 72 9/7:(10)
Jetstream 3 Hybrid: IM Jl 72 9/7:(11)
Hunting Percival Jet Provost 2: test bed: PAM O 74 7:115
Provost T.1: Shuttleworth Trust: PAM O 74 7:115
OR-65-2 Owl Racer: "Ricochet," North Weald, Aug 1971: Aero Ja 72 37/432:46-47
Pitts Special S-2A: Rothmans Aerobatic Team, 1974; 5 var: Aero S 74 39/464:491-495
Rollason Beta: 3 var: Aero Jl 71 36/426:364-368
Rollason D-62B Condor: 6 var: Afx Je 72 13/10:539-540
Short Skyliner: company demonstrator, Nepal, 1974: PAM Ja 75 8:125
Sikorsky S-58T: Bristow, North Sea oil well operations: AN 21 Mr 75 3/21:9
Sikorsky S-61N: BEA: Afx S 71 13/1:26-31
Thruxton Jackaroo: 3 var: Sc Ap 75 6/67:188-189
Jackaroo crop sprayer: prototype: Sc Ag 75 6/67:188-189

(U.K. Military--Helicopter)

Westland AH.1 Scout: Advanced Rotary Wing Flight, Army Air Corps, Middle Wallop: AN 8 Je 73 2/2:8-9
Scout: Empire Test Pilot's School, Boscombe Down: AN 8 Je 73 2/2:8-9

Westland HAS. 1 Wasp: 706 Sqn, RN, Culdrose: AN 8 Je 73 2/2: 8-9
Westland Wessex Mk. 1: SAR Flight, HMS Ark Royal, 1970: AN 18 Ag 72 1/7:14
Wessex HC. 2: Gulf Communications & SAR Flight, Sharjah: AN 21 Mr 75 3/21:9
Wessex HC. 2: 103 Sqn: AN 4 O 74 3/9:9
Westland Whirlwind HAR 10: 22 Sqn, AN 4 O 74 3/9:9
Westland Aérospatiale Gazelle HT. 1: CFS: AN 4 O 74 3/9:8
Westland Aérospatiale Puma HC. 1: 33 Sqn: AN 4 O 74 3/9:8

(U. K. Military--Jet)

(Bombers)
BAC Canberra B. 2: Leuchars, Sept 1972: IM N 73 10/11-12:8
Canberra B. 2: 10 Sqn, Suez: Afx O 73 15/2:97
Handley Page Victor K. 1: 214 Sqn: AN 4 O 74 3/9:8
Hawker Siddeley Vulcan B. 2: 230 OCU: AN 4 O 74 3/9:8-9

(Fighters)
BAC Lightning F. 2A: 92 Sqn, RAF Gutersich, Germany, 1973: AN 29 Mr 74 2/22:14
Lightning F. 2A: 92 Sqn, RAF Gutersich, Germany, 1974: IM Ja 75 11/1:13; add My 75 11/3:3
Lightning F. 3: 5 Sqn: AN 4 O 74 3/9:8
Lightning F. 6: 11 Sqn: AN 4 O 74 3/9:8
Canadair CL-13 Sabre Mk 4: 92 Sqn, Linton-on-Ouse, 1954: AE Ap 72 2/4:204
De Havilland Sea Vixen: FAA Museum, HMS Heron, May 1974: PAM Jl 74 9:152
Sea Vixen FAW. 1: 890 Sqn, HMS Ark Royal, 1964: AN 28 S 73 2/10:8
Sea Vixen FAW. 1: 892 Sqn, HMS Centaur, 1963: AN 28 S 73 2/10:8
Sea Vixen FAW. 2: 892 Sqn, HMS Hermes, 1966: AN 28 S 73 2/10:8
Sea Vixen FAW. 2: 899 Sqn, HMS Eagle, 1964: AN 28 S 73 2/10:8
Sea Vixen FAW. 2: 899 Sqn, HMS Eagle, 1970: AN 28 S 73 2/10:9
Sea Vixen FAW. 2: Royal Navy Air Yard, Sydenham, Belfast: AN 28 S 73 2/1:9
Sea Vixen FAW. 2: "Simon's Sircus," RNAS Yeovilton, 1968: AN 28 S 73 2/1:9
De Havilland Vampire FB. 5: Honiley wing, 1953-54: IM My 75 11/3:10
Vampire NF. 10: 23 Sqn, 1951-54: MW D 72 1/4:186-187
Gloster Javelin Fighter Test Sqn, Boscombe Down, Sept 1974: IM My 75 11/3:3
Javelin F(AW). 6: 85 Sqn: AN 1 Mr 74 2/20:7
Javelin F(AW). 7: 64 Sqn, 1958-60: AN 1 Mr 74 1/20:7
Javelin F(AW). 9R: 60 Sqn, June 1967: AN 1 Mr 74 2/20:7
Gloster Meteor F. 8: 74 Sqn: Sc D 72 3/12:647
Meteor NF. 11: 29 Sqn, Acklington, 1957: AN 25 My 73 2/1:9

III. Color Patterns

Meteor NF.11: 68 Sqn, Kirkbride: AN 25 My 73 2/1:9
Meteor NF.11: 85 Sqn: Sc D 72 3/12:648
Meteor NF.12: 85 Sqn, Church Fenton: AN 25 My 73 2/1:9
Meteor NF.12: 153 Sqn: AN 25 My 73 2/1:9
Meteor NF.14: 25 Sqn: AN 25 My 73 2/1:9
Meteor NF.14: 264 Sqn, Middleton St. George, 1957: AN 25 My 73 2/1:9
McDonnell Douglas Phantom: 43 Sqn: PAM O 75 11:193
Phantom: 43 Sqn, Leuchars: PAM O 75 11:193
Phantom: Phantom Training Flight, Leuchars: PAM O 75 11:193

(Strike)
BAC TSR-2: 1st prototype: AN 30 Mr 73 1/23:8-9
TSR-2: 2nd prototype: AN 30 Mr 73 1/23:8-9
Hawker Siddeley Buccaneer: 1st prototype: MW S 72 1/1:42
Buccaneer: 5th prototype: MW S 72 1/1:43
Buccaneer S.1: 735 Sqn, Lossiemouth: MW S 72 1/1:43
Buccaneer S.2: 208 Sqn, RAF Honington, Suffolk, Dec 1974: AN 11 Jl 75 4/3:15
Buccaneer S.2: 237 OCU: AN 4 O 74 3/9:8-9
Buccaneer S.2: 800 Sqn, HMS Eagle, 1968: MW O 72 1/2:97
Buccaneer S.2: 801 Sqn, HMS Victorious, 1967: MW O 72 2/1:9
Hawker Siddeley Harrier FGA.9: TWU: AN 4 O 72 2/1:9
Harrier GR.1: 4 Sqn: AN 4 O 74 3/9:8
Harrier GR.1: 4 Sqn, Wildenrath, Germany: AE Ag 71 1/3:145
Harrier GR.1A: 3 Sqn, RAF Wildenrath, Germany, 1973: AN 29 Mr 74 2/22:14
Hawker Siddeley Hunter: now in RAF Museum: AE Ap 74 6/4:199
Hawker Siddeley Kestral FGA.1: 1966: MW Ap 73 1/8:434
Hawker Siddeley P.1127: 1st prototype: MW F 73 1/6:325
P.1127: Prototype: MW Ap 73 1/8:434
P.1127: Development Harrier: MW Ap 73 1/8:434
Hawker Siddeley Seahawk: 804 Sqn, Suez Campaign: PAM Ap 75 9:152
McDonnell Douglas Phantom: 2 Sqn, Laarbruch, at Lahr CFB, May 1974: RT Ja 75 8/1:8
Phantom: 17 Sqn, 2 ATAF, May-June 1974, CFB Baden-Soelingen: RT Ja 75 8/1:8
Phantom FG.1 (F-4K): 43 Sqn, Leuchars, 1972: AN 29 Mr 74 2/22:14
Phantom FGR.2: 17 Sqn: AE S 71 1/4:200
Phantom FGR.2: 17 Sqn: AN 4 O 74 3/9:8
Sepecat Jaguar GR.1: 6 Sqn: AN 4 O 74 3/9:9
Jaguar S.06: strike prototype: AE Jl 71 1/2:93

(trainers)
BAC Canberra T.4: 231 OCU: AN 4 O 74 3/9:8-9
Canberra T.11: 85 Sqn: AN 4 O 74 3/9:8
BAC Jaguar T.2: Jaguar OCU: An 4 O 74 3/9:9
BAC Jet Provost T.1: Central Flying School aerobatic team: PAM O 74 7:114
Jet Provost T.3: 1 FTS: AN 4 O 74 3/9:8
Jet Provost T.4: "Gemini" aerobatic team, 3 Flight Training

Aircraft

School, Leeming, 1973: AN 22 Je 73 2/3:10
Jet Provost T.4: "Macaws," RAF College of Air Warfare, 1973: AN 22 Je 73 2/3:8+
Jet Provost T.5: "Linton Blades," 1 Flight Training School, Linton-on-Ouse, 1973: AN 22 Je 73 2/3:10
Jet Provost T.5: "Poachers," RAF College, Cranwell, 1973: AN 22 Je 73 2/3:8+
Jet Provost T.5: RAF College: AN 4 O 74 3/9:8
Jet Provost T.5: "Red Pelicans," Central Flying School, 1973: AN 22 Je 73 2/3:10
BAC Lightning T.4: 74 Sqn, June 1960: Afx Jl 75 16/11:648-649
Lightning T.5: 23 Sqn: AN 4 O 74 3/9:8
De Havilland Sea Vixen FAW 1: 766 (Training) Sqn, RNAS Yeovilton, 1969: AN 28 S 73 2/10:8
Gloster Javelin T.3: 46 Sqn, Odiham, 1955: AN 1 Mr 74 2/20:7
Gloster Meteor T.7: Station Flight, West Raynham, 1956: Sc D 72 3/12:647
Hawker Siddeley Dominie T.1: RAF College: AN 4 O 74 2/20:7
Hawker Siddeley Gnat T.1: 4 FTS: AN 4 O 74 3/9:8
Gnat T.1: "Red Arrows" Central Flying School, 1973: AN 22 Je 73 2/3:9-10
Hawker Siddeley Harrier T.2: 233 OCU, Wittering: MW F 74 2/6:309
Harrier T.4: 20 Sqn: AN 4 O 74 3/9:9
Hawker Siddeley Hunter T.7: 4 FTS: AN 4 O 74 3/9:8
Hunter T.7: 65 Sqn: Afx Mr 72 13/7:385
Hunter T.7: 92 Sqn: Afx Mr 72 13/7:384-385
Hunter T.7: 208 Sqn: Afx Mr 72 13/7:384
Hunter T.7: 229 Sqn: Afx Mr 72 13/7:383

(Other Aircraft)
BAC Canberra PR.7: 13 Sqn: AN 4 O 74 3/9:8-9
Canberra PR.9: 13 Sqn: AN 4 O 74 3/9:8-9
BAC VC-10: 10 Sqn: AN 4 O 74 3/9:8
Gloster Meteor PR 10: Sc D 72 3/12:647
Meteor TT.20: Sc D 72 3/12:648
Hawker Siddeley Comet C.4: 216 Sqn: AN 4 O 74 3/9:8-9
Hawker Siddeley Nimrod MR.1: 203 Sqn: AN 4 O 74 3/9:8-9
Messerschmitt Me 262B-1a: stated Italy WW2J Jl 75 2/4:12; cor Ja 76 3/1:36

(U.K. Military--Prop)

(Bombers)
Fairey Barracuda Mk III: 815 Sqn, Eglinton, 1951: AN 4 Ja 74 2/16:9
Fairey Firefly AS 7: Afx My 73 14/9:492-493
Short Stirling IV: 570 Sqn, Sept 1945, 2 var: IM N 74 10/19:7
Westland Wyvern: prototype: AN 7 Jl 72 1/4:8
Wyvern: Clyde-powered prototype: RT Je 71 4/6:70
Wyvern S.4: 830 Sqn, Suez: RT Je 71 4/6:70

III. Color Patterns   302

(Cargo & Transport)
Avro Anson I: 61 Gp Communications Flight, RAF Kenley, Surrey, 1951: Q Ja 71 6/1:13
Anson C. 19: RAF Transport Command Communications Unit, 1960: AN 26 O 73 2/12:8-9
Bristol Britannia C. 2: 511 Sqn: AN 4 O 74 3/9:9
De Havilland Canada DHC-2 Beaver AL. 1: 132 Flight, AAC, Netheraven, Wilts, early 1970: IM O 72 9/10:4
Fairey Barracuda Mk. III: Admiral's barge, HMS Vengeance, 1948: AN 4 Ja 74 2/16:9
Fairey Gannet COD. 4: 849 Sqn, RNAS Brawdy: AN 8 Ag 75 4/5:7
Handley Page Hastings C. 1A: 48 Sqn, Far East Air Force: AN 5 S 75 4/7:7
Hastings C. 2: RAF Flying College, Manby, 1951: AN 5 S 75 4/7:7
Hawker Siddeley Andover C. 1: 46 Sqn: AN 4 O 74 3/9:8
Andover CC. 2: Queen's Flight: AN 4 O 74 3/9:8
Hawker Siddeley Argosy E. 1: 115 Sqn: AN 4 O 74 3/9:9
Hawker Siddeley Devon C. 2: 207 Sqn: AN 4 O 74 3/9:8
Hunting Pembroke C. 1: 60 Sqn: AN 4 O 74 3/9:9
Lockheed Hercules C. 1: Lyneham Wing: AN 4 O 74 3/9:9
Short Belfast C. 1: 53 Sqn: AN 4 O 74 3/9:9
Vickers Valetta C. 2: RAF Flying College: AN 24 Ja 75 3/17:10
Vickers Viking C. 2: King's Flight: AN 24 Ja 75 3/17:10

(Electronics)
Fairey Firefly AEW. 1: D Flt, 849 Sqn: Afx N 75 17/3:160-161
Fairey Gannet AEW. 3: prototype: AN 8 Ag 75 4/5:7
Gannet AEW. 3: 849 Sqn: AN 8 Ag 75 4/5:7
Hawker Siddeley Shackleton AEW. 2: 8 Sqn: AN 4 O 74 3/9:9

(Fighters)
De Havilland Sea Hornet: 730 Sqn, Ford: MW F 74 2/6:289
Sea Hornet F. 20: 728 Sqn (Fleet Requirements Unit), Hal Far, Malta, 1953: MW F 74 2/6:289
Sea Hornet F. 20: 801 Sqn, Arboath, attached to 806 Sqn, North America, 1948: MW F 74 2/6:289
Sea Hornet F. 20: 801 Sqn, Ford, 1947: MW F 74 2/6:289
Sea Hornet F. 21: 809 Sqn, HMS Eagle, 1953: MW F 74 2/6:291
Fairey Firefly FR Mk. IV: 825 Sqn, HMS Ocean, at Kimpo, Korea, early 1950s: Q Ap 73 8/2:90-91
Grumman Hellcat II: FAA: MW F 74 2/6:320
Hawker Tempest Mk II: 20 Sqn, Agra, India, 1946, Wilson: RT My 75 8/5:52
Supermarine Spitfire Mk XVI: 601 (County of London) Sqn, RAux AF, 1946: AN 2 Mr 73 1/21:9

(Trainers)
Avro Anson T. 1: FAA: Afx Mr 71 12/7:360-361
Anson T. 20: 3 ANS, RAF Thornhill, 1948: AN 26 O 73 2/12:8-9
Anson T. 21: 23 RFS, Usworth: AN 26 O 73 2/12:8-9
Avro Lincoln: Bomber Command Training Unit, West Freugh, 1957: AN 28 Je 74 3/2:10

De Havilland Tiger Moth: Cambridge University Air Squadron: AN 28 N 75 4/13:8-9
Tiger Moth: Oxford UAS, 2 var: AN 28 N 75 4/13:8-9
De Havilland Canada DHC 1 Chipmunk: Birmingham UAS, 1969: AN 28 N 75 4/13:9
Chipmunk: London UAS, 1957: AN 28 N 75 4/13:9
Chipmunk: Nottingham UAS, 1965: AN 28 N 75 4/13:9
Chipmunk: Oxford UAS, 1952: AN 28 N 75 4/13:9
Chipmunk: Oxford UAS, 1958: AN 28 N 75 4/13:9
Chipmunk: St. Andrews UAS, 1962: AN 28 N 75 4/13:9
Chipmunk: Southampton UAS, 1963: AN 28 N 75 4/13:9
Chipmunk: UAS std & badges of all University Air Squadrons: AN 28 N 75 4/13:9; add 23 Ja 76 4/17:12
Chipmunk T. 10: AN 4 O 74 3/9:9
Chipmunk T. 10: Cambridge UAS, Oct 1971: IM Ja 74 10/13-14:3
Chipmunk T. 10: 2 FTS, Church Fenton, 1971: IM Ja 74 10/13-14:3
Chipmunk T. 10: "Blue Chips," 2 Flight Training School, Church Fenton, 1973: AN 22 Je 73 2/3:9-10
De Havilland Canada DHC 2 Beaver AL. 1: Adv. Fixed Wing Flight, School of Army Aviation, Middle Wallop, 1970: IM O 72 9/10:4; cor Ja 73 10/1:11
Fairey Barracuda Mk V: 753 Training Sqn, Lee-on-Solent, 1948: AN 4 Ja 74 2/16:9
Handley Page Hastings T. 5: SCBS: AN 4 O 74 3/9:8
Hunting Percival Provost I: RAF Central Flying School: AN 15 N 74 3/12:9
Provost I: RAF College, Cranwell: AN 15 N 74 3/12:9
Provost I: test flying, Luton, prior to delivery to Muscat/Oman: AN 15 N 74 3/12:9
North American Harvard II: Bristol University Air Sqn: AN 28 N 75 4/13:8-9
Harvard II: FAA: Afx Je 71 12/10:526
Scottish Aviation Bulldog: Oxford UAS, 1974: AN 28 N 75 4/13:9
Bulldog: RCA CFS, early 1973: IM Jl 75 11/4:5
Bulldog: Southampton UAS, 1974: AN 28 N 75 4/13:9
Bulldog: 2 FTS "The Bulldogs," summer 1974: IM Jl 75 11/4:5
Bulldog: T. 1: Central Flying School, Little Rissington: AE Ag 73 5/2:204
Bulldog T. 1: 2 FTS: AN 4 O 74 3/9:8
Bulldog T. 1: 5 FTS: AN 4 O 74 3/9:8
Vickers Valetta T. 3: No. 1 Air Navigation School: AN 24 Ja 75 3/17:10
Vickers Varsity T. 1: No. 1 Radio School, RAF Locking: AN 24 Ja 75 3/17:10
Varsity T. 1: College of Air Warfare, Manby: AN 24 Ja 75 3/17:10
Varsity T. 1: 5 FTS: AN 4 O 74 3/9:9
Varsity T. 1: RAF College, Cranwell: AN 24 Ja 75 3/17:10
Vickers Wellington T. Mk X: RAF Museum: Sc N 74 5/62:593-595
Westland Wyvern T. 3: RT Je 71 4/6:70

III. Color Patterns

(Other Aircraft)
Avro Lincoln: Naid ducted spinner turboprop testbed: AN 28 Je 74 3/2:10
Lincoln: Napier icing research rig: AN 28 Je 74 3/2:10
Lincoln: RAF Signals Command: AN 28 Je 74 3/2:10
Lincoln: radar test modification, RAE Farnborough: AN 28 Je 74 3/2:10
Handley Page Hastings Met.1: 202 Sqn, Coastal Command: AN 5 S 75 4/7:7

(United Nations)

SAAB J 29B Tunnan: F 22, Swedish Voluntary Air Component in Congo: AN 11 My 73 1/26:9
Westland Wessex HC.2: RAF in Cyprus: AN 21 Mr 75 3/2:9

(U.S. Civil)

(Airliners)
Boeing 727: Continental Airlines: IM Mr 71 8/3:6-7
Boeing 727: Northeast: IM Mr 71 8/3:6-7
Boeing 727: Pacific Southwest: IM Mr 71 8/3:6-8
Boeing 727: Western: IM Mr 71 8/3:6-7
Boeing 727: Wien Consolidated: IM Mr 71 8/3:6-7
Boeing 727-222: United, old livery: Q O 72 7/4:156
Boeing 727-222: United, new livery: Q O 72 7/4:156
Boeing 727-222: United, new colors, old lettering: Q O 72 7/4:156
Boeing 727 stretch: United "Stars & Stripes" livery: Q O 72 7/4:156
Boeing 747: United Airlines: Q Ap 72 7/2:80
Convair CV-990: Alaska Airlines: Q Jl 6/3:33
CV-990: American Airlines: Q Jl 71 6/3:33
CV-990 Modern Air, ex-American Airlines, charter line: Q Jl 71 6/3:30
CV-990: Northeast, ex-American Airlines: Q Jl 6/3:30
McDonnel Douglas DC-9-30: Eastern Airlines: AN 12 Jl 74 3/3:9
DC-9-30: Hawaiian Airlines: AN 12 Jl 74 3/3:9
DC-9-31: Ozark Airlines: PAM Ag 74 6:83
DC-9-31: Hughes Air West: PAM Ag 74 6:83
DC-9-31: North East Airlines: PAM Ag 74 6:83

(Coast Guard)
Grumman HU-16 Albatross: Mobile: Q Ap 72 7/2:72
HU-16B: Mobile: AN 29 N 74 3/13:10
HU-16D: Windsor, Ont, Aug 1972: RT My 74 7/5-6:65
HU-16E: Elizabeth City, 1971: RiS Mr 73 3/1:85
HU-16E: Kodiak: RiS Mr 73 3/1:85
HU-16E: Port Angeles, WA: RT Ap 72 5/4:41
HU-16E: Quonset Point: RT Ap 72 5/4:41
HU-16E (UF-2G): Salem: RiS Mr 73 Mr 73 3/1:85

UF-2G: Salem: RT Ap 72 5/4:42
Sikorsky HH3F: San Diego, May 1971, Preston: Q Ap 72 7/2:72

(Fire Fighting)
Beechcraft T-34A Mentor: U.S. Forestry Service, spotter aircraft: IM N 74 10/11-12:16
Grumman AF-2 Guardian: IM Jl 75 11/4:21
Grumman F7F Tigercat: Santa Barbara Airport: Q Ap 74 9/1:26
Grumman TBM Avenger: Aerial Applicators, Salt Lake City Airport: Q Ap 74 9/1:26
TBM-3: Nevada company unknown: IM Mr 75 11/2:11
TBM-3: Aerial Applicators, Salt Lake City; IM Mr 75 11/2:11
TBM-3: Hemet Valley Flying Service, CA: IM Mr 75 11/2:11
TBM-3: Johnson Flying Service, MN: IM Mr 75 11/2:10
TBM-3: TBM, Inc, CA: IM Mr 75 11/2:10
Lockheed P2V-5F Neptune: Rosenbalm Aviation, Bedford, OR: Q Jl 74 10/1:26
North American T-28D Trojan: U.S. Forestry Service spotter aircraft: IM N 74 10/11-12:16

(NASA)
Boeing B-52 Stratofortress: X-15 tests, mother ship, Edwards AFB, 1959: MW S 73 87/3:24
Cessna T.37B Tweet: Edwards AFB, CA, 1974: RiS Mr 75 3/1:45
Douglas C-133A: Apollo Recovery Vehicle tests, NAF El Centro, late 1960s: Q Ja 75 10/3:98
Hawker Siddeley XV-6A Kestral: Q Ja 75 10/3:97
LTV F-8 Crusader: Digital Fly-by-Wire, Flight Research Center: Q Ja 75 10/3:98
Critical Wing Crusader: Flight Research Center, 1971, 3 var: Q Ja 75 10/3:128-129
Lockheed F-104G Starfighter: lifting body chase plane: RT Ag 75 8/8:95; cor F 76 9/2:27
Lockheed T-33: Flight Research Center: Q Ja 75 10/3:97
Lockheed U-2C: Earth Survey: Q Ja 75 10/3:97
U-2: 1971: AM Jl 72 75/1:33
Lockheed YF-12: high speed research: Q Ja 75 10/3:98
Martin B-57: Viking Space Probe Parachute Tests: Q Ja 75 10/3:98
Martin WB-57F: Earth Survey, Houston TX: Q Ja 75 10/3:98
North American P-51 Mustang: Q Ja 75 10/3:96
Northrop F-15 Reporter (P-61 recon): 2 var, Ames, early 1950s: Q Ja 75 10/3:96
Northrop T-38 Talon: 2 var: Q Ja 75 10/3:97
Republic F-84F Thunderstreak: 1953: Q Ja 75 10/3:97
Vertrol CH-46C: jointly with Army: Q Ja 75 10/3:98

(Private)
Bede BD-5J: 3 var, factory demonstration aerobatic team: RT Je 75 8/6:71
BD-5J: USAF markings: RT Je 75 8/6:71; add S 75 8/9:105
Boeing B-29: Confederate Air Force: IM N 73 10/11-12:26

III. Color Patterns

B-29: "Fertile Myrtle," Oakland Airport, 1973: IM N 73 10/11-12: 26
De Havilland Canada DHC-2 Beaver: Alaska Civil Air Patrol: Boeing Field, Seattle WA, Aug 1971: Q O 73 8/4:222
Douglas DC-3: Abbotsford Air Show, Aug 1973, Bede: RT D 73 6/12:147
El Chuparosa: 1959, Hegey: Aero Jl 72 37/438:392-394
Grumman F8F-2 Bearcat: Christopher: AN 10 N 72 1/13:10
Hawker Sea Fury Mk. 11: Royal Navy pattern: Palo Alto CA, 1972, Saunders: RT Ja 73 6/1-2:1
Knight Twister Imperial: Oshkosh, June 1970, Payne: AM Ap 74 78/4:48
Liberty Sport: 1966, Liberty: MAN Ag 71 83/2:29
McDonnell Douglas DC-9-30: Heffner: AN 12 Jl 74 3/3:9
Miller JM-2: Marble Falls TX, March 1974, Frazee: MAN O 75 91/4:67
North American AT-6: PAM Jl 75 10:169
Harvard: (RAF 600 Sqn Hurricane pattern), Vancouver WA, 1972, Ross: RT Je 72 5/6:63
North American F-100C: Flight Test Research: RiS Jl 75 3/2:84
Piper Cherokee 140: EAA Fly-In, Oshkosh, Aug 1971: Q Ja 74 9/1:27
Pitts S-2A Special: Shreveport LA, Cole: MAN Je 74 88/6:34
Ryan STA Special Super 200: Ottumwa, GA, Sept 1969, Gosney: MAN S 71 83/3:26
Waco CTO Taperwing: 1964 airshows, Lyjak: MAN Ag 75 91/2: 26-27

(Racers)
Bell Airacobra "Mr. Mennen," Reno Air Races, 1972, Slovak: PAM Mr 75 9:145
Cobra II (mod P-39Q): Thompson Trophy winner, 1946, Johnston: Sc Mr 75 6/66:127
Bell Kingcobra: 1972 unlimited racer: PAM O 74 7:105
Boeing 720: Allman Brothers Band "Band Wagon," Lewis B. Wilson Airport, Macon GA: RT S 75 8/9:106
Cassutt Model 2: Ft. Wayne, IN, July 1960, Cassutt: RC My 73 10/5:60-61
De Havilland Mosquito: 1949 Bendix Trophy Race, Stallings: RT N 74 7/11:130; cor F 75 8/2:14
Goodyear FG-1D Corsair: 1946 Bendix Trophy race, Call: Sc Ja 75 6/64:39
Grumman F8F Bearcat: Reno races: RT N 73 6/11:130
Bearcat: "AbleCat," Reno Air Races, 1969: RT F 74 7/2:21
Hawker Sea Fury FB Mk. 11: 1967 Reno Air Race, Taylor: RT Ja 73 6/1-2:15
Sea Fury FB Mk. 11: racing mod, Mojave Air Race, 1971, Cooper: RT Ja 73 6/1-2:16
Sea Fury FB Mk. 11: ex RAN, 1972 Reno Air Race, Hamilton, ex VH-BOU: RT Ja 73 6/1-2:16
Sea Fury: racing mod, 1970 racing colors, Cooper: RT Ja 73 6/1-2:15
Lockheed P-38-L-5 Lightning: 1946 Thompson Trophy race: RT N

74 7/11:130; cor F 75 8/2:14
Long LA-1: "P-Shooter," 1948 Goodyear races, Johnson: RC O 72 9/10:60-61
Long LA-1: "P-Shooter," 1949 Goodyear races, Johnson: RC O 72 9/10:60-61
Little Gem: 1951-53 Goodyear races, Miller: RC Mr 73 10/3:58-59
Little Gem: 1954-57 Goodyear races, Miller: RC Mr 73 10/3:58-59
Mace R-2 Shark: 1969 Formula 1 races, Mace: Aero N 71 36/430:637
North American AT-6: racer mod, Cleveland air race, 1947: IM S 71 8/9:16
North American P-51D Mustang: 1967 Nationals, Reno, Weiner: RT N 74 7/11:130
P-51D: 1948 Thompson Trophy, Johnson: RT N 74 7/11:130; cor F 75 8/2:14
P-51D: unlimited racers, 3 var: PAM Ja 74 4:53-54
OR-65-2 Owl Racer: "Pogo," Alford: Aero Ja 72 37/432:46-47
Owl Racer: Formula 1, St. Louis, Aug 1961, Alford: AM Ap 71 72/4:23-24
Rivets: Formula 1: AM F 72 72/2:24-25

(U. S. Military--Helicopter)

Bell TH-1G Huey Gunship: 9 Infantry Div, Ft. Lewis, WA: Q Ja 74 9/1:7
Bell UH-1 Iroquois: UH-1: C Coy, 227 Avn Btn, Bien Hoa, Oct 1969: Q Ap 74 9/2:88
UH-1: C Coy, 227 Avn Btn, Bien Hoa, Jan 1970: Q Ap 74 9/2:89
UH-1B: 1 Pltn, Btry C, 2 Btn, 20 Artillery, 1 Air Cav, An Khe, Nov 1966: Q Ap 71 6/2:22
UH-1B: 62 Avn Coy, Vinh Long, March 1965: Q Ja 72 7/1:25-26
UH-1B: 114 Avn Coy, Vinh Long, March 1965: Q Ja 72 7/1:25-26
UH-1B: 114 Assault Helicopter Coy, Vinh Long, 1966: Q Ap 71 6/2:24
UH-1H: Coy A, 25 Avn Btn: Q Ap 71 6/2:23
UH-1H: 95 Med, Da Nang, 1969: Q Ap 71 6/2:23
Boeing-Vertol UH-46 Sea Knight: 1 Med, Da Nang, 1969: Q Ja 71 6/1:14
Hughes OH-6A Cayuse: North Dakota NG, May 1973: RT Ap 74 7/4:43
Kaman H-2 Seasprite: USS Kitty Hawk, Oct 1967, Doane: Q Ap 73 8/2:92
Kaman UH-2: HC-4: Q Ap 73 8/2:93
UH-2A: USS Springfield: Q Ap 73 8/2:93
Piasecki HUP-2 Retriever: HU-1, USS Shangri-la, 1958: Q Ap 72 7/2:64

III. Color Patterns 308

(U. S. Military--Jet)

(Boeing)
B-47 Stratojet: static display, Plattsburgh AFB, NY: Q Ap 73 8/2: 96
B-47: 303 BW, 1965 Bombing Competition winner: Q Ap 73 8/2: 96; cor Jl 73 8/3:175
B-50A: 43 BW, Davis Monthan, Feb 1949: Q Ja 72 7/1:20-21
B-50D: 341 BS, 97 BG, Giggs AFB, TX, 1948: Q Ja 72 7/1:20-21
B-52G: Barksdale AFB, LA, 1971: Q O 71 6/4:20-21
T-43A (737-200 navigation trainer): RT N 74 7/11:131

(Cessna)
A-37A Dragonfly: 604 SOS, 3 TFW, Bien Hoa AB, Vietnam, late 1967: RiS Mr 75 3/1:46
A-37A: 604 SOS, 3 TFW(CK), Bien Hoa AB: RiS Mr 75 3/1:46
A-37A: 604 SOS, 3 TFW(EK), Bien Hoa AB, 1968, Wilson: RiS Mr 75 3/1:46
A-37B: USAF std: RiS Mr 75 3/1:43
A-37B: 8 AS, 3 TFW(CF), Bien Hoa AB: RiS Mr 75 3/1:46
A-37B: 90 AS, 3 TFW(CG), Bien Hoa AB: RiS Mr 75 3/1:46
A-37B: 104 TFS, 175 TFG, Maryland ANG, Baltimore MD: RiS Mr 75 3/1:46
A-37B: 138 TFS, 174 FG, New York ANG, Syracuse NY: RiS Mr 75 3/1:46
A-37B: 514 AS, 4410 CCTW(IK), England AFB: RiS Mr 75 3/1:46
A-37B: 603 SOS, 1 SOW(AF), Hurlburt Field, 1970: RiS Mr 75 3/1:46
A-37B: 4532 CCTS, 1 SPW(II), Hurlburt Field: RiS Mr 75 3/1:46
T-37 Tweet: std, 1,000th delivered: RT Ap 71 4/4:43
T-37: std stencils: Q Ja 72 7/1:16-19
T-37B: USAF std: RiS Mr 75 3/1:34
T-37B: ATC Laredo AFB TX: RiS Mr 75 3/1:45
T-37B: ATC Laredo AFB TX, 1972: RiS Mr 75 3/1:34
T-37B: 12 FTW, Randolph AFB TX, 1972: RiS Mr 75 3/1:34
T-37B: 14 FTW, Columbus AFB, MS, 1972: Ri S Mr 75 3/1:34
T-37B: 29 FTW, Craig AFB, AL: RiS Mr 75 3/1:45
T-37B: 71 FTW, Vance AFB, OK, 1974: RiS Mr 75 3/1:34

(Chance Vought, LTV)
A-7 Corsair II: Luke AFB: Q Ap 72 7/2:71
A-7: Nellis AFB: Q Ap 72 7/2:71
A-7: VA-46, USS Kennedy: Q Ja 73 8/1:13
A-7: VA-122: Q Ap 72 7/2:71
A-7: VA-146: Q Ap 72 7/2:71
A-7: VA-147: Q Ap 72 7/2:71
A-7A: Naval Missile Center, Point Mugu, CA: IM N 75 11/6:9
A-7A: USNATC, Cold Lake, Alta, winter 1970: RT N 71 4/11:125
A-7A: VA-105, USS Saratoga, 1971: IM N 75 11/6:19
A-7B: VA-72, USS John F. Kennedy, April 1970: IM N 75 11/6:20
A-7B: VA-93, USS Midway: IM N 75 11/6:18

Aircraft

A-7B: VA-153, USS Oriskany, April 1972: IM N 75 11/6:17
A-7C: VA-82, USS America, Oct 1974: IM N 75 11/6:18
A-7C: VA-82, USS America, Schoeffel: IM N 75 11/6:21
A-7C: VA-86, USS America, Oct 1974: IM N 75 11/6:20
A-7D: 57 Fighter Weapons Wing, Nellis AFB: AN 12 Ap 74 2/23:8
A-7D: 333 TFTrS, 355 TFW, Davis-Monthan AFB, Jan 1973, Burke: RiS Sp 73 1/3:98
A-7D: 333 TFTrS, 355 TFW, Kelly AFB, Feb 1972: RiS Sp 73 1/3:98
A-7D: 354 TFS, 355 TFW, Davis-Monthan AFB, Jan 1973: RiS Sp 73 1/3:98
A-7D: 354 TFS, 355 TFW, Kelly AFB, Feb 1972, Costello: RiS Sp 73 1/3:98
A-7D: 355 TFW, Haeffner: AN 12 Ap 74 2/23:9
A-7D: CO, 355 TFW, Haeffner: RiS Sp 73 1/3:96
A-7D: 355 TFW, Panama Canal: RiS Sp 73 1/3:96
A-7D: 357 TFS, 255 TFW, Davis-Monthan AFB: Q Ap 72 7/2:71
A-7D: 356 TFS, 354 TFW, Korat, Thailand, Jan 1973: IM N 75 11/6:17
A-7D: 357 TFS, 355 TFW, Davis-Monthan AFB, Jan 1973, Penney: RiS Sp 73 1/3:99
A-7D: 357 TFS, 355 TFW, Kelly AFB, before 1972, Lacey: RiS Sp 73 1/3:98
A-7D: 358 TFS, 355 TFW, Davis-Monthan AFB, Jan 1973, Myrick: RiS Sp 73 1/3:99
A-7D: 358 TFS, 355 TFW: RiS Sp 73 1/3:99
A-7D: 366 TFW: AN 12 Ap 74 2/23:9
A-7D: 366 TFW, 1974: IM N 75 11/6:18
A-7E: VA-8: USS Forrestal: AN 12 Ap 74 2/23:8
A-7E: VA-12, USS Independence: Q Ap 72 7/2:70
A-7E: VA-25, March 1970, Orrik: IM N 75 11/6:17
A-7E: VA-27 "Royal Maces": AN 12 Ap 74 2/23:9
A-7E: CO, VA-66, USS Independence: Q Ap 72 7/2:70
A-7E: VA-94, USS Coral Sea, April 1973: IM N 75 11/6:20
A-7E: CO, VA-97, USS Enterprise: AN 12 Ap 74 2/23:9
A-7E: VA-192, USS Kitty Hawk: IM N 75 11/6:19
YA-7H: Andrews AFB, Dec 1972: Q Ja 73 8/1:13
YA-7H: NAS Dallas, 3 var: Q O 74 10/2:56-58
F8 Crusader: fin markings for all USN squadrons so equipped, 30 var: IM N 71 8/11:11+
F8C: USS Oriskany: IM N 71 8/11:6
F8E: USS Hancock: IM N 71 8/11:6
F8U-1: VF-11, CAGroup 1, USS F.D. Roosevelt, spring 1961: Q Jl 71 6/3:5
RF-8G: VFP-63: IM N 71 8/11:7
RF-8G: VFP-63, USS Hancock, 1971: AN 26 D 75 4/15:9
RF-8G: VFP-63, USS Midway, Oct 1971: AN 26 D 75 4/15:9
RF-8G: VFP-63, Det. 2, USS Roosevelt, early 1973: AN 26 D 75 4/15:9
RF-8G: CO, VFP-106 Reserve Sqn, NAF Washington DC, Andrews AFB, MD, 1975: AN 26 D 75 4/15:9
RF-8G: CO, VFP-306, NAF Washington, DC, Andrews AFB, MD,

III. Color Patterns

1975: AN 26 D 75 4/15:9
TF-8A: LTV modification or F8U-1T trainer, USN: RT S 71 4/9:105
TF-8A: Naval Air Test Center: IM N 71 8/11:7

(Convair, General Dynamics)
B-58 Hustler: 43 BW, Davis-Monthan AFB (MASDC), Nov 1971: Q Ja 73 8/1:28
B-58: 43 BS, 43 BW, now at USAF Museum, Wright-Patterson AFB, OH: Q Ja 73 8/1:27
B-58: 305 BG, Mitchell Field, Milwaukee WI: Q Ja 73 8/1:28
B-58: 305 BW, Bunker Hill (now Grissom) AFB, IN, 1968: Q Ja 73 8/1:27
B-58: 305 BW, 40 Combat Wing, 2 AF: Q Ja 73 8/1:27
F-102 Delta Dagger: California ANG: RT Mr 75 8/3:35
F-102: Idaho ANG: RT Je 73 6/6:67
F-102: North Dakota ANG, Moose Jaw, Alta: RT Ag 72 5/8:91
F-102A: 317 FIS, 1969: RiS N 72 1/2:54-55
F-102A: Washington ANG: Q Jl 72 7/3:86
F-102A-20-CO: 196 FIS (Ontario) California ANG, 1968: RiS N 72 1/2:57
F-102A-45-CO: 40 FIS, Yokota AB, Japan, 1961: RiS N 72 1/2:59
F-102A-50-CO: 186 FIS, Montana ANG, 1971: RiS N 72 1/2:57
F-102A-50-CO: 431 FIS, Prestwick, Scotland, 1964: Ri S N 72 1/2:59
F-102A-55-CO: 32 FIS, Soesterberg, Holland, 1963: RiS N 72 1/2:56
F-102A-55-CO: 32 FIS, Soesterberg, Holland, 1965: RiS N 72 1/2:58
F-102A-60-CO: 122 FIS, Louisiana ANG, 1965: RiS N 72 1/2:57
F-102A-60-CO: 152 FIS, Arizona ANG, 1969: RiS N 72 1/2:57
F-102A-60-CO: 525 FIS, Bitburg AB, Germany, 1959: RiS N 72 1/2:59
F-102A-60-CO: 525 FIS, Soesterberg AB, Holland, 1965: RiS N 72 1/2:59
F-102A-65-CO: 111 FIS, Texas ANG, 1969: RiS N 72 1/2:57
F-102A-65-CO: 118 FIS, 103 FG, Connecticut ANG, Bradley IAP, Windsor Locks: Q O 74 10/2:75
F-102A-65-CO: 157 FIS, South Carolina ANG, 1972: RiS N 72 1/2:57
F-102A-65-CO: 194 FIS (Fresno) California ANG, 1971: RiS N 72 1/2:57
F-102A-65-CO: 509 FIS, Clark AB, Philippines, 1960: RiS N 72 1/2:58
F-102A-75-CO: 64 FIS, Paine Field, WA: RiS N 72 1/2:59
F-102A-70-CO: 175 FIS, South Dakota ANG, 1961: RiS N 72 1/2:56
F-102A-70-CO: 176 FIS, Wisconsin ANG, 1971: RiS N 72 1/2:57
F-102A-75-CO: 64 FIS, Paine Field, WA: RiS N 72 1/2:59
F-102A-75-CO: 118 FIS, Connecticut ANG, 1971: RiS N 72 1/2:57
F-102A-75-CO: 159 RIS, Florida ANG: RiS N 72 1/2:56
F-102A-75-CO: 326 FIS, 1966: RiS N 72 1/2:54-55

Aircraft

F-102A-75-CO: 326 FIS, Richards Gebaur AFB, MO, 1965: RiS N 72 1/2:59
F-102A-80-CO: 11 FIS, 1960: RiS N 72 1/2:58
F-102A-80-CO: 18 FIS, Wurtsmith AFB, MI, 1958: RiS N 72 1/2:59
F-102A-80-CO: 59 FIS, Goose Bay, Lab, 1964: RiS N 72 1/2:57
F-102A-80-CO: 178 FIS, North Dakota ANG, 1971: RiS N 72 1/2:57
F-102A-90-CO: CO, 123 FIS, Oregon ANG, 1969, McGrady: RiS N 72 1/2:58
F-102A-95-CO: 82 FIS, Travis AFB, CA, 1962: RiS N 72 1/2:59
F-102A-95-CO: CO, 116 FIS, Washington ANG, Nelco: RiS N 72 1/2:58
F-102A-95-CO: 460 FIS, Portland, OR, 1958: RiS N 72 1/2:59
F-106 Delta Dart: 5 FIS, Minot ND: RT O 72 5/10:113
F-106: 5 FIS, Minot AFB, My 1970: RT Je 71 4/6:71
F-106A-75-CO: 186 FIS, Montana ANG, 1972: RiS Su 73 1/4:132
F-106A-75-CO: 186 FIS, Montana ANG, Great Falls, MT, 1972: RiS Su 73 1/4:132
F-106A-85-CO: 498 FIS, McChord AFB, WA, c.1965: RiS Su 73 1/4:133
F-106A-85-CO: 539 FIS, McGuire AFB, NJ: RiS Su 73 1/4:133
F-106A-90-CO: 95 FIS, Dover AFB, DE, 1965: RiS Su 73 1/4:131
F-106A-90-CO: 95 FIS, Dover AFB, DE, 1972: RiS Su 73 1/4:131
F-106A-100-CO: 5 FIS, Minot AFB, ND, 1969: RiS Su 73 1/4:130
F-106A-100-CO: 73 FIS, 1963: RiS Su 73 1/4:133
F-106A-100-CO: 94 FIS, Selfridge AFB, MI, 1964: RiS Su 73 1/4:130
F-106A-100-CO: 4750 Test Sqn, Air Defense Weapons Center, Tyndall AFB, FL, 1972: RiS Su 73 1/4:133
F-106A-105-CO: 5 FIS, Minot AFB, ND, 1965: RiS Su 73 1/4:130
F-106A-105-CO: 5 FIS, Minot AFB, ND, 1972: RiS Su 73 1/4:130
F-106A-105-CO: 94 FIS, Selfridge AFB, MI, 1964: RiS Su 73 1/4:131
F-106A-110-CO: 27 FIS, Loring AFB, ME, 1969: RiS Su 1/4:130
F-106A-110-CO: 83 FIS, Hamilton AFB, CA, 1971: RiS Su 73 1/4:130
F-106A-110-CO: 318 FIS, McChord AFB, WA: RiS Su 73 1/4:132
F-106A-120-CO: 49 FIS, Griffis AFB, NY, 1972: RiS Su 73 1/4:128-129
F-106A-120-CO: 84 FIS, Hamilton AFB, CA, 1967: RiS Su 73 1/4:130
F-106A-120-CO: 84 FIS, Hamilton AFB, CA, 1971: RiS Su 73 1/4:130
F-106A-120-CO: 438 FIS, Kinross AFB, MI: RiS Su 73 1/4:132
F-106A-125-CO: 2 FIS, Wurtsmith AFB, MI, 1971: RiS Su 73 1/4:130
F-106A-125-CO: 1 FIS, Duluth, MN, RiS Su 73 1/4:130
F-106A-125-CO: 11 FIS, Duluth MN, 1962: RiS Su 73 1/4:130
F-106A-125-CO: 87 FIS, Sawyer AFB, MI, 1971: RiS Su 73 1/4:130
F-106A-125-CO: 87 FIS, Sawyer AFB, MI, 1972: RiS Su 73 1/4:130

III. Color Patterns 312

F-106A-130-CO: 329 FIS, George AFB, CA, 1964: RiS Su 73 1/4:132
F-106A-131-CO: 11 FIS, Duluth MN, 1967: RiS Su 73 1/4:130
F-106A-131-CO: 48 FIS, Langley AFB, VA, 1969: RiS Su 73 1/4:130
F-106A-131-CO: 318 FIS, McChord AFB, WA, 1972: RiS Su 73 1/4:132
F-106A-131-CO: 456 FIS, Grand Forks AFB, ND, 1972: RiS Su 73 1/4:132
F-106A-135-CO: 460 FIS, Castle AFB, CA, 1962: RiS Su 73 1/4:133
F-106B-90-CO: 101 FIS, Boston, 1972: RiS Su 73 1/4:128-129

(Grumman)
A-6A Intruder: NAS Oceana: Q Su 75 10/4:158
A-6A: VA-95, USS Coral Sea, Whidbey Island NAS: Q Su 75 10/4:158
A-6A: VA-115, USS Midway, Barber's Point NAS: Q Su 75 10/4:156
A-6A: VA-145, USS Ranger, Whidbey Island NAS: Q Su 75 10/4:157
A-6A: VM (AW) 242: Q Su 75 10/4:158
A-6A: VMA (AW) 533: Q Su 75 10/4:157
NA-6a: NATC Pax River: Q Su 75 10/4:158
F9F Cougar: USS Boxer, early 1950s: Q Ap 73 8/2:89
F9F-8P: VFP-61, USS Shrangi-la, 1958: Q Ap 72 7/2:62-63
TF-9J Cougar: Naval Aerospace Recovery Facility, El Centro, 1965-69, 2 var: Q Ja 71 6/1:15
F11F-1 Tiger: VA-156, USS Shrangi-la, 1958: Q Ap 72 7/2:62
F-14 Tomcat: prototype 1X: Q Jl 72 7/3:91
F-14: prototype 2, Transpo 72, Dulles Airport MD, 1972: Q Jl 72 7/3:92
F-14: suitability trials, USS Independence (CVA-62): Q Jl 72 7/3:92
F-14: test aircraft, June 1972: Q Ja 73 8/1:51
F-14: VF-124, first operational: Q Ja 73 8/1:51; cor Jl 73 8/3:174
F-14A: VF-124, NAS Miramar: MAN Ap 74 88/4:73

(Lockheed)
A-11: first in USAF: RT N 73 6/11:131
C-141 Starlifter: 63 MAW, Clark Field, Philippines, FEB 1973: RT Ap 73 6/4:42
F-80 Shooting Star: 96 Sqn, 1 FIG; RT F 75 8/2:20
F-80A-10-LO: 61 FS, 56 FG, 1958, Westfall: RiS N 72 1/2:41
F-80B-LO: 94 FS, Ladd Field, AK, 1947: RiS N 72 1/2:46
F-80B-LO: Ohio ANG: RiS N 72 1/2:45
F-80B-1-LO: Air Training Command, Luke AFB, 1953, Hill: RiS N 72 1/2:43
F-80C: 15 TRS, 67 TRG, Kimpo, early 1950s, 3 var: Q Ap 73 8/2:83+
F-80C-5-LO: Alaska: RiS N 72 1/2:43
F-80C-5-LO: Anchorage, AK, "Operation Sweetbriar," 1950: RiS

N 72 1/2:46
F-80C-10-LO: Korea, 1952: RiS N 72 1/2:45
F-80C-10-LO: 35 RBS "Black Panthers," 8 FBG "Hobo Wing," K-13, Suwon, South Korea, 1952, Keeler: RiS Ag 72 1/1:25
F-80C-10-LO: 56 FG, Selfridge Field, 1949: RiS N 72 1/2:46
F-80C-10-LO: 144 F/BS, Alaska ANG: RiS N 72 1/2:45
F-80C-12-LO: 181 F/BS, Texas ANG: RiS N 72 1/2:46
F-80C-12-LO: 185 F/BS, Oklahoma ANG: RiS N 72 1/2:45
F-80C-12-LO: 187 F/BS, Wyoming ANG: RiS N 72 1/2:45
F-80C-12-LO: 334 FS, Andrews Field, MD, 1947: RiS N 72 1/2:46
P-80: Okinawa, 1947, 3 var: Q Ap 72:44
P-80A-LO: RiS N 72 1/2:43
P-80B: 94 FS, early 1948: MW Ja 73 1/5:261
P-80B-LO: prob 94 FS: RiS N 72 1/2:43
P-80C: 67 Training Group, Kimpo, late 1948: MW Ja 73 1/5:261
P-80C: 155 TRS, 67 TRG, Kimpo, 1950: Q Ap 72 7/2:58
P-80C: 155 TRS, 67 TRG, Kimpo, 1952: Q Ap 72 7/2:59
QF-80 (drone): USAF: RiS N 72 1/2:45
RF-80A: 15 TRS, 67 TRG, Kimpo, early 1950s; 6 var: Q Ap 73 8/2:82+
RF-80A-15-LO: 155 TRS, 67 TRG, Kimpo, 1952 2 var: Q Ap 72 7/2:57
TV-1 (P-80C): NAS Oakland: RiS N 72 1/2:43
YP-80A: England, 1944: RiS N 72 1/2:45
QF-104A Starfighter drone: AF Systems Command, 1960: RiS W 74 2/2:59
T-33 Thunderbird or T-Bird: 474 TFW, Barksdale AFB, June 1970: Q Jl 72 7/3:100
T-33: 68 FIS, E Flt, Japan, 1955: Q Jl 72 7/3:10
T-33A: Air Weapons Development Center, Barksdale AFB, April 1970: Q Jl 72 7/3:103
T-33A: Laon AFB, France, 1958: Q Jl 72 7/3:102
T-33A: Texas ANG, Bergstron AFB, Aug 1967: Q Jl 72 7/3:103
T-33A: 21 Composite Wing, Alaskan Air Command, Elmendorf AFB, 1969-70, Piccirillo: Q Jl 72 7/3:103
T-33B: USMC Flight Section HW, USMC, Washington: Q Jl 72 7/3:101
T-33B: Utility Sqn One, NAS Barber's Point, HI, 1963-64, Fink: Q Jl 72 7/3:102
DT-33B: in-flight drone control: Q Jl 72 7/3:102

(Martin)
B-57B Canberra: 8 TBS, Randolph AFB, TX, spring 1969: Q O 71 6/4:33
B-57B: 71 BS, 38 BW, Laon, France, July 1957: Q O 71 6/4:33
B-57B: 822 BS, 38 BW, Laon, July 1957: Q O 71 6/4:33
B-57C: 405 BS, 38 BW, Laon, July 1957, trainer version: Q O 71 6/4:33
RB-57F: 58 Weather Recon Sqn, Kirtland AFB, NM: Q Jl 73 8/3:172-173

III. Color Patterns   314

(McDonnell-Douglas)
A-3B Skywarrior: NARF: Q Ja 71 6/1:16-17
A3D-2: VAH-4, USS Shangri-la, 1958: Q Ap 72 7/2:62-63
A-4 Skyhawk: VA-23, Patrick: Q Jl 72 7/3:114
A-4: VMA-223, Osegura: Q Jl 72 7/3:114
A-4A (A4D-1): VA-113, flight demonstration team, USS Shangri-la, 1958, Cormier: Q Jl 72 7/3:115
A-4B: Fleet Composite Sqn 1, NAS Barber's Point, HI, Fink: Q Jl 72 7/3:116
A-4B: NARF: 2 var: Q Ja 71 6/1:18
A-4B: Navy & Marine Reserve, NAS Jacksonville, mid-1960s: RiS Mr 75 3/1:21
A-4B: N&MR, NAS New Orleans, mid 1960s: RiS Mr 75 3/1:18
A-4B: N&MR, NAS Norfolk, mid 1960s: RiS Mr 75 3/1:18
A-4B: N&MR, NAS New York: RiS Mr 75 3/1:19
A-4B: VMA-332, c.1964: RiS Mr 75 3/1:15
A-4B: VMA-533: RiS Mr 75 3/1:20
A-4C: H&MS-15, Detachment N, DVSG-57, USS Hornet: RiS Mr 75 3/1:19
A-4C: VMA-131: RiS Mr 75 3/1:21
A-4C: VMA-131(R), NAS Willow Grove, mid 1972: RiS Mr 75 3/1:18
A-4C: VMA-133, NAS Alameda: RiS Mr 75 3/1:15
A-4C: VMA-133(R), NAS Alameda: RiS Mr 75 3/1:20
A-4C: VMA-134: RiS Mr 75 3/1:20
A-4C: VMA-134, NAS Los Alamitos, mid 1970: RiS Mr 75 3/1:18
A-4C: VMA-142, NAS Jacksonville: RiS Mr 75 3/1:18
A-4C: VMA-214: Q Jl 72 7/3:117
A-4C: VMA-223, Detachment T, DVSG-55, USS Yorktown: RiS Mr 75 3/1:19
A-4C: VMA-242, MCAS Cherry Point, May 1963: RiS Mr 75 3/1:18
A-4C: VMA-322(R), NAS South Weymouth, mid 1971: RiS Mr 75 3/1:18
A-4D-1: VA-43: Q Jl 72 7/3:115
A-4D-1: VA-113: Q Ap 72 7/2:62
A-4D-1: VMA-211, c.1957: RiS Mr 75 3/1:15
A-4D-2: Quantico, VA: RiS Mr 75 3/1:16
A-4D-2: SOES, Quantico VA, 1962: RiS Mr 75 3/1:16
A-4D-2: VMA-225, USS Essex, Atlantic Fleet, c.1960: RiS Mr 75 3/1:14
A-4D-2: VMA-331, MCAS Cherry Point, early 1960s: RiS Mr 75 3/1:18
A-4D-2N: VMA-225, USS Shangri-la, c.1960: RiS Mr 75 3/1:20
A-4E: FCS-1 (VC-11): Q Jl 72 7/3:116
A-4E: NAS Miramar, Jan 1975: RiS Mr 75 3/1:17
A-4E: VMA-121, Ubon RTAFB, Thailand, 1968: RiS Mr 75 3/1:14
A-4E: VMA-211: RiS Mr 75 3/1:20
A-4E: VMA-322 (Reserves): Robertson ANGB, St. Louis, mid 1974: RiS Mr 75 3/1:16
A-4E: CO, CAW 7, VMA-331, USS Independence, 1970: RiS Mr 75 3/1:19

Aircraft

A-4E: VMA-332, c.1964: RiS Mr 75 3/1:15
A-4F: Blue Angels: Q Ap 74 9/2:62
A-4F: VA-22, Ashmore: Q Jl 72 7/3:117
A-4F: VA-153, USS Coral Sea, Norton: Q Jl 72 7/3:116
A-4F: VA-192, Gureck: Q Jl 72 7/3:117
A-4F: VMA-214: RT Je 73 6/6:67
A-4F: CO, VMA-223, Spring 1972, Laezo: RiS Mr 75 3/1:14
A-4L: NAR flight demonstration team, NAS Glenview IL, Bentley: Q Jl 72 7/3:115
A-4L: VMA-124(R), NAS Memphis, late 1973: RiS Mr 75 3/1:17
A-4L: VMA-142(R): Mc Coy AFB, late 1972: RiS Mr 75 3/1:17
A-4L: MARTD Glenview (VMA-543), late 1973: RiS Mr 75 3/1:17
A-4L: VMA-543, NAS Glenview, 1971: RiS Mr 75 3/1:21
A-4M: USMC, Cold Lake, Alta, winter 1970: RT N 71 5/11:125
A-4M: VMT-203, late 1970: RiS Mr 75 3/1:17
A-4M: VMA-214, MCAS El Toro, mid 1973, Newton: RiS Mr 75 3/1:17
A-4M: VMA-324, MCAS Beaufort MD, 1971: AE F 72 2/2:100
NA-4B: NATF: Q Jl 72 7/3:114
TA-4B: MARS, NAS Los Alamitos, 1968: RiS Mr 75 3/1:21
TA-4B: N&MR, North Weymouth, late 1969: RiS Mr 75 3/1:21
TA-4B: shared VMA-133(R) & VMA-141(R), NARTU Alameda, early 1970: RiS Mr 75 3/1:19
TA-4B: VMA-543, NAS Glenview, 1969: RiS Mr 75 3/1:14
TA-4F: CO, H&MS-11, June 1970: RiS Mr 75 3/1:20
TA-4F: H&MS-11, NAS Atsugi: RiS Mr 75 3/1:19
TA-4F: H&MS-12, NAS Atsugi, mid-1971: RiS Mr 75 3/1:21
TA-4F: CO, H&MS-14, Hammong: RiS Mr 75 3/1:16
TA-4F: H&MS-15: RiS Mr 75 3/1:17
TA-4F: H&MS-15: RiS Mr 75 3/1:20
TA-4F: H&MS-24: RiS Mr 75 3/1:21
TA-4F: H&MS-31, Randolph AFB, 1969: RiS Mr 75 3/1:21
TA-4F: H&MS-32, NCAS Beaufort, mid-1970: RiS Mr 75 3/1:18
TA-4F: H&MS-33, mid 1972: RiS Mr 75 3/1:14
TA-4F: H&MS-37, MCAW El Toro: RiS Mr 75 3/1:19
TA-4F: VA-45, Hayworth: Q O 71 6/4:4
TA-4F: VMT-103, MCAS Yuma: RiS Mr 75 3/1:15
TA-4J: USN test unit: Q O 71 6/4:5
TA-4J: VA-43, Colgan: Q Jl 72 7/3:116
TA-4J: VA-127: Q Jl 72 7/3:115
TA-4J: VT-21, NAS Kingsville: AE F 72 2/2:100
TA-4J: VMT-103: Q Jl 72 7/3:115
TA-4J: VMT-203, c.1971: RiS Mr 75 3/1:16
EB-66C Destroyer: 39 TEWS, 36 TFW: Q Ja 73 8/1:44
F2H-1P Banshee: VMJ-1, Phoang, Korea, 2 var: Q Ap 73 8/2:89
F2H-2: NAS Oakland, July 1959: AN 15 Mr 74 2/21:10
F2H-3: std: AN 15 Mr 74 2/1:10
F2H-3: first USN "-3": AN 15 Mr 74 2/21:9
F2H-4: NAS Oakland, Sept 1959: AN 15 Mr 74 2/21:8
F2H-4: VMF(N)-533, Sept 1955: AN 15 Mr 74 2/21:8
F3H-2N: VF-114, USS Shangri-la, 1958: Q Ap 72 7/2:62-63
F3H-3: Naval Missile Center, Cold Lake, Alta, winter 1959: RT Jl 74 7/7:69

III. Color Patterns

F3H-3: Point Mugu, Cold Lake, Alta, winter 1959: RT Jl 74 7/7: 69
F-4 Phantom II: OT&EF: IM Ja 71 8/1:10-11
F-4: 347 TFW, late 1968, 3 var: Q Ap 71 6/2:4
F-4: Thunderbirds: Sc F 75 6/65:86
F-4A: NARF: Q Ja 71 6/1:16-17
F-4B: VF-51, USS Coral Sea: Afx S 74 16/1:31
F-4B: VF-74: Sc S 71 2/9:468
F-4B: VF-143: Sc S 71 2/9:466
F-4B: VF-161: Sc O 71 2/10:530
F-4B: VF-213: Sc N 71 2/9:610
F-4B: VMFA-115: Sc N 71 2/9:608
F-4B: VMFA-122: Sc N 71 2/11:612
F-4B: VMFA-321, MARTD Andrews, McLeran, bi-centennial pattern: Q Au 75 11/1:52
F-4B: VMFA-323: Sc S 71 2/9:469
F-4B: VX-4; Point Mugu Naval Missile Center: Q O 74 10/2:86
F-4C: 81 TFW, Bentwaters, 1972: Afx S 72 14/1:29
F-4D: 22 TFS, 36 TFW: Q Ja 73 8/1:44
F-4D: 23 TFS, 36 TFW, Germany, March 1966: Q Ja 73 8/1:44
F-4D: 53 TFS, 36 TFW: Q Ja 73 8/1:44
F-4D: 555 TFS, 432 TFW, Udorn, Thailand, Aug 1972, Ritchie: RT Jl 73 4/7:75
F-4E: 32 TFS, Europe: AN 7 Mr 75 3/20:9
F-4E: 34 TFS, 388 TFW: AE S 71 1/4:200
F-4E: CO, 307 TFS, Udorn, Thailand, Oct 1972: RT F 74 7/2:16
F-4E: 338 TFW, Korat, Thailand, in ferry, Guam, Nov 1968, Douglas: RT Ag 72 5/8:72; cor & add N 72 5/11:122
F-4E: 625 TFS, 36 TFW: Q Ja 73 8/1:44
F-4E: 4530 TFS, 1 TFW, McDill AFB, 1970: Q Jl 71 6/3:20-22
F-4J: Blue Angels: Sc Mr 73 8/1:44
F-4J: CO, CAG-9, USS Constellation, May 1972, Eggert: Q Ja 74 9/1:42
F-4J: VF-96, USS America: Afx S 74 16/1:31
F-4J: VF-96, USS Constellation, Cunningham: Q Ja 74 9/1:42
F-4J: VF-101, bi-centennial pattern: Q Au 75 11/1:52
F-4J: VF-114, USS Kitty Hawk: Afx S 74 16/1:31
F-4J: VX-4, Point Mugu Naval Missile Center, Cawley: Q O 74 10/2:86
F-4J: VX-4, Point Mugu Naval Missile Center, Harter: Q O 74 10/2:86
QF-4B: drone, VX-4, Point Mugu Naval Missile Center: Q O 74 10/2:86
RF-4B: VMCJ-2: AE S 71 1/4:200
RF-4C-20MC: 30 TRS, 10 TRW, Alconbury, 1972, Wicker: Afx S 72 14/1:29
F-15 Eagle: two-tone grey std: IM N 75 11/6:10
F-15: two-tone grey std: Q Su 75 10/4:154-155
F-101 Voodoo: North Dakota ANG, Wold Chamberlain Field, St. Paul-Minneapolis, summer 1970: Q O 72 7/4:126
F-101B: 18 TIS, 24 AD, ADC, Cold Lake, Alta: RT Mr 72 5/3:32
F-101B: 60 TFS, Langley AFB, June 1970: MW Mr 73 1/7:364-365

Aircraft

F-101B: 98 FIS, 52 FW, ADC, Dover AFB, DE, 1966: RiS Au 73 2/1:20-21
F-101B: 125 FIG, Florida ANG, Sept 1970: RT N 73 6/11:125
F-101B: 125 FIG, Florida ANG, May 1973: RT N 73 6/1:125
F-101B: 111 FITS, Texas ANG, Ellington AFB, 1972: RiS Au 73 2/1:26
F-101B: 132 FIS, Maine ANG, Bangor Intl Airport, 1971: RiS Au 73 2/1:26
F-101B: 322 FIS, Kingsley Field, OR: RiS Au 73 2/1:26
F-101B: 444 FIS, Charleston AFB, 1966: RiS Au 73 2/1:26
F-101B-60-MC: 98 FIS, Suffolk AFB, Long Island, NY, 1974: RiS Au 73 2/1:25
F-101B-70-MC: 445 FIS, Davis-Monthan AFB: RiS Au 73 2/1:26
F-101B-80-MC: 60 FIS, Otis AFB, MA, 1968: RiS Au 73 2/1:25
F-101B-80-MC: 83 FIS, Hamilton AFB, CA: RiS Au 73 2/1:25
F-101B-80-MC: 87 FiS, Lockbourne AFB, OH, 1966: RiS Au 73 2/1:25
F-101B-85-MC: 59 FIS, 52 FW, Kingsley Field, OR, 1968: RiS Au 73 2/1:24
F-101B-85-MC: 116 FIS, Washington ANG, Spokane, 1970: RiS Au 73 2/1:25
F-101B-90-MC: 13 FIS, Glascow AFB, MT, 1968: RiS Au 73 2/1:24
F-101B-100-MC: 2 FIS, 52 FW, Suffolk Co. AFB, Long Island, NY, 1965: RiS Au 73 2/1:24
F-101B-100-MC: 75 FIS, Dow AFB, ME, 1967: RiS Au 73 2/1:25
F-101B-100-MC: 75 FIS, Dow AFB, ME, 1968: RiS Au 73 2/1:25
F-101B-100-MC: 179 FIS, Minnesota ANG, 1973, Gatlin: RiS Au 73 2/1:26
F-101B-100-MC: 437 FIS, Oxnard AFB, CA, 1963: RiS Au 73 2/1:26
F-101B-100-MC: 437 FIS, Oxnard AFB, CA, 1967: RiS Au 73 2/1:26
F-101B-105-MC: 15 FIS, Davis-Monthan AFB, AZ: RiS Au 73 2/1:24
F-101B-105-MC: 84 FIS, Hamilton AFB, CA, 1967: RiS Au 73 2/1:25
F-101B-110-MC: 18 FIS, Grand Forks AFB, ND, 1963: RiS Au 73 2/1:24
F-101B-110-MC: 18 FIS, Glascow AFB, MT, 1968: RiS Au 73 2/1:24
F-101B-110-MC: 29 FIS, Malstrom AFB, MT, 1966: RiS Au 73 2/1:24
F-101B-110-MC: 49 FIS, Griffiss AFB, NY, 1968: RiS Au 73 2/1:24
F-101B-110-MC: 62 FIS, Sawyer AFB, MI, 1969: RiS Au 73 2/1:25
F-101B-115-MC: 60 FIS, Otis AFB, MA, 1970: RiS Au 73 2/1:25
F-101C: 81 TFW, South Ruislin, England, 1961: Q O 72 7/4:126
RF-101C-40-MC: 363 TRW, Shaw AFB, SC, "Operation Sun Run," Nov 1957, Schrecengost: RiS Sp 73 1/3:100
RF-101C-40-MC: 363 TRW, Shaw AFB, SC, "Operation Sun Run,"

III. Color Patterns 318

    Nov 1957, Sweet: RiS Sp 73 1/3:100
F4D Skyray: Naval Test Pilot School, NAS Patuxent River, Aug 1968: Q O 74 10/2:71
F4D: USNR, NAS Olanthe: Q O 74 10/2:70
F4D: VF-102, Stenetee: Q O 74 10/2:70
F4D: VF-102, April 1961, Stenetee: Q O 74 10/2:70
F4D: ADC, VFAW-3, San Diego, 1960, Nankiuil: Q O 74 10/2:71
F4D: VMF(AW) 531: Q O 74 10/2:70
F4D-1: USS Lexington: AN 4 Ap 75 3/22:9
F4D-1: NATC drone control: Q O 74 10/2:86
F4D-1: VFAW-3, Norad: AN 4 Ap 75 3/22:9
F4D-1: VMF(AW)-114: AN 4 Ap 75 3/22:9
F4D-1: VMF-115, 2 var: AN 4 Ap 75 3/22:9
FH-1 Phantom I: "Flying Leathernecks" demonstration team, Cherry Point, NC, summer 1947: Q O 73 8/4:233
FH-1: NATC, 3 var: Q O 73 8/4:229-230
FH-1: prob Reserve Sqn, Floyd Bennett Field, NY, Gould: Q O 73 8/4:231
FH-1: VF-17A, Carrier Suitability Trials, USS Saipan, 1948: Q O 73 8/4:230
FH-1: VF-17A: NAS Glenview IL, July 1948: Q O 73 8/4:229
FH-1: VMF-122: Q O 73 8/4:231
FH-1: VMF-122, July 1948: Q O 73 8/4:229
FH-1: VMF-122, NAAS Sufley Field, Pensacola, FL, 1948: Q O 73 8/4:229
FH-1: VMF-122, NAS New York, Oct 1949: Q O 73 8/4:231
XFD-1: prototype: Q O 73 8/4:229

(North American Rockwell)
EF-100-5-NA: Wright Air Development Center, ARDC: RiS Jl 75 3/2:85; cor Ja 76 3/3:162
F-86A-1 Sabre: 71 FIS, 1 FIW, 1949: RiS Sp 74 2/3-4:101
F-86A-5: 4 FIW, 1951: RiS Sp 74 2/3-4:101
F-86A-5: 17 FIS, 1 FIW, 1949: RiS Sp 74 2/3-4:101; cor Mr 75 3/1:24
F-86A-5: 94 FIS, 1 FIW, 1949: RiS Sp 74 2/3-4:101; cor Mr 75 3/1:24
F-86A-5: 116 FS, 1951: RiS Sp 74 2/3-4:101
F-86A-5: 123 FS, Oregon ANG: RiS Sp 74 2/3-4:104; cor Mr 75 3/1:24
F-86A-5: 191 FIS, Utah ANG, RiS Sp 74 2/3-4:101
F-86A-5: 197 FIS, Arizona ANG: RiS Sp 74 2/3-4:101
F-86A-5-NA: 58 FIS, RiS Sp 74 2/3-4:104
F-86D: std: RiS Sp 74 2/3-4:112
F-86D: 31 FIS, 4702 ADW, 1954: RiS Sp 74 2/3-4:114
F-86D: 97 FIS, 4706 ADW: RiS Sp 74 2/3-4:113
F-86D-5: 27 FIS: RiS Sp 74 2/3-4:112
F-86D-10: unit unknown, McDonnell AFB: RiS Sp 74 2/3-4:117
F-86D-25: 94 FIS, George AFB, 1954: RiS Sp 74 2/3-4:117
F-86D-25: 159 FIS, Florida ANG: RiS Sp 74 2/3-4:117
F-86D-30: 37 FIW: RiS Sp 74 2/3-4:114
F-86D-30: 37 FIS, 14 FIW, Ethan Allen AFB, VT: RiS Sp 74 2/3-4:114

F-86D-30:   97 FIS, 1953: RiS Sp 74 2/3-4:113; cor Mr 75 3/1:24
F-86D-30:   465 FIS, 1953: RiS Sp 74 2/3-4:112
F-86D-35:   unit unknown: RiS Sp 74 2/3-4:117
F-86D-35-NA: 31 FIS, Moses Lake, WA, 1953, Heatley: Q O 71 6/4:10
F-86D-35:   68 FIS, 1958-59: RiS Sp 2/3-4:117
F-86D-35:   182 FIS, Texas ANG: RiS Sp 74 2/3-4:116
F-86D-35:   257 FIS: RiS Sp 74 2/3-4:116
F-86D-35:   513 FIS, 406 FIW, Phalsbourg, France: RiS Sp 74 2/3-4:113; cor 86 FIW: Mr 75 3/1:24
F-86D-40:   63 FIS, 56 FIW: RiS Sp 74 2/3-4:115
F-86D-40:   326 FIS, 328 FIW, Grandview AFB, MO, 1954: RiS Sp 74 2/3-4:114
F-86D-40:   Texas ANG: RiS Sp 74 2/3-4:116
F-86D-45:   16 FIS, 51 RIW, Okinawa, 1956: RiS Sp 74 2/3-4:115
F-86D-45-NA: 40 FIS, Yokota AB, Japan, Walsh: Q O 71 6/4:11
F-86D-45:   56 FIW, 1955: RiS Sp 74 2/3-4:115
F-86D-45:   440 FIS, 531 FIW, 1956: RiS Sp 74 2/3-4:114
F-86D-45:   512 FIS, 406 FIW: RiS Sp 74 2/3-4:113
F-86D-45:   520 FIS, 530 FIW, "Geiger Tigers": RiS Sp 74 2/3-4:115; cor Mr 75 3/1:24
F-86D-50-NA: 4 FIS, Misawa AB, Japan, 1959, Pelter: Q O 71 6/4:11
F-86D-50:   4 FIS, Misawa, Japan, 1959: RiS Sp 74 2/3-4:113
F-86D-50:   14 FIS, 53 FIW: RiS Sp 74 2/3-4:114
F-86D-50:   35 FIW: RiS Sp 74 2/3-4:116
F-86D-50:   40 FIS, Komaki, Japan: RiS Sp 74 2/3-4:116
F-86D-50:   94 FIS, Selfridge AFB, 1955: RiS Sp 74 2/3-4:117
F-86D-50:   157 FIS, South Carolina ANG: RiS Sp 74 2/3-4:113
F-86D-50:   512 FIS, 406 FIW, 1953: RiS Sp 74 2/3-4:113
F-86D-55:   95 FIS; RiS Sp 74 2/3-4:115
F-86D-55-NA: 97 FIS, Wright Patterson AFB, 1955, Lane: Q O 71 6/4:11
F-86D-55:   108 FIS, Illinois ANG: RiS Sp 74 2/3-4:116
F-86D-55:   125 FIS, Oklahoma ANG: RiS Sp 74 2/3-4:117
F-86D-55:   127 FIS, Kansas ANG: RiS Sp 74 2/3-4:117
F-86D-60:   unit unknown, 1955: RiS Sp 74 2/3-4:117; cor Mr 75 3/1:24
F-86D-60:   56 FIW, 1955: RiS Sp 74 2/3-4:115
F-86D-60:   prob 49 FIS: RiS Sp 74 2/3-4:114; cor Mr 75 3/1:24
F-86D-60:   83 FIS, 529 ADW, 1959: RiS Sp 74 2/3-4:115
F-86D-60:   127 FIS, Kansas ANG, McConnel AFB: RiS Sp 74 2/3-4:117
F-86D-60:   194 FIS, California ANG, 1964: RiS Sp 74 2/3-4:117
F-86D-60:   331 FIS, Webb AFB, TX: RiS Sp 74 2/3-4:116
F-86D-60-NA: 520 FIS, Gieger Field, WA, 1956, Reynolds: Q O 71 6/4:10
F-86D-60:   Texas ANG: RiS Sp 74 2/3-4:116
F-86E-1:   4 FG, Kimpo, pos 1952: Q Ap 73 8/2:87
F-86E-1:   199 FS, Hawaii ANG: RiS Sp 74 2/3-4:108
F-86E-5-NA: 25 FS, 51 FW: RiS Sp 74 2/3-4:104
F-86E-10-NA: Flight Test Center, Edwards AFB: RiS Sp 74 2/3-4:107

III. Color Patterns 320

F-86E-10-NA: 119 FS, New Jersey ANG: RiS Sp 74 2/3-4:108
F-86E-10-NA: 144 FS, Alaska ANG: RiS Sp 74 2/3-4:108
F-86E-10-NA: 325 FS, 327 FW, "Sabre Knights," Hamilton AFB, CA: RiS Sp 74 2/3-4:106
F-86E-15-NA: Flight Test Center, Edwards AFB: RiS Sp 74 2/3-4:108
F-86E-15-NA: 120 FS, Colorado ANG, 1955: RiS Sp 74 2/3-4:108
F-86E-15-NA: 127 FS, Michigan ANG: RiS Sp 74 2/3-4:108; cor Jl 75 3/2:94
F-86F-10-NA: 120 FS, "Minute Men," Colorado ANG: RiS Sp 74 2/3-4:106
F-86F-15-NA: 335 FIS, Moore: RiS Sp 74 2/3-4:102-103
F-86F-25-NA: unit unknown, Wiesbaden, Germany, 1955, 2 var: RiS Sp 74 2/3-4:107; cor: 416 FBS, 21 FBW, Chambley Field, France, & 531 FBS, 21 FBW: MR 75 3/1:24
F-86E-25-NA: AF Logistics Command: RiS Sp 74 2/3-4:106
F-86F-25-NA: 4520 CCTW, Nellis AFB, NV, 1960: RiS Sp 74 2/3-4:106; cor Mr 75 3/1:24
F-86F-30-NA: unit unknown: RiS Sp 74 2/3-4:107
F-86F-30-NA: unit unknown, prob aerobatic: RiS Sp 74 2/3-4:106
F-86F-30-NA: "Skyblazers" aerobatic team, 1956: RiS Sp 74 2/3-4:205
F-86F-30: 12 FBS, 18 FBW, Osan AB: RiS Sp 74 2/3-4:104
F-86F-30-NA: 16 FS, 51 FW, 1954: RiS Sp 74 2/3-4:104
F-86F-30-NA: 35 FBS: RiS Sp 74 2/3-4:104
F-86F-30-NA: 44 FS, Formosa, 1954: RiS Sp 74 2/3-4:105
F-86F-30-NA: 50 FG, Germany, 1955: RiS Sp 74 2/3-4:106
F-86F-30: 67 FBS, 18 FBW, 1955: RiS Sp 74 2/3-4:104
F-86F-30-NA: 81 FS, 50 FG, Germany: RiS Sp 74 2/3-4:106
F-86F-30-NA: 311 FBS, 58 FBW, Korea, 1953: RiS Sp 74 2/3-4:105
F-86F-30: 334 FIS, 1953, Parr: RiS Sp 74 2/3-4:102-103
F-86F-30: 336 FIS, Hall: RiS Sp 74 2/3-4:102-103
F-86F-30-NA: 390 FBS, 366 FBW, 1955: RiS Sp 74 2/3-4:105
F-86F-30-NA: 720 FDS, 11 AD, Alaska, 1954: RiS Sp 74 2/3-4:107
F-86F-30-NA: 3595 CCTW, Nellis AFB, 1955: RiS Sp 74 2/3-4:107; cor Mr 75 3/1:24
F-86F-35-NA: "Skyblazers," 48 FW, 1955, 2 var: RiS Sp 74 2/3-4:105
F-86H: std camouflage: RiS Sp 74 2/3-4:109
F-86H-1-NH: 131 TFS, Massachusetts ANG, 1965: RiS Sp 74 2/3-4:111
F-86H-1-NH: 167 FS, West Virginia ANG; RiS Sp 74 2/3-4:110
F-86H-1-NH: 3595 CCTW, Nellis AFB, 1956: RiS Sp 74 2/3-4:111
F-86H-5-NH: 34 FS: RiS Sp 74 2/3-4:110
F-86H-5-NH: 101 TFS, Massachusetts ANG, 1963: RiS Sp 74 2/3-4:110
F-86H-5-NH: 119 TFS, New Jersey ANG, 1965: RiS Sp 74 2/3-4:111
F-86H-5-NH: 138 FBS, New York ANG, 1964: RiS Sp 74 2/3-4:111
F-86H-5-NH: 198 FIS, Puerto Rico ANG: RiS Sp 74 2/3-4:111

F-86H-10-NH: unit unknown: RiS Sp 74 2/3-4:111
F-86H-10-NH: 11 FIS, 1955: RiS Sp 74 2/3-4:109
F-86H-10:   115 FS, California ANG, 1960:   RiS Sp 74 2/3-4:111
F-86H-10-NH: 121 FS, DC ANG: RiS Sp 74 2/3-4:110
F-86H-10-NH: 136 FS, New York ANG: RiS Sp 74 2/3-4:111
F-86H-10-NH: 142 FS, Delaware ANG: RiS Sp 74 2/3-4:109; cor Mr 75 3/1:24
F-86L-55:   95 FIS, 4710 ADW: RiS Sp 74 2/3-4:115
F-86L-56-NA: 56 FIS, Wright Patterson AFB, 1953, Askelson: Q O 71 6/4:11
QF-86H-10-NH: navy drone: RiS Sp 74 2/3-4:110
RF-86A: 15 TRS, Kempo, Williams: IM N 73 10/11-12:9
RF-86A: 15 TRS, 67 TRG, Kimpo, 1952, 2 var: Q Ap 73 8/2:85
RF-86A: 15 TRS, 67 TRG, Kimpo, late 1952: Q Ap 73 8/2:85
RF-86A: 15 TRS, 67 TRG, Kimpo, late 1952, Burkhart: Q Ap 73 8/2:85
RF-86A-5:   15 TRS, 67 TRG, Kimpo Afld, Korea, 1952: Q Ap 72 7/2:56
FJ-1 Fury (carrier version of Sabre): VF-51, NAS North Island: AN 14 N 75 4/12:7
FJ-2:   VMF-334, base unknown: AN 14 N 75 4/12:7
FJ-2:   VMF-235, MCAS Iwakuni, Japan: AN 14 N 75 4/12:7
FJ-3:   VC-3, base unknown: AN 14 N 75 4/12:7
FJ-3:   VF-33, base unknown: AN 14 N 75 4/12:7
FJ-3:   VF-143, USS Constellation: AN 14 N 75 4/12:7
FJ-3:   VF-173: IM Mr 74 10/(15):11
FJ-3:   VU-3: IM Mr 74 10/(15):11
FJ-3:   GMGRU-1, USS Shangri-la, 1958: Q Ap 72 7/2:62-63
FJ-4B: VA-126, NAS Miramar: AN 14 N 75 4/12:7
FJ-4B: VMA-223, MCAS El Toro: AN 14 N 75 4/12:7
F-100-85-NH Super Sabre: 21 TFS, 31 TFW or 413 TFW: RiS Jl 75 3/2:78
F-100-85-NH: 307 TFS, 31 TFW: RiS Jl 75 3/2:78
F-100-85-NH: 308 TFS, 31 TFW, George AFB, 1959: RiS Jl 75 3/2:78
F-100A-5-NA: 188 TFS, Missouri ANG: RiS Jl 75 3/2:88
F-100A-10-NA: 152 FIS, Arizona ANG: RiS Jl 75 3/2:87
F-100A-15-NA: 344 FBS, 479 FBW: RiS Jl 75 3/2:82
F-100A-15-NA: 435 FBS, 479 FBW: RiS Jl 75 3/2:82
F-100A-20-NA: Air Force Logistics Command: RiS Jl 75 3/2:84
F-100A-20-NA: 118 FIS, Connecticut ANG: RiS Jl 75 3/2:87
F-100A-20-NA: 436 FBS, 479 FBW, 1955: RiS Jl 75 3/2:82
F-100A-21-NA: 152 FIS, Arizona ANG, 1965: RiS Jl 75 3/2:87
F-100C-NA: 32 TFS, 36 TFW, 1958: RiS Jl 75 3/2:75
F-100C-1-NA: 120 TFS, Colorado ANG: Ris Jl 76 3/2:87; cor Ja 76 3/3:162
F-100C-1-NA: 120 TFS, Kansas ANG, 1967: Ri S Jl 75 3/2:87
F-100C-1-NA: 121 TFW, DC ANG, 1960: Ri S Jl 75 3/2:87
F-100C-1-NA: CO, 452 FBS, 322 FBW, Foster AFB, TX: RiS Jl 75 3/2:79
F-100C-2-NA: 119 TFS, New Jersey ANG, 1965: RiS Jl 75 3/2:87
F-100C-2-NA: 152 TFS, Arizona ANG, 1972: RiS Jl 75 3/2:89

III. Color Patterns 322

F-100C-2-NA: 188 TFS, 31 TFW, New Mexico ANG: RiS Jl 75 3/2:89
F-100C-5-NA: pos CO, 4 TFW: RiS Jl 75 3/2:73
F-100C-5-NA: 188 TFS, 31 TFW, New Mexico ANG: RiS Jl 75 3/2:86
F-100C-10-NH: 7272 ABW, Wheelus AB, Libya, 1959, target tug: RiS Jl 75 3/2:83; cor Ja 76 3/3:162
F-100C-10-NH: 7272 TFTW, 1965, target tug: RiS Jl 75 3/2:83
F-100C-15-NA: 451 FBS, 322 FBW, Foster AFB, TX: RiS Jl 75 3/2:79
F-100C-20-NA: 45 FDS, 316 ADW, North Africa, mid 1950: RiS Jl 75 3/2:75
F-100C-20-NA: 127 TFS, Kansas ANG, 1969: RiS Jl 75 3/2:89
F-100C-20-NA: 166 TFS, Ohio ANG, 1972: RiS Jl 75 3/2:89
F-100C-20-NA: 4758 DSES (ADC), Edwards: RiS Jl 75 3/2:83
F-100C-21-NA: 162 TFW, New York ANG, 1967: RiS Jl 75 3/2:87
F-100C-25-NA: "Skyblazers": RiS Jl 75 3/2:85
F-100C-25-NA: 21 FBS, 413 FBW, George AFB: RiS Jl 75 3/2:80
F-100C-25-NA: 23 TFS, 36 TFW, 1959: RiS Jl 75 3/2:75
F-100C-25-NA: 53 TFS, 36 TFW: RiS Jl 75 3/2:70
F-100C-25-NA: 121 TFS, DC ANG, 1971: RiS Jl 75 3/2:87
F-100C-25-NA: 124 TFS, Iowa ANG: RiS Jl 75 3/2:87
F-100C-25-NA: 127 TFS, Kansas ANG, 1962: RiS Jl 75 3/2:87
F-100C-25-NA: CO, 435 FBS, 479 FBW: Ri S Jl 75 3/2:82
F-100C-25-NA: CO, 413 FBW, George AFB, 1955: RiS Jl 75 3/2:80
F-100C-25-NA: 461 TFS, 36 TFW, 1959: RiS Jl 75 3/2:75
F-100D: Thunderbirds: RiS Jl 75 3/2:85
F-100D: 308 TFS, 31 TFW, Sept 1969: Q Ja 72 7/1:38
F-100D-5-NA: Missile Command: RiS Jl 75 3/2:84
F-100D-15-NA: CO, 48 TFS, 48 TFW: RiS Jl 75 3/2:77
F-100D-15-NA: 48 TFW, Chaumont AB, France, 1956, Smith: RiS N 72 1/2:67
F-100D-15-NA: 494 TFS, 48 TFW: RiS Jl 75 3/2:86
F-100D-20-NA: ARDC, Edwards Flight Test: RiS Jl 75 3/2:84
F-100D-20-NA: 35 TFS, 8 TFW: RiS Jl 75 3/2:74
F-100D-25-NA: CO, 20 TFW, RAF Wethersfield: RiS Jl 75 3/2:72
F-100D-25-NA: CO, 49 TFW: RiS Jl 75 3/2:76
F-100D-25-NA: 72 TFS, Clark Field, Philippines, 1958: RiS Jl 75 3/2:81
F-100D-25-NA: 110 TFS, Missouri ANG, McConnell AFB, 1973: RiS Jl 75 3/2:89
F-100D-25-NA: 416 TFS, 3 TFW, Bien Hoa, Vietnam, 1966: RiS Jl 75 3/2:73
F-100D-25-NA: 416 TFS, 21 TFW, 1962: Ri S Jl 75 3/2:74
F-100D-25-NA: 510 FBS, 405 FBW: RiS Jl 75 3/2:81
F-100D-30-NA: 8 TFS, 8 TFW: RiS Jl 75 3/2:73
F-100D-30-NA: 21 TFW: RiS Jl 75 3/2:74
F-100D-30-NA: 90 TFS, 3 TFW: RiS Jl 75 3/2:86
F-100D-30-NA: 164 TFS, Ohio ANG, 1972: RiS Jl 75 3/2:89
F-100D-30-NA: 416 TFS, 37 TFW: RiS Jl 75 3/2:86
F-100D-30-NA: 429 TFS, 474 TFW: RiS Jl 75 3/2:80

F-100D-30-NA: 615 TFS, 35 TFW: RiS Jl 75 3/2:86
F-100D-40-NA: 405 FBW, Oct 1956: RiS Jl 75 3/2:80
F-100D-45-NA: 10 TFS, 50 TFW, Hahn AB, Germany, 1960: RiS Jl 75 3/2:76
F-100D-45-NH: 48 TFW, RAF Lakenheath, UK, 1962: RiS Jl 75 3/2:77; cor Ja 76 3/3:162
F-100D-45-NH: 493 TFS, 48 TFW: RiS Jl 75 3/2:86
F-100D-45-NH: 509 FBS, 405 FBW, Langley AFB, VA: RiS Jl 75 3/2:81; cor Ja 3/3:162
F-100D-45-NH: 511 FBS, 405 FBW: RiS Jl 75 3/2:81
F-100D-45-NH: Iowa ANG, 1974: RiS Jl 75 3/2:89
F-100D-50-NA: 454 FBS, 323 FBW, Bunker Hill AFB, IN, 1957: RiS Jl 75 3/2:79
F-100D-50-NA: 531 TFS, 21 TFW, 1962: RiS Jl 75 3/2:74
F-100D-51-NA: 118 TFS, Connecticut ANG, 1975: RiS Jl 75 3 /2:89
F-100D-55-NH: 81 TFS, 50 TFW, Toul/Rosieres AB, France, 1959: RiS Jl 75 3/2:76
F-100D-55-NH: 308 TFS, 20 TFW: RiS Jl 75 3/2:72
F-100D-60-NA: 77 TFS, 20 TFW, 1958: RiS Jl 75 3/2:72
F-100D-60-NA: 79 TFS, 20 TFW: RiS Jl 75 3/2:72
F-100D-60-NA: 107 TFS, Michigan ANG: RiS Jl 75 3/2:89
F-100D-60-NA: 612 TFS, 401 TFW, Langley AFB, 1959: RiS Jl 75 3/2:81
F-100D-60-NA: Zero launch test aircraft, 1958: RiS Jl 75 3/2:85
F-100D-61-NA: 113 TFS, Indiana ANG, 1974: RiS Jl 75 3/2:89
F-100D-65-NA: 390 FBS, 366 FBW, England AFB: RiS Jl 75 3/2:78
F-100D-66-NA: Armament Development Test Center, Eglin AFB, 1971: RiS Jl 75 3/2:84
F-100D-66-NA: 162 TFS, Ohio ANG, 1973: RiS Jl 75 3/2:89
F-100D-70-NA: Nellis AFB: RiS Jl 75 3/2:84
F-100D-70-NA: 65 FWS, 35 FWW: RiS Jl 75 3/2:86
F-100D-70-NA: 381 TFS, 27 TFW, Tan Son Nhut, Vietnam, 1965: RiS Jl 75 3/2:75
F-100D-70-NA: 309 TFS, 31 TFW: RiS Jl 75 3/2:86
F-100D-70-NA: 355 TFS, 31 TFW: RiS Jl 75 3/2:86
F-100D-70-NA: 416 TFS, 31 TFW: RiS Jl 75 3/2:86
F-100D-70-NA: 417 TFS, 50 TFW: RiS Jl 75 3/2:76
F-100D-70-NA: 429 FBS, 474 FBW: RiS Jl 75 3/2:80
F-100D-70-NA: 430 FBS, 474 FBW: RiS Jl 75 3/2:80
F-100D-70-NA: 478 FBS, 474 FBW: RiS Jl 75 3/2:80
F-100D-70-NA: 612 TFS, 35 TFW: RiS Jl 75 3/2:86
F-100D-75-NA: CO, 474 FBW: RiS Jl 75 3/2:80
F-100D-75-NA: 481 FBS, 27 FBW: RiS Jl 75 3/2:74
F-100D-80-NH: 307 FBS, 31 FBW: RiS Jl 75 3/2:78
F-100D-80-NH: 308 FBS, 31 FBW: RiS Jl 75 3/2:78
F-100D-80-NH: 352 TFS, 354 TFW: RiS Jl 75 3/2:82
F-100D-85-NH: CO, 27 FBW: RiS Jl 75 3/2:74; cor Ja 76 3/3:162
F-100D-85-NH: 31 TFW, Aviano, 1960: RiS Jl 75 3/2:79
F-100D-85-NH: 309 FBS, 31 FBW: RiS Jl 75 3/2:78
F-100D-85-NH: 356 TFS, 354 TFW, Aviano, 1960: Ris Jl 75 3/2:82

III. Color Patterns

F-100D-85-NH: 531 TFS, 3 TFW: RiS Jl 75 3/2:86
F-100D-85-NH: 523 FBS, 27 FBW: RiS Jl 75 3/2:74
F-100D-86-NA: 352 TFS, 35 TFW: RiS Jl 75 3/2:86
F-100D-86-NA: 614 TFS, 35 TFW: RiS Jl 75 3/2:86
F-100D-90-NA: 7 TFS, 49 TFW: RiS Jl 75 3/2:76
F-100D-90-NA: 8 TFS, 49 TFW: RiS Jl 75 3/2:76
F-100D-90-NA: CO, 18 TFW: RiS Jl 75 3/2:71
F-100D-90-NA: 36 TFS, 8 TFW: RiS Jl 75 3/2:73
F-100D-90-NA: 44 TFS, 18 TFW: RiS Jl 75 3/2:72
F-100D-90-NA: CO, 48 TFW, Smith: RiS Jl 75 3/2:77
F-100D-90-NA: 48 TFS, Texas ANG, 1975: RiS Jl 75 3/2:71
F-100D-90-NA: 48 TFW, Lakenheath UK, 1962: RiS Jl 75 3/2:77
F-100D-90-NA: 48 TFW, William Tell Scheme, 1958, Smith: RiS N 72 1/2:67
F-100D-90-NA: 67 TFS, 18 TFW, 1963: RiS Jl 75 3/2:72
F-100D-90-NA: 128 TFS, Georgia ANG: RiS Jl 75 3/2:89
F-100D-90-NA: 182 TFS, Texas ANG, 1975: RiS Jl 75 3/2:71
F-100D-90-NA: 493 TFS, 48 TFW: RiS Jl 75 3/2:77
F-100D-90-NA: 492 TFS, 48 TFW, 1959: RiS Jl 75 3/2:77
F-100D-90-NA: 494 TFS, 48 TFW: RiS Jl 76 3/2:77
F-100D-90-NA: 494 TFS, 48 TFW, Chaumont, France, 1956: RiS Jl 75 3/2:77
F-100D-91-NA: 510 TFS, 3 TFW: RiS Jl 75 3/2:86
F-100F-1-NA: 524 TFS, 27 TFW: RiS Jl 75 3/2:86; cor Ja 76 3/3:162
F-100F-2-NA: 120 TFS, Colorado ANG: RiS Jl 75 3/2:88
F-100F-10-NA: CO, Nellis AFB: RiS Jl 75 3/2:84
F-100F-10-NA: CO, 8 TFW: RiS Jl 75 3/2:73
F-100F-10-NA: 31 TFW: RiS Jl 75 3/2:78
F-100F-10-NA: 50 TFW, 1960: RiS Jl 75 3/2:76
F-100F-10-NA: 119 TFS, 113 TFW: RiS Jl 75 3/2:86
F-100F-10-NA: 306 TFS, 31 TFW: RiS Jl 75 3/2:86
F-100F-10-NA: 310 TFS, 354 TFW: RiS Jl 75 3/2:86
F-100F-10-NA: 524 FBS, 27 FBW: RiS Jl 75 3/2:74
F-100F-10-NA: 532 TFS, 27 TFW, 1965: RiS Jl 75 3/2:75
F-100F-10-NA: 353 TFS, 354 TFW, 1959: RiS Jl 75 3/2:82
F-100F-10-NA: 356 TFS, 354 TFW: RiS Jl 75 3/2:86
F-100F-10-NA: 356 TFS, 475 TFW: RiS Jl 75 3/2:83
F-100F-10-NA: 614 TFS, 401 TFW: RiS Jl 75 3/2:81
F-100F-10-NA: 615 TFS, 401 TFW: RiS Jl 75 3/2:81
F-100F-10-NA: 492 TFS, 48 TFW: RiS Jl 75 3/2:86
F-100F-11-NA: 166 TFS, Ohio ANG, 1966: RiS Jl 75 3/2:87
F-100F-15-NA: Aerospace Medicine Div, Brooks AFB, TX, Det. 1, 6570 ABG, 2 var: RiS Jl 75 3/2:85
F-100F-15-NA: Kirkland AFB, 1972: RiS Jl 75 3/2:84
F-100F-16-NA: 110 TFS, Missouri ANG: RiS Jl 75 3/2:88
F-100F-16-NA: 112 TFW, Ohio ANG: RiS Jl 75 3/2:89
F-100F-20-NA: 617 TFS, 37 TFW: RiS Jl 75 3/2:86
F-100F-65-NA: 522 TFS, 27 TFW: RiS Jl 75 3/2:86
F-107A: prototype, Edwards AFB & Air Force Museum: Q Ja 73 8/1:43
RA-5C Vigilante: RVAH-3, NAS Albany, GA: Q Ap 72 7/2:45
RA-5C: RVAH-6, USS America, Thompson: Q Ap 72 7/2:46

RA-5C: RVAH-9:   NS Rota, Spain, July 1971:   Q Ap 72 7/2:47
RA-5C: RVAH-12, USS America, Dec 1970:   Q Ap 72 7/2:45
RA-5C: RVAH-12: USS Independence, July 1971:   Q Ap 72 7/2:45
RA-5C: RVAH-13, USS America, Mediterranean, 1971:   Q Ap 72 7/2:46
RA-5C: RVAH-14, USS Kennedy, Mediterranean, 1971:   Q Ap 72 7/2:47
T-39A Sabreliner: AF Communications Service, Europe: AN 7 D 73 2/15:8
T-39A SAC VIP & Communications: AN 7 D 73 2/15:8
T-39A: 3 AF, Europe, 1961:   AN 7 D 73 2/15:8-9
T-39D: NAS Glynco IL: AN 7 D 73 2/15:8-9
T-39D: 2 Marine Air Wing, Cherry Point: AN 7 D 73 2/15:8

(Northrop)
F-89D Scorpion: South Dakota ANG, Sioux Falls, SD: RT S 73 6/9:95
N156F Freedom Fighter: prototype: Q Jl 74 10/1:11
T-38 Talon: Thunderbirds: IM Mr 75 11/2:21
T-38A: Thunderbirds, 1974:   RT O 74 7/10:112; cor Ja 75 8/1:2; reply My 75 8/5:50
T-38A: Thunderbirds, 1974:   RiS Sp 74 2/3-4:157; cor Jl 75 3/2:94
T-38A: US Navy Fighter Weapons School, NAS Miramar, 1974-75:   RT S 75 8/9:106

(Republic)
F-84:   Illinois ANG, 1958:   Q Au 75 11/1:43
F-84F: Illinois ANG, 1958, Norman: Q Au 75 11/1:43

(Foreign Manufacturers)
Canadair CF-86 Sabre: US markings while transfering from RAF to Italian AF: RT N 71 4/11:126
F-86E-6 (CL-13 Mk2):   104 FBS, Maryland ANG: RiS Sp 74 2/3-4:108
Hawker Siddeley AV-8A (Harrier GR Mk 50):   USMC,   AE Ag 71 1/3:145

(U.S. Military--Prop)

(Bombers)
Boeing B-29:   19 BG, Kimpo, Japan, June 1952, Perry: Q Ap 73 8/2:90-91
Douglas A-1E Skyraider: Vietnam, 1967:   Q O 71 6/4:16
A-1H: Thailand, 1969:   Q O 71 6/4:16
A-1H: VA-25, USS Coral Sea, autumn 1966:   Q O 72 7/4:149
A-1H: 518 FBS, Tan Son Nhut, 1965, Keeler: RiS Ag 72 1/1:25
A-1H-5:   VA 52, USS Ticonderoga, spring 1967:   Q O 72 7/4:149
A-1H-5:   CO, VA 52, USS Ticonderoga, ACAW 19:   Q O 72 7/4:149
AD-5N Skyraider: VAAW-35, USS Shangri-la, 1958:   Q Ap 72 7/2:63

III. Color Patterns 326

AD-5W: VAW-11, USS Shangri-la, 1958: Q Ap 72 7/2:63
AD-6: VA-115, USS Shangri-la, 1958: Q Ap 72 7/2:63
Douglas A-26 Invader: Miho Base, early 1950s: RT S 74 7/9:107
A-26: Miho Base, early 1950s, Howe: RT S 74 7/9:107
A-26: 12 TRS, Kimpo, early 1950s: Q Ap 73 8/2:90
A-26: 34 BS, Korea, 8 var: Q Ap 73 8/2:90-91
A-26A: 609 Special Operations Sqn, 46 SOW, Nakhon Phanom, Thailand: Afx Mr 72 13/7:379
Douglas B-26B Invader: Iwakuni, Jan 1953: Afx Mr 72 13/7:378
B-26B: 13 BS, 3 BW, Korea: Afx Mr 72 13/7:378
B-26B: 17 BW, Korea, 1951-52: IM D 71 8/10:8
B-26B-45-DL: 4 ATAF, Germany, 1954: Afx Mr 72 13/7:378
B-26B-55/56 DL: 47 BW, Sculthorpe, Norfolk, 1955: Afx Mr 72 13/7:379
B-26C: Langley AFB, May 1965: IM D 71 8/12:9
B-26C: prob 425 BG: IM O 71 8/10:9
B-26C: 729 BS, 452 BG, Pussan, Korea, May 1951-May 1952: IM O 71 8/10:8
Grumman AD-4W Avenger: VMC-3: Afx N 75 17/3:160
North American AJ-1 Savage: VC-6, USS Yorktown: AN 25 Jl 75 4/4:9
AJ-1P: VCP-61 or VAP-62: AN 25 Jl 75 4/4:9
AJ-2: VAH-11: AN 25 Jl 75 4/4:9

(Electronic Warfare)
Grumman E-1B (WF-2) Tracer: CVSG-53 with VAW-11, USS Ticonderoga: AN 22 D 72 1/16:10
Grumman E-2 Hawkeye: RVAW-110, NAS North Island: Q Ja 73 8/1:34
E-2: VAW-113, USS Constellation: Q Ja 73 8/1:33
E-2: VAW-115, USS Midway: Q Ja 73 8/1:34
E-2: VAW-122, USS America: Q Ja 73 8/1:35
E-2A: prototype, NATC: Q Ja 73 8/1:32
E-2A: RVAW-120: Hampton Beach VA, Dec 1968: Q Ja 73 8/1:35
E-2A: CAW-126, USS Forrestal: Q Ja 73 8/1:32
E-2A: VAW-112, CAW 9, USS Enterprise, off Oahu, Feb 1969: Q Ja 73 8/1:32
E-2A: VAW-113, NAS North Island, March 1971: Q Ja 73 8/1:35
E-2A: VAW-114, USS Kittyhawk: Q Ja 73 8/1:34
E-2A: VAW-116, USS Coral Sea: Q Ja 73 8/1:35
E-2A: VAW-124, USS America, Sept 1970: Q Ja 73 9/1:34
E-2B: VAW-114, USS Kitty Hawk: Q Ja 73 8/1:34
E-2B: VAW-123, USS Saratoga, NAS North Island, March 1971: Q Ja 73 8/1:32
E-2B: VAW-125, USS John F Kennedy, Mediterranean, 1970-71: Q Mr 73 8/2:74
Lockheed AP-2E Neptune: Army 1 Radio Research Coy, Cam Ranh Bay, Vietnam: Q Jl 74 10/1:31
AP-2H: Davis-Monthan AFB, Sept 1971: Q Jl 74 10/1:35
AP-2H: NAS Patuxent River, July 1969: Q Jl 74 10/1:34
OP-2E: Obsron 67, Nakkon Phanom, Thailand: Q Jl 74 10/1:33
RP-2E: Army 1 Radio Research Coy: Q Jl 74 10/1:31

Aircraft

(Fighters)
Chance Vought AU-1 Corsair: Naval Air Reserve Sqn, Akron: Afx N 71 13/3:134
F4U-4: VMA-332, Korea, 1951: Afx N 71 13/3:134
F4U-4B: VMF 214, USS Sicily, Aug 1950: Afx N 71 13/3:134
F4U-5N: VC-3, USS Princeton, Korea, 1953, Bordelou: Afx N 71 13/3:134
Douglas AC-47 mini-gun ship: 4 SOS, 14 SOW, Bien Hoa: Q O 72 7/4:135
Fairchild AC-119G mini-gun ship: 440 TAW, Milwaukee Armed Forces Day, May 1969: Q Jl 71 6/3:17
Grumman F6F Hellcat: std camouflage for NAS aircraft, June 1952: Q Jl 73 8/3:161
F6F-5: std for aircraft attached to utility sqns, May 1950: Q Jl 73 8/3:159
F6F-5: NRS, Dallas: Q Jl 73 8/3:165
F6F-5: Oakland NAS, Feb 1949: Q Jl 73 8/3:160
F6F-5: USNR, Dallas NAS: Q Jl 73 8/3:163
Grumman F7F-3N Tigercat: VMF(N)-533: Q Ap 72 7/2:68
F7F-3N: VMF(N)-542, 2 var: Q Ap 72 7/2:68-69
F7F-4N: 33 HQ Sqn, Kimpo: Q Ap 73 8/2:88
Grumman F8F-1: CO, AG 19, USS Boxer, Cook: Q Ja 73 8/1:30
F8F-1: Glenview NAS, IL: Q Ja 73 8/1:30
F8F-1: VF-72, USS Leyte, 1949-50, Clarke: AE F 73 4/2:96
F8F-2: Air Group 19 Cook: AN 10 N 72 1/13:10
F8F-2: USN Reserve, Denver CO: AE F 73 4/2:96
F8F-2: USS Midway, Richardson: Q Ja 73 8/1:30
F8F-2: VU-7 Miramar NAS, early 1950s: AN 10 N 72 1/13:10
North American F-82 Twin Mustang: 68 FS, 2 var, Korea, 1950: Q Ja 71 6/1:30-31
North American P-51D Mustang: Illinois ANG, 1947: Q Au 75 11/1:42
North American P-51D-NA-30-Q Mustang: 27 Ftr Esc Wing (SAC), 5 AF, Feb 1953, Donovan: RT F 75 8/2:14
Northrop P-61B-20 Black Widow: 68 FS, 314 Air Div: Q O 72 7/4:143
Republic P-47D Thunderbolt: Puerto Rico ANG: RT Je 71 4/6:65
F-47D-30-RA: 527 FS, 86 FG, Neubiberg, Germany, 1948-49: Q Ja 72 7/1:27

(Reconnaissance, Observation & Light Strike)
Cessna O-1E Bird Dog: 19 TASS, Bien Hoa, c.1964: Q Ap 74 9/2:57
O-1E: 21 TASS, Feb 1967, Wilbanks: Q Ap 74 9/2:58
O-1G: 19 TASS, Bien Hoa, late 1965: Q Ap 74 9/2:56
O-1G: 21 TASS, Qui Nhon Province, June 1969, Byers: Q Ap 74 9/2:56
Consolidated RB-36H: 28 SRW, Ellsworth AFB, SD, 1952: Q Ja 74 9/1:24-25
Curtiss SC-1 Seahawk: USS Providence (CL 82), 1947, Roth: AM N 74 74/11:84
De Havilland Canada U-1B Otter: NARF: Q Ja 71 6/1:18
Douglas AC-47 speaker bird: 9 SOS, 14 SOW, Bien Hoa: Q O 72

III. Color Patterns

7/4:135
Douglas EA-1E: Da Nang, 1967: Q O 71 6/4:16
Grumman US-2B: NAF Washington, DC, 1975, bicentennial pattern: Q Au 75 11/1:51
US-2B: VC-10, bicentennial pattern: Q Au 75 11/1:51
Grumman OV-1 Mohawk: Barksdale AFB, LA: Q O 73 8/4:208
OV-1: McChord AFB, Tacoma WA, July 1970, 2 var: Q O 73 8/4:210
OV-1: McChord AFB, Tacoma WA, Sept 1971: Q O 73 8/4:210
OV-1: 131 Avn Coy, Phu Bai, Vietnam, Wilkins: Q O 73 8/4:210
OV-1: 226 Avn Coy, 11 Air Assault Sqn, Little: Q O 73 8/4:209
OV-1A: MASDC, David-Monthan AFB, AZ, Sept 1971: Q O 73 8/4:209
OV-1A: 74 Avn Coy, Tan Son Nuut, 1968: Q O 73 8/4:208
OV-1B: U.S. Army, German: AN 15 F 74 2/19:8-9
OV-1B: 23 Special Warfare Aviation Detachment, Vietnam: AN 15 F 74 2/19:9
OV-1B: 131 Avn Coy, Phu Bai, Vietnam, March 1970: Q O 73 8/4:209
OV-1C: Ft. Lewis, WA, May 1971: Q O 73 8/4:208
OV-1C: USN Test Pilot School, Ft. Eustis, VA, April 1972: Q O 73 8/4:208
OV-1D: 7 Army: AN 15 F 74 2/19:9
YOV-1: Pax River, July 1966: Q O 73 8/4:209
ROV-1-GR: NATC, Pax River, Aug 1964: Q O 73 8/4:209
Grumman S-2E Tracker: CVSG-59 with VS-38, USS Hornet: AN 22 D 72 1/16:10
North American F-6D (P-51D photo recon): 155 TRS, 67 TFG, Kimpo, 1952: Q Ap 72 7/2:57
North American OV-10 Bronco: std: RiS Ag 72 1/1:7
OV-10: std camouflage: RiS Ag 72 1/1:11
OV-10A: 19 TASS, Tan Son Nhut, Sept 1970: RiS Ag 72 1/1:12
OV-10A: 20 TASS, Da Nang, Dec 1970, Crawford: RiS Ag 72 1/1:13
OV-10A: 549 TASS, Hurlburt Field, Sheppart AFB, TX, Oct 1971: RiS Ag 72 1/1:12
OV-10A: VAL-4 (UM-15): RiS Ag 72 1/1:13
OV-10A/1: VAL-4, USN, Vieng Tau, Vietnam, 1968: Q Ja 75 10/3:114
OV-10A/1: VAL-4, Vung Tau, Vietnam, 1970: Q Ja 75 10/3:114
OV-10A/1: VMO-2, Columbus OH, Aug 1971: Q Ja 75 10/3:114
OV-10A/1: VS-41, North Island CA, 1968: Q Ja 75 10/3:114
OV-10A/2: 4410 CCTW, Elgin AFB, FL, 1968: Q Ja 75 10/3:114
OV-10A-20-NH: 19 RASS, Tan Son Nhut, Nov 1970, Rivers: RiS Ag 72 1/1:12
OV-10A-35-NH: prob 19 TASS: RiS Ag 72 1/1:11
OV-10A-35-NH: 19 TASS with 1 Cav Div, Tan Son Nhut, May 1970, Schwalm: RiS Ag 72 1/1:13
OV-10A-40-NH: 20 TASS, Tan Son Nhut, May 1970: RiS Ag 72 1/1:11
OV-10A-40-NH: 23 TASS, Tan Son Nhut: RiS Ag 72 1/1:13
OV-10A-40-NH: 23 TASS, Tan Son Nhut, May 1970: RiS Ag 72 1/1:12

OV-10A-40-NH: CO, 504 TASG, Tan Son Nuut, May 1970: RiS Ag 72 1/1:12
North American LT-6G: 6147 Tactical Control Group, Korea 1952: Afx Je 71 12/10:531
North American SNJ-3: NAS Corry, 1952: Afx Je 71 12/10:526
North American T-6 Texan: RAC, Kimpo, early 1950s: Q Ap 73 8/2:91
North American YAT-28E: turboprop prototype: Q Ja 73 8/1:11
YAT-38E: 2nd prototype, Elgin AFB, 1964: MAN Ja 75 90/1:58
YAT-28E: production model, unit unstated: Q Ja 73 8/1:11
North American YOV-10D: gunship mockup mod of Bronco: Q Ja 75 10/3:114
YOV-10D: USMC, Vietnam, 1970: Q Ja 75 10/3:111

(Search & Rescue)
Consolidated PBY-5A: no national markings, San Francisco CA, 1948: RT D 72 5/12:142
Grumman HU-16B Albatross: MATS: RT Ap 72 5/4:40
HU-16B: MATS: RiS Mr 73 3/1:79
HU-16B: SAC: RT Ap 72 5/4:40
HU-16B: SEA, 2 var: RiS Mr 73 3/1:79
HU-16B: USAF: RT Ap 72 5/4:40
HU-16B: USAF: RiS Mr 73 3/1:82
HU-16B: USAF serial but no lettering: RT Ap 72 5/4:41
HU-16B: USAF with Pan-Am emblem: RT Ap 72 5/4:40
HU-16B: USAF, 1971: RiS Mr 73 3/1:82
HU-16B: USAF, SAC: RiS Mr 73 3/1:79
HU-16B: USN, Kodiak: RT Ap 72 5/4:41
HU-16B: 304 Air Rescue Sqn, Alaska, May 1964: RiS Mr 73 3/1:82
HU-16B: 354 TFW: RiS Mr 73 3/1:82
HU-16D: USN, Agana, 1972: RiS Mr 73 3/1:79
HU-16C: Brunswick NAS: RT Ag 73 6/8:88
HU-16C: US Naval Mission to Peru: RT Ag 73 6/8:88
Lockheed DP-2E Neptune: NAF China Lake: Q Jl 74 10/1:28
DP-2E: VC-5, Naha AFB, Okinawa, March 1971: Q Jl 74 10/1:29
DP-2E: VC-8, Scott AFB, Aug 1966: Q Jl 74 10/1:28
NP-2H: Naval Air Test Center, Pax River, March 1973: Q Jl 74 10/1:31
P1V-7 Neptune: VP-18, Dow AFB, Nov 1960: Q Jl 74 10/1:7
P-2E: VP-772, NAS Los Alamitos: Q Jl 74 10/1:26
SP-2H: std USN: Q Jl 74 10/1:22-24

(Trainers, Utility, & Drones)
Cessna O-1E Bird Dog: 4408 Combat Crew Training Sqn, Hooley Field FL, Dec 1968: Q Ap 74 9/2:57
TL-19D Bird Dog: California NG, Van Nyys, 1959: Q Ap 74 9/2:58
TL-19D: Ft. Rucker AL, 1968: Q Ap 74 9/2:58
Cessna O2A: Illinois ANG, 1970: Q Au 75 11/1:44
Cessna U-3B (Cessna 310): Illinois ANG, 1969: Q Au 75 11/1:44
Chance Vought F4U-4 Corsair: VMJ-1 hack, Kimpo, 1952: Q Jl 73 8/3:175

III. Color Patterns 330

De Havilland Canada L-20A Beaver: US Army red & white, pre-1962 std: IM O 72 9/10:4
L-20A-DH: arctic std, 51 serial: IM O 72 9/10:6
L-20A-DH: SAC, 1952 serial: IM O 72 9/10:6
U-6 Beaver: USAF std: RiS W 74 2/2:46
U-6: Minnesota NG, Wold Chamberlain Field, Minneapolis-St. Paul, Aug 1970: Q O 73 8/4:220
U-6: 20 TFW, Bentwaters, England, 1969: RiS W 74 2/2:46
U-6A: US Army std, 1971: RiS W 74 2/2:54
U-6A: US Army National Guard std, 1972: RiS W 74 2/2:54
U-6A: 3 var: RiS W 74 2/2:50-51, 55
U-6A: Army, c.1970: RiS W 74 2/2:54
U-6A: c.1957: RiS W 74 2/2:50
U-6A: c.1972, 3 var: RiS W 74 2/2:51-55
U-6A: Airfield A-10, Korea, 1964: RiS W 74 2/2:49
U-6A: Alabama NG, 1972: RiS W 74 2/2:55
U-6A: Arizona NG, 1972: RiS W 74 2/2:55
U-6A: Army Flight Training School, Ft. Rucker AL, May 1969: RiS W 74 2/2:51
U-6A: 18 Div (Airborne): RiS W 74 2/2:55
U-6A: Electronics Command, 1970: RiS W 74 2/2:57
U-6A: Ft. Hood TX, March 1965: RiS W 74 2/2:54
U-6A: 40 Armored Div, California NG, 1959: RiS W 74 2/2:56
U-6A: 45 Div, Oklahoma NG, 1972: RiS W 74 2/2:55
U-6A: Idaho NG, Boise, May 1971: Q O 73 8/4:221
U-6A: Iowa NG, 1961: RiS W 74 2/2:56
U-6A: MASDC, Davis-Monthan AFB, AZ, Sept 1971, 2 var: Q O 73 8/4:221
U-6A: Minnesota NG, 1969: RiS W 74 2/2:57
U-6A: Missouri NG, 1961: RiS W 74 2/2:56
U-6A: Montana NG, 1972: RiS W 74 2/2:55
U-6A: NAS El Centro, CA, 1972: RiS W 74 2/2:55
U-6A: Nebraska NG, 1960: RiS W 74 2/2:56
U-6A: 90 Div, 1972: RiS W 74 2/2:55
U-6A: 92 SBW, Fairchild AFB, May 1970: RiS W 74 2/2:51
U-6A: North Carolina NG, 1960: RiS W 74 2/2:56
U-6A: North Dakota NG, 1960: RiS W 74 2/2:56
U-6A: Ohio NG, 1960: RiS W 74 2/2:56
U-6A: Oklahoma NG, 1960: RiS W 74 2/2:56
U-6A: San Jose, CA, Dec 1967: RiS W 74 2/2:50
U-6A: 76 Aviation Gp, California NG, 1971: RiS W 74 2/2:57
U-6A: South Dakota NG, 1972: RiS W 74 2/2:50
U-6A: USN Test Pilot School, March 1973: Q O 73 8/4:220
U-6A: US Naval Test Pilot School, NAS Patuxent River MD, 1966: RiS W 74 2/2:55
U-6A: Washington NG, Grey Field, 1970: RiS W 74 2/2:55
U-6A: Wisconsin NG, 1969: RiS W 74 2/2:57
YL-20 Beaver: pos Korea, early 1950s: RiS W 74 2/2:54
Douglas TB-26B-45-DL: 4 Tow Target Sqn, George AFB, CA, June 1957: IM O 71 8/10:3
Grumman F6F: VU-1 (drone operation) UTRON-1, Bonham AFB, Kauai, Hawaii, May 1950: Q Jl 73 8/3:162
F6F-3 Drone: Bikini A-Bomb tests: PAM O 75 11:183

Aircraft

F6F-3 Queen: Bikini A-Bomb tests: PAM O 75 11:183
Grumman HU-1T Albatross: USS Naval Academy navigation & electronics trainer: RT Ag 73 6/8:88
Grumman OV-1A Mohawk: Army trainer: AN 15 F 74 2/19:8-9
Lockheed RB-69 Neptune: USAF navigation & ECM trainer: Q Jl 74 10/1:30
North American T-6: Illinois ANG, 1947: Q Au 75 11/1:44
North American AT-28D Trojan: 4407 CCTS: Q Ja 73 8/1:11
North American T-28: Illinois ANG, 1956: Q Au 75 11/1:44
T-28A: Q Ja 73 8/1:10
T-28A: USAF, Andrews AFB, Washington, DC: AN 19 S 75 4/8: 8-9
T-28B: NAF Washington DC, 1975: Q Au 75 11/1:44
T-28B: NARF: Q Ja 71 6/1:18
T-28B; station hack, Naval Air Facility, Andrews AFB, Washington DC, Marines: AN 19 S 75 4/8-9
T-28B: training sqn 3, NAAS Whitting Field FL, April 1962, Beatty: Q Ja 73 8/1:10
T-28B: VA-45 "Blackbirds," instrument training: AN 19 S 75 4/8: 8-9
T-28C: training sqn 5, NABasic Training Command Carrier Qualification Sqn, USS Lexington: Q Ja 73 8/1:10
T-28C: VT-5, NAS Pensacola, deck landing training, USS Lexington: AN 19 S 75 4/8:9
North American TB-25B Mitchell: Instrument School, Moodey AFB, GA, 1954: IM S 71 8/9:14

(Transports & Tankers)
Boeing C-97 Stratofreighter: MATS, 1948: AN 20 Jl 73 2/5:14
KC-97G: 9 ARS, 9 BW, Mt. Home AFB, 1962: AN 20 Jl 73 2/5: 14
De Havilland Canada C-7A Caribou: 451 TAS, 483 TAW, Bien Hoa, 1971: Q Jl 73 8/3:155
C-7A: 458 TAS, 483 TAW, Cam Ranh Bay, Dec 1971, Bob Hope Christmas Tour: Q Jl 73 8/3:154
C-7A: 536 TAS, 483 TAW, Cam Ranh Bay, Sept 1971: Q Jl 73 8/3:155
C-7A: 908 TAG, AF Reserve, Maxwell AFB, AL, May 1973: Q Jl 73 8/3:154
Douglas C-47 Dakota: Illinois ANG, 1951: Q Au 75 11/1:44
Douglas C-47J: NARF: Q Ja 71 6/1:16-17
Douglas R4D-3 Skymaster: USN Oceanographic Survey Unit, Project Magnet: AN 18 Ap 75 3/23:7
Douglas SC-54 Skymaster: USAF, Prestwick, 1965: AN 18 Ap 75 3/23:7
VC-54: Washington ANG: AN 18 Ap 75 3/23:7
Fairchild C-119G: Cold Lake, Alta: RT Mr 72 5/3:32
Grumman C-1A (TF-1) Trader: VR-24, Naples to USS John F. Kennedy, 6 Fleet, Mediterranean: AN 22 D 72 1/16:10
Grumman C-2A Greyhound: VRC-50: Q Ja 73 8/1:38
Lockheed Constellation: MATS, Pusan, Korea, 1951: RT My 75 8/5:59
Noorduyn Norseman JA-1: USN 1946: RT D 72 5/12:140

III. Color Patterns

Norseman UC-64: late 1940s or early 1950s: RT D 72 5/12:140

(U. S. Military--Helmets)

(LTV A-7 Corsair II pilots)
333 TFTr Sqn, 355 TFW, 1972-73: RiS Sp 73 2/3-4:98
354 TFS, 355 TFW, 1972-73: RiS Sp 73 2/3-4:98
357 TFS, 355 TFW, 1972-73: RiS Sp 73 2/3-4:99
358 TFS, 355 TFW, 1972-73: TiS Sp 73 2/3-4:99

(Uruguay Military)

Grumman F6F-3: navy, Isla Libertad, late 1950s: AI S 75 9/3: 148
Martin PBM-5: AN 17 Ag 73 2/7:7

(Venezuela Military)

Northrop CF-5A: RT Mr 74 7/3:32

(Vietnam, North, Military)

MiG-17: 4 var: RT Je 71 4/6:64; cor N 71 4/11:122
MiG-17F: 2 var: IM Jl 74 10/(17):13
MiG-17F: 1971: AE D 72 3/6:312
MiG-21FP: RT Je 71 4/6:64; cor N 71 4/11:122
MiG-21PFM (Fishbed F): RT N 72 5/11:122

(Vietnam, South, Military)

Cessna A-37B Dragonfly: 516 FS: RiS Mr 75 3/1:46
A-37A: 524 FS: RiS Mr 75 3/1:46
Cessna O-1 Bird Dog: unit unknown: Q Ap 74 9/2:58
Douglas A-1E Skyraider: KD 23, Bien Hoa, 1967: Q Jl 71 6/3:16
A-1H: 23 Sqn, Bien Hoa, 1967, 2 var: Q Jl 71 6/3:17
A-1H: 518 FBS, Tan Son Nhut AB, 1965, Keeler: RiS Ag 72 1/1:25
Grumman F8F-1B Bearcat: Bien Hoa: AN 10 N 72 1/13:10
F8F-1B: 514 FS, 1956: AE F 73 4/2:96
North American F-100D-70-NA Super Sabre: 3 FG, Bien Hoa, 1965, Keeler: RiS Ag 72 1/1:25
North American T-28: Q Au 75 11/1:5
T-28C: 1st Air Commando (U. S.), Bien Hoa, 1963, Shank: Q Au 75 11/1:5
T-28C: 1st Air Commando, Bien Hoa, 1963-64, Gorski: Q Au 75 11/1:4
T-28C: 1st Air Commando, Bien Hoa, 1963-64, 5 var: Q Au 75 11/1:5

Northrop F-5A: 522 Sqn, 23 Wing, Bien Hoa: AE Je 72 2/6:324

(Vietnam, United, Military)

Morane Saulnier MS 500 Criquet (Fi 156C): 1 Air Observation Sqn, Nhatrang, late 1951: AI Ap 75 8/4:200

(Yugoslavia Civil)

McDonnell-Douglas DC-9-30: Pan Adria: AN 12 Jl 74 3/3:9

(Yugoslavia Military)

Messerschmitt BF 109G-6: AE S 71 1/4:211
MiG 21 MF: AI N 75 9/5:248

(Zaïre Military)

Aermacchi MB. 326B: AN 16 F 73 1/20:10

(Zambia Military)

Aermacchi MB. 326B: AN 16 F 73 1/20:10
De Havilland Canada DHC-2 Beaver: IM O 72 7/10:6

ARMOR

GENERAL

Color

Armor Markings on American Tanks in Korea: AFV Jl 74 4/11: 4-9+
Black Star: Contemporary U.S. Armor Camouflage: Q W 75 11/2:91-(100)
British Army Vehicle Colour Schemes & Markings of WW-II: see separate listing, following
Classification of Bridges: bridge rating plates, WW-II: MW F 73 1/6:303
Command Flags & Pennants of the SS: all units: MW Je 73 1/10: 522-523+

III. Color Patterns   334

Current Colours: British: MM D 74 4/12:746-748
Dodge WC series Military Truck Registration Numbers: AFV Mr 74 4/10:13
German Panzer Insignia & Markings: Polish campaign: AFV Mr 72 3/7:20-21
Modern U.S. Army 4-Color Camouflage: AFV S 75 5/6:32-35+
Numbering U.S. Army Vehicles: 1930-1950: registration code: AFV D 72 3/12:22-23
Pennents & Guidons of the German Army: WW-II code: IM O 71 8/10:10-11
RAF Armoured Car Insignia: roundels & pennants: MM Ap 72 2/4:202
What Color?: German WW-II armor: Q O 73 8/4:242

(British Army Vehicle
Color Schemes & Markings of WW-II) [all MM]

1939: Ja 74 4/1:33-35
European Area, 1939-42: Mr 74 4/3:148-151
Desert War 1940-43: Ap 74 4/4:192-195
Vehicle Disguises of the Desert War: My 74 4/5:272-273
India, Burma, & Far East, 1941-45: Je 74 4/6:320-321+
D-Day & NW European Campaigns: Jl 74 4/7:404-406+
Miscellaneous Colour Schemes: Ag 74 4/8:460-462
Miscellaneous Markings: S 74 4/9:543-545+
Nationality, Air Recognition Signs, Special Use Signs, Names, Instructions, Etc.: O 74 4/10:591-593
Arm of Service & Tactical Signs: N 74 4/11:697-700
Formation Badges: D 74 4/12:768-770+

Heraldry

Canadian Armored Corps: all 29 units, unit signs (2 to 4 each): RT D 75 8/12:135; cor Mr 76 9/3:30
DAK Stencil: full size vehicle stencil: WW2J S 75 2/5-6:52
German Organization Chart Symbols: AFV Ja 75 5/2:34-35+
German Panzer Badges: unit badges: AFV Ja 72 3/5:21
Military Insignia (part of series started Sc O 69 1/1): U.S. & German WW-I markings: Sc Ja 71 2/1:54-56
Tactical Markings of the Waffen SS: divisional badges: AFV Mr 73 4/3:14-16; My 73 4/4:10-11; Je 73 4/5:10-11+; Ag 73 4/6:14-15; S 73 4/7:20-21+; N 73 4/8:10-11

APCs & ICVs

M106: VII Corps: Q W 75 11/2:(100)

M-113: U.S. std: MM Mr 75 5/3:155
M-113: U.S. std 4-color camouflage: AFV S 75 5/6:35
M113: standard U.S. camouflage: Q W 75 11/2:95
M113: Ft. Hood: Q W 75 11/2:(99)
M113: VII Corps, 4/73 Armor: Q W 75 11/2:(100)
M577 armored command post: standard U.S. camouflage: Q W 75 11/2:94
M-113: U.S. std 4-color camouflage with table of colors for all areas: RiS Jl 75 3/2:98-99
M-113 A1: U.S. 7 Army, Germany: AFV Mr 74 4/10:20-22
M-113 ACAV with supplemental armor & armament: RiS Jl 75 3/2:98
Saracen: Ulster, 9 var: RT Ag 74 7/8:91-92; S 74 7/9:98-99
Universal Carrier: U.K., 56 Recon Btn, Recon Corps, 78 Infantry Div, Tunisia, Sept 1942: AFV Je 75 5/5:28-29
Universal Carrier: Le Regiment de Maisonneuve, 5 Bgd, 2 Canadian Infantry Div, England, March 1943: AFV Je 75 5/5:28-29+

ARMORED CARS

BA-32: Finnish: Q Ja 75 10/3:105
BA-32: Finland 7 Independent Armored Car Coy, 1941: Q Ja 75 10/3:105
M-8: U.S. 48 Const Sqn, 2 Const Rgt, Occupied Germany, 1948: AFV F 75 5/3:28-29+
M-8: U.S. C Troop, 82 Cav Recon Sqn, 2 Armd Div, "Operation Cobra," July 1944: AFV F 75 5/3:28-29+
Marmon Herrington "Breda Car" Mk II: U.K. North Africa, 1941: MM Je 75 5/6:351
SdKfz 232 Puma: Polish campaign: MM Mr 75 5/3:171
SdKfx 232 Puma: 3 Schw, Kradschutzen-Abteilung "Grossdeutschland," Russia, 1942: AFV Jl 72 3/9:20-21

ARTILLERY

7.7 cm Feld-Kanone 96m/A: German, 1914: MW Ja 73 1/5:262
7.7 cm Feld-Kanone 96m/A: German, 1917-1918: MW Ja 73 1/5:262

HALF-TRACKS

M-3: U.S., "Operation Torch," North Africa: IM My 72 9/5:4
M-14: Canadian Midland Rgt, Feb-April 1944, Prince Rupert, B.C.: RT Mr 75 7/3:34

III. Color Patterns

M-14: Canadian Midland Rgt, June 1944, Colwood Camp, B.C.: RT Mr 74 7/3:34
SdKfz 250/9: 2 Komp, SS Panzer-Aufklärungs-Abteilung 11, Dec 1943, Eastern front: AFV O 71 3/2:24-25+
SdKfz 251/1D: unit unknown, surrendered to U.S. in Austria, May 1945: AFV S 73 4/7:12-13
SdKfz 251/9D: 5(schwere) Kompanie, Panzer Aufklärungs-Abteilung 2, Normandy, 1944: AFV S 73 4/7:12-13

SELF-PROPELLED ARTILLERY

ASU-85: Polish 6 PDPD, invasion of Czechoslovakia, 1968: Q Jl 73 8/3:169
ASU-85: Russia parade stds: Q Jl 73 8/3:169
Ekranami (Finnish KV-1 mod): Q Ap 74 9/2:77
Ha-to: Japanese, 300mm mortar: Q O 73 8/4:219
Jagdpanzer 38(t) Hetzer: Germany, May 1945: AFV F 73 4/2:22-23
Jagdtiger: unit unknown, southern Germany, 1945: Q Su 75 10/4:138
Jagdtiger: unit unknown, Dec 1945: Q Su 75 10/4:138
Jagdtiger: captured March 1945, now at Aberdeen Proving Ground: Q Su 75 10/4:138
KV-1-M42: Finnish unit unknown, 1944: Q Ap 74 9/2:76
KV-1-M42: Finland, Portinhoikassa, 1944: Q Ap 74 9/2:76
M7B1 Priest: hull name grafitti, U.S., North Africa: Q Ja 71 32
M109: Israel, 1972: Q Au 75 11/1:49
M109: U.K., 176 Bty, 39 Medium Rgt, BAOR, Germany: Q Au 75 11/1:48
M109: U.S. standard camouflage: Q W 75 11/2:95
M109: Q Au 75 11/1:49
M109 (155mm howitzer): Fort Sill, OK, June 1972: RiS Ag 72 1/1:33
M109: 2nd/6th Field Artillery, Germany, 1974: Q Au 75 11/1:48
M109: A Bty, 14 Field Artillery, 2 Armd Div, 1974: Q Au 75 11/1:48
M109: A Bty, 1 Btn, 84 Field Artillery, Vietnam: Q Au 75 11/1:49
M109A1: 7 Army, Germany, 1974: Q Au 75 11/1:48
M163: standard U.S. camouflage: Q W 75 11/2:97
M163: Ft. Hood: Q W 75 11/2:(99)
Marder III: German, Utrecht, Netherlands, spring 1945: RT Ap 72 5/4:37
175mm T235 gun: U.S., Fort Sill, OK, June 1972: RiS Ag 72 1/1:33
Obus autopropulsado de 155/32 (M109A1): Spain, Brunette Armd Div: Q Au 75 11/1:49
Panzerjäger Tiger (P): Panzer Abteilung 654: Q Ja 74 9/1:4
Panzerjäger Tiger (P): 2 Btn, Panzer Abteilung 654, c. Kursk: Q Ja 74 9/1:4

SAV M/43: Sweden, camouflage, 1943: RT Ag 73 6/8:92
Semovente da 75/18 su scafo M 42: Italian, Parma, Sept 1943:
    AFV Jl 74 4/11:24-25
StuG III: Finnish: Q Ja 75 10/3:109
StuG III: Finnish, 1960: Q Ja 75 10/3:109
StuG III: Finnish, Ryn. Tyk. P, 1944: Q Ja 75 10/3:109
StuG III: Malmedy Bulge, 1944, disguised as U.S. 5th Armd Div:
    Q O 74 10/2:60
Stu III Ausf G: 9 Schw, PzRgt 24, Russia, autumn 1943: AFV D
    72 3/12:28-29
StuHb 42 (Hetzer): Finnish: Q Ja 75 10/3:109
StuPz 43 Brummbär: German: RT Ja 71 4/1:11
Sturmtiger (SturmPanzer VI): German, 2 var: Q Ja 74 9/1:6

SOFTSKINS

Austin K2 Ambulance: 8 USAAF, England: RT N 73 7/11:129
Chevrolet C30 (4x4) 30 cwt, GS truck: 58 MTC, Udine, northern
    Italy, 1946: Sc Ap 71 2/4:198
Ford Jeep: 67 Army Field Artillery Btn, HQ Coy, 3 Armd Div,
    Camp Polk LA, 1942: AFV My 72 3/8:24-25
Kfz. 1/20 K2s schwimmwagen: Canadian, captured near Caen, 1944:
    RT My 75 8/5:49
Leyland Retriever wireless lorry: British, Desert War: MM Ap
    74 4/4:194
M151: standard camouflage: Q W 75 11/2:95
M548: Ft. Hood: Q W 75 11/2:(99)
Volkswagen Type 82: Nachrichten-Regt, Pz. Armee-Afrika, Tunisia,
    spring 1942: AFV Je 73 4/5:20-21
Volkswagen Type 82: SS Div (mot) Wiking, Russia, summer 1942:
    AFV Je 73 4/5:20-21

TANKS

(General)

Cruiser Mk 1 North Africa: std camouflage: Afx Jl 75 16/11:636
M-60 Medium Tank & Variants: std camouflage: AFV S 74 4/12:
    13
Sherman: 1942 regulation markings: Q Ja 74 9/1:13

(Australia)

Carro Armato Tipo M.13/40: 6 Asl Cavalry, North Africa, 1940:
    AFV O 71 3/2:9

III. Color Patterns

(Austria)

M-24 Chaffee: 1949-1950: Q O 74 10/2:50

(Canada)

Centurion Mk 4: B Sqn, 8 Cdn Hussars, DFB Petawawa, 1970: RT F 72 5/2:24
Centurion Mk 5: CFB Wainwright, summer 1971, in storage: RT N 71 4/11:124
Churchill I: Three Rivers Rgt (12 C.A.R.) (C Sqn + HQ Sqn), Oct 1941-March 1943: RT N 75 8/11:125
Churchill III: Three Rivers Rgt (12 C.A.R.) (C Sqn + HQ Sqn), Oct 1941-March 1943: RT N 75 8/1:125

(China)

Chi-Ha: Red Army, 1947-1949: Q Ap 74 9/2:61

(Czechoslovakia)

JS 2: Prague, 1945: Q Jl 74 10/1:9
Lt Vz 35: 1938: MW D 73 2/4:188
T-34/85A: Q Ap 72 7/2:79
T-34/85A: 1 Independent Tank Bgd, USSR, Aug 1945, 2 var: RT Ja 75 8/1:1

(Egypt)

T-34/85B1: 1967: Q Ap 72 7/2:79

(Finland)

BT-42: Independent Heavy Tank Rgt, 1941: Q Ja 75 10/3:105
Pz IV: post war: Q Ja 75 10/3:109
Pz IV H Nelonen: June 1944: Q Ja 75 10/3:109
T-26: Q Ja 75 10/3:102
T-26A: 3 Ps. P: Q Ja 75 10/3:102
T-26B: Q Ja 75 10/3:102
T-26E: 1941: Q Ja 75 10/3:102
T-26E: Viipuri, 1944: Q Ja 75 10/3:102
T-26E: 3 Tank Coy, 1941: Q Ja 75 10/3:102
T-26Lh (OT-130): Q Ja 75 10/3:102
T-26S: Q Ja 75 10/3:102
T-28M mod 1940: Heavy Tank Rgt, 1941: Q Ja 75 10/3:105
T-34 mod 1941: 1950s: Q Ja 75 10/3:105
T-34/76C1 Sotka: captured 1943: Q Ap 72 7/2:79
T-34/85: 2 var: Q Ja 75 10/3:105

Armor

T-34/85B1 Sotka: post war: Q Ap 72 7/2:79

(France)

M4A2 Sherman: 2 Div Blindée, Paris Victory Parade, 1945, Leclerc: Q Ja 74 9/1:19
M-24 Chaffee: Algers, 1962: Q O 74 10/2:50
M-24: 1 Rgt de Chasseurs, Pho Nho Quan, Vietnam, Nov 1953, Henri: Q O 74 10/2:50
M-24 Rhino: 1 Rgt de Chas: Q O 74 10/2:50
M-24 Rhino: 1 Rgt de Chas, pos Dien Bien Phu, Vietnam: Q O 74 10/2:50

(Germany)

M-48A2 Patton: 3 PzDiv, I German Corps, Germany, late 1950s: AFV F 72 3/6:20-21
PT-76: DDR Marine: Q Jl 73 8/3:169
Panther: PzBgd 150, disguised as U. S. M-10, Battle of the Bulge, 1944: Q O 74 10/2:62
Panzer II Ausf B: 3 Btn, Light Tank Coy, 25 PzRgt, 7 PzDiv, Russia, 1942: AFV Ap 75 5/4:25
Panzer II Ausf B: 8 Coy, 2 Btn, 5 PzRgt, 5 Light Div, Tripoli, 1941: AFV Ap 75 5/4:25
Panzer III Ausf F: 15 PzDiv, 8 Rgt, Libya, May 1941: AFV Ja 74 4/9:20-21+
Panzer III Ausf F: 21 PzDiv, 1 Zug, 6 Komp, II Abteilung, PzRgt 5, North Africa, Nov 1941: AFV Ja 74 4/9:20-21+
Panzer IV Ausf E: North Africa, 1942: Q Ap 71 6/2:34
Panzer IV Ausf F1: Russia, 1942, 2 var: Q Ap 71 6/2:35
Panzer IV Ausf H: 1 Zug, 8 Komp, PzRgt 26, 26 PzDiv, 3 Pz-Gren-Div, Anzio, Feb 1944: AFV Mr 73 4/3:20-21
Panzer VI Tiger I: Russian front, Wittman, 2 var: Q Jl 73 8/3: 148
Panzer VI Tiger I: Russian front: Q O 73 8/4:238
Panzer VI Tiger I: 1 SS Liebstandarte Adolf Hitler, 2 var: Q O 73 8/4:240-241
Panzer VI Tiger I: 501 Heavy Tank Btn, Tunisia: Q O 73 8/4: 239
Panzer VI Tiger II (H): ex 1 SS PzDiv, captured in Ardennes: Q Su 75 10/4:138
Panzer VI Tiger II (H): 1 SS PzDiv, Ardennes, 1944: Q Su 75 10/4:140
Panzer VI Tiger II (H): 2 Komp CO, Operation Panzerfaust, Budapest, Oct 1941: AFV D 74 5/1:26-27+
Panzer VI Tiger II (H): CO, 2 Coy, 502 Heavy Tank Btn, Ardennes: Q Su 75 10/4:140
Panzer VI Tiger II (H): 2 Coy, prob Kampfgruppe Peiper, Ambleve Valley, Battle of the Bulge: Q Su 75 10/4:140
Panzer VI Tiger II (H): 3 Komp, Schwere-SS-Panzer-Abt 501 "LSSAH," Ardennes, Dec 1944: AFV D 74 5/1:26-27+

III. Color Patterns

Panzer VI Tiger II (H): 3 Coy, Btn unknown: Q Su 75 10/4:140
Panzer VI Tiger II (P): captured in Ardennes, 1945: Q Su 75 10/4:141
Panzer VI Tiger II (P): 3 Coy, 1 Plt, gunnery range, 1944: Q Su 75 10/4:141
Panzer VI Tiger II (P): 3 Coy, 3 Plt, same Btn (unstated) as above: Q Su 75 10/4:141
PanzerBefehlswagen III Ausf E: I Abt, PzRgt 5, Afrika Korps 21, Tobruk, 1942: AFV Mr 71 2/12:8-9
Panzerkampfwagen "Valentine": I PzRgt 7, Tunisia, Nov 1942-Jan 1943: AFV N 71 3/3:10-11
T-34/76C1: captured by Grossdeutschland Div, 1943: Q Ap 72 7/2:79

(Hungary)

T-34/85A: 1959 uprising: Q Ap 72 7/2:79

(Israel)

Centurion: before Yom Kippur War: Q O 74 10/2:74
Centurion: Six Day War: Q O 74 10/2:74
Centurion: Negev, before 1967 war: 3 var: Q O 74 10/2:73
Centurion: Sheikh Zuweid, Six Day War: Q O 74 10/2:74
Panturion: Golan Heights, 1973 war: Q O 74 10/2:74
Panturion: Kuneitra-Damascus road, Yom Kippur War: Q O 74 10/2:74
Panturion: Sinai front, 1973: Q O 74 10/2:74
Panturion: Syrian front, Yom Kippur War, 4 var: Q O 74 10/2:73
Patton: 1 Coy, T/01 Btn, Tal's Ugda, 1967: Q Jl 74 10/1:38
Patton: 2 Coy, T/01 Btn, Rafah operation with Z Parachute Bgd, 1967: Q Jl 74 10/1:38
Patton: 2 Coy, T/01 Btn, Sheikh Zuweid, 1967: Q Jl 74 10/1:39
Patton: 3 Coy, T/01 Btn, Bir Rud Salim, 1967: Q Jl 74 10/1:38
Patton: S/14 Btn, Bir Gafhafa, 1967, 2 var: Q Jl 74 10/1:39
Patton: S/14 Btn, Tal's Ugda, 1967: Q Jl 74 10/1:39

(Italy)

M-13/40: 133 Div Corazzata "Litorio," North Africa, Feb 1942: AFV Ja 72 3/5:18-19+
M-24 Chaffee: 13 Tank Btn, Folgore Infantry Div, Sicily, 1964: Q O 74 10/2:50
T-34/76A4: captured in Russia, 1942: Q Ap 72 7/2:79

(Japan)

Chi-Ha: unit unknown, Manchuria, 1942: Q Su 75 10/4:165

Armor

Chi-Ha: unit unknown, northern Manchuria, 1945: Q Su 75 10/4: 165
Chi-Ha: naval landing force, Palau Islands: Q Ap 74 9/2:61
Chi-Ha: maneuvers with 285 Infantry Coy, Manchuria, 1944: Q Su 75 10/4:163
Chi-Ha: Army Cavalry School, Chiba: Q Su 75 10/4:165
Chi-Ha: Army Field Artillery School, Chiba: Q Su 75 10/4:165
Chi-Ha: Army Tank School, Chiba: Q Su 75 10/4:165
Chi-Ha: Army Youth Tank School: Q Su 75 10/4:165
Chi-Ha: Special Naval Landing Force: Q Su 75 10/4:163
Chi-Ha: 1 Armd Div, 1 Tank Rgt, 3 Coy, Kanto gun garrison, northern Manchuria, 1944: Q Su 75 10/4:163
Chi-Ha: 1 Tank Rgt, 3 Coy, Burma, 1941: Q Su 75 10/4:163
Chi-Ha: 1 Armd Div, 5 Tank Rgt, Manchuria, 1944: Q Su 75 10/4:163
Chi-Ha: 1 Armd Div, 9 Tank Rgt, Saipan, June 1944: Q Su 75 10/4:163
Chi-Ha: CO, 4 Coy, 6 Tank Rgt, Malaya, 1941-42, Chimade: Q Su 75 10/4:163
Chi-Ha: 5 Tank Btn, 2 var: Q Ap 74 9/2:61
Chi-Ha: pos 5 Tank Rgt: Q Su 75 10/4:165
Chi-Ha: 7 Tank Rgt, Saipan, 1944, 2 var: Q Ap 74 9/2:61
Chi-Ha: 9 Rgt: Q Ap 74 9/2:61
Chi-Ha: 9 Tank Rgt, Saipan: Q Su 75 10/4:163
Chi-Ha: 9 Tank Rgt, pos 4 Coy, Saipan: Q Su 75 10/4:163
Chi-Ha: 9 Tank Rgt, 6 Coy, Saipan: Q Su 75 10/4:163
Chi-Ha: 23 Tank Rgt, Manchuria, 3 var: Q Su 75 10/4:165
Chi-Ha: 23 Tank Rgt, Manchuria; 1942: Q Ap 74 9/2:61
Chi-Ha Special: 2 Coy CO: Q Ap 74 9/2:61
Ha-Go (Type 95): 1944: Q W 75 11/2:57
Ha-Go: 1 Tank Rgt, Singapore, 1942: Q W 75 11/2:57
Ha-Go: 2 Coy, 13 Tank Rgt, Northern China, 1944: Q W 75 11/2:58
Ha-Go: 3 Coy, 1 Tank Rgt, Kanto-gun Garrison, Kwantung Army, northern China: Q W 75 11/2:57
Ha-Go: 5 Tank Rgt: Q W 75 11/2:58
Ha-Go: 6 or 7 Special Naval Landing Force, Makin (near Tarawa), 1943: Q W 75 11/2:58
Ha-Go: 7 Tank Rgt, Philippines, 1942: Q W 75 11/2:57
Ha-Go: 8 Tank Rgt: Q W 75 11/2:57
Ha-Go: 14 Infantry Divisional Tank Coy, Peleliu, Sept 1944: Q W 75 11/2:57
Ha-Go: 18 Infantry Rgt, Tinian, July 1944: Q W 75 11/2:57
Ha-Go: with 285 Infantry Rgt, Manchuria, 1944: Q W 75 11/2:58
Ha-Go: Army Youth Tank School, Chiba: Q W 75 11/2:57
Ha-Go: Kwantung Army: Q W 75 11/2:58
Ha-Go: Tank School attached to 23 Tank Rgt: Q W 75 11/2:58
M-24 Chaffee: 1957: Q O 74 10/2:51

(Jordan)

Centurion: against PLF, border war of 1970: Q O 74 10/2:74

III. Color Patterns 342

(Korea, South)

M-24 Chaffee: c.1955: Q O 74 10/2:51

(Pakistan)

M-24 Chaffee: Q O 74 10/2:51
M-24: Dacca, Indo-Pakistani war over Bangladesh: Q O 74 10/2: 51

(Poland)

Cromwell Mk VII: 1 Polish Armd Div, 10 Mounted Rifle Rgt, Normandy, 1944: AFV N 73 4/8:20-21
JS 1: 2 WO Army, 1 Army Corp, 1 Bgd, 9 Btn, 6 Coy: Q Jl 74 10/1:9
JS 2: 1944: RT F 71 4/2:20
JS 2: 1 WP: Q Jl 74 10/1:9
M4A1 Sherman: 1 Szw, 2 Pulk Panc, 1 Dyw Panc, 1945: Q Ja 74 9/1:16
M4A1: HW Szw, 1 Pulk Panc, 1 Dyw Panc, Netherlands, 1945: Q Ja 74 9/1:6
M4A2: 1 Pulk UK, 2 Bry Panc, 1944: Q Ja 74 9/1:14
M4A2: 1 Szw, 2 Pluton, 2 Bry Panc, Monte Cassino, 1944: Q Ja 74 9/1:14
M4A2: 2 Bry Panc, Italy, 1944: Q Ja 74 9/1:14
M4A2: 2 Bry Panc, Palestine, 1943: Q Ja 74 9/1:14
M4A2: 4 Pulk, 2 Bry Panc, Italy, 1944: Q Ja 74 9/1:14
M4A4: 1 Dyw Panc, Battle of Maczuga, Falaise Gap, Sept 1944: Q Ja 74 9/1:16
M4A4: 2 Szw, 1 Pulk Ulanow, Krechowieckich, 2 Dyw Panc, Italy, 1945: Q Ja 74 9/1:14
PT-76: Maritime Defense Unit, 1972: Q Jl 73 8/3:149
T-34/76C1: Wojska Polskiego, 1944: Q Ap 72 7/2:79
T-34/85B2: UN duty in Cyprus, 1960: Q Ap 72 7/2:79

(Rumania)

Lt Vz 35: Eastern front, 1942: MW D 73 2/4:188

(Spain, Nationalist)

BA-10: MW N 73 2/3:141
BT-5: captured: MW N 73 2/3:141
CV-33: Italian unit, 2 var: MW N 73 2/3:141
Panzer IB: 3 var: MW N 73 2/3:141
PanzerBefehlswagen IB: Condor Legion: MW N 73 2/3:141
T-26: 6 var: MW N 73 2/3:144

Armor

(Spain, Republican)

BA-10: MW N 73 2/3:141
BT-5: MW N 73 2/3:141
CA 2 (M18) Schneider: defence of Cuartel de Montana: MW N 73 2/3:141
FT-17: MW N 73 2/3:141
T-26: 6 var: MW N 73 2/3:144

(USSR)

JS 2: Q Ja 71 6/1:2
JS 2: Guard's Tank Army, Prague: Q Jl 74 10/1:9
JS 2: Lelyushenko's 4th Guard's Tank Army, Berlin: Q Jl 74 10/1:9
KB-85: Q Jl 74 10/1:8
KV-1 mod 41: Q Ap 74 9/2:76
KV-1 mod 42: Q Ap 74 9/2:76
KV-8 (flamethrower var): Q Ap 74 9/2:77
M4A2: Q Ja 74 9/1:19
M4A2: 1945: Q Ap 74 9/2:76
PT-76: Marines, 1970: Q Jl 73 8/3:169
T-34/76A1: Q Ap 72 7/2:79
T-34/76A2: Q Ap 72 7/2:79
T-34/76A3: Q Ap 72 7/2:79
T-34/76B: Battle of Stalingrad: Q Ja 71 6/1:2
T-34/76B1: Q Ap 72 7/2:79
T-34/76B2: Q Ap 72 7/2:79
T-34/76B3: Q Ap 7/2:79
T-34/76B3: post photo: Q Ap 72 7/2:79
T-34/76C1: 2 var: Q Ap 72 7/2:79
T-34/76C1: pattern incomplete: Q Ap 72 7/2:79
T-34/76C1: winter: Q Ap 72 7/2:79
T-34/76C1: CO, winter: Q Ap 72 7/2:79
T-34/76C1: 5th Army, Stalingrad area, 1942, posed: Q Ap 72 7/2:79
T-34/76C3: posed: Q Ap 72 7/2:79
T-34/76D: Q Ja 71 6/1:2
T-34/85: Hungary, 1954: Q Ja 71 6/1:2
T-34/85-1: winter, 1944: Q Ja 71 6/1:2
T-34/85A: River Spree, 1945: Q Ap 72 7/2:79
T-34/85B1: Berlin, 1945, with bedspring aplique armor: Q Ap 72 7/2:79

(U.K.)

A.10 Cruiser: HQ sec, B Sqn, 3 Royal Tank Rgt, 2 Armd Div, Greece, 1941: AFV Mr 72 3/7:10-11
Centurion Mk 3: C Sqn, King's Royal Irish Hussars, Korea: MM Je 74 4/6:339

III. Color Patterns

Centurion Mk 3: 8 King's Royal Irish Hussars, 29 Br Infantry Bgd, Korea, 1951, Strachan: AFV O 72 3/11:24-25+
Centurion Mk 5: B Sqn, Queen's Bays, Libya: MM Je 74 4/6:339
Cromwell Mk VII: Armd Observation Post, 5 Royal Horse Artillery, 17 Armd Div, Normandy, 1944: AFV N 73 4/8:20-21
Cruiser Mk IVa: North Africa: Afx My 75 16/9:538
Lee Mk I: MM Ag 74 473
Lee Mk I: North Africa: MM Ag 74 4/8:472
Lee Mk I: North Africa, 1943: MM Ag 74 4/8:473
M3 Stuart: 8 King's Royal Irish Hussars, Egypt, July 1941: AFV S 74 4/12:14-15
M4A1 Sherman II: 4 Troop, A Sqn, 3 County of London Yeomanry, Normandy, summer 1944: AFV Ja 73 4/1:24-25
M4A2 Sherman: 1 Guard's Mechanized Corps, 9 Guard's Tank Bgd, 49 Tank, Germany, 1945: Q Ja 74 9/1:19
M4A3 Sherman: A Sqn, 3 County of London Yeomanry, 4 Armd Bgd, Sept 1943: AFV S 71 3/1:10-11
Mk IV: HMS Excellent, 1940: RT My 71 4/5:54
Mk VIb Light Tank: 1 Btn, Royal Tank Rgt, 4 Amd Bgd, Egypt, June 1940: AFV F 71 2/11:4-5
Matilda Mk II: HQ Troop, B Sqn, 50 Royal Tank Rgt, England, 1941: AFV 4/6:16-17
Matilda Mk II: D Sqn, 7 Royal Tank Rgt, Bardia & Tobruk, Jan 1941: AFV Ag 73 4/6:26-27
Tank, Medium Mk. A Whippet: WW-I: RT F 71 4/2:13

(U. S.)

Firefly VC (M4 A4): hull name graffiti, D-Day: Q Ja 72 7/1:32
M3 Lee: early star: MM Ag 74 4/8:473
M3 Lee: solid bogies: MM Ag 74 4/8:472
M3 Lee with M2 75mm gun: MM Ag 74 4/8:473
M3 Lee: 1 Armd Div, 14 Armd Rgt, 2 Btn, D Coy, Battle of Tebourba, Algeria, Nov 1942: AFV Ja 75 5/2:24-25
M3 Lee: 3 Armd Div, 32 Armd Rgt, 2 Btn, G Coy, Tank 2, Jan 1942: AFV Ja 75 5/2:24-25
M4 (105mm howitzer): unit unstated, Invasion of Okinawa, 1945: Q Ja 74 9/1:17
M4 (105mm howitzer): 4 Armd Div, Contentin Peninsula, July 1944: Q Ja 74 9/1:17
M4A3 dozer: 3 Engineer Btn, advance on Seoul, March 1951: AFV Jl 74 4/11:9
M4A3 w/M1A1 dozer blade: Korea, Q Ja 74 9/1:17
M4A3E8 Sherman: hull name graffiti, 1944: Q Ja 72 7/1:32
M4A3E8: hull name graffiti, Remagen: Q Ja 72 7/1:32
M4A3E8: hull name graffiti, Germany, 1945: Q Ja 72 7/1:32
M4A3E8: hull name graffiti, 1944: Q Ja 72 7/1:32
M4A3E8: 7 Cav, Coy B, Korea 1951: Q Ja 74 9/1:19
M4A3E8: 64 Tank Btn, Sokchon-ni, Korea, March 1951: AFV Jl 74 4/11:7
M4A3E8: 2 Ptn, Tank Coy, 65 RCT, March 1951, Williamson: AFV Jl 74 4/11:8

M4A3E8: 70 Tank Btn, A Coy, 1 Ptn, 1 Sec, 2 Tank, Japan, 1951: Q Ja 74 9/1:19
M4A3E8: C Coy, 72 Tank Btn, 2 Infantry Div, Korea, June 1951: AFV D 71 3/4:12-13; add Jl 72 3/9:8
M4A3E8: 89 Tank Btn, Korea, 1951, 2 var: Q Ja 74 9/1:19
M4Ae/8: Coy C, 89 Medium Tank Btn, "Rice's Red Devils," Han River, Korea, March 1951: AFV Jl 74 4/11:6
M-24 Chaffee: Rhine River, 1945: Q O 74 10/2:50
M-24: 1955: Q O 74 10/2:51
M-24: Korea, summer 1950: Q O 74 10/2:50
M-24 (90mm): France, late 1960s: Q O 74 10/2:50
M-48A2: Korea, mid 1960s: Q Ap 73 8/2:102
M60A1 & A2: standard four-color camouflage: Q W 75 11/2:93
M60A1: Ft. Hood: Q W 75 11/2:(99)
M-60A1 battle tank: Fort Sill, OK, June 1972: RiS Ag 72 1/1:33
M60A1: Ft. Hood, Nov 1973: Q W 75 11/2(99)
M60A1: 4/73 Armor, VII Corps, 2 var: Q W 75 11/2:(100)
M-60A1: B Coy, 5/68 Armor, NATO, Germany, present: AFV S 72 3/10:20-21
M-60A1: 1 Btn, 72 Armor, Korea 1971: AFV My 73 4/4:28-29
M-60A1: 1 Btn, 73 Armor, Korea 1971: AFV My 73 4/4:28-29
M60A2: 1 Armd Bgd, 2 Armd Div, winter scheme, Ft. Hood: Q W 75 11/2:(99)
M60A2: 2 Armd Bgd, desert scheme, Ft. Hood: Q W 75 11/2:(99)
M551 Sheridan: Q W 75 11/2:95
M551: 1 Mech Cav Div, Ft. Hood, 1974: Q W 75 11/2:(99)
M551: VII Corps: Q W 75 11/2:(100)

(Vietnam, North)

PT-76: 1971: Q Jl 73 8/3:169
T-34/85B1: training unit, 1970: Q Ap 72 7/2:79
T-60: 1971: Q Jl 73 8/3:169

(Vietnam, South)

M-24 Chaffee: Tan Son Nhut: Q O 74 10/2:51
M-24: 3 Recon Sqn, Tan Son Nhut airfield, 1972: Q O 74 10/2:51

AUTOMOBILES

(Cars)

BRM P.180: 1972 Formula 1 season: Sc F 73 4/2:138
Chevrolet Camaro: Group Two season, 1972, Gardner: Sc Jl 74 5/58:388

III. Color Patterns   346

Eifelland March 721: South African Formula 1 race, 1972, Stommlen: Sc Ap 73 4/4:285
Ferrari 312 B3: Monaco, 1973, Ickx: Sc N 73 4/11:766
Jaguar SS.100: all factory colors (12 exterior, 1-6 interiors each, 2-3 tops each): Sc N 71 2/11:601
Lola T330: Formula 5000, 1973, Barclasy, Shell, & Haggar colors: Sc S 73 4/9:631
MG Midget series TD: all factory colors (5 exterior, 1-3 interiors each): Sc O 72 3/10:551
March 721 Ford: South African Formula 1 race, 1972, Williams: Sc Ap 73 4/4:283-284
Matra Simca 670: Le Mans winner, 1974, Larrousse & Pescarolo: Sc Ap 75 6/67:168+
McLaren M20: Can-Am, 1971 Hulme: Sc Je 73 4/6:426+
Porsche Carrera RS: Austrian 1,000km, 1972: Sc O 73 4/10:702-703

(Carriages)

Marlborough's Coach: MM S 73 3/9:603

(Trucks)

GM series 450 tractor & Texaco fuel trailer: New York International Airport: RCS Je 75 1/2:31

FIGURES

Samurai: armor plate colors for Japanese armor: MM S 73 3/9: 591
Some Authentic Colours for Your Samurai Models: S&L (Je 75) 8: 8-9
Tartans: 42nd, Gordon Highlanders, Cameron of Erracht (79th Highlanders); MacKenzie: S&L (F 75) 6:24

MISSILES

V-2: in factory, operational variant, Germany, end of WW-II: RT Je 73 6/6:65
V-2: on launch stand, prob Peemuende, test variant: RT Je 73 6/6:65

RAILROAD

Amtrak Passenger Cars: MR Ag 74 41/8:40-42
CN's "Circus Cars": contemporary billboard cars, cpph: RMC Ap 72 40/11:46-47
Delaware & Hudson 2000 hp Alco PA: RMC S 71 40/4:26; cor N 71 40/6:54
Imperial type 4-42 passenger coaches: New York Central, Pennsylvania, Illinois Central, Southern Pacific, Golden State (SO & Rock Island), Overland (SP, UP, C&NW), Union Pacific, Atlantic Coast Line, Canadian National, National of Mexico, & Long Island: colors & names: MR Je 75 42/6:48
SP Daylight 4-8-4: MR Ap 72 39/4:42-45
Santa Fe Alco PA: RMC S 71 40/4:27; cor N 71 40/6:54
Peerbolte Onion Sets Reefer: MR Ag 71 38/8:35
Yakima Interurban Streetcar Lines: NMRA Mr 75 40/7:14

SHIPS

(General)

RN Colours: present ships: Sc N 73 4/11:762-764
Royal Malaysian Navy Fast Patrol Boats: IM Ja 72 9/1:5
U.S. Navy Battleship Colours of WW-II: Sc Je 75 6/69:280-281
Warship Camouflage: British WW-II: MM Jl 73 3/7:438-439

(Individual--Civil)

SS Canberra: IM F 73 10/2:1
Mayflower: IM Je 71 8/5:5-6

(Individual--Naval)

HMS Amazon: IM Mr 75 11/2:3
Bennington/Bon Homme Richard/Antietam: Q Au 75 11/1:17
HMS Defender: China, 1937: Q Jl 74 10/1:14
Essex: Q Au 75 11/1:14
HMS Fly: October 1943, modified Peter Scott camouflage scheme: MM Jl 73 3/7:438
Franklin/Bunker Hill: Q Au 75 11/1:16-17
USS Hornet: Sc My 75 6/68:248
Intrepid/Hornet/Hancock: Q Au 75 11/1:15; cor W 75 11/2:55

III. Color Patterns

HMS Leander: IM S 75 11/5:8-11
Lexington: Q Au 75 11/1:11
Moskva: 1975: IM Jl 75 11/4:18
HIJMS Nehoni: 21 Destroyer Div, 1 Dest. Sqn, Yangtzee-Whanpoo Operation, Aug 1937: Q Ap 74 9/2:80-81
HMS Pangbourne: 1942, early Western Approaches two-color scheme: MM Jl 73 3/7:438
Randolph: Q Au 75 11/1:16
HMS Rattlesnake: 1943, 1942 Admiralty Light Disruptive scheme: MM Jl 73 3/7:438
Yorktown/Ticonderoga/Wasp/Shangri-La: Q Au 75 11/1:14-15

(Heraldry)

German Naval Heraldry: WW-II battleship arms & flags: MM Ap 71 1/4:192-194

SPACE VEHICLES

Kosmos Rocket Markings: IM My 73 10/5:9

SIGNS

Billboards from the Past: Coca-Cola in O, HO, N: MR D 75 42/12:78
Billboards Used in the 1920s & 1930s: MR S 75 42/9:57
Common Railroad Signs: crossing, speed, yard, whistle, etc. in O, HO, N, pph: MR F 75 42/2:44-45
Modern Billboards & Signs: MR F 75 42/2:46
Signs for Model Co-ops: MR S 73 40/9:58
Signs for Structures & Streetcars; agricultural products: O, S, HO, TT, N: MR Je 72 39/6:43
Signs for the Layout: traffic signs & one billboard: O, HO, N: MR D 72 39/12:62
Store Signs & Billboards: MR Ja 73 40/1:66

IV. NON-SCALE MODELS

AIRCRAFT

FREE FLIGHT

Gliders

(A-1)

Bazoom 2: MAN Jl 74 88/6:8
David: AM D 72 75/6:29-31
Gob: all balsa: FM Ap 71 409:27-29
Gullnik: MAN N 73 87/5:17-18+
Little Hinney: Aero Mr 72 37/434:158-160
Mike's A-1: sp: MAN N 75 91/5:19
SAM A-1: MAN Mr 73 86/3:11-13+
Santana: AM Je 71 72/6:32-33+
Starstream A-1: Aero F 74 39/457:96
Starstream: sp: AM Ap 74 78/4:110
Starstream: all balsa: MAN F 75 90/2:17-19+
Tadpole: all balsa: MAN Ap 75 90/4:19
Tri-Star: Aero Ag 71 36/427:434-435
Wee Kee Wee: all balsa: Aero O 72 37/441:571-573

(A-2)

Banzai Machine: catapult with outdoor hand-launched glider lines
   (uses loophole in rules: FM Mr 73 76/3:32-35
Classic: Aero Je 37/437:316-318
Dragmaster: MAN S 72 85/3:8
Dragmaster: calm air: MAN My 73 86/5:17-19+
Draw Dip II: sp, windy weather: AM O 72 75/4:61; N 72 75/5:58
Dry Fly: sp: AM D 71 73/6:28
Gambit: turbulent air: FM N 71 416:28-31
Gran Zot: Aero Jl 71 36/426:358-359
Go-Bird: sp: MAN Mr 75 90/3:19
HS 3: sp: MAN Ap 72 84/4:8

IV. Non-Scale 350

Happy Hooker: sp: MAN Jl 73 87/1:8
Hopper: sp: MAN Jl 73 87/1:8
Lead Zepplin: FM Ag 71 413:38-41
Leading Lady: sp: Aero O 75 40/477:925-928
Led Zepplin: sp: Aero Ja 71 36/420:44
Loner: Aero Jl 74 39/462:350-352
Ochroma Pyramidale: FM Ag 75 78/8:26-29
Poacher: FM Ja 72 418:35-37
Quest: MAN Ja 72 84/1:12-14+
S. P. L.: sp, all balsa: MAN Mr 72 84/3:8
Sam 7: sp: MAN F 72 84/2:8
732: sp: Aero D 75 40/179:1047
Sharkie: sp: AM My 71 72/5:42
Skyhawk: sp: AM Mr 71 72/3:36
Sunshot V: sp: Aero S 75 40/476:851-852
Thermal Pig: sp: MAN O 71 83/4:8
Woodstock: sp, still air: MAN Ap 72 84/4:8
nameless: Allnut, sp: Aero D 75 40/179:1045
nameless: Deubel, sp: MAN Je 75 90/6:16
nameless Dvorak, sp 1971 World champ: MAN Ja 72 84/1:8
nameless: Procházka, sp: MAN Ag 71 83/2:8

(Open Class)

Big Dad: Aero Jl 73 38/450:358-360

(Other Towline)

Charisma: all foam: AM F 73 76/2:58-60+
Crofter: all balsa, sport/trainer: Aero Je 73 38/449:319
May Morning: trainer: Aero Je 75 40/473:324-325+
Rainbow: all balsa, auto-rudder, 3' wingspan: Aero Jl 72 37/438: 372-374
Sand Baby: sport: MAN S 74 89/3:11-13+
Schweizer I-29: all balsa, profile trainer: AM N 71 73/5:47-49+
Snoopy: Rogallo-wing: Aero Ag 72 37/439:451-452
Stag: unconventional wing planform: AM Je 74 86/6:34-36
Victory III: flying wing: MAN My 71 82/5:17-19+
Wing Thing: true flying wing (no vertical surfaces): AM My 71 72/5:42

(Catapult)

A-4 Skyhawk: profile delta: FM D 72 75/12:26-27
Akrobat: profile aerobatic monoplane: AM S 71 73/3:48-49+
B-47: profile: Aero F 73 38/445:92
Banzai Machine Mk II: FM Mr 73 76/3:32-35
Cata-Strofic: DT: MAN Ap 74 88/4:17-19+
Catastrofic: sp, using recording tape bracing on geodetic wing: MAN Jl 71 83/1:9

Thermus: all balsa: FM N 73 76/11:37-39
Viggen: profile: AM Mr 73 76/3:23
nameless: Sotich: MAN Ap 71 82/4:9

(Outdoor Hand Launched)

(Competition)
Bo-Weevil: DT: AM O 72 75/4:21-23
Drifter: AM S 71 73/3:47
Easy Rider: MAN Jl 73 87/1:17-19+
Face Saver: turbulent wind, DT: FM Ag 74 77/8:46-49
Flic: sp: MAN My 73 86/5:8
Lunchbox: MAN S 75 92/3:11-12+ Maxwell: sp: AM My 74 78/5: 87
Monster: Aero D 72 37/443:710+
Mrs. Beasley: AM Ja 73 76/1:60
Oklahoma Backroom Dancer: sp: MAN 71 82/2:8
Slick Stick: AM O 73 77/4:60-61
Tribute: Aero Ja 71 36/420:36-37
20/20: FM Ap 73 76/4:27-29
Under Dog: FM Ag 73 76/8:28-30
Zweibox: MAN F 75 90/2:15

(Sport)
Bonanza: profile lightplane: AM Ja 71 72/1:15+
Czech Glider: hang glider (with pilot): AM Je 74 78/6:76-77+
Jr's Pride: full fuselage, sl: AM Ag 73 77/2:34-35
Me 163B-1A: profile: AM My 73 76/5:36
Mustang: profile P-51D fighter: AM Ja 71 72/1:15+

(Indoor Hand Launched)

(Competition)
Driftwould: AM S 72 75/3:44
Hi Sweep Jr.: sp: MAN Ag 73 87/2:8
Penn Central: sp, low ceiling: MAN F 74 88/2:8
Rubber Arm Special: AM Ap 74 78/4:20
Super Sweep 22: sp: MAN Ag 73 87/2:8
Supersweep: AM S 74 78/9:33-37+ ; O 74 78/10:57-59+
Supersweep 22: sp, first to do 1:30: AM Je 73 76/6:18
Thantos: sp: AM S 73 77/3:66
nameless: 1975 Nats winner, sp: MAN O 75 91/4:16

(Sport)
Red Baron: rolled tube structure, sheet cover, all paper: AM Je 72 74/6:60-61
Thing: Wedge-shape lifting body: AM D 72 75/6:40-41+

IV. Non-Scale

Rubber

(Coupe d'Hiver)

Beau Coupe: FM Ja 74 77/1:28-31
Garricoupe: Aero Je 72 37/437:330+
Lucky Pierre: adjustable wing & prop offset: FM S 72 75/9:32-35
Maxwell Mk II: sp: AM My 74 78/5:87
Mugwump: MAN Ag 73 23/272:12-14+
Octagon Coupe: sp: MAN D 73 87/6:8
Splatter: sp: MAN D 71 83/6:8
Super Coup: sp: AM Ag 74 78/8:96
Union Jack Frost: geodedic wing: MAN Ag 71 83/2:11-13+
Winter Herald: Aero O 75 40/477:900-901
nameless: sp: AM Ja 71 72/1:39
nameless: sp, Garrigou: MAN F 73 86/2:278
nameless: Sauvage, 1971 CdH champ: Aero My 71 36/424:254-255

(Wakefield)

Automat: MAN Ap 71 82/4:11-13+
Citadel: sp: AM Ap 71 72/4:42
Clodhopper: 1938: Aero Ap 73 38/447:192-193
Finnegans Wake: sp: AM Jl 71 73/1:40
Groovy Tuna: sp: MAN Jl 75 91/1:24
Hesitator: MAN My 74 88/5:11-13+
Monarch: sp: MAN Ag 75 91/2:14
No. 72-9: sp: AM F 74 78/2:20
Parastar: 1938: Aero S 74 39/464:470-472
Reliant: variable stab & rudder: AM My 73 76/5:32-35+
Sakitumi: AM S 71 73/3:53-55+
Stratowake II: MAN F 72 84/2:17-19+
Vitar 2: Aero My 75 40/472:281-284
Wing Wiggler: variable angle of attack, sp: AM Ap 73 76/4:64
Woodwake: sp, all balsa: MAN O 75 91/4:15
nameless: sp: 1969 Dutch champ: Aero Ja 71 36/420:44
nameless: sp, Allen: MAN Mr 71 82/3:8
nameless: Fillon, 1937 winner: Aero Mr 74 39/458:126-128
nameless: Greaves, sp: Aero D 75 40/479:1026

(Unlimited)

Blimp: sp: AM Ja 73 76/1:64
Draft Dodger: FM Ap 75 78/4:32-36
Fairy Unlimited: AM Ja 74 78/1:28-29+
Lube Tube: CdH size: Aero D 71 36/431:672-673
Roamer: AM Mr 74 78/1:28-29+
Silver $: MAN Ja 71 82/1:8
Super Arrow: sp, trainer lines: AM O 71 73/4:40
Supreme: AM O 72 75/4:33-36+

Aircraft

Tubestake: FM D 75 78/12:19-22
Twin Fin: FM Je 73 76/6:40-43
Ugly Duckling: sp: AM Ja 75 75/1:79
nameless: Batiuk: MAN Ja 73 86/1:11-13+
nameless: White, sp: AM Ap 71 72/4:43

(Unlimited Class II)

2+ 2: FM Ja 75 78/1:30-33

(Open Class)

Licorice Stick: Aero N 74 39/466:596-598
Licorice Stick: MAN My 75 90/5:19
Predator: Aero D 73 38/455:674-675+
Windy: sp: MAN D 75 91/6:23
nameless: Nobbs, sp: MAN S 71 83/3:9

(Speed)

Brokenspar Bird: sp: MAN S 75 91/3:24
Dash Dip Mk I: sp: MAN Ag 74 89/2:9
Quail: sp: MAN F 75 90/2:16
Sizzle Stick: MAN N 74 89/5:11-13+

(Sport)

Auntie-Q: twin-engine pusher, Peoli-style: MAN Ja 71 82/1:11-13+
Canard Drop-Off: drops rubber & prop, launches parasitic glider, DT, 1-blade prop: AM F 72 74/2:26-27+
Candice: canard: Aero Ap 72 37/435:211-212
Clodhopper II: trainer, all balsa half-size Wakefield: AM F 73 76/2:52-53+
Fli-Wing: flying wing tractor, sport: Aero S 74 39/464:486+
Foo: 1938 endurance: MAN Je 72 84/6:9
Long Tom: all balsa, plastic prop, short wingspan, long fuselage, trainer: AM Je 72 74/6:52-53+
Mosquito: all balsa, small field: MAN Mr 72 84/3:12-13+
O-Fungle: annular wing: AM Ja 73 76/1:52-53+
Pepe the Sport: all balsa: MAN S 75 91/6:10-12+
Profile Peanut Pitts Special: all balsa biplane: AM S 72 75/3:56-57+
Stringless Wonder: kite-shaped: AM Ap 71 72/4:44-45+
Tailup: pusher canard: AM My 71 72/5:44-45+
Tenderfoot Tom: with large profile cowboy on fuselage: AM Jl 72 75/1:54-57
Yako: pusher canard: AM D 71 73/6:44-45+
nameless: twin-engine tilt-wing convertaplane: Aero N 74 39/466: 614-615

IV. Non-Scale   354

(Cabin)

Baby Biplane: oc biplane trainer: AM O 71 73/4:46-49+
Bi-Star: biplane sport: Aero D 73 38/455-702+
Black Corsair: sl: MAN Mr 74 88/3:11-13+
Cheechack: tail prop, conventional configuration: Aero Ap 71 36/423:298+
Curlew: high performance sport with DT, can adapt to CdH: AM S 73 77/3:68-70+
Orlik: Aero F 71 36/421:76
Scamper, Jr.: pusher with ventral rudder: MAN O 71 83/4:11-13+
Tangerine: AM Ap 73 76/4:60-62+
Whippet: FM Jl 73 76/7:36-39

(Profile & Stick)

Pogo: sport/trainer, ROG, STOL, stick: AM Mr 71 72/3:16-17
Profile Porter: Pilatus Turboporter profile trainer: AM Je 73 76/6:56-57+
Super Sleek Streek: all balsa, stock power, trainer: AM Je 71 72/6:50-51+
Tail Winder 2: stick canard: MAN Jl 75 91/1:11-13+
Tee-Bipe: all balsa biplane, Northern Pacific motor & wing parts, trainer: AM Ja 74 78/1:56-57+
Tenderford Trimotor: triple stick sport/trainer: AM Ag 71 37/2:48-49+

(Indoor B)

EZB: sp: Aero O 75 40/477:923
Easy '72: sp: MAN Ja 73 86/1:8
Flit: Easy B: Aero My 75 40/472:287
Little Willie Mk II: Easy B: Aero F 71 36/421:199
Puck: micro, half-size 65cm FAI: Aero 71 36/421:200-201

(Indoor D)

Bandersnap: microfilm stick: AM Ja 71 72/1:34-37+
Big D: MAN My 75 90/5:11-13+
Slithery Dee: MAN Jl 71 83/1:16-19+

(Indoor FAI)

FAI Tandem: tandem wing: AM Ag 73 77/2:30-32+
Rafter Rattler: Aero Jl 72 37/438:390-391
Red Baron: biplane, sp: FM N 72 76/11:49
Time Machine: 65cm rule: Aero Ja 73 38/444:30-31
Top Cat 200: sp: FM N 73 76/11:48
nameless: Czechowski, world champ: Aero F 75 40/469:104

(Indoor Paper Stick)

Junior Jackpot: MAN F 73 86/2:17-19+

(Indoor Cabin)

Fat Cat IV: MAN F 74 88/2:17-19+
Junior Jackpot: MAN F 73 86/2:17-19+

(Indoor, Manhattan Formula)

Stoneybrook Special: MAN My 75 90/5:18

(Pennyplane)

Denny's Penny: sp: MAN Jl 72 84/1:8
Denny's Penny: sp: MAN O 72 85/4:8
Duffer Dip: sp: AM Ag 71 73/2:45
Lucky Penny: AM Mr 75 75/3:48-50+
1¢ Plane: sp: MAN O 72 85/4:8
Penny Auntie: sp: MAN O 72 85/4:8
Penny Auntie II: MAN Jl 72 84/1:18-19+
Penny from Heaven: MAN Je 75 90/6:17-19+
Penny Plain: sp: MAN Je 71 82/6:8
Penny Wise: Aero Je 71 36/425:321
Pennyplane: sp: MAN Ap 75 90/4:19
Philadelphia Penny: sp: MAN Je 74 88/6:9
Plain Penny: MAN Jl 72 84/1:17-19
Plain Penny: sp: MAN O 72 85/4:8
nameless: Cailliau: AM F 73 76/2:68
nameless: Jaecks: AM F 73 76/2:68
nameless: Jaecks: AM My 74 78/5:41

(Indoor Sport, Trainer)

Tyromin: trainer: AM Mr 74 76/3:34
nameless: Fedor, matchbox helicopter: AM Ap 71 72/4:42+

Rocket

(Competition)

Canned Heat: MAN Ag 75 91/2:17-19
Cheap Thrills: all balsa: AM S 73 77/3:66
Firefly: sp: AM My 74 78/5:41
Jet-TEXan: sp: AM Je 71 72/6:34

IV. Non-Scale

Jetex I: sp: AM O 72 75/4:63
Jetset: Aero Ap 72 37/435:210+
Micro-Mini-Pearl: sp: MAN O 74 89/4:23
Puff-A-Long: sp: MAN D 72 85/6:8
Sundancer: sp: AM Ja 74 78/1:26
Zip Dip 150 Mk III: sp: Aero Ja 71 36/420:45

(Payload)

Chicken Ship: Aero Je 71 36/425:322

(Sport)

Cheechack: Aero Ap 71 36/423:198+

Electric

Sparky: Mabuchi A-1: Aero D 75 40/479:1038

Gas

($\frac{1}{2}$A Competition)

Bad Medicine: FM Mr 75 78/3:30-33
Cuddy: Aero O 73 38/453:550-551
Daytripper Mk 5: sp: MAN Jl 75 91/1:24
Doubloon: Aero Jl 75 40/474:722-723
Fire Wagon: AM My 71 72/5:14-15
Grand Funk 320: sp: AM S 74 78/9:62
$\frac{1}{2}$A Maverick: MAN My 72 84/5:17-19+
Medicine Man: FM F 74 77/2:26-30
Micro-Mini-Pearl: .02, sp: MAN O 74 89/4:23
Mini-Pearl: sp: MAN D 71 83/6:8
Sirocco: FM Ja 73 76/1:27-29
Sprinkle: .02: MAN Ja 74 88/1:11-13
Tornado: FM My 71 410:40-43
Upper Crust: AM Je 74 77/6:20-22+
Wizrod 350: hybrid of Wizard & Ramrod: AM Jl 72 75/6:34-36+

($\frac{1}{2}$A Payload/Cargo)

Forty Plus: cargo: AM O 71 73/4:28
Go Cargo: FM My 74 410:33-35
Pay-Triot: MAN S 71 83/3:17-19+
Pay-Up: AM Ja 72 74/1:32-33+

Aircraft

(½A Sport)

American Hawk Mystery Ship: all balsa, CdH lines: AM O 73 77/4:22-23+
Cheechack: cabin: Aero Ap 71 36/423:198+
Dandylion: .02-.049, all balsa: FM O 72 75/10:35-37
Delphinium: profile porpoise: Aero N 75 40/478:975-978
IFO: .02 flying saucer: AM Jl 71 73/1:24-25+
Little Deer: competition configuration: Aero F 71 36/421:77
Oini: .02 flying wing: Aero Je 73 38/449:318
Quarter Pint: .02 sport/trainer: AM Ap 72 74/4:26-27+
SBD Dauntless: .02 profile: AM Ap 71 72/4:20-21+
Shingleship: .01 hydrofoil ROW: FM S 75 78/9:42-45
Sundowner: .02: Aero N 71 36/430:624-626
Tenderfoot Tom: with profile cowboy on fuselage: AM Jl 72 75/1:54-57+
Thomas Morse Scout S4-C: .01/.02 profile, all balsa: MAN Ja 75 90/1:11-13+
Throwback: .02, Old Timer lines: FM N 74 77/11:45-48
Wildcat: .02 profile F4F: MAN F 71 82/2:16-17+

(A Competition)

Bad Medicine: FM Mr 75 78/3:30-33
Dixielander: sp: AM D 72 75/6:52
Dixielander: SMAE Open Power: MAN S 71 83/3:8
Dixielander: SMAE Open Power, sp: MAN Jl 72 84/1:9
Easy Rider: SMAE Open Power: MAN Ag 72 85/2:12-14+
Fire Wagon: AM My 71 72/5:14-15
Flying Burrito Brother: FM Je 71 411:42-45
Jubilee: Old Timer profile: FM Ap 74 77/4:32-35
Medicine Man: FM F 74 77/2:26-30
Pearl 450: FM F 72 75/11:27-30
Rambunctious: FM F 72 419:22-27
Scrambler: MAN Je 72 84/6:12-14+
Star Seeker: FM Mr 74 77/3:23-27

(A Radio Assisted)

Hi-Ball: sp: MAN S 72 85/3:32
nameless: sp, Mathis, II channel: AM Jl 72 75/1:21-22+

(FAI Power)

Alegro: sp: MAN F 72 84/2:8
Andromeda: variable camber: Aero Jl 72 37/438:384
Big Boy IV: AM Je 74 78/6:64-67+
Excelsior: FM Jl 72 75/7:23-26
Excelsior: sp: MAN Ap 75 90/6:16
FAIman: AM O 71 73/4:16-17+

IV. Non-Scale

Gambrinus 2000: sp: MAN Mr 73 76/3:8
Half-Nog: sp: Aero Ja 71 36/420:45
Meta-Nemesis: sp, variable camber: Aero Ja 72 37/437:338
Moonraker: MAN Mr 75 90/3:11-13+
Par FAI: FM S 75 78/9:26-31
Pearl 450: FM N 72 75/11:27-30
Pulemjot: sp: MAN Mr 74 88/3:9
Square V: sp: MAN Je 75 90/6:16
Strutter 7: sp: MAN Ag 75 91/2:16
Supper Flap Cream: sp, variable camber: Aero Jl 72 37/438:386
Suspense III: MAN Ap 73 86/4:11-15+
Uncle Remus: sp, 1975 world champ: MAN D 75 91/6:23
Veterano: sp: MAN O 73 87/4:8
Zingo: FM Ag 72 75/8:29-33
nameless: Taylor, sp: MAN Mr 71 82/3:8

(B Competition)

Excelsior C Special: FM F 73 76/2:38-42
Flying Burrito Brother: FM Jl 71 412:42-45
Jubilee: with profile Old Timer lines: FM Ap 74 77/4:32-35
Maxi-Pearl: FM D 73 76/12:36-40
Pearl Duster BC: MAN Ja 74 88/1:8
Pearl 450: FM N 72 75/11:27-30
Rambunctious: FM F 72 419:22-27
Scrambler: MAN Je 72 84/6:12-14+
720 Turn: AM Ja 73 75/6:30-32+
Skystreak: FM Ja 71 406:28-32
Star Seeker: FM Mr 74 77/3:23-27

(B Radio Assisted)

nameless: II: MAN Mr 73 86/3:32

(C Competition)

Excelsior C Special: FM F 73 76/2:38-42
Forté: Aero My 74 38/460:228-229
Hysteria 1000: FM Mr 71 408:25-29
Lipstick C: FM O 71 415:28-31
Maxi-Pearl: FM D 73 76/12:36-40
Pearl Duster BC: MAN Ja 74 88/1:8
Rambunctious: FM F 72 74/5:22-26
Satellite 1000: AM My 72 74/5:22-25
Scrambler: MAN Je 72 84/6:12-14+
Shocer: sp: MAN S 74 89/3:27
Skystreak: FM Ja 71 406:28-32
nameless: Brodersen, sp: MAN Ap 73 86/4:8

Aircraft

(D Competition)

Maxipearl: FM D 73 75/12:36-40
Rambunctious: FM F 72 419:22-26

Old Timer

Brooklyn Dodger: B, DT added, ignition engine: AM D 71 73/6: 16-17+

Miniatures

So-Long: .02, original 1940 B cabin: AM Je 72 74/6:20-21+
Wedgy: .02, original 1940 B: AM Mr 74 78/3:70-71

Other Than Airplanes

(Autogyro)

Twin Gyro: $\frac{1}{2}$A, twin rotor: Aero Mr 75 40/470:144-145+

(Helicopter)

Boomerang: $\frac{1}{2}$A competition: AM Ap 74 78/4:75-76+
Charybdis: .01, one blade rotor with engine on counterbalance: AM O 72 75/4:55-57+
Lynx: r, profile sport: Aero N 74 39/466:612-614
Minicopter: sp, indoor sport/trainer: AM Ap 74 78/4:20
Pearl Copter: r, indoor: MAN Mr 72 84/3:8
Puddle Jumper: r, profile sport: RCS S 75 1/5:28-31+
Unicopter: r, sport: AM My 73 76/5:54-56+
Whirlybird: r, indoor, contra-rotating rotors: MAN Je 74 88/6: 17-19

(Lighter-Than-Air)

Midair: sl hot air balloon: Aero Ja 72 37/432:28-32
Paraballoon: cleaner bag thermal-rider: AM Jl 71 73/1:44-45+

(Ornithopter)

Delta-Belle: sp, large fixed wing: AM O 71 73/4:57
Shear Delight: double flap, with large fixed area: MAN Ap 72 84/4:12-14+
Wingfoot: Aero F 72 37/433:88-93

IV. Non-Scale

Kit Construction

Asteroid A/1: Aero O 73 38/453:544-545+; N 73 38/454:614-615+; D 73 38/455:676-679; Ja 74 39/456:24-26; F 74 39/457:86-87; My 74 39/460:230-231+
Back to Square One: the Mercury Swan glider: Aero Ja 73 38/444:20-21; F 38/445:79+; Mr 73 38/446:137-139; Ap 73 38/447:194-197; My 73 38:448:250-251+; Je 73 38/449:306-307; Jl 73 38/450:384-386
Mercury Mentor: r FF Sport/trainer: Aero My 75 40/472:274-276; Je 75 40/473:338-340; Jl 75 40/474:732-734

TETHER AIRCRAFT

Rubber

Midget Mustang: stick fuselage, Skeeter prop & bearing: MAN Mr 74 88/3:14
Rivets: stick fuselage, Skeeter prop & bearing: MAN Mr 74 88/3:14
Shoestring: stick fuselage, Skeeter prop & bearing: MAN Mr 74 88/3:14
Swee'Pea: stick fuselage, Skeeter prop & bearing: MAN Mr 74 88/3:14

(Electric (Round the Pole)

Spitfire: profile: Aero Ap 74 38/459

CONTROL LINE AIRCRAFT

Combat

(AMA)

Apteryx: C, foam wing: AM Ag 72 75/2:15+
Bosta: C, eliptical wings: AM O 73 77/4:80-82+
Fox Feathers: C: MAN D 71 83/6:12-14+
George: $\frac{1}{2}$A: MAN Ja 73 86/1:17-19
Hornet 3: A: Aero Ap 74 38/459:174-175
Killer: C: AM S 71 73/3:26-27+
Matador: FM Jl 75 78/7:44-47
Mini-Nemesis: $\frac{1}{2}$A: MAN Jl 75 91/1:25-27
Mongoose: C: FM Mr 73 76/3:25-28
Nemesis II: C: AM Ag 72 75/2:14+
Orchrist: A: Aero O 71 36/429:550-552

Aircraft

Phantasy: AM Ja 75 75/1:48-49
Raven: A: MAN Je 71 82/18-20
Scorpion: AM My 73 76/5:42-43+
Scrambler: C: MAN Ja 72 84/1:17-19+
Snip: ½A: MAN Ap 74 88/4:14
Toothpick: C: AM Ja 71 72/1:24-25+
Tyrantula II: C: MAN Jl 71 182/7:11-13+

(FAI)

Firefly: Aero My 75 38/460:266-268
Iron Butterfly: FM Mr 72 420:29-31
Ironmonger: sp: Aero D 72 37/443:684-685+
Pink Panther: Aero O 73 38/453:542-543
Squeeze-Banger: AM Ap 72 13/8:40-42+
T-Bird: Aero My 72 37/437:256-258

(Slow Combat)

AEG G-IV: twin ¼A profile: AM My 74 78/5:35-40+
Bristol Monoplane: ½A profile: AM My 74 78/5:35-40+
Clipper: FM Ag 74 77/8:34-36
De Havilland DH-10: twin ¼A profile: AM My 74 78/5:35-40+
Falcon Hunter: ½A: MAN Ap 74 88/4:11-16+
Junkers J-IX: ½A profile: AM My 74 78/5:35-40+
Pfalse Fighters: vss Pfalz or SE5A: ½A/A: Aero Ag 73 38/451: 445
Sky Fire: ½A: FM My 75 78/5:26-29
Spider: C: FM N 73 76/11:40-43

Exhibition

ThunderFlash: C, rLG, throttle, bomb drop: Aero Ag 72 37/439: 440-443

Speed

(½A)

Bounty Hunter: AM Ap 73 76/4:51
Mighty Mouse: .01: MAN O 74 89/4:24-25
Sweet Leilani: MAN Ap 75 90/4:11-13+

(FAI)

Challenger I: sp: Aero O 72 37/441:578
Kingfisher: Aero S 75 40/476:842-843+

IV. Non-Scale

(B)

Piped Bee: AM F 75 40/469:44-48+

(C)

Monza: Aero N 72 37/442:647
White Fright: Aero S 73 38/452:499

(Jet)

Sidewinder: MAN F 71 82/2:11-13+

(Proto-Speed B)

Aquarius: MAN N 72 85/5:17-19+

(FAI Team Race)

Heaton Ross: flying wing for windy weather: Aero Je 75 40/473: 349
Hotrok: MAN Je 75 90/6:11-13+
Moskito 1974: Aero D 74 39/467:666-668
Parrot: Aero My 74 38/460:252
Sapovolov Onufrienko: Aero Je 75 40/473:350
Simple Sprint: Aero O 74 39/465:532-534
Tiger Mirage: FM My 72 422:24-28
Timeta: sp: Aero Jl 71 36/426:377-378
Turtle IV: Aero N 73 38/454:608-610+
XFW-3: flying wing: Aero Je 75 40/473:348
nameless: Safler & Kodytek: Aero My 72 37/438:269-271

(B Team Race)

Montezuma's Revenge: Aero F 75 40/469:110

(Slow Rat Race)

Sizzler II: C: MAN D 74 89/6:16-18+

(Goodyear Race)

Cassutt Boo-Ray: Aero F 72 37/433:102-103
Cosmic Wind/Ballerina: MAN Ag 72 85/2:17-19+
Falcon: MAN N 74 89/5:22-24+
Lil Rebel: AM My 72 74/5:36-38+
Little Gem: Aero F 72 37/433:102-103
Miss San Bernardino: Aero F 74 40/469:82-83+
Pitts Special: biplane: AM F 75 75/2:44-48+

Plum Crazy: Cassutt: FM Je 73 76/6:44-47

(Goodyear Race Profile)

Bonzo: A: MAN F 72 84/2:12-13+
Deerfly/Shoestring: $\frac{1}{2}$A/A: Aero S 74 39/464:487+
Mike Argander Special: A/B: Aero Je 73 38/449:304-305+
Ol Blue: A: Aero N 75 40/478:962-963
P-Shooter: A: MAN S 75 91/3:25-27+
Rivets: A: FM Ja 71 496:33+
Whitmann Buster: A: AM N 71 73/5:28-29+

Stunt

($\frac{1}{2}$A)

Falcon Hunter: MAN Ap 74 88/4:11-16+
Kittywasp: vss P-40: Aero Je 71 36/425:323
Pinto: FM D 72 75/12:34-36

(A)

Macchi C. 202: profile: AM Mr 73 76/3:24-25+
Martin Baker MB5: profile: Aero D 75 40/479:1024-1025+
Mirabilis: Aero Jl 74 39/461:271
Reaction: Aero O 71 36/429:568-569

(Twin A)

Me-110: profile: Aero N 72 37/442:616-619
Mosquito: profile: Aero N 72 37/442:616-619

(B)

Citabria: profile: FM Ap 73 76/4:32-36
Humbug: semi-flying wing configuration, no flaps: MAN Ja 71 82/1:16-19+
Macchi C. 202: profile: AM Mr 73 76/3:24-25+
Metaphor I: profile: FM Ja 75 78/1:19-25
Thrift: Aero Ag 75 40/475:782-783
Zlin Akrobat Stunter: profile: MAN N 71 83/5:17-19+

(Twin B)

Me-110: profile: Aero N 72 37/442:616-619

IV. Non-Scale

Mosquito: profile: Aero N 72 37/442:616-619

(C)

Akromaster: AM N 74 74/11:29-34
Astarte: FM Je 75 78/6:20-25
Avenger: AM Jl 74 78/7:51-55+
Be-Witched: double boom: FM Jl 72 75/7:19-21
Bell Airacobra: Aero Ag 73 38/451:418-420
Bishop: FM S 74 77/9:19-22
Citabria: profile: FM Ap 73 76/5:36-40
Cobra: AM F 71 72/2:16-19+
Commodore: sp: Aero F 73 38/445:76-78
Continental: MAN Mr 71 82/2:11-13+
Dancing Girl Mk II: sl biplane: MAN F 75 90/2:11-13+
Das Kraut: WW-I lines, auto-rudder: AM Mr 74 78/3:48-50+
Excalibur II: profile: FM S 73 38/451:418-420
F-4 Phantom: AM Je 71 72/6:14+
F-8 Crusader: AM Je 71 72/6:15+
F-14 Tomcat: FM Ja 72 418:22-25
Fly Baby: FM O 72 75/10:25-28
Genesis: FM F 74 77/2:20-25
Hurricane: FM Ag 73 76/8:34-37
Kawasaki Ki-61 Hein: profile: AM Ja 75 75 /1:40-47+
Kawasaki Ki-61 Kai C Hein: rLG: AM Ja 75 75/1:40-47+
Kittyhawk: vss P-40: Aero D 74 39/467:660-662
Loriot: sl: Aero Je 74 39/461:290-292
Macchi C-202: FM O 74 77/10:32-35
Magister: profile: FM Ag 71 413:27-29
Marut: AM O 71 73/4:35-37+
Metaphor I: profile: FM Ja 75 78/1:19-25
Miss Dara: FM D 73 76/12:21-24
Miss Jill: profile: FM D 75 78/12:47-49
Miss Lexington: AM O 74 74/10:52-55+
Mustunt I: profile: AM F 73 76/2:30-36+
Mustunt III: sl competition: AM F 73 76/2:30-36+
Nimrod III: MAN S 72 85/3:11-13+
Nimrod V: Aero S 72 37/440:498-500+
Old Glory: FM F 71 407:42-45
P-40: FM Je 72 423:36-39
P-51 Mustang Stunter: MAN My 75 90/5:22-24+
P-51B Stunter: FM F 75 78/2:19-22
Panic: FM Ap 75 78/4:23-27
Pea-Shooter Stunter: vss P-26: FM Mr 74 77/3:440-433
Scorpio: FM Mr 75 78/3:38-42
Shoestring: FM S 71 414:38-41
Skyraider: FM Mr 72 420:24-28
Spirit of Saginaw III: profile: FM Ja 73 76/1:21-23
Spitfire Mk XVI: AM Ag 73 77/2:60-63+
Stiletto: MAN Je 74 88/6:11-13+
Stuka: profile: MAN Je 73 86/17-19+
Stunt Machine: FM D 71 417:30-33

Aircraft

Sundance Stunter: FM N 75:78/11:24-30
Sunshine: FM Jl 74 77/7:26-29
Sweet Pea: V-tail: AM N 72 75/5:46-48+
T-38 Talon: FM Ap 74 77/4:24-29
Thunderchief: vss F-105: FM My 73 76/5:36-40
U-2: FM O 73 76/10:36-39
United: FM Ap 72 421:18-22
Volunteer: FM Jl 73 76/7:20-23
Vulcan: FM Je 71 411:32-36
Yak 9D: Aero F 71 36/421:72-74
Zlin Akrobat Stunter: profile: MAN N 71 83/5:17-19+

Trainer/Sport

($\frac{1}{2}$A)

Red Baron: trainer: MAN My 72 84/6:15
Card Shark: sport stunt: MAN D 72 85/6:12-13+
Chicago Model Masters' Trainer: all balsa: MAN Ag 71 83/2:17-19+
Dancer: fixed slat: AM F 71 72/2:14-15+
F-105F: profile: MAN Ja 75 90/1:17-19+
Flying Outhouse: AM Ap 74 78/4:66-69+
Fokker D-7: sport profile: AM Mr 74 78/3:34-36
Fokker Triplane: AM Mr 74 78/3:34-36
Fokker Triplane: MAN S 73 87/3:12-13+
Milk Carton Special: stuntable, made from milk carton material, stapled: AM Mr 71 72/3:32-33+
Nifty Novice: monoplane or biplane: AM Ja 72 74/1:42-43+
Pfal-se Fighter: Pfalz or SE-5: sport: Aero Ag 73 38/451:445
Skyfire: stunt trainer: FM My 75 78/5:26-29
Sopwith Camel: sport profile: AM Mr 74 78/3:34-36
Sopwith Tripe: AM Mr 74 78/3:34-36
Sopwith Triplane: MAN S 73 87/3:12-13+
Spirogyra: stunt trainer: Aero O 72 37/441:570+
Student Trainer: AM S 73 77/3:56-57+
Super Sabre Trainer: profile: AM My 72 74/5:51-53
Tuffer: .02, profile: MAN F 74 88/2:12-13+
Two for the Show: stunt trainer biplane: AM Mr 72 74/2:23-25
Ukie Snoopy Doghouse: sport, doghouse on conventional planform: MAN D 73 87/6:11-12
Volksplane: MAN Jl 74 89/1:17-19
Witch Craft: sport, witch on broom: AM N 75/5:52-53+

(A)

Jay Pee: sport: Aero Ap 73 38/447:206+
Nifty Novice: monoplane or biplane trainer: AM Ja 72 74/1:42-43+
Pfal-se Fighter: Pfalz or SE5a: Aero Ag 73 38/447:445

IV. Non-Scale 366

Spirogyra: stunt trainer: Aero O 72 37/441:570+
Trojan Tenderfoot: profile T-28, trainer: AM F 74 78/2:56-57+
Vertigo: VTO flying wing biplane: AM S 72 75/3:61-63+

(Twin A)

Heinkel He 219: profile: FM My 74: 77/5:30-33
OV-10A Bronco: profile sport: MAN Jl 73 87/1:13-14+

(B)

Boeing F4B-3: profile sport: FM D 74 77/12:42-45
Citabria: profile: AM Ap 73 76/4:32-36
Dutchess: sl sport biplane: Aero Ag 74 39/463:410-411
Erocoupe: sport profile: FM Je 74 78/6:35-37
Fireball: ignition engine, first U-Control aircraft: AM D 71 73/6: 14-15+
Flying Fortress: castle configuration with drawbridge wings: AM Ag 71 73/2:30-31+
T-19: trainer monoplane or biplane: AM D 73 77/6:61-63+
Vertigo: VTO flying wing biplane: AM S 72 75/3:61-63

(C)

Boeing F4B-3: sport profile: FM D 74 77/12:42-45
Chance Vought Skimmer: profile (single engine on fuselage) flying pancake: AM Je 72 74/6:32-34
Citabria: profile: FM Ap 73 77/4:32-36
Ercoupe: profile sport: FM Je 74 77/6:35-37
Mangler: profile sport: FM My 71 410:30-32
Mustunt II: stunt trainer, sl: AM F 73 76/2:30-36+
Paper Cub: cardboard (model kit cartons) construction: AM Ap 74 78/4:32-35+
Touch and...: throttle, lights, tail-drag or trike LG: MAN Mr 72 86/3:17-19+

(Triple C)

BV P-170: profile of German light bomber experiment: AM F 72 74/2:20-21+

Autogyro

Otto the Giro: B/C: MAN Ja 74 88/1:17-19

Aircraft

RADIO CONTROL

Category I

(Glider)

Capstan: all balsa sport, vss Slingsby Type 49: AM Ag 72 75/2: 30-31+
Charisma: sport, all foam: AM F 73 76/2:58-60+
Chobham Hawk: slope or thermal: Aero Je 71 36/425:304-306
Clod Nine: all balsa: RC Ja 72 9/1:51
Jaguar: thermal or slope: Aero S 71 36/428:502-503
Little Cirrus: slope or thermal, sl: RC N 71 8/11:20-27
Tadpole: sport trainer: RC S 74 11/9:38-42+
Tourmaline: slope or thermal, sl: Aero O 72 37/441:558-560

($\frac{1}{2}$A)

Ace High: powered sailplane, stock foam wings: AM S 71 73/3: 32-33+
Bf-109: vss sport: RC Ap 73 10/4:28-30+
Capstan: .02, all balsa powered sailplane: AM Ag 72 75/2:30-31+
Hurricane: vss sport: RC Ap 73 10/4:28-30+
Javalaero: powered glider: RC My 73 10/5:37-41+
Littlest Stick: .01: RC N 75 12/64-69
MMS-1: .01 flying airfoil, sport: MAN Ag 73 87/2:31-33+
P-38: vss single engine profile with foam wings: AM S 71 73/3: 32-33+
P-51: vss sport: RC Ap 73 10/4:28-30+
Pluto: amphibian lines but ground only: RC F 75 12/2:42-45+
Skyphonic: sport: AM Jl 73 77/1:56-57+
Skyrider: powered sailplane: RC Ag 75 12/8:49-51
nameless: rigid airship: MM D 71 1/2:643-644

(A)

Little Snort: sport: MAN Je 72 84/6:48-50+
Pronto: sport: MAN Ag 72 85/2:26-28+
Thor: sport/trainer: AM Ap 73 76/4:44-45

(B)

Pronto: sport: MAN Ag 72 85/2:26-28+
Royal Rudder-Bug: sport update of Good's original RC Competition: AM My 74 78/5:50-53+

(C)

Royal Rudder-Bug: sport update of Good's original RC Competition: AM My 74 78/5:50-53+

IV. Non-Scale

Category II

(Glider, Slope)

Albatross: MAN Je 74 88/6:26+
Bolero: Aero Ja 74 38/456:22-23
Centurion: RC D 72 9/12:26-29+
Clod Nine: all balsa: RC Ja 72 9/1:51
Delta Diamond: double delta: AM Jl 73 77/1:30-32+
Giant Prancer: pod & boom: FM F 71 407:36-40
Hi-Pro: T or regular stab, sl: AM O 71 73/4:19+
Little Plank: flying wing, elevon control: RC My 72 9/5:18-23+
Long Islander: FM D 73 76/12:26-29
98.6: V-tail: FM O 75 78/10:27-32
Phoebe: vss Bölkow Phoebus: FM O 74 77/10:50-52
Ridge Runner II: a&e: RC S 75 12/9:40-46+
Silent Squire: RC F 75 12/2:31-35+
Spirit of Freedom: FM O 72 75/10:20-24
Sweeper: flying wing, foam or built-up: RCS D 75 1/8:30-33
Tourmaline: sl: Aero O 72 37/441:558-560
Windfree: sl: RC Je 72 9/6:18-23+
Windhover: RC O 75 12/10:24-31+

(Glider, Thermal)

Albatross: MAN Je 74 88/6:26+
Aquila: spoiler, Standard class: RC My 75 12/5:40-47+
Astro-Jeff: spoilers: AM Ag 74 78/8:19-23+
Barracuda: RC Ag 73 12/8:18-22
Bolero: Aero Ja 74 38/456:22-23
Bommel: flap, FAI: FM My 75 78/5:35-40
Centurion II: RC Ag 74 11/8:24-31+
Eclipse: V-tail, 16' wingspan: AM O 74 74:20-25
Esprit: RC Ag 71 8/8:36-43+
Giant Prancer: FM F 71 407:36-40
Gulf Coaster: MAN F 75 90/2:33-36+
Hi-Pro: T or regular stab, sl: AM O 71 73/4:19+
Jonathan Livingston Sailplane: rLG, spoiler: RCS Ap 75 11/1:46-50+
Little Plank: flying wing, elevon control: RC My 72 9/5:18-23+
Long Islander: FM D 73 76/12:26-29
Maxisailer: RC Ja 71 8/1:16-19+
Monarch: V-tail: RC N 74 11/11:34-37+
Monterey: sl: RC Ap 71 409:30-33
Nebula: flap & spoiler: AM F 74 78/2:28-32+
98.6: V-tail: FM O 75 78/10:27-32
Orange Julius: sl: RC Mr 71 8/3:22-27
Phoebe: vss Bölkow Phoebus: FM O 74 77/10:50-52
Pro-Soarer: flap or variable camber: FM F 75 78/2:23-29
Quasoar: rLG, flap, spoiler, 12' wingspan: FM S 72 75/9:37-40
Sabre Soar: FM Ap 71 409:30-33

Aircraft

Silent Squire: RC F 75 12/2:31-35+
Slingby Skylark 4: RC Mr 73 10/3:31-41+
Snoopy: RC N 72 9/11:33-39
Specialist V: V-tail: RC F 72 9/28-31+
Spirit of Freedom: FM O 72 75/10:20-24
Standard Plank: flying wing: RC Jl 75 12/7:40-43+
Tern: flap: AM Jl 74 78/7:18-22+
Thermal Hopper: 10' wingspan: FM Je 72 423:19-23
Tourmaline: sl: Aero O 72 37/441:558-560
The Weird One: canard: FW Je 75 78/6:26-31; power pod: Jl 75 78/7:33
Wild Blue: 100" wingspan, folds to fit suitcase: FM Jl 74 77/7: 19-25

(Glider, Sport, Stunt, & Unstated)

Delta Diamond: aerobatic double delta: AM Jl 73 77/1:30-32+
Flexi-Flier: Rogallo hang-glider: AM Ap 74 78/4:21-24+
Illusion: swept flying wing: FM N 72 75/11:32-35
Max Fly: spoilers: AM S 74 78/9:43-46
Peregrine: a&e, V-tail, racing & stunt: AM O 71 73/4:18+
Pfalz Alarm: sport: AM Mr 75 75/3:26-29+

(Electric)

Bushmaster: Astro-25: AM O 74 74/10:61-64
Electra-Fli: Astro-10: AM N 73 77/5:20-22+
Electraglide 62: Astro-05, powered sailplane: RC Ag 75 12/8:24-29+
Jr. Electra Fli: Astro-02: RCS S 75 1/5:22-25
Tom Swift: Astro-10: RC D 73 10/12:25

($\frac{1}{2}$A)

All Star: sl oc sport biplane with stock foam wings: RC Jl 72 9/7:24-30+
Bizzy Bee: sport: RC O 74 11/10:32-34
Bf-109: vss sport: RC Ap 73 10/4:28-30+
Hafadussin: sport, foam wing: RC F 75 12/2:38-40
Half A Chaos: sport/pylon: RC Jl 75 12/7:32-37+
Half A Stick: sport/pylon: RC Jl 75 12/7:32-37+
Honker: sport: RC Je 73 10/6:38-41+
Hot Dawg: sport racer, stock foam wings: RC Je 74 11/6:18-21+
Hurricane: vss sport: RC Ap 73 10/4:28-30+
Joy Stick: stunt/Sport pylon: RC Ap 75 12/4:38-41+
Little Plank: elevon, flying wing, powered glider: RC My 73 9/5: 18-23+
P-51: vss sport: RC Ap 73 10/4:28-30+
Pacer: small field stunt: AM Ag 74 11/1:26-30+
Scooter: pusher pod-and-boom sport: RC D 75 12/12:64-68+

IV. Non-Scale 370

Skyphonic: stunt: AM Jl 73 77/1:56-57+
Sprinter: a&e, V-tail sport: FM Mr 72 420:32-35
Standard Plank: flying wing powered glider: RC Jl 75 12/7:40-43+
Thunderbird: sport, delta, foam wings: RC Ag 71 8/8:44-46
Tiny Tee: a&e sport, pylon engine, T-tail: MAN F 71 82/2:43-46+
2T: trainer: AM Mr 72 74/3:38-39+
Whizard: stunt, sport: RC Ja 74 11/1:26-27+

(Twin $\frac{1}{2}$A)

Ju-88: rLG, vss: RC O 73 10/10:51-55+

(Quad $\frac{1}{2}$A)

Three Channel B-24: .02: AM O 73 77/4:44-46+

(A)

All Star: sl, oc sport biplane with stock foam wings: RC Jl 72 9/7:24-30+
BT-70: trainer: RC My 71 8/5:16-19+
Baby Buzzard: scaled down Old Timer Free Flight: RC My 74 11/5:18-21+
Bippi-Bipe: sport biplane: AM N 71 73/5:20-21+
Bristol Spadport: foam wing sport: AM Mr 74 78/3:19-24+
Fokker Heinschmitt: foam wing sport, vss D. VII: AM Mr 74 78/3:19-24+
Honker: sport: RC Je 73 10/6:38-41+
Honker Bipe: sport biplane: RC Mr 74 11/3:30-32+
Hot Dawg: sport racer, stock foam wings: RC Je 74 11/6:18-21+
Joy Stick: stunt/sport pylon: RC Ap 75 12/4:38-41+
Kwick Stick I: trainer: RC N 73 10/11:40-47+
Little Plank: elevon, flying wing, powered glider: RC My 72 9/5:18-23+
Mark 1 Trainer: MAN Mr 73 86/3:42-43+
Migga-Bipe: sport biplane: MAN Ag 71 83/2:41-43+
Pronto: sport: MAN Ag 72 85/2:26-28+
Puddle Jumper: flying boat, optional wheels: RC Jl 73 10/7:18-21+
Quickie: sport: RC D 72 9/12:22-25+
The Real Thing: sport: RC Ag 73 10/8:23-27
Rumplestadt C Type: sport, somewhat WW-I lines, stock foam wings: RC My 71 8/5:16-19+
Sneaky Pete: a&e sport: MAN Ap 75 90/4:50-52+
Sopwith Triplane: sport: RC Ja 72 9/1:30-33+
Sprinter: a&e, V-tail sport: FM Mr 72 420:32-35
Standard Plank: flying wing powered glider: RC Jl 75 12/7:40-43+
Tiny Tee: a&e, pylon engine, T-tail: MAN F 71 82/2:43-46+
VM1W: trainer: RC O 72 9/10:22-25+
The Weird One: canard powered sailplane: FM Je 75 78/6:26-31;

Aircraft

Jl 75 78/7:33
Wimpy: sport, Old Timer lines: RC Ja 75 12/1:18-21+

(B)

Buzzard Bombshell: RC adaptation of 1940 Old Timer free flight:
  RC F 73 10/2:30-39+
DH-4: sport biplane: MAN Ja 73 86/1:26-29
Eyesore: powered glider flying wing with camera: FM Ag 75 78/8:
  32-39
Flymobile: wheel or float LG, trainer: AM F 75 75/2:60-63+
Honker Bipe: sport biplane: RC Mr 74 11/3:30-32+
Kwik Stick I: trainer: RC N 73 10/11:40-47+
Madge: flying boat, pylon engine, sl: FM My 72 422:37-41
Playboy Sr.: RC sport version of 1941 pylon free flight: RC My
  75 12/5:24-31+
Pronto: sport: MAN Ag 72 85/2:26-28+
Quickie Bipe: sport: RC O 75 12/10:41-44+
Royal Rudder-Bug: sport update of Good's original RC Competition:
  AM My 74 88/5:50-53+
Rumpler C-5: sport biplane: MAN Ja 73 86/1:26-29
STOL: flap/slot: MAN N 74 89/5:30+
Wimpy: sport, Old Timer lines: RC Ja 75 12/1:18-21+

(C)

Big Flapper: sl sport: AM F 72 74/2:14-17
Buzzard Bombshell: RC adaptation of 1940 Old Timer free flight:
  RC F 73 10/2:30-39+
Cardboard Stick: foam wing, corrugated cardboard fuselage & tail,
  sport: RC Jl 74 11/7:32-35+
Ducted Fan Heinkel He-162: a&e sport: FM N 75 78/11:34-40
Fat Porter: profile: RC Ap 75 40/8:32-37+
Madge: flying boat, pylon engine, sl: FM My 72 422:37-41
Mini Smog Hog: 3/4 size Smog Hog, tail-dragger or trike LG:
  MAN Ag 73 10/2:42-43+
Playboy Sr.: RC sport version of 1941 pylon free flight: RC My
  75 12/5:24-31+
Royal Rudder-Bug: sport update of Good's original RC competition:
  AM My 74 88/5:50-53+
Seaweed: seaplane, inverted fin for water rudder, sport: FM Mr
  75 78/3:18-26
Snoopy's Doghouse--Revised: updated version of flying doghouse:
  MAN Ap 71 82/4:48-49+
Super Sauder #5: rLG, sign towing: MAN Ap 73 86/4:43+
Weekend Warrior: a&e, boxy twin-fin sport: RC N 71 8/11:28-30

(Twin C)

Toadstar: camera, all foam construction, 16' wingspan: AM Mr 74
  78/3:60-65+

IV. Non-Scale

Category III

(Glider)

Ibex: flap, scale, Standard Class: RCS Jl 75 1/3:19-23+
Ladybird Mk 2: slope/aerobatic: RC Jl 73 10/7:31-33+
Phase One: slope: MAN Je 73 86/6:46-47+
Yankee Soar: thermal, 16' wingspan: FM O 71 415:19-23

(Electric)

Electra 225: twin Astro 25: RCS D 75 1/8:53-56

($\frac{1}{2}$A)

Centerfire: sport: RC Ap 71 8/4:22-25+
Half A Chaos: sport/pylon: RC Jl 75 12/7:32-37+
Honker: sport: RC Je 73 10/6:38-41+
Pacer: small field stunt: AM Ag 74 78/8:26-30+

(A)

All Star: sl oc sport biplane with stock foam wings: RC Jl 72 9/7:24-30+
BD-4: trainer: RCS N 75 1/7:26-31+
Bump: sport/trainer: RC My 71 8/5:22-27+
DDT: Goodyear lines, sport: FM F 72 419:30-32
Fokker D-VII: sport biplane: RC S 73 10/9:18-21+
Grasshopper: Goodyear lines: RC N 74 11/11:38-41
Honker: stunt: RC Je 73 10/6:38-41+
Hump: sport/trainer: RC My 71 8/5:22-27+
King Foo: trainer: MAN Ja 75 90/1:30-34+
Li'l Steaker: sport: RCS Ap 75 1/1:11-14+
Mark I Trainer: MAN Mr 73 86/3:42-43+
Pegasus: sport, with carrying case holding plane, transmitter, tools, fuel, etc: AM My 72 74/5:48-50+
Quickie: sport: RC D 72 9/12:22-25+
Snoopy: sport/trainer: AM D 72 75/6:48-49+
Styros XV: sport: RC Jl 75 12/7:24-31+
Tall Texan: foam wing sport: RC D 73 10/12:18-22+

(B)

BD-4: trainer: RCS N 75 1/7:26-31+
BD-6: trainer: RC Ag 75 12/8:32-39+
BD-VI: vss sport: FM S 75 78/9:19-25
Bokkie: stunt/sport: RC F 71 8/2:22-25+
Curlew Mk II: concave hull flying boat, sl: RC Ag 72 9/8:22-27+
DDT: Goodyear lines, sport: FM F 72 419:30-32

Aircraft

Divider: RC D 74 11/12:38-42+
Frantique: sport, open fuselage: AM My 73 76/5:26-28
Frantique Too: sport: RC Ap 71 8/4:16-19+
Grasshopper: Goodyear lines, sport/stunt: RC N 74 11/11:38-41
Das Mini Stik: miniature Ugly Stik, stunt: RC O 73 10/10:22-25+
Miss Crescent City: stunt: MAN N 73 87/5:34-37
Miss Playmate: tandem oc, sl, stunt: RC S 71 8/9:30-33+
New Era II: stunt: RC Ja 71 8/1:28-31
New Era III: sport/stunt: RC Je 75 12/6:48-55+
Osker: flying boat: AM Je 74 78/6:25-28
Quasimodo: sport: AM O 72 75/4:48-49+
RCM Sportster: sl advanced trainer: RC N 73 10/11:49-53
Royal Rudder-Bug: sport update of Good's original RC Competition: AM My 74 88/5:50-53+
Seasquare GT: Quickfloat with wings, pylon & tail: AM N 74 74/11:45-49+
Simple Fly: trainer, foam wing: AM Je 71 72/6:26-27+
Snoopy: sport, open frame fuselage, doghouse at wings: RC D 73 10/12:26-29+
Super Clean: rLG stunt trainer, sl: MAN D 73 87/6:27-30+
Whiplash: advanced trainer: AM N 74 74/11:39-43

(Twin B)

Waco PG-2 Power Glider: ss troop glider with no interior detail: MAN F 72 84/2:27-29+
Doublet: sl sport: MAN O 73 87/4:27-30+

(B Helicopter)

Polecat: RC Ag 74 11/8:46-57+; mods O 74 11/10:51-52
Anita III: RCS N 75 1/7:8-9+

(C, Sport)

Acro-Fury: vss Hawker Fury from Acro-Star: RC Ag 74 11/8:32-34
Aero Sport: sl: AM S 74 78/9:26-31+
Afrit: sl biplane: MAN Ja 72 84/1:26-29+
Big Flapper: sl: AM F 72 74/2:14-17
Cardboard Stick: all cardboard: RC Jl 74 11/7:32-35+
Cheapmunk: ss Chipmunk from Sig CL kit: RC N 71 8/11:31-33
Cold Duck: rLG: RC Je 71 8/6:24-27+
Desperado: twin-cylinder, flaps, powered glider: FM S 74 77/9:34-39
Dreamer: sl oc biplane: FM Je 72 423:46-49
Fat Porter: extra large profile fuselage: RC Ap 75 12/4:32-37+
Flicon: Sr. Falcon wing: FM S 75 78/9:46-49
Foam Fli: all foam: MAN Ja 71 82/1:33-35+

IV. Non-Scale

Frantique: open fuselage: AM My 73 76/5:26-28
Frantique Too: RC Ap 71 8/6:24-27+
Galloping John mod: biplane: MAN Mr 75 90/3:54-56+
Grouper: stock foam wings: AM Ap 71 72/3:14+
Gull: gull-wing: FM Je 73 76/6:26-29
Henchman 40: stunt trainer: MAN F 74 88/2:26+
Jolly Roger: RC Jl 74 11/7:18-21+
Kwick-Stick: open crutch fuselage: RC N 73 10/11:40-47+
Mark 20: wheels, floats, ski LG: FM Ap 71 409:22-26
Mighty Barnstormer: sl parasol lines, oc: RC My 72 9/5:28-31+
Mini Smog Hog: 3/4 size Smog Hog, tail drag or trike LG: MAN Ag 73 87/2:42-43+
Miss Playmate: tandem oc, sl: RC S 71 8/9:30-33+
Miss Scarlett: gag "Confederate" a/c with 24 pdr naval cannon & plastic fruit pilot: RC S 71 8/9:16-21
Quasimodo: AM O 72 75/4:48-49+
RC Modular: modular construction to replace damaged parts quickly: MAN Je 74 88/6:39-41+
RCX4: bat-wing, cabin: AM Ap 72 74/4:32-34+
Raider: vss Skyraider: FM Mr 71 408:34-37
Rodeo: vsl biplane: RC F 75 12/2:18-22+
Royal Rudder-Bug: update of Good's original RC Competition: AM My 74 78/5:52-53+
Sea Vixen: vss boom jet: FM N 72 75/11:39-42
Senior Telemaster: RC O 75 12/10:56-63+
Silver Asteroid: FM Ap 72 421:40-42
Southern Belle: sl homebuilt lines, oc: RC Mr 72 9/3:30-34
Sparrow: twin-cylinder engine, flaps, video tape camera: AM S 73 77/3:43-50+
Strikemaster: RC Mr 74 11/3:18-22+
Sundowner: rLG, ducted fan, vss Phantom: AM Jl 74 79/7:27-31
Super Goose: swept-forward flying wing: AM F 73 76/2:27-29+
Super Kaos, Jr.: RC Ap 74 11/4:26-32+
Super Saucer #5: rLG, sign towing flying saucer: MAN Ap 73 86/4:43+
Supercoupe II: vss Aerocoupe: MAN Jl 73 87/1:27-29+
Valley Flyer: RC F 71 8/2:16-21
Victor: FM Ag 71 413:22-26
Wayfarer: sl biplane: RC F 72 9/2:24-27+
Weekend Warrior: minimal plan: RC N 71 8/11:28-30
X-2D Sharpshooter: MAN S 73 87/3:45-47+

(C, Rise Off Water)

Mark 20: FM Ap 71 409:22-26
Osker: flying boat: AM Je 74 78/6:41-44+
Platypus: flying boat: AM My 71 72/5:20-21+
Seasquare: Quickfloat with wings, pylon & tail: AM N 74 74/11:45-49
Skip Jack: single float & tips: FM Ja 71 406:24-27
nameless: rLG; 3v, sec, but no struc: RCS Ap 75 1/1:25

(Twin C)

Outlaw II: RCS S 75 1/5:46-50
Preventer: rLG, flap: MAN My 75 90/5:30-34+
Ugly Twin: RC Ja 75 12/1:22-27

(Stunt, Biplane)

Acro Fury: vss Hawker Fury mod to Acro Star: RC Ag 74 11/8: 32-34+
Acro Star: RC Ap 73 10/4:31-41
Furee: MAN O 74 89/4:30+
Great Lakes Trainer: radial & inline cowls: MAN Ag 74 89/2:26+
Hiperbipe: FM N 74 77/11:26-30
Knight Twister Imperial: RCS Ag 75 1/4:46-50
Mallard: rLG: AM O 74 74/10:41-44+
Pitts S-1A: MAN Ap 74 88/4:28-31+
Pitts Special: RC My 73 10/5:26-32+
Rodeo: RC F 75 12/2:18-22+
Senior Aero Sport: scale: AM Mr 75 75/3:18-22+
Sunray: shoulder upper wing, inverted gull lower: RC Mr 75 12/3:24-31+

(Stunt, Fixed LG)

A-6 Intruder: MAN Mr 71 82/3:30-34+ ; Ap 71 82/4:42-43+
Akromaster: AM N 74 74/11:29-34
Avanti: RC My 74 11/5:24-29+
Brazen Raven: FM My 71 410:24-29
Cajun Queen: AM Mr 73 76/3:19-22+
Camus: AM D 71 73/6:20-21+
Cardinal: AM F 72 74/2:28-29+
Configurator 3: AM D 74 74/12:40-45
Desperation III: MAN F 71 82/2:30-33+
Dragonette: sl with homebuilt lines: AM Ap 72 74/4:48-49+
Eclipse: RCS Je 75 1/2:22-25+
Ekko: AM Mr 71 72/3:50-51+
El Gringito: sl: RC F 73 10/2:18-20
Imitator: FM Ja 72 418:30-34
Indy 500: CL stunt lines: FM O 71 415:42-45
Joey: foam wing: FM Ag 72 75/8:37-40
Little Bird: AM Mr 72 74/3:20-22+
Mach VIII: RC S 73 10/9:22-25+
Mark 20: FM Ap 71 409:22-26
Mickey Moustang: RC Mr 73 10/3:23-25
Moonrock: delta: FM My 73 76/5:41-44
Morris HF: foam wing & stab: RC Ag 72 9/8:18-21+
Mr. Slick: RC F 72 9/2:18-23
Mustang-X: vss P-51: MAN D 72 85/6:26-29+
New Era II: RC Ja 71 8/1:28-31
Northern Eagle: FM S 73 76/9:34-38

IV. Non-Scale   376

Pathfinder: MÅN My 73 86/5:27-29+
Pegasus: RC Je 71 8/6:16-21+
Quickie Mk 4: foam wing & nose: AM Jl 72 75/1:40-41+
Ragnarok: MAN D 74 89/6:37-41
Renegade: stunt trainer: RCS Je 75 1/2:19-21
Silver Asteroid: FM Ap 72 421:40-42
Super Kaos, Jr.: RC Ap 74 11/4:26-32
Sweetater: MAN F 73 86/2:40-43
Taurisimo: modified from Tauri to low wing: RC N 71 8/11:66-68+
Texas Twister: RC Ap 73 10/4:42-45+
Tiger Panzer: RC S 72 8/9:28-34
El Tigre: AM Jl 74 78/7:74-77
Tiger Tail: MAN Mr 72 84/3:26-30+

(Stunt, rLG)

Banshee: FM S 71 414:23-26
Belaire Mk 2: RC N 74 11/11:46-53+
Cold Duck: RC Je 71 8/6:24-27+
Compensator: MAN Ja 74 88/1:27+
CompTaur: MAN Jl 75 91/1:30-33+
Dirty Birdy: RC Je 75 12/6:32-37+; Jl 75 12/7:64-65+
Don Juan II: RC N 71 8/11:16-19
Dragon Fli: AM Ja 71 72/1:18-19+
Ekko Mk III: MAN Ap 74 88/4:47-49
Escapade: windy conditions: FM Ag 72 75/8:20-24
Faimeister: FM Jl 72 75/7:32-36
Fakir I: AM My 74 78/5:43-48+
Fakir II: AM My 74 78/5:49
Friendship I: AM My 73 76/5:19-22+
Gator Flea: MAN Mr 75 90/3:30-33+
Hot Pants: sl: AM S 72 75/3:22-27+
Mach 1: MAN Je 73 86/6:27-30+
Marabu Mk 3: MAN Jl 72 85/1:26-30
Migi Ball: MAN Ag 72 85/2:43+
Mura: RC Je 73 10/6:30-37+
Novi Arrow: AM Je 74 78/6:16-21
Panzer D20: MAN My 72 84/5:26-29+
Phantom I: RC N 73 10/11:62-65+
Phoenix 5: AM Jl 71 73/1:16-17+
Pisces: AM S 73 77/3:36-37+
Prairie Duster: AM Je 73 76/6:40-42+
Rampant: tandem LG, wire wing skids: FM Jl 4/12:32-36
Saturn: MAN O 75 91/4:30-33+
Sequel: AM Ja 75 90/1:28-34; F 75 90/2:26-30
Shrike: fiberglass fuselage, foam wing & tail: AM Ja 74 78/1:19-21+
Star Trek: foam wings, plywood fuselage: RC S 74 11/9:32-37+
Super Home Brew: MAN Ag 73 87/2:27+
Super Kaos: RC My 73 10/5:18-25+
Super Sicroly II: flaps: MAN My 74 88/5:26+

Aircraft

Superstar: RCS Jl 75 1/3:46-49
Tailgater: FM Jl 73 76/7:26-29
Thunder Panzer: RC N 75 12/11:40-45
Utopia: MAN Mr 73 86/3:27-29+
Viper: rough weather: AM Ja 73 76/1:35-40+
Warlock: AM N 72 75/5:42-45+
Warlord: AM O 73 77/4:27-30+
Yankee: AM S 74 78/9:51-54+

(Trainers)

Cadet: flaps, oc, parasol wing, STOL: MR Mr 71 408:20-24
Dennymite: corrugated cardboard: AM N 71 73/5:32-35+
MAN Trainer 40: MAN N 75 91/5:42-45+
RCM Trainer, Jr.: RC Je 74 11/6:32-39+; Jl 74 11/7:41-44+
Scooter: quickly-built, minimal plans: RC Je 71 8/6:58-59
Simple Fly: foam wings: AM Je 71 72/6:26-27+
Spinks Akromaster: AM Je 74 78/6:40-45+
Tycho 400: altimeter to keep below 400': FM D 72 75/12:22-25
Tutor: MAN Je 75 90/6:30-33+

(C Helicopters)

Runway Sweeper: RC Je 74 11/6:48-56+; Jl 74 11/7:36-40+
S.S.P. Helicopter: trainer: AM Ag 72 75/2:50-53; improvements: N 72 75/5:65-70; Mr 73 76/3:42-45
2B: tube fuselage: AM My 72 74/5:65; Ag 72 75/2:65; S 72 75/3:43; Ja 75 75/1:130

(D)

Sr. Aero Sport: biplane: AM Mr 75 75/3:18-22+

Combat

RC-Guillotine: B II a&e, CL design: AM F 71 72/2:24+
RC-Voodoo: B II a&e, CL design: AM F 71 72/2:25+

Pylon Racers

(FAI Pylon (III))

Bobcat: MAN F 73 86/2:26-29
Firecracker: rLG, foam wings: AM Ja 72 74/1:14-15+

IV. Non-Scale 378

Hot Canary: biplane: AM Ag 71 73/2:18+
Minnow II: rLG: MAN N 71 83/5:32-35+
Miss Canada: RCS Ap 75 1/1:18-21+
Mustang: modified P-51 racer: RC Ap 72 9/4:20-27
Pete: Howard racer: MAN Jl 71 83/1:26-29+
Phoney Folkerts: AM Jl 74 78/7:43-46
Pogo: AM Ag 71 73/2:19+
Susie Q: vss P. 40Q: FM Mr 72 420:18-23

(15-500 (III))

Cardboard 500: all cardboard: RC Ja 75 12/1:39-43+
Gee Tee I: RC D 75 12/12:32-37
nameless: RC O 73 10/10:18-21+

(Formula I (III))

BooRay: RCS Ag 75 1/4:20-24
Cassutt Racer: MAN My 71 82/5:30-33+
Cosmic Wind: MAN N 72 85/5:32-35+
Denight Special: AM Je 72 74/6:26-27+
Hot Canary: biplane: AM Ag 71 73/2:18+
Miss San Bernadino: RCS O 75 1/6:22-25+
Pogo: AM Ag 71 73/2:19+
Shark: MAN O 71 83/4:26-28+

(Formula II (III))

Dee-Kay Special: FM Je 71 411:38-41
Firecracker: rLG, foam wing: AM Ja 72 74/1:14-15+
Hot Canary: biplane: AM Ag 71 73/2:18+
Minnow II: rLG: MAN N 71 83/5:32-35+
Pogo: AM Ag 71 73/2:19+
Susie Q: vss P. 40Q: FM Mr 72 420:18-23

($\frac{1}{2}$A Goodyear (II))

Bonzo: RC Ag 71 8/8:16-19+
Cassutt: RC Ag 71 8/8:16-19+
Nothin' Special: a&e, V-tail: FM My 75 78/5:19-25
Upstart: stock foam wing: RC My 71 8/5:28-29+

(Open Pylon (III))

BS Mach 1A: MAN Je 71 82/6:41-43+
Blue Flame: FM Ap 73 76/4:20-25
Swinger: RCS Ag 75 1/4:52-55+
Victor: FM Ag 71 413:22-26

(Quarter Midget (III))

El Bandito: RC Jl 73 9/7:23-25+
Bonzo II: MAN My 74 88/5:46-48
Cassutt Special: RC Je 71 8/6:22-23+
Caudron C-460: RC Ap 75 12/5:18-21+
Deju Vu: MAN S 74 89/3:32-34+
Dick Ohm Special: RC F 72 9/2:36-37
Hot Canary: RC My 72 9/5:47
Li'l Pogo: MAN F 72 84/2:35-37+
Me-109: FM F 73 76/2:43-46
Minnow: MAN D 75 91/6:51-53+
Miss Paranoia: AM D 74 74/12:20-25
Missy Dara: AM Ap 74 78/4:48-62+
Ole Tiger: AM Ag 73 77/2:20-21
Ole Tiger: RC F 72 9/2:36-37
Shoestring: RC F 72 9/2:36-37
Shoestring: RC Je 72 9/6:40-41+
Spirit of St. Louis: RC My 72 9/5:24-27
X-2D Sharpshooter: MAN S 73 76/9:45-47+
XP-40Q Snafu: RC O 72 9/10:43-45+

(Quickie 200)

Quickie 200: ½A II: RC Je 75 12/6:24-27

(Quickie 500)

Quickie 500: C III: AM D 72 75/6:36-39+

(Sport Pylon (½A))

Hafadussin: II, 2 var, foam wings: RC F 75 12/2:38-40
Half A Chaos: II/III: RC Jl 75 12/7:32-37+
Half A Stick: I/II: RC Jl 75 12/7:32-37+
Hot Dawg: II: RC Je 74 11/6:18-21+
Joy Stick: II: RC Ap 75 12/4:38-41+
LIT Special: II, pod & boom: FM Ag 74 77/8:19-23
Little Mulligan: II, high wing: RC Mr 72 9/3:35-38
Super Chip: II a&e: RCJa 72 9/1:34-37+

Improving Ready-To-Fly

Custom Techniques for Plastic & Fiberglass ARF's: RC Jl 71 8/7:25
How Cheap Can It Get: converting Eldon RTF glider to RC I: AM D 71 73/6:26-27
RC Superstar: souping the Mattel SuperStar: AM Ap 74 78/4:70-72+

IV. Non-Scale 380

Super Tune Your Super Stunter: Cox Bf-109E Super Stunter: MAN O 74 89/4:14-16+

Kit Modification

Acro-Fury: vss Hawker Fury from Airtronics Acro-Star: RC Ag 74 11/8:32-34+
Converting Keil Kraft Nieuport to Electric Round the Pole: Aero S 75 40/476:856-857
Cougar Slope Cat: RC II slope glider from Midwest Super Combat Streak CL: AM Mr 75 75/3:30
Detailing the SE5A: superdetailing Top Flight SE5A: AM O 73 77/4:72-73
Dick's Dream: conversion of RC design to electric power: AM S 74 78/9:40-41+
DuBro Hughes 500: helicopter: RC S 75 12/9:72-77+; cor O 75 12/10:156
Focke Wulf 190: converting Guillow rubber FF to electric tether: Aero Ap 71 36/423:188
Fortune Hunter: FF adapted for RC retrieval: AM Jl 72 75/1:20-22+
Helicopter Training Fuselage: to save wear on kit fiberglass: RC N 74 11/11:18-23
Improve Your Hughes 300: Du Bro helicopter: RC Ag 74 11/8:35-37+
Little Lightning: ½A RC III vss P-38 (engine in nose) from Guillow P-38 FF rubber: AM Ja 75 75/1:62-64
Low Wing Ugly Stick: RC S 71 8/9:45
Micro Mold Lark: helicopter: RC S 75 12/9:72-77+; cor O 75 12/10:156
Miniature Sport RC: converting FF to RC: AM F 75 75/2:21-24
Miss America: Howie Keefe's unlimited racer from Top Flight P-51: RCS N 75 1/7:22-25+
Modified Shoestring: stunt trainer to pylon trainer: RC N 74 11/11:60-61
Mods to a Cirrus: Cirrus glider souping: MAN Mr 72 84/3:36-38+
Mods to Du Bro 300 helicopter: MAN Mr 74 88/3:49-50
Mods to a Galloping John: full house mod to 1960s biplane: MAN Mr 75 75/3:54-56+
My Electric Powered Jenny: adding Mattel SuperStar engine to Sterling rubber kit: MAN Ap 73 86/4:48-49+
Piper L-4B Grasshopper: from Sig Piper Cub J-3: RCS Je 75 1/2:55-57
Pronto: modifying kit for easy travel: RC O 73 10/10:31-35+
Shark: from Hughes 300 helicopters: RC Jl 75 12/7:47-49+
Sterling E: adaptation of kit line to flying scale competition standards: Aero F 74 39/497:97-98
Super Cirrus: mods to Graupner Cirrus: RC Je 75 12/6:29-10
Superbird: shaft-drive conversion of Du-Bro 505 helicopter: AM D 73 77/6:43-50

Swing Blades for Du Bro 505 helicopter: RC O 74 11/10:52
Tailpiece: detachable fin for Nimrod stunt: Aero Ap 75 40/471: 217-219
Taurismo: Tauri to low wing: RC N 71 8/11:66-68+
Top Flite Mustang Mods: RC F 75 12/2:50-52
Twin Mustang: from two Ralvin quarter midget P-51s: RCS Jl 75 1/3:32-33
Ugly American: Ugly Stick to pack better for travel: RC Je 71 8/6:30-31
Wee Bonnie Lass: Kwick Stick mods: RC My 75 12/5:64-65

Kit Construction

Airplanes

Birdi Hobby Enterprises T-20: C III trainer: RC S 75 12/9:60-61+; O 75 12/10:75-77+; N 75 12/11:46-47+
Hobie Hawk: RCS S 75 1/5:71-74
Quickie 500 with electric power: RCS O 75 1/6:19-21+
Stirling Gazariator: C III trainer: RC Ap 75 12/4:52-55+; My 75 12/5:60-61+

Helicopters

Building the Bell Huey Cobra: RC Jl 72 9/7:31-39+; Ag 72 9/8:28-35+; S 72 9/9:35-42+
Building the Du Bro Hughes 500: RC Ap 73 10/4:18-27; My 73 10/5:51-59+
Du Bro Shark: RC Mr 74 11/3:25-28+
Du Bro Shark: RC N 74 11/11:62-65+
Du Bro Whirlybird 505: RC Ja 75 12/1:58-61+
Kalt Hughes 500: RC O 75 12/10:33-38+; N 75 12/11:56-61+
Kavan Jet Ranger: RC Ag 73 10/8:42-49+; S 73 10/9:26-33+
Micro Mold Lark: RC S 75 12/9:72-77+; cor O 75 12/10:156
RC Circa 1972: Du Bro Whirlybird 505: RC Mr 72 9/3:20-29
RCM Builds the Tri-Star: RC D 75 12/12:72-76
Schluter Heli-Baby: RC O 75 12/10:64-71+

IV. Non-Scale

BOATS

FREE RUNNING

Power

(Electric)

B-Liner: racer: MB Je 72 22/258:247+
Birdie II: straight runner: MB Ja 73 23/265:12-13

(Gas)

Birdie II: straight runner: MB Ja 73 23/265:12-13

(Outboards)

Tom Tit: e, runabout: MB D 73 87/6:517-520+

Sail

($\frac{1}{2}$ Meter)

Shortbow: MB S 71 21/249:373

(International A)

Challenge: MB Jl 71 21/247:276-278
Clockwork Orange: MB Ap 73 24/279:144-145
Hoyden: MB Jl 73 23/271:278-279
Huron III: MB N 72 22/263:470-471
Kia Kia: MB Je 74 24/281:210-211
Lightfoot: MB Ag 74 14/283:318-319
Lowlander: MB F 73 23/266:72-73
Mini A: MB Ap 71 21/244:154-155
Moderation: MB D 74 24/287:540

(Marblehead)

Aquaplane: Marblehead adaptation of Plane Jane: MB D 72 22/264: 524-525+
Cinque: MB O 72 22/262:426-427+
Genie: simplified construction: MB D 73 23/276:510-513; Ja 74 24/277:25-28; Mr 74 14/178:88-90; Ap 74 24/279:128-130+ ; My 74 24/280:172-174; Je 74 24/281:228-229; Jl 74 24/282:276-277+ ;

Ag 74 24/283:336
Nerang: MB O 72 22/262:426-427+
Sailplane II: MB Ag 72 22/260:328-329+
Turi: MB My 74 24/280:163+
247: MB Jl 75 25/294:393; Ag 75 25/295:411-412; S 75 25/296: 268-269

(36" Restricted)

Gosling: MB My 73 23/269:195-197; Je 73 23/270:232-234+; Jl 73 23/271:284-285+
Playaway: MB N 75 25/298:570-572
Square One: ultra-simple construction: MB Ja 71 21/241:21-23+; F 71 21/242:70-71; Mr 71 21/243:108-109; Ap 71 21/244:164-165

(10-Rater)

Cochin: constant chine: MB S 72 22/261:382-383
Cracker: MB My 71 21/245:198-199+
Ranger: MB Ap 74 24/283:124

(Sport)

Birkenhead: One-Design catamaran: MB N 71 21/251:452-453
Cair Andros: vane control ketch, fiberglass hull: MB O 75 25/297:533-535; N 75 25/298:588-589; D 75 25/299:656-658
Eowyn of Rohan: vane control ketch: MB Mr 74 24/278:78-80
Gosling: MB My 73 23/269:195-197; Je 73 23/270:232-234+; Jl 73 23/271:284-285+
Sail Foil: hydrofoil sport: MB Je 74/281:206-207
Sailboard: scrapbin sailboat: MB Ap 75 25/291:188-189
Sir William Petty's Catamaran: vss Simon & Jude, 1662 British: MB Ja 74 24/277:30-31
Splinter: 12" long vane-control yacht: MB F 75 25/290:77-81
Thames Sailing Barge: vss, mizzen boom controls rudder: MB Jl 74 24/282:258-259+

Tether--Competition

(Inboard)

Rodeo: C: MB My 74 24/280:169
nameless: MB Je 74 24/281:212

IV. Non-Scale

(Air Drive)

Komet 4:   MB My 74 24/280:168

Radio Control

(Electric)

(Speed)
Arrow: 100W flattie: MB O 72 22/262:423
Lidia II: 1 kilo flattie: MB Jl 74 24/282:278-279

(Sport)
HMS Hornblower: free lance battleship: MB F 75 25/289:74-76
Radio-Active: oar-powered & steered dingby: MB Ja 71 21/241: 14-15+ ; F 71 21/242:54-56
Rakituma: twin motor, single prop, ss New Zealand crayfishing boat: MB Je 71 21/242

(Steering)
nameless: F3E: MB D 74 24/287:532-533

(Submarines)
Resolution class Polaris sub: ss: MB D 72 22/264:506-507+
Type XXIC U-Boat: MB D 72 22/264:506-507+

(Gas)

(Air Drive)
FM Airboat: B, water rudder, throttle: FM Ap 75 78/4:62-65

(Inboard--speed)
Aurora: C sl offshore lines: MB Ag 74 24/283:310-311
Blue Streak III: modifications to flattie kit for multi-boat racing: MB S 71 21/249:354-355
EZVee: C, offshore lines: FM S 74 77/9:59-62
Foamy: B flattie, foam block construction: FM N 74 77/11:59-62
Force 3: A/B sl multi-boat: MB Mr 72 22/255:104-105; Ap 72 22/256:167
Fusilier: A/B multi-boat: MB Je 73 23/270:246-247+
Miss Misty: A/B hydroplane: RC Jl 74 11/7:24-29+
Musketeer: C multi-boat: MB Jl 71 21/247:268-269
Onetahua: $2\frac{1}{2}$-5cc offshore: MB F 73 23/266:56-57
Polywog: B flattie: FM F 75 78/2:59-62
Quarter Crackerbox: A, Quarter Midget flattie: FM Ag 75 78/8: 59-63
Red Devil: C, F1-V15 European record-holder: MB Ap 71 21/244: 151
Screwdriver: 10cc offshore: MB N 71 21/251:448-449+

Cars

Sniper: ½A/A multi-boat: MB D 72 22/264:518-520+
Stiletto SK 40: C skiboat: MB My 72 22/257:106-207

(Inboard--steering)
Blue Streak: modifications to flattie kit for naviga: MB S 71 21/249:354-355
Musketeer: C: MB Jl 71 21/247:268-269
Sniper: ½A/A: MB D 72 22/264:518-520+

(Sail)

Ariel: sl sport cruiser: RC F 73 10/2:40-46+
Comet: sl cruising catamaran: MB My 72 23/257:194-196; Je 72 23/258:252; Jl 72 23/258:289-290
Critter: Marblehead: AM Jl 73 77/1:72-76+
Electra XII: RM Class: MB Jl 75 25/294:336-339; Ag 75 25/295:411-412; S 75 25/296:468-469
Genie: Marblehead, simplified construction: MB D 73 23/276:510-513; Ja 74 24/277:25-28; Mr 74 24/278:88-90; Ap 74 24/279:128-130+; My 74 24/280:172-174; Je 74 24/281:228-229; Jl 74 24/282:276-277+; Ag 74 24/283:336
Gosling: 36" Restricted: MB My 73 23/269:195-197; Je 73 23/270:232-234+; Jl 73 23/271:284-285+
Radio Solent: Solent class: MB D 71 21/252:497-499+; Ja 72 21/253:18-20; F 72 21/254:62-64; Mr 72 23/255:118-119; Ap 72 23/256:156-157; My 72 23/257:190-191+
Rio: 10-Rater: MB Ja 75 12/1:20-21+
Sea Foam: foam bead hull: RC D 75 12/12:69-71+
247: Marblehead: MB Jl 75 25/294:393; Ag 75 25/295:411-412; S 75 25/296:268-269
nameless: 8' catamaran, sport: MB My 75 25/292:234-235

Kit Construction

Dumas Shelly Foss Tug: RCS N 75 1/7:44-48+
Graupner Optimist: RC Sail: MB My 71 21/245:202-203+; Je 71 21/246:227-229
Nylet Moonraker: RC Marblehead: MB Je 74 24/281:214-215; Jl 74 24/282:266-267+; Ag 74 24/283:330-331+; S 74 24/284:284

CARS--RADIO CONTROL

(Motorcycles)

Motor X: ½A, side car optional: MAN F 74 88/2:39-41+

IV. Non-Scale 386

(ROAR Racers)

Electric Race Car: Black & Decker utility motor conversion of Jerobee RC racer: RC D 75 12/12:56-59
Hopping Up Heath's Spectre RC Car: modifications to chassis & engine: FM Ap 71 409:41
The Simple Machine: independent rear suspension, belt drive: MAN N 72 85/5:47-49+

(Sport)

RC SuperStar Car: converting free-running electric car to RC: AM Mr 75 75/3:56-57
Snow Bird: C RC air drive, ski: MAN Ap 72 84/4:43+

ROCKET

(Altitude)

Delta Mark IV: D, triangular cross-section: AM S 71 73/3:18-19+

(Boost Glider)

Cheechako: $\frac{1}{2}$A 6-2, delta: AM F 72 74/2:44-45+; cor Mr 72 74/3:52
Delta Katt: sp: Aero Ja 73 38/444:43
Skydancer: D RC II a&e, dropping power pod: AM Mr 71 72/3:14-15+

(Pay Load)

Atur: B/C: AM Ag 72 75/2:38-39

V. ARTICLES

CONSTRUCTION

MATERIALS

(Adhesives)

ACC For Bonding Model Parts: using cyanoacrylate: MR N 72 39/
   11:74-77
Adhesives: AM S 73 77/3:40
And Now for a Sticky Subject: flying model cement: Aero Jl 73 38/
   450:363-365
Cold Facts on Hot Glue: MR N 75 42/92-93
Epoxy Resin Glues: Aero My 74 39/460:238
Hot Stuff: cyanoacrylate: RC F 75 12/2:2+
Modifying White Glue for Specific Adhesions: mixes for wood ties,
   plastic ties, & cardboard: NMRA Ap 71 36/8:10
The Truth About Adhesives: glues for RC aircraft: RC F 74 11/
   2:53-56+

(Covering)

Mylar: AM O 72 75/4:52-54+
Solarfilm: evaluation & application techniques: RC Jl 71 8/7:30-
   31+
Super MonoKote Techniques: application: MAN Ap 71 83/2:46-48+

(Electronic Components)

Choosing & Using Diode Rectifiers: MR N 72 39/11:72-73
Heat Sinks for Transitors: chart, wd: MR Ja 75 42/1:70-73
Miniature Lamp Bulbs: MR Ja 74 41/1:78-79

(Metal)

Aluminum: how to join by brazing, soldering, & gluing: RC F

V. Articles

73 10/2:16
Anodizing: protecting aluminum: Aero My 74 39/460:238-240
Bending Sheet & Wire Stock: Aero F 74 39/457:83-85
Better Performance at Little Cost: soldering track & wire: MR S 71 38/9:31
Chemical Colouring of Metals: other than aluminum: Aero My 74 39/460:238-240
Cuttlefish Moulds: use for metal casting: MW O 73 2/2:86
An Etching Gimmick: rub-on transfer as etch resist, for making thin brass letters & numbers: NMRA Jl 72 37/11:42
Fuel Tank Making: Aero Mr 74 39/458:146-148
Grab Irons Made Easy: NMRA S 75 41/1:60
Handtool Use: Aero Ja 74 39/456:33-36
Hard Soldering: Aero Mr 74 39/458:146-148
How to Make Parts with Brass: MR Jl 71 38/7:44-46
Inexpensive Etching: using india ink for resist material, ammonium persulfate for etch: RMC O 71 40/5:42
Insect Pins: use in static scale: RT N 72 5/11:123
Introduction to Castings for Scratchbuilding: making brass patterns, etched details: MR Ja 73 40/1:79-84
Loco Cab Construction: sheet brass technique: RMC O 71 40/5: 40-41
Metal Cowling: CerroBend mold & vibrator-hammered aluminum sheet: AM S 74 78/9:21
Metal Work: sharpening knives, oil stone care, drilling balls, wire cabane struts, engine turning, drilling slots: Aero Ag 74 39/463:416-417+
Metric Coarse Thread: introduction to metric threads: MB F 73 23/266:58-59
Model Deterioration: how to prevent "metal disease" corrosion: Afx My 73 14/9:497
Modelling Ships in Tinplate: MB F 72 22/254:68-70
Notes on Photoetching: designing pattern to reduce area to be etched: MR Jl 71 38/7:72-73
Opening a Neat Loop in the End of a Small Coil Spring: NMRA Ag 73 38/12:41
Piano Wire: how to form & join: Aero Mr 74 39/458:146-148
Raised Letter Signs & Builders Plates: from photo-offset plates: MR Ap 71 38/4:50
Riveting: Aero My 74 39/460:238-240
Simulated Chain: braiding wires to resemble chain: NMRA Ja 75 40/5:65
Soldering: tools & techniques: RC Je 74 11/6:44-45+; Jl 74 11/7:45-49+
Steel Construction: tinplate construction of ship models: MB Ja 72 22/253:68-71
Stirrup Step Gimmick: made from stamped ladder stock: NMRA Mr 74 39/8:29
Tapping & Dieing: Aero Je 74 39/461:298-299+
Trolley Wire: correct scale size for various scales: NMRA O 71 37/2:11
Vacuum De-Airing: for better casting: MR S 75 42/9:68-70

Construction

(Plastics)

ABCs of Fiberglass: AM Ag 74 78/8:51-53
Acrylic Plastic for Modelbuilding: MR Jl 75 42/7:70-73
Advanced Fiberglass Mold Construction: RC S 72 9/9:52-57+
Building a Fiberglass Cowl the Easy-est Way: RC Ap 72 9/4:58+
Buy & Fly: laminate bending process for ARF construction: RC N 75 12/11:70-72
Cast & Stretch Molding: Afx Ja 73 14/5:261
Epoxy-Cast Detail Parts: silicone & resin casting: RMC Mr 75 43/10:34-35
Fiberglass: female molds: RC Jl 73 10/7:39-42+
Fiberglass & Foam Techniques: for formula racer aircraft: RC S 71 8/9:38-41+
Fiberglassing Wings: RC S 74 11/9:16
Fibreoptics for Modellers; MM N 75 5/11:657-658
Foam: use in fuselage construction & other applications: RC Ap 75 12/4:43-44+; My 75 12/5:70-71+; Je 75 12/6:67-69+
Foam Board: foam & paper construction material: RC Ag 74 11/8:58-59
Foam Techniques: use of high density foam: AM F 73 76/2:44-51+
Glass Reinforced Plastics: how to use: Aero S 73 38/452:501-503
Introduction to Castings for Scratchbuilding: silicone & resin: MR Ja 73 40/1:79-84
Make It Easy: shock absorbtion in flying models, silicone: Aero Ja 74 39/456:51
Model Deterioration: how to prevent reaction between vinyl & styrene model parts: Afx My 73 14/9:497
Modeling with Fiber Optics: MR Ap 73 40/4:52-58
Plastics: Show & Tell: see separate listing, immediately following
Plastruct Petro/Chem Refinery Kits: use of industrial planning model materials in railroad: RMC My 71 39/12:39-41
Self-Hardening Sealants for Axles & the Like: MR My 71 38/5:64-65
Simple Mould-Making: Silicone molds & resin casts: MM N 74 4/11:696
Stretching Sprue: how-to: Afx N 72 14/3:132
Styrene Fabrication: ladders & boxcar ribs, technique applicable to many repeated shapes: NMRA Ap 74 39/9:44-45
Vacuum De-Airing for Better Casting: MR S 75 42/9:68-70
Vacuum-Forming: including trouble-shooting chart: PAM Ja 75 8:131
Vacuum Molding Made Easy: RC aircraft applications: RCS S 75 1/5:51+
What Is Polystyrene?: IM Mr 75 11/2:19
Why Not Plastic/: use of polystyrene sheet in operating boat construction: MB Je 75 25/293:283-284

(Plastics: Show and Tell) [all RC]

Polystyrene: F 73 10/2:6+

High Impact Styrene: Mr 73 10/3:6+
Acrylics: Ap 73 10/4:6+
Nylon: My 73 10/5:6+
Polypropylene: Je 73 10/6:6+
Polyethylene: Jl 73 10/7:6+
Polycarbonate: Ag 73 10/8:50+
Fluropolyments: nylon-glass: S 73 10/9:39+
Identification Chart & Conclusion: O 73 10/10:57+

(Wood)

Balsa: grain, density, cutting: RC Ag 73 10/8:36-41+
More About Balsa & How to Work With It: glued-up balsa sheet preparation: RC N 73 10/11:38-39+
To Sand It Better: balsa sanding technique: FM My 75 78/5:41-43

(Miscellaneous)

Another Look at Lichen: MR N 74 41/11:86-87
Bargains: low-cost sources for standard model building supplies: RC Mr 73 10/3:67+
Carbon Fibre Reinforcement: Aero Ap 72 37/435:196-198
Casting Structures from Plaster: RMC F 74 42/9:29-33
Dentists Use Hydrocal: dental plaster: NMRA Jl 72 37/11:54
Dyeing Sawdust: with fabric dye, for scenery material: RMC S 73 42/4:48-49
Foliage Materials--Use a Variety: sources: RMC Ap 71 39/11:28-31
Modeling with Strathmore: RMC Jl 73 42/2:44-45
Shock Absorber Color Code: bungee color codes for dating 1969-1974: AM My 74 78/5:40
Silicone Rubber Tubing: FM Ag 72 75/8:16-17
Strathmore, a Versatile Construction Material: MR Je 74 41/6:81-84
Teflon-Loaded Lubricants: MR Mr 75 42/3:35
Try Cardboard: corrugated cardboard as a balsa substitute: AM N 72 75/5:31-32+
Use Clay to Build Models: potters clay: MR S 73 40/9:61-63
Wood Nut Wing Mount Bolt: wing mounting hardware: RC Ap 73 10/4:48-49

AIRCRAFT--OPERATING

<u>General</u>

General Techniques

A-2 Construction: catahooks, fuselage joints: Aero Jl 75 40/474:

Construction

724-725

Aerial Movie Making: techniques & modifications to a/c for 8mm movie making: RC Je 71 8/6:72-75
Aerodynamic Balancing: RC Je 75 12/6:31
Balancing Made Easy: calculating weight amount & distribution in aircraft: RC Ag 74 11/8:60
Building Better Bipes: RC stunt biplanes: RCS Je 75 1/2:46-48+ ; Jl 75 1/3:55-57+
Build a Little Better: Aero Je 72 37/437:319-321
Cheaper by the Dozen: production-line techniques in model plane construction: MAN Ja 75 90/1:53-55
Combat Hints: construction techniques: Aero Mr 74 40/470:170-171
Construction Techniques for Formula Racers: use of fiberglas & foam: RC S 71 8/9:38-41+
A Few Ideas Utilising a Band Saw: use in flying model construction: Aero My 75 40/472:284
Fiberglass: female molding techniques: RC Jl 73 10/7:39-42+
Foam Techniques: high density foam construction: AM F 73 76/2: 44-51+
Full Length Surface Hinges from Monokote: RC S 71 8/9:44
Interface Design: plastic joining techniques: RC Mr 73 10/3:110
Laminated Structures: Aero F 74 39/457:81-82
Letters to a Young Modeller: basic construction: Aero Jl 74 39/462:357-359; Mr 75 40/470:160-161
Lighten the Load: keeping weight down in CL stunt: Aero Ja 74 39/456:28-29
The Lost Wax Process: paraffin for molding fiberglass into odd configurations: FM Ag 72 75/8:34-36
Mass Production: FM Ag 75 78/8:43-48
Motorized Modelling: use of buzz saw to mass-produce parts: Aero Mr 72 37/434:164-166
Surface Detailing: rivets, panel lines, fabric tape, canopy details: RC D 72 9/12:12+
Ten Steps to Lining up Your Plane: trammelling: RC F 71 8/2: 36-37

Strengthening

Carbon Fibre Reinforcement: Aero Ap 72 37/435:196-198
Combat Hints: strength without undue weight for combat CL: Aero Mr 75 40/470:170-171
Laminated Structures: Aero F 74 39/457:81-82
Superstructure: construction to resist damage: RC N 71 8/11:36-37

Flying Scale

Best Airplane for Scale RC: how to match design with rules: RC D 71 8/12:12+
CL Scale: panel lines, rivets, toggle switches: MAN Mr 73 86/3: 21-23+

V. Articles

Cockpit: design & construction for flying scale: AM S 74 78/9:16-17+
Cockpit Detail: RC Ja 72 9/1:12+; Mr 72 9/3:12+
Detailing the SE5a: AM O 73 77/4:72-73
Fairey Youngman flaps: design of Fairey Firefly flaps: AM Ap 74 78/4:44
Flying Scale Models: see separate listing, immediately following
Framed: vacuum-forming cockpit frames: AM Ag 74 78/8:64
Instrument Panels: flying scale instrument panels: RC My 72 9/5:12+
Light Blinker for Wingtip Lights: AM Ag 73 77/2:66
Lighted Instrument Panels: AM Ag 71 73/2:42
Lightweight Flying Scale: all balsa free flight: Sc S 71 2/9:485-489
Little Time to Spare? Modify a Kit: conversions for stand-off scale: RCS Je 75 1/2:55-57
Metal Plate Seams: metal panel lines in three-dimensions: MAN S 71 83/3:30+
PPP: Polystyrene & paper pilots: crew for flying scale: Aero F 75 40/469:100
Pilot Detailing: painting techniques for RC pilot figures: RCMr 71 8/3:28-31
Scale Antenna Ties: antenna splicing for prototypes: AM F 72 74/2:50
Scale Sliding Canopies: RCN 75 12/11:54
Simulated Fabric Covering: AM Ag 74 78/8:64
Throttled Cat: how to throttle CL PBY or other twin: Aero Je 71 36/425:327

(Flying Scale Models) [all Aero]

Introduction: MR 71 36/422:153-155
Selection of Prototype: aerodynamic suitability: Ap 71 36;423:153-155
Design Features: overall configuration & power plant: My 71 36/424:250-253
Fuselage Construction: Je 71 36/425:310-313
Rigging & Wing Attachment: Jl 71 36/426:380-383
Wing & Tailplane Construction: Ag 71 36/427:436-439
Covering the Airframe: S 71 36/428:496-498
Applying the Finish: O 71 26/429:558-560
Important Detail Parts: props, cowls, engine details: N 71 26/430:619-622
Important Details: cockpit, pilots, guns, landing gear, lacing: D 71 26/431:678-681
Initial Test Flying: Ja 72 37/432:18-21
Contents: F 72 37/433:94-96
Conclusion: Mr 72 37/434:154-156

Helicopter

5' Hiller Rotor: sp: AM S 72 75/3:43
Fuselage Design: box to inclose all components: AM N 72 75/5: 65-66
Hiller Type Rotor Head: AM N 71 73/5:38
Tubie's Tail Rotor, Drive & Control: AM Ag 72 75/2:65
2-B Helicopter Drive System: AM My 72 74/5:65

Repair

Bilgri Patching & Covering Methods: microfilm: AM Mr 71 72/3: 25-27
Custom Techniques for Plastic & Fiberglass ARFs: RC Jl 71 8/7: 25
Repair: Aero Ap 71 36/423:208-210; My 71 36/424:264-266
Repairs: Aero Jl 73 36/450:384-386
Super Fireball: restoring spark-ignition CL: MAN Jl 75 91/1:17-19+
Tire Repair: fixing flat non-inflatable pneumatic tires: RC S 71 8/9:51

Components

Fuselage

Advanced Fiberglass Mold Construction: male mold: RC S 72 9/9: 52-57+
Another Way to Make a Cowl: 1/32" plywood & resin: RC Je 74 11/6:58-59
Building a Fiberglass Cowl: RC Ap 72 9/4:58+
Building on a Tube: tube-core fuselage construction: RC S 74 11/9: 64-65
Catahook & Fuselage Joint: Aero Jl 75 40/474:724-725
Circular Towhooks: 3 variants: Aero Jl 75 40/474:730-731+
Cockpit Canopies: RC F 71 8/2:14+
Coupe Motor Tubes: CdH: Aero D 74 39/467:681-683
Crutch Fuselage: Aero D 73 38/455:676-679
Easy Way to Face Nose Blocks: faring cowl to prop/spinner unit: RC Ag 75 12/8:67
Hatch Latch: how to make: RC S 74 11/9:117
The Fancy Towhooks: for circular tow: FM Ja 74 77/1:41-47
Fiberglass Cowlings: RC S 73 10/9:6+
Fiberglass Fuselage: MAN O 75 91/4:17-19+
Foam Techniques: high density foam construction: AM F 73 76/2:44-51+
Fuselage Bracing: indoor motor tube bracing: AM O 72 75/4:64
Fuselage Construction: Aero Je 71 36/425:310-313
How to Make Windshields: for open cockpits: RC Je 74 11/6:57

V. Articles

Indoor Wing Sockets: how to build: AM Mr 71 72/3:37
Installing Canopies over Monokote: RC Je 73 10/6:58
Lightweight Cockpit Interiors for stunters: ss fittings for flying non-scale: FM F 75 78/2:38-44
Molded Balsa Ply: sheet balsa plywood fuselage made over solid core: RC Je 71 8/6:38-41+
Molded Wing Saddles: from silastic: RC Je 71 8/6:42
Nordic Boom Flex Joint: break-away fuselage joint for nordic crashes: AM Je 71 72/6:34
PPP... Polystyrene & Paper Pilots: Aero F 75 40/469:100
Pilot: modeling crew for flying models: AM Mr 75 75/3:12-13
Protecting Fuselage from Rubber Lubricant: Aero Ja 75 40/468:47
Rolled Plywood Booms: for FF & RC fuselages: Aero Ja 74 39/456:43-44
Splicing & Steaming Square Balsa Strips: Aero F 73 38/445:79+

Landing Gears

Almost Round: working spoked wheels: FM Ag 71 413:36-37
Aluminum Skis: RC Mr 75 12/3:46-47+
Antique or Old Timer Floats: for ROW Old Timer conv: RC My 75 12/5:31
Aqua-Vent Floats: twin float with air introduced to break suction: AM S 72 75/3:38-41+
Ball Bearings for RC Landing Gear: RC 75 12/10:39
Bent Wire Tip-Skids: for team racers: Aero Mr 74 39/458:153
Build Your Own Retractable Gear: plans: RC Ja 71 8/1:32-37+
Carrier Hook: for carrier event: AM O 72 75/4:60-61
Detachable Nose Skids for Team Racers: Aero Je 74 39/461:293
Easy Wire Bending: for accurate landing gear struts: RC Mr 74 11/3:58
Floats: sl for RC helicopters: RC My 74 11/5:30-33
Handyman's Retracts: Pneumatic system: AM D 74 74/12:68-71
LG Doors: actuator for doors open only during LG movement: AM S 73 77/3:22-23
Make Your Own Retracts: AM Ja 72 74/1:16-17+
Pick Up That Dragging Tail: retracting tail wheels: AM Mr 75 75 /3:113
Plywood Skis: RC Mr 74 11/3:58-59
Positive, No-Load Mechanical Brake: elevator actuated, tire rotation powered: RC Je 71 8/6:44-45
Quick Float: flat single float for ROW: AM My 73 76/5:62-64+
RCM Floats: Edo type for RCM Trainer: RC Ap 74 11/4:49-51+
ROS: ski construction: RC F 73 10/2:48-49+
Real Retracts for the Phony Folkerts: AM Jl 74 78/7:47-48+
Retract Mods 90° Swing: MAN Mr 75 90/3:57-58+
Retractable Floats: RCS Ap 75 1/1:22-25+
Retractable Gear Doors: AM My 74 78/5:72
Retracting Gear Doors: AM My 74 78/5:72-74+
Retracts: RC Ag 73 10/8:30+
Shaft Collars: wheel retainers: AM Je 73 76/6:18
Shock Absorbing Nose Wheel Linkage: RC Je 71 8/6:44

Simple Effective Mechanical Brakes: drag on tire: RC F 71 8/2: 35
Skis: plywood & foam designs: MAN Mr 74 88/3:33
Snow Ski: balsa: AM Mr 74 78/3:46
Tail-Draggers; RC S 75 12/9:12+
Wheel Pants: plywood & foam: RC S 75 12/9:53
Wing Gear Retraction: RC Je 71 8/6:28-29
Wire Spoke Wheels: how to make: MAN Mr 72 84/3:78-79+

Power Mounting

Auxiliary Power Pod: A, for powered gliders: FM Ap 74 77/4: 36-37
Kraft Hayes Glass Filled Engine Mount: how to use beam mounting bracket: RC My 74 11/5:10
Power Pod for T.W.O.: A: FM Jl 75 78/7:33
Snoopy Goes Electric: modifying for electric power: RC F 75 12/2:26-29

Wing & Stab

Aluminum Wings: offset printing plates skin material: AM Ap 73 76/4:40-41+
Burying Leadouts: for control line wings: Aero N 73 38/454:632-633
D-Tube Construction: sparless, sheet balsa-covered construction: AM Mr 71 72/3:36
Dethermalizer: pop-up stab construction: Aero Je 73 38/449:306-307
Easy to Make Wood & Metal Wing Struts: RC Jl 74 11/7:57
Easy Wing Struts: detachable wing braces: RC Jl 72 9/7:46
Fiberglassing Wings: RC S 74 11/9:16
Flying Wire Fabrication: working wing rigging: RC F 75 12/2:41
Foam Techniques: high density foam construction: AM F 73 76/2: 48-51+
Foam Wing Construction for Combat: MAN Je 71 82/6:20
Full Length Control Hinges from Monokote: RC S 71 8/9:44
Glass Fibre Wing Fillets: Aero Mr 71 12/7:138
Hollo-Foam Wings: commercial item: RC Ja 75 12/1:46-50+
Insetting: wood, LGs, bellcranks, etc. in foam wings: Aero Jl 75 40/474:747
Kit Wing Construction: Aero O 73 38/453:544-545+
Magnum 400: variable pitch wing: RCS Ap 75 1/1:54-56
Moulded Leading Edges: Aero Ap 74 39/459:186-187+
Reinforcing Wing Center Sections: RC D 75 12/12:44
Rib & Multi-Spar Construction: Aero Mr 73 38/446:137-139
Rib Wings: Aero N 73 38/454:614-615+
Robert Hinge Point: hinge mounting techniques for various applications: RC Je 72 9/6:62
Sandwitched Ribs: for tapered wings: AM Jl 74 78/7:24
Sheet Construction: all balsa wings: Aero Mr 74 39/458:140-142

V. Articles

Sliced Ribs: indoor rib layout: AM S 71 73/3:43
T-Tail: hinge & linkage for T-tail sailplanes: RC Ja 71 8/1:21
Tail Bracing: indoor: AM S 72 75/4:45
Warps--How to Avoid 'Em: Aero F 75 40/469:94
Wing & Stab Construction: AM Ag 71 73/2:45; S 71 73/3:46
Wing & Tailplane Construction: Aero Ag 71 36/427:436-439
Wing Bracing for Beginner Models: indoor wings: AM My 72 74/5:61; Je 72 74/6; Jl 72 75/1:44-45; Ag 72 75/2:59
Wing Rigging: peanut scale: AM Jl 72 75/1:45

ARMOR--OPERATING

RC Elephant: power & control using Mecanno treads: MM Ja 73 3/1:36-38

BOATS--OPERATING

General

Bow Fender for Model Yachts: silicone & wire: MB Ja 75 25/288:23
Bow Fenders for RC Tugs: FM F 75 78/2:64-65
Capitol Ships in Miniature: operating warship construction: MB Jl 72 22/259:286-287+
SY Cardella: cardboard hull for steam yacht: MB Jl 75 25/294:333-335+
Casting Yacht Ballast: keel weight making: MB Ap 73 23/267:163-164
Functional Ventilators: MB My 75 25/292:242-243
Glass-Fibre Lifeboat Model: techniques: MB N 73 23/275:462-463+; D 73 23/276:514-516; Ja 74 24/277:18-19; Mr 74 24 279:86-87
High Performance Hydros: waterproofing the antenna lead: RC Ag 75 12/8:66
Making a Hull for Eppleton Hall: all metal working ship hull construction: FM My 74 77/5:59-61
Model Racing Yacht Construction: see separate listing, immediately following
Modelling Ships in Tinplate: MB F 72 22/253:68-70
New Fawn: scale power construction: FM Je 74 77/6:64-65
Notes on Metal Ship Construction: metal hull making: MB F 73 23/266:64-65
Plastic Building from Scratch: use of foam & styrene sheet in operating boats: MB Ag 75 25/295:415+
Railings Aboard Ship: FM D 74 77/12:63
Round Hulls in Wood: rib & plant construction for extreme tumblehome Marbleheads: MB N 74 24/286:472-474

Sails & Masts: masts with grooves for sail lufts: FM Ag 74 77/8:59-62
Scratch Building RC Sail Yachts: RC Ag 73 10/8:31-35+; S 73 10/9:56-59+; O 73 10/10:59+
Steel Construction: tinplate construction technique: MB Ja 72 22/253:68-71
Tornado: racing yacht techniques: MB S 71 21/249:356-357
Vibration: how to damp in boats: FM S 74 77/9:63

(Model Racing Yacht Construction) [all MB]

[series started in Je 70]
Keel Casting: two piece: Ja 71 21/241:16-17
Fittings: mast slide, mast bands, spreaders, gooseneck, metal mast: F 71 21/242:61-65
Mast & Booms: Mr 71 21/243:116-119+
Erection: mast, jib horse, rudder & fittings, spinaker, hardware: My 71 21/245:186-189
Vane Gears: qualities, details of moving carriage system: Je 71 21/246:236-239
Vane Gears: break-back system: Jl 71 21/247:286-288
Vane Feathers, Sychronous Sheeting, Sails, & Spinnakers: Ag 71 21/248:324-326
Sail Making: S 71 21/249:370-372
Checking All-Up Weight & Trim: O 71 21/250:415-418
Alignment: N 71 21/251:458-460
Conclusion: D 71 21/252:512-513

Repair

Repairing a Fiberglass Boat: FM F 74 77/2:64-65

Sails

Double Luff Sails: MB S 73 23/273:380-381
Making a Spinnaker: MB S 73 23/273:377
Sailmaking: MB Ap 71 21/244:164-165
Sails: intro to sail construction: MB O 72 22/262:435-436+
Sails: RC O 73 10/10:59+

RAILROAD--OPERATING

Layouts

Arm Rests: to prevent leaning on layout: RMC F 75 43/9:42-43
Beverage Holders: to keep off of layouts: RMC F 75 43/9:43
Brandywine Transit Co.: MR My 75 42/5:5054; Jl 75 42/6:60-64;

S 75 42/9:72-76; N 75 42/11:80-81
Building the Bantam & Cycloid RR: MR Ap 75 42/4:74-75; My 75 42/5:72; Je 75 42/6:72-73
Charles Small's LG&B TT: Gm outdoor: MR Ap 72 39/4:58-65
Design for Foldaway Layout: MR N 74 41/11:92-93
Dust Covers: RMC F 75 43/9:42
Easing the Tops & Bottoms of Grades: plotting transitions: MR N 74 41/11:79-81
East Glasstop: N gauge coffee table: see separate listing, immediately following
Experiences with Suspended Layouts: NMRA Jl 73 38/11:11-12
Fairmount Traction Co.: the vertical module: traction unit that inserts into regular layout: RMC D 74 43/7:46-47
Fold-Away Model Railroad Platform: mat, 2-6x14 layout folds into wall: RMC D 73 42/7:37-41
Kinnickinnic Railway & Dock: see separate listing, following
Marquette & Independence: MR D 75 42/12:62-68; to be continued
A Modular Switchback Trackplan: hiding the joints: RMC S 73 42/4:46-47
NTRAK: modular layout to be built at shows from 8' sections prebuild by modelers: NMRA F 74 39/7:16-18
Pieces of Sunset: modular layout construction: MR N 73 40/11:68-70
Rochester Regional RR: MR F 74 41/2:55-58; Mr 74 41/3:56-61
Scenic Modules: as dioramas before ultimate incorporation into layout: RMC O 75 44/5:40
Site Labels: RMC F 75 43/9:43
Space-Saving Control Panel: slide-out, tilt-up: RMC Ap 72 40/11:48-49
Takeout Layouts: removeable module for exhibitions: MR Je 73 40/6:56-57
Three in One Benchwork: with built-in storage below: MR O 72 39/10:63-64
Truss Module Framework: girders of $\frac{1}{2}$" square wood for frame: NMRA My 75 40/9:36-37
Try a Trundle Layout: MR N 73 40/11:59
Under-Layout Space Usage: workbench, mat: RMC Ja 71 39/8:44-45
Ups & Downs of the Frances Lines: suspended layout: NMRA Jl 73 38/11:13-18
Whatta Way to Spend a Sunny Afternoon!: outdoor O gauge construction: RMC S 75 44/4:40-43
You Can Take it With You--the Whole Railroad: modular construction: MR Je 74 41/6:60-63

(East Glasstop) [all MR]

[series started in 1970]
Laying Track: Ja 71 38/1:66-71
Up & Over: bridge, trestle, & tunnel: F 71 38/2:53-57
Wiring: MR 71 38/:51-54
Scenery & Structures: Ap 71 38/4:30-35

Construction

(Kinnickinnic Railway & Dock) [all MR]

Benchwork: Ja 72 39/1:60-64
Track, Switch Machines & Ground Throw Switchstands: F 72 39/2: 51-54
Wiring: MR 39/3:52-57
Hard Shell Terrain: My 72 39/5:36-39
Color, Foliage, & Details: Jl 72 39/7:36-40

Lighting

Blacklight Magic: intro to use of ultraviolet: MR O 71 38/10:35
Diode Lightning for Locomotives & Cars: wd, steady lighting: MR My 74 41/5:61
Dome Flasher for Locomotives or Cabooses: wd, mat, pph: MR Ap 73 40/4:72-73
Dozens of Streetlights: jig construction using grain-of-wheat bulb & conducting stand: MR Ja 75 40/1:64-65
Flashing Lights Plus: wd: NMRA Ag 75 40/12:50; cor N 75 41/3: 70
Install Working Headlights: for locomotives: MR Jl 73 40/7:66
Lighting the Layout: MR N 74 41/11:90-91
Lights & Markers for Cars: MR Mr 73 40/3:38+
Modeling with Fiber Optics: MR Ap 73 40/4:52-58
Practical Layout Lighting: Christmas tree bulbs & dimmers: MR Jl 74 41/7:51
Using PFM Miniature Bulbs to Make Classification Lights: RMC Je 73 42/1:43-44
A Working Track Diagram: for inside signal tower, fiberoptics: MR Jl 74 41/7:62

Operating Scenery/Accessories

Operating Clamshell Bucket: MR My 73 40/5:80
Road Vehicle Operation: methods for powering cars in layouts: MR Je 71 38/6:73
Working Windmill: motor under, from Campbell windmill & scrap watch gears: NMRA S 74 40/1:22-23

Rolling Stock

Construction

Achieving that "Sway Back" Look: old cable-truss cars: RMC S

V. Articles

75 44/4:52-54
Another Drop in the Bucket: concealing track cleaners under scale rolling stock: NMRA N 75 41/3:56-57
Another Way to Finish Monitor Roof Ends: NMRA S 73 39/1:24
Average Modeler, Above-Average Model: techniques: MR D 73 40/12:84-88
Basic House Car Construction: MR Ja 72 39/1:70-71
Boiler, Frame, & Cylinder Fastening Methods for Model Steam Locos: MR Ja 72 39/1:81-83
Build Your Printed Side Bulletin Reefer from what you have handy: NMRA Ja 74 39/5:59
CP Unit Coal Gondola: silicone molding: MR O 71 38/10:38-39
Diaphragms: beveled striker plate edges to prevent catching on curves: NMRA Jl 75 40/11:27
Easiest Detailing: detailing caboose with stock parts: MR D 73 40/12:71
Epoxy-Cast Detail parts: rubber molds for N passenger car steps: RMC Mr 75 43/10:34-35
Loco Cab Construction: brass techniques: RMC O 71 40/5:40-41
The Locomotive You Wanted but Couldn't Get: converting locos with styrene sheet: MR O 74 41/10:40-43+
Logs from Balsa: timber line loads: RMC Jl 73 42/2:49
Magnetic Couplers for O scale: MR My 72 39/5:62-65; Je 72 39/6:58-59; Ag 72 39/8:58-59
Making Car Roofs Removeable: MR S 71 38/9:73-76
Messiness with a Flair: clutter detail inside rolling stock: MR Mr 75 42/3:49
Modeling Modern Cabooses: MR Je 74 41/6:42-43
Modifying Ready-to-Run Passenger Cars: RMC Mr 71 38/10:42-44
Moveable Draft Gear for Long Cars: to prevent derailment on curves: MR N 75 42/11:56
Niles Interurban in N Scale: scratchbuilding with commercial parts: RMC O 71 40/5:27-28
Scrap Iron Load for a Gondola: metal bales from aluminum foil: RMC Je 72 41/4:41
Scratch Building Reefers: NMRA D 72 38/4:23
Scratchbuilder's Locomotive Kinks: how to fit a motor into a tight space: MR Mr 74 41/3:48-49
Scratchbuilding N Scale Passenger Cars: RMC Ap 72 40/11:24-27
Sliding Box Car Doors: NMRA Ja 73 38/5:20
Sunset Valley's Neat Cabeese: free lance conversions, how to: MR Jl 73 40/7:38-39
3' Caboose EBT Style: RMC My 74 42/12:31-34
Walthers Fine Passenger Car Kit: improvements in windows & roof hold-down: NMRA Je 75 40/10:46
What About the Works Underneath: into to loco conversions in the working parts: MR Mr 75 42/3:41

Kit Improvement

Kitbashing Big Juice Jacks in N Scale: large electric loco conversions in N: RMC Ag 75 44/3:54-55

Construction

Loco with Double Chain Drive: MR O 71 38/10:68-69
Making the Ready to Run more Ready: MR Je 74 41/6:66-72
Modifying the IHB 0-8-0: increasing motor size: MR S 71 38/9: 36-41
Observation Interior Observations: NMRA Ap 75 40/8:42+
Posidrive for Suydam: for gas-electric car: NMRA Ja 74 39/5: 20-21
Reducing Oversize Flanges: how to, with a small lathe: MR Mr 75 42/3:52
Regearing the Roundhouse Diesel: for better slow speed performance: NMRA O 72 38/2:227
Regearing the Roundhouse Switcher: NMRA Je 74 39/11:20-21
Regearing a Wagner Inch-66 Truck: to take 65% grade: NMRA Ag 75 40/12:58-59
Slow Down Speedy Suydam: regearing: NMRA Ag 73 38/12:11-12
Track Slider Pickup: from printed circuit board material: NMRA D 75 41/4:24
Truck Centering Springs for Locos: MR Mr 71 38/3:40-42
Uni-Drive Compact Locomotive Drive Unit: NMRA S 75 41/1:31-33
Weighting Cars: for better track-keeping: MR My 73 40/5:77-79
Why Side Rods will Bind: improving locos: MR F 71 38/2:67-68

Signaling Equipment

Slow Semaphore: control system for slow movement of semaphore arm: MR Mr 74 41/3:76

Track

Better Performance at Little Cost: track alignment: MR O 71 38/10:33
Building a Spring Switch: RMC S 74 43/4:54-55; O 74 43/5:52-53
Detailing the Right of Way: track, ballast & trackside detailing: MR Ap 74 41/4:36-38
Foam Tape Roadbed: RMC Ja 71 39/8:46-48
How to Build Switchstands: MR Mr 75 42/3:50-51
Insulated Frogs: NMRA My 71 36/9:18
Jig-Made Epoxy-Mounted Switches: MR Mr 73 40/3:36-37
Keeping in Line: tracklaying: NMRA O 75 41/2:46-48
London's Benchwork & Tracklaying: MR My 73 40/3:36-40
On Track & Ballast: RMC D 73 42/7:51-54
Operational Large-Scale Switch Stands: RMC Ap 75 43/11:54-56
Rail & Ballast: NMRA Ag 73 38/12:18-20
Rail Expansion Joints: bridges, etc.: RMC F 75 43/9:44-45
Simulating Prototype Trackway: MR Jl 73 40/7:30-33
A Split Derail: RMC Jl 74 43/2:37
Superelevation: NMRA Je 73 38/10:26-27
A System for Handlaying Track: curved turnout construction: MR

V. Articles 402

Je 75 42/6:62-63
Traction Roadbed: 4 variants, dim: NMRA F 75 40/6:60
Wye Polarity: wiring: NMRA D 72 38/4:33
Yardsticks and Matches: yardstick roadbed & matchstick ballast filler: NMRA O 75 41/2:56

Traction

Axle Hung Motor Drive: NMRA My 75 40/9:31-32
Bob Hegge Builds a Brill Combine: mat: RMC O 72 41/5:30-36
Catenary on the Idaho Midland: overhead electric: MR Je 71 38/6: 40-42
Deck-Roof City Street Car: exploded sk, sec: NMRA My 74 39/10: 18
Double Jointed Drawbars: traction couplers: NMRA Ag 72 37/13: 43
Hanging Catenary for Pantograph & Bow Collectors: MR O 73 40/10:56-60
Having Fun with Belts & Bands for Traction: NMRA D 73 39/4:42-43
Improving Trolley Pole Operation: shoe construction: NMRA Mr 73 38/7:51
Improving Trolley Pole Tracking: mods: NMRA F 74 39/7:29+
Magnetic Couplers in Radial Mounts: traction couplers: NMRA Ap 75 40/8:56-57
Make Your Own Trucks: NMRA Ja 73 38/5:25
Making Built-Up Old Time Street Car Bodies: NMRA N 72 38/3:11
Method of Making Rod or Bar Window Guards: NMRA S 72 38/1:32
Overhead Wire for Pole Trolleys: MR Mr 75 42/3:56-61
Pantographs that Work Smoothly: MR My 74 41/5:37-39
Power for Open Bench Trolleys: NMRA Mr 72 37/7:39
Problem of Couplers for HO Traction: NMRA Ag 74 39/13:22-23
Shoe & Frog for Trolley: RMC Jl 71 40/2:46
Trolley Pole Reverse with a Single Pole: moving pole reverses polarity: NMRA My 75 40/9:33-34

Turntables

Automatic Turntable Indexing: MR Mr 73 40/3:50-51
Display Motor Drive for Turntable: NMRA N 73 39/3:44-45
Turntable Operating Mechanism: wd: NMRA Ja 75 40/5:41-44+
Unbreakable Turntable: metal construction: NMRA O 73 39/2:39-40
A Unique Turntable Bearing: aircraft control cable pulley, built-in motor & control: NMRA Ag 72 37/13:22-24

Yard Equipment

Box Car Under Repair: being sheathed, with equipment: NMRA My 71 36/9:34-35
Modeling Pallets for Shipments: trackside clutter: MR Ja 74 41/1:80-81
Railway Ice Specifications: dimensions of blocks: MR N 75 42/11:114

Miscellaneous

Catenary on the Idaho Midland: overhead electric: MR Je 71 38/6:40-42
Inexpensive Turnout Control: blade of spdt knife switch actuates turnout by weighted string and signal by circuit: MR F 71 38/2:85
Piece-Part Approach to Locomotive Scratchbuilding: built-up details rather than simulated basic shape: MR S 74 41/9:67-70
Solid Telltales: all-metal construction: NMRA Ja 74 39/5:25

STATIC SCALE

General

Back to Baseics: model decorated base design & construction: MM Mr 75 5/3:152-153
Cardboard Modelling: techniques: Sc Mr 71 2/3:124-127; Jl 71 2/7:351-353
Casting Spackle: how to use spackling plaster: FuS W 74 1/2:41-42
Cuttlefish Moulds: MW O 73 2/2:86
Detailing Transparencies: lights: RiS Ag 72 1/1:27
Finish & Detailing: IM N 72 8/11:2-3
Insect Pins: uses as modeling material: RT N 72 5/11:123
Moulding: Plasticine & resin: MM O 74 4/10:589
Non-Dioramic Display Bases: decorative base mountings for aircraft: RiS Sp 74 2/3-4:121-123
Parts: liquid masker as mold compound: RT D 72 5/12:141
Parts: molding parts from polyester with latex (plaster backed) molds: RT D 72 5/12:141
Plastic Card: use in conversions & scratch-building: Afx N 73 15/3:152
The Pyrogravure: how to use: MM D 73 3/12:834-835
Rivet-Making: for armor: MM Jl 75 5/7:424
Simple Mould Making: Plasticine & resin: MM N 74 4/11:696
Stretch-Forming--the Poor Man's Vacuform: RT Jl 75 5/7:78

Uncle Freddie Shovels It Up: bleach for plastic model paint stripping: RT Ja 75 8/1:3
What is Photo-Etching: Method of making very small detailed parts: Sc N 73 4/11:773-775

Aircraft

Agricultural Aircraft: conversion techniques: Afx O 71 13/2:80-82
Attention to Details: cockpits: Sc Mr 71 2/3:128-131
Cerro-Safe: low melting point metal to weight tricycle gear aircraft: RiS N 72 1/2:69
Custom-Built Exhausts: superdetailing molded-on exhausts: IM N 74 10/19:16
Detailing Aircraft Model Cockpits: WW2J Jl 75 2/4:22-23
Detailing Transparencies: aircraft lights: RiS Ag 72 1/1:27
Detailing Wheel Wells: RiS Su 73 1/4:134
Details: instrument panels, consoles, seat belts, & ordinance: RT N 73 6/11:123
The Inside Story: cockpit detailing: AI N 74 7/5:245
Large Scale Canopy: detailing techniques: RT Ja 74 7/1:3
Making Gun Troughs: in fuselages: RT O 73 6/10:120
Modeling the Biplane: superdetailing techniques: RiS Au 73 2/1:32-33
Motorizing Model Aircraft: to spin props for display or photography: Afx S 75 17/1:31-34
1/24 Flier: operating controls in 1/24 scale aircraft: RT Je 73 6/6:63/64
Perpetuating the Pristine: care of models after completion, repairs: AE O 73 5/4:195
Prop Bending: factors affecting bending of props in gear-up landings: RT My 73 6/5:49
The Question of Suitable Support: LG superdetailing: AE S 74 7/3:135
Rigging Biplanes: IM Je 72 9/6:15
Scratch-Building--Why Not?: see separate listing
Whittle or Waffle?: intro to plastic conversions: AN 4 Ag 72 1/6:14
Wing Fences: accurate construction on plastic models: RiS Ag 72 1/1:32

(Scratch-Building) [all IM]

What It Can & Can't Do: Ap 72 9/4:1-2
Features of Plastic: selecting a subject: My 72 9/5:1-2+
Solid Fuselage Carving: Je 72 9/6:1-3
Vacuum Moulding Fuselages: Jl 72 9/7:2-4
Wing Construction Techniques: Ag 72 9/8:2-3
Surface Details, Biplane Rigging: S 72 9/9:2

Armor

APC & How to Scratchbuild 'Em in Large Scale: MM Ja 72 2/1: 34-35
BMW R-75: scratch motorcycle techniques: Sc Ja 72 3/1:22-29
8th Army in the Desert: see separate listing under scale plans, figures, armies & under history, armies
Elmer's Treads: scratchbuilding tank treads from plaster molds & white glue: Q Ja 73 8/1:41
Guns: muzzle brakes: RT Ja 72 5/1:11
Hinges that Work: AFV F 71 2/11:21
M-3 in 1/32: techniques: MM N 73 3/11:744-745
Modeling Armor in Wood: scratch techniques: AFV Je 75 5/5:33-36+
On the Grand Scale: scratch artillery: MM N 72 2/11:580-582
Plastic AFV: kit construction techniques: MM O 73 2/11:580-582
Scratch-Building Larger Scale AFVs: MM O 71 1/10:504-505+
Scratchbuilding Large Scale Tanks: Afx Ap 75 16/8:465-469; My 75 16-9:536-540
Scratchbuilding Period Guns: intro to muzzle-loading artillery: MM Ap 72 2/4:184-187; My 72 2/5:246-247
The Tank That Never Was: scratch techniques in Maus model: Fus Su 74 1/4:42-44+
WW-I Machine Gun Combination: scratch techniques for motorcycles: MM Mr 71 1/3:126-129
Working Door Lock: 1/35 & larger: Sc Je 72 3/6:318
Working Doors for Tamiya Kübelwagen: AFV N 71 3/3:27+

Ancient & Medieval Weaponry

Making a Siege Tower: Afx My 71 12/9:460-461
Medieval Guns & Cannons: Afx N 71 13/3:148-149
Medieval Siege Artillery: Afx Je 71 12/10:516-517
Medieval Siege Weapons: Afx Jl 71 12/11:592-593
More Medieval Siege Equipment: Afx O 71 13/2:78-79

Automobiles

Carlton Racing Cycle: 1/8 scratch techniques: Sc D 74 5/12:644-645
Classics in Metal: assembling die cast car kits: Sc Je 73 4/6:438-439
Motoring History in Card: cycle & car engine techniques: Sc My 73 4/5:317+
Superdetailing Model Cars: Afx Ja 73 14/5:287
Trucks of the '40s: conversions using Matchbox & AHM ready-built trucks: RMC S 72 41/4:37

V. Articles

Bridges

Bash a Bridge: conversion techniques: MR O 73 40/10:54-55
Trestle Bridges: Afx D 71 13/4:196-197; Ja 72 13/5:154-155

Diorama

Bandai Possibilities: 1/48 armor designs, armor diorama construction: MM Jl 73 3/7:452-454
Basic Stonework Effects for Layouts & Dioramas: MW N 73 2/3: 147-148
Box Dioramas: small forced-perspective dioramas for figures: MM Jl 72 2/7:346-347
Circa Thirty Display: railroad & traction diorama with lighting & slide projectors: MR Ap 75 42/4:52-56
The Complete Diorama Builder: excluding anachronisms, selecting materials, techniques: WW2J My 75 2/3:102-107
Details for Desert Dioramas: German vehicle breakdown types: WWE N 74 1/6:185+
Diorama Walls: brick & stone simulation: RiS Ag 72 1/1:34
Dioramas with Buildings: MW Jl 73 1/11:597-598+
Improving the Scene: construction hints: Sc O 74 5/10:529
Is Your Railroad a Ghost?: figures in a layout: NMRA Ag 73 38/12:41
Mini-Diorama Bases: Afx O 71 13/2:92-93
Modeling in the Meantime: dioramas until pike space is obtained: NMRA F 75 40/6:7-12
RAF Aerodrome: design & construction: Sc Mr 75 6/3:138-141; Ap 75 5/4:194-197
Settings for the 8.8 cm Flak 36: several diorama designs: MW My 73 1/9:476-478
Small Base Figure Dioramas: Afx N 73 15/3:148
Snow & Stuff: winter diorama construction: RT S 73 6/9:103

Figures

Anatomy of a Prize-Winning Figure: posing-conversions of lead figures: Fus Au 73 2/1:35-36
Byzantine conversions: mail, helmets, standards, weapons: MM Mr 73 3/3:152-153
Byzantine Strategos: conversion techniques: MM My 71 1/8:396-397
Cast Your Own Figures: silicone mold making: MM O 72 2/10: 545-548
Cast Your Own Horses: silicone rubber mold making: MM D 72 2/12:670-672
Ceramics for the Military Modeller: large figures from ceramic

Construction

clay: MM Je 72 2/6:306-310
Dreaded Rot: priming to prevent metal corrosion: MM N 73 3/11: 770; Ja 74 4/1:36; F 74 4/2:134
Fiddling with Romans: Roman conversions from Airfix figures: MM Ja 72 2/1:14-15
Figure Building on a Budget: MM Mr 72 2/3:146-147
Figure Conversion: Airfix horse & rider posing techniques: MM F 74 4/2:92-95
Figure Painting: RT Mr 74 7/3:31+
Fleshing it Out: face painting: RT Ag 74 7/8:89
How to Paint Tartans: MM Je 71 1/6:299-300
Improve Your Converting Technique: knees & elbows, kilts, edged weapons: S&L (D 75) 11:8-9
Japan in the Age of War: 15-17th Century Japanese armor: MM Jl 71 1/7:342-343
Making Your Own Figures in Plasticine, Clay & Isopon: S&L Jl 74 2:18
Metal Figure Kit: construction techniques: MM S 73 3/9:594-597
The Model Railroad's Population: use of figures in model railroading: MR S 75 42/9:39+
Model Soldiers: conversions from dissimilar materials: Afx Je 72 13/10:565+
Modelling Japanese Samurai of the 12th Century: MM F 71 1/2:76-79
Painting Faces: over 54mm scale: MM Je 75 5/6:346-347
Painting a Landsknecht: MM Ag 72 2/8:417-419
Painting Techniques: preparation, slight conversion to more realistic poses: MM F 73 3/2:82-83; brushes, paints, working area, painting faces, toning, dry toning: Mr 73 3/3:144-146
The Plastic Warrior: converting Airfix 20mm figures: MM Jl 71 1/7:346-347
Plasticine Figure Modelling: Sc Ap 72 3/4:196-197+
Sassanid Persian Clibanarii: conversion techniques: MM My 71 1/5:237-238
Simulated Leather: 54mm techniques: MM My 73 3/5:298
Slings & Arrows: Airfix 20mm to ancient archers & slingers: MM O 72 2/10:516-517+
Thracians: Airfix 20mm to ancient mercenaries: MM F 72 2/2:70-71
Tips on Figure Modelling: superdetailing & re-posing horses in plastic: IM My 74 10/(16):14
Painting Military Miniatures: techniques & materials: MM D 71 1/12:629-630

Scenery

Backgrounds

Build a Backdrop Collage: three-dimensional backdrops: RM O 75 42/10:66-68

V. Articles

Photos for False Fronts: NMRA S 71 37/1:32-33
Speaking of Backgrounds: intro to backdrop painting: NMRA Ap 71 36/8:29

Terrain

Adding Culverts: NMRA Ap 75 40/8:24
Bandai Possibilities: snow, ice, sand, earth: MM Jl 73 3/7:453-454
Casting Rocks from Plaster: rubber mold: RMC D 74 43/7:59-61; Ja 75 43/8:39-41
Cheap Lightweight Scenery for Portable Layouts & Dioramas: MW Mr 73 1/7:371-372
Ever Make a Mistake? Correct It: remodeling hard-shell scenery: NMRA My 75 40/9:40-41
From the Dark of the Tunnel: criteria for having tunnels, basic design: RM Jl 73 40/7:29
Lightweight Scenery: urethane foam: RMC Jl 74 43/2:40-43
Mining in Miniature: small operation mine tunnel faces: Afx O 71 13/2:94
Non-Supportive Tunnel Liners: to hide inside of terrain shell: NMRA Je 71 36/10:39
Plastic Pike: styrofoam terrain: NMRA Ag 72 37/13:44-45
Realistic Roads for your Layout: asbestos furnace cement for paving: MR D 75 42/12:84
Scenery & Foliage Texturing: rock: MR S 74 41/9:56-63
Scenery the McCrary Way: NMRA S 71 37/1:34-35
Short Course in Scenery: paper & plaster shell: RMC Jl 72 41/2:32-33
Sudden Scenery: screen-supported scenery: MR Ag 71 38/8:49-53
The Whole Blasted Railroad: modeling Mt. Rushmore: MR Mr 75 42/3:63-65

Vegetation

All About Lichen: finding, collecting & processing for model vegetation: RMC S 75 44/4:34-37; installation techniques: O 75 44/5:44-47
Bandai Possibilities: grass, trees: MM Jl 73 3/7:453-454
Building Trees with Picture Wire: MR Ja 74 41/1:44-45
Cactus: Sgauaro from pipe cleaners: MR My 71 38/5:75
Citrus Grove: NMRA D 74 40/4:50-51
Foreground Scenery: NMRA D 74 40/4:22-26
Grass from Brush Bristles: RMC O 74 43/5:30-31
Growing Vines: RMC Ag 74 43/2:30-33
Hanging Vines: RMC Mr 75 43/10:32-33
A Lonesome Pine: RMC Ap 73 41/11:31-33
Make Better Trees from Bought Ones: MR Ja 73 40/1:64-65
Marvelous Moss: preserving moss for model vegetation: MR Je 73 40/6:67-68
Modeling Trees: MR Jl 72 39/7:72-75

Mr. Lukesh Revisited: palm trees with feathers: MR Ag 75 42/8: 44-45
Preparing Sorgum Trees: MR Ag 72 39/8:61
Realism in Model RR Scenery: use of plants for model vegetation: NMRA Je 74 39/11:28-30
Scenery & Foliage Texturing: vegetation: MR S 74 41/9:56-63
Scenery the McCrary Way: NMRA S 71 37/1:34-35
Speedy Tumbleweed: NMRA Mr 71 36/7:10
Trees: from Spirea: RMC D 73 42/7:50
Trees are Thousands: getting variety in layout trees: MR Ag 73 40/8:33
Walls of Ivy: RMC O 75 44/5:57-58

Water

How to Build a Waterfall: cotton, waxed paper, & spray fixative: MR D 75 42/12:81-83
Scratchbuild a Waterfall: silicone sealer: MR Jl 73 40/7:43
Two Ways to Simulate Water: epoxy resin or varnish: RMC D 73 42/7:35-36

Miscellaneous

Hiding Joints in Scenery: MR N 73 40/11:97
Let's Study Scenery: colors, order of work progress: MR F 75 42/2:43
Model Scenery is Important: MW S 72 1/1:41+
Scenery Made Simple: Afx Ag 71 12/12:646-647

Ship

The Art of Small Scale Waterline Ship Modeling: Sc Ja 71 2/1: 33-35
MS Clan MacDonald: 1/600 waterline techniques: MB O 72 22/262: 436-437
Cowl Ventilators: how to make from metal or paper: MB Ja 75 25/288:17-19
Cutty Sark: rigging clipper ships: Sc Ag 75 6/8:382-385
Deadeyes & Shrouds: MB Ag 72 22/260:332
Don't Man the Boats: displays without figures: MB F 71 21/242: 57
Hamburg Class Destroyer: paper ship techniques: Sc O 71 2/10: 540-541; N 71 2/11:620-621
Internal Lighting of Ship Models: MB Ap 71 21/244:152-153
Learning from the Museum: construction for display: MB Jl 74 24/282:265
Marine Modelling: building cardstock Schleswig-Holstein in plastic card: Sc Ap 73 4/4:256-257+

Model Fishing Gear: MB Ap 71 21/244:142-145; My 71 21/245:206
Modern Steamers: small scale techniques: MB D 74 24/287:520-522
Period Ship Hints: sailing ship construction techniques: MB My 71 21/245:210; cor S 71 21/249:375
Planked Decks: RT Jl 71 4/7:80-81
Rigging: superdetailing: Sc Je 72 3/6:314-317
Sailing Ship Models: superdetailing techniques: IM Ja 71 8/1:14+
Shortening Sail: mounted sails on static scale sailing ships: MB N 71 21/251:460-462
Simple Rigging Improvement: waxing: Sc S 75 6/9:465
Simplified Warship Construction: MB Je 72 258:248-250
Small Scale Ship Modelling: 1/32": 1' techniques: MB Ja 72 22/253:14-15+
Warship Portholes: 1/6":1' techniques: MB Ja 72 22/253:28-29
Warships in 1/1200 Scale: detailing: MW Je 73 1/10:548-549
Waterline Bases: realistic water for waterline models: MM Ag 72 2/8:398

Structures--

Buildings

Aging Boards & Shingles: MR Ap 71 38/4:46-47
Being Your Own Contractor: scratch techniques: NMRA Ja 71 36/5:6-8
Brick Texturing: RMC Je 75 44/1:6
Casting Structures from Plaster: RMC F 74 42/9:29-33
The Concept of Kitlancing: intro to kit structure conversion: RMC D 72 41/7:58-63
Damaged Buildings: Afx F 72 13/6:316-317
Detail Your Interiors with a Camera: flats from color transparencies as interiors: MR Jl 73 40/7:40-42
Fitting a Modern Passenger Platform: lights & signs: MR Ap 73 40/4:71-72
Foreground Scenery: buildings: NMRA D 74 40/4:22-26
The Gingerbread House: making molding, repeated shapes, pph: MR N 73 40/11:71-77
How to Build a Freight House for One's Own Pleasure: NMRA Ag 75 40/12:11-14
How to Make Neat Signs: matching signs to buildings, weathering signs: MR Ag 73 40/8:43-45
Kunzelmann Builds a Roundhouse: MR F 72 39/2:65-68
Logos: signs from magazine pictures: NMRA Sp 75 40/8:53
Making Good Structures Better: mild superdetailing of kit structures: MR Ja 74 41/1:62-63
Modifying Kit Structures: MR My 75 42/5:38-39
Modular Structure Assembly: use of MDG wall material: MR F 74 41/2:60-65
New Houses from Old: wargaming houses from Airfix trackside buildings: Afx D 72 14/4:201+

"Novelty" (cove) siding: from clapboard siding: RMC D 72 41/7: 91
Railroad Structures of the Steam Diesel Era: station construction: NMRA O 73 39/2:53-58
Scenery the McCrary Way: corrugated metal, building sidings: NMRA S 71 37/1:34-35
Shingling Made Easy: Scotch Adhesive Transfer Tape No. 465 for adhesive: NMRA Je 75 40/10:44-45
Small City Terminal: NMRA Mr 74 39/8:38-39
Small Scale Model Buildings: intro to techniques in 1/150: Sc O 75 6/10:492-495
A Small Station Building: English style passenger: Afx O 72 14/2:90-93
Station Signs: O, S, HO, N samples: NMRA Ag 75 40/12:33-35
Structures from History: individually glazed windows: MR Ja 71 38/1:56-59
Trackside Saloon: exploded sk: NMRA S 75 41/1:46-47

Other Than Buildings

Add Signal Detail to Your Right of Way: trackside equipment: MR Je 75 42/6:66-71
Billboards from Matchbook Covers: MR S 74 41/9:52
Bronze Statue for Albion: from figures of a larger scale: MR N 75 42/11:82
Color Signs from Black or White Dry Transfers: using transfer as mask: RMC Jl 75 44/2:50-52
Modeling a Chain Link Fence: gate types, barbed wire toppings, bracing: RMC Ag 75 44/3:44-47
N Scale Scratch-Building Tips: RMC N 73 42/6:32-33
Retaining Walls from Ties: RMC O 74 43/5:31-33
Signs from Catalogs & Other Sources: MR D 72 39/12:63-64

<u>Wargames Models</u>

Building a Sand Table: AFV F 71 2/11:6-7
Sand Table Fortifications: AFV N 71 3/3:26; D 71 3/4:22
Sand Table Terrain: AFV S 71 3/1:22+; O 71 3/2:29

V. Articles   412

CONTROL

AIRCRAFT

Free Flight

Autorudder & Dethermaliser: Aero Ja 74 39/456:24-26
Brackencroft Brake: Aero O 75 40/477:922
Bring 'Em Back Alive: retrieval gimmicks: Aero Ap 75 40/471: 213+
Denney DT: beer can aluminum spoiler, for hand-launched gliders: MAN O 75 91/4:15
Do-It-Yourself Dethermalizer Fuse: cotton string & potassium nitrate: Aero F 75 40/469:109+
Glider Flying 1975: outdoor hand-launched: Aero My 75 40/472: 286-287
K&W Brake: engine brake: Aero O 75 40/477:(921)
Kerr Brake: engine brake for FAI power: MAN N 75 91/5:19
Poor Man's Seelig: four functions from camera timer: MAN Ap 71 82/4:8
Programmed Return of Magnet Steered Gliders: Aero My 71 36/424:246+
Raux/Bailey Brake: Aero O 75 40/477:922
Twin Engine FF Scale Control: engine pressure actuates aileron & rudder: Aero My 74 39/460:242-243

Control Line

Carrier Controls: bellcranks & hook controls: MAN S 72 85/3:14
Control Handle: dowel & coat hanger: AM Ap 71 72/4:37
Dutch Handle Grouper: handle to group lines for safety in team racing: Aero Ap 75 40/471:225
FAI Combat Handle: Aero Ja 72 37/432:36-37
Grouper: MAN My 75 90/5:27
Groupers: three types: AM D 74 74/12:50
Hand on Chest Team Race Handle: Aero N 75 40/478:972-973
Improved Bellcrank: modified Roberts three-line, for CL scale: AM Mr 73 76/3:64
Make It Easy--Bent Wire Horns: how to make control horns: Aero D 73 38/455:693
Navy Carrier Throttles: types & use: MAN F 74 88/2:14-16+
Profile Carrier Control System: left flap deflects more than right to keep lines tight at slow speed: MAN D 75 91/6:15
Reeves Bellcrank: throttle & elevator bellcrank: Aero Jl 72 37/

438:403-404
Squeeze Handle: control line handle with squeeze throttle control:
   Aero Jl 72 37/438:403-404
Throttle Handle: sp: AM N 72 75/5:61
Tinplate Control Horns: Aero Ja 75 40/468:41
The Year of the Grouper: Aero O 74 39/465:554-555

Radio Control

ASW-17 Spoiler: RC My 75 12/5:22
Altimeter: balloon operating throttle to keep under 400' ceiling:
   FM D 72 75/12:22-25
Backwards is Sometime Better: alternate stick system: RC Ag 74
   11/8:66
Control Linkages: AM F 71 72/2:49+
Control Mixer: for V-tail servos: RC Ag 75 12/8:30
Easy Aileron Servo Connection: permanently linked push-rods: RC
   N 72 9/11:10
Electrostatic Autopilots: pitch & roll stabilizer: FM F 73 76/2:
   20-29
Elevons Another Way: improved sliding tray design: RC Ag 75 12/
   8:58-59
Equipment Selection Guide: combining RC components for specific
   needs: RC N 72 9/11:22-23+
Non-Linear Servo Output: RCS S 75 1/5:6+
Nullifying Device for Kavan Jet Ranger: prevent over-control: RC
   S 75 12/9:65
Pre-Flight Procedures for Your RC Model: AM F 73 76/2:24
Programmed Manoeuvers? push-button on transmitter for rate of
   roll: MAN O 73 87/4:31
Pushrod Installations: AM Ja 71 72/1:30+
RC System Adjustment: AM Ag 73 77/2:65
Roger's Rocker: elevon control without moving servo block: RC Mr
   73 10/3:53+
Sailplane Speed Brakes: adding spoilers to two-channel system: RC
   Ap 73 10/4:52-53
Servo Mechanical Configurations: RC S 75 12/9:6+
Single Stick Developments: all four controls on one stick, contoured
   case: RC F 72 9/2:38-39
Throttle Control Switch: for separate throttle setting for starting
   twin engine, synchronized in flight: RC N 74 11/11:54-55+
Tow Hook: releasable tow hook for RC gliders (coupled to down
   elevator): RC D 71 8/12:61
Transmitter Stick Configurations: RC F 72 9/2:58-61
Vibration...and How to Keep It Out of Your Radio: mounting: RC
   Ap 72 9/4:50-51+

V. Articles 414

BOATS

Free Running

An Integrated Circuit Timer: for engine run: MB My 75 25/292: 229+
Staying on Course: light-actuated auto-pilot for boat models: MB Ja 75 25/288:14-16
Timing Mechanisms: for cutting engines of straight-runners: MB Ja 75 25/288:16+

Vane Control

Break Back Vane Gear: MB Jl 71 21/247:286-288
Epicyclic Vane Gear: MB Ap 75 25/291:186-187
First Time Out: trimming yachts for the first time: MB S 72 22/261:390-391
Moving Carriage Gear: MB Je 71 21/246:236-239
Simple Moving Carriage Vane Gear: Meccano gears: MB Ap 71 21/244:148-149
Simple Non-Self Tacking Vane Gear: for 30-45" yachts: MB Jl 72 22/259:296-297
Simple Vane Gear: self-taking, guying: MB D 72 22/246:514-515

Radio Control

General

Four From Two: four functions on two channels: MB Jl 75 25/294:348-349
Making Servos Do More Work: circuit breaker for electric power, RC breaker reset, line cast-off: FM Ja 74 77/1:59-61

Power

Adjustable Trim Tabs: MB Ja 74 24/277:29
Electric Motor Control: pulsed speed control: MB Jl 71 21/247:274-275; Ag 71 21/248:317-318
High Performance Boating: waterproof radio gear: RC D 75 12/12:55+
High Performance Hydros: antenna routing: RC Ag 75 12/8:66
Motor Control System: for electric boats: MB Ag 75 25/295:414-415
Motor Controls for Model Boats: FM Ag 73 76/8:32-33
Motor Tuning: RC needle valve control: MB S 73 23/273:271

Control

Simple Reversing Baffle: deflector behind prop for reverse (horizontal when not in use): FM F 74 77/2:62
Tiller & Throttle Linkage: MB Ja 71 21/241:38+

Sail

Canadian RC Yachts: winch motors: MB My 73 23/269:188-189
Easy Proportional Sheet Winch: MB Je 75 25/293:281-282
My Twopenn'orth on Winches: MB D 75 25/299:641-644
Proportional Sail Winch: no wipers: MB Ag 73 76/8:32-33
Proportional Sail Winch: MB Ap 73 23/268:150-151
Proportional Sail Winch: MB D 74 24/287:524-527+
Proportional Sail Winch Mechanism: microswitch with feedback: MB Jl 74 24/282:260-261
RC Sheeting Systems: chain drive: MB O 72 22/262:425
Sheet Control: MB Ag 74 24/283:330-331+
Sheet Control: RC Je 73 10/6:64-65+
Sheet Control for RC Yachts: connects to stock servo: MB Mr 73 23/267:104-105
Sheeting Systems for RC Yachts: MB Ap 72 22/256:156-157
Some Observations on Radio Controlled Yachts: MB Ap 71 21/244:150+
Two Lightweight Sail Winches: conversion of Horizon servo for sheets: MB S 72 22/261:380-381
Ultra-Simple Sheeting System: MB Mr 73 23/267:105

RADIO CONTROL EQUIPMENT

General

Batteries: AM D 73 77/6:74
Digital Encoder: how it works: AM Je 71 72/6:30+
Interference & You: AM My 74 78/5:58
Pulse Proportional: 1972: survey of the market: RC D 72 9/12:6+
Systems Effectiveness: evaluating radio quality: RC Ja 75 12/1:16+
Transmitter Interference: transmitter switch key to avoid two on same frequency: RC F 72 9/2:16
Trouble?: trouble-shooting RC equipment: FM S 71 414:42-44
Trouble Shooting & Trouble Avoidance: AM D 72 75/6:8

Construction

AAM Commander: two channel digital system, IC: AM Ap 72 74/

V. Articles

    4:50-53+; My 72 74/5:40-43+; Je 72 74/6:48-51+; Jl 72 75/1: 50-53+
AAM 8-Channel Commander Receiver/Decoder: AM Je 73 76/6:28-31+; cor Jl 73 77/1:20
AAM 3-4 Channel Transmitter Conversion: AM F 74 78/2:68-70+
Buddy Box: modifying Heathkit: RC Ja 71 8/1:20+
Decoder for AAM Commander: AM D 73 77/6:62-63
Dorffler Micro FET IC Receiver: ultra-light for two channels, receiver & decoder: FM Ap 72 421:27-31
Dorffler II Becomes a IV: adding two channels to Dorffler Micro FET IC receiver: FM S 72 75/9:36
Heath Servo for Retract Gear: modification: RC F 71 8/2:31-33+
Homebuilt Proportional Servo: for boat operation: MB S 71 21/249:366-367
Modifying S4A Servos for Retracts: RC Ap 72 9/4:54-55
More Versatile Heath: converting three channel to single stick: MAN My 71 82/5:48-49+
RCM World: six channel digital proportional system: RC O 73 10/10:40-50; N 73 10/11:18-32; D 73 10/12:36-44; Ja 74 11/1:32-39; F 74 11/2:44-52; Mr 74 11/3:44-45; Ap 74 11/4:33-39; My 74 11/5:34-39
SCS Decoder Conversion: Cannon C525 or D525 or Heath GD 247 converted to IC: AM F 75 75/2:35-37
Servo-Driven Switcher for Proportional Systems: accessory cascade switch: MB Jl 72 22/259:295+
Winch Actuator for Small Yachts: MB S 71 21/249:374

Parts

Build a Two Channel Brick for the Ace Digital Commander: RC N 72 9/11:24-26+
Building the Heath Full House Plus Three: RC O 72 9/10:26-32
Cold Duck Retract Servo Wiring: RC Je 71 8/6:28-29
Converting 9v Dry Cell Transmitter to NiCd Cells: RC Ap 75 12/4:45
Frequency Selector Switch Guard: to prevent accidental change of frequency: AM S 71 73/3:41-42
Linear Servo Extension Arm: to match throttle throw: RC O 72 9/10:6+
Making Boat & Transmitter Covers: FM Mr 74 77/3:70
Modeler's Muff: for hands & transmitter in cold weather: RC S 75 12/9:16
Quick Change Servo Tray: to change RC unit from one plane to another: RC S 71 8/9:62

RAILROAD

Accessories (Electrical)

Automatic Locomotive Light Control: steady light regardless of speed: NMRA Ag 71 36/13:38-39
Contact Protection: electrical switch contacts, wd: NMRA S 75 41/1:41
Digital Fast Clock: wd: NMRA My 72 37/9:14-16
Echos Add to Sound Effects: MR D 73 40/12:42-43
Electronic Bell: wd, sound effect: NMRA Mr 74 39/8:26-28
Fast Clocks: external electrical power of spring clocks through setting knob: NMRA Je 74 39/11:8-10
A Few Easy Lights for Your Layout: street lights: NMRA N 71 37/3:35
Flashing Light Plus: wd, crossing flashers: NMRA Ag 75 40/12:50-52; cor N 75 41/3:70
Flashing Lights Put Pizazz in Your Railroad Scene: transistorized blinker circuit control: NMRA O 71 37/2:6-7
Highway Flasher Produces Cold Light: LEDs, wd: MR F 71 38/2:42-43
Illuminated Track Diagram: using ultra-violet, control panel: MR My 75 42/5:66-67
Inexpensive Panel Lights: grain of wheat in eyelet sockets: NMRA Je 72 37/10:29
Protect Your Power Supply: preventing accidentally leaving power on: NMRA F 71 36/6:38
Residential Gas Lamps: 1v, det, pph: NMRA F 75 40/6:44-45; medicine capsule lens: S 75 41/1:29
Sound for Geared Locomotives: RMC Ja 72 40/8:33-35
Street Lamp: SP Depot, San Francisco, Aug 1968: 1v, det: NMRA Ja 74 39/5:17
Tender Speaker for Noise Effects: phonograph pick-up, track transmission: MR Ja 71 38/1:62b-63

Circuitry

The Case for 24 Volts Restated: NMRA Ap 72 37/8:29
Circuit Breaker: wd, for control panel: NMRA Mr 74 39/8:30
Electrical & Electronics: see separate listing, immediately following
Heating Effects of DC: circuit heating: NMRA Mr 72 37/7:42-44
Hot Wire: intro to railroad wiring: MR Ja 74 41/1:70-71
Self-Restoring Overload Protection: wd: NMRA S 71 37/1:42
Wiring Your First Layout: MR Ap 75 42/4:40-43

V. Articles 418

(Electrical & Electronics) [all NMRA]

[introductions to model railroad electrical subjects, most include wiring diagrams or function charts]
Dirty Track Problems: Ja 71 36/5:22
Pulsed Power for Transistor Throttles: F 71 36/6:14
Cab Control: Mr 71 36/7:20
Understanding Transistors: Ap 71 36/8:15
Turnouts & Shorting: My 71 36/9:20
Constant Current & Constant Voltage Throttles: Je 71 36/10:13
Testing Diodes & Transistors with an Ohmmeter: Jl 71 36/10:9
Blocks & Sections: Ag 71 36/13:11
Bridge Rectifiers: S 71 37/1:12
Light-Emitting Diodes: O 71 37/2:10
Pulse Power: N 71 37/3:17
24 Volts: D 71 37/4:20
Speedometer: Ja 72 37/5:18
Reading Wiring Diagrams: connections, non-connections, & commons: F 72 37/6:12
Capacitators: Mr 72 37/7:19
Signals with Transistors: Ap 72 37/8:16
Twin T Three Color Signals: My 72 37/9:28
National Electrical Code: Je 72 37/10:19
Walkaround Control: Jl 72 37/11:11
Sound Systems: Ag 72 37/13:13
24 Volts: S 72 38/1:12
Understanding Transistors: O 72 38/2:22
Volts, Amps, & Watts: N 72 38/3:20
X Section: how to wire: D 72 38/4:19
Trouble Shooting Transistor Throttles: Ja 73 38/5:16
Reversing Loops: F 73 38/6:12
Route Selection: setting several turnouts with one switch: Mr 73 38/7:25
Prototype Traction Power: Ap 73 38/8:22; cor Ag 73 38/12:21
Computer Cab Control: use of shared-time computers for pike operation: Je 73 38/10:23
Current-Limiting Throttles: Jl 73 38/11:31
Diodes for Constant Lighting: Ag 73 38/12:21
Flux & Solder: S 73 39/1:16
Choosing Integrated Circuits: O 73 39/2:27
Operational Amplifiers: uses in model railroad circuitry: N 73 39/3:25
Ultrasonic Lighting: using sound as light power source: D 73 39/4:27
Electrical Problems at Turnouts: F 74 39/7:15
Lamps for Protection: lamp as a variable resistor: Mr 74 39/8:21
Trouble-Free Wiring: Ap 74 39/9:21
Sound from Locomotives: My 74 39/10:39
Multiplexing: separate signal on each half-wave: Je 74 39/11:16
Schematics: introduction: Jl 74 39/12:15
Section vs. Block: Ag 74 39/13:14
Heat Sinks: S 74 40/1:13

Trouble Shooting: O 74 40/2:35
Delaware Cab Control: N 74 40/3:15
Prototype Power Control: D 74 40/4:27
Light Emitting Diodes: F 75 40/6:13
Walkaround Cab Control: Ap 75 40/8:60; My 75 40/9:12
Integrated Circuits: Je 75 40/10:10+ ; Jl 75 40/11:26
Electrical Destruction: effect of over-voltage: Ag 75 40/12:24
Change in Direction: integrated circuits & computer cab control:
    S 75 41/1:27
Reducing the Rat's Nest: computer cab control as way to reduce
    wires under layout: O 75 41/2:24-25
Precautions with Integrated Circuits: N 75 41/3:52-53
Integrated Circuit Counters & Counter Applications: D 75 41/4:25

Control Circuitry

Basics of Two-Train Operation: RMC My 71 39/12:42-43
A Better Switch Machine Power Supply: SCR circuit, wd, mat:
    RMC Ja 73 41/8:35-37; wd, mat: F 73 41/9:31-33; cor Jl 73
    42/2:10-11
Cab Control on the New Rock Island: NMRA Ag 75 40/12:7-10
Carrier Train Control: multitrain operation without blocks, wd:
    NMRA Mr 72 37/7:23
The Case for Dual Polarized Feeder Wiring: wd: MR Ag 73 42/1:
    74-77
Command Control for Easy Operation: carrier wave control, re-
    quirements: MR Ag 71 38/8:31
Computer Cab Control: function charts but no wd, how it works:
    NMRA N 74 40/3:28-30+
Control & Scenery on the Allegheny Route: Canandaigua Southern:
    MR Mr 71 38/3:61-68
First On Locks Out: multiple cab control: NMRA Mr 72 37/7:27-
    29
Follow the Train: walkaround control module & control post (block)
    modules: MR Ap 75 42/4:37
Lamps That Remember: turnout indicator lamps without turnout
    contact, wd: MR O 73 40/10:61-64
Lazyman's Thought for Wye Control: wd: NMRA Ag 72 37/13:52
Local Operations Control: control at junctions: NMRA Jl 73 38/
    11:42
Model Train Control Methods: varieties: MR Ja 72 39/1:73-78;
    F 72 39/2:71-75
Most Needed Improvement for Many Layouts: wiring blocks for
    two power packs: MR Mr 73 40/3:33
Non-Priority Cab Control Systems: from contest: NMRA My 71
    36/9:14-15; add Jl 71 36/11:7
One Button Ladder Control: wd: MR Ag 75 42/8:72-74
Operation by Zone Control: separate control panel for high intensity
    traffic areas only:(MZL): MR F 74 41/2:66-71; cor Ap 74 41/
    4:86; Ap 74 41/4:68-71; master panels, wd: My 74 41/5:61-64;

indicating train location: O 74 41/10:66-69
1 Pole x 2 Throws = 3 Aspects: double throw single pole signal switch: NMRA N 72 38/3:37; Local Operations Control: control at junctions: NMRA Jl 73 38/11:42
Route Selection with Fewer Diodes: MR N 71 38/11:68
Separated Return Loop Control: MR Mr 74 41/3:41
Transistorized 4-Car Trolley Control System: wd: NMRA Mr 71 36/7:16
A Turn Lever for Switch Machine Control: mat, rotary panel switch: MR F 74 41/2:44
Two Reverse Switches?: direction switch & reverse switch saves confusion at loops & wyes: wd: NMRA Ja 75 40/5:30
Water Level Simulator: cab meter to indicate fill time, wd: NMRA Jl 74 39/12:36-37

Detectors

Approach Indicator Lamps: wd: MR My 72 39/5:60-61
CAPY Detection in Phoenix: wd, differences with NMRA & Twin-T: MR Ap 73 40/4:45
An Economical & Sensitive Track Detector: tells if train is in block, wd: NMRA Mr 72 37/7:23
Light Beams Detect Trains: wd: MR S 73 40/9:59-60
Op Detection Circuit: wd, op amps: MR Ag 73 40/8:65-67
Optical Detector: wd: RMC D 74 43/7:67-69
Track Contacts: how to make & use for detectors or actuators: MR My 73 40/5:52-53
Train Detection Made Easy: wd: NMRA Jl 75 38/11:42
Train Situation Indicator: wd, mat, lightbeam/photoelectric cell: MR D 73 40/12:82-83
Twin-T Circuit: wd, twin transistor detector: MR O 72 39/10:80-84

Lighting Control

Build an SSF Generator: wd, for constant lighting: MR D 71 38/12:60-64
Constant Lighting--or Separate Control of Two Motors: wd, pulse system: MR S 74 41/9:74-75

Ramps

Electromagnet Uncoupling Ramp: MR N 71 38/11:65
Retractable Ramp for Any Scale: MR F 71 38/2:58-59

Roving Uncoupling Ramps: moveable ramp: MR Ag 73 40/8:58-59

Signals

Adding Three-Color Signals: wd: MR Ap 72 39/4:37-39
Automatic Train Control Scheme with Tricolor Signals: wd, mat: MR O 75 42/10:76-77
Coded Control of Signals: one-wire/diode: MR S 71 38/7:58
LED Searchlight Signals: wd, mat: RMC D 75 44/7:70-73
Mechanism for a Searchlight Signal: MR F 73 40/2:60
Three-Color Signals on the TSL: wd: MR Je 72 39/6:60-61
Three Color Signals with One Lamp: 2v, cd, wd: MR D 74 41/12:78
Two Color Signal Lighting: wd: MR S 71 38/9:64-65
What Do You Want--Proper Cab Signals or Faulty Operation?: wd, intro: NMRA Je 71 36/10:36-37
Working Mars Light: wd: MR Mr 75 42/3:74-77

Switch Machines

Crimp-Link Switch Machine Installation: MR D 74 41/12:61
Improved Hand Throw Switch Stand: NMRA Ja 72 37/5:20-21
Inexpensive Ground Throws: NMRA Ap 73 38/8:35
Installing HO Ground Throws: RMC Ap 74 42/11:28-29
Modified "Slanser" Ground Throw: NMRA D 73 39/4:46-47
Mounting Quadrant Action Switch Machine to Layout: NMRA My 75 40/9:38-39
Non-Critical Throw Rods: telescopic tubing: NMRA Mr 74 39/8:15
Operational Large-Scale Switch Stands: construction & use: RMC Ap 75 43/11:54-56
A Simple Turnout Control Mechanism: MR Je 75 42/6:57
Switch Machine Power Supply with Snap Regardless of Load--Almost: NMRA Ag 74 39/13:15
Turnout Drive Mechanism: NMRA D 71 37/4:19-20
What Ever Happened to Rotary Switch Machines? reviving old system with permag motors: NMRA My 72 37/9:28-29

Throttles & Walkaround Controls

Advanced Solid State Throttle: wd, mat: NMRA Ja 73 38/5:19-20
Another Go Around for Walkaround: intro to advantages: MR Je 74 41/6:29
Converting a Live-Steam Air Brake Casting for Solid State Throttle Use: RMC N 75 44/6:42-43

An Evolving Throttle: wd, mat: NMRA N 74 40/3:40-44
Follow the Train: walkaround control module & control post (block) modules: MR Ap 75 42/4:37
An Improved Conventional Throttle: $\frac{1}{2}$ to full wave power, wd: RMC O 73 42/5:40-41; cor F 74 42/9:10-11
More Power from Throttles: booster to 8 amps: wd: MR Mr 73 40/3:62-63
PRR-NJB's Walkaround Controls: MR S 72 39/9:50-53; cor N 72 39/11:18
Packaging the Walk-Around Throttle: modes: NMRA F 75 40/6:49-50
Practical Throttle Handle: wafer switch & pot: MR Jl 71 38/7:58
Quarter-Size Locomotive Cab Controls: 2v, cd, pph, cpph: RMC O 75 44/5:48-56
The SST/7: a second-generation solid-state throttle: wd, mat: RMC S 75 44/4:55-59; O 75 44/5:34-35+
A Throttle for Easy Walkaround Control: wd, mat: MR Ja 75 42/1:74-77
Transistor Throttle with a Future: wd: MR Je 75 42/6:52-56
Walk-Around Throttle: wd: RMC D 73 D 73 42/7:48-49
Walkaround Control: requirements for design: MR Ja 72 39/1:33

DESIGN

AIRCRAFT

Aerodynamics

All Control Systems

CG: how to find center of gravity: RC Je 75 12/6:12+
Delta Design: Aero F 71 36/421:88-90
Ducted Fans & Delta Data: FM S 74 77/9:26-33
Effect of Wind on Altitude: RC Ag 74 11/8:6+

Free Flight

About that Vertical Tail: MAN S 71 83/3:14-16+
Airfoil Aerodynamics: Aero Je 73 38/449:327-328
Free Flight Technicalities: state of the art in A-2 glider hardware: Aero D 75 40/479:1044-1047
Mysteries of Flight: pitch control: Aero D 73 38/455:694-695
The Ultimate Rubber Ship: unlimited rubber category: AM S 72 75/3:30-33+
Under Dog Airfoil: FM Ja 74 77/1:48

Wakefield Developments: state of the art: Aero D 73 38/455:684-687
What's All the Flap About?: Aero My 72 37/436:262-264

Control Line

Bipes for Stunt: design conjecture for CL stunt competition design: AM Je 73 76/6:38-39
Build a Bipe: Aero Jl 74 39/462:365-367
CL Stunt Design: MAN Ag 73 87/2:22-23+
Class B TR: state of the art in B Team Racing in New Zealand: Aero Je 75 40/473:328-329
Go For Broke: stunt design: AM Mr 73 76/3:28-33+
How to Build a Better Mouse: mouse racer planform design: MAN Jl 72 85/1:23+
Longitudinal & Static Stability: (started in MAN S 70): MAN Ja 71 82/1:156-157
Stunt Theory: how it is affected by aerodynamics: Aero Mr 71 36/422:156-157
What is a Modern Team Racer: design trends: Aero Je 75 40/473: 348-350

Radio Control

About That Vertical Tail: MAN S 71 83/3:14-16+
Basic Sailplane Design: see separate listing
Birds Do It: aerodynamic parameters of birds & sailplanes: RC N 75 12/11:79+
Drag & Flutter: control hinge design: RC Ag 73 10/8:55+
Drag Reduction: see separate listing
Drag Reduction Techniques for Modelers: AM F 75 75/2:68-69; Mr 75 75/3:66+
Flutter: control surface flutter & how to cure it: FM Ap 71 409: 45-48
How to Design a Glider: math for planform design: RC N 73 10/11:12+
Let's Customize: keeping ARFs from looking alike: MAN F 71 82/2:48+
A New Look at RC Seaplane Design: AM O 74 74/10:46-49+
Practical Aerodynamics: see separate listing
Radio Controlled Flight & Airfoils: RC N 71 8/11:45-49
Rx for Flutter: control surface flutter & how to cure it: RC S 71 8/9:37+
Sailplanes versus Wind: wind & penetration requirements: RC D 74 11/12:61+; Ja 75 12/1:36+
Stability & Control of RC Aircraft: RC D 71 8/12:56-57
Stand-Off Scale Design: RC Ag 74 11/8:16+
Theory of Model Helicopter Flight: RC S 75 12/9:38-39+
Understanding Your Aircraft: effect of wind & trim of aircraft on flight characteristics: RC S 73 10/9:12+
Why Airplanes Fly: basic aerodynamics as applied to RC models:

V. Articles

RC Ag 75 ·12/8:69+
Wing Loading: RC D 75 12/12:12+

(Drag Reduction) [all RCS]

Induced drag, profile drag & effects of scale: Ap 75 1/1:16-17+
Effect of scale: Jl 75 1/3:14-15+
Effect of model parts: Ag 75 1/4:14-15+
The clean fuselage: S 75 1/5:3+
Control/flap drag reduction: O 75 1/6:30-31
Induced drag: N 75 1/7:12-13
Reducing parasitic drag: D 75 1/8:10-11
series continues

(Practical Aerodynamics) [all RC]

Primary axes, angle of attack: Jl 73 10/7:36-37+
G forces, banking, stalls: Ag 73 10/8:16+
Control surface effect: S 73 10/9:34-35+
Engine/propeller combination: O 73 10/10:56+

(Basic Sailplane Design) [all RC]

The Basic Forces: F 73 10/2:54+
Calculating Performance: Mr 73 10/3:16+
Design Effects: force factors & computerized sailplane performance
    data: Ap 73 10/4:16+
Airfoils: Je 73 10/6:50-51; Jl 73 10/7:65+
Design Details: Ag 73 10/8:53+
Handling Qualities: S 73 10/9:41+
Stability: O 73 10/10:58+
Design comparison of several commercial designs: N 73 10/11:72+
Spoilers, design comparison of commercial sailplanes: Ja 74 11/1:
    16+
More Tests: Mr 74 11/3:56-57+

Airfoils

Benedek B-6407-e: Aero Ap 75 40/471:212
Benedek B-6456-f: Aero N 75 40/478:966
Clark Y: Aero Ap 72 37/435:206
E58/Mod 7,6: AM S 74 78/9:62
E59/Mod 7,6: AM S 74 78/9:62
E374/Mod 4,10: AM Jl 74 78/7:62
E385/Mod 4,10: AM Jl 74 78/7:62
E385/Mod 7,6: AM S 74 78/9:62
E387/Mod 4,10: AM Jl 74 78/7; RCS Ag 75 1/4:14
Equiangular Sections: tangentials, set of 12: Aero Je 72 37/437:
    331-332 & insert

GF-6: MAN Jl 71 83/1:8
GF-6 modified: AM D 71 73/6:28
GF-6 stab: AM D 71 73/6:28
Kaczanowski GF-6 Original: AM D 71 73/6:28
Monson M-4: AM Mr 72 74/3:42
MacDonald: Aero Ap 75 40/471:212
NACA 0009: RC Je 73 10/7:50
NACA 2412: RC Je 73 10/7:50
NACA 2415: MAN Jl 71 83/1:23
NACA 4409: RC Je 73 10/7:51
NACA 4410: AM Jl 74 78/7:62
NACA 4412: RC Je 73 10/7:51
NACA 6412: RC Je 73 10/7:51
NACA 7306: AM S 74 78/9:62
NACA 7406: AM S 74 78/9:62
NACA 7506: AM S 74 78/9:62
RAF 15: Aero Ap 72 37/435:206
633018: MAN Je 71 82/6:22
TE 123-650L: modified NACA 4309, some co-ordinates: RC Mr 74 11/3:57
nameless: propeller airfoil for rubber power: Aero S 75 40/476: 495

Performance

"Best" Airplane: getting most points in RC scale competition: RC D 71 8/12:12+
Calculating Glider Performance: AM Mr 72 74/3:46-47
Weight/Power Predictions: AM My 74 78/5:60; Ag 74 78/8:64+

Components

Fuselage

Flying Boat Hull Design: RC Ag 73 10/8:12+
Pilot: modeling crew for flying models: AM Mr 75 75/3:12-13
Vent That Fuse: greenhouse effect in RC fuselages & effect on radio components: RC O 73 10/10:6+

Landing Gear

Birth of a Landing Gear: shock absorbing: RC Jl 72 9/7:47-48+
Design: ROW design: FM F 71 407:46-48
Float Design: RC Ag 73 10/8:12+
Hydrofoils: for unsticking ROW floats: MAN Jl 74 89/1:50+
Landing Gear: design for small free flight: AM F 71 72/2:36
New Look at RC Seaplane Design: AM O 74 74/10:46-49+
Retract Gears: design considerations for scale rLG: RC Ag 72 9/8:14+

V. Articles 426

Retracts: design of aircraft to take rLG: RC Ag 73 10/8:30+
Retracts Revisited: designs: AM Ja 72 74/1:46-49
Show a Leg: CL team racer design: Aero F 73 445/82-84
Uneven Retraction: one landing gear retracts before the other--for scale effect: RC Jl 71 8/7:8+
Up & Twist LG; working rLG of difficult type: RC Ag 71 8/8:8+

Power Systems

CO_2 Reborn: modifying rubber designs to CO_2 piston: Aero Mr 72 37/434:137-140
Converting to Electric: criteria for conversion: RCS O 75 1/8:3+
Designing a Ducted Fan: AM F 71 72/2:42-44+
Ducted Fans & Delta Data: AM S 74 77/9:26-33
Engine Mountings: AM Ag 72 75/2:62
On Engine Vibration: mounting design to minimize effect: FM N 71 416:44-46
Power Pods for Soaring Purists: parachute dropping engines: FM Ag 73 76/8:48-49

Wing & Stab

About that Wing: aerodynamics of wing design: MAN My 73 86/5: 14-15+
Ailerons, Flaperons, Variable Camber Airfoils: designing & using: RC Je 72 9/6:16+
Burying Leadouts: CL leadout design: Aero N 73 38/454:633-634
Calculating Incidence Angles: RC Jl 73 10/7:38+
Computer Designed Airfoils: programming details: Aero F 74 39/457:93-95
Converting to Flaperons: variable-aileron connecting design: RC Je 72 9/6:63-64+
Drag Reduction Techniques: AM F 75 75/2:68-69; Mr 75 75/3:66+
Reynolds Numbers Made Easy: RC S 74 11/9:12+
Skinny Lifters: thin versions of std airfoils to reduce drag: AM D 74 39/467:85-86
Two-Part Models: control links in removeable parts: Aero N 75 40/478:974
Turbulator Design: Aero N 73 38/454:627
Variable Incidence Tailplanes: Aero My 72 37/436:279-281
The Warp that Wins: importance of tip washout: RCS Jl 75 1/3: 8; add O 75 1/6:4+

Control Systems

Free Flight

Bring 'Em Down Alive: DT: AM D 72 75/6:3:68

The Fancy Towhooks: circular tow: FM Ja 74 77/1:41-47
Flapped Wings: variable camber: Aero Je 75 40/473:351-353
Hand Launch Glider DT: AM Mr 72 74/3:43
Magnet Flying Developments: magnetic-controlled sailplanes: Aero S 72 37/440:508-509
Maxi-Dethermalizer: pop-up wing for rubber stick: MAN F 74 88/2:8
Programmed Return of Magnet-Steered Gliders: Aero My 71 36/424:246+
Stab-Actuated Auto-Rudder: AM Mr 74 78/3:68
Towhooks: design of glider towline releases: AM S 72 75/3:45-46+
Variable Incidence Tailplane: Aero Mr 71 36/422:146
Variable Incidence Tailplane: Aero Je 75 40/473:351-353
Variable Incidence Tailplanes: Aero My 72 37/436:279
Wakefield Auto-Everything: auto-rudder & stab: AM S 71 73/3:44

Control Line

Asymetrical Thrust: use of spoilers to counter gyroscopic precession: Aero Mr 71 36/422:156-157
LE Spoilers: ultra-slow flight for non-scale carrier event: MAN Ag 73 87/2:22-23+

Radio Control

Ace Plug-In Radio Installation: twin actuator, removeable system: RC Jl 75 12/7:38
Component Mounting: AM N 72 75/5:8
Converting to Flaperons: variable aileron connecting design: RC Je 72 9/6:63-64+
Coupled Flap-Elevators: CL stunt technique for RC stunt: AM Ag 71 73/2:22-24+
Elevon Control: servo linkage: RC My 72 9/5:23
Elevons & Flaperons: electronic & mechanical connection methods: RC F 73 10/2:22+
Flaperons for Quarter Midget: RC D 74 11/12:34
Flaps? Why Not: installation not requiring elevator trim change: MAN Ap 74 88/4:50+
Integral Flap-Aileron Torque Rod Installation: RC N 72 9/11:27-28
Moving Servo: flaperon, air brakes, etc.: AM Jl 74 78/7:68
On Engine Vibration: protecting RC components: FM N 71 416:44-46
Padre's Parachute: chute fail-safe recovery system: MAN O 71 83/4:43-47+
Plug-In Spoiler System: RC O 74 11/10:56-57
RC Glider Dethermalizer: stab pop-up rather than spoilers: AM Je 74 78/6:30-31+
RCM Looks Ahead: ultra-small scale RC sets using present technology: RC Je 73 10/6:42/45+
Rattle-Proof Pushrod Exits: RC S 73 10/9:40
Roger's Rocker: twin-control mixer: RC Mr 73 10/3:53+

V. Articles   428

Servo Mount: sliding mounts for moving servo in V-tail control:
    RC O 72 9/10:86
Servos: mounting & connecting: AM Ja 73 76/1:10
Simple Detachable Coupled Ailerons: for CAR: RC Ap 74 11/4:
    48
Split Rudder Dive Brake System: servo mounting: AM My 73 76/
    5:18
Steering Diodes for LG Retract Control: AM S 72 75/3:42
Tilted Sticks: 45° angle sticks on transmitter for elevron control:
    MAN F 71 82/2:29
V-Tail Control for Single Channel Sailplanes: uses one pushrod:
    RC Je 72 9/6:46
Water Ballast: use in RC sailplanes: RC O 74 11/10:16+

Non-Standard Types

Autogyros

Some Experiments with Model Autogyros: Aero F 75 40/469:85-89

Flying Scale

Airfoils in Scale Aircraft: RC D 74 11/12:62-63+
Cockpit: design & construction for flying scale: AM S 74 78/9:
    16-17+
Fairey Firefly V: how an RC scale model is developed: AM N 73
    77/5:73-76+
Fuselage Types: RC F 75 12/2:56-57+
New Math: formula for computing scale/weight/power for flying
    scale: AM My 74 78/5:60
To Scale or Not to Scale: airfoil deviation in competition scale:
    RCS Je 75 1/2:6+
Source of Scale Detail: use of static scale plastic kits as proof-of-
    scale: FM O 75 78/10:48-49
Stand-Off Scale Design: RC Ag 74 11/8:16+; cor RC D 74 78/9:16-
    17+
Twin: twin engine free flight design: Aero Mr 73 38/446:165-
    168
2+2=4 Approximately: use of pocket computers in designing odd-
    scales to fit shelf components: RC S 74 11/9:18+

Helicopters

Basics of Helicopter Flight: helicopter aerodynamics: MAN Ag 72
    85/2:48-50+
Designing RC Helicopters: AM Mr 71 72/3:42-44+
Hiller Rotor Hub for 5' Rotor: AM N 71 73/5:38
2b: tube fuselage design for crash protection: AM My 72 74/5:
    65; Ag 72 75/2:65; S 72 75/3:43

Kitting

Rib Die Cutter: RC Je 71 8/6:50-51

BOATS

Aerodynamics of Yacht Sails: MB D 73 23/276:532-533+ ; Ja 74 24/277:36-37
Bones: effect of bow on bow wave formation: MB Jl 72 22/259: 297-298
Bulbous Bows in the A Class? racing yacht hull design: MB Mr 74 24/278:72-73
Electric Motor Control: MB Jl 71 21/247:274-275
Fin Depth: MB Je 75 25/293:289
High Performance Hydros: drive line & running gear design: RC Jl 75 12/7:44-46+
Hydroplanes in France: contemporary tether competition design: MB My 74 24/280:168-169; Je 74 24/281:211-212+
It Ain't Easy Being Big: problems of 8' RC aircraft carrier: FM Jl 75 78/7:62
Lateral Control: keel design & stability: started MB D 70; MB Ja 71 21/241:28-29; F 71 21/242:72-73; Mr 71 21/243:120-122
Multi-Boat Design: considerations of class in boat design: MB F 72 22/254:60-61
Multi-Spray Rail Designs: power speed hulls: MB Jl 73 23/271: 281-282
Multiple Spray Rails: rudder, CG, depth of V: MB O 73 23/274:418
RC Speed & Multi-Racing Design: MB Jl 72 22/259:278-280
Radio Speed Under the 80 dB Limit: factors & applications: MB O 74 24/285:414-417
Riding Plates for Hydros: stern hydrofoils for low speed running: FM O 74 74/10:65
Sail Aerodynamics: MB My 74 24/280:181-182
Sails: intro to sail principles & design: MB O 72 22/262:435-436+
Sheeting Systems for RC Yachts: MB Ap 72 22/256:156-157
Speed and How to Obtain It: prop, boat, performance: MB Ap 73 23/268:167+ ; Ag 73 23/272:324; S 73 23/273:418
Stability: MB Je 75 25/293:292-293
Starting to Build: math of scale boats: MB Jl 74 24/282:262-263
Submarining: design problems of working submarine models: MB My 72 22/257:188-189+
Tank Tests of Model Yacht Hulls: Red Herring vs. Clockwork Orange: MB Ag 73 23/272:325-326
Trim Tabs: on power boat transom: MB D 72 22/264:512-513
Una-Rig: single sail on rotating mast: MB F 75 25/289:88
Wing-Ding: rigid airfoil for RC Marblehead mast & sail: MB S 74 24/284:370-372

V. Articles 430

RAILROAD

Layout

(General)

Add a Branch Line: MR My 71 38/5:29
Add a Shoo Fly: temporary by-pass: NMRA Jl 75 40/11:41
Basic Layout Design: Afx F 72 13/6:315+
Basic Layout Planning: Afx Mr 72 13/7:390-391; Ap 72 13/8:434+
Cab Control of Locomotives: track patterns: NMRA Mr 71 36/7: 20
A Case for Mixed Gauges: use of smaller scale for forced perspective: NMRA O 71 37/2:42-43
The Challenge of Plausibility: HOn3, On20" & On3 in same layout: RMC Ag 73 42/3:30-35
The Christmas Tree Set: small layouts: Afx Ja 73 14/5:268-269
The Competing Railroad: one solution to doubled mainlines: MR Jl 74 41/7:29
Cubicle Railroads: designing into 6x9 office cubicle space: MR My 75 42/5:40-43
Curves Without Radii: long flowing curves: NMRA Je 75 40/10:52
Developing a Railroad Concept: NMRA D 73 39/4:20-23
Don't Waste Aisle Space: using wasted space for sidings: MR Ag 74 41/8:39
Double Crossing RR: X-chaped layout with four themes, connections with 270° tunnels: MR Jl 74 41/7:45-47
The Elegant Back Door: a Paired Industries Trackplan: buildings with track under, to pass through backdrop: RMC My 74 42/12:36-37
An Evolving Yard: MR N 71 38/11:62-65
From the Dark of the Tunnel: criteria for having tunnels, basic design: MR Jl 73 40/7:29
Gaps & Feeders in Blind Faith: MR Jl 72 39/7:52-54
A Great New Railroad: progress report: NMRA Ap 72 37/8:40-41
A Great New Railway: designing a large club layout: NMRA Ap 71 36/8:12-13
How About a Kickback Hump Yard?: MR S 74 41/9:52
How Large is a Model RR Layout?: formulation of maximum layout for available space: NMRA N 71 37/3:10-11; add Je 72 37/10:30-31
Layouts in Modular Sections: MR Ja 72 39/1:66-69
The Limitless 4x8: use of dividing backdrops to enlarge scope of small layout: RMC D 74 43/7:34+
"Maxi-dioramas" on the John Galt Line: use of two-sided scenery rather than hidden tracks: RMC Ja 74 42/8:34-35
A Model of the Model Railroad: use of model to design pike: NMRA Mr 71 36/7:31-32
Model Railroading Underworld: use of under-bench area of layout: MR F 72 39/2:37
Modular Layout Sections Tailored for the Garage: 15" wide modules

Design

for shelf layouts: RMC Ag 75 44/3:52-53
A Modular Switchback Trackplan: hiding the joints: RMC S 73 42/4:46-47
Narrow Gauge for Beginners: layout ideas: MW O 72 1/2:88-89+
One Answer to Dust: removeable scenery & structures to permit vacuum cleaning: MR S 73 40/9:42
Over the River & Through the Woods: scenery planning: MR Jl 75 42/7:39
Planning a Roundhouse: MR F 72 39/2:69-70
Pop Top Access Hole: raising mountain peak: RMC Je 75 44/1:40-41
Russel Cook's LC&J RR: large size layout designed for moving: MR S 71 38/9:32-35
The Scenery's the Thing: RMC D 75 44/7:62-65
Scenic Modules: as dioramas before ultimate incorporation into layout: RMC O 75 44/5:40
Simple Steps in Beginning a New Layout: MR S 74 41/9:33
Start with a Layout Like This?: 4x8 layout designing: MR D 73 40/12:54-57+
Station Locations: where to put them: RMC Ja 72 40/8:48-49
Super Benchwork: high layout to provide workspace under: RMC N 74 43/6:52-53
Switchbacks: NMRA Mr 74 39/8:45
Track Planning for Small Spaces: MR D 74 41/12:83-86
Train Operation Versus Power Packs: designing layout circuitry: MR Ja 71 38/1:60-61
A Town is More than Structures: arrangement of buildings: MR My 73 40/5:48-51
Using Spirals to Save Space: RMC Jl 74 43/2:44-45
Walkaround Operation: designing for walkaround: MR My 72 39/5:31

(Long Dimension Under 10')

[HO gauge unless otherwise stated]
Arcade & Attica: 4x10: NMRA N 74 40/3:19
Blue Ridge Mining: 4x8: RMC D 73 42/7:46-47
Calamity & Uproar: 8x8: NMRA Jl 73 38/11:12
Carbon County Railroad: 6x10, 1 foot wide through most of L shape: RMC Ja 71 39/8:54-55
Central Michigan: 4x8 in gauge N: MR N 72 39/11:68
Compact Layout Folds Away: 3x5 in N gauge, mat, const: MR Ja 73 40/1:70-72
East Broad Top Railroad: 6x10 in Sn3 gauge: NMRA Ja 73 38/5:30
Epithet Creek RR: $2\frac{1}{2}$x8: MR Je 72 39/6:54
Fairmount Traction: 3-4x3-9: RMC D 74 43/7:47
Gold Reef Railroad: 4x8 mine & mill with aerial tram: NMRA Ag 74 39/13:35
Grovers Corners, Thronville & White River: 4-6x8-4: MR Ap 75 42/4:42
Grunt & Clumsum RR: 9x9: RMC F 71 39/9:31

V. Articles 432

Jonstown & West Summit RR: 2x4 in N gauge: MR F 75 42/2:64
Louisville & Nashville: 4x8: MR Ag 75 42/8:71
North Fork Railroad: 8x8: NMRA Ag 72 37/13:23
Pig & Whistle Transit: 5x10 commuter outside third rail: MR Ag 72 39/8:51
Port-A-Pike Operation in Limited Space: $1\frac{1}{2}$x6: NMRA F 72 37/6: 6-9; wiring Mr 72 37/7:8-11+
Rochester Regional RR: 5x10: MR Ja 74 41/1:46
Rochester Regional: 2-6x5 in N gauge: MR F 74 41/2:40
Rubble Creek & Thunder Mine: 4x8: MR Ap 74 41/4:67
Short Hills & Eastern: 6x9, 2 level with rail ferries: MR My 75 42/5:43
Southhaven: 3x8 in N gauge: MR D 72 39/12:53
Strasburg Railroad: 5x10: NMRA Ja 74 39/5:42
Sunset Canyon: MR D 74 41/12:94
Swansea Electric Railway: 3x8 traction: RMC F 71 39/9:48-49
Terminal Central: 5x9: MR O 73 40/10:44-45
Test Rrack No. 1:4x8: MR Mr 74 41/3:55
Titusville Railroad: 5x9: NMRA Je 74 39/11:14
Twin Peaks Logging Company: 4x8 in HOn3: RMC Ap 71 39/11: 48-49
United Maryland Railroad & Canal Co.: 6x8: RMC Mr 71 38/10: 48-49
The Utah Railway: 4x8: RMC Jl 72 41/2:40
Valley Western: 6x9 in N gauge: MR My 75 42/5:42
White Pass & Yukon: 5x10: NMRA Ja 75 40/5:27
Wilburn Southern: 4x8 coal hauler: NMRA F 74 39/7:28
A World in My Lap: 3x5-6 in Z gauge: MR O 75 42/10:42
nameless: 3x3 in N gauge: RMC Ja 73 41/8:47

(Long Dimension 10' to 20'; Short, Under 10')

Alaska Railroad: 8x13: NMRA Mr 74 39/8:12
Allegheny Central: 6x11 + 3x9 reversing loop: NMRA Ja 72 37/5: 26
Brandywine Transit: 3x12 traction: MR My 75 42/5:50-51
Burlington Northern: 9x16: MR Mr 75 42/3:80
Canadian National: 6x15-6: RMC D 72 41/7:32
Cascade Northern: 5x15: MR Jl 73 40/7:68-69
Cedar Valley: 6x11 switching line: MR Je 74 41/6:74
Chama: 10x12: NMRA Je 73 38/10:40
D&W Valley: 9-6x14: MR N 71 38/11:47
Deer Creek Route: 10x13: MR Ag 72 39/8:65
Ft. Worth & Brazos: 10x15 in N gauge: NMRA S 75 39/1:35
Fremont, Elkhorn & Missouri Valley RR: 10x12 mining: NMRA Jl 72 37/11:25
Hetch Hetchy: 10x12: NMRA O 74 40/2:42
Kinnickinnic Railway & Dock: 10x16: MR Ja 72 39/1:61
Lehigh & Ohio: 5-$4\frac{1}{2}$x13-$9\frac{1}{2}$: MR D 72 39/12:49
Mann's Creek RR: 9x18: MR Jl 72 39/7:31
Marquette & Independence RR: 4x14: MR D 75 42/12:62
Narragansett Pier RR: 10x14: MR S 74 41/9:43

Design

New Jersey Northern: 9-6x15: NMRA O 73 39/2:46
Pacific Electric: 8x16 in O traction: MR Mr 73 40/3:53-57
Peace River Railroad: 6-9x19: NMRA D 72 38/4:12
Rowland Springs: 10x15: MR Je 74 41/6:45
Sagatukett River: 10x15 in std or ng: MR Mr 72 39/3:61
Saranac & Wolf Pond: 6x16-6: MR Ja 75 42/1:53
Sierra Santa Fe: 8x13: MR Jl 74 41/7:49
Skagit River RR: 4 layouts connected in 10x12: NMRA Mr 73 38/7: 7-10
Southern Pacific Coast RR: 10x15: NMRA Ap 72 37/8:7-8
Tennessee Southern: 5-6x15: MR Jl 71 38/7:59
Termite Timber: 6x11-3 logging: MR Ja 75 42/1:55
Troll & Elfin: 6x11: RMC Jl 73 42/2:31
Tupper Lake & Faust Junction: 10x15-9 with 3x5 helix extension: MR Mr 75 42/3:72
Union Central: 5x12: MR S 71 38/9:52
Union Metropolitan Transit: 6x12: MR S 72 39/9:38
Vicksburg & Eastern: 6x12: MR S 72 39/9:38
Watkins, Walford, & Western: 9x11 in N gauge: MR N 74 41/11: 94
Yosemite Valley Model Track Plan: 8x15: NMRA D 74 74 40/4:18
nameless: 12x14 modular, portable in two station wagons: MR D 73 40/12:63

(Both Dimensions 10' to 20')

Ashville & Augusta Connecting Ry: 12x17: MR Ap 71 38/4:48
B&M Still River Division: 10-3x14 in N gauge: RMC F 74 42/9:39
Bay Point & Clayton Valley: 15-6x19-6: MR Ag 73 40/8:49
Central Indiana: 18x19 std & ng: MR Je 72 39/6:32
Fox River Grove RR: 12x12: MR F 75 42/2:64
Green Valley Railroad: 12x12: NMRA S 72 38/1:17
Kaw Valley: 15x20 traction: MR F 72 39/2:41
L&N RR: 12x15 double level: MR N 72 39/11:64-65
Live Oak, Perry & Gulf: 16x16: NMRA Ag 73 38/12:32-33
Mad River Navigation Ry: 14-9x20: RMC My 73 40/5:55
New Jersey Northern: 12x18: MR F 73 40/2:52
Oriana Line: 11x12: RMC O 73 42/5:43
Ottumwa Central: 16-6x20: MR My 74 41/5:43
Pacific Coast Railway: 12x18: NMRA D 73 39/4:22
Palouse & Lewiston Air Line RR: 14x19; MR Ja 74 41/1:67
Pine Valley RR: 16-6x19-9; MR My 74 41/5:41
Quanta RR: 13-8x20 double level in three stages of development: MR Je 71 38/6:54-55
Reader RR: 20x20: NMRA O 73 39/2:23
Rio Grande & San Juan: 18-9x20 in Sn$3\frac{1}{2}$ gauge: MR O 71 38/10: 47
Rossadora Western: 15x19: MR F 74 41/2:47
Schuykill Haven & Mine Hill: 10-3x12-9: NMRA S 73 39/1:14
South Pacific Coast RR: 15x20: NMRA Ap 72 37/8:7-9
Trott Run Railroad: 11x11: NMRA Je 73 38/10:24
Union Railroad: 15x17: NMRA N 73 39/3:14

Wagner County Railroad: 11x12: RMC O 71 40/5:49
Washington, Idaho, & Montana Ry: 12x14: MR S 75 42/9:45
Whiskytown & Shasta: 16x16: NMRA Jl 73 38/11:10
Wind River & Northern: 11x15: MR Ja 73 40/1:50
Yancy RR: 10-6x13: MR Ag 74 41/8:39

(Long Dimension Over 20'; Short, Under 20')

Allegheny & Ohio: 12-6x26: MR Jl 75 42/7:68
California Central: 14x55: NMRA N 75 41/3:35-38
Central States Electric/Seaboard & Western: 15x25 rail & traction: RMC Jl 71 40/2:26-30
Chesapeake & Allegheny: 12x36: MR Je 73 40/6:37
Dover Hill Western: 15-6x22-6 expandable from 6x14 to multi-level: MR Ag 75 42/8:40-43
East Broad Top: 18x30: MR D 71 38/12:54-55
CP&BS: 17x24: RMC N 74 43/6:37
Glencoe Skokie Valley: 18x24: MR Ag 72 39/8:44-45
Gorre & Daphetid II: 6-6x20-6 with 3x14 extension: MR Ap 73 40/4:39
Great Lakes Western: 17x41: MR Ag 71 38/8:39
Kinzua Creek Lumber Co.: 6x26: RMC Jl 75 44/2:42-43
L&N: 16-4x23: RMC Ag 74 43/2:42
Lake Forest & Scagattville: 19-6x20-8: MR N 73 40/11:51
New York Central: 13x64 in O & O traction: MR Ja 72 39/1:55
Ohio, Michigan, & South Shore: 12-3x38-6: MR Mr 75 42/3:46
Pacific Coast Railway: 18x32: NMRA Mr 75 40/7:32-33
Penn Creek Valley: 15x25: RMC N 75 44/6:50
Plymouth: 17x32: MR F 73 40/2:40
Reading & Western: 12x22: RMC My 75 43/12:39
St. Clair Northern: 17x35: MR S 73 40/9:39
Shasta Southern: 15-6x25-6 traction: MR Ap 73 40/4:49
Sierra Railroad: 15x20-6: NMRA D 73 39/4:21
Simpatico: 12x22, std, ng, & traction: MR Jl 74 41/7:32
South Shore: $2\frac{1}{2}$x162 in O traction (can be bent or spiraled): NMRA Je 75 40/10:27
Spud Valley Club: 16x48: RMC D 71 40/7:43
Texas & Rio Grande Western: 14-6x46-6: RMC O 74 43/5:35
Thunder Valley: 11x24 in HOn3, On20", & On3 combined: RMC Ag 73 42/3:30
WUT: 8x22 portable: MR N 72 39/11:61
Weird & Wonderful: 18-6x45: RMC O 72 41/5:40-41
Western Maryland, Elkins Division: 15x22: NMRA Ap 74 39/9:14-15
Woodland Valley & Western: 12x28: MR Ap 75 42/4:60
nameless: 8x28: MR D 74 41/12:66

Design

(Both Dimensions Over 20')

Apache Mining & Tombstone Valley & Eagle Rock Gulch: 20x28-8: MR N 71 38/11:40
Black Hills Railroads: 25x45 mining: NMRA Jl 72 37/11:27-28
Canadaigua Southern: 24x36 + 18' tunnel in 1' diameter pipe outside: MR Ja 71 38/1:46-47
Canadaigua Southern II: 24x36: MR Ja 71 38/6:31
Chattahoochee Valley: 27x40: MR D 73 40/12:74-75
Gorre & Daphetid III: 24x32: MR Ap 73 40/4:40
Grand Valley: 23x26: RMC Je 75 44/1:33
Laurel, Christon, & Johnsville: 20x22-8 portable: MR S 71 38/9:33
Millcreek Road: 28-6x35-6 in O & On3: MR Je 71 38/6:31
MoPac/Santa Fe: 24x40: RMC Mr 75 43/10:37
Oregon Division: 40x60: MR S 73 40/9:54-55
Pacific Southern: 42x60: RMC S 74 43/4:49
Rock Island Retiree's Railroad: 22x22: NMRA Jl 75 40/11:11
Sierra Pass Revisisted: 21x35 double level in O gauge or less: MR My 72 39/5:42-47
South Oakland County: 32x44: MR Mr 74 41/3:38
South Troy, English & Wickliffe Ry: 27x30: MR N 75 42/11:51
Spare Time Lines: 23x40: MR O 73 40/9:52
Stony Creek & Western: 26-8x32: RMC Ap 75 43/11:35
Vermont Granite Railroads: 22-6x32-6 irregular in two rooms: MR O 75 42/10:58-59
Yosemite Valley Track Plan: 20x22: NMRA O 71 36/2:36-37

Layout Modules

Add-On for a Christmas Layout: engine terminal module: 6x2-5: MR D 73 40/12:50
Bitter Creek Jct: corner module: RMC N 73 42/6:50
Dual Gauge Transfer Terminal: Placerville, Consumnes, & Eastern: 2-5x9: MR My 71 38/5:35
Epithet Creek Gets a Terminal: 2-6x5-6: MR O 72 39/10:67
Iota: End of a Very Short Line: 1-5x4-8, yard: RMC My 72 40/12:44-45
North Conway: 2x8, pph: MR Je 71 38/6:62-65
Plan for an Engine Terminal: 2x12: MR O 71 38/10:41
Scenic Construction for Larger Scale Layouts: station & water tower: MW Jl 73 1/11:604-605+
Stop Gap Falls on Mescal Lines: 3x6, mine, canyon & scenic lift: RMC Ja 75 43/8:46-52; F 75 43/9:52-55
Switching the Mill at Lake Edith: 5-3x9, yard: RMC Mr 74 42/10:51-53
Timesaver: 2x6 yard or operating yard puzzle, wd: MR N 72 39/11:66-68

V. Articles   436

Outdoor

Lake George & Boulder: 40x60 Gm: MR Ap 72 39/4:59
Michigan Traction System: battery-powered traction outdoor layout: dimensions unstated, approximately one acre: MR Ap 74 41/4:58-59
Pennsylvania Live Steamers: 250x480: MR S 71 38/9:56
nameless: 105x115 live steam: RMC My 73 41/12:33
nameless: 180x350, 4 3/4 & $7\frac{1}{2}$ inch dual gauge live steam: RMC My 73 41/12:33
nameless: 75x150 in O gauge: RMC S 75 44/4:41

Other

Build an Electric Utility: power generating & transmitting facilities in layouts: MR Jl 75 42/7:43-49
The Case for Catenary: overhead electric line system: NMRA O 72 38/2:37-42
Modern Car Design: free-lancing rail motor cars: NMRA Ag 75 40/12:46-47
Outline for Locomotive Model Design: NMRA Ja 71 36/5:40-41; F 71 36/6:18-20
Similitude & Model Railroading: scalelike operations: NMRA S 72 38/1:30-32; O 72 38/2:16-19; N 72 38/3:14-15; comment D 72 38/4:49
Study Reveals Superiority of Rotating Trolley Wheel: NMRA S 73 38/1:25-26
Toluca Motor Truck: design of power truck for traction or rail car: NMRA O 71 37/2:16

Trackside Components

Model Mines for Railway Layouts: Afx S 71 13/1:24

SCENERY

Animation with Dignity: operating components without gimmicky appearance: MR Je 71 38/6:29
Putting Rail to Work of the Layout: prototype practice using rail as structural material: MR O 71 38/10:65-67
Save Space by Selective Compression: foreshortening: MR Jl 71 38/1:31

STRUCTURES

Retail Coal Dealers: RMC D 75 44/7:38-44

Structures from History: translating into models: MR Ja 71 38/1: 56-59
The Urban Scenery of Severna Park: translating prorotype buildings into layout: MR D 75 42/12:54-58

DRAFTING TECHNIQUES

Airfoil Scaling: convergent line nomograph technique for enlarging or reducing: RC Je 72 9/6:42-43
Building from Magazine Plans: drafting equipment & how to use: RC F 74 11/2:56+
Building Front Short-Cut: using slide for scaling buildings: RMC Ja 75 43/8:45
Drawing: intro to drafting techniques, particularly as applies to magazine drawings: RT Jl 72 5/7:80-81
Drawing Tapered Wing Ribs: proportional dimensioning for taper: RC Mr 73 10/3:61-62
Fuselage Lofting: for flying scale: RC F 75 12/2:56+
Making Templates from Scale Drawings: auxiliary angle projections: AFV Ag 73 4/6:22-25
Painless Parts for Planes from Plans: making full-size templates: FM Mr 73 10/3:46-48
Photo Enlarging Three-Views at Home: using slide projector & paper: RC Jl 71 8/7:52-53
Preparation of Line Drawings: basic marine drafting: MB My 75 25/292:230-231
Shelling Out for Peanuts: photo copying with slide projector & paper: AM F 75 75/2:53-54
2+2=4...Approximately: pocket computers in scaling: RC S 74 12/9:18+
Working with Scale Drawings: making own scale rule by divided diagonal method: RMC F 71 39/9:50-51

ENGINES & PROPS

ELECTRIC MOTORS

General

Assemble a Gear Drive: Dumas gears for electric RC boats: FM Jl 74 77/7:63
Cooling: problems in aircraft use: RC Ma 74 11/1:29
Dump Charging: quick-charging technique for flying batteries: RC Mr 75 12/3:53+

Electric Flight Motors: intro to type, market survey: AM Jl 73 77/1:22-26+
Electric Motor Control: MB Jl 71 247:274-275; Ag 71 21/248:317-318
Electric Motor Switching: servo operated: MB Je 71 21/246:242-243
Electric Power--Try It: intro to aircraft power: RC D 73 10/12:23-24+
Electric Power for Model Boats: MB N 74 24/286:476-477; D 74 24/287:530-531; Mr 75 25/290:124-125
Electromotive Power Plants: intro to aircraft uses: AM Mr 74 78/3:56-57+
The Intricacies of Electric Power: AM N 73 77/5:66+
Motor Magnets & How to Charge Them: how permanent magnet motors work: MR S 72 39/9:59-61
Simple Speed Control from Digital Receivers: MB Je 71 21/246:224-226
A Quiet Revolution: intro to aircraft power: RC D 73 10/12:23-24+; Ja 74 11/1:28-31+
The Sound of Things to Come: application in aircraft power: AM Ja 73 76/1:24-26
Throttles: for radio control electric aircraft: RC Jl 75 12/7:83+
Wiring Electric Aircraft for Charging: RCS D 75 1/8:19

Construction

An Electri-Flying Dream: rewind from car windshield washer motor: AM Ag 74 78/8:114-115; S 74 78/9:40-41+
Glider Power Pod: modification of SuperStar: AM Ja 73 76/1:25

Tuning & Souping

An Electri-Flying Dream: windshield washer motor rewinding: AM Ag 74 78/8:114-115; add S 74 78/9:40
Motor Magnets & How to Charge Them: MR S 72 39/9:59-61
A Quiet Revolution: matching prop to motor in electric aircraft: RC Ja 74 11/1:28-31+

INTERNAL COMBUSTION

General

The Care of Small Engines: .15 & smaller, principally Cox: RC F 74 11/2:27-30+
Glow Motors for Combat: use in event: Aero D 74 39/467:673-675

Engines

Monolith: Russian team racing engine: Aero Ap 75 40/471:222-223
The Power Scene: installation, trim, tuning, props in boats: MB S 73 23/273:370-372; props: O 73 23/274:417-418

Design

Ducted Fans & Delta Data: RM S 74 77/9:26-33
Next Generation: futuristic concepts in model glow engine design: RC O 72 9/10:8+
RPM Control: throttle for control line engines: AM Mr 72 74/3: 29-31+
Twin .71: external gearing for two Super Tigre 60, 65, or 71, for boats: MAN Ja 72 84/1:42-43+
Veco .19 Outboard Motor: conversion from Veco .19 aircraft engine: FM Ap 74 77/4:59-62

Construction

To the Rear March: converting McCoy 19 to spark ignition: AM S 73 77/3:52-53+

Conversions

Build a Veco .19 Outboard Motor: from Veco 19 aircraft engine: FM Ap 74 77/4:59-62
Diesel Conversion Heads: MAN My 75 90/5:16
Hop Up that Veco .19: McCoy conversion kit: FM Je 75 78/6:63-65
K&B 15 to Diesel: MAN My 75 90/5:16+
Model Engine Recoil Starter: for McCoy 19 or 29 engines: RCS D 75 1/8:12-13+
Rossi 15 to Diesel: MAN My 75 90/5:16+
ST G15 to Diesel: MAN My 75 90/5:16+
To the Rear March: McCoy 19 to spark ignition: AM S 73 77/3: 52-53+

Cooling

Conversion of Aero Engines for Marine Use: water cooling modifications, throttles: MB Ap 73 23/268:162-163
Scale Cooling: design of flying scale for adequate cooling: RC My 72 9/3:10+

V. Articles

Exhaust

Adjustable Noise Level Pipe: add-on for tuned pipe to reduce noise level: MB Je 75 25/293:297
Build Your Own Exhaust Throttles: FM My 75 78/5:59-62
Exhaust Pressure & How to Use It: RC F 74 11/2:35+
Getting Down to 80 dB Noise Output: boats; MB Mr 73 23/267:121
½A Tuned Pipe: AM Ja 72 74/1:38
A Hidden Muffler for Scale Models: spin-flow, some back-pressure: FM Jl 71 413:47
A Loss in RPM: muffler design to avoid loss of power: FM Ap 72 421:39
Mini-Pipes: formula for small, taperless tuned pipes: Aero My 75 40/472:292
More on Tuned Pipes: MB Ag 73 23/272:329
Muffler Construction: brazing technique: RC S 71 8/9:42-44
Next Generation: theory of muffler design for experimentation: RC O 72 421:39
Noise--Again: muffling design: MB Jl 74 24/282:273
Pressure Tap for Tuned Pipes: pressurizing fuel system tap: MB O 73 23/274:419
Reflector Silencers: tuned pipe design & formula: MB Ja 75 25/288:24
Silencing Tips: exhaust port change & expansion area mufflers: MB My 74 24/280:169
The Story of How the Muffler Got its Bad Name: RC Ag 74 11/8:120-123
Tuned Pipe Silencers: current design trends: MB Ap 74 24/279:116-118
What's All the Noise About: muffling power boats: FM Je 74 77/6:62-63
Wooden Muffler: how to build: RC Je 74 11/6:46-47

Fuel System

Carrier Fuel Control: Aero Ap 73 38/447:200
Chicken Hopper: team race tank for control line: Aero O 71 36/429:557
Clunk Tank Improvement: AM F 71 72/2:39
Custom Fuel Tanks for RC: flim hardener bottle for clunk tank: RC Ag 75 12/8:88
Fuel Filter & Valve: cuts out carb for filling: AM Mr 71 72/3:39
Fuel Lines: for formula racers: RC S 71 8/9:78-79
High Performance Throttles: control line carrier equipment for boat engine control: FM O 75 78/10:59-61
Lion or Lamb: O&R carb modification: MB S 74 24/284:368-369+
Metal Pressure Feed Tank: wedge with crankcase pressure: Aero F 75 40/469:111

Navy Carrier Throttles: MAN F 74 88/2:14-16+
Outwitting Murphy's Law: fuel tank design & use: AM N 74 74/11: 88-91
Pendulum Throttle Control: for FF scale: Aero Mr 73 38/446:167
Pressurized Fuel Systems: pressure for pylon racers: RC Ja 71 8/1:10+
RPM Control: 3-speed control for control line: AM Mr 72 74/3: 29-31+
Simple Fuel Tank Float Valve: for distance flights using feed tank: RC Je 72 9/6:44
Stunt Tank: how to make: Aero Ja 75 40/468:40-41
Surgical Tube Tank: pacifier-type: Aero F 75 40/469:111
Tanks for B Team Racers: pressure & squeeze-bottle refueling systems: Aero Mr 75 40/470:149
Team Race Tank: Aero My 72 37/436:269+
Throttle Pushrod Systems: for radio control: AM Ap 72 74/4:20
Uniflow Tank: team race fuel tank: Aero Ja 71 36/420:38

Ignition

Airborne Glow Plug Supply: in-air plug heating from battery: RC D 74 11/12:57-58
Cheap Fuel: spark ignition as alternative to glow fuel costs: FM F 71 407:32-33
Epoxied "Fireball" Glow Plugs: improving stock glow plug: Aero Je 75 40/473:330-331
Shielded Ignition for Old Timers: for RC application: MAN F 75 90/2:56-58
Spark Ignition Shielding: adapting spark engines to radio control: MAN D 72 85/6:34
To the Rear March: converting glow to spark: AM S 73 78/9:52-53+

Noise

Mandatory Mufflers: RC My 72 9/5:3
Measurement of Noise Level: MB Ja 74 24/277:33-34
Noise--Again: measurement problems: MB Jl 74 24/282:273
Noise & Vibration: vibration-damping mounts: MB O 74 24/285: 433
Noise, Mufflers, & Fields: RC Ap 75 12/4:2+
Noise Notes: MB Ja 75 25/288:24
Protect Your Hearing: noise & hearing loss: AM D 73 77/6:64+
Quietness of Model Boats: MB Ag 74 24/283:327-328; S 74 24/284:382

V. Articles

Troubleshooting

Carbon & Varnish: what it is & how to prevent it: RC Mr 73 10/3:10+
Northfield-Ross Engines: troubleshooting, maintanence: FM Ag 72 75/8:46-49

Tuning & Souping

Care & Feeding of Cox TC .049 Engines: correcting defects in cylinders: MAN F 73 86/2:9+
Compression Ratios for Glows: compression ratio vs. nitromethane content in fuel: Aero Jl 75 40/474:747
Elementary Engine Rework: intro to souping: MAN Ja 74 88/1:14-16+
½A Tuning: MAN Jl 72 88/1:23+
Jets: selection of metering jet, souping: MAN F 71 82/2:12+
K&B 6.5cc SR II: improving within the limits of remaining "stock": MAN N 75 91/5:48-50+
Motor Tuning: basic glow engine tuning: MB S 73 23/273:371
Reversing Rotation: K&B for carrier, prevents torque affecting take-off: MAN Ap 73 86/5:22-23+
Super Tune Your Super Stunter: MAN O 74 89/4:14-16+

RUBBER

Cartridge Loading for Rubber Motors: Aero Ap 75 40/471:209-212
Free Flight Bearings: thrust bearing types: MAN N 75 91/5:25-27+
Geared Rubber: advantages of gearing: AM O 73 77/4:52
Knot Trouble?: rubber knot tying for indoor planes: AM Ag 71 73/2:45
Lubrication & Preparation: Aero Jl 74 39/461:372-374
Pirelli Parameters: graph from determining motor size: AM Jl 71 73/1:41
Pretensioning: Aero Je 74 39/461:306-307+
Running In: Aero N 74 39/466:606-607
Winding: Aero Ag 74 39/462:435-437

STEAM

Flash Steam Propulsion--With No Moving Parts: putt-putt: MB F 75 25/289:69-71

Engines

FUEL

B Team Race Glow Fuels: Aero Je 74 39/461:293-295
Cheap Fuels: ignition engine fuel: FM F 71 407:32-34; My 71 410: 36-38
Compression Ratios for Glows: compression ratio vs. nitromethane content in fuel: Aero Jl 75 40/474:747
Cumene-Base Fuel: B team race fuel: Aero Je 75 40/473:329
Fuel Mixture: for RC Flying: RC F 73 10/2:2+
Hot Fuel: for CL carrier: MAN My 75 90/5:90
Jet Fuel: MAN F 71 82/2:12
Long Range Fuel: B team race fuel: Aero My 75 40/472:289
Medium Range Fuel: B team race fuel: Aero My 75 40/472:289
Mild Fuel: for CL carrier event: MAN My 75 90/5:90
New Zealand Record Fuel: B team race fuel: Aero My 75 40/472:289
Oil: lubricating oil for model engines: Aero My 73 38/448-252
Racing Fuels: chemistry & formulae: FM Ag 74 77/8:31-32
Short Range Fuel: B team race fuel: Aero My 75 40/472:289
Two Stroke Oils--Their Analysis: MAN My 74 88/5:14-18+

PROPELLERS

Rubber

Adjustable-Pitch Prop for Pennyplane or Easy B: AM Jl 71 73/1:41
Airscrews en Masse: see separate listing, immediately following
Blade Outline: making outline rib for microfilm props: AM D 71 73/6:29
Don Edison Prewind Loading & Holding Device: Wakefield prop hub: AM Jl 72 75/1:44
Rubber Prop Design: laying out accurate blanks: AM Jl 74 78/7:68-69
Single Blade Propeller Carving: Aero My 75 40/472:274-276
Tube Clamp: for holding adjustable pitch prop blades on hub: AM My 72 74/5:60-61

(Airscrews en Masse) [all Aero]

With a Tin Can: bent sheet blades: Je 73 39/449:312-315
With a Wooden Mould: bent sheet blades: Jl 73 38/450:373-375
Attaching the Hubs: folding blades: Ag 73 38/451:424-425
Carved from Block: design, blanks, airfoils: S 73 38/452:494-495
Carved from Block: finishing: O 73 38/453:558-560

V. Articles 444

Gas

About Scale Props: for flying scale: RCS D 75 1/8:4+ ; cor Mr 76 1/11:26
About That Prop: aerodynamics of propellers: MAN Jl 73 87/1: 15-16+
Formula I Racing Prop: modifying stock props: RC F 74 11/2:10
Making Your Own Masters for Glass-Fibre Props: Aero Mr 75 40/470:147-148
Moulding Carbon Fibre Propellers: construction: Aero My 72 37/436:284-287
Prop Selection Criteria: MAN S 74 89/3:35
Propellers: selection & use in radio control: AM My 71 72/5:49+
The Super Prop?: design, modifying stock wood props: MAN Ap 72 84/4:48-49+
What's the Pitch: finding pitch, gauge & table: MAN Mr 75 90/3: 14-16+
Working up GFRP Props: improving fiberglass props: Aero Ap 74 38/459:180-182

Boat

Cavitation: what it is & effect on launching hydroplanes: FM Ja 75 78/1:64
Drive Systems: inboard power boats: FM Mr 75 78/3:59-61
An Easy Brass Stuffing Box: from aquarium valve: FM O 75 78/10:65
Gear Box: for Taplin Twin: MB Ja 74 24/277:24
Props: speed & slippage in power boat props, charts of size & speed: FM Ag 75 78/8:64-65
Props: J.G. propellers: MB O 73 23/274:417-418
Time, Speed & RPM Tables: speed prediction: MB Je 73 23/270: 167+
Two Times four--the Hard Way: cast working boat propeller making: MB Mr 74 24/278:70-71

FINISH

COLOR CHIPS

Afrika Korps Sand Yellow: AFV Mr 71 2/12:9
Blue: USAF: IM N 75 11/6:10
Blue 2-6 or 202-101: Canadian insignia blue: RT F 71 4/2:15

British Bronze-Green: std post-WW-II armor: AFV O 72 3/11:24
British Dark Green: basic WW-II European color: AFV N 73 4/8: 20
British Light Earth: armor, Feb 1941: AFV S 71 3/1:11; AFV Mr 72 3/7:11
British Smoke Gray: AFV Ag 73 4/6:26
Brown #30117: U.S., present: AFV Mr 74 4/10:20
Bundeswehr Green-Gray: present: AFV F 72 3/6:20
CAF Post-Unification Green: Canadian vehicles: RT Ja 71 4/1:2
Camouflage Off-White: German WW-II: AFV O 71 3/2:25
Dark Green: German WW-II camouflage: AFV D 74 5/1:26
Dark Olive Drab: U.S. armor, present: AFV S 72 3/10:20
Desert Yellow or Sand: British WW-II: AFV S 74 4/12:15
Field Drab 30118: U.S. four-color camouflage, present: AFV S 75 5/6:34
Forest Green 43079: U.S. four-color camouflage, present: AFV S 75 5/6:34
German Dark Brown: WW-II camouflage: AFV F 73 4/2:22
German Green Camouflage Overspray: WW-II: AFV S 73 4/7:13
German Mountain Parka Brown: WW-II uniform: Fus W 74 1/2:5
German Sand: Europe 1943-1945: RT Ja 72 5/1:2
German Shelter Camouflage Dark Brown-Black: WW-II: Fus Sp 74 1/3:32
German Shelter Camouflage Dark Tan: WW-II: Fus Sp 74 1/3:32
German Shelter Camouflage Light Brown-Gray: WW-II: Fus Sp 74 1/3:32
German Shelter Camouflage Light Tan: WW-II: Fus Sp 74 1/3:32
Green 3-213 or 503-301: Canadian army aircraft: RT Mr 71 4/3:26
Green #34127: U.S. present: AFV Mr 74 4/10:20
Grey 1-209: Canadian aircraft: RT My 71 4/5:50
Grey 1-217: Canadian aircraft: RT My 71 4/6:62
High Reflectance Grey: USAF, 1975: IM N 75 11/6:10
Insignia or Chrome Yellow: AFV My 73 4/4:28
Insignia Orange: British WW-II armor squadron marking color: AFV Ja 73 4/1:24
Insignia Yellow FS 33538: U.S. WW-II: AFV F 75 5/3:28
Italian Gray-Green: WW-II uniform: Fus Au 73 1/1:12
Italian Sand-Yellow: North Africa, 1940s: AFV Ja 72 3/5:18; Jl 74 4/11:24
Khaki: Egyptian aircraft, present: RT Jl 71 4/7:77
Light Olive Green: U.S. WW-II: AFV Je 75 5/5:28
Low Reflectance Grey: USAF, 1975: IM N 75 11/6:10
Mediterranean Light Blue: British WW-II: AFV F 71 2/11:4
Olive: Egyptain aircraft, present: RT Jl 71 4/7:77
Olive Drab: U.S. WW-II: AFV D 71 3/4:14; Ja 75 5/2:24
Panzer Blue-Gray: main German WW-II gray: AFV Jl 72 3/9:20; AFV Ap 75 5/4:24
Robin's Egg Blue: U.S. early WW-II vehicle registration numbers: AFV My 72 3/8:24
Sahara Gelb: AFV Ja 74 4/9:20
Sand 30277: U.S. four-color camouflage, present: AFV S 75 5/6: 34

Sand Brown #34127: U.S., present: AFV Mr 74 4/10:20
Sand Tan Primer: German early WW-II factory-finish color: AFV
   N 71 3/3:13; D 72 3/12:28; Mr 73 4/3:20
Sky Blue: Egyptain aircraft, present: RT Jl 71 4/7:77
Swedish "Blue": very dark bluish-gray, present: RT Je 72 5/6:
   62
Swedish "Green" or "Brownish Green": present: RT Jl 72 5/7:74
Swedish "Light Blueish Gray": present: RT Ag 72 5/8:86
Zinc Chromate Primer: Canadian aircraft: RT Ap 71 4/4:38

COLOR MIX

   Aircraft

            (Czechoslovakia--Pre WW-II)

Khaki (Olive Green): Humbrol: IM Ag 71 8/8:11
Svetle Modra (Light Blue): Humbrol: IM Ag 71 8/8:11

                (Germany--WW-II)

00 Wasserhall: Humbrol: IM Mr 72 9/3:2
01 Silber: Humbrol: IM Mr 72 9/3:2; Sc Ag 72 3/8:436
02 RLM Grau: Humbrol: IM Mr 72 9/3:2; Sc Ag 72 3/8:436
04 Gelb: Humbrol: IM Mr 72 9/3:2; Sc Ag 72 3/8:436
21 Weiss: Humbrol: IM Mr 72 9/3:2; Sc Ag 72 3/8:436
22 Schwarz: Humbrol: IM Mr 72 9/3:2; Sc Ag 72 3/8:436
23 Rot: Humbrol: IM Mr 72 9/3:2; Sc Ag 72 3/8:436
24 Dunkelblau: Humbrol: IM Mr 72 9/3:2; Sc Ag 72 3/8:436
25 Hellgrun: Humbrol: IM Mr 72 9/3:2; Sc Ag 72 3/8:436
26 Braun: Humbrol: IM Mr 72 9/3:2; Sc Ag 72 3/8:436
27 Gelb: Humbrol; IM Mr 72 9/3:2; Sc Ag 72 3/8:436
28 Weinrot: Humbrol; IM Mr 72 9/3:2; Sc Ag 72 3/8:436
61 Dunkelbraun: Humbrol: IM Mr 72 9/3:3; Sc Ag 72 3/8:436
62 Grun: Humbrol: IM Mr 72 9/3:3; Sc Ag 72 3/8:436
63 Hellgrau: Humbrol: IM Mr 72 9/3:3; Sc Ag 72 3/8:436
65 Hellblau: Humbrol: IM Mr 72 9/3:3; Sc Ag 72 3/8:436
66 Schwarzgrau: Humbrol: IM Mr 72 9/3:3; Sc Ag 72 3/8:436
70 Schwarzgrun: Humbrol: IM Mr 72 9/3:3; Sc Ag 72 3/8:436
71 Dunkelgrun: Humbrol: IM Mr 72 9/3;3; Sc Ag 72 3/8:436
72 Grun: Humbrol: IM Mr 72 9/3:3; Sc Ag 72 3/8:436
73 Grun: Humbrol: IM Mr 72 9/3:3; Sc Ag 72 3/8:436
74 Dunkelgrau: Humbrol: IM Mr 72 9/3:3; Sc Ag 72 3/8:436
75 Mettelgrau: Humbrol: Sc Ag 72 3/8:436
76 Hellgrau: Humbrol: IM Mr 72 9/3:3; Sc Ag 72 3/8:436

(Italy--WW-II)

Azzuro Paludo (Pale Blue): Humbrol: IM Ap 73 10/4:8
Giallo (Yellow): Humbrol: IM Ag 73 10/4:8
Grigio Azzur (Light Blue Grey): Humbrol: IM Ag 73 10/4:8
Grigio Chiaro (Light Grey): Humbrol: IM Ap 73 10/4:8
Sabbia (Sand): Humbrol: IM Ap 73 10/4:8
Verde Medio (Medium Green): Humbrol: IM Ap 73 10/4:8
Verde Scuro (Dark Green): Humbrol: IM Ap 74 10/4:8

(Japan--WW-II)

Dark Green A1: Modelcolour: RT F 75 8/2:21
Olive Green A/N2: IR: RT F 75 8/2:21
Medium Green A3: IR: RT F 75 8/2:21
Light Green A/N4: IR: RT F 75 8/2:21
Light Grey Green A5: IR: RT F 75 8/2:21
Dark Grey A6: IR: RT F 75 8/2:21
Medium Grey A7: IR: RT F 75 8/2:21
Medium Blue Grey A8: IR: RT F 75 8/2:21
Light Grey A9: Modelcolour: RT F 75 8/2:21
Light Blue Grey A10: IR: RT F 75 8/2:21
Dark Brown A11: IR: RT F 75 8/2:21
Medium Brown A12: Humbrol: RT F 75 8/2:21
Red Brown A13: Floquil: RT F 75 8/2:21
Light Earth A/N14: Humbrol & IR: RT F 75 8/2:21
Ivory Yellow A15: Humbrol & IR: RT F 75 8/2:21
Medium Yellow A16: IR: RT F 75 8/2:21
Deep Yellow A17: IR: RT F 75 8/2:21
Transluscent Blue A18: Testors: RT F 75 8/2:21
Red Orange A19: IR: RT F 75 8/2:21
Weathered Red A20: IR: RT F 75 8/2:21
Fresh Red A21: IR: RT F 75 8/2:21
Dark Blue A22: IR: RT F 75 8/2:21
Medium Blue A23: Humbrol & IR: RT F 75 8/2:21
Blue Black A24: Humbrol: RT F 75 8/2:21

(Israel)

Brown 30219: Humbrol: IM Ja 73 10/1:11
Green 34227: Humbrol: IM Ja 73 10/1:11
Pale Blue 35622: Humbrol: IM Ja 73 10/1:11
Yellow 33531: Humbrol: IM Ja 73 10/1:11

(USSR)

Dark Earth Brown: Humbrol: IM Ap 71 8/4:14
Dark Earth Brown: Pactra: IM Ag 72 9/8:12
Dark Olive Green: Humbrol: IM Ap 71 8/4:14
Dark Olive Green: Pactra: IM Ag 72 9/8:12

Light Grey: Pactra: IM Ag 72 9/8:12
Pale Blue: Humbrol: IM Ap 71 8/4:14
Pale Blue: Pactra: IM Ag 72 9/8:12

(U. K. & Commonwealth--WW-I)

Black: Humbrol: IM N 71 8/11:3
Clear Varnish: Humbrol: IM N 71 8/11:3
Light Grey: Humbrol: IM N 71 8/11:3
N1VO Dark Green: Humbrol: IM N 71 8/11:3
PC10 Khaki-Green: Humbrol: IM N 71 8/11:3
Roundel Blue: Humbrol: IM N 71 8/11:3
Roundel Red: Humbrol: IM N 71 8/11:3
Roundel White: Humbrol: IM N 71 8/11:3

Armor

Black #37038: U.S. present: Floquil: AFV Mr 74 4/10:20
British Bronze Green: post WW-II: Floquil: AFV O 72 3/11:24
British Dark Green: WW-II Europe: Floquil: AFV N 73 4/8:20
British Light Earth: 1941: Floquil: AFV S 71 3/1:11; AFV Mr 72 3/7:11
British Smoke Gray: Floquil: AFV Ag 73 4/6:26
Brown #30117: US present Floquil: AFV Mr 74 4/10:20
Bundeswehr Green-Gray: present: Floquil: AFV F 72 3/6:20
Camouflage Off-White: German WW-II: Floquil: AFV O 71 3/2:25
DAK Sand-Yellow: Floquil: AFV Mr 71 2/12:9
Dark Green: German WW-II camouflage: Floquil: AFV D 74 5/1:26
Dark Olive Drab: U.S. present: Floquil: AFV S 72 3/10:20
Dessert Yellow or Sand: British WW-II: Floquil: AFV S 74 4/12:15
Field Drab 30118: U.S. contemporary 4-color camouflage: Floquil: AFV S 75 5/6:34
Forest Green 34079: U.S. contemporary 4-color camouflage: Floquil: AFV S 75 5/6:34
German Dark Brown: WW-II camouflage: Floquil: AFV F 73 4/2:22
Green #34127: U.S. present: Floquil: AFV Mr 74 4/10:20
Green Camouflage Overspray: German WW-II: Floquil: AFV S 73 4/7:13
Insignia or Chrome Yellow: U.S. WW-II markings: Floquil: AFV My 73 4/4:28
Insignia Orange: British WW-II squadron markings: Floquil: AFV Ja 73 4/1:24
Insignia Yellow FS 33538: U.S.: Floquil: AFV F 75 5/3:28
Italian Sand-Yellow: North Africa, WW-II: Floquil: AFV Ja 72 3/5:18; Jl 74 4/11:24
Light Olive Green: British WW-II: Floquil: AFV Je 75 5/5:28

Mediterranean Light Blue: Floquil: AFV F 71 2/11:4
Olive Drab: U.S.: Floquil: AFV D 71 3/4:13; Ja 75 5/2:24
Panzer Blue-Gray: WW-II: Floquil: AFV Jl 72 3/9:20; Ap 75 5/4:24
Robin's Egg Blue: U.S. early WW-II registration numbers: Floquil: AFV My 72 3/8:24
Sahara Gelb: German WW-II North Africa: Floquil: AFV Ja 74 4/9:20
Sand 30277: U.S. Contemporary 4-color camouflage: Floquil: AFV S 75 5/6:34
Sand Brown #30277: U.S.: Floquil: AFV Mr 74 4/10:20
Sand Tan Primer: German early WW-II factory finish: Floquil: AFV N 71 3/3:13; AFV D 72 3/12:28; AFV Mr 73 4/3:20; Q O 73 8/4:242
Sand Tan Primer: Poly S: Q O 73 8/4:242
Sand Tan Primer: Pactra: AFV Mr 73 4/3:20

Figures

German Mountain Troop Parka Brown: WW-II: Floquil: Fus W 74 1/2:5
German Shelter Camouflage Light Brown-Gray: WW-II: Floquil: Fus Sp 74 1/3:32
German Shelter Camouflage Light Tan: WW-II: Floquil: Fus Sp 74 1/3:32
German Shelter Camouflage Dark Brown-Black: WW-II: Floquil: Fus Sp 74 1/3:32
German Shelter Camouflage Dark Tan: WW-II: Floquil: Fus Sp 74 1/3:32
Italian Gray-Green: uniform, WW-II: Floquil: Fus Au 73 1/1:12

Ships

5-H Haze Gray: USN, WW-II, Humbrol: Q Au 75 11/1:12
5-N Navy Blue: USN, WW-II, Humbrol: Q Au 75 11/1:12
5-P Pale Gray: USN, WW-II, Humbrol: Q Au 75 11/1:12
5-S Sea Blue: USN, WW-II, Humbrol: Q Au 75 11/1:12
20-B Deck Blue: USN, WW-II, Humbrol: Q Au 75 11/1:12

COVERING

Bilgri Patching & Covering Methods: microfilm: AM Mr 71 72/3: 25-27
Covering & Doping: Aero Ap 73 38/447:194-197

Fiberglass Covering: use of fiberglass in place of silk & dope: RC Jl 73 10/7:16+
Modes in Appearance: tissue finishing for CL stunt: AM Jl 73 77/1: 60-61+
Mylar: use of covering material: AM O 72 75/4:52-54+
Patches: patchwork surface pattern from scrap MonoKote: RC Ap 74 11/4:22-24
Pouring & Covering with Microfilm: AM F 71 72/2:32-35
Solarfilm: evaluation & techniques: RC Jl 71 8/7:30-31+
Super Monokote: MAN Ag 71 83/2:46-48+
Techniques of Covering & Finishing with Solarfilm: RC S 72 9/9: 43-47+

DETAILS

Applying Decals: IM My 74 10/(16):3
Applying Mylar Numerals: AM Mr 74 78/3:53
Assemble Your Own Custom Decals: blank decal & dry-transfer: MR D 73 40/12:53
Custom Decals: how to make: RC Je 71 8/6:57
Discourses on Decals: applying to matt surfaces: Sc Ag 74 5/8: 442
Dry Transfer Application: getting more accurate spacing: NMRA Ap 72 37/8:37
Evaluating Decal Base Coatings: improvements on water: Sc My 75 6/5:221
Flying Scale Details: RC S 73 10/9:16+
Masking Stencils That Work: construction & use: RC O 72 9/10: 48-49
Matting Transfers: Afx N 72 14/3:132
Reflectorized Safety Striping: from Scotchlite: RMC F 74 42/9: 52-53
Spray Painting Signs: with stencils: RMC Ja 74 42/8:47-50
Surface Detailing: rivets, panel lines, fabric tape, canopy frames: RC D 72 9/12:12+
You Can Create Your Own Decals: decal kit for pressure-sensitive letters: RC Mr 72 9/3:46-47

PAINT

General

The Acceptable Finish: RC F 71 8/2:34
Boiler Jacket Color: early locomotives: NMRA Je 71 36/10:17; add N 71 37/3:45
Checkerboards: layout & masking checkerboard cowls: RT F 75 8/2: 23

Finish

Color Mixing: RC D 70 7/12; Ja 71 8/1:14+
Colors: Fed. 595 numbers for USAAF, USN, RAF, RN, Luftwaffe colors: RC Ja 73 10/1:6+
Detailing: painting checkerboards, lettering, etc. in flying scale: RC O 73 10/10:16+
Detailing & Painting Warships: IM Mr 75 11/2:18
The Eye of the Beholder: problems of matching colors in print: AE O 74 7/4:195
Facets of Professional Finishing: preparation for painting, painting, detail finish: RMC Ag 71 40/3:24-29
Finish: intro to scale finishing: RC O 72 9/10:87-89
Finish & Detailing: scale-like finish for static models: IM N 72 9/11:2-3
Finesse in Finishing: static scale technique: AE Ag 72 3/2:89
In Search of the Perfect Paint: for figures; Fus Sp 75 2/1:39-41
It's Easy When You Know How: figure painting techniques: S&L (F 75) 6:32
Luftwaffe Camouflage: how to do: Afx S 75 17/1:37-40
Military Camouflage Color Application: applied to flying scale: RC Ag 73 10/8:70+
Miniature Figure Painting: shading & its application: Fus Au 73 1/1:33-34
Model Finishing: preparing surface & applying paint: Aero D 74 39/467:678-680+; Ja 75 40/468:37-39
Multi-tone "Natural" Finish: bare aluminum finish for aircraft models: Sc Ja 73 4/1:24-25
Paint for Performance: finish design for orientation of RC aircraft: AM S 74 78/9:50+
Paint Like a Pro: spraycan dope finishes for flying models: RC F 74 11/2:23-26+
Paint Removal: de-painting plastic models: RT Ja 75 8/1:3
Paint Selection for Flying Scale: intro: RC Ja 73 10/1:6+
Painting Diesel Switchers: MR Jl 74 41/7:36-40
Painting a Figure: Afx Jl 72 13/11:622-623
Painting & Finishing Ship Models: old time vessels: IM Ja 75 11/1:16
Painting Modern Warships: IM My 75 11/3:15-16
Painting the Western Pacific Outside-Braced Cupola Caboose: NMRA Ap 74 39/9:48-50
Painting Without Tears: intro to figure painting, selection of brushes, paint types: S&L (Ap 75) 7:23
Paints: clear flat for static scale: MM My 75 5/5:298
Pearl Finish: how to get: AM Ag 73 77/2:68
Perfect Finish with a Brush: use of long-flow epoxy paints: AM Je 72 74/6:29-31+
Perfecting the Paint Job: plastic scale finish: AE My 73 4/5:251+
A Place for Lace: lace paint patterns for aircraft: FM F 72 419:41-43
Question of Scale Colour: matching color to "look right": Sc Je 75 6/6:270-271+
Quick Silver: applying silver paint by brush, spray can, & airbrush: IM Mr 74 10/(15):12
RLM Colours Equivalents: Humbrol matching: Sc Ag 72 3/8:436

V. Articles   452

Shading & Its Application: miniature figure painting: Fus Au 73 1/
   1:33-34
Ship Model Paint: selection & application: Sc Je 72 3/6:315-316
Techniques with Paint: mixing, use in armor: AFV S 73 4/7:11
Techniques with Paints: AFV S 73 4/7:11
Tinting Tips: formulae for avocado, gold, light brown, orange,
   purple, turquoise, burgandy, & gray using five basic colors:
   AM Ja 72 74/1:34
Tips on Mixing Paint: eyedropper measuring, etc.; AFV Mr 71 2/
   12:30

   Airbrushes

The Air Brush & the Innocent: introduction to use: IM Ja 75 11/1:
   11
Air Brush Technique: NMRA Mr 71 36/7:27
Airbrush Afterthoughts: how to use: Afx S 73 15/1:22-23
Airbrush Artistry: use of airbrush: Sc O 71 2/10:555-557+
Airbrush Techniques: AN 2 F 73 1/19:14-15
Airbrush Techniques: PAM Ap 74 5:66-67
Fine Spraying: MR F 73 40/2:88
Introducing the Airbrush: Afx My 72 13/9:502-503+
Multicolor Painting: MR Jl 75 42/7:34-35
Painting with an Airbrush: MR Jl 74 41/7:38-39

WEATHERING

Aging Boards & Shingles: MR Ap 71 38/4:46-47
Aging With Chalks: pastels: MR D 72 39/12:46-48+
Aging Wood Cars: MR O 72 39/10:56-57
Finishing Espee Steam Power: NMRA My 74 39/10:30-33
Weathering: flak damage & gas stains: IM S 71 8/9:6
Weathering Armor Models: AFV Ap 75 5/4:35
Weathering for Realism: boat weathering: FM S 74 77/2:64-65
Weathering Techniques: static scale aircraft: RiS Ag 72 1/1:30-
   31
Weathering with a Brush: MR O 75 42/10:61-63
Whether to Weather: aircraft weathering: Afx Jl 72 13/11:592-593

MISCELLANEOUS FINISHING

Bricks: how to make realistic: RMC F 75 43/9:56-57
An Easy Way to Custom Letter Cars: paper sides using dry transfer masters & felt-tip colored copy for rolling stock sides:

RMC N 75 44/6:61-63
Uses of Rub 'n Buff: RMC Ap 75 43/11:48-49

HISTORY--AIRCRAFT

GENERAL

Aerobatics--Skill or Strength: Lockheed Trophy vs. World Championship styles: AN 7 F 75 1/13:13
British Aircraft in Belgian Colours: AN 18 Ap 75 3/23:4-6
The Crop Dusters: AN 5 S 75 4/7:6
The Fight for the Skies: Air Superiority Development: AE Je 73 4/6:267-281
Fighter Spectrum: contemporary fighter development: AE Je 71 1/1:5-8+; Jl 71 1/2:74-78
Front Office Evolution: cockpits: AE F 72 2/2:63-67; Je 72 2/6: 291-294; N 72 3/5:237-240; Ap 73 4/4:188-191; O 73 5/4:172-176; AI Ag 74 7/2:84-87
Horsas Make Good Henhouses: present use for WW-II gliders: AN 25 Jl 75 4/4:6-7
Italy to England in Three Days: SR.1 airship ferry, 1918: AE F 73 4/2:84-88
Lamps Illuminated: multi-purpose, destroyer-based USN helicopters: AE Ap 73 4/4:169-174
Lend Lease Flying Boats: Coronado & Mariner in RAF service: AN 15 N 74 3/12:4
Mistel: PAM Ja 75 8:126-130
Oil Rig Aviation: servicing off-shore drilling platforms: AN 15 F 74 2/19:12-13
Pulham Pigs: RAF airships: AN 13 O 72 1/11:7
The Rise & Demise of a Weapon: military gliders: AE Mr 72 2/3: 126-134+; Ap 72 2/4:207-212; My 72 2/5:250-253; Je 72 2/6: 318-322
Samaritan Sea Kings: SAR in Norway, Germany, & Denmark: AN 10 N 72 1/13:13
Tank Busting Aircraft of the Luftwaffe: Fus Sp 75 2/1:6-11
Tutors with Teeth: Military Trainers & Light Attack Aircraft: AI Je 75 8/6:269-284
USAAF Aircraft Nicknames: individual aircraft: WWE S 74 1/5: 139+

AIR BASES

RAF Acklington: AN 16 F 73 1/20:4-5

V. Articles 454

Airfields of the 8th Air Force: complete list: WWE Ja 75 2/1: 13-15
Brigands, Balliole & Meteors: RAF North Luffenham in the Fifties: AN 28 N 75 4/13:4-5
Barksdale AFB: HQ or 2 AF: AN 13 D 74 3/14:6
Cherry Point: USMC: AN 7 D 73 2/15:4-5
RAF Cosford: AN 1 F 74 2/18:12-13
RAF Debden: AN 8 D 72 1/15:8-9
RAF Driffield: AN 21 Mr 75 3/21:4-6
RAF Duxford: AN 12 O 73 2/11:10-11
For Post Graduates Only: RAF Manby: AN 19 Ja 73 1/18:6
Gottesmore: RAF: AN 18 Ja 74 2/17:6
Grafton Underwood: 8th Air Force WW-II base: WW2J My 72 2/3: 82-83
Haldon Aerodrome: AN 14 S 73 2/9:6
RAF Halton: training base: AN 24 N 72 1/14:11
Hurlburt Field: Elgin AFB satellite field: AN 27 Ap 73 1/24:10-11
Kirtland AFB: research: AN 17 Ag 73 2/7:6
RAF Leuchars: AN 12 O 73 2/1:4-5
Malta--Holiday Isle or Military Base: RAF base: AN 9 Ag 74 3/5:4-5+
RAF Newton: AN 6 Jl 73 2/4:10
RAF North Coates: AN 13 O 72 1/11:12-13
Parachute Support Unit: RAF Hullavington: AN 30 Mr 73 1/23:11
Portage la Prairie: CAF training base: AN 11 My 73 1/26:10-11
San Francisco Coast Guard Air Station: AN 1 N 74 3/11:7
HMS Siskin--the Concrete Carrier: AN 9 Je 72 1/2:11
So You Want to Fly a Sea King: RNAS Culdrose: AN 4 Ag 73 1/6:4-5
Swing-Wing Birds of Pease: Pease AFB, NH: AE Ja 72 2/1:7-11
Too Many Airfields: survey of U.K. military airfields: AN 14 S 73 2/9:10
Yeovilton: AN 7 Jl 72 1/4:7

AIR BATTLES & CAMPAIGNS

Achtung Moskito: German night fighter operations: RT S 74 7/9: 104; My 75 8/5:56-57
Against Enemy & Elements: air operations in Mesopotamia, 1915-1918: AN 9 Je 72 1/2:12-13
Battle of Britain Units: sqn, base, a/c type, code letters (some serial number, code letter, sqn, & pilot's name): Q Ja 73 8/1:49
The Battle of the Flying Bomb: AN 18 Ag 72 1/7:4-6
Bomber Raced Down Path of Bullets to Blast a U-Boat: contemporary news account: WWE Ja 75 2/1:6
The Bombing of Japan: WWE N 74 1/6:174-175
Bombs by Balloon: Japanese use of robot balloon bombs in WW-II: AE F 74 6/2:79-83
Broken Wings... Broken Hopes: defense of the Reich: RT F 72 5/2:22

China Incident: AE Ap 73 4/4:198-199
Conflict over the Carpathians: Hungarian-Slovak war, 1939: AE S 71 1/4:180-183
Emil Versus the Luftwaffe: Yugoslavia invaded: AE S 71 1/4:209-211
Gallipoli Carriers: carrier operations in Turkey, WW-I: AN 13 O 72 1/11:6-7
High Flying Raiders: Ju 86P high altitude bombing & Mosquito counter-measures: AN 18 O 74 3/10:4-5
The Holy Day Air War: Yom Kippur War: AE My 74 6/5:240-252
Insatz. 39: NJG 6 Engagement: RT S 71 4/9:101+; cor N 71 4/11:122
Journal of an Air War: India-Pakistan, 1971: AE Ap 72 2/4:177-183+
A Ju 88 Mystery: British acquire first Ju 88R-1 nightfighter: AI D 75 9/6:282
Lucky Bastards Club: three combat incidents by B-25 radio operator: WW2J S 75 2/5-6:8
Ludwig Viktor Strikes Again: RT D 71 4/12:137
A Night Hawk Spreads His Wings: Weinmann, NJG 6: RT N 73 6/11:124; F 75 7/2:17
An OS2U Gets a Zero: Kingfisher combat incident: WWE Mr 74 1/2:52
The Parson's Nose Remembers: account of child's first V-1 sightings: RT Ap 74 7/4:39; My 74 7/5-6:51-52
Portugal's Forgotten War: Guinea-Biseau: AE F 72 2/2:59-62+
Post-Mortem on an Air War: India-Pakistan, 1971: AE My 72 2/5:227-232+
Prelude to a Mission: USAAF, WW-II: AN 30 Mr 73 1/23:10-11
Steve Ritchie gets His Fifth: first Vietnam War ace: RT Jl 74 7/7:74
Supporting a "Sensitive" War: British involvement in South Yemen: AE S 72 3/3:115-119
Thirty Seconds over Sargodha: Indo-Pakistan war of 1965 engagement: AE Je 71 1/1:16-19
The Undeclared War: 1939 Russo-Japanes border war: AE My 73 4/5:245-250; Je 73 4/6:294-296; Jl 73 5/1:26-29+
Unternehmen "Bodenplatte" The Final Gamble: January 1945, last German air offensive: AI Ja 75 8/1:29-32+
War in the Northwest: RCAF Alaskan campaign, 1942-1943: RT Je 71 4/6:67; S 71 4/9:99; F 72 5/2:17; Ag 72 5/8:88+
Was It Necessary to Drop the Atom Bomb on Japan? reasons pro & con at the time: WWE N 74 1/6:176+

AIR FORCES

Nations

Air Commandos in Action: British Navy helicopter operations: Afx

V. Articles

Ag 74 15/12:698-699
Air National Guard Units, 1973: aircraft flown & bases: AE Ap 73 4/4:177
The Arab Professionals: Jordan: AI S 75 9/3:111-117
Arabian Fledgling: Royal Saudi AF: AE Je 72 2/6:301-308
Army Aviation 1974: U.K.: AN 15 F 74 2/19:4-5
Asiatic Air Cover: Japan: AE Ag 73 5/2:67-73+
At Home with the Fleet Air Arm: Afx Jl 74 15/11:646+
Australian Air Power: AE Mr 74 6/3:109-114+
Aviazione della RSI: Q Ja 75 10/3:116-122
Belgium's Air Arm, Today & Tomorrow: AI D 75 9/6:267-274
Black Knights of Ramstein: USAF in Europe: AN 22 Ag 75 4/6: 6-7
Canadian Military Aviation Today: AI Ap 75 8/4:163-169+
Current Swiss Air Force Aircraft Types: AN 19 S 75 4/8:6
Diamond Dutch: AN 3 Ag 73 2/6:4-5
Diamond for the Dutch: 60th Anniversary Royal Netherlands AF: AE Jl 73 5/1:23-25+
Eighth Air Force Tactical Development: Aug 1942-May 1945: WWE Mr 74 1/2:28-30
European Commitment: USAF in NATO: AN 2 F 1/19:10-11
A Facelift for the Luftwaffe: aircraft & tactics: AE F 72 2/2:68-71
Far Eastern Threesome: U.K., Australian, & New Zealand combined operations: AE Ja 74 6/1:17-18+
Fighters of the RAF: AE S 71 1/4:191-196+
Finland's Air Force: AN 23 Ag 74 3/6:10
Fleet Air Arm in War & Peace: Afx O 74 16/2:101-103+; N 74 16/3:158-160+; D 74 16/4:238-242; Ja 75 16/5:309+; F 75 16/6:347-348+
The Flying Leathernecks: U.S. Marine Corps Today & Tomorrow: AI Ag 75 9/2:61-66+
French Air Force, 1938-40: Q W 75 11/2:59
Fuerza Aerea Facelift: Argentina: AE Ag 72 3/2:72-77
Germany's Quiet Birdmen: 1922-1933 German pilot training in Russia: AM Ja 75 75/1:52-57+
Half Decade & Air Defence: Singapore: AE O 73 5/4:158-162+
Harvards of the SAAF: South African training in the 1950s: Afx N 71 13/3:139+
Iberian Air Cover: Spain: AI Jl 74 7/1:14-18+
Indian Ocean Air Power: India's carrier forces: AE D 72 3/6: 275-281
Irish Air Corps: 1922 to present: Q Jl 73 8/3:141-143
Israel, Preparing for the Next Round: AE D 71 1/7:343-350
It Ain't 'Arf Hot Mum: RAF in India, WW-II: AN 23 Ag 74 3/6:4-5
Jets in the Spanish Air Force: AN 17 O 75 4/10:12-14
Jungle Fliers of the Rubber State: Malasian AF: AE Ag 71 1/3: 147-151
Mais Alto: Portuguese AF: AN 22 Ag 75 4/6:4-5+
NATO: Airforces, equipment, & bases: AN 7 Mr 75 3/20:4-13
Oil Well Top Cover: Rumanian AF: AE Je 71 1/1:25-35+
The Paradox of Japan's Maritime Wings: AI My 75 8/5:222-227+
The Planes in Spain: AN 21 F 75 3/19:14

Quantity or Quality? the Indian Dilemma: AI O 75 9/4:170-179
RAF Germany: U.K. NATO bases: AN 23 N 73 2/14:12-13
Royal Air Force 1974: survey of equipment & bases: AN 4 O 74 3/9:4-13
Royal Air Force Today & Tomorrow: AE Ap 74 6/4:159-169
SAAF Dakotas: South African transports in 1950s & '60s: Afx Ap 72 13/8:435-442+
Stronger Sealegs: Soviet naval aviation: AE Je 74 6/6:271-277+
The Sultan's Defenders: Oman: Afx Ag 75 16/12:717+
Sweden's Air Defences: AN 31 O 75 4/11:4-6
Switzerland's Air Force: AN 19 S 75 4/8:4-5
Third USAF in Britain: AN 7 Jl 73 1/4:4-6
Topsails for the Armada: Spain: AE N 73 5/5:211-215
Tree Top Warriors: Pakistani Army Aviation: AE O 72 3/4:167-170
Turkish AF: AE Jl 71 1/2:63-66
U.S. Coast Guard: aircraft operations: AN 1 N 74 3/11:3-6
U.S. Coast Guard at War: AN 1 N 74 3/11:12-13
Venezuela Refurbishes Her Aerial Sombrero: AE S 73 5/3:118-124+
Winged Springbok: South African AF: AE Mr 73 4/3:111-116

Organization Charts

Eighth Air Force, May 1942: WWE Mr 74 1/2:29
Eighth Air Force, Aug 1942: WWE Mr 74 1/2:30

Unit Histories

Ambassadors in Blue: USAF Thunderbirds: Fus Mr 75 3/1:32-34+
Aussies in England: 455 & 452 Squadrons, RAAF: AN 20 Jl 73 2/5:6-7
CEAM: French test unit: AN 8 D 72 1/15:4-5
Canada's Snowbirds: aerobatic team: AN 17 Ag 73 2/7:11
Chivenor's Anniversary: 229 OCU: AN 15 F 74 2/19:7
Comet Squadron Disbands: 216 Sqn, RAF: AN 25 Jl 75 4/4:5
Condor Legion: MW F 73 1/6:301-302; Ap 73 1/8:404-409; My 73 1/9:462-465; Ag 73 1/12:638-639
Danish Transports: 721 Esk: AN 17 O 75 4/10:15
Douglas Dauntless in RNZAF Service: 25 Sqn: IM S 74 10/(18):4-7
8 Sqn (BR) RCAF: RT F 72 5/2:258-269+
81 Tactical Fighter Wing: AN 13 O 72 1/11:13
Escadrille Lafayette: AN 21 F 75 3/19:4-6
F-111s in the Midlands: 79 Tactical Fighter Sqn, USAF in U.K.: AN 7 D 73 2/15:5
Ferry Squadron, RAF: AN 6 Jl 73 2/4:4-5
First with the Jaguar: 7 Escadrille de Chasse: AN 29 S 72 1/10:4-5

He Who Dares: RAF Sqn 603: Sc My 74 5/56:258-259+
Jasta 5: Sc N 71 2/11:587-589
Jungle Lift Experts: 103 Sqn, helicopters: AN 10 My 74 2/25:4-5
Lady Moe: 96 Bomb Group, USAAF mascot: AN 4 Ja 74 2/16:4
Look... No Hands: 728 Sqn drone missile targets: AN 14 S 73 2/9:4-5
Lossimouth Gannetry: Gannets of 849 Sqn, FAA: AN 27 D 74 3/15:7
Luftwaffe Transport Squadrons: post WW-II: AN 27 O 72 1/12:11
Night Hawks of the South Pacific: USN night-flighter unit: WWE N 74 1/6:172
No. 7 Squadron's Anniversary: AN 26 Jl 74 3/4:16
No. 23 Sqn: Havoc I (Intruder) 1941: MW Mr 73 1/7:377; Lightning F3 & F6, 1964-1973: O 73 2/2:82-83
No. 781 Sqn--the Navy's Airline: FAA: Afx Je 75 16/10:573-574
Normandie-Niemen Fighter Regiment: Q Ja 72 7/1:9
Normandie-Niemen Rgt: AN 12 Ap 74 2/23:4-5
111 Grupe (Kampfgeschwader 3): RT Ap 71 4/4:39+
Operation Thursday: Air Support for Wingate's Chindits: 1 Air Commando Group: AN 3 O 75 4/9:4-7
Patrouille de France is 20: aerobatic team: AN 6 Jl 73 2/4:11
Puerto Rico Air Guard: AN 12 O 73 2/11:6
RAF Aerobatic Teams, 1973: AN 22 Je 73 2/3:8-10
RAF Squadron Directory: all to date, paragraph on each: AE Ap 74 6/4:179-189
Scanning the Seas: 543 Sqn, RAF: AN 14 S 73 2/9:11
Second Air Commando Group, Burma: Q Jl 71 6/3:12-13
Senior RAF Squadron: 6 Sqn: AN 1 Mr 74 2/20:6
Sentai 74: 1 Sen, WW-II: RT Mr 75 8/3:29
7 Air Division, USAF: AN 24 N 72 1/14:4-5
67 Aerospace Rescue & Recovery Sqn, USAF: Afx Mr 75 16/7:402-403+
Southampton University Air Squadron: AN 2 F 73 1/19:13
3 Squadron Gladiators & Bulldogs: Sc F 71 2/2:90-91
36th Tactical Fighter Wing, USAF: Q Ja 73 8/1:45
355 Tactical Fighter Wing, USAF: RiS Sp 73 1/3:95-97
368 Fighter Squadron at War: AN 18 Ja 74 2/17:7
University Air Squadrons: AN 28 N 75 4/13:6-7
Wasp Squadron: 829 Sqn, Royal Navy: AN 8 Je 73 2/2:7
Wessex over the Vineyards: 18 Sqn helicopters: AN 14 Je 74 3/1:10-11
Whiskey Four: Netherlands aerobatic team: AN 16 F 73 1/20:13

AIR RACES & AIR SHOWS

Air Races at Reno: AN 29 N 74 3/13:4-5
A Day Out with Rothmans: Pitts Special aerobatic team: AI Ag 74 7/2:64-67
Safety at Air Displays: AN 10 My 74 2/25:7
They Fly Pitts Specials: Rothman's aerobatic team: AN 11 My

History--Aircraft

73 1/26:13
200 mph Volkswagen: Formula V aircraft racing: AM F 74 78/2: 52-55+
Unlimited Racing with the Hot Ships: AE My 72 2/5:240-241

AIRCRAFT--Individual

Pre World War I

Edsel's Folly: 1909 Ford monoplane: AM My 72 74/5:32-33+
Voisin of 1909: Sc N 72 3/11:596-599

World War I

Airco DH 2: 1915 pusher scout: Sc Je 72 3/6:320-323
Albatross D.V & D.Va: 1917 German fighters: Sc S 72 3/9:489-493
Avro 504K: AM Jl 71 73/1:28-31+
Avro 504K: 1913 trainer: Sc My 75 6/5:216
Avro 504K-L: AN 27 D 74 3/15:8-9
Brandenburg C.I: AN 20 S 74 3/8:8-9
Bristol F.2B: AN 12 O 73 2/11:7-9
DFW C.V: 1918 German two-seat observation: Sc Mr 71 2/3:147-149
DH 9: Sc O 75 6/10:484-485
De Havilland DH.4: 16 My 75 3/25:8-9
De Havilland DH 10 Mk III: AN 14 Je 74 3/1:8-9
Fokker D.VII: Sc F 74 5/2:84-88
Fokker D.VIII: AN 9 Je 72 1/2:8-9
German Army P-Type Zepplins: MM Je 71 1/6:304-309
Handley Page's Bloody Paralyser: Type O series: AE Ag 73 5/2: 74-81
Hansa Brandenburg D.I: Sc Ag 74 5/59:414-419
LVG C.VI: 1918 two-seat photo recon: Sc Ja 73 4/1:27-31
Morane Saulnier N: 1914 French monoplane fighter: Sc N 72 3/11: 588-590
Nieuport 17: AN 6 Jl 73 2/4:8-9
Nieuport 28C-1: AN 21 F 75 3/19:8-9
Pfalz D.III: IM S 73 10/9:2-6
Pfalz D.VIII: 1918 German fighter: AM Jl 73 77/1:40-41+
The Red Baron's Aircraft: modeler's guide to Manfred von Richthofen's aircraft: Sc Ap 73 4/4:258-264
La Recherche du Lepere: U.S. two-seat fighter: AM S 74 78/9: 18+
Roland D.II: 1917 German fighter: Aero Mr 73 37/434:149-151
Rumpler C.IV: Sc F 75 6/65:72-75
Siemens-Schukert Flies Again: replication of WW-I fighter: MAN

V. Articles

  Ja 72 84/1:15-16+
 Sopwith Camel: MAN D 75 91/6:24-26
 Sopwith Snipe: AE Ap 74 6/4:190-195+; Je 74 6/6:289-299
 Sopwith Triplane: AN 8 D 72 1/2:8-9
 Tony's Wild Weekend: acceptance trials of Fokker D. VII: RCS S 75 1/5:32-34+
 Tops in Trainers: Avro 504K, 1914: AM Jl 71 73/1:28+

 Between World Wars

                    Civil

 The Airliner that Went to War: Junkers Ju 86: AE Ja 72 2/1:25-31
 Ansett's Fokker Phoenix: AI D 75 9/6:303-307
 The Blitz: Heinkel He 70: AI F 75 8/2:76-80+
 Bücher Bü 131B Jungmann: 1934 German trainer: Aero F 74 39/457:89-91
 Circle the World: Winnie Mae Vega: RCS N 75 1/7:32-34+
 The Cloak & Dagger: Bellanca Irish Swoop racer/warplane: AM Ag 72 75/2:40-43+
 Commercial Condor: Focke Wulf Fw 200 airliner: AE Ja 73 4/1:22-29
 Curtiss R3C-1&2: biplane racers of 1925: AM Je 73 76/6:52-55+
 DH 85 Leopard Moth: 1933 lightplane: Aero Jl 73 38/449:378-380
 DH 88 Comet: 1934 distance racer: Aero D 72 37/44:703-707
 DH Hornet Moth: 1934 cabin biplane: Aero O 71 36/429:563-566
 De Havilland DH 71 Tiger Moth: 1927 King's Cup racer: Aero My 74 39/460:245-248
 Dornier Do-X: 1926 twelve-engine flying boat: Aero F 71 36/421:84-87
 Douglas DC-5: late 1930s airliner: AN 9 N 73 2/13:12
 The Fokker Fours: F-11 four-engine airliners: AE N 71 1/6:292-296
 Folkerts Speed King: 1930s Thompson racers: AM F 73 76/2:40-43
 Gee Bee Z: racer: RCS Ag 75 1/4:32-34+
 Gere Sport: 1927 homebuilt: AM My 71 72/5:32
 Handley Page Airliners: 0/400 variants: Afx Ap 71 12/8:410-411+
 Incredible Hawk: 1930 Thompson racer: AM O 71 73/4:28-31+
 Iron Annie: Junkers Ju 52 tri-motor airliner: AM My 73 76/5:72-75+
 It Happened in Hanger 4: Rouffaer Model R-6 homebuilt design, 1936: AM O 74 74/10:35-39
 Junkers Ju 86: AN 18 Ag 72 1/7:7-10
 Knight Twister: 1928 racing biplane: AM Ap 74 78/4:46-48+
 Lockheed Sirius: 1929 two-place monoplane: AM Ap 73 76/4:20+
 Lockheed 12A: AE My 72 2/5:261-267+
 Loughead Sport Biplane: 1920, first Lockheed: AM O 72 75/4:46-47+
 Lublin R XVIb: 1932 Polish ambulance/light airliner: Aero Mr 75

40/470:151-153
Parnell Pixie III: 1924 lightplane: AN 24 N 72 1/14:6-7
The Plane that Had it All: Northrop Gamma, 1932: AM Mr 71 72/3:28-31+
Roscoe Turner's Wedell-Williams: AM Ja 71 72/1:20-23+
Short Fairey Tale: Short S.32 airliner: AE S 72 3/3:144-150
Stagger Wing Beech Model 17: lightplane: RCS Jl 75 1/3:52-54
Those Versatile Vultees: Vultee V-1 airliner: AE Jl 72 3/1:27-32+
Tiger Moth: trainer: AM Ap 72 74/4:28-31+
Tingnissartoq: Lindbergh's Lockheed Sirius: RCS Ap 75 1/1:30-34+
Travel Air 5000 "Woolaroc": 1927 California-Hawaii race winner: Aero Ap 72 37/435:221-224
Trusty Tri-Motor: Ju 52/3m: AI Ag 74 7/2:76-83
Unlucky Seven: DH Albatross: 1935 4-engine airliner: AE My 73 4/5:234-240+

Military

Armstrong Whitworth Atlas: RT D 75 8/12:139
Armstrong Whitworth Siskin: in Canadian service: RT N 75 8/11:130-131
Armstrong Whitworth Siskin IIIA: Sc My 71 2/5:229-231
Bf 163: Messerschmitt STOL, beat by Storch: Sc Ap 71 2/4:174-177
Blackburn Cubaroo: 1924 torpedo-bomber prototype: Afx F 74 15/6:352-354
Boeing P-26: WWE Ja 74 1/1:16+
Brewster Buffalo: MW O 73 2/2:68+ ; D 73 2/4:179-184
Bristol 138A: 1935 British high-altitude research aircraft: Afx N 74 16/3:175-176+
The Bulldog Breed: Bristol Bulldog: AE Ja 73 4/1:30-32; F 73 4/2:91-95
Caudron Renault CF 714: 1938 French fighter: Aero Je 71 36/425:314-317
Chance Vought C-143: carrier fighter prototype: AE O 72 3/4:199-200
Christmas Fantasy: Bullet sesquiplane experiment: AE D 73 5/6:293-295+
Dewoitine D.500: 1932 French fighter: AN 13 Ap 73 1/24:4-5
Dutch Digression: D. XXIII, CLT fighter: AE F 74 6/2:69-75
The Early Cats: PBY-1 through -4: Q W 75 11/2:74-81
End of an Era... Polikarpov's Chaika: AE Je 71 1/2:9-15
Epitome of an Era: Gloster Gladiator: AE Mr 73 4/3:125-136
Fairey Seafox: Sc S 75 6/72:444-449
Fairey IIIF: AN 9 N 73 2/13:8-10
Fiat C.R.32: AN 18 Ja 74 2/17:8-9
Fiat C.R.32s in Spain: Spanish Civil War: Q Ja 74 9/1:43
Fledgling Fighter: early Bf 109s: AE N 71 1/6:323-328
Focke Wulf Fw 56 Stösser: AN 2 F 73 1/19:7-9
Gallic Verve--Vintage Style: MS 230 parasol fighter: AE Ag

V. Articles   462

72 3/2:82-85
Gloster Gladiator: Sc Ag 73 4/8:549-551
Goldfinch: Focke-Wulf Fw 44 Stieglitz: RCS Je 75 1/2:26-27+
Halfway House Fokker: D. XXI: AE Ag 71 1/3:152-159
Handley Page Heyford: AN 32 Ag 2/8:7-9
Hawker Tomtit: Sc Ja 74 5/1:16-17
Heinkel He 51: RT Mr 71 4/3:27
Heinkel He 51: WWE N 74 1/6:178-182
Heinkel He-51 Fighter: MW Je 73 1/10:518-521; Jl 73 1/11:573-576
Heinkel's Prettiest Biplane: He 51, 1935: AM D 72 75/6:32-35+
Last Belligerent Biplane: Avia B. 534: AI Jl 74 7/1:25-35
Last Bipe Fighter: Grumman F3F series: AM D 71 73/6:22-25+
The Mower: Fokker G. 1: AI O 74 7/4:178-182; N 74 7/5:239-244; D 74 7/6:286+
PZL-23A & B Karas: 1934 Polish light bomber: Aero O 72 37/441: 574-577
A Plane for All Seasons: Boeing F4B/P-12/100 series: RCS O 75 1/6:32-34+
Mr. Polikarpov's Short Little Ugly Fella: I-16: AM Je 74 78/6: 58-60+
Saro London II: AN 9 Ag 74 3/5:8-9
Southampton: Sc Ag 73 3/8:549-551
Das Sturzkampfflugzeug von Junkers: Ju-87 pre-war development: RCS D 75 1/8:26-29+
Swedish Harts: Hawker Harts in Swedish Service: AN 14 S 73 2/9: 7
Tale of a Saga, the Last of the Hawk Biplanes: F11C: AE O 72 3/4:194-198
Ubiquitous Hawk: Hawk 75: AE N 71 1/6:307-314; D 71 1/7:374-378; Ja 72 2/1:47-52
Vickers Vimy & Vernon: AN 17 O 75 4/10:8-10
Wings in Memory: Curtiss & the Hawks: WWE Jl 74 1/4:105-?

World War II--Civil

Civil

End of an Era: Armstrong Whitworth Ensign airliner: AE F 72 2/2:75-83

World War II--Military

(Australia)

Antipodean Finale: Commonwealth CA-15 fighter design: AE O 72 3/4:178-180
Boomerang: AE F 72 2/2:91-98
CA-1 Wirraway: Aero Ja 73 38/44:39-41

History--Aircraft

(Finland)

Violent Finnish Wind: VL Pyörremyrsky: AE O 71 1/5:273-275

(France)

Gallic Guardian: MS 406: AE S 73 5/3:130-136; O 73 5/4:183-188

(Germany)

Arado Ar 96: AN 27 Ap 73 1/25:8-9
Arado Ar 234B Blitz: Aero Mr 72 37/434:148-153
Blitz: Arado 234 jet bomber: AM Je 72 74/6:22-25+
Dornier Do 17: AN 9 Je 72 1/2:7-10
Dornier 217 Fighter: AI S 75 9/3:129-132+
Dornier's Arrow: AN 18 Ag 72 1/7:12-13
Fiesler Storch: MW Ja 73 1/5:233; F 73 1/6:292
First Jet Fighter: Heinkel He 280: AE Ap 72 2/4:184-188
Focke Wulf Fw 189: MW Ag 73 1/12:630; S 73 2/1:32
Focke Wulf Fw 190: WWE S 74 1/5:126-129; N 74 1/6:169; Ja 75 2/1:21
From Magdenburt to Saxonwold: South African National War Museum's Me 262: AI Ap 75 8/4:195-198
Heinkel He 59: ASR: AN 24 N 72 1/14:8-10
Heinkel He 162 Volksjager: AN 29 Mr 74 2/22:8-9
Heinkel He 219 Uhu: AN 23 Ag 74 3/6:8-9
Junkers Ju 52/3m g4e (MS): minesweeping variant: AN 3 O 75 4/9:8-9
Junkers Ju 86: AN 18 Ag 72 1/7:7-10
Junkers Ju 88: AN 3 Ag 73 2/6:7-9
Junkers Ju 188: Sc Je 75 6/69:284-285
Luftwaffe's Arrow: Do 355 Pfeil: Sc Jl 75 6/70:348
The Messerschmitt Classic: Bf 109: WWE Ja 74 1/1:9; Mr 74 1/2:31
Messerschmitt Bf-109 Specifications: prototypes; B-0, 1&2; C-0: WWE Ja 74 1/1:12-13
Messerschmitt 110: MW O 72 1/2:69; N 72 1/3:120; D 72 1/3:175
Messerschmitt Me 262: WW2J Jl 75 2/4:8-13
Natter: AE S 71 1/4:203-208

(Italy)

The Caproni that Nearly Joined the RAF: Caproni 311: AE Jl 71 1/2:95-103
Centauro--the Final Fling: Fiat G. 55: AE My 74 6/5:233-239+
Italian Kingfisher: CANT Z 1007bis: AE My 72 2/5:272-273
Lightning from Lombardy: Macchi C. 200 Saetta: AE Ja 72 2/1:17-24+
Macchi C. 202 A.S. Folgore: 1940 fighter: Aero Je 72 37/437:334-336
Reggiane Re. 2001 Falco II: AN 11 Jl 75 4/3:13

V. Articles 464

Savoia Marchetti SM 82 Marsupiale: AN 13 Je 75 4/1:8-9

(Japan)

Bombs by Balloon: robot balloon bombers: AE F 74 5/2:79-83
Kawasaki Ki-61 Hein: AN 1 F 74 2/18:809
Mitsubishi J2M3 Raiden: AE Jl 71 1/2:67-73+
Nakajima Demonology: Ki. 44 Shoki: AE Jl 72 3/1:17-25
Nipponese Uniquity: Kawanishi Shiden "George": AE Ap 73 4/4: 178-186
An Oriental Swallow: Kawasaki Hein: AI Ag 75 9/2:75-78+
Slayer of Dragons: Kawasaki Ki. 45 Toryu: AE N 73 5/5:225-229; D 73 5/6:276-281
Turbojets over Tokyo Bay: Kikka jet fighter design: AE My 72 2/5:268-271

(Sweden)

J-22: RT Mr 71 4/3:33
SAAB J-21 series: boom pusher fighter: AM F 71 72/2:25-31+
Sweden's Stop Gap Fighter: J-22: IM My 74 10/(16):9 (reprint of RT)

(USSR)

Devil's Broomstock: BI rocket fighter experiment: AE D 73 5/6: 282-286+
First of the Yaks: Yak-1: AI Je 75 8/6:297-304
Ilyushin Il-2: Sc Ap 74 5/55:192-198
Lavochkin La-4FN: 1941 fighter: Aero Ap 71 36/423:190-193
Lavochkin La-7: 1944 fighter: Aero Ap 71 36/423:190-193
Lisunov Li-2: armed, license-built DC-3: AN 12 D 75 4/14:8-9
MiG-3: AE O 71 13/2:252-260
Second Generation of Yaks: Yak 3-9: AI N 75 9/5:229-240+
Soviet Piston/Ramjet Development: Su-5: WW2J S 75 2/5-6:30
To Berlin by Night: Yermoleyev Yer-2 bomber: AE O 72 1/5:181-183+
Yakovlev Yak 9: 1940 fighter: Aero D 71 36/431:696-699

(U.K.)

Airborne Jeep: Rotabuggy experiment: AE My 72 2/5:273
Airspeed Oxford: in Canadian service: RT O 75 8/10:116+
Airspeed Oxford 10: AN 13 D 74 3/14:8-9
Avro Lincoln B. 2: AN 28 Je 74 3/2:8-10
Beaufighter: AE Ja 74 6/1:25-32+; Mr 74 6/3:124-130
Beauforts Down Under: RAAF service: AN 20 Jl 73 2/5:10-11
Boulton Paul Defiant: AN 10 My 74 2/25:8-10

History--Aircraft

Bristol Beaufighter: AN 13 Ap 73 1/24:8-10
Bristol Bombay: transport/bomber: AN 23 73 2/14:8-9
CAM-Ship Hurricanes: cargo ship catapult fighters: Afx My 74 15/9:510-511
Captured Stirling: AN 29 N 74 3/13:5
Çoldiz Cock: prison escape glider, 1944: Sc Ap 74 5/55:206-207
Fairey Albacore: AN 22 Ag 75 4/6:8-9
Fairey Barracuda Mks I-V: AN 4 Ja 74 2/16:8-9
Firefly: AE Mr 72 2/3:139-147; Je 72 2/6:309-315
Floatfires?: float var of Spitfire: RT Ja 71 4/1:9-10
Greatest Prop Fighter: Martin Baker MB 5: AM My 71 72/5:16-19
Hawker Tempest: Sc F 73 4/2:92-100
Last of the Ansons: Mks 19-22: AN 26 O 73 2/12:8-9
A More Violent Hurricane: Hawker Typhoon: AE Ag 72 3/2:91-98
The Mosquito in RAAF Service: AN 20 Jl 73 2/5:4-5
Sea Hurricane: PAM O 75 11:184
Short Stirling: AN 19 Ja 73 1/18:7-10
Supermarine Spitfire Mks IX & XVI: AN 2 Mr 73 1/21:8-9
Vickers Wellington: AN 4 Ag 72 1/6:7-10
Westland Lysander: WWE Jl 74 1/4:100-?
Westland Lysander Mks I-III: AN 27 Je 75 4/2:8-9
Westland Welkin: AN 28 S 73 2/10:10-11
Westland Whirlwind: AE Jl 73 5/1:30-36

(U.S.)

Airacobra: P-39: AM S 73 77/3:24-27+
Calamatous Cobra: P-39: AE Ag 71 1/3:134-143
Chance Vought F4U Corsair: WW2J My 75 2/3:90-101
Consolidated PBY Catalina: AN 1 N 74 3/11:8-10
Curtiss Hawk 75: particularly those in French service: Sc N 72 3/11:601-604
Curtiss P-40 Series: AN 6 S 74 3/7:8-10
Curtiss SB2V Helldiver: IM Mr 75 11/2:6
Do You Want to Buy a Liberator: ex Indian AF, ex RAF: AN 12 O 73 2/11:4-5
Don't Call Her Jug: P-47: AM S 72 74/3:32-35+
Douglas Boston & A-20 Havoc: AN 30 My 75 3/26:8-9
Douglas C-54 Skymaster: AN 18 Ap 75 3/23:7-9
Douglas TBD-1 Devastator: WWE My 74 1/3:71+
East Indies Catalinas: PBY in Dutch Service, WW-II & after: AN 13 Je 75 4/1:4-5
Fiasco or Foretaste?: B-17G in RAF service: AI D 74 7/6:279-285
Goodby Gooney Bird: C-47: AN 4 Ag 72 2/6:10
Grumman Avenger in Royal Navy Service, 1943-1945: IM Je 73 10/6:4-7
Grumman F4F Wildcat: AN 7 F 75 3/18:8-9
Grumman TBM-3 Avenger: AN 27 O 72 1/12:8-10
Kingfisher: scout: AM N 71 73/5:16-19+
Last of a Breed: Curtiss Seahawks (last catapult scout is USN service): AM N 74 74/11:78-84+

V. Articles 466

Martin B-26 Marauder: PAM Ap 75 9:146-147
Martin B-26 Marauder: Sc My 73 4/5:331-335
Martin PBM Mariner: AN 17 Ag 73 2/7:7-9
Mustang: P-51 series: AM Mr 72 75/3:34-37+
P-38--Best of the Twins: AM Ap 71 72/4:28-31+
Ryan ST's Ugly Cousin: PT-21 & 22: AM Ag 71 73/2:32-35+
Saga of the OQ-2A Drone: target: AM Mr 71 72/3:18-21
Second Patches: B-17G: FM S 73 76/9:46-49
Unknown Dakotas: military DC-3: AN 12 D 75 4/14:4-6
Vought Corsair: Afx S 71 13/1:12+ ; N 71 13/3:132+
Vought Kingfisher: Afx Ap 72 13/8:423-427
The Widow: P-61: AE Je 71 1/1:44-50

Post World War II

(Australia Civil)

Australian Wanderer: GAF N 22 Nomad: executive: AE Je 73 4/6:282-286
Transavia PL-12-U Airtruk: crop duster: PAM O 73 3:33

(Austria Civil)

MB-31: Electromotor Aircraft: electric powered glider: AM My 74 78/5:70-71+

(Brazil Civil)

Bandeirante: Embraere EMG-110, light airliner: AE Je 74 6/6: 284-288+

(Brazil Military)

Neiva & the Universal: trainer/light attack: AI My 75 8/5:228-232+

(Canada Civil)

De Havilland U-6A/L-20/DHC 2 Beaver: RiS W 74 2/2:44-45
Going to Blazes: Canadair CL-215 fire bomber: AI O 75 9/4:163-169+
STOL Comes Quietly: DHC-7: AE D 72 3/6:282-286+
Saunders ST. 28: modification of DH Heron light airliner: AN 16 My 75 3/25:7
Twin Otter: AI F 75 8/2:65-68+

(Canada Military)

The (Almost) Flying Saucer: Avro Avrocar: AE Je 74 6/6:300-302
Recollections of the Canadair Sabre: AE Ap 72 2/4:196-203
Tilt-Wings in Transition: Canadair CL-84: AE N 73 5/5:207-210+

(Czechoslovakia Civil)

Brouček W-01: 1970 homebuilt: Aero My 71 36/424:242-244

(Denmark Civil)

Keeping the KZs Airworthy: lightplanes: AN 1 N 74 3/11:16

(France Civil)

Concorde, the Evolution of an SST: AE S 71 1/4:184-190
Dassault/Breguet Mercure: short-haul jet: AE Mr 72 2/3:119-125
Fournier RF-5: 1966 powered sailplane: Aero Je 73 38/449:308-311
The Jodel Revolution: homebuilt: AE My 72 2/3:119-125
Truth About the Concorde: AN 30 Mr 73 1/23:4-5

(France Military)

Arsenal VB 10...un Chasseur Variament Unique: design started 1939, prototype completed 1946: AE Jl 71 1/2:79-82
Dassault Flies a Kite: Mirage: AE Je 71 1/1:21-24+
Ferocious Feline: Jaguar: AE S 72 3/3:120-128+
Jaguar: Sc Je 73 4/6:401-407
Jaguar into Service: operational: AE O 73 5/4:189-191
Mirage F: AE Ap 72 2/4:171-176
The Multi-Mission Mirage F: AI Je 75 8/6:285-288+
Sepecat Jaguar: Aero Ja 71 36/420:26-32

(Germany Civil)

VFW 614: 1971 small airline jet: AE D 71 1/7:367-372

(Germany Military)

Alpha Jet: AI O 74 7/4:167-173
They Call It the Tornado: Panavia 200 strike: AN 18 O 74 3/10:6
Transall Production Ends: AN 22 D 72 1/16:11
VFW-Fokker VAK 191B: AE Ap 72 2/4:189-190+

V. Articles

(India Military)

Harnessing the Storm Spirit: Marut: AE My 73 4/5:215-222
Storms over Jodhpur: HF-24 Marut: AN 16 Mr 73 1/22:6-7

(Israel Military)

Arava: STOL utility: AE F 74 6/2:55-61+
Young Lions, Old (Copy) Cats...and the Games People Play: Kfir fighter: AI S 75 9/3:139-142

(Italy Military)

Aermacchi MB.326: trainer: AN 16 F 73 1/20:8-10
Fiat G.91: AN 1 Mr 74 2/20:4-5

(Japan Civil)

For Businessmen with the Yen: Mitsubishi Mu-2 turboprop executive: AE N 73 5/5:216-224

(Japan Military)

Kawasaki C-1, Japan's Mini-Starlifter: AI Jl 75 9/1:7-10+
Mitsubishi T-2: AI Ap 75 8/4:170-176

(Netherlands Civil)

Fellowship Finds a Slot: Fokker turboprop airliner: AE F 73 4/2:63-68

(Poland Civil)

S.4 Kania 3: 1951 glider tug experiment: Aero S 71 36/428:504-506
TS 8 bies: 1955 trainer: Aero Ja 75 40/468:29-32

(Sweden Military)

SAAB J-29: AN 11 My 73 1/26:8-9
SAAB J-35 Draken: AN 26 Jl 74 3/4:8-10
SAAB 37 Viggen: AN 31 O 75 4/11:8-9
Sweden's Muscular Minimus: SAAB Supporter/Safari: AI Ja 75 8/1:13-17+
Swedish Hocus Pocus: SAAB-MFI 17: 1974 trainer, lightplane, light attack: AM D 74 74/12:27-35
Thor's New Hammer: SAAB 37 Viggen: AM Ja 74 78/1:64-67+

History--Aircraft

(Switzerland Civil)

Revolution in Aerobatics--the Acrostar: AM Ag 71 73/2:26-28+

(Switzerland Military)

Tow by Turboprop: turbo conversion of C-3603 fighter to C-3605 target tug: AE S 72 3/3:142-143

(USSR Civil)

Yak 18PB & PS: 1966 aerobatic: Aero Mr 71 36/422:139-143

(USSR Military)

The Billion Dollar Bomber: Tu-4, B-29 copy: AE Jl 71 1/2:104-107; Ag 71 1/3:160-163; S 71 1/4:214-218; O 71 1/5:263-268
Cambodia to Cuba: MiG-17: AE D 72 3/6:301-311
First of the Many: MiG 9, Yak 15 & 17 jets: AI N 7/5:232-238+
Il-28, A Soviet Canberra: AE D 71 1/7:351-356
India & the MiG-21: AE Jl 73 5/1:7-14
MiG-19 (Farmer): AN 18 O 74 3/10:8-9
MiG-21: AE Ag 71 1/3:121-127
Mikoyan MiG-15: AN 14 S 73 2/9:8-9
Two Decades of Twenty-One: MiG-21: AE My 74 6/5:226-232
Yakovlev's Lightweight--Yak-23: AE My 73 4/5:229-233

(U.K. Civil)

The Abandoned Executive: Handley Page Jetstream: AN 19 Ja 73 1/18:11
Airbus: AI S 74 7/3:127-134
The Airliner That Nobody Wanted: Miles Marathon: AN 5 S 75 4/7:4-5
Ajep Wittman Tailwind: recent U.K. mod of pre-WW-II U.S. lightplane design: Aero N 72 37/442:633-636
Big Bus, European Style: Airbus A300B: AE Ag 72 3/2:65-71+
Britain's Best Seller: Islander: AN 8 Ag 75 4/5:10-11
British Bulldog, Scottish Accent: Scottish Aviation Bulldog lightplane: AE Ag 73 5/2:59-66
Concorde, the Evolution of an SST: AE S 71 1/4:184-190
Ex-Service Chipmunks: civil survey: AN 4 Ap 75 3/22:16
Executive Excellence: HS-125: AE N 72 3/5:231-236
Fairwell to the First Airbus: Vickers Vanguard: AN 18 O 74 3/10:11
Feederjet Formula: HS 146: AE Ja 74 6/1:19-24
5,000 Miles for Lunch!: Concorde: AN 17 O 75 4/10:4-5
From Islander to Trislander: AE O 71 1/5:239-244
The Four Pronged Trident Three: 4-engine trident: AE Jl 71 1/2:87-90+
HS 141, The Airport Shrinker: AE Je 71 1/1:39-43

Jupiter: record-holder in man-powered flight: Aero Mr 73 38/446:
141-143+; Ap 73 38/447:214-216; My 73 38/448:257-259; Je 73
38/449:324-325
Rollason Beta: 1964 Formula 1 racer: Aero Je 71 36/425:364-368
Rolls Royce Flying Bedstead: jet VTOL testbed: Afx Mr 75 16/7:
416-420
SA Bulldog: IM Jl 75 11/4:6-7
The Silent Solents: flying boats stored at San Francisco: AN 22
D 72 1/16:7
Stretching the 111: BAC One-Eleven: AN 16 My 75 3/25:11
Thruxton Jackaroo: 1957 4-place conversion of DH Tiger Moth: Sc
Ap 75 6/4:186-189
Trislander, the First Five Years: AI Jl 75 9/1:16-18+
Truth About the Concorde: AN 30 Mr 73 1/23:4-5

(U. K. Military)

BAC Lightning F. 6: Sc F 71 2/2:84-88
BAC Strikemaster: AN 26 Ap 74 2/24:8-9
BAC TSR-2: AN 30 Mr 73 1/23:8-9
The Buccaneer Story: MW S 72 1/1:42-45; O 72 1/2:95-98; N 72
1/3:154-156; D 72 1/4:198-200
Fairey Firefly: AM N 73 75/5:72+
Fairey Gannet: AN 8 Ag 75 4/5:8-9
The Fighter That Failed: Supermarine Swift: AN 26 Ap 74 2/24:
4-5+
First Lightnings: English Electric: AN 10 Ja 75 3/16:4-6+
Fly with a Sting: Folland Gnat: AI Ag 74 7/2:68-75
Gloster Javelin: AN 1 Mr 74 2/20:7-9
HS 1182: HS Hawk prototype: AE My 73 4/5:223-228
Handley Page Hastings C. Mk 1: AN 5 S 75 4/7:7-9
The Harrier & VTOL Flight: abandoned prototypes: MW F 73 1/6:
324-326; P1127 & Kestral: Ap 73 1/8:433-437; Harrier: My
73 1/9:489-492; Harrier in RAF service: Jl 73 1/11:593-595
The Harrier Needs No Runway: AM Je 71 72/6:22-25
Harrier Training Aircraft: MW F 74 2/6:307-308
Hawk in the Sun: HS Hawk: AI D 74 7/6:268-269
Hawk Update: AI Ag 75 9/2:88-90
Hawker Siddeley HS 1182 Hawk: Afx D 74 16/4:226-230+
Hawker Siddeley's Mighty Hunter: Nimrod: AE D 73 5/6:259-267
Hellohawk: HS Hawk trainer: AN 6 S 74 3/7:13
Hunting Percival Provost: AN 15 N 74 3/12:6-9
Jaguar: AM Ja 72 74/1:20-21+
Jaguar on the Line: RAF operational: AN 28 Je 74 3/2:6-7
Jump-Jet Made for Two: Harrier trainer: AE My 72 2/5:223-230+
Last of the Hastings: Handley Page 4-engine transport: AN 14 Je
74 2/22:4
Last of the Line: Jet Provost: AN 18 Ja 74 2/17:4-5
Mastery in Marine Harrying: Harrier in USMC service: AE F 73
4/2:59-62
Meteor Night Fighters: AN 25 My 73 2/1:7-9
Nimrod Sampled: AN 29 Mr 74 2/22:6

History--Aircraft

Percival Prentice T. Mk. I: AN 7 F 75 3/18:4-6
Petter's Midget Masterpiece: Folland Gnat: AN 20 S 74 3/8:4-5
Saro Skeeter: AN 28 Je 74 3/2:4-5
Scottish Aviation Bulldog: IM Jl 75 11/4:6-7
Sea Fury: Trainer: PAM Ja 75 8:132
Sepecat Jaguar: Aero Ja 71 36/420:26-32
The Shackleton Goes on For Ever: AN 29 Mr 74 2/22:4-5
Sharper Claws for the RAF: Jaguar in British service: AE Je 74 6/6:278-283
Strikemaster: AE Mr 73 4/3:117-120+
Vickers Valetta & Varsity: AN 24 Ja 75 3/17:8-10
Vixen Valediction: AN 28 S 73 2/10:7-9
Westland Wyvern T. Mk. 3:   1950 target tug: AN 7 Jl 72 1/4:8

(U.S. Civil)

BD-5:   homebuilt: FM My 73 76/5:30-34
Bowers Fly-Baby Biplane: Aero D 75 40/479:1049
The Cassutt Story: racer: MAN My 74 88/5:36-37+
Cessna's Past Masters: Cessna Airmaster: AM My 74 78/5:62-64+
El Chuparosa: 1959 ultra-light homebuilt biplane: Aero Jl 72 37/438:392-394
Double Deck Fly Baby: homebuilt biplane: AM O 73 77/4:74-77+
FM Rides the Blimp: Goodyear blimp: FM S 74 77/9:46-48
Ibex: sailplane: RCS Jl 75 1/3:24-25
Infectious Mite: Mooney Mite, 1951 single-seat lightplane: AM Mr 75 75/3:51-54+
Mace R-2 Shark: 1969 Formula 1 racer: Aero N 71 36/430:636-638
McDonnell Douglas DC-9:   AN 12 Jl 74 3/3:8-9
Miss America & Howie Keefe: air show P-51 racer: RCS N 75 1/7:21+
Mizar: Cessna Skymaster/Ford Pinto cross: Sc Ja 74 5/1:47
Mr. Bede's Dreamboat: BD-5:   AE F 73 4/2:69-72+
Nelson Bumblebee: powered variant of Baby Bowlus sailplane: RCS D 75 1/8:20-21
OR-65-2 Owl Racer: 1969 Goodyear racer: Aero Ja 72 37/432:44-48
Owl Racer: Formula 1:   AM Ap 71 72/4:22-24+
Piper Cherokee: Sc D 75 6/75:612-616+
Pitts S-2A Special: aerobatic biplane: Aero S 74 39/46:491-485
Pitts Special: AM D 73 77/6:25-28+
RCM Visits the Pitts Factory: Afton Wyoming: RC My 73 10/5:33-36
RCM Visits War Aircraft Replicas: $\frac{1}{2}$-size sports planes on WW-II fighter designs: RC Je 74 11/6:40-43+
Rainbow: 1946 airliner prototype: AM N 71 73/5:44-46+
Rivets: 1964 Formula 1:   AM F 72 74/2:22-25+
The Second Coming: NASA U-2 operations: AM Jl 72 75/1:30-33+
Stephens Akro: aerobatic light monoplane: AM Ag 73 77/2:40-44
Tenth Dimension: McDonnell Douglas DC-10:   AE D 73 5/6:268-275+

V. Articles 472

Thorp T-18 Tiger: 1964 homebuilt: Aero F 72 37/433:81-83
Tristar--Through Tribulation to Triumph: AE Jl 73 5/1:15-22+
Tristar Without Tears: AN 12 Jl 74 3/3:12-13
200 mph Volkswagen: Wittman V, formula V racer: AM F 74 78/2:52-55+

(U.S. Military)

(Fighters & Strike)
Banshee: in Canadian service: RT O 73 6/10:116
Between DAF & Daimler: NF5 in Dutch service: AE Jl 72 3/1:7-10
Blackbirds over the Black Sheds: SR-71: Afx N 74 16/3:150-152
A Cat for Dogfighting: Northrop F5E Tiger II: AE O 72 3/4:184-191
Cobra Concept: Northrop P-530 experiment: AE Ag 72 3/2:59-64
Convair F-102 Delta Dagger: RiS N 72 1/2:120-124
Convair F-106 Delta Dart: RiS N 72 1/2:120-124
Corsair II: 1965 strike: AM Ja 71 72/1:44-47
Day of the Eagle: F-15: AE Mr 74 6/3:115-123
Dogfighter Supreme: Tomcat: AE Ja 74 6/1:7-16+
Douglas F4D-1 Skyray: AN 4 Ap 75 3/22:8-9
F8F Bearcat: AN 10 N 72 1/13:8-10
F-14 & F-15: AE Mr 72 2/3:115-118+
FH-1 Phantom: Q O 73 8/4:226-228
Facing the Axe?: Northrop A-9A & Fairchild A-10A: Ae Ja 73 4/1:7-11
Fairchild A-10A: AE My 74 6/3:115-123
Grumman's First Swinging Cat: XF10F Jaguar: AI Mr 75 8/3:125-133+
Hot Rod: Douglas Skyhawk: AM S 71 73/3:28-31+
The Hun: North American F-100 Super Sabre: RiS Jl 75 3/2:56-68; cor Ja 76 3/3:162
LTV A-7 Corsair II: AN 12 Ap 74 2/23:8-9
LTV Corsair II^2: 2-seat variant: Q O 74 10/2:54-55
Lancer: Lockheed jet fighter experiment: AE S 71 1/4:175-179
Lightweight Fighter: YF-16: AI Ag 74 7/2:59-63+
Lockheed F-80 Shooting Star: RiS N 72 1/2:40-44
Lockheed's Lone Ranger: YF-12 & SR-71: AI O 74 7/4:159-166+
Marine Corps Skyhawk: RiS Mr 75 3/1:4-13
McDonnell F2H-3 & 4: AN 15 Mr 74 2/21:8-10
McDonnell F-101B Voodoo: RiS Au 74 1/4:120-124
New Vertical Approach: Rockwell XFV-12A strike experiment: AE F 74 6/2:64-68
North American F-86 Sabre: RiS Sp 74 2/3-4:84-96
North American Fury: AN 14 N 75 4/12:7
Northrop's New Fighter Generation: YF-17: AE Mr 74 6/3:105-108+
Not So Ancient Mariner: McDonnell Douglas A-4 Skyhawk: AE D 71 1/7:359-366
Pirates Ashore: Air Force use of Corsair II: AE Ag 71 1/3:128-132

Phantom: Sc Jl 71 2/7:354-362
Phantom Fighters: in RAF service: AN 25 Jl 75 4/4:16
Sabre Ks & Vespas: in Italian service: AN 27 Je 75 4/2:16
Starfighter with Iron Crosses: F-104G in Luftwaffe service: AN 19 Ja 73 1/18:4-5
Super Spads for the USAF: Northrop YA-9A & Fairchild YA-10A: AE F 72 2/2:72-73
USAF F-15 Eagle: Sc F 75 6/65:65-66
Untossed Pancake: XF5U-1: AE Je 73 4/6:287-293
Vought A-7 Corsair: IM N 75 11/6:14-15
YC-15: STOL performer for the eighties: AI D 75 9/6:275-280

(Other Aircraft)
A-37 Dragonfly & T-37 Tweet: RiS Mr 75 3/1:31-37
AMST--Advancing the STOL Art: Boeing YC-14: AE S 73 5/3: 116-117+
AWACS: A Better Balloon: Boeing EC-137/E-3A (Boeing 707): AI Ja 75 8/1:18-23
AWACS in Europe: EC-137D: AN 2 My 75 3/24:12
Air Skimmer Project X-28A: 1970 ultra-light seaplane experiment: AE N 72 3/5:251-252
B-1: AE Jl 72 3/1:11-16
B-1: AI F 75 8/2:59-64+
B-1 Testing Time: AI Jl 75 9/1:14-15
B-47 Remembered: Q Ja 73 8/1:31
Biafra's Invaders: A-20: AN 22 Je 73 2/3:6
Boeing's Military Twin: 737 navigation trainer T-63A: AE S 73 5/3:111-115
Bronco, the Willing Workhorse: OV-10A: AE O 71 1/5:231-236
Cessna's Cut-Price Combateer: A-37 Dragonfly: AI My 75 8/5: 215-221
Cessna's For Citizen Airmen: A-37 in Air National Guard service: AE Ap 73 4/4:175-177+
Douglas SC-54 Searchmaster: SAR: AN 4 Ja 74 2/16:10-11
Fixer, Finder, Striker: S-3A Viking: AI Jl 74 7/1:5-13
Grumman HU-16 Albatross: AN 29 N 74 3/13:8-10
Grumman HU-16B Albatross: RiS Sp 73 1/3:76
Grumman OV-1 Mohawk: AN 15 F 74 2/19:8-9
Grumman S-2 Tracker & variants: AN 22 D 72 1/16:8-10
The Labours of Hercules: AI N 74 7/5:224-230+ ; D 74 7/6:270-278+
Lockheed Neptune: AN 26 O 73 2/12:4-6
North American AJ-2 Savage: AN 25 Jl 75 4/4:8-9
North American OV-10 Bronco: RiS Ag 72 1/1:4-6+
North American T-28 Trojan: AN 19 S 75 4/8:8-9
North American T-39 Sabreliner: AN 7 D 73 2/15:8-9
OV-1 Mohawk: Q O 73 8/4:207
Orion: AWS Star Performer: AI S 9/3:118-123+
P-2 Neptune: Q Jl 74 10/1:18
Photo Crusaders: RF-8: AN 26 D 75 4/15:6-7
RAF's Superforts: Washingtons: AN 22 Je 73 2/3:4-5
Rockwell Buckeye: T-2A trainer: AE O 73 5/4:163-169
Super Gooney Bird: C-117D variant of C-47: AN 16 My 75 3/25:4-6

Superglider from the Skunk Works: U-2: Q O 73 8/4:216
Variations on a Tanker Theme: AN 26 Jl 74 3/4:6
Vigilante, the Eyes of the Fleet: North American RA-5C: AI N 75 9/5:215-258+

Helicopters

Superior Sub-Hunter: SH-3 variants: AE N 72 3/5:223-230+ ; D 72 3/6:287-291
UTTAS: Boeing Vertol YUH-61A & Sikorsky YUH-60A helicopter transports: AI Ag 75 9/2:67-74
Westland Lynx: AE Je 72 2/6:283-290
Westland Scout/Wasp: AN 9 Je 72 2/2:8-9
Westland Aerospatiale Puma: Afx Ap 73 14/8:424+

Separate Listings

(Aircraft of the RAF) [all AN; 3v sil, brief background]

Aerospatiale Puma: 3 Ag 73 2/6:12
Armstrong Whitworth Whitley: 18 Ag 72 1/7:11
Avro Shackleton AEW. 2: 17 Ag 73 2/7:12
BAC Canberra: 6 Jl 73 2/4:12
BAC Jet Provost: 27 Ap 73 1/25:12
BAC Lightning: 22 Je 73 2/3:12
BAC VC-10 C. Mk. 1: 19 Ja 73 1/18:12
Bristol Britannia: 2 Mr 73 1/21:12
DHC-1 Chipmunk T. Mk. 10: 13 Ap 73 1/24:12
De Havilland DH 104 Devon: 20 Jl 73 2/5:12
Fairey Battle: 9 Je 72 1/2:6
Handley Page Victor: 10 N 72 1/13:12
Hawker Hunter FGA Mk. 9: 11 My 73 1/26:12
Hawker Hunter T. Mk. 7: 13 O 72 1/11:10
Hawker Siddeley Andover C. Mk. 1: 24 N 72 1/14:12
Hawker Siddeley Argosy: C. 1: 25 My 73 2/1:12
Hawker Siddeley Buccaneer S. Mk. 2: 27 O 72 1/12:12
Hawker Siddeley Comet C. Mk. 4: 8 Je 73 2/2:12
Hawker Siddeley Dominie T. Mk. 1: 16 F 73 1/20:12
Hawker Siddeley Gnat T. Mk. 1: 16 Mr 73 1/22:12
Hawker Siddeley Harrier GR. 1: 31 Ag 73 2/8:12
Hunting Provost T. Mk. 1 (prop): 4 Ag 72 1/6:12
Royal Aircraft Factory SE 5a: 7 Jl 72 1/4:12
SAL Jetstream T. Mk. 1: 12 O 73 2/11:12
Scottish Aviation Bulldog T. Mk. 1: 14 S 73 2/9:12
Sepecat Jaguar GR. 1: 28 S 73 2/10:12
Short Belfast: 8 D 72 1/15:10
Westland Sioux: 2 F 73 1/19:12

History--Aircraft

Westland Wessex HC. Mk. 2:   30 Mr 73 1/23:12
Westland Whirlwind HAR Mk. 10:   22 D 72 1/16:12

(Aircraft of the USA) [all AN; 3v sil, brief background]

Boeing B-52 Stratofortress: 26 O 73 2/12:12
Boeing KC-97E/L Stratofreighter: 10 My 74 2/25:12
Boeing KC-135 Stratotanker: 21 My 75 3/21:12
Cessna O-2:   27 D 74 3/15:12
Cessna T-37/A-37:   9 Ag 74 3/5:11
Convair F-102 Delta Dagger: 18 Ja 74 2/17:10
Convair F-106 Delta Dart: 1 F 74 2/18:10
Convair T-29 & C-131:   15 Mr 74 2/21:12
Fairchild C-123B Provider: 16 My 75 3/25:12
General Dynamics F-111:   12 Ap 74 2/23:10
Kaman HH-43 Huskie: 14 Je 74 3/1:12
LTV A-7 Corsair II: 4 Ja 74 2/16:10
Lockheed C-5A Galaxy: 6 S 74 3/7:12
Lockheed C-130 Hercules: 1 Mr 74 2/20:10
Lockheed C-140B Jetstar: 25 Jl 75 4/4:12
Lockheed C-141 Starlifter: 29 N 74 3/13:12
Lockheed EC-121:   12 Jl 74 3/3:10
Lockheed F-104 Starfighter: 23 N 73 2/14:10
Lockheed SR-71:   13 Je 75 4/1:12
Lockheed T-33A: 18 O 74 3/10:12
Lockheed U-2:   15 F 74 2/19:10
Martin B-57:   7 D 73 2/15:10
McDonnell Douglas C9A Nightingale: 24 Ja 75 3/17:12
McDonnell-Douglas F-4 Phantom: 29 Mr 74 2/22:10
Northrop T-38 Talon & F-5:   26 Ap 74 2/24:12
Republic F-105 Thunderchief: 9 N 73 2/13:6
Rockwell T-29 Sabreliner: 7 F 75 3/18:12

(The Civil Scene) [all AN; 3v sil, brief background]

Aero Commander: 7 Jl 72 1/4:12
Aero 45 & Aero 145:   27 Je 75 4/2:12
Aerospatiale (Nord) N. 262 Fregate: 15 N 74 3/12:12
Airbus Industries A. 300B: 21 F 75 3/19:12
Aviation Traders Carvair: 29 Mr 74 2/22:10
BAC One-Eleven: 10 Jl 73 2/5:12
Beechcraft Model 18:   30 Mr 73 1/2:12
Beechcraft 35 Bonanza: 13 Ap 73 1/24:12
Boeing 707:   22 Je 73 2/3:12
Boeing 727:   15 F 74 2/19:10
Boeing 737:   1 F 74 2/18:10
Boeing 747:   12 Ap 74 2/23:10
Cessna Citation: 22 D 72 1/16:12
Cessna 170, 172, & 175:   11 My 73 1/26:12
Cessna 310:   10 N 72 1/13:12
Cessna 400 series: 2 Mr 73 1/21:12

V. Articles

Dassault Mystere 20 executive: 4 Ag 72 1/6:12
De Havilland DH. 82A Tiger Moth: 31 Ag 73 2/8:12
De Havilland DH 104 Dove: 24 N 72 1/14:12
De Havilland Canada DHC-6 Twin Otter: 14 S 73 2/9:12
Dornier Do. 28: 28 Je 74 3/2:12
Douglas DC-8: 7 D 2/15:10
Fokker F. 28 Fellowship: 25 My 73 2/1:12
Gates Lear Jet: 18 Ag 72 1/7:11
Grumman American AA-5 Traveler: 13 D 74 3/14:14
Grumman Gulfstream I: 16 Mr 73 1/22:12
Grumman Gulfstream II: 27 O 72 1/12:12
HFB 320 Hansa: 19 Ja 73 1/18:12
Hawker Siddeley Comet: 4 Ja 74 2/16:10
Hawker Siddeley HS 125: 9 Je 72 1/2:6
Hawker Siddeley HS. 748 Series 200: 12 O 73 2/11:12
Hawker Siddeley Trident: 6 Jl 73 2/4:12
Hughes Model 500: 26 Jl 74 3/4:12
IAI Commodore Jet Eleven 23: 16 F 73 1/20:12
Ilyushin Il-62: 26 Ap 74 2/24:12
Lockheed Tristar: 1 Mr 74 2/20:10
McDonnell Douglas DC-9: 9 N 73 2/13:6
McDonnell Douglas DC-10: 18 Ja 74 2/17:10
Mooney M. 20: 23 Ag 74 3/6:12
North American-Rockwell Sabreliner: 2 F 73 1/19:12
Partenavia P. 68: 20 S 74 3/8:12
Piper PA-23 Aztec: 13 O 72 1/11:10
Piper PA-31 Navajo: 27 Ap 73 1/25:12
Piper Seneca: 8 D 72 1/15:10
SUD Caravelle: 26 O 73 1/12:12
Short SC. 7 Skyvan: 3 Ag 73 2/5:12
Sikorsky S-61L & N: 18 Ap 75 3/23:12
Socata (Aerospatiale) Rallye: 10 My 74 2/25:12
Tupolev Tu-104: 17 Ag 73 2/7:12
Tupolev Tu-134A: 8 Je 73 2/2:12
VFW-Fokker F. 27 Friendship: 28 S 73 2/10:12
VFW Fokker VFW 614: 10 Ja 75 3/16:12
Vickers Viscount: 15 Mr 74 2/21:12
Victa Airtourer: 30 My 75 3/26:12
Zlin Z-326 Trener Master: AN 22 Ag 75 4/6:12

(New & Revised Silhouettes) [all AN; 3v sil, brief background]

Dassault Super Etendard: AN 26 D 75 4/15:12
General Dynamics F-16: AN 5 S 75 4/7:12
McDonnell Douglas/Northrop F. 18: AN 22 Ag 75 4/6:12
Mikoyan MiG-25 Foxbat B: AN 14 N 75 4/12:10
Panavia 200 MRCA: AN 17 O 75 4/10:6

Prototype Flight Characteristics

Assessing an Anachronism: Ju 87: AI Jl 74 7/1:19-24
Audacious Arrow: Dornier Pfeil: AE Ja 73 4/1:16-21
Bell Aracobra: AE Ag 71 1/3:143+
Bf-109G: AE Je 73 4/6:297-302
Bf 110: AE O 73 5/4:177-181
Bristol Beaufighter: AE Mr 74 6/3:130-132
Bronco: OV-10A: AE O 71 1/5:236-238+
Brush with Exoticism: Me 163 Komet: AE S 72 3/3:129-136
Condor, an Elegant Improvisation: bomber version: AI S 74 7/3: 143-150
Curtiss P-40: AI Ag 74 7/2:95-99
Dissimilar Pair--Beaufort & Botha: AI S 75 9/3:124-128
Fairey Battle: AE Ag 72 3/2:86-87+
Flying the Airspeed Horsa: glider: AE Ap 72 2/4:213-216
Flying the Consolidated Liberator: AE F 72 2/4:213-216
Flying the Douglas Twins: Boston/Havoc: AE D 71 1/7:379-383
Flying the Eye: Fw 189: AI O 74 7/4:183-189
Flying the Flying Suitcase: Handley Page Hampden: AE S 71 1/4: 197-199+
Flying the Geodetic Giant: Wellington: AE My 73 4/5:241-244
Flying the Harassing Hudson: AE D 72 3/6:292-294
Flying the Pregnant Pencil: Dornier Do 217: AI My 75 8/5:233-236+
Flying the Trent-Meteor: AE Mr 72 2/3:135-138+
Flying the Wooden Wonder: Mosquito: AE N 71 1/6:319-322
Flying Vertically: Harrier T. 4: AN 23 N 73 2/14:6-7
Fritz of All Trades: Junkers Ju 88: AI D 75 9/6:281-282+
Gloster Gladiator: AE Mr 73 4/3:136-137
The Grievous Griffin: Greif: AI Ap 75 8/4:177-184
Handley Page O/100: AE Ag 73 5/2:81-83
Heinkel He 111H-1: AE N 73 5/5:231-238
Heinkel's Nocturnal Predator: He 219: AI Jl 75 9/1:23-29
Iron Annie from Dessau: Junkers Ju 52: AI O 75 9/4:180+
The Illbegotten Albermarle: AI F 75 8/2:81-83
Like Greased Lightning: Arado Ar 234 Blitz: AE F 73 4/2:73-81
MS 406: AE Ag 73 5/3:136+
Mastering Heinkel's Minimus: He 162 Volksjäger: AE Je 72 2/6: 295-300
Mastering the Mosquito: AN 29 Mr 74 2/22:7
N1K1-J Shiden "George": AE Ap 73 4/4:186-187
Nimrod Sampled: AN 29 Mr 74 2/22:6
No Harbinger of Summer: Me 262: AE N 72 3/5:241-248
Northrop A-17A Nomad: AE Ag 72 3/2:87+
One Pup & a Few Problems: restored Sopwith Pup: AN 26 Ap 74 2/24:7
RA-5C Vigilente: AI N 75 9/5:259
Rockwell T-2C Buckeye: AE O 73 5/4:169-171
SAAB-Scania Safari/Supporter: AI Ja 75 8/1:24-28
Stuka: Ju-87D: AN 18 O 74 3/10:12
Tiffie Airborne: Typhoon: IM O 73 10/10:13-14

V. Articles 478

Westland Lysander: AE Jl 72 3/1:33-35
Westland Whirlwind: AE Jl 73 5/1:36-39
A Wild, Wild Cat: Grumman Jaguar: AI Mr 75 8/3:141-146+

Surviving Examples

Fairey Battle: Sc Ja 71 2/1:37-39
Fairey Survivors: other than Battle: Sc Ja 71 2/1:37-39
The Last of the Lancs: Afx Ag 72 13/12:674-676+
Schneider Survivors: Schneider Trophy Racers: AI N 75 9/5:244-247

AIRLINES

AER Turas: AN 15 Mr 74 2/21:5
Air Anglia: AN 17 Ag 73 2/7:4-5
Air Bahama: AN 8 Je 73 2/2:6
Air Canada: AN 11 My 73 1/26:4-6
Air Pegasus: charter airline: AN 27 Ap 73 1/25:6
Airline of the Cedar Tree: Middle East Airlines, Lebanon: AI O 74 7/4:174-177+
Aviation in the Norwegian Arctic: AN 7 F 75 3/18:7+
BEA Helicopters: AN 8 D 72 1/15:12
Bahama Island Air Services: airlines serving islands: AN 8 Je 73 2/2:11
Braathens SAFE to Spitsbergen: AN 25 Jl 75 4/4:4-5
Bristow's Helicopter Operations: AN 21 Mr 75 3/21:7
British Air Ferries: AN 22 D 72 1/16:4-5
British Airways...the first fifty years: AI O 75 9/4:186-192; N 75 9/5:223-228+
Brymon Aviation: AN 20 S 74 3/8:14
CP Air: AN 25 My 73 2/1:10-11
Casair Aviation: air taxi: AN 31 Ag 73 2/8:6
Corvette Joins Air Alpes: AN 15 N 74 3/12:5
Dan-Air Expands: AN 18 Ag 72 1/7:15
The End of an Era--27 Years of BEA: Afx D 73 15/4:230-231
European Airlines: see separate listing
40-Year Old Newcomer: British Caledonian Airways: AE O 72 3/4:171-177
Helicopters in Hong Kong: Hong Kong Air: AN 28 N 75 4/13:10
India Airlines: AN 30 Mr 73 1/23:6-7
Indian Aviation: Air India: AN 16 Mr 73 1/22:4-6
Linjeflyg Aktiebolag (LIN): AN 31 O 75 4/11:12-13
Loganair: AN 6 Jl 73 2/4:6-7
Merlot Aviation: charter/small airline: AN 31 Ag 73 2/8:4-5
Merpati Nusantara: Indonesian: AN 2 F 72 1/19:6
North Sea Rig Helicopter Operations: oil well service: Afx My 75

16/9:514-515+
STOL: Airtransit Twin Otter use in Ottawa--Montreal run: AN 21 Mr 75 3/21:11
Sabena Half Century: AN 2 Mr 73 1/21:4-5
A Sheep with Five Legs: Martinair: AE Mr 73 4/3:121-124+
Survey of U.K. Operators: AN 31 Ag 73 2/8:10-11
Swift Aire: Canadian charter service: AN 8 D 72 1/15:13
Swissair & the DC-9-50: AN 2 My 75 3/24:11
There's Nothing Like the Heron: Peters Aviation, European charter: AN 7 D 73 2/15:6
United Kingdom Air Traffic Control: air operations: AN 27 Ap 73 1/25:4-5
World Airline Fleets: see separate listing

(World Airline Fleets) [all AN]

Aer Lingus: 26 Jl 74 3/4:13
Aero Lineas Argentinas: 26 Jl 74 3/4:13
Aeroflot: 12 O 73 2/11:13
Aeromexico: 1 Mr 74 2/20:11
Aeronaves Alimentadoras: 15 Mr 74 2/21:13
Air Afrique: 6 Jl 73 2/4:13
Air France: 17 Ag 73 2/7:13
Air Inter: 6 S 74 3/7:12
Air Inter: 30 My 75 3/26:13
Air Jamaica: 1 F 74 2/18:11
Air Malawi: 8 Ag 75 4/5:13
Air New Zealand: 20 Jl 73 2/5:13
Air Niugini: 25 Jl 75 4/4:13
Air Zaire: 28 Je 74 3/2:13
Alitalia: 20 Jl 73 2/5:13
All Nipon Airways: 21 Mr 75 3/21:13
Austrian Airlines: 13 D 74 3/14:15
Avianca-Columbia: 20 S 74 3/8:13
Balair: 9 Ag 74 3/5:13
Braniff International Airways: 29 N 74 3/13:13
British Airline Survey 1974: all U.K. carriers: AN 12 Jl 74 3/3: 4-7+
British West Indian Airways: 9 Ag 74 3/5:13
Burma Airways: 17 O 75 4/10:11
CAAC: 15 Mr 74 2/21:13
Ceskoslavenske Aerolinie: 9 N 73 2/13:7
China Air Lines: 26 Ap 72 2/24:13
Compania Mexicana de Aviacion: 26 Ap 74 2/24:13
Condor Flugdienst GmBh: 31 Ag 73 2/8:13
Continental Airlines: 21 F 75 3/19:13
Cruzeiro: 1 F 74 2/18:11
Delta Airlines: 18 Ja 74 2/17:11
Eastern Airlines: 28 N 75 4/13:13
Egyptair: 2 My 75 3/24:13
Finnair: 10 Ja 75 3/16:13
Flying Tiger Line: 1 N 74 3/11:14

Garuda Indonesian Airways: 12 Jl 74 3/3:14
Ghana Airways: 17 O 75 4/10:11
Iberia (Lineas Aereas de Espana SA): 14 S 73 2/9:13
Interflug: 7 D 73 2/15:11
JAT--Jugoslovenski Aerotranport: 1 Mr 74 2/20:11
Japan Airlines: 18 O 74 3/10:13
Lan-Chile: 14 N 75 4/12:13
Lineas Aereas Paraguayas: 29 Mr 74 2/22:11
Linjeflyg: 14 Je 74 3/1:13
Lot-Polskie Linie Lotnicze: 7 D 73 2/15:11
Lufthansa: 3 Ag 73 2/6:13
Middle East Airlines: 7 F 75 3/18:13
National Airlines: 7 D 73 2/15:11
New Zealand National Airways: 29 Mr 74 2/22:11
Nordair: 15 F 74 2/19:11
Olympic Airways: 12 Ap 74 2/23:11
Overseas National Airways: 27 D 74 3/15:13
Pacific Southwest Airlines: 3 O 75 4/9:13
Pan American: 26 O 73 2/12:13
Pelita Air Service: 31 O 75 4/1:14
Philippines Airlines: 24 Ja 75 3/17:13
Qantas Airways: 15 Mr 74 2/21:13
Royal Air Maroc: 22 Ag 75 4/6:13
SAHSA Service Aereo de Honduras: 12 D 75 4/14:15
SAM Columbia: 27 Je 75 4/2:13
SATA (SA de Transport Aerien): 23 Ag 74 3/6:13
Sabena: 10 My 74 2/25:13
Saturn Airways: 12 Ap 74 2/23:11
Saudi Arabian Airlines: 15 N 74 3/12:13
Singapore Airlines: 28 Je 74 3/2:13
South African Airways: 29 Mr 74 2/22:11
Spantex: 6 S 74 3/7:12
Sterling Airways: 4 Ap 75 4/2:13
Suidwes Lugdiens: 5 S 75 4/7:13
TOA Domestic Airlines: 16 My 75 3/25:13
Texas International Airlines: 26 D 75 4/15:13
Thai Airways: 23 Ag 74 3/6:13
Trans World Airlines (TWA): 23 N 73 2/14:11
Transair: 23 Ag 74 3/6:13
Transavia Holland NV: 31 Ag 73 2/8:13
TransMediterranean Airways: 18 Ap 75 3/23:13
Turkish Airlines: 4 Ja 74 2/16:11
UTA Union de Transports Aeriens: 6 Jl 73 2/4:13
United Air Lines: 28 S 73 2/10:13
Varig: 7 Mr 75 3/20:14
Wardair: 13 Je 75 4/1:13
Western Airlines: 11 Jl 75 4/3:16

(European Airlines) [all AN 2 My 75 3/24]

ATI (Aero Transport Italiani): p10
Aeromaritime: p5

Aeropa: p10
Air Alpes: p5
Air Champagne Ardenne: p5
Air Charter International: p5
Air France: p4-5
Air Inter: p5
Air Limousin: p5
Air Littoral: p5
Air Paris: p5
Alisarda: p10
Alitalia: p10
Bavaria: p7
Catair: p6
Condor: p7
Euralair: p6
Europe Aero Service: p6
Europe Air Charter: p6
General Air: p7
Germanair: p7
Hapag Lloyd: p7
Itavia: p10
LTU (Lufttransport Unternehmen): p10
Lufthansa: p6-7
OLT (Ostfriesische Lufttransport): p10
SAM (Societe Aerea Mediterranea): p10
Touraine Air Transport: p6
Transportes Aeriens Reunis: p6
UTA (Union de Transports Aeriens): p6
Uni Air: p6
Vargas Aviation: p6

AIRPORTS

Exeter Airport: AN 1 F 74 2/18:7
Gravesend: AN 1 Mr 74 2/20:12-13
Kirmington: AN 12 Ap 74 2/23:6
New Developments at Bristol: AN 4 Ja 74 2/16:6
Oil Rig Aviation: Dyce Airport, Aberdeen, Scotland: AN 15 F 74
 2/19:12-13
Southend: AN 22 D 72 1/16:6-7
Speke: Liverpool International: AN 10 N 72 1/13:11
Sumburgh & the HS 748: North Sea Scotland airport: AN 22 Ag 75
 4/6:10
Tegel Replaces Templehof: West Berlin: AN 15 N 3/12:1

V. Articles

BIOGRAPHY

Godwin Brumowski: Austro-Hungarian fighter pilot, thumbnail: Q Au 75 11/1:39
Conquest of the Skies: see separate listing
Franz Gräser: Austro-Hungarian fighter pilot, thumbnail: Q Au 75 11/1:39
From Liberators to Mustangs: Harold Hagerman: AN 17 Ag 73 2/7:10
John Keeler (Col. USAF): RiS Ag 72 1/1:24-26
Frank Linke-Crawford: Austro-Hungarian fighter pilot, thumbnail: Q Au 75 11/1:39
Miss America & Howie Keefe: RCS N 75 1/7:21+
One Man Air Force: Don Gentile: AN 27 O 72 1/12:14
RC or RPV?: Don Lowe: RCS D 75 1/8:14-15
The Red Baron: Manfred von Richthofen: S&L (Ap 75) 7:24-25
Col. Stanton T. Smith, Jr.: RiS N 72 1/2:66-68

(Conquest of the Skies) [all MAN--cartoon]

[started S 70 81/3]
James McCudden: WW-I ace: D 70 81/6; Ja 71 82/1:14-15
Louis Bleriot: English Channel crossing: F 71 82/2:22-23
Edward O'Hare: WW-II naval ace: Mr 71 82/3:16-17
Amelia Earhart: women's distance record-holder: Ap 71 82/4:18-19
Joseph Michel Montgolfier: pioneer ballonist: Je 71 82/6:16-17

DIRECTORIES

RAF Aircraft Directory: current aircraft in use: AE Ap 74:179-189
Soviet Aircraft Directory: NATO code, type, brief description: AN 11 Jl 75 4/3:4-12
United States Coast Guard Aircraft Data List: AN 1 N 74 3/11:10

DOWNED AIRCRAFT, SURVIVAL, ESCAPE, RESCUE

August Escapade: mid-air collision between P-47 & B-24: AN 3 O 75 4/9:8
The Big Search: largest SAR operation: AN 2 Mr 73 1/21:6-7
CQ, CQ, CQ: radioman's account of B-25 in Pacific storm: WWE Mr 75 2/2:40-41
Hairbreadth Tom (Moorer): PBY crew survival: WWE Ja 75 2/1:23

Lady Be Good: Q Ja 72 7/1:12-14
The Luftwaffe's Last Liberator: German B-24 is shot down during ferry: AN 3 O 75 4/9:10-11
The Last Flight of the Heavenly Daze: RAF shoots down crewless B-24: AN 10 N 72 1/13:6
The Last Mission: Mosquito pilot's escape attempt from Netherlands: RT Ag 73 6/8:90; Q Jl 71 6/3:23
S. Missing on Duisburg Raid: 16 April 1943: RT S 75 8/9:108
Search & Rescue in Scotland: AN 7 D 73 2/15:12
Sidelights on a Bf 109: first captured by Allies (Nov 1939): PAM O 75 11:187
Was There a Saboteur in the RFC? accidents at Waddinton, 1917: AN 15 Mr 74 2/21:11

FLYING FULL-SIZE AIRCRAFT

Aerobatics--The King of Sports: AN 28 Je 74 3/2:12
The Dying Art of Visual Navigation: AN 9 Ag 74 3/5:12
Sidelights on Tugging, 1945: glider tugs in WW-II: PAM Ap 75 9: 154

MANUFACTURING

Aerospace Industry in France: AN 39 My 75 3/26:4-6
Australian Aircraft Industry: CAC, HDH, & GAF: AN 17 O 72 1/12:6
British Aerospace 74: what each company is doing: AI S 74 7/3: 111-126
Cessna's French Empire: AN 21 F 75 3/19:7
Cessna's 100,000th Single Engined Aircraft: AN 5 S 75 4/7:10
Douglas' Long Beach Production Line: AN 10 N 72 1/13:4-5
Fifty Years & Avicar: CASA: AE Ap 73 4/4:163-168+
French Aircraft Industry: AN 8 Je 73 2/2:4-5
Hurricanes Canada: Canadian Car & Foundry Co. Ltd. production: RT O 72 5/10:115
India's Aircraft Industry: HAL: AN 16 Mr 73 1/22:10
License to Build: Japanese & Russian-built DC-3: AN 12 D 75 4/14:10-11
Long Beach '75: McDonnell Douglas: AN 12 D 75 4/14:12-13
Lyulka, a Soviet Pioneer: jet development: AE N 71 1/6:297-300
The Man Who Collects Prentices: Aviation Traders civil conversions: AN 30 My 75 3/26:10-13
Pilatus Flugzeugwerke AG: AN 19 S 75 4/8:10-12
Robin Revolution: French lightplanes: AN 2 F 73 1/19:4-5
60 Years of Fairey Aircraft: AN 8 Ag 75 4/5:4-6
Spinal Cord of Indian Air Defence: HAL: AI Ja 75 8/1:7-12+; F 75 8/2:69-75+

V. Articles 484

Sweden's Aerospace Industry: AN 31 O 75 4/11:10-12
Wasmer Aviation: French lightplanes: AN 9 N 73 3/19:7
Where Did Our Light Aircraft Industry Go Wrong?: AN 24 Ja 75 3/17:7

PHOTOGRAPHIC STUDIES (Not Accompanied by Plans)

A-4 Skyhawks: AN 1 Mr 74 2/20:16
Albatross in detail: RT S 75 8/9:102-103
Anson Miscellaneousy: AN 26 O 73 2/12:16
Argonauts & North Stars: AN 28 N 75 4/13:16
BAC Canberra in RAF service: AN 24 N 72 1/14:16
Beechcraft Model 18: AN 29 N 74 3/13:7
Boeing B-52: AN 26 Jl 74 3/4:7
Boeing 707: AN 8 D 72 1/15:16
Brewster 339D Buffalo: Q Su 75 10/4:174
Canberra Cavalcade: IM My 74 10/(16):8-9
Consolidated Catalina: AN 13 Je 75 4/1:16
Constellations & Warning Stars: AN 17 O 75 4/10:16
Curtiss C-46 Commando: AN 16 F 73 1/20:16
De Havilland DH 82A Tiger Moth: AN 18 O 74 3/10:7
De Havilland DH 89A Dragon Rapids: AN 29 Mr 74 2/22:16
De Havilland Canada Chipmunk F.10: AN 12 Ap 74 2/23:16
Every Air Force Has One!: C-47 Dakota: AN 12 D 75 4/14:16
F-84 Thunderstreak in Close Up: Afx Jl 74 15/11:653-654
Fairchild C-119 Packet: AN 22 Ag 75 4/6:16
Grumman Goose: AN 21 F 75 3/19:16
Grumman Hu-16 Albatross: AN 27 Ap 73 1/25:16
Hawker Siddeley Argosy: AN 3 O 75 4/9:16
Hawker Siddeley Buccaneer: AN 18 Ap 75 3/23:16
Ilyushin Il-18 Coot: AN 7 F 75 3/18:16
Lockheed Neptune: AN 16 My 75 3/25:16
Lockheed's T-Bird: AN 5 S 75 4/7:16
NA T-6 International Trainer: AN 23 N 74 2/14:16
PBY: early var: Q W 75 11/2:80-81
Rockwell Commander: AN 30 My 75 3/26:16
Sea Venom: PAM O 73 3:inside both covers
U-2: Q O 73 8/4:217
Valiant--the First V-Bomber: AN 27 O 72 1/12:16

PRIVATE AVIATION

Aviation News Goes Up, Up & Away: hot-air ballooning: AN 28 S 73 2/10:6
Beromünster: Lucerne flying club: AN 19 S 75 4/8:12
Civil Aviation in Western Israel: AN 20 S 74 3/8:12
Island Hopping Holiday: Bahamas by lightplane: AN 8 Je 73 2/2:10

History--Aircraft

Jamaican Balloon Flight: aviation in Jamaica: AN 13 Je 75 4/1:6-7
The Man Who Collects Prentices: Aviation Traders civil restoration of military trainers: AN 30 My 75 3/26:10-11
Mix Oil & Aircraft: between wars oil company aviation: MAN Ag 71 83/2:14-16+
Rise & Fall of the British Light Aeroplane: AE Ag 73 5/2:90-95+; S 73 5/3:125-129+
Time to Spare? Go by Air: cross-country ferry of Piper Cub: RCS Je 75 1/2:51-52+

RESEARCH & DEVELOPMENT

Advancing the Harrier: jet VTOL work: AE F 74 6/2:53-54
Annals of the Polymorph, a Short History of V-G: variable geometry: AI Mr 75 8/3:134-140; Ap 75 8/4:185-188+; My 75 8/5:149-157
Canadair's STOL Story: AE Ja 72 2/1:12-16
Germany by a Short Nose: gas turbine engine research: AE Ag 72 3/2:78-81
Lifting Bodies...a new shape for the 21st century: AN 10 Ja 75 3/16:7
Look...No Hands: Firefly drones in missile testing: AN 14 S 73 2/9:4-5
Man Power Achievements: state of the art in man-powered flight: Aero My 72 37/436:260-261
On the Other Side of Farnborough Airfield: RAE: AN 23 Ag 74 3/6:6
Project Skywards: towed jeep autogyro experiments: AI Jl 75 9/1:19-22
RPVs: drones in research: RC N 75 12/11:12
Rolls Royce Flying Bedstead: Afx Mr 75 16/7:416-420
Silent Stars for Stealthy Spies: Lockheed low-noise-level light plane experiments: AE Ja 73 4/1:13-15
Tailess Tailpiece: German flying wing development, written by Lippisch: AE S 72 3/3:136-138+
Variable Geometry Today: swing wings & such: AI Mr 75 8/3:111-124

TACTICS

Breeding Better Dogfighters: AI N 74 7/5:211-217
VIFF--The Agility Factor: use of vertical thrust features of VTOL jets for increased maneouverability: AI D 74 7/6:263-267+

V. Articles

TRAINING

Always Ready, Rarely in Action: CAA fire training school at Stanstead: AN 26 Ap 74 2/24:10-11
Biggen Hill: RAF Training Command: AN 15 Mr 74 2/21:6
Chopper Training: Ternhill RAF: AN 24 Ja 75 3/17:4-5
First Stages in Flying Training: Church Fenton & Chipmunks: AN 14 Je 74 3/1:6-7
Henlow Bedfordshire: Officer Cadet Training Unit: AN 10 My 74 2/25:11+
New Look for RAF's Flying Training: AN 18 Ap 75 3/23:10
No. 4 Flying Training School: AN 20 S 74 3/8:6-7
Plotting to Kill: Observer School of Fleet Air Arm: AN 29 N 74 3/13:6
Rhodesian Reminiscenses: WW-II Commonwealth Air Training Plan: AN 26 O 73 2/12:10-11
T-Birds & Tigers: Danish military flying training: AN 10 Ja 75 3/16:16
Wings!: Linton-on-Ouse training base: AN 26 Jl 74 3/4:4-5

USE IN MOVIE MAKING

Hell's Angels Meet the Dawn Patrol: pre-WW-II aerial movies: Sc Jl 73 4/7:476-485
Lisunov's Wellington: Wellington replica made from DC-3 (Li-2): AE F 73 4/2:82-83
The Red Baron: Sc Ja 72 3/1:29

WEAPONS

Air to Air Rockets: German WW-II: WW2J S 75 2/5-6:40-43
Aircraft Gunsights: WWE Ja 75 2/1:11
American Aircraft Bombs 1917-1974: RiS Sp 74 2/3-4:126-149

HISTORY--ARMOR

CATEGORY SURVEYS

General

The Alvis FV 600 Range of Fighting Vehicles: MM Ap 71 1/4:

195-197
The Armor of Israel: AFV Ja 74 4/9:4-14+
Armor of the Russo-Finnish Wars: Q Ja 75 10/3:103-109
The Armoured Vehicles in the 1980s: A&W Mr 73 4/40:42; My 73 5:23-26
The Arms of the Canuck: weapons of the Canadian Army, 1939-1945; list: RT Ap 74 7/4:38
The CVR(T) Family: Scorpion, Spartan, Scimitar, Samaritan, etc.: A&W Mr 74 10:36-38
Centurion Variants: funnies on Centurion chassis: A&W N 73 8:20-22
First World War Depoisoners: mobile water purification facilities: MM N 72 2/11:597-598
French Armoured Vehicles: A&W 73 7:53-58
History & Development of Czechoslovak Armored Fighting Vehicles: AFV O 71 3/2:10-13; N 71 3/3:4-8+; D 71 3/4:8-9
Main Armoured Vehicles Used in the Yom Kippur War: both sides: A&W My 73 5:poster
New Vehicles for the Italian Army: armored cars, softskins, APC & ICV: A&W Mr 73 4:23-27
Satory '73: French weapon systems: A&W Jl 73 6:39-50
Scorpion Family: Afx D 74 16/4:246-247
Swiss Armoured Vehicles: A&W Mr 73 4:31-39

APCs, ICVs, ARVs, & Funnies

Comparison of Armored-Infantry Support Vehicles of WW-II: AFV Je 73 4/5:17+
The Funnies: see separate listing
Sherman ARVs: tank recovery vehicles of WW-II on Sherman chassis: MM Je 73 3/6:354-357
Sweden's Personnel Carriers: A&W Jl 74 12:20-26
Swedish AFVs: armored recovery vehicle 82, armored personnel carrier 302, bridgelayer 941: MM N 71 1/11:583-585

(The Funnies) [all MM]

Introduction: historical background, where used, when by types, units: Ap 71 1/4:182-188
Churchill AVRE Fascine & Sledge: My 71 1/5:232-236
Churchill Carpet-Layer type C: Je 71 1/6:292
Terrapin Amphibious Truck: Jl 71 1/7:256-257
Buffalo Carpet-Layer: Ag 71 1/8:410-414
Buffalo Mk 4 Assault Landing Craft: Ag 71 1/8:410-414
Buffalo Mk 2, 17 pdr Anti-Tank Gun Carrier: S 71 1/9:466-468
Buffalo Mk 2 Assault Landing Craft: S 71 1/9:466-468
Churchill Bridge Layers: folding & towed: O 71 1/10:512-521
Churchill VII Crocodile Flamethrower: with trailer: N 71 1/11:572-574

V. Articles

Sherman Crab Mine Clearer: D 71 1/12:634-537
Gutted Carrier: Bren carrier converted to tracked trailer: Ja 72 2/1:36-37
Grant CDL: armored floodlight: F 72 2/2:72-74+
Ram Kangaroo: APC: Mr 72 2/3:126-128+
Churchill AVRE with Log Carpet: Ap 72 2/4:190-192
Conger: rocket-launched hose in gutted carrier for mine clearing: My 72 2/5:224-226
Churchill Ark Mk I: short bridge using tank as permanent part of structure: Je 72 2/6:278-281
Skid Bailey Bridge & Churchill AVRE Pusher: Jl 72 2/7:365-367
Armoured Bulldozer: S72 2/9:462-463
Centaur Dozer: O 72 2/10:523-524
Sherman DD Tank: amphibious modification of Sherman: N 72 2/11:604-608
Bullshorn Plough & Porpoise: mine clearer & floating equipment sledge: D 72 2/12:648-650
Conclusion: miscellaneous demolition, bridging, & mine clearing devices: Ja 73 3/1:42-43

Armored Cars

Armoured Cars in the Desert: MM Je 75 5/6:350-353; Jl 75 5/7: 399-401; add F 76 6/2:110-111
Armored Cars of the RAF: see separate listing
Armoured Vehicles for Reconnaissance & Raids in Depth: A&W S 75 19:22-26
German Late-War Armored Cars: AFV D 74 5/1:16-17
To Battle in a Rolls: Rolls Royce armored cars: AFV Mr 74 4/10:4-8+ ; Ja 75 5/2:6-11

(Armored Cars of the RAF) [all MM]

Introduction: F 72 2/2:93-94
Improvised Armoured Vehicles, 1940-1945: Mr 72 2/3:144-145
Middle East Operations, 1920s & 1930s: Ap 72 2/4:200-202
Rearmament & Experiment: My 72 2/5:236-239
Second World War, North Africa & Middle East: Je 72 2/6:290-293
WW-II UK Defence, the War in Europe & the Far East: Jl 72 2/7:353-355
Post WW-II Armoured Cars: Ag 72 2/8:420-422

Half Tracks

Seek, Strike, & Destroy: U.S. tank destroyers: AFV ?; F 71 2/11:18-20; S 71 3/1:23-25; N 71 3/3:20-22

Artillery

Anti-Tank Weapons: survey of guns & missiles: A&W N 75 20:45-54
Armoured Vehicles & Small Calibre Automatic Cannons: A&W My 74 11/18:20
The Carronade: history of short muzzle-loading naval guns: MM My 71 1/5:258-259
New Infantry Support Weapon--20mm or 25mm?: current development for ICVs: A&W Jl 73 6:25-26
Russian Medium Artillery: contemporary: A&W S 73 7:25-26
Soviet Union's Rocket Launchers: A&W S 74 13:25-26
A Visit to Oerlikon: A&W Jl 74 12:37-45

Self-Propelled

American Assault Guns of World War Two: WW2J My 75 2/3:84-89; Jl 75 2/4:20-21

[all MM following]
World War I Beginnings: F 71 1/2:82-85
Wasp: F 71 1/2:85
German WW-II Development: assault guns, Hommel: Mr 71 1/3:130-133
German Equipment on Captured Chassis: Ap 71 1/4:204-206
German Siege Guns: My 71 1/5:244-247
Russian & Italian: Je 71 1/6:296-298
British: Jl 71 1/7:369-371
U.S.: Ag 71 1/8:422-424
NATO: S 71 1/9:473-475; O 71 1/10:528-530
Rocket Launcher Variants in Contemporary Use: N 71 1/11:564

Small Arms

History of Czechoslovak Military Pistols: Fus Sp 74 1/3:17-19+; Su 74 1/4:20-23
MAB 38/49: carbine: A&W 73 8:18-19
Multibarrel Firearms: S&L (F 75) 6:25
Russian Infantry Weapons of WW-II: Heavy Machine Guns: Afx Ap 72 13/8:430-431
A Visit to the FN: A&W Ja 73 3:35-37

Softskins

Bedford 30 cwt & 3 ton Vehicles of 1939-1945: MM Ap 73 3/4:239-241

V. Articles

Bedford Vehicles of WW-II: British army trucks: MM Ag 71 1/8: 402-404
Motorcycles in the U.S. Army: contemporary experimental use of cycles: AFV Ja 73 4/1:12-13
Soviet Artillery Tractors & Transporters: AFV S 75 5/6:17-19
A Visit to Berliet: trucks: A&W My 73 5:46-50

Tanks

Austria's Own Tracked Vehicles: A&W Ja 73 3:19-21
British AA Tanks: WW-II: AFV D 71 3/4:20
The Coming of the Tanks: reminiscenses of tank in 1916: S&L Jl 74 1:19
The Chosen Tanks: Israeli Sherman variants: A&W My 74 11:45-52
Development of French Tanks: A&W Mr 74 10:51-58
French Armour Takes a Wrong Turning: between Wars French design: A&W My 74 11:53-59; Jl 74 12:53-58
Panzerwaffe: A&W My 73 5:51-58; Jl 73 6:51-58
Some Considerations for a Reconnaissance Vehicle: AFV S 74 4/12:22-23
Soviet Heavy Tanks of the Great Patriotic War: Q Jl 74 10/1:4-6
Steam Power for Tanks: past & future: AFV Ap 75 5/4:6-12
Swedish AFVs: light tank 91: MM N 71 1/11:583-585
Tank Tales: WW-I tank operations from crew member's viewpoint: S&L Ag 74 3:9; (O 74) 4:8-9; (D 74) 5:5+
When Tanks Were Called Combat Cars: mechanization of U.S. Army 1925-1940: AFV Ap 75 5/4:18-21+

Accessories & Details

Blackout Lights: WW-II station-keeping systems: AFV Mr 73 2/12:13
Classification of Bridges: WW-II Allied bridge sign system: MW F 73 1/6:303
German Military Semaphore Signals, 1939-1945: visual communication apparatus: MW Ja 73 1/5:253
Ostkette: track width extensions, German, WW-II: AFV F 73 4/2: 15
Sand Shields: purpose: Afx S 75 5/6:56

INDIVIDUAL TYPES

APCs & ICVs

AMX-10: French ICV: A&W S 73 7:27-34

AMX-10P: 1969 ICV: MM D 74 4/12:762-764
Alvis Saracen: A&W S 75 19:35-42
BMP 76 PB: Russian ICV: A&M My 74 11:22-24
BTR-60: Russian: A&W Ja 75 15:24-26
Belfast Saracens: RT Ag 74 7/8:91
Berliet VXB: French APC: A&W Ja 75 15:35-42
FV-432: British ICV: A&W N 72 2:35-36
Fiat 661: Italian wheeled APC: A&W Mr 75 16:33-42
GKN Sankey AT-104 internal security vehicle: AFV S 75 5/6:29-31; add Ja 76 5/7:4+
LVTP-7 series: amphibious APC landing craft: MM F 74 4/2:84-86
Late-War Armored LVTs: LVT(A) 4&5: AFV Ja 73 4/1:4-9
The Loyd Carrier: MM Jl 73 3/7:449-457
M-113: A&W Ja 74 9:25-28
M-113: RiS Jl 75 3/2:95-99
Marder: 1950s West German ICV: AFV D 71 3/4:10-11+
Marder: A&W N 73 8:27-34
Marder: German ICV: MM D 72 2/12:666-668
Mowag Tornado: Swiss ICV: A&W My 74 11:25-36
Ram Kangaroo: RT Ag 75 8/8:92
Stalin Tank Missile Carriers & ARVs: Afx F 71 12/6:312-313
Unimog UR 416: ICV: A&W S 73 7:21-23
VAB Saviem: French wheeled APC: A&W Jl 74 12:27-36

ARVs & Funnies

FV-180 CET: engineer combat vehicle: A&W S 75 19:20-21
A Lepe of Leopards: funnies on Leopard tank chassis: MM F 72 2/2:88-93
M31 Tank Recovery Vehicle: WW2J Jl 75 2/4:14-17
Remote Control Tank K-3: WWE S 74 1/5:132
Sherman ARVs: MM Je 73 3/6:354-357

Armored Cars

AC Armoured Cars 1915: MM Ja 75 5/1:42-43
Alvis Saladin: A&W My 75 17:35-42
An Armoured Car for the Belgian Gendarmerie: FN 4 RM/62: A&W Mr 73 4:18-19
Commando: in Vietnam war: AFV S 71 3/1:4-8
The Commando: A&W Ja 73 3:22-24
French Armoured Cars: Panhard AML series: MM Ja 72 2/1:28-32
M-20 Armored Utility Vehicle: AFV Ja 75 5/2:19+
Panhard M-4, M-6, & M-8: 4-, 6-, & 8-wheeled French: A&W Mr 74 10:25-34

V. Articles   492

SdKfz 222: WW2J S 75 2/5-6:32-34
Shortland: armored Land Rover: MM Ag 73 3/8:528-530
Unimog UR 416: gun & missile armed var: A&W S 73 7:21-23

Artillery

AT-3 Sagger Anti-Tank Missile: Russian: A&W N 75 20:20
Big Bertha: MM My 75 5/5:270-272
Bofors FH-77: field howitzer: Q W N 75 20:29-30
Bofors 40/70: Swedish anti-aircraft gun: A&W S 74 13:27-36
British 6" 26 Cwt howitzer Mk I: Fus Sp 75 2/1:24-29+
18 pdr Mk I Field Gun: British WW-I: MW Je 73 1/10:536-539
FH-70 gun/howitzer: UK-German-Italian field piece: A&W My 75
   17:11-13
Flakvierling 38: WWE Mr 75 2/2:50-54
German 88mm Gun: MM F 73 3/2:106-107
HOT: anti-tank missile: A&W Jl 75 18:35-42
The Hazemeyer Gun: radar-controlled AA, primarily ship-board:
   MM Ap 73 3/4:236-239
Luftwaffe Gets the Rh202: automatic AA: A&W Mr 73 4:28-30
M-693: Weapon of Today: 20mm automatic: A&W N 72 2:20-22
Men Against Tanks: individual Anti-tank Weapons in the German
   Wehrmacht: AFV S 73 4/7:4-6
Men Against Tanks: Panzerfaust: AFV Ag 73 4/6:10-12+
Oerlikon 25mm: A&W Jl 73 6:22-24
Oerlikon 35mm: Swiss anti-aircraft gun: A&W Ja 75 15:17-21
Rocketmen of 1814: Congreve rocket: MM Mr 73 3/3:162-163; Ap
   73 3/4:216-217
7. 7cm Feld-Kanone 96n/A: 1914 German field gun: MW Ja 73 1/
   5:262-265
Soviet RPG-7 Rocket Launcher: 1960s descendent of Panzerfaust:
   Fus Su 74 1/4:27-29

Half Tracks

American Half-Tracks: see separate listing, immediately following
Finland's M3 Halftrack Conversions: AFV Je 75 5/5:20-23
Kleines Kettenkrad: AFV N 71 3/3:24-25
The 7.62 cm Russian Pak 36(r) mounted on the German 5-ton Half-
   track: AFV Mr 71 2/12:26
T-12/M-3 Halftrack: AFV S 72 3/10:4-7+; O 72 3/11:14-17+; D
   72 3/12:4-7
U.S. Half Tracks: IM My 72 9/5:2
White Half-tracks: in Canadian service: RT Mr 75 8/3:34

History--Armor

(American Half-Tracks) [all Afx]

Introduction: Je 71 12/10:534-535
Personnel Carriers: Jl 71 12/11:590-591
Multiple Gun Motor Carriages: Ag 71 12/12:634-635+; S 71 13/1: 40-41
Miscellaneous Types: O 71 13/2:70-71

Self-Propelled Artillery

Flakpanzer 38t: AFV Mr 72 3/7:9
Ha-To: Japanese 300mm mortar: Q O 73 8/4:218
Ha-To: WWE N 74 1/6:172
JPZ 4-5: West German tank destroyer: MM Je 73 3/6:372-375
Lancia 3RC & DA 90/53: MM D 73 3/12:827-828+
M-36 Tank Destroyer: AFV Mr 71 2/12:4-7
M-107/M-110: A&W Ja 73 3:27-33
Marder 38 in Action: AFV D 72 3/12:17+
155 GCT: on AMX 30 chassis: A&W N 74 14:35-42
An Original Self-Propelled Gun: Bofors VK-155 L/50: A&W N 73 8:26
Panzerjäger Ib mit 4.7 cm PAK(t): AFV S 71:20-21
SdKfz 138 Marder III: AFV O 71 3/2:4-6
SU-76: AFV Jl 72 3/9:15
2 Pdr Anti-Tank Gun Portee: 1940 carried artillery: MW S 73 2/1:28-31
Vest Pocket Artillery: Bison: AFV F 73 4/2:17-19+
West Germany's Tank Killer: JPz 4-5: A&W Mr 74 10:22-24

Small Arms

The Baker Rifle: MM N 74 4/11:671+
Beaumont Adams model 1855: British military revolver: S&L Ag 74 3:21
Beretta BM 59 FAL: Italian rifle: A&W S 74 13:20-24
The Blunderbuss: MM Ja 75 5/1:39-40
Boys Anti-Tank Rifle: Fus Au 73 1/1:22-25
British #82 Gammon Grenade: WWE Ja 75 2/1:7
The Brown Bess: musket: MM Jl 74 4/7:411-412
The Charleville: French musket: MM S 74 4/9:526-527
Colt CMG-2: light machine gun: A&W Jl 73 6:20-21
Degtyarev MG: MM O 74 4/10:599-601
FN Minimi: Belgian light machine gun: A&W S 75 19:18-19
FN's FAL: rifle: A&W My 73 5:18-22
Fallshirmjäger Gewehr 42: MM Je 74 4/6:330-331+
Ferguson Rifle: 1776 breachloading flintlock: MM S 75 5/9:538-539+; add Mr 76 6/3:157

V. Articles

A French Revolution: MAS 5.56 assault rifle: A&W Ja 74 9:18-19
Galil Assault Rifle: Israel: A&W Jl 75 18:16-19
The Gatling Gun: S&L (Je 75) 8:5-8
German Anti-Personnel Stick Grenades: WWE S 74 1/5:130-131+
German Sniper Rifles Kar 98k with ZF-41: rifle & telescopic sight: Fus Au 73 1/1:16-17+
Hunting Tanks with a Mortar: Danish 51mm Madsen anti-tank mortar: Fus W 74 1/2:24-27+
"Kentucky" Long Rifle: MM S 75 5/9:550-552
MG-42/MG-3: NATO: A&W Mr 73 4:43-52
Machinengewehr 34: MM Jl 74 4/7:396-399+
Men Against Tanks: introduction: AFV Je 73 4/5:12-13; Panzerfaust: Ag 73 4/6:10-12+; Raketenpanzerbusche: S 73 4/7:4-6
Navy Colt, model 1851: S&L Jl 74 2:14-15
No. 69 Bakelite Grenade: U.S. WW-II: WWE Mr 74 1/2:44-45
The Rifle of the French Army: MAS 49/56: A&W N 72 2:18-19
SIG 540/542 Assault Rifle: A&W Jl 74 12:18-19
SIG MG710-3: German machine gun: A&W Mr 74 10:18-21
Something for the Infantry: Falconet 24mm grenade launcher: A&W Ja 74 9:20-22
Spanish American War Gatling: RiS Au 2/1:30-31
Sterling Sug Machine Gun: A&W N 74 14:18-19
Stoner 63A1 System: light machine gun: A&W S 73 7:18-20
U.S. Pineapple Grenade (Mk II): WW2J S 75 2/5-6:50
Walther P.38: MM Ja 74 4/1:38-50
A Weapon for the Jungle: Colt M-16 Commando: A&W Ja 73 3:18
The XM 175 Grenade Launcher: Fus Sp 74 1/3:6-9

Softskins

Alvis Stalwart: British amphibious truck: MM Je 71 1/6:315-317
Austin K6 Breakdown Gantry: light recovery truck: MM My 73 3/5:288-291
BMW Motorcycle Variants in WW-II: AFV D 72 3/12:16
Bedford QL Army Fire Service Tender with Dennis Trailer Pump: MM F 73 3/2:92-95
Canadian Artillery Tractor: Chevrolet CGT: AFV S 75 5/6:21
Dodge Military Trucks: $\frac{1}{2}$, 3/4 ton, 1939 to present: AFV Ag 73 4/6:4-8
Flextrac Nodwell Dynatrac: fully tracked truck & powered trailer, amphibious: MM Ag 72 2/28:430-432
Henschel Dreiachs Kraftwagen type 33D1: 1934 German 6x4 truck: Sc Jl 73 4/7:488-489
Kubelwagen: 1939 German utility car: Sc Ag 71 2/8:402-406
Kurogane Type 95 4x4 scout car "Black Medal": MM Ap 75 5/4:231
M-584 Tracked Cargo Carrier: AFV Mr 73 4/3:4-7; My 73 4/4:12-15
Mobile Pigeon Loft: British WW-I wagon: MM S 72 2/9:490
Mobile VHF D/F Unit: RAF, 1948-1950: MM Ag 71 1/8:394+

495 History--Armor

Pink Panther: post 1960 SAS Land Rover: MM D 72 2/12:674-675; Ja 73 3/1:39-41
Scammell Pioneer: prime mover: MM Mr 73 3/3:154-156
Soviet ASU-85 Assault Gun: AFV S 73 4/7:17
Special Air Service & Its Jeeps: MM Ag 72 2/8:412-416+; S 72 2/9:485-487
Sweden's Army Snow Vehicles: Volvo BV 202 Snowcat: MM Mr 71 1/3:150-152
Vickers/Clyno Combination: 1915 machine gun motorcycle: MM Mr 71 1/3:126-129
XM-761: experimental U.S. military truck: MM O 72 2/10:538-541

Tanks

A.13 Cruiser in the Western Desert: AFV S 72 3/10:24-25
British WW-I Medium D Tank: 1919: MM Mr 71 1/3:139-141
Centurion: A&W Jl 73 6:27-34
Centurion III: IM My 73 10/5:2-4
Centurion Mk III: MM My 73 3/5:299-301; add S 73 3/9:620-621
Char B1: Afx Mr 71 12/7:356-357
Chi-Ha Type 97: Japanese medium: Q Su 75 10/4:159
Churchill: in Canadian service: RT N 75 8/11:124
Falcon: AA tank: A&W My 73 5:27-34
French Char B1 Tank: AFV F 72 3/6:15-17
German Disguised Panthers (to resemble U.S. M-10 tank destroyers): AFV D 74 5/1:22-23
German Panzerkampfwagen I: AFV F 75 5/3:16-21
Ha-Go Type 95 Light Tank: Q W 75 11/2:56
Japanese Type 95 Light Tank: AFV My 73 4/4:17+
Ka-Mi Type 2: Japanese amphibious tank variant of type 98 light tank: AFV My 72 3/8:15-17
Ka-Mi Type 2: WWE Ja 75 2/1:16-20
L40 Da 47/32 Semovente: Italian tankette: MM F 75 5/2:108
A Lepe of Leopards: Leopard tank & variants: MM F 72 2/2:88-93
M-3A1 Medium Tank: Lee/Grant: AFV S 72 3/10:15
M-18 Hellcat: AFV S 71 3/1:15-18
M-24 Chaffee: AFV O 71 3/2:16-19+
M-48: A&W N 72 2:27-34
M-60A-2: U.S.: A&W N 75 20:22-23
MBT-70 Kpz 70: US-German heavy tank: A&W S 74 13:37-44
The Maus That Almost Roared: German ultra-heavy tank: AFV Mr 71 2/12:14-17
PT-76: Russian amphibious recon tank: A&W N 72 2:23-26
Panzerkampfwagen IV: design & development: MW S 72 1/1:8-10
PzKpfw IV: early models: MW N 72 1/3:116-117; early production models: Ja 73 1/5:266-268; later production models: Mr 73 1/7:360-361
Ram I & II: Canadian Sherman variants: RT Je 75 8/6:67

V. Articles

The Russian T-35 Heavy Tank: five turret, 1933: AFV My 73 4/4: 19-22
STB type 74: Japanese 1974 tank: A&W N 75 20:55-62
The Scorpion Family: Afx N 71 13/3:146-147; D 71 13/4:216-217
Short History of the PzKw III Tank: IM F 72 9/2:2
Soviet PT-76 Recon Tank: AFV Jl 74 4/11:14-17
Summary of Leopard I Tank Development: West Germany, 1957-- present: AFV 4/12:17
Supertank: the Story of the M-6 Heavy Tank: AFV Ja 73 4/1:14-19
Tank, Medium, M-45, Pershing: AFV Ag 73 4/6:16
Tank S: Swedish turretless tank: AFV F 71 2/11:13-17
Tiger I: WWE Ja 74 1/1:7+ ; Mr 74 1/2:37
A Yank Tank in the Desert: M-3 Stuart: AFV Ja 74 4/9:26-27

Photographic Studies (Not Accompanied by Plans)

American Half-Tracks: White M3 variants: Afx F 72 13/6:330-331
Chieftain in Close Up: Afx Ag 71 12/12:648-649
Coles Crane in Close Up: Afx Je 72 13/10:547-548
Crusader Close-up: Afx F 72 3/6:310-311+
Daimler Mk I Armoured Car: AFV S 75 5/6:16
Daimler Scout Cars: MW F 73 1/6:298-299
Down the Hatch of a Churchill II: AFV Jl 74 4/11:10-11+
GAZ-67: AFV Jl 74 4/11:12
Hanomag SdKfz 251/1C Aberdeen Proving Grounds; 251/7D Patton Museum, Ft. Knox, KY: AFV S 73 4/7:14-15
M-5 Stuart light tank, City Park, South Gate, GA: AFV N 73 4/8: 12-14
M109 SP Howitzer: Q Au 75 11/1:50
Matilda Close-up: Afx S 73 4/7:17-18
Montgomery's M3A5 Grant Command Tank: AFV Ap 75 5/4:26-27
Scorpion in Close Up: Afx Mr 75 16/7:411-415
SdKfz 250/0 Reconnaissance halftrack: AFV D 74 5/1:24
45mm model 37, model 42: Q Au 75 11/1:20+
7/5cm KuK 37 gun on SdKfz 251/9: AFV Mr 74 4/10:16-17
75mm Pack Howitzer M1A6, 1943: WWE Mr 74 1/2:46
Type 95 Kyu-Go light tank, Schofield Barracks, Oahu: AFV My 73 4/4:23

Sketches (Not Accompanied by Plans)

Armored Car 6x6, 76mm Gun, Saladin Mk 2: AFV N 73 4/8:22-23
BMW R/75 motorcycle & side car: RiS N 72 1/2:61
M42 Duster: RiS Au 73 2/1:34-35
M113: RiS Jl 75 3/2:96-97

History--Armor

SPECIFICATIONS

APCs, ICVs, ARVs & Funnies

Alvis FV 603 Saracen: MM Ap 71 1/4:197
Alvis FV 604 Regimental Command Vehicles: MM Ap 71 1/4:197
Alvis FV 610 Regimental/Brigade/Division Command Vehicle: MM Ap 71 1/4:197
Carrier, Universal, T16: AFV S 73 4/7:22
LVT(A) 4 & 5: 1944 U.S. amphibious landing craft: AFV Ja 73 4/1:9
LVTP-7: amphibious APC landing craft: MM F 74 4/2:86
Pbv 301, 302: Swedish APC: A&W Jl 74 12:26
Remote Control Tank K-3: WWE S 74 1/5:132
Tank Recovery Vehicles M31 series: WWE S 74 1/5:132-133

Armored Cars (& Half-Track)

AEC Mk I: MM Je 72 2/6:291
Alvis FV 601 Saladin: MM Ap 71 1/4:197
Alvis Straussler Type A: MM My 72 2/5:236
Beaverbug Standard type D: MM Jl 72 2/7:354
Beaverette Standard type C: MM Jl 72 2/7:254
Car, Armored, Light, M8: Greyhound: AFV N 73 4/8:27
Carrier, Personnel, Half-Track, M3: AFV My 73 4/4:9
Commando Armored Cars: AFV S 71 3/1:8
Humber Mk II: MM Je 72 2/6:291
Humber Mks III & IIIa Recon Car: MM Ag 72 2/8:422
Lancia Armoured Car: RAF, 1930s: MM Ap 72 2/4:201
Otter Mk I, Recon Car: MM Ag 72 2/8:422
Panhard M-4, M-6, M-8: French 4, 6, & 8 wheeled: A&W Mr 74 10:34
Rolls Royce Standard Type A: MM My 72 2/5:236
SdKfz 222: WW2J S 75 2/5-6:32-34
SdKfz 234/1&2 Puma: AFV D 74 5/1:19
Shortland: armored Land Rover: MM Ag 73 3/8:530

Artillery

German AP40 Tungsten Shot: AFV N 73 4/8:17
German 88mm Ammunition: all variants: AFV O 72 3/11:20-23
German 5cm Ammunition: AFV My 73 4/4:4-6
German 7.5cm Ammunition: all variants: AFV F 73 3/6:4-8
German 3.7cm Ammunition: AFV My 73 4/4:4-6
German 12.8cm Ammunition: AFV S 73 4/7:8-10

Performance Charts for 90mm M-3 gun & armor-piercing ammo:
AFV N 71 3/3:21
7.7cm Feld-Kanone 96 n/A: German WW-I field gun: MW Ja 73
1/5:263-265

Self-Propelled Artillery

Carriage, Motor, 90mm Gun, M36B1: AFV Je 73 4/5:9
Ha-To: 300mm mortar: Q O 73 8/4:218
Ha-50: WWE N 74 1/6:172
Jagdpanzer 38(t) Hetzer: MW F 73 1/6:305
M19A1: twin 40mm tracked carriage gun: AFV Mr 73 4/3:12
M-36 Carriage, Motor, 90mm: U.S. medium tank/tank destroyer:
AFV F 73 4/2:9
M-36 Tank Destroyer: AFV Mr 71 2/12:5-6

Small Arms

Beretta BM 59 FAL: rifle: A&W S 74 13:24
Danish Madsen 51mm Mortar: Fus W 74 1/2:26
Degtyarev MG: DT 1929, DTA 1944, FP 1928, DPM 1944: MM O
74 4/10:601
Sterling Submachine Gun: A&W N 74 14:19

Softskins

Alvis FV 622 Stalwart: MM Ap 71 1/4:197
Alvis FV 652 Salamander fire crash tender: MM Ap 71 1/4:197
Dynatrac XM-571, SSV, RAT: MM Ag 72 2/8:432
XM-761, M35A2: trucks: MM O 72 2/10:540

Tanks

Armor Versus Shot Confrontation: penetration, deformation, etc.:
AFV My 72 3/8:7-9+ ; Jl 72 3/9:9-11+
Centurion: Mks 1, 3, 5, 13: A&W Jl 73 6:34
Centurion Mk III: firepower specs of all guns, small arms, grenades, etc.: MM My 73 3/5:301
FV.101 Scorpion CVR(T) FS: Afx N 71 13/3:147
German Tank Gun Performance: MM Ag 71 1/8:424
Ka-Mi Type 2: Japanese amphibious tank variant of type 98 light

tank: AFV My 72 3/8:15-17
Light Tank 38 M Toldi, 1939: Hungarian var of Swedish Landsverk L-60 (from 38(t)): WWE My 74 1/3:66-67
M3 Stuart: AFV Ja 74 4/9:27
M-3A1 Medium Tank, Lee Mark II: 1942: AFV S 72 3/10:18
M4A3E2 Sherman: AFV F 71 2/11:25-26
M18 Hellcat: AFV S 71 3/1:18
M-18 Carriage, Motor, 76mm: medium tank: AFV Ja 73 4/1:31
M-24 Chaffee: AFV O 71 3/2:17
T-35: 1933 Russian heavy tank with five turrets: AFV My 73 4/4:21
M-45 Tank, Medium (Pershing): AFV Ag 73 4/6:17
MBT-70 Kpz 70: U.S.-German: A&W S 74 13/44
Maus: AFV Mr 71 2/12:14-17
Medium Tank 40 M Turan I, 1940: Hungarian medium tank: WWE My 74 1/3:66-67
Montreal Locomotive Works Tank, Cruiser, Grizzly I: RT O 74 7/10:110
PT-76: Russian recon tank: AFV Jl 74 4/11:17
Panther: MM D 75 5/12:728
PzKpfw IV: Ausf A, B, C, D, E, F1, F2, G, H, J: MW Mr 73 1/7:361
Pz 58, 61, 68: Swiss tanks: A&W Mr 73 4:39
Ram I & II: RT Je 75 8/6:67
Skink AA: on Grizzly hull: RT F 75 8/2:18
Tiger I: WWE Mr 74 1/2:37

HISTORY--ARMY

ARMS MANUFACTURERS

British Defence Industry in the Land Sector: A&W My 75 17:14-26
Italian Producers of Ground Defence Systems: A&W Mr 75 16:15-32

ARMY HISTORIES

Argentine Army: A&W S 73 7:39-42
The Armor of Israel: AFV Ja 74 4/9:4-14+
Army of the Ancien Regime: A&W Mr 74 10:59-66; My 74 11:59-66
Austrian Army in the Napoleonic Wars: S&L (D 75) 11:12-13
British Army in the Seven Years War: S&L (O 75) 10:4-6
The British Army: A&W My 75 17:27-34
Canadian Armed Forces: A&W S 73 8:46-52

V. Articles 500

Canadian Armored Corps in WW-II: RT D 75 8/12:134+
Dervish Army at Omdurman, 1898: S&L (F 75) 6:18-19
The Eastern Alliance: Warsaw Pact: A&W Jl 74 12:48-52; S 74 13: 45-50
Eaters of Men: Zulu of 1879 period: MM My 74 4/5:262-264; Je 74 4/6:322-324
Egyptian Army Today: A&W S 75 19:30-34
French Infantry 1900-1914: MW F 74 2/6:297-299
French Paratroops: A&W Ja 73 3:54-58; Mr 73 4:53-58
The Italian Army: A&W Mr 75 16:43-50
Italy's Marines: A&W Ja 73 3:41-44
Johnnie Reb of 1861: MM Ja 75 5/1:25-27; cor Mr 75 5/3:154-155; Je 75 5/6:336
Jordanian Army: A&W N 75 20:39-41
KNL, the Long-Haired Brigade: Dutch conscript forces: A&W Mr 74 10:46-50
Knights & Medieval Warfare: Henry V: MM Ap 75 5/4:225-227; cor Je 75 5/6:336; add Ag 75 5/8:468
Landsknechts: German mercenaries, 16th century: MM D 73 3/12: 811
The Modern U.S. Army: AFV Je 75 5/5:6-14
Ninja: MM Mr 75 5/3:148-149; Ap 75 5/4:232-233
Plains Indians: MM Jl 74 4/7:392-395
Prussian Infantry in the Waterloo Campaign: S&L (D 74) 5:2-3; (F 75) 6:10-11; (Ap 75) 7:10-12; (Je 75) 8:22-23
Prussian Infantry under Frederick the Great: A&W Ja 73 3:59-66
The Red Army: A&W Ja 75 15:27-34
The Russian Soldier: see separate listing
Samurai: MM S 73 3/9:588-591
Soldier of Pharoic Egypt: S&L (Ap 75) 7:4-6; (Je 75) 8:14-16; (Ag 75) 9:?-?; (O 75) 10:14-15; cor (O 75) 10:32-33; (D 75) 11:10-11
Successors of William Tell: Swiss army: A&W Ja 73 45-53
U.S. Cavalry in the Indian Wars: MM O 74 4/10:613-617; N 74 4/11:672+; cor F 75 5/2:89
Z'va Haganah: Israel: A&W S 72 1:?; N 72 2:45-51

(The Russian Soldier) [all WWE]

Peculiarities as a Type: Ja 74 1/1:5-6
Command Eschelons: Mr 74 1/2:33-35+
The Commissar: My 74 1/3:63-64
Combat Arms: infantry, artillery, armored forces, horse cavalry: S 74 1/5:124-125+
Battle Techniques: Ja 75 2/1:4-5+

History--Army

BATTLES & CAMPAIGNS

Pre World War II

The Battle of Bunker Hill: MM S 75 5/9:542-544
Battle of Crecy: S&L (Ap 75) 7:18-22; (Je 75) 8:24-25
The Battle of the Granicus: Alexander vs. Darius, 334 BC: MM N 73 3/11:750-753
The Battle of the Holy Island: Battle of Miyajima, 1594: S&L Ag 74 3:10-11
The Battle of Kadesh, 1288 BC: MM O 75 5/10:606-608; N 75 5/11: 664-665+; cor Ja 76 6/1:17; Mr 76 6/3:156-157
Battle of Marathon: MM Jl 74 4/7:386-388+
The Battle of Minkata-Ga-Hara, 1572: S&L (O 74) 4:16-17
Battle of Montebello, April 1859: A&W Ja 74 9/59:68
Battle of Nagashino, 1575: S&L (D 74) 5:10-11+
Battle of Pydna, 168 BC: MM Mr 75 5/3:160-163; cor Je 75 5/6: 337
Battle of Shizu-Ga-Take, 1583: S&L (F 75) 6:6-7+
Battle of Vimeiro: Penusular War: S&L Je 74 1:13-14
Bombardment of Hartlepool: as seen in 1914 by a schoolgirl: S&L Ag 74 3:12
Campaign in Fruili, 1809-1813: A&W Jl 73 6:59-66; S 73 7:59-66
The Fight for the Standard: capture of 45th's Eagle by Ewart & 105th's by unknown: S&L Ag 74 3:16-17
Isandhlwana: Jan 1879 Zulu War battle: MM Je 75 5/6:355+; Jl 75 5/7:418-421
More Cuckoos for Chelsea: Eagle capturing in the Peninsular War: S&L (O 75) 10:11-13
Rennaissance Warfare: see separate listing in Static Scale Figures
Retreat to Corumnna: Penusular War: S&L Jl 74 2:6-7; cor S&L (F 75) 6:21
The Russo-Turkish War of 1853: A&W Mr 73 5:59-67
The Spanish Civil War: MW N 73 2/3:139-142
Tank Versus Tank: first tank battle, 1918: AFV O 72 3/11:10-11
Tel-el-Kebir, 1882: Egypt: S&L Je 74 1:7-8
Two Minutes at Marengo: 1800: A&W Mr 73 4:59-66
Warfare in the Age of Marlborough: see separate listing, immediately following

(Warfare in the Age of Marlborough) [all MM]

The Character of the Age: My 73 3/5:275-277
Pattern of Strategy: Je 73 3/6:387-389
Siege: fort design & attacking tactics: Jl 73 3/7:460-462
Battle: Ag 73 3/8:517-519
Pattern of Command & Staff Work: S 73 3/9:602-604

V. Articles

World War II

The Admiral & the Afrikakorps: Sir Walter Cowan, 18th Indian Cavalry Rgt: AFV Mr 73 4/3:9+

Anzio, the Soft Underbelly of Europe: AFV O 72 3/11:4-8; D 72 3/12:12-15+; Ja 73 4/1:20-23+; F 73 4/2:28-31+; Mr 73 4/3: 28-32; My 73 4/4:32-36; S 73 4/7:29-32; N 73 4/8:28-31+; Mr 74 4/10:28-31

Armoured Cars in the Desert: MM Je 75 5/6:350-353; Jl 75 5/7: 399-401

Battered Hulks & Cockleshells: British Armor in the Defense of Crete: AFV Mr 72 3/7:4-6+

The Battle for Kursk: WWE Ja 75 2/1:8-10; Mr 75 2/2:62-64

Charge of the Light Brigade: battle near Siegfried Line: AFV N 71 3/3:33

Defense of Sicily, 15th Panzer-Grenadier Division: AFV Ja 72 3/5: 22-23+; F 72 3/6:12-14; Mr 72 3/7:12-14; My 72 3/8:21-23+

Eighth Army in the Desert: see separate listing in Static Scale Figures

The First Days of the Belgian Invasion: A&W N 74 14:49-55

German Invasion of Poland: MW Ap 73 1/8:417-419

Heinz Guderian & the Drive for Moscow: AFV F 71 2/11:8-10

KV-1: 4th Tank Bgd defense of Moscow: RT Ap 73 6/4:39

The Last Gasp of the Waffen SS: operations in Hungary & Austria: WWE Mr 75 2/2:42-48; disc WW2J S 75 2/5-6:46-47; reply Mr 76 3/2:30-31; add & cor My 76 3/3:50

Libya 1940: Start of the Desert War: AFV O 71 3/2:7-9

Lost & Found: SU-76i in Pripyat Marsh campaign: AFV Je 73 4/5:28-29

Marder 38 in Action: incident in autumn 1943 on Eastern Front: AFV Je 73 3/12:28-29

Men Against Tanks: PAK 38 against T-34: AFV S 72 3/1:9+

1941: Attack on Yugoslavia: A&W Ja 75 15:49-55; Yugoslave Campaign: A&W My 75 17:49-55

Normandy D Plus 3: AFV O 71 3/2:14

On to Bizerte: unplanned first entry to Bizerte: AFV Mr 71 2/12: 27

Operation Griffon: PzBgd 150 in Malmedy attack, Dec 1944; Q O 74 10/2:59-61

Operation Sealion: planned invasion of Britain: Afx Je 75 16/10: 596-600; Jl 75 16/11:642-644; Ag 75 16/12:694+; S 75 17/1:17-18+; O 75 17/2:82-84+; cor O 75 17/2:82-84+; cor O 75 17/2: 124; N 75 17/3:142-143; F 76 17/6:365-366; cor & add N 75 17/3:178; cor & add Ap 76 17/8:483-484

Operation Weseruebung (Invasion of Norway): A&W Jl 75 18:49-55; S 75 19:49-54

Rearguard: 1941 Defense of Greece: Fus Au 73 1/1:8-9+

Salerno: AFV Mr 71 2/12:18-20; N 71 3/3:9-11; D 71 3/4:18-19

Stop Thrust: Arras, 1940: AFV Mr 71 2/12:10-11

Swanning into the Blue: British armored car operations during Operation Crusader: AFV F 72 3/6:4-7+

The Tunisian Campaign: A&W N 73 8:51-55; Ja 74 9:53-58

Velikiye Luki: a Miniature Stalingrad: 1942 siege: WW2J Jl 75 2/4:4-6
When the Wheat Ripened: Russian front, August 1944: AFV O 71 3/2:26-27

Post World War II

Arab-Israeli War of 1973: AFV D 74 5/1:4-13+
Blunted Sword: Jordanian Armor in the 1967 Sinai War: AFV S 71 3/1:12-14; O 71 3/2:20-22+
Delta Ambush: U.S. Action in Mekong Delta, Vietnam, 1968-72; Fus Sp 75 2/1:12-14+
NVA Easter Offensive of 1972: Vietnam: AFV Je 73 4/5:28-29
Tanks of Dien-Bien-Phu: AFV D 71 3/4:4-6
Yom Kippur War: A&W N 73 8:35-50
Yom Kippur War: Egyptian front: AFV S 74 4/12:4-8+; F 75 5/3: 6-10

BIOGRAPHY

Correspondent: War Zone: Ernest Hemingway in WW-II: WWE My 74 1/3:78
Correspondent: War Zone--Pacific War Reporters: WWE Jl 74 1/4: 111
Giap, Guerrilla Genius: A&W N 72 2:40-44
Making of a Marshal: Gouvion St. Cyr: S&L (Je 75) 8:21
Michel Wittmann: SS Panzer Obersturmführer: AFV Ja 72 3/5:4-9

EQUIPMENT

Army Paybooks: Third Reich: Fus Au 73 1/1:4-7
First World War Depoisoners: portable water purification units: MM N 72 2/11:597-598
From Scarlet to Khaki: British field uniforms, 1857 to WW-I: S&L (D 75) 11:18-21
German Mountain Troop Field Clothing: Fus W 74 1/2:4-6+
Helmets & Headdresses Through the Ages: ancient to medieval: S&L Jl 74 2:22-23; Ag 74 3:22-23; (D 74) 5:16-17; (F 75) 6:12-13; cor (O 74) 4:(3)
Introduction of Plate Armour: MM Je 75 5/6:358-359
Ladies from Hell: British military tartans & kilts: S&L (F 75) 6: 22-24
Once Upon a Time There was a Simple Bonnet: headgear: A&W S 74 13:57-66

V. Articles 504

FORTIFICATIONS

Channel Isle Fortifications: MM F 74 4/2:126-127
German Fortifications in Jersey: those still remaining: Afx Ja 75 16/5:307-309
Maginot: the Useless Colossus: A&W N 72 2:53-58

MOVIES

Waterloo: Columbia/Mosfilms: MM Ja 71 1/1:18-21

ORGANIZATION CHARTS

Larger Than Regiment

Afrika Korps: WWE S 74 1/5:142+
Afrika Korps Panzer Regiments: AFV Ja 73 4/1:29
German Forces, Attack on Yugoslavia: A&W Ja 75 15:51
German Panzer-Aufklärungs (armored recon division) 1945: AFV Mr 73 4/3:24-26
Hungarian Armor: WW-II: AFV S 74 4/12:10-12+
Italian Armoured Division: June 1940: A&W S 74 13:53
Italian Armoured Division: 1942: A&W S 74 13:56
Italian Armoured Division: 1943: A&W S 74 13:57
Italian Forces, Attack on Yugoslavia: A&W Ja 75 15:51
Luftwaffen Feld Divisionen: internal units of each division: WWE N 74 1/6:165+
Respective Battalions & Divisions to which the Tiger I Belonged: internal organization: WWE Mr 75 1/2:37
Soldiers of Pharaoric Egypt: S&L (Ap 75) 7:5
Soviet Army Order of Battle: June 1944: Fus Au 73 1/1:18-21+; W 74 1/2:20-23; Sp 74 1/3:20-22
Soviet Army Order of Battle: Aug 1944: Fus Su 74 1/4:14-17+
Tanks of Dien-Bien-Phu: order of battle: AFV D 71 3/4:6
U.S. Army Armor-Cavalry Units: units, btns, & sqns, unit of assignment: AFV S 75 5/6:36-37+
U.S. Army Infantry Divisions, WW-II: number, nickname, sub-unit numbers: Fus Sp 74 1/3:14-16
Yugoslavian Cavalry Division: A&W Ja 75 15:54
Yugoslavian Forces: Attack on Yugoslavia: A&W Ja 75 15:52
Yugoslavian Infantry Division: A&W Ja 75 15:53

Regiment or Lower

(Egypt)

Soldiers of Pharaoric Egypt: S&L (Ap 75) 7:5

(Germany; sil)

Jagdpanzer-Kompanie (Jagdpanzer 38): Nov 1944: AFV O 72 3/11: 26-27
Panzer-Aufklärunge-Kompanie "C": 1944, SdKfz 250: AFV F 71 2/11:26-27
Panzer-Aufklärunge-Kompanie (KRAD): Nov 1943, motorcycle recon: AFV Je 73 4/5:24-26
Panzer-Aufklärunge-Kompanie (Volkswagen): Nov 1944: AFV F 75 5/3:30-32
Panzer Fliegerabwehrzug (2cm Flak 38): Feb 1944: AFV S 72 3/10:22-23
Panzer-Funklenk-Kompanie: 1944, heavy & robot tank unit: AFV Ja 72 3/5:24-25
Panzerjäger-Kompanie: April 1945, half-track anti-tank unit: AFV My 72 3/8:26-27
Panzer-Kompanie "Panther" (frei Gliederung): Nov 1944: AFV Ja 74 4/9:25
Panzer-Kompanie Panzer IV (frei Gliederung): Nov 1944: AFV Jl 74 4/11:28-29
Panzerspäh-Kompanie "A" (frei Gliederung): Nov 1944, Puma: AFV Jl 74 4/11:28-29
Panzerspäh-Kompanie "B": March 1944: AFV D 74 5/1:30-31
Schnelle Panzerjäger-Kompanie: Nov 1943: AFV Je 75 5/5:642
Schwere-Panzer Kompanie: 1943, mixed heavy & medium tanks: AFV Mr 72 3/7:22-23+
Schwere-Panzer Kompanie: 1944-1945, PzKpfw VI Königstiger: AFV N 72 3/3:28-29
Schwere-Panzerjäger-Kompanie: March 1944, Jagdpanther: AFV Jl 72 3/9:24-25
Stabskompanie Eines Panzer-Abteilung (frei Gliederung): April 1944, tank btn HQ: AFV Ja 73 4/1:26-28
Tiger I Units: 1942-1943: WWE Mr 74 1/2:36
Tiger I Units: 1944-1945: WWE Mr 74 1/2:35

(India; sil)

Infantry Reconnaissance Sqn of 1944: AFV F 73 4/2:25-27+
Reconnaissance Rgt HQ: 1943: AFV My 73 4/4:26-27

(USSR)

Armored Train Division: late 1930s, individual train: AFV Ja

V. Articles

74 4/9:23
Guards Rocket Artillery Regiment: AFV Je 75 5/5:15
Heavy Tank "Breakthrough" Rgt: AFV N 73 4/8:7
Independent Tank Battalion: winter 1942-43: AFV F 75 5/3:11
Self-Propelled Artillery Rgt: summer 1944, JSU-152: AFV Ja 74 4/9:15
Self-Propelled Artillery Rgt: summer 1944, SU 76: AFV Ag 73 4/6:9
Self-Propelled Artillery Rgt: summer 1944, SU-85: AFV D 74 5/1: 15
Tank Brigade: summer 1944, btn & coy: AFV Mr 74 4/10:9
Tank Regiment: summer 1944: AFV Ap 75 5/4:32-34+

(U.K.; sil unless otherwise stated)

Armored Division; type 1939, no sil: AFV O 71 3/2:30-31
Armoured Division: Autumn 1940, no sil: Afx Jl 75 16/11:642
Infantry Division: 1940, no sil: Afx Jl 75 16/11:643
Light Tank Sqn 1940 Mk IV light tank: AFV N 73 4/8:7
Matilda Tank Company: 1938-1941: AFV D 71 3/4:26-27
Motor Machinegun Brigade: June 1940, no sil: Afx Jl 75 16/11: 643
Motorized Infantry Battalion: 1940, no sil: Afx Jl 75 16/11:643
Mountain Artillery: 1879-1885, mule & camel mounted 7 pdr, no sil: MW F 74 2/6:332
Stuart Tank Sqn; 1942: AFV Mr 71 2/12:25-24

(U.S., sil unless otherwise stated)

Armored Cavalry Howitzer Battery: March 1975, 155mm self-propelled: AFV S 75 5/6:26-28
Armored Cavalry Troop: 1973: AFV S 74 4/12:28-30+; cor D 74 5/1:2; Ja 75 5/2;4: F 75 5/3:4
Infantry Regiment Tank Company: 1950: AFV D 72 3/12:24-25
Light Tank Battalion: 1942, HQ & HQ Coy: AFV Ja 75 5/2:28-31
Mechanized Cavalry Reconnaissance Troop of 1940: AFV Ag 73 4/6:28-30+
Mechanized Rifle Company: Nov 1970: AFV Ap 75 5/4:17
Medium Tank Company, 1944: AFV F 72 3/6:26-27
Reconnaissance Troop (mechanized): March 1943: AFV Mr 74 4/10: 24-26+
Tank Destroyer Gun Company: 1944-1045, half-track: AFV S 71 3/1:24-25
T/O&E Ranger Infantry Battalion: 1944, duty, rank & arms, no sil: Fus Su 74 1/4:24-26

TACTICS

Amphibious Operations: Central Pacific: WW2J S 75 2/5-6:10-15

Aztec Warfare: S&L Je 74 1:15
The Beginnings of Tank Warfare: A&W N 75 20:63-69
Castles Under Siege: MM Ap 75 5/4:216-217
Heinz Guderian on Armored Forces: AFV S 74 4/12:20-21; Ja 75 7/2:26-27+; F 75 5/3:14-15+
Infantry Versus Soviet Tanks: German, WW-II: AFV D 71 3/4:15-17
Techniques of Indirect Fire by Tanks during WW-II: AFV S 75 5/6: 6-12; add Ja 76 5/7:4
Thus Fought Napoleon: A&W N 73 8:56-66

UNIT HISTORIES

Anti-Partisan Forces of the Third Reich: WW2J Jl 75 2/4:31-33; S 75 2/5-6:48-50
Brandenburg Formations of WW-II: MW F 74 2/6:324-327
Cacciatori delle Alpi, 1859: Garibaldi's unit: A&W Jl 74 12:59-66
Chasseurs Britannique: S&L (D 74) 5:14-15; add S&L (F 75) 6:20
8072 Tank Battalion: AFV D 72 3/12:10-11+
Essex Regiment in WW-II: Fus Su 74 1/4:30-31
1st Armoured Car Regiment (Wimmera Rgt): AFV Ja 74 4/9:29+
Flemish Volunteers of the Third Reich: WWE Jl 74 1/4:92-?
The Forgotten Fifteenth: 15th Infantry, U.S. Army, around Tientsien, China, 1912-1938: RiS Sp 74 2/3-4:150-154
The 4th SS Police Division: WWE N 74 1/6:177+
From Texas to Salerno, the 141 Infantry Rgt: WW2J S 75 2/5-6: 4-7
Guards Camel Regiment in the River War 1884-1889: S&L (D 74) 5:4
Highland Regiments in the War of Independence: MM S 75 5/9:532-533
Imperial Regiments in the Zulu War of 1879: MM Jl 74 4/7:389-381; Ag 74 4/8:457-459+
Italian Armoured Divisions in World War II: A&W S 75 13:51-58
Jägers: Prussian Army, 1813 onwards: S&L (D 74) 5:28
Japanese Snipers: WWE N 74 1/6:167
Louisiana Tigers: Wheat's Battalion, CSA Zouaves: Fus W 74 1/ 2:32-35
Luftwaffe Field & Para Divisions: land units: WWE My 74 1/3:65+
Navy Beach Parties: work in initial landing & in restoring harbors: WWE Ja 74 1/1:10+
Organization & Equipment of the Irish Army: Afx Mr 74 15/7:408-410; add My 74 15/9:540-541
Polish Winged Hussars c. 16th-18th Century: S&L (D 75) 5:8
The Royal Artillery: A&W Ja 74 9:40-45
Six Day War Pattons: Tal's Ugda (division), 1967: Q Jl 74 10/1: 37
610th Tank Destroyer Battalion: AFV Ja 72 3/5:12-14
Special Air Service: MM Ag 72 2/8:412-416; S 72 2/9:485-487
363 Infantry Regiment in Combat: 1943-1945: Fus Sp 74 1/3:10-11+

V. Articles   508

Tigers at the Front: Schwere Panzer Abteilung 503 in Feb 1943:
   WW2J S 2/5-6:20-21
A True Land Battleship: Soviet Armored Trains: AFV Ja 74 4/9:
   22-23+
U.S. 1st Cavalry: AFV F 72 3/6:8-9
U.S. Seventh Army: A&W My 73 11:40-45
Upper Number U.S. Armored Divisions in WW-II: 10, 11, 12, 13:
   AFV Ag 73 4/6:13+; 14, 16, 20: AFV S 73 4/7:28+
Women's Volunteer Reserve: British, WW-I: Afx S 73 15/1:30-31

HISTORY--AUTOMOBILES

GENERAL

Auto-Union 1934-1939 Grand Prix racers: Sc D 71 2/12:645-649
Bombardier Snowmobiles from Canada: Sc Je 72 3/6:341
Ford Turbine Engine: Sc My 74 5/56:274-277
RFB (Lippisch) X 113Am Aerofoil Boat: Aero S 73 38/452:488-490
   [surface effect vehicle]

RACERS

   Formula 1

AFV Shadow: Sc F 75 6/65:82-85
BRM P.180: Sc F 73 4/65:135-136
Brabham BT 42: Sc My 74 5/56:251-255
JPS 9: Sc D 74 5/63:646-649
John Player Special: Sc Je 72 3/6:332-334
Lola T370: Sc Ja 75 6/64:12-15
March Formula 1: Sc My 73 4/5:283-285
March 711: Sc Je 71 2/6:309-312; Sc My 73 4/5:358-361
McLaren M20: Sc Je 73 4/6:426-429
McLaren M23: Sc Jl 73 4/7:502-505
McLaren M23: Texaco-Marlboro, 1974: Sc Mr 75 6/66:130-135
TS 7: 1969: Sc Ja 71 2/1:22-25
Tecno: Sc Ja 74 5/1:40-43
Tyrrell 006: Sc S 74 5/60:496-499

   Grand Prix

Alfa-Romeo T33TT: Sc Ja 73 4/1:59-61

Alfa-Romeo T33/12: Sc Je 75 6/69:301-303
da Tomaso Pantéra: Sc Mr 73 4/3:171-172
Ferrari 312 B3: Sc My 75 6/68:240-243
Gulf Mirage Long Tail: Sc Ag 73 4/8:558-560
Matra Simca 670: 1974 Le Mans: Sc Ap 75 6/67:169-171
Porsche 917/30: Sc O 74 5/61:545-547
Surtees TS 16: 1974-1975: Sc S 75 6/72:452-455
Type C Jaguar: Sc Ag 73 4/8:556-558
Tyrrell 007: Sc Jl 75 6/70:342-345

Other

BMW CSL: stock car: Sc D 73 4/12:840-841+
Chevrolet Camaro: Gran Tourismo: Sc Jl 74 5/58:386-388+
Jabford 1172: sporting trials: Sc Jl 71 2/7:363-365
Lancia Stratos: 1973 road racer: Sc Ag 75 6/71:398-401
Lola T330: Formula 5000: Sc S 73 4/9:629-630
McLaren M.16: 1971 Indianapolis: Sc S 71 2/9:482-484
Porsche Carrera: Gran Tourismo: Sc O 73 4/10:702-704
Proteus Bluebird: Absolute Speed: Sc Je 74 5/51:328-331
Renault Alpine A 364: Formula 3: Sc Mr 73 4/3:173-174
Trojan 6101: Formula 5000: Sc Mr 74 5/54:162-165

TRUCKS

American La France Ladder Chief: aerial ladder fire truck: Sc Ja 72 3/1:32-33
Pyrene Pathfinder: airport crash truck: Sc Ja 74 5/1:20-22+

HISTORY--MISSILES

BAC ET-316 Rapier: SAM: A&W Ja 73 3:25-26
Crotale: SAM: A&W My 73 5:35-39
German V-1 Flying Bomb: Fus Sp 74 1/3:26-29
Komoran: ASM: AN 7 Jl 72 1/4:9
Lance: SSM: A&W N 74 14:24-27
The Swingfire Hits Out: SSM: A&W S 73 7:35-38
V-2 Terror Weapon: history, operations of field units: MM Jl 73 3/7:446-448

HISTORY--MODELING

GENERAL

Aerospace Technology: and how RC models are used in research: RC F 75 12/2:23-25
Air Power: pneumatic toy trains: NMRA N 72 38/3:35-36
Autopilot in Project Teleplane: Hill's autopilot: AM Ag 73 76/8: 12-13+
Dateline: Ft. Campbell, KY: drone anti-aircraft gun targets: RC Ja 75 12/1:28-30+
Development of a Wakefield: background to Vitar II: Aero Ap 75 40/471:220-221; My 75 40/472:281-284; Je 75 40/473:344-346
Flash Steam Propulsion--With No Moving Parts: putt-putt engined toy boats & their application to models: MB F 75 25/289:69-71
Flies Like a Bird: development of falcon-shaped glider: Aero Jl 74 39/462:362-364
Milestones of Progress: history of model aircraft engines: MAN Ag 74 89/2:14-16+ ; S 74 89/3:14-17+
Modelling in the '20s: cardstock models: Sc O 75 6/10:508-509; add D 75 6/75:508-509
The Nordics: evolution of towline glider competition models: FM Jl 72 75/7:27-31
Project Teleplane: models in recon drone development: AM Jl 73 76/7:12-14+
RC Circa 1937: RC Mr 72 9/3:18-19+
RC Helps Hit the Spot: parachute research: MAN S 71 83/3:46-47
An RC RPV: RC model converted to drone TV testbed: AM Ja 73 76/1:58-59+
RMD'S History in Models: loco type: MR O 72 39/10:51-55
Rags to Riches: model building incident gets job: FM Je 74 77/6: 48
Something Other than Sunday Flying: drone research: RC D 72 9/12:36-40+
Uncle Sam's Plastic Air Force: WW-II identification-training models: AM S 73 77/3:54-55+
The Walt Billett Loving Cup: U.S. hobby industry Flying Eight Ball trophy: FM Mr 74 77/2:49-50
The World Beaters: evolution of free flight power competition models: FM My 72 422:29-34

BIOGRAPHIES

The Artistry of John Turnbull: aircraft mini-dioramas: Fus Sp

74 1/3:38-40
As I Knew Willis Nye: scale drawings of aircraft: MAN N 71 83/ 5:11+
Bill Hearne: figures, scratch aircraft & vehicles: Sc My 72 3/5: 266-267
Bob Gieseke: control line champ: AM Ja 75 75/1:22-26
Bob Hegge Interviews Bill Clouser: fine-scale railroading: MR Mr 71 38/3:55-60
Car Models by Wingrove: Sc My 73 4/5:346-349
Charles Parker: armor & figures: Fus Su 74 1/4:37-40
Don Skinner: armor: Sc Je 72 3/6:318-319
Fred Henderson: aircraft: Sc D 72 3/12:656-657
The Good Bros., 37 Years Later: RC pioneers: MAN Jl 75 91/1: 48-49+
Harold McEntee: RC pioneer: MAN Mr 72 84/3:11+
An Insight: Miroslav Nemecke: pattern modeler for Kovozavody Prostejov: Sc F 74 5/2:89
John Allen: Gorre & Daphetid RR: MR Ap 73 40/4:35-44
John Cuiffo: figures: Sc Ap 72 3/4:196-197+
Look at Phil Kraft: RC equipment & competition: RCS S 75 1/5: 14-15+
The Models of Jack Cassin Scott: scratch figures: MM My 74 4/5: 252-253
Models of John Cuiffo: figures: MM D 74 4/12:749
Owen Fee: large scale figures: Sc O 72 3/8:535-537
RCM Visits Lou Casale: all-metal flying scale models: RC Ag 73 10/8:56-57+
Rod Holland: ships, aircraft & figures: Sc Jl 72 3/7:388-389
Scale Perfection: Gerald Wingrove, car models: Sc N 74 5/62: 606-608

PLANT TOURS

AAM Visits the Engineer, Lou Ross: Ross Engines: AM Je 72 74/ 6:36-37
Chez Heller: plastic kits: MW Je 73 1/10:545-547
Ed's Covina Hobby Center: visit to a retail hobby store: RC Je 73 10/6:47-49+
FM Visits Duke's Place: Fox engines: FM Ap 72 421:32-33
Heller: plastic kits: Sc Jl 72 3/7:376-378
Hinchliffe Models: 20 & 30mm metal figures: MM F 73 3/2:78-79+
Historex: plastic figures: MM F 71 1/2:96-99
Humbrol: paint & cement: Sc F 75 6/65:90-91
An Insight: Kovozavody Prostejov, plastic kits: Sc F 74 5/2:89
K&B: engines: MAN O 75 91/4:46-48+
Lanierland: Lanier Industries, airplane kits: MAN S 71 85/3:36-38+
The Lewis's Live-Steam Heritage: Little Engines: MR Je 72 39/ 6:35-37

V. Articles

Lifting the Lid on Humbrol: paint & cement: Aero F 75 40/469: 90-91
Matchbox: Sc D 75 6/75:604-605
Matchbox Magic: IM S 75 11/5:18
Milman Engineering: spoked wheels for scale aircraft: MAN Je 72 84/6:46-47
Nitto: plastic kits: Sc O 74 5/61:536-537
The Northfield-Ross Engines: FM Ag 72 75/8:46-49
RCM Visits Bob & Doris Rich: Goldberg kits field reps: RC Ag 75 12/8:72-73+
RCM Visits Du-Bro Products: control links, helicopter kits: RC Mr 72 9/3:54-55+
RCM Visits Duke Fox: engines: RC Mr 73 10/3:42-43+
RCM Visits Hobby People: mail order supply house: RC Mr 71 8/3:48+
RCM Visits K&B: engines: RC Ja 73 10/1:42-44
RCM Visits Millers Hobby Shop: RC S 71 8/9:35-37
RCM Visits Sky Glas Fabricators & Hobby World: RC Ag 74 11/8: 39-43+
Revellations: Revell, UK, plastic kits: Sc Ja 74 5/1:54-55
Series 77: metal 77mm figures: MM Ja 73 3/1:44-45
Skyland Models: display model manufacturer: Sc Ag 73 4/8:541-543
Taking a Look at Humbrol: paint & cements: MB F 75 25/289:94
Tamiya: plastic kits: MW Mr 73 1/7:354-355
Tamiya: plastic kits: Sc S 74 5/60:482-485
A Visit to Helmet Products: 54mm metal figures: MM F 73 4/2: 88-89
Visit to Micro-Mold: diorama bases: Sc Jl 73 4/7:466-467+
A Visit to Rom-Air: retracting landing gear mechanisms: FM Mr 73 76/3:47-48
We Visit Aviomodelli: RC kits: MAN Mr 74 88/3:40-41
We Visit Kavan RC Helicopters: MAN Je 72 84/6:35-37
We Visit William Bros: flying scale details, static scale kits, parts: MAN Jl 74 89/1:35-37
We Visit Supertigre: engines: MAN F 74 88/2:50-52+
What a Vista: Kraft RC systems: FM Ag 71 413:44-47

RECORD ATTEMPTS

Almost 200: 1971 attempt on RC speed record: FM Ag 71 413: 42-43
An Electric Record?: RC closed-circuit distance for electric power (but no category exists): FM Je 72 423:24-25
The Endless Hover: helicopter endurance record: AM O 74 77/9:5
Flight of Operation Skyhook: Giertz RC endurance record: MAN D 74 89/6:52-55+
Krainock Does it Again: RC sailplane distance record: AM Ja 75 75/1:84+
Not Fast Enough: 1972 attempt to RC glider speed record: MB Ja

73 23/265:44-46
A Piranha Set the Record: RC seaplane straight-line distance, 1970: FM Ap 71 409:19-21
Seaplane Records Wrested from the Russians: close-circuit, straight-line distance, endurance: FM My 73 76/5:45-49
Spirit of California: RC car speed record: MAN F 75 90/2:41-43+
27,000' It's Catbird Country: 1970 attempt at RC altitude record: FM Ja 71 406:18-23
World Records: Sept 1971 Soviet FAI record onslaught: Aero Jl 72 37/488:375-379

USE IN MOVIES

Agent X-13 Does His Thing: RC model in film: AM S 72 75/3:18
Hindenburg: RC/cable airship in movie: RC Je 75 12/6:40-47
Jonathan Livingston Seagull: RC gulls in movie: RC N 73 10/11: 35-37
Much Ado About Something: incident in Jonathan Livingston Seagull filming: RC N 73 10/11:34
Zepplin: MM Je 71 1/6:309

HISTORY--MUSEUMS

GENERAL

Beaulieu: auto & ships: Sc Ap 71 2/4:182-184
Hull City & County Museums: transport & maritime: Sc O 71 2/8:532-534
Italian National Museum of Science & Technology: Sc F 75 6/65:87
Royal Scottish Museum: Sc D 74 5/63:665-667
Twenty-One Years On: Derby museum models by Maurice Brett: Sc Je 72 3/6:342-345
United Kingdom's Museums Guide: AN 4 Ap 75 3/22:4-7+
Wings & Wheels: Santee SC transportation museum: FM My 72 422:42-43

AVIATION

ABC to USA: tour of Smithsonian, Confederate Air Force, Miami International Airport: AN 13 D 74 3/14:12-13
Air Force Museum: Dayton OH: FM Ap 74 77/4:41-45

Air Museum, Schiphol Airport, Amsterdam: RCS O 75 1/6:9+
Another Look at Wreckovery: finding vintage aircraft wrecks: AN 18 Ja 74 2/17:12
Australian Naval Aviation Museum: AN 14 N 75 4/12:15
Aviation Memorials: UK monuments: AN 12 Ap 74 2/23:13
Back to Base: Dornier Do 24 at Friedrichshafen: AE Ja 72 2/1: 43-45
Behind the Shuttleworth Scene: restoration work: AN 4 Ap 75 3/22:10-11
Brussels Air Museum: AN 7 Mr 75 3/20:16
Canada's National Aeronautical Collection: FM Ap 73 76/4:42-45
Canadian Air Museum Visited: PAM O 74 7:106-107
Cole Palen's Rhinebeck: WW-I period air show: Sc Ja 72 3/1:12-17
The Confederate Air Force: WWE S 74 1/5:134-136; N 74 1/6:166
The Confederates: Confederate Air Force, Harlingen TX: Sc Ja 73 4/1:17-19
DC-3 Installed in Smithsonian: AN 12 D 75 4/14:7
Duxford: Imperial War Museum/East Anglian Aviation Society: AN 26 Jl 74 3/4:15
Family Air Museum in Australia: AN 5 S 75 4/7:15
Fleet Air Arm Museum: Yeovil: Sc Ag 71 2/8:426-428
From Aero to Zlin: Prague Air Museum: AI N 74 7/5:218-227
German Helicopter Museum: Buckeburg: AN 14 Je 74 3/1:15
The Great Danes: Danish Air Museum: AE S 71 1/4:212-213
Italy's Secret Museum: Vigna di Valle: AN 22 Ag 75 4/6:15
A Kingfisher Comes Home: USS North Carolina restoration: AE N 71 1/6:335-336
Lucerne Air Museum: AN 19 S 75 4/8:7
Lysander First Flight: restoration & flight of California Lysander: AI Ja 75 8/1:34-36
Movieland of the Air: Tallmantz, Orange County Airport, CA: AM S 71 73/3:14-17+
La Musée de l'Aire: French national air museum: FM Ap 72 421: 36-38
Museum of Army Flying: ex-Army Air Corps Museum, Middle Wallop: AN 2 Mr 73 1/21:10
The Museum That Never Opens: Swedish Air Force Collection, Malmslätt: AN 31 O 75 4/11:6-7
National Aeronautical Collection: Canada: Afx Ap 71 12/8:400-401
National Aeronautical Collection: Canada: RT D 73 6/12:135+
New RAF Museum: Afx Ja 73 14/5:244-245
Newark Air Museum: Winthrop aerodrome, Notts: Sc Je 71 2/6: 288-289
Palem: Indian Air Force museum: AN 16 Mr 73 1/22:13
Planes of Fame: California air museum: Sc My 75 6/68:244-245; disc Jl 75 6/7:339; N 75 6/74:547
RAF Museum Takes Shape: AE Je 71 1/1:51-52
Restoration of Pfalz D.XII: AN 13 Je 75 4/1:15
Royal Air Force Museum: Hendon: Sc D 72 3/12:670-671
Silver Hill: Smithsonian storage & restoration facilities: AI Jl 75 9/1:32-35
Smithsonian Institution: Air & Space Museum: Sc D 71 2/12:666-670

History--Museums

Smithsonian's Hidden Air Museum: Silver Hill: FM D 71 417:40-41
Strathallan: Scottish air museum: AN 10 My 74 2/25:15
To Fly or Not to Fly: flying vs. static aircraft collections (prototype size): AN 9 Je 72 1/2:4-5
A Very Private Collection: Jean Salis (fils) collection, La Ferte-Alais: AI O 75 9/4:193-196
What Happened to the Nash Collection: AN 4 AP 75 3/22:11
Wright-Patterson Air Force Museum: Afx F 73 14/6:298-299
Wroundabout the RAF Museum: AE Ap 74 6/4:197-200
Yesterday's Air Force: Ontario CA: AE D 72 3/6:300

MARITIME

Etona: Australian Anglican mission steamer restoration, Murray River: MB Mr 75 25/290:130-132; Ap 75 25/291:184-185
National Maritime Museum: MM S 71 1/9:444-445
Preservation of WW-II Ships: current situation in USN mothball fleet: WWE S 74 1/5:141
U-505 Chicago's Submarine: Sc D 74 5/63:654-659

MILITARY

Artillery at the Rotunda: Woolwich: MM My 71 1/5:255-257
Artillery Museum Re-Opened to Public: Rotunda at Woolwich: Afx Je 75 16/10:580+
British Cavalry Helmets: Birmingham Museum of Science & Technology: MM My 74 4/5:249
Cheshire Military Museum: Chester: MM D 72 2/12:680-681
Developments at APG: Aberdeen Proving Ground, MD: MM D 72 2/12:647
Dorset Military Museum: Dorchester: MM My 72 2/5:228-229
An Echo of Glory: Military Vehicle Conservation Group: MM N 71 1/11:586-587
Finland's Armor Museum: AFV Je 75 5/5:16-19+
Infantry in Rome: Museo Storico dell'Arma della Fanteria: A&W N 73 8:70
Military Museums of Shrewsbury: MM Je 73 3/6:376-377+
National Army Museum: Chelsea: MM Ja 72 2/1:20-22
Parachute Regiment & Airborne Forces Museum: Aldershot: MM Mr 71 1/3:144-146
RAC Tank Museum: Bovington: MM Jl 71 1/7:344-345; Ag 71 1/8: 416-417
Royal Armoured Corps Tank Museum: WWE Jl 74 1/4:96-?
Scottish United Services Museum, Edinburgh: MM F 71 1/8:416-417
Visit the Royal Marines Museum: Afx D 75 77/4:234-236
A Visit to the Royal Armoured Corps Museum: Bovington: AFV Mr 74 4/10:14-15

V. Articles 516

York Castle: MM Mr 72 2/3:132-133
Yugoslav People's Army Military Museum, Kalmegdan, Belgrade:
   MM Mr 73 3/3:148-149

RAILROAD

Swindon: Sc S 71 2/9:471-473
Trolley Travel to Perris: Orange Empire Trolley Museum: NMRA
   Ap 71 36/8:18-19

HISTORY--POLITICAL

Denmark During the Occupation: WW2J S 75 2/5-6:39
He Saw Hitler Rise to Power: early relations between Hitler &
   Mussolini: WWE Mr 74 1/2:44
Nazi Atrocities Come to Light: post-war news account of Greek
   concentration camp: WWE Ja 75 2/1:11+

HISTORY--RAILROAD

ACCIDENTS & DISASTERS

A Remarkable Boiler Explosion: extreme distance of pieces: NMRA
   Ag 72 37/13:29
Trains 1, Trucks 0: wreck: NMRA Ag 74 39/13:32-33

INCLINE RAILWAYS

Funiculi, Funicula: intro to funicular railways: MR F 73 40/2:35
Mount Beacon in Autumn: NMRA Ap 38/8:7-9
The Mount Low Line: NMRA Ap 71 36/8:6-9

EQUIPMENT (Other Than Rolling Stock)

ACI: automatic car identification system & equipment: NMRA D

74 40/4:42-43
A Box Office: semi-trailer offices: RMC My 74 42/12:44
Down by Mitchell Yard: sk, pph, site, yard clutter: MR My 73 40/5:60-61
Europe's New Automatic Coupler: UIC, to replace chain-and-bumper system in 1979: MR Ap 73 40/4:46-47
Flange Greaser: NMRA D 73 39/4:53
Grand Central Station: New York City: NMRA Mr 74 39/8:35-37
Horseshoe Curve Revisited: Pennsylvania curve near Altoona: NMRA S 75 41/1:44-45
Locomotive Bells: NMRA F 74 49/7:38-39
Locomotive Whistles: NMRA F 74 39/7:36-37
Milwaukee's Stowell Yard: MR Ja 72 39/1:50-53
Old Mike and His Single Stall Engine House: NMRA Ja 75 40/5:45-47
Relay Boxes: NMRA Ap 75 40/8:52
Roundhouse Details & Clutter: NMRA D 73 39/4:12-15
Southern Pacific's New West Colton Classification Yard: NMRA Mr 74 39/8:16-18
Third Rail Detail: outside third rail: NMRA Jl 71 36/11:8
Trackside Industries: RMC Ja 71 39/8:33-38
Water Columns & Steel Tanks: NMRA F 71 36/6:11
Wooden Bridges & Railroad Loggers: NMRA N 73 39/2:50-53+
Yard Structures: MR Jl 75 42/7:85+

EQUIPMENT MANUFACTURERS

Electro-Motive 50 Years of Power: diesel locomotives: RMC Ja 73 41/8:40-41

OPERATIONS

General

Amtrak No. 1: confusion before November 1971 with five "No. 1" trains: RMC Je 72 41/1:37
Auto-Train: MR D 74 41/12:48-53
Catching & Throwing the Mail: flying mail exchanges: NMRA O 71 37/2:14-15+
Common Carrier Logger: western rail lines: NMRA Ja 72 37/5:38-42; F 72 37/6:18-22
Employee Timetables: MR N 75 42/11:68-70
The Fast Mail: evolution of mail transport by rail: NMRA Jl 74 39/12:38-40
Firing a Steam Locomotive: NMRA F 75 40/6:41-42
Horseshoe: Penn Central track near Altoona: RMC S 72 41/4:46-48

V. Articles 518

The Hustlin' Hostlers: engine preparation before run: NMRA D 75 41/4:52-54
Illinois Central Railroad Locomotive Servicing Facilities at Dyersburg: NMRA Ja 75 40/5:32
Kick the Dead Lion: superiority of steam over diesel: NMRA Mr 74 39/8:40-41
Labbe on Logging: log line operation: NMRA Je 71 36/10:6-8
Logging Camps on Wheels: rail-transported camps: NMRA S 75 41/1:7-18
Logging Road to Main Line Junctions: NMRA My 72 37/9:30-31
Milk Trains, Milk Cars & Creameries: RMC Je 74 43/1:26-30
On a Fast Freight Through Arkansas: NMRA F 75 40/6:50-51+ ; My 75 40/9:39
Poling & Push Poles: MR F 75 42/2:87-91
Prototype Steam Locomotive Controls: RMC O 75 44/5:52-53
Railroads in the Mountains: MR O 74 41/10:34-39
Railway Signaling: see separate listing immediately following
Rebuilding Steam Locomotives: shop practice: NMRA Ag 75 40/12:54-56
Refrigerator Car Ice: MR N 75 42/11:113-117
Rotary Snowplow Special: Cumbres & Toltec: NSG Mr 75 1/1:32-35
SP 8799 Train Simulator: training device: NMRA Ag 71 36/13:14-15
Standard Hand Signals: MR Ja 73 40/1:62
Steam Lives on the Burlington Northern: tie-treating plant shunt engines charged from stationary boiler, no fire in locos: MR O 75 42/10:78-80
South Durham on the Norfolk Southern: yard operations: MR Je 74 41/6:54-56
Tender Capacity: calculating prototype capacity: MR O 73 40/10:78-80
Trailing Logs: dragging logs between rails rather than on cars: NMRA N 71 37/3:18-19
Trains--Grains & Rawhide: Pendleton Oregon rail operations: NMRA D 75 41/4:37-43
Tuckahoe Jct: RMC Ja 75 43/8:56-58
Turntables for Freight Yards: for 4-wheel European boxcars: Afx My 72 13/9:501
White Light at Yamato: detection equipment: NMRA Ap 75 40/8:48-51
Why So Fast? Great Northern speed limits for classes: NMRA Jl 75 40/11:30-31+
Wrecker--Defender of the Main Line: NMRA Je 75 40/10:38

Railway Signalling [all NMRA]

Early Days: Ja 71 36/5:20; F 71 36/6:15
Early Automatic Blocks: MR 71 36/7:21
Modern Block Systems: Ap 71 36/8:16+
Interlocking Signals: My 71 36/9:36

History--Railroad

Mechanical Locking Bed: Ag 71 36/13:34-36
Electro-Mechanical Interlocking: F 72 37/6:28-29
Electric Locking: Ap 72 37/8:22
Railroad Signals: My 72 37/9:26
Interlocking Signals Today: Je 72 37/10:22
Interlocking Circuitry: Jl 72 37/11:13
Automatic Train Control: Ag 72 37/13:25
Traffic Control Systems: S 72 38/1:22
Car Retarders: O 72 38/2:19
Hot Box Detection: N 72 38/3:17
Automatic Car Identification: D 72 38/4:30

Military

Panzer Draisine: self-propelled German railway "tank": AFV N 73 4/8:18-19
A True Land Battleship...Soviet Armored Trains: AFV Ja 74 4/9: 22-23+

Regional

Brazil: traction & railroads, variety of types: NMRA My 75 40/9:26-27
Heart of the Black Hills Narrow Gauge Country: NMRA Jl 72 37/11:29-36
Narrow Gauge in New Zealand: NSG S 75 1/4:14-24
Railroading in the Netherlands: NMRA Je 71 36/10:27-30
Rails at the Border: Mexico: RMC My 74 42/12:38-43
Switzerland's Railways: NMRA Ja 73 38/5:9-11
Three Gauge Country: standard, narrow & midget; Sonoma County CA: NMRA F 74 39/7:46-50
Vermont Granite Railroads: quarry lines: MR O 75 42/10:52-60

RAIL LINES

Alaska Railroad: NMRA Mr 74 39/8:7-13
The American Freedom Train: NMRA O 75 41/2:25-26+
Amtrak: End of an Era: RMC O 71 40/5:20-26
Ann Arbor: Ann Arbor Railroad: RMC N 73 42/6:38-45
Arcade & Attica Railroad: NMRA N 74 40/3:18-24
Bangor & Aroostock: Maine potato line: NMRA F 75 40/6:26-31
Big Creek & Telocast RR: logging: NMRA S 73 39/1:46-50
Black River & Western: NJ shortline: NMRA Jl 75 40/11:34-37
Caboose Mixed to Ivyland: New Hope & Ivyland: RMC Je 71 40/1: 34-39
Cass: Geared Loco Haven: Cass WV shortline: RMC Ag 72 41/3: 38-45

V. Articles

Cedar Point Amusement Park: 3'ng, 2 miles: NMRA Je 71 36/10: 14-15
Chattahooche Valley's short line: MR D 73 40/12:72-76
Clinchfield: Mountain Climber of the East: Blue Ridge mountains: NMRA Je 75 40/10:7-11+
Deep in the Heart of Texas: Moscow, Camden & San Augustine RR & Carter locomotive graveyard: NMRA F 71 36/6:34-37
Durango Colorado & Denver & Rio Grande: NMRA S 71 37/1:21-27
East Broad Top: MR D 71 38/12:70-75; cor F 72 39/2:15
East Broad Top Railroad: 3'ng: NMRA Ja 73 38/5:31-51
Ferrocarril del Pacifico de Nicaragua: NMRA Jl 74 39/12:28-30
Four Routes into Plymouth: Plymouth Michigan C&O junction: MR F 73 40/2:38-41
Golden Memories of a Silver Train: Chicago to San Francisco on Burlington's California Zephyr: RMC D 72 41/7:50-57
Graham County Railroad: NMRA Je 74 39/11:32-37
Hetch Hetchy Railroad: NMRA S 74 40/1:32-46; O 74 40/2:43-46
High Country Railroad: Colorado tourist line: NMRA Ag 75 40/12: 18-19
Kaslo Curiosity: barge-connected branch of CP: RMC Je 73 42/1: 24-27
The Kite Route: Denver & Interurban Railway: NMRA D 75 41/4: 7-12
La Salle & Bureau County: RMC Jl 72 41/2:24-28
Lake Erie, Franklin & Carion RR: NMRA Mr 75 40/7:22-25
Last of the All Steam Mixed Trains: Reader Railroad: NMRA Mr 71 36/7:6-8
Last Steam Shortline: Edgmoor & Manetta, SC: RMC Mr 72 40/ 10:30-34
Laurel Line Electric Locomotives: RMC S 72 41/4:43-44
Live Oak Perry & Gulf: NMRA Ag 73 38/12:22-25
Maynesburg & Washington RR: NMRA Ja 71 36/5:10-14
NP's P&L Branch Operation: MR Ja 74 41/1:64-68
Narragansett Pier RR: MR S 74 41/9:37-43
Narrow Gauge in Washington: industrial lines in Washington state: NMRA O 75 41/2:57-60
Newfoundland Railway: NMRA N 75 41/3:41-49
Ogden Mine Obituary: mixed-train line: NMRA S 72 38/1:7-9
One-Horse Short Line: Wagner County RR: RMC O 71 40/5:48-49
150 Years of the D&H: RMC Ag 73 42/3:38-45
Pacific Southern: RMC S 74 43/4:44-51
Pittsburg & Shawmut: coal hauling: NMRA F 74 39/7:55-60
Poughkeepsie's Unusual Rapid Transit: New Paltz & Wallkill Valley RR: NMRA Ap 75 40/8:8-15
Quebec, North Shore & Labrador Railway: NMRA O 75 41/2:30-34
Red Combine to Moscow: Moscow, Camden & San Augustine: RMC D 71 40/7:31-36; add My 72 40/12:6-7+
Reflections on the Abingdon Branch: RMC S 75 44/4:44-51
Remember the Pittsburg & West Virginia?: NMRA Jl 75 40/11:20-24
Roscoe, Snyder & Pacific: NMRA S 72 38/1:38-40
St. Louis-Southwestern (Cotton Belt): RMC Je 72 41/1:24-30
Santa Fe's Unit Sulphur Train: melted sulfur: NMRA Ag 73 38/12: 48-50

History--Railroad

Skagit River RR: NMRA Mr 73 38/7:11-17
Skaneateles Short Line: RMC F 73 41/9:38-41
Speed Quarry Railroad: meter gauge in America: cement limestone quarry: NMRA S 75 41/1:24-25+
Spokane, Portland & Seattle: RMC Ap 71 39/11:32-37; My 71 39/12:20-24
Strasburg Railroad--Try, Try Again: Pennsylvania shortline: NMRA Ja 74 39/5:37-41
Sumpter Valley Gets a New Start: NSG N 75 1/5:28-29
Twilight of the Electrics: Milwaukee Road: RMC Mr 74 42/10:34-41
Union Railroad: steel industry: NMRA N 73 39/3:7-10
Virginia & Truckee Railroad: NMRA Ja 75 40/5:49-54
Washington, Idaho & Montana Ry: MR S 75 42/9:40-46
West Virginia Operations of the Western Maryland: NMRA My 74 39/10:7-14
Western Maryland Railway: NMRA Ap 74 39/9:8-13
Western Pacific: RMC N 72 41/6:38-45
What Amtrak Means to Model Railroaders: MR Ja 72 39/1:34-39
White Pass & Yukon: NMRA Ja 75 40/5:26-28
Milwaukee Road's Kingsbury Branch: MR Ap 75 42/4:52-57
Winchester & Western: MR O 74 41/10:44-47
Yancey RR: MR Ag 74 41/8:33-38
Yosemite Valley RR: NMRA D 74 40/4:7-17

ROLLING STOCK

Alco's Stillborn Prototype, the Black Maria: RMC Je 75 44/1:30-32
All About Sharks: Baldwin diesels: RMC My 72 40/12:34-37
American Railroad Ditchers: American Hoist & Derick steam shovels: NSG Jl 75 1/3:14-29
B&O's West Virginia Mallets: RMC S 74 43/4:36-41; O 74 43/5:44-47
Ballast Shouldering Cars: NMRA Jl 72 37/11:22-23
Beloit's Biggies & Babies: Fairbanks-Morse Trainmasters & Baby Trainmasters: RMC Jl 75 42/2:24-27
Big Boats: Union Pacific's GE U50c: diesels: RMC Jl 75 44/2:35-36
Big Power & Little: 4-8-4 locomotives: NMRA N 72 38/3:12-13
Boston Bogies: 2-4-0: NSG My 75 1/2:26-27
Bucyrus Erie Class 200-17½ Railway Crane: sk, dim, pph of assembly line: NMRA Ag 72 37/15:8-12
Colonie Kitbash: 2-10-0 prototype conversion: RMC Jl 73 42/2:41-43
D&RGW Narrow Gauge Work Cars: NMRA D 75 41/4:26-31
The Different Dash 2s: EMD miscellaneousy: RMC My 75 43/12:29-33
EBT's Mike: 2-8-2 ng: RMC N 75 44/6:56-60
EMD--Giant of Dieseldom: NMRA S 74 40/1:7-11

V. Articles

East Broad Top 35-ton Triple Hopper: RMC F 74 42/9:54-56
Electromotive F 45: diesel locomotive: MR D 75 42/12:69-71
The Enduring GG1: RMC D 75 44/7:52-61; continues
Est-ce le Train à Chicago?: Amtrak French-built Turboliner: RMC Je 74 43/1:40-42
The First Denver & Rio Grande Freight Cars 1871-1872: NSG My 75 1/2:12-17
4-8-2s of the Norfolk & Western Ry: MR N 74 41/11:52-58
A 4-4-2 Passenger Car?: 4 double bedroom, 4 compartment, 2 drawing room: MR Je 75 42/6:47-49
Gauge Cocks: NSG N 75 1/5:46-47
International's Custom Cabooses: MR Je 74 41/6:35-39
It's Canada for C-Liners: diesel locos: RMC Jl 71 40/2:20-24
Liberation Mikado: post WW-II French 2-8-2: MR Jl 73 40/7:48-52
Logging Mallets: NSG S 75 1/4:28-31; N 75 1/5:44-45
MLW's new M420: diesel: RMC D 74 43/7:55-58
Maine Two-Foot Flatcars: ng: RMC Jl 71 40/2:20-24
New Haven's EMD FL9s: RMC O 72 41/5:43-45
O&W's Light 400s: diesel: RMC Ap 72 40/11:36-41
One-of-a-Kind: Alco's DL 103b: diesel: RMC Ag 75 44/3:40-41
PA Postlude: diesel: RMC Ag 71 40/3:30-37; S 71 40/4:23-28
Passenger Cars of the White Pass & Yukon: RMC Ap 75 43/11:40-43
Pioneer: Burlington Zephyr: RMC F 71 39/9:24-26
Products of the Marion Steam Shovel Company: NMRA O 72 38/2:11-15
SW 1: diesel: RMC Ag 74 43/2:46-51
SW-1 The Little Giant: diesel switcher: RMC Jl 74 43/2:32-35
3 Truck Steeple Cabs?: traction: NMRA Jl 72 37/11:24
Valve & Fittings: NSG S 75 1/4:32-33
Watson Manufacturing Co., Springfield MA: traction equipment: NMRA Ag 74 39/13:24-30
Way Cars: caboose: NMRA Ja 74 39/5:7-15
Where 4-8-4s were Poconos: Lackawanna use: RMC F 74 42/9:44-47
Wood Chip Hoppers: NMRA My 74 39/10:42-43
Work Trains: NMRA Je 72 37/10:8-12
Zeitler Gasoline Power Truck: replaced passenger car truck to make rail motor car: NMRA Je 75 40/10:53

TRACTION & RAPID TRANSIT

Apple Country Interurban: Yakima WA: NMRA Mr 75 40/7:12-14
BART: Bay Area Rapid Transit, CA: NMRA Mr 75 40/7:53-55
Canmore Mines: traction mine line: NMRA Ap 75 40/8:34-36
Kaw Valley: MR F 72 39/2:38-41
San Francisco Bay Area Rapid Transit Now and Then: NMRA My 71 36/9:32-33
San Francisco's Cable Cars: NMRA Jl 72 37/11:18-19
South Shore at Gary, Indiana: NMRA Je 75 40/10:22-27

HISTORY--SHIPS

GENERAL

Civil

Bristol Channel Steamers: MB My 73 23/269:198-200
Canal Narrow Boats: British horse & self-propelled barges: MB Jl 73 23/271:276-277
Clyde Ferries: MB Ja 73 23/265:14-17
Clyde Puffer: MB Ja 74 24/277:24-27
Deep Sea Fisheries: MB Jl 75 25/295:330-332+; Ag 75 25/296:390-392+; S 75 297:454-457; O 75 25/297:538-540; N 75 25/298:581-585; D 75 25/299:644-646; continues
Early English Catamarans: 17th century: MB Mr 73 23/267:117-118
Flying Duck: Clyde river tugs: MB D 73 23/276:523-527
Modern Mini-Cobles: cartop versions of sea-going utility boat design: MB My 71 21/245:190-191
Modern Shipping: construction & usage of modern freighters: MB Jl 71 21/247:279-281+
Raised Quarterdeck Coasters: MB O 72 22/262:418-421
Single Hatch Coasters: MB Mr 73 23/267:110-113
Small Pleasure Steamers: mostly paddle: MB D 72 22/264:508-511
Steamers of the Northern Isles: Scottish island vessels: MB Ap 73 23/168:156-159
Thames Penny Steamers: pedestrian ferries & excursion boats: MB Jl 72 22/259:274-277
Three Island Steamers: MB Ag 73 23/272:328-331

Naval

Armed Fishing Trawlers of WW-II: MB D 71 21/252:495-496
British Destroyers: A, I, & J classes: MB Ap 72 22/256:158-159+
British Destroyers: M, V & W, R & S (modified to T) classes: MB O 73 23/274:426-427
Class of '44: Essex Class carriers with the Pacific Fleet: Q Au 75 11/1:7
The Deutschlands: pre-WW-I German battleship class: MM Ja 71 1/1:38-41
Fleet Minesweepers of WW-II: U.K.: MM Ag 72 2/8:408-411+; S 72 2/9:469-473+; O 72 2/10:528-532; N 72 2/11:588-591; D 72 2/12:656-658; Ja 73 3/1:32-35
Flower Class Corvette: MB O 71 21/250:408-409

V. Articles 524

Flower Class Corvettes: MM S 73 3/9:598-601; O 73 3/10:669-672;
  N 73 3/11:747-749+; D 73 3/12:816-818
German Pocket Battleships: Sc Ap 72 3/4:200-207
Motor Torpedo Boats: MM Ag 74 4/8:465-467; S 74 4/9:534-535;
  O 74 4/10:605-608; N 74 4/11:680-685; D 74 4/12:755-757; Ja
  75 5/1:35-36
Naming of United States Naval Vessels: WW-II practice: WWE N
  74 1/6:176
RAF High Speed Rescue Launches: MB Je 75 25/293:286-288; Jl
  75 25/294:341-344+; Ag 75 25/295:401-404+; S 75 25/296:461-465
S Class Submarines: British WW-II: Sc Ap 75 6/4:180-183
Salvage Tugs: particularly Saint Class of WW-II: MB Mr 72 22/
  255:109-111
T Class Submarines: British WW-II: Sc Mr 75 6/3:118-121
Tugs in Wartime: MB Ag 72 22/260:323-325; S 72 22/261:372-375
U & V Class Submarines: British WW-II: Sc My 75 6/5:230+
U.S. Naval Nomenclature: letter code & type: WWE Ja 75 2/1:6
U.S. Navy Ship Type Designations: letter code: MB D 71 21/252:547+
When Pepys Visited the Tyne: 1662 account of Stuart yachts: MB
  F 73 23/266:78-79

INDIVIDUAL

  Civil

Anonity: coastal tanker: 1945: MB F 72 22/253:21-23+
RRS Bransfield: Antarctic research ship: Sc Je 72 3/6:328-331
Brighton: cross-channel steamer: 1903: MB My 72 22/257:197-200
Britain's Last Steam Dredger: Mannin: MB F 73 23/266:74-75
Channel Queen: well-deck steamer, 1912: MB Ap 72 22/256:149-151
Coleraine: fire-fighting tug: Sc O 71 2/10:538-539
Delta 28: 1966-1969 offshore racers: Sc S 71 1/9:490-492
Dutchess of Kent: 1897 paddle steamer: MB Ja 72 22/253:21-23+
Five Paddle Tugs Named Stag: MB Mr 74 24/278:76-77+
Flying Duck: tug: MB D 73 23/276:523-527
Grangemouth: 1908 east coast (U.K.) passenger/cargo: MB N 72
  22/263:463-465
Hector: 1945 cargo-passenger liner: MB Je 72 22/258:232-234
Hotspur: 1897 twin-screw dock tug: MB F 73 23/266:66-69
Isle of Man Steamer Victoria: MB S 73 23/273:373-376
Juno: 1898 Clyde paddle steamer: MB Je 72 22/258:241-244
Lloydsman: ocean tug: Sc F 73 3/2:110+
Mikkel mols: Danish ferry: Sc My 71 2/5:237
Nandhimitre: MB Mr 75 25/290:125-127
Paddle Steamer Marmion: Clyde steamer: MB O 73 23/274:422-425+
Paddle Tug Chieftain: MB Jl 73 23/271:286-289
QED: first screw-driven iron ship: MB Jl 73 23/271:291-292
SS Shengking: MB N 74 24/286:478-479
Song of Norway: Norwegian cruise liner: Sc Ap 72 3/4:220-222

History--Ships

Totnes Castle: River Dart paddle steamer: MB N 73 23/275:473-475
Tyne Ferry Mona: 1903: MB Je 73 23/270:241-243

Naval

(Austro-Hungary)

Helgoland: 1914 cruiser: MB Ag 71 21/248:322-323
Tatra: 1917 destroyer: MB Ag 71 21/248:322-323
Viribus Unitis: 1912 battleship: MB F 73 23/266:70-71

(Brazil)

Minas Gerais: 1919 battleship: MB F 72 22/254:72-73

(France)

Jeanne d'Arc: 1964 helicopter cruiser: MM S 71 1/9:456-460
Jean de Vienne: 1936 cruiser: MB Mr 74 24/278:82-84
Le Terrible: 1936 destroyer: MB Mr 74 24/278:82-84

(Germany)

Admiral Scheer & Admiral Graf Spee: 1939 pocket battleships: MB Ja 75 25/288:31-32
Deutschland 1933/Lutzow 1945: pocket battleship: MB Ja 75 25/288:31-32
German Pocket Battleships: Deutschland/Lutzow & Scheer: Sc Ap 72 3/4:200-207
Gneisenau: 1938 battle-cruiser: MB S 71 21/249:368-369
SMS Königsberg: 1907 cruiser: MB O 74 24/285:434
Lebrecht Maass: 1937 destroyer: MB Mr 71 21/243:112-114
Mainz: 1909 cruiser: MB Mr 73 23/267:114-115
Prinz Eugen: 1938 heavy cruiser: MB Mr 71 21/243:112-114
Roeder Class Destroyers: 1938-1941: MB S 72 22/261:384-385+
Schleswig-Holstein: 1908 battleship, 1930 training ship: MB Ap 74 24/279:132-133
Stettin: 1907 cruiser: MB Mr 73 23/267:114-115
Tirpetz: 1941 battleship: MB S 73 23/273:378-379+
SMS Von der Tan: 1910 battle-cruiser: MB Mr 72 22/255:116-117

(Italy)

Attilio Regolo: 1942 cruiser: MB Ja 74 24/277:30-31
Conte di Cavour: 1915 battleship: MB Ag 74 24/283:328-329

Conte di Cavour: 1938 battleship: MB S 74 24/284:378-379
Curatone: 1924 destroyer: MB Ja 72 22/253:24-25
Dante Alighieri: 1913 battleship: MB Jl 73 23/271:290-291
Eritrea: 1935 colonial sloop: MB Jl 71 21/247:282-283
Guiseppe Garibaldi: 1901 armored cruiser: MB Jl 72 22/259:292-293
Guiseppe Miraglia: 1927 seaplane carrier: MB Jl 71 21/247:282-283
Leone: 1924 destroyer: MB Ja 72 22/253:24-25
Luigi Cadorna: 1933 Cruiser: MB Ja 71 21/241:24-25+
Pisa: 1909 armored cruiser: MB Jl 72 22/259:292-293
Pola: 1932 cruiser: MB Ja 73 23/265:24-26
San Marco: 1956 destroyer, converted from Attilio Regolo: MB Ja 74 24/277:30-31
Trento: 1933 cruiser: MB Ja 71 21/241:24-25+
Turbine: 1927 destroyer: MB Ja 72 22/253:24-25
Zara: 1931 cruiser: MB Ja 73 23/265:24-26

(Japan)

Aoba: 1927 heavy cruiser: MB N 71 21/251:454-455
Ashigara: 1929 heavy cruiser: WWE S 74 1/5:141
Hatsushimo: 1934 destroyer: MB My 73 23/269:202-203
Hiei: 1914 battleship: MB My 71 21/245:204-205
Hiryu: 1939 aircraft carrier: MB N 73 23/275:470-472
Kako: 1926 heavy cruiser: MB N 71 21/251:454-455
Kumano: 1937 battleship: MB N 72 22/257:202-203
The Mystery of Midget D: submarine recovered off Pearl Harbor with no trace of crew: WW2J My 75 2/3:80-81
Nagato: 1920 battleship: MB Ap 75 25/291:182-183+; My 75 25/292:238-240
Oi: 1921 cruiser: MB Je 74 24/281:220-221
Yamagumo: 1938 destroyer: MB My 73 23/269:202-203
Yamashiro: 1917 battleship: MB My 72 22/257:202-203
Yubari: 1923 cruiser: MB Je 74 24/281:220-221

(Sweden)

Plajad: MTB class: Sc N 72 3/11:607

(USSR, Russia)

Aurora: 1903, cruiser which opened October Revolution: MB Ag 73 23/272:334-335
Aurora: MM N 71 1/11:580-581
Chervonaya Ukraina: 1927 cruiser: MB Ag 73 23/277:334-335
Kashin: missile destroyer class: Sc Ja 72 3/1:43
Kildin: destroyer class: Sc F 72 3/2:93
Knyaz Souvorov: 1905 battleship: MB Ag 72 22/260:338-339+
Komar: 1960 torpedo boat class: Sc My 72 3/5:263
Kotlin: destroyer class: Sc Mr 72 3/3:149

History--Ships

Krivak: 1971 destroyer escort class: Sc Ag 72 3/8:443
Krupny: 1967 destroyer class: Sc Ag 71 2/8:433
Marat: 1939 battleship, rebuilt from Petropavlovsk: MB F 71 21/242:68-69
Moskva: helicopter cruiser: MM Jl 71 1/7:348-352
Osa: missile patrol boat class: Sc Jl 72 3/7:383
Petropavlovsk: 1919 battleship: MB F 71 21/242:62-69
Potemkin: 1903 battleship: MM My 73 3/5:306-312; Je 73 3/6: 364-365

(U.K.)

Albion: commando carrier: MM O 71 1/10:522
Arethusa: 1914 & 1936 destroyers: MB My 74 24/280:175-177
Ark Royal: 1937 aircraft carrier: MB Ap 71 21/244:156-157+
Black Swan Class Sloops: Afx N 71 13/3:128-130+; D 71 13/4:210-211
Blake: command helicopter cruiser, 1961: MM D 71 1/12:647-648
British Power Boat 64' HSL: high speed rescue launch: MB O 75 25/297:520-523
Caesar: 1944 destroyer: MM Jl 72 2/7:348-352
Chatham: 1912 cruiser: MB D 74 24/287:535
Chester: 1914 four-stack cruiser: MB F 72 22/257:60-67
Devastation: first British battleship without sails: MB My 71 21/245:200-201
Fal: river class frigate: MB O 74 24/285:426-427
Goliath: 1900 battleship: MB N 74 24/286:482-483
Good Hope: 1902 armored cruiser: MB O 71 21/250:410-411+
Iron Duke: 1916 battleship: MB O 72 22/262:428-430
Natal: 1907 armored cruiser: MB O 71 21/250:410-411+
Rattlesnake: 1943 Algerine class minesweeper: MB Ap 72 22/256: 162-163
Rattlesnake: MM Je 73 3/6:368-371+
River Class Frigates: Afx Je 71 12/10:512-515+; Jl 12/11:568-570+
Rodney: 1927 battleship: MB Ap 73 23/268:154-155
63' BPB type 2: Air-Sea Rescue launch: MB Jl 75 25/294:341-344+
Thornycroft 67' High Speed Launch: ASR: MB Ag 75 25/295:401-404+
Vickers Vedette: frigate class: MB D 75 25/299:632-633
Weymouth: 1911 cruiser: MB N 74 24/286:483

(U.S.)

Alabama: 1942 battleship: MB Je 71 21/246:234-235
Arizona: 1916 battleship: MB D 72 22/264:526-527
Arkansas: 1912 battleship: MB Jl 74 24/282:274-275
Bagley: destroyer: WW2J Jl 75 2/4:18-19
Baltimore: 1943 heavy cruiser: MB Je 72 22/258:244-245
Dixie: destroyer tender: MB D 71 21/252:506-507+
Essex: 1942 aircraft carrier: MB Je 73 23/270:244-246
USS Heron: small seaplane tender: WW2J S 75 2/5-6:9

V. Articles 528

Porter: 1937 destroyer: MB D 73 23/276:528-530
Salt Lake City: 1929 heavy cruiser: MB D 73 23/276:528-530
San Francisco: heavy cruiser: WWE My 74 1/3:69
Terror: 1942 mine layer: MB D 71 21/252:506-507+
Wyoming: 1912 battleship: MB Je 75 25/294:290-291

MISCELLANEOUS

Movies

Hispaniola: ship used for Disney's 1950 "Treasure Island": MB D 75 25/299:647-651

Naval Incidents (Non-Combat)

Treasure of Corregidor: USS Trout's gold cargo: WWE N 74 1/6: 172+

Operations

Deep Sea Fisheries: MB Jl 75 25/294:330-332; Ag 75 25/295:390-392+; S 75 25/296:454-457; O 75 25/297:538-540; N 75 25/298:581-585; D 75 25/299:644-646 [continuing]
Deep Sea Towage: MB Jl 74 24/282:268-272; Ag 74 24/283:322-326; S 74 24/284:373-378; O 74 24/285:428-429; N 74 24/286:484-487+
Feat of Tyne Towage: William rescues Brotherly Love in storm: MB D 74 24/287:545
Modern Shipping: trends in design & cargo handling: MB Jl 71 21/247:279-281+

Photographic Studies

Devonshire & Other Counties: IM My 75 11/3:18-21

Sea Battles

Action off Koh Chang: Jan 1941: WW2J Jl 75 2/4:7
Battle of Koh Chang Bay, Jan 1941: Vichy France vs. co-belligerent Thailand: MB D 75 25/299:665
Battle of the Atlantic: MB Jl 75 25/294:346-348; Ag 75 25/295:406-408; S 75 25/296:466-467+; O 75 25/297:530-532; N 75 25/298:586-587+
Battle of the River Plat: MB Ja 75 25/288:30-32; F 75 25/289:82-83+; Mr 75 25/290:136-137
Hai-Yang Island: Sino-Japanese War of 1894: Fus Sp 75 2/1:16-20+

Japanese Attack on the West Coast of Canada's Vancouver Island:
    Estevañ Light shelling: WWE My 74 1/3:61
The Königsberg Incident: WW-I, off East Africa: MB O 74 24/
    285:434-435; N 74 24/286:482-483; D 74 24/287:534-535
The Last Heavy Gun Naval Duel: Aleutians: WWE S 74 1/5:137+

HISTORY--SPACE VEHICLES

Space Shuttle: Afx My 72 13/9:496-497

HISTORY--MISCELLANEOUS

Coal Yard & Conveyor Details: photo study: RMC Ap 73 41/11:26-27
The Lombard: snow half-track with locomotive steam plant: NMRA
    N 74 40/5:7-12
Mills & Milling: RMC N 71 40/6:36-37
Spar Trees & Rigging Slingers: full details for highline act: NMRA
    O 74 40/2:22-28

INTRODUCTIONS

AIRCRAFT

General

Let's Scratch Build: using published plans: RC Ap 74 11/4:25+
Playing with Toy Airplanes?: why of flying models: MAN D 71
    21/252:11+

Free Flight

A Case for Sport Free Flight: FM Jl 71 412:24-25
Development of Chaperoned Free Flight: RC retrieval of competition aircraft: AM Jl 72 75/1:20-22+
The Fascinating World of Indoor Modeling: AM Mr 73 76/3:12-13+

V. Articles

World Indoor Championship Technicalities: one gram FAI: Aero D 72 37/443:693-695

Control Line

ABCs of Speed: AM Ap 73 76/4:50-52+
Combat: plane & engine, fuel, training: MAN F 73 86/2:21-23
Carrier Facts: intro to carrier event: MAN S 72 85/3:14-15+
Carrier Models: Aero Ap 73 38/447:198-200
Electric Round the Pole Flying: Aero Ap 74 39/459:189-192
Fly Speed: Aero S 73 38/452:496-500
Getting Started in Aerobatics: AM Jl 73 77/1:48-50+
Indoor on a String: rubber-powered tether: MAN Mr 74 88/3:14-16+
FAI Team Racing: MAN My 75 90/5:22-23+
Speed: MAN O 73 87/4:22-23+
Stunt: MAN Jl 73 87/1:22-23+
Stunt Flying Made Easy: FM O 75 78/10:45-48
What's the Word on Goodyear?: profile racing: Aero F 71 36/421: 94-97; Mr 71 36/422:148-151

Radio Control

Born Free: RC sailplanes: RC Mr 73 10/3:54-57
Fly a Glider & Have Fun: catapult-launched RC sailplanes: RC My 74 11/5:22+
Flying the RC Helicopter: RC My 74 11/5:23+
Getting Started in RC: see separate listing, immediately following
Getting Your RC License: FM Ja 74 77/1:65
Half A Midget Pylon Racing: RC My 71 8/5:30
Half A RC: state of the art in category I: RC D 75 12/12:77-79
Hover: helicopters: RC F 74 11/2:57-58+
How I Got Started in RC: MAN Ag 74 89/2:38-40+
Introduction to Radio Control: Aero F 72 37/433:84-87
A Lady Looks at Pattern Flying: MAN D 75 91/6:56-57+
Miniature Sport RC: $\frac{1}{2}$A, particularly .01 & .02: AM F 75 75/2: 21-24
Quarter Midget: MAN Mr 72 84/3:42
Quarter Midget Pylon Racing: RC My 71 8/5:20
RC Helicopter Game: RC F 73 10/2:26-29+
RC Kibitzer: instructing beginner pilots: MAN D 72 85/6:47+
Radio Control Combat: AM F 71 72/2:22-23
Rudder Only, an Answer to the [cost] Crunch: RC Ap 75 12/4:60-61
Scratch-Building RC Helicopters: RC Jl 74 11/7:36-40+
Soaring for Records: FAI glider distance record attempts: AM Ja 75 75/1:85+

Understanding Radio & Flying More: intro to 6 meter band: RC O 74 11/10:62
Understanding Thermal Soaring without Mathematics: RC My 75 12/5:67
What Is Radio Control?: RC S 71 8/9:64-65

(Getting Started in Radio Control) [all AM]

[series started Ag 67]
Pushrod Installations: Ja 71 72/1:30+
Control Linkages: F 71 72/2:49+
Suggestions from the Pros: Ap 71 72/4:50+
Propellers: selection, balance, & maintenance: My 71 72/5:49+
Digital Encoder: Je 71 72/6:52
Digital Receiver: Jl 71 73/1:42+
Servo Electronics: Jl 71 73/1:42+
Gliders: Ag 71 73/2:54+
Index: O 71 73/4:54
Stunting with Rudder Only: F 72 74/2:18+
Throttle Pushrod Systems: Ap 72 74/4:20
Stunting with Rudder & Elevator Only: My 72 74/5:20+
Glow Plugs, Choice & Care: Je 72 74/6:16+
Trainer Aircraft Design: Jl 72 75/1:12+
Selecting First RC Model: Ag 72 75/2:12+
Choosing a Radio: S 72 75/3:12+ ; O 72 75/4:12
Component Installation: N 72 75/5:8
Malfunction Symptoms: D 72 75/6:8
Component Placement & Connection: Ja 73 76/1:10
Pre-Flight Procedures: F 73 76/2:24
Build or Buy a Radio: Mr 73 76/3:10; Ap 73 76/4:58
Test Equipment & Its Uses: My 73 76/5:68
Back to Basics: Je 73 76/6:26
Basic Questions & Answers: Jl 73 77/1:44
How Various Parts of the RC System are Adjusted: Ag 73 77/2:65
What You Probably Never Wanted to Know About Adhesives: S 73 77/3:40
Visibility & Model Control: O 73 77/4:34
Batteries: D 73 77/6:74
Wife's Eye View: Ja 74 78/1:74
Support Equipment for RC Flying: F 74 78/2:38
Laws, Rules, Regulations, & The Modeler: Mr 74 78/3:74
Proper Dress for RC: AP 74 78/4:52+
Interference & You: a Glitch in Time: My 74 78/5:58
Buying Used Equipment: Je 74 78/6:54
How Many Channels: Jl 74 78/7:38
Learning to Fly: Ag 74 78/8:36
Plugs: electrical components: S 74 78/9:32+
Cost of Ownership: small aircraft as trainers: O 74 74/10:18
Nickel Cadmium Batteries: N 74 78/11:18+ ; D 74 74/12:10
What is a Good Radio: evaluating equipment: Ja 75 75/1:38+ ; Mr 75 75/3:40+

V. Articles

Flying Scale

All About Peanuts: MAN O 75 91/4:22-24+
CL Scale: MAN Mr 73 86/3:21-23+
Getting Into Peanut Scale: AM Ag 72 75/2:34-36+
Stand-Off Scale: RC D 73 10/12:16+
What Is Sport Scale?: RC Ag 74 11/8:16+

BOATS

Boating for Beginners: MB N 75 25/298:595; D 75 25/299:659-660
Choice of a Boat: sail racing classes: MB Ag 72 22/260:340-342
Concerning Sailing: RC sail: FM F 74 77/2:63
Is F Hydro for You?: large power boats: FM Ja 75 78/1:65
Glossary of Nautical Construction Terminology: AM Jl 73 77/1:82+
Let's Go Sailing: vane-control yacht racing: MB Jl 72 22/259:284-285; Ag 72 22/260:340-342; S 72 22/261:390-391; O 72 22/262:435-436+
Model Ships are Fun: RC sport boats: RCS Ap 75 1/1:61-63
Or Have You Tried RC Racing?: sail: MAN Jl 73 87/1:35-37+
RC Boating: AM Je 72 74/6:64-65
The RC Revolution in Model Yachting: MB Mr 75 25/290:133-136; Ap 75 25/291:175-177
RC Yachting: U.S. & U.K.: MB My 73 23/269:204-206; Je 73 23/270:248-250
RC Yachting: RC sail classes in U.S.: RC My 73 10/5:70+
So You Want to Go Boat Racing?: FM My 75 78/5:63
When One Man's Hobby is Another Man's Sport: multi-boat racing: MB My 75 25/292:232-233

CARS

Introduction to RC Cars: RCS Je 75 1/2:49-50+
Most Asked Questions About RC Cars: RCS N 75 1/7:49-51+
The RC Sport that Went Underground: ROAR: AM O 73 77/4:12-13+
The Unlimiteds Are Here: 1/8 scale RC racing cars: AM Ag 74 78/8:47+

RADIO CONTROL

Avoid the Crowd, Use Six Meters: intro to ham frequencies: RC S 71 8/9:35

Getting Started in Radio Control: see separate listing under aircraft radio control
NiCd Memory Effect: what it is, how it works: RC D 75 12/12:6+

RAILROAD

The Basics of Steam: see separate listing, immediately following
Brassbashing: intro to brass loco conversions: MR My 74 41/5: 52-57
Everything You Didn't Want to Know About Model Railroading: RMC D 74 43/7:32-33
Finescale Rolling Stock: intro to Protofour scale: Afx F 71 72/6: 310-311
Fitting the N Pieces into the Puzzle of the Scales: advantages of N gauge: MR O 74 41/10:33
Gauge: name, ratio, length of scale, foot, std track gauge, ng: MR D 73 40/12:41
Getting Started in This Hobby: MR D 74 41/12:79-82
Getting Started with Good Wiring: MR N 71 38/11:66-67
Good Modeling on a Budget: low cost materials: MR Ag 72 39/8: 27
The Imported Brass Caboose: intro to the type: NMRA F 74 39/1: 7-13
Indian Valley Railroad: 2' gauge live steam large scale layout: NMRA S 71 37/1:36-38
Irish Mail Millennium: backyard pump-power railroad: NMRA Je 73 38/10:14-17
The Joys & Challenges of $\frac{1}{2}$" Scale Traction: $2\frac{1}{2}$" gauge: NMRA F 72 37/6:32-35
Live Steam--Missouri Style: RMC My 73 41/12:30-35
A Look at N Gauge: Afx Ja 71 12/5:238-239; Mr 71 12/7:344-346+
Mechanical & Magnetic Couplers: MR Je 72 39/6:70b-74
Modeling a Foreign Prototype: NMRA Ap 75 40/8:25
Narrow Gauge for Beginners: MW O 72 1/2:88-89
Narrow Gauge Modeling: MR My 71 38/5:54-55
On3 Times Ten: intro to $2\frac{1}{2}$" scale live steam: NMRA F 71 36/6: 6-8
Photos Can Prove the Models: superdetailing, what editors look for: MR F 71 38/2:35
Picking a Railroad Name: rules & suggestions for prototype-sounding name: MR Ap 75 42/4:68-71
Railroads and the Circus: circus railroad modeling: NMRA S 73 39/1:7-13
Road Names & Numbers: realism in model practice: RMC D 75 44/7:74+
Röwa Close Coupling: European system for more scale-like distance between passenger cars: MR Mr 74 41/3:62-63
Shortline Modeling Tips: track rolling stock mods: RMC D 71 40/ 7:37-38
Small Scale Traction Modeling: N gauge: Mr Ja 75 42/1:78-79

So You Want to Dieselize: additions to yard equipment needed: NMRA Jl 75 40/11:40
Some Notes on Diesels for Model Railroaders: MR Mr 72 39/3:34-40
Starter Course in Model Railroad Building: tables, trackbed, scenery: MR D 71 38/12:66-69
30" Gauge--Fact & Fiction: intro to narrow gauge form: NMRA Ag 75 40/12:60
Watch Out N, 1/400th Is On the Way: experiments with ultra-microscopic railroads: NMRA D 71 37/4:24
What's That Name Again?: model railroad line names: NMRA Ap 75 40/8:47
Wild River Scenic Railway: 12" gauge electric 4-6-2 line: NMRA Jl 74 39/12:7-11
Work Cars--Prototype Style: converting old style cars to work cars: MR D 74 41/12:87-88

(The Basics of Steam) [all RMC]

Frame & Wheels: N 71 40/6:42-44
Cylinders: F 72 40/9:43-45
Valve Gear: S 72 41/4:40-42
Boilers: F 73 41/9:50-53
External Details: S 73 42/4:53-56
Tenders: O 74 43/5:54-57

ROCKETS

Rockets: FM F 72 419:18-21

STATIC SCALE

Armor Modelling in 1/48 Scale: AFV D 74 5/1:28
Back to Baseics: model base design: MM Mr 75 5/3:152-153
Castles in Card: Sc F 72 3/2:84-86
Cesare Milani on Series 77: 77mm metal figures: MM S 71 1/9:461-463
Collecting Waterline Ship Models: intro to subject: Sc Mr 73 4/3:200-201
Consider Dioramas: realism: Sc Ja 75 6/1:22-25
Enticement: figures: MM Ja 71 1/1:25-28
Have You Stopped Beating Your Wife: vacuum-formed kits: AI S 75 9/3:149
Hot Rods: static scale categories: IM Je 71 8/6:13; Jl 71 8/7:4-6
If You Can't Beat 'Em... woman's first model kit: AN 4 Ja 74 2/16:14
The Interesting World of Flats: Fus Sp 74 1/3:34-36

Modeling in 1/87: HO armor: AFV S 72 3/10:18+
Modelling a Secret Air Force: conversions to lesser-modeled Air Forces, example: Egypt: Afx N 72 14/3:140-142
Modelling from Vacuform Kits: Afx Jl 74 15/11:632+
Modelling Japanese Samurai of the 12th Century: MM F 71 1/2:76-79
Modern Steamers: intro to a subject for modeling: MB D 74 24/287:520-522
On the Grand Scale: large scale artillery: MM N 72 2/11:580-582
Samurai: intro to figure modeling subject: MM S 73 3/9:587-597
Scenery is Important: railroad & diorama: MW S 72 2/1:41+
Those Other Models: flats: MM My 73 3/5:292
Warships in 1/700 Scale: waterline: MW Jl 73 1/11:599+
Warships in 1/1200 Scale: MW Je 73 1/10:548-549

MISCELLANEOUS

Confessions of a Reggie Spotter: plane spotting: AN 9 Ag 74 3/5:13
Go Fly a Kite: kite types & performance: AM F 72 74/2:64+
How Safe from Theft are Your Models?: reducing the chances: RMC Ja 75 43/8:53; add My 75 43/12:5
I've Logged 20,000 Registrations: intro to plane spotting: AN 20 S 74 3/8:10
Metric Conversions: MR Ag 75 42/8:8-
Metrics Are Coming: application to modeling: NMRA S 74 40/1:51
Model Railroader Scale Model Conversion Tables: fraction, decimal inches & millimeters; prototype maters to scale inches & millimeters; bridge & structure clearances--tangent track; prototype feet & inches to scale inches & millimeters: MR Ap 74 41/4:49-52
Screw, Drill, & Wire Size to scale dimension in Z, N, TT, HO, OO, S, O (1/48 & 1/45), & 7mm: MR Ag 74 41/8:45-48
Spot Check: plane spotting: PAM Ja 74 4:57
Thermals: how they are formed & how to use them: AM My 73 76/5:30
Weather to Fly or Not: meteorology: AM Je 74 78/6:73-75

OPERATING TECHNIQUES

AIRCRAFT

Free Flight

Circular Tow: Nordic launching techniques: Aero Jl 75 40/474:

V. Articles

730-731+ ; Ag 75 40/475:784-786+ ; S 75 40/476:858-859; O 75 40/477:925-928
From Theory to Trophy: outdoor hand-launch glider technique & physical conditioning: FM Mr 73 76/3:39-41
Getting It All Together: tuning $\frac{1}{2}$A competition aircraft & engines: MAN Ap 72 84/4:15-16+
Glider Trimming: towliner adjustments: Aero My 74 39/460:230-231+
How to Fly a Low-Wing Model: trim for FF scale: AM Mr 71 72/3:37+
One Blade Prop Winding & Trimming: Aero Jl 75 40/474:732-734
Pre-Flight Checks: adjustments & trimming: Aero My 73 38/448:250-251+
Programmed Return of Magnet Steered Gliders: Aero My 71 36/424:245
Tow Line Knots: RC Ag 71 8/8:57

Tether

Electric Round the Pole Aerobatic flying: Aero S 75 40/476:855-856

Control Line

ABCs of Speed: AM Ap 73 76/4:50+
Effects of Wind: on take-off & pit positions: Aero My 74 39/460:254-255
Get the Best from Your FAI Racer: Dutch World Champ techniques: Aero O 73 38/453:561-564
Stunt Flying Made Easy: FM O 75 78/10:45-48
Wind Flying: advanced techniques in whip-power flying: AM S 72 75/3:20-21

Radio Control

Aircraft Towing: towhook design & mounting for aircraft towing sailplane: RC Je 72 9/6:49
Basic RC Aerobatics: category I techniques: Aero Mr 71 36/422:136-137
A Few Notes on Trimming: aerobatics: RC S Ag 75 1/4:4
Flight Training Seminar: RC helicopter flight training: RC Mr 75 12/3:39-42+ ; Ap 75 12/4:50+ ; Je 75 12/38-39+ ; Jl 75 12/7:39+ ; Ag 75 12/8:62+ ; S 75 12/9:38-39+ ; N 75 12/11:73-75+ ; article continues
Flying Proficiency Program: RC Jl 75 12/7:22+
How to Go Faster: formula 1 pylon tips: AM F 75 75/2:39-40+

How to Set Up & Use the Hi-Start: elastic launch catapult technique: RC S 73 10/9:43-46+
Learning to Fly Helicopters: RC My 74 11/5:33+
Learning to Fly the S.S.P.: RC helicopter: AM S 72 75/3:50-55
Loncevak: how to do it with RC planes: MAN Jl 74 89/1:44-45
Notes on that First Flight: RC Je 74 11/6:16+
On Launching Gliders: FM Ag 71 413:10
On One: flying techniques for twin engine aircraft with one engine out: AM Mr 71 72/3:40
Pre-Flight: check-out: RC My 73 10/5:12+
Pulse Rudder-Only Flying Technique: AM Ap 71 72/4:32-35
Pylon Racing the Easy Way: 12 ways to psyche out opponent before race: RC N 74 11/11:12+
RC Kibitzer: instructing beginning pilots: MAN D 72 85/6:47+
RCM Flight Training Course: see separate listing, immediately following
Roll, Roll, Roll: how to: RCS D 75 1/8:34
Sailplane Aero Tow: RC model towing RC sailplane: AM Mr 75 75/3:34-36
Straight Up: early RC helicopter operations: MAN Jl 72 88/1:35-39+
Stunting with Rudder & Elevator: AM My 72 74/5:20+
Stunting with Rudder Only: AM F 72 74/2:18+
Tail Dragger Take-Offs: RC Ja 74 11/1:6+
10 Easy Ways to Crash: maintenance: RC Jl 74 11/7:16+
Thermal Finding: RC sailplanes: RCS S 75 1/5:9+
The Three Turn Spin: how to do it with the usual nose-heavy trim of aerobatic craft: RCS O 75 1/6:26
Vision & the RC Pilot: maintaining contact with the craft: RC Mr 73 10/3:8+
What Makes a Good RC Pilot: AM Mr 74 78/3:6+

(RCM Flight Training Course) [all RC]

What is Radio Control: S 71 8/9:64-65
Radio Controlled Flight & Airfoils: N 71 8/11:45-49
Flight Stability & Control of RC Aircraft: D 71 8/12:56-57
Selection of Radio Equipment: Ja 72 9/1:56-57+
Transmitter Stick Configurations: F 72 9/2:58-61+
Shop Tools & Accessories: Mr 72 9/3:48-49+

BOATS

Inside Story--Sailing: MAN Ag 72 87/2:38-39
Let's Get Started: engine starting procedures for model power boats: FM Jl 73 76/7:51-52
Some Observations on Radio Controlled Yachts: MB Ap 71 21/244:150+
Working to Windward: RC yacht tactics: MB D 75 25/299

V. Articles

CARS [all RCS]

Introduction: Je 75 1/2:49-50+
Selecting the Car: Jl 75 1/3:10+
Selecting the Radio: Ag 75 1/4:8+
Starting: S 75 1/5:7+
Learning to Drive: O 75 1/6:8+
Tuning for Racing: N 75 1/7:10+
The First Race: D 75 1/8:8+
[series continues]

RAILROAD

Layout Operation

The Brakeman on the Yellow Extra: way-freight operations on single-track mainline: MR Ja 73 40/1:56-57+
Cargo Operation: MR Mr 74 41/3:66+
The Day Time Almost Ran Out on the Virginia & Ohio Railroad: problem of dying battery on fast clock: NMRA My 71 36/9:37
Dispatcher on the Sunset Valley: responsibilities in club layout: MR N 75 42/11:72-79
Flying Switch Operations: MR Ja 74 41/1:42
An HO Layout Under the Sun: outdoor operation: NMRA Jl 71 36/11:24-25
How Long Should a Train Be: matching train length to layout size: MR O 72 39/10:37
Industrial Interaction for the Small Layout: NMRA Ag 75 40/12:48-49
Make Mine Passenger Operation: intro to operations: MR N 74 41/11:66
Model Railroading Learned in a 12"=1' Loco Cab: realism of procedure: NMRA Ap 71 36/8:20-21
Model Railroading with Shay Lokies: MR My 71 38/5:30-32
On Operating a Scale Narrow Gauge Layout: without timetables: NMRA My 72 37/9:34-35
Operating Systems: a form to end all forms: dispatcher's log & routing form: NMRA Ja 75 40/5:58-60
Operating the Lazy Creek Rd: work order system: NMRA S 71 37/1:14
Operating the Rock Island: poster time-table: NMRA Jl 75 40/11:14-16
Operating Your Model Railroad: MR N 75 42/46-49
Operation by Trial & Error: large pike operations: NMRA Ja 72 37/5:26-29
Operation Comes After the Surgery: basic operation: MR N 75 42/11:45
Operation on the New Jersey Northern: NMRA O 73 39/2:46-47

Operation Royal George: industrial operations: MR My 73 40/5: 62-66
Operations on the Kinnickinnic Railway & Dock Co.: switching operations involving rail ferry: MR F 73 40/2:56-59
Over the Waves, or There are Ferries at the Bottom of Our Basement: ferry on cart: NMRA N 74 40/3:26-27
Passenger Train Operation: from prototype: NMRA Ag 72 37/13: 38-39+
Plugboard for Scheduling: routing on pegboards instead of graph paper: NMRA Ag 73 38/12:13
Pre-Planned Dispatching: RMC Ag 74 43/2:42-45
Refinements for CCT Car Forwarding: coded tacks for routing: MR Jl 72 39/7:41
The Tab System John Allen Used: color coded tabs on cars: MR F 75 42/2:67-71
A Time Table of the Sierra, Cajon & Pacific: NMRA N 73 39/3: 40-43
Train Orders on the Rock Island: NMRA O 71 37/2:34
Uncoupling on a Grade: stop to prevent loose cars from rolling: NMRA Je 73 38/10:39
Unit Trains & Their Modeling: MR O 71 38/10:36-38
Waybills on the Car: waybill coding methods: MR N 75 42/11:86-89
What Amtrak Means to Model Railroaders: MR Ja 72 39/1:34-39
Why Not Run a Commuter Train?: NMRA O 71 37/2:11

Maintenance

Easy Dollar-Model-In-A-Minute Projects for Everyone: pike maintenance: MR N 72 39/11:43

Troubleshooting

Improving Operating Reliability: train wheel & rail contact problems: NMRA Mr 73 38/7:20-21
Locomotive Performance Analysis: troubleshooting locos with ammeter: MR Ag 74 41/8:27
Locomotive Short Circuits: how to find: RMC F 71 39/9:36-37
Oops! It's Off the Track: Troubleshooting derails: MR Ja 75 42/1:45

SAFETY

CL Handle Safety Thongs: MAN Ag 71 83/2:23
How Many Times?: crash prevention by better pre-flight inspection

V. Articles   540

    & construction: FM F 75 78/2:50
Incident over New York: airspace violation: FM Ja 72 418:19-21
Is Safety a Dull Subject?: safety in model construction: MR Mr 72 39/3:34-40
Model Fuel in Closed Cars: fire hazard: RCS S 75 1/5:2
Over 400 Foot & the FAA: clearance procedures: AM Ja 74 78/1:116
Visibility: color for RC planes: FM My 71 410:38
Vision & the RC Pilot: eyes, aircraft visibility as they affect safety: RC Mr 73 10/5:8+
Why Did I Crash? FM O 72 75/10:49-51

WEATHER

Weather or Not: probability of accuracy for given forecasts: RCS Ag 75 1/4:7+

STANDARDS & TECHNICAL INFORMATION

NMRA RECOMMENDED PRACTICES

Electrical: NMRA D 71:37/4:25
Standards for N scale: MR S 71 38/9:48-50

NMRA STANDARDS

Electrical: NMRA Ja 73 38/5:7-8
Fine Standards: NMRA Ja 73 38/5:9

NMRA TECHNICAL INFORMATION

Bridge Designs: Ja 74 39/5:29-36; Ap 74 39/9:29-36
Car Clearances on Curves--Traction: Mr 71 36/7:41-42
Code of Rules, City Traction Operation: Ja 73 38/5:55-56
Commercial Buildings of the 1850-1880 Period: D 75 41/4:57-60
Curve Data for Model RRs: Ag 75 40/12:36
Drawings, Scale; Enlargements & Reductions: S 72 38/1:43
Grade Tables: S 74 40/1:59-60
Interurban Operating Rules: Signals: Ja 73 38/5:57-58
Lowcost Diodes & Rectifiers: Ja 71 36/5:15

Lowcost SCRs, Unijunction Transistors & Zener Diodes: Ja 71 36/5:17
Lowcost Transistors: Ja 71 36/5:16
Nomographs for Determining Siding Capacity: S 75 41/1:58
Passenger Cars--Lightweight, Painting, Decal & Interior Detail: see separate listing
Portable Layout Modules: Ap 72 37/8:27-28
Scale Equivalents of Steel Pipe: chart: My 75 40/9:43
Timetable Work Sheets: S 73 39/1:55-57
Track Layouts: Traction, City Car Barns & Yards: D 71 37/4:27-28
Traction Car Wiring: Ag 71 36/13:23-26
Wiring for Traction Overhead & Rail: Jl 72 37/11:39-41
Wooden Trestle Bridges: Je 75 40/10:47-50; Ag 75 40/12:65-66; S 75 41/1:61-62

(Passenger Cars--Lightweight; Painting, Decal & Interior Detail) [all NMRA]

Canadian National 2 Compartment-2 Bedroom-Buffet Lounge: F 73 38/6:49
Great Northern "Empire Builder" Baggage-Dormitory: Mr 73 38/7:56
Great Northern "Empire Builder" Baggage-Mail: Mr 73 38/7:55
Great Northern "Empire Builder" Diner: Ap 73 38/8:50
Great Northern "Empire Builder" 8 Duplex Roomette-4 Double Bedroom-4 Section: MR 73 38/7:57
Great Northern "Empire Builder" 48 Seat Chair Car: Mr 73 38/7:58
Great Northern "Empire Builder" Lunch Counter-Lounge Car (Ranch Car): Ap 73 38/8:49
Great Northern "Empire Builder" 6 Roomette-5 Double Bedrooms-2 Compartments: Ap 73 38/8:50
Great Northern "Empire Builder" 16 Duplex Roomette-4 Double Bedroom: Mr 73 38/7:58
Great Northern "Empire Builder" 60 Seat Chair Car: MR 73 38/7:56-57
Illinois Central Cafe-Lounge: N 74 40/3:57
Illinois Central Diner: 6 var: N 74 40/3:58-60
New York Central 56 Seat Chair Car: F 73 38/6:49
Northern Pacific 56 Seat Chair Car: F 73 38/6:50
Pennsylvania 5 Bedroom-Bar-Lounge: F 73 38/6:51
Pennsylvania 4 Bedroom-4 Compartment-2 Drawing Room: F 73 38/6:51
Pennsylvania 10 Roomette-6 Bedroom: F 73 38/6:50
Southern Pacific Articulated Chair Cars "The Daylight": Je 73 38/10:58
Southern Pacific Baggage Car: Ap 73 38/8:52
Southern Pacific Baggage "The Daylight": Je 73 38/10:57
Southern Pacific Chair Car "The Daylight": Je 73 38/10:58
Southern Pacific 40 Seat Chair Car "The Cascade": Jl 73 38/11:56
Southern Pacific 4 Compartment-4 Double Bedrooms-2 Drawing Rooms

"The Lark": Jl 73 38/11:58
Southern Pacific Parlor Car "The Daylight": Jl 73 38/11:56
Southern Pacific 10 Roomette-5 Double Bedroom "The Lark": Je 73 38/10:57
Southern Pacific 10 Roomette-6 Bedroom "The Cascade," "The Lark": Jl 73 38/11:55
Southern Pacific 13 Double Bedroom "The Lark": Je 73 38/10:59
Southern Pacific 12 Double Bedroom "The Cascade": Je 73 38/10:59
Southern Pacific Triple Unit Diner "The Cascade": Jl 73 38/11:55
Southern Pacific Triple Unit Diner" The Coast Daylight": Je 73 38/10:56
Southern Pacific Triple Unit Diner "The Lark": Ap 73 38/8:52
Southern Pacific 22 Roomette "The Lark": Ap 73 38/8:51
Southern Railway Chair-Lounge: N 74 40/3:56
Southern Railway Diner: N 74 40/3:54
Southern Railway Diner: N 74 40/3:55
Southern Railway Diner-Lounge: N 74 40/3:56
Southern Railway Dinette-Coach: N 74 40/3:54
Southern Railway 5 Double Bedroom-Buffet-Lounge-Observation: N 74 40/3:57
Southern Railway 1 Master Bedroom-2 Drawing Rooms-Buffet Lounge: N 74 40/3:55
Southern Railway Tavern-Lounge-Observation: N 74 40/3:55
Southern Railway Tavern-Lounge-Observation: N 74 40/3:56
Union Pacific Baggage Car: F 73 38/6:52
Union Pacific Baggage-Dormitory: Mr 73 38/7:54
Union Pacific Baggage-Postal: Mr 73 38/7:53
Union Pacific Cafeteria Lounge: Mr 73 38/7:53
Union Pacific 44 Seat Chair Car: Mr 73 38/7:55
Union Pacific 4 Bedroom-12 Roomettes: Mr 73 38/7:54
Union Pacific 5 Bedroom-Bar-Lounge-"Redwood Lounge": Mr 73 38/7:53
Union Pacific 4 Double Bedroom-6 Roomette-6 Section: F 73 38/6:52

STANDARDS OTHER THAN NMRA

Correctly-Scaled Wheel & Track Standards for HO: Protofour translated to HO: NMRA O 73 39/2:45
Overhead Construction: NMRA N 71 37/3:39
Pole Standards, in Traction Lines: for wood & metal poles: NMRA Ap 71 36/8:22
Protofour Policies: several finescale standards: MR Ag 75 42/8:54-57
Recommended Wheel & Track Standards for 3/16" Scale: proposed S gauge standards: NMRA S 73 39/1:28

TEST EQUIPMENT

AIRCRAFT

Beam Scale Calibrations: weights & calibration for Go-No-Go Scale: AM F 73 76/2:68-69
Flying Models Dynamometer: see separate listing, immediately following
Go-No-Go Scale: balance beam scale for one gram FAI or pennyplane: AM Ja 73 76/1:65
How Fast Does Your Airplane Fly?: doppler correction for audio tach: FM O 72 75/10:48-49
Let's Build a Tach: reflected light: RC Ja 71 8/1:38-41
Mixture Control Meter: fuel mix indicator: RC Ja 74 11/1:56-59
One Gram Balance: go/no go, for FAI indoor: MAN Je 71 82/6:8
Pitch-Gauging Props the Cheap Way: ruler & paper: Aero Ap 74 39/459:181-182
Poor Modeler's Scale: 1 oz to 21 lb beam scale: AM D 74 77/12: 36-38
ProTach: how to make: RC Jl 75 12/7:72-79
Range & Altitude Finder: uses known dimension of plane, triangulation: RC Mr 73 10/3:49+
Scale: deflected piano wire: AM Jl 71 73/1:86
Tachometers: history of model engine tachs: RC Ag 74 11/8:10+
Torque Meter: for indoor rubber: AM Ja 71 72/1:38; My 71 72/5: 43
Watch the Birdie: FAI speed trap: FM Mr 72 420:45-47

(Flying Models Dynamometer) [all FM]

Concepts & Principles: work, power, torque, horsepower, energy, efficiency: Je 73 76/6:21-23
Power Absorption Unit: Je 73 76/6:23
Torque Measuring System: Je 73 76/6:23-25
Conducting a Test: Atmospheric Correction Factors for BHP (corrected HP): Jl 73 76/7:44-46
Analyzation of Dynamometer Test Results: Jl 73 76/7:46-48
Energy Flow: Jl 73 76/7:48
Air & Fuel Flow Rate Measurement: Jl 73 76/7:48-49
Air Flow Measurement System: Jl 73 76/7:50
Volumetric Efficiency: Ag 73 76/8:38-40
Air-Fuel Ratio: Ag 73 76/8:40-41
Specific Fuel Consumption: Ag 73 76/8:41
Brake Thermo-Efficiency: Ag 73 76/8:41-42
Brake Mean Effective Pressure: Ag 73 76/8:42
Analysis of Air/Fuel Flow: Ag 73 76/8:43-46
Instrumentation Construction: Ag 73 76/8:47

V. Articles 544

BOATS

A Useful Tuning & Sailing Aid: sailing & wind directions computer for adjusting vane control: MB Jl 72 22/259:280-281

ELECTRONIC

Ammeters, Voltmeters, Which? Both!: meters built into track circuitry: NMRA D 72 38/4:15
Cab Ammeters: wd: NMRA Ja 71 36/5:22
Electronic Flight Timer: 5-16 minutes: RC Ag 73 10/8:28-19+
Electronic Fuel Gauge: timer for RC aircraft as approximate battery life indicator: RC Mr 74 11/3:34-39+
Expanded Scale Voltmeter: RC O 75 12/10:72-74
Fancy Box: continuity checker: RC F 73 10/2:50-51+
Field Strength Meter: RC Jl 73 10/7:34-35+
Heath Servo Simulator: servo tester, how to use: MAN S 71 83/3:42-43+
Micro-Mini-Field Kit: volt/ammeter, field strength meter: RC D 73 10/12:47-51+
Mini Flight Pack Checker: battery charge meter, plugs into charging jack: RC Ap 74 11/4:45-51; mods S 74 11/9:2
NiCd Tester: RC Mr 72 9/3:50
POD: pulse omission detector, for Heath transmitter: AM Jl 71 73/1:39
Plug Tester: Aero N 74 39/466:599
RC Battery Tester: RC N 74 11/11:16
RC Control Movement Indicator: for translating rotary to linear motion on servos: RC Ja 72 9/1:47+
A Sensitive Ammeter for Your Pike: wd: NMRA O 71 37/2:30-31; cor Ja 72 37/5:46-47
Servo Analyst: RC S 74 11/9:50-54; mods S 75 12/9:2
Simple Glow Plug Checker: flashlight circuitry tester: RC F 75 12/2:62
Test Instruments for RCers: intro to equipment: MAN Je 71 82/6:48-50+
Testing Diodes & Transistors with an Ommeter: NMRA Jl 75 36/10:9
Testing Nickel Cadminum Batteries: RC F 73 10/2:58
Transistor Tester: wd: NMRA Jl 17 36/11:9
Universal Crystal Checker: RC Jl 73 10/7:29-30+
Versatile Test Power Pack: for checking motors, components or track: NMRA Je 75 40/10:43
Watch It: wd, volt/ammeter tester for glow-plug dry cells: Aero Ja 73 38/444:28

METEOROLOGICAL

AAM Weathermaster: wind speed, direction, pressure: AM Jl 74 78/7:40-41+ ; Ag 74 78/8:48-49+
Anemometer: ping pong ball, fish line, protractor, level, & chart: AM F 72 74/2:33
Blowing Bubbles: bubble generator for thermal detection: Aero N 75 40/478:965
RCM Wind Meter: four cups & Mabuchi motor as generator: RC Mr 73 10/3:62
Reading the Skies: weather forecasting by clouds: Aero N 71 36/430:616-618
A Simple Telltale: wind direction indicator for yacht racing: MB N 75 25/298:580
Weather or Not: probability of accuracy for given forecasts: RCS Ag 75 1/4:7+
Wind Direction Indicator: AM Ap 72 74/4:58
Windicator: deflected vane (ping pong ball) direction & speed: RC Ag 75 12/8:86-87

RAILROAD

A Compact Engine Test & Break-In Track: wd: NMRA O 73 39/2:42-44
An Electronic Tractometer: drawbar pull: NMRA N 75 41/3:60
How Much Can Your Loco Pull?: traction meter: NMRA S 74 40/1:30-31
Locomodometer: odometer on loco, for measuring track distances: NMRA Jl 73 38/11:37
Locomotive Test Track: dynamometer: MR Ag 71 38/8:66-67
Scale Speed Measurements: speedometer: NMRA My 71 36/9:38
Steam Engine Rating: locomotive tractive effort, car rolling ease: NMRA D 74 40/4:40-41
What's That Car's RF: testing rollability factor; wd, det: NMRA Ap 75 40/8:54-55

TOOLS

ACCESSORIES

Battery Chargers

BCRC Charger: RC F 73 10/2:53

V. Articles 546

Battery Charger-Discharger: RC My 73 10/5:42-50
Battery Chargers: requirements & types: MB Mr 75 25/290:124-125
DC to DC Charger for Electric Flight: car or cycle battery-powered recharger for motor batteries: AM Ja 74 78/1:39+
Ebenezer Scrooge Special: low cost battery recharger: 110v to 9v: RC My 74 11/5:49-51
Fast Charging Ni-Cads: RCS S 75 1/5:12-13
Inexpensive Battery Charger: from HO power pack: FM Jl 74 77/7:43-45
Make-It: Aero Ag 74 39/463:440+
Nicad Charger for your Car: using lighter socket: RC S 73 10/9:36-37
Nickel Cadmium Battery Service & Power Supply: recharger, starter battery, etc.: RC Ag 72 9/8:36-42
RCS Cycle Charger: wd, mat: RCS Jl 75 1/3:26-30; cor S 75 1/5:19

Field Boxes

AAM Glowdriver: glow plug pulser for starting flooded engines, 12v motorcycle battery: AM Jl 74 78/7:56-57
Atomic Field Kit: fuel tank, pump, plug batteries, tools: RC O 74 11/10:40-45+
Black Box Replacement: twin lead mount, on/off switch, test light--mounts directly on $1\frac{1}{2}$v dry cell: AM Ja 71 92/1:40
Build a Plywood Sailboat Stand: beach cradle: FM My 74 77/5:62
Complete Field Box: includes fuel pump, plug tester, storage: MAN Mr 71 82/3:41+
Custom Flight Box: sealed power, power converter, fast charger; from commercial parts: RC N 75 12/11:36-38
Electric Jetex Ignitor: AM Ja 75 75/1:79
Field & Pond Tote Box: MAN Mr 75 90/3:78
Field Box: modified from Goldberg Field Box: RC Ag 75 12/8:12+
Field Kit: with battery charger: Aero O 74 39/465:540+
Field Kits for Compact Cars: to fit Beetle trunk; two pieces--essentials & extras: FM N 74 77/11:40-44
Flight Box: field box: RC O 75 12/10:78
Folding Sailboat Stand: holds keel weight in transit: FM Ap 75 78/4:61
Fuel Pump: bicycle pump-charged sealed gallon plastic container: RC S 75 11/9:20+
Handy Flight Caddy: collapsible-leg field box: RC Ap 74 11/4:40-41
Make It: glow battery from one cell of car battery: Aero Jl 74 39/462:353
MicroMini Field Kit: glow plug battery, meters, accessories, on wrist or in pocket: RC D 73 10/12:47-51+
NFFS Fuse Light: DT service box--lighter, fuse, rubber band & pin storage: MAN F 73 86/2:8

One Tripper: field box with starter, fuel pump, etc.: RC Jl 72 9/7:40-45
Removable Power Module: light duty glow plug battery for $\frac{1}{2}$A separable from main box: RC Ag 75 12/8:16+
Starter Battery & Plug Tester: Aero N 74 39/466:599
Toter: field box on wheels, pull cart: RC F 73 10/2:23-25+
Transmitter Stand: rack to hold transmitter when not in use: FM Ap 74 77/4:70
12v DC-DC Converter: 12, 6, 3, 1$\frac{1}{2}$v power pack from 12v battery for starter, pump, plugs, etc: RC D 72 9/12:52-55+
12v Fueling System: fuel pump from truck windshield washer: RC F 73 10/2:8
12 volt Battery: modifying 12v starter battery for aircraft pit needs: RC My 75 12/5:38-39
Winning Pit Strategy: Organize: model boat pit box, description but no plans: FM Je 75 78/6:62

Glider Launching Equipment

AAM Glider Winch: battery powered: AM Ap 73 76/4:66-67+
Airfoiler 12v Winch System: RC Ag 75 12/8:63
Can Winch: Hi-Start catapult: RC Je 71 8/6:32-33+
Contork Winch: variable speed towline winch: RC Jl 73 10/7:48-55+
Electric Winch for Gliders: RC Ap 71 8/4:34-37
Glider Tow Methods with Pulleys: manual power for RC sailplane launching: MAN My 74 88/5:34
Glider Winch: from clamp-on, hand-powered grinding wheel: Aero F 74 39/457:86-87
Hi-Start Reel & Driver: RC S 74 11/9:58-60+
LSF Winch: portable, battery-powered sailplane winch: MAN My 73 86/5:46-47+
Low Cost Hi-Start: surgical rubber & fishing line: FM F 75 78/2:49
Rapid Winches: continuous loop system for ground-handling speed in RC glider launching: FM S 72 75/9:50-51
Poor Man's Wench: towline winch, manual: MAN Ag 75 91/2:52-53
Sailplane Launch Chute: for hi-start launchers: RC Ag 75 12/8:76
Soaring Boom: hi-start: RC Jl 74 11/7:22+
Something New in Power Pods: wing mounted to keep fuel out of radio: FM N 75 78/11:42-44
To Launch a Glider: electric glider winch: FM O 73 76/10:44-46
Towline Retrieval Chute: FM My 71 410:39
Towline Winch: RC F 72 9/2:46
Winch-Launch Pulley: so pilot can operate winch: AM Jl 71 73/1:39

V. Articles 548

Model Display & Storage

Box It: design & construction of carrying boxes for model aircraft: Aero N 72 37/442:626-628
Boxes: design & construction of model storage boxes: AM F 73 76/2:69
Building Wall Display Cases with Picture Frames: NMRA D 72 38/4:16-17
Cased Displays & Their Presentation: construction, lighting: MM D 75 5/12:740-741
Corrugated Carrying Cases: foam lined transport boxes: NMRA Ja 73 38/5:18
Economical Rolling Stock Storage: templates: NMRA Ap 75 40/8:44-45
Making Boat & Transmitter Covers: FM Mr 74 77/3:70
Space Saving Modelling: half-models on wall plaques: Afx Je 72 13/10:553

Modelborne Accessories

Aerial Movie Making: RC Je 71 8/6:72-75
Airborne Airspeed Indicator: telemetric: RC Ag 72 9/8:44-47+
Airborne Angle of Attack Indicator: telemetric, for finding stall angle, best glide angle, etc: RC Ag 72 9/8:44-47+
Airborne Cylinder Head Temperature Gauge: telemetric: RC Ag 72 9/8:44-47+
Airborne Fuel Gauge: telemetric: RC Ag 72 9/8:44-47+
Airborne G Sensor: telemetric: RC Ag 72 9/8:44-47+
Airborne Movies: RC glider-mounted movie camera: RC Ag 75 12/8:64-65+
Airborne RPM Indicator: telemetric: RC Ag 72 9/8:44-47+
Bomb Dropping Mechanism: Aero F 74 39/457:99
Build Your Own G-Meter: AM Ag 74 78/8:56
Club Flying Banner: RC towed: AM F 71 72/2:40
Combat--A Knotty Problem: combat streamers: Aero My 73 38/448:254-255
Drag Chute: low-throttle actuated, for RC drag racers: AM Ja 71 72/1:43
It's a Small World Down Below: camera attachment for RC Planes: FM Mr 74 77/3:19-22
Light Flasher: for strobe on flying scale: wd, mat: RCS S 75 1/5:68
Low Fuel Level Indicator: for helicopters: RC D 74 11/12:56-57
Rhinebeck Bomb: WW-I style bomb for semi-scale planes: MAN O 71 83/4:31
Rocket: operating scale rocket, airborne, electric firing: MM Ja 73 3/1:37-38
Simple Parachute Dropper: external, actuated by full left rudder: RC Je 71 8/6:43

Streamer Clips: for combat: Aero F 74 39/457:101
Thermal Sensor: rate of climb indicator: RC F 72 9/2:48-51
Towing Bridle: for power towing of gliders, forms own drag chute: FM Jl 71 412:44-45

Railroad

A Compact Rail Cleaner: attaches to one truck: for sharp curve layouts: MR My 75 42/5:56
Digital Fast Time Clock: mods to Heath GC-1005 clock: MR N 74 41/11:82-84
One Man's Battle Against Dirty Wheels: cleaner-moistened foam on track: MR D 75 42/12:80

Starters

Make It Easy--Hot Thumb: Aero D 74 39/467:669
Quick & Easy Car Starter: modified bicycle frame for RC cars: MAN Ag 71 83/2:74
RCM 12v Starting System: RC Ja 72 9/1:38-39+; cor My 72 9/5:4

Stooges

Easy Driver: rubber winding stooge from snow shovel: AM F 74 78/2:21
Gust Restraining Device: towline stooge: AM Je 72 74/6:58
One Man Launcher for Combat: MAN S 75 91/3:18-19+
Rubber Techniques: winding stooges: Aero Mr 75 40/470:154-155
Stooge: from hinge parts: MAN D 75 91/6:15
Stooges: three designs for control line: AM Je 71 72/6:37

Winders

Indoor Winder: from flywheel toy motor gears: AM F 72 74/2:32
Rubber Techniques: Aero Ag 74 39/463:435-437

V. Articles   550

CAMERAS

Modeler's Camera with Roll-Film Holder: 35mm film, pin-hole lens, HO eye-level appature: MR Ag 73 40/8:50-58

CHARTS & NOMOGRAPHS

Balsa Weight: 3" & 4" sheets: Aero Jl 71 36/426:356
Grams per Square Decemetre to Ounces per Square Foot Loading Scale: Aero Jl 72 37/438:363
Inches into Decimals of a Foot: conversion table: RT Ja 73 7/5-6:21
Metrication in the A Class: boat rules: MB Ja 73 23/265:20-21
Nomograph for Determining Siding Capacity: NMRA Tech Info: NMRA S 75 41/1:58
1/32 Scale Conversion Chart: scale feet & inches to model inches: Sc Je 73 4/6:419
Power Loading: graph: RC S 74 11/9:63
Prop Pitch, RPM, Highest Probable Speed: chart: MAN Je 73 84/6:23
Prop Selection Criteria: chart: MAN S 74 89/3:35
RPM: musical pitch & RPM chart: MB Ag 73 23/272:327
Scale Conversion Nomograph: prototype dimension, scale dimension, scale: AFV D 71 3/4:25+
Time, Speed, RPM: table for boats: MB Je 73 23/270:251
Wing Loading: graph: RC S 74 11/9:62

DRAFTING TOOLS

Drafting Board Conversion: 2x3 foot board for 21" roll paper: RC Ag 75 12/8:31
El Cheapo Peanut Proportional Dividers: AM Ja 74 78/1:40; My 74 78/5:6
Home-Built Projector for Enlarging Scale Drawings: 35mm slides: Afx Jl 72 13/11:603
Simple Gadget for Drawing Elliptical Sailplane Cross Sections: square for trammelling: RC N 75 12/11:76-78
Turnout Template: for layout planning: NMRA N 73 39/3:54-55

GLOSSARIES

Colors: Czech to English translations: WWE N 74 1/6:186
Terms Often Confused: model railroad terms: NMRA F 73 38/6: 42-43

HAND TOOLS

Commercial

Better Models with a Surface Plate: MR Jl 74 41/7:34-35
Budget Tools for Model Makers: adapting common objects for model work: Sc O 75 6/73:490-491
Ferroequinologist Metrology: metalurgy & tool quality: NMRA Jl 71 36/11:14
Files: RT S 75 8/9:99
Engraving Tools: use of hand gravers in modeling: MW S 73 2/1: 42
How Hammers Work: using: MR S 72 39/9:75-78
Meet the Dentist's Spoon: MR O 74 41/10:55
Modeler's Saws: razor, jeweler, hacksaw, homemade handsaw: MR Ap 74 41/4:80-82+
A New Source of Tools for Model Railroading: dental tools: MR Ap 75 42/4:62-65
Of Tweezers & Model Railroading: NMRA Ag 71 36/13:19
Screwdrivers: MR N 72 39/11:84+
Shop Tools & Accessories: RC Mr 72 9/3:49+
Taps & Dies: intro, tap & clearance drills for 2 to 00 sizes: MR Ja 74 41/1:89-91
Tools: basic for plastic static scale: RiS Jl 75 3/2:93-94
Tools Without Tears: basic plastic kit modeling tools: AE Je 73 4/6:303
Working with Magnifiers: Sc Ag 75 6/71:397

Jigs

Add to Your Roster: jigs for making flat cars & gondola sides on assembly-line: NMRA Jl 72 37/11:48
An Adjustable Driver Quartering Jig: MR Ja 71 38/1:44
Alignment Jig: trammeling jig: RC F 73 10/2:55-57+
Assembling Kadee N scale Couplers: tool for assembly: MR My 73 40/5:75-76
Ball Drilling Jig: Aero Ag 74 39/463:417
Build it Straight: tube & angle jigs for fuselage construction: Aero Je 74 39/461:308-309
The Builder's Building Board: pinning board (same as Superboard): RC N 71 8/9:34
Cutting Jig for Switch Ties: RMC Jl 75 44/2:56
Grab Iron Template: jig for making: NMRA D 74 40/4:58
Handy Dandy Notcher: razor saws & spacer: AM Ag 74 78/8:64
Holder for Sharpening Small Drills: NMRA Mr 75 40/7:46-47
Improving the Rolling Qualities of Car Trucks: smoothing journal box hole: NMRA Mr 72 37/7:12-13
Prop Frame: for covering microfilm propeller blades: AM F 72

74/2:33
RCM Fuselage Jig: RC F 72 9/2:34-35+
Roadbed by the Mile: jig for cutting curved trackbed for large club layouts: MR Je 75 42/6:64-65
Simple Aileron Jig: for measuring control surface throw: RC S 75 12/9:69
Superboard: pinning board (same as Builder's Building Board): AM S 71 73/3:40
Taper Boom Form: dowel & paper form for indoor motor booms: MAN F 71 82/2:8
Taper Boom Mandrill: for outdoor rubber, includes graph for dimensions: AM Ap 71 72/3:42
Truck Drilling Jig: for Backshop trucks & Unimat drill: NSG N 75 1/5:24
Tube Cutting Made Easy: guide for perpendicular cutting of tubes: NMRA Je 71 36/10:38-39
Turn Out Turnouts by the Dozens: MR Jl 72 39/7:46-51
Undercamber Planking: for sheeted undercambered wings: AM Mr 71 72/3:36
Wing Building Jig: Aero D 74 39/467:676-677
Wing Jig: shim for dihedral, storage rack for finished wings: Aero Je 74 39/461:296-297

Make Your Own

Balsa Stripper: variable (including taper) stripping straightedge: AM Ja 74 78/1:27
Build a Clamp: monkey wrench shape, rubber band tensioner: NMRA S 75 41/1:59
A Complete Torch Soldering System: propane/compressed air: RMC Mr 75 43/10:29-31
Cutter: razor blade guillotine for cutting ties: NMRA S 75 41/1:59
Engraving Tools: making hand graver: MW S 73 2/1:42
Locomotive & Car Rerailer: NMRA D 75 41/4:61
Modeler's Saws: commercial & home made handsaws: MR Ap 74 41/4:76-78
Modeler's Tap Wrench: plans: NMRA S 72 38/1:19-20
Paper Dispenser: adding machine roll for epoxy mixing: RC F 73 10/2:21+
RCM Caster Knife: modifying X-Acto #16 to swivel: RC Je 74 11/6:66
Scribed Siding: for N gauge buildings, making tool: NMRA F 72 37/6:31
Simple Surface Gauges: MR Ag 72 39/8:60
Snap-r-Keeper Removal Tool: for RC pushrods: RC N 75 12/11:39
Strip Cutter: for narrow strips of paper, uses scissors for blade: NMRA Ja 73 38/5:24
Third Hand: clamp for holding during covering with Mylar: AM Mr 75 75/3:24

A Versatile Surface Gauge: MR N 71 38/11:69-71
Wood Strippers: indoor balsa stripper & jig for tapered spars: AM Je 71 72/6:35

POWER TOOLS

Commercial

The Calculator, Your Next Tool: WW2J Jl 75 2/4:28
Lathe Tool Post Modifications: rocker tool holder from stock Sherline & Unimat European style rests: MR S 75 42/9:67
Machining in Miniature: Sherline or Unimat operation: MR S 75 42/9:66-67
Minicalculator: Tool for Modeling: intro & how-to for various functions: MR Ja 75 42/1:84-87
A Most Useful Tool: drill press: MR S 73 40/9:74-77
Power Tools for the Hobbyist: intro to various power tools: MAN F 71 82/2:40-43+
The Pyrogravure: MM D 74 3/12:834-835
Shop Tools & Accessories: intro: RC Mr 72 9/5:48-49+
A Simple Air Brush System: mods to Humbrol Spray Gun to take Humbrol tinlets: Afx Ag 71 12/12:663+
The Small Electronic Calculator as a Model Railroading Aid: scale, grade, speed: NMRA D 74 40/4:40-41

Make Your Own

Balsa Finisher: thickness sander for sheet balsa: RC Jl 71 8/7: 42-44+
Carbon Rod Soldering: welding rods for soldering without excess: NMRA Ap 73 38/9:56-57; improved handle: Ag 74 39/13:34
Complete Torch Soldering System: propane bottle fuel, aquarium air pump, torch from ball point pen cartridge: RMC Mr 75 43/10:29-31
The D Bit, Poor Man's Reamer: NMRA D 73 39/4:45
Foam Cutter: transformer & nichrome wire: Aero Jl 75 40/474: 735
Foam Cutter: MAN My 72 84/5:39
Humbrol Tinlet Paint Stirrer: Afx D 72 14/4:197
I Made My Airbrush: shop cleanout blowpipe & tubing: MR Jl 71 38/7:62-63
Locating Holes Accurately: micrometer head for Unimat: MR Ag 74 41/8:60-61
Moisture Trap Coil: for airbrush compressor: RMC S 71 40/4: 30-31
Motor Magnet Remagnetizer: wd: MR S 72 39/9:60-61

One Man Foam Cutter: resistor wire cutter for polystyrene: RC F 74 11/2:34
Oven for Setting Epoxy Joints & Castings: mat: MR Ap 74 41/4:46
Paint Compressor: fridge compressor, freon tank, & other scraps: RC My 72 9/5:48-50
Paint Mixer: AM S 72 75/3:44
A Powered Saw for Small Parts: model buzz saw: MR Mr 75 42/3:78-79
RFI Suppressor for Moto-Tool: RC S 72 9/9:95
Rip Fence: for small jig saw: RC O 72 9/10:52; reprint RC Mr 75 12/3:65
Traub's Wheel Collet: for turning wheels without disturbing quartering: MR Jl 72 39/7:55
Unimat Way Clamp: to increase way stiffness: NSG N 75 1/5:24
Vacuum Cleaner Attachment: for cleaning models with regular vacuum cleaner: Afx Je 73 14/10:546
Vacuum Former: RT Ja 71 4/1:4-5
Vacuum Machine: for plastic sheet vacuum-forming: Sc D 72 3/12:642-643

WORKBENCHES

Basic Workshop: card table set-up for RC aircraft: RC Ja 74 11/1:109-112
Humbrol False Lid: for scraping brushes without having paint run into rim: Afx F 73 14/6:310
Jack's Workbench: MR Ap 72 39/4:53-57
Junion/Open Bench: folding workbench: AM Ag 71 73/2:25
Paint Brush Box: Afx Ap 73 14/8:444
A Place for Every Tinlet: Humbrol paint can holder: Sc Mr 75 6/68:137
Portable Workshop & Carrying Case: MR Mr 75 42/3:68-69
Under-Layout Space Usage: mat: RMC Ja 71 39/8:44-45
Work Tray for Apartment Dwellers: 3v, mat: RMC Mr 74 42/10:44
Workbox for Home or Vacation: plans, templates, mat: portable workshop: MR O 74 41/10:56-57

WORKSHOPS

Balsa Storage & Wing Racks for your Shop: RC Ag 75 12/8:68
One Man's Shop: MR Jl 75 42/7:76-77
Work Area: workbench & surrounding area: RiS Mr 75 3/1:22

MISCELLANEOUS

Helicopter Training Pole: training device: RC Mr 75 12/3:38-42+
Polarized Sun Screen: for watching aircraft near sun: RC Ag 71 8/8:57
Table Top Helicopter Trainer: servo-operated tilt board & ball: RC S 74 11/9:55-57+
Taxi Dolly: for helicopter training: RC Je 75 12/6:38-39+

WARGAMING

CONSTRUCTION

First Take a Biscuit Tin: Gladiator game: MM Ag 73 3/8:520-521+
A Heavy Weavy Weapons Wargames Sight: determining dice value by sighting frontal area: MM N 75 5/11:680
How to Avoid a Mini Arms Race: equipping for model wargaming: AFV My 72 3/8:20

PLAYING

Aerial Warfare: see separate listing
Battle of Ben Het: tank battle in Vietnam jungle: AFV D 71 3/4:24
Battle of the Granicus: Alexander vs. Darius: MM N 73 3/11:750-753; D 73 3/12:829-831; Ja 74 4/1:32; disc My 74 4/5:258; Jl 74 4/7:408-409; S 74 4/9:532; O 74 4/10:589-590; D 74 4/12:761
Battle of Marathon: MM Jl 74 4/7:386-388+ ; Ag 74 4/8:468-470+
Battle of Pydna: rules: MM Ap 75 5/4:207-209
Battle of Waterloo: order for battle for club wargames: MM Ag 75 5/8:490; rules S 75 5/9:528-530
Board Games, Paper Games, & Combinations: intro to types: A&W N 72 2:68
Board Wargames: see separate listing
Bridge Battle: WW-II skirmish: AFV Mr 71 2/12:28
Commando Attack on Bridge: AFV N 71 3/3:30+
Congreve Rockets System: wargame effect: MM My 73 3/5:297-297
Choosing an Ancient Wargames Army: balancing forces: S&L Jl 74 2:13; disc (O 74) 4:13-14; (D 74) 5:12
Elizabethan Sea Dogs: S&L (D 74) 5:22-23; (F 75) 6:14-15
First Take a Biscuit Tin: Gladiator wargame: MM Ag 73 3/8:

V. Articles

520-521+
How to Play a Napoleonic Wargame: basic rules: Afx My 72 13/9: 482-483+
How to Steel a Set of Rules: adapting wargame rules to new situations: AFV Jl 72 3/9:26
Micro Tank Warfare: visibility, tank destroyers, concealment, concealed defence: S&L Je 74 1:19-20
Infantry Versus Soviet Tanks: field of view & fire: AFV D 71 3/4:16-17
Move & Fire: model armor game with single & multiple shot rules: AFV Ja 72 3/5:26+ ; F 72 3/6:24+
The Napoleonic Wargame: see separate listing
Napoleonic Wargaming: point system for balancing armies: Afx Ap 75 16/8:472
Napoleonic Wargaming--Playing Solo Games: Afx My 75 16/9:521-522
Napoleonic Wargaming Skirmishers & Melees: Afx Je 75 16/10:601-602
The New Look in Ancient Wargaming: MM F 71 1/2:86-87
Operation Sea Lion--the Non-Invasion: Afx Je 75 16/10:596-600; Jl 75 16/11:642-644; Ag 75 16/12:694+ ; S 75 17/1:16-18+ ; cor F 76 17/6:365-366; add My 76 17/9:543
Persian Army: intro for wargaming: S&L (O 74) 4:18-19; (D 74) 5:13
Running Land & Air Battles: see separate listing
Schizophrenic Wargaming: supply problems: AFV Mr 71 2/12:21-22+
Team Play in Amphibious Exercise: A&W Ja 73 3:68
A Touch of Fantasy: intro to sources: S&L (O 74) 4:10-11
Wargames for the Young Enthusiast: see separate listing
Wargames for the Younger General: see separate listing
Wargaming Operation Sealion: Afx D 75 17/4:228+
Writing Wargame Rules: MM My 75 5/5:292-293; disc Ag 75 5/8: 468-469
The World of Wargaming: Napoleonic: see separate listing
World War I Aerial Combat: S&L (O 75) 10:18-19; (D 75) 11:14-15

SEPARATE LISTINGS

Aerial Warfare [all MM]

The Models & Equipment: S 72 2/9:474-476
The Game: rules: O 72 2/10:536-537+
Aerial Campaigns: comparative scoring, aircraft performance: N 72 2/11:584-585; chronology, ground defense: D 72 2/12:678-679
Modifying Rules for Free-Lance Designs: Ap 73 3/4:213

Wargaming

Board Wargames [all MM]

Introduction: N 73 3/11:736-737
Sampling of Commercially-Available Games: Ja 74 4/1:24-25+
Combat Unit Effectiveness: balancing of luck & skill: Mr 74 4/3: 132-133+
Movement: My 74 4/5:260-261
Equipment: Jl 74 4/7:400+
Conclusions: S 72 4/9:538-539+

Napoleonic Wargame [all MM]

Introduction: weaponry & tactics of the period: Mr 71 1/3:136+
Infantry: preliminary points, company & battalion size, space required, etc: Ap 71 1/4:180-181
Infantry Movement: speed, spacing of skirmishers: My 71 1/5:248-249
More About Infantry: line, column, & square & their development: Je 71 1/6:300-301
Light Infantry: use of skirmishers: Jl 71 1/7:361-362
Cavalry: survey of equipment & tactics of the period: Ag 71 1/8: 419-420
Cavalry: speed & movement: S 71 1/9:451-452; O 71 1/10:531-532
Cavalry Charge: N 71 1/11:562-563
Musketry: intro to the weapon & its use in the period: D 71 1/2: 656+
Effectiveness of Musket Fire: Ja 72 2/1:42/43
Musket Fire Effectiveness Against Moving Targets: F 72 2/2:86-87
Functions of Light Infantry: Mr 72 2/3:142-143
British Riflemen: Ap 72 2/4:180-181
Hand to Hand Combat: infantry: My 72 2/5:232-233
Infantry Melee: Je 72 2/6:288-289
Infantry Melees, Special Situations: Jl 72 2/7:341-342
Cavalry in Action: Ag 72 2/8:404-405
Charging Cavalry Against Stationary Infantry: S 72 2/9:466-467
A Few Loose Ends: situations not covered by the rules: O 72 2/10:534-535
Artillery--the Backgrounds: basics of period artillery: N 72 2/11: 578-579
Artillery--the Roundshot: D 72 2/12:662-663
The Howitzer Shell: Ja 73 3/1:46-47; disc Mr 73 3/3:166; Ap 73 3/4:205; Jl 73 3/7:444-445
Artillery--Canister: F 73 3/2:76-77
Artillery--the Final Points: Mr 73 3/3:164-165
Morale: Ap 73 3/4:211-213; cor My 73 3/5:278

V. Articles   558

Running Land & Air Battles [all A&W]

Introduction: Mr 73 4:68
Moves: My 73 5:69
Fire Effectiveness: Jl 73 6:70
Distances, Value, Range: S 73 7:70
Replenishment, Logistics: N 73 8:68
Preparation, Combat: Ja 74 9:70-72
Repairs, Positions, Batteries: Mr 74 10:68-69
Bases, Transport: My 74 11:68-69
Weather, Ships & Aircraft: Jl 74 12:68-69
Sea Depth, Aircraft Carriers & Hellicopter Carriers, Support Ships: S 74 13:68
Minelaying & Sweeping, Landing Ships, Aircraft, Anti-Coast Fire & Air Attacks: N 74 14:44-45
Damage & Repair of Harbors & Airfields, Submarines, Torpedos: Ja 75 15:44-45
Concealed Positions, Air & Naval Search: Mr 75 16:52-53
Surface Raiders, Amphibious Operations, Saboteurs, Rescue Operations: My 17:44-45
Nuclear Weapons: Jl 75 18:48
Special Naval Units, Duration of Simultaneous Events: S 75 19:44-45
Anti-Missile Missiles, Midget Submarines, Aircraft/Helicopter Action, Emergency Landing/Ditching: N 75 20:74
[series continues]

Wargames for the Young Enthusiast [all S&L]

Knightly Combat--Fight to the Death: (O 74) 4:45
Knightly Combat--The Tournament: Ag 74 3:6; cor (O 74) 4:5
U.S. Civil War: Je 74 1:10-11; Jl 74 2:10-11

Wargames for the Younger General [all MM]

WW-II Rules: O 73 3/10:682-683
Artillery Fire: N 73 3/11:760+
Tanks, Tank Guns, & Armoured Cars: D 73 3/12:820-821
Infantry: Ja 74 4/1:50-51
Flame Throwers, Grenades, Mortars, & Anti-Tank Weapons: F 74 4/2:82-84
Mines & Aircraft: Mr 74 4/3:152-153
General Notes: Ap 74 4/4:210-211
Aid to Realism: My 74 4/5:275-276

World of Wargaming [all MW]

Time-Space Ratios: S 72 1/1:38-39
The Line & Mixed Order: O 72 1/2:99-100
The Column: N 72 1/3:118-119
The Skirmishing Line: D 72 1/4:174+
The Square: Ja 73 1/5:240-241
Cavalry Tactics: F 73 1/6:318-319
Engineer Services: Ap 73 1/8:410-411
Artillery: My 73 1/9:486-487

MISCELLANEOUS

CLUB ORGANIZATION & OPERATION

Clipped Wings: Prison model club: MAN Ag 72 85/2:15-16+
Concept for a Club: planning large club layouts: RMC My 71 39/12:36-38
Model Railroad Clubs: NMRA F 73 38/6:19+
Model Railroading in France: NMRA Jl 71 36/11:10-11
R/C For the Masses: model air show to raise club funds: RC S 71 8/9:47-50
Small Meetings: local clubs: NMRA Mr 74 39/8:44
Those Magnificent Young Cons & Their Flying Machines: Models in prison: AM Jl 74 78/7:14-15+
Twelve Ways to Kill an Association: members' responsibilities: NMRA F 71 36/6:3

COLLECTING

The Art of Pass Exchanging: model railroad line passes: NMRA Ja 74 39/5:23
Builder's Plates & Bells are Where you Find 'Em: NMRA My 72 37/9:41-42
The Case for Collecting Models: railroad particularly: MR Ja 71 38/1:11-13
The Case for Tinplate Restoration: locomotives: RMC D 71 40/7:47-48; Ja 72 40/8:46-49
Collecting Scale Model Railroad Equipment: NMRA Mr 71 36/7:22
Engine Collecting: MAN S 75 91/3:15+
The Great Pass Race: design of model rail line passes: NMRA N 75 41/3:55+
How & Why of Pass Exchanging: NMRA N 75 41/3:54

V. Articles

Nazi Military Relics, Real Thing or Reproduction?: problems of determining: WWE Ja 75 2/1:12+
Numismatics & Philately: WW-II stamps & occupation currency: WWE Mr 74 1/2:32
Posters of WW-II: WWE S 74 1/5:144
Renovating Die-Casts: restoring collector's toy cars: Sc Jl 73 4/7:468-470
Santa Fe Roster of Bob Kjellander: RMC O 73 42/5:51-57
The Solid: MM Mr 75 5/3:150-151
The Starting Collector: railroad models: RMC S 71 40/4:40-41
Those Other Models: flats: MM My 73 3/5:292
The Tin Soldier: flats: MM S 74 4/9:522-524
When I Was a Boy: model aircraft engines: FM Ap 75 78/4:40-45

CONTESTS

Boat

Masterboard for Multi-Boat Racing: frequency & order: MB My 73 12/269:192-193

Flying

Contest Procedure Guide for RC Pylon Racing: RC Jl 72 9/7:58+
How We Did It: running a contest: MAN Ap 71 82/4:34+
How We Did It: running a contest: RC Ap 74 11/4:20-21+
One on One: pyramid challenge contests: RC D 75 12/12:22
Quarter Midget: contest operation: RC My 72 9/5:14+
The Unsung Workers: need for better participation in meet operation: FM Ag 74 77/8:3

Static Scale

Model Competitions & the Judges: contest operation: Sc Mr 72 3/3:152-154

HUMOR [see also VI. REVIEWS; Parodies]

A Beginner's Guide to Contest Flying: design & operation "Advice": AM Ap 74 78/4:26+
Curtiss-Wright CW-21B: satire on radical multi-kit conversions:

RT S 73 6/9:97
Ferrous Frog: water-seeking missile: RT Ap 74 7/4:39; Jl 74 7/7:71
Flotchillator Assy: optical Illusion: NMRA Ap 71 36/8:11
Food for Thought: period war rations to accompany wargames: MM Jl 73 3/7:445
From the Grass: "needed" new equipment items for RC sport flying: RC S 75 12/9:22+
From String to Wire...to RC: progress through control systems: MAN N 71 83/5:48-50+
German Secret Weapons: the Buchem Spinne: 3v, struc, pat, col, launcher: WW2J S 75 2/5-6:36-37
How to Dress for the Sport: flying modeler clothing: AM Ap 74 78/4:52+
How to Phly a Phantom: steps before catapult launch: IM My 75 11/3:3
I Am Not a Buff: railfans & their priorities on fan trips: NSG N 75 1/5:36
Iron Beaver: wood-seeking missile: RT Ap 74 7/4:39; Jl 74 7/7:71
The Long & the Short of It: problem of multiplicity of wargame figure scales: S&L (O 75) 10:17
Model Railroading as a Vice: MR D 75 42/12:114-115
Middle Earth, Outer Space & Inner Misgivings: fantasy wargaming from "any book": S&L (Je 75) 8:20
Model Mulling: "advice column" letters about modelers: RCS Ap 75 1/1:(17)
The Noble Art of Desk-Drawer Modeling: model building during office hours: MR Je 73 40/6:19-22
Racing or Chasing?: views of pit crew in RC pylon race: RCS Je 75 1/2:34
Roger, Wilco, Over & Out: an improbable personal recollection, mostly during Torch: WWE My 74 1/3:60+
SMASH: account of first lessons in RC flying: RC Ap 74 11/4:16+
Scale Bees: problems of realistic bee hives on HO layouts: MR F 74 41/2:45
The Story & Men Behind BDAE: designing RC plane: MAN Je 75 90/6:42-45+
Superdetailing the Avon 4-4-2: Avon aftershave bottle, parody on super-detailing articles, NMRA Ap 75 40/8:22+
There's a Prototype for Everything: prototype use of thumbtack car waybills: MR Ap 74 41/4:76-78
Tuthill on Metrication: cartoon collection on metric model railroading: RMC N 75 44/6:46-47
12 oz Beverage Container: NMRA Unstandard: parody on NMRA Standards: NMRA Ap 74 39/9:7
Vacationing with a Model Railroader: non-modeling wife's guide to survival: MR O 75 42/10:90-91
Whirlybird a la Parisien: RC helicopter demonstration at trade show: AM Je 74 78/6:37-39
Zero Displacement Engine: technical details of high speed engine: AM Ag 71 73/2:29

V. Articles 562

MODEL BUILDING CLASSES

Isn't It Time for School: club-operated classes in RC modeling & flying: AM Mr 72 74/3:26-28+
Pied Piper of Peralta: training system for kids: MAN Ap 74 88/4: 11+
Teaching Aeromodelling: for adults: Aero Ja 74 39/456:52-53
Try It...You'll Like It: aviation class for kids: MAN Ag 73 87/2: 15-16
Where Are the Juniors?: Coffee Air Foilers program: MAN My 71 82/5:14-16+

MODEL FACILITIES

Circle Marker: line marker for pavement: AV My 72 74/5:62-63
Construction of a Lake: MB Je 74 24/281:216-217
A Dream Field: Keystone Clippers: FM N 71 416:38-39
Hillman Model Air Park: Pittsburgh: AM Mr 71 72/3:10-11+
Lima Area Radio Kontrol Society Story: LARKS airfield: AM O 73 77/4:112+
Make Your Own Concrete Carrier Deck: MAN Jl 74 89/1:15-16
Make Your Own Pylons: for RC pylon racing: RC F 71 8/2:39
Modeler's Miracle in Madison: WI, parks: AM S 72 75/3:28-29
Mow the Field: robot lawn mowers: RC F 75 12/2:70
Optical Tracking Station Mk II: transit for triangulating downed aircraft: AM D 72 75/6:53+
Portable Transmitter Pound & Official's Stand: RC O 72 9/10:53-56
Practice Carrier Deck: four cable deck: AM Ja 73 76/1:63
ROAR National Race Tracks: course design: MAN Jl 72 85/1:33
Scatter Pylon Signal Lights: replaces green flag: AM Mr 71 83/2: 49-50+
Self-Destruct: PR & site keeping: MAN S 73 87/3:28-29
Simplified Electric Two Minute Clock: for pylon racing: MAN Ag 71 83/2:49-50+
Success in Mahwah: Mahwah NJ model park: FM Ap 73 76/4:50-51
There We Were in Court: neighbor action against flying site: RC Ja 75 12/1:38+
To Share an Airfield: use of municipal airport for model flying: FM Ap 74 77/4:46-48

MODELING IN EDUCATION

Aerospace--Grade School Level: MAN Mr 71 82/3:19-20+
Logical Thinking Skills Development Program: 5th grade rail layout: MR D 75 42/12:86-94

Now--The Schools: use of model aircraft & rockets in curriculum: MAN Jl 72 88/1:15-16+
Rail Transportation project: use of model railroads as part of school curriculum: MR Ja 75 42/1:90-91

NON-MODELS

Flying With Your Model: shipping hints for shipping by airline: RC Ag 71 8/8:20+
How to Fly a Model: transport by airliner: AM Ag 74 78/8:24+
Instant Boomerang: four-blade X: Aero Ag 71 36/427:448
Jet Set Modeler: crating flying models for air shipment: AM Jl 72 75/1:29
Learning from the Museum: display techniques: MB Jl 74 24/282: 265
Make Your Own Christmas Cards: with help of local instant printer shop: NMRA O 75 41/2:49
Mow the Field: wind-up tether self-propelled power mower guide: RC F 75 12/2:265
Sculptured Metal Art Trophies: soldered wire & wood base: RC Jl 74 11/7:50-51
Why Not Try a Boomerang: fiberglass boomerang design & construction: Aero Ja 71 36/420:39-41

PHOTOGRAPHY

Amateur Aviation Photography: how to photograph aircraft: AN 25 My 73 2/1:6
A Change of Scene: projected backgrounds for model photographs: NMRA Mr 75 40/7:48-49
Chasing Trains with a Camera: NMRA Mr 75 40/7:42-45
Check All the Angles: NMRA Jl 75 40/11:7-8
Effective Use of Lighting: for figures: Fus Sp 75 2/1:42-45+
Give Impact to Your Pictures: NMRA F 75 40/6:32-34
Guide to Model Photography: see separate listing, immediately following
HO Snow Scene: how to pose model: MR Je 73 40/6:70
Let's Clamp Down on Model Photography: C-Clamp monopod, how to make: NMRA N 75 41/3:64-65
The Lost Hudson: photographing model loco with full-scale rail yard background: MR F 74 41/2:48-51
Photo Enlarging Three-Views at Home: copy photography & tracing projected slides: RC Jl 71 8/7:52-53
Photograph Your Models Easily: MR Mr 72 39/3:68-71
Photographing Your Model: table-top photography for plastic scale: AM O 71 73/4:24-25+
RAF Steeple Claydon: use of photography in model research for

V. Articles

diorama composition: Sc Ag 75 6/71:407
A Real Snow Job: overlay print for falling snow: RMC Ja 75 43/8:34-35
Special Effects: masks, backgrounds & props: Sc My 75 6/68:225-227

(Guide to Model Photography) [all MW]

Basic Equipment: F 73 1/6:310-311+
Taking the Picture: Ap 73 1/8:426-428
Background & Staging: Jl 73 1/11:588-594
Special Effects: D 73 2/4:194-198

PUBLIC RELATIONS

Col. Betkey's Flying Circus: RC air show team: RCS Jl 75 1/3:(34-35+)
5 in 75: PR program using maximum number of people for minimum amount of time: MAN Jl 75 91/1:10+
Modeling and the Marriage: PR at home: MR D 71 38/12:60-64
Police Story: PR involving local police: RC D 75 12/12:80-81+
Put Your Club on TV--Free: use of public service spots: RMC N 71 40/6:46-49
SPARKS Thunderchickens: four plane RC aerobatic team: MAN S 73 77/4:20+
Sailing Indoors: RC sailing demonstration at boat show: FM Ap 74 77/4:63
Self-Destruct: PR & site keeping: MAN S 73 87/3:28-29
So You Think Your Club can Arrange a Flying Display: control line demonstration: Aero Ap 74 39/459:178+
Swift Wings Fly: March of Dimes fund-raising show: RC O 72 9/10:46-47
Tactics & Strategy for Married Model Railroaders: introducing wives to hobby: MR D 74 41/12:90-92
Uplift: Key City Prop Twisters (Abilene, TX) program: AM O 73 77/4:20+
Using a Show to Gain Public Support: static display in shopping center & TV meet: AM Ap 74 78/4:18+
What Is Your Club Doing to Improve Public Relations: RC S 74 11/9:66-67+

RESEARCH [also see PHOTOGRAPHY, p. 563]

About Maps & Railfanning: how to find it: NMRA N 74 40/3:51-53
Another Solution--Bulletin Binding: post binder: NMRA Ja 75 40/5:30

Architectural Sources: bibliography: NMRA F 74 39/7:22-24
Bind Your Own Bulletins: basic bookbinding: NMRA Ap 74 39/9: 24-25
Building a Box of Facts: card cataloging of specific model research data: AFV Ja 72 3/5:29
Comments on the Needs of World War 2 History: problems of viewpoint & bias, gaps in present coverage: WWE N 74 1/6:185
An Effective System of Note Retrieval: card catalog system, abstracts of articles: AFV My 72 3/8:28
Finding Orders of Battle: AFV Jl 74 4/11:13; S 74 4/12:9; D 74 5/1:14
A Guide to Military Research: choosing sources: AFV D 71 3/4:24
How Many Apples in an Orange: German vs. British tanks lost statistics: AFV My 73 4/4:30
How to Get 10,000 Words from One Picture: photo-interpretation: AFV F 72 3/6:28
The Individualization Urge: developing a reference library without running out of space: AE Ja 74 6/1:33
It is Written...Somewhere: card cataloging library data: AFV Mr 72 3/7:26
It's Official: use of official histories: AFV S 73 4/7:23
Mag-Bin: box for magazines: NMRA Ap 74 39/9:25
Microfilm as a Research Tool: AFV N 73 4/8:15
Napoleonic Military Uniform Research: Afx O 75 17/2:87+
Personal Color Mixture Index: making a color chip file while mixing paint: MR Ap 71 38/4:29
Photo Finding: AM S 74 78/9:68
Project 603--An Account of An Exercise in Model-Making: research for collection: IM N 73 10/11-12:14-15; Ja 74 10/13-14:19-21+
The Research Gambit: basic aircraft research: AM O 71 73/4:32-34+
Research Sources: libraries & museums as document sources: AFV Ag 73 4/6:31-32
Scale Ship Models: reference sources for last century of British ships: MB N 71 21/251:450-451
Shelling Out for Peanuts: camera for copying plans: AM F 75 75/2:53-54
A Source of Scale Detail: use of static scale plastic kits as flying scale proof-of-scale: FM O 75 78/10:48-49
Timelines: use & how to make: AFV Je 73 4/5:31-32
Try a 5 Foot Ruler: scale reference for photographing prototypes: MR F 73 40/2:54-55

RULES

Discussion

Clockwork Orange & the Future of the A Class: mock turtle prob-

lems: MB Ap 73 23/268:145-146
FAI Team Race Rule Change Proposals: Aero S 74 39/464:499
Is It Ethical?: plastic-only rule in IPMS competition: AE F 73 4/2:97
Scale Boat Event: MB Ap 72 22/256:168-170
3D 3-Views: arguments favoring allowing plastic kits as proof-of-scale documentation in flying scale competition: RCS S 75 1/5:4+
To Overtake Is Illegal?: FAI combat rule loophole: Aero Ja 74 39/456:51; cor Mr 74 39/458:153-154; Je 75 40/473:326; O 75 40/377; loophole sealing proposal N 75 40/478:971
Turtle or Mock Turtle: finer points of A class sail boat turtle-deck rules: MB Jl 73 23/271:279-280
What Ever Happened to Formula I: suggested rule changes: RC My 71 8/5:32-35+
What the H... Is Sport Scale? RC Ag 74 11/8:61+
Which Way Rat-Race: variations on rules: Aero Jl 75 40/474:745

Official

AMA Helicopter: AM Je 73 76/6:24
FAI Pattern: RC stunt: MAN Ap 74 88/4:34-35+
FAI RC Aerobatic K Factors: AM Ap 74 78/4:110
FAI CL: revised (1970) pattern: Aero My 71 36/424:267-269
FAI RC Pattern: AM Ag 74 78/8:4-5+
FAI Scale K Factors in RC, CL & FF Scale: Aero Ap 73 38/447:218-219
Fly the Schedule: FAI CL stunt: Aero Jl 73 38/450:369-372; Ag 73 38/451:447-449
MYA "A" Class Rules: changes in sail event: MB My 75 25/292:237
Metrication in the A Class: rules in metric for sail: MB Ja 73 23/265:20-21
Naviga Rule Changes: boat steering event: MB Jl 72 22/259:294
RC Rule Changes: MPBA power boats: MB Ap 73 23/268:148

Unofficial

A-6: indoor rubber: MAN S 75 91/3:24
Bay Area Quarter Midget: MAN My 71 82/5:39-40+
CL Pattern: stunts with bottoms under 18": AM Ag 74 78/8:65+
The Continental Pattern: RC stunt, choose 2/3 of manoeuvers, with K factors: FM Jl 75 78/7:34-35
Electric Competition: electric aircraft: AM Ag 74 78/8:65+
15-500 Pylon: RC class: RC S 73 10/9:19
Fun Events: RC stunts: AM Ag 74 78/8:65
$\frac{1}{2}$A Beginner's Event: stunt, balloon, mouse, combat, blindfold stunt,

streamerless combat: MAN Jl 72 88/1:79-80
½A Midget Pylon Racing: RC My 71 8/5:31
Helicopter Performance: for RC helicopters: FM S 72 75/9:48-50
Junior Free-for-All: free-flight: MAN O 71 83/4:8
Not-Too-Scale: free flight "stand way off" scale: MAN O 71 83/4: 8-9
Peanut Scale, Miami Variant: Aero My 75 40/472:162-165
Pennyplane: rule proposals: MAN Jl 75 91/1:92+
Peralta Balloon Breaking: MAN Ap 74 88/4:53
Peralta .049 Proto Speed: MAN Ap 74 88/4:53
Peralta Rubber Free Flight: MAN Ap 74 88/4:53
Peralta Team Racing: MAN Ap 74 88/4:53
Quarter Midget: MAN Je 73 86/6:41-42+
Quarter Midget Pylon Racing: RC My 71 8/5:21
Quickie 200 Races: ½A simplified pylon: RC Je 75 12/6:28
Radio Control Combat: AM F 71 72/2:23
Radio Old Timer: FM O 72 75/10:60
Regatta with a Difference: Naviga: MB D 73 23/276:530
SMAK ½A Weight-Lifting: CL cargo event: MAN Jl 72 88/1:78-79
SMAK Mouse Racing: MAN Jl 72 88/1:23
Scramble: rules for WW-II scale meet: RC Je 72 9/6:4+
Simulated Bird Flight: competition for RC gas ornithopter design: Aero D 72 37/443:716-717
Slope Slalom: RC sailplane event: RC N 74 11/11:31
Sport Stunt: with semi-scale biplanes: RC Jl 74 11/7:104+
Star C: RC sail yacht: MB My 72 22/257:201
WW-I Scramble: semi-scale WW-I aircraft pylon race with aerobatic manoeuvers in each lap: RC Jl 73 10/7:22+
Water Polo: beach ball & RC power boats: MB S 74 24/284:361

MISCELLANEOUS

Brass from Japan: inflation & the brass locomotive market: MR Mr 73 40/3:64-69
Can You Spot the Potential Good Customer: how to spot a good hobby store: RCS N 75 1/7:72b
How to Protect Yourself from Mail Order Rip-Off: NMRA N 74 40/3:25
Making a Modelmaker: commercial modeling: Sc D 73 4/12:818-820
Printing for the Model Railroader: preparing copy for job printers: NMRA Ja 75 40/5:48
Riding the Cab--Through Television?: possible TV camera in model loco: RMC Ap 75 43/11:29
Which Switch Is Which? switching puzzle in three-dimensions: NMRA D 74 40/4:56-57

VI. REVIEWS

BOOK REVIEWS

AIRCRAFT

Air Battles

(Pre World War II)

Aces High, the War in the Air over the Western Front, 1914-1918, by Alan Clark, Fontana, 1974: S&L (D 75) 11:31
At War with the Bolsheviks, by Robert Jackson, Tom Stacey: Allied Intervention: AE D 73 5/6:301; AN 7 D 73 2/15:11
La Aviacion en la Guerra de España, 3 vols, by Salvador Rello, Liberia y. Editorial San Martin, Madrid: AE D 72 3/6:315; vol. 4: AE My 73 4/5:259
Fighting the Flying Circus, by Eddie V. Rickenbacker, Bailey Bros. & Swinfen, Folkestone: AI O 74 7/4:202; Afx Je 74 15/10:600
The Origins of Strategic Bombing, by Neville Jones, William Kimber, London: AI O 74 7/4:202
They Shall Not Pass, by Bruce Palmer, Doubleday, NY: Spanish civil war: AE F 72 2/2:86
The War in the Air, 1914-1918, by Jack Woodhouse & G. A. Embleton, Almark, New Malden: MM Mr 75 5/3:159
Who Killed the Red Baron?, by P. J. Carisella & James W. Ryan, White Lion: S&L (Ap 75) 7:26-27

(World War II)

Air Defence of Great Britain, by John R. Bushby, Ian Allan, Shepperton: AE Je 74 6/6:312; Afx N 74 16/3:190
Air War over France, 1939-1940, by Robert Jackson, Ian Allan, Shepperton: AI D 75 9/6:310
Als Deutschlands Damme Brachen, by Helmut Euler, Motorbuch Stuttgart: AN 2 My 75 3/24:14-15
Arctic War Birds, by Stephen E. Mills, Superior, Seattle, 1971:

Alaska defence: WWE Mr 74 1/2:49
Attacks on the Tirpitz, by Gervais Frere-Cook, Ian Allen, Shepperton: AE Mr 74 6/3:149
Battle of Britain, by Bruce Robertson, J. W. Caler, CA: AE Ag 71 1/3:146; AN 25 My 73 2/1:15; Afx F 72 13/6:339
The Battle Over the Reich, by Alfred Price, Ian Allan, Shepperton: AE My 74 6/5:164; Afx Je 74 15/10:600
Bomber Pilot, by Leonard Cheshire, White Lion, London: AI Ag 74 7/2:102
The Bombing of Nuremberg, by James Campbell, Doubleday, Garden City, NY: WWE N 74 1/6:170
Carrier Operations in WW-II, 2 vols., by David Brown, Ian Allan, Shepperton: Afx My 75 16/9:554
Double Strike/The Epic Air Raids on Regensburg-Schweinfurt, August 17, 1943, by Edward Jablonski, Doubleday, Garden City, NY: WWE My 74 1/3:75
Fight for the Sky, by Douglas Bader, Sedgwick & Jackson, London: AE Mr 74 6/3:149; Afx Mr 74 15/7:421; AM F 75 75/2:421; S&L (D 75) 11:30
Fighters Over Tunisia, by Christopher Shores, Hans Ring & William N. Hess, Neville Spearman, London: Afx Jl 75 16/11:668
La Guerra Aerea in Africa Settentrionale, by A. Borgiotti & G. Gori, STEM-Mucchi, Modena, 1940-1941: AN 3 Ag 73 2/6:15; RT Mr 73 6/3:37; 1942-1943; AE F 74 6/2:98; AN 3 Ag 73 2/6:16; Afx Ja 74 15/5:315; RT Ag 73 6/8:93
Japan's World War II Attacks on North America, Smithsonian Institution, U.S. Government Printing Office, Washington: balloons: WWE N 74 1/6:171
Mediterranean Air War, vol. 1, by Christopher F. Shores, Ian Allan, Shepperton: AE Ap 73 4/4:204
Middle East Air War, Midland Counties Aviation Society, Solihull, Warwick: AN 15 F 74 2/19:15
The Nurenberg Raid, by Martin Middlebrook, Penguin, London: AI Jl 74 7/1:49
Outraged Skies, by Edward Jablonski: RT F 72 5/2:21
Pearl Harbor Attack, by Arnold S. Lott & Robert F. Sumrall, Leeward, Pompton Lakes, NJ, 1974: WW2J S 75 2/5-6:22
Pictorial History of the Mediterranean Air War, by Christopher Shores, Ian Allan, Shepperton, vol. 1: Afx Ap 73 14/8:455; vol. 2: Afx Mr 74 15/7:421; Afx Ag 74 15/12:723; vol. 3: AI Jl 74 7/1:49; Afx Ag 74 15/12:723
The Poltava Affair, by Glenn B. Infield, Macmillan, NY: WWE Ja 74 1/1:11
Safe as Houses, Wimbledon 1939-1945, by Norman Plastow, John Evelyn Society, Wimbledon: V-Bombs & Blitz: AN 31 Ag 73 1/8:15
Schweinfurt: Disaster in the Skies, by John Sweetman, Pan/Ballantine, London: Afx S 74 16/1:52
Tragic Victories, vol. 2, by Edward Jablonski: RT O 71 4/10:117
We Were There at the Battle of Britain, by Clayton & K. S. Knight, Bailey Bros. & Swinfen, Folkestone, Kent: Afx Ap 74 15/8:479
World War II Fighter Conflict, by Alfred Price, Macdonald & Jane's, London: Afx D 75 17/4:242; Sc D 75 6/75:596

(Post World War II)

Air War Over Korea, by Robert Jackson, Ian Allan, Shepperton: AI Ag 74 7/2:102; Afx Mr 74 15/7:421
And Kill Migs, by Lou Drendel, Squadron/Signal, Warren MI: Vietnam: AI Ap 75 8/4:207
Smash Four...Smash Five, by John R. Beaman, pvt: IM S 73 10/9: insert; RT Ag 73 6/8:85

Air Forces

(General)

World's Air Forces, by David Wragg, Osprey, Reading, Berks: Afx D 71 13/4:223; RT N 71 4/11:129

(Australia)

Aircraft of the RAAF, by G. Pentland & Peter Malone, Kookaburra, Melbourne: Afx Mr 72 13/7:389
Men & Machines of the Australian Flying Corps 1914-1919, by Charles Schaedel, Kookaburra, Melbourne: AN 7 Jl 72 1/4:15; Afx D 72 14/4:225; Sc Jl 72 3/7:379-380
Mission Vietnam, by George Odgers, Australian Government Publishing Service, Canberra: AI F 75 8/2:93

(Canada)

Wings of the Canadian Armed Forces, by Roy Thompson, pvt, Halifax, NS: WWE Ja 75 2/1:28

(Czechoslovakia)

Czechoslovakian Air Force 1918-1970, by Zdenek Titz, Aircam, Osprey, Reading, Berks: Afx S 71 13/1:20+; Afx F 72 16/6:339; Sc F 72 3/2:101

(Denmark)

Danish Military Aviation, G. L. Kongevej, Copenhagen: Afx Ap 72 13/8:452

(Finland)

Suomen Ilmavoimien Lentokoneet 1939-1972, by Kalevi Keskinen, pvt, Helsinki: AE Me 73 4/3:138; Afx Ja 73 14/5:282; RT O 75 8/10:110

(France)

French Air Force, vol. 1, 1909-1940, by Andre van Haute, Ian Allen, Shepperton: AI O 74 7/4:202
French Military Aviation, comp Paul A. Jackson, Midland Counties Publications, Leicestershire: AI N 75 9/5:255; AN 22 Ag 75 4/6:10
Pictorial History of the French Air Force, by Andre van Haute, Ian Allan, Shepperton: Afx S 74 16/1:52

(Germany)

Birth of the Luftwaffe, by H. Schlephake, Ian Allan, Shepperton: AE N 71 1/6:318; Afx S 71 13/1:20
Die Deutsche Luftwaffe, 1939-1945, by Adolf Galland, Karl Ries, & R. Anhert, Podzun, Dorhein: Afx Ja 71 12/5:251
Dora Kurfurst und rote 13, vol. IV, by Karl Reise, Jr., Dieter Hoffmann, Mainz: AE Ag 71 1/3:146
The Luftwaffe, by Roger James Bender: MM Je 73 3/6:390
Luftwaffe Airborne & Field Units, by Martin Windrow, Osprey, Reading: Afx F 73 14/6:337-338
The Luftwaffe at War 1939-1945, by Adolph Galland, Karl Ries, & R. Anhert, Ian Allan, Shepperton, AE O 72 3/4:207; Afx Ag 72 13/12:685-686
Luftwaffe in Action, vol. 1, by Uwe Feist & Mike Dario, Squadron/Signal, Redbridge, Essex: Afx S 72 14/1:48
Luftwaffe in Action, vol. 4, by Uwe Feist, Squadron/Signal, Warren MI: AN 28 S 73 2/10:15
Luftwaffe Story 1935-1939, by Karl Ries, Dieter Hoffmann, Mainz-Ebershelm: AI D 74 7/6:305
The New Luftwaffe in Action, by Peter Doll & Hermann Dorner, Squadron/Signal, Warren MI: AE Je 74 6/6:312; AN 10 My 74 2/25:7; RiS W 74 2/2:75
Pictorial History of the German Army Air Service, 1914-1918, by Alex Imrie, Ian Allan, Shepperton, Middx: Afx Jl 71 12/11: 589+
The Straits of Messina, by Johannes Steinhoff, Andre Deutsch, London: AE Jl 72 3/1:51; Afx N 71 13/3:163
Unsere Luftwaffe, Carl Schunemann, Bremen: Sc S 71 2/9:500

(Italy)

Dimensions Cielo: RT D 72 5/12:136
L'Aeronautica Nazionale Republicana, vol. 1, by Nino Arena, STEM-Mucchi, Modena: AI O 74 7/4:202; Afx O 74 16/2:116-117

(Japan)

Japanese Army of Wings of the Second World War, Light Corp., Tokyo: AE D 72 3/6:316

VI. Reviews

Japanese Military Aviation--A Pictorial History, by Eiichiro Sekigawa, Ian Allan, Shepperton: Sc S 75 6/72:441
Pictorial History of Japanese Military Aviation, by Eiichiro Sekigawa, Ian Allan, Shepperton: Afx Jl 75 16/11:668

(New Zealand)

RAAF & RNZAF in the Pacific, by Rene Francillon, Aero, Fallbrook, CA: Afx Mr 71 12/7:357+; Sc F 71 2/2:74

(Philippines)

50 Years of the Philippine Air Force, by F. A. Aquino, Jr., F. C. Vasalli, & A. A. Anido, John W. Caller, CA: AE S 73 5/3: 149; RT S 72 5/9:105

(Poland)

History of the Polish Air Force 1918-1968, by Jerzy B. Cynk, Osprey, Reading, Herts: MW S 72 1/1:39

(USSR)

The Red Falcons, by Robert Jackson, Clifton Books, Brighton: AE Ag 71 1/3:146; AN 18 Ag 72 1/7:14; Sc Ap 71 2/4:208
The Soviet Air Force in World War II: trans Leland Fetzer, Doubleday, NY: AE Jl 73 5/1:43

(U.K.)

Aircraft of the Royal Air Force, by Owen Thetford, Putnam, London: AE Jl 71 1/2:91
Challenge in the Air, by Bryan Philpott, MAP, Hemel Hempstead, Herts: Sc Jl 71 2/7:347
Flying Navy, Fleet Air Arm, by Richard E. Gardner, Almark, New Malden, Surrey: Afx F 72 15/6:339
Pictorial History of the Fleet Air Arm, by John D. R. Rawlings, Ian Allan, Shepperton: Afx F 74 15/6:367
Pictorial History of the RAF, vols. 2&3, by John W. R. Taylor & Philip J. R. Moyes, Ian Allan, Shepperton: AE Je 71 1/1:15; Afx Ja 71 12/3:263; IM Ap 71 8/4:15; Sc Jl 71 2/7:345-346
2 Group RAF, A Complete History 1936-1945, by Michael J. F. Bowyer, Faber & Faber, London: AI D 74 7/6:306; AN 1 N 74 3/11:15; Afx Mr 75 16/7:441

(U.S.)

Aces & Wingmen, by Danny Morris, Neville Separman, London: 8th

AF: AI D 75 9/6:310; AN 4 Ap 75 3/11:14; Afx S 75 17/1:55
Air Corps, by Joe V. Mizrahi, Sentry Books, CA: AE Mr 72 2/3: 154
Carrier Fighters, by Joe V. Mizrahi, Sentry Books, CA: AE Mr 72 2/3:154
5th Air Force Story, by Kenn C. Rust, W. E. Hersant, London: AI Je 75 8/6:305; Afx Mr 75 16/7:441-442; Sc Ja 75 6/64:33
Flying Army, the Modern Air Arm of the U.S. Army, by W. E. Butterworth, Doubleday, NY: AE Mr 72 2/3:155
Pictorial History of the USAF, by David Mondey, Ian Allan, Shepperton: Sc Ja 72 3/1:44-45
2nd Tactical Air Force, by Christopher Shores, Osprey, Reading, Berks: AE S 71 1/4:224; Afx Mr 71 12/7:357; RT Ap 71 4/4: 46; Sc Ap 71 2/4:203
USAF Today, by Chris Pocock & Colin Smith, West London Aviation Group, Eastcote, Middx: AI Jl 75 9/1:30; AN 30 My 75 3/26: 14
United States Army Air Force, vol. 2, Osprey, Reading, Berks: Afx F 74 15 6:367
United States Naval Aviation, 1910-1970, ed Lee M. Pearson, U.S. Government Printing Office, Washington: AE N 71 1/6:318

Air Shows & Races

Aerobatic Teams 1950-1970, by Richard Ward, Arco, NY: AE Jl 72 3/1:154; RT Ag 71 4/8:93; RT Ag 72 5/8:93; Sc O 71 2/10: 559-560; vol. 2: Afx Ag 72 13/12:686
Aerobats in the Sky, by John W. Underwood, Heritage Press, CA: AE D 73 5/6:301
Airshow, by Bill Johnson, Superior, Seattle: AE Jl 72 3/1:52
Baling Wire, Chewing Gum & Guts, the Story of the Gates Flying Circus, by Bill Rhode, Kennikat Press, Port Washington, NY: AE F 73 4/2:89
British Racing & Record-Breaking Aircraft, by Peter Lewis, Putnam, London: AE Je 71 1/1:20; Afx Ap 71 12/8:428
Racing Planes & Air Races 1971, by Reed Kinert, Aero, Fallbrook CA: AI F 75 8/2:93-94; Afx Ja 71 12/5:251; Afx Ap 75 16/8: 498; Sc Ja 75 6/64:33
Red Arrows, by Ray Hanna, Balfour, Photo Precision, Huntingdon: AN 9 N 73 2/13:15; Afx Je 74 15/10:600
Schneider Trophy, by David Mondey, Robert Hale, London: AI O 75 9/4:205

Airlines

Aeroflot--Soviet Air Transport since 1923, by Hugh MacDonald, Putnam, London: AI My 75 8/5:260; AN 21 F 75 3/19:15; Afx Jl 75 16/11:668; Sc Je 75 6/69:294

VI. Reviews 574

Air Travel, by Kenneth Hudson, Adams & Dart, Bath: AE Ap 73 4/3:205

Airlines & Airliners, VHF Supplies, Hounslow, Middx: IM Ja 71 8/1:16

Airlines of the United States since 1914: by R. E. G. Davies, Putnam, London: AE Ja 73 4/1:46; AN 13 O 72 1/11:15; Afx D 72 14/4:225

Airline Pilots: A Study in Elite Unionization, by George E. Hopkins, Harvard University Press, Cambridge, MA: Airline Pilots' Association: AE Mr 73 4/3:139

Annals of Aviation in Iceland 1917-1928, by Arngrimut Sigurdsson, AESKAN, Reykjavik: AE D 73 5/6:315-316

British Independent Airlines & Operators since 1946, by T. Merton Jones, LAAS International: AE F 73 4/2:89

Channel Silver Wings, by Ian Scott-Hall & George Behrend, Jersey Artists, Jersey: AE Ja 73 4/1:46-47

A Dream of Eagles: the Story of the New York, Rio & Buenos Aires Line, by Ralph A. O'Neil, Houghton Mifflin, Boston: AE Mr 74 6/3:149-150

The El Al Story, by Arnold Sherman, Valentine Mitchell, London: AN 14 S 73 2/9:15

Ernest K. Gann's Flying Circus, by Ernest K. Gann, Macmillan, NY: airline piloting: AI Jl 75 9/1:31

Forty Years of Air Transport in Northern Ireland, by John W. Swann, Ulster Folk & Transport Museum: AE O 72 3/4:207

Handling the Big Jets, by D. P. Davies, ARB Technical Publications, Cheltenham: AE Ag 72 3/2:102

Imperial Airways Pilot's Handbook & General Instructions, 1924, Ducimus, London: AI Jl 75 9/1:31

The Munich Air Disaster, by Stanley Williamson, Faber & Faber, London: AE D 73 5/6:301

Observer's World Airlines & Airliners Directory, by William Green & Gordon Swanborough, Frederick Warne, London: AI N 75 9/5:255

Safety Last, by Brian Power-Waters, Millington: PAM Ap 75 9:157

The Sky Pirates, by James A. Arey, Scribners, NY: AE Ag 72 3/2:103

The Skyjacker, His Flights of Fantasy, by David G. Hubbard, Macmillan, NY: AE Ag 72 3/2:103

Biographies

Aces Full, by Robert Grinsel, Sentry, Northridge CA, 1974: WW-II: WW2J S 75 2/5-6:23

Aeronauts & Aviators, by Christopher Elliott, Terence Dalton, Lavenham, Suff: AE Je 71 1/1:20; AE Ja 72 2 /1:42

Air Adventures, by Graeme Cook, Macdonald & Jane's, London: Afx Jl 74 15/11:662

Air Command, by Raymond Collishaw, William Kimber, London:

autobiography: AI Je 75 8/6:305
Aircraft Pioneer, by Lawrence James Wackett, Angus & Robertson, Sydney & London: AE D 72 3/6:315
Airship Pilot No. 28, by T. B. Williams, William Kimber, London: autobiography: AI Mr 75 8/3:155
Barnes Wallis, by J. E. Morpurgo, Penguin: AE Mr 74 6/3:150
The Black Eagle, by John Peer Nugent, Stein & Day, NY: Hubert Julian: AE D 71 1/7:358
Bomber Pilot 1916-1918, by C. P. O. Bartlett, Ian Allan, Shepperton: Sc D 74 5/63:650
Bush Pilot with a Brief Case, by Ronald A. Keith, Doubleday, NY & Toronto: Grant McConachie: AE D 73 5/6:300
Captains & Kings, by Neville Birch & Alan Bramson, Pitman: AE Ja 73 4/1:46
Combat Report, by Bill Lambert, William Kiber, London; autobiography: AE Ap 74 6/4:211
The Eighth Sea, by Frank T. Courtney, Doubleday, NY: autobiography: AE D 72 3/6:315
The Father of the British Airships, by Alec McKinty, William Kimber: T. E. Willows: AE F 73 4/2:90
Flight Path, by Frank T. Courtney, William Kimber, London: autobiography: AN 7 D 73 2/15:15
Flying Between the Wars, by Allen Wheeler, G. T. Foulis, Henley-on-Thames: autobiography: AE Ag 72 3/2:102
Flying Fury, by James T. B. McCudden, Bailey Bros. & Swinfen: autobiography: AI O 74 7/4:202; Afx Jl 74 15/11:662
Flypast, by Arthur Gould Lee, Jarrolds: autobiography: AN 13 D 74 3/14:7
The Forgotten Pilots, by Lettice Curtis, G. T. Foulis, Henley-on-Thames: AE Ja 72 2/1:42
Glenn Curtiss: Pioneer of Flight, by C. R. Roseberry, Doubleday, NY: AE D 72 3/6:315
Glider Pilot, by Peter Champion, MAP, Hemel Hempstead, Herts: AI Jl 74 7/1:49
Gunner's Moon, by John Bushby, Ian Allan, Shepperton, Middx: AE Ja 73 4/1:47; AN 16 F 73 1/20:15; Afx O 72 14/2:105
Hour of Gold, Hour of Lead: Diaries & Letters 1929-1932, by Anne Morrow Lindbergh, Harcourt Brace Jovanovich, NY & London: AE F 74 6/2:97
Igor Sikorsky, by Frank J. Delear, Dodd, Mead, NY: AE D 71 1/7:358
Last Post, by Spike Mays, Eyre Methuen, London: AE Ap 74 6/4:211
Off the Beam, by Robert Chandler, David Rendel, London: AE Je 71 1/1:20
The Riddle of Richard Pearse, by Gordon Ogilivie, A. H. & A. W. Reed, Wellington & London: AE Je 74 6/6:312
Ryan, the Aviator, by William Wagner, McGraw Hill, Maidenhead: AE Je 72 2/6:323
The Skyline is a Promise, by Tom Browne, Rondo, Liverpool: AE Mr 72 2/3:155
Sopwith, the Man & His Aircraft, by Bruce Robertson, Harleyford, Letchworth, Herts: Afx Mr 71 12/7:357

Wiley Post, his Winnie Mae & the World's First Pressure Suit, by
 Stanley R. Hohler & Bobby H. Johnson, U.S. Government Print-
 ing Office, Washington: AE Je 72 2/6:323
Winged Warfare, by William A. Bishop, Bailey Bros. & Swinfen,
 Folkestone, Kent: autobiography: Afx Ag 75 16/12:727
Wings God Gave My Soul, by Joseph W. Noah, pvt, Alexandria VA:
 George E. Preddy: AI Mr 75 8/3:155; IM Mr 75 11/2:17
Wings of War--An Airman's Story of the Last Year of WW-I, by
 Rudolph Stark, Arms & Armour, London: Afx D 73 15/4:249

Color Patterns

ANA Standard Aircraft Colors 1943-1970, Modeler's Journal, Oak-
 land, CA: RT S 72 5/9:106
Aircraft Markings of the World 1912-1967, by Bruce Robertson,
 Harleyford, Letchworth, Herts: AN 16 F 73 1/20:15
Bf 109 Fuselage Markings, 1940, by Michael Payne, pvt, Salisbury,
 Wilts: vol. 1: Afx Jl 74 15/11:662; PAM Ja 74 4:53; WWE
 Mr 75 2/2:65; vol. 2: Afx D 74 16/4:257; PAM Jl 74 6:96;
 WWE Mr 75 2/2:65
Boeing B-17 Flying Fortress, by Rober A. Freeman, Camouflage &
 Markings, Ducimus, London: Sc Jl 72 3/7:380-381
Bombing Colours, British Bomber Camouflage & Markings 1914-
 1937, by Bruce Robertson, Patrick Stephens, London: AE Ja
 73 4/1:46; Afx S 72 14/1:47; RT O 72 5/10:111
Bombing Colours, 1937-1973, by Michael J. F. Bowyer, Patrick
 Stephens, Cambridge: AE My 74 6/5:164; AN 7 D 73 2/15:15;
 Afx N 73 15/3:179; IM O 73 10/10:insert
Bristol Beaufighter, by James Goulding, Camouflage & Markings,
 Ducimus, London: RT Mr 71 4/3:34; Sc Je 71 2/6:302
British Aircraft in USAAF Service 1942-1945, by R. Freeman,
 Camouflage & Markings 21, Ducimus, London: AN 28 S 73 2/
 10:15; Sc O 73 4/10:673
Boulton Paul Defiant, by R. C. Jones, Camouflage & Markings,
 Ducimus, London: RT Mr 71 4/3:34; Sc Je 71 2/6:301
Camouflage & Markings, Ducimus Books, London: series review:
 Afx Ja 71 12/5:251
Civil Aircraft Markings, 1971, by J. W. R. Taylor, Ian Allan, Shep-
 perton: AI O 75 9/4:206; Afx Je 71 12/10:533+; Afx O 75 17/2:
 122; Sc Je 71 2/6:301
Coleurs, Immatriculations et Camouflage des Republic F-84F, by
 Jacques de Kimpe, pvt: AN 9 N 73 2/13:15
De Havilland Mosquito, Camouflage & Markings, Ducimus, London:
 Sc F 71 2/2:72
Douglas Boston/Havoc, Camouflage & Markings, Ducimus, London:
 RT O 71 4/10:117; Sc Jl 71 2/7:346
Erflogsmarkeierungen der Deutschen Luftwaffe 1936-1945 (rudder
 markings): Sc Ap 71 2/4:207-208
Fighter Command Blenheims, Camouflage & Markings, Ducimus, Lon-
 don: RT Ja 71 4/1:12

Fighting Colours 1937-1975, by M. J. F. Bowyer, Patrick Stephens, Cambridge: AN 18 Ap 75 3/23:15; IM Mr 75 11/2:17

Italian Air Force Camouflage in World War II, Le Macchine e la Storia-Profile, STEM-Mucchi, Modena: AI D 75 9/6:308

JP Aircraft Markings 73, by F. E. Bucher & U. Klee, Editions JP, Zurich: airlines: AN 31 Ag 73 2/8:15

Lockheed P-38 Lightning, Camouflage & Markings 18, Ducimus, London: RT N 72 5/11:131

Luftwaffe Camouflage & Markings, by Kennedy Merrick, Kookaburra, Dandenong, Vic: vol. 1: AI D 74 7/6:305; Afx D 73 15/4:249; Sc Ag 74 5/59:441; WWE Ja 74 1/1:111

Luftwaffe Camouflage & Markings--Bombers 1940, Osprey: MW N 72 1/3:160

Luftwaffe Camouflage & Markings Schemes, vols. 1 & 2, by Martin Windrow, Aircam S6 & S8, Osprey, Reading, Berks: Sc Ja 72 3/1:45

Luftwaffe Camouflage of WW-II, by Bryan Philpott, Patrick Stephens, London: AI D 74 7/6:308; AN 28 N 4/13:12; Afx S 75 17/1:54

Luftwaffe Colour Schemes & Markings, vols. 1 & 2, by Martin Windrow, Osprey, Reading, Berks: Afx Jl 71 12/11:589

Luftwaffe Fighter, Bomber, & Marine Camouflage & Markings, 1940, Aircam, Osprey, Reading, Berks: Afx Ja 74 15/5:316; Sc O 73 4/10:672

Markings & Camouflage Systems of the Luftwaffe Aircraft in WW-II, vol. 4, by Karl Ries, Dieter Hoffmann: AE D 72 3/6:315; Sc N 72 3/11:586-587

Markings of the Aces--8th USAF, book 1, by Theodore R. Bennett, Kookaburra: Sc F 71 2/2:74

Martin B-26 Marauder, by Roger A. Freeman, Camouflage & Markings, Ducimus, London: Sc Jl 72 3/6:380-381

North American B-25 Mitchell, by Roger A. Freeman, Ducimus, London: WWE N 74 1/6:170

North American P-51 & F-6 Mustang, Camouflage & Markings 16, by Roger A. Freeman, Ducimus, London: AN 9 Je 72 1/2:15; RT Jl 72 5/7:84; Sc Jl 72 3/7:380-381

RAF Camouflage of WW-II, by Michael J. F. Bowyer, Patrick Stephens, Cambridge: Afx D 75 17/4:242; IM N 75 11/6:25

RAF Fighter Command Northern Europe, 1936-1945, by James Goulding & Robert Jones, Camouflage & Markings, Ducimus, London & Doubleday, NY: AE O 71 1/5:245; Sc Ja 71 2/1:17-18

Republic F-84F Thunderstreak in Belgium Service 1955-1971, Colours, Markings & Camouflage, by Jacques de Kimpe, Brussels: Sc Jl 74 5/58:358

Republic P-47 Thunderbolt, by Roger A. Freeman, Camouflage & Markings, Ducimus, London: AE Jl 71 1/2:91; RT Ap 72 5/4:45; Sc Jl 72 3/7:380-381

Spitfire Markings of the RAAF, by Frank Smith & Peter Malone, Kookaburra, vol. 1: AN 7 Jl 72 1/4:15; Sc F 71 2/2:75; vol. 2: MW S 72 1/1:39; RT O 72 5/10:117; Sc Je 72 3/6:336; WWE N 74 1/6:192

Tomahawk, Airacobra & Mohawk, by R. C. Jones, Camouflage & Markings, Ducimus, London: Sc O 71 2/10:559

USN Color Schemes & Markings, 1911-1950, by Bill C. Kilgrain,

pvt, Dartmouth, NS: RT S 75 8/9:101
World Airline Insignia, by Humphrey Wynn, Hamlyn, London: AN 27 Ap 73 1/25:15

Companies

Amphibian: The Story of the Loening Biplanes, by Grover Loening, New York Graphic Society, Grenwich CN: AE F 74 6/2:97
Armstrong Whitworth Aircraft since 1913, by Oliver Tapper, Putnam, London: AE Jl 73 5/1:43; AN 13 Ap 73 1/24:15; Afx My 73 14/9:511-512
Avro--an Aircraft Album, by E. A. Harbin & G. A. Jenks, Ian Allan, Shepperton: AE Jl 73 5/1:43; Afx Je 73 14/10:565-566
Beagle Aircraft, Midland Counties Aviation Society Research Group, Hinckley, Leich: AI Jl 75 9/1:30; AN 29 N 74 3/13:15
Boeing--An Aircraft Album, by Kenneth Munson & Gordon Swanborough, Ian Allan, Shepperton: AE Je 72 2/6:51; Afx Je 72 13/10:569
Bristol--An Aircraft Album, by James D. Oughton, Ian Allan, London: AN 14 S 73 2/9:15
Bristol Aircraft Since 1910, by C. H. Barners, Putnam, London: AE Je 71 1/2:20
Cessna Guidebook, by Mitch Mayborn & Bob Pickett, Flying Enterprise, Dallas: AI Jl 74 7/1:49
The Curtiss Hawks, by Page Shamburger & Joe Christy, Wolverine Press, Kalamazoo MI: AI Ag 74 7/2:102
The Douglas Commercial Story, ed Peter Berry, Air Britain, Saffron Walden, Essex: AE Mr 72 2/3:154
Fairey Aircraft Since 1915, by H. A. Taylor, Putnam, London: AE Je 74 6/6:312; AN 29 Mr 74 2/22:15; Afx Jl 74 15/11:662
First 500--A Production History of the Islander, Trislander, & Defender, B. N. Historians, Egham, Surrey: AI Jl 75 9/1:30; AN 7 Jl 73 3/18:14
Flying Wings of Northrop, by Leo J. Kohn, Aviation Publications, Milwaukee WI: AI D 75 9/6:308
Fokker Portfolio, Avia, Amsterdam: AE F 73 4/2:89
Gloster Aircraft since 1917, by Derek N. James, Putnam, London: AE Ag 71 1/3:146; Afx Jl 71 12/11:589
Hawker--An Aircraft Album, by Derek N. James, Ian Allan, Shepperton: AE F 73 4/2:90
Hawker Aircraft since 1920, by Francis K. Mason, Putnam, London: Afx My 71 12/9:470
Hawker Siddeley Aviation 1909-1972, Historian Publications, Kogarah, Australia: AN 6 Jl 73 2/4:15
Heinkel--An Aircraft Album, by P. St. John Turner, Ian Allan, Shepperton: AE Jl 71 1/2:91; Sc F 72 2/2:73
Heinkel und Seine Flugzeuge, by Heinz J. Nowarra, J. F. Lehmanns, Munchen: AN 5 S 75 4/7:12
History of Beech Aircraft, by William H. McDanniel, McCormig Armstrong: AE Ag 72 3/2:102

Junkers--An Aircraft Album, by P. St. John Turner & H. J. Nowarra, Ian Allan, Shepperton: AE Je 72 2/6:323; Afx O 71 13/2:105
Lightning in the Skies, the Story of Israel Aircraft Industries, by Arnold Sherman, Stone, London: AN 10 My 74 2/25:7
McDonnell Douglas, pvt by the Company: WWE N 74 1/6:192
Messerschmitt--An Aircraft Album, by J. Richard Smith, Ian Allan, Shepperton: AE O 71 1/5:245; Afx S 71 13/1:33; Sc D 71 2/12:671
Messerschmitt, Aircraft Designer, by Armand van Ishaven, Doubleday, Garden City, NY, 1975: WW2J S 75 2/5-6:22
Miles Aircraft since 1925, by Don L. Brown, Putnam, London: Afx My 71 12/9:470
Robey Aircraft Productions, by John Walls, Aero Litho, Lincoln: AI Ag 75 9/2:86; AN 21 F 75 3/19:15; Afx Je 75 16/10:612
Ruston Aircraft Production, by John Walls, Aero Litho, Newark, Notts: AI O 74 7/4:202; AN 18 O 74 3/10:15; Afx S 74 16/1:52
Sopwith--The Man & His Aircraft, by Bruce Robertson, Air Review, Letchworth: AE Je 71 1/1:20; Afx Mr 71 12/7:357; Sc Ap 71 2/4:208
To Join With the Eagles, by Murray Rubenstein & Richard M. Goldman, Doubleday, NY: Curtiss-Wright: AI F 75 8/2:93; Afx Ja 75 16/5:384; AM Mr 75 75/3:14; RT O 74 7/10:117; RiS Sp 74 2/3-4:159; WWE Ja 75 2/1:28
Vickers Turbine Transports, by D. A. Dorman & A. E. Eastwood, LAAS International, Bracknell, Berks: AI D 74 7/6:306
The Wight Aircraft, by Michael H. Goodall, Gentry Books: Afx Mr 74 15/7:422; Sc Ja 75 6/64:33

Development

The Achievement of the Airship, by Guy Hartcup, David & Charles, Newton Abbot, Devon: AN 2 My 73 3/24:14
Airliners since 1946, by Kenneth Munson, Blandford, London: Sc D 75 6/75:596
British Naval Aircraft Since 1912 (3rd ed), by Owen Thetford, Putnam, London: Afx D 71 13/4:223+
The Dragonflies, by Robert Jackson, Arthur Barker, London: rotarywing: Afx Je 72 13/10:569
Early Aviation at Farnborough, vol. 1, Balloons, Kites, & Airships, by Percy B. Walker, Macdonald, London: Afx S 71 13/1:33
Encyclopedia of Air Warfare, by Christopher Chant, Richard Humble, John F. Davis, Donald Macintyre & Bill Gunston, Salamander, Spring Books, London: AI Jl 75 9/1:30
Fighter, a History of Fighter Aircraft, by John Batchelor & Brian Cooper, Macdonald, London: AN 15 F 74 2/19:16; RCS Jl 75 1/3:62; Sc Jl 74 5/58:358
Flying Boats & Seaplanes Since 1910, by Kenneth Munson, Blandford, London: Afx D 71 13/4:223+
Forgotten Fighters & Experimental Aircraft, 2 vols. by Peter M.

Bowers, Arco, NY: AE O 72 3/4:207
Historic Airships, by Peter W. Brooks, Hugh Evelyn, London: Afx Jl 73 14/11:633-624
History of Air Power, by Basil Collier, Macmillan, NY: WWE N 74 1/6:171
The Lightplane, a Pictorial History 1909-1969, by John W. Underwood & George B. Collinge, Heritage Press, Glendale CA: Afx Ag 71 1/2:629
Polish Aircraft 1893-1939, by Jerzy B. Cynk, Putnam, London: AE O 71 1/5:245; Afx O 71 13/2:75+; Afx Je 72 13/10:569
Project Cancelled, by Derek Wood, Macdonald & Jane's, London: British military aircraft: AI N 75 9/5:254-255
Rebirth of European Aviation, by Charles H. Gibbs-Smith, HMSO, London: effect of Wrights on European aviation development: AI S 75 9/3:151
Russian Aircraft Since 1940, by Jean Alexander, Putnam: Sc N 75 6/74:569
United States Military Aircraft Since 1908, by Gordon Swanborough & Peter M. Bowers, Putnam: Afx Je 72 13/10:569

Directories

Air Distances Manual, TATA & IAL, Southhall, Middx: AI Ja 75 8/1:33
Airlines & Airliners, VHF Supplies, Hounslow, Middx: western jets before 1970: IM Ja 71 8/1:16
Australian Aviation Year Book 1974, by John Stackhouse, Pacific Yearbooks, Sydney: AI O 74 7/4:202
Balloons Around the World--A Register of Hot Air & Gas Balloons, by A. K. Jenkinson, pvt, London: AI O 75 9/4:206; AN 18 O 74 3/10:15
British Airline Fleets: AVSOC Publications, C. R. Shepheard, Farnham, Surrey: Afx Ap 72 13/8:452
British Aviation, ed Peter Lockhart, AVSOC, Farnham, Surrey: AE Mr 73 4/3:139
British Civil Aircraft Registers, by Peter W. Moss, Air Britain, Saffron Walden, Essex: AE Ja 73 4/1:47; AN 18 Ag 72 1/7:14
British Isles Airfield Guide, by Merseyside Society of Aviation Enthusiasts, Liverpool: AN 26 O 73 2/12:15; Afx Ap 72 13/8:452
British Military Aircraft Serials, by Bruce Robertson, Ian Allan, Shepperton: AE Mr 72 2/3:154; Afx Mr 72 13/7:389
Cadet Corps Airframes, Midland Counties Aviation Society, Oadby, Leics: AN 30 My 75 3/26:14
Civil Aircraft Registers of France, ed S. D. Partington, Air Britain, Saffron Walden, Essex: AN 22 Je 73 2/3:15
Civil Aircraft Registers, Southern Europe & Mediterranean, ed David Partington, Air Britain, Saffron Walden: AE Mr 73 4/3:139
Civil Aircraft Registers of West Germany, ed David Partington, Air Britain, Saffron Walden: AN 20 S 74 3/8:10

Belgium, Netherlands, Luxembourg 1973, LAAS International, Dagenham, Essex: AN 22 Je 73 2/3:15

Denmark, Finland, Iceland, Norway, Sweden, 1973, LAAS International, Dagenham, Essex: AN 31 Ag 73 2/8:15

Europa 75, by A. B. Eastwood, LAAS International: AN 25 Jl 75 4/4:12

Fleet Operators 1974, by Jim Birch, Air Britain, Saffron Walden: AN 18 O 74 3/10:15

Flight Directory of British Aviation, 1974, Kelley's Directories: AI O 74 7/4:202

Flight International Airports Guide, ed Roy Allen, IPC Business Press, Kingston-upon-Thames: AI D 74 7/6:306

France 1973, LAAS International, Dagenhem, Essex: AN 22 Je 73 2/3:15

Interavia ABC, Interavia, Geneva: government agencies & manufacturers: AI Ag 75 9/2:86

JP Airline Fleets 74, by F. E. Bucher & U. Klee, Airline Publications, Hounslow: AI Mr 75 8/3:155

JP Airline Fleet 75, by F. E. Bucher & U. Klee, Editions JP, Zurich: AN 27 Je 75 4/2:10

Jet Airliners of the World, ed J. R. Birch, Air Britain, Saffron Walden, Essex: AI O 75 9/4:206

LAAS Civil Aircraft Registers, LAAS International, Usbridge: AN 25 Jl 75 4/4:12

UK & Eire Civil Registers, 1972, comp B. Wormersley, Air Britain, Saffron Walden, Essex: AE Mr 73 4/3:139

UK & Eire Commercial Airports, by P. St. John Turner, Airline Publications: AI Je 75 8/6:305; AN 20 S 74 3/8:10

US Navy Serials 1941-1972, Merseyside Aviation Society, Liverpool: AN 27 Ap 73 1/25:15

US Register Review 1975, by Daniel Willink, Runway Six Nine, Bath: AI Jl 75 9/1:31; AN 13 Je 75 4/1:10

United Kingdom & Eire Civil Registers, ed Bernard Martin & Peter Crittle: AN 23 Ag 74 3/6:5

United States Air Force Serials 1946-1974, comp Peter A. Danby, Merseyside Aviation Society: AN 6 S 74 3/7:15; AN 14 N 75 4/12:12

Vintage Aircraft Directory, 1975, ed Gordon Riley, Battle of Britain Prints, London: Afx N 75 17/3:177

World Airline Record, comp & pub Roadcap & Assoc, Chicago: AE My 75 6/5:259

World Airliner Registrations, by Gordon Swanborough, Ian Allan, Shepperton: AE Jl 71 1/2:91; Afx Ag 71 12/12:629; Sc Jl 71 2/7:346

World Airliner Registrations, by David Mondey, Ian Allan, Shepperton: AI F 75 8/2:94; Afx Je 75 15/10:612-613

Engines

The Aero Manual, 1910, by the staff of The Motor, David & Charles reprint: AE Ja 73 4/1:46

Aircraft Engines of the World 1970, by Paul H. Wilkinson, pvt: AE Jl 72 3/1:52

Album of OX-5 Aircraft, Antique Airplane Association, Ottumwa IO: Sc Ja 71 2/1:14-15

Guide to Pre-1930 Aircraft Engines, comp M. S. Rice, Aviation Publications: AE D 73 5/6:301

The Power to Fly, by L. J. K. Setright, George Allen & Unwin, Hemel Hempstead: AE S 71 1/4:224

Schweizerische Strahlflugzeuge und Strahltriebwerke, by Georges Bridel, Berkhrshause der Schweiz, Lucerne: AI Ag 75 9/2:86

General Aircraft

(General; Several Periods)

Aeronautica Militare Italiana 1923-1973, by Alberto Mondinci & Benedetto Pafi, Etas Compas: AE F 74 6/2:98

Aircraft, by Kenneth Munson, Macdonald, London: AE Mr 72 2/3:155

Aircraft--A Picture History, by Maurice Allward, Pan Books: AE Mr 72 2/3:154-155

Aircraft of the RAAF 1921-1972, by Geoffrey Pentland & Peter Malone, Kookaburra: Sc Ag 72 3/8:448

American Flying Boats, by G. R. Duval, D. Bradford Barton, Truro, Corn: Afx Je 75 16/10:612; Sc Ja 75 6/64:33

Australian Military Aircraft 1909-1971, Australian War Memorial, Canberra: AI Je 75 8/6:305

L'Aviation Française 1914-1940, by E. Moreau-Berillon: Sc Je 72 3/6:336

Bomber, by Len Deighton, Jonathan Cape, London: Afx Ap 71 12/8:428

British Bombers Since 1914, by Peter Lewis, Putnam, London: AI Mr 75 8/3:154-155

British Civil Aircraft Since 1919, by A. J. Jackson, Putnam, London: AE Ap 73 4/4:204; AI D 74 7/6:306; AN 2 Mr 73 1/21:15; vol. 1-3: AN 18 O 74 3/10:15

British Fighters Since 1914, by Peter Lewis, Putnam, London: AI Mr 75 8/3:154-155

British Flying Boats, by G. R. Duval, D. Bradford Barton, Truro, Corn: Afx D 74 16/4:256; Sc Jl 71 2/7:359

British Gliders, ed P. H. Butler, Merseyside Society of Aviation Enthusiasts, Liverpool: AN 25 Jl 75 4/4:12; Afx Ja 71 12/5:251

British Gliders & Sailplanes, 1922-1970, by Norman Ellison, Adams & Charles Black, London: AE S 71 1/4:223

Carrier Fighters, by David Brown, Macdonald & Jane's, London: Afx Ag 75 16/12:727; IM Jl 75 11/4:19; Sc S 75 6/72:441

Encyclopedia of Japanese Aircraft 1900-1945, Orion Books, Tokyo: IM Je 73 10/6:insert

Encyclopedia of Japanese Aircraft, vol. 6, Imported Aircraft, 1900-1945, by Tadashi Nozawa, Shuppan Kyodo, Tokyo: AE O 72 3/4:206

Encyclopedia of U.S. Military Aircraft, 2 vols, by Robert Casari, pvt, Chillicothe OH: AE N 71 1/6:318; vol. 3: AE S 73 5/3:149; vol. 4: AI D 74 7/6:306

Europa Vliegt!, by Hugo Hooftman, Cockpit, Bennekom, Holland: AN 8 D 72 1/15:11

Flying Boats & Seaplanes since 1910, by Kenneth Munson, Blandford, London: AE S 71 1/4:224

Fighter, by Brian Cooper & John Batchelor, Macdonald, London: MM Ap 74 4/4:188

Flyghistroisk Revy, Swedish Aviation Historical Society, Gothenburg: AI O 75 9/4:205; AN 18 Ap 75 3/5:14

Flying Combat Aircraft of the USAAF-USAF, ed Robin Higam & Abigail Siddall, Iowa State University Press, Ames IA, 1975: WW2J S 75 2/5-6:22

Helicopters & Other Rotorcraft since 1907, by Kenneth Munson, Blandford, London: AE F 74 6/2:98; AN 14 S 73 2/9:15

The Jet Age, by Bill Gunston, Arthur Barker: AE Mr 72 2/3:155

The Lightplane, by John W. Underwood & George B. Collinge, Heritage Press, Glendale, CA: AE Jl 71 1/2:91

RAAF Aircraft 1921-1971, Aviation Historical Society of Australia, Sydney: AE Ja 72 2/1:42

Russian Aircraft since 1940, by Jean Alexander, Putnam, London: AI N 75 9/5:254; AN 5 S 75 4/7:12; Afx S 75 17/1:54-55

Sea Wings, by E. A. Jablonski: RT O 72 5/10:115

U.S. Pursuit Aircraft, by G. R. Duval, D. Bradford Barton, Truro, Corn: Afx Je 75 16/10:612; Sc Jl 75 6/70:337

United States Military Aircraft since 1908, by Gordon Swanborough & Peter M. Bowers, Putnam, London: AE O 72 3/4:206

World Flying Boats, by Geoff Duval, D. Bradford Barton, Truro, Corn: AI O 75 9/4:205; Sc Jl 75 6/70:337

Zeldame Villegtulfogotos, by Hugo Hooftman, Cockpit, Bennekom, Holland: AN 27 O 72 1/21:15

(Pre World War I)

Early Flying Machines, 1799-1909, by Charles Gibbs-Smith, Eyre Methuen, Andover, Hants: AI O 75 9/4:205

The First Aeroplanes, by Percy B. Walker, Macdonald & Jane's, London: British developments: AI S 75 9/3:151

Jane's Historical Aircraft 1902-1916, Macdonald, London: AE Mr 73 4/3:138; AN 8 D 72 1/15:11; AN 18 Ja 74 2/17:15; Afx Ap 73 14/8:476

(World War I)

Aircraft & Fliers of the First World War, by Joseph A. Phelan, Patrick Stephens, Cambridge: AI Je 75 8/6:305; AN 27 D 74 3/15:15; Afx N 74 16/3:189; IM Ja 75 11/1:16; Sc Ja 75 6/1:33

VI. Reviews

Aircraft of WW-I, by Kenneth Munson, Ian Allan, Shepperton, 1967: A&W Ja 73 3:13

Bombers 1914-1939, by Bryan Cooper & John Batchelor, Macdonald & Jane's, London: Afx N 74 16/3:190

The Clouds Remember: the Aeroplanes of WW-I: by Leonard Bridgman & Oliver Stewart, Arms & Armour, London: AE F 73 4/2:90; Afx F 73 14/6:338

Early Military Aircraft of the First World War, 3 vols, Flying Enterprises, Dallas: AE N 71 1/6:318

Encyclopedia of U.S. Military Aircraft, Aircraft of WW-I, vol. 1, by Robert Casari, pvt, Chillicothe OH: AE Jl 72 3/1:51; vol. 12, the WW-I Production Program: AE My 74 6/5:164

German Aircraft of the First World War, by Peter Gray & Owen Thetford, Putnam, London: AE Ag 71 1/3:46; Afx My 71 12/9:470; RT Ap 71 4/4:46

Ideas & Weapons, Exploitation of the Aerial Weapon by the United States During World War I, by I. B. Holley, Jr., Archon Books, Hamden CN: AE Jl 72 3/1:52

Jane's Historical Aircraft 1902-1916, Macdonald, London: AE Mr 73 4/3:148; AN 8 D 72 1/15:11; AN 18 Ja 74 2/17:15; Afx Ap 73 14/8:455

Military Aircraft of Australia, 1909-1918, by Keith Isaacs, Australian War Memorial, Canberra: AE O 72 3/4:206

War Birds: Military Aircraft of the First World War in Colour, Macdonald & Jane's, London: Sc F 75 6/65:71

Warplanes of the First World War, Fighters, vol. 4&5, by J. M. Bruce, Macdonald, London: AE Je 72 2/6:323; Afx Je 72 13/10:569

(Between World Wars)

Airliners Between the Wars 1919-1939, by Kenneth Munson, Blandford, London: AE F 73 4/2:90; AN 27 O 72 1/12:15; Afx F 73 14/6:338

Bombers 1914-1939, by Bryan Cooper & John Batchelor, Macdonalds & Jane's, London: Afx N 74 16/3:190

Jane's All the World's Aircraft, 1938, ed C. G. Grey & Leonard Bridgeman, David & Charles Reprint, London: AE Mr 73 4/3:138

U.S. Pursuit Aircraft 1918-1936, by G. R. Duval, D. Bradford Barton, Truro, Corn: AI O 75 9/4:205

(World War II)

American Bombers of WW-II, vol. 1, by Roger A. Freeman, Hylton Lacey, Windsor: AN 2 Mr 73 1/21:15

American Fighters of WW-II, vol. 2, Men & Machines: RT S 72 5/9:99; Sc D 72 3/12:654-655

Arctic War Birds, by Stephen E. Mills, Superior, Seattle: AE Jl 72 3/1:52; WWE Mr 74 1/2:49

L'Aviation Française 1939-1940, by Gaston Botquin, Rossel, Brussel:

Sc Jl 5/58:358

British Fighters of World War 2, vol. 1, by Francis K. Mason, Hylton Lacy, Windsor, Berks: Afx Ja 71 12/5:251

Bombers 1939-1945, by Bryan Cooper & John Batchelor, Macdonalds & Jane's, London: AN 9 Ag 74 3/5:14; Afx N 74 16/3:190

Fifty Fighters, 1938-1945, by Richard War, Aircam S17 & 18, Osprey, Reading, Berks: Afx Je 74 15/10:600; RiS Sp 74 2/3-4: 158

French Fighters of WW-II, Men & Machines: RT My 72 5/5:51

German Aircraft of the Second World War, by J. R. Smith & Antony Kay, Putnam, London: AE My 73 4/5:358-359; AN 10 N 72 1/13:13; Afx N 72 14/3:164-165

German Combat Planes, by Ray Wagner & Heinz Nowarra: RT D 71 4/12:145

German Fighters of World War 2, vol. 2, by Martin Windrow, Hylton Lacy, Windsor, Berks: Afx Ja 71 12/5:251

Jane's All the World's Aircraft 1945-6, ed Leonard Bridgman, David & Charles, Devon: AE Je 71 1/1:20

Luftwaffe Bombers in Action, by Use Feist, Squadron/Signal, Warren MI: AN 2 Mr 73 1/21:15

Luftwaffe in Detail, by IPMS-Canada, Ottawa: IM D 71 8/12:insert

Military Aircraft 1939-1945, by Roy Cross, Hugh Evelyn, London: AE F 72 2/2:86; Afx O 71 13/2:75; Sc O 72 3/10:552-553

RAF Righters of WW-II, by Alan W. Hall, Patrick Stephens, Cambridge: AI Ag 75 9/2:87; Afx My 75 16/9:553; IM My 75 11/3: 9; PAM Ja 75 8:136; Sc Jl 75 6/70:337

Das Waren die Deutschen Kriegsflugzeuge, 1935-1945, by Ulrich Elfrath, Podzun, Dorhein: AI D 74 7/6:306

(Post World War II)

Gli Aerie X, by Nico Scarlato, Delta, Parma: AN 26 D 75 4/15: 14

Aircraft Annual 1972, ed J. W. R. Taylor, Ian Allan, Shepperton: Afx Ja 72 13/5:255

Aircraft 1973, ed J. W. R. Taylor, Ian Allan, Shepperton: AE F 73 4/2:89; Afx N 72 14/3:165-166; Afx Je 75 16/10:612

Aircraft 1974, ed John W. R. Taylor, Ian Allan, Shepperton: Afx D 73 15/4:249

Aircraft 75, ed J. W. R. Taylor, Ian Allan, Shepperton: AI Je 75 8/6:305; Sc Ja 75 6/64:32

Aircraft of the Indian Air Force, by Pushpindar Singh Chopra, English Book Store, New Delhi: AI Jl 75 9/1:31; AN 25 Jl 75 4/4:12

Aircraft of the Vietnam War, by Lou Drendel, Arco, NY: AE F 72 2/2:84

Aircraft Seventy-One: ed John W. R. Taylor, Ian Allan, Shepperton: Afx Ap 71 12/8:409

Airliners Since 1946, by Kenneth Munson, Blandford, Poole, Dorset: AI D 75 9/6:309; AN 14 N 75 4/12;12; PAM O 75 11:197

Attack Aircraft of the West, by Bill Gunston, Ian Allan, Shepperton: Afx O 75 17/2:122

VI. Reviews

Les Avions du Monde, by Robert J. Roux, Editions La Rivière, Paris: AN 18 Ap 75 3/23:15
Biz-Jet 73, by B. Gates, Airline Publications, Hounslow, Middx: AN 19 Ja 73 1/19:13
Biz-Jet 75, by Brian Gates, Airline Publications, Hounslow, Middx: AN Ja 75 3/16:15
Bombers of the West, by Bill Gunston, Ian Allan, Shepperton: AI Jl 74 7/1:49; Afx Mr 74 15/7:421
Civil Aircraft, by Garry May, Lutterworth, Guildford: AI Jl 75 9/1:31
Civil Aircraft of the World, by John W. R. Taylor & Gordon Swanborough, Ian Allan, Shepperton: AI Jl 75 9/1:30; Afx Ag 72 13/12:686
Fighters in Service, by Kenneth Munson, Blandford, London: AI D 75 9/6:309; Sc D 75 6/75:596
Jane's All the World's Aircraft, 1971-72, ed John W. R. Taylor, Jane's Yearbooks, London: AE F 72 2/2:84
Jane's All the World's Aircraft, 1972-73, ed John W. R. Taylor, Sampson Low, Marston: AE Ja 73 4/1:47
Jane's All the World's Aircraft, 1973-74, ed John W. R. Taylor, Sampson Low, Marston: AE My 74 6/5:164
Jane's All the World's Aircraft, 1974-75, ed John W. R. Taylor, Macdonald & Jane's, London: AI F 75 8/2:95; AN 26 D 75 4/15:14; Sc Je 75 6/69:294
Military Aircraft of the World, by John W. R. Taylor & Gordon Swanborough, Ian Allan, Shepperton: AE O 71 1/5:245; Afx N 73 15/3:179-180; Sc F 72 3/2:100
Military Transport & Training Aircraft, Jane's Pocket Books, ed John W. R. Taylor, Macdonald & Jane's, London: AI D 74 7/6:306
Moderne Kampfflugzeuge in Westeuropa, by Peter Doll, J. F. Lehmanns, Munich: AN 22 Ag 75 4/6:10
RAF Jet Bomber Flypast, by Philip J. R. Moyes, Ian Allan, Shepperton: Afx Ag 74 15/12:723
RAF Jet Fighter Flypast, by P. J. R. Moyes, Ian Allan, Shepperton: Afx F 73 14/6:338
Ship & Aircraft of the U.S. Fleet, 9th ed, by John S. Rowe & Samuel L. Morison, Naval Institute Press, Annapolis: AE Ag 72 5/2:102; Afx My 72 13/9:487
The World's Airliners, by John Stroud, Bodley Head, London: Afx Jl 71 12/11:589
The World's Fighters, by H. F. King, Bodley Head, London: Afx Jl 71 12/11:589
World's Strike Aircraft, by H. F. King, Putnam, London: Afx My 73 14/9:511

Identification

Airplanes of the World, by Douglas Rolfe & Alexis Dawydoff, William Kimber, London: Afx Ag 71 12/12:623+

Civil Aircraft of the World, by J. W. R. Taylor & Gordon Swanborough, Ian Allan, Shepperton: AE O 72 3/4:207; Afx My 75 16/9:554

Civil Airliner Recognition, by John W. R. Taylor, Ian Allan, Shepperton: AI O 75 9/4:206; Afx S 71 13/1:20

Commercial Transport Aircraft, ed John W. R. Taylor, Jane's Pocket Books 3, Macdonald & Jane's, London: AE Je 74 6/6:312; AN 29 Mr 74 2/22:15; Afx My 74 15/9:539

Enthusiast's Guide to British Aviation, ed Peter Lockhart, AVSOC, Farnham, Surrey: Afx Mr 73 14/7:399-400

House's Guide to Light Aircraft, 1973, ed Alexander Barrie, House Information Services: AE D 73 5/6:300

Jane's Pocket Book of Light Aircraft, Madconald & Jane's, London: Sc D 75 6/75:596

Light Plane Recognition, by John W. R. Taylor, Ian Allan, Shepperton: AI Ag 75 9/4:206; Afx Ag 72 13/12:686

Major Combat Aircraft, ed John W. R. Taylor, Jane's Pocket Books 2, Macdonald & Jane's, London: AE Je 74 6/6:312; AN 29 Mr 74 2/22:15

Major Combat Aircraft, ed John W. R. Taylor, Jane's Pocket Books 4, Macdonald & Jane's, London: Afx Ap 74 15/8:479

Military Aircraft of the World, John W. R. Taylor & Gordon Swanborough, Ian Allan, Shepperton: Afx S 71 13/1:33

Military Transport & Training Aircraft, ed John W. R. Taylor, Jane's Pocket Books 5, Macdonald & Jane's, London: Afx D 74 16/4:256

Observer's Basic Civil Aircraft Directory, by William Green & Gordon Swanborough, Frederick Warne, London: AI Mr 75 8/3:155; Afx Ap 75 16/8:498; Sc F 75 6/65:71

Observer's Basic Military Aircraft Directory, by William Green & Gordon Swanborough, Frederick Warne, London: AE My 74 6/5:164; Afx Ap 74 15/8:479

Observer's Book of Aircraft, by William Green, F. Warne, London: AI Jl 75 9/1:30-31; Afx Je 71 12/10:533+

Observer's Soviet Aircraft Directory, comp William Green & Gordon Swanborough, Frederick Warne, London: AI My 75 8/5:260; Afx Je 75 16/10:612

The World's Bombers, by H. F. King, Bodley Head, London: Afx Mr 72 13/7:389

The World's Civil Marine Aircraft, by John Stroud, Bodley Head, London: AN 5 S 75 4/7:12

The World's Helicopters, by Joan Bradbrooke, Bodley Head, London: AN 3 O 75 4/9:12; Afx Je 72 13/10:569

Individual Aircraft

Comparisons

Bf-109E-3 vs. Spitfire IA, Fighter Combat Comparison 2, Tacitus, Teaneck NJ: AE N 73 5/5:250

Curtiss P-40CC vs. Mitsubishi A6M2, Fighter Combat Comparison 1, Tacitus, Teaneck, NJ: AE Ap 73 4/4:205

Publication Surveys & Collections

Action Profiles, Profile, Windsor, Berks: AN 19 Ja 73 1/18:13
Aeroplani d'Italia, Giorgio Melocchi, Milan: Sc Ja 71 2/1:15
Aircraft in Profile, vol. 2, Profile, Windsor, Berks: Afx Mr 73 14/7:400
Aircraft in Profile, vol. 11, Profile, Windsor: MW F 73 1/6:331
Aircraft in Profile, vols. 12 & 13, Profile, Windsor: Afx Ag 74 15/12:724
Aircraft in Profile, vol. 14, ed Charles W. Cain, Doubleday, Garden City, NY, 1975: AI Ag 75 9/2:87; AN 13 Je 75 4/1:10; WW2J S 75 2/5-6:22
Flying Wartime Aircraft, ed Hugh Bergel, David & Charles, Newton Abbot, Devon: Ferry pilot's instruction booklets: Sc Ja 75 6/64:33
...In Action series, Squadron/Signal, Warren MI: AE D 73 5/6:300
Luftfahrt-Geschichte 1-8 series, Schmidt-Publickation, Stuttgart: AN 9 Ag 74 3/5:14; Afx O 73 15/2:116; RT Ag 73 6/8:93
Pilot's & Flight Engineer's Notes, survey of reprints: Afx Mr 72 13/7:389+

By Periods

(World War I)

De Havilland DH9A, by Chaz Bowyer, Profile 248, Windsor, Berks: AN 2 Mr 73 1/21:15; Afx Jl 73 14/11:623

(Between World Wars)

Boeing P-26 Peashooter, by Edward T. Maloney, Aero, Fallbrook CA, 1973: Afx Ap 74 15/8:479; Sc Ag 74 5/59:441; WWE Mr 75 2/2:65
Brewster B-239 ja Humu, by Kalevi Keskinen, Kari Stenman, & Laus Niska, Helsinki: AE S 71 1/4:224; AN 39 My 75 3/26:14; Sc Ja 71 2/1:13
Brewster Buffalo, by Chris Shores, Profile 217, Windsor, Berks: Sc Ja 71 2/1:17
Bristol Bulldog, by Alfred Granger, Data Plans 2, Visual Art Productions, Oxford: AN 12 O 74 2/11:15; Afx My 74 6/5:539
Bristol F2B Fighters, RAF 1918-1932, Profile 237, Windsor, Berks: RT Ag 72 5/8:95; Sc O 72 3/10:555
Bücker Bü 131 Jungmann: Profile 222, Windsor, Berks: RT Mr 71 4/3:34
DC-3, by Arthur Pearcy, Ballantine: AN 12 D 75 4/14:7
Fokker D. XXI, by Kalevi Keskinnen, Kari Stenma, & Klaus Niska, Tietotoes, Helsinki: AN 10 Ja 75 3/16:15; RT Je 75 8/6:62;

Sc Ja 75 6/64:33

Hawker Woodcock/Danecock Series, by A. Granger, Data Plans 1, Taurus, Oxford: AE Jl 73 5/1:43; AN 25 My 73 2/1:15

The Hindenburg, by Michael M. Mooney, Dodd, Mead, NY: AE Ag 72 3/2:103

IK Fighters (Yugoslavia), by Sime I. Ostric & Cedomir J. Janic, Profile 242, Windsor, Berks: Afx Je 73 14/10:565

Lubin R.XIII Variants, Profile 231, Windsor, Berks: RT Ja 72 5/1:4; Sc Ag 72 3/8:449

PZL P.37 Los, by Jerzy B. Cynk, Profile 258, Windsor, Berks: AN 1 F 74 2/18:15

Ryan Broughams & Their Builders, by William Wagner, W. E. Hersant, London: AI F 75 8/2:94-95; Afx Ap 75 16/8:498; Sc Ja 75 6/64:33

Udet (BFW) U-12 Flamingo variants, by Armand van Ishoven, Profile 157, Windsor, Berks: AN 29 Mr 74 2/22:15

Vickers Wellesley Variants, by Norman Barfield, Profile 256, Windsor: AN 1 F 74 2/18:15

(World War II)

(Germany)

The Augsburg Eagle (Fw 190), by William Green, Macdonald, London: AE F 72 2/2:85-86

Dornier Do 17Z/Junkers Ju 88A-4, by Kalevi Keskinen, pvt, Helsinki: AE S 71 1/4:224; Sc Ja 72 3/1:44

Dornier Do 217 variants, by Alfred Price, Profile 261, Windsor, Berks: AN 20 S 74 3/8:10

FW 190A-8 Aircraft Handbook, technical manual trans by George G. Hopp, Valkyrie, Ottawa: AI D 75 9/6:309; AN 10 My 74 2/25:7; Afx Ag 74 15/12:723-724; PAM O 74 7:117; Sc N 75 6/74:569; WWE My 74 1/3:75-76

Fiesler Fi 156 Storch, by Richard P. Bateson, Profile 228, Windsor, Berks: Sc Jl 72 3/7:381

Focke Wulf Fw 190 in Action, by Jerry L. Campbell, Squadron/Signal, Warren MI: AI Ag 75 9/2:87; RiS Jl 75 3/2:102

Heinkel He 111 in Action, by Uwe Feist, Squadron/Signal, Warren MI: AN 27 Ap 73 1/25:15

Heinkel He 177 Greif, Profile 234, Windsor, Berks: RT Je 72 5/6:66; Sc Ag 72 3/8:449

Heinkel He-219 Uhu, by Richard P. Pateson, Profile 219, Windsor, Berks: RT F 71 4/2:15+; Sc F 71 2/2:73

Junkers Ju 52 in Action, Squadron/Signal, Warren, MI: AN 26 O 2/12:15

Junkers Ju 87 Stuka, by G. Borelli, A. Borgiotti, R. Caruana, G. Pini, & C. Gori, STEM-Mucchi, Modena: AI Ja 75 8/1:33; AN 9 Ag 74 3/5:14; Afx O 74 16/2:116

Junkers Ju 88 in Action, by Uwe Feist, Squadron/Signal, Warren MI: AI Ag 74 7/2:202

Junkers Ju 287, by Thomas H. Hitchcock, Monogram Aviation, Acton MA: RiS Jl 75 3/2:101; Sc Jl 75 6/70:337

Junkers Ju 288, by Thomas H. Hitchcock, Monogram Aviation, Ac-

ton MA: RiS Jl 75 3/2:101
Junkers Ju 290, by Thomas H. Hitchcock, Monogram Aviation, Acton MA: Sc O 75 6/73:506
Messerschmitt Bf 109B, C, D, E, by Francis K. Mason, Aircam, Osprey, Reading, Berks: Afx Ag 73 14/12:682; Sc O 73 4/10: 672-673
Messerschmitt Bf 109B, C, D, E, F, G in Luftwaffe & Finnish Service, Aircam 43, Osprey, Reading, Berks: Afx S 74 16/1:53
Messerschmitt Bf 109F-G in Luftwaffe & Foreign Service, by Francis K. Mason, Aircam, Osprey, Reading, Berks: Afx Ag 73 14/12:682; Sc O 73 4/10:672-673
Messerschmitt Bf 109 Luftwaffe Experten, Aircam 42, Osprey, Reading, Berks: Afx S 74 16/1:53
Messerschmitt Bf 109 versions B to E, by Roy Cross & Gerald Scarborough, Patrick Stephens, London: AE My 73 4/5:258; AN 10 N 72 1/13:13; Afx N 72 14/3:164; MW D 72 1/4:211
Messerschmitt 'O-Nine' Gallery, by Thomas H. Hitchcock, Monogram Aviation, Acton MA: AI D 74 7/6:305-306; WWE My 74 1/3:76
Messerschmitt Me 163 Komet, Profile 225, Windsor, Berks: Afx D 71 13/4:227; RT S 71 4/9:98; Sc O 71 2/10:560
Nights of the Black Cross, by Joseph Mizrahi, Aviation Books: Bf 109 & Fw 190: AM F 75 75/2:14+
Rocket Fighter (Me 163 Komet), by William Green, Ballantine, NY: AE Ag 71 1/3:224
Stuka at War, by Peter C. Smith, Ian Allan, Shepperton, Middx: Afx Ap 71 12/8:428; Sc Jl 71 2/6:346
Stuka: Junkers Ju 87, by Richard P. Bateson, Ducimus, London: AE My 73 4/5:259

(Italy)
Caproni Reggiane Re 2001 Falco II, Le Macchine e la Storia-Profile, STEM-Mucchi, Modena: AI D 75 2/6:308
Caproni Reggiane Re 2001 Falco II, Re 2002 Ariete, & Re 2005 Sagittario, by John F. Brindley, Profile 244, Windsor, Berks: AN 19 Ja 73 1/18:13; RT D 72 5/12:139
Macchi MC 202 Folgore, Le Macchine e la Storia-Profile, STEM-Mucchi, Modena: AI D 75 2/6:308
Savoia Marchetti SM 79 Sparviero, Le Macchine e la Storia-Profile, STEM-Mucchi, Modena: AI D 75 2/6:308

(Japan)
Aichi D3A (Val) & Yokosuka D4Y (Judy), Profile 241, Windsor, Berks: AN 27 O 72 1/12:15; RT N 72 5/11:126
Kawanishi Flying Boats, Profile 233, Windsor, Berks: RT Ap 72 5/4:66; Sc Ag 72 3/8:449
Kawanishi N1K Kyofu/Rex & Shinden/George, by Rene J. Francillon, Profile 213, Windsor, Berks: Sc Ja 71 2/1:17
Kawasaki Ki 48-I/II Sokei, comp Richard M. Bueschel, Aircam, Osprey, Reading, Berks: Afx S 72 14/1:47-48
Kawasaki Ki 61/Ki 100 Hein: by Richard M. Bueschell, Aircam 21, Osprey, Reading, Berks: Afx S 71 13/1:20+; Sc F 72 3/2:101
Ki 27a & b, Manshu Ki 79: Aircam, Osprey, Reading, Berks: RT

Ja 71 4/1:12

Mitsubishi A6M5 to A6M8 Zero-Sen, by M. C. Richards & Donald S. Smith, Profile 236, Windsor, Berks: Sc O 72 3/10:506

Mitsubishi, Nakajima G3M1/2/3, Kusho L3Y1/2 in Japanese Naval Air Service, by Richard M. Bueschel, Aircam, Osprey, Reading, Berks: Afx Je 73 14/10:565

Nakajima Ki 27A-B Manshu Ki 79A-B, by Richard M. Bueschell, Aircam 18, Osprey, Reading, Berks: Sc F 71 2/2:73

Nakajima Ki-44 Shoki (Tojo), by John F. Brindley, Profile 255, Windsor, Berks: AN 28 S 73 2/10:15; MW Ja 74 2/5:268; RT D 71 4/12:134

(USSR)

Petlyakov Pe-2, Profile 216, Windsor, Berks: RT My 71 4/5:51; Sc S 71 2/9:500

(U.K.)

Airspeed Oxford, Profile 227, Windsor, Berks: RT Ja 72 5/1:9

Avro Anson Mks I, II, III, IV & X, by Alan W. Hall & Eric Taylor, Almark, New Malden: MW S 72 2/1:52

Avro Manchester, by Chaz Bowyer, Profile 260, Windsor, Berks: AN 10 My 74 2/25:7; Afx Jl 74 15/11:662

The Blackburn Shark, by Carl Vincent, Canada's Wings, Stittsville, Ont: AI Ag 75 9/2:86-87; AN 21 Mr 75 3/21:12; Afx Ap 75 16/8:498; IM My 75 11/3:9; RT Ja 75 8/1:3; Sc Je 75 6/69:294; WW2J S 75 2/5-6:22

Bristol Blenheim IV, by James D. Oughton, Profile 218, Windsor, Berks: Sc Ja 71 2/1:17

De Havilland Mosquito, vol. 1, comp Richard Ward, Aircam, Osprey, Reading, Berks: Afx S 72 14/1:47-48

Fairey Barracuda Mks I/V: Profile 240, Windsor, Berks: Afx Mr 73 14/7:400; RT O 72 5/10:115

Fairey Fulmar Mks I & II, by David Brown, Profile 254, Windsor, Berks: AN 14 S 73 2/9:15

Fairey Swordfish, by Ian G. Scott, Profile 213, Windsor, Berks: Sc Ja 71 2/1:16-17

Handley Page Halifax Crash Log, Warplane Wreck Investigation Group, Wigan, Lancs: AN 13 Je 75 4/1:10; Afx Jl 75 16/11:668

Hawker Hurricane, by Bruce Robertson & Gerald Scarborough, Patrick Stephens, Cambridge: AI D 74 7/6:306; AN 26 Jl 74 3/4:5; Afx Je 74 15/10:599; Sc Ag 74 5/59:440-441

Hawker Hurricane Described, by Francis K. Mason, Kookaburra, Dandenong, Vic: Sc Ja 71 2/1:12; WWE N 74 1/6:171

Hawker Hurricane, by Bruce Robertson & Gerald Scarborough, Patrick Stephens, Cambridge: AI D 74 13/6:339; AN 26 Jl 74 3/4:5; Afx Je 74 15/10:599; Sc Ag 74 5/59:440-441

Hurricane at War, by Chaz Bowyer, Ian Allan, Shepperton: AI O 75 9/4:206; Afx Ap 75 16/7:441; Sc Je 75 6/69:294

Hurricane Special, by Maurice Allward, Ian Allan, Shepperton, Middx: AI D 75 9/6:309

The Lancaster At War, by Mike Garbett & Brian Goulding, Ian Allan, Shepperton: AE Ja 72 2/1:41; Afx N 71 13/3:138+; Sc F 72 3/2:102

Malta Spitfire, by George Buerling & Leslie Roberts, Arms & Armour, London: AN 26 O 73 2/12:15

Miles Magister, by G. H. R. Johnson, Newark Air Museum, Newark, Notts: AE Je 72 2/6:323

Mosquito, by C. Martin Sharp & Michael J. F. Bowyer, Faber & Faber: AE F 72 2/2:84; Afx N 71 13/3:138

Mosquito at War, by Chaz Bowyer, Ian Allan, Shepperton: AE Mr 74 6/3:149; Afx Mr 74 6/3:421-422; Sc Jl 74 5/58:359

Mosquito, Wooden Wonder, by Edward Bishop, Ballantine, NY: AE Ag 72 3/2:52; WWE Mr 74 1/2:49-50

Pilot's Notes: Spitfire, Hurricane, Mosquito, Wellington, Lancaster, reprints of WW-II pilot's manuals, Sapphire, Essex: AE F 72 2/2:86

Seafire, by David Brown, Ian Allan, Shepperton: AE S 73 5/3:149; Afx Ag 73 14/12:682

Short Stirling Remembered, Visual Art Productions, Oxford: AN 26 Jl 74 3/4:5; Afx D 74 16/4:256; WW2J Jl 75 2/4:35

Spitfire, by Roy Cross & Gerald Scarborough, Patrick Stephens: AE F 72 2/2:86; AN 17 Ag 73 2/7:11; Afx Ja 72 13/5:255; MW Jl 73 1/11:587; RT Je 73 6/6:61; Sc O 72 3/10:553

Spitfire at War, by Alfred Price, Ian Allan, Shepperton: AI Mr 75 8/3:154; Afx Mr 75 16/7:441; Sc Je 75 6/69:294

Spitfire Special, by Ted Hooten, Ian Allan, Shepperton: AE Jl 72 3/1:52; AN 9 Je 72 1/2:15; Afx Je 72 13/10:546; Sc O 72 3/10:552

The Story of a Lanc, comp Brian Goulding, Mike Garbett & John Partridge, RAF Scampton, Lincoln: Afx D 74 16/4:256-257

Supermarine Seafire (Merlins), by Len Bachelor, Profile 221, Windsor, Berks: Afx My 71 12/9:470; RT Mr 71 4/3:34; Sc Je 71 2/6:334

Supermarine Spitfire, by Peter Moss, Ducimus, London: AE Jl 71 1/2:91; Sc F 72 2/2:75

Supermarine Spitfire (Griffons) Mks XIV & XVIII, by L. J. Bachelor, Profile 246, Windsor, Berks: AN 8 D 72 1/15; RT F 73 6/2:24

Supermarine Walrus I & Seagull Variants, by David Brown, Profile 224, Windsor, Berks: Sc Jl 71 2/7:334

Typhoon & Tempest at War, by Arthur Reed & Roland Beamont, Ian Allan, Shepperton: AI F 75 8/2:95; AN 15 N 74 3/12:15; Afx F 75 16/6:384; Sc Ja 75 6/64:32

Wellington Special, by Alec Lunsden, Ian Allan, Shepperton: Afx Ap 75 16/8:498

Westland Whirlwind, by Bruce Robertson, Kookaburra: Sc F 71 2/2:74

(U.S.)

B-17B-H, by Ernest R. McDowel & Richard Ward, Aircam 15, Osprey, Reading, Berks: Sc Ja 71 2/1:16

B-17 in Action, by Steve Birdsall, Squadron/Signal 12, Warren MI: AI Mr 75 8/3:155; AN 15 F 74 2/19:15

B-24 Liberator in Action, by Steven Birdsall, Squadron/Signal, Warren MI: AI D 75 9/6:308; Afx O 75 17/2:122; RiS Jl 75 3/2:103

B-24D, by Steve Birdsall, Eagle Aviation, NJ: AE D 72 3/6:316
The Dakota, by Arthur Pearcy, Jr., Ian Allan, Shepperton, Middx: AE Ja 73 4/1:47; Afx D 72 14/4:225-226
Dakota I-IV, by Arthur Pearcy, Jr., Profile 220, Windsor, Berks: RT Ja 71 4/1:12; Sc Ap 71 2/4:206-207
Douglas R4D Variants (USN DC-3/C-47), by Arthur Pearcy, Jr., Profile 249, Windsor, Berks: AN 2 Mr 73 1/24:15; MW My 73 1/9:495
Douglass TBD-1 Devastator, by B. R. Jackson & T. E. Doll, Aero, Fallbrook, CA: Afx Ap 74 15/8:479; WWE My 74 1/3:75
Flying Fortress, by Edward Jablonski, Sidgwick & Jackson: AI Mr 75 8/3:155
Grumman Hellcat, by Richard M. Hill & Richard Ward, Aircam 19, Osprey, Reading, Berks: Afx Jl 71 12/11:589; RT F 72 5/2:21; Sc Je 71 2/6:301
Grumman TBF/TBM Avenger, by B. R. Jackson & T. E. Doll, Aero, Fallbrook, CA: Afx Mr 71 12/7:357+
Lockheed Hudson Mks I-VI, by Christopher F. Shores, Profile 253, Windsor, Berks: AN 22 Je 73 2/3:15
Log of the Liberators: An Illustrated History of the B-24, by Steve Birdsall, Doubleday, NY: AE F 74 6/2:98
Martin Maryland & Baltimore, Profile 232, Windsor, Berks: RT Mr 72 5/3:33; Sc Jl 72 2/10:560
Mustang at War, by Roger A. Freeman, Ian Allan, Shepperton: AI F 75 8/2:95; Afx Mr 74 15/7:421-422; Afx Ja 75 16/5:232; Afx Jl 75 16/11:667-668
P-40 Kittyhawk in Service, by Geoffrey Pentland, Kookaburra, Dandenong, Vic, 1974: WW2J S 75 2/4-5:22
P-51 Mustang, by G. Borelli, A. Borgiotti, C. Gori, & G. Pini, STEM-Mucchi, Modena: AE F 74 6/2:98; AN 28 S 73 2/10:15; Afx S 73 15/1:54; RT Je 73 6/6:69
P-51 Mustang, by Roy Cross & Gerald Scarborough, Patrick Stephens, London: AE N 73 5/5:250; AN 17 Ag 73 2/7:11; Afx Je 73 14/10:565; MW Jl 73 1/11:587; RT Je 73 6/6:61; WWE N 74 1/6:170
Republic P-47 Thunderbolt Described, pt. 1, by Geoff Duval, Kookaburra, Dandenong, Vic: WWE N 74 1/6:171; pt. 2: Sc Ja 71 2/1:12-13
Republic Thunderbolt in Action, by Gene B. Stafford, Squadron/Signal, Warren MI: AI Ag 75 9/2:87; RiS Jl 75 3/2:102
Stearman Guidebook, by Mitch Mayborn & Peter M. Bowers, Flying Enter-Prise, Dallas: AE Ag 72 3/2:102-103
The Story of the PBY Catalina, by Ray Wagner, Flight Classics: Afx Ap 74 15/8:479
Supplement to Grumman TBF/TBM Avenger, by B. R. Jackson & T. E. Doll, Aero, Fallbrook, CA: Afx Ag 71 12/12:623
The Unknown Mustangs (P-51A), by John R. Beaman, pvt, Greensboro NC: IM S 75 11/5:14; RT S 75 8/9:99; Sc N 75 6/74:569
Vought F4U-1/7 Corsair, Aircam 23, Osprey, Reading, Berks: RT Jl 71 4/7:75; Sc O 71 2/10:560
Vought Sikorsky OS2U Kingfisher, by T. E. Doll & B. R. Jackson, Profile 251, Windsor, Berks: AN 18 Ag 72 1/7:14; Afx S 72 14/1:48; RT N 72 5/11:131; Sc D 72 3/12:655

VI. Reviews 594

(Post World War II--Civil)

Aerospatiale/BAC Concorde, by Norman Barfield, Profile 250, Windsor, Berks: AN 17 Ag 73 2/7:11; Afx Ja 74 15/5:316
BAC One-Eleven, by D. Dorman, LAAS International, Luton Beds: AN 8 D 72 1/15:11
Boeing 707 & 720, ed John A. Whittle, Air Britain, Saffron Walden, Essex: AE Ap 73 4/4:205; AN 19 Ja 73 1/18:13
Boeing 747, pt. 1, comp Jim Lucas, Airline Publications, Hounslow, Middx: AE F 72 2/2:86; AN 19 Ja 73 1/18:13; pt. 2: AN 21 Mr 75 3/19:15
The Concorde Fiasco, by Andrew Wilson, Penguin, London: AE Mr 74 6/3:150
Convair Transports CV240-990, by A. B. Eastwood, LAAS International, Luton, Beds: AN 27 Ap 73 1/25:15
DC-10, comp Jim Lucas, Airline Publications, Hounslow, Middx: AN 1 F 74 2/18:15
The Douglas DC-6 & DC-7 Series, comp John A. Whittle, Air Britain, Saffron Walden: AE Mr 72 2/3:154
Faster Than the Sun, Photographic Record of Concorde Prototypes, Image in Industry/British Aircraft Corp, Weybridge, Surrey: AE F 73 4/2:89; Afx Ap 73 14/8:455
The Great Gamble: the Boeing 747, by Laurence S. Kuter, University of Alabama, Tuscaloosa AL: AI Mr 75 8/3:154
Hawker Siddeley 748, by Harry Holmes, Airline Publications, Hounslow, Middx: AN 26 Jl 74 3/4:5
Hawker Siddeley Trident, by Jim Lucas, Airline Publications, Hounslow, Middx: AN 13 Ap 73 1/24:15
Herald, Airline Publications, Hounslow, Middx: AE F 72 2/2:86
History of the Short SC-7 Skyvan, Mersyside Aviation Society & Ulster Aviation Society, Liverpool: AN 27 Je 75 4/2:10
Howard Hughes H-4 Hercules, by D. D. Hatfield, John W. Caler: AE Ag 72 3/2:103; RCS Ag 75 1/4:68
The Lockheed Constellation, by M. J. Hardy, David & Charles, Devon: AE N 73 5/5:250; AN 17 Ag 73 2/7:11; Afx Ag 73 14/12:682
McDonnell Douglas DC-8, ed John A. Whittle, Air Britain, Saffron Walden: AE Ap 73 4/4:204-205; AN 24 N 72 1/14:15
Nord 262 & Fregate, by T. Thompkins, Airline Publications, Hounslow, Middx: AN 19 Ja 73 1/18:13
Skyvan, ed B. Tomkins, Airline Publication, Staines, Middx: AE O 71 1/5:245
Super Constellation, comp Peter J. Marson, Airline Publications, Hounslow, Middx: AN 1 F 74 2/18:15
747--Story of the Boeing Super Jet, by Douglas J. Ingells, Aero, Fallbrook CA: AE Ja 72 2/1:41-42
Those Incomparable Bonanzas, by Larry A. Ball, McCormick-Armstrong, KA: AE Jl 72 3/1:51
VC-10, by Jim Lucas, VHF supplies, Hounslow, Middx: IM Ja 71 8/1:16
Vickers Viscount 700, by P. St. John Turner, Airline Publications, Hounslow, Middx: AN 14 Ap 73 1/24:15

Book--Aircraft

(Post World War II--Military)

A-4 Skyhawk in Action, by Lou Drendel, Squadron/Signal, Warren MI: AN 12 O 73 2/11:15

A-7 Corsair II in Action, by Lou Drendel, Squadron/Signal, Warren MI: AI D 75 9/6:308; Afx O 75 17/2:122; RiS Jl 75 3/2:103

Boeing B-52A/H Stratofortress, by Peter M. Bowers, Profile 245, Windsor, Berks: AN 19 Ja 73 1/18:13; Afx F 74 15/6:368; RT F 74 7/2:24

The C-5A Scandal, by Berkeley Price, Houghton Mifflin, Boston: AE N 71 1/6:318

Canadair Sabre, by G. Joos, Aircam 20, Osprey, Reading, Berks: RT Ja 72 5/1:3+; Sc Je 71 2/6:302

Dassault Mirage Variants, Profile 230, Windsor, Berks: RT Ja 72 5/1:9; Sc Jl 72 3/7:381

De Havilland Venom, by Roger Lindsay, pvt, Cleveland, England: AI O 74 7/4:202; AN 28 Je 74 3/2:16; Afx O 75 17/2:122; PAM O 74 7:116

English Electric Lightning in RAF & Foreign Service, Aircam 37, Osprey, Reading, Berks: Afx My 73 14/9:511

F-4 Phantom, by Richard Gardner, Almark, New Malden, Surrey: Sc Ja 71 2/1:15

F-8 Crusade in Action, by Lou Drendel, Squadron/Signal, Warren MI: AN 2 Mr 73 1/21:15

F-100 Super Sabre in Action, by Lou Drendel, Squadron/Signal, Warren MI: AN 17 Ag 73 2/7:11

F-105 Thunderchief in Action, by Lou Drendel, Squadron/Signal, Warren MI: AI Ja 75 8/1:33; AN 20 S 74 3/8:10; IM Mr 75 11/2:16; RiS Sp 74 2/3-4;161

F-106 Delta Dart in Action, by Don Carson & Lou Drendel, Squadron/Signal, Warren MI: AI Ja 75 8/1:33; AN 23 Ag 74 3/6:5

General Dynamics F-111A to F & FB111A, by Kurt H. Miska, Profile 159, Windsor, Berks: Afx O 74 16/2:116

Grumman A-6 Intruder in Action, by Lou Drendel, Squadron/Signal, Warren MI: AI D 75 9/6:308; Afx O 75 17/2:122; RiS Jl 75 3/2:103

Grumman A6A Intruder & EA-6B Prowler, Profile 252, Windsor, Berks: Afx N 74 16/3:190

A History of the Douglas Skyraider AEW-1, British Aviation Research Group: AI Ag 74 7/2:102; AN 10 My 74 2/25:7; Afx Ag 74 15/12:722-723; IM Mr 74 10/(15):12; Sc Jl 74 5/58:359

A History of the Westland Wyvern, Blackbushe Aviation Research Group: AE D 73 5/6:301; AN 14 Ap 73 1/24:15; Afx Ap 74 15/8:479; RT F 74 7/2:15

LTV A-7A/E Corsair II, Profile 239, Windsor, Berks: Afx S 72 14/1:48; RT S 72 5/9:99; Sc D 72 3/12:655

Lockheed C-130 Hercules, by Paul St. John Turner, Profile 223, Windsor, Berks: IM Ap 71 8/4:15

Lockheed Herculese, by Lars Olausson, pvt, Satenas, Sweden: AN 12 D 75 4/14:7

Lockheed 382 L-100 Hercules, by B. Thompkins, Airline Publications, Hounslow, Middx: AN 19 Ja 73 1/18:13

Martin B-57 Night Intruders & General Dynamics RB-57F, by David

VI. Reviews

A. Anderton, Profile 247, Windsor, Berks: AN 16 F 73 1/20: 15
McDonnell F-4 Phantom II, vol. 2, Aircam, Osprey, Reading, Berks: Afx N 74 16/3:190
McDonnell-Douglas A-4 Skyhawk, comp Richard Ward & Richard M. Bueschal, Osprey, Reading, Berks: Afx Ap 72 13/8:452
Mikoyan MiG 21 Variants, by John Brindley, Profile 238, Windsor, Berks: Afx S 72 14/1:48; RT S 72 5/9:99
Republic F/RF-84F Thunderstreak/Thunderflash, by Ernest R. McDowel, Aircam 14, Osprey, Reading, Berks: Sc Ja 71 2/1:15-16
Republic F-105, by Robert D. Archer, Aero, Fallbrook CA: Afx Ja 71 12/5:251
Republic F-105 Thunderchief, Profile 226, Windsor, Berks: RT O 71 4/10:117; Sc F 72 3/2:100
Sabre F-86A-L, Aircam, Osprey, Reading, Berks: Afx Ap 71 12/8:428
Shackleton Mks 1-4, Profile 243, Windsor, Berks: AN 27 O 72 1/12:15; RT N 72 5/11:126
Vought F8 Crusader, comp Richard Ward & Arthur L. Schoeni, Aircam, Osprey, Reading, Berks: Afx Ja 73 14/5:282

Lighter-Than-Air

The Age of the Airship, by Edward Horton, Sedgwick & Jackson, London: Afx O 73 15/2:116
Airship, a History, by Basil Collier, Hart-Davis, MacGibbon: AI Ap 75 8/4:207; AN 13 D 74 3/14:7
Airships, by Henry Veaubois & Carlo Deman, Macdonalds & Jane's, London: AI Je 75 8/6:305; Sc D 74 5/63:650
Balloons & Airships, by Lennard Ege & Otto Frello, Macmillan, NY, 1974: WWE Ja 75 2/1:26
Historic Airships, by Peter W. Brooks, Hugh Evelyn: Sc Jl 74 5/58:674
Hot Air Ballooning, by Christine Turnbull, Speed & Sport Publications, London: AE S 71 1/4:224
Illustrated History of Airships, by A. F. L. Deeson, Spurbooks, Bourne End, Bucks: AI Ap 75 8/4:207
Proceedings of the Interagency Workshop on Lighter Than Air Vehicles, ed Joseph F. Vittek, MIT Press, Cambridge MA, 1935: AI O 75 9/4:205
The Romance of Ballooning, Edit SA, Lausanne, Patrick Stephens, London: AE Mr 72 2 /3:154

Military Operations

Air Power, by Robin Higam, Macdonald, London: AE Ja 73 4/1:47

Aircraft Versus Submarine, by Alfred Price, William Kimber, London: AN 26 O 73 2/12:15
L'Aviation de Chasse Française 1918-1940, by Jean Cuny & Raymond Danel, Editions La Rivière, Paris: AN 18 Ap 75 3/23:15
Black Lysander, by John Nesbitt-Dufort, Jarrolds, London: Special Service missions: AI D 75 9/6:309
Bombs Away!, ed Stanley M. Ulanoff, Doubleday, NY: AE Mr 72 2/3:155; RT Mr 72 5/3:33
Carrier Operations in World War II, vol. 2, The Pacific Navies, by David Brown, Ian Allan, Shepperton: AI Ja 75 8/1:33
Clouds of Fear, by Roger Hall, Bailey Bros. & Swinfen, Folkestone: AI D 75 9/6:308; AN 28 N 75 4/13:12
Encyclopedia of Air Warfare, by Christopher Chant, Richard Humble, J. F. Davies, Donald Macintyre & Bill Gunston, Salamander, London: Sc O 75 6/73:506
Fighter Tactics & Strategy 1914-1970, by Edward H. Sims, Cassel, London: Afx Je 72 13/10:569
Fighters Over Tunisia, by Christopher Shores, Hans Ring, & William H. Ness, Neville Spearman, London: AI D 75 9/6:309-310
Flight to Freedom, by Baron Michel Donnet, Ian Allan, London: Belgian pilot's escape: AI Ap 75 8/4:207
The Glider War, by James E. Mrazek, Robert Hale, London: AI N 75 9/5:255
Gunslingers in Action, by Lou Drendel, Squadron/Signal, Warren MI: helicopter gunships in Vietnam: AI Jl 74 7/1:49; RiS W 74 2/2:75
A History of Aerial Warfare, by J. W. R. Taylor, Hamlyn, Feltham: AI Je 75 8/6:305; Sc O 75 6/73:506
Leaflet Operations in the Second World War, by James M. Erdmann, University of Denver, Denver CO: AE Ag 71 1/3:146
Lucht Spionage, Akenreeks Beeld Encyclopedia Alkmaar: Sc S 71 2/9:500
Photo Reconnaissance, by Andrew J. Bookes, Ian Allan, Shepperton: Afx Ag 75 16/12:727
The Sergeant Escapers, by John Dominy, Ian Allan, Shepperton: NCO prison escapes, WW-II: AI F 75 8/2:93
Six Months to Oblivion, by Werner Girbig, Ian Allan, Shepperton: Operation Bodenplate: AI D 75 9/6:308
Spies in the Sky, by John W. R. Taylor & David Mondey, Ian Allan, Shepperton: AE Ap 73 4/4:205; AN 16 F 73 1/20:15; Afx F 74 6/2:368
Wings of War, by Rudolph Start, Arms & Armour, London: AN 9 N 74 2/13:15
World Military Aviation, by Nickolaus Krivinyi, Arms & Armour, London: Afx F 74 15/6:368

Pioneering Aircraft, Records, & Epics

Aircraft--The Story of Powered Flight, by John Young & Peter Shep-

ard, Ward Lock: AN 22 Je 73 2/3:15
British Racing & Record-Breaking Aircraft, by Peter Lewis, Putnam, London: AE Je 71 1/1:20
British Flying Boats, by G. R. Duval, D. Bradford Barton, Truro: AE Ag 74 15/12:102; Afx Ap 71 12/8:428
Clipped Wings, by Ian & Ralph Ormes, William Kimber, London: AE N 73 5/5:250; AN 17 Ag 73 2/7:11
Conquerors of the Air, by Heiner Emde, Patrick Stephens, Cambridge: Afx N 73 15/3:180
The Conquest of the Air, by Frank Howard & Bill Gunston, Pall Elek, London: AE Ap 73 4/4:204
Daffodil & Golden Eagle, by Jonathan Yeatman, Granada/Paladin, St. Albans: Sahara by balloon: AI Ja 75 8/1:33
The Deltoid Pumpkin Seed, by John McPhee, Farrar, Straus & Giroux: lifting bodies: AM Ag 74 78/8:4
Early Aviation at Farnborough, by Percy B. Walker, Macdonald, London: AE D 71 1/7:358; vol. 2: Afx Jl 75 16/11:668
Flight Fever, by Joseph Hamlen, Macmillan, NY: trans-Atlantic: AE F 72 2/2:84-85; RT S 71 4/9:98
First Across, by Richard K. Smith, Naval Institute Press, Annapolis MD: NC-4: AE Jl 73 5/1:43; Sc Jl 74 5/58:358-359
The Fort Air Tours 1925-1931, by Lesley Forden, Nottingham Press, Alameda, CA: AE F 74 6/2:98
Flight Before Flying, by David W. Wragg, Osprey, Reading, Berks: 1783-1903 flights: Afx S 74 16/1:53
Flight Through the Ages, by C. H. Gibbs-Smith, Hart-Davis, MacGibbon, London: Afx Ag 75 15/12:727; Sc Jl 75 6/70:337
Giants in the Sky, a History of the Rigid Airship, by Douglas H. Robinson, G. T. Foulis, London: AE N 73 5/5:250
Great Pioneer Flights, by Oliver Tapper, Bodley Head, London: AN 19 S 75 4/8:15
Guinness Book of Air Facts & Feats, by John W. R. Taylor, Michael J. H. Taylor, & David Mondey, Guinness Superlatives: AE Ap 74 6/4:211; Afx Mr 71 12/7:357; RT My 71 4/5:51
History of Aviation, ed John W. R. Taylor & Kenneth Munson, New English Library, London: AN 31 Ag 73 2/8:15
History of Aviation Aircraft Identification Guide, ed John W. R. Taylor & Kenneth Munson, New English Library, London: AN 31 Ag 73 2/8:15
Man-Powered Flight, by Keith Sherwin, MAP, Hemel Hempstead, Herts: AE F 72 2/2:85
The Madrid-Manila Flight, by Eduardo G. Gallarza & Joaquin Loriga Taboada, Philippine Airlines, Manila: AE F 72 2/2:86
Ocean, Poles & Airmen: the First Flights over Wide Waters & Desolate Ice, by Richard Monteague, Random House, NY: AE Ja 72 2/1:41
Pioneer Days of Aviation in Jersey, by J. Edouard Slade, pvt, vol. 1, Ludwigshafen am Rhein, vol. 2 Mannheim: AN 18 Ag 72 1/7:14
The Schneider Trophy Races, by Ralph Barker, Chatto & Windus, London: AE F 72 2/2:85
Supersonic Flight--Breaking the Sound Barrier & Beyond: the Story of the Bell X-1 & Douglas D-558, by Richard P. Hallion, Mac-

millan, NY: AE S 73 5/3:149
The Time Shrinkers, by David Jones, David Rendel, London: AE F 72 2/2:84
Veteran & Vintage Aircraft, by Leslie Hunt, Garnstone, London: AE Jl 71 1/2:99; AI D 74 7/6:306; Afx Ap 71 12/8:409; Afx Ag 74 15/12:722; Sc Ag 74 5/59:441

Private Flying

Associated Ground Subjects, Flight Briefing for Pilots, vol. 4, by N. H. Birch & A. E. Bransom, Putnam, London: AI Je 75 8/6:305
Aviation Law for Pilots, by S. E. T. Taylor & H. A. Parmar, Crosby Lockwood Staples, London: AN 9 Ag 74 3/5:14
Check Pilot, by N. H. Birch & A. E. Bramson, Pitman, London: multiple-choice quiz: AE Je 74 6/6:312
Enthusiast's Guide to British Aviation, ed. Peter Lockhard, AVSOC, Farnham, Surrey: AN 13 O 72 1/11:15
Flying Light Aircraft, by David Oglivy, Adam & Charles Black, London, AN 8 D 72 1/15:11
Flying the Old Planes, by Frank Tallman, Doubleday, NY: AM Jl 74 78/7:8
Flying the VOR, by Alan Bramson & Neville Brich, IAL: AI O 75 9/4:206
Ground Studies for Pilots, by S. E. T. Taylor & H. A. Parmar, Crosby Lockwood Staples, London: for commercial license: AN 7 F 75 3/18:14
Hang Glider Flight Log, Aviation Book Co., Glendale, CA: AI Ag 75 9/2:87
Hang Gliding, by Dan Poynter, Parachuting Publications, North Quincy MD: AI Ag 75 8/4:207
Kiting, by Dan Poynter, Parachuting Publications, Santa Barbara CA: AI Je 75 8/6:305
Private Pilot's Dictionary & Handbook, by Kirk Polking, Arco, NY: AI Je 75 8/6:305
Radio Aids to Navigation, Flight Briefing for Pilots, vol. 3, by N. H. Birch & A. E. Bransom, Putnam, London: AI Je 75 8/6:305
True Flight, by Herman Rice, True Flight, San Jose, CA: hang gliders: AI Ag 75 9/2:87
Yesterday's Wings, by Peter Bowers, AOPA, Washington, DC: flying antique planes: AI Ag 75 9/2:87

Regional Aviation

Annals of Aviation in Iceland 1917-1928, by Arngrimur Sigurdsson, AESKAN, Rekjavik: AE D 73 5/6:515-516

Flightpath South Pacific, by Ian Driscoll, Whitcombe & Tombes, Christchurch, NZ: AN 7 D 73 2/15:15
Scotland Scanned '75, ed A. R. Benzies, Central Scotland Aviation Group, Edinburgh: AN 2 My 75 3/24:14

Training

Observer & Navigation Training since 1914, by C. G. Jefford, RAF Finingley, Concaster, Yorks: AE Ja 73 4/1:47; Afx Mr 73 14/7:399
Trained to Intrude, by Richard Gentil, Bachman & Turner, London: WW-II: AI Ap 75 8/4:207

Unit Histories

Aces of the Eighth, by Gene B. Stafford & William N. Hess, Squadron/Signal, Warren MI: AI Jl 74 7/1:49; AN 29 Mr 74 2/22:15; RiS W 74 2/2:74
Before the Storm (RAF Bomber Command), by Robert Jackson, Arthur Barker, London: Afx Je 72 13/10:569
Carrier Air Groups: HMS Eagle, vol. 1, by David Brown, Hylton Lacy, Windsor, Berks: AN 19 Ja 72 1/18:13; Afx F 74 15/6:368; RT D 72 5/12:139
Challenge in the Air, by Brian Philpott, MAP, Hemel Hempstead, Herts: Air Training Corps: Afx Je 71 12/10:542
The Cherry Blossom Squadrons, Hogoromo Society, trans Hobuo Ashai & ed Andrew Adams, Ohara Publications, Los Angeles: WWE S 74 1/5:143
Condor Legion, by Peter Elstob, Ballantine, Westminster, MD: AE Ap 74 6/4:211
The Debden Eagles, by Garry L. Fry, W. E. Hersant, London: 4th Fighter Group, USAAF: AE D 71 1/7:358; Afx D 71 13/4:223; Sc O 71 2/10:558-559
Divine Thunder, by Bernard Millet, Macdonald, London: Kamakazi units: AE Ja 72 2/1:42
Duxford: Its First Year of War, by Michael J. F. Bowyer, East Anglian Aviation Society, Hutington: airfield: AN 15 N 74 3/12:15; Afx Ag 74 15/12:722
Duxford Diary, East Anglian Aviation Society, Royston, Herts: AN 8 Ag 75 4/5:13
Famous Fighter Squadrons of the RAF, vol. 1, Men & Machines, by James J. Halley, Hylton Lacy & Profile, Windsor, Berks: Afx Mr 72 13/7:389; RT Jl 72 5/7:75; Sc Je 72 3/6:336
Famous Maritime Squadrons of the RAF, by James J. Halley, Hylton Lacy Windsor: AN 22 Je 73 2/3:15
The Fireball Outfit, by Ken Blakeborough, Aero, Fallbrook CA: 457th Bomb Group: Afx Ap 71 12/8:409+

Flying at Hendon, by Clive R. Smith, Routledge & Kegan Paul, London: to 1920: AI S 75 8/3:151
The Flying Elephants, the History of the No. 27 Squadron RFC/RAF 1915-1969, by Chaz Bowyer, Macdonalds, London: AE Ja 73 4/1:46; Afx F 73 14/5:338
The 458 Bombardment Group (Heavy), by George A. Reynolds, pvt, Birmingham AL: WWE N 74 1/6:170
The Friendly Firm, by Wilfred Russell, 194 Squadron RAF Association, London: AE Ap 73 4/4:204; AN 8 D 72 1/15:11
History of No. 15 Squadron RAF, by N. J. Roberson, 15 Sqn, RAF Laarbruch: AN 4 Ap 75 3/22:14
A History of Woodvale, by Aldon P. Ferguson, Merseyside Aviation Society, Liverpool: AN 7 F 75 3/18:14
I Fear No Man, by Douglas Tidy, Macdonald: 74 Squadron RAF: AE Ap 73 4/4:204; AN 2 F 72 1/19:15
Kampfgeschwader "Edelweiss," by Wolfgang Dietrich, Ian Allan, Shepperton: AI D 75 9/6:309; Afx Ag 75 16/12:727-728
Lincolnshire Air War, 1939-1945, by S. Finn, Aero Litho, Lincoln: aerodromes: AE D 73 5/6:300; AN 31 Ag 73 2/8:15; Afx D 73 15/4:249; WWE Mr 75 2/2:66
Luftwaffe Airborne & Field Units, by Martin Windrow, Osprey, Reading, Herts: MW F 73 1/6:291
Martlesham Heath, by Gordon Kinsey, Gerence Dalton, Lavenham, Suffolk: AN 13 Je 75 4/1:10
Naval Eight, ed E. G. Johnstone, Arms & Armour, London: AE S 73 5/3:300; Afx Jl 73 14/11:623; MW Ag 73 1/12:627; Sc S 73 4/9:625
Nothing Heard After Take-Off--a Short History of No. 7 Squadron RAF, 1914-1974, Newquay, Corn: AI Ag 75 9/2:87; AN 7 Mr 75 3/20:15; Afx Je 75 16/10:612
104th Aero Squadron, by John W. Stuart Gilchrist et al, John W. Caler: AE D 72 3/6:316
110 Squadron History, by Elwyn D. Bell, Air Britain, Saffron Walden, Essex: AE Mr 72 2/3:154
Pacific Sweep, 5th & 13th Fighter Commands in WW-II, by William N. Hess, Doubleday, Garden City, NY, 1974: WWE Ja 75 2/1:28
Royal Air Force Unit Histories, by J. J. Halley, Air Britain, Saffron Walden, Essex: AI Ag 74 7/2:102
Squadrons of the RAF & FAA, AVSOC, Farnham, Surrey: Afx Ap 72 13/8:452
The Story of the 609 Squadron, by Frank H. Ziegler, Macdonald, London: AE S 71 1/4:223; Afx Ag 71 12/12:629
Twenty-One Squadrons--the History of the Royal Auxiliary Air Force, 1925-1957, by Leslie Hunt, Garnstone, London: AE Mr 73 4/3:138-139; AN 8 D 72 1/15:11; Afx Ja 73 14/5:282
Twice Vertical, by Michael Shaw, Macdonald, London: No. 1 Squadron, RAF: AE Ja 72 2/1:41
White Rose Base, by Brian J. Rapier, Newark, Notts: Yorkshire aerodromes: AE S 73 5/3:149; AN 25 My 73 2/1:15; Afx My 73 14/9:512; MW My 73 1/9:487+; WW2J Jl 75 2/4:35
The Yoxford Boys, by Merle C. Olmstead, Aero, Fallbrook CA: 357 Fighter Group: Afx F 72 13/6:339

Miscellaneous

Air Facts Reader, ed Leighton Collins, Air Facts Press, NY: anthology of Air Facts magazine articles, 1939-1946: AI D 75 9/6:310

Armament of British Aircraft, 1909-1939, by H. F. King, Putnam, London: AE Mr 72 2/3:155; Afx F 72 13/6:339; Sc My 72 3/5:254

Aviator's World, by Michael Edwards, David & Charles, Newton Abbot, Devon: careers in aviation: AI Ja 75 8/1:33

Beyond the Tumult, by Barry Winchesters, Allison & Busby, London, war prisoners: Afx F 72 13/6:339

The Cutting Air Crash, a Case Study in Early Aviation Policy, by Nick A. Komans, U. S. Government Printing Office, Washington, DC: AI S 75 9/3:151

The Dangerous Sky, by Douglas H. Robinson, G. T. Foulds, Henley-on-Thames: aviation medicine: AI Ag 74 7/2:102

Economic Regulation of Domestic Air Transport: Theory & Policy, by George Douglas & James C. Miller, Brookings Institution, Washington, DC: AI O 75 9/4:206

FAA Historical Fact Book, A Chronology, 1926-1971, U.S. Government Printing Office, Washington, DC: AI O 75 9/4:206

Flying Combat Aircraft, ed Robin Higham & Abigail Siddall, Iowa State University Press, Ames IO: U.S. types from WW-II to present, flying chracteristics: AI D 75 9/6:310

The Guns of the Royal Air Force, 1939-1945, by G. F. Wallace, William Kimber, London: AN 2 Mr 73 1/21:15; Afx F 74 15/6:368

Instruments of Flight, by Marvyn Siberry, David & Charles, Newton Abbot, Devon: Afx O 74 16/2:116

Know Aviation, by Francis Mason & Martin Windrow, George Philip, London: AN 12 O 73 2/11:15; Afx Ja 74 15/5:316

Most Probable Position: A History of Aerial Navigation to 1941, by Monte Duane Wright, University of Kansas Press, Lawrence KA: AE F 74 15/6:97-98

Runway, by John Godson, Scribners, NY: Anchorage DC-8 crash: AI F 75 8/2:95

The Wit of the Air, by Kenneth Wolstenholme, Leslie Frewin, London: anthology: AE Ap 73 4/4:204

Wrecks & Relics, ed Ken Ellis, Merseyside Aviation Society, Liverpool: AN 15 N 74 2/23:15

ARMOR

General

Antique Arms & Armour, by Frederick Wilkinson, Arms & Armour, London: MM Ap 73 3/4:244

Armoured Fighting Vehicles of the World, by Christopher F. Foss, Ian Allan, Shepperton: MM S 71 1/9:479-480; MM Mr 75 5/3: 158; Sc F 72 3/2:101; 2nd ed: A&W Mr 75 16:56

Armoured Fighting Vehicles of the World, vol. 4, American AFVs of WW-II, ed Duncan Crow, Profile, Windsor, Berks: AFV Ja 73 4/1:30; vol. 5, German AFVs of WW-II: AFV N 73 4/8:16; MM O 73 3/10:668; MW F 73 1/6:331

Arms & Armour, by Aldo Cimarelli, Orbis: MM O 73 3/10:668

Atlante Mondaile dei Mezzi Corazzati 1945-73, col. 4, by Nicola Pignato: AFV Ja 74 4/9:28

British & Commonwealth AFVs 1940-46, ed Duncan Crow, Profile, Windsor, Berks: AFV My 72 3/8:18; Sc Je 71 2/6:302-304

British & Commonwealth Armoured Formations 1919-1946, by Duncan Crow, Profile 2, Windsor, Berks: Afx Ag 72 13/12:687; MM Ag 72 2/8:428-429; MW S 72 1/1:39

Directory of Wheeled Vehicles of the Wehrmacht, ed Chris Ellis, Ducimus, London, 1974: WWE Ja 75 2/1:65-66

Fighting Vehicles, by Peter Chamberlain & Chris Ellis, Hamlyn, Feltham: MW Mr 73 1/7:345

German Explosive Ordnance, vol. 1, Bombs, Rockets, Grenades, Mines, Fuses, & Igniters; Normount: WWE N 74 1/6:170-171

German Secret Weapons, by Brian Ford, Pan/Ballantine, London: Afx Ap 75 5/4:499

German Tanks & Armoured Vehicles, 1914-1945, by B. T. White, Ian Allan, Shepperton, 1971: A&W N 72 2:13

Guide to Combat Weapons of Southeast Asia, ed Donald B. McLean, Normount, Forest Grove, OH: AFV S 72 3/10:19

Hellcat, Long Tom, & Priest, by Robert J. Icks, Profile 26, Windsor, Berks: Sc Jl 71 2/7:345

History of Armoured Forces & Their Vehicles, by Richard M. Ogorkiewicz, Arms & Armour, London: A&W Jl 75 12:15

Illustrated Arsenal of the Third Reich, by Donald B. McLean, Normount, Wickenburg AZ: AFV Mr 74 4/10:27; WWE N 74 1/6: 171

Jane's Pocket Book of Modern Tanks & Armoured Fighting Vehicles, ed Christopher Foss, Macmillan, NY, 1974: AFV Ap 75 5/4: 13; Afx D 74 16/4:157; MM Ag 74 4/8:476

Jane's Weapons Systems, 1974-1975, ed R. T. Pretty & D. H. Archer, Macdonald & Jane's, London: AI Jl 75 9/1:31

Japanese Combat Cars, Light Tanks, & Tankettes, by Tomio Hara, Profile 54, Windsor, Berks: Afx D 73 77/6:149; MM My 73 3/5:314

Japanese Tanks, Tactics, & Antitank Weapons, ed Donald B. McLean, Normount: WWE My 74 1/3:76

Le Material de l'Armée de Terre Française, by Jean Gabriel Jeudy, Crepin-Leblond, Paris, 1972: A&W My 73 5:13

Mechanical Traction in War, by Otfried Layrtz, David & Charles reprint, 1900: MM S 73 3/9:615

Modern Tanks & Armoured Fighting Vehicles, by Christopher F. Foss, Macdonald & Jane's, London: Afx S 74 4/12:54

Observer's Army Vehicles Directory to 1940, by Bart H. Vanderveen, Frederick Warne, London: A&W Mr 75 16:56; Sc F 75 6/65:71

VI. Reviews

The Observer's Fighting Vehicle Directory, by Bart H. Vanderveen, Frederick Warne, NY, 1969: AFV O 71 3/2:23; IM Mr 75 11/2:17; MM My 73 3/5:314; MM Ja 75 5/1:31
Portrait of Power; a Photo-History of U.S. Tank & Self-Propelled Artillery, by G. B. Jarrett & J. J. Icks, Normount, Forest Grove OR: AFV Jl 72 3/9:18
Shottesbrooke, by Nick Rogers, John Carter: military vehicle ralley, 1972: MM Ap 73 3/4:243-244
Tanks & Other Armoured Fighting Vehicles, 1900-1918, by B. T. White, Blandford, London: A&W My 73 5:13
Tanks & Transport Vehicles, WW-II, ed Bart H. Vanderveen, Olyslager Auto Library, Frederick Warne, London: Afx Ap 75 5/4: 498; MM Ja 75 5/1:24+; Sc F 75 6/65:71; WW2J S 75 2/4-5:23
U.S. Military Vehicles of WW-II, by E. J. Hoffschmidt & W. H. Tantum IV, WE Inc., Old Greenwich CN: AFV Mr 71 2/12:23
Vehicles of the German Wehrmacht, TLO Publications, Egham, Surrey: Afx F 72 3/6:346; MM D 71 1/12:666
Veicoli Speciali de Regio Esercito Italiano nella Seconda Guerra Mondaile, by Guilio Benussi, Intergest, Milan, 1973: A&W Jl 74 12/14
WW-2 Fact Files, by Peter Chamberlain & Terry Gander, Arco, NY, 1975: series review: WW2J S 75 2/5-6:23
Weapons & Equipment of the Israeli Armed Forces, by Raid Ashkar & Ahmed Khalidi, Institute for Palestine Studies, Beirut, 1971: AFV D 71 3/4:23
West of Alamein, ed Joseph V. Mizrahi, Sentry Books, Northridge CA, 1971: AFV D 71 3/4:23

APCs & ICVs

Armoured Personnel Carriers--a Survey, by N. W. Duncan, Profile 64, Windsor, Berks: Afx Jl 74 15/11:664
Carrier, by Peter Chamberlain & Chris Ellis, Profile 14, Windsor, Berks: MM F 71 1/2:105-106; Sc Ja 71 2/1:18
FV 432, Profile 53, Windsor, Berks: MM Mr 73 3/3:170; MW Mr 73 1/7:345
Landing Vehicles Tracked, by Robert J. Icks, Profile 16, Windsor, Berks: Sc F 71 2/2:75
Making Tracks, British Carrier Story 1914 to 1972, by Peter Chamberlain & Chris Ellis, Profile, Windsor, Berks, 1973: AFV Jl 74 4/11:31; Afx Mr 74 15/7:422; MM Ja 74 4/1:54; WWE S 74 1/5:143

ARVs & Funnies

British ARVs & Transporters, by Peter Chamberlain & Nigel Duncan, Profile 35, Windsor, Berks: Afx O 71 13/2:75; RT S 71

4/9:98
The Funnies, by Geoffrey W. Futter, MAP, Hemel Hempstead, Herts: Afx Mr 75 16/7:442; MM F 75 5/2:88; WW2J S 75 2/5-6:22-23

Armored Cars

Armored Cars, Profile 21, Windsor, Berks: RT Ja 71 4/1:12
Commando, Twister & High Mobility Vehicles, by C. F. Foss, Profile 62, Windsor, Berks: Afx Jl 74 15/11:664
Ferrets & Fox, Profile 44, Windsor, Berks: RT Ag 72 5/8:95
German Armoured Cars, by N. W. Duncan, Profile 33, Windsor, Berks: MM D 71 1/2:664+; RT N 71 2/7:346-347
German Armoured Cars of WW-II, by John Milsom & Peter Chamberlain, Arms & Armour, London: Afx Ap 75 16/8:498-499; MM Mr 75 5/5:158-159; WW2J Jl 75 2/4:34
Marmon Herrington & Alvin Straussler Armoured Cars, Profile 30, Windsor, Berks: RT Ja 72 5/1:4
Panhard Armoured Cars, Profile 39, Windsor, Berks: RT F 72 5/2:21; RT O 72 5/10:115
Russian Armoured Cars to 1945, by John Milsom, Profile 60, Windsor, Berks: Afx D 73 15/4:250
Saladin Armoured Car, by Michael Norman, Profile 27, Windsor, Berks: RT N 71 4/11:127; Sc Jl 71 2/7:346-347
U.S. Armoured Cars, by Robert Icks, Profile 40, Windsor, Berks: RT Je 72 5/6:71

Artillery

Anti-Tank Weapons, by Peter Chamberlain & Terry Gander, Macdonald & Jane's, London: Afx Mr 75 16/7:442
Artillery, by John Batchelor & Ian Hogg, Macdonald, London: Afx Ja 71 12/5:263; MM Jl 73 3/7:465
Artillery of the World, by Christopher F. Foss, Ian Allan, Shepperton: Afx S 74 16/1:54; A&W N 74 14:48; MM O 74 4/9:626
British Artillery Weapons & Ammunition 1914-1918, by Ian Hogg & L. F. Thurston, Ian Allan, Shepperton: MM Jl 73 3/7:465; MW F 73 1/6:291+
Discovering Artillery, by R. J. Wilkinson-Latham, Shire Publications, Aylesbury, Bucks: Afx My 72 13/9:522; MM My 72 2/5:227
Field Rocket Equipment of the German Army, 1939-1945, by T. J. Gander, Almark, London, 1972: WW2J S 75 2/4-5:22
Firepower-Weapons Effectiveness on the Battlefield, 1630-1850, by B. P. Hughes, Arms & Armour, London: MM Mr 75 5/3:158
French Napoleonic Artillery, by Michael Head, Almark, New Malden: Afx Ja 71 12/5:263; MM Ap 71 1/2:105

German Anti-Aircraft Gun Material, TM E9-369A, Inco reprint, Burbank CA & Deutschland Ordinance, San Jose, CA: WWE Mr 74 1/2:50; Military Arms Research reprint, San Jose CA, 1972: AFV Mr 72 3/7:24; MM Ap 75 5/4:244

German Anti-Tank Weapons, Profile 21, Windsor, Berks: Afx F 74 15/6:368-369

German Artillery of 1914-1918, by David Nash, Almark, New Malden: MM F 71 1/2:105

German 88mm Anti-Aircraft Gun, Military Arms Research Service, San Jose, CA: Afx Mr 72 13/7:389; S&L Ag 74 3:28

The Great Art of Artillery, by Casimir Simienowicz, reprint, Scholar Press, Wakefield, Yorks: S&L Je 74 1:21

Guns: an Illustrated History of Artillery, ed J. Jobe, Patrick Stephens, London: Afx O 71 13/2:75

History of Artillery, by Ian V. Hogg, Hamlyn, Feltham, Middx: MM F 75 5/2:88

Japanese Artillery, ed Donald B. McLean, Normount: WWE My 74 1/3:76

Pictorial History of Artillery--Light Field Guns, by Franz Kosar, Ian Allan, Shepperton: Afx Ag 74 15/12:724; MM Je 74 4/6:333

Rail Gun, by John Batchelor & Ian Hogg, MAP, Hemel Hempstead, Herts: Afx Ag 73 14/12:683

Recoilless Anti-Tank Weapons, Profile 21, Windsor, Berks: Afx F 74 15/6:368-369

Round Shot & Rammers, by Harold L. Peterson, Arms & Armour, London: Afx Je 75 16/10:613; MM Ag 74 4/8:476

Edged Weapons

Discovering Edged Weapons, by J. Wilkinson-Latham, Shire Publishing, Aylesbury, Bucks: Afx My 72 13/9:522; MM My 72 2/5:227

Edged Weapons of the Third Reich, by Frederick J. Stephens, Almark, New Malden: MW D 72 1/4:211

European Edged Weapons, by Terence Wise, Almark, New Malden: Afx D 74 16/4:257; MM Je 74 4/6:333; S&L Je 74 1:21

Italian Fascist Daggers, Frederick J. Stephens, Military Publications: Afx Je 72 13/10:546

Japanese Sword Blades, by Alfred Dobree, Arms & Armour, London: MM F 75 5/2:88

Pictorial History of Swords & Bayonets, by R. J. Wilkinson-Latham, Ian Allan, Shepperton: Afx S 73 15/1:54; MM My 73 3/5:313

Half-Tracks

German Halftracks in Action, by Uwe Feist & Kurt Rieger, Squadron/

Signal, Warren MI, 1972: AFV O 72 3/11:31; A&W Mr 74 10: 13
German Semi-Tracked Vehicles, pt. 3, by Peter Chamberlain & Hillary Doyle, Bellona 2: Sc Jl 72 3/7:380
Half Tracks, by Bart H. Vanderveen, Olyslager/Warne, Frederick Warne, London: MM Ap 71 1/4:210; MM Jl 73 3/7:464
NSU Kettenkrad, via Modelbau und Militaria: MM D 74 4/12:772
Panzer-Grenadiers Halbkettenfahrzeuge, Almark, New Malden: Afx Ap 72 13/8:452
Panzerspähwagen in Action, by Uwe Feist & Mike Dario, Squadron/ Signal, Warren MI: AFV Ja 73 4/1:30
Schützenpanzerwagen in Action, by Uwe Feist & Kurt Rieger, Squadron/Signal, Redbridge: AFV S 72 3/10:19; Afx S 72 14/1:48; A&W Ja 74 9:13
SdKfz 250/252/253, by Eric Clark, MAFVA, Southport, Lancs: WWE N 74 1/6:192
SdKfz 251, by Walter Spielberger & SdKfz 250 by Peter Chamberlain & Hilary L. Doyle, Profile 57, Windsor, Berks: Afx O 73 15/2:117; MM S 73 3/9:614

Self-Propelled Artillery

Elefant & Maus, by Walter Speilburger & J. Milsom, Profile 61, Windsor, Berks: Afx Jl 74 15/11:664
German Self-Propelled Weapons, by Peter Chamberlain & H. L. Doyle, Profile 55, Windsor, Berks: Afx Ja 74 15/5:317
Missile Armed Armoured Vehicles, by R. M. Ogorkiewicz, Profile, Windsor: Afx Ag 73 14/12:683
Modern Artillerie 1&2, Akenreeke Beeld Encyclopedia Alkmaar: Sc S 71 2/9:499-500
Panzerjäger in Action, by Uwe Feist & Mike Dario, Squadron/Signal, Warren MI: AFV S 73 4/7:27
Selbstfahrlafette Loraine SdKfz 135/1, by J. D. Barnes & D. M. Pearce, Recon Publications, San Jose, CA, 1972: AFV S 73 4/7:27; WWE Mr 74 1/2:50

Small Arms

Armalite Weapons, Profile 22, Windsor, Berks: Afx Ja 74 15/5: 317; MW S 73 2/1:45
Astra Pistols & Revolvers, Profile 15, Windsor, Berks: Afx My 73 14/9:512
British & American Infantry Weapons of WW-II, by A. J. Barker, Arms & Armour, London: Afx Je 73 14/10:566; Sc S 73 4/9: 624
Colt Fixed Cylinder Cartridge Revolvers, Profile 20, Windsor, Berks: Afx F 74 15/6:368-369

VI. Reviews

Colt Percussion Revolvers, Profile 16, Windsor, Berks: Afx Ag 74 15/12:724; Afx O 74 16/2:117

Combat Weapons--Hand Guns & Shoulder Arms of WW-II, by Brian Burrell, Spurbooks, Bourne End, Bucks: MM My 74 4/5:277; S&L Jl 74 2:20

Early Enfield Arms--Muzzle Loaders, Profile 14, Windsor, Berks: Afx My 73 14/9:512

Enfield Arms, the Early Breech-Loaders, Profile 18, Windsor, Berks: Afx Ja 74 15/5:317; MM My 73 3/6:314

Firearms--the History of Guns, by Frederick Wilkinson, Orbis, London: MM Ag 73 3/8:538-539

Flintlock Guns & Rifles, by F. Wilkinson, Arms & Armour, London: MW Ag 71 1/8:417-418

German Infantry Weapons of World War II, by A. J. Parker, Arms & Armour Press, London: Afx Je 73 14/10:566; Sc S 73 4/9:624

German Pistols & Revolvers 1871-1945, by Ian V. Gogg, Arms & Armour, London: Afx N 71 13/3:138

Guide to United States Machine Guns, by Konrad F. Schreier, Jr. Normount, Wickenburg AZ: AFV D 72 3/12:20

Infantry Weapons of the World 1975, ed J. I. H. Owen, Brassey's, London: MM Mr 75 5/3:159

Jane's Infantry Weapons 1974, ed F. W. A. Hobart, Jane's Yearbooks, London: A&W S 75 19:48; 1975: Afx My 75 16/9:554-555

Japanese Infantry Weapons, ed Donald B. McLean, Normount: WWE My 74 1/3:76

Machine Guns, by Peter Chamberlain & Terry Gander, Macdonald & Jane's, London: Afx Mr 75 16/7:442; MM Mr 75 5/3:159

The Mauser 1896, Profile, Windsor, Berks: Afx Jl 73 14/11:624

Military Pistols & Revolvers, by I. V. Hogg, Arms & Armour, London: MM Ja 71 1/1:47-48

Military Small Arms of the 20th Century, by Ian Hogg & John Weeks, Arms & Armour, London: MM F 74 4/2:99

Pictorial History of the Sub-Machine Gun, by F. W. A. Hobart, Ian Allan, Shepperton, 1973: Afx Ap 74 15/8:480; A&W Jl 74 12:14; Sc My 72 3/5:254

Russian Infantry Weapons of WW-II, by A. J. Barker & John Walter, Arms & Armour, London: MM Ag 71 1/8:418

Russian Sub-Machine Guns, by F. W. A. Hobart, Profile 12, Windsor, Berks: Afx D 72 14/4:226

Small Arms Ammunition, Profile Special, Windsor, Berks: Afx My 74 15/9:539

Small Arms Identification & Operation Guide--Eurasian Communist Countries, FSTC-CW-07-03-70, by Harold E. Johnson, U.S. Army Foreign Science & Technology Center, Burbank CA: Fus Sp 74 1/3:24

Small Arms in Profile, vol. 1, Profile, Windsor, Berks: Afx Je 74 15/10:601; MM F 73 3/2:112; MW F 73 1/6:331

Small Arms of the World, by Joseph E. Smith, Arms & Armour, London: Afx Jl 74 15/11:663

Smith & Wesson Tip-up Revolvers, Profile 17, Windsor, Berks: Afx Ja 74 15/5:317; MM Mr 73 3/3:170

Soviet Rifles & Carbines, Identification & Operation, ORD17-101, Inco reprint, Burbank CA: WWE Mr 74 1/2:50

U.S. Cartridge Company's Collection of Firearms, WE Inc. facsimile, NY: Afx Ap 72 13/8:447

United States Single Shot Martial Pistols, 1776-1945, by Charles Winthrop Sawyer, WE Inc, NY: Afx Ap 72 13/8:447

Webbley & Scott Automatic Pistols, by A. J. R. Cormack, Profile 1, Windsor, Berks: Afx N 71 13/3:138

Softskins

AD 748872: Concise Automotive Manual, trans 1972: AFV My 73 4/4:18

British ARFs & Transporters, by Peter Chamberlain & Nigel Duncan, Profile 35, Windsor, Berks: Afx O 71 13/2:75

Directory of Wheeled Vehicles of the Wehrmacht, ed Chris Ellis, Ducimus, London: Afx O 74 16/2:116; MM O 74 4/10:624; Sc D 74 5/12:650

JPES 56726: Concise Handbook of Soviet Motor Vehicles & Trailers, by D. V. Chaban, trans 1972: AFV My 73 4/4:18

German Military Transport of WW-I, by John Milsom, Arms & Armour, London: WW2J Jl 75 2/4:35

German Military Transport of WW-II, by John Milsom, Arms & Armour, London: Afx Jl 75 16/11:668; MM Je 75 5/6:363

Jeep, Clymer Publications: MM Ja 72 2/1:40-41

The Jeep, by Bart H. Vanderveen, Olyslager Auto Library, Frederick Warne, NY, 1971: Afx O 71 3/2:23; MM Ap 71 1/4:209-210; MM Jl 73 3/7:464

Mechanized Warfare in Color, military transport of WW-I, by Chris Ellis & Denis Bishop, Macmillan, NY, 1970: WWE Ja 75 2/1:27

Militarfahrzeug, by W. J. Spielberger & Uwe Feist, Aero, CA: Afx S 71 13/1:49

The Military Jeep Complete, ed Dan R. Post, Post Motor Books, Arcadia CA: AFV My 72 3/8:18

Military Transport of WW-II, by Chris Ellis & Dennis Bishop, Blandford, London: A&W Jl 73 6:15

The Observer's Army Vehicle Directory to 1940, by B. H. Vanderveen, Frederick Warne, NY, 1973: AFV Ap 75 5/4:13; Afx Mr 75 16/7:442

Volkswagen for the Wehrmacht, 1939-1945, reprint of TM E9-803 German Volkswagen by Post Era Books, Arcadia CA: AFV O 72 3/11:31

Willys Jeep Manual TM9-803, War Dept, 1944: MM My 73 3/5:313

Tanks

(General)

Armor in Action, by Uwe Feist & Mike Dario, Squadron/Signal, Warren MI, 1973: A&W My 73 5:13

Encyclopedia of Tanks, by Duncan Crow & Robert J. Icks, Barrie & Jenkins, London: AFV S 75 5/6:20; Afx Ag 75 15/12:728; MM Ag 75 5/8:48; WW2J Jl 75 2/4:34

50 Famous Tanks, by George Bradford & Len Morgan, Ian Allan, Shepperton, 1967: A&W Ja 73 3:13

The Great Tanks, by Chris Ellis & Peter Chamberlain, Hamlyn, Feltham, Middx: Afx Jl 75 16/11:668; MM Je 75 5/6:363

Guinness Book of Tank Facts & Feats, ed Kenneth Macksey, Guinness Superlatives, Enfield, Middx: Afx F 73 14/6:337

Pictorial History of Tanks of the World 1915-1945, by Peter Chamberlain & Chris Ellis, Arms & Armour, London: Afx F 73 14/6:336-337; MM Ja 73 3/1:51; MW Ja 73 1/5:268

Tank, by Kenneth Macksey & John H. Batchelor, Ballantine, NY: AFV S 71 3/1:27; MM F 71 1/2:105

The Tank, by Douglas Orgill, Heinemann, 1970: MM F 71 1/2:104

Tank Data 3, by Harold E. Johnson, WE Inc, Old Greenwich CN & Patrick Stephens, London, 1972: Afx Mr 73 14/7:400; A&W N 73 8:13; MM Mr 73 3/3:157

Tank Force, by Kenneth Macksey, Pan/Ballantine, London: Allied, WW-II: Afx Ap 74 15/8:480

Tanks: An Illustrated History of the Armoured Fighting Vehicle, by A. Halle & Carlo Demand, Edita of Lausanne: Afx Jl 71 12/11:606

(France)

AMX-30 Battle Tank, by R. M. Ogorkiewicz, Profile 63, Windsor, Berks: Afx Jl 74 15/11:664

Chars Hotchkiss H35, H 39, & Souma S35, Profile 36, Windsor, Berks: RT Ja 72 5/1:4

French Infantry Tanks, part 1, by James Bingham, Profile 58, Windsor, Berks: MM S 73 3/9:614

(Germany)

British & German Tanks of WW-I, by Peter Chamberlain & Chris Ellis, Arms & Armour, London, 1969: A&W S 73 7:13

Elefant & Maus, by Walter Speilburger & J. Milsom, Profile 61, Windsor, Berks: Afx Jl 74 15/11:664

German Heavy Tanks 1930-1945, by Peter Chamberlain & Chris Ellis, Ducimus, London: Afx Je 71 12/10:533; RT Ja 71 4/1:12; Sc O 71 2/10:561

German Tanks of WW-II, by Terry Gander & Peter Chamberlain, Patrick Stephens, Cambridge, 1975: Afx Jl 75 16/11:668; A&W

N 75 20:73; MM Ag 75 5/8:488
German Tanks of WW-II, by F. M. von Senger und Etterlin, trans
J. Lucas, Arms & Armour, London: Afx Ja 74 15/5:601; MM
My 74 4/5:277
Leichte Panzers in Action, by Uwe Feist & Mike Dario, Squadron/
Signal: RiS Sp 74 2/3-4:161
Panther in Action, by Bruce Culver & Don Greer, Squadron/Signal,
Warren, MI: AFV Je 75 5/5:27; IM Jl 75 11/4:19; RiS Jl 75
3/2:102
Panzer: German Armor, 1935-1945, by Peter Stahl, Die Wehrmacht,
Stanford CA: Afx Ap 71 12/8:437
Panzer in Russland, by Horst Scheibert & Ulrich Elfrath, Podzon,
Dorheim: AFV F 73 4/2:14
Panzer III, 1935-1945, by Beneditto Pafi, STEM-Mucchi, Modena:
AFV S 74 4/12:31
Panzer III in Action, by Uwe Feist, Squadron/Signal, Vancouver,
B.C., 1972: AFV Ja 72 3/5:28; A&W Ja 74 9:13
Panzerkampfwagen: German Combat Tanks 1939-1945, by J. Williamson, Almark, New Malden: Afx Ap 74 15/8:480; MM S 73
3/9:615; MW S 73 2/1:45
Panzerkampfwagen in Action, by Uwe Feist & Mike Dario, Squadron/
Signal 1972: A&W S 73 7:13
Panzerkampfwagen I & II, by N. W. Duncan, Profile 14, Windsor,
Berks: MM F 71 1/2:105-106; Sc Ja 71 2/1:18-19
Panzerkampfwagen 38(t) & 35(t), by John Milsom, Profile 22, Windsor, Berks: Sc Ap 71 2/4:75
PzKpfw IV in Action, by Bruce Culver, Squadron/Signal, Warren MI:
AFV S 75 5/6:20
PzKpfw VI Tiger I & Tiger II Kingtiger, by Peter Chamberlain &
Chris Ellis, Profile, Windsor, Berks: Afx D 72 14/4:226
Tiger I & II, by Peter Chamberlain & Chris Ellis, Profile 48,
Windsor, Berks: MW D 72 1/4:211
Tiger I in Action, by Uwe Feist & Norm E. Harms, Squadron/
Signal, Warren, MI: AFV D 74 5/1:25

(Italy)

Fronte Terra Carri Armati vol. 1, Edizioni Bizzarri, Roma: Afx
F 74 15/6:368
Italian Tanks & Fighting Vehicles of WW-II, by Ralph Riccio, Pique
Publications, Henley-on-Thames, Oxon: Afx O 75 17/2:123;
MM O 75 5/10:605

(Japan)

Imperial Japanese Tanks, 1918-1945, by Paul M. Roland, Bellona,
Langley, Herts, 1975: AFV S 75 5/6:20; MM O 75 5/10:605;
Sc N 75 6/74:569
Japanese Medium Tanks, by Tomio Hara, Profile 49, Windsor,
Berks: MW F 73 1/6:291

(Sweden)

S Tank, by R. M. Ogorkiewicz, Profile 28, Windsor, Berks: Afx S 71 13/1:49; RT My 71 4/5:51; Sc O 71 2/10:561

(USSR)

Czolg Ciezki IS, by Janusz Magnunski, Warsaw: Sc Jl 75 6/70:337
PT-76 Light Amphibious Tank & Variants, by Christopher Foss, Profile 65, Windsor, 1974: AFV Ap 75 5/4:13
Russian BT series Tank, Profile 37, Windsor, Berks: RT Ja 72 5/1:4
Russian T34, by J. M. Brereton & Michael Norman, Profile 47, Windsor, Berks: Afx O 72 14/2:107
Russian Tanks 1900-1907, by John Milsom, Arms & Armour, London: MM Mr 71 1/3:159-160
Soviet Combat Tanks 1939-1945, by Peter Chamberlain & Chris Ellis, Almark, New Malden: MM Ap 71 1/4:207
Soviet Panzers in Action, by Uwe Feist, Squadron/Signal Publications, Warren MI: AFV Je 75 4/5:16
Soviet T-54, 55, 62, Profile, Windsor, Berks: RT Mr 71 4/3:26

(U.K.)

British & German Tanks of WW-I, by Peter Chamberlain & Chris Ellis, Arms & Amour, London, 1969: A&W S 73 7:13
British Armour in Action, by Norm E. Harms & Steve Clayton, Squadron/Signal, Warren MI: AFV S 74 4/12:31; RiS Sp 74 2/3-4:162; WWE S 74 1/5:143
British Tanks 1946-1970, by RAC Tank Museum, Bovington, Dorset: MM F 72 12/10:533
Chieftain & Leopard, vols. 1&2, by Michael Norman, Profiles 18 & 19, Windsor, Berks: Sc Ja 71 2/1:19
The Churchill Tank, by Peter Chamberlain & Chriss Ellis, Arms & Armour London, 1971: AFV F 72 2/11:22; Afx N 71 13/3:138; Afx Je 73 14/10:566; MM Ag 74 4/8:417-418; WWE Ja 75 2/1:27
The Churchill, by Bryan Perret, Ian Allan, Shepperton: Afx Je 75 16/10:613; MM O 74 4/10:624; WWE Mr 75 2/2:65
Conqueror Heavy Gun Tank, Profile 38, Windsor, Berks: RT Je 72 5/6:71
Cromwell & Comet Tanks, by James Bingham, Profile 25, Windsor, Berks: Afx Je 71 12/10:533; IM Je 71 8/6:17; RT Ap 71 4/4:46; Sc Jl 71 2/7:344-345
Matilda, by Bryan Perret, Ian Allan, Shepperton: MW F 74 2/6:323
The Valentine in North Africa, by Bryan Perrett, Ian Allan, London, 1972: AFV My 73 4/4:18

(U.S.)

Light Tanks M22 Locust & M24 Chaffee, by Robert Icks, Profile 46, Windsor Berks: Afx O 72 14/2:107; RT S 72 5/9:99
M4 Medium (Sherman) Tank, Profile 29, Windsor, Berks: Afx S 71 13/1:49; Sc O 71 2/9:561
M6 Heavy Tank & M26 Pershing, by Robert J. Icks, Profile 32, Windsor, Berks: MM D 71 1/12:664; RT N 71 4/11:129
M47 Patton, by Robert J. Icks, Profile 52, Windsor, Berks: MW Mr 73 1/7:345
M-48, M-60, by Robert Icks, Profile, Windsor, Berks: RT Mr 71 4/3:26
M103 Heavy Tank & M41 Light Tank (Walker Bulldog), Profile 41, Windsor, Berks: RT Jl 72 5/7:84
Pershing--A History of the Medium Tank T20 Series, by R. P. Hunnicutt, Feist Publications, 1971: AFV N 71 3/3:23; Afx N 71 13/3:138
The Sherman, an Illustrated History of the M4 Medium Tank, by Peter Chamberlain & Chris Ellis, Arco, NY, 1969: RiS W 74 2/2:66
Sherman Tank 1941-45, by Chris Ellis & Peter Chamberlain, Almark: MM Ja 71 1/1:48-49; RiS W 2/2:66

Color Patterns & Markings

American Military Camouflage & Markings 1939-1945, by Terence Wise, Almark, New Malden: Afx S 73 15/1:56; A&W Ja 74 9:13; MM Ag 73 3/8:538; MW Ag 73 1/12:663
Armor Camouflage & Markings, North Africa 1940-1943, by George R. Bradford, pvt: AFV Ja 72 3/5:27; MM Ag 74 4/8:476; RT D 71 4/12:145
British Military Markings, 1939-1945, by Peter Hodges, Almark, New Malden: AFV N 71 3/3:23; Afx Jl 71 12/11:606; Sc D 71 2/12:671
Cavalry & Yeomanry Badges of the British Army, 1914, by F. Wilkinson, Arms & Armour, London: Afx Mr 74 15/7:422; MM F 74 4/2:98
Formation Badges of WW-II--Britain, Commonwealth, & Empire, by Howard N. Cole, Arms & Armour, London: Afx Mr 74 15/7:422
Military Vehicle Markings, by Terence Wise, MAP, Hemel Hempstead, Herts: Afx My 72 13/9:522
Military Vehicle Markings, part 2: tactical signs & national identification marks, by Terrence Wise, MAP, Hemel Hempstead, Herts: Afx Je 73 14/10:566; MM Ap 73 3/4:244-245; MW Ap 73 1/8:411
Wehrmacht Camouflage & Markings, 1939-1945, by W. J. K, Davies, Almark, London, 1972: AFV Je 73 4/5:16; Afx F 74 15/6:369; A&W Mr 73 4:13
Wehrmacht Divisional Signs, 1938-1945, by Theodor Hartmann, Almark, New Malden: MM Ap 71 1/4:208

ARMY

Biography

Hitler & His Generals, the Hidden Crisis, Jan-June 1938, by Harold C. Deutsch, University of Minnesota Press, Minneapolis: WWE S 74 1/5:143

Hitler's Generals, by Richard Humble, Doubleday, Garden City, NY: WWE N 74 1/6:171

Master of Spies, by Frantisek Moravec, Doubleday, Garden City, NY, 1975: autobiography: WW2J Jl 75 2/4:35

Patton, a Study in Command, by H. Essame, Scribners, NY, 1974: WWE Mr 74 1/2:50

Rommel, by Charles Douglas-Home, Saturday Review Press, NY: WWE Ja 74 1/1:14

Strictly Personal, by John S. D. Eisenhower, Doubleday, Garden City, NY: WWE S 74 1/5:143

Covert Operations

The Battle for Twelveland, by Charles Whiting, Leo Cooper, London: WW-II spy: MM S 75 5/9:527

Codeword: Direktor, by Heinz Hohne, Pan, London: Afx Je 74 15/10:601

Encyclopedia of Espionage, by Ronald Seth, Doubleday, Garden City, NY: WWE My 74 1/3:75

Game of Foxes, by Ladislas Farago, David McKay, NY, 1971: WWE Mr 74 1/2:49

Hitler's Spies & Saboteurs, by Charles Wighton & Günther Peis, Award Books (org Holt, Rinehart & Winston, 1958): WWE Mr 75 2/2:66

Master of Spies, by Frantisek Moravec, Doubleday, Garden City, NY, 1975: WW2J Jl 75 2/4:35

The Navajo Code Talkers, by Doris A. Paul, Dorrance, Philadelphia: WWE Ja 74 1/1:11

A Secret War, Americans in China, 1944-1945, by Oliver J. Caldwell, Arcturus Paperbacks, Southern Illinois University Press, Carbondale, IL, 1972: WW2J Jl 75 2/4:35

Secrets of the Fascist Era, by Howard McGaw Smyth, Southern Illinois University Press, Carbondale, IL: compiling Italian documents: WW2J Jl 75 2/4:75

Fortifications

Architecture of Aggression, by Keith Mallory & Arvid Ottar, Archi-

tectural Press, London: MM N 73 3/11:763; MW F 74 2/6:323
Fire & Stone, the Science of Fortress Warfare 1660-1860, by Christopher Duffy, David & Charles, Newton Abbot, 1975: A&W S 75 19:48
Forts & Castles, by Terence Wise, Almark: MW Mr 73 1/7:381

Heraldry

Army Badges & Insignia of World War II, by Guido Rosignoli, Blandford, London: Fus W 74 1/2:30+; IM S 75 11/5:14; MW Ja 73 1/5:268; book 2: S&L (D 75) 11:32
British Cavalry Standards, by Dino Lemonofides, Almark, New Malden: MM F 72 2/2:75
British Infantry Colours, by Dino Lemonofides, Almark, New Malden: Afx Ap 71 12/8:429; MM Jl 71 1/7:368
British Military Colours, by Dino Lemonofides, Almark, New Malden: Sc Jl 71 2/7:347
Cap Badges of the Canadian Officer Training Corps, by Roy Thompson, pvt, Halifax, NS: WWE Ja 75 2/1:26-27
Discovering British Military Badges & Buttons, by R. J. Wilkinson-Latham, Shire, Aylesbury, Bucks: Afx My 73 14/9:512
Flags & Banners of the Third Reich, by A. S. Walker, R. G. Hickox, C. Farlowe, Almark, New Malden: Afx Ap 74 15/8: 480; A&W My 74 11:13; RiS Sp 74 2/3-4:159; WW2J Jl 75 2/4: 34
Flags & Standards of the Third Reich, by Brian Leigh Davis, Macdonald & Jane's, London: AI O 75 9/4:206; Afx Je 75 16/10: 613; MM Ap 75 5/4:218
Headress Badges of the British Army, by A. L. Kipling & H. L. King, Frederick Muller, London: MM Ag 73 3/8:539
Heraldry of the World, by Carl Alexander von Volborth, ed D. H. B. Chesshyre, Macmillan, NY, 1974: WWE Ja 75 2/1:27
Insignia of the Third Reich, by John H. Angolia, Ducimus Books, London: MM F 75 5/2:88
Military Badges & Buttons, by R. J. Wilkinson-Latham: MM Ap 73 3/4:245
Military Insignia of Cornwall, by D. E. Ivall & Charles Thomas, Penwith Books, Redruth, Corn: MM Ap 75 5/4:233
Observer's Book of British Awards & Medals, by E. C. Joslin, Frederick Warne, London: MM Ja 75 5/1:24
Observer's Book of Heraldry, by Charles Mackinnon, Frederick Warne, London: MM My 72 2/5:227
Piccolo Picture Book of Flags, by Valerie Pitt, Pan: MM Ap 73 3/4:245
Regimental Badges, by T. J. Edwards, Charles Knight, London: MM O 74 4/10:625
Ribbons & Medals, the World's Military & Civil Awards, ed H. Taprell Dorling, L. F. Guill & Francis K. Mason, Doubleday, Garden City, NY: WWE N 74 1/6:192
Waffen SS, Its Divisional Insignia, by C. Beadle & Theodore Hart-

mann, Key Publications, Bromley, Kent: Afx N 71 13/3:138; MM D 71 1/2:664

Land Battles & Wars

(General)

Almanac of Liberty, A Chronology of American Military Anniversaries from 1775 to Present, by Benjamin F. Schemmer, Macmillan, NY, 1974: WWE Mr 75 2/2:65
Dictionary of Battles 743 BC to Present, by Thomas Harbottle & George Bruce, Stein & Day, Briarclife Manor, NY: WW2J Jl 75 2/4:35
Encyclopedia of Military History from 3500 BC to Present, by R. E. Dupuy & T. N. Dupuy, Macdonald: Afx Je 71 13/10:546; MW S 72 1/1:52
Famous Land Battles, by Donald Kneebone, Frederick Muller: MM Mr 71 1/3:159
Famous Tank Battles from World War I to Vietnam, by Robert J. Icks, Profile, Windsor, Berks: AFV D 72 3/12:20; Afx Ag 73 14/12:682; MM My 73 3/5:313; MW Je 73 1/10:515
Guinness History of Land Warfare, by Kenneth Macksey, Guinness Superlatives, Enfield, Middx: MM Ja 74 4/1:54
The Relentless Verity, Canadian Military Photographers since 1885, by Peter Robertson, University of Toronto Press, Toronto: RT Ja 74 7/1:2; WWE My 74 1/3:76
The Universal Soldier, ed Martin Windrow & Frederick Wilkinson, Guinness Superlatives: Afx D 71 13/4:227

(Ancient to 1700)

Battle of Tewkesbury, 4th May 1471, by P. W. Hammond, R. G. Shearing & G. Wheeler, Municipal Offices, Tewkesbury, Glos: Afx Ag 72 13/12:686
Battle of Tewkesbury, May 4th 1471, by B. Linnell, pvt, Tewkesbury, Glos: Afx Ag 72 13/12:686
Discovering Famous Battles--Ancient Warfare, by Jeff Fletcher, Shire, Tring: MM My 74 4/5:277-278
The English Civil War--A Military Handbook, ed John Tucker & Lewis S. Winstock, Arms & Armour, London: Afx N 72 14/3:166; MM N 72 2/11:610-611; MW N 72 1/3:159-160
The English Civil War 1642-1651, by R. Potter & G. A. Embleton, Almark, New Malden: Afx S 73 15/1:54+; MM Ag 73 3/8:538
Great Battles--Agincourt, by Charles Knight, Almark, New Malden: MM Ap 75 5/4:218; S&L (Ap 75) 7:33
History of the Battle of Agincourt, by Sir Harris Nicolas, Muller facsimile 1827: MM Ap 71 1/4:207
Marlborough's Campaigns, by I. F. W. Becken, Shire, Aylesbury, Bucks: Afx N 73 15/3:180; MM Jl 73 3/7:465

Military History of Tewkesbury, by B. Linnell, pvt, Tewksbury, Glos: Afx Ag 72 13/12:686
An Accurate & Interesting Account of Heroes in the Campaign Against Quebec In 1775, by John Joseph Henry, reprinted from 1812, E. P. Publications, Wakefield, Yorks: S&L Jl 74 2:20
The American War of Independence 1775-1783, ed John Williams, Invasion, London: MM Ja 75 5/1:31; S&L (O 74) 4:29
Jacobite Rebellion, by Hilary Kemp, Almark, New Malden: S&L (D 75) 11:30
La Marsigliese in Liguria, by Antonino Ronco, Edizioni Tolozzi, Genoa, 1973: A&W Mr 74 10:13

(Napoleonic)

Britain at Bay--Defence Against Bonaparte 1803, by Richard Glover, George Allen & Unwin, Hemel Hempstead, Herts: MM F 74 4/2:98
History of the Late War Between Great Britain & the United States of America, by David Thompson, reprint of 1832, E. P. Publishing, Wakefield, Yorks: S&L (O 74) 4:29-30
Napoleon's Conquest of Prussia 1806, by F. Loraine Petre, Arms & Armour, London: Afx N 72 14/3:166; MM N 72 2/11:611; MM Ja 73 3/1:52; MW D 72 1/4:211
Napoleon's Last Campaign in Germany 1813, by F. Loraine Petre, Arms & Armour, London: MM N 74 4/11:702
The Peninsular War, by R. J. Wilkinson-Latham, Shire, Aylesbury, Bucks: Afx N 73 15/3:180
The Peninsular War 1807-1814, by Michael Glover, David & Charles, Newton Abbot, Devon: MM Ag 74 4/8:477
A Voice from Waterloo, by Edward Cotton, E. P. Publishing, Wickfield, Yorks, facsimile 1849: MM My 74 4/5:277
Waterloo, by Henry Lachouque, Arms & Armour, London: Afx Ag 75 16/12:728; MM Ag 75 5/8:488-489; S&L (Je 75) 8:29
Wellington's Masterpiece--the Battle & Campaign of Salamanca, by J. P. Lawford & Peter Young, George Allen & Unwin, Hemel Hempstead, Herts: MM F 74 4/2:98
The Years of Napoleon, by C. A. Embleton & C. J. Hunt, Almark, New Malden: MW Mr 73 1/7:345+

(1820-1914)

Afghan Campaign 1878-1880, by Sidney Shadbolt, J. B. Hayward, London: S&L (D 75) 11:31
American Civil War, by Arthur H. Booth, Frederick Muller: MM Mr 71 1/3:158-159
The American Civil War, by C. J. Hunt & G. A. Embleton, Almark, New Malden: MM O 74 4/10:624; S&L (O 74) 4:28
Civil War Handbook, by William H. Price, Civil War Research Associates, 1961: MM Jl 71 1/7:367
The Emperor's Sword, by Noel F. Busch, Gallery Press, Liverpool: Russo-Japanese War: S&L (D 75) 11:28

First Bull Run 1861, by Peter Davis & H. John Cooper, Charles Knight, London: Afx O 71 13/2:75
Omdurman, by Philip Ziegler, Collins, London: MM N 73 3/11:763
Rorke's Drift--a Victorian Epic, by Michael Glover, Leo Cooper, London: MM Je 75 16/10:363
South African Campaign of 1879, by J. B. Mackinnon & S. H. Shadbolt, J. B. Hayward, London: S&L (D 75) 11:31
Victoria's Wars, by I. F. W. Beckett, Shire, Aylesbury, Bucks: MM Mr 75 5/3:158

(World War I)

Battle for the Bundu, by Charles Miller, Macmillan, NY, 1974: Fus Su 74 1/4:34
History of World War I: ed A. J. P. Taylor, Octopus Book, London: S&L (D 74) 5:26
Purnell's History of the World Wars Special, serial review: RiS W 74 2/2:77
Tank Battles of WW-I, by Bryan Cooper, Ian Allan, Shepperton: Afx S 74 16/1:53; MM Je 74 4/6:333
The Western Front 1914-1918, by D. Banting & G. A. Embleton, Almark, New Malden: S&L (O 74) 4:29

(Between World Wars)

Days of Emperor & Clown, the Italo-Ethiopian War 1935-1936, by James Dugan & Laurence Lefore, Doubleday, Garden City, NY: WWE Ja 74 1/1:4
And I Remember Spain, ed Murray A. Sperber, Macmillan, NY, 1974: WWE Ja 75 2/1:26
Revolution & Civil War in Spain, by Pierre Broue & Emile Temime, MIT Press, Cambridge MA: AI Ap 75 8/4:207
The Sino-Japanese War 1937-1941, by Frank Dorn, Macmillan, NY, 1974: WWE Ja 75 2/1:28

(World War II)

The Battle for Crete, by S. W. C. Pack, Ian Allan, Shepperton: AE Mr 74 6/3:149; MW Ja 74 2/5:270
The Battles for Cassino, by E. D. Smith, Ian Allan, Shepperton, Surrey: MM N 75 5/1:667; S&L (D 75) 11:29
Bir Hacheim--Desert Citadel, by Richard Holmes, Pan/Ballantine, London: Afx Je 75 16/10:613
Bloody River, the Real Tragedy of the Rapido, by Martin Blumenson, Houghton Mifflin, Boston, 1970: WWE Ja 75 2/1:26
A Bridge at Arnhem, by Charles Whiting, Futura, London: Afx S 75 17/1:55-56
A Bridge To Far, by Cornelius Ryan, Hamish Hamilton, London: Afx S 75 17/1:55-56
The Bruneval Raid, Flashpoint of the Radar War, by George Millar,

Doubleday, Garden City, NY, 1975: WW2J Jl 75 2/4:35
Cassino, by Dominick Graham, Pan/Ballantine, London: Afx Ja 75 16/5:323
Code Word Barbarossa, by Burton Whaley, MIT Press, Cambridge MA: AFV F 75 5/3:13
A Concise Encyclopedia of the Second World War, by Alan Reid, Osprey, Reading: Afx Mr 75 16/7:442; MM Ap 75 5/4:233
D-Day, by Warren Tute, Macmillan, NY: Afx Jl 75 16/11:669; WWE S 74 1/5:143
Eyewitness History of WW-II, vol. 4, Victory, by Abraham Brothberg, Bantam, NY, 1966: WWE Mr 74 1/2:50
The Fall of Eban Emael, Prelude to Dunquerque, by James E. Mrazek, Robert B. Luce, Washington: AE Mr 73 4/3:139
The German Invasion of Crete, by Peter Stahl, A. A. Johnston, Langport, Som: MW S 73 2/1:45
Die Grosse Offensive 1942 Zeil Stalingrad, by H. Scheibert & W. Haupt, Podzun, Dorheim: AFV Mr 73 4/3:27
History of World War II, ed A. J. P. Taylor, Octopus Books, London: S&L (D 74) 5:26
Hitler's Last Offensive, by Peter Elstob, Macmillan, NY, 1971: Ardennes: WWE Mr 74 1/2:49
Illustrated Book of WW-II, by Peter Simkins, Sedgwick & Johnson (hardcover) & Pan (paperback): Afx Ja 74 15/5:316; MM Jl 73 3/7:464
Kreta--the German Invasion of Crete, by Peter Stahl, A. A. Johnston, Langport, Som: Afx N 73 15/3:180
Line of Departure, Tarawa, by Martin Russ, Doubleday, Garden City, NY, 1975: WW2J My 75 2/3:115
The Ninety Days, by Thomas N. Carmichael, Vernard Geis Associates, 1971: Summer 1942: WWE Mr 74 1/2:50
Not in Vain, by Ken Bell, C. P. Stacey, & Kildare Dobbs, University of Toronto: WWE Ja 74 1/1:11
Notes from the Warsaw Ghetto, by Emmanuel Ringelblum, trans Jacob Sloan, Schocken Books, NY: WW2J Jl 75 2/4:35
Operation Sealion, by Richard Cox, Thornton Cox, London: MM Mr 75 5/3:159
Les Poches de l'Atlantique, by Jacques Mordal, Presses de la Cité, Paris, 1965: WW2J Jl 75 2/4:34-35
Purnell's History of the World Wars Special, serial review: RiS W 74 2/2:77
The Race for the Rhine Bridges, by Alexander McKee, Souvenir, London: Afx Jl 71 12/11:606; MM My 71 1/5:252
Salerno, by David Mason, Pan/Ballantine, London: Afx Ap 75 16/8:499
The Second World War, pt. I & II, by Liliane & Fred Funcken, Ward Lock: S&L (D 75) 11:29
Siege & Survival, the Oddyssey of a Leningrader, by Elena Skrjabina, Southern Illinois University, Carbondale IL, 1971: WW2J Jl 75 2/4:35
Swastika at War, by Robert Hunt & Tom Hartman, Leo Cooper: Sc S 75 6/72:441; Doubleday, Garden City, NY, 1975: WW2J 75 2/4-5:22
Through Mud & Blood, by Bryan Perrett, Robert Hale, London: Afx

VI. Reviews

O 75 17/2:123
The Tigers are Burning, by Martin Caidin, Hawthorn, NY: Kursk: WWE My 74 1/3:76
Weapons & Warfare, ed Angus Hall, Phoebus, London: WW2J S 75 2/5-6:23

(Post World War II)

Seven Fireflights in Vietnam, by John Albright, John A. Cash, & Allan W. Sandstrum, Office of the Chief of Military History, U.S. Army, Washington: AFV N 73 4/8:26
When God Judged & Men Died, a Battle Report of the Yom Kippur War, by Arnold Sherman, Bantam Books, NY, 1973: AFV Mr 74 4/10:27

Strategy & Tactics

British Generalship in the Twentieth Century, by E. K. G. Sixmith, Arms & Armour, London, 1970: WWE Mr 75 2/2:65
The Politics of Torch, by Arthur Layton Funk, University of Kansas Press, Lawrence KS, 1974: WWE Ja 75 2/1:28

Uniforms

(General)

America's Fighting Men, by Peter Copeland & Harold L. Peterson, New York Graphic Society, NY: Afx O 72 14/2:107
Argyll & Sutherland Highlanders, by William McElwie, Osprey, Reading, Berks: Afx O 72 14/2:106
An Assemblage of Indian Army Soldiers & Uniforms, by Michael Glover & Chater Paul Chater, Perpetua, Farnham, Surrey: Afx My 74 15/9:539; MM F 74 4/2:98-99
Battle Dress, by Frederick Wilkinson, Business Signatures, Enfield, Middx: Afx O 71 13/2:75
The Buffs, by Gregory Blaxland, Osprey, Reading: Afx O 72 14/2:106
Cavalry Uniforms, by Robert & Christopher Wilkinson-Latham, Blandford, London: MM Jl 74 4/7:384
Ceremonial Uniforms of the World, by Jack Cassin-Scott & John Fabb, Stephen Hope: S&L Jl 74 2:28
Coldstream Guards, by Charles Staddon, Almark, New Malden: MM Ag 73 3/8:538; MW O 73 2/2:81
Cossacks, by Albert Seaton, Osprey, Reading: Afx F 73 14/6:337
The Dress of the Royal Artillery, by D. Alastair Campbell, Arms & Armour, London: A&W N 73 8:13

Discovering British Military Uniforms, by Arthur Taylor, Shire, Aylesbury, Bucks: Afx My 72 13/9:522
Discovering French & German Military Uniforms, by Arthur Taylor, Shire, Aylesbury, Bucks: Afx Jl 74 15/11:662-663; MM My 74 4/5:277
L'elmetto Italiano, 1915-1971, Intergest, Milan: MM Je 75 5/6: 362
15th King's Hussars, Dress & Appointments, 1759-1914, by Alan Kemp, Almark, London, 1972: A&W My 73 11:13
French Army Regiments & Uniforms, by W. A. Thornburn, Arms & Armour, London, 1971: Revolution to 1870: A&W N 72 2:13
Infantry Uniforms, including Artillery & Other Supporting Corps of Britain & the Commonwealth, 1742-1855, by Robert & Christopher Wilkinson-Latham, Blandford, London, 1972: A&W My 73 11:13; MM Jl 74 4/7:384; 1855-1939, 1970: A&W My 73 11:13
Key Uniform Guides, Arms & Armour, London: series review: MM Ag 74 4/8:476
The Life Guards, by Charles Stadden, Almark, New Malden, 1971: A&W Ja 73 3:13
Life Guards, Dress & Appointments, 1660-1914, comp A. H. Bowling, Almark, New Malden: Afx F 72 13/6:346
Military Dress of North America 1665-1970, by Martin Winrow & Gerry Embleton, Ian Allan, Shepperton: Afx Je 74 15/10:601; MM Ja 74 4/1:98; MW F 74 2/6:323; S&L Jl 74 2:20
Military Fashion, by John Mollo, Barry & Jinkins: MM O 72 2/10: 544
Military Uniforms, by J. B. R. Nicholson, Orbis, London: MM Ag 73 3/8:538-539
Regiments of Foot, by H. L. Wickes, Osprey, Reading: MM D 74 4/12:777
Regiments of Scotland, Aerial Press, London: MW Ja 73 1/5:268
The Royal Artillery, by W. Y. Carman, Osprey, Reading, Berks: Afx Je 73 14/10:566
Royal Scots Greys, by Charles Grant, Osprey, Reading, 1972: A&W Ja 73 3:13
Scots in Uniform, by Douglas N. Anderson, Holmes McDougal: S&L (Ap 75) 7:33
Scottish Military Uniforms, by Robert Wilkinson-Latham, David & Charles, 1975: A&W N 75 20:73; S&L (Ap 75) 7:33
Scottish Regiments & Uniforms 1660-1914, by A. H. Bowling, Almark, London, 1972: A&W Mr 73 10:13; MM F 72 2/2:75
A Short History of Japanese Armour, by Russell Robinson, HM Stationery Office, London: S&L (Ap 75) 7:32
Soviet Army, by Albert Seaton, Osprey, Reading: Afx F 73 14/6: 337-338
Stahlheim, by Floyd R. Tubbs, A. A. Johnson, Langport, Som, & Sky Books, NY: Afx Mr 72 13/7:389; WW2J Jl 75 2/4:35
30th Punjabis, by James Lawford, Osprey, Reading: Afx O 72 14/ 2:106
Uniformi Dell'Accademia Militare, by P. Giannatasio, Corporazione Arti Grafiche, Rome: A&W Ja 75 15:48
Uniformi Della Guardia di Fianza, by P. Giannatasio, Corporazione Arti Grafiche, Rome: A&W Ja 75 15:48

VI. Reviews 622

Veccie Uniformi Della Fanteria, by P. Giannattasio, Corporazione Arti Grafiche, Roma, 1972: A&W Ja 73 3:13

(Pre 18th Century)

The Armour of Imperial Rome, by H. Russell Robinson, Arms & Armour, London: Afx S 75 17/1:55; MM My 75 5/5:277; S&L (O 75) 10:26
Arms & Armour, by Aldo Cimarelli, Orbis: MM O 73 3/10:668
Uniforms of Marlborough's War, by Frank Wilson & Arthur Kipling, Charles Knight, London: Afx Je 71 12/10:535; MM Jl 71 1/7: 367

(18th Century)

The British Army in North America 1775-1783, by Robin May, Osprey, Reading, Berks: S&L (D 75) 5:26
The Colouring Book of Soldiers from the American Revolution, Imrie-Risley, NY: MM Mr 74 4/3:143
George Washington's Army, by Peter Young, Osprey, Reading, Berks: Afx O 72 14/2:106
Uniforms of the American, British, French, & German Armies in the War of the American Revolution 1775-1783, by Charles M. Lefferts, WE Inc reprint, NY: Afx Ap 72 13/8:447
Uniforms of the American Revolution, by John Mollo & Malcolm McGregor, Blandford, MM Ap 75 5/4:218; S&L (Ap 75) 7:32
Uniforms of the Seven Years War--Prussia, comp J. Braithwaite, Uniform Reference 1, Greenwood & Ball, Thornaby-on-Tees: MM F 75 5/2:102; S&L (F 75) 6:30
Uniforms of the War of the American Revolution, by Charles M. Lefferts, WE Inc: Sc Je 72 3/6:336
Uniforms Worn During 1740-1760, by Arthur Kipling, Charles Knight, London: Afx F 75 16/6:384; MM O 74 4/10:625

(Napoleonic)

Anthologie de l'Uniforms, series 1er Empire, No. 1: Grenadiers à Pied de la Garde Imperiale, by Liliane & Fred Funcken, Editions Funcken, Brussels: Afx O 72 14/2:106
Arms & Uniforms of the Napoleonic Wars, 2 vols, by Liliane & Fred Funcken, Ward Lock, London: Afx F 74 15/6:369; MM Ap 73 3/4:243; pt 1 only: MM F 74 4/2:99; pt 2 only: MM Ja 73 3/1:53
The Austro-Hungarian Army of the Napoleonic Wars, by Albert Seaton, Osprey, Reading, Berks: Afx Jl 73 14/11:624
Blucher's Army 1813-1815, by Peter Young, Osprey, Reading, Berks: Afx Je 73 14/10:566
British Cavalry, by John Mollo, Waterloo Uniforms 1, Historical Research Unit, London: Afx Ap 74 15/8:480; MM S 73 3/9:539; MW Ja 74 2/5:268

L'Esercito del Regno Italico, by Stefano Ales, Intergest, Milan:
1812: S&L N 74 14:48
Foot Regiments of the Imperial Guard, by Michael G. Head, Almark,
London: A&W S 73 7:13; MW Jl 73 1/11:587
Imperial Guard of Napoleon Bonaparte, Aerial Press, London: MW
Ja 73 1/5:268
Military Dress of the Peninsular War, by Martin Windrow & Gerry
Embleton, Ian Allan, Shepperton: Afx N 74 16/3:190; MM O
74 4/10:625
Regiments at Waterloo, by Rene North, Almark, New Malden: Afx
Je 71 12/10:533
The Russian Army of the Napoleonic Wars, by Albert Seaton, Osprey, Reading, Berks: Afx Jl 73 14/11:624
Uniforms of the Napoleonic Wars 1796-1814, by Jack Cassin-Scott,
Blandford: MM Ja 74 4/1:53-54
Uniforms of the Peninsular War, by Arthur Kipling, Charles Knight,
London: Afx Je 72 13/10:546
Uniforms of Waterloo in Colour, by Philip Haythornwaite, Blandford:
MM Ap 75 5/4:218; S&L (Ap 75) 7:33

(1820-1914)

Album de la Artilleria Espanola en 1862, by Alfonso de Carlos,
Madrid, 1972: A&W My 73 5:13
American Civil War Cavalry, by Michael Blake, Almark, London,
1973: A&W S 73 7:13; MW My 73 1/9:495
American Civil War Infantry, by Michael Blake, Almark, New Malden, Surrey: Afx F 71 12/6:328
The American War 1812-1814, by Philip R. N. Katcher, Osprey,
Reading, Berks: S&L (D 74) 5:26
British Artillery, by Robert Wilkinson-Latham, Crimean Uniforms
2, Historical Research Unit: MM My 74 4/5:278
British Infantry, by Michael Barthrop, Crimean Uniforms 1, Historical Research Unit: MM O 74 4/10:626
Crimean Uniforms: British Infantry, by Michael Barthrop, Historical Research Unit, 1974: S&L (D 74) 5:27
Cuirassiers & Heavy Cavalry, by D. S. V. Fosten, Almark, New
Malden, Surrey: Afx D 73 15/4:249-250; IM Ag 73 10/8:insert; MM S 73 3/9:615; MW S 73 2/1:45
Dress Regulations 1846, Arms & Armour reprint of Crimea war
manual: MM Ag 71 1/8:418
Foot Guards Regiments, 1880-1914, comp A. H. Bowling, Almark,
New Malden: Afx F 72 13/6:346
Hussars & Mounted Rifles--Uniforms of the Imperial German Cavalry 1900-1914, by D. H. Hagger, Almark, New Malden: MM N
74 4/11:701; S&L Ag 74 3:28; S&L (O 74) 4:28
Indian Cavalry Regiments, 1880-1914, by A. H. Bowling, Almark,
New Malden: Afx Je 71 12/10:533

(World War I)

Arms & Uniforms: the First World War, by Liliane & Fred Funcken,

Ward Lock, London: S&L (O 74) 4:29
German Artillery 1914-1918, by David Nash, Almark, London, 1971: A&W N 72 2:13
German Infantry 1914-1918, by David Nash, Almark, Edgward, Middx: Afx O 71 13/1:75

(World War II)

Afrika Korps, by Peter Chamberlain & Chris Ellis, Wehrmacht Illustrated 1, Almark, New Malden: Afx F 71 12/6:328
Army Uniforms of World War 2, by Andrew Mollo & Malcolm McGregor, Blandford & Macmillan, NY, 1974: MM Ja 74 4/1:53-54; WWE Ja 75 2/1:26
Colour Guide to German Army Uniforms 1933-1945, by J. L. de Smet, Arms & Armour, London: Afx Jl 74 15/11:663; MM My 74 4/5:277
Fakes & Frauds of the Third Reich, by Freiherr von Mollendorf, Die Wehrmacht: Afx Mr 72 13/7:389; MM Ja 71 1/1:47
German Army Uniforms & Insignia, 1933-45, by Brian L. Davis, Arms & Armour, London: Afx F 72 13/6:346; MM Ja 72 2/1:45
German Combat Uniforms, by S. R. Gordon Douglas, Almark: Afx Ja 71 12/5:263; MM F 71 1/2:104-105; MM Ap 71 1/4:208-209
German Military Combat Dress, 1939-1945, by Chris Ellis, Almark, New Malden: Afx S 73 15/1:56; MM Ag 73 3/8:538; MW Jl 73 1/11:587
Japanese Army Uniforms & Equipment 1935-1945, by Roy Dilley, Almark, London, 1970: A&W N 72 2:13; A&W S 73 7:13
Kreigsmarine Uniforms, by Peter Stahl, A. A. Johnston, Langport, Som: Afx N 73 15/3:180
Luftwaffe Uniforms, by Peter Stahl, A. A. Johnston, Langport, Som: Afx N 73 15/3:180
Naval, Marine, & Air Force Uniforms of WW-2, by Andrew Mollo, Blandford, London: AN 12 D 75 4/14:7; IM N 75 11/6:25
Panzer Divisions, by Martin Windrow, Osprey, Reading: Afx My 73 14/9:512
L'Uniforme et les armes des soldats de la guerre 1939-1945, by Liliane & Fred Funcken, Casterman Books, Paris: Afx F 73 14/7:336; A&W Jl 74 12/14
Uniforms of the Luftwaffe 1939-1945, by Matthew Cooper, Almark, New Malden: MM Ag 74 4/10:624; WW2J Jl 75 2/4:35
Uniforms of the Royal Armoured Corps, by Malcolm Dawson, Almark, New Malden: MM N 74 4/11:701; S&L (D 74) 5:27
Uniforms of the SS, vol. 6: Waffen SS Clothing & Equipment, by Andrew Mollo, Historical Research Unit, London, 1972: Afx My 73 14/9:512; Fus Sp 74 1/3:24+; MM Mr 73 3/3:157; MW My 73 1/9:459
Uniforms, Organization & History of the Afrika Korps, by Roger James Bender & Richard D. Law, pvt, Mountain View, CA: WWE Ja 74 1/1:14
United States Army Uniforms 1939-45, by Roy Dilley, Almark, New Malden, Surrey: Afx N 72 14/3:166; A&W Ja 74 9:13; MW S

72 1/1:39
Waffen SS, by D. S. V. Fosten & R. J. Marrion, Almark, Edgward, Middx: Afx Ag 71 12/12:657; MM O 71 1/10:532

(Post World War II)

The Naval Officer's Uniform Guide, by J. B. Castano, Patrick Stephens, Cambridge: U.S.: Afx Je 75 16/10:613

Units

(General)

Airborne to Battle, by Maurice Tugwell, William Kimber, London: MW O 72 1/2:103
Armies of the American Wars 1753-1815, by Philip Katcher, Osprey, Reading: S&L (D 75) 11:32
British Hussar Regiments, 1805-1914, by A. H. Bowling, Almark: MW N 72 1/3:160
Commandos, by Mar Fiament, Balland, Paris, 1972: A&W My 73 5:13
Durham Light Infantry, by William Moore, Leo Cooper, London: S&L (O 75) 10:26
41st Artillery, by A. Giachi, STEM-Mucchi, Modena: Italian, 1915-1952: A&W My 75 17:48
French Foreign Legion, by Martin Windrow, Osprey, Reading, Berks: MM S 71 1/9:480
Gunners at War: a Tactical Study of the Royal Artillery in the Twentieth Century, by Shelford Bidwell, Arms & Armour, London, 1970: WWE Ja 75 2/1:26
The Gurkha Rifles, by J. B. R. Nicholson, Osprey, Reading, Berks: S&L (D 74) 5:26
History of Armoured Forces & Their Vehicles, by Richard M. Ogorkiewicz, Arms & Armour, London: A&W Jl 73 6:15
History of the Regiment of Artillery, Indian Army, ed D. K. Pelit: MM Mr 73 3/3:157
History of the Scottish Regiments, by W. P. Paul, Scottish Military Collectors Society, Glasgow: Afx Je 75 16/10:613; S&L (F 75) 6:30
Household Cavalry Regiment, by Roy Manser: S&L (D 75) 11:28
Men-At-Arms Series, Osprey, Reading, Berks: Afx Ag 74 15/12: 724; MM Jl 74 4/7:463
I Paracadutisti, by Nino Arena, STEM-Mucchi, Modena: Afx My 74 15/9:539; RT Ja 72 5/1:22
The Royal Dragoons, by R. J. T. Hills, Leo Cooper, Knight: MM Ja 73 3/1:52
Royal Green Jackets, by Christopher Wilkinson-Latham, Osprey, Reading, Berks: S&L (D 75) 11:31
Royal Wiltshire Yeomanry, vol. 3, 1907-1967, by J. R. I. Platt,

VI. Reviews

Garnstone: MM Ja 73 3/1:51-52
16th/5th Queen's Royal Lancers, by James Lowe, Leo Cooper: MM
    My 73 3/5:314
The Tewkesbury Volunteers 1750-1950, by B. Linnell, Tewkesbury,
    Glos: MW Ag 73 1/12:627
Tracing the Regiments, by Edgar Letts, pvt, Marblethorpe, Lincs:
    Afx F 74 15/6:369
U.S. Armor--Cavalry, by Duncan Crow, Profile, Windsor, Berks:
    AFV Je 73 4/5:16; Afx Jl 73 14/11:624; MM Jl 73 3/7:464;
    MW Jl 73 1/11:587
U.S. Cavalry, by John Selby & Michael Roffe, Men-at-Arms, Hippocrene Books, NY: Fus Su 74 1/4:34+

(Ancient to Renaissance)

The English Civil War Armies, by Peter Young, Osprey, Reading,
    Berks: Afx S 73 15/1:54
Medieval European Armies, by Terence Wise, Osprey, London:
    Afx D 75 17/4:242; S&L (D 75) 11:31
Renaissance Armies 1480-1650, by George Gush, Patrick Stephens,
    Cambridge: Afx N 75 17/3:177; IM N 75 11/6:26; S&L (D 75)
    11:32

(18th Century)

American Soldiers of the Revolution, by Alan Kemp, Almark, New
    Malden, Surrey: Afx My 72 13/9:522; MM Ag 72 2/8:428
Armies of the American Revolution, by Ian V. Hogg & John Batchelor, Leo Cooper, London: MM Jl 75 5/7:427; S&L (D 75) 11:
    29
The British Army in the American Revolution, by Alan Kemp, Almark, New Malden, Surrey: Afx Je 74 15/10:601
King George's Army 1775-1783: A Handbook of British, American,
    & German Regiments, by Philip R. N. Katcher, Osprey, Reading, Berks: Afx O 73 15/2:117
Navies of the American Revolution, by Anthony Preston, David Lyon
    & John H. Batchelor, Leo Cooper, London: S&L D 75 11:29

(Napoleonic)

Attack the Colour! The Royal Dragoons in the Peninsular & at
    Waterloo, by A. E. Clark-Kennedy, Research Publishing, London: MM Ag 75 5/8:489
The Black Brunswickers, by Otto von Pivka, Osprey, Reading,
    Berks: Afx Jl 73 14/11:624
The British Soldier in the Napoleonic Wars 1793-1815, by Antony
    Brett-James, Macmillan: MM Mr 71 1/3:158
La Cavalleria di Linea Italica 1796-1814, by G. Galliani, G. R.
    Parisini, G. M. Rocchiero, Interconair, Genoa, 1973: A&W
    73 6:15

1815, the Armies at Waterloo, by Ugo Pericoli, Sphere Books, London: MM D 73 3/12:832
L'Esercito del Regno Italico, by Stefano Ales, Itnergest, Milan: 1812: A&W N 74 14:14
The French Imperial Army, by Richard Riehn, Imrie/Risley, Merrick, NY: MM Ja 71 1/1:47
French Napoleonic Line Infantry, by Emir Bukhari, Almark, New Malden, Surrey: Afx Ap 74 15/8:480; MM My 74 4/5:278
The King's German Legion, by Otto von Pivka, Osprey, Reading, Berks: Afx D 74 16/4:257
Men of Waterloo, by John Sutherland, Frederick Muller, 1966: MM Mr 71 1/3:47
Napoleon's Army, by H. C. B. Rogers, Ian Allan, Shepperton: Afx N 74 16/3:190; MM O 74 4/10:625-626
Napoleon's Artillery, by Robert Wilkinson-Latham, Osprey, Reading, Berks: S&L (D 75) 11:31
Napoleon's German Allies (1): Westfalia & Kleve-Berg, by Otto von Pivka, Osprey, Reading, Berks: Afx Ag 75 16/12:728
Napoleon's Polish Troops, by Otto von Pivka, Osprey, Reading, Berks: S&L (D 74) 5:26
The Prussian Army 1808-1815, by David Nash, Almark, New Malden, 1972: A&W Mr 73 4:13; MM Ap 73 3/4:244; MW Mr 73 1/7: 381
Regiments at Waterloo, by Rene North, Almark, New Malden, Surrey: MM S 71 1/9:478; MM O 71 1/10:533
Soldiers of the Peninsular War, by Rene North, Almark, New Malden, Surrey: MW S 72 1/1:52
Spanish Armies of the Napoleonic Wars, by Otto von Pivka, Osprey, London: Afx D 75 17/4:242

(1820-1914)

American Civil War Infantry, by Michael Blake, Almark, London, 1970: A&W N 72 2:13; MM Ap 71 1/4:207; MM O 71 1/10:533
The Army of the Duchy of Sicily 1850-1860, by Stefano Ales, Integest, Milan: MM S 75 5/9:527
The British Army from Old Photographs, by Boris Mollo, J. M. Dent, London: MM Je 75 5/6:362
Honour the Light Brigade, by William M. Lummis & K. C. Wynn, J. B. Hayward: S&L (D 75) 11:29
Stonewall Brigade, by John Selby, Osprey, Reading, Berks: MM S 71 1/9:480
Twenty-Five Years in the Rifle Brigade, by William Surtees, Muller reprint, 1833: MM Mr 73 3/3:157
The Victorian & Edwardian Army from Old Photographs, by John Fabb & W. Y. Carman, B. T. Batsford: MM Je 75 5/6:362
The Victorian Army in Photographs, by David Clammer, David & Charles, Newton Abbot, Devon: Afx Jl 75 16/11:668-669; MM Je 75 5/6:362
With the Camel Corps Up the Nile, by Count Gleichen, E. P. Publishing, Wakefield, W. York: MM N 75 5/11:667

VI. Reviews 628

(World War I)

Austro-Hungarian Infantry 1914-1918, by J. S. Luchas, Almark, London, 1973: A&W S 73 7:13
Hussars & Mounted Rifles, by D. H. Hagger, Almark, London: German cavalry: A&W Ja 75 15:48

(World War II--Allied)

British Airborne Troops, by Barry Gregory, Macdonald & Jane's, London: AI Mr 75 8/3:154; Afx Ap 75 16/8:499; MM D 74 4/12:777
Chindit, by Michael Calvert, Pan/Ballantine, London: Afx Ag 74 15/12:724; MM Ag 74 4/8:476
Commando, by Peter Young, Pan/Ballantine, London: Afx Ap 74 15/8:480
The 1st & 2nd Yugoslavian Tank Brigades, 1943-1945, Anthony's Originals, Los Angeles, CA: WWE Mr 75 2/2:66-67
The Raiders, by Arthur Swinson, Pan/Ballantine, London: LRDG, SAS: Afx S 74 16/1:53-54; MM Je 74 4/6:333
The 79th Armoured Division, Hobo's Funnies, by Nigel Duncan, Profile, Windsor, Berks: AFV Jl 72 3/9:18; Afx Ag 72 13/12:687; MW S 72 1/1:39
TD, a Brief History of the 899th Tank Destroyer Battalion, ed David R. Haugh, Recon, San Jose, CA, 1970: AFV F 73 4/2:14; WWE Mr 74 1/2:50
U.S. Airborne Forces Europe 1942-1945, by Brian L. Davis, Arms & Armour, London: Afx Ap 75 16/8:499; MM Mr 75 5/3:158

(World War II--Axis)

Afrika Korps, by Bruce Quarrie, Patrick Stephens, Cambridge: Afx D 75 17/4:242; IM N 75 11/6:25; S&L (D 75) 11:32
Afrika Korps 1941-42, by Peter Chamberlain & Chris Ellis, Almark, New Malden, Surrey: MM Ap 71 1/4:207
Afrikakorps--An Illustrated History, by Peter Stahl, A. A. Johnston, Langport, Som: Afx N 73 15/3:180
The East Came West, by Peter J. Huxley-Blythe, Caxton, Caldwell, ID, 1968: Cossacks in the German Army: WWE N 74 1/6:170
Fallschirmjaeger in Action, by Uwe Feist, Norman Harms, Ron Volstadt, Squadron/Signal, Warren MI, 1973: A&W Mr 74 10:13; AN 28 S 73 2/10:41; Fus Au 73 1/1:41
Gebirgejager, by Peter Chamberlain & Chris Ellis, Almark, New Malden, Surrey: MW Ap 73 1/8:411
German Airborne Troops, by Roger Edwards, Macdonald & Jane's, London: Afx Je 75 16/10:613; Doubleday, Garden City, NY, 1974: WWE Mr 75 2/2:66
German Army Handbook, 1939-1945, by W. J. K. Davies, Ian Allan, Shepperton, 1972: A&W Mr 73 1/7:13
German Parachute Forces 1935-1945, by Brian L. Davis, Arms & Armour, London: Afx Ap 75 16/8:499; MM Mr 75 5/3:158

Hitler Youth, by F. J. Stephens, Almark, New Malden, Surrey:
 Afx My 74 15/9:539
Hitler's Elite: Leibstandarte SS, by James Lucas & Matthew Cooper,
 Macdonald & Jane's, London: Afx D 75 17/4:242-243; MM S
 75 5/9:527
Hitler's Guard, Leibstandarten SS Adolf Hitler, by James J. Weingartner, Southern Illinois University Press, Carbondale IL,
 1974: WWE Ja 75 2/1:27
Hunters from the Sky, by Charles Whiting, Stein & Day, NY, 1974:
 AI O 75 9/4:205; Fus Sp 75 2/1:15+
Japanese Army of WW-II, by Philip Warner, Osprey, Reading,
 Berks: Afx Ja 74 15/5:316-317
Japanese Parachute Troops, ed Donald B. McLean, Normount: WWE
 My 74 1/3:76
Organizationbuch der NSDAP (1943 ed), Military Press: MW O 72
 1/2:103
Panzer Divisions, by Martin Windrow, Osprey, Reading, Berks:
 Afx My 73 14/9:512; A&W Mr 75 16:56; A&W My 75 17:48
Panzer Divisions of WW-II, by H. B. C. Watkins & Duncan Crow,
 Profile, Culver City, CA: AFV D 74 5/1:25
Panzer-Grenadier-Division "Grossdeutschland," by Horst Scheivert,
 Podzun, Dorheim, 1973: AFV Ja 74 4/9:28
Political Leaders of the NSDAF, by L. Milner, Almark trans of
 1943 German manual: A&W Mr 73 1/7:4:13; MW N 72 1/3:160
Uniforms, Organization & History of the Afrikakorps, by Roger
 James Bender & Richard D. Law, pvt, Mountain View, CA:
 MM Mr 74 4/3:143; WWE Ja 74 1/1:14
Waffen SS, by Roger James Bender & Hugh Page Taylor: MM Je
 73 3/6:390
Waffen SS in Action, by Uwe Feist, Norman Harms & Ron Volstad,
 Squadron/Signal, Warren MI: AFV Ja 74 15/5:28; Fus W 74
 1/2:30
Wehrmacht Illustrated series, Almark, London, 1972-1973: A&W
 Mr 74 10:13
Wenn alle Bruder schweigen, Munin Verlag: MM D 74 4/12:772

Miscellaneous

A Casebook of Military Mystery, by Raymond Lamont Brown, Patrick
 Stephens: occult: S&L (O 74) 4:28
Classical Bujutsu, by Conn F. Draeger, Phaidon: MM Jl 73 3/7:
 463
The German Army Handbook, 1939-1945, by Denis Bishop & W. J. K.
 Davies, Arco, NY, 1973: WW2J S 75 2/4-5:23
Military Origins, by Lawrence Gordon, Kaye & Ward: traditions:
 MM Jl 71 1/7:367-368
A Practical Guide for the Light Infantry Officer, by T. H. Cooper,
 Muller facsimile: MM Ap 71 1/4:207
Storia e Linguaggio dei Correspondenti di Guerra, by Glauco Licata,
 Buido Maino, Milan, 1972: A&W Jl 73 6:15

VI. Reviews

ASTRONOMY

Star & Planet Spotting, by Peter Lancaster Brown, Blandford, London: Al Je 75 8/6:305

AUTOMOBILES

General

American Trucks of the Early Thirties, Olyslager, Frederick Warne: Afx S 75 17/1:56; Sc Je 75 6/69:294
American Trucks of the Late Thirties, Olyslager, Frederick Warne: Afx S 75 17/1:56
British Cars of the Early Forties, Olyslager, Frederick Warne: Sc S 73 5/59:440
British Cars of the Early Thirties, Olyslager, Frederick Warne: Sc S 73 4/9:625
British Cars of the Late Forties, Olyslager, Frederick Warne: Sc Jl 74 5/58:359
British Cars of the Late Thirties, Olyslager, Frederick Warne: Sc S 73 4/9:625
British Lorries 1900-1945, by C. F. Klapper, Ian Allan, Shepperton: MW Ja 74 2/5:268
History of the Hants & Dorset Motor Services Ltd., by Colin Morris, David & Charles, Newton Abbot, Devon: Afx O 74 16/2: 117
In the Age of Motoring, by Ronald Barker & D. B. Tubbs, Patrick Stephens, London: Afx S 71 13/1:657
London Buses, Ian Allan, Shepperton: Afx Je 71 12/10:542
Observer's Book of Commercial Vehicles, Olyslager, Frederick Warne: Sc Ja 72 3/1:45; Sc F 75 6/65:71
Observer's Book of World Automobiles, Frederick Warne: Sc Ja 71 2/1:19
Prototype 1968-1970, by Mike Twits, Roger Taylor, & David Windsor, Pelham, London: Racing: Afx Ap 71 12/8:437
The Vintage Alvis, by Peter Hull & Norman Johnson, David & Charles, Newton Abbot, Devon: Sc Ag 74 5/59:440

Horse-Drawn

An Assemblage of 19th Century Horses & Carriages, by William Francis Freelove & Jennifer Lang, Perpetua, London: S&L (D 75) 11:32

Individual

Jaguar D-Type, Profile 11, Windsor, Berks: Afx Jl 74 15/11:664-665; MW Ja 74 2/5:270
Ruston Hornsby Cars 1923, Ruston Paxman Diesels, Lincoln: Afx F 75 16/6:385
246 SP 330 P4 Ferraris, by Paul Brère, Profile 1, Windsor, Berks: MW D 72 1/4:211

Traction

British & American Steam Carriages & Traction Engines, by William Fletcher, David & Charles, Newton Abbot, Devon: Afx F 75 16/6:385
A Century of Traction Engines, by W. P. Hughes, David & Charles, Newton Abbot, Devon: Afx O 71 13/2:105
The Complete Traction Engineman, by E. C. Kimbell, Ian Allan, Shepperton: MW F 74 2/6:323
Old Far Tractors, by Philip A. Wright, David & Charles, Newton Abbot, Devon: MW O 72 1/2:103
Steam on the Road, by David Brugess Wise, Hamlyn: MW Ag 73 1/12:627
Steam Traction Engines, Ruston Paxman Diesels, Lincoln: Afx F 75 16/6:385
Traction Engines & Steam Vehicles in Pictures, by Anthony Beaumont, David & Charles, Newton Abbot, Devon: Afx Ag 73 14/12:682
Traction Engines Past & Present, by Anthony Beaumont, David & Charles, Newton Abbot, Devon: Afx O 75 17/2:123

MISSILES & SPACE VEHICLES

Field Rocket Equipment of the German Army 1939-1945, by T. J. Gander, Almark, 1972: A&W N 73 8:13
Jane's Weapons Systems 1972-73, ed R. T. Pretty & D. H. R. Archer, Jane's Yearbooks, London: AE Mr 73 4/3:138
Jane's Weapons Systems 1973-74, ed R. T. Pretty & D. H. R. Archer, Sampson Low Marston, London: AE Ap 74 6/4:211
Missiles, Jane's Pocket Book, comp Ronald Pretty, Macdonald & Jane's, London: AI D 75 9/6:308; Sc N 75 6/74:569
Missiles of the World, by M. J. Taylor & J. W. R. Taylor, Ian Allan, Shepperton, 1972: AE F 73 4/2:89; Afx Mr 73 14/7:399; A&W N 72 2:13
Observer's Book of Manned Spaceflight, by Reginald Turnill, Frederick Warne: AE D 73 5/6:301; AI O 75 9/4:205; Afx My 74 15/9:539

Observer's Book of Unmanned Spaceflight, by Reginald Turnill,
   Frederick Warne, London: AI Ja 73 8/1:33
Our World in Space, by Isaac Asimov, Patrick Stephens, Cambridge:
   Afx Jl 74 15/11:665
Robot Explorers, by Kenneth Gatland, Blandford, London: AE D 73
   5/6:301
A Source Book of Rockets, Spacecraft & Spacemen, by Tim Furniss,
   Ward Lock, London: Afx S 74 16/1:52
Spies in the Sky, by John W. R. Taylor & David Mondey, Ian Allan,
   Shepperton: AE Ap 74 6/4:205; Afx F 74 15/6:368; AN 16 F
   73 1/20:15

MODELS

General

Airbrushing for Modellers, by Richard Goldman & Murray Ruben-
   stein, 1974: RT Je 75 8/1:9; RiS Mr 75 3/1:50
Handbook of Model Planes, Cars & Boats, by Bill Winter: RCS Ag
   75 1/4:67
Model World, ed Peter Riding, BBC Publications, London: Afx Jl
   75 16/11:667; IM Jl 75 11/4:19
Modelling with Balsa, by Ron Warring, Stanley Paul, London: Afx
   Ap 74 15/8:479-480

Aircraft

Airfoil Sections, by John Malkin, MAP, Hemel Hempstead, Herts:
   Aero D 71 36/431:710
The Art & Technique of Soaring, by Richard A. Worlters, McGraw-
   Hill: AM O 74 74/10:124-125
Building & Flying Scale Model Aircraft, by Walter A. Muscaiano,
   Herman: AM Ja 75 75/1:18
Flying Hand-Launched Gliders, by John Kaufman, William Morrow:
   AM Mr 75 75/3:14+
Flying Scale Models of WW-II, comp E. I. Coleman, CA: Sc S 75
   6/72:441
How to Make & Fly a Paper Aircraft, by Ralph Barnaby, John Mur-
   ray: Aero D 71 36/431:562
The Know How Book of Flying Models, Useborne, London: Afx My
   75 16/9:554
Make Your Hobby Model Aircraft, by Brian Philpott, Purnell, Maid-
   enhead, Berks: Afx N 75 17/3:177
Modern Aeromodelling, by R. G. Moulton, Faber & Faber, London:
   Afx My 75 16/9:554
Radio Control Model Aircraft, by Robert Lopshire, Macmillan: AM

D 74 74/12:18
Transistorized Radio Control for Models, by D. W. Aldrige, W. Foulsham, Slough, Bucks: Afx Je 74 15/10:600
The World of the Model Aircraft, by Guy R. Williams, Andre Deutch, London: AE Mr 74 6/3:150

Boats

Model Sail & Power Boating by Remote Control, TAB Books: RCS Ag 75 1/4:67-68

Railroads

Atlas Kingsize Railroad Plan Book, by John Armstrong & Thaddeus Stepek, Atlas, Hillside, NJ: RMC F 73 40/9:20-21
Bassett-Lowke Railways: RMC Ap 71 39/11:17
Bridges & Trestle Handbook for Model Railroaders, by Paul Mallery, Builders Compendium, Cossayuna, NY: NMRA Je 73 38/10:10
Clockwork, Steam & Electric--the History of Model Railways up to 1939, by Gustav Reder, trans C. Hamilton Ellis, Ian Allan, Shepperton: Afx Jl 74 15/11:664
Collector's Guide to Lionell Trains, 2 vols, by Tom McComas & James Tuohy, TM Productions, Wilmette, IL: MR D 75 42/12: 40-42
Color Treasury of Model Trains; or Model Trains, Railroad in the Making, by Gerald Pollinger, Instituto Geographico de Agostini, Novarra, Italy: MR Ap 74 41/4:18
Diesel & Electric Locomotive Painting & Lettering Diagram Book, New Haven RR Technical Information Assn, Montgomery AL: NMRA Je 73 38/10:11
Easy to Build Model RR Freight Cars: 24 "Dollar Car" Projects, by Model, Railroader, Kalmbach, Milwaukee, 1971: MR Mr 72 39/3:6-7; NMRA My 72 37/9:22
HO Engine Manual, by Harold Mellor, pvt, Saddle River, NJ: NMRA N 74 40/3:13; RMC N 74 43/6:15
HO Railroad That Grows, by Lynn H. Westcott, Kalmbach, Milwaukee: NMRA Je 73 38/10:10
How to Go Railway Modelling, by Norman Simmons, Patrick Stephens, London: Afx My 72 13/9:487+; Afx Ag 75 16/12:728; RT Ag 72 9/8:95
Illustrated HO Brass Caboose Checklist 1960-1973, Ladd Publications, Jacksonville, IL: MR O 74 4/10:29; NMRA Jl 74 39/12:16
Lettering Guide for Early Colorado Narrow Gauge Freight Cars, by William M. Cohen, Rocky Mountain Region, NMRA, Denver, CO: RMC N 71 40/6:18
The Model Railroading Handbook, by Robert Schleicher, Chilton, Radnor PA, 1975: MR D 75 42/12:40; NMRA D 75 41/4:21; NSG N 75 1/5:6-7

Model Railway Engines, by J. E. Minns, Wiedenfeld & Nicholson, London: Afx My 71 12/9:470

Model Traction Handbook for Model Railroads, by Paul Mallery & Steven Mallery, Vane A. Jones, Indianapolis, IN, 1974: MR S 75 42/9:21; NMRA My 75 40/9:13; NMRA Jl 75 40/11:25

Model Trains... Railroads in the Making, Orbis, London: Afx My 74 15/9:539-539; NMRA Ap 73 38/8:19

Modelbahn vor der Kamera, by Von Vernd Schmid, Alba, Düsseldorf: MR Ja 74 41/1:19

N Gauge Model Railways, by Michael Andress, Almark, New Malden, Surrey: Afx Jl 72 13/11:602

N Scale Primer, by Russ Larson, Kalmbach, Milwaukee: NMRA O 74 40/2:37

Narrow Gauge Model Railways, by Michael Andress, Almark, New Malden, Surrey: Afx D 71 13/4:223

1972 Decal Catalog & Railroad Lettering Manual, Walthers, Milwaukee WI: RMC F 73 41/9:24

1001 Model Railroading Ideas, Delta Magazine, Los Angeles, CA: NMRA Ag 72 37/13:21

Practical Electronic Projects for Model Railroaders, by Peter J. Thorne, Kalmbach, Milwaukee, WI, 1974: MR Mr 75 42/3:17+; NMRA My 75 40/9:13

Rails Around the Rectory: the Story of the Cadeby Light Railway, by E. R. Boston, Book House, Loughborough, Leics: Afx Ja 74 15/5:317

Restoration Parts for the Train Collector, by Dick Wheeler, Model Engineering Worlds, Monrovia, CA: RMC S 75 44/4:17

S Gauge Building & Repair Manual, ed Don Heimburger, S Gaugian, Tolono, IL: NMRA Ja 75 40/5:8

So You Want to Build a Live Steam Locomotive, by Joseph Foster Nelson, Wildwood, Cadillac, MI: MR My 75 42/5:19-20

Traction Guidebook for Model Railroaders, ed Mike Shafer, Kalmbach, Milwaukee: NMRA N 74 40/3:13

Traction Handbook (Traction Plan Index, vol. 1), comp Blair Foulds & NMRA Traction Committee, NMRA, Canton, OH: NMRA Ap 73 38/8:19; RMC Ap 73 41/11:26

200 & 1 Model Locomotives, by William J. Lenoir, pvt, Tampa, FL: RMC Ja 72 40/8:19

World Locomotive Models, by George Dow, Arco, NY: NMRA Mr 74 39/8:9

The World of Locomotive Models, by George Dow, Arco, NY: MR Ja 74 41/1:18-19

The World of Model Trains, by Guy R. Williams, Putnams, NY: NMRA My 71 36/9:21

Static Scale

General

Discovering Modelling for Wargames, by Dennis Teague, Shire,

Aylesbury, Bucks: Afx O 73 15/2:117; MM Ag 73 3/8:538
How to Go Advanced Plastic Modelling, by Chris Ellis, Patrick Stephens, London: Sc Ap 71 2/4:203+
How to Go Plastic Modelling, by Chris Ellis, Patrick Stephens, London: AN 28 S 73 2/10:15; Afx Ag 73 14/12:682; IM Jl 73 10/7:insert; MM Ag 73 3/8:539; MW O 73 2/2:81; RT Ag 73 6/8:91; Sc O 73 4/10:673
Making & Improving Plastic Models, by Bryan Philpott, David & Charles, Newton Abbot: AN 21 Mr 75 3/21:12; IM Mr 75 11/2:16; MM My 75 5/5:276; PAM Ja 75 8:136
Plastic Modelling, by Gerald Scarborough, Patrick Stephens, Cambridge: Afx My 74 15/9:538; AN 28 Je 74 3/2:16; MM Jl 74 4/7:384; RT Jl 74 7/7:71
Scale Models in Balsa, by W. M. Colbridge, Arthur Barker, London: Afx Ap 72 13/8:452

Aircraft

Aircraft Modelling, by Bryan Philpott, Patrick Stephens, Cambridge: Afx My 74 15/9:538; MM Jl 74 5/7:384; RT Jl 74 7/7:71
Calling All Spitfires--A Scale Modeller's Guide to the Spitfires in 1/72 Scale, by John R. Beaman, Jr., G. W. Jones, London: Afx O 74 16/2:116; IM N 73 10/11-12:insert; PAM Ap 74 5:75; RT Mr 74 7/3:31; (revised edition): IM My 75 11/3:9
How to Make Model Aircraft, by Chris Ellis, Hamlyn, Feltham, Middx: Afx My 75 16/9:554; Sc Ja 75 6/64:33
Model Aircraft, by Toby Wrigley & Philip O. Stearns, Orbis: Afx My 73 14/9:511; Afx F 74 15/6:367; AN 16 F 73 1/20:15; IM D 72 9/12:insert; MW Ja 73 1/5:268; Sc Ja 73 4/1:45
Plastic Scale Model Aircraft, by W. R. Matthews, Almark, New Malden, Surrey: AE F 72 2/2:85; Afx D 71 13/227; Sc F 72 3/2:99-100
Scale Model Aircraft in Plastic Card, by Harry Woodman, MAP, Hemel Hempstead, Herts: IM N 75 11/6:25

Armor

Military Modelling, by Gerald Scarborough, Patrick Stephens, Cambridge: Afx N 74 16/3:189
Scale Model Fighting Vehicles, by Kenneth M. Jones, Almark, New Malden, Surrey, 1972: Afx N 72 14/3:166; A&W My 73 5:13
Tank & AFV Modelling, by Gerald Scarborough, Patrick Stephens, Cambridge: Afx My 75 16/9:553; IM My 75 11/3:9; MM Je 75 5/6:363

Automobiles

Building Model Trucks, by Phil Jensen, Patrick Stephens, Cambridge: Afx Jl 74 15/11:664; IM My 74 10/(16):13
Collecting & Constructing Model Buses, by Michael Andress &

VI. Reviews

David Armitage, Ducimus, London: Afx Jl 75 16/11:667

Figures

Beginner's Guide to Military Modelling, by Roy Dilley, Pelham, London: Afx Ap 75 16/8:499; IM Ja 75 11/1:11; MM N 74 4/11:702
The Book of the Continental Soldier, by Harold L. Peterson, Stackpole, Harrisburg, PA: IM D 72 9/12:insert
Collecting Model Soldiers, by John G. Garratt, David & Charles, Newton Abbot, Devon: Afx My 75 16/9:554; MM Je 75 5/6:363; S&L (Je 75) 8:29
Collector's Guide to Model Tin Figures, by Erwin Ortmann, Studio Vista, London: MM N 74 4/11:702
How to Make Model Soldiers, by Phillip O. Stearns, Hamlyn, Feltham, Middx: Afx Ja 75 16/5:323; MM D 74 4/12:772; RiS Mr 75 3/1:50; S&L (F 75) 6:30
Making Model Soldiers of the World, by Jack Cassin-Scott, Stephen Hobe, London: Afx Mr 74 15/7:422; MM D 73 3/12:832; S&L Jl 74 2:20
Military Modelling, by Donald Featherstone, Kay & Ward, London: Afx Ap 71 12/8:429
Military Modelling, by Gerald Scarborough: IM Mr 75 11/2:16; S&L (D 74) 5:27
The Model Soldier Manual, by Peter J. Blum, A. A. Johnston, Langport, Som: MM Ja 71 1/1:50
Model Soldiers, Orbis: MM Je 72 2/6:283
Model Soldiers, by Peter Blum, Arms & Armour, London: Afx F 72 13/6:346; MM Ap 72 2/4:195+; Sc O 72 3/10:554-555
Model Soldiers, by W. Y. Carman, Charles Letts, London: Afx Mr 74 15/7:442; MM My 73 4/5:313; MW Ag 73 1/2:627
Model Soldiers, by John G. Garratt, Seeley Service, London: MM Ja 71 1/1:47
Model Soldiers for the Connoisseur, by John G. Garratt, Weidenfeld & Nicholson, London: Afx Je 73 14/10:566; IM Ap 73 10/4:insert; MM My 73 3/5:313
Models in the Making, by Jack Cassin-Scott, Blandford, London: Afx Mr 74 15/7:422
Modelling Miniature Figures, ed Bruce Quarrie, Patrick Stephens, Cambridge: Afx My 75 16/9:553-554; MM Ag 75 5/8:488; IM Mr 75 11/2:16; S&L (Je 75) 8:29
Scale Model Soldiers, by Roy Dilley, Almark, New Malden, Surrey: Afx Jl 72 13/11:602; A&W My 73 14/9:13; MM Jl 72 3/7:368

Ships

Discovering Ship Models, by Norman Boyd, Shire, Tring, Herts: Afx F 72 13/6:346
Henry Huddleston Rogers Collection of Ship Models, U.S. Naval Institute Press: Afx Jl 72 13/11:602
Lusci's Ship Model Builder's Handbook, by Vincenzo Lusci: Afx Jl 72 13/11:602

Modelling Ships in Bottles, by Jack Needham, Patrick Stephens,
　　London:　Afx O 72 14/2:105
Ship Models, by C. Fox Smith, Conway Maritime Press:　Afx D 72
　　14/4:226
Warship Modelling, by Peter Hodges, Patrick Stephens, Cambridge:
　　Afx Jl 75 16/11:667; MM Ag 75 5/8:488; Sc O 75 6/73:506
Waterline Ship Models, by John Bowen, Conway Maritime Press:
　　Afx D 72 14/4:226

Structures

Architectural & Interior Models, by Sanford Hohauser, Van Nostrand
　　Reinhold, NY:　NMRA Jl 72 37/11:15
Scale Model Buildings, by Michael Andress, Almark, New Malden,
　　Surrey:　Afx Je 74 15/10:600-601; MM Ag 74 4/8:477; S&L Je
　　74 1:21

Tools & Materials

Cerro Bend Casting, by Bill Coffey, Finelines Reprint 1, Finelines,
　　Los Altos, CA:　RMC N 73 42/6:18
Concerning Saws, Spear & Jackson, Wednesbury, Staffs:　Afx Ap 74
　　15/8:479
Creative Plastics Techniques, by Claude Smale, Van Nostrand Reinhold, NY:　PAM Jl 74 6:95-96
Plastics, by J. Harry Dubois & Frederick W. Hohn, Van Nostrand
　　Reinhold, NY:　PAM Ja 75 8:137
Tools for Electronic Assembly & Precision Mechanics, Jensen Tools
　　& Alloys, Phoenix AZ:　AFV Mr 74 4/10:27

MUSEUMS

Aircraft Museums Directory, comp Gordon Riley, Battle of Britain,
　　London:　Afx Mr 75 16/7:441; Sc Jl 75 6/70:337
Guide to the Battlefields of Britain & Ireland, by Howard Green,
　　Constable, London:　MM Ja 74 4/1:53
A Guide to Military Museums, by Terence Wise, MAP, Hemel Hempstead, Herts:　Afx My 72 13/9:522
Light Railways, Steamers, & Historic Transport, by Avon Anglia,
　　Bristol:　Sc S 75 6/72:441
Museum & Preserved Aircraft in Australia, comp & pub by AHSA,
　　Sydney:　AE D 73 5/6:301
Museums & Galleries in Great Britain & Ireland, by ABC Travel
　　Guides, Dunstable, Beds:　MM O 73 3/10:668
Skyfame & Its Aircraft, by Geoffrey Body, Skyfame Museum, Gloucestershire:　AE Ap 73 14/8:205

Warplanes Return No. 2, by Brian Rapier, Air Museum, Yorks, restorations: AE F 73 4/2:89-90

POLITICS

Adolph Hitler, by Colin Cross, Berkeley Publications, NY, 1973: WWE Mr 74 1/2:49
Arms Trade with the Third World, Stockholm International Peace Research Institute, Penguin, London: AI Ag 75 9/2:86
On War, by Manus I. Midlarsky, Free Press, NY, 1975: WW2J Jl 75 2/4:35
The Pattern of Soviet Power, by Edgar Snow, Random House, NY, 1945: WW2J Jl 75 2/4:34
Russia & the West Under Lenin & Stalin, by George F. Kennan, Little, Brown, Boston, 1961: WW2J Jl 75 2/4:35

RAILROADS

General

The Age of the Railway, by Harold Perkin, Drake, NY: NMRA N 73 39/3:26-27
All Aboard!... The Railroad Trains that Build America, by Mary Elting, Four Winds, NY: NMRA S 71 37/1:28
All Kinds of Trains, by Ron White, Grosset & Dunlap, NY: NMRA Jl 73 38/11:39
Along an Open Track, comp Ed & Sally Kochanek, North Shore Publishers, Prospect Heights IL: NMRA Ag 73 38/12:34
The American Railroad, Harpers 1874, Builder's Compendium, Cossayuna, NY: NMRA D 72 38/4:11
Car Names, Numbers, & Consists, by Robert J. Wayner, pvt, Ansonia Station, NY: MR N 72 39/11:15
Compendium of Signals, by R. F. Karl: MR S 72 39/9:10
The Great Trains, by Edita Lausanne, Crown Publishers, NY: NMRA O 74 40/2:36
Guinness Book of Rail Facts & Feats, by John Marshall, Guinness Superlatives, Enfield, Middx: Afx My 73 14/9:512-513; MR Ag 74 41/8:14
Herb's Hot Box of Railroad Slang, by J. Herbert Lund, pvt, Chicago, IL, 1975: NMRA D 75 41/4:20-21
Jane's World Railways, 1970-1971, ed Henry Sampson, McGraw-Hill, NY: NMRA O 71 37/2:21
Jane's World Railways, 1974-1975, ed Paul Goldsack, Franklin Watts, NY, 1975: NMRA N 75 41/3:17
Lenahan's Locomotive Lexicon, by Lenahan, Locomotive Lexicon, Chicago: MR Ag 75 42/8:18

Locomotive Dictionary 1906, facsimile, Newton K. Gregg, Kentfield, CA: RMC N 72 41/6:20
The Lore of the Train, by C. Hamilton Ellis, Grosset & Dunlap, NY: NMRA Ag 73 38/12:35
More Classic Trains, by Arthur D. Durbin, Kalmbach, Milwaukee, 1974: NMRA Mr 75 40/7:21
Narrow Gauge Nostalga, by George Turner, Trans-Anglo, Costa Mesa CA: MR F 72 39/2:11-12
Portrait of the Rails, comp Don Ball, Jr., New York Graphic Society, Greenwich CT: NMRA Ag 73 38/12:35
The Pullman Scrapbook, ed Robert J. Wayner, Ansonia Station, NY, 1971: articles from Pullman News: NMRA N 72 28/3:23
The Railroaders, Time/Life, Little Brown, Boston, MA, 1974: in western expansion: NMRA N 74 40/3:14
Railroads...An American Journey, by Don Ball, Jr., New York Graphic Society, Boston, 1975: NMRA S 75 41/1:28
Railroads USA...Steam Trains to Supertrains, by C. B. Colby, Coward-McCann, NY, 1970: NMRA N 71 37/3:39
Rails to the Setting Sun, by Charles S. Small, Kigei, Tokyo: ng, world-wide: MR Ap 72 39/4:8
Railway World Annual, ed G. M. Kichenside, Ian Allan, Shepperton, Middx: Afx D 71 13/4:223
Railway World Annual, ed Alan Williams, Ian Allan, Shepperton, Middx: Afx O 72 14/2:105
Railways & War Before 1918, by D. Bishop & K. Davies, Macmillan, NY: MW O 72 1/2:103; NMRA Jl 73 38/11:39
Railways & War Since 1971, by D. Bishop & K. Davis, Blandford, London, 1974: Afx O 75 17/2:123; MM My 75 5/5:276; WW2J S 75 2/4-5:22
Railways at the Zenith of Steam 1920-1940, by O. S. Nock, Macmillan, NY: NMRA Je 71 36/10:21
Railways in the Formative Years 1851-1895, by O. S. Nock, Macmillan, NY: NMRA Ja 74 39/5:24
Railways in the Modern Age, since 1963, by O. S. Nock, Blandford, London: Sc D 75 6/75:596
The Spectacular Trains, by John Everds, Hubbard, Northbrook, IL: NMRA Jl 74 39/12:17
Steam Powered Passenger Trains of Yesteryear 1971, comp E. T. Mitchell, pvt, Paoli, PA, 1971: NMRA Mr 73 37/7:21
Steel Rails & Iron Men, by Frederick G. Harrison, Books Unlimited, Indian Rocks Beach, FL: NMRA O 71 37/2:21
Steel Rails to Victory...a Photographic History of Railway Operations During WW-II, by Ron Ziel, Hawthorn Books, NY: NMRA Je 71 36/10:21
The Streamline Era, by Robert Reed, Golden West, San Marino, CA, 1975: NMRA N 75 41/3:16
Trains, Grosset All-Color Guide, by John Day, Grosset & Dunlap, NY: NMRA My 71 36/9:21
Trains Seventy One, ed G. M. Kichenside, Ian Allan, Shepperton, Middx: Afx F 71 12/6:303
When the Steam Railroads Electrified, by William D. Middleton, Kalmbach, Milwaukee, WI, 1975: NMRA N 75 41/3:17

VI. Reviews 640

Biographies

The Great Persuader, by David Lavender, Doubleday, Garden City NY: California rail pioneers: NMRA Ja 71 36/4:42
Iron Wheels & Broken Men, by Richard O'Connor, Putnam, NY: railroad barons: NMRA D 73 39/4:18-19
Life on a Locomotive, by George Williams, Howell North, Berkeley CA, 1971: Buddy Williams, engineer on C&NW: NMRA F 72 37/6:43; RMC F 72 40/9:21
The Morleys, by Norman Cleaveland, C. Horn, Albuquerque, NM: Raton Pass surveyors: NMRA Jl 73 38/11:39
'Ritin' & Railin', by Brooks Pepper, West Virginia Hillbilly, Richwood WV, 1974: personal-journalism column of ex-B&O dispatcher: NMRA D 74 40/4:20
Steam Was My Calling, by E. S. Beavor, Ian Allan, Shepperton: shed master: Afx D 75 17/4:243
Steaming Up!, by Samuel M. Vauclain, Golden West, San Marino CA: autobiography of head of Baldwin Locomotives: NMRA N 73 39/3:26

Logging

Ghost Lumber Towns of Central Pennsylvania, by Benjamin F. Klein, Jr. pvt, Lancaster, PA: MR Ja 71 38/1:7
Logging Along the Denver & Rio Grande, by Gordon S. Chappell, Colorado Railroad Museum, Golden, CO: NMRA Ap 72 37/8: 38-39
Logging Railroads in Pennsylvania--a Series, by Walter Casler, Ben Kline & Thomas Taber III, Strasburg, PA: NMRA O 71 37/2:20
Pine Across the Mountain, by Robert M. Hanft, Golden West, San Marino, CA: McCloud River Line, Mt. Shasta: NMRA D 71 37/4:14-15
Pitch Pine & Prop Timber, by Benjamin F. G. Kline, Jr., pvt, Strasburg, PA, 1971: South-central Pennsylvania: NMRA F 72 37/6:43
The Roddie Line, by Harvey Huston, pvt, Winnetka, IL, 1972: NMRA D 72 38/4:10
Sawmills Among the Derricks (Pennsylvania logging lines), by Thomas T. Taber, F. G. Kline, Jr., Lancaster, PA: NSG S 75 1/4:8
Seattle Car & Foundry Catalog, Pro Custom Hobbies, Catonsville, MD, 1975: logging equipment: NMRA O 75 41/2:38
Tionesta Valley, by Walter Casler, pvt, Corry, PA: Pennsylvania: NMRA D 73 39/4:19
Wildcatting on the Mountain, by Benjamin F. Klein, Jr., pvt, Lancaster PA: MR Ja 71 38/1:7

Memorabilia & Literature

Adirondack Vistas, comp Ed Gardner, pvt, Mountain Top, PA, 1974: timetables & postcards: NMRA Ap 75 40/8:26-27
All Time Catalogue of Interurban & Street Railway Books & Bulletins, comp by Raymond F. Radway, pvt, Detroit MI: bibliography: NMRA Jl 72 37/11:15
Central New England, comp Ed Gardner, pvt, Mountain Top, PA, 1974: timetables & postcards: NMRA Ap 75 40/8:26-27
Collecting Railroad & Trolley Timetables as a Hobby, by Edward G. Gardner, pvt, Wilkes-Barre, PA: NMRA Je 73 38/10:11
Collecting Railroad Station Postcards--Pennsylvania, by Lloyd M. Noseworthy, Bethlehem, PA: RMC My 73 41/12:17
Erie Pictorial, comp Ed Gardner, pvt, Mountain Top, PA, 1974: timetables & postcards: NMRA Ap 75 40/8:26-27
Go Great Western: A History of GWR Publicity, by Roger Burdett Wilson, David & Charles, Newton Abbot, Devon: Afx My 71 12/9:463
Railbook Bibliography 1948-1972, comp F. K. Hudson, Specialty Press, Ocean N. J.: NMRA Jl 75 38/11:39
Railroad Collectables, by Neil S. Uteberg, pvt, Edinburg, TX: NMRA N 73 39/3:27
Railroad Collectables--A Price Guide, by Howard Johnson, LW Promotions, Gas City, IN: NMRA Jl 74 39/12:16-17
Railroads of the Trans-Mississippi West, comp Donovan L. Hofsommer, Wayland College, Plainview TX, 1974: bibliography: NMRA Mr 75 40/7:38

Rail Fans & Rail Travel

All Aboard with E. M. Frimbo, by Rogers E. M. Whitaker, Grossman, NY, 1974: NMRA S 75 41/1:29
Baxter's USA Train Travel Guide, by Robert Baxter, Rail-Europe, Alexandria, VA, 1974: NMRA Mr 75 40/7:21+
Chronicles of Boulton's Siding: by Alfred Rosling Bennet, reprint David & Charles, Newton Abbot, Devon: Afx S 71 13/1:33+
Commuter Railroads, by Patrick C. Dorin, Superior, Seattle: NMRA Ag 71 36/13:31
Crofutt's Trans-Continental Tourist, by George A. Crofutt, Potsdam Associates, Boston, 1975: NMRA O 75 41/2:38
Europe by Rail, by Hank Stansbury, Great Outdoors, St. Petersburg, FL, 1971: NMRA Mr 72 37/7:21
400,000 Miles by Rail, by Burt C. Blanton, Howell-North, Berkeley, CA, 1972: NMRA D 72 38/4:10
High Iron, 1971, Quadrant, NY: RMC F 72 40/9:21
High Iron, '72, ed Howard Pincus, Quadrant, NY: NMRA Jl 73 38/11:38
Maken's Guide to Mexican Train Travel, by James C. Maken, Le Voyageur, Irving, TX: NMRA S 74 40/1:12

VI. Reviews 642

The Pacific Tourist, ed Frederick E. Shearer, Bounty/Crown, NY, 1970: 1870 railroad guide: NMRA F 71 36/6:27

Riding the Rails, by Michael Mathers, Gambit, Boston, MA: hobos: NMRA Jl 74 39/12:17

A Railfan's Guide to Nebraska, by William F. Rapp, J. B. Publishing, Crete, NE: NMRA Jl 73 38/11:38

1974 Railfan Directory (US & Canada), Overland Chapter NRHS, Oak Park, IL: railfan clubs: NMRA D 74 40/4:21

Railway Enthusiast's Handbook, 1971-72, ed Geoffrey Body, David & Charles, Newton Abbot, Devon: Afx S 71 13/1:33; MW N 72 1/3:160

Second Diesel Spotter's Guide, Kalmbach Books, Milwaukee, WI: RMC S 73 42/4:18

1972 Steam Passenger Service Directory, Empire State Railway Museum, Middletown, NY: RMC Ag 72 41/3:20

1973 Steam Passenger Service Directory, Empire State Railway Museum, Middletown, NY: RMC S 73 42/4:18

1975 Steam Passenger Service Directory, Empire State Railway Museum, Middletown, NY: RMC N 75 44/6:21

The Way to Go, by Thomas C. Southerland, Jr. & William McCleery, Simon & Schuster, NY, 1973: NMRA Ja 75 40/5:8

Rail Lines

General

Shortline Railroad Series, Stephen Greene, Brattleboro, VT: NMRA Ap 71 36/8:42

By Countries

(Argentina)

British-Owned Railways in Argentina, by Winthrop R. Wright, University of Texas, Austin, TX: NMRA Ap 75 40/8:27

(Australia)

All Stations West, by G. H. Fearnside, Bailey Bros. & Swinfen, Folkestone, Kent: Sydney-Perth Standard Gauge Railway: NMRA N 71 37/3:38

(Canada)

Canadian Pacific Railway, by Patrick C. Dorin, Superior, Seattle, 1974: MR Jl 75 42/7:17; NMRA Ap 75 40/8:26

Gold Rush Narrow Gauge... White Pass & Yukon, by Cy Martin,

Trans-Anglo Books, Costa Mesa, CA: NMRA Mr 71 36/7:19
History of the Canadian National Railways, by G. R. Stevens, Macmillan, NY: NMRA S 73 39/1:15

(U. K.)

The Aberford Railway, by Graham S. Hudson, David & Charles, Newton Abbot, Devon: Afx Jl 71 12/11:589
Brunel & After: the Romance of the Great Western Railway, by Archibald Williams, Patrick Stephens, London: Afx Ap 72 13/8:452
Great Western Album No. 2, by R. C. Riley, Ian Allan, Shepperton: Afx Ap 71 12/8:429
Lancashire & Yorkshire Railway, by John Marshal, David & Charles, Newton Abbot, Devon: Afx Jl 72 13/11:602
Picture History of the Somerset & Dorset Railway, by Robin Atthill, David & Charles, Newton Abbot, Devon: Afx F 71 12/6:303
Salute to the LMS, by Cecil J. Allen, Ian Allan, Shepperton: Afx Je 72 13/10:546
Twixt Rail & Sea, by W. G. Chapman, Patrick Stephens, London: GWR docks in South Wales: Afx Jl 71 12/11:589

(U. S.)

Arcade & Attica Railroad, by Edward A. Lewis, Baggage Car, Arcade, NY, 1972: MR Mr 73 40/3:16; NMRA O 73 39/2:21
BART--Off & Running, by joseph A. Strapac, Chatham, Burlingame, CA: NMRA Je 73 38/10:10
The Black River & Western Story, by Virginia Smith, Quadrant, NY: NMRA Jl 74 39/12:16
The Blackstone Valley Line, by Edward A. Lewis, Baggage Car, Strasburg, PA, 1974: NMRA Ap 75 40/8:27
The Burlington in Transition, by Bernard Corbin & Joseph Hardy, pvt, Red Oak, IO: NMRA Ag 71 36/13:30-31
CZ: The Story of the California Zephyr, by Karl R. Zimmermann, Starrucca Valley, Starrucca, PA: RMC Je 73 42/1:19-20
Chesapeake Beach Railway, by Ames W. Williams, Meridian Sun, Alexandria, VA, 1975: NMRA D 75 41/4:20-21
Ginder & Smoke, by Doris D. Osterwald, Western Guideways, Lakewood, CO: D&RGW Silverton: NMRA Je 73 38/10:11
The Colorado Road, by F. Hol Wagner, Jr., Intermountain Chapter NRHS, Denver, CO: MR My 72 39/5:5; NMRA D 71 37/4:15
Crossties over Saluda, by John F. Gilbert & Grady Jefferys, Crossties, Raleigh, NC: RMC Jl 72 41/2:22
Crystal River Pictorial, by Dell McCoy & Russ Collman, Sundance, Denver, CO: NMRA Ag 73 38/12:35; RMC D 73 42/7:17
The Dublin & South Eastern Railway, by W. Ernest Shepherd, David & Charles, North Pomfret, VT, 1974: NMRA F 75 40/6:23
Edaville Story, by William K. Viekman, Edaville RR, South Carver, MA, 1971: NMRA F 72 37/6:42
The Erie-Lackawanna Story, by Paul Carleton, D. Carleton Rail

Books, River Vale, NJ, 1975: NMRA S 75 41/1:28-29
The Far Out Island Railroad, by Clay Lancaster, Pleasant, Nantucket, MA, 1972: Nantucket RR: NMRA O 73 39/2:21
Gilpin Gold Train, by Mallory Hope Ferrell, Pruett, Boulder, CO, 1970: Shay ng: MR N 71 38/11:6; NMRA Ag 71 36/13:30; RMC O 71 40/5:18
The Golden Spike, ed David E. Miller, University of Utah, Salt Lake City: Southern Pacific: NMRA Ag 74 39/13:18
Gone but Not Forgotten, by Richard F. Palmer, Central New York NRHS, Marcellus, NY: Marcellus & Otisco Lake Ry: NMRA Jl 73 38/11:38
Grass Between the Rails, by Denny Rehder & Cecil Cook, Waukon & Mississippi Press, Des Moines, IO: Waukon Branch of Milwaukee Road: NMRA D 73 39/4:19
Hetch Hetchy & Its Dam Railroad, by Ted Wurm, Howell-North, Berkeley, CA: NMRA Ap 74 39/9:18
The Hiawatha Story, by Jim Scribbins, Kalmbach, Milwaukee, WI, 1970: NMRA F 71 36/6:26; RMC Ja 71 39/8:18
History of the Atcheson, Topeka & Santa Fe, by Keith L. Bryant, Jr., Macmillan, NY, 1975: NMRA O 75 41/2:38-39
History of the Lehigh & New England, by Randolph L. Kulp, Lehigh Valley NRHS, Allentown, PA: NMRA Je 74 39/11:13; RMC F 74 42/9:17
History of the Louisville & Nashville, by Maury Klein, Macmillan, NY: NMRA Ag 73 38/12:34
History of Passenger & Through Car Service, Pennsylvania RR 1849-1947, comp Douglas Wornom, Owen Davies, Chicago, IL, 1974: NMRA F 75 40/6:23
Hollywood in the Mother Lode, by Larry Jensen, pvt, Burbank, CA: NMRA N 73 39/3:27
Homage to the Santa Fe, by Merle Armitage, Manzanita, Yucca Valley, CA, 1973: NMRA D 74 40/4:21
Iron Horse Rambles 1959-1964 (Reading), by William S. Young, Railroading Magazine, Lanesboro, PA: RMC Jl 73 42/2:19
Journey to Amtrak, ed Harold A. Demonson, Kalmbach, Milwaukee, WI, 1972: NMRA D 72 38/4:11; RMC D 72 41/7:23
The Last Whistle, by Jack R. Wagner, Howell-North, Berkeley, CA, 1974: Ocean Shore RR: MR Jl 75 42/7:17-18; NMRA Mr 73 40/7:39
The Milwaukee Road Under Wire, by Karl R. Zimmermann, Quadrant, NY: NMRA S 74 40/1:12
Milwaukee Road--West, by Charles R. & Dorothy M. Wood, Superior, Seattle, 1972: MR D 72 39/12:15; NMRA Mr 73 38/7:137
The Missabe Road, by Frank A. King, Golden West: MR F 74 41/2:20
Mother Lode Shortline, Chatham, Burlingame, CA: Sierra RR: NMRA My 71 36/9:21; RMC N 71 40/6:18
Nachez Route...A Mississippi Central Rail Album, by David S. Price & Louis R. Saillard, Mississippi Great Southern Chapter NRHS, Hattisburg, MS, 1975: NMRA D 75 41/4:21
Narrow Gauge in a Kingdom, by Jay Conde, Glenwood, Fleton, CA, 1971: Hawaiian RR: NMRA F 72 37/6:43
The Narrow Gauge Silverton Train, by Jack H. Douglas, pvt, Salt

Lake City: NMRA Je 73 38/10:11
Narrow Gauge to Cumbres, by Doris B. Osterwald, Western Guideways, Lakewood, CO: Cumbres & Toltec Scenic RR: NMRA Jl 73 38/11:38; RMC Ja 73 41/8:25
The Next Station Will Be, vol. 3 (Greenwood Lake Division of the Erie RR), Railroadians of America, Roselle Park, NJ, 1975: NMRA D 75 41/4:21
Norfolk & Western Steam, by Ron Rosenberg, Quadrant, NY: NMRA Ja 74 39/5:24; RMC My 73 41/12:16-17
Norfolk Southern Railroad, by Richard E. Prince, pvt, Omaha, NE: NMRA Ag 73 38/12:35
On the Main Line... The Pennsylvania Railroad in the 19th Century, by Edwin P. Alexander, Clarkson N. Potter, NY: NMRA Ja 72 37/5:15
The Philadelphia, Marlton & Medford RR 1881-1931, ed William J. Coxey, West Jersey NRHS, Oaklyn, NJ: NMRA Jl 74 39/12:17
Pike's Peak Cog Road, by Morris W. Abbott, Golden West, San Marino, CA, 1972: NMRA D 72 38/4:10
The Railroad That Died at Sea, by Pat Parks, Stephen Greene, Brattleboro, VT: Florida East Coast's Key West Extension: NSG S 75 1/4:6
Rails North (Lehigh Valley), comp Albert J. Kallfelz, Richard F. Palmer, Frederick W. Wengenroth & Frank M. Klock, Central New York NRHS, Marcellus NY: NMRA Jl 73 38/11:38; RMC Ag 72 41/3:20
Rails to Carry Copper, by Gordon Chappell, Pruett, Boulder, CO: Magma: MR Ap 75 42/4:18; NMRA Ag 74 39/13:18
Rails to the Blue Ridge: Washington & Old Dominion RR, by Herbert H. Harwood, Jr., Pioneer American Society, Fall Church, VA: NMRA Mr 71 36/7:18
The Railroad That Ran by the Tide, by Raymond J. Feagans, Howell-North, Berkeley, CA: Ilwaco Ry: MR D 72 39/12:15
Railroads in the Streets of Syracuse, Central New York NRHS, Marcellus, NY: NMRA Jl 73 38/11:38
Railway to the Moon, by Glen M. Kidder, pvt, Acton, MA: Mt. Washington, NH: NMRA Ap 71 36/8:42
The Rainbow Route, by Robert B. Sloan & Carl A. Skowronski, Sundance, Denver, CO: NSG My 75 1/2:9
A Ramble into the Past on the East Broad Top Railroad, by Frank Kyper, East Broad Top RR, Rickhill Furnace, PA: NMRA N 72 38/3:22
Redwoods, Iron Horses, & The Pacific, by Spencer Crump, Trans-Anglo, Costa Mesa, CA: California & Western: MR D 71 38/12:13+
Ride the Sandy River, by L. Peter Cornwall & Jack W. Farrell, Pacific Fast Mail, Edmonds, WA: MR D 73 40/12:22; NMRA D 73 39/4:19; RMC O 73 42/5:14
Rio Grande Pictorial, by Dell A. McCoy & Russ Collman, Sundance, Denver, CO: NMRA My 72 38/3:22
Rio Grande to the Pacific, by Robert A. LeMassena, Sundance, Denver, 1974: NMRA Ag 75 40/12:18
The Road to Paradise, by William Moedinger, pvt, Lancaster, PA, 1971: Strasburg RR: NMRA F 72 37/6:42

VI. Reviews

Rock-A-Bye Baby, by Thomas T. Taber III, pvt, Muncy, PA: Rockaway Valley RR: NMRA Je 73 38/10:11

SP&S, The Northwest's Own Railway, by Charles & Dorothy Wood, Superior, Seattle: MR N 74 41/11:26

Saga of the Soo, by John A. Gjevre, pvt, Moorhead, MN: NMRA N 73 39/3:27

Short Haul to the Bay, by James N. J. Henwood, Stephen Greene, Brattleboro, VT: Narragansett Pier RR: NSG S 75 1/4:6

Silver San Juan, by Mallory Hope Ferrell, Pruitt, Boulder, CO: MR F 74 41/2:20; NMRA Ap 74 39/9:18-19; RMC Ap 75 43/11:15-17

Spokane, Portland & Seattle Ry, by Charles & Dorothy Wood, Superior, Seattle, 1974: NMRA Ja 75 40/5:8

Steam Trains of the Soo, by Leslie V. Suprey, pvt, Fortuna, CA: NMRA N 71 37/3:38

Stemwinders--The Laurel Highlands, by Benjamin F. G. Kline, Jr., pvt, Lancaster, PA: NMRA Ap 74 39/9:19

Stone Mountain Scenic Railway, by Frederick G. Harrison, Books Unlimited, Indian Rocks Beach, FL: NMRA Mr 74 39/8:19

36 Miles of Trouble, by Victor Morse, Stephen Greene, Brattleboro, VT: West River, VT: NSG S 75 1/4:6

Three Foot Rails, by Gary Morgan, Little London Press, Colorado Springs, CO: Colorado Central RR: NMRA Mr 75 40/7:21

Through Covered Bridges to Concord, by Edgar T. Mead, Jr., Stephen Greene, Brattleboro, VT: Concord & Claremont: NSG S 75 1/4:6

To the Mountains by Rail, by Manville B. Wakefield, Wakefair, Grahamsville, NY: New York, Ontario & Western: NMRA Je 71 36/10:10

Trail of the Zephyrs, by Robert P. Olmstead, pvt, Woodridge, IL: NMRA Ja 72 37/5:16; RMC F 72 40/9:21

Trains to Russian River, by Fred A. Stindt, pvt, Redwood City, CA: Northwestern Pacific: NMRA N 74 40/3:13

Ulster & Delaware, by Gerald M. Best, Golden West, San Marino, CA, 1972: NMRA N 72 38/3:22

Unitah Railway, by Henry E. Bender, Jr., Howell-North, Berkeley, CA: NMRA Ag 71 36/13:30-31; RMC Ja 72 40/8:19

Vermont's Covered Bridge Road, by Edward A. Lewis, Baggage Car, Strasburg, PA, 1974: St. Johnsbury & Lamille County RR, ME: NMRA My 75 40/9:13

Wellsville, Addison & Galeton RR, by Edward A. Lewis, Baggage Car, Arcade, NY, 1971: NMRA O 73 39/2:21; RMC Ja 73 41/8:24

The Welsh Highland Railway, by Charles E. Lee, David & Charles, North Pomfret, VT, 1974: NMRA F 75 40/6:22

Winchester's Forgotten Railway, by Roger Arcara, Quadrant, NY: NMRA Je 73 38/10:11

The Wreck of the Penn Central, by Joseph R. Daughen & Peter Binzen, Little, Brown, Boston, MA: NMRA F 72 37/6:43

Book--Railroad

Regional

California's Railroad Era 1850-1911, by Ward McAfee, Golden West, San Marino, CA: NMRA F 74 39/7:42

Colorado Railroads, by Tivis E. Wilkins, Pruett, Boulder, CO: NMRA Je 75 40/10:17

Continental Railway Handbook: West Germany, by W. J. K. Davies, Ian Allan, Shepperton: Afx Je 72 13/10:546

East Carolina Railway, by Henry C. Bridgers, Jr., T&E Publishers, Louisville, KY: NMRA D 73 39/4:18

Ghost Railroads of Indiana, by Elmer G. Sulzer, Vane A. Jones, East Indianapolis, IN: NMRA Je 71 36:10:21; RMC Mr 71 38/10:14

Highland Railway Album, by Anthony J. Lambert, Ian Allan, Shepperton, Middx: Afx D 75 17/4:243

History of Railways in Britain, by Frank Ferneyhough, Osprey, London: Afx N 75 17/3:177

Hungarian Railroads, by P. M. Kalla-Bishop, Drake, NY: NMRA S 74 40/1:12

Just a Few Lines, by Paul Jennings, Guinness Superlatives, London: English railways: Afx Ja 71 12/3:163

The Lunatic Express...An Entertainment in Imperialism, by Charles Miller, Macmillan, NY: British East Africa: NMRA Je 72 37/10:27

Mallets to Mogul, by Robert L. Hogan, Chatham, Burlingame, CA: tourist trains on the Pacific Coast: NMRA My 74 39/10:16

Metre Gauge Railways in South & East Switzerland, by John Marshal, David & Charles, North Pomfret, VT, 1974: NMRA F 75 40/6:22

Metre Gauge Steam in India, by Louis T. Cerny, pvt, New Lenox, IL, 1974: NMRA F 75 40/6:23

New Mexico's Railroads, by David F. Myrick, Colorado Railroad Museum, Golden, CO: NMRA O 71 37/2:20

New Zealand Railway Scrapbook, New Zealand Model Railway Guild, Wellington: MR O 72 39/10:32

Michigan's Railroad Scene, by R. Craig Rutherford & Raymond Sabo, pvt, Sterling Heights, MI, 1973: NMRA O 73 39/2:20

Narrow Gauge Railways of Canada, by Omer Lavallee, Railfare, Montreal: NMRA Ag 73 38/12:34-35

The Northern Counties Railway, 2 vols., by J. R. L. Currie, David & Charles, North Pomfret, VT, 1974: NMRA F 75 40/6:22

Railroads of Canada, by Robert F. Leget, Drake, NY: NMRA S 74 40/1:12

Railway History in Pictures--Ireland, by Alan McCutcheon, David & Charles, Newton Abbot, Devon: Afx Ap 71 12/8:428

Railway History in Pictures--Wales & Welsh Border, by H. C. Casserley, David & Charles, Newton Abbot, Devon: Afx Ap 71 12/8:429

Railways of Canada, J. M. & Edward Trout, Coles, Rexdale, Ont, 1975: NMRA Ag 75 40/12:29

Railways of Rhodesia, by Anthony H. Croxton, David & Charles, North Pomfret, VT, 1973: NMRA Ja 75 40/5:9

Railways to India, by J. N. Westwood, David & Charles, North

VI. Reviews

Pomfret, VT, 1975: NMRA Ag 75 40/12:28
A Regional History of the Railways of Great Britain, vol. 3, by
  H. P. White, David & Charles, Newton Abbot, Devon: Afx O
  71 12/8:105
Rip Van Winkle Railroads, by William F. Helmer, Howell-North,
  Berkeley, CA: Catskill Mountains: NMRA Je 71 36/10:20
Roaring Fork Valley, by Len Shoemaker, Sundance, Denver, CO:
  Colorado: NMRA O 74 40/2:36-37
South American Steam, ed Roy Christian & Ken Mills, pvt, Aptos,
  CA: NMRA Ap 72 37/8:38
Stations West, by Edwin D. Culp, Caxton Printers, Caldwell, ID,
  1973: Oregon: NMRA O 73 39/2:20-21
Steam in the Andes, by Brian Fawcett, Bradford Barton, Truro,
  Cornwall: NMRA Ap 74 39/9:19
Steam on the Veld, by A. D. Durrant, A. A. Jorgensen, & C. P.
  Lewis, Ian Allan, Shepperton: Afx Jl 72 13/11:602+
Steam Railroads of Central New York, by Kenneth J. Hojnacki, Central New York Chapter NRHS, Martisco Railway Station Museum,
  NY: RMC Mr 74 42/10:21
Sugar Trains, by Jesse C. Conde, Glenwood, Felton, CA: narrow
  gauge in Hawaii: NMRA O 74 40/2:37
Train Watcher's Guide to Chicago, by John Szwajkart, pvt, Brookfield, IL: NMRA N 73 39/3:26
Vancouver Island Railroads, by Robert D. Turner, Golden West,
  San Marino, CA: NMRA D 73 39/4:18
When Steam Was King, by W. W. Steward, A. H. & A. W. Reed,
  New Zealand: New Zealand lines: NMRA Je 71 36/10:20
Yankees Under Steam, ed Austin N. Stevens, Yankee Inc., Dublin,
  NH: New England: NMRA Ap 72 37/8:39
title unstated, by Tivie E. Wilkins, Pruett, Boulder, CO: history
  of Colorado railroads: NSG Mr 75 1/1:13

Traction

Blue Ridge Trolley, by Herbert H. Harwood, Jr., Golden West:
  Hagerstown & Frederick: MR D 75 42/12:42
The Cable Car in America, by George W. Hilton, Howell-North,
  Berkeley, CA: MR Mr 72 39/3:5; NMRA Je 72 37/10:27
Cars of the Sacramento Northern, Interurban Special 32, Ira Swett,
  South Gate, CA: MR Mr 73 10/3:16
Cars Stop Here, by John A. Haney, Tucson Corral of the Westerners, Tucson, AZ: NMRA Jl 72 37/11:15
Change at Park Street Under, by Brian J. Cudahy, Stephen Greene,
  Brattleboro, VT, 1971: Boston subway: NMRA Ap 73 38/8:18;
  NSG S 75 1/4:6
Chicago Surface Lines, by Alan R. Lind, Transport History Press,
  Park Forest, IL, 1974: NMRA Mr 75 40/7:20
Cincinnati & Lake Erie Interurban, by Jack Kennan, Golden West,
  San Marino, CA, 1974: MR O 75 42/10:20+; NMRA Mr 75 40/
  7:20-21
Cincinnati Streetcars--Millcreek Valley Lines, by Richard M. Wagner & Roy J. Wright, Wagner Car Co., Cincinnati, OH: NMRA

S 72 37/1:28
Cincinnati Streetcars 1912-1922, by Roy J. Wright & Richard M. Wagner, pvt, Wyoming, OH: MR Mr 74 41/3:18; NMRA Jl 74 39/12:16
Corner of Hickory & Third, by Lawrence Meloling, Central New York NRHS, Marcellus, NY: NMRA Jl 73 38/11:38
Dayton Covington & Piqua Traction Co., by William Reed Gordon & Richard M. Wagner, Trolley Talk, Wyoming, OH: MR O 74 41/10:28
Elmira & Chemung Valley Trolleys in the Southern Tier, by William R. Gordon, pvt, Rochester, NY: NMRA Ag 72 37/13:21
The End of the Penny Section, by Grahame Stewart, Charles E. Tuttle, Rutland, VT: New Zealand traction: NMRA Ap 74 39/9:19
The Era of Streetcars & Interurbans in Winnipeg, by Herbert W. Blake, pvt, Winnipeg, Man: NMRA N 74 40/3:13
The Era of Streetcars in Winnipeg 1881-1955, by Herbert W. Blake, pvt, Winnipeg, Man: MR Ja 72 39/1:12
Heavy Traction 1922-1941, Train Shed Cyclopedia, Newton K. Gregg, Novato, CA: RMC Ap 74 42/11:13-14
Historic Cars of the Seashore Trolley Museum, ed O. R. Cummings, New England Electric Railway Historical Society, Kennegunkport, ME: RMC Mr 72 40/10:20
Horsecars, Cable Cars & Omnibuses, by John H. White, Jr., Dover, NY, 1974: MR D 75 42/12:40; NMRA Ap 75 40/8:27
Interurbans of Utah, by Ira L. Swett, Interurbans, Cerritos, CA, 1974: NMRA D 74 40/4:21
Iowa Trolleys, Central Electric Railfans Assn, Chicago, MR Je 75 42/6:18
Jamestown & Chataqua Lake Trolleys, Fenton Historical Society, Jamestown, NY: NMRA O 75 41/2:38
The Last Line, Pelican Publishing, Greta, LA, 1973: New Orleans streetcars: NMRA D 74 40/4:21
London Trams in Camera, by Julian Thompson, Ian Allan, Shepperton: Afx O 71 13/2:105
The Los Angeles Railway, by Steven L. Easlon, pvt, Anaheim, CA: NMRA Jl 74 39/12:16
Market Street Railway Revisited, ed Ira Swett, Ira Sweet, South Gate, CA, 1972: NMRA Ap 73 38/8:18
McGraw Electric Railway Directory 1924, Wagner Car Co., Cincinnati OH: streetcar lines: NMRA Mr 71 36/7:18
McGraw Electric Railway List--August 1918, Harold E. Cox, Forty Fort, PA: all lines in USA: NMRA Ag 72 37/13:21
Mile High Trolleys, by Jones, McKeever, Wagner, & Forrest, Pruett, Boulder, CO, 1975: Denver Tramways, Denver & Intermountain Interurban: NMRA Ag 75 40/12:28; NSG Jl 75 1/5:17
Montreal's Electric Streetcars, by Richard M. Binns, Railfare, Montreal, 1974: NMRA Ja 75 40/5:9
1905 John Stephenson Electric Railway Car & Truck Catalog, facsimile Glenwood, Felton, CA: MR Ja 73 40/1:11
Ninety Years of Buffalo Railways, by William R. Gordon, pvt, Rochester, NY: NMRA S 71 37/1:28

Ohio Trolley Trails, by Harry Christainsen, Transit House, Euclid, OH: Cincinnati & Lake Erie: NMRA Ag 72 37:21; RMC Jl 72 41/2:22

The Old Park Trolley: Fairmount Park Philadelphia: NMRA Jl 75 40/11:42-46

100 Years of Capital Traction, by LeRoy O. King, Jr., pvt, Dallas, TX: Washington, DC: MR Mr 74 41/3:18; NMRA N 73 39/3:26

The Overlook Route, by William R. Gordon & Richard M. Wagner, Trolley Talk, Wyoming, OH, 1972: Dayton, Covington & Piqua: NMRA Mr 73 38/7:37

Passengers Must Not Ride on Fenders, by Filey, Howard, & Weyerstrahs, Green Treet, Toronto, Ont, 1974: NMRA O 75 41/2:38

Piedmont & Northern, by Thomas T. Fetters & Peter W. Swanson, Jr., Golden West, San Marino, CA: NMRA Mr 75 40/7:20

Rapid Transit Boston: Transit Boston 1850-1970, by Bradley H. Clarke, Boston Street Railway Assn, Cambridge, MA: NMRA Jl 72 37/11:15

The Red Arrow, by Ronald DeGraw, Haveford Press, Haverford, PA, 1972: Philadelphia Suburban Transportation System: MR Mr 73 40/3:15-16; NMRA Ap 73 38/8:19

Rochester, Lockport & Buffalo Railroad 1908-1931, by William R. Gordon, pvt, Rochester, NY: NMRA S 71 37/1:28

Sacramento Northern Album, Interurban Special 34, Cerritos, CA: MR D 73 40/12:23-24

Saskatchewan's Pioneer Streetcars, by Colin H. Hatcher, Railfare, Montreal, 1971: Regina Municipal Railway: NMRA Ap 73 38/8:18

South Shore...Quincy to Boston Rapid Transit, by Bradley H. Clarke, Boston Street Ry, Cambridge, MA: NMRA Mr 73 38/7:37

System of Steam Street Railways of Philadelphia, comp Harold E. Cox, pvt, Forty Fort, PA: NMRA Jl 72 37/11:15

TM, by Joseph M. Canfield, Central Electric Railfans Assn, Chicago, IL: RMC N 72 41/6:18

Third Rails, Pantographs & Trolley Poles, by William Reed Gordon, pvt, Rochester NY: NMRA Ag 74 39/13:18

The Trackless Trolleys of Boston, by Bradley H. Clarke, Boston Street Railway Assn, Cambridge, MA: NMRA Jl 72 37/11:15

Trackless Trolleys of the Fitchburg & Leominster St. Ry, by Bradley H. Clarke, Boston Street Ry Assn, Cambridge, MA, 1975: NMRA D 75 41/4:21

The Trolley...Triumph of Transport, by William Moedinger, Applied Arts, Lebanon, PA, 1971: NMRA Ap 73 38/8:18

Trolleys Down the Mohawk Valley, by William R. Gordon & Robert D. Mowers, pvt, Rochester, NY: NMRA S 71 37/1:28

Trolleys of the Gem City (Erie, PA), by Kenneth C. Springurth, pvt, Erie, PA: RMC Mr 71 38/10:14

Trolleys of the Pennsylvania Dutch Country, by John D. Denney, Jr., pvt, Columbia, PA: NMRA Ja 71 36/5:42

Two Ohio Tractions, by Richard & Birdella Wagner, Trolley Talk, Wyoming, OH, 1974: NMRA Mr 75 40/7:20

White Front Cars of San Francisco, by Charles A. Smallwood, Ira

Swett, South Gate, CA, 1972: Market Street Railway, Co.:
NMRA Ap 73 38/8:18
Who Made Our Streetcars Go, by Michael R. Farrell, Baltimore
NRHS, Baltimore, MD: Baltimore Transit: MR Ap 75 42/4:
18a; NMRA F 74 39/7:42

Rolling Stock

Cars

Amtrak Car Spotter, Wayner Publications, Ansonia Station, NY:
NMRA N 74 40/3:14
Boxcars, Railroad Car Journal 1, Kratville Publications, Omaha,
1971: RMC Ja 72 40/8:19
Burlington Northern Passenger Cars, by Charles A. Rudiesel, Car
Publications, White Bear Lake, MN, 1974: NMRA D 74 40/4:21
Cabooses, Railroad Car Journal 4, ed George R. Cockle, Kratville,
Omaha, NE: RMC N 72 41/6:18+
Car Builder's Cyclopedia 1940, Kalmbach, Milwaukee, WI, 1973:
NMRA O 73 39/2:20
Car Builders' Dictionary 1906, by Newton K. Gregg, Kentfield, CA,
1971: NMRA Mr 72 37/7:20-21
Car Builder's Dictionary 1888, by Newton K. Gregg, Kentfield, CA:
NMRA O 71 37/2:20-21
Cars, Scales, Gates, Train Shed Cyclopedia, Navato, CA: NMRA
Jl 75 10/11:25
Chesapeake & Ohio Freight Cars, by Dean Freytag & Ted Wetterstroem, C&O Historical Society, Ashland, OH, 1974: NMRA N
74 40/3:14
Chesapeake & Ohio Freight Cars Prior to 1945, D&T Enterprises,
Columbus, OH: RMC Ag 75 44/3:18
Dimensions & Classifications of Freight Car Equipment on the New
York Central, George R. Cockle & Assoc, Omaha, NE, 1975:
NMRA Je 75 40/10:17
The Domeliners, by Patrick C. Dorin, Superior, Seattle: NMRA D
73 39/4:18
From Zephyr to Amtrak... A Guide to Lightweight Cars & Streamliners, comp David Randall, Prototype Publications, Park Forest,
IL, 1972: NMRA D 72 38/4:10-11
The LMS Coach 1923-1957, by R. J. Essery & D. Jenkinson, Ian
Allan, Shepperton: Afx My 71 12/9:463
Lettering Guide for Early Colorado Narrow Gauge Freight Cars, by
William M. Cohen, Denver, CO: NMRA Je 71 36/10:21
Milwaukee Road Freight Cars, Normandie House, Chicago, IL:
NMRA N 74 40/3:14
1970 Car & Locomotive Cyclopedia, Simmons-Boardman, NY, 1970:
NMRA F 71 36/6:26-27
Passenger Cars, comp Newton K. Gregg, Train Shed Cyclopedia,
Novato, CA, 1973: NMRA O 73 39/2:20
Passenger Cars 1943, Train Shed Cyclopedia, Navato, CA: NMRA

VI. Reviews

Ja 75 40/5:9
Passenger Train Cars of the Santa Fe 1870-1971, vol. 1, Railcar Press, La Mirada, CA: MR Mr 74 41/3:17
Passenger Train Equipment of the Santa Fe 1870-1971, vol. 1, Head End Cars, by Joseph W. Shine & Frank M. Ellington, Railcar Press, Colfax, IO: NMRA Ap 74 39/9:18; RMC Je 75 44/1:14
Pullman Co. List of Cars 1950, Wayner Publication, Ansonia Station, NY: NMRA N 74 40/3:14
The Railroad Car Builders Pictorial Dictionary, by Matthias N. Forney, Dover, NY, 1975: NMRA Je 75 40/10:17
Railway Service Cars 1928-1943, Train Shed Cyclopedia, Navato, CA: NMRA Jl 75 10/11:25
Refrigerator Cars, Railroad Car Journal 2, ed George R. Cockle, Kratville, Omaha, NE, 1971: RMC Ap 72 40/11:18
Rotary Snow Plows, Specialty Press, Ocean, NY: RMC F 75 43/9:19
Santa Fe Diesels & Cars, Wayner Publication, Ansonia Station, NY: NMRA N 74 40/3:14
Southern Pacific Equipment Circular #14, comp Richard K. Wright, pvt, Oakhurst, CA: NMRA Je 73 38/10:10

Locomotives

(General)

French Steam Locomotives, 1840-1950, by Graham Clover, Barry Rose, Little London, Chichester, Sussex: MR D 75 42/12:43
GWR Engines, Names, Numbers, Types & Classes: David & Charles, Newton Abbot, Devon: Afx Jl 71 12/11:589
Lenahan's Locomotive Lexicon, by John Lenahan, Locomotive Lexicon, Chicago, IL, 1974: NMRA Je 75 40/10:17
Loco Profiles, Profile Publications, Windsor, Berks: NMRA Ja 72 37/5:16
Locomotives in My Life, by Don Wood, Audio-Visual Designs, Earlton, NY: MR D 75 42/12:42
Locomotives in Profile, vol. 1, ed Brian Reed, Profile, Windsor, Berks: Afx D 71 13/4:223
Locomotives in Profile, vol. 2, ed Brian Reed, Doubleday, NY: Afx Je 74 15/10:601; MW F 73 1/6:331; NMRA Ap 74 39/9:19
North British Locomotives: a Catalogue of Narrow Gauge Locomotives, 1912, David & Charles reprint, Newton Abbot, Devon: Afx Ja 71 12/5:263
Railways in the Transition from Steam 1940-1965, by O. S. Nock, Macmillan, NY, 1975: NMRA Je 75 40/10:16-17

(Diesel)

Diesel Electric Locomotives, Train Shed Cyclopedia, Novato, CA: NMRA Je 75 40/5:9
The Diesel Years, by Robert P. Omsted, Golden West, San Marino, CA, 1975: NMRA N 75 41/3:16-17

Book--Railroad

Our GM Scrapbook, from Trains Magazine, Kalmbach, Milwaukee, WI: NMRA My 72 37/9:22
The Second Diesel Spotter's Guide, by Jerry A. Pinkepank, Kalmbach, Milwaukee, WI: NMRA N 73 39/3:27

(Steam)

Development of the Locomotive Engine, by Angus Sinclair, MIT Press, Cambridge, MA: NMRA Ag 71 37/1:28
Early American Steam Locomotives, by John H. White, Jr., Dover, NY: NMRA S 73 39/1:15
Famous Steam Locomotives, by Richard J. Cook, BofLE, Cleveland, OH, 1974: NMRA My 75 40/9:13
The Golden Age of Steam, by O. S. Nock, St. Martins Press, NY, 1974: NMRA Mr 75 40/7:39
The Iron Horse, America's Steam Locomotive, by Henry B. Comstock, Thomas Y. Crowell, NY: NMRA My 72 37/9:22
Locomotive Cyclopedia 1925, Newton K. Gregg, Novato, CA: NMRA Jl 74 39/12:16
Locomotive Cyclopedia 1938, Train Shed Cyclopedia, Novato, CA, 1974: NMRA Mr 75 40/7:21
Locomotive Cyclopedia 1941, facsimile, Kalmbach, Milwaukee: MR S 72 39/9:8
Locomotive Dictionary 1908, facsimile, Newton Gregg: MR S 72 39/9:6
The Majesty of British Steam, by George F. Heiron, Ian Allan, Shepperton: Afx N 74 16/3:190
Pocket Encyclopedia of British Steam Locomotives, by O. S. Nock, Dover, NY: MR D 73 40/12:24
The Railway Steam Enthusiast's Handbook, ed Geoffrey Body, David & Charles, North Pomfret, VT: NMRA F 75 40/6:22
Say, Grandpa, What's the Story on these Big Engines, by Frederick G. Harrison, Books Unlimited, Indian Rocks Beach, FL: NMRA Mr 74 39/8:19
The Search for Steam, by Joe G. Collins, Howell-North, Berkeley, CA: MR D 72 39/12:15; NMRA Ag 73 38/12:34; RMC Ja 73 41/8:25-26
The Shay Locomotive: Titan of the Timber, by Michael Koch, World Press, Denver, CO: RMC Ag 72 41/3:20
Shays & Other Geared Locomotives, Train Shed Cyclopedia 34, Newton K. Gregg, Novato, CA: NMRA D 75 41/4:20
Southern Steam Specials, by Mike Eagleson, Ron Ziel, Camelback Publishing, Mt. Arlington, NJ, 1971: NMRA F 72 37/6:42-43
Steam in Camera 1898-1959, ed Patrick Russell, Ian Allan, Shepperton: Afx Je 72 13/10:546
Steam in the Landscape, by Kenneth Wescott Jones, Dover, NY: NMRA F 74 39/7:42
Steam Locomotive, by W. A. Tuplin, Scribner's, NY, 1974: NMRA Mr 75 40/7:29
Steam Locomotives 1938, Train Shed Cyclopedia, Novato, CA: NMRA Ja 75 40/5:9
Steam Locomotives of the Eastern European Railroads, by A. E.

Durrant, Drake, NY: NMRA O 74 40/2:36
Streamlined Steam, by Eric H. Archer, Quadrant, NY: NMRA Je 73 38/10:11; RMC Ja 73 41/8:24-25
Twilight of Steam, Colin D. Garratt, Dover, NY: NMRA F 74 39/7:42
Twilight of Steam Locomotives, by Ron Ziel, Grosset & Dunlap, NY: NMRA Mr 71 36/7:18
The Twilight of World Steam, by Ron Ziel & Mike Eagleson, Grosset & Dunlap, NY: NMRA Jl 74 39/12:17
When Steam was King, by W. W. Stewart, A. H. & A. W. Reed, Wellington, NZ: RMC Ag 71 40/3:17
The World of the Steam Locomotives, by Gustav Reder, Putnam, NY, 1974: NMRA Mr 75 40/7:39
World Steam in Action, by Harold Edmonson, Ian Allan, London, 1970: NMRA Mr 72 37/7:21
World Steam Locomotives, by James G. Robbins, Arco, NY: NMRA N 74 40/3:13

(Individual)

America's Bi-Centennial Queen--Engine 4449, by Richard K. Wright, pvt, Oakhurst, CA, 1975: NMRA Ag 75 40/12:29
Articulated Locomotives, by Lionel Wiener, Kalmbach, Milwaukee: MR Ap 71 38/4:7
Austrian 2-8-4, Profile 29, Windsor, Berks: Afx My 73 14/9:513
BR Class 9 2-10-0, by Brian Reed, Profile 33, Windsor, Berks: Afx F 74 15/6:370
The Brighton Gladstones, by Brian Reed, Profile 32, Windsor: Afx Ja 74 15/5:317
The Caledonian 4-4-0, Profile 34, Windsor, Berks: Afx D 74 16/4:257
The Deltics, by Cecil J. Allen et al, Ian Allan, Shepperton: MW O 72 1/2:103
The Fairlie Locomotive, by Rowland A. S. Abbott, David & Charles, Newton Abbot, Devon: RMC Ag 72 41/3:20-21
The 4-10-2: Three Barrels of Steam, by James E. Boynton, Glenwood, Fulton, CA: MR Ja 74 41/1:19; NMRA My 74 39/10:16
Fowler Locomotives, by Brian Haresnape, Ian Allan, Shepperton: Afx Je 74 15/10:601
German Austerity 2-10-0, Profile 18, Windsor, Berks: NMRA Ja 73 38/5:53
Gresley A4s, Profile 19, Windsor, Berks: Afx Je 72 13/10:546
Gresley Pacifics 1922-35, by O. S. Nock, David & Charles, North Pomfret, VT: NMRA F 75 40/6:22
Jones Goods & Indian L, Profile 17, Windsor, Berks: Afx D 71 13/4:223; NMRA Ja 73 38/5:53
King of the Railway Locomotives, facsimile of 1927 British Railways: King Class 4-6-0: Afx Jl 71 12/11:589; MR O 71 38/10:5+
Lima Super Power, by C. P. Atkins & Brian Reed, Profile 31, Windsor, Berks: Afx Je 73 14/10:568
Locomotion (first locomotive on a public railway), by Brian Reed, Profile 25, Windsor, Berks: Afx N 72 14/3:167

The Mallet Locomotive, by A. E. Durrant, Arco, NY, 1975: NMRA S 75 41/1:28
Pennsylvania Duplexii, by Brian Reed, Profile 24, Windsor, Berks: Afx N 72 14/3:167
RHD Locomotives, by Brian Reed & George A. Barlow, Profile, Culver City, CA: 15" gauge: NMRA Ag 74 39/13:18
The Shay Locomotive, by Michael Koch, World Press, Denver, CO: NMRA D 71 37/4:14
South African 4-8-2, by Brian Reed, Profile 36, Culver City, CA: NMRA Je 74 39/11:13
Standardized Locomotives Built for the USRA, Specialty Press, Ocean, NY: RMC F 75 43/9:19
Stanley Black Fives, by John F. Clay & J. Cliffe, Ian Allan, Shepperton: MW O 72 1/2:103
Union Pacific 4-12-2, Profile 16, Windsor, Berks: Afx D 71 13/4:223

(Lines)

British Railway Locomotives 1948-1950, Ian Allan, Shepperton, Middx: Afx D 72 14/4:226
Burlington Northern Motive Power 1971, by F. Hol Wagner, Jr., Motive Power Series, Denver, CO: RMC My 72 40/12:19
Burlington Northern 1972 Annual, comp F. Hol Wagner, Jr., Motive Power, Denver, CO: NMRA Je 73 38/10:10-11
Canadian National Steam Power, by Anthony Clegg & Raymond F. Corely, Railfare, Montreal: MR N 74 41/11:25-26
Chicago & Northwestern Power, by Patrick C. Dorin, Superior, Seattle: MR Mr 73 40/3:18-19; NMRA Jl 73 38/11:39
The Early Motive Power of the Baltimore & Ohio Railroad, by J. Snowden Bell, Glenwood, Felton, CA, 1975: NMRA D 75 41/4:21
Fight Four Forty Four, Union Pacific, Omaha, NE: NMRA N 73 39/3:27
GWR Steam, by O. S. Nock, David & Charles, Newton Abbot, Devon: MW S 72 2/1:39+
Great Western Stars, Castles & Kings, 2 vols, by O. S. Nock, David & Charles, North Pomfret, VT: NMRA F 75 40/6:22
The Hiawathas, by Brian Reed, Profile 26, Windsor, Berks: Afx F 74 15/6:370
Locomotives of the East Broad Top Railroad, Railroading Magazine, Starrucca, PA: RMC Ap 72 40/11:18
Locomotives of the Empire Builder, by Charles F. Martin, Normandie House, Chicago: Great Northern: MR S 72 39/9:10; NMRA N 72 38/3:22
Locomotives of the LB&SVR, part 2, Railway Correspondence & Travel Society, Rugeley, Staffs: Afx S 72 14/1:48
Locomotives of the South African Railways, by Bernard Zurnamer, pvt, Bainsvlei, South Africa: MR Ja 71 38/1:7; MW My 73 1/9:487
Milwaukee Road Locomotives, Normandy House, Chicago, IL: NMRA N 74 40/3:14

VI. Reviews 656

New Haven Diesel Locomotive, Rail Diesel & Gas Electric Cars Diagram Book, New Haven Technical Information Assn, Montgomery, AL: RMC S 71 40/4:15
Pennsy Steam & Semaphores, by Fred Westing, Superior, Seattle, 1974: NMRA Mr 75 40/7:39
Portrait of an Engine, SP Cab Forward 4294, by Joseph J. Bothman, pvt, Kirkwood, MO, 1974: NMRA F 75 40/6:23
Riding the Limited's Locomotives, by Howard G. Hill, Superior, Seattle, 1972: NMRA O 73 39/2:31
The Santa Fe Big Three, by S. Kip Farrington, Jr., David McKay, NY: NMRA Jl 73 38/11:39
Santa Fe Diesels & Cars, Wayner Publications, Ansonia Station, NY: NMRA N 74 40/3:14
Santa Fe's Diesel Fleet, by Joe McMillan, Chatham Publications, Burlingame, CA, 1975: NMRA N 75 41/3:17
Southern Pacific Locomotives & Tenders, Pacific Lines, ed Richard K. Wright, pvt, Oakhurst, CA: NMRA Mr 74 39/8:19
Southern Pacific Mallets, by Brian Reed, Profile 28, Windsor, Berks: Afx F 74 15/6:370
Southern Pacific Motive Power 1971, by Joseph A. Strapac, Chatham, Burlingame, CA: MR Mr 73 40/3:19; RMC Ap 72 40/11:18
Southern Pacific Motive Power Annual 1972, by Joseph A. Strapac, Chatham, Burlingame, CA, 1973: NMRA O 73 39/2:21
Southern Pacific 1970 Motive Power Annual, by Joseph A. Strapac & Karl R. Koening, Chatham, Burlingame, CA: RMC Ap 71 39/11:16-17
Southern Railway System Steam Locomotives & Boats, by Richard E. Prince, pvt, Omaha, NE: RMC Mr 72 40/10:20
Steam Locomotives of the East African Railway, by R. Ramaer, David & Charles, North Pomfret, VT: NMRA F 75 40/6:23; vol. 2, by D. F. Holland, David & Charles, Newton Abbot, Devon: Afx Jl 72 13/11:602+
Swendon Steam, 1921-1951, by Kenneth J. Cook, Ian Allan, Shepperton: Afx S 74 16/1:54-55
Union Pacific Streamliners, by Harold E. Ranks & William W. Kratville, Kratville, Omaha, NE: MR N 75 42/11:102-105; NMRA S 75 40/1:21; NMRA N 75 41/3:16

Manufacturers

Baldwin Locomotive Works Catalog 1910, Specialty Press, Ocean, NY: NMRA S 73 39/1:15
Canadian Car Builders Series, Ontario Scenic Railway Historical Assn, Scarborough, Ont: Canadian traction equipment manufacturers: NMRA N 73 39/3:26
Narrow-Gauge Locomotives--Baldwin Catalog 1877, University of Oklahoma, Norman, OK, 1967: NMRA Je 75 40/10:17
1925 Shay Locomotive Catalog, facsimile, Old Line Publishers, Milwaukee, WI: RMC Je 72 41/1:20
Philadelphia Passenger Car Plans, comp George W. Metz, pvt, Haverton, PA: NMRA Ag 72 37/13:21

Seattle Car & Foundry Catalog 1913, facsimile, Northwest Short Line, Seattle: MR Jl 75 42/7:18; NSG Mr 75 1/1:12
The Story of Eadystone, Glenwood, Felton, CA, 1974: Baldwin Locomotive: NMRA Ja 75 40/5:9

Traction & Rail Cars

Edwards Gasoline Rail Cars Model 10, Old Line Publishers, Milwaukee, MI: NMRA N 71 37/3:38-39
Edwards Gasoline Rail Cars Model 20, Old Line Publishers, Milwaukee, MI: NMRA N 71 37/3:38-39
Electric Motor Cars, by Newton K. Gregg, Novato, CA, 1974: NMRA Ap 75 40/8:26
Electric Motor Cars 1888-1928, Train Shed Cyclopedia, Novato, CA: NMRA Jl 75 10/11:25
Electric Railway Cars & Trucks, 1905 Catalog, Glenwood, Felton, CA, 1972: NMRA Mr 73 38/7:37
Four Wheel Drive Railroad Equipment, Old Line Publishers, Milwaukee, WI: NMRA Mr 72 37/7:20-21
The Liberty Bell Route's Heavy Interurban Cars, NRHS, Allentown, PA: NMRA S 71 37/1:28
Mack Rail Cars, Old Line Publishers, Milwaukee, WI, NMRA Mr 72 37/7:20-21
250 HP Power-Gas Electric Car: Old Line Publishers, Milwaukee, WI: NMRA Mr 72 37/7:20-21

Miscellaneous

The Compendium of Signals, by R. F. Karl, the Builder's Compendium, Cossayuna, NY: NMRA Ap 72 37/8:38
Electric Railway Dictionary, by Rodney Hitt, Newton K. Gregg, Novato, CA, 1972: NMRA S 72 38/1:16
Fontaine Fox's Toonerville Trolley, comp Herb Galewitz & Don Winslow, Scribners, NY, 1973: NMRA O 73 39/2:20
No Performance Today, by Warren A. Reeder, Jr., Hammond Historical Society, Hammond, IN: 1918 circus train wreck: NMRA Je 75 40/10:17
Railfacts & Feats, by John Marshal, Two Continents, NY: NMRA N 74 40/3:14
Railway Accidents of Great Britain & Europe, by A. Schneider & Armin Mase, David & Charles, Newton Abbot, Devon: Afx Jl 72 13/11:602
Railway Stamps, by Howard J. Burkhalter, American Topical Assn, Milwaukee, WI: NMRA Ap 72 37/8:38
Signals & Signal Symbols, Train Shed Cyclopedia, Novato, CA, 1974: NMRA Mr 75 40/7:21
The Tay Bridge Disaster, by John Thomas, David & Charles, Newton Abbot, Devon: Afx Jl 72 13/11:602
Tragedy at Eden, by Dow Helmers, pvt, Pueblo, CO: bridge col-

lapse on Missouri Pacific, 1904: NMRA N 71 37/3:38

RESEARCH AIDS

Aircraft, Engines, & Airmen: A Selective Review of the Periodical Literature, 1930-1969, ed August Hanniball, Scarecrow, Metuchen, NJ: Afx Jl 72 13/11:620
A Dictionary of Modern War, by E. Luttwak, Allen Lane/Penguin: AE F 72 2/2:85
Dictionnaire Technique Aérospatiale, French-English, English-French, Gauthier-Villars, Paris: AE O 72 3/4:207
Imperial Russian Army, A Bibliography of Regimental Histories & Related Works, comp & ed M. Lyons, Stanford University, Stanford, CA, 1968: Fus Sp 74 1/3:24
Military Dictionary: German-English/English-German TM 30-506, reprint Inco Military Books, Burbank, CA, 1964: AFV Ja 72 3/5:28; WWE Mr 74 1/2:49
Scale Plastic Kits of the World 1973, IPMS-UK, MAP, Hamel Hempstead: AE D 73 5/6:292; Afx F 74 15/6:367; IM Ag 73 10/7: insert; MW Ja 74 2/5:268; RT Ag 73 6/8:91
Tracing the Regiments, by Edgar Letts, Brackenhurst, Mablethorpe, Lincs: MW Mr 73 1/7:381
Walther's 1973 Military Miniatures Catalog, William K. Walthers, Milwaukee, WI: AFV O 72 3/2:31; Fus Au 73 1/1:41
World War II at Sea, a Bibliography of Sources in English, by Myron J. Smith, Scarecrow, Metuchen, NJ: WW2J S 75 2/5-6:23

SHIPS

Naval Battles & Wars

The Attacks on the Tirpitz, by Peter Dickens, Ian Allan, Shepperton: Afx S 74 16/1:480
Battle of the Atlantic, ed Andrew Kershaw, Phoebus, London, 1975: WW2J S 75 2/5-6:23
Battle of the River Plate, by Geoffrey Bennett, Ian Allan, Shepperton: Sc Jl 72 3/7:379
Hitler's Naval War, by Cajus Bekker, trans Frank Ziegler, Doubleday, Garden City, NY: Fus Sp 75 2/1:15; WW2J Jl 75 2/4:34
Loss of the Bismark, by B. B. Shofield, Ian Allan, Shepperton: Sc Jl 72 3/7:379
Narvik, Battles in the Fjords, by Peter Dickens, Ian Allan, Shepperton: Afx S 74 16/1:54
The Naval War Against Hitler, by Donald Macintyre, Scribners, NY, 1971: WWE Mr 74 1/2:50
Night Action Off Cape Matapan, by S. W. C. Pack, Ian Allan, Shep-

perton: Sc My 72 3/5:265
Pursuit: the Chase & Sinking of the Battleship Bismarck, by Ludovic Kennedy, Viking, NY, 1974: WW2J My 75 2/3:115
Scapa Flow 1919, by Friedrich Ruge, Ian Allan, Shepperton: MW F 74 2/6:323

Navies

Pictorial History of the Royal Navy, vol. 1, 1816-1880, by Anthony J. Watts, Ian Allan, Shepperton: MM Ap 71 1/4:209; vol. 2: 1880-1914: Sc F 72 3/2:99
The Royal Navy in Old Photographs, by W. P. Trotter, J. M. Dent, London: MM Jl 75 5/7:427; Sc S 75 6/72:441
Unser Flotte, Carl Shunemann, Breman: Sc S 71 2/9:500

Ships

Civil

British Paddle Steamers, by Geoffrey Body, David & Charles, Newton Abbot, Devon: Afx F 71 12/6:303
Cunard White Star Quadruple Screw Liner Queen Mary, Patrick Stephens, London: Afx O 72 14/2:105
Cutty Sark, by Noel C. L. Hackney, Patrick Stephens, Cambridge: Afx N 74 16/3:189; Afx D 74 16/4:256; IM Ja 75 11/1:16; RT Ja 75 8/1:9; Sc Je 75 6/69:294
Fast Sailing Ships, by David MacGregor, Nautical Publishing, Lymington, Hants: MB O 73 23/274:428-429
The French Line Quadruple-Screw Turbo-Electric Liner "Normandie," intro & epilog by Leslie Reade, Patrick Stephens, London: Afx Je 72 13/10:569
Sailing Barges, by Frank G. G. Carr, Conway Maritime Press, Patrick Stephens, London: Afx S 71 13/1:49
Sailing Boat Recognition, by P. W. Blandford, Ian Allan, Shepperton, Middx: Afx Ap 71 12/8:409
Ships Seventy-One, by David A. Parsons, Ian Allan, Shepperton: Sc Ap 71 2/4:206
The Victorian Summer of the Clyde Steamers 1864-1888, by Alan J. S. Paterson, David & Charles, Newton Abbot, Devon: MW S 72 1/1:39
White Star Liners Olympic & Titanic, facsimile of 1911 "Shipbuilder," Patrick Stephens, Cambridge: Sc N 75 6/74:569

VI. Reviews 660

Naval

(General)

Battleships & Battlecruisers 1905-1970, by Siegfried Breyer, Doubleday, Garden City, NY: WWE Ja 74 1/1:4
Battleships of World War I, by Antony Preston, Arms & Armour, London: Afx Je 73 14/10:568; MM Jl 73 3/7:463; Sc S 73 4/9:624-625
The Great Age of Sail, Edit SA, Lausanne: Afx Je 71 12/10:533
The Illustrated History of the Submarine, by Edward Horton, Doubleday, Garden City, NY: WWE Ja 75 2/1:27
Jane's Fighting Ships 1973-74, ed, John E. Moore, Jane's: MM S 73 3/9:612
The Liberty Ships, by L. S. Sawyer & W. H. Mitchell, David & Charles, Newton Abbot, Devon: Afx F 71 12/6:303
Q-Ships & Their Story, by E. Keble Chatterton, Conway Maritime Press reprint of 1922: Afx Ja 73 14/5:283
Steam at Sea, by K. T. Rowland, David & Charles, Newton Abbot, Devon: Afx F 71 12/6:303
Warships & Navies, 1973, ed Anthony J. Watts, Ian Allan, Shepperton, Middx: Afx N 72 14/3:167
Warship Identification, by E. C. Talbot-Booth & David G. Greenman, Ian Allan, Shepperton: Afx N 71 13/3:163; Sc My 72 3/5: 165
Warships in Profile, vol. 2, ed John Wingate, Profile, Windsor, Berks: Afx Je 73 14/10:568; MM Ap 73 3/4:245; WWE Ja 74 1/1:14
Warships in Profile, vol. 3, ed Antony Preston, Doubleday, Garden City, NY, & Profile, Windsor, Berks: Afx Ag 74 15/12:724; WWE S 74 1/5:143
Weyer's Warships, 1971, U.S. Naval Institute: Afx Je 71 12/10: 533
Weyer's Warships of the World 1973, by Gerhard Albrecht, U.S. Naval Institute Press: Afx My 73 14/9:513

(France)

French Warships of WW-II, by Jean Labayle Couhat, Ian Allan, Shepperton: Sc S 71 2/9:500
Le Vaisseau de 74 Cannon, by Jean Houdriot, Editions de Quatre Seigneurs, Grenoble: MM My 74 4/5:278

(Germany)

KM Admiral Graf Spee, Profile 4, Windsor, Berks: MM Jl 71 1/7:253-254; RT Mr 71 4/3:34
SMS Emden, by Friederich Forstmeier, Profile 25, Windsor, Berks: Afx F 74 15/6:368
German Schnellboot, Profile 31, Windsor, Berks: Afx O 74 16/2: 117; MM S 73 3/9:614; MW O 73 2/2:81

German Warships 1939-1945, by W. D. G. Blundell, Almark, New Malden, Surrey: Sc My 75 6/68:265
Hitler's High Seas Fleet, by Richard Humble, Pan/Ballantine: MM Ap 72 2/4:199
KM Prinz Eugen, by D. Paul Schmalenbach, Profile 6, Windsor, Berks: Sc S 71 2/9:499
Sea Raider Atlantis, by Ulrich Wohr & A. V. Sellwood, Pinnacle, NY (org Atlantis, T. Werner Laurie, 1955): WWE S 74 1/5: 143
U-Boats Under the Swastika, by J. P. Mallmann Showell, Ian Allan, Shepperton: Afx O 73 15/2:116-117
U-Boote im Ensate, by Bodo Herzog, Podzun, Dorheim: Afx F 71 12/6:303

(Italy)

Caio Duilio class Battleships, Orizzonte Mare 2, Edizioni Bilzarri, Roma: MM Ap 73 3/4:243

(Japan)

Japanese High Seas Fleet, by Richard Humble, Pan/Ballantine: Afx Ap 75 16/8:499; MM Ag 74 4/8:476
Japanese Naval Vessels Survived, Orion Books, Tokyo: IM Je 73 10/7:insert
Yamato & Musashi Battleships, Profile 30, Windsor, Berks: MM Mr 73 3/3:170; MW Ap 73 1/8:411

(USSR & Russia)

Review of Warships of the Imperial Russian Navy, by V. M. Tomitch, B. T. Publishers: MM My 71 1/5:252-253
The Russian Fleet, by René Greger, Ian Allen, Shepperton: Afx Jl 72 13/11:622-623
The Russian Fleet 1914-1917, by René Greger, Ian Allan, Shepperton: Sc Jl 72 3/7:379

(U.K. --General)

Army & Navy Illustrated Jubilee Review of the Fleet 1897, Arms & Armour facsimile, London: MW D 72 2/4:211
British Battle Cruisers, by Peter C. Smith, Almark, New Malden, Surrey: MW Mr 73 1/7:345
British Escort Ships, by H. T. Lenton, Macdonald & Jane's, London: Afx Mr 75 16/7:442
British Warships 1914-1919, by F. J. Dittmar & J. J. Colledge, Ian Allan, Shepperton: Afx D 72 14/4:226; Sc S 73 4/9:624
British Warships 1975, by J. W. Goss, Marinart, Deal, Kent: Sc O 75 6/73:506

VI. Reviews 662

British Warships of the Second World War, by Alan Ravan & John
   Roberts, Conway Maritime Press: Afx Mr 72 13/7:404; MM O
   72 2/10:544
Deadnaught: A History of the Modern Battleship, by Richard Hough,
   Patrick Stephens, Cambridge: Afx N 75 17/3:177
Introduction to RAF High Speed Rescue Launches 1938-1945, by John
   Prichard, pvt, Ware, Herts: Afx O 75 17/2:123
Royal Navy Battleships 1895-1946, by W. D. G. Bludell, Almark,
   New Malden, Surrey: MW Je 73 1/10:515
Royal Navy Coastal Forces 1939-1945, by A. J. D. North, Almark,
   New Malden, Surrey: Afx N 72 14/3:167; MW O 72 1/2:103
Royal Navy Warship Drawings, by Norman A. Ough, Neptune, Lon-
   don: Afx O 75 17/2:123; MM S 75 5/9:527; Sc O 75 6/73:506
Royal Navy Warships, 1939-1945, by W. G. D. Blundell, Almark,
   New Malden: Afx N 71 13/3:163; Sc F 72 3/2:99
Ships of the Royal Navy, by W. D. G. Blundell, Almark, New
   Malden: Sc Jl 71 2/7:499
Warships of the British & Commonwealth Navies, by H. T. Lenton,
   Ian Allan, Shepperton: Afx F 72 13/6:346; Sc My 72 3/5:265

(U. K. --Individual)

Abdiel Class Fast Minelayers, by Tom Burton, Profile 38, Wind-
   sor, Berks: MM Mr 74 4/3:143
Battle Class Destroyers, by Peter Hodges, Almark: MM My 71 1/
   5:253; Sc S 71 2/9:499
HMS Belfast, by John Wingate, Profile 4, Windsor, Berks: Afx Ap
   73 14/8:456; MM F 73 3/2:112; MW F 73 1/6:331
HMS Cambelltown, by John Wingate, Profile 5, Windsor, Berks:
   Afx Je 71 12/10:533; IM Je 71 8/6:17
Carrier Air Groups: HMS Eagle, by David Brown, Hylton Lacy,
   Windsor, Berks: Afx F 74 15/6:368; RT D 72 5/12:139
HMS Cavalier, Profile 32, Windsor, Berks: MM My 73 3/5:314
HMS Cossack & Other Tribals, Profile 2, Windsor, Berks: IM Mr
   71 8/3:16; RT Ja 71 4/1:12; Sc Ap 73 4/4:207
Dido Class Cruisers, Ensign 2, Bivouac, London: Afx Ag 74 15/
   12:725; MM S 73 3/9:615; MW O 73 2/2:81; RiS W 74 2/2:77
HMS Dreadnought, by John Wingate, Profile 1, Windsor, Berks:
   Afx F 71 12/6:303; RT Ja 71 4/1:12
HMS Eagle, Profile 35, Windsor, Berks: Afx D 74 16/4:257; MM
   S 73 3/9:614
Flower Class Corvettes, Ensign 3, Bivouac, London: Afx Ag 74
   15/12:725; MM S 73 3/9:615; MW O 73 2/2:81; RiS W 74 2/
   2:77
HMS Furious, by C. A. Jenkins, Profiles 23 & 24, Windsor, Berks:
   Sc S 73 4/9:624
HMS Hesperus, Profile 20, Windsor, Berks: Afx S 72 14/1:48
HMS Illustrious, Profile 10 & 11, Windsor, Berks: Afx N 71 13/
   3:163; RT Je 73 5/6:71
Invincible Class, by John A. Roberts, Warship Monographs, Mari-
   time Press: Afx O 72 14/2:105
King George V, Ensign 1, Bivouac, London: Afx Ag 74 15/12:724-

725; MM F 73 3/2:112; MW Mr 73 1/7:345
Queen Elizabeth Class, by John Campbell, Warship Monographs, Maritime Press: Afx O 72 14/2:105
Queen Elizabeth Class Battleships, by Alan Raven & John Roberts, Ensign 4, Bivouac, London: MM My 75 5/5:277
Send Her Victorious, by Michael Apps, William Kimber, London: AE F 73 4/2:90
The Tribals, by Martin H. Brice, Ian Allan, Shepperton: Afx F 72 13/5:339
Tribal Class Destroyers, by Peter Hodges, Almark, New Malden, Surrey: Afx F 72 13/6:339+; Sc My 75 6/68:264-265
Vosper 70' MTB, by David Cobb, Profile 7, Windsor, Berks: Sc O 71 2/10:560-561

(U.S.)

USS Alabama, Ship's Data, Leeward Publications: MM N 74 4/11: 703
American Destroyer Escorts of WW-II, by Peter Elliott, Almark, New Malden, Surrey: Afx Ap 75 16/8:499
American Gunboats & Minesweepers, by H. T. Lenton, Macdonald & Jane's, London: Afx Mr 75 16/7:442; MM Mr 75 5/3:159
American Steel Navy, by John D. Alden, Patrick Stephens, London: Afx F 73 14/6:338
USS Barb, Profile 34, Windsor, Berks: Afx S 74 16/1:54
Cruise of the Lanikai, by Kemp Tolley, U.S. Naval Institute Press, Annapolis, MD: WW-II schooner: WWE My 74 1/3:75
USS Enterprise, Profile 15, Windsor, Berks: RT Je 72 5/6:71
Ghost of the Java Coast, by Walter G. Winslow, Coral Reef Publications, Satellite Beach, FL: USS Houston: WWE N 74 1/6:171
USS Hornet, by W. H. Cracknell, Profile 3, Windsor, Berks: MM My 71 1/5:253-254; Sc Je 71 2/6:300-301
USS Indianapolis, Profile 28, Windsor, Berks: MW F 74 2/6:323
USS Mississippi, Profile 39, Windsor, Berks: Afx Jl 74 15/11:664
USS North Carolina, Ship's Data, Leeward Publications: MM N 74 4/11:703
Ships & Aircraft of the U.S. Fleet, by John S. Rowe & Samuel L. Morison, Naval Institute Press, Annapolis, MD: AE Ag 72 3/2:102; Afx My 72 13/12:487
United States Warship Camouflage 1939-1945, by Chris Ellis, Kristall Productions, Henley-on-Thames, Oxon: Afx S 75 17/1:55; MM Ag 75 5/8:489

STRUCTURES

Board Street Station, 1881-1952, comp Harry Albrecht, pvt, Clifton Heights, PA, 1972: Philadelphia station: NMRA N 72 38/3:23
Building & Structures, Train Shed Cyclopedia, Novato, CA, 1973: NMRA O 73 39/2:20; RMC Je 73 42/1:18-19

VI. Reviews

Buildings & Structures of American Railroads 1893, Train Shed Cyclopedia, Novato, CA: NMRA Ap 75 40/8:26
Caerphilly Castle, by W. G. Chapman, facsimile, Patrick Stephens, London: Afx F 71 12/6:328
Canal Enthusiasts' Handbook No. 2, ed Charles Hadfield, David & Charles, Newton Abbot, Devon: Afx Jl 74 15/11:664
New England Country Depots, by Edward A. Lewis, Baggage, Car, Arcade, NY: NMRA S 73 39/1:15
The Next Station...: NMRA Ja 75 40/5:9
The Next Station Will Be, Railroadians of America, Rahway, NJ: 1910 stations: NMRA N 73 39/3:27
Palliser's Model Homes 1878, Glenwood, Felton, CA: NMRA Jl 73 38/11:38
The Vanishing Depot, by Ranulph Bye, Livingston Publishing, Wynnewood, PA: NMRA O 74 40/2:36

WARGAMES

Battles

The Alma, by Henry Harris, Charles Knight, London: Afx F 72 13/6:346; MM F 72 2/2:75
The American Civil War 1862, by Terence Wise, Battles for Wargamers 1, Bellona, Hemel Hempstead, Herts: Afx O 72 14/2: 106
Armies & Enemies of Ancient Egypt & Assyria, by Alan Buttery, Wargames Research Group, Goring-by-Sea, Sussex: Afx F 75 16/6:384; MM O 74 4/10:624-625; S&L (D 75) 5:26
Armies & Enemies of Imperial Rome, by Phil Barker, Wargames Research Group, Goring-by-Sea, Sussex: Afx Ag 72 13/12:687; MM Jl 72 2/7:369
Armies of the Greek & Persian Wars, by Richard Nelson, War Games Research Group, Goring-on-Sea, Sussex: MM O 75 5/10:605
Armies of the Macedonian & Punic Wars, by Phill Barker, War Games Research Group, Goring-on-Sea, Sussex: Afx Ja 72 13/5:255; MM Ja 72 2/1:40
Battle of Fontenoy, by Charles Grant: S&L (D 75) 11:28
Battle of Salamis, by Richard B. Nelson: S&L (D 75) 11:28
Battle of Tewkesbury, a Roll of Arms, by Geoffrey Wheeler, Gloucester Group, Cliftonville, Kent: Afx My 72 13/9:522
Battle of Waterloo, by B. J. Hurren: S&L (D 75) 11:28
Battles for Wargamers, WW-II: Tunisia, by Terence Wise, MAP, Hemel Hempstead, 1973: AFV Jl 74 4/11:31; Bellona: MM Ap 74 4/4:188
Blenheim, by D. S. V. Fosten, Almark, New Malden, Surrey: S&L (D 75) 11:29
Borodino 1812, by E. R. Holmes, Charles Knight, London: MM Jl 71 1/7:368; MM S 71 1/9:479

Chancellorsville, by H. John Cooper, Knights Battles for Wargames, London: Afx Ap 73 14/8:456; MM Ja 73 3/1:52
Dettingen 1742, by Michel Orr, Charles Knight, London: MM Jl 72 2/7:369
Flodden 1513, by Charles Knightly, Almark, New Malden: MM Ag 75 5/8:488; S&L (Je 75) 8:28
Leipzig, by Per-Eric Jannson, Almark, New Malden, Surrey: S&L (D 75) 11:29
Minden, by Howard N. Cole, Knights Battles for Wargamers, London: Afx Ap 73 14/8:456; MM Ja 73 3/1:52; MW F 73 1/6:331
The Peninsular War 1813, by Terence Wise, Bellona, Hemel Hempstead, Herts: MM Ap 74 4/4:188
Poitiers, by Donald Featherstone, Knights Battles for Wargamers, London: Afx Ap 73 14/8:456; MM Ja 73 3/1:52; MW F 73 1/6:331
Saratoga 1777, by John Sweetman, Charles Knight, London: MM Jl 71 1/7:368; MM S 71 1/9:479
2nd Punic War, by Terence Wise, MAP, Hemel Hempstead, Herts: Afx Ap 73 14/8:456; MM Ja 73 3/1:52; MW F 73 1/6:331
Tank Battles in Miniature: A Wargamer's Guide to the Western Desert Campaign 1940-42, by Donald F. Featherstone, Patrick Stephens, Cambridge: Afx N 73 15/3:180; MM N 72 2/11:610; MM D 73 3/12:832
Tank Battles in Miniature 2, Wargamer's Guide to the Russian Campaign, by Bruce Quarrie, Patrick Stephens, Cambridge, 1973: Afx S 75 17/1:53; A&W Mr 74 10:13; S&L (Je 75) 8:28
Vitoria 1813, by J. P. Lawford, Charles Knight, London: MW F 74 2/6:323
The Wargame, ed Peter Young, Cassell, London: ten battles: Afx D 72 14/4:226
World War II in the Western Desert, by Terence Wise, Battles for Wargamers 2, Bellona, Hemel Hempstead, Herts: Afx N 72 14/3:167

Playing

The Ancient Wargame, by Charles Grant, Adam & Charles Black, London: MM Jl 74 4/7:384
Ancient Wargaming, by Phil Barker, Patrick Stephens: MM N 75 5/11:667; S&L (O 75) 10:26
Battle Notes for Wargamers, by Donald F. Featherstone, David & Charles, Newton Abbot, Devon: Afx F 74 15/6:369
Battles with Model Soldiers, by Donald Featherstone, David & Charles, 1970 reissue: MM Jl 72 2/7:368-369
Discovering English Civil Wargaming, ed John Turnstill, Shire, Aylesbury, Bucks: MM Ag 73 3/8:538
Hsian Ch'i, by Terence Donnelly, Wargames Research Group, Birmingham: Chinese version of go: MM Jl 75 5/7:427
Little Wars, by H. G. Wells, Arms & Armour reprint from 1913: MM Mr 71 1/3:158

VI. Reviews

Modern War in Miniature, by Michael F. Korn, M&J Independent Research, Lawrence, KA: AFV D 72 3/12:20

The Napoleonic Wargame, by Charles Grant, MAP, Hemel Hempstead, Herts: MM Ja 74 4/1:53

The Napoleonic Wargame, by F. W. Jeffrey, Almark, New Malden, Surrey: MM Ap 75 5/4:218; S&L (Ap 75) 7:32

Napoleonic Wargaming, by Charles Grant, MAP, Hemel Hempstead, Herts: Afx F 74 15/6:369-370

Napoleonic Wargaming, by Bruce Quarrie, Patrick Stephens, Cambridge: IM Ja 75 11/1:11; S&L (D 74) 5:26

Naval Wargames--World War I & II, by Barry J. Carter, David & Charles, Newton Abbot, Devon: Afx S 75 17/1:54; MM My 75 5/5:276

Practical Wargaming, by C. F. Wesencraft, Elmfield Press, Leeds: MM N 74 4/11:702-703; S&L (O 74) 4:28-29

SUTC Referee's Rule Book, by Michael F. Korn, Limpex, Mountain View, CA: AFV Mr 73 4/3:27

Sea Battle Games, by P. Dunn, MAP, Hemel Hempstead, Herts: MM Ap 71 1/4:207-208

Sea Battles, by Michael Sanderson, David & Charles, Newton Abbot, Devon: MM My 75 5/5:276

Setting up a Wargames Campaign, by Tony Bath, Wargames Research Group, Birmingham: MM N 73 3/11:763

Skirmish Wargaming, by Donald F. Featherstone, Patrick Stephens, Cambridge: Afx O 75 17/2:121; S&L (D 75) 11:31

Solo Wargaming, by Donald Featherstone, Kaye & Ward, London, 1973: Afx Je 73 14/10:566+; A&W N 73 8:13; MM Ja 73 3/1:52; MW F 73 1/6:331; MW Je 73 1/10:515

Venture Simulation in War, Business, & Politics, by Alfred H. Hausrath, McGraw-Hill: MM Jl 72 2/7:369

Warfleets of Antiquity, by R. B. Nelson, Wargames Research Group, Goring-by-Sea, Sussex: Afx S 73 15/1:56; MM Je 73 3/6:390

The Wargame, by Charles Grant, Adam & Charles Black: Afx Ja 72 13/5:255; MM D 71 1/12:662-663

The Wargame, ed Peter Young, Cassell: MM Ja 73 3/1:51

Wargames Through the Ages, 3000BC to 1500AD, by D. F. Featherstone, Stanley Paul, London: MM Ap 72 2/4:199

Wargames Through the Ages, vol. 2, 1420-1783, by Donald F. Featherstone, Stanley Paul, London: MM Ag 74 4/8:477

Wargames Through the Ages, vol. 3, 1792-1859, by Donald F. Featherstone, Stanley Paul, London: Afx N 75 17/3:176; MM Je 75 5/6:362-363

MISCELLANEOUS

The American West, by Robin May & G. A. Embleton, Almark, New Malden, Surrey, 1973: Afx Je 74 15/10:601; A&W My 74 11/13; MM My 74 4/5:278

Collecting Meccano Dinky Toys, comp Ronald Turni, Cranbourn, London: Sc Ja 75 6/64:33

Gunfighters, Time-Life: S&L (D 75) 11:29
More There I Was..., by Bob Stevens, Aero, Fallbrook, CA, 1974: air force cartoons, songs, & miscellaneous WW-II humor: WWE Ja 75 2/1:27
Posters of World War Two, by Denis Judd, St. Martin's, NY: WWE Ja 74 1/1:11+
Sears, Roebuck 1902 Catalog, facsimile by Bounty Books, Crown Publishers, NY: RMC F 71 39/9:14
The Wild West, by Robin May, Independent Television Books, London: MM S 75 5/9:527
World War II Military Currency, by Raymond S. Toy & Carlton F. Schwan, pvt, Portage, OH, 1974: WWE Mr 75 2/2:66

ENGINE REVIEWS
sil unless otherwise stated

ELECTRIC MOTORS

Astro-Flight Astro 10: no sil AM Mr 73 76/3:65; AM Jl 73 77/1: 24-25; AM O 77/4:38; AM N 73 77/5:66+
Astro-Flight Astro 10 Marine: no sil FM Mr 74 78/3:64-65
Astro-Flight Astro 25: no sil AM Mr 73 76/3:65; AM Jl 73 77/1: 24-25
Galler Alpha Power: AM Jl 73 77/1:24-25
Graupner Electroprop: AM Jl 73 77/1:24-25
Hobbymax Seven & Five Pole DC Motors: no sil MR Mr 73 40/3: 28
Kroker Seahorse: no sil MB D 75 25/299:639-640
M-7: MB Mr 74 24/278:85+
Mabuchi A-1: no sil Aero D 75 40/479:1052-1053
Marx Hectoperm Special: no sil MB Ja 72 22/153:26-27
Mattel Signal Command: AM Jl 73 77/1:24-25
Mattel SuperStar: AM Jl 73 77/1:24-25
Monogram E: no sil Aero D 75 40/479:1052
Rail Craft Motors: no iron in armature: no sil MR Ag 72 39/8: 19-20
Sea Pup: AM Jl 73 77/1:24-25
Sea Ram: AM Jl 73 77/1:24-25
Sea Wasp: AM Jl 73 77/1:24-25
Urei EMF 040: AM Jl 73 77/1:24-25

VI. Reviews

INTERNAL COMBUSTION

($\frac{1}{2}$A)

Cox Black Widow (.049): no sil AM Jl 74 78/7:36; Aero Ag 74 39/463:412-413; MAN Je 74 88/6:20+
Cox Pee-Wee .020: MAN D 75 91/6:46+
Cox TD .049: no sil AM S 74 78/9:49
OTM .048 Kolibri: diesel: MAN S 75 91/3:38+
Quickstart Wasp: Aero Jl 71 36/426:369-371

(A)

Cosmic 15: no sil AM My 73 76/5:52
Cox TD .09: no sil AM S 74 78/9:49
Enya 19-V & 19 TV: MAN F 72 84/2:20+
Enya 19-V BB: Aero N 74 39/466:604-605; MAN Jl 74 89/1:20+
Fox .15 RC: Aero Mr 71 36/422:128-129
Fox 15 RC Marine: MB N 71 21/251:445-447
Fox .19, 1974: Aero Ap 74 38/459:176-177; MAN My 74 89/1:20+
K&B .15 RC series 72: MAN Je 73 86/6:20+
K&B 15 Schnuerle port: no sil AM Mr 73 76/3:50
Kumah AM-25: diesel: scale & dim sil Aero S 75 40/476:850
McCoy 19 series 21: Aero Je 75 40/473:332-333; MAN N 72 85/5: 16+; MAN Mr 74 88/3:20+
O.S. Pet III (.09): Aero Ap 72 37/435:208-209; MAN S 71 83/3:20+
Rossi R-15 Normale: Aero F 73 38/445:88-89; Aero D 73 38/455: 706-707; MAN Mr 73 86/3:20+
Super Tigre G.15-F1: Aero Je 71 36/425:308-309
Super Tigre G.15 RC: Aero Mr 75 40/470:156-157; MAN D 74 89/6:19+
Super Tigre G-20-15 RC 70-71 series: Aero Ag 72 37/439:453-454; MAN Jl 71 83/1:20+
Taipan .15 TBR RC: MAN Jl 75 91/1:47+
Taipan 2.5 BR RC: Aero Ag 75 40/475:806-807
Veco .19 RC series 71: Aero F 72 37/433:97-99; MAN D 71 83/6: 20+
Veco 19-V: Aero Je 72 37/437:328-329

(B)

Fox .25: Aero O 72 37/441:568-569; MAN Jl 72 85/1:20+
Fox .29: Aero Jl 73 38/450:376-377; MAN My 73 86/5:20+
Kosmic 23RC: no sil AM D 73 77/6:70
Micron 5cc 2 cyl: sil only MAN N 73 87/6:6
O.S. Graupner Wankle .30: Aero D 72 27/443:700-702; no sil FM Ag 71 413:50-51; MAN Ap 72 84/4:20+; exploded drawing RC F 71 8/2:10+
O.S. Max 20: Aero O 73 38/453:556-557
O.S. Max .20 RC: MAN Je 72 84/6:20+

O. S. Max 25 & 25 RC: MAN Ap 74 88/4:20+
Super Tigre G21-45 RC: MAN Ag 73 87/2:20+
Taipan 3.5 BB R/C: Aero My 73 38/448:262-263; MAN O 73 87/4: 20+
Taipan 21: AM N 73 77/6:64

(C--Marine)

K&B Stallion 35 RC Marine: no sil MB N 71 21/251:447
K&B 40 series 71 marine conversion: MB Jl 73 23/271:282-283
OPS Speed 60 RC Marine: MB Je 72 22/258:238-240
Super Tigre G 60 RC Marine: MB Mr 71 21/243:105-106

(C--RC)

Bernhardt HB-61: MAN Je 74 88/6:47+
Enya .60F: MAN Ja 75 90/1:52+
Enya .60 III B: no sil AM Jl 73 77/1:68; MAN Ap 73 86/4:20+
Enya .60 III B8: MAN Ap 73 86/4:20+
Fox .36RC (1973): MAN Ja 74 88/1:20+
Fox .40RC: MAN Mr 72 84/3:20+; no sil MAN O 75 91/4:38+
Fox .59 RC: MAN My 71 82/5:20+
Fox Eagle 60 RC: MAN D 72 85/6:20+
Fox Hawk .60: MAN Mr 75 90/3:53+
HB 60 RC: no sil AM Ap 74 78/4:40
HP 40 R.PR: MAN N 73 87/5:16+
HP .61 F RC: no sil AM S 73 77/3:76; MAN Ap 71 82/4:20+
Hirtenberger HP .40F-RC: MAN Ap 74 88/4:46+
K&B 40-A: Aero F 74 39/456:79-80+; MAN F 74 88/2:20+
K&B 40 S Schneurle: no sil AM D 73 77/6:70
K&B 40 RC series 70F: MAN Ja 71 82/1:20+
K&B 61 series 75: MAN N 75 91/5:46-47+
K&B 61 with Perry Pump carb: MAN N 75 91/5:46-47+
MRC Webra Speed .61 RC: MAN Mr 74 88/3:48+; MAN My 75 90/5:48+
MRC YS 60 RC: MAN S 73 87/3:20+; RC My 74 11/5:54-55
Merco .61 RC Mk IV: no sil AM Ag 74 78/8:40; MAN D 73 87/6:20+
Northfield-Rosspower 4: four cylinder: MAN S 72 85/3:16-17+
OPS .40-SLA: MAN Ap 75 90/4:53+
OPS Project 40: no sil FM Mr 74 77/3:62-63
OPS Ursus .60RC: MAN F 73 86/2:20+
OPS Ursus .60 Series 74: MAN My 74 88/5:35+
O.S. Max 40H RC: no sil AM Mr 74 78/3:42
O.S. Max 40RC: MAN Jl 73 87/1:20+
O.S. Max .60F: MAN Ja 75 90/1:52+
O.S. Max H 60F GP: MAN Je 71 82/6:15+
Ross .60 Twin: AM O 74 74/10:83-84
Ross Black Demon 61: no sil FM O 74 77/10:47-48
Ross Custom 61 Schneurle: no sil FM O 74 77/10:47-48
Rossi .60 RC: MAN Ag 72 85/2:20+

VI. Reviews

Super Tigre G20/15 RC: Aero Ag 72 37/439:453-454
Supertigre ST. 51 RC: MAN Jl 74 89/1:46+
Supertigre G. 60 RC Bluehead: AM Je 74 78/6:61+ ; MAN N 71 83/5:16+
Testors McCoy . 40 RC series 21: MAN My 72 84/5:20+
Veco 61 RC: AM Je 74 78/6:50+
Webra . 40 RC: MAN O 71 83/4:20+
Webra . 61 Blackhead: no sil AM Mr 74 78/3:44; MAN N 74 89/5:19+
YS 60 RC: no sil AM Ja 74 78/1:36

(C--Other Than RC)

Fox . 40 RC: MAN O 75 91/4:38+
Fox 59 Stunt: Aero N 71 36/430:627-629
Fox 78: MAN O 74 89/4:22+
K&B Torpedo 40R series 71: MAN Ag 71 1/8:20+
McCoy . 35 Series 21: MAN Je 75 90/6:41
McCoy . 40 series 21: MAN Ja 72 84/1:20+
O. S. Max H40-S: Aero Ja 71 36/420-421+ ; MAN F 71 82/2:47+
O. S. Max 40SR: Aero S 74 39/464:496-497; MAN S 74 89/3:25+
O. S. Max . 60 F-SR: MAN Ag 75 91/2:46+
O. S. Max . 80: MAN Ja 73 86/1:20+
Super Tigre X-40: no sil AM Mr 75 75/3:61+
Super Tigre Saturn . 60: MAN Mr 71 82/3:18+

JETS

Terbocraft P-80 Jet-Stick: no sil RC Ag 71 8/8:47+
Thermo-Jet J3-200: no sil AM Ja 74 78/1:34; no sil RC Jl 74 11/7:53+

KIT REVIEWS (1)--STATIC SCALE

SUBJECT REVIEWS

Battle of Britain: survey of existing kits of 1/72 aircraft: PAM Jl 75 10:164+
Miniature Figures of the American West: Fus W 74 1/2:37-39
Miniature Navies: 1/1200 modern ships: MM Je 72 2/6:296-298
Modelling Marlborough's Wars: MM My 72 2/5:247-249
Space Model Survey: Sc Ag 74 5/59:420-425
Warships in 1:700 Scale: MW Jl 73 1/11:599+
Warships in 1/1200 Scale: MW Je 73 1/10:548-549

AIRCRAFT

Range Reviews

Airframe 1/72 Aircraft: Afx Ja 71 12/5:268
Airmodel 1/72 vacuum: AN 27 Je 75 4/2:11
Aurora KB Collectors Series: WW-I & between wars, 1/48: IM Ap 73 10/4:insert
Eidai Lightplanes: 1/72: AE O 73 5/4:196; IM S 73 10/9:insert; MW Ja 74 2/5:276+; Sc N 73 4/11:776-777
Ge-Li: cardboard aircraft: AN 30 My 75 3/26:7
Heller 1/72 Musée Range: Afx Ag 71 12/12:654
Helmet Battle of Britain Aircraft: 1/350: Sc D 75 6/75:620
Horizon Conversions: 1/32 vac conversion kits: RT Jl 75 8/7:75
Imai 1/144 Aircraft: RiS Sp 74 2/3-4:162
The Lesneys: Matchbox 1/72: AE Je 73 4/6:305; RiS Su 73 1/4: 139
Matchbox Aircraft: 1/72: Afx Jl 73 14/11:622
Microscale 1/48 Collector Classics: RiS Jl 75 3/2:101
Miniature Aircraft vacuum-formed canopies, 1/72 & 1/48: RiS Jl 75 3/2:101
Polific Airmodel: 1/72 vac: AN 16 F 73 1/20:14-15
Revell 1/144: (P-40E, F4F, SBD-5, P-39Q): Sc Jl 74 5/7:389-390
Revell 1/144: (Hurricane, Typhoon, Tempest, Spitfire): Afx Ja 74 15/5:315; AN 31 Ag 73 2/8:14; IM S 73 10/9:insert; MW O 73 2/2:103; RiS Au 73 2/1:14; Sc O 73 4/10:706
Revell 1/144: (Bf 109E, Me 262A, Fw 190A, Ju 87B): Afx Ja 74 15/5:315; MW Ja 74 2/5:274
Revell Collector's Choice: changes in re-relase models: PAM O 73 3:163
Sutcliffe (Harrow, Bombay, Hendon, & Ju 390A): 1/72 vac: AN 11 My 73 1/26:14
Sutcliffe 1/72 vac: IM Jl 73 10/7:insert

World War I

(Allies)

Airfix Avro 504K: 1/72: Sc My 75 6/5:218
Airfix Sopwith Pup: 1/72: AI Jl 75 9/1:37; Afx Je 75 16/10:572; AN 2 My 75 3/24:15; PAM Ap 75 9:142; Sc Je 75 6/6:272
Airframe Morane: 1/72 vac: Sc Ja 71 2/1:46
Artiplast/Merit Avro 504K: 1/48: Sc My 75 6/5:218
Aurora Breguet 14: 1/48: RT Ja 73 6/1-2:3; Sc Mr 74 5/3:169
Aurora DH 10A: 1/48: Sc Mr 74 5/3:170
Aurora Nieuport 28: 1/48: Sc Mr 74 5/3:169
Aurora Sopwith Triplane: 1/48: RT Ja 73 6/1-2:3; Sc Mr 74 5/3: 170

VI. Reviews

Frog Vickers Vimy Mk IV: 1/72: AI F 75 8/2:88; AN 18 O 74 3/10:10
Fuji Nieuport 17: 1/72: Sc Je 73 4/6:422
Fuji SE5A: 1/72: Sc Je 73 4/6:422
Fuji Sopwith Camel: 1/72: Sc Je 73 4/6:422-423
Fuji Spad XIII: 1/72: Sc Je 73 4/6:423
Hawk Nieuport 17: 1/48: IM Ag 72 9/8:insert
Laird DH 6: 1/?? vac: Sc S 74 5/9:500
Lindbergh Curtiss Jenny: 1/48: Afx Ja 71 12/5:266
Merit/Aurora Camel: 1/48: IM Ap 72 9/4:5
Rareplanes Sopwith Snipe: 1/72 vac: AN 8 Je 73 2/2:14; RiS Su 73 1/4:140
Rareplanes Thomas-Morse Scout: 1/72 vac: AN 20 Jl 73 2/5:14; RiS Su 73 1/4:138
Revell Sopwith Camel: 1/72: Afx D 75 17/4:241; IM Ap 72 2/4:5; Sc Ag 75 6/8:412
Revell Sopwith Camel: 1/28: IM Ap 72 9/4:5
Revell Nieuport 17: 1/72: IM Ag 72 9/8:insert

(Central)

Airfix Albatros D. V: 1/72: AI O 75 9/4:197; IM Je 72 9/6:10; Sc S 72 3/9:494-495
Airframe Phonix D. 1: 1/72 vac: Sc D 71 2/12:676; Sc My 72 3/5:280-281
Airframe Siemens Schuchert D. 3: 1/72 vac: Sc Ja 71 2/1:46
Aurora Albatros C. III: 1/48: Sc Mr 74 5/3:170
Aurora/Merit Albatros D. III: 1/48: IM Je 72 9/6:10
Aurora Fokker D. VIII: 1/48: IM Ja 73 10/1:13
Aurora/Merit Fokker Dr. 1: 1/43 (nom 1/48): Sc Ja 72 3/1:48
Aurora Fokker E. III: 1/40 (nom 1/48): RT Ja 73 6/1-2:3; Sc Mr 74 5/3:169
Aurora Fokker F. V (ex D. VIII): 1/48: Sc Mr 74 5/3:170
Aurora Gotha G. V: 1/48: Sc Mr 74 5/3:170
Aurora Halberstadt Cl. II: 1/48: Sc Mr 74 5/3:170
Aurora Pfalz D. III: 1/48: Sc Mr 74 5/3:169
Elvin Albatros D. V: 1/72: Sc S 72 3/9:494-495
Fuji Albatros D. III: 1/72: Sc Je 73 4/6:421-422
Fuji Fokker D. VII: 1/72: Sc Je 73 4/6:422
Renwal Albatros D. V: 1/72: AI O 75 9/4:197; Sc S 72 3/9:494-495
Revell Albatros D. III: 1/72: Sc Ap 73 3/4:260
Revell Fokker D. VII: 1/72: IM Ja 73 10/1:13
Revell Fokker Dr. 1 Triplane: 1/72: Afx D 75 17/4:241; Sc Ap 73 4/4:262; Sc Ag 75 6/8:412

Kit--Static

Between World Wars

(Czechoslovakia Military)

KP Avia B35: 1/72: AI O 75 9/4:200; RiS Jl 75 3/2:102; Sc Je 75 6/6:299; WW2J Jl 75 2/4:28
KP Avia B-534: 1/72: AE S 71 1/4:201; AE D 73 5/6:288-289; Afx F 73 14/6:342; IM Ap 71 8/4:2-3; RT My 71 4/5:56; Sc O 71 2/10:542-543
KP Letov Š. 328 Smolik: 1/72: AE D 73 5/6:288-289; AN 28 S 73 2/10:14; Afx O 73 15/2:114-115; IM Je 73 10/6:insert; RT Jl 73 6/7:79; Sc D 73 4/12:845

(France Military)

Heller Morane Saulinier 225: 1/72: AE N 72 1/6:255; Sc O 72 3/10:556-557
Heller Morane Saulinier 230: 1/72: AE N 72 1/6:255; Sc O 72 3/10:556-557

(Germany Civil)

Airframe Blohm und Voss Ha 139: 1/72 vac: Afx Ag 71 12/12: 654+; RT O 71 4/10:115
Airmodel Bf 108 Taifun: 1/72 vac: Sc Ag 74 5/8:448
Airmodel Bücker Jungmann: 1/72 vac: AN 28 N 75 4/13:11
Otaki Do-X: 1/144: AI O 74 7/4:195+; Sc Ja 75 6/1:11

(Germany Military)

Airfix Henschel Hs 123: 1/72: Afx F 71 12/6:291; RT Ja 71 4/1: 12; Sc Ja 71 2/1:45
Airframe Ju 87A: 1/72 vac conv: AN 12 O 73 2/11:14
Airmodel Dornier Do 23G: 1/72 vac: IM Mr 72 9/3:insert
Airmodel Focke Wulf Fw 56 Stösser: 1/72: AN 27 Je 75 4/2:11
Airmodel Focke Wulf Fw 58 Weihe: 1/72 vac: IM O 72 9/10:insert
Airmodel Heinkel 42C: 1/72 vac: IM Mr 72 9/3:insert
Airmodel Heinkel He 60: 1/72 vac: AN 28 N 75 4/13:11
Airmodel Junkers Ju 87A: 1/72 vac: AN 12 O 73 2/11:14
Hasegawa Heinkel He 51B-2: 1/72: Afx Ap 71 12/8:430; Afx Ag 74 15/12:716; MW Je 73 1/10:518; Sc O 71 2/10:550
Italaerei Henschel Hs 126: 1/72: AI F 75 8/2:86; Afx Ja 74 15/5:314; AN 7 D 73 2/15:14; AN 22 Ag 75 4/6:11; IM Jl 73 10/7:insert; IM Ja 74 10/13-14:insert; PAM Jl 74 6:92; RT Ag 73 6/8:85; Sc O 74 5/61:550-551
Italaerei Junkers Ju 86D: 1/72: AN 19 S 75 4/8:15; Sc N 75 6/74: 571
Matchbox Henschel HS 126: 1/72: AI Jl 75 9/1:37; AI D 75 9/6: 299+; IM Jl 75 11/4:14; PAM Jl 75 10:163; Sc O 75 6/73:515

Rareplanes Heinkel He 51: 1/72 vac: MW Je 73 1/10:518
Rareplanes Henschel Hs 126B-1: 1/72 vac: Sc O 71 2/10:542

(Italy Civil)

Delta Macchi Castoldi MC 72 Schneider racer: 1/72: AE F 74 6/2:88; RT O 72 5/10:111; RiS N 72 1/2:48; Sc My 74 5/5:246-247
Delta Savoia Marchetti S. 55X: 1/72: RiS Au 73 2/1:37

(Italy Military)

Delta Campini Caproni turbojet: 1/72: RT D 73 6/12:134; RiS Au 73 2/1:37
Italaerei Fiat CR 32: 1/50: AI D 74 7/6:295
Supermodel Fiat CR 32: 1/72: AE F 74 6/2:88-89; AI D 74 7/6:295; AN 12 Ap 74 2/23:14; RT D 73 6/12:134; RiS Au 73 2/1:36; Sc Ag 75 6/8:410

(Poland Military)

Revel PZL P. 11c: 1/72: AE S 73 5/3:140
Ruch PZL P. 11c: 1/72: AE S 73 5/3:140

(USSR Military)

Frog SB-2: 1/72: AE Ja 74 6/1:36
Heller Polikarpov I-153: 1/72: PAM O 75 11:194; RiS Jl 75 3/2:102; Sc O 75 6/10:517
KP Polikarpov Po-2: 1/72: IM S 75 11/5:13
Revell Polikarpov I-16 Ishak: 1/72: AE Mr 72 2/3:152

(U. K. Civil)

Airframe Short Mercury: 1/72 vac: AN 17 O 75 4/10:14
Frog Vickers Vimy, Alcock & Brown: 1/72: RT Jl 74 7/7:70
Rareplanes DeHavilland Dragon Rapide: 1/72: Afx Ap 74 15/8:476
Sutcliffe Short Maia: 1/72 vac: AN 17 O 75 4/10:14

(U. K. Military)

Airfix Bristol Bulldog: 1/72: Afx F 71 12/6:291; RT Ja 71 4/1:12; Sc Ja 71 2/1:43-44
Airframe Vickers Wellesley: 1/72 vac: Sc Ap 73 4/4:254
Airframe Westland-Hill Pterodactyl Mk I: 1/72: RT Je 71 4/6:72
Frog Gloster Gladiator II: 1/72: AE Ap 74 6/4:204; AN 6 Jl 73 2/4:14; RiS W 74 2/2:73

Frog Shark: IM Jl 73 10/7:5-6; Sc My 71 2/5:252-255
Matchbox Armstrong Whitworth Siskin IIIA: 1/72: AI D 75 9/6: 299; AN 22 Ag 75 4/6:11; RiS Jl 75 3/2:163; Sc Je 75 6/6:298
Matchbox Gloster Gladiator: 1/72: AE Je 73 4/6:305; AE Ap 74 6/4:204; AN 6 Jl 73 2/4:14; Sc Jl 73 4/7:495; Sc Ag 73 4/8: 546-548
Matchbox Hawker Fury I: 1/72: AE Je 73 4/6:305; AN 8 Je 72 1/2:14; AN 2 Mr 73 1/21:14; RT Je 73 6/6:69; Sc Ap 73 4/4:254
Rareplanes Hawker Fury: 1/72 vac: Sc Ap 73 4/4:254
Sutcliffe Blackburn Iris: 1/72 vac: AI S 75 9/3:150
Sutcliff Blackburn Perth: 1/72 vac: AI S 75 9/3:150
Sutcliff Saro London: 1/72 vac: Sc N 74 5/11:612
Sutcliff Supermarine Scapa: 1/72 vac: AI S 75 9/3:150
Sutcliff Supermarine Southampton II: 1/72 vac: AI S 75 9/3:150
Sutcliff Supermarine Stranraer: 1/72 vac: Sc N 74 5/11:612

(U.S. Civil)

Entex Douglas DC-3: 1/100: Sc Mr 75 6/3:142
Greenback Castle Ryan M-1: 1/72: AE My 72 2/5:258; RT Jl 72 5/7:83; Sc O 72 3/10:567
Lindbergh Lockheed Vega Winnie Mae: 1/48: Afx Ja 71 12/5:266
Monogram Douglas DC-3: 1/77: Sc Ag 75 6/8:408
Monogram Ford tri-motor: 1/77: Sc Jl 75 6/7:360
Nitto Douglas DC-3: 1/100: AI O 74 7/4:197-198
Williams Boeing 247: 1/72: AE F 74 6/2:89; AN 12 O 73 2/11: 14; RT O 73 6/10:108; Sc S 73 4/9:604-605

(U.S. Military)

Airfix Brewster Buffalo: 1/72: AE F 73 4/2:98; Afx N 72 14/2: 127; AN 10 N 72 1/13:14; MW Je 73 1/10:552-553; MW D 73 2/4:179
Hasegawa Boeing P-12E: 1/32: AE F 72 2/2:99; Sc Ag 71 2/8: 434-436+; Sc D 71 2/12:658-659+; Sc Jl 73 4/7:491-492
Hasegawa Boeing P-26: 1/32: Ris Sp 74 2/3-4:159
Hasegawa Curtiss BF2C-1: 1/32: AE F 72 2/2:99; IM My 71 8/5:4; Sc Ag 71 2/8:434-436+, cor S 71 2/9:461
Matchbox Boeing P-12E: 1/72: AE Je 73 4/6:305; AN 2 Mr 73 1/21:14; Sc My 73 4/5:354
Matchbox Brewster Buffalo: 1/72: AN 11 Jl 75 4/3:15; IM Jl 75 11/4:15; PAM Ja 75 8:122; Sc O 75 6/10:516
Monogram Douglas TBD-1 Devastator: 1/48: AI My 75 8/5:246
Rareplanes Curtiss A-8 Shrike: 1/72 vac: AI Jl 74 7/1:44; Sc Je 74 5/6:336
Rareplanes Martin B-10: 1/72 vac: AI Jl 74 7/1:44; AI Ag 74 7/2:91; Afx Ap 74 15/8:476; AN 28 S 73 2/10:14; RiS W 74 2/2:75
Rareplanes Republic P-43A Lancer: 1/72 vac: AE Mr 73 4/3:149; AN 27 O 72 1/12:13
Rareplanes Seversky P-35: 1/72 vac: AN 19 Ja 73 1/18:15

Sutcliffe Martin B-10: 1/72 vac: IM Ag 73 10/8:insert
Tamiya Brewster Buffalo: 1/48: RiS Sp 74 2/3-4:158; Sc O 74 5/
  10:548-549
Williams Martin B-10: 1/72: AI O 74 7/4:197; Sc S 74 5/9:502;
  Sc F 75 6/2:92

World War II

(France)

Heller Bloch MB 152: 1/72: AE F 74 6/2:92
Heller Breguet 693: 1/72: AE My 73 4/5:253
Heller Dewoitine D. 520: 1/72: AI My 75 8/9:243
Heller Dewoitine D. 520: nom 1/50: AI My 75 8/9:243
Heller Morane MS 406: 1/72: Afx Ja 72 13/5:281
Heller Potez 540: 1/72: AE N 72 3/5:255

(Germany Bombers)

Airfix Dornier Do 17E/F: 1/72: AE Ap 73 4/4:194; Afx D 72
  14/4:221; MW Mr 73 1/7:382; RT Ap 73 6/4:37; RiS Sp 73 1/3:
  101; Sc My 73 4/5:357
Airfix Heinkel He 111H-20: 1/72: Sc S 71 2/9:475-477
Airmodel Arado Ar 232: 1/72 vac: IM O 72 9/10:insert
Airmodel Arado Ar 240A-02: 1/72: AN 28 N 75 4/13:12
Airmodel Dornier Do 18: 1/72 vac: IM Ja 72 9/1:9
Airmodel Junkers Ju 388: 1/72 vac conv from Matchbox Ju 188:
  AI Ag 75 9/2:94; Afx O 75 17/2:118
Frog Dornier Do 17Z-2: 1/72: AE D 71 1/7:386; Afx O 71 13/2:
  100; IM Jl 71 8/7:insert; Sc O 71 2/10:546-548
Frog Junkers Ju 88A-4: 1/72: IM My 71 8/5:11
Frog Heinkel 111H1/H6: 1/72: AE Ag 72 3/2:90; AN 18 Ag 72 1/
  7:14; IM Je 72 9/6:insert; MW S 72 1/1:50; RT Jl 72 5/7:75;
  Sc S 72 3/9:405-406
Heller Junkers Ju 87B: 1/72: AE Ap 73 4/4:194; Afx 14/9:506;
  MW Ap 73 1/8; RiS Sp 73 1/3:102
Italaerei Ju 188: 1/72: AI Je 75 8/6:296; AN 25 Jl 75 4/4:11;
  PAM Ja 75 8:122-123; RiS Mr 75 3/1:50; Sc Ap 75 6/67:176;
  Sc Je 75 6/69:288-289
Lindberg Arado Ar 234 Blitz: 1/72: Sc Ap 72 3/4:225
Matchbox Heinkel He 111H: 1/72: AI D 75 9/6:302; IM S 75 11/
  5:17; PAM O 75 11:182; Sc D 75 6/75:618
Matchbox Junkers Ju 87 G1/D3 Stuka: 1/72: AI D 75 9/6:299; AN
  22 Ag 75 4/6:11; Sc O 75 6/72:515
Matchbox Junkers Ju 188: 1/72: AI Je 75 8/6:296; Afx Ag 75 16/
  12:726; AN 7 F 75 3/18:11; IM My 75 11/3:13; PAM O 74 7:
  103-104; Sc F 75 6/65:94
Matchbox Messerschmitt Me 262: 1/72: AN 11 Jl 75 4/3:15
Revell Junkers Ju 87D-5/G-2: 1/72: PAM O 75 11:183
Sutcliffe Junkers Ju 290: 1/72 vac: AN 26 O 74 2/12:13

Kit--Static

(Germany Fighters)

(Reaction)
Airfix Messerschmitt Me 262: 1/72: AN 18 Ag 72 1/7:14
Frog Heinkel He 162A: 1/72: AE Mr 73 4/3:149; AN 8 D 72 1/15:14
Frog Messerschmitt Me 262A: 1/72: AE O 72 1/5:203-204; AE F 73 4/2:98; Afx O 72 14/2:101; AN 22 D 72 1/16:15; IM Ag 72 9/8:insert; MW O 72 1/2:159; MW N 72 1/3:159; Sc N 72 3/11: 615-616
Hasegawa Messerschmitt Me 163 Komet: 1/32: AE Mr 74 6/3:138; AN 29 Mr 74 2/22:14; IM N 73 10/11-12:insert; IM Ja 74 10/13-14:insert
Hasegawa Messerschmitt Me 262A Schwalbe: 1/32: AE F 73 4/2:98; AN 8 D 72 1/15:14; AN 22 D 72 1/16:15; MW S 73 2/1:48
Heller Messerschmitt Me 262B-1a/U1: 1/72: PAM O 75 11:194
Matchbox Me 262A-2a: 1/72: PAM Ja 75 8:122; Sc Ap 75 6/67: 177
Revell Me 262-1a: 1/72: Afx Ja 73 14/5:280-281
Revell Me 262A/IA Schwalbe: 1/32: AE N 72 3/5:255+; Sc N 72 3/11:616-618
Revell Me 262B-1a/U1: 1/32: AE N 72 3/5:255+; AN 13 D 74 3/14:10; Sc D 74 5/63:672
Tamiya Me 163B Komet: 1/100: MW Mr 73 1/7:383
Tamiya Me 262A Schwalbe: 1/100: Afx Je 73 14/5:281; MW Mr 73 1/7:383

(Single Engine)
Airfix Messerschmitt Bf 109E: 1/24: AE F 72 2/2:99+; Afx Ja 72 13/5:248; IM N 71 8/11:insert; Sc Ja 72 3/1:46-47
Airmodel Messerschmitt Bf 109B-2: 1/72 vac conv from Revell Bf 109E: AE Mr 74 6/3:136; IM O 71 8/10:insert
Frog Focke Wulf Ta 152H: 1/72: AI Jl 74 7/1:44; Sc F 71 2/2: 102
Frog Messerschmitt Bf 109E: 1/72: AE F 73 4/2:98
Frog/Hasegawa Messerschmitt Bf 109E: 1/32: AE F 73 4/2:98; Afx Jl 73 14/11:618; AN 8 D 72 1/15:14; Sc My 73 4/5:355-356
Fujimi Focke Wulf Fw 190A-6-9A & D-9: 1/50 (nom 1/48): AE S 71 1/4:201-202; Sc O 71 2/10:549-550
Fujimi Messerschmitt Bf 109G/K: 1/48: AE Jl 72 3/1:45; Sc Jl 73 4/7:493-494
Hasegawa Focke Wulf Fw 190: 1/32: MW S 73 2/1:48; Sc N 72 3/11:618
Hasegawa Focke Wulf Fw 190A: 1/72: RiS Jl 75 3/2:101
Hasegawa Focke Wulf Fw 190D-9: 1/72: AI O 75 9/4:197+; RiS Jl 75 3/2:103
Heller Focke Wulf Fw 190A-8/F-8: 1/72: PAM O 75 11:194
Heller Messerschmitt Bf 109E-3/E-4: 1/72: PAM O 75 11:194; RiS Mr 75 3/1:49
Heller Messerschmitt Bf 109F: 1/72: AE N 72 3/5:255; MW N 72 1/3:158-159

Jo-Han Messerschmitt Bf 109F/G: 1/72: AN 10 My 74 2/25:14; PAM Ja 74 4:53; RT Ja 74 7/1:12
Matchbox Focke-Wulf 190: 1/72: AE Jl 73 5/1:46; AN 13 Ap 73 1/24:14; Sc My 73 4/5:354-355
Matchbox Messerschmitt Bf 109E: 1/72: AI Jl 74 7/1:44; Afx Je 74 15/10:596; AN 12 Ap 74 2/23:14; IM Ja 74 10/13-14:insert; PAM Ja 74 4:53; RiS Sp 74 2/3-4:162; Sc My 74 5/56:281
Otaki Messerschmitt Bf 109G: 1/48: AI N 75 9/5:250
Revell Focke Wulf Fw 190A-6/R6: 1/72: AN 27 Je 75 4/2:11
Revell Focke Wulf Fw 190D: 1/32: AE O 72 3/4:203; MW O 72 1/2:101; Sc O 72 3/10:558+
Revell Messerschmitt Bf 109E: 1/72: AE Mr 74 6/3:136; Afx D 75 17/4:240; AN 27 Je 75 4/2:11

(Twin Engine)
Airmodel Messerschmitt Bf 109Z: 1/72 vac conv from Frog or Jo-Han Bf 109H-1: AI Ag 75 9/2:94; Afx O 75 17/2:118
Frog Dornier Do 335 Pfeil: 1/72: AI Jl 75 9/1:37+; AN 18 Ap 75 3/23:11; IM My 75 11/3:13; Sc Ap 75 6/67:177; Sc Jl 75 6/70:358
Frog Messerschmitt Bf 110G: 1/72: AE O 71 1/5:272; Afx Ag 71 12/12:656; IM Je 71 8/6:3; Sc S 71 2/9:498
Lindberg Dornier Do 335A Pfeil: 1/72: IM S 72 9/9:1-2
Matchbox Junkers Ju 188: 1/72: AN 7 F 75 3/18:11; Afx Ag 75 16/12:726; PAM O 74 7:103-104; RT Jl 75 8/7:83; Sc F 75 6/65:94; Sc Je 75 6/69:289
Matchbox Messerschmitt Me 410: 1/72: PAM O 75 11:192
Monogram Dornier Do 335 Pfeil: 1/48: AI S 74 7/3:138; Afx O 74 16/2:114; IM My 74 10/(16):12; Sc Ap 75 6/67:177
Revell Junkers Ju 88C-6c nightfighter: Afx F 75 16/6:382+; IM S 74 10/(18):10-11; PAM Jl 74 6:92; Sc D 74 5/63:671
Revell Heinkel He 219 Uhu: 1/72: AE My 74 6/5:255; Afx My 74 15/9:535; Sc Ap 74 5/55:222
Revell Messerschmitt Bf 110C: 1/32: Afx N 75 17/3:174; IM S 75 11/5:12; PAM O 75 11:192
Revell Messerschmitt Bf 110G: 1/32: AI Ag 74 7/2:91+; Afx N 74 16/3:184-185; RiS Sp 74 2/3-4:159; Sc N 74 5/62:614-615

(Germany Other)

Airfix Arado Ar 196A-3: 1/72: IM Ag 72 9/8:1-2
Airfix Blohn und Voss BV 141B: 1/72: Afx Ja 71 12/5:234; IM Ja 71 8/1:1; Sc Ja 71 2/1:42
Airfix Fiesler Fi 156 Storch: 1/72: AI Ap 75 8/4:201; IM Ap 72 9/4:1
Airframe Henschell Hs 132: 1/72 vac: AN 31 Ag 73 2/8:14
Airmodel Heinkel He 111Z: 1/72 vac conv from Frog He 111: AN 24 N 72 1/14:14
Airmodel Heinkel He 115: 1/72 vac: AN 4 Ag 72 1/6:14-15
Airmodel Messerschmitt Me 321/323 Gigant: 1/72 vac: AN 16 Mr 73 1/22:14
Italaerei Gotha Gö 242A Lastensegle/Gö 244: 1/72: AI S 74 7/3:

138; PAM Ap 75 9:144; RiS Sp 74 2/3-4:158; Sc Ag 74 5/59: 447-448
Matchbox Heinkel He 115: 1/72: AI D 75 9/6:302; IM N 75 11/6: 24; Sc D 75 6/75:618

(Italy)

Airfix Fiat G. 50: 1/72: AE Je 74 6/6:304
Airfix Savoia Marchetti SM 79 Sparviero: 1/72: AI D 75 9/6:299
Artiplast Macchi MC 200 Saetta: 1/48: IM D 71 8/12:insert; Sc Ja 72 3/1:47-48
Artiplast Macchi C. 200 Saetta: 1/50: AE D 71 1/7:386
Artiplast Macchi C. 202 Folgore: 1/50: AI O 74 7/4:197
Artiplast Reggaine Re 1000 Falco: 1/50: AI Ag 75 9/2:91
Artiplast Savoia Marchetti SM 79 Sparviero: 1/50: AI D 75 9/6: 299
Frog Fiat G. 55 Centauro: 1/72: AE Ja 73 4/1:42; Afx F 73 14/6:334; Sc Ja 73 4/1:44
Italaerei Cant Z 501: 1/72: AI Mr 75 8/3:150; AN 27 D 74 3/15: 10; RiS Sp 74 2/3-4:161; Sc F 75 6/65:96
Italaerei Cant 2501: 1/72: Sc Ja 75 6/64:35
Italaerei Caprioni Ca 311: 1/72: Sc S 75 6/72:464
Italaerei Caprioni CA 313/Ca 314: 1/72: AE Ja 72 2/1:32+; Afx F 72 13/6:340+; Afx N 73 15/3:170; IM Ap 71 8/4:4
Italaerei Fiat BR 20: 1/72: Sc N 73 4/11:779
Italaerei Reggaine Re 2000 Falco: 1/72: Afx Ja 71 12/5:264; Sc Mr 71 2/3:155
Italaerei Reggiane Re. 2002 Ariete: 1/72: RT Jl 71 4/7:75
Rareplanes Breda Ba 65: 1/72 vac: IM Ap 72 9/4:insert
Revell C. 202 Folgore: 1/72: AI O 74 7/4:197
Supermodel Cant Z1007: 1/72: RT Jl 72 5/7:76
Supermodel Cant Z1007bis Monoderiva: 1/72: AE O 72 3/4:204; Afx D 73 15/4:243; AN 11 My 73 1/26:14; IM S 72 9/9:insert; IM Ap 73 10/4:insert; RiS Ag 72 1/1:16; Sc Ja 74 5/1:50
Supermodel Fiat G. 55S Silurante: 1/72: Afx D 73 15/4:248; RT Ja 73 6/1-2:22
Supermodel Macchi C. 205 Veltro: 1/72: AI Jl 75 9/1:40; Sc O 75 6/73:513
Supermodel Reggaine Re 200 Falco: 1/72: AI Ag 75 9/2:91
Supermodel Savoia-Marchetti SM 81 Pipestrello: 1/72: PAM Jl 74 6:82; Sc O 73 4/10:705-706

(Japan Bombers)

Hasegawa Mitsubishi G4M1 Mk II "Betty": 1/72: Afx O 73 15/2: 112+; Sc Ag 72 3/8:451
Imai Kawasaki Ki-48 Shiki "Lily": 1/144: MW Jl 73 1/11:608
LS Aichi D4Y3 "Judy": 1/72: RiS Mr 75 3/1:50
LS Mitsubishi G3M "Nell": 1/72: Afx N 73 15/3:174+
Mania Mitsubishi Ki-51 "Sonia": 1/72: RiS Sp 74 2/3-4:161
Mania Nakajima B5N2 "Kate": 1/72: IM Jl 73 10/7:insert; PAM

Ap 75 9:144; RiS Su 73 1/4:140
Nichimo Mitsubishi Ki 51 "Sonia": 1/48: AI My 75 8/5:246; RiS Mr 75 3/1:49
Nichimo Nakajima B5N2 "Kate": 1/48: AE Je 72 2/6:326; RT Ap 72 5/4:45
Nitto Nakajima B5N2 "Kate": 1/72: IM N 72 9/11:insert
Revell Mitsubishi Ki. 21 "Sally": 1/72: RiS Jl 75 3/2:102
Revell Nakajima Ki-49 "Helen": 1/72: RiS W 74 2/2:77
Revell Yokosuka P1Y1/2 Ginga: 1/72: AE O 73 5/4:196; AI N 74 7/5:248; AN 12 O 73 2/11:14; Sc O 73 4/10:711

(Japan Fighters)

Fujimi Mitsubishi A6M2 "Zeke": 1/48: Sc D 73 4/12:847
Hasegawa Aichi E13A1 "Jake": 1/72: Afx Ap 74 15/8:476-477; Sc Ag 73 4/8:571
Hasegawa Kawasaki Ki. 61 "Tony": 1/72: AI N 74 7/5:248; RiS W 74 2/2:73
Hasegawa Mitsubishi A6M2, A6M3, A6M5 "Zeke": 1/72: Afx O 73 15/2:112+; Sc D 73 4/12:847
Hasegawa Mitsubishi A6M5 "Zeke": 1/32: AE Ja 73 3/1:42-43; AN 19 Ja 73 1/18:14; IM Mr 72 9/3:insert; Sc N 72 3/11:615
Hasegawa Nakajima Ki. 43 "Oscar": 1/32: AI Jl 74 7/1:44; RiS W 74 2/2:74; Sc Jl 74 5/58:389
Hasegawa Nakajima Ki. 44 "Tojo": 1/72: IM Mr 74 10/(15):9; PAM Jl 74 6:92; RiS W 74 2/2:73
Heller Mitsubishi Zero 52: 1/75 (nom 1/72): AE Ap 73 4/4:194; RiS N 72 1/2:47
Jo-Han Mitsubishi Zero/Rufe: 1/72: AN 10 My 74 2/25:14; IM Ja 74 10/13-14:insert; RiS W 74 2/2:73
Mania Mitsubishi Ki. 51 "Sonia": 1/72: AI N 74 7/5:245
Mania Nakajima Ki. 27 "Nate": 1/72: AI Jl 75 9/1:37; RT Mr 71 4/3:34
Mania Nakajima Ki. 27 "Nate": 1/48: RiS Jl 75 3/2:102
Matchbox Mitsubishi A6M3 Model 22 Zero: 1/72: AE Jl 73 5/1:47; PAM O 73 3/36; Sc Jl 73 4/7:495+
Nichimo Kawasaki Ki 45 "Nick": 1/48: RiS Jl 75 3/2:103
Nichimo Kawanishi N1K2 Shinden-Kai "George": 1/35: AE F 72 2/2:101
Otaki Kawanishi N1K1J Shinden "George": 1/48: Q Ja 73 8/1:40
Otaki Kawasaki Ki 61-I Hein "Tony": 1/48: Q Ja 73 8/1:40; Sc D 72 3/12:676-678
Otaki Kawasaki Ki. 100: 1/48: AI Mr 75 8/3:150; RiS Sp 74 3/3-4:159
Otaki Nakajima Ki. 43 "Oscar": 1/48: AI Ag 75 9/2:94; IM Je 72 9/6:insert
Otaki Nakajima Ki. 44 "Tojo": 1/72: RiS Sp 74 2/3-4:159
Otaki Nakajima Ki. 44 Shoki "Tojo": 1/48: AI Mr 75 8/3:150
Revell Kawasaki Ki. 45 Kai Toryu "Nick": 1/72: AE Ag 72 3/2:90; Afx F 73 14/6:336; AN 19 Ja 73 1/18:14; IM S 72 9/9:insert; MW Jl 73 1/11:606
Revell Kawasaki Ki. 61 Hein "Tony I": 1/32: AE Ag 73 5/2:98; AI

N 74 7/5:245+; Afx S 73 15/1:52+; AN 25 My 72 2/1:14; IM S 72 9/9:insert; Q Ja 73 8/1:39; Sc D 72 3/12:676-678
Revell Mitsubishi Zero: 1/144: MW Ag 73 1/12:661
Revell Mitsubishi Raiden "Jack": 1/32: AE Ap 72 2/4:205-206; IM Ja 72 9/1:9-10; Sc Jl 71 2/7:374-375; Sc Mr 72 3/3:172-173
Revell Nakajima Ki. 43-I "Oscar": 1/72: AI Jl 75 9/1:36
Revell Nakajima Ki. 43 "Oscar": 1/32: Afx Ap 75 16/8:497; Sc O 74 5/61:553
Revell Nakajima Ki. 44 Shoki "Tojo": 1/144: MW Ag 73 1/12:661
Revell Yokosuka P1Y1/2 Ginga "Frances": 1/72: AE O 73 5/4:196; AI N 74 7/5:248; AN 12 O 73 2/11:14; Sc O 73 4/10:711
Tamiya Kawasaki Ki. 61-II Hein "Tony": 1/50: AI N 74 7/5:248
Tamiya Mitsubishi A6M2 Zero: 1/48: RiS Su 73 1/4:140; Sc Mr 74 5/54:168-169
Tamiya Mitsubishi J2M3 Raiden "Jack": 1/48: IM My 74 10/(16):13; RiS W 74 2/2:77
Tamiya Nakajima A6M2N "Rufe": 1/48: AE Mr 74 6/3:138+; Afx Ja 74 15/5:314; RiS Su 73 1/4:140
Tamiya Nakajima Ki. 84 Hayate "Frank": 1/48: AE Je 72 2/6:326; AE Ap 73 4/4:194; IM Je 72 9/6:insert; Sc Ja 73 4/1:42-43
Tomy Nakajima Ki. 84 "Frank": 1/32: RiS Su 73 1/4:140

(Japan Other)

LS Mitsubishi L3M1: Afx N 73 15/3:176
LS Type 93 "Willow": 1/72: RiS Sp 74 2/3-4:159
Nitto Willow: 1/32: AE Ja 74 6/1:36; Sc O 73 4/10:707+
Otaki Yokosuka K5Y1 Type 93 Willow: 1/48: AE S 73 5/3:140; RiS Sp 73 1/3:101

(USSR)

Heller Yak-3: 1/72: RiS Jl 75 3/2:102
Heller Yak-9: 1/72: PAM O 75 11:194
Italaerei Lavochkin La 5FN: 1/72: Afx F 74 15/6:363; Sc F 74 5/2:117
KP Ilyushin Il-10/B-33: 1/72: AE Mr 72 2/3:152+; IM Ja 72 9/1:10-11; RT Mr 72 5/3:33; Sc My 72 3/5:260-261
KP Lavochkin La-7: 1/72: AE Mr 74 6/5:256; Afx My 74 15/9:535-536; PAM Jl 74 6:91; RT Jl 74 7/1:2; RiS W 74 2/2:77; Sc Ap 74 5/4:225
Moscow Yak-3: 1/50: AE My 72 2/5:258; Sc Jl 73 4/7:492-493
Nichimo Yak 9D: 1/65: IM Ap 71 8/4:14
Rareplanes La 5 FN: 1/72 vac: IM Ap 72 9/4:insert
unnamed USSR manufacturer Yak-3: 1/72: Sc Jl 73 4/6:492-493

(U.K. Bombers)

Airfix De Havilland Mosquito Mks II, VI, XVII: 1/72: AE Ap 73

4/4:194; Afx Ja 73 14/5:252; AN 19 Ja 73 1/18:14; MW My 73 1/9:493; PAM Ap 74 5:73; RiS Sp 73 1/3:103; Sc Ag 74 5/8: 438-439
Airfix Fairey Battle: 1/72: AE Ag 72 3/2:89-90; Sc Ja 71 2/1:26
Airfix Short Stirling I/III: 1/72: IM F 72 9/2:1
Crown Avro Lancaster: 1/144: RiS Jl 75 3/2:101
Frog Bristol Beaufort II: 1/72: AE Jl 71 1/2:94
Frog Bristol Blenheim: 1/72: AE Ap 74 6/4:201
Frog Fairey Barracuda: 1/72: Sc F 71 2/2:104-105
Frog Fairey Swordfish: 1/72: AE Mr 74 6/3:138; AN 15 F 74 2/19:14; IM Ja 74 10/13-14:insert; PAM Jl 74 6:91; RiS W 74 2/2:74; Sc F 74 5/2:116; Sc Mr 74 5/3:146
Matchbox Vickers Wellington Mk X: 1/72: AI D 75 9/6:302; IM N 75 11/6:23-24; Sc D 75 6/75:619
Monogram De Havilland Mosquito: 1/48: IM D 71 8/12:13+
Revell Mosquito Mk IV: 1/32: AE O 72 3/4:203; MW Ja 73 1/5: 270
Sutcliffe Avro Lincoln: 1/72 vac: Afx Ag 74 15/12:718-719
Tamiya Lancaster: 1/48: AI N 75 9/5:250; AN 3 O 75 4/9:15; PAM Jl 75 10:177; RiS Jl 75 3/2:103

(U. K. Fighters)

Airfix Hawker Hurricane: nom 1/72 (less): AE S 72 3/3:151; Afx Ag 72 13/12:649; Afx S 72 14/1:10; IM Ag 72 9/8:insert; Sc S 72 3/9:503-504
Airfix Hawker Hurricane I: 1/24: AE F 74 6/2:89; AN 1 F 74 2/18:14; IM S 73 10/9:insert; IM Ja 74 10/13-14:insert; MW Ja 74 2/5:274; Sc Ja 74 5/1:26-28
Airfix Supermarine Spitfire Mk IA: 1/24: AE Je 71 1/1:38; Afx Ja 71 12/5:235+; Afx D 73 15/4:210; IM F 71 8/2:1-4; RT F 71 4/2:15; Sc F 71 2/2:98-100
Airfix Supermarine Spitfire Vb: 1/72: AI My 75 8/5:243+; Afx Ap 75 16/8:488; AN 10 Ja 75 3/16:10; IM Mr 75 11/3:12; PAM O 74 7:117; RT Je 75 8/6:62; RT Jl 75 8/7:83; WW2J Jl 75 2/4: 29
Frog De Havilland Hornet F3: 1/72: AE Jl 71 1/2:94; Afx Jl 71 12/11:598; Sc My 71 2/5:260-262
Frog Hawker Hurricane: 1/72: IM D 72 9/12:1
Frog Hawker Tempest: 1/72: Sc F 73 4/2:101
Frog Hawker Typhoon: 1/72: AI O 75 9/4:200; Afx O 75 17/2: 120; AN 8 Ag 75 4/5:15; IM Jl 75 11/4:13; PAM Jl 75 10:162; Sc O 75 6/73:516
Frog Spitfire VIII/IX: 1/72: AI F 75 8/2:88; AN 18 O 74 3/10: 10; IM N 74 10/19:10; PAM O 74 7:102; Sc Ja 75 6/64:20-21
Fujimi Spitfire Mk Vb/Vc:◄1/50 (nom 1/48): AE N 71 1/6:317; IM N 71 8/11:insert; Sc My 72 3/5:286+
Hasegawa Spitfire Mk I: 1/72: AI Mr 75 8/3:150; AN 21 Mr 75 3/21:10; IM My 75 11/3:14; PAM Jl 75 10:176; Sc Je 75 6/69: 299
Heller Spitfire I: 1/75 (nom 1/72): AE Ja 73 4/1:42; RiS N 72 1/2:47; Sc Jl 73 4/7:494

Heller Spitfire Vb: 1/72: PAM O 75 11:194; RiS Mr 75 3/1:49
Matchbox Bristol Beaufighter Tf Mk X: 1/72: AN 4 O 74 3/9:15; IM Mr 74 10/(15):9
Matchbox Hawker Hurricane IIc: 1/72: AE F 74 6/2:92; AN 26 O 73 2/12:14; IM Ja 74 10/13-14:insert; MW Ja 74 2/5:276; RT O 73 6/10:108
Matchbox Hawker Tempest Mk VI & II: 1/72: AI Je 75 8/6:296; AN 24 Ja 75 3/17:11; IM Mr 75 11/2:15; PAM O 74 7:103; Sc F 75 6/65:95
Matchbox Spitfire IX: 1/72: AE Jl 73 5/1:46; AN 2 Mr 73 1/21:14
Rareplanes Fairey Fulmar: 1/72 vac: AI Jl 75 9/1:36-37; AI D 75 9/6:298-299; Afx Je 75 16/10:611; Afx D 75 17/4:241; AN 16 My 75 3/25:15; RiS Jl 75 3/2:103
Revell Bristol Beaufighter: 1/32: AE Ap 74 6/4:201+; Afx Je 74 15/10:596; RiS W 74 2/2:73
Revell Hawker Hurricane: 1/32: AE My 74 6/5:256; Afx Jl 71 12/11:598; Afx S 74 16/1:48; Sc Ap 74 5/4:222
Revell Hawker Tempest Mk V: 1/72: Sc F 73 4/2:101
Revell Hawker Typhoon Ib: 1/32: AE D 73 5/6:289+; Afx Ap 74 15/8:474; AN 23 N 73 2/14:14; Sc N 73 4/11:778; Sc F 74 5/2:78-79

(U. K. Other)

Airfix Westland Lysander: 1/72: Afx N 72 14/3:127
Airmodel Tandem-Wing Lysander: 1/72 vac conv from Frog Lysander: AI Ag 75 9/2:94; Afx O 75 17/2:120
Matchbox Supermarine Walrus Mk 1: 1/72: AI O 74 7/4:198; Afx O 74 16/2:114; PAM O 74 7:102; Sc Ag 74 5/59:436-437
Matchbox Westland Lysander: 1/72: AN 20 Jl 73 2/5:14; Sc Jl 73 4/7:495

(U. S. Bombers)

Airfix Douglas A-26 Invader: 1/72: Afx D 71 13/4:227
Airfix Martin B-26B-25 Marauder: 1/72: Afx N 73 15/3:140; AN 1 Mr 74 2/20:14; IM S 73 10/9:insert; RT D 73 6/12:145; Sc F 74 5/2:116
Airfix North American B-25H/J: 1/72: AI S 74 7/3:135
Aurora Martin B-26D Marauder: 1/48: Sc My 73 4/5:335-336
Crown Boeing B-17G: 1/144: RiS Jl 75 3/2:101
Crown Consolidated B-24J: 1/144: RiS Jl 75 3/22:101
Entex/Marusan Boeing B-29 Superfortress: 1/100: Sc Mr 75 6/66:144
Frog Grumman Avenger I (TBM-1): 1/72: IM Je 73 10/6:4-6
Frog Grumman Avenger II: 1/72: AE Ag 73 5/2:97-98; Afx F 74 15/6:363; AN 8 Je 73 2/2:14; Sc Ag 73 4/8:571-573
Frog Martin Maryland: 1/72: AE Mr 74 6/3:138; AN 15 F 74 2/19:14; IM Ja 74 10/13-14:insert; RiS W 74 2/2:73; Sc My 74 5/56:280
Matchbox SB2C-1 Helldiver: 1/72: Afx D 74 16/4:252; AN 20 S 74

VI. Reviews 684

3/8:11; IM S 74 10/(18):10
Monogram Boeing B-17G: 1/48: Afx N 75 17/3:173; AN 14 N 75 4/12:11+; Sc N 75 6/74:570; Sc D 75 6/75:598-603; WW2J S 75 2/5-6:29
Nichimo (org Monogram) Douglas SBD-4 Dauntless: 1/72: Sc My 71 2/5:240-241
Rareplanes Northrop A-17: 1/72 vac: IM Ap 72 9/4:insert
Revell Boeing Fortress IIA: 1/72: AE N 72 3/5:257; Afx Jl 72 13/11:628; IM Jl 72 9/7:insert; Sc Jl 72 3/7:402
Revell Boeing B-17E: 1/72: AE N 72 3/5:257
Revell Boeing B-29 Superfortress: 1/135: AE My 74 6/5:253+; Afx My 74 15/9:535; Sc Ap 74 5/55:222-223
Revell Douglas A-20C Havoc: 1/72: Sc Jl 74 5/7:390
Revell Martin B-26B Marauder: 1/72: AE My 74 6/5:255; Afx My 74 15/9:535; Sc My 73 4/5:336
Revell North American B-25B Mitchell: 1/48: AI S 74 7/3:135+

(U.S. Fighters)

(Carrier-Based)
Frog Chance Vought F4U-1D Corsair: 1/72: AE Ag 72 3/2:90; AN 9 Je 72 1/2:14; IM Je 72 9/6:insert; Sc S 72 3/9:405
Frog Grumman F4F-3 Wildcat IV: 1/72: AE Ja 73 4/1:40+; Afx My 73 14/9:510; AN 10 N 72 1/13:14; IM N 72 9/11:insert; Sc Ja 73 4/1:43-44; Sc Mr 73 4/3:164-165
Frog Grumman F6F-3 Hellcat: 1/72: AE D 71 1/7:386; Afx N 71 13/3:156+
Frog Grumman F6F: 1/32: Afx Jl 73 14/11:618
Fujimi F6F-5: 1/48: Sc F 73 4/2:130-132
Hasegawa Grumman F6F-3/F6F-5 Hellcat: 1/32: AE Je 73 4/6: 303+; AI S 75 9/3:149-150; AN 16 Mr 73 1/22:14; IM S 72 9/9:insert
Matchbox Chance Vought F4U-4 Corsair: 1/72: AI Jl 74 7/1:44; Afx Je 74 15/10:596: AN 12 Ap 74 2/23:14; RiS Sp 74 2/3-4: 162; Sc My 74 5/56:280
Matchbox Grumman F6F Hellcat: 1/72: AI S 75 9/3:149; Afx Ja 75 16/5:322; AN 20 S 74 3/8:11; IM Jl 74 10/(17):16
Monogram Grumman F6F-5: 1/48: AI S 75 9/3:149
Revell Chance Vought F4U-1D Corsair: 1/72: Afx D 75 17/4:240; Sc Ag 75 6/71:410
Revell Chance Vought F4U-1: 1/32: AE N 73 5/5:242; Afx Ja 71 12/5:264; Afx D 73 15/4:244; Sc F 71 2/2:96; Sc N 73 4/11: 788
Revell Grumman F4F-4B Wildcat IV: 1/72: Sc Mr 73 4/3:164-165
Revell Grumman F4F-4: 1/32: AE My 74 6/5:256

(Land-Based Single Engine)
Airfix North American P-51D Mustang: 1/72: Afx Ja 75 16/5:318-319; AN 27 D 74 3/15:10; PAM O 74 7:103; RiS Mr 75 3/1:50
Airfix North American P-51D: 1/24: AE Mr 73 4/3:147+: AI Ap 75 8/4:201; Afx D 72 14/4:219-220; AN 22 D 72 1/16:14; MW Ap 73 1/8:439; Sc Ja 75 6/64:36

Kit--Static

Airfix Republic P-47 razorback: 1/72: PAM O 75 11:190
Airmodel Republic XP-47H: 1/72 vac conv from razorback P-47: AI Ag 75 9/2:94; Afx O 75 17/2:118
Bandai North American P-51D Mustang: 1/24: Sc O 73 4/10:710-711
Frog Republic P-47D Thunderbolt: 1/72: AI Jl 75 9/1:40; AN 4 Ap 75 3/22:14; IM My 75 11/3:13; PAM O 75 11:190; Sc My 75 6/68:249
Hasegawa North American P-51D: 1/72: AI Ap 75 8/4:201; Afx S 75 17/1:51; AN 25 Jl 75 4/4:11; IM Jl 75 11/4:15; PAM O 75 11:192; Sc Je 75 6/69:300; cor O 75 6/73:511; D 75 6/75:596; Jl 76 7/82:350
Hasegawa North American P-51D: 1/32: AE D 73 5/6:289+; AN 28 S 73 2/10:14
Hasegawa Republic P-47D: 1/72: Afx Je 75 16/10:610; AN 7 F 75 3/18:11; PAM O 74 7:103; Sc My 75 6/69:160; PAM O 75 11:190
Hawk North American P-51D: 1/48: Sc Mr 72 3/3:136-137
Heller Curtiss P-40E: 1/72: AE N 72 3/5:255
Heller North American P-51D: 1/72: PAM O 75 11:194
Heller Republic P-47N: 1/72: PAM O 75 11:194
Jo-Han Republic P-47D: 1/72: AN 10 My 74 2/25:14; PAM Ap 74 5:67; PAM O 75 11:190; RiS Au 73 2/1:36
Lindberg North American P-51B/C: 1/72: Sc Mr 72 3/3:134
Matchbox North American P-51D: 1/72: AE F 74 6/2:92; AN 9 N 73 2/13:14; MW Ja 74 2/5:276; RT O 73 6/10:116; RiS Au 73 2/1:37; Sc D 73 4/12:845+
Matchbox Republic P-47: 1/72: IM My 75 11/3:13; PAM O 74 7:103; PAM O 75 11:190; Sc My 75 6/68:252
Monogram North American P-51B/C: 1/72: AI Ja 75 8/1:44; IM Ag 71 8/8:15; Sc Mr 72 3/3:134-138
Monogram North American P-51B: 1/48: AI Ja 75 8/1:43
Monogram North American P-51D: 1/32: AE D 74 5/6:289+
Nichimo North American P-51D: 1/48: AE F 72 2/2:101; Sc Mr 72 3/3:137-138
Otaki Curtiss P-40E Warhawk: 1/48: AI F 75 8/2:88
Otaki North American P-51D: 1/48: AI F 75 8/2:88; Sc My 75 6/68:251
Revell Bell P-39 Airacobra: 1/72: Afx D 75 17/4:240; Sc Ag 75 6/71:411
Revell Curtiss P-40E: 1/72: Afx D 75 17/4:240; Sc Ag 75 6/71:410-411
Revell North American P-51B Mustang III: 1/32: AI Ja 75 8/1:44; Sc Mr 72 3/3:138-139; Sc Ap 72 3/4:198-199
Revell Republic P-47D Thunderbolt: 1/72: Afx D 75 17/4:240; Sc Ag 75 6/71:410
Revell Republic P-47D Razorback: 1/32: AE Ap 72 2/4:206; AI Mr 75 8/3:147

(Twin Engine)
Airfix Lockheed P-38F Lightning: 1/72: AE Ja 73 4/1:42; Afx O 72 14/2:67; IM N 72 9/11:insert; Sc D 72 3/12:675
Airfix Northrop P-61 Black Widow: 1/72: IM Je 72 9/6:3-4

Airframe Grumman XF5F-1 Skyrocket: 1/72 vac: RT O 71 4/10: 117; Sc D 71 2/12:676
Airframe Grumman XP-50: 1/72 vac: Afx S 72 14/1:46
Aurora Northrop P-61 Black Widow: 1/48: AE Je 71 1/1:37
Monogram Lockheed P-38: 1/48: AI Je 75 8/6:293+
Monogram Northrop P-61 Black Widow: 1/48: AI Ap 75 8/4:199
Rareplanes Bell XFM-1 Airacuda: 1/72 vac: Afx Ag 73 14/12:678; AN 8 Je 73 2/2:14; RiS Su 73 1/4:141
Revell P-38J Lightning: 1/32: AE Je 71 1/1:37-38; Afx S 71 13/1: 42+ ; Sc Je 71 2/6:368-372

(U.S. Other)

Monogram Chance Vought OS2U-3 Kingfisher: 1/48: IM Mr 71 8/3:4
Rareplanes Beech C-45: 1/72 vac: AI Jl 74 7/1:44; AN 29 Mr 74 2/22:14; RiS W 74 2/2:75
Rareplanes Stinson L-5A Sentinel: 1/72 vac: AE Jl 73 5/1:47; AN 13 Ap 73 1/24:14
Revell Consolidated RAF Catalina: 1/72: AE N 72 3/5:257; Afx Jl 72 13/11:628; IM Jl 72 9/7:insert; Sc Jl 72 3/7:402
Sutcliffe Curtiss C-46 Commando: 1/72 vac: AN 28 S 73 2/10:14; IM Ag 73 10/8:14

Post World War II

(Canada)

Airfix De Havilland Canada DHC-2 Beaver: 1/72: AE My 72 2/5: 258; Afx Mr 72 13/7:364; RT F 72 5/2:21; Sc Ap 72 3/4:225-230, cor D 72 3/12:660

(France Civil)

Laird Fournier RF4: 1/?? vac: Sc S 74 5/60:500
Nitto Concorde: 1/100: AE Jl 72 3/1:43; Sc Mr 73 4/3:170

(France Military)

Airfix Super Mystere B2: 1/72: AE S 72 3/3:151; Afx S 72 14/1: 11; IM Ag 72 9/8:insert; MW D 72 1/4:210; RT S 72 5/9:106
Airmodel Fouga Magister: 1/72 vac: AN 18 F 74 2/17:14
Frog Dassault Mirage IIIE/O: 1/72: AI O 75 9/4:200; Afx O 75 17/2:121; AN 8 Ag 75 4/5:15; IM S 75 11/5:13; PAM Jl 75 10: 162; Sc N 75 6/74:571
Heller Sepecat Jaguar E Trainer: 1/50: AE N 71 1/6:317; Afx Ap 71 12/8:430

Heller Sud Transall C.160: 1/72: AE Ja 74 6/1:36
Matchbox Dassault Mirage II: 1/72: Afx F 75 16/6:384; PAM Jl 74 6:91; Sc Ja 75 6/64:37
Matchbox Dassault-Breguet/Dornier Alpha Jet 501: 1/72: AE Je 73 4/6:305; AN 13 Ap 73 1/24:14; Sc My 73 4/5:355
Revell Dassault Mirage: 1/32: AI Jl 74 7/1:41+; Afx F 75 16/6: 380; IM Mr 74 10/(15):8-9; IM N 75 11/6:23; Sc Jl 74 5/58: 374-376

(Germany Civil)

Airmodel Dornier Do 27 STOL: 1/72 vac: IM Ja 72 9/1:9-10
Matchbox Dornier Do 28D Skyservant: 1/72: Afx Ap 75 16/8:494; AN 29 N 74 3/13:11; IM S 74 10/(18):insert

(Germany Military)

Matchbox Dassault-Breguet/Dornier Alpha Jet 501: 1/72: AE Je 73 4/6:305; AN 13 Ap 73 1/24:14; Sc My 73 4/5:355

(Japan Civil)

Eidai Fuji FA 200 Aero Subaru: 1/72: IM N 72 9/11:insert
Hasegawa Mitsubishi MU-2: 1/72: Sc Ap 75 6/67:179
Marui Aero Subaru: 1/36: AE Ja 74 6/1:36
Nichimo Fuji FA 200 Aero Subaru: 1/48: Sc Ap 74 5/55:224
Nichimo Fuji FA 200: 1/20: AE D 72 3/6:314; MW D 72 1/4:173
Otaki Mitsubishi Mu-2: 1/72: MW F 74 2/6:331

(Japan Military)

Hasegawa Fuji T-1A: 1/72: AE O 72 3/4:204; IM O 71 8/10:insert; Sc Je 72 3/6:348
Hasegawa Shinmeiwa PS-1 or SS-2: 1/72: AE O 71 1/5:272; Afx N 71 13/3:156; IM My 71 8/5:3-4

(Sweden Military)

Airfix SAAB J35-F Draken: 1/72: AE Jl 71 1/2:94; Afx Ag 71 12/12:62; IM Ap 71 8/4:2; RT Jl 71 4/7:74; Sc Jl 71 2/7:276
Airfix SAAB Viggen: 1/72: Afx O 71 13/2:66; Sc S 71 2/9:494
Hasegawa SAAB Viggen: 1/72: Afx Ap 74 15/8:476
MAS Saab J-29: 1/72 vac: RT Mr 72 5/3:33

(USSR Civil)

Nitto Tu 144: 1/144 (nom 132): Afx D 72 14/4:224

VEB Antonov An-12: 1/100: AE My 74 6/5:256
VEB Ilyushin Il-18: 1/100: AE Ja 74 6/1:36
VEB Tupolev Tu-144: 1/100: AE S 71 1/4:202
VEB Tupolev Tu-154: 1/100: AE My 74 6/5:256
VEB Yak 40: 1/100: IM My 71 8/5:3

(USSR Military)

Airfix Ilyushin Il-28: 1/72: IM Ja 74 10/13-14:26
Hasegawa MiG 17D/E Fresco: 1/67 (nom 1/72): AN 30 Mr 73 1/23:14; IM N 72 9/11:insert; RT Ag 75 8/8:89; RiS N 72 1/2:47; Sc O 73 4/10:712
Heller MiG 19: 1/72: MW Ja 74 2/5:274
Heller MiG 21: 1/72: IM Jl 73 10/7:insert; MW O 73 2/2:102; Sc O 73 4/10:712
KP MiG 17PF: 1/72: AI Ja 75 8/1:44; AN 15 N 74 3/12:10; IM S 74 10/(18):10; RT Ag 75 8/8:89; RiS Mr 75 3/1:49; Sc N 74 5/62:613-614
KP MiG 19: 1/72: AE Mr 73 4/4:149; Afx D 72 14/4:224; AN 13 O 72 1/11:14; IM N 72 9/11:insert; MW Je 73 1/10:554; RT S 72 5/9:98; Sc Ja 74 5/1:51
Matchbox MiG 21: 1/72: AI S 74 7/3:138; AI N 75 9/5:249-250; Afx S 74 16/1:48; IM Mr 74 10/(15):9; PAM Ap 74 5:68; RT Jl 74 7/7:81; Sc S 74 5/60:501
Nitto Tu 144: 1/144 (nom 1/132): Afx D 72 14/4:224
Revell MiG 21: 1/32: AI F 75 8/2:86+; Afx Mr 75 16/7:438+; IM Ja 75 11/1:14-15; Sc Ap 75 6/67:178
Tamiya Ilyushin Il-28: 1/100: Afx Ja 71 12/5:266; IM Ja 74 10/13-14:24+
Tamiya MiG-15 & F-86F Sabre: 1/100: AE Ja 73 4/1:43; IM Je 72 9/6:insert; RiS Sp 74 2/3-4:96; Sc My 72 3/5:289
VEB Tu-20 Bear: 1/100: AI D 75 9/6:298; IM S 75 11/5:13

(U.K. Civil)

Airfix A300 Airbus: 1/144: IM N 75 11/6:22
Airfix Short Skyvan: 1/72: AI O 75 9/4:200; Afx S 75 17/1:11; AN 5 S 75 4/7:11; IM S 75 11/5:12; Sc O 75 6/73:502-503
Airmodel Vickers Viking/Valleta: 1/72 vac conv from Airfix Wellington: AN 15 N 74 3/12:10
Matchbox Hawker Siddeley HS 125: 1/72: AN 24 Ja 75 3/17:11
Nitto Concorde: 1/100: AE Jl 72 3/1:43; Sc Mr 73 4/3:170

(U.K. Military)

(Jet)
AirConversion Hawker Hunter T. 7: 1/72 conv from Hunter: AE F 73 4/2:98; AN 7 Jl 72 1/4:15
AirConversion Hawker Siddeley Harrier T2: 1/72 conv from Harrier: AE F 73 4/2:98; AN 24 N 72 1/14:14; RiS Sp 73 1/3:102

Airfix BAC Canberra: 1/72: Afx Ja 74 15/5:280; AN 9 Ag 74 3/5:10; IM S 74 10/(18):10; PAM O 74 7:102; RiS Sp 74 2/3-4: 158; Sc N 74 5/62:614
Airfix BAC Strikemaster: 1/72: Afx O 74 16/2:86; AN 8 Je 73 2/2:14; AN 9 Ag 74 3/5:10; IM N 74 10/19:10-11; MW N 73 2/3: 158; Sc Ja 75 6/64:37
Airfix Gloster Meteor III: 1/72: Afx Ja 71 12/5:235
Airfix Hawker Siddeley Gnat T. Mk I: 1/72: Sc F 74 5/2:115
Airfix Hawker Siddeley Harrier: 1/24: AI Ja 75 8/1:44; Afx Ap 74 15/8:446; AN 23 Ag 74 3/6:11
Airfix Hawker Siddeley Hawk: 1/72: AN 26 D 75 4/15:11; PAM O 75 11:180
Airframe De Havilland DH 108 Swallow: 1/72: AN 7 D 73 2/15:14; IM Ag 73 10/8:insert; MW Ja 74 2/5:274
Frog BAC Canberra B. Mk 8 or 12: 1/72: AE Ja 74 6/1:36; AN 9 N 73 2/13:14; IM S 73 10/9:insert; MW Ja 74 2/5:274; RiS W 74 2/2:73; Sc Ja 74 2/6:30-32
Frog De Havilland Vampire Mk 5: 1/72: AE O 71 1/5:272; Afx S 71 13/1:44; Sc S 71 2/9:496-497
Frog De Havilland Venom: 1/72: AE N 73 5/5:242; AN 31 Ag 73 2/8:14; IM Ag 73 10/8:insert; MW Ja 74 2/5:274; MW F 74 2/6:330; RiS Au 73 2/1:37; Sc O 73 4/10:711-712
Frog Gloster Javelin FAW 9/9R: 1/72: AI Je 75 8/6:296; Afx Ag 75 16/12:724; AN 18 Ap 75 3/23:11; IM My 75 11/3:13; PAM Ja 75 8:122; Sc Jl 75 6/70:332-333
Frog Hawker Hunter FBA 9: 1/72: AI N 74 7/5:248; Afx S 74 16/1:48; AN 28 Je 74 3/2:11; IM Mr 74 10/(15):9; RiS Sp 74 2/3-4:158-159; Sc Ag 74 5/59:450
Frog Hawker Siddeley Buccaneer S2: AE O 72 3/4:202; Afx O 72 14/2:101; IM Ag 72 3/2:insert; Sc D 72 3/12:680
Frog Sepecat A. 2/T. 2 Jaguar: 1/72: AI O 74 7/4:197; Afx O 74 16/2:114; AN 26 Jl 74 3/4:71; IM My 74 10/(16):11; PAM Jl 74 6:90; Sc S 74 5/60:501
Hasegawa BAC Lightning F. Mk 6: 1/72: Afx S 73 15/1:52
Hasegawa Hawker Siddeley Harrier: 1/72: Afx S 73 15/1:52
Hawk Supermarine Swift F. Mk 4: 1/72: AI O 74 7/4:198
Heller BAC/Sepecat Jaguar: 1/50: AE N 71 1/6:317
Matchbox BAC Strikemaster: 1/72: AE Jl 73 5/1:47; AN 8 Je 73 2/2:14; Sc Jl 73 4/7:494-495
Matchbox BAC (S) Jaguar: 1/72: AN 20 S 74 3/8:11; IM Mr 74 10/(15):9; PAM Jl 74 6:90-91; Sc Ag 74 5/59:450
Matchbox Folland Gnat T. Mk I: 1/72: AE F 74 6/2:92; Afx Jl 74 15/11:660; AN 23 N 74 2/14:14; RT O 73 6/10:116; Sc F 74 5/2:115-116
Matchbox Hawker Siddeley Buccaneer S2B: 1/72: AN 18 O 74 3/10:10; IM N 74 10/19:11; Sc Mr 75 6/66:145
Matchbox Hawker Siddeley Harrier: 1/72: AI S 74 7/3:138; Afx Ag 74 15/12:718; AN 20 S 74 3/8:11; IM Mr 74 10/(15):9; PAM Ap 74 5:68; Sc S 74 5/60:502
Matchbox Hawker Siddeley Hawk: 1/72: PAM O 75 11:180
Prodimex Saunders Roe SR. 53 rocket: 1/72: PAM Ja 75 8:124
Revell Hawker Siddeley Harrier GR Mk IA: 1/32: AE N 73 5/5: 242; AN 14 S 72 1/4:15

VI. Reviews 690

Reyhex BAC Canberra Mk 11: 1/72 conv for Airfix Canberra: AN 21 Mr 75 3/21:10
Sutcliffe TSR-2: 1/72 vac: AI S 75 9/3:150
Tamiya Hawker Siddeley Buccaneer S Mk 2: 1/100: Afx F 72 2/2:342; IM O 71 8/10:insert; Sc Ap 72 3/4:226-227
Tamiya Hawker Siddeley Harrier: 1/48: AE Jl 72 3/45; Afx Mr 73 14/7:396; Sc Jl 72 3/7:400

(Prop)
Airfix Fairey Firefly Mk 5: 1/72: AE Mr 73 4/3:149; Sc My 73 4/5:362-364
Airfix Scottish Aviation Bulldog: 1/72: AI Ag 75 9/2:91+; Afx Jl 75 16/11:628; AN 13 Je 75 4/1:10; Sc Ag 75 6/71:408
Airframe Hunting Percival Provost: 1/72 vac: Afx O 72 14/101; AN 13 O 71 1/11:14; IM D 72 9/12:insert; MW O 72 1/2:63
Airmodel Blackburn Firebrand: 1/72 vac: AI Ag 75 9/2:94; Afx O 75 17/2:120
Airmodel Gannet AEW 3: 1/72 vac conv from Frog Gannet ASW: Afx N 73 15/3:174; AN 27 Ap 73 1/25:14; MW Ja 73 1/5:230
Frog Fairey Firefly F.Mk 1: 1/72: Afx F 73 14/6:334
Frog Westland Wyvern: 1/72: IM F 71 8/2:4-5; Sc F 71 2/2:102+; Sc My 71 1/5:262
Rareplanes Supermarine Spiteful: 1/72 vac: AE N 72 3/4:257; Afx Ag 72 13/12:684; IM Jl 72 9/7:insert

(U.S. Civil)

Airfix McDonnell Douglas DC-9-30: 1/144: Afx N 74 16/3:171+; PAM O 74 7:102; Sc Ja 75 6/64:35
Airfix Piper Cherokee Arrow II: 1/72: Afx O 74 16/2:87; AN 4 O 74 3/9:15
Aurora Boeing 737: 1/72: AN 4 Ap 75 3/22:14
Aurora McDonnell Douglas DC-9: 1/72: AN 4 Ap 75 3/22:14
Aurora McDonnell Douglas DC-10: 1/144: AE Ag 71 1/3:168; Afx Ja 71 12/5:268
Bandai Cessna 150: 1/48: Sc D 74 5/63:672
Eidai Cessna 172: 1/72: AN 3 Ag 73 2/6:14
Entex McDonnell Douglas DC-9-40: 1/100: PAM O 74 7:102; Sc Mr 75 6/66:142-143
Entex Hughes HK-1 or H-4 Hercules (Spruce Goose): 1/200: Sc N 74 5/62:612-613; WWE Ja 74 1/1:16
Entex Lockheed L-1011 Tri-Star: 1/100: Sc Mr 75 6/66:143
Heller Boeing 747: 1/125: AE Je 72 2/6:325-326
Marui Cessna 172: 1/35: AE N 73 5/5:239+; AN 3 Ag 73 2/6:14; IM Ja 71 8/1:2
Marui Piper Cherokee 140: 1/36: AE Ja 74 6/1:36; RiS Su 73 1/4:144
Nichimo Cessna 172 Skyhawk: 1/48: AI F 75 8/2:88
Nichimo Cessna 172 Skyhawk: 1/20: AE N 73 5/5:239+
Nitto Boeing 727-200: 1/100: AE Ja 73 4/1:42; Sc F 73 4/2:127
Nitto Boeing 747: 1/200: AE D 72 3/6:314; AE Ja 73 4/1:43
Nitto Boeing 747: 1/100: Sc My 73 4/5:344

Nitto Douglas DC-8: 1/200: AE D 72 3/6:314
Nitto Douglas DC-8-62: 1/100: IM My 71 8/5:2; Sc Mr 73 4/3: 169-170
Nitto Lockheed L-1011 TriStar: 1/100: AI O 74 7/4:198
Nitto McDonnell Douglas DC-9-40: 1/100: AI O 74 7/4:198
Nitto McDonnell Douglas DC-10: 1/100: AE Ag 73 5/2:98
Rareplane Super Constellation: 1/72 vac: AI My 75 8/5:246; AN 27 D 74 3/15:10; RiS Mr 75 3/1:50
Revell Boeing 747: 1/144: Afx Ap 75 16/8:496; IM N 74 10/19:11; IM Mr 75 11/2:15
Revell Boeing 747 Cutaway: 1/144: Sc S 74 5/60:500
Revell Douglas DC-7: 1/144: Afx O 75 17/2:121; PAM Jl 75 10/174
Revell Douglas CD-8 Super 61: 1/144: AE Ja 73 4/1:42; Sc Mr 71 2/3:155
Revell Lockheed L1049 Super Constellation: 1/144: Afx O 75 17/2: 121; PAM Jl 75 10:174
Revell Lockheed L-1011 Tri-Star: 1/144: AE My 74 6/5:256; Afx F 75 16/6:380-381; AN 13 D 74 3/14:10
Revell McDonnell Douglas DC-10: 1/144: AN 19 Ja 73 1/18:15

(U. S. Military--Jet)

(Bell)
Rareplanes P-59B Airacomet: 1/72 vac: IM Mr 71 8/3:1

(Boeing)
Tamiya B-52D Stratofortress: 1/100: Afx Ja 71 12/5:266; Afx D 74 16/4:155; IM S 74 10/(18):10; Sc Ag 74 5/59:446-447

(Cessna)
Aurora T-37B: 1/48: RiS Mr 75 3/1:44
Hasegawa A-37A: 1/72: RiS Mr 75 3/1:44

(General Dynamics, Convair)
Airfix F-111A: 1/72: Sc Je 71 2/6:194-197
Airfix RB-57: 1/72 vac: AN 15 Mr 74 2/21:14
Revell F-111A/B: 1/72: IM Jl 72 9/7:1
Revell F-111E: 1/72: Sc Je 71 2/6:294-297

(Grumman)
Airmodel F9F Panther: 1/72 vac: AN 13 O 72 1/11:14
Monogram F-14A Tomcat: 1/72: AE O 71 1/5:270+; IM Jl 71 9/7:insert; MW F 74 2/6:331; Sc N 71 2/11:616

(LTV, Chance Vought)
Airfix A-7 Corsair II: 1/72: Afx Ag 72 13/12:649; AN 9 Je 72 1/2:14; RT Ag 72 5/8:93; Sc S 72 3/9:508-509
Matchbox Corsair II: 1/72: AI Ag 74 7/2:94; AN 12 Ap 74 2/23: 14; Sc My 74 5/56:179

(Lockheed)
Airfix F-80C: 1/72: Afx O 74 16/2:87; AN 29 N 74 3/13:11; RiS Sp 74 2/3-4:158; Sc F 75 6/65:92
Otaki C-5A Galaxy: 1/144: AE Ja 72 2/1:32; Afx F 72 13/6:342
Revell F-104 Starfighter: 1/64: IM S 75 11/5:12; PAM O 75 11: 192
Revell YF-12A: 1/72: Sc D 74 5/63:662-663

(McDonnell Douglas)
Airfix F-4 Phantom: 1/72: AE Ja 72 2/1:34; IM O 71 8/10:insert
Airfix F-4B Phantom: 1/72: Sc S 71 2/9:465-466
Airframe RF-4: 1/72 resin conv from F-4 Phantom: AN 29 Mr 47 2/22:14; IM Mr 74 10/(15):8
Airmodel B-66: 1/72 vac: AN 6 Jl 73 2/4:14
Airmodel F2H-2P Banshee: 1/72 vac: AN 15 Mr 74 2/21:14
Airmodel XF-85 Goblin: 1/72 vac: AI Ag 75 9/2:94; Afx O 75 17/2:118+
Armtec F-101B Voodoo: 1/72 vac conv from Hasegawa RF-101C: AN 30 My 75 3/26:7
Frog A-4 Skyhawk: 1/72: Sc S 71 2/9:497-498
Fujimi TA-4F Skyhawk: 1/50: AE F 72 2/2:101
Hasegawa A-4F Skyhawk: 1/72: AE N 71 1/6:317; IM Jl 71 8/7: insert
Hasegawa F-4C Phantom: 1/90: Afx F 71 12/6:322
Hasegawa F-4E Phantom: 1/72: Sc Je 73 4/6:424-425
Hasegawa/Frog F-4K/M: 1/72: Sc S 71 2/9:470
Hasegawa F-15 Eagle: 1/72: AI Mr 75 8/3:150; Sc D 74 5/63: 670; Sc F 75 6/64:67+
Hasegawa F-101 Voodoo: 1/72: Afx 74 15/6:366
IMC RF-4B/C: 1/72 "battle-damaged": Sc S 71 2/9:466+
Matchbox F-4M/K: 1/72: AI D 75 9/6:302; IM N 75 11/6:23; Sc D 75 6/75:620
Monogram F-15 Eagle: 1/72: Afx Mr 75 16/7:437-438; IM N 74 10/19:10; Sc D 74 5/63:670; Sc F 75 6/65:67+
Otaki F-4J Phantom II: 1/144: Sc My 72 3/5:286
Revell Blue Angels Aerobatic Team (four Phantoms): 1/72: AE N 72 3/5:257; Afx Je 72 13/10:572; IM Jl 72 9/7:insert; Sc Jl 72 3/7:402
Revell F-4B: 1/72: Sc S 71 2/9:470
Revell F-4J: 1/32: AE F 73 4/2:97-98; Afx Mr 73 14/7:398; Afx Ag 73 14/12:680; AN 25 My 73 2/1:14; IM N 75 11/6:23; Q Ja 73 8/1:39; RiS N 72 1/2:48; Sc Ja 73 4/1:44-45
Revell F-15 Eagle: 1/72: AI Mr 75 8/3:150; Afx Mr 75 16/7:437-438; AN 13 D 74 3/14:10; Sc D 74 5/63:670; Sc F 75 6/65:67+
Revell RF-4E Phantom: 1/32: AN 25 My 73 2/1:14
Revell Thunderbird Phantoms: 1/??: IM Mr 75 11/2:15
Reyhex: RF-4: 1/72 conv from Airfix Phantom: AN 21 Mr 75 3/21:10
Tamiya F-4E Phantom II: 1/72: Sc S 71 2/9:470
Tamiya F-4K/M: 1/100: Afx Ja 71 12/5:266; AN 27 O 72 1/12:13
Tamiya F-4K/M: 1/72: Sc S 71 2/9:470

(North American Rockwell)
Airfix F-86D Sabre: 1/72: AN 26 D 75 4/15:11
Airfix RA-5C Vigilante: 1/72: AE D 71 1/7:385
Airmodel F-86D fuselage for Frog F-86 Sabre: 1/72 conv: Afx Ag 71 12/12:654
Entex B-1: 1/144: AI O 74 7/4:198
Fuji F-86D Sabre: 1/48: RiS Sp 74 2/3-4:98-99
Hasegawa F-86F-40 Sabre: 1/72: RiS Sp 74 2/3-4:96-97
Hasegawa F-86F: 1/32: AE S 73 5/3:140; AN 20 Jl 73 2/5:14; MW Ag 73 1/12:661; RiS N 72 1/2:48; RiS Sp 74 2/3-4:96-97; Sc Jl 73 4/7:496-499
Lindberg F-86A Sabre: 1/48: Afx My 73 14/9:510; RiS Sp 74 2/3-4:97-98
Rareplanes FJ-1 Fury: 1/72 vac: Sc S 75 6/72:342
Tamiya F-86F Sabre & MiG-15: 1/100: AE Ja 73 4/1:43; IM Je 72 9/6:insert; RiS Sp 74 2/3-4:96; Sc My 72 3/5:289

(Northrop)
Matchbox F-5A: 1/72: AE F 74 6/2:92; Afx Jl 74 15/11:660; AN 23 N 73 2/14:14

(Republic)
Airfix F-84 Thunderstreak: 1/72: Afx Jl 74 15/11:630; AN 28 Je 74 3/2:11; IM Ja 74 10/13-14:insert; PAM Ap 74 5:68; RiS Sp 74 2/3-4:158; Sc S 74 5/60:501
Italaerei F-84F & RF-84F: 1/72: AE Je 72 2/6:326; Afx Jl 73 14/11:622; IM Mr 72 9/3:insert; Sc My 72 3/5:286
Rareplanes F-84G Thunderjet: 1/72 vac: Afx Ap 74 15/8:476; PAM Ap 74 5:68
Tamiya F-105 Thunderchief: 1/100: IM My 74 10/(16):11; Sc Ag 74 5/59:446-447

(U.S. Military--Prop)

Airfix Cessna O-1 or L-5 Bird Dog: 1/72: AE Jl 73 5/1:46; AN 25 My 73 2/1:15; IM Jl 73 10/7:insert; MW Ag 73 1/12:660; RT Ag 73 6/8:91; RiS Su 73 1/4:144
Airfix Douglas AC-47 gunship: 1/72: AE O 73 5/4:196; Afx S 73 15/1:16; AN 17 Ag 73 2/7:14; Sc S 73 4/9:644
Airmodel Boeing KC-97 Stratocruiser: 1/72 vac conv from Airfix B-29: AN 27 O 72 1/12:13; AN 20 Jl 73 2/5:14
Airmodel North American T-28 Trojan: 1/72 vac: AN 6 Jl 73 2/4:14
Airmodel Vought XF5U-1 Skipper: 1/72 vac: MW N 73 2/3:158
Eidai Cessna O-2: 1/72: RiS Su 73 1/4:142+
Frog SP-2H Neptune: 1/72: AE Ag 73 5/2:97-98; Afx F 74 15/6:366-367
Fujimi Grumman E-2A Hawkeye: 1/72: Sc Mr 71 2/3:150-152
Hasegawa Beechcraft T-34A Mentor: 1/72: AI Ag 74 7/2:94; AN 26 Jl 74 3/4:11; IM Ja 74 10/13-14:insert; RT Ag 74 7/8:86; RiS Au 73 2/1:37
Hasegawa Grumman S2F-1 (S-2A) Tracker: 1/72: AN 17 O 75 4/

10:14; RiS Jl 75 3/2:103; Sc D 75 6/75:620-621; add F 76 7/ 77:83
Hasegawa/Minicraft Lockheed P2V-7 (P-2H) Neptune: 1/72: AE N 73 5/5:242; Afx F 74 15/6:366-367; AN 8 Je 73 2/2:14; AN 26 O 73 2/12:14; Q Ja 73 8/1:34; RiS N 72 1/2:47; Sc Je 73 4/6: 420
Hasegawa Martin Marlin: 1/72: AE O 72 3/3:204
Hawk North American OV-10A: 1/48: IM O 72 9/10:1
Monogram North American F-82 Twin Mustang: 1/72: AE Ap 74 6/4:204; Afx Mr 74 15/7:420-421; AN 18 Ja 74 2/17:14; IM N 73 10/11-12:insert; Sc Ap 74 5/55:223
Rareplanes C-121 Super Constellation: 1/72 vac: AN 27 D 74 3/ 15:10; RiS Mr 75 3/1:50
Revell Lockheed KC-130 Hercules: 1/140: AE My 74 6/5:255; Afx My 74 15/9:535
Revell Lockheed Orion: 1/144: AE My 74 6/5:255; Afx My 74 15/ 9:535

Helicopters

Airfix SA 330 Puma: 1/72: AE Jl 73 5/1:46; Afx Je 73 14/10:561; AN 22 Je 73 2/3:14; IM Je 73 10/6:insert; MM Jl 73 3/7:426- 427; Sc Jl 73 4/7:490
Airfix Westland-Sud Aviation SA341 Gazelle: 1/72: AE Je 74 6/6: 305; Afx Ap 74 15/8:447; AN 15 Mr 74 2/21:14; IM Ja 74 10/ 13-14:insert; Sc Ap 74 5/55:224
Airframe Westland Sea King German ASR: 1/72 vac conv from Si- korsky Sea King: AN 30 Mr 73 1/23:14; RT Je 73 6/6:65
Airmodel Westland Dragonfly: 1/72: Afx Ja 74 15/5:314-315
Frog Westland Lynx: 1/72: AI Ag 75 9/2:94; AN 13 Je 75 4/1: 10; IM Jl 75 11/4:15; Sc S 75 6/72:462
Fujimi Sud Alouette III: 1/50: AE S 71 1/4:201-202; IM Je 71 8/6:2-3
Hasegawa/Minicraft Bell UH1-D: 1/72: IM Jl 71 8/7:insert; Sc O 71 2/ 10:548-549
Heller SA 541 Gazelle: 1/50: Sc Ap 74 5/55:224
Matchbox Bell 209 Hueycobra: 1/72: AE Jl 73 5/1:47; cor F 74 6/2:92; AE O 73 5/4:196; AN 11 My 73 1/26:14; PAM O 73 3: 36; Sc Ag 73 4/8:570
Matchbox Lynx: 1/72: Afx Ap 75 16/8:494; AN 24 Ja 75 3/17:11; IM N 74 10/19:11; Sc D 74 5/63:671
Nichimo Hughes 500 civil: 1/20: AI N 74 7/5:248; Sc Ja 75 6/64: 36
Rareplanes Bell 206 Jet Ranger: 1/72 vac: AI Mr 75 8/3:150; Sc F 75 6/65:93
Revell Hughes OH-6A Cayuse: 1/32: AE Ag 71 1/3:144; Sc Jl 71 2/7:372
Revell Piasecki YH-16A: 1/96: IM S 75 11/5:12; PAM O 75 11: 192
Reyhex Sea King mods: 1/72 conv: AN 18 Ap 75 3/23:11
Reyhex Sikorsky HH-3F Pelican: 1/72 conv from Revell or Aurora

HH-3E: AN 21 Mr 75 3/21:10
Richard Kohnstam Bell Huey Cobra AH-1G: 1/87: IM Ap 71 8/4:3
Roco Bell Iroquois UH-1D: 1/87: IM Ap 71 8/4:3
Roxkopf MBB Bo 105: 1/100: AE Mr 74 6/3:138
Tamiya Hughes 500 Cayuse: 1/48: RiS Su 73 1/4:138; Sc F 73 4/2:127-128
Tamiya Hughes (Kawasaki-built) civil 500: 1/48: Sc F 73 4/2:127-128
Tamiya Sikorsky CH 54 Sky Crane: 1/100: AE Je 74 6/6:305; IM Jl 73 10/7:insert; MW Ja 74 2/5:272
Tamiya Sikorsky SH3-A/D Sea King: 1/72: Sc D 71 2/12:675
Tamiya Vertol 107: 1/100: Sc D 71 2/12:675-676
VEB Mil Mi-10K: 1/100: AE Je 74 6/6:305; IM My 71 8/5:3

Accessories

Airmodel Cockpit Canopies: 1/72 range view: Afx Ja 71 12/5: 264+
Bare Metal pitot tubes & gun barrles: 1/72: RT My 74 7/5:50
Frog Spin-A-Prop Motors: Afx O 71 13/2:96+
Horizon Conversions: external aircraft stores, 1/32 vac: RiS Su 73 1/4:140
Model Accessories instrument panels: 1/72, 1/48, 1/32: RiS Sp 73 2/3-4:101
Tandair: drop tanks for Revell 1/32 Phantom: vac: Afx Ja 75 16/5:320; AN 15 N 74 3/12:10; RT Ap 75 8/4:39; Sc Ja 75 6/64:40
Weapons Shop: contemporary 750 lb bomb: 1/32: RiS W 74 2/2:75
Weapons Shop: F-4 droptanks, P-38 intakes & droptanks: 1/35: RiS Au 73 2/1:38

ARMOR

Range Reviews

Armtec AFV Accessories: 1/76: Afx Je 71 12/10:544
Bandai AFVs: 1/48: Afx S 73 15/1:51; Afx Je 75 16/10:608
Building Plastic Pistols: L&S 1/1 handguns: MM Ag 75 5/8:463-465
Cannon AFVs: 1/300: S&L (O 74) 4:23
Edison on Guns: Replica 1/1: MM Ag 71 1/8:400-401
France Jouets Rifles: 1/5: Afx Je 71 12/10:543-544
GHQ Microarmor: Jagdtiger, Firefly, GMA $2\frac{1}{2}$ ton truck & British Infantry: 1/285: WW2J S 75 2/5-6:26
Hinchliffe Cannons: 1/76: Afx Ja 71 12/5:272
Historex AFV Accessories: 1/32: Afx D 72 14/4:225

VI. Reviews 696

Kirk AFVs: ·1/300: Afx Ag 72 13/12:684; Afx Ap 74 15/8:478
Max Vehicles: 1/35 softskins: Afx Jl 75 16/11:664+
Micro Miniatures for Armour Enthusiasts: 1/285: MM Ag 72 2/8: 426-427
The Mini-Tank Range: 1/87 assembled models: MM Ja 71 1/1:32-33
Modeling Bandai's Shermans: 1/48: AFV Je 75 5/5:38-39
Monogram Armor Series: 1/34 (nom 1/35): MM My 73 3/5:319
Replica 1/1 small arms: MM Jl 71 1/7:353-355

APCs, ICVs, ARVs & Funnies

Minitanks Leopard ARV: 1/76: Afx Ag 72 13/12:684-685
Nitto Alligator LVT(A)5: 1/25: Sc Ja 71 2/1:47
Tamiya M113: 1/35: MM O 74 4/10:595; MM N 74 4/11:692-694

Armored Cars

Airfix Reconnaissance Set: 1/76: Afx Ja 75 5/2:219; IM My 75 11/3:12-13; RT Jl 75 8/7:83; Sc F 75 6/65:97; WWE Mr 75 2/2:69
Bandai Daimler Mk I: 1/48: Afx N 75 17/3:174
Clark Daimler Mk I: 1/76 resin: Afx F 74 16/6:363
Fujimi SdKfz 222: 1/76: Afx Mr 75 16/7:438; MW F 74 2/6:330; RiS Su 73 1/4:141
Matchbox Humber: 1/76: MM My 75 5/5:303
Matchbox Puma SdKfz 234/2: 1/76: IM Jl 75 11/4:14; Sc S 75 6/72:462
Matchbox Puma SdKfz 234/4: 1/76: Afx N 75 17/3:173; MM N 75 5/11:662; WW2J Jl 75 2/4:29
Max M3A1 White Scout Car: 1/35: AFV F 75 5/3:12
Midori SdKfz 232: 1/40: Afx F 74 73/6:364+
Midori SdKfz 312: 1/40: IM Ja 73 10/1:insert
Monogram SdKfz 232 Puma: 1/32: AFV Ja 75 5/2:32; MM O 75 5/10:616
Renown Daimler Dingo: 1/76: MW Ap 73 1/8:439-440
Tamiya Daimler Dingo: 1/35: MM Ap 73 3/4:231-233; MW O 72 1/2:101-102
Tamiya M8 Greyhound: 1/35: MM F 71 1/2:108-109; Sc F 71 2/2:106
Tamiya Saladin: 1/35: Afx Je 71 12/10:544; Sc Ja 72 3/1:50
Tamiya SdKfz 222: 1/35: Afx S 75 17/1:51-52; RiS Jl 75 3/2:101; WW2J S 75 2/5-6:26-27
Tamiya SdKfz 223 Radio Car: 1/35: WW2J S 75 2/5-6:28
Tamiya SdKfz 232 Puma: 1/35: Afx O 74 16/2:112+; MM Mr 75 5/3:169-171; RiS Sp 74 2/3-4:161; S&L (D 74) 5:21

Artillery

Bandai Flak 18: 1/48: RiS Su 73 1/4:142
Bandai Pak 75mm: 1/48: Afx F 75 16/6:381
Busler 12 pound Napoleon & casson with limbers: 54mm: Fus W 74 1/2:36
Fujimi 88mm Flak AT-AA Gun: 1/76: MM Jl 73 3/5:318-319
H. L. Pearson 13" land mortar c.1790: 1/8: MM My 73 3/5:318-319
Hasegawa 88 Flak 18: 1/72: Afx D 74 16/4:254
Hasegawa 155mm Long Tom: 1/72: RiS Sp 73 1/3:103
Hinchliffe Armstrong 10 pdr: 1/32: MM N 73 3/11:738
Hinchliffe 7.2" howitzer: 25mm: Afx O 73 17/2:115
Hinchliffe 6 barrel, 1" bore, Gatling Gun, 1865: 54mm: S&L (D 74) 5:20
Hinchliffe 2.75" Rifle Muzzle-Loading Screw Gun: 54mm: S&L (D 74) 5:20
Hinchliffe 2.75" Rifle Muzzle-Loading Screw Gun: 54mm: S&L (D 74) 5:20
Italaerei Pak 40: 1/35: Afx Je 74 15/10:598; IM N 73 10/19:insert
Lemarks 8.8cm shell: 1/1: Afx Ap 75 5/5:282-283; RT Jl 75 8/7:83
Mantua English Caronade of 1778: 1/??: MM Ap 71 1/4:211
Marine Model 6 pound James Cannon 1841: 1/16: MM S 73 2/1:623
Max Six Pounder: 1/35: WW2J Jl 75 2/4:29
Nitto 37mm PAK: 1/35: Afx N 74 16/3:186
Palmer 75mm Field Gun: 1/9: MW Jl 73 1/11:606
Pocher 1914 Krupps Field Gun: 1/20: MM Ap 71 1/4:211
Superior 5cm PAK 38: 1/32 metal: AFV F 71 2/11:20
Tamiya 88mm Flak 36/37: 1/35: Afx F 73 14/6:334; MM F 73 3/2:105-107
Tamiya Pak 40/L46: 1/35: MM O 75 5/10:594-595
Tamiya Pak 40 7.5cm: 1/35: Afx S 75 17/1:51
Tamiya 6 pdr: 1/35: Afx Ja 71 12/5:268
Tamiya 25 pdr: 1/35: MM My 75 5/5:282-283; RT Jl 75 8/7:83

Half Tracks

Airfix SdKfz 250/3: 1/76: IM N 75 11/6:22
Airfix SdKfz 250/3 Leichter-Schutzenpanzerwagen: 1/32: AFV S 75 5/6:13; Afx D 75 17/4:201; WW2J Jl 75 2/4:28
Airfix SdKfz 251: 1/32: Afx S 73 15/1:16
Bandai Schutzenpanzerwagen SdKfz 251/1 Hanomag: 1/48: Afx S 73 15/1:51; IM Ja 73 10/1:16
ESCI SdKfz 251: 1/72: AFV Ap 75 5/4:36-37; Afx Mr 75 16/7:438
Fujimi SdKfz 251/1 or /10: 1/76: Afx Mr 75 16/7:438; MW F 74 2/6:330; RiS Su 73 1/4:741

Hasegawa Quad 20mm Flak on SdKfz 7: 1/72: Afx D 74 16/4:254
Hasegawa SdKfz 7: 1/72: Afx S 74 16/1:50
Hasegawa 37mm Flak on SdKfz 7: 1/72: Afx D 74 16/4:254
Hinchliffe SdKfz 251: 1/76 metal: MW My 73 1/9:494
Matchbox M-16 halftrack: 1/76: Afx N 75 17/3:173; IM Jl 75 11/
  4:14; MM N 75 5/11:662; Sc S 75 6/72:462
Midori SdKfz 250/3 & /10: 1/40: Afx Ja 72 13/5:282; IM D 71 8/
  12:insert
Midori SdKfz 250/9: 1/40: Afx F 74 15/6:364+
Monogram M3A1 APC halftrack: 1/35: WWE S 74 1/5:150
Nitto SdKfz 2 Kleines Kettenkraftrad: 1/35: MM Ap 74 4/4:206-
  207; RiS Au 73 2/1:37
Nitto SdKfz 250/3: 1/35: WWE S 74 1/5:151
Nitto SdKfz 251/1: 1/35: Afx My 73 14/9:506+
Rico SdKfz 250/3: 1/35: MM Jl 75 5/7:432
Tamiya SdKfz 2 Kleines Kettenkraftrad: 1/35: Afx F 74 15/6:366;
  MM Ap 74 4/4:206; RiS Au 73 2/1:36
Tamiya SdKfz 7: 1/35: AFV Mr 72 3/7:29; Afx S 72 14/1:44; Afx
  N 72 14/3:162; IM O 72 9/10:insert; MM D 72 2/12:664-665;
  MW D 72 1/4:210; RiS Ag 72 1/1:16
Tamiya SdKfz 7/1 20mm Flakvierling: 1/35: AFV Je 75 5/5:37;
  MM Ag 75 5/8:479; RiS Jl 75 3/2:101; WW2J S 75 2/5-6:26
Tamiya SdKfz 251: 1/35: AFV My 73 4/4:37; MM Jl 73 3/7:456-
  457+; MW Jl 73 1/11:606-607; RiS Su 73 1/4:139

Self-Propelled Artillery

(Germany)

Armtec Hetzer: 1/76: Afx Ja 72 13/5:281-282
Bandai Hetzer: 1/48: MM N 73 3/11:764-765
Bandai Hummel: 1/30: MM Ag 73 3/8:542-543
Bandai Jagdpanther: 1/48: RiS Sp 74 2/3-4:159
Bandai Jagdtiger: 1/48: MM Ag 74 4/8:483-484; Q Su 75 10/4:
  137; RiS Au 73 2/1:36
Bandai PzH Auf Gw.II Wespe: 1/48: Afx S 73 15/1:51; IM Ja 73
  10/1:insert; MM Mr 73 3/3:167; MW Ag 73 1/12:660; Sc My 73
  4/5:353-354
ESCI Elefant: 1/72: MM N 75 5/11:681-683
ESCI Hetzer: 1/76: IM Jl 75 11/4:14
ESCI Hummel: 1/72: AFV Ap 75 5/4:36-37; RiS Mr 75 3/1:49
ESCI Marder III: 1/72: AFV Ap 75 5/4:36-37; IM Jl 75 11/4:15
Fujimi Elefant: 1/76: Afx N 74 16/3:185-186
Fujimi Hetzer: 1/76: AFV D 72 3/12:27; Afx D 72 14/4:222; MM
  Mr 73 3/12:50; Sc N 72 3/11:610-611
Fujimi Jagdtiger: 1/76: Afx D 72 14/4:222; MM Ja 73 3/1:50;
  MW Mr 73 1/7:383; Q Su 75 10/4:137
Fujimi SU-85: 1/76: Afx My 75 16/9:550+
Italaerei Elefant: 1/35: MM My 75 5/5:303; cor Ja 76 6/1:17; RiS
  Mr 75 3/1:50; S&L (D 74) 5:21; WWE Mr 75 2/2:67-68

Italaerei Hetzer: 1/35: Afx Je 73 14/10:562; IM N 73 10/11-12: insert; MM Jl 73 3/7:432-433; MW My 73 1/9:493; RT Ja 73 6/1-2:22
Italaerei Panzerjager 38(t) Marder III: 1/35: Afx S 74 16/1:48+; IM N 73 10/11-12:insert; RT Ag 73 6/8:84; RiS Au 73 2/1:38
Matchbox Wespe: 1/76: Afx O 75 17/2:120; IM Jl 75 11/4:15; MM N 75 5/11:662; Sc S 75 6/72:462
Monogram Ostwind: 1/32: MM N 75 5/11:661
Otaki Jagdpanther: 1/48: MM O 73 3/10:690
Otaki Schutzenpanzer Marder: 1/48: MM O 73 3/10:690
Rico Jagdpanther: 1/76: MW Je 73 1/10:552
Tamiya Jagdpanther: 1/35: Afx Ja 73 14/5:280; MM D 72 2/12: 676-677; MW Mr 73 1/7:382
Tamiya KV-IIB: 1/35: MM N 75 5/11:678-679
Tamiya Marder II: 1/35: WW2J S 75 2/5-6:28-29
Tamiya Sturmgeschutz III: 1/35: Afx N 72 14/3:160; MM D 72 2/12:668

(Italy)

Italaerei Semovente M 40: S&L (D 74) 5:21

(Japan)

Fujimi Type 1 Ho Ni tank destroyer: 1/76: RiS Jl 75 3/2:102

(USSR)

Fujimi KV-1: 1/76: Afx D 72 14/4:222
Fujimi KV-2: 1/76: Afx D 72 14/4:222; MM Ja 73 3/1:50; Q Jl 74 10/1:5; Sc My 73 4/5:351-352
Ogonek JSU-152: 1/30: Q Jl 74 10/1:5-7
Tamiya KV-1C: 1/35: Afx Ja 75 16/5:322; Q Jl 74 10/1:7; RT Ap 73 6/4:43; RiS N 72 1/3:48; Sc N 72 3/11:611-614

(U.S.)

Tamiya M-10 tank destroyer: AFV Ap 75 5/4:37; MM N 75 5/11: 662-663
Tamiya M-36 Jackson: 1/35: MM Ag 73 3/8:526-527

Small Arms

H&R Vickers 303 machine gun: 1/32: MM S 74 4/9:549
LS Luger Model P.08 Parabellum pistol: 1/1: MW N 72 1/3:158

VI. Reviews

Softskins

(Canada)

Clarks Chevrolet 30 cwt LRDG truck: 1/76 resin: MM F 73 3/2: 99-101
Max CMP Chevrolet light truck & 6 pdr gun: 1/35: AFV Je 75 5/5:37+; RiS Jl 75 3/2:103
Max CMP Quad & 6 pdr AT gun: 1/35: WW2J Jl 75 2/4:29
Tamiya Quad: 1/35: Afx Ag 75 16/12:726; MM F 75 5/2:104-105; RT Jl 75 8/7:83; RiS Mr 75 3/1:49-50

(Germany)

Airfix Reconnaissance Set: 1/76: Afx Ja 75 16/6:319; IM My 75 11/3:12-13; RT Jl 75 8/7:83; Sc F 75 6/65:97; WWE Mr 75 2/2:69
Bandai Opel Maultier halftrack truck: 1/48: IM Ja 73 10/1:insert
Bandai PKW K1 Kubelwagen: 1/48: IM Ja 73 10/1:insert: MM 73 3/3:167; Sc My 73 4/5:353
ESCI BMW R75 motorcycle & sidecar: 1/9: Afx Ag 72 13/12:682; IM N 72 9/11:insert; Sc Ag 72 3/8:450-541
ESCI Zundapp KS 750: 1/9: Afx Jl 74 15/11:657
Fujimi BMW motorcycle & side car: 1/76: Afx N 74 16/3:186
Fujimi Kommanderwagen: 1/32: Sc F 73 4/2:124
Fujimi Kubelwagen: 1/76: Afx N 74 16/3:186
Hasegawa BMW 75/R: 1/72: Afx N 74 16/3:186; RiS Au 73 2/1: 37
Hasegawa Kubelwagen: Afx N 74 16/3:186; RiS Au 73 2/1:37
Italaerei Opel Blitz: 1/35: RiS Mr 75 3/1:50
Marui Mercedes Benz Type C4/W31 staff car: 1/35: RT Jl 75 16/11:80
Minitanks Opel Blitz: 1/87: Afx Jl 75 16/11:664
Modakit Kubelwagen: 1/76: Afx Jl 73 14/11:620
Tamiya BMW R. 75 motorcycle & sidecar: 1/35: Afx N 72 14/3: 160; IM O 72 9/10:insert; MM D 72 2/12:644-646; MW D 72 1/4:211; RiS N 72 1/2:60
Tamiya BMW R. 75 & Zundapp KS 750 motorcycles: Afx D 73 15/4: 248; MW N 73 2/3:157-158
Tamiya Horch Kfx 69: 1/35: WW2J S 75 2/5-6:69-70
Tamiya Kubelwagen: 1/35: MM F 71 1/2:108
Tilt Mercedes-Benz Cr/W31 S. gl. Pkw: 1/35: RiS W 74 2/2:74

(Japan)

Hasegawa Fuel Truck: 1/72: Afx N 74 16/3:184; AN 4 O 74 3/9: 15; RiS W 74 2/2:74
Hasegawa Hucks Starter Truck: 1/72: Afx N 74 16/3:184; AN 4 O 74 3/9:15; RiS W 74 2/2:74
Hasegawa Isuzu TX-40 Fuel Truck: 1/72: Sc Ja 75 6/64:36

(U. K.)

Airfix Humber Snipe staff car: 1/32: Afx D 72 14/4:220; Sc F 73 4/2:128-130
Airfix RAF Recovery Set: 1/76: Afx Je 73 14/10:561; AN 22 Je 73 2/3:14; IM Je 73 10/6:insert; MM Jl 73 3/7:443; Sc Jl 73 4/7:490-491
Airfix RAF Refueling Set: 1/76: RT F 71 4/2:15; Sc Ja 71 2/1: 49-50
Bandai Austin K5 3-ton 4x4 truck: 1/48: Afx N 75 17/3:174
Lasset GS Wagon: 54mm metal: Afx Jl 71 12/11:598
Renown Bedford 15cwt truck: 1/76 metal: Afx Ag 72 13/12:582; MM Jl 72 2/7:371-372; MW S 72 2/1:51

(U. S.)

Bandai M12 gun motor carriage: 1/48: WWE Mr 75 2/2:69-70
Bandai M30 cargo carrier: 1/48: WWE Mr 75 2/2:69-70
Bandai Willys Jeep: 1/48: WWE S 74 1/5:151
Hasegawa GMC CCKW-353 cargo truck: 1/72: Afx N 75 17/3:174
Hasegawa GMC Dump Truck: 1/72: Afx N 75 17/3:174
Hasegawa GMC Gasoline Truck: 1/72: Afx N 75 17/3:174
Hasegawa Jeep: 1/72: RiS Sp 73 1/3:103
Max Dodge WC-51 3/4 ton weapons carrier: 1/35: AFV S 74 4/12:33
Max Dodge WC-62 1½ ton personnel carrier: 1/35: AFV Ap 75 5/4:37
Max Dodge T214 WC-56/57 Command Reconnaissance Car: 1/35: WW2J My 2/3:109
Max Dodge 3/4 ton Command & Recon Truck: 1/35: AFV S 75 5/6:13
Max M-6 37mm Anti-tank gun carriage: AFV Ja 75 5/2:32
Max M8A1 Tractor, Trailer & 155mm Howitzer: 1/35: MW S 72 1/1:50
Nitto Willys Jeep: 1/24: Afx S 72 14/1:46
Tamiya Amphibious Jeep: 1/35: MM F 75 5/2:110
Tamiya Willys Jeep: 1/35: AFV My 72 3/8:30; Afx N 72 14/3: 160+; MM F 73 3/2:102-104; RiS Ag 72 1/1:16

Tanks

(Canada)

Matchbox Sherman Firefly: 1/76: Afx O 74 16/2:112; IM My 74 10/(16):13; Sc D 74 5/63:671

(France)

Heller AMX-13: AFV S 75 5/6:13

Raretanks Souma S 35: 1/76 vac: Afx Je 71 12/10:554
Riko AMX-30: 1/76: MW Je 73 1/10:552

(Germany)

Airfix Leopard: 1/76: Afx Ja 71 12/5:234; Sc Ja 71 2/1:49
Airfix Panzer IV F1/F2: 1/76: AFV O 71 3/2:33; Afx Ag 71 12/ 12:622; IM Ap 71 8/4:5-6; MM Je 71 1/6:312; Sc Je 71 2/6: 283-284
Airfix PzKpfw VI Tiger I Ausf E (late production): 1/76: IM O 71 8/10:13+ ; Q Su 75 10/4:137
Aurora Royal Tiger (Henschel turret): 1/48: Q Su 75 10/4:137
Bandai Heuschrecke 10. 5cm leichte FH 18/6 auf GW IV: 1/30: AFV O 71 3/2:34; MM Ag 71 1/8:409
Bandai PzKpfw IV Ausf H: 1/48: WWE N 74 1/6:187
Bandai Panther G: 1/24: MW Ja 73 1/5:272
Bandai Panzer IV Ausf G: 1/30: Sc Je 71 2/6:285
Bandai PzKpfw VI Königstiger (Porsche turret): 1/48: MM N 73 3/11:765; Q Su 75 10/4:137
ESCI PzKpfw III Ausf M: IM N 74 10/19:10
Fujimi PzKpfw VI Königstiger: 1/76: AFV F 72 3/6:29; Afx D 72 14/4:222; IM Mr 72 10/3:insert; MM Ja 73 3/1:49; Q Su 75 10/ 4:137; RT F 72 5/2:21; Sc My 72 3/5:288
Hasegawa Panther G: 1/72: Afx S 74 16/1:50
Hasegawa Tiger I: 1/72: Afx S 74 16/1:50
Matchbox Panther: 1/76: IM N 74 10/19:11; MM N 74 4/11:687- 688
Matchbox Panzer III Ausf L: 1/76: IM My 75 11/3:13
Monogram PzKpfw IV Ausf I: 1/32: MM D 71 1/12:616; add Ja 72 2/1:13
Nichimo PzKpfw IV Ausf G: 1/30: MM S 71 1/9:453-455; Sc O 71 2/10:544-545
Nichimo Tiger II Ausf B: 1/35: WW2J S 75 2/5-6:29
Nitto Tiger I Ausf E (std production): 1/76: Q Su 75 10/4:137
Otaki PzKpfw III: 1/35: Afx Ap 71 12/8:432
Tamiya Panther Ausf A: 1/25: Afx Ja 73 14/5:28+; MW Ja 73 1/5: 270-271
Tamiya Panzer III: 1/35: Afx Ap 71 12/8:432
Tamiya PzKpfw II Ausf F/G: 1/35: AFV D 71 3/4:29; Afx O 71 13/2:98; MM D 72 2/12:668; MW Je 73 1/10:553; Sc N 71 2/ 11:619
Tamiya PzKpfw IV Ausf H: 1/35: RiS Jl 75 3/2:101
Tamiya Royal Tiger: 1/35: Q Su 75 10/4:137

(Italy)

Italaerei M 13/40:135: AFV Ja 74 4/9:33; IM N 73 10/11-12:insert
Tamiya M 13/40: 1/35: IM My 47 10/(16):12; RiS Sp 74 2/3-4: 161

(Japan)

Airfix Chi-Ha: 1/76: Afx N 74 16/3:174; IM N 74 10/19:11; Q Su 75 10/4:162; RiS Mr 75 3/1:49; Sc O 74 5/10:554; WWE S 74 1/5:151
Fujimi Chi-Ha: 1/76: Afx Je 75 16/10:610; Q Su 75 10/4:162
Fujimi Shinhoto Chi-Ha: 1/76: RiS Jl 75 3/2:102; WW2J Jl 75 2/4:29
LS Type 3: 1/50: RiS Su 73 1/3:139
LS Type 97: 1/50: RiS Su 73 1/3:139
Tamiya Type 61 JSDF tank: 1/35: MM F 71 1/2:109-110

(Sweden)

Tamiya S tank: 1/48: MM My 71 1/5:241

(USSR)

Airfix Josef Stalin III: 1/76: Q Jl 74 10/1:7
Aurora JS-III: 1/48: Q Jl 74 10/1:7
Bandai T34/76: 1/48: AFV F 75 5/3:12+
Espewe PT 76: 1/87: Q Jl 73 8/3:168
Fujimi T-34/76A: 1/76: Afx Ap 75 16/8:496; IM My 74 10/(16): 13
Fujimi T-34/85: 1/76: Afx My 75 16/9:552
ITC PT 76A: 1/32: Q Jl 73 8/3:168
Moscow Toy & Model Plastics T-34: 1/35: Sc Mr 72 3/3:166+
Ogonek KB-85: 1/32 (nom 1/30): Q Jl 74 10/1:7; Sc S 74 5/5: 478-479
Roskopf PT 76: 1/100: Q Jl 73 8/3:168
Tamiya T-34: 1/48: MM My 73 1/5:241
Tamiya T-34/76 (1943): 1/33 (nom 1/35): AFV Ap 75 16/8:36; MM N 75 5/11:678-679; RiS Mr 75 3/1:49; WW2J My 75 2/3: 110; cor S 75 16/9:552

(U. K.)

Airfix Chieftain: 1/76: IM Ap 71 8/4:5; MM Je 71 1/6:311-312; Sc Je 71 2/6:282-283
Airfix Cromwell Mk IV: 1/32 ready-assembled: Afx S 73 15/1: 16; RT Ag 73 6/8:86
Airfix Crusader II or III: 1/76: AFV Ja 72 3/5:29; Afx Ja 72 13/5:149; IM N 75 11/6:22
Airfix Crusader III: 1/32: Afx D 75 17/4:201
Airfix Matilda: 1/76: Afx N 73 15/3:140; MM N 73 3/11:764; MW D 73 2/4:213
Airfix Scorpion: 1/87: Afx Ap 75 16/8:488
Armtec M3A1 Lee: 1/76 vac conv from Airfix Lee: Afx F 74 15/6:364
Armtec M4A1 Sherman: 1/76 vac conv from Airfix Sherman: Afx

F 74 15/6:364
Bandai Matilda: 1/48: MM N 75 5/11:660-661
Fujimi Matilda Mk III: 1/76: Afx O 73 15/2:115; MM Jl 73 3/7: 408; MW D 73 2/4:213; RiS Sp 73 1/3:103
Fujimi Valentine: 1/76: Afx S 74 16/1:50-51; RiS Au 73 2/1:36
Matchbox A34 Mk I Comet: 1/76: Afx Ag 75 16/12:726; Sc Ap 6/67:179; WW2J Jl 75 2/4:28
Modakit Cromwell: 1/76: Afx S 73 15/1:54; MM F 73 3/2:110
Nichimo Chieftain: 1/35: MM Ap 71 1/4:212-213
Tamiya Centurion Mk III: 1/35: Afx Je 71 12/10:544; Afx My 73 14/9:510; IM My 71 8/5:3; MM Ag 71 1/8:408-409; MW Jl 73 1/11:607
Tamiya Centurion Mk III: 1/25: IM Ja 73 10/1:insert; IM My 73 10/5:insert; MM My 73 3/5:302-303; MM Je 74 4/6:337-338; MW Jl 73 1/1:607
Tamiya Matilda Mk II: 1/35: Afx Ja 74 15/5:312+; IM Jl 73 10/7:insert; MW O 73 2/2:102; RiS Su 73 1/4:138

(U.S.)

Airfix M-551 Sheridan: 1/76: Afx S 72 14/1:10; cor N 72 14/3: 127
Armtec M3A1 Lee cast hull & sand shields: 1/76 vac conv from Airfix Lee: RT Mr 73 6/3:24
Armtec M4A1 Sherman cast hull & sand shields: 1/76 vac conv from Airfix Sherman: RT Mr 73 6/3:24
Bandai M4A3 Sherman: 1/48: Afx Ap 75 16/8:494; RiS Au 73 2/1: 38; WWE S 74 1/5:151
Bandai M60A1: MM Ja 73 3/1:26
Fujimi M4A3 105mm HVSS Sherman: 1/76: Afx Je 73 14/10:562; MM Jl 73 3/7:468
Hasegawa M3 Stuart: 1/72: MM D 73 3/12:836; MW Je 73 1/10:552; RiS Su 73 1/4:141
Hasegawa M4A3E8 Sherman: 1/72: Afx Ja 75 16/5:320
Hasegawa M-24 Chaffee: 1/72: Afx N 74 16/3:186; IM Ja 75 11/1:15; MM N 74 4/11:686
MAZ M4 Sherman conversion: 1/76: AFV Mr 74 4/10:33
Monogram M3 Medium, Lee & Grant: 1/32: Afx Mr 75 16/7:437; IM Ja 74 10/13-14:insert; MM Ag 74 4/8:471-473; RT Mr 74 15/7:27; Sc Jl 74 5/58:372-373
Monogram "Screeming Mimi" (Sherman Calliope): 1/32: MM N 75 5/11:660
Nichimo M4A1 Sherman: 1/35: AFV Jl 74 4/11:33; MM Ja 75 5/1:46-47; cor Mr 75 5/3:154
Otaki M60 Super Patton: 1/50: Sc D 72 3/12:674
Revell M4 Sherman: 1/36 (nom 1/40 or 1/35): WWE S 74 1/5: 150
Tamiya M3 Grant: 1/35: RiS Sp 74 2/3-4:158; S&L (D 74) 5:18
Tamiya M3 Lee: 1/35: MM N 74 4/11:687; WWE N 74 1/6:187
Tamiya M3 Stuart: 1/35: MM F 75 5/1:103; RiS Sp 74 2/3-4:158; S&L (D 74) 5:18
Tamiya M4 Sherman RCT: 1/16: MM Je 75 5/6:164+

Kit--Static

Tamiya M-41 Walker Bulldog: 1/35: Afx Ja 71 12/5:268
Tamiya M60A1: 1/48: MM My 71 1/5:241-242
Tamiya M60A1: 1/35: Afx My 71 12/9:490; MM F 71 1/2:107;
   Sc Mr 71 2/3:155-157
Tamiya M60A1E1: 1/48: MM My 71 1/5:241-242
Tamiya M551 Sheriden: 1/35: Afx O 71 13/2:98+ ; IM My 71 8/5:
   5-7; MM D 72 2/12:665+
Tamiya Main Battle Tank 71: 1/48: Afx D 72 14/4:225

Accessories

Range Reviews

Armtec Accessories: 1/76: AFV N 71 13/3:34
Squadron Armor Model Accessories: AFV S 71 3/1:28

Individual Sets

Armour Accessories German WW-II, packs, weapons: 1/35: MW
   Ag 73 1/12:661
Armtec AFV Accessories: 1/76: IM F 71 8/2:7
Armtec British Weapons: 1/76: RT My 74 7/5-6:50
Armtec German Spare Track Sections: 1/76: MM Mr 71 1/3:147
Armtec German Vehicle Breakdown Equipment: 1/76: MM Mr 71
   1/3:147
Armtec Jerry Cans: 1/48: RT Mr 73 6/3:24
Armtec PAK 7.5cm AT gun: 1/76 metal: RT Mr 73 6/3:24
Armtec Tow Chain: 1/48: MM Mr 71 1/3:147; RT Mr 73 6/3:24
Bandai Field Accessories: 1/48: Afx F 75 16/6:382
Historex AFV Parts: 1/35: Sc Ja 71 2/1:47+
Seagull Models barbed wire: 1/32: Afx My 72 13/9:512
Tamiya Barricade: 1/35: Afx Ag 74 15/12:718
Tamiya Jerry Cans: 1/35: Afx Ag 74 15/12:718
Tamiya Sand Bags: 1/35: Afx Ag 74 15/12:718

AUTOMOBILES

Animal-Powered

APAG Logging Wagon: HO: NSG N 75 1/5:6

Motorcycles

Airfix Honda 750: 1/8: Afx Ap 74 15/8:446

VI. Reviews

Airfix Suzuki Cyclone: 1/8: Afx Ja 75 16/5:318
Hasegawa BMW R 75/5: 1/10: Sc D 71 2/12:676-677
Hasegawa BMW R. 75/5 with side car: 1/10: Sc Je 72 3/6:347-348
Hasegawa Yamaha 250 DTI: 1/10: Sc N 71 2/11:618
Heller BMW R60/5 French Gendarmerie: 1/8: MW Mr 73 1/7: 345; MW Ap 73 1/8:439
Heller BMW 75/5: 1/8: Afx Je 72 13/10:572
Heller Laverda 750: 1/8: Sc Ja 74 5/1:51-52
Heller Norton: 1/8: Afx Jl 73 14/11:618
Heller Norton Commando 750: 1/8: MW O 73 2/2:103
Heller Norton Roadster 750: 1/?: Sc O 73 4/10:707; Sc Ja 74 5/1:52
Heller Norton 750 Commander Hi-Rider: 1/8: MW Mr 73 1/7:345; MW Ap 73 1/8:439
Nagano Kawasaki 750RS: 1/8: Sc N 75 6/74:572
Protar DKW Grand Prix 350: 1/6: Afx O 71 13/2:98
Protar DKW 350: 1/9: Sc My 72 3/5:273+
Protar Gilera 500: 1/9: Sc N 73 4/11:779
Protar Greeves Challenger: 1/6: Afx Ap 71 12/8:430
Protar Husqvarna 400 Cross: 1/9: Sc Ja 73 4/1:52-53
Protar Laverda SF 750: 1/9: Sc N 73 4/11:774
Protar Moto BMW 500: 1/9: Sc N 71 2/11:618
Protar Norton Commando 750: 1/9: Afx Jl 74 15/11:658+
Pyro Harley Davidson Electra-Glide: 1/16: Sc Mr 71 2/3:157; Sc Jl 71 2/7:378-379
Pyro Harley Sho-Go Cycle: 1/16: Sc Mr 71 2/3:157
Revell BMW R75/5: 1/8: IM Ag 73 10/8:insert; MW S 73 2/1:48
Revell BMW R75/5 police issue: 1/8: Afx D 74 16/4:252; Sc Jl 73 4/7:486
Revell Chain Gang: 1/12: Sc Ag 74 5/59:448+
Revell Harley Davidson Electra-Glide: 1/8: Sc Jl 71 2/7:378-379
Revell Harley Davidson "Knucklehead" Drag Bike: 1/8: IM Jl 72 9/7:insert
Revell Harley Davidson police bike: 1/8: MAN F 71 82/2:21+
Revell Honda "Super Sport": 1/8: IM Mr 72 9/3:1-2
Revell Husqvarna: 1/12: IM Ag 73 10/8:insert; MW Ag 73 1/12: 660; Sc Jl 73 4/7:486
Revell Kawasaki Drag Bike: 1/8: Sc D 71 2/12:678
Revell Kawasaki Mach III: 1/12: IM Jl 72 9/7:insert; Sc S 73 4/9:643
Revell Kawasaki Mach III: 1/8: Sc S 73 4/9:643
Revell Kawasaki Street Racer: 1/12: MW Ja 74 2/5:272; Sc Ja 74 5/1:51
Revell "Rough Rider" Chopper: 1/12: IM Jl 72 9/7:insert
Revell Street L'Eagle: 1/12: IM Ag 73 10/8:insert
Revell Suzuki motocross: 1/12: IM Jl 75 11/4:14
Revell Triumph Drag Bike: 1/8: IM Ag 73 10/8:insert; Sc Jl 73 4/7:486
Revell Yamaha 250 DTI "Trials" bike: 1/12: IM Jl 72 9/7:insert
Tamiya BMW R75/5 police: 1/6: MW D 73 2/4:213
Tamiya Dax Honda 70 Export: 1/6: Sc My 72 3/5:284-286
Tamiya Honda CB 750: 1/6: Afx Ap 71 12/8:430

Passenger Cars

Airfix Austin Maxi: 1/32: RT Jl 71 4/7:74
Airfix Austin Mini: 1/32: Afx Ag 71 12/12:622
Airfix Beach Buggy: 1/32: Afx O 72 14/2:66-67; IM O 72 10/10: insert
Airfix Bond Bug: 1/32: Afx Ja 72 13/5:249
Airfix $4\frac{1}{2}$ litre Bentley: 1/12: Afx Ja 72 13/5:248; IM N 71 9/11: insert
Airfix Morris Marina 1.8TC: 1/32: Afx S 72 14/1:10-11; IM O 72 10/10:insert
Airfix 1930 supercharged Bentley $4\frac{1}{2}$ litre: 1/12: Sc Mr 72 3/3: 168-170
Airfix 1927 Lincoln Roadster: 1/25: Afx Jl 75 16/11:628; IM S 75 11/5:12; Sc Ag 75 6/71:409
Airfix Vauxhall Prince Henry: 1/32: Afx Ja 72 13/5:249; Sc Ap 72 3/4:227
Auto Replica Amilcar: 1/43 metal: Sc S 75 6/72:450-451
Bandai Alfa Romeo Gran Sport: 1/12: Sc O 71 2/10:543-544
Bandai Bugatti Royale: 1/16: MW Ja 73 1/5:230-231
Bandai Mercer Raceabout: 1/16: Sc Ja 73 4/1:49-51
EMK 1895 Panhard Coupe: 1/32: Sc O 71 2/10:546
Europe Model Panhard 1895 Coupe: 1/32: Afx N 71 13/3:158
Europe Model Panhard 1905 Tonneau Roi des Belges: 1/32: Afx N 71 13/3:158
Grand Prix Rover BRM: 1/43 metal: Sc S 75 6/72:451
Heller Renault 16: 1/20: IM N 71 8/11:1; IM Ja 72 9/1:3
Jo-Han Javelin/AMX: 1/25: IM O 72 10/10:insert
Jo-Han Mercedes 500K: 1/25: Afx F 75 16/6:381; IM Jl 71 9/7:1
Matchbox Aston Martin Ulster: 1/32: IM S 75 11/5:17; Sc D 75 6/75:619
Matchbox Jaguar SS100: 1/32: IM S 75 11/5:17
Midori 1907 Pechino-Paragi: 1/20: Sc D 71 2/12:678+
Monogram 1930 Ford A Coupe: 1/24: Sc Jl 75 6/70:360
Monogram Mercedes Benz 540 K: 1/??: Afx Ag 73 14/12:680
Monogram Packard Boat-Tail Speedster: 1/24: Sc D 75 6/75:621
Nakamura Mercury Cougar: 1/20: Sc Mr 72 3/3:171-172
Penguin Citroen 2CV: 1/20: Sc S 73 4/9:642-643
Pocher 1935 Mercedes Benz Cabriolet 500K: 1/8: Sc Ag 74 5/59:424-425
Renwal 1930 Packard Victoria: 1/48: MR O 75 42/10:26
Revell Gypsy Dune Buggy: 1/25: Sc Ja 72 3/1:49-50
Revell Porche 914 sports car: 1/25: IM Jl 72 10/7:insert
Rio Duesenberg SJ Torpedo Phaeton 1934: 1/43: Sc Ja 71 2/1:50
Rio 1908 Thomas Flyer: 1/43: Sc Ja 71 2/1:50
Tamiya Datsun 240Z: 1/12: Afx Mr 74 15/7:419-420; MW Ja 74 2/5:276
Tamiya Datsun 240ZG: 1/12: Afx Jl 74 15/11:658
Wills Finecast Austin 7: 1/24 metal: Afx F 74 15/6:363-364
Wills Finecast 1928 $4\frac{1}{2}$ litre Le Mans Bentley: 1/24 metal: Sc Mr 72 3/3:146-148
Wills Finecast 1934 Super Aero Morgan: 1/24 metal: Sc My 72 3/5:274-275

VI. Reviews

Racing Cars

Airfix Maserati Indy: 1/32: Afx Je 73 14/10:561; Sc Jl 73 4/7: 491
Airfix Porsche 917: 1/32: Sc Je 72 3/6:351
Heller Brabham BT 33: 1/24: Sc N 73 4/11:777-778
Heller Ferrari 330-P4: 1/24: IM My 71 8/5:7+ ; Sc O 71 2/10: 545
Heller McLaren Grand Prix: 1/24: IM D 71 8/12:insert
Heller Matra: 1/24: Sc O 71 2/10:545-546
Lindberg Exterminator: 1/??: Afx Ag 74 15/12:719
Midori 1907 Pechino Parigi Itala: Afx Ja 72 13/5:282
Nichimo Shelby Cobra GT 500: 1/16: Sc F 71 2/2:100; Sc Mr 73 4/3:166+
Revell 1950 Austin Drag Sedan: 1/25: Sc N 71 2/1:616+
Revell Big Daddy: 1/25: IM Mr 75 11/2:15; Sc Mr 75 6/66:145
Revell Eastern Raider: 1/??: Afx Je 75 16/10:611
Revell Garlit AA Fuel Dragster: 1/??: IM Jl 75 11/4:14
Revell Mickey Thompson's Grand Am Funny Car (Revelleader): 1/16: Afx My 75 16/9:549; Sc Jl 74 5/58:391
Revell Racing Porsche 911: 1/25: IM Jl 72 9/7:insert; IM O 72 3/10:insert
Revell Porsche 915/6: 1/25: Afx Mr 73 14/7:454
Revell Praying Mantis: 1/16: Afx My 75 16/9:550; Sc Ap 74 5/55: 223
Revell Tony Nancy Dragster: 1/16: Afx F 73 14/6:333-334
Revell Tony Nancy "The Loner": 1/16: Sc F 73 4/2:123-124
Solido Ferrai 512 S: 1/43: Sc Ja 71 2/1:50
Tamiya Ferrari 312B: 1/12: Afx Ja 72 13/5:284; Sc Ja 72 3/1: 18-21+
Tamiya John Player Special Lotus 72D: 1/12: Sc Ja 74 5/1:32-33
Tamiya Lola T-70: 1/12: Afx Ja 71 12/5:266+
Tamiya McLaren 8A: 1/18: Afx Jl 71 12/11:600
Tamiya McLaren M23: 1/12: Sc My 75 6/66:134-136
Tamiya Tyrrell-Ford F1: 1/25: Afx O 73 15/2:112; MW Jl 73 1/11:607-608

Ready-Assembled

Bachmann Heavy Construction Equipment: N: RMC My 72 40/12: 57-58
Boyd Scale Vehicles: N: MR Jl 71 38/7:21
Gescha Earthmoving Equipment: 1/50: MR F 74 41/2:33-34
Harbutt's Plasticene Period Vehicles: HO: RMC S 72 41/4:60+
Märklin Volkswagen Station Wagon: 1/43: MR Je 73 40/6:29
Miniature-Toys Container Transporter Truck: S: MR Ap 74 41/4: 27
Miniature-Toys Container Transporter Truck & Trailer: S: MR Ap 74 41/4:27

Scale Structures Steam Road Roller: HO: RMC Ap 74 42/11:58+
Ulrich Tractor-Trailers: HO: RMC Mr 74 42/10:59
Walthers Semi-Trailer Trucks: HO: MR Jl 73 40/7:21
Walthers Tractor & Van: HO: RMC Jl 72 41/2:53-54

Tractors

Scale Structures Steam Traction Engine: Case: HO & O: NSG Mr 75 1/1:13

Trucks & Trailers

AMT American La France Ladder Chief: 1/25: Sc Ja 72 3/1:33-35
AMT Autocar DC 9964B Dump Truck: 1/25: MW Ja 74 2/5:272+
AMT Ford LNT 800 Snow Plough: 1/??: IM N 73 10/11-12:insert
AMT Ford LNT 8000 Tractor: 1/25: Afx N 71 13/3:156
AMT Fruehauf F tandem-axle semi-trailer: 1/43: Sc O 74 5/61: 552-553
AMT Fruehauf Model FB Trailer: 1/25: Afx Je 72 13/10:570+
AMT Fruehauf semi-trailer: 1/25: Afx Je 71 12/10:543
AMT Fruehauf Tanker Trailer: 1/25: Sc D 75 6/75:593
AMT GMC Astro 95 & Lowboy Trailer: 1/25: Afx Jl 72 13/11:630
AMT Kenworth K.123 trailer tractor: 1/43: Sc O 74 5/61:552-553
AMT Peterbuilt Cabover: 1/25: Afx Je 71 12/10:543
AMT Peterbuilt Wrecker: 1/25: Afx Jl 72 13/11:630
AMT White Road Boss: 1/25: IM Mr 75 11/2:15-16; Sc D 75 6/75:592-593
Bandai Ford T Stake Truck: 1/16: Sc Ag 75 6/71:408-409
Jordan Model T Fire Truck: 1/87: IM S 74 10/(18):11
IMC Dodge/Fargo L 700 & flatbed trailer: 1/25: Sc D 72 3/12: 666-669
Kohnstam RAF-type Leyland Lorry: between world wars, 00 cardboard: Afx N 73 15/3:178
Lindberg earth-moving vehicles: O & S: RMC Je 75 44/1:48-49+
Lilliput Miniatures LGOC ST class bus: 1/76 cardboard: Afx Ag 74 15/12:718; MW Ja 73 1/5:271
Monogram Mack Bulldog truck, 1926: Sc D 74 5/63:672
Riko 1920 Type S London Bus: 1/76 cardboard: Afx Ag 74 15/12: 718

Engines

Airfix Four Stroke Engine: no scale or specific prototype: Afx N

72 14/3:127; IM D 72 9/12:insert
Cannon AH&D Boiler: HO: MR S 75 42/9:28; NSG Mr 75 1/1:12
Cannon Caterpiller engine: for stationary uses: NSG Mr 75 1/1: 12
Cannon Dolbeer Donkey Engine: HO: MR O 72 39/10:27-28
Cannon Hoist & Derrick Donkey Engine: HO: MR Ap 74 41/4:30; RMC My 74 42/12:54-59
Charles H. Brommer mill engine: O: MR Ap 75 42/4:25
Keystone Locomotive portable horizontal boiler: HO: RMC D 74 43/7:74-75
Model Masterpieces horizontal boiler: NSG Jl 75 1/3:7
Rio Grande horizontal boiler: HO: NSG N 75 1/5:7
Scale Structures engine & boiler: HO: MR My 73 40/5:21
Scale Structures power machinery, stationary steam engine supplies: HO: MR S 71 38/9:27-28
Town Models hoist engine boiler: O: MR O 74 41/10:20+
Williams 80hp Le Rhone rotary engine: 1/6: Sc F 71 2/2:94-95
Williams Pratt & Whitney Wasp: 1/8: Sc O 75 6/73:516
Williams Wright J5 Whirlwind: 1/6: Sc Ag 72 3/8:428-429

FIGURES [metal, unless otherwise stated]

Subject Reviews

Miniature Figures of the American West: Fus Au 73 1/1:42-44+; W 74 1/2:37-39+
Modeling Marlborough's Wars: MM My 72 2/5:247-249

Range Reviews

(Smaller Than 20mm)

Laing 15mm wargame figures: Afx S 73 15/1:52
Miniature Figurines: Afx D 73 15/4:244+; MM My 71 1/5:250-251
Peco N Gauge figures: 1/160: Afx F 71 12/6:324

(20-30mm)

Bygone Wars: Hinchliffe ancients: 25mm: MM Je 73 3/6:362-363+
Edward Suren "Willie": 30mm: MM S 71 1/9:450-451
Greenwood & Ball: 25mm Garrison ancients: MM N 72 2/11:586-587
Hinchliffe: 25mm: MM F 72 2/2:95-96; MM Ag 72 2/8:406-407; MW O 72 1/2:101
Les Higgins: 25mm: MM Ap 72 2/4:174-175

Kit--Static

Hinchliffe Vikings, English Civil War: 25mm: Afx D 73 15/4:246-247
Jacklex/Silver Cross: 20mm: MW Ja 73 1/5:270
K&L figures: HO: RMC Je 72 41/1:56+
Mini-Figs: 25mm: Afx Mr 72 13/7:398
Minifigs: 25mm strips: Afx Ag 73 14/12:680-681
Minifigs Ancients: 25mm: Afx Ja 73 14/5:281
Minifigs Macedonian & Punic Wars: 25mm: Afx Mr 73 14/7:398
Minifigs Samurai & Mongols: 25mm: Afx Je 73 14/10:564
Minitanks: WW-II & personality: Afx Jl 75 16/11:664
Minot British Napoleonic: 30mm: MW S 73 2/1:49
Minot French Napoleonic Infantry: 30mm: MW N 73 2/3:158
Phoenix in '73: 25 & 30mm: MM My 73 3/5:294-295
SS people: HO: NSG My 75 1/2:8-9
SEGOM: 25mm plastic: MM S 72 2/9:464-465
Spencer-Smith American Revolution: IM Mr 75 11/2:15
Tradition: 25mm: MM Je 74 4/6:316-317
Warrior: 30mm: MM Jl 71 1/6:360-361
Willy Landsknechts: 30mm: MW S 73 2/1:49

(30-54mm)

Cannon 19th century civilian: 1/48: MR Jl 73 40/7:20-21
Lee Town human figures: 1/48: MR D 75 42/12:38; NSG S 75 1/4:10
Scale Railway figures: O: MR Jl 75 42/7:30
Stephen Poole civilians: 42mm: Sc Ja 75 6/64:40

(54mm)

Airfix: plastic: Fus W 74 1/2:45
Battles Long Ago: Elastolin Renaissance, plastic: MM Je 72 2/6: 284-286+
Britains British Infantry: WW-II, polyvinylchloride: MM Ag 73 3/8:543-544
Ensign early 20th century British mess-dress: Afx Ap 74 15/8: 474+; Afx Je 74 15/10:584-586; MW N 73 2/3:157; S&L (O 75) 10:28
Garrison: MM Ja 71 1/1:57-58
Greenwood & Ball gladiators: MM F 73 3/2:108-109
Les Higgins: MM Mr 71 1/3:142-143
Hinchlifee Si-Fi: mythical: MM Je 75 5/6:366
Historex: plastic: MM Mr 72 2/3:140-141
Hitler's Toymakers: Elastolin 1930s & 1940s production: MM S 71 1/9:476-478
JAC: MM Mr 72 2/3:167-168
Lamming Miniatures: MM F 71 1/2:93-94
Lasset 54mm Figures: Afx Mr 72 13/7:398; MW Je 73 1/10:554
Lasset Dervish Army 1898: Afx Jl 72 13/11:626
Lasset German Army WW-I: S&L (D 74) 5:20
Lasset German Soldiers: Afx S 72 13/1:42

VI. Reviews

Lasset Prussian Army 1815: S&L (D 74) 5:20
Minitanks: WW-II & personality: Afx Jl 75 16/11:664
Little Generals: Fus W 74 1/2:43+
Omdurman 1898: Greenwood & Ball: MM Jl 73 3/7:458-459+
Phoenix in '73: MM My 73 3/5:294-295
Rose Miniatures: MM Mr 72 2/3:124-125
SEGOM: plastic: Fus W 74 1/2:44
Sanderson gladiators: MW Je 73 1/10:552
Squadron/Rubin: one line each in large collection: RiS Sp 74 2/3-4:160
Standish: MM Jl 72 2/7:356-357
Starlux First Empire: 55mm: Afx S 71 13/1:44+
Starlux Napoleonics: finished: MM Ag 71 1/8:392-393
Trophy Miniatures: MM N 72 2/11:596-597
Valda: MW F 73 1/6:330
Valiant: MM Ag 72 2/8:402-403; MM Ap 73 3/4:208-209

(Over 54mm)

Charles Stadden: 90mm: MM Je 71 1/6:313-314; MM D 71 1/12: 652-654
The Greeks: Series 77: MM S 72 2/9:482-484
Hinchliffe Napoleonic: 75mm: MW F 74 2/6:330
Sentry Box: 120mm: MM O 71 1/10:526-527
Series 77: 77mm: MM Ap 71 1/4:178-179
Series 77 German Imperial Cavalry: 77mm: S&L Ag 74 3:25-26
Series 77 16th century landsknechts: MM Ja 72 2/1:44-45; MM My 72 2/5:247-249
Series 77 Stage 10: English Civil War: 77mm: MM Ag 73 3/8: 514-516
Something Traditional: Tradition mounted figures, 90mm one-off, finished: MM My 75 5/5:278-279
Warneford: 300mm: MM N 71 1/11:570-571

(Unknown Scales)

Pyro Dinosaurs: Sc Jl 71 2/7:380
Revell Animals: Afx Ag 75 16/12:726

Figures

(Smaller Than 20mm)

LaBelle engineer & fireman: N: RMC O 75 44/5:72-73

(20-30mm)
[plastic, unless otherwise stated]

Airfix Air Cavalry: 1/76: Sc O 71 2/10:548-549

Airfix American Astronauts: 1/72: Afx O 71 13/2:66
Airfix American War of Independence Troops: 1/76: Afx O 71 13/2:66
Airfix Australian Infantry, WW-II: 1/76: Afx S 75 17/1:11
Airfix Grenadier of the French Imperial Guard: 1/76: Afx Ap 75 16/8:489
Airfix High Chaparral figures: 1/76: Afx Ja 71 12/5:234
Airfix Japanese Infantry: 1/76: MM F 71 1/2:107-108
Airfix RAF Personnel: 1/72: Afx D 72 14/4:221; AN 8 D 72 1/15:14; MW Ag 73 1/12:660
Airfix station platform detail & people: RMC Ja 74 42/8:70
Airfix USAF Personnel: 1/76: Afx Jl 74 15/11:631; AN 9 Ag 74 3/5:10; Sc O 74 5/61:553
Airfix U.S. Paratroops, WW-II: 1/76: Afx D 75 17/4:202
Airfix Waterloo British Airtillery: 1/76: Afx O 72 14/2:66; MW Je 73 1/10:553
Airfix Waterloo British Cavalry (Hussars): 1/76: MW Je 73 1/10:554; Sc Jl 72 3/6:405
Airfix Waterloo British Grenadiers: 1/76: IM O 71 8/10:insert
Airfix Waterloo British Infantry: 1/76: Afx O 72 14/2:66; MW Je 73 1/10:553
Airfix Waterloo French Artillery: 1/76: MW Je 73 1/10:554
Airfix Waterloo French Cuirassiers: 1/76: MW Je 73 1/10:554
Airfix Waterloo French Infantry: 1/76: IM O 71 8/10:insert; MW Je 73 1/10:554
Airfix Waterloo Highland Infantry: 1/76: MW Je 73 1/10:553
Almark British WW-II infantry: 20mm: MM F 73 3/2:110-111; reply Mr 73 3/3:168
Fujimi German Infantry: 1/76: Afx D 72 14/4:222
Garrison English Civil War pikeman attacking: 25mm metal: S&L Jl 74 2:26
Garrison French Napoleonic Grenadier at high porte: 25mm metal: S&L Jl 74 2:26
Garrison Geonoese Crossbowman readying: 25mm metal: S&L Jl 74 2:26
Garrison Hoplite: 25mm metal: MM Jl 71 1/7:353; S&L Jl 74 2:26
Hinchliffe Elephant Gun: 20mm metal: Afx Jl 72 13/11:626
Hinchliffe French Napoleonic Field Forge: 25mm metal: Afx O 72 14/2:102
LaBelle engineer & fireman: HO: RMC O 75 44/5:72-73
Minifig elephant: 20mm metal: MM Jl 71 1/7:355
Minitanks American Troops: 1/76: Afx Ag 72 13 /12:685
Minitanks German Troops: 1/76: Afx Ag 72 13/12:685
Minitanks Tank Crews: 1/87: Afx S 71 13/1:44
Preiser Luftwaffe: 1/72: AN 1 Mr 74 2/20:14

(30-54mm)

Bandai American Infantry: 1/48: Afx F 75 16/6:382
Bandai German Infantry: 1/48: Afx F 75 16/6:382
Bandai German Sappers: 1/48: Afx F 75 16/6:382
Selley Martin standing & working figures: 1/48: RMC O 75 44/5:76+

VI. Reviews 714

(54mm Individual--Metal)

Cameo Churchill: 1/32: MW Je 73 1/10:553
Cameo Adolph Hitler: S&L Ag 74 3:26
Cameo Robert E. Lee: S&L Jl 74 2:26
Cameo Musolini: S&L Je 71 1:16
Cameo George Patton: S&L Jl 74 2:26
Cameo Manfred von Richthofen: Sc O 74 5/61:535; S&L Je 74 1:16
Cameo Teddy Roosevelt: S&L Ag 74 3:26
Coronet Northwest Mounted Police: Afx Jl 75 16/11:666
Coronet Sir John Plessis: Afx Jl 75 16/11:666
Coronet Squire: Afx Jl 75 16/11:666
Covington Sir Roget de Trumpington: RiS Ag 72 1/1:16
Frontier Ali Pasha (pirate): Fus Su 74 1/4:45
Frontier German Policeman: paramilitary: MW N 73 2/3:159
Frontier King John with Magna Charta: Fus Su 74 1/4:45
Frontier Nigerian Infantryman 1890: Fus Su 74 1/4:45
Frontier Vatican Swiss Guard with standard: Fus Su 74 1/4:45
Helmet Hussar: Afx D 73 15/4:248
Hinchliffe American Civil War Artilleryman: Afx Je 75 16/10:611
Lasset Blucher: S&L (Ap 75) 7:28
Lasset Omdurman Mounted Figures (British & Dervish): Afx O 72 14/2:66
Lasset 21st Lancers, 1898: MW S 72 1/1:50; MW O 73 2/2:102
Old Guard Ballister & Crew: MM O 73 3/10:689
Old Guard French Officer & Indian: MM F 74 4/2:95-96
Phoenix Hussar Dancing with Lady: S&L (F 75) 6:26
Phoenix mounted Ironside (English Civil War): MM Je 73 3/6:378-379
Phoenix Royalist cuirassier: MM O 73 3/10:664
Phoenix Young Winston (Churchill): MW O 73 2/2:102-103
Sanderson Roman Beggar: Afx Mr 72 13/7:398
Sanderson Roman Bidding Customer: Afx Mr 72 13/7:398
Sanderson Cavalier & Tavern Wench: S&L Jl 74 2:26
Sanderson Viking "girlie": Afx S 71 13/1:42
Soldat German Paratroop Officer: Fus Su 74 1/4:45
Soldat SS Soldier in parade dress: Fus Su 74 1/4:47
Trophy Earl of Essex, mounted with falcon: MM N 74 4/11:687
Trophy Samurai Archer: MM Je 73 3/6:378-379

(54mm Individual--Plastic)

Airfix American Soldier of 1775: Afx N 74 16/3:171; MM D 74 4/12:752; S&L (F 75) 4:24
Airfix British Grenadier of 1776: Afx D 75 17/4:202
Airfix British 10th Hussar: Afx Ja 72 13/5:249; MM Ja 72 2/1:16-18
Airfix 42nd Highlander: IM Ag 72 9/8:insert; MW F 73 1/6:330
Airfix French Cuirassier: Afx Ja 75 16/5:319; IM My 75 11/3:12; MM Ja 75 5/1:48; cor Mr 75 5/3:156; S&L (O 74) 4:24
Airfix French Grenadier of the Imperial Guard: Afx N 73 15/3:140; MM N 73 3/11:764; MW N 73 2/3:157

Airfix French Line Infantry, 1815: Afx S 75 17/1:11; IM S 75 11/ 5:12; S&L (O 75) 10:27
Airfix George Washington: Afx Ap 75 16/8:488-489; IM My 75 11/ 3:12; S&L (F 75) 6:28
Airfix 95th Rifleman, 1815: Afx O 74 16/2:86; IM My 74 10/(16): 11; MM S 74 4/9:549-550
Airfix Polish Lancer: Afx D 73 15/4:210; IM S 73 10/9:insert; IM Ja 74 10/13-14:insert; MM D 73 3/12:272
Airfix Scot Grey: Afx D 72 14/4:220; IM D 72 9/12:insert; MM Ja 73 3/1:21; MW F 73 1/6:330
Airfix 2nd Coldstream Guard: Afx Ja 72 13/249; MM Ja 72 2/1:16-18
Historex Guard Engineer (Sapeur): Afx Jl 72 13/11:626
Historex Gun Team & Limber: MM Ap 72 2/4:193-195; My 72 2/5: 244-245; Je 72 2/6:304-305
Historex Imperial Guard Scout: Afx Jl 72 13/11:626
Historex Mamelukes: Afx N 74 16/3:186; MM O 73 3/10:684-685; MW F 74 2/6:330
Historex Military Forge: MM D 74 4/12:752; S&L (F 75) 6:26
Historex Napoleon: MW F 73 1/6:330
Historex Scots Grey: MM My 72 2/5:230-231
Historex stretched & Jumping horses: Afx My 74 15/9:536
Tamiya Wehrmacht mounted infantry: Afx S 75 17/1:51

(54mm Sets)
[plastic unless otherwise stated]

Airfix Australian Infantry: MM F 73 3/2:110
Airfix British 8th Army Troops: 1/32: Afx D 75 17/4:201-202
Airfix British Infantry, 1815: MW N 73 2/3:157
Airfix British Paratroopers: 1/32: Afx Ag 72 13/12:649
Airfix Cowboys & Indians: Afx Je 75 16/10:572; MM Je 75 5/6:366
Airfix Footballers (soccer): 54mm: Afx Ag 72 13/12:649
Airfix U.S. Paratroops, WW-II: 1/32: Afx D 75 17/4:202
Almark German Panzer Grenadiers 1939-1945: MM F 71 1/2:110-111
Almark Japanese Infantry 1939-1945: MM F 71 1/2:111
Almark U.S. WW-II Troops: Afx Jl 71 12/11:598+
Ensign well vignette: metal: S&L (D 75) 11:24
Historex Regimental Band of the Imperial Guard 1804-1812: IM Ap 71 8/4:6
Italaerei Panzer Artillerie-Rgt Grossdeutschland: RiS Mr 75 3/1: 50
Sanderson press gang: metal: S&L Ag 74 3:14-15
Tamiya Afrika Korps figures: 1/35: Afx O 71 13/2:98; IM N 71 8/11:16-17
Tamiya American tank crew: Sc F 71 2/2:106
Tamiya British Eighth Army troops: Afx N 74 16/3:186; IM My 74 10/(16):11; RiS W 74 2/2:74
Tamiya British Infantry: 1/35: Afx Je 71 12/10:543
Tamiya Fallschirmjäger: 4 in set: Afx N 72 14/3:160; MW D 73 2/4:211

VI. Reviews 716

Tamiya German Artillery Troops: IM N 73 10/11-12:insert; RiS
    W 74 2/2:74
Tamiya German Assault Troops: Afx N 74 16/3:186
Tamiya German Machinegun Troops: WW2J Jl 75 2/4:29
Tamiya Russian Infantry: Afx D 73 15/4:248
Tamiya U.S. Army Infantry: MW D 73 2/4:211

(77mm)

Hinchliffe Italian Death Volunteer, 1917: S&L (O 75) 10:28
Hinchliffe Panzer Grenadier: Afx Je 75 16/10:610-611
Hinchliffe Tambour de Fusiliers: 75mm: MM O 73 3/10:665; MW
    O 73 2/2:102
Imrie-Risley American Civil War Confederate Infantryman: RiS W
    74 2/2:75
Series 77 RAF & German Pilots: 1/24: Afx O 71 13/2:98; MM S
    73 3/9:625; RiS Au 73 2/1:37
Series 77 Turkish camel trooper 1453: MM Ja 74 4/1:28-29+
Tamiya German Figures: 1/25: Afx D 74 16/4:254; WW2J My 75
    2/3:108

(Over 77mm)

Airfix Anne Boleyn: 1/12: Afx Ja 74 15/5:318; Sc F 75 6/65:97
Airfix Queen Elizabeth I: 1/12: Afx D 75 17/4:202
Airfix Show Jumper: 1/8?: Afx S 75 17/1:11
Hinchliffe Taisho: 6" Saburai general: MM S 73 3/9:591-593
Sentry Box Royal Scots Dragoon Guards Drum Horse: 120mm: S&L
    (D 75) 11:25
Tamiya motor racing team: 1/12: Sc Jl 75 6/70:359
Tradition French Imperial Grenadier Garde: 90mm: S&L (Ap 75)
    7:28

Accessories

Lasset Military Accessories: 54mm WW-II German, French Napo-
    leonic: Afx My 72 13/9:514; MW O 72 1/2:102
Top Brass German insignia & decorations: 1/32 etched brass: MM
    F 73 3/2:111; RT My 73 6/5:48

MISSILES & SPACE VEHICLES

Airfix SAM II "Guideline": 1/76: Afx Jl 74 15/11:630-631; Sc Ap
    74 5/55:225
Airfix Saturn IB rocket: 1/144: Afx Ag 71 12/12:623; RT Jl 71 4/
    7:74

Airfix Vostok: 1/144: Afx Ja 71 12/5:235; IM F 71 8/2:10; Sc Mr 71 2/3:153
Aurora Starship Enterprise: 1/???: Afx Jl 72 13/11:628+
Eidai V-2 & launching equipment: 1/72: MM S 74 4/9:548-549; Sc S 74 5/60:502
Heller Command & Service Module, Apollo Cabin: 1/95: IM F 71 8/2:10
Heller Lunar Module: 1/100: Afx Je 72 13/100:574; IM F 71 8/2:10
Revell V-2 rocket: 1/70: AN 25 My 73 2/1:14; IM O 72 9/10:insert; Sc Ag 73 4/8:571

RAILROAD (Non-Operating)

Airfix BR Mogul: 1/76: RT Jl 71 4/7:74
MicroModels Locos: 1/??? cardstock range review: Sc Je 73 4/6:434-435
Peacock Paperkit Bluebell: O17 cardstock: Sc Jl 72 3/7:393+

SHIPS

Range Reviews

Aoshima waterline: 1/700: MW Jl 73 1/11:607
Ensign: 1/1200: Afx Ag 73 14/12:678
Fleetline British Warships: 1/1200 metal: MW Jl 73 1/11:608
Heller Cadet series: 1/1200: MW O 73 2/2:102
Miniature Navies: 1/1200: MM Je 72 2/6:296-299
Revell Destroyers: MW O 72 1/2:102
Revell 720 series warships: 1/720: MW S 72 1/1:51
Saito 1/1000 waterline: Sc Ja 74 5/1:52
Tamiya Torpedo Boats: semi-scale line using same hull: Afx S 71 13/1:42
Tamiya waterline series warships: 1/700: Afx Ja 72 13/5:284; Afx F 74 15/6:364; MW S 72 1/1:51; MW D 72 1/4:210
Wiad Harbour Craft: HO wl: Afx Je 72 13/10:570

Powered

Civil

Airfix Great Western: 1/126: IM N 72 9/11:1
Ensign SS Amora: 1/1200 metal three island tramp steamer (armed

VI. Reviews 718

& unarmed var): S&L Jl 74 2:28
Ensign SS Avoceta: 1/1200 metal freightliner: S&L (Je 75) 8:32
Ensign MV British Endurance: 1/1200 metal, 1937 tanker: S&L Ag 74 3:27
Ensign British motor coaster: 1/1200 metal: S&L Ag 74 3:27
Engisn SS Galway: 1/1200 metal cross-channel passenger cargo: S&L (Je 75) 8:32
Ensign Isle of Guernsey: 1/1200 metal channel island ferry: S&L (O 74) 4:22
Ensign Nixie: 1/1200 metal turn-of-century steam yacht: S&L (Jl 74) 2:28
Ensign MV Pacific Coast: 1/1200 metal British coaster: S&L Ag 74 3:27
Ensign pilot cutter: 1/1200 metal: S&L Ag 74 3:27
Entex Titanic: 1/350: Sc S 75 6/72:463
Heller Lenine: 1/400 nuclear-powered icebreaker: Sc Ja 72 3/1: 52
Heller Pourquoi-Pas?: 1/100 exploration ship: IM My 71 8/5:insert; Sc Jl 71 2/7:372-373
Revell Robert E. Lee: 1/???: Afx Mr 75 16/7:440
Revell Russian "Spy Trawler": 1/??: IM Je 71 8/6:4
Revell Taurus: 1/??: Afx Mr 75 16/7:440

Naval

(France)

Heller FS Clemenceau: 1/400: IM My 71 8/5:7
Heller Maille Breze: 1/400: Afx D 71 13/4:228

(Germany)

Airfix Bismark: 1/1200: Afx Ap 74 15/8:446-447; IM N 73 10/11-12:insert; Sc Je 74 5/57:337
Airfix Graf Spee: 1/600: Afx D 71 13/4:227; IM Ap 72 9/4:insert; Sc D 71 2/12:680-681; Sc Ap 72 3/4:208
Airfix Prinz Eugen: 1/600: Afx Ap 75 16/8:488; IM Mr 75 11/2: 15; Sc Ap 75 6/67:176
Airfix Rommel: 1/600: Afx O 71 13/2:66
Aoshima Bismark: 1/700: Sc D 74 5/63:671
Darnell U-47: 1/??: MM N 75 5/11:682
Ensign Maass class destroyer: 1/1200 metal: S&L (O 74) 4:22
Frog Tirpitz: 1/450: Afx My 71 12/9:489
Heller Gneisenau: 1/400: Sc Ja 74 5/1:52-53
Heller Scharnhorst: 1/400: Sc Ja 74 5/1:52-53
Jade Schieswig Holstein: 1/250 cardstock: MM Ja 71 1/1:42-43
Revell Blücher (org Prinz Eugen): 1/72: IM Ag 73 10/8:insert; Sc S 73 4/9:644
Revell Gneisenau: 1/570: IM N 75 11/6:22
Revell Scharnhorst: 1/5700: IM N 75 11/6:22
Revell Tirpitz: 1/600: IM S 72 9/9:15

Revell U47: 1/125: IM My 75 11/3:14
Airfix Prinz Eugen: 1/600: Afx My 75 16/9:549; IM Mr 75 11/3: 14; Sc Mr 75 6/66:145
Schreiber type VIIc U-Boat: 1/200 cardstock: Sc Ja 72 3/1:41
Tamiya Gneisenau: 1/700: Sc D 75 6/75:619
Wilhelmshaven Hamburg: 1/250 waterline cardstock: Sc O 71 2/10:540-541

(Japan)

Aoshima Hiryu: 1/700: Sc My 73 4/5:357
Aoshima Kagero: 1/700: Sc My 75 6/68:250
Aoshima Katori: 1/700: Sc My 75 6/68:250
Aoshima Nagato: 1/700: Sc Je 73 4/6:424
Ensign Fubuki class destroyer: 1/1200 metal: S&L (F 75) 6:28
Ensign I-40 class submarine: 1/1200 metal: S&L (O 74) 4:22
Fujimi Kongo: 1/700: Sc Je 73 4/6:423
Fujimi Nagara: 1/700: Q Ja 73 8/1:40
Hasegawa Hayanami: 1/700: MW My 73 1/9:493-494
Hasegawa Hushashi: 1/450: Sc Ag 72 3/8:454
Hasegawa Yamato: 1/450: Sc Ag 72 3/8:454
Nichimo Ashigara: 1/500: WWE S 74 1/5:141
Nichimo I-19: 1/200: Sc F 73 4/2:90-91
Tamiya Fubuki: 1/700: Afx F 74 15/6:364
Tamiya Harusame: 1/700: Q Ja 73 8/1:39
Tamiya I-16 & I-58: 1/700: IM Ap 73 10/4:insert; Sc Ag 73 4/8: 570
Tamiya Junyo: 1/700: Afx S 74 16/1:51; Sc O 73 4/10:706-707
Tamiya Kumano: 1/700: MW D 72 1/4:210
Tamiya Mushashi: 1/700: Sc Ja 72 3/1:49
Tamiya Shinano: 1/700: MW D 72 1/4:210; Sc Je 73 4/6:424
Tamiya Shiratuyu: 1/700: Afx F 74 15/6:364
Tamiya Taiho: 1/700: Sc My 73 4/5:357
Tamiya Tama: 1/700: Afx Jl 74 15/11:660
Tamiya Ukikaze: 1/300: IM Je 71 9/6:3-4
Tamiya Yahagi: 1/700: Sc Mr 73 4/3:170

(Malaysia)

Tamiya Perkasa: Afx F 72 13/6:340; IM Ja 72 9/1:10; IM Mr 72 9/3:13+; Sc N 71 2/11:613-616

(USSR)

Aurora Moscow: 1/600: Afx F 72 13/6:340; Afx D 73 15/4:210; IM Je 71 8/6:3; Sc F 74 5/2:116
Heller Aurora: 1/400: MM N 71 1/11:579+; Sc Ja 72 3/1:49

(U.K.)

Airfix Amazon: 1/600:   Afx D 72 14/4:221; MB Ja 73 23/265:18; Sc F 73 4/2:91
Airfix Belfast: 1/600:   Afx Ja 74 15/5:280; Sc F 74 5/2:116-117
Airfix Hood: 1/1200:   Afx Ap 74 15/8:446-447; IM N 73 10/11-12: insert; Sc Je 74 5/57:337
Airfix Manxman: 1/600:   Afx Mr 72 13/7:364; IM Ap 72 9/4:insert; Sc Mr 72 3/3:170-171
Airfix Narvik: 1/600:   Afx Jl 75 16/11:628; IM S 75 11/5:12; Sc Jl 75 6/70:359
Airfix tribal class destroyer: 1/1200:   Afx Ap 75 16/8:489; Sc Ap 75 6/67:176
Airfix Vosper MTB: 1/72:   Afx Ag 72 13/12:648; IM S 72 9/9:3+; MW S 72 1/1:50; RiS Ag 72 1/1:15; Sc Ag 72 3/8:452-453
Fleetline Ajax: 1/1200 metal: Sc Je 75 6/69:300
Fleetline floating dock: 1/1200 metal: S&L (Je 75) 8:32
Fleetline Robert Middleton (1940): 1/1200 metal admiralty coastal supply vessel: S&L (Je 75) 8:32
Ensign Ark Royal: 1/1200 metal: S&L (F 75) 6:28
Ensign Exeter: 1/1200 metal: S&L (F 75) 6:28
Ensign Narvik class destroyers: 1/1200 metal: S&L (D 75) 11:27
Ensign Ulster Monarch as LSI: 1/1200 metal: S&L (D 75) 11:27
Frog Tiger: 1/417 (nom 1/500):   Afx F 71 12/6:324
Frog Vanguard: 1/440:   Afx My 71 12/9:489; IM F 71 8/2:5
Revell Bligh: 1/250:   Afx Jl 72 13/11:628; IM Je 72 9/6:insert; Sc Jl 72 3/7:402
Revell Campbelltown: 1/240:   Afx Jl 72 13/11:628; IM Je 72 9/6: insert; Sc Jl 72 3/7:402-403
Revell Duke of York: 1/570:   Afx N 75 17/3:173-174; IM S 75 11/5:13
Revell King George V: 1/570:   IM Ja 75 11/1:14; Sc Mr 75 6/66:144
Revell Prince of Wales: 1/570:   Afx N 75 17/3:173-174; IM Jl 75 11/4:12; Sc O 75 6/73:516
Tamiya Nelson: 1/700 waterline: Sc Ja 75 6/64:34-35

(U.S.)

Aoshima North Carolina: 1/700:   Sc My 75 6/68:250
Aoshima Washington: 1/700:   IM Ja 75 11/1:15
Hasegawa Essex: 1/700:   Afx My 75 16/9:552
Hasegawa Hancock: 1/700:   Afx My 75 16/9:552
Hasegawa South Dakota & Alabama: 1/700:   Sc N 75 6/74:570
Model Figures & Hobbies Buckley class destroyer: 1/1200 metal: S&L (O 75) 10:30
Model Figures & Hobbies Casablanca: 1/1200 escort carrier: S&L (O 75) 10:30
Otaki Missouri: 1/350:   Afx Ap 73 14/8:452; Sc Ag 72 3/8:453
Revell Burton Island: 1/287:   Afx Ag 74 15/12:716+; Sc Jl 74 5/7: 369
Revell Defiance (org Tacoma): 1/131:   Afx Jl 73 14/11:622; IM Ag

73 10/8:insert
Revell Flasher: 1/179: IM Je 71 8/6:5
Revell Growler (org Flasher), 1/179: Afx Jl 73 14/11:620; IM Ag 73 10/8:insert
Revell Intrepid (org Essex, org Franklin): 1/720: Sc Jl 74 5/58: 369
Revell Montrose: 1/370: Afx Ag 74 15/12:716+; Sc Jl 74 5/7:369
Revell PT 207, 212: 1/97: IM Ja 71 8/1:4
Revell Olympia: 1/232: IM Jl 75 11/1:15
Revell Pine Island: 1/424: Afx Ag 74 15/12:716+; Sc Jl 74 5/7: 391
Revell Tacoma: 1/131: IM Je 71 8/6:4-5
Revell Wasp: 1/546: Afx N 74 16/3:185
Tamiya Hornet: 1/700: Sc My 75 6/68:248

Sail

Airfix St. Louis: 1/???: Afx Ja 74 15/5:280
Airfix Wasa: 1/???: Afx S 72 14/1:11
Heller Alcyon: 1/150 schooner: Sc Ja 72 3/1:50+
Heller Le Mataro: 1/76: Afx My 72 13/9:514
Heller Osberg Ship: 1/60? Viking: Afx My 72 13/9:512; IM Ap 72 9/4:insert
Heller Pamir: 1/150: Afx Ja 73 14/5:278; IM D 72 9/12:insert; MW Mr 73 1/7:345
Heller Le Phenix: 1/175: Afx S 71 13/1:42
Heller Carrack Pinta: 1/??: Afx My 71 12/9:490
Heller La Sirene: 1/75: Afx S 71 13/1:42
Neptune Royalist: 1/48 brig: MW S 73 2/1:48-49
Pyro USS Alliance: 1/200 1777 frigate: Sc Je 71 2/6:285-286
Revell Elizabethan Man O' War: 1/??: IM Jl 75 11/4:13
Revell Spanish Galleon: 1/???: Sc N 74 5/62:612
Revell Thermopylae: 1/96: Afx My 71 12/9:489; IM Ap 71 8/4:3

Unpowered Vessels & Research Devices

Aurora Sealab III: 1/??: Afx F 71 12/6:324
Fine Scale steam pile driver barge: HO: RMC F 73 41/9:56-59

Fittings

Ensign 1/1200 accessories: Afx O 73 15/2:115

VI. Reviews

STRUCTURES

Range Reviews

AHM Railroad Structures: HO: MR N 72 39/11:35-36
Card Modelling: survey of cardstock buildings: Sc Ap 72 3/4:214-217
Life-Like Scale Houses: HO: MR Jl 71 38/7:25

Bridges

AHM deck truss: HO: MR F 72 39/2:26+; RMC O 72 41/5:55-56
AHM life bridge: HO: MR S 73 40/9:28-29
AHM operating rolling lift bridge: N: RMC N 75 44/6:84-86
AHM pedestrian overpass: HO: RMC F 73 41/9:64
AHM through plate girder: HO: MR F 72 39/2:26+
AHM plate girder: HO: RMC O 72 41/5:55-56
AHM Warren pony truss: HO: MR F 72 39/2:26+
AHM Trestle Set: HO: RMC Jl 72 41/2:54
AHM Warren through truss: HO: RMC O 72 41/5:55-56
Cal-Scale timber trestle: N: RMC D 75 44/7:83+
Campbell through timber truss bridge: N: MR My 72 39/5:22; RMC Jl 73 42/2:54-55
Geiger deck girder swing bridge: HO: RMC Mr 72 40/10:54+
Hi Rail trestle: O: MR F 74 41/2:25-26
Lambert deck girder bridge: HO: MR Je 71 38/6:26
Mil-Scale 65' covered bridge: N: MR D 71 38/12:29
Pacific Model Supplies (New Zealand) three span pony truss: HO-O: MR Jl 71 38/7:20
Russel Mobi-Models rolling lift bascule bridge: HO: MR O 71 38/10:29-30
San Juan Howe pony truss bridge: O: MR N 74 41/11:36+
Scale Structures deck girder bridge: HO: RMC My 72 40/12:58+
Scale Structures wood truss bridge: HO: RMC S 73 42/4:63-64
Sierra Southern timber trestle: HO, HOn3, N: MR S 72 39/9:22-24

Building Parts

(Exterior)

Arkay stripwood & scale lumber: HO: MR F 75 42/2:31
Campbell corrugated material: HO: MR D 71 38/12:30+
Champion Decal brick & stone sheets: HO & O: MR Ja 74 41/1:25+; RMC N 75 44/6:89-90

Durango structure details: RMC O 75 44/5:79-81
Durango Victorian chimney: HO: MR D 74 41/12:33
Dyna-Model scratchbuilders supplies: HO: RMC D 72 41/7:78-80
Faller steel girders: HO/OO: MW O 72 1/2:210
Fotocut fire escapes: HO: RMC D 74 43/7:81-82
Grandt separate-frame windows: HO: RMC Jl 75 44/2:63-64
Instant Rivet: MR D 71 38/12:41
Kibri platform canopy: HO & N: MR D 72 39/12:35
Model Die Casting stone building & kitbashing components: HO: RMC Ap 74 42/11:55-57
Model Hobbies brick paper: O & HO: RMC Jl 73 42/62
Model Hobbies building paper: N, HO, O siding paper: RMC S 72 41/4:57-58
Model Hobbies structure parts & accessories: working hinges, roof ventilators, wooden steps, medium window castings: HO: RMC N 72 41/6:75-77
Model Railroad Supplies brick & stone: N, TT, HO, & S: MR O 72 39/10:27
No-Lo structural material: plastic siding sheet: RMC D 72 41/7: 71
Northeastern scratchbuilder's materials: N: MR Ap 75 42/4:32-33
Scale Railway plastic siding, masonry & rivet sheets: RMC S 75 44/4:61-62
Scale Structures embossed cut stone material: HO: RMC D 74 43/7:84-85
Simpson corrugated paper siding & roofing: O: RMC N 72 41/6: 74-75
Williams corrugated aluminum sheeting: HO & O: RMC Ap 72 40/11:58+

(Interior)

SS Dorothy's House furnishings: HO: NSG My 75 1/2:9
Scale Structures blacksmith's equipment: HO: MR Je 74 41/6:25
Scale Structures shop machinery: HO: MR My 71 38/5:17-18
Mountain States carpets: NSG Jl 75 1/3:7

Buildings

Sets

AHM Cutout Cardstock Buildings: 1930s: 5&10 cent store, small gas station, Victorian house, pool hall: HO: RMC D 72 41/7:74
AHM Cutout Cardstock Buildings: 1930s: large railroad station, large mercantile block: HO: RMC D 72 41/7:74
AHM Cutout Cardstock Buildings: Old West: jail, bank, church, city hall: HO: RMC D 72 41/7:74
AHM Cutout Cardstock Buildings: Old West: station, blacksmith,

general store, saloon: HO: RMC D 72 41/7:74
Model Die Casting western structures: HO: MR S 73 40/9:26

Commercial

AHM Busy Bee department store: HO: MR Je 74 41/6:18-19; RMC N 74 43/6:72+
AHM Emporium department store: HO: MR Je 74 41/6:18-19
AHM hardware store: HO: MR Mr 75 42/3:24-25; RMC Mr 75 43/10:57-58
AHM service station: HO: MR Ag 71 8/8:26-27; MR D 73 40/22:29; RMC N 71 40/6:63
AHM undertaker: HO: MR Mr 75 42/3:24-25
Campbell cigar store: HO: RMC Ap 71 39/11:60-61
Campbell laundry: HO: RMC Ap 71 39/11:60-61
Campbell saloon & store: HO: MR Jl 74 41/7:18-19
Con Cor hotel: HO: MR Mr 75 42/3:31
Con Cor restaurant: HO: MR O 75 42/10:28+
Durango Perkins Products: HO: NSG My 75 1/2:9
Dyna-Model country grocery store: HO: RMC O 72 41/5:54-55
Fine Scale garaga: HO: MR Ap 75 42/4:31-32; RMC Ag 75 44/3:58-59
Heljan store & apartment building: HO: MR Ag 71 38/8:22-23; "Watch Repair Shop": RMC S 71 40/4:48-49
Historical Scale Miniatures false-front store: HO: RMC Ap 73 41/11:56+
JMC commercial buildings: N modules: MR O 73 40/10:26-27
Muir saloon & gun shop: HO: MR S 75 42/9:31-32
Placer, Nevada, & El Dorado Bonanza saloon & dance hall: HO: RMC Ja 73 41/8:65-66
Placer, Nevada, & El Dorado hardware store: HO: MR N 72 39/11:38+
Scale Structures country store: HO: MR F 71 38/2:20
Scale Structures drug store: HO: MR Ja 72 39/1:20-21
Structure Co. false-front store: HO: RMC Jl 75 44/2:59-60+
Structure Co. York's store: HO: NSG S 75 1/4:9
Sugar Pine supply store: HO: MR My 75 42/5:28-29
Suydam Bekins Storage warehouse: HO: RMC My 73 41/12:54-55
Timberline photographer's home & studio: HO: RMC My 71 39/12:49
Wabash Valley brick barber shop: HO: RMC My 74 42/12:58-59+

Houses

AHM Aunt Millie's house: HO: MR Ag 74 41/8:21-22
AHM Cape Cod house & garaga: N: MR N 74 41/11:43
AHM Farmhouse: N: MR O 74 41/10:24-25
AHM Farmhouse: HO: MR S 72 39/9:28
AHM Ma's Place boarding house: HO: RMC F 72 40/9:54+
AHM ranch houses: N: RMC S 75 44/4:71-72
Airfix Battle of Waterloo Farm House: OO/HO: MW Ap 73 1/8:440

Kit--Static

Faller Lean-To add-on: OO: Afx Ja 75 16/5:322
Campbell farmhouse: HO: MR S 73 40/9:20
Chapman Le Haye Sainte: 1/72 cardstock: Afx Jl 71 12/11:60
Classic Miniatures red-light district houses: HO: MR O 75 42/10:31
Historical Scale Miniatures house: HO: MR Ap 72 39/4:23-24
Historical Scale Miniatures Bridgeport house: HO: RMC Ap 73 41/11:55-56
Historical Scale Miniatures 1890 period "Queen Anne" house: HO: RMC Je 72 41/1:50+
101 Productions Victorian house: O: MR F 75 42/2:28
Structure Co. mountain cabin: NSG N 75 1/5:7
manufacturer unstated (2 distributors) house & garage: Z: MR Ap 75 42/4:32

Industries

AHM printing company building: HO: MR F 74 41/3:28-29
AHM processing plant: HO & N: MR Ap 73 40/4:20
AHM Ramsey Journal building: HO: RMC F 72 40/9:54+
Bordertown blacksmith shop: HO: RMC Ap 72 40/11:56-57
Campbell dinghy shop: HO: MR D 75 42/12:34-35
Campbell gold or silver mine: HO: RMC My 75 43/12:52-53
Campbell grain elevator: HO: MR F 74 41/2:21-22
Campbell gristmill: HO: MR O 72 39/10:20
Campbell manufacturing company: HO: MR Jl 73 40/7:21-22
Campbell mine structures: HO: MR Mr 75 42/3:27+
Campbell waterwheel grist mill & sluiceway: HO: RMC N 73 42/6:66-68
Con Cor grain elevator: N: MR Jl 74 41/7:20+
Con Cor pickle factory: HO: MR N 72 39/11:23
Con Cor slaughterhouse: N: MR Ag 75 42/8:23-24
Dyna-Model blacksmith shop: HO: RMC O 72 41/5:54
Dyna-Model slaughterhouse: HO: RMC F 74 42/9:66+
Dyna-Model stockyard & holding pens: HO: RMC N 73 42/6:71+
Faller water mill: HO: MW Ja 74 2/5:276
Fine Scale coal & fuel distributing facility: HO: RMC D 73 42/7:60+
Fine Scale fuel company: HO: MR Mr 73 40/3:20
Fine Scale coal bunker: HO: RMC D 71 40/7:60-61
Heljan pickle works & loading facility: HO: RMC Ja 74 42/8:61-62
Life-Like brick factory building: HO: RMC Ap 74 42/11:52+
Life-Like manufacturing building: HO: MR Mr 74 41/3:28-29
Life-Like operating log dump & mill: HO: RMC D 74 43/7:82+
Quality Craft factory: N: MR Ja 73 40/1:27
Quality Craft grain storage elevator: N: RMC D 74 43/7:78+
Quality Craft lumber company: HO: MR D 71 38/12:30; RMC Ag 72 41/3:55
Quality Craft modern warehouse: HO: RMC Jl 71 40/2:49-50
Quality Craft warehouse or factory: HO: MR Jl 71 38/7:26
Railhead grain elevator: N: MR Je 74 41/6:24-25

VI. Reviews 726

Railhead industrial building: N: MR F 74 41/2:23
Scale Structures oil loading facility: HO: RMC F 74 42/9:61-62
Suncoast concrete grain elevator: HO: RMC Je 72 41/1:53-54
Suydam Warehouse: HO: MR Jl 72 39/7:22-23
Timberline container warehouse: HO: MR Je 73 40/6:27-29
Timberline grain elevator: HO: MR Ja 73 40/1:34
Timberline Mine Structure: HO: MR Ap 73 40/4:24-25
Vau-Pe factory: HO: MR Ag 73 40/8:18-19
Vollmer freight warehouse: HO: MR Ja 71 38/1:34b
Vollmer oil refinery structures: HO: RMC Je 72 41/1:50
Wabash Valley grain elevator: HO: RMC Ap 73 41/11:54-55
Williams storage tank facility: HO: RMC Ja 72 40/8:56

Railroad Stations

AHM "Arlee" depot: N: RMC Mr 74 42/10:66
AHM combination station: N: MR Ap 74 41/4:25
AHM combination station: HO: MR Je 71 38/6:25-26
AHM freight station: HO: MR Je 75 42/6:16-17
AHM freight station & transfer shed: HO: RMC O 73 42/5:68+
AHM passenger station: HO: MR Ja 73 40/1:29-30
Campbell combination station: HO: RMC S 71 40/4:43-44
Campbell produce shed: HO: MR Ag 73 40/8:27
Campbell wayside freight station: HO: MR F 71 38/2:28+
Durango station: HO: MR O 75 42/10:34-35
Dyna-Model passenger station: RMC O 72 41/5:54-55
Fine Scale flagstop station: HO: MR Ag 72 39/8:21
Fine Scale truck or wagon terminal: HO: MR Ja 71 38/1:26
Fine Scale two-story combination station: HO: RMC Ag 74 43/2: 53-56
LeMay prefab freight station & loading dock: HO: MR F 74 41/2:30+
Lionel freight house: O: RMC Ap 75 43/11:68-69
Model Hobbies freight platform & passenger shelter: HO: RMC D 71 40/7:67-68
Revell/AHM freight station: HO: RMC N 73 42/6:75-76
"S"cenery flagstop station: S: MR F 73 40/2:20-21; RMC Ja 74 42/8:66+
Scale Structures Victorian station: HO: MR Jl 71 38/7:18-19
Suncoast freight house: O: MR Ap 73 40/4:26-27
Suncoast wood frame depot: O: RMC Ag 71 40/3:52-54
Timberline combination depot: HO: RMC N 75 44/6:73-75+
Vollmer old-time station: HO: RMC Je 73 42/1:50-51
Vollmer passenger station: HO: MR Mr 73 40/3:24; RMC F 74 42/9:57-58
Williams loading facility: HO: MR S 71 38/9:22-23; RMC S 71 40/4:45-46

Roundhouses, Sheds, etc.

Campbell handcar house & supply shed: HO: MR Ja 75 42/1:41; RMC O 72 41/5:54

Campbell one-stall engine house: HO: RMC N 75 44/6:81-82+
Con-Cor roundhouse: HO: MR My 73 40/5:21-23
Durango handcar shed: HO/HOn3 (handcar included): NSG N 75 1/5:8-9
Fine Scale car repair shop: HO: MR My 71 38/5:19-20; RMC My 71 39/12:52-54
Fine Scale roundhouse: HO: MR Je 74 41/6:18
Fine Scale two-stall engine house: HO: NSG S 75 1/4:7; RMC O 74 43/5:60+ ; RMC D 75 44/7:78+
Heljan enginehouse: O: MR D 75 42/12:35
JMC brick roundhouse: HO: RMC F 74 42/9:58-59
Mill-Scale freight car repair shed: N: MR Ja 71 38/1:28
Model Hobbies single-stall engine house: HO: RMC Jl 72 41/2:54+
Model Masterpieces Como roundhouse: HO: NSG Mr 75 1/1:14
San Juan Engineering engine house: O: NSG S 75 1/4:10
Scale Structures roundhouse: HO: MR S 73 40/9:19
Timberline enginehouse: HO: MR S 73 40/9:19

Shanty & Signal

AHM interlocking tower: HO: MR D 71 38/12:32-33; RMC F 72 40/9:54+ ; RMC Ag 72 41/3:54-55
Airfix interlocking or signal tower: OO: RMC N 73 42/6:69-70
Placer, Nevada & El Dorado shanty: O: MR My 73 40/5:31
Scale Structures crossing shanties: HO: MR My 74 41/5:26-28
Scale Structures Victorian crossing shanties: HO: RMC S 75 44/4: 62+
Vollmer signal tower: HO: MR D 72 39/12:39-40

Other

AHM church: HO: MR S 73 40/9:27-28; RMC D 74 43/7:71-72
AHM firehouse: HO: MR Mr 72 39/3:24
AHM single-stall firehouse: HO: RMC F 72 40/9:54+
Airfix control tower: 1/87: AI S 75 9/3:150-151; Afx Jl 75 16/11: 628; AN 30 My 75 3/16:13; Sc Jl 75 6/70:358
Bellona Niseen huts: 1/76: Afx N 72 14/3:162
Bellona Roman fort: 1/76: Afx N 72 14/3:162
Campbell country schoolhouse: HO: MR F 72 39/2:29+ ; RMC Ja 73 41/8:62-63
Campbell shed under construction: HO: RMC O 72 41/5:54
Campbell sheriff office: HO: MR Ag 71 38/8:24
Fujimi Uji-Byodoin Hooh-Do temple: 1/???: Sc Jl 71 2/7:379
Historical Scale fire station: HO: MR Mr 71 38/3:30
Historical Scale Miniatures Los Angeles Masonic Lodge: HO: RMC D 71 40/7:60-62
Modakit airfield control tower: 1/72: AN 27 O 72 1/12:13; Sc Je 73 4/6:423
Modakit Nissen hut: 1/72: Afx Ja 71 12/5:264; IM F 71 8/2:5-6; MM Mr 71 1/3:147-148; Sc Je 71 2/6:286+
Monte Enterprises Alamo: 1/120 cardstock: Sc Ja 72 3/1:52

Nanco police &' fire station: N: RMC Ag 72 41/3:56
Real Life sheriff's office & jail: HO: RMC Mr 71 38/10:59-60
Simpson portable lumber camp utility cabin: HO: RMC Ja 72 40/8: 66
Sugar Pine courthouse: HO: NSG S 75 1/4:10
Sugar Pine firehouse: HO: NSG S 75 1/4:10
Suncoast logging camp (house, derrick & cable house): HO: MR Ag 71 38/8:25-26; RMC N 71 40/6:56-57
Timberline "Boot Hill" graveyard: HO: RMC Ap 71 39/11:56+

Non-Buildings

Docks

Campbell wharf: HO: RMC Mr 71 38/10:56+

Water Tanks

Campbell northern water tank: HO: RMC D 73 42/7:58-60
Campbell water tank & tool shed: HO: MR Ap 73 40/4:21
Campbell wood water tank: HO: MR D 73 40/12:34+
Durango Q&TL water tank: HO: NSG S 75 1/4:6
Fine Scale water tank & toolshed: HO: MR D 74 41/12:31-32; RMC F 75 43/9:60+
Hetch Hetchy water tank: HO: NSG N 75 1/5:7
Model Hobbies water tank: HO: RMC Jl 71 40/2:52-53
Pacific Model water tank: HO: MR Ja 71 38/1:29+
Scale Structures water tank: HO: MR D 72 39/12:30
Simpson Pacific & Idaho Northern water tank: HO: NSG N 75 1/5:6
Simpson Rio Grande hillside water column: HO: RMC F 71 39/9: 62+
Vintage Diamond Springs water tank: HO: NSG Jl 75 1/3:7

Yard Structures

AHM coaling stage: HO: MR Mr 73 40/3:27
AHM coaling tower: HO: RMC Ag 73 42/3:54-55
AHM diesel servicing facilities: HO: MR Ja 74 41/1:22+
AHM sand & pump house with oil tank: HO: RMC D 74 43/7:75-76+
AHM sand house: HO & N: RMC My 71 39/12:54
AHM trackside maintenance buildings: HO: RMC Jl 74 43/2:58-59
Cannon engine oil facility: O: MR My 73 40/5:29-30
CaPart junkyard detail: HO: MR My 74 41/5:26
Grandt Line coal chute gate: O: MR My 73 40/5:27-28
Model Hobbies yard accessories: HO: several buildings: RMC Je 71 40/1:45
Scale Structures cinder conveyor: HO: MR Je 73 40/6:23-24

Scale Structures steel coaling tower: HO: MR Ag 73 40/8:23-24
Steward diesel locomotive facilities: N: MR F 72 39/2:19+; RMC O 72 41/5:61-62
Steward oil pumphouse & oil tank: N: MR My 72 39/5:21
Vintage Denver, South Park & Pacific coaling platform: HO: NSG Jl 75 1/3:6-7

Miscellaneous

AIM tunnel portals: HO: MR O 73 40/10:24-25; RMC Mr 74 42/10:60-61
Airfix station platform detail & people: HO: RMC Ja 74 42/8:70
Airfix telegraph poles & cable reels: OO: RMC N 73 42/6:68-69
Alexander Scale Models tunnel portal: N: RMC Ja 72 40/8:59
Brawa Powered Roadway Set: N: MR Je 71 38/6:24
Campbell timber tunnel portal: N: MR Mr 71 38/3:26-27; RMC Ap 71 39/11:58
Charles Brommer oiler: O: NSG Jl 75 1/3:6
Charles Brommer screw jacks: O: NSG S 75 1/4:6
Coffee Table stone tunnel portal: N: RMC Mr 72 40/10:60
Fine Scale signs for all scales: MR N 74 41/11:38+; RMC Je 75 44/1:54+
Keystone jill-poke log unloader: HO: RMC My 75 43/12:53-56
Keystone logging line detail: saws, axes, pevees: HO: NSG N 75 1/5:10
Mil-Scale snowsheds: HO & N: MR N 71 38/11:30-31
Model Hobbies phone boxes & poles: HO: RMC Ag 71 40/3:54
Mountain States telephone booth: O: MR N 75 42/11:39; NSG Jl 75 1/3:7
Phoenix Barrel Organ: 1/24 metal: Sc Je 75 6/69:300
Railhead Billboard: N: MR O 73 40/10:30
Revell Funfdekker: WW-I aircraft caricatures: Sc D 72 3/12:680
Röwa container crane: MR N 71 38/11:28-30
SS clutter details: station carts, etc.: HO: NSG My 75 1/2:8-9
Scenery Products wood tunnel portal: O: RMC Ap 71 39/11:61
Selley-Martin highway signs: O: RMC Ja 74 42/8:69-70
Selley-Martin pipe valves: RMC D 73 42/7:68
Selley-Martin vending machines: HO & O: RMC N 71 40/6:57-58
Stewart car washing facility: N: RMC My 73 41/12:54-56+
Tom Littlefield signs: NSG N 75 1/5:6
Tyco electric & telegraph poles: HO: MR F 73 40/2:26
Vollmer Overhead Traveling Crane: N: MR F 71 38/2:24

KIT REVIEWS (2)--OPERATING SCALE

AIRCRAFT

Surveys

Scale Kit Guide: RC Ja 73 10/1:38-39

Free Flight

Graupner Junior: A-1: Aero Je 74 39/461:316-318
Guillow Ju-87B Stuka: r scale: FM Ag 71 413:30-32
Keilkraft Aquarius: A-2: Aero F 73 38/445:80-81
Kelston Swift: towline trainer: Aero Ag 75 40/475:787-788
Mattel SuperStar: e ARF: Aero D 72 37/443:686-687
Midwest Super Sniffer Sportster: $\frac{1}{2}$A old timer: FM Ja 72 418:45-47
Performance Kits Wasp Wings: A sport: Aero Mr 73 38/446:152-153
RAI Buzzard Bombshell: C old timer: FM My 71 410:54-55
Sig Cub: r trainer: FM F 71 407:30-31

Control Line

Cox Super Stunter: $\frac{1}{2}$A RTF trainer: AM O 74 77/4:84
Dumas Smoothie: C stunt: Aero Je 75 40/473:336-337
Mick Tiernan Anduril: A FAI combat: Aero Ap 75 40/471-472:214-215
Midwest P-51 Mustang: B/C stunt trainer: FM Ap 71 409:42-44
Midwest P-63 King Cobra: C sport-stunt profile: Aero Ag 74 39/463:414-415
Midwest Snorky: B trainer: MAN Ap 72 2/4:17-19+
Pegasus Models Warlord: C combat: Aero Jl 72 37/438:387-388
Pegasus Models Minilord: $\frac{1}{2}$A combat: Aero My 73 48/448:260-261
Scientific Little Mercury: $\frac{1}{2}$A trainer: FM D 71 417:42-43
Sig Super Chipmunk: C stunt: FM Ag 74 77/8:28-30
Sterling Eindecker: $\frac{1}{2}$A trainer: MAN O 71 83/4:14-15+
Sterling Thunderjet: $\frac{1}{2}$A trainer: MAN O 71 83/4:14-15+
Sterling Piper Cub: $\frac{1}{2}$A trainer: MAN O 71 83/4:14-15+

Radio Control

ARF

Carol Craft Splinter: C III: AM Jl 71 73/1:27+
Casburn Fun-Fli: C III: RC Ag 71 8/8:6+
Dee Bee Eyeball: C III: MAN Ap 71 82/4:46-47+
Hobby Lobby Ready Bird 23: B II: RC Ag 73 10/8:51-52+
Lanier Colt: C III: AM Mr 72 74/3:18+ ; FM F 72 419:38-40
Lanier Invader: C III: MAN D 73 87/6:47-49+
MRC Cessna Cardinal: C III: AM O 74 74/10:85; RCS Jl 75 1/3: 50+
Pilot Box Fly: B II: MAN F 73 84/2:34-36+ ; RC F 73 10/2:52+
Pilot Cavalier: C III: MAN Ag 71 83/2:34-37+
Pilot Cherokee: A/B II: RC N 71 8/11:42
Pilot Five Star: C III: AM Jl 72 75/1:18+ ; FM Ap 72 421:34-35
Pilot Super Star: C III: AM O 74 74/10:83
Reddi-Flite Dragon Fli: C III: AM Ja 72 74/1:52+

Gliders

Airtronics Aquila: II: RC D 75 12/12:45
Astro-Flight Monterey: II slope/thermal: FM O 71 415:40-41
Astro-Flight AWS-17: II thermal: FM D 74 77/12:46-47; MAN Jl 74 89/1:38-40; RC Ap 74 11/4:62-63; RC F 75 12/2:53
Ace High: ½A pod I sport: MAN Ap 72 84/4:37-39+
Airtronic Grand Esprit: II spoilers thermal: MAN Je 73 86/6:37-39+ ; RC Ag 75 12/8:83
Airtronics Mini-Olympic: II slope: RC N 71 12/11:59-62+
Airtronics Super Questor: RC F 75 12/2:36
Beltz Pokey 808: II: MAN D 75 91:6:47-49
Canyon Schweizer 1-26: II ARF: AM Je 71 72/6:19+ ; FM Jl 71 412:30-31; MAN Jl 71 83/2:41-43+
Craft-Air Drifter: II: RC Ja 75 12/1:62-63
Cecil Haga Legion Air: II spoilers, competition: RC Ap 75 12/4: 49+
Competition Models Easy Riser: II: RC N 75 12/11:81
Dodgson Todi: II CAR flaps slope/thermal; aerobatic: AM Mr 75 75/3:61+ ; RC O 72 9/10:78+
Dumas Hi-Pro: II thermal: AM Jl 74 78/7:37
Earl Wolsleger ASW-15: II scale: RCS Jl 75 1/3:50
Graupner Cumulus 2800: II: AM N 73 77/5:64; FM N 71 416:40-42
Graupner Hi-Fly: II: AM S 74 78/9:49
Glasflugel 604: II thermal: RC Jl 74 11/7:52+
Haga Legion-Air: II spoilers, thermal: RCS Ag 75 1/4:74+
Hobie Hawk: II competition: AM Je 74 78/6:51; MAN S 75 91/3: 49+ ; RC Ap 75 12/4:59+
Hobie Hawk (pre-production): RC Ap 74 11/4:52-53
House of Balsa Nomad: I sport: RC F 74 11/2:43+
House of Balsa Nomad Two: II: RC O 75 12/10:105+
J&J American Eagle: I thermal: FM Ag 72 75/8:44-45

VI. Reviews

JEF's Friends Western Wind: II sport: RC Ag 75 12/8:55
JP Dart: II thermal: FM O 72 75/10:32-33; RC Ja 73 10/1:57+
JP Javelin: II thermal: MAN Ag 74 89/2:47-49+ ; RC D 74 11/12: 29
MALco Eagle: II spoilers: MAN Ag 75 91/2:39-41+
MS Avatar 72: I slope/thermal: RC O 72 9/10:50-51; RCS S 75 1/5:26+
MS Curio: II: RC Mr 75 12/3:37
Mark's Models Windfree: II thermal: AM F 74 78/2:64
Model Dynamics Gryphon: II flying wing: AM Ag 74 78/8:41+ ; RC S 71 8/9:58-61
Multiplex E-1: twin e with folding props, sport: MAN Je 75 90/6: 38-40
Peerless-Kyosho Cirrus 3000: II sport: RC Ag 75 12/8:60
Performance Flight Systems Rubber Ducky: II/III sport: RC N 75 12/11:55+
Pierce Arrow: II sport: RC Ja 75 12/1:44-45+
Pilot Thermul: A/B pod II thermal/slope: AM Je 73 76/6:64; FM N 71 416:40-42
Pro-Model Apollo: II V-tail: RC Mr 75 12/3:44
Soarcraft Diamant: II optional spoilers: RCS O 75 1/6:70
Soarcraft Libelle: II scale: RC S 73 10/9:38+
Southwest Sailplanes Doodler: II thermal: RC D 72 9/12:62+
Superior Boss-T: II CAR flaps: RC Ja 75 12/1:56-57
Svenson Schleicher K8B: II scale/thermal: FM Mr 71 408:44-46
T&H Gull: II spoiler: RC Je 74 11/6:61+
T&H Hi Jacker: II CAR: RC N 75 12/11:84
Zaic Eastwind: II thermal: RCS Jl 75 1/3:79

Helicopters

Aristo-Craft Hegi DS-22 Enstrom: C: MAN N 73 87/5:47-49+
Du-Bro Hughes 500: D: FM S 73 76/9:42-45; MAN My 73 86/5:37-39+
Du-Bro Shark: D: FM Ja 75 78/1:26-29
Du-Bro Tri-Star: C, interchangeable fuselages (Hughes 500, Scorpion, Shark): RC My 75 12/5:56-59; RCS N 75 1/7:66
Du-Bro Whirlybird 505: B: AM N 72 75/5:17+ ; FM D 72 75/12: 41-43; MAN S 72 85/3:42-43+
Graupner Bell 212 Twin Jet: C: MAN Ja 74 88/1:47-50+
Kalt Bell Huey Cobra: C: AM My 73 76/5:52; FM F 73 76/2:47-50
Lenco 100: C: MAN Ag 74 89/4:35-37+
MRC Heli-Baby: C: RCS S 75 1/5:27+
MRC/Kavan Bell Jet Ranger: C: AM N 73 77/5:64; FM Jl 74 77/ 7:40-42; MAN S 73 87/3:36-38
Micro-Mold Lark: A/B: RCS Jl 75 1/3:51+

Pylon Racers

Ace Upstart: $\frac{1}{2}$A II $\frac{1}{2}$A pylon: MAN Mr 72 84/3:46-48+

Francis Product Shark: C II formula 1: MAN Mr 72 84/3:39-40
House of Balsa Shoestring: A II quarter midget: MAN F 75 90/2: 38+
JEM Quick One: B/C III sport pylon: AM S 74 78/9:49
Miss Dara: C II (s&e) formula 1: AM Ag 73 77/2:56
Models West Two-Bits: A III quarter midget trainer: RC Je 74 11/6:60+
Prather Little Toni: C III formula 1: AM Mr 75 75/3:60+; MAN Jl 75 91/1:41-43+; RC D 75 12/12:87; RCS Ag 75 1/4:74-75
RC Kits F8F: A II quarter midget: AM F 74 75/2:64
Sky-Glas Fabricators Miss Cosmic Wind: quarter midget: FM D 75 78/12:23-27
Spickler Aeromodels Quickie 500: C II quickie 500: MAN My 75 90/5:42-44+; RC S 75 12/9:52

Scale & Semi-Scale

Aero Precision AT-6 Texan: C III scale: FM S 74 77/9:23-25
Aerotec Albatros D. Va: semi: FM Ap 72 421:54-55
Astro-Flight RF-4 Fournier: A II semi: MAN Ja 72 84/1:47-49+
Bob Holman Pitts Special: C/D III scale: RCS S 75 1/5:27
Concept Models Fleet 1930: C III scale: RCS N 75 1/7:64
D&B P-51 Mustang: C III rLG scale: MAN D 74 89/6:42-44+
Dave Platt Spitfire: C III rLG semi: RC F 75 12/2:54
Dave Platt T-28: C III scale: FM Je 75 78/6:40-44
Flite-Glas P-51 Mustang: C III rLG flaps, scale: MAN Ag 73 87/2:47-49+
Flyline Curtiss Robin: $\frac{1}{2}$A II scale: RCS O 75 1/6:69
Goldberg Skylark: twin B III semi: RC Jl 71 8/7:6+
Hand Crafted Me-109: C III semi: FM Jl 73 76/7:24-25
Hot Line Comanche: C III semi: MAN Ag 72 85/2:35-37+
Hot Line Mooney Chapparel: C III rLG scale: MAN My 71 82/5: 34-37+
Kyosho AD-6 Skyraider: C III semi: MAN D 71 83/6:35-37+
Midwest P-63 King Cobra: semi: MAN F 75 90/2:26-27+
Midwest Pitts Special: C III biplane semi: MAN O 75 91/4:52-54+; RC D 75 12/12:63+
Midwest Super Chipmunk: A/B III ARF semi: AM O 73 77/4:38; RC Ap 73 10/4:50-51+
Royal Cessna 310G: twin C III semi: AM Ap 74 78/4:40
Royal Fw 190A: C III scale: AM F 74 78/2:66
Royal Oscar: C III scale: MAN Mr 73 86/3:35-37+
Royal Victor P-68: twin C III scale or semi: RCS N 75 1/7:65
Sig Kwik Built Chipmunk: C III semi: AM S 74 78/9:48
Sig Ryan STA: C III flaps, scale: MAN O 72 85/4:36-38+
Sig Yak 18: C III scale: RC Ja 71 8/1:12+
Soarcraft Libelle: g II scale: RC S 73 10/9:38+
Span Aero J-3 Piper Cub: C III scale: MAN N 72 85/5:42-43+
Stafford Sperry Messenger: C III scale: AM Je 74 78/6:50
Sterling Fokker D. VII: C III semi: AM D 72 75/6:18+
Sure Flight Aeronca Champ: A II semi: RCS O 75 1/6:71
Sureflight P-39 Aircobra: A/B III semi: RC Ag 75 12/8:75

VI. Reviews 734

Top Flite P-39 Airacobra: C III semi: AM Jl 74 78/7:36
Top Flite P-40 Warhawk: C II semi: MAN Ja 73 86/1:45-47+
Top Flite P-51 Mustang: C III semi: AM My 72 74/5:14+; FM Ag 72 75/8:44-45
Top Flite SE-5a: C III semi: AM F 74 77/2:66+
VK Corben Super Ace: C II CAR/III semi: AM Ja 74 78/1:36; RC O 74 89/4:55
Westcoast Phantom II: C III scale: FM F 75 78/2:30-32

Sport

Ace Pacer: ½A/A II a&e: RC Ap 75 12/4:66+
Astro Flite Bushmaster: e II: RCS Ap 75 1/1:6
Casburn Super Lucky Fly: C III: RC Ap 75 12/4:67
Chuck Gill Powerhouse: C II, conversion of old timer free flight: RC N 75 12/11:83+
Competition Models Paper Tiger: C III: MAN Ap 71 82/4:40-41+
Fibre Foam Mini-Stick: A III: RC D 73 10/12:52-53
Gee Bee Mallard: B II flying boat: RC D 74 11:54-55
Goldberg Skylark: twin B III: RC Jl 71 8/7:6+
Hobby Shack Citabria: ½A/A II: RC F 75 12/2:37
King Wavemaster: C III flying boat: RC Ag 73 10/8:54+
Kraft Wingmaster: C II flying wing: AM Ja 74 78/1:36; MAN F 74 88/2:35-37; RC S 73 10/9:48+
MRC Cessna 177: C III: MAN Mr 75 90/3:50-52+; RC N 74 11/11:32-33
Midwest Cardinal Squire: C III: RC F 75 12/2:55
Midwest Strikemaster: B/C III: FM Mr 75 78/3:34-36
Midwest Sweet Stick: B/C III: AM Ag 73 77/2:56
Mile High Joy Stick: ½A II: RC D 75 12/12:83
Model Dynamics Shriek: B/C II flying wing: AM Ag 74 78/8:41+; MAN N 74 89/5:44-46+; RC Jl 73 10/7:44-47+
Ralvin J-Bipe: C III biplane: FM S 75 78/9:31-34
Rand Little Hawk: A/B III: MAN Jl 71 83/1:35-37+; RC N 71 8/11:42-43
Senior Telemaster: C III: RC Ap 73 10/4:46-47+
Shell Fly: C III: AM O 71 73/4:52+
SkyGlas A6 Intruder: C III: AM Ja 73 76/1:20+
Southern Bobcat: B/C III: FM My 74 76/5:43-45
Stafford Weekender: C III: MAN D 72 85/6:36-38
Strato 210: C III: MAN N 73 87/5:38-40+
Sure Flite Aeronca Champ: A II: RCS O 75 1/6:71
Texas Models Big Daddy: C III: MAN S 72 85/3:34-36+
Top Flite Contender: C II: FM Ja 71 406:38-39
Warehouse Systems Strato 210: B/C III: AM 74 78/4:42

Stunt

Ace Whizard: ½A II: MAN Ja 75 90/1:47+
Airborne Associates Hi-Lo: C III rLG: AM Mr 73 76/3:50; MAN Je 73 86/6:43-45+

Airborne Associates Nutcracker: C III: AM S 73 77/3:76
Airborne Associates Phoenix-six: C III rLG: MAN Ja 75 90/1:38-40+
Airborne Associates Troublemaker: C III: MAN S 74 89/3:41-43+
Airtronics Acro-Star: C III biplane: AM Ap 74 78/4:40; MAN Je 74 88/6:36-38+
Allied Hobbies Integra: C III rLG: MAN D 75 91/6:39-41+ ; RC Ap 75 12/8:48
Better Built Super Cuda: C III: AM Jl 74 78/7:37
Bridi Super Kaos: C III: MAN Ag 75 91/2:43-45+
Casburn Super Lucky Fly: C III: RC Ap 75 12/4:67
FliteGlas Gladiator: C III: AM Ja 74 78/1:34
Flite Line Skooter II: B/C II: MAN Je 72 84/6:41-43
G. B. Glas Products Lightning B: C III: RCS Jl 75 1/3:51+
Hobby Shack Spinks Acromaster: B/C III: AM Ag 74 78/8:40
Hobby Enterprises Kaos: C III: MAN F 72 84/2:38-41+
J&J Banshee: C III: MAN My 73 86/5:43-45
J&J Eyeball: C III: MAN Je 71 82/6:38-40+
J&J Trouble Maker: C III: FM Ap 74 77/4:38-40
MRC Blue Angel: C III rLG: MAN Ap 74 88/4:38-40+
Midwest Mach 1: C III rLG: MAN Jl 73 87/1:38-40+
Midwest Pitts Special: C III biplane: MAN O 75 91/4:52-54+
Mini-Flite Cutlass Supreme: C III rLG: MAN O 73 78/4:37-39+
PB Products T2-A: C III rLG: MAN Mr 74 88/3:35-37+
Pro-Line Competition Six: C: AM Mr 74 76/3:50
Sig Komet with Goldberg retracts: C III rLG: AM F 73 76/2:16+
Southern Tiger Tail: C III: AM Mr 74 78/3:44; MAN Ja 73 86/1:35-37+
Svenson Wayfarer: C III biplane: AM Je 74 78/6:50; RC D 73 10/12:45-46+
Top Flite Contender: C III: MAN Mr 72 82/3:38-40+
Top Flite Nobler: C III: MAN F 71 82/2:37-39+
World Engines Hawk 460: C III: MAN Ap 73 86/4:36-38+

Trainer

Bridi Basic Trainer: B III: MAN O 74 89/4:53-55+
Bridi Dart Cart: C III: MAN O 74 89/4:42-44
Bridi T-20: A III: RCS Ap 75 1/1:6-7
Cam-Craft (Midwest in U.S.) Easy Flyer: C III: RCS Ag 75 1/4:75+
Custom Models Primer: B III: AM N 73 77/5:60
Dee Bee Cardinal: B II: AM Ag 71 73/2:53+ ; MAN Ja 72 84/1:36-38+
Goldberg Ranger 42: e/$\frac{1}{2}$A/A I/II/III: RCS Ap 75 1/1:5-6
Hot Line Sierra: C III: FM Ja 73 10/8:51-52+
J-Craft: C III: AM Je 72 74/6:14+
Micro-Flite Hoss Fly: B III: RC Ja 75 12/1:52-53
Midwest Cessna Cardinal: $\frac{1}{2}$A/A III: RC F 75 12/2:63
Mini-Flite A.T.: B III: RC Mr 75 12/3:45
Pilot Junior Box Fly: B/C III: AM Ap 73 76/4:34; RC F 73 10/2:52

VI. Reviews 736

RC Kits Acro Trainer: C III: FM F 75 78/2:45-47
Sterling Fledgling: D/C III: FM Ap 73 76/5:43-45
Sterling Gazariator: C III: MAN Je 75 90/6:46-48+ ; RC Ap 75 12/4:52-55+ ; RC My 75 12/5:60-61+
Sterling SL-62 Lancer: C III stunt trainer: AM D 73 77/6:70; FM O 75 78/10:24-26
Strato 210: C III stunt trainer: MAN N 73 87/5:38-40+
Tidewater Pronto: e/A/B II: AM Ag 74 78/8:40; FM Jl 75 78/7: 48-50; RC D 72 9/12:56-57+
Timely Models Chili Pepper: B/C II: RC F 75 12/2:49

ARMOR

Tamiya Sherman RCT: 1/16 scale tank: MAN O 75 91/4:39-41+ ; RC S 75 12/9:54-55+

AUTOMOBILES--Radio Control

Aristo Craft Fuji Motorcycle: B: MAN Ap 73 86/4:38-40+
Curtis Car: B: AM My 71 72/5:52+
Delta Dash II SL: B: AM D 73 77/6:68
Jerobee Comando: $\frac{1}{2}$A: MAN Jl 72 85/1:40-42; RC F 71 8/2:32-33+
Jerobee .049 Fast & Fun: $\frac{1}{2}$A McLaren: AM D 71 73/6:42+
Kyosho McLarrcn Mk 8A: B: MAN My 71 82/5:46-47+
Kyosho racing cycle with side car: A: RCS S 75 1/5:26+
MCE Sidewinder Indy Wedge: B: AM Ap 71 72/4:49+ ; MAN Ja 71 82/1:39-40
Mach 12 RC: $\frac{1}{2}$A: AM Jl 73 77/1:68

BOATS--Radio Control

Power

Dumas Atlas Van Lines Hydroplane: $\frac{1}{2}$A & C var scale hydroplane: FM My 73 76/5:50
Dumas Deep Vee 400: C: FM My 74 77/5:63-65
Dumas Li'l Swamp Buggy: $\frac{1}{2}$A I air drive: AM Mr 75 75/3:61
Dumas SKdaddle 20: C ski boat: AM N 71 73/5:40+
Dumas Wood Deep Vee 60: C ski boat: FM O 75 78/10:62-64
Ed Fisher Li'l Northwind: B hydroplane: FM O 74 77/10:62-64
Fibo Craft Sport Fishing Skiff: e/A sport: FM Ag 74 77/8:64-65
Hughey Li'l Hughey: B hydroplane: MAN My 74 88/5:38-40+
JVS Hydro: B hydroplane: FM Ja 75 78/1:62-63
Mini-Flite MiniVee: B runabout: FM Ap 74 77/4:64-65

Octura White Heat 4-60: C hydroplane: MAN My 72 84/5:41-43+
Octura Wildcat Tunnel Hull: C hydroplane: FM D 75 78/12:59-61; MAN N 75 91/5:78/12:59-61
Precision Boat Crapshooter: C hydroplane: FM Ap 75 78/4:59-61
Schuco-Hegi submarine: e submergable: FM F 75 78/2:63
Scientific Sport Fisherman: e sport scale: FM Mr 75 78/3:62-63
3D Models Hustler: C hydroplane: FM Jl 75 78/7:63-65

Sail

Graupner Optimist: MB My 71 21/245:202-203+
Peerless/Kyosho Newport: FM Je 75 78/6:59-61
Shadow Yachts Shadow: 50/800 class: FM N 75 78/11:59-60
Vortex SB-1: MAN F 72 84/2:47-49+
Vortex Soling M: Soling class: AM Jl 74 78/7:36; FM Mr 73 76/3:29-31; MAN Ag 73 87/2:36-38+

RAILROAD

Range Reviews

Amro HOn2½ European narrow gauge trains: RMC Ja 72 40/8:56-58
Graham Farish coaches: N: Afx Je 72 13/10:574
LGB 1:22.5 Scale Railways: Gm: Afx O 71 13/2:96
Rivarossi HO: Afx N 71 13/3:169
Rivarossi O Gauge Equipment: Afx Ja 72 13/5:281
Ye Olde Huff-n-Puff Old Time freight cars: HO: MR My 71 38/5:20-21

Complete Trains

BART Models BART train: HO: MR Ag 74 41/8:16-17
Märklin passenger train: Z: MR Ja 74 41/1:27-28
Nickel Plate Zephyr 9900: 3 unit streamliner: MR O 72 39/10:28-30
Stewart Products Mine Train Set: overhead electric & 3 dump cars: Hon3, Sn27", or On20": MR Je 71 38/6:21

European Rolling Stock

Graham-Parish N gauge van: Afx Je 71 12/10:543

Lilliput Modelbahn Deutsche Bundesbahn class T-38 4-6-0: HO:
 RMC Ag 72 41/3:62
Peco LMS brake van: N: Afx Ap 73 14/8:452+
Three Aitch wagon: O: Afx My 71 12/9:489

Freight Cars

(Boxcars)

AHM boxcar: O: MR Ja 71 38/1:34+
AHM 50' double door boxcar: HO: RMC Mr 72 40/10:56-57
AHM 40' steel boxcar: O: RMC Ja 71 39/8:64+
AHM Southern all-door boxcar: HO: RMC Ja 73 41/8:70
AHM ventilated boxcar: HO: RMC O 73 42/5:67-68
Alamosa Car Shop/Tomalco D&RGW 3000 series box car: HOn3:
 NSG S 75 1/4:9
Ambroid aircraft component boxcar: HO: RMC Ja 72 40/8:66+
Ambroid Burlington 60' insulated boxcar: HO: MR Jl 71 38/7:19
Ambroid ribbed-side boxcar: HO: MR N 71 38/11:34-35
American Tortoise high-cube boxcar: MR F 75 42/2:31-32
Atherarn 40' grainloading boxcar: HO: RMC Ja 71 39/8:62-63
Atlas boxcar: O: MR My 72 39/5:24
Atlas Hy-Cube boxcar: N: RMC F 71 39/9:64-65
Atlas L&N 40' boxcar: O: RMC My 72 40/12:56
Blackhawk boxcar: HO: MR Ap 74 41/4:20-21
Con Cor boxcar: N: RMC My 72 40/12:58
Coronado boxcar: On3: MR Ja 71 38/1:32-33
East Penn Southern all-door boxcar: O: MR Ja 72 39/1:30; RMC
 Ja 73 41/8:63-64
Kadee boxcar: N: MR Jl 73 40/7:24-25; MR Jl 75 42/7:26+
Kadee double door boxcar: N: MR O 73 40/10:24-25
Kadee 1½ door, double-sheathed boxcar: N: RMC Ap 75 43/11:
 64+
Kadee 1½ door, outside braced boxcar: N: RMC Ap 75 43/11:64+
Kadee single-door, double sheathed boxcar: N: RMC Ap 75 43/11:
 64+
Kadee steel boxcar: N: RMC Ja 74 42/8:57+
Kar-Line New England boxcars: HO: RMC Mr 72 40/10:56-57
Kar-Line Rutland steel boxcar: HO: RMC F 73 41/9:62-63
Kris Col. Carstens 40' boxcar: O: RMC N 71 40/6:62
Kris "Shalom" boxcar: O: RMC Ja 72 40/8:58
LaBelle Old Time boxcar: HO: MR F 71 38/2:27
Life-like thrall door boxcar: HO: MR N 75 42/11:34+
Lykens Valley baby hy-cube boxcar: O: RMC Mr 71 38/10:58-59
Nickel Plate automobile boxcar: HO: MR N 73 40/11:29
Poly Mold Maine boxcar: HOn2: RMC My 72 40/12:57
Prototype 40' boxcar: HO: MR Ag 75 42/8:26
Quality Craft box car: N: MR Ja 73 40/1:27
Quality Craft 90' Vert-A-Pac auto car: HO: MR Ag 71 38/8:21-22
Quality Craft UP high cube boxcar: O: MR O 71 38/10:22-23

Quality Craft Weyerhaeuser all-door boxcar: N: RMC F 75 43/9: 66-68
Quality Craft Weyerhaeuser all-plug-door boxcar: HO: RMC Mr 72 40/10:58
Rail Line D&RGW 3000 series box car: HOn3: NSG N 75 1/5:6
Sandy River Car Shops SR&RL box car: On2: NSG S 75 1/4:8
Suncoast Santa Fe panel boxcar: HO: MR My 71 38/5:25-26; RMC S 71 40/4:46+
Train-Miniature Centennial boxcars: HO: MR N 74 41:11:29
Train Miniatures 50-ton ARA boxcars: HO: RMC Ap 73 41/11:62+
Train-Miniature 40' boxcar: HO: MR Mr 73 40/3:24-25
US Hobbies 50' boxcar: O: MR Ap 71 38/4:23-24
US Hobbies 50' plug door boxcar: O: MR Ja 72 39/1:30
Walthers Waffle-side boxcar: O: MR N 72 39/11:30+
Ye Old Huff-n-Puff truss-rod boxcar: HO: MR D 71 38/12:30

(Cabooses)

AHM Chessie caboose: HO: RMC Je 74 43/1:57
AHM extended vision cupola caboose: HO: RMC N 72 41/6:70
Ambroid NKP wood caboose: HO & O: RMC My 73 41/12:54-56+
Atherarn Extended-Vision Caboose: HO: MR Ag 73 40/8:19-20
Atlas Caboose: O: MR F 72 39/2:32+
Atlas 4-wheel caboose: O: MR Ja 73 40/1:28
Car Shop C&O wood caboose: HO: MR S 74 41/9:18d+
Car Shop brass caboose: HO: RMC N 73 42/6:65-66
Gem IC wood caboose: HO: RMC S 72 41/4:56-57
Hallmark drover's caboose: HO: MR S 74 41/9:26+
Hallmark wood caboose: HO: MR N 74 41/11:34
Kadee wood caboose: N: MR N 75 42/11:28-29; RMC N 75 44/6: 86
Nickel Plate brass O&W caboose: HO: RMC Je 72 41/1:56
Nickel Plate brass Soo Line caboose: HO: RMC N 72 41/6:77
Nickel Plate caboose: HO: MR Jl 72 39/7:23-24; MR N 73 40/11: 38+
Nickel Plate "Eastern" steel caboose: HO: RMC F 74 42/9:64+
Nickel Plate Milwaukee bay window caboose: HO: RMC Je 74 43/ 1:50
Nickel Plate Reading caboose: HO: MR S 73 40/9:22
Nickel Plate Soo Line caboose: HO: MR N 72 39/11:34-35
Pacific Fast Mail narrow-gauge caboose: HOn3: MR O 75 42/10: 26
Quality Craft East Broad Top caboose: HOn3: RMC Ap 75 43/11: 59+
Quality Craft wood caboose: O: MR S 75 42/9:24
Springtown "Eastern" steel caboose: O: RMC S 75 44/4:77

(Flat Cars)

AHM flatcar: O: MR Ag 71 38/8:24-25
Athearn 85' trailer flatcar with containers: HO: MR My 71 38/5: 22-23

VI. Reviews 740

Kadee flatcar: N: RMC Ap 75 43/11:64+
Keystone Locomotive log car: HO: RMC My 74 42/12:57-59
Liberty Models wood flatcar: O: MR Mr 73 40/3:26; RMC O 73 42/5:63-65
Robb Flatcar: HOn3: MR Ag 71 38/8:26-27
Quality Craft 64' bulkhead flat car: HO, O: MR Ja 71 38/1:26
Scale Craft bulkhead flatcar: HO: MR Je 72 39/6:23; RMC F 72 40/9:60
Scale Craft 68' finger rack flatcar: HO: MR N 71 38/11:31-32
Scale Railway Monson two-foot gauge flatcar: On2: RMC D 72 41/7:66-67
Scale Railway 2' flat car: On2: RMC Je 74 43/1:53-54
Scotia Scale truss-rod flatcar: HO: MR My 72 39/5:26-27
Simpson Products flat car: O: RMC Jl 71 40/2:52
Tomalco idler flatcar: On3: MR Je 74 41/6:23-24
Walthers circus flatcar: O: RMC Jl 72 41/2:58+

(Gondolas)

AHM gondola: O: RMC Ja 71 39/8:64+
Atlas Great Northern 52' gondola: O: RMC My 72 40/12:56
Kadee gondola: N: RMC Ap 75 43/11:64+; add My 75 43/12:52
Prototype gondola: HO: MR Ag 71 38/8:25
Quality Craft bathtub gondola: HO: MR Ag 73 40/8:28-29
Robb drop-bottom gondola: HOn3: MR D 73 40/12:28-29
Simpson Products gondola: O: RMC Jl 71 40/2:52
Suncoast MoPac 45' gondola: HO & O: RMC O 75 44/5:78-79
Tomalco D&RG gondola: HOn3: RMC Jl 74 43/2:54-55
Valley Works high-side gondola: On3: MR Je 71 38/6:25
Walthers open-side gondola: O: MR D 72 39/12:37-38
Wisconsin Central gondola: S: MR F 74 41/2:26-28

(Hoppers)

AHM covered hopper: HO: MR Ag 75 42/8:27-28
Ambroid three-bay hopper: HO & O: RMC Ag 75 44/3:56
Athearn hopper, 34', 3 side vars: MR O 73 40/10:27-29
Athearn open top twin hopper: HO: RMC S 73 42/4:62-63
Athearn Pullman-Standard 54' covered hopper: HO: MR Je 71 38/6:24-25
Atlas triple hopper: N: MR S 75 42/9:28-29; RMC N 75 44/6:88-89
Con-Cor hopper car: N: RMC My 72 40/12:58
MRC twin hopper: N: RMC D 71 40/7:66
Model Die Casting drop-bottom sand & gravel hopper: HO: MR S 74 41/9:20+; RMC Je 74 43/1:50-51
Quality Craft coal hopper: O: MR Mr 72 39/3:25+
Ulrich Triple hopper: HO: MR Ag 73 40/8:25-26

Kit--Operating

(Mine & Ore Cars)

Atlas ore car: O: MR O 72 39/10:24+; RMC Ja 73 41/8:64-65
Grandt Line mine car & track: Sn1½: MR Mr 73 40/3:22-23
Grandt Line ore car: On2: MR Ja 72 39/1:29-30
Scale Structures mine car: HO: MR N 71 38/11:28

(Reefers)

Ambroid modern refrigerator car: HO: RMC Ap 71 39/11:58-59
Ambroid Olympis beer refrigerator car: O: MR Je 75 42/6:27-28
Ambroid refrigerator car: HO: MR Ap 73 40/4:20-21
Ambroid 36' refrigerator car: HO: RMC O 75 44/5:82+
Con Cor Budweiser beer reefer: HO: RMC Je 71 40/1:49
Con Cor refrigerator car: N: MR O 72 39/10:22; RMC My 72 40/12:58
Model Die Casting 50' express refrigerator car: HO: MR F 71 38/2:22; RMC Ap 71 39/11:59-60
Model Die Casting truss-rod beer reefer: HO: RMC Ag 72 41/3:56+
Roanoke Shops beer reefer: HO: RMC S 71 40/4:44
Simpson D&RGW refrigerator car: On3: NSG N 75 1/5:6
Tomalco refrigerator car: HOn3 & On3: MR D 71 38/12:42
Train-Miniature double-sheathed wood 40' reefer: HO: MR Ja 73 40/1:35
Train-Miniature "Wine-Maker" reefer: HO: RMC Mr 72 40/10:54
Walthers mechanical reefer: HO: MR F 73 40/2:19-20

(Special Purpose)

AHM integral-cover steel-coil car: MR O 72 39/10:20+
AHM United States Railway Equipment 100-ton coil car: HO: RMC Ja 73 41/8:70-71
Buckeye Pollock hot metal car: HO: MR Je 73 42/1:58
Keystone log car: HOn3: NSG N 75 1/5:10
Keystone log car: O: RMC Ja 72 40/8:62-63
Walthers barrel & wooden ware car: O: MR O 72 39/10:23-24

(Stockcars)

AHM bi-level stock car: HO: RMC F 72 40/9:62
Atlas stockcar: N: RMC F 71 39/9:64-65
Kadee despatch stockcar: N: MR O 74 41/10:23-24
Train-Miniature stockcar: HO: MR Ap 74 41/4:28-29
Train-Miniature wood stock car: HO: RMC Ap 72 40/11:56-57
Tomalco stockcar: Sn3: MR Jl 73 40/7:22-23
Wisconsin Central stockcar: S: MR Jl 72 39/7:22

(Tank Cars)

Lee Town B&SR tank car bodies: On2: RMC Je 72 41/1:54+
MRC 3-dome tank car: N: RMC D 71 40/7:66
Narrow Gauge Car Shop 3' gauge tank car: HOn3: RMC N 74 43/6:68-69
Nickel Plate milk tank car: HO: MR Ja 74 41/1:34+
Rio Grande Westside Lumber tank car: ??: NSG Mr 75 1/1:14-15
Scale Railway Tank Car: On2: RMC Je 74 43/1:53-54
Westside narrow-gauge tank car: On3: MR Je 75 42/6:30-31
Wisconsin Central tank car: S: MR Mr 74 41/3:25-26

Non-Revenue & Special

AHM track-cleaning car: HO: RMC Ag 72 41/3:60
AHM work car: HO: RMC Ja 74 42/8:62-63
Al Ellis velocipede: O: MR D 75 42/12:38
Athearn museum car "Fredon": HO: RMC Ag 73 42/3:55-56
Custon Brass NKP dynamometer car: HO: RMC Ag 74 43/2:58+
Durango Handcar: HO: MR Ja 74 41/1:34; NSG Jl 75 1/3:9; RMC Mr 75 43/10:62+
Durango Handcar: On3: MR N 74 41/11:42
Hallmark Santa Fe dynamometer car: HO: MR Mr 74 41/3:22-23; RMC Ja 74 42/8:59-60
Nickel Plate rotary snowplow: HO: MR My 72 39/5:22-23
Precision Models D&RGW flanger: HOn3: MR My 74 41/5:21-22
Red Ball 70' steel circus flat car: HO: RMC S 74 43/4:08
SS RGS Ford inspection car: O & On3: RMC Mr 74 42/10:62-63
Scale Structures tractor-locomotive: O: MR Mr 74 41/3:24-25
Selly-Martin handcar: O: MR Ap 74 41/4:29-30; RMC Jl 74 43/2:57-58
Selly-Martin Light yard rip-track crane: HO: RMC Mr 74 42/10:58-59
Soho Harriman business car: HO: RMC Ja 75 43/8:64+
Steward 25-ton crane: N: MR Ag 75 42/8:30-31
Sunshine rail & tie car: S: MR N 73 40/11:34
Sunshine tool & office car: S: RMC Jl 74 43/2:55-56
Tomalco D&RGW work gondola: Sn3: RMC D 71 40/7:70-72
Walthers circus car sleeper-kitchen: HO: MR Ag 72 39/8:23
Walthers U.S. Army hospital car: HO: MR F 74 41/2:29-30; RMC F 75 43/9:74-76
Ye Olde Huff-n-Puff bunk car: HO: RMC My 75 43/12:56+

Passenger

(General)

AHM Lakawanna passenger car: HO: RMC Jl 74 43/2:61

AHM old-time passenger car: HO: MR Ag 74 41/8:15
Athearn standard passenger cars: HO: RMC D 71 40/7:64
Labelle passenger car 1887: HOn3: MR Ap 74 41/4:26-27
Westwood Sumpter Valley passenger train: kit makes 2 of 4 possible var: HOn3: MR S 71 38/9:25-27

(Coach)

AHM standard coach: HO: RMC Jl 72 41/2:62-63
Alco Pennsylvania MP-54 MU cars: HO: RMC F 73 41/9:60+
Arnold Rapido gallery commuter coach: N: MR Mr 75 42/3:24
Baldwin Model Locomotive lightweight coach: O: RMC N 73 42/6: 70-71
Baldwin Model Locomotive streamlined passenger coach: O: RM Ap 73 40/4:28-29
Con Cor streamlined coach: HO: RMC O 71 40/5:58
JMC Delaware & Hudson coach: HO: RMC D 72 41/7:77-78
Model Die Casting Harriman coach: HO: RMC Je 73 42/1:51-52
Model Die Casting 34' Overton passenger car: HO: RMC My 72 40/12:60+
Nickel Plate 87' coach: HO: MR Ap 74 41/4:24
Nickel Plate Osgood Bradley passenger car: HO: RMC Mr 74 42/10:65-66
Nickel Plate UP modernized chair car: HO: RMC D 73 42/7:68+
Northwest Short Line Ohio River & Western coaches: HOn3: NSG My 75 1/2:8
Poly Mold coach: HOn2/HOn2½: RMC Jl 75 42/2:55-56+
Soho Harriman chair car: HO: RMC Ja 75 43/8:64+
Soho Harriman coach, 4 or 6 wheel trucks: HO: RMC Ja 75 43/8:64+
Tomalco coach: Sn3: MR My 72 39/5:21-22
Ulrich Sierra coach: HO: RMC O 75 44/5:73+

(Diners)

Athearn streamline diner: HO: RMC Ja 72 40/8:68
Con-Cor streamlined diner: HO: RMC O 71 40/5:58
JMC Delaware & Hudson diner: HO: RMC D 72 41/7:77-78

(Front-End Cars)

AHM standard combine: HO: RMC Jl 72 41/2:60+
AHM smooth-side baggage car: HO: RMC Je 73 42/1:54
AHM standard combine: HO: RMC Jl 72 41/2:62-63
All Nation North Shore combine: O: MR O 75 42/10:31-33
Ambroid 60' baggage-express car: HO: MR F 72 39/2:24+
Athearn streamline Budd baggage car: HO: RMC Ja 72 40/8:68
Athearn streamline RPO car: HO: RMC Ja 72 40/8:68
LaBelle combine: HO: MR O 73 40/10:31-32
Model Die Casting Harriman baggage: HO: RMC Je 73 42/1:51-52

VI. Reviews 744

Nickel Plate 63' baggage car: HO: MR Ap 74 41/4:24
Poly Mold combine: HOn2/HOn2½: RMC Jl 73 42/2:55-56+
Pro Custom period baggage car: HO: RMC Jl 72 41/2:58
Pro Custom period postal car: HO: RMC Jl 72 41/2:58
Rivarossi baggage-RPO car: HO: RMC Ja 71 39/8:64
Quality Craft express mail car: HO: MR F 71 38/2:30
Soho Harriman baggage-express: HO: RMC Ja 75 43/8:64+
Soho Harriman baggage/RPO: HO: RMC Ja 75 43/8:64+
Soho Harriman combine: HO: RMC Ja 75 43/8:64+
Tomalco baggage-coach: Sn3: MR My 72 39/5:21-22
Ulrich Sierra combine: HO: RMC O 75 44/5:73+
Walthers Sierra combine: O: MR N 75 42/11:25

(Observation, Lounge)

AHM standard open platform observation: HO: RMC Jl 72 41/2: 62-63
Athearn streamline observation car: HO: RMC Ja 72 40/8:68
Athearn streamline Vista-dome: HO: RMC Ja 72 40/8:68
Con-Cor streamlined dome car: HO: RMC O 71 40/5:58
Con-Cor streamlined observation car: HO: RMC O 71 40/5:58
JMC Delaware & Hudson dome car: HO: RMC D 72 41/7:77-78
JMC Delaware & Hudson observation: HO: RMC D 72 41/7:77-78
Model Die Casting Harriman observation: HO: RMC Je 73 42/1: 51-52
Nickel Plate SSW-NYC&W observation: HO: RMC S 74 43/4:62
Nickel Plate Vista-dome buffet lounge: HO: RMC N 74 43/6:64-66
Soho parlor car: HO: MR D 72 39/12:36-37
Westwood Canadian Pacific dome car, 1902: HO: MR Jl 71 38/7: 26-27

(Sleepers)

AHM duplex sleeping car: HO: RMC Ja 72 40/8:58; RMC F 72 40/ 9:61-62
AHM IC 1930s duplex sleeper: HO: RMC Jl 72 41/2:60+
AHM standard Pullman: HO: RMC Jl 72 41/2:62-63
Con-Cor slumbercoach: N: MR Je 74 41/6:20-21
Nickel Plate 16 section sleeper: HO: RMC N 74 43/6:64-66
Pro Custom period sleeping car: HO: RMC Jl 72 41/2:58
Western Railcraft wood pullman car: N: RMC O 75 44/5:68-69

Locomotives

(Motive Power Performance Review) [all NMRA]

AHM ATSF Pacific 4-6-2: HO: Mr 75 40/7:19+
AHM-Rivarossi Pacific 4-6-2: HO: Ap 74 39/9:17

Alco Alco C-628: HO F 73 38/6:22
Alco PRR B-1 electric switcher: HO: O 73 39/2:18
Alco General Electric U-33C: HO: My 71 36/9:28
All Nation EMD F-7: O: F 74 39/7:21
Athearn F-45: HO: O 74 40/2:40; F 75 40/6:40
Atlas ATSF SD-24 diesel: HO: Jl 75 10/11:8-9
Atlas EMD F-9 diesel: O: N 72 38/3:26
Bachman Union Pacific 4-8-4: N: Ag 72 37/13:36
Berg NSWGR C.36 4-6-0 (European couplers): HO: Mr 73 38/7:24
Bowser Pennsylvania L-1 Mikado (2-8-2): HO: D 75 41/4:36
Central Locomotive Works EMD GP-35: O: N 75 41/3:28-29
Comparative Testing of the Modified Roundhouse Old Timer Diesel: O 72 38/2:27
Con-Cor Union Pacific SD-45: N: Ja 73 38/5:26
Custom Brass CMSP&P EP-2 B1 Polar Electric: O: O 75 41/2: 27+
Custom Brass Long Island G-53sd 4-6-0: Je 75 40/10:21
Custom Brass NYC class P-2 Electric: HO: Ag 75 40/12:21
GEM Reading 88a 0-6-0 Camelback: HO: F 71 36/6:28
Hallmark ATSF 2-8-0: HO: My 74 39/10:41
Hallmark Baldwin Centipede diesel: HO: D 71 37/4:11
Hallmark MKT H-3A Pacific 4-6-2: HO: Mr 71 36/7:17
Hobbytown Yard Switcher power chassis kit: HO: Ja 71 36/5:21
LMB UP class 9000 4-12-2: HO: S 71 37/1:20
Lambert Penn H6sb 2-8-0: HO: Ap 75 40/8:18
Model Die Casting box cab diesel: HO: Ja 75 40/5:15
Model Die Casting old timer diesel: HO: My 72 37/9:21
Model Power Santa Fe Alco FA-2: HO: N 74 40/3:35
Nickel Plate Hiawatha Atlantic: HO: S 72 38/1:13
Northwest Short Line GE EF-4 Little Joe: HO: Ag 73 38/12:10
Northwest Short Line Norfolk & Western class E2A 4-6-2: HO: D 72 38/4:14
Northwest Short Line Sierra Railway 2-8-0: HO: D 74 40/4:29
Pacific Fast Mail ATSF 2-8-4 Berkshire: HO: Ja 74 39/5:19
Pacific Fast Mail C&O 2-6-6-2 H-6: HO: F 75 40/6:25
Pacific Fast Mail Climax class C: HO: Mr 72 37/7:16
Pacific Fast Mail D&RGW 4-6-0: HO: N 73 39/3:18
Pacific Fast Mail Ma & Pa 2-8-0: HO: Jl 74 38/12:31
Pacific Fast Mail Santa Fe 2-10-4: HO: Ap 71 36/8:17
Pacific Fast Mail Western Pacific 4-8-2: HO: Je 73 38/10:18
Perfect Scale Baldwin DS-14: HO: Ap 73 38/8:23
Red Ball 2-6-0 Camelback: HO: O 71 37/2:13
Rivarossi SP cab forward 4-8-8-2: HO: Ja 72 37/5:22
Roundhouse Pennsylvania 4-4-2 Ebs Atlantic: S 75 41/1:21
Suydam PE "Electra" switcher: HO: Jl 72 37/11:16
Suydam San Berdoo Twelve Coach (interurban): HO: D 73 39/4:26
Tomalco D&RGW C-16 2-8-0: Sn3: Je 71 36/10:18
Tyco Santa Fe Mikado 2-8-2: HO: Mr 74 39/8:14
US Hobbies ATSF Northern 4-8-4: O: Je 72 37/10:18
US Hobbies L&N 2-8-4: O: S 73 39/1:17
US Hobbies SD-45 diesel: O: N 71 37/3:12-13
Westside Climax class A: HO: Jl 73 38/11:21
Westside D&RGW C-16 2-8-0: HOn3: Jl 71 36/11:13

VI. Reviews 746

Westside Heisler: O/On3: Ag 71 36/13:16
Westside SP T-31 4-6-0: HO: Ap 72 37/8:14
Westside Southern Pacific 4-10-2: HO: Je 74 39/11:12

Diesel

(N Gauge)

Atlas EMD Cow & Calf: MR My 71 38/5:24
Atlas Diesel Switcher: MR Ap 73 40/4:29-30
Atlas GP9: MR F 75 42/2:27
Atlas GP-30 Diesel: MR My 75 42/5:30-31
Con Cor F3: MR Ap 75 42/4:28-29
Con Cor PB Units: RMC D 71 40/7:70
Con Cor SD 45 Diesel: MR Ap 72 39/4:21-22
Con Cor U50 four truck diesel: MR Ja 74 41/1:22; RMC S 75 44/4:70-71
Minitrix FM switcher: MR S 74 41/9:24-25
Rivarossi EMD TR 12 (SW 1200) Cow & Calf: RMC Je 71 40/1:46

(HO Gauge)

AHM E8 passenger diesel: MR Ag 74 41/8:19
AHM EMD FT: MR F 75 42/2:29-30
AHM EMD GP18: RMC Ag 74 43/2:52-53
AHM SP Alco RS2: RMC Ja 74 42/8:63-64
AHM unpowered diesel units: RMC Ja 72 40/8:62
Alco Alco Century 628: RMC Ap 73 41/11:58+
Alco Alco 100 hp T6: RMC Ap 74 42/11:50-51
Alco Alco RS2 & RS3: RMC Jl 73 42/2:58+
Alco Century 630: RMC O 74 43/5:58-59
Alco DL-702: MR Je 74 41/6:20
Alco EMD switcher: MR Ja 72 39/1:25-26
Alco General Electric U33C: RMC Ja 71 39/8:68
Alco RSD 12 (DL702): RMC O 74 43/5:58-59
Alco road switcher: MR Ap 74 41/4:19-20
Athearn Baldwin S-12 switcher: MR Jl 74 41/7:16-17
Athearn EMD FP 45 & F 45 diesels: MR Mr 74 41/3:20-21
Athearn GE U30B: MR Mr 72 39/3:28
Athearn's SW?: SW7 (nom SW1500): RMC O 71 40/5:46-47
Athearn 1776 diesel: MR Ja 73 40/1:25-26
Atlas EMD GP 38: RMC N 75 44/6:80-81
Atlas Hi-Nose EMD SD 24: RMC Mr 75 43/10:66+
Atlas SD24: MR Ap 75 42/4:26-28
Atlas SD 35 road diesel: MR My 75 42/5:24-25; RMC S 75 44/4:76-77
Bachmann EMD 1750 hp F8A: RMC Ja 71 39/8:68-70
Bachmann GP40: MR My 71 38/5:17-18
Cary E6 body casting: MR Ag 71 38/8:20
Cary EMD E6A: RMC S 71 40/4:44-45
Cary EMD E6B: RMC O 71 40/5:57-58

Kit--Operating

Cary EMD Phase 1 F3 body: RMC Mr 75 43/10:64-66
Custom Brass poling car: MR D 74 41/12:37-38
Gem GP40: MR D 72 39/12:31-32+
Gem SDP 40F: MR O 74 41/10:18d+
Hallmark Alco passenger diesel: MR Jl 71 38/7:20-21
Hallmark Baldwin road switcher: MR O 75 42/10:33-34
Hallmark EMD E5: RMC O 72 41/5:56-57+
Hallmark T&NO P-14 "Sunbeam": RMC Je 74 43/1:51-53
Hobbytown Alco PA drive: RMC N 71 40/6:58+
Hobbytown Alco PA 2000 hp diesel: RMC D 71 40/7:62+
Life-Like Alco Century 628: MR Ag 73 40/8:16+ ; RMC Mr 74 42/10:63-65
Life-Like RS11/DL701: RMC Ag 73 42/3:58+
Lionel Alco diesel: MR Ag 75 42/8:24-26
Lionel G07: MR S 75 42/9:30-31
Merzbach Alco FA2 diesel: RMC Mr 72 40/10:60+
Merzbach dual purpose diesel: MR Ja 72 39/1:26+
Model Die Casting 1925 diesel: MR Je 72 39/6:19
Model Power Alco FA1/FB1: RMC F 74 42/9:59-60
Model Power Baldwin RF16 Shark: MR Ag 72 39/8:22-23; RMC S 72 41/4:59-60
Nickel Plate EMD F3 Phase Two: RMC D 74 43/7:70
Perfect Scale Baldwin road switcher: RMC F 73 41/9:56
Westside industrial switcher: RM D 71 38/12:34

(S Gauge)

Locomotive Workshop GE 44-ton diesel: RMC Ag 75 44/3:62-64
Model Power EMD E7 passenger unit: RMC S 74 43/4:58

(O Gauge)

All Nation FM power unit: MR N 73 40/11:31
Atlas F9 diesel: MR Jl 72 39/7:18-20; RMC My 72 40/12:54+
Atlas industrial switcher: MR Ap 73 40/4:30-31
Central Locomotive Alco freight diesel: MR N 73 40/1:36-38
Central Locomotive 200 hp Alco PA1: RMC S 73 42/4:64-66+
Locomotive Workshop Baldwin RF16 sharknose: RMC Ag 71 40/3: 49-50
Pacific Fast Mail diesel-mechanical switcher: On3: MR Mr 72 39/3:28+
R&M PCC body kit: MR Jl 71 38/7:25-26

Electric

AHM GG-1: HO: RMC O 71 40/5:56-57; RMC Jl 72 41/2:53
Alco DD1: MR Ap 71 38/4:23
Alco General Electric 2-D+D-2: HO: RMC Mr 74 42/10:59-60
Arnold Rapide GG-1: N: MR D 71 38/12:38-40; RMC N 71 40/6: 60-61

VI. Reviews

Bachmann Amtrak Metroliner: HO: MR Jl 75 42/7:24+
Custom Brass NYC Oil-Electric: HO: MR Je 72 39/6:20-21
Master Model boxcab electric body: HO: MR F 74 41/2:32
Merker + Fischer Electric Locomotive: HO: MR S 71 38/9:21-22
Nickel Plate C+C: HO: MR My 74 41/5:18-20
Nickel Plate CSS&SB electric locomotive: HO: RMC Jl 75 44/2: 68-69
Northwest Short Line Milwaukee Road class EP-4 electric: HO: MR Je 73 40/6:25-26

Steam

(Smaller Than HO Gauge)

Bachmann 4-8-4 Northern: N: MR My 72 39/5:25-26
Gem 4-4-0: TT: MR N 73 38/11:35-36
Graham Parish GWR tank engine: N: Afx Ag 71 12/12:656
Rocky Mountain ten wheeler: N: MR S 72 39/9:20-22

(HO Gauge)

AHM 4-4-0: MR O 73 40/10:22
AHM 0-6-0 switcher: MR O 71 38/10:22-23
AHM 0-6-OT: MR Je 39/6:20; RMC F 73 41/9:63-64
AHM IC 4-6-0: MR O 71 38/10:26+
AHM AT&SF 4-6-2: MR Ap 75 42/4:23-24
AHM USRA Heavy Pacific 4-6-2: MR F 73 40/2:29-31
AHM NYC streamlined Hudson 4-6-4: MR Mr 72 39/3:21; RMC Ap 72 40/11:57-58
AHM 0-8-0 switcher: MR D 71 38/12:28-29
AHM Centennial 759 2-8-4: RMC Jl 72 42/2:53
AHM Lehigh & Hudson River/Boston & Maine 4-8-2: RMC My 71 39/12:50+
Atlas 0-4-0 switcher: MR My 73 40/5:25-26
Bachmann B&O 0-4-OT switcher: MR Mr 71 38/3:23; RMC My 71 39/12:49-50
Bowser Pennsylvania 2-8-0: MR Mr 71 38/3:23-24+
Gem Pennsylvania 2-10-2: MR My 75 42/5:23-24
LMS Princess Elizabeth 4-6-2: HO gauge/00 scale: RMC Je 71 40/1:50
Lambert Pennsylvania 2-8-0: MR D 73 40/12:25
Life Like PRR A-3 class 0-4-0: RMC Ap 72 40/11:60+
Life Like Pennsy 4-6-0: MR F 72 39/2:19
Model Die Casting 0-6-0 switcher: MR Mr 73 40/3:20-22
Model Die Casting Pennsylvania 4-4-2: MR Jl 75 42/7:20-21
Model Masterpieces tender tank body: HOn3: RMC S 75 44/4:72-74
Nickel Plate CB&Q ten wheeler 4-6-0: MR Je 75 42/6:23-24
Northwest Short Line two-truck shay: MR N 73 40/11:28-29
Pacific Fast Mail CN 4-8-4: MR F 73 40/11:28-29
Pacific Fast Mail Denver & Salt Lake 2-6-6-0: RMC F 71 39/9:58+

Pro Custom USRA steam locomotive cab: MR N 75 42/11:25-26; NSG Jl 75 1/3:6
Proscale Cabs light USRA locomotive cab: RMC D 75 44/7:82-83
Tyco Mikado 2-8-2: MR Ja 75 42/1:32-36
US Hobbies Vanderbilt tender: MR Jl 73 40/7:19-20
Westside Baldwin 4-6-0: HOn3: NSG My 75 1/2:9-10
Westside SP T-31 4-6-0: RMC Jl 72 41/2:62
Westside SP Harriman P-1 4-6-2: RMC D 75 44/7:88-89+
Westside 2-8-0: HOn3: MR S 71 38/9:21
Westside Cotton Belt/SP 4-8-4: RMC D 72 41/7:74-77
Westside 4-10-2 three-cylinder engine: MR O 71 38/10:24+
Westside D&RGW 3700 series 4-6-6-4: RMC F 72 40/9:62

(Larger Than HO Gauge)

AHM 0-6-0T: 1/45: MR S 72 39/9:25-26
AHM 0-8-0 switcher: O: MR Ap 71 38/4:21
LGB 0-6-2T: Gm: MR D 73 40/12:30
Pacific Fast Mail 4-6-0: On3: MR Ag 73 40/8:15-16
Pacific Fast Mail 2-8-0 Consolidation: O: MR D 71 38/12:36+
Rivarossi V&T "Genoa" 4-4-0: O: RMC Ja 74 42/8:56-57
Rivarossi 0-8-0 Indiana Harbor Belt class U-4A: O: Sc My 71 2/5:259-260
US Hobbies 13-ton Shay: On3: NSG My 75 1/2:10-11
Westside 2-truck Heisler: O/On3: MR N 71 38/11:27-28

Traction

Copetown IRR high-speed interruption: O: MR F 75 42/2:33+
Fairfield streetcar: HO: MR Jl 74 41/7:24-25
Fairfield Brooklyn & Queens streetcar: HO: MR O 71 38/10:23-24; RMC N 72 41/6:71-72+
Franklin Boston type 4 trolley: O: MR Jl 71 38/7:24; RMC O 71 40/5:55-56
Franklin differential dump car: O: MR F 71 38/2:26-27; RMC Ja 71 39/8:70-71
Northwest Short Line Brill streetcar: HO: MR Ja 74 41/1:30-32
Pacific Traction streetcar body: O: MR Je 72 39/6:22
Precision Brass Birney car: O: MR N 74 41/11:30-31
Q-Car CSL streetcar: Q: MR O 74 41/10:25-26
R&M Industry PCC car: O streamlined streetcar: RMC Jl 71 40/2:50+
Soho LARY streetcar: HO: MR S 71 38/9:24
Suydam Interurban freight motor: HO: MR D 73 40/12:30-31+
Western Railcraft interurban express motor body: N: RMC F 75 43/9:66-68
William J. Clouser North Shore combine: O: RMC O 73 42/5:59+

VI. Reviews

Rail Cars

Custom Brass RDC-1 coach: HO: RMC Ap 74 42/11:50-51
Jouef Sentinel-Cammel steam railcar: HOn$2\frac{1}{2}$: RMC Jl 71 40/2:53-54
Lee Town rail bus chassis & power unit: On3: NSG N 75 1/5:8
Lima Locomotive rail inspection car: O: MR Jl 73 40/7:18
Nickel Plate Motor Car: MR D 72 39/12:34
Q-Car Manhattan Elevated car: Q body: MR Je 75 42/6:25
Scale Structures automobile inspection car: HO/HOn3: RMC My 73 41/12:62

Parts

(Couplers)

Atlas automatic coupler: O: MR Jl 72 39/7:21
Back Shop coupler pocket: O: MR N 72 39/11:32+
Kadee scale coupler conversions: N: MR Jl 38/7:27-28
Kadee scale coupler repair kit: N: MR Ja 71 38/1:34
Terrier Fox coupler: working scale UIC (new European) automatic coupler: MR Ap 73 40/4:46-47

(Drive Systems)

Grandt delrin gears with steel shafting: right angle drives: MR My 75 42/5:29-30
Northwest Short Line brass & delrin gears: NSG Mr 75 1/1:12
Northwest Short Line worm & gear sets: MR Jl 75 42/7:32
Stephen Poole drive wheels: HO: MR Ag 74 41/8:20
Walthers power truck set: HO: MR Ja 72 39/1:22-24

(Exterior Details)

AHM accessory details: HO: RMC N 74 43/6:69+
Alexander Scale diesel detailing parts: HO: MR D 75 42/12:29-30
Back Shop detail castings: NSG N 75 1/5:8
Back Shop handrail posts: O: MR F 75 42/2:31
Back Shop headlights: O: NSG My 75 1/2:8
Back Shop locomotive details: HO: NSG My 75 1/2:6
Back Shop 3 cylinder Shay cylinders: O: NSG S 75 1/4:6
Cannon steam pump: O: MR F 74 41/2:26
Capitol Specialties roofwalks: HO: MR F 74 41/2:24
Cary locomotive fittings: HO: MR Ja 73 40/1:31
Charles Brommer feedwater pump: O: MR O 75 42/10:35
Charles Brommer pump: O: NSG Jl 75 1/3:6
Con-Cor coal load: N: MR Jl 75 42/7:30-31

Con-Cor fluted car roof: HO passenger: MR S 73 40/9:24
Custom Railway steam locomotive number plates: HO: MR D 71 38/12:32
Detail Associates diesel detail parts: HO: MR S 75 42/9:25-26
Durango caboose windows: HOng: MR Ja 75 42/1:38
Durango rolling stock details: RMC O 75 44/5:79-81
G. I. Models full-width diaphragms: HO: MR My 75 42/5:27-28
Gemini brake cylinders & air cocks: O: NSG Jl 75 1/3:7
Gemini details for Mich-Cal log cars: On3: NSG N 75 1/5:7
Gemini locomotive parts: O: MR S 75 42/2:31
Holgate & Reynolds air conditioning unit: HO: MR My 75 41/5:20
Lee Town Car Steps: O: MR Jl 73 40/7:23
Lee Town Climax domes: ? scale: NSG Mr 75 1/1:13
Lee Town snowplow: HO & O: NSG Mr 75 1/1:13
Lee Town tender water hatch: O: MR Ag 75 42/7:32
Liberty Models roofwalks: HO & S: MR Mr 73 40/3:24; HO: RMC O 73 42/5:66-67; S: RMC N 71 40/6:62
Precision Scale locomotive detail parts: NSG N 75 1/5:9-10
Precision Scale steam locomotive detail parts: O: RMC Ap 75 43/11:62-64
Precision Scale rolling stock details: NSG Mr 75 1/1:12
Precision Scale steam locomotive parts: On3 & HOn3: NSG Jl 75 1/3:8
Q-Car traction air compressor: Q: MR Ag 74 41/8:17; MR D 75 42/12:26
Roller Bearing Models hopper loads: HO: MR Mr 74 41/3:22
Quality Craft scratch-builder's ladder stock: HO: RMC O 72 41/5:62-63
Rio Grande steam shovel bucket: HO: NSG N 75 1/5:7
Salem Model Railroad coal hopper load: HO: MR My 74 41/5:20
Scale Railway detail parts: On2: RMC Mr 71 38/10:59
Selley-Martin pipe valves: RMC D 73 42/7:69+
Tomalco narrow gauge queenposts: HO: RMC D 74 43/7:73
Tomalco passenger car detail parts: HOn3: RMC F 75 43/9:70+
Utah Pacific locomotive detail parts: HO: RMC S 74 43/4:65-66+

(Interior Details)

Back Shop oil firebox door: O: MR N 73 40/11:38
Durango rolling stock details: HO: RMC O 75 44/5:79-81
Model Traction Supply fare box & controllers: HO: RMC D 72 41/7:74
Precision Scale oil firebox door: O: MR My 74 41/5:23+
Q-Car traction car seats: Q: MR F 75 42/2:30
Q-Car traction car seats: Q: MR O 75 42/10:28
Scale Railway parlor car castings: On2: RMC Ag 72 41/3:62-63
Selley-Martin combine interior detail & figures: HO: RMC S 74 43/4:62

(Lighting)

Alexander Scale removable marker lamps: HO: RMC Ja 74 42/8:64

VI. Reviews 752

Back Shop headlights: HO: MR Ag 75 42/8:28
GH working marker lights: HO: MR F 72 39/2:22-23
Modeltronics directional headlight control: MR N 74 41/11:43
RK car lighting unit: constant brightness components: MR Ja 75 42/1:36
RK directional headlight control: MR S 74 41/9:26
Scale Locomotives caboose marker lights: 1/8: MR D 73 42/12: 30-31
Scale Structures station platform lamps: HO: NSG Jl 75 1/3:7
Suydam hollow illuminated marker lamps: HO: RMC Je 74 43/1:56
Utah Pacific working marker lights: HO: MR O 74 41/10:22

(Trucks)

Ace passenger trucks: O: MR Ag 72 39/8:23
Ace six-wheel passenger trucks: O: MR Je 72 39/6:22-23
Central Valley streamlined passenger trucks: MR Ja 75 42/1:40
Gemini Pacific Car & Foundry arch-bar truck: On3: NSG N 75 1/5: 7
Grandt narrow-gauge freight truck: On3: MR Je 73 40/6:28
KTM trucks: O: MR Ap 71 38/4:21-22
Kadee D&RGW arch-bar trucks: HO: RMC F 75 43/9:72+
Kadee passenger truck: N: MR Je 73 40/6:29
Kar-Line Bettendorf: HO: RMC D 74 43/7:72-73
Kemtron diesel truck sideframes: HO: RMC Ja 73 41/8:68+
Lindberg freight trucks: HO: MR Ja 73 40/1:30
Nickel Plate freight car truck: HO: RMC N 72 41/6:70-71
Precision Scale trucks: O: NSG N 75 1/5:9-10
Robb C&S Bettendorf trucks: HOn3: NSG My 75 1/2:8
Robb D&RGW Bettendorf trucks: HOn3: NSG My 75 1/2:8
Scale Railway Equipment freight trucks: On3: MR F 74 41/2:28
Tomalco D&RGW prototype trucks: HOn3: RMC S 72 41/4:56
Wabash Valley Traction side frames: HO: MR Mr 71 38/3:28
Walthers Archbar trucks: O: MR S 72 39/9:26-27
Walthers passenger trucks: HO: MR O 73 40/6:29
Walthers power truck set: HO: MR Ja 72 39/1:22-24

Control Systems

Codar Electronics transistor throttle: MR S 72 39/9:28-29
Cor-Cor switch machine: MR F 71 38/2:32
Digitrack 1600: 16 train command control system: MR Ag 72 39/8:37-40
Don Fowler trackside electrical switch: MR S 72 39/9:24-25
Eda Electronics handheld transistor throttle: MR F 73 40/2:27-28
Fyffe Electronics solid state throttle: MR N 71 38/11:32+
GB Electronics momentum throttle: MR Jl 71 38/7:22
GH Products switch machine illuminated Superbutton: MR D 75 42/12:24-25

Kit--Operating

Hammant & Morgan power pack: MR N 72 39/11:28
Jelco indicator lamp driver: MR Ja 72 39/1:21-22
Jelco switch control module: MR Je 72 39/6:19
Ken's Custom Builders lamp brilliance control: MR Jl 75 42/7:28-29
Ketterman's bellows-operated train whistle: RMC N 74 43/6:66+
MEC optoelectronic train detector: MR Mr 74 41/3:27
Model Rectifier power pack: HO & N: MR D 71 38/12:40-41
Pacific Fast Mail steam locomotive sound & lighting simulator: MR Jl 72 39/7:16-18
Power Systems series 200 transistor cabtrollers: RMC Ja 72 40/6: 64-66
Power Systems transistor throttle pack: MR D 72 39/12:40-41
Power Systems walkaround solid state throttle: RMC Je 75 44/1: 47-49
Precision Scale transistorized control module: RMC S 73 42/4:58-59+
Precision Scalespeed throttle: MR Mr 72 39/3:21-22
QMR turnout control switch: MR D 75 42/12:29-30
RK constant-brilliance lighting unit for cars: MR Ja 75 42/1:36
RK flasher unit: MR Je 71 38/6:23
Solitronic diesel horn sound system: MR My 71 38/5:23
Tenshodo switch machine: MR S 71 38/9:24
Tom Hunt steam locomotive sound system: MR F 72 39/2:28-29
Tork solid state throttle: RMC O 71 40/5:58+
Tri-Delt switch machine control products: MR F 71 38/2:21-22
Trionyx Electronics grade-crossing signal circuits: MR F 71 38/2: 23-24
Trionyx Electronics lamp flasher circuit: MR Mr 71 38/3:28
Utah Pacific diesel chime horn: HO: MR O 74 41/10:26
Walthers electric meters: voltmeter & ammeter: MR Jl 75 42/7: 31-32
Zimmerman TORK throttle: HO or N: MR O 71 38/10:21-22

Signals

AHM signal set: HO: MR Ag 74 41/8:23
APAG branchline crossing gate: HO: NSG N 75 1/5:6
CaPart crossing signal: HO: MR S 73 40/9:23-24
Custom Photo/Graphics cantilever signal bridge: HO: MR D 74 41/12:34+
Custom Photo/Graphics three-color signals: HO: MR D 74 41/12: 32-33
Custom Photo Service signal bridge: HO: MR Ap 72 39/4:27
Don Fowler crossing gate: HO: MR N 73 40/11:32-33
JMC flashing crossing signals: HO & N: MR Mr 75 42/3:25-26
Scale Structures train order board: HO: MR O 75 42/10:30; NSG Jl 75 1/3:7
Walthers crossing signal: O: MR F 74 41/2:34
Walthers flasher unit: RMC Mr 74 42/10:61-62

VI. Reviews 754

Walthers highway crossing signal: HO: RMC Je 74 43/1:56-57

Track

AHM dual gauge crossing: N & HO: RMC Jl 74 43/2:52+
AHM insulated plastic railjoiners: HO: RMC My 72 40/12:62
AHM spur siding set: HO: RMC D 72 41/7:72-73
AIM bridge abutments & wings: MR Ag 73 40/8:26
AIM instant roadbed: HO or S, O: MR Ap 74 41/4:22
AIM masonary retaining walls: HO: MR My 74 41/5:22-23
Alexander Scale Models ground throw switch stand: O: RMC Je 71 40/1:46+
Atlas No. 6 remote-control turnout: MR Ja 71 38/1:32
Atlas turnouts: O: MR N 72 39/11:23+
B&H scenic materials: ballast: N: MR D 75 42/12:31
Bachmann manual & remote turnouts: N: RMC D 71 40/7:72-73
Bachmann turnouts: N: MR F 71 38/2:31-32
CaPart switchpoint heater parts: HO: RMC My 74 42/12:52
Caboose Industries ground-throw switchstand: RMC O 75 44/5:69+
GH switch machine mounting kit & contact set: MR D 74 41/12: 37; RMC D 75 44/7:91-92+
Grandt Switchstand: O: MR My 75 42/5:29
Highball model ballast: RMC D 73 42/7:64+
Hughes large scale track materials: Gm & No. 1 gauges: MR S 73 40/9:24-26
John's Lab track ballast & adhesives: RMC D 72 41/7:66-68
LaBelle ground throws: N: MR Jl 75 42/7:29
Lima turnout: MR Je 71 38/6:22
Lind street railway track: HO: MR Mr 74 41/3:30
Nickel Plate code 100 flexible track: HO: RMC Ja 73 41/8:67-68
Nickel Plate flexible track: HO: MR Ja 73 40/1:32-33
Nickel Plate turnouts: HO: MR S 73 40/9:27
Precision Scale cast switch components: HO: MR Ag 73 40/8:22-23
Pritchard curved turnouts: N: MR Ag 72 39/8:20
Railcraft code 55 rail: NSG S 75 1/4:7
Railcraft ties: N: NSG S 75 1/4:7
Railcraft turnouts: HOn3: NSG S 75 1/4:7
Right-'O-Way code 100 rail: HO: NSG My 75 1/2:8
Shinohara code 100 turnouts: HO: MR Ja 72 39/1:24
Simpson code 100 turnouts: On3: NSG S 75 1/4:8
Smith & Son ballast & coal: RMC Je 75 44/1:56+
Sommerfeldt catenary supplies: HO: MR My 71 38/5:24-25
Timberline switch ties & template: HO: MR D 72 39/12:36
Tru-Scale pre-fabricated turnouts: HO: RMC Ap 72 40/11:62

Turntables

Con-Cor manual turntable: MR Ja 74 41/1:29
Heljan manual turntable: N: RMC Jl 74 43/2:59-61
Model Masterpieces D&RGW turntable: HO: MR N 75 42/11:29-31+
Sierra Railroad turntable: HO: NSG S 75 1/4:8-9

REVIEWS OF OTHER PRODUCTS

ADHESIVES

Aron Alpha #201 Quick-Set: cyanoacrylate: AFV D 71 3/4:30
Cyanoacrylates & RC: Zap cyanoacrylate filler for balsa: RC Je 75 12/6:16
Durafix: cyanoacrylate: MR Jl 74 41/7:18
Hot Stuff: cyanoacrylate: RC F 75 8/2:2+
Loctite Cyanoacrylate: MR Ag 73 40/8:27-28
Micro Metal Foil Adhesive: Sc N 75 6/74:570
Microweld: AN 11 My 73 1/26:14
Permabond: cyanoacrylate: RT Ag 73 6/8:94
S-Dine: cyanoacrylate: RMC Ag 71 40/3:50+
William Dixon Duradix: cyanoacrylate: MR Jl 74 41/7:18

COVERING

Permagloss Coverite: mylar: RC Ag 75 12/8:48+
Solarfilm: RC Jl 71 8/7:30-31+

FINISH

Airfix enamel paints: RT Je 73 6/6:69
Authenticolour WW-II German armour colors: RT S 72 5/9:98
Bare Metal: metal paint: AE O 71 1/5:272; Afx Je 71 12/10:544+; RT Je 73 6/6:65
Continental Monarch CMMC model railroad paint: RMC F 75 43/9:62+
Drumhead Un-Paint: paint remover: MR Mr 75 42/3:33-34
ESCI Russian: errors in tank graffiti decals: RT My 73 6/5:51+; cor Je 73 6/6:60
Evreka Model Paint: MR Ag 73 40/8:20-21; MR Ag 75 42/8:28
Floquil Polly-S weathering medium: RMC Ag 75 44/3:54+

VI. Reviews 756

Floquil wood stain: RMC O 74 43/5:59-60
Frisk Air Cans: for airbrushes: Sc D 72 3/12:678-679
Harris Finishes: lacquers: MR Ap 72 39/4:24
Hobby Black: FM S 72 75/9:55
Humbrol Authentic Sprays: spray cans: Afx S 75 17/1:52
Krasel plastic cement & plastic filler putty: RMC Ap 74 42/11: 57-58
Liqu-a-Plate: Afx Jl 73 14/11:620
Marglotex Ulrich 410M paint: MR Jl 71 38/7:23
Metal Paint: RT Je 72 5/6:69
Micro Kristal-Kleer: small window-making solution: Sc N 75 6/74: 570
Micro Quick Silver: putty: AN 12 O 73 2/11:14
Midland Central dry pigment: NSG N 75 1/5:8
Pactra Authentic International Colours: IM S 75 11/5:13
Pactra Paints: Afx D 75 17/4:240
Paints: evaluation of blotching characteristics of varnishes: MM My 75 5/5:298
Perfect Paint: R&S Hobby Products: RC Ag 75 12/8:56-57+; RCS Ag 75 1/4:19
Polly S Paint: AFV D 71 3/4:29; MR Je 71 38/6:21; RMC S 71 40/ 4:43-44
Quality Craft Paint Drying Additive: MR My 73 40/5:30
Quality Craft Wash Away Paint Remover: MR Ja 75 42/1:38-39
RAC Distributing Metal Blackening Chemical: MR Ap 72 39/4:25
Revell Enamel Paints: IM Ja 75 11/1:14
Scale Metal: metal foil: RM Mr 71 4/3:34
Scale Model Products lacquer: MR Mr 75 42/3:33
Scalecoat sanding sealer: RMC Ja 73 41/8:66-67
Terry Westbrook wood aging solution: RMC Ag 74 42/11:57-58
Testors Plaspray Dullcote: PAM O 74 7:117

SCENERY MATERIALS

AIM plaster rock castings: RMC Je 73 42/1:52+
Action Boulders: MR Ap 73 40/4:25
Adventure Scale Miniatures old oak tree: HO: MR N 74 41/11:29-30
Adventure Scale Miniatures tree kits: HO: RMC Ap 75 43/11:57-59
Architectural Models trees & scenic materials: RMC Jl 72 41/2:63
Atlantic Modelers ground scenic foam texture: RMC Ag 75 44/3: 58-59+
Busch Instant Scenery: spray-on foam in colors: MR Ap 71 38/4: 22
Campbell fir tree: RMC Ap 73 41/11:64
Campbell pine trees: O to N: MR S 72 39/9:27
Cherry Glen tree stumps: MR Ja 73 40/1:33; RMC S 73 42/4:57-58
Con-Cor lichen: RMC Ja 72 40/8:68+
Con-Cor ready-made trees: HO & N: RMC F 72 40/9:60-61

D&R rock castings: MR Mr 74 41/3:26
George Kendrick Tru-Trees: RMC Jl 75 44/2:64+
HO-West landscape background scenes: HO: RMC Jl 75 44/2:57-59
Highball ballast, ore, & coal material: MR Ap 72 39/4:22; RMC D 73 42/7:64+
Highball grass & earth: HO & N: MR Ja 73 40/1:32
ISLE natural rock castings: RMC Je 74 43/1:48-49
ISLE scenery material "Mountains in Minutes": RMC F 72 40/9: 56+
John's Lab ballast: N, HO, O: MR Mr 72 39/3:22+
Micro-Mold terrain: 1/300, for wargames: Afx S 74 16/1:51
Miniature Realism deciduous & evergreen trees: RMC My 74 42/12:52-55
National Cellulose "Sculptamold" scenery material: RMC F 74 42/9:60-61
Q-Car jacks & highway cones: O: MR Je 75 42/6:28+
Real Models barbed wire: 54mm & 25mm: MM Mr 71 1/3:148; separate strands: MM My 71 1/5:240
Riko diorama sets: 1/76: Afx Je 74 15/10:598-599
Scale Structures tree stumps: RMC O 75 44/5:81-82
Scale World rock castings: RMC Mr 75 43/10:58-59
Scenic Architectural trees: MR Ja 75 42/1:39; RMC S 75 44/4:77-78
Schaer Ready-to-Use trees: MR S 73 40/9:19
Sha-heen trees: RMC Ja 73 41/8:63
Terra-Tex scenic material for weeds: MR My 73 40/5:23
Woodland Scenics trees: NSG N 75 1/5:9

TOOLS

Airbrushes & Accessories

Badger airbrush: MM Je 73 3/6:394-395; MW S 73 2/1:46-47; Sc Ap 72 3/4:223-224
Badger 100XF airbrush: Afx S 73 15/1:22-23; PAM Ja 75 8:136-137
Campbell-Hausfeld MD 1033 Hornet air compressor: PAM Ja 75 8:137
DeVilbiss Models A & E airbrushes: PAM Jl 74 6:94-95
Precision Spray Booth: with exhaust fan: MR Ap 71 38/4:24-25
Scalecoat Paints adjustable painting stand: MR Jl 71 38/7:22; RMC D 71 40/7:66-67
Wold airbrush: MR Ap 72 39/4:28

Aircraft Flight Equipment

AeroTrend Flyin' Box: RC Ja 73 10/1:58+

VI. Reviews 758

Flight Life: charger: MAN N 74 89/5:56-57+
Flyte Box: charger, fuel pump, plug tester, battery: RC Mr 74 7/3:29+
Goldberg Handi-Tote: field box: FM Ap 75 78/4:37
In-Flyte Flyte Box: electronic field box: RC Mr 74 11/3:29+
Pro Models Super Charger: battery charger: RC Ap 75 12/4:16
Sonic Tronics Challenger: starter: RC F 72 9/2:62
Sullivan Hi-Tork starter: RC My 74 7/5:16+
Super Cycle: discharger/Charger: RC Je 75 12/6:62-63
Totemaster: field box, fuel pump, starter, voltmeter, battery: FM Ag 73 76/8:26-27; RC S 73 10/9:49
World Engines Multipurpose Battery Charger XA007: MAN O 72 85/4:46-47+

Cleaners (Ultrasonic)

Branson Ultrasonic Cleaner: MR Ap 71 38/4:25-26; MR Ag 73 40/8:21-22; RMC D 72 41/7:80
Electromation Components ultrasonic cleaner: MR N 73 40/11:31-32
Heath ultrasonic cleaner kit: FM O 74 77/10:42-43; MAN D 74 89/6:56-57; MR S 74 41/8:18d
L&R ultrasonic cleaning unit: MR Ja 73 40/1:24

Hand Tools

Agostine's Machine Shop work mat: MR F 73 40/2:25
Bench Model Caddy: fuselage holder for adjustments at workbench: RC Mr 74 11/3:33+
Con-Cor small parts case: MR S 75 42/9:33
Jim Crockett Replicas copy cutter: sheet cutting jig: MR Ja 74 41/1:26
NMRA Scale Converter: circular slide rule: MR Ap 72 39/4:26-27
Nickel Plate wheel puller & press: RMC O 71 40/5:56
Northwest Short Line calibrated stripwood cutting jig: HO: NSG N 75 1/5:8; RMC Ja 75 43/8:73-74+
PAV Vernier & Dial Calipers: MR My 71 38/5:21-22
Precision rivet embosser: MR Je 71 38/6:23
Pro-Custom soldering torch: blowpipe & tablet fuel: RMC Mr 72 40/10:60
RCM Solarfilm Cutter: plastic covering cutting jig & heated iron holder: RC S 74 11/9:49+
Simpson small T-Square: RMC F 71 39/9:65
Special Development dry-transfer burnisher: MR Jl 74 41/7:19; RMC Ja 75 43/8:77
Stanley knives: PAM O 75 11:197
Stanley utility knife: RC Je 74 11/6:6+
Walthers Micro-Measure: S, HO, O, N, TT, 1/32, 1/100, & mm scales on clear rule: RMC Ag 72 41/3:55-56

Jigs

Creekmore bench model caddy: holding rack for construction or adjustments: RC Mr 74 12/5:33+
Custom Craft miter sander: dihedral sanding jig: RM Ag 75 78/8: 30-31
Frank R. Marshal, Jr. HO & HOn3 track gauges: MR Mr 75 42/3:32-33
Keeler rail turnout jig: HO: MR Ag 71 38/8:20-21
Prather drill jig: drill guide for cast beam mounts: RC Je 74 11/6:10
RCM Fuselage Building Jig II: RC F 75 12/2:58-59
RCM Wing Jig II: RC N 74 11/11:28-29+
Ramex tie & track gauge: HO & HOn3 track laying jig: MR Je 74 41/6:22; RMC Ja 75 43/8:63-64
Scale Railway track gauge: On2: RMC Mr 71 39/10:59
Tom's Hobby Aids layout planning kit: HO track templates: MR Ap 74 41/4:21-22

Power Tools

Adcola soldering iron: Afx Ap 73 14/8:452
Dremel Moto-Flex tool: MR N 75 42/11:37-38
Dremel variable-speed motor tool: MR Ja 74 41/1:34; RMC N 75 44/6:86+
Micron miniature drill press: MR Jl 72 39/7:24
Mining & Chemical Products styrene injection molding machine: AN 10 Ja 75 3/16:10
Petite Precision Drills: hand power drill: IM Mr 75 11/2:16
Ploton Pyrogravure: MM D 74 4/12:753
Precision Power Tool: hand grinder: MW Ag 73 1/12:660-661
Pyrogravure: MM D 73 3/12:834-835
Sherline lathe: MR S 74 41/9:18a; RMC Ag 75 44/3:66+
Taig Micro-Lathe: RC D 75 12/12:60-62+
X-Acto motor hand tool: RMC Ja 72 40/8:63-64

Test Equipment

GH drawbar tractometer: railroad power tester: MR Jl 74 41/7:22-23
Heath Servo Simulator: servo tester: FM N 71 416:54-55; MAN S 71 83/3:42-43+; MAN My 74 88/5:49-50+
Misjon Flite Life: NiCd battery tester: FM N 74 77/11:32-33; MAN N 74 89/5:56-57+; RC Ag 74 11/8:44-45+
Model Rectifier VOM Multitester: MR Jl 71 38/7:23; Ag 71 38/8:23

VI. Reviews

Power CYT: battery condition indicator: RCS Je 75 1/2:33
Pulse Comparator: MAN Je 74 88/6:48-50+
T-Meter: for indoor rubber torque reading: MAN My 71 82/5:8-9
Telecraft Flight Pacer: timer on RC transmitter: FM Ag 73 76/ 8:31

RADIO CONTROL

Complete

Ace Commander: FM Mr 72 420:48-50
Blue Max System: FM Mr 71 72/3:41-43
Blue Max Mk II: AM Jl 72 77/1:18+; MAN Jl 72 85/1:50-52
Cannon Grand Prix: 6 channel: AM S 74 78/9:48
Cannon Three Channel Mini-Flite digital: MAN N 71 83/5:43+
Cannon Tini-Block: 2 channel: AM Ap 74 76/4:34
Cannon two-channel ultra-light (3 3/4 oz): RC Ja 73 10/1:40-41+
Climax 2 Function Digital Marine: MB S 71 21/249:380+
Deans Radio: car & boat: AM N 71 73/5:40+
Dembros Star-Flite: AM Ag 73 76/8:56; RC Jl 73 10/7:43+
Digiace 4 Channel: AM Je 71 72/6:19+; MAN Jl 71 83/1:35-37+; RC S 71 8/9:36
EK Little Red Brick: AM Ag 71 73/2:53+; FM O 75 78/10:33-35
Futuba FP-2D: 4 channel: AM Ag 74 78/8:41+
Futuba FPS-6D: AM O 74 78/10:84+
HP 1+1: proportional digital: RC Ap 72 9/6:58-59+
Hobby Lobby 4: AM Mr 72 74/3:18+; RC N 71 8/11:414
Hobby Lobby 5 channel: RC D 72 9/12:41+
Hobby People Phoenix: 4 channel: AM My 72 74/5:14+
Hobby Shack Cirrus: two channel: AM S 73 77/3:76; RC F 73 10/2:47+
Kraft Five Channel: AM Ap 73 76/4:34
Kraft KB2B: MAN My 71 82/5:46-47+
Kraft Systems series 71: RC Ap 71 8/4:26-27+
Kraft series 72: AM D 72 75/6:16+; RC Jl 72 9/7:49-50+
Kraft series 73 KP-5B: 5-7 channel: AM Jl 73 77/1:68
Kraft Three Channel Sport: AM O 73 77/4:38
Larson 5: AM Ja 72 74/1:52+
MRC F-170 Digital: MAN Mr 71 82/3:38-39+; RC Ap 71 8/4:32-33
MRC F-713 System: MAN Ja 72 84/1:36-38+
MRC F-724 Single Stick: four channel: FM Ap 73 76/4:30-31
MRC Mk V: four channel: RC D 73 10/12:54-55+
MRC Mk V: five channel: AM Mr 74 78/3:44
MRC Master Mk VIII: FM S 74 77/9:40-41; RC Je 73 10/6:52-54+
Micro-Avionics Digital & PS-5 Servo: MAN Ag 71 83/2:34-37+
Micro-Avionics 4 channel & MPS-4 IC servo: AM Mr 71 72/3:24+
Min-X Astromite 72: AM Ja 71 72/1:31+
Orbit Custom Six Single Stick: AM Ja 73 76/1:18+

Orbit Five Channel Sport: AM Ap 74 78/6:51+
Orbit Hawk Three Channel: AM F 74 78/1:64; FM Jl 74 77/7:64-65
Orbit Micro Avionics: 5 channel: AM Je 73 76/6:68
Orbit 72 Compact: RC N 72 9/11:29-30
Orbit Single Stick: MAN Ap 71 82/4:40-41+
Pro Line Challenger: 5 channel: AM Je 74 78/6:51+
Pro Line Competition Six: 6 channel: AM O 73 77/4:40
RC Manufacturing series 800: four channel: RC Je 72 9/6:58-59+
RS Systems 6 channel digital: RC Mr 74 11/3:40-43+
RS-6D Dual Sticks: 4 channel: AM N 73 77/5:60
RS Systems: three channel: RC D 72 9/12:20-21+
Royal Apollo Two Channel: AM D 73 77/6:68
Royal Sport series 1975: FM S 75 78/9:35-37
Silvertone Mk VII: AM N 72 75/5:16-17+; RC My 71 8/5:38+
Simprop Alpha 2007: 7 channel: AM Jl 74 78/7:37+
Space Commander C-45: 4 channel: AM Je 72 74/6:14+
Tower 5: RC Ap 74 11/4:42-44+
Velvet Touch: Citizen-Ship six channel: FM O 72 75/10:43; FM Jl 75 78/7:42-43
World Engines Delux Migit: 3 channel: RC Ap 72 9/4:62

Control Components

MD-3 Super Driver: electric boat motor control: RC F 71 8/2:38+
Servo Sentry: failsafe for RC power boats: FM S 75 78/9:64-65

Kits

Ace Digital Commander 1-8 Flite-Pack: 2 channel: AM Je 73 76/6:64; FM Ap 75 78/4:28-31
Heath GD-57: three channel digital: MAN O 71 83/4:33-35+
Heath GDA-1057-1: three channel: AM D 73 77/6:68; FM O 73 76/10:31-33
Heath Full House Plus Three: RC O 72 9/10:26-32
Heath Mini-Servo: FM N 71 416:32-33
Heathkit 8 Channel: AM F 73 76/2:14+; FM Ja 73 76/2:40-41+
Heathkit Pack 17: FM N 75 78/11:31-33
Heathkit 3 Channel: AM F 71 73/2:54+
Royal Classic Digital: AM Jl 71 73/1:27+

Servos

Bantam servo: RC N 71 8/11:38-40

EK Logitrol Super Pro: AM My 73 76/5:53; RC S 75 12/9:70-71+
Goldberg: AM Ja 74 78/1:34
Heath's Mini-Servo: FM N 71 416:32-33
Kraft KPS 14, 15, 15H, & 16: AM N 73 77/5:60
Orbit: AM Ja 74 78/1:34
World Engines: AM F 74 78/2:66

WARGAMES

Surveys

North Africa Wargames: survey of commercial games: WWE N 74 1/6:183

Components

Hinchliffe System 12: bases & roads for wargame layouts: MM Ap 75 5/4:219-222

Individual Games

Anzio: Avalon Hill: Afx My 75 16/9:552-553
Bar-Lev: Conflict: Afx N 74 16/3:189; S&L (Ap 75) 7:7
Battle of Britain: Renwal: WWE Mr 74 1/2:47
Battle of Britain: Simulations: Afx N 75 16/7:440
Battle of Hue: Conflict: S&L (Ap 75) 7:26-27
Battlewagon Salvo: Zocchi: WWE Mr 75 2/2:58
Blue & Gray: Simulations: Shiloh, Antietam, Gettysburg, Chickamauga: S&L (O 75) 10:34
Chaco: Simulations: Afx F 75 16/6:385
Coral Sea: Game Designers: S&L (O 75) 10:35
Crimea: Game Designers: S&L (D 75) 11:23
D-Day: Avalon Hill: WWE S 74 1/5:142
Decline & Fall: Wargames Research Group: S&L (Je 75) 8:17
Diplomacy: Phimar: S&L (O 75) 10:27
Drang Nach Osten: Game Designers: 1941-52 eastern front: AFV Mr 74 4/10:23+
Dunkirk: Guidon: AFV F 72 3/6:29; Afx Jl 74 15/11:661
Eagles: Game Designers: Afx O 74 16/2:115
El Alamein, Battles in North Africa 1942: Simulations: AFV N 73 4/8:16+
Epaminodas: Philmar board game: S&L (D 75) 11:25
Frigate: Simulations: Afx D 74 16/4:255
Guerilla: Maplay: S&L (D 75) 11:23
Jerusalem: SDC: S&L (D 75) 11:23
Kasserine Pass: Conflict: Afx N 74 16/3:189
Kasserine Pass: Zocchi: WWE My 74 1/3:80
Kingmaker: Philmar: War of the Roses: S&L (F 75) 6:27; S&L (Je 75) 8:17

Marine: Jagdpanther: S&L (O 75) 10:34-35
Mercenary: Gamesters: Afx Jl 75 16/11:666-667
Modern Battles: Quadrigame: Wurzburg, Mukden, Golan, Chinese
   Farm: S&L (D 75) 11:22
Napoleon: Simulations: Afx Ja 75 16/5:324
Narvik: Game Designers: Afx Jl 75 16/11:667; S&L (D 75) 11:22
Omaha: JagdPanther: WWE Ja 75 2/1:24
Overlord: Conflict: Afx D 74 16/4:255
Patrol: Simulations: Afx Jl 75 16/11:666
Poland 1939: JagdPanther: WWE My 74 1/3:80; cor S 74 1/5:157
Pre-Seventeenth Century Tactical Games System: SPI: Afx S 75
   17/1:52+
Prochorovka: JagdPanther: WWE Ja 75 2/1:24
Quebec 1759: Gamma 2: Afx D 73 15/4:243
Railway Rivals: D.G. Watts: 19th century rail barons: S&L (O
   75) 10:35
Richthofen's War: Avalon Hill: MM Ag 73 3/8:539
Rommel: Loren Sperry: AFV Ag 73 4/6:8+
Search & Destroy: SPI: Afx Ag 75 16/12:726-727
Seastrike: Wargames Research Group: Afx S 74 16/1:51; S&L (D
   74) 5:20
Seelowe: Simulations: Afx S 74 16/1:51-52
1776: Avalon Hill: Afx Jl 74 15/11:661
Sinai: S&T: Afx Ag 74 15/12:722
Sinai: Simulations: S&L (Ap 75) 7:7
Stalingrad: JagdPanther: WWE Ja 75 2/1:24
Star Force: Simulations: Afx Mr 75 16/7:440
Tactics II: Avalon Hill: Afx Mr 74 15/7:420
Tarawa: JagdPanther: WWE Ja 75 2/1:24
Third Reich: Avalon Hill: Afx Ap 75 16/8:497
Torgu: Game Designers: 1760: S&L (O 75) 10:34
Triplanetary: Simulations: Afx D 74 16/4:255
War of 1812: Gamma 2: Afx D 73 15/4:243
World War One: Simulations: S&L (D 75) 11:22-23

MISCELLANEOUS

Clean Track track cleaning cloth: RMC S 75 44/4:65+
Du-Bro Universal Muffler: RC Ja 73 10/1:16
Falcon Safety Products compressed gas model cleaner: freon duster:
   RMC My 75 43/10:59+
GMC sculptured metal art trophies: RC Jl 74 11/7:50-51
Gel/Cell: rechargeable "dry cell" for starters: RC Ag 75 12/8:
   22
Goldberg retract gear: RC Je 72 9/6:54+; RC Mr 73 10/3:50-52
Golden Foam: shock absorber: RC O 72 9/10:14-15+
Instant Rivet: AFV O 71 3/2:33; RT Je 71 4/6:63
Labelle multi-purpose synthetic oils: lubricant for electric motors
   & railroad rolling stock: RMC S 75 44/4:68+
Micro Lite fiber optics kit: RMC Ja 71 39/8:71

VI. Reviews 764

Modeltronics subminiature connectors: MR Mr 75 42/3:31-32
Multi-Purpose Battery Charger XA007: MAN O 72 85/4:46-47+
Quiet Tone Muffler: RC Mr 72 9/3:39
Robart Hinge Point: control surface hinge: RC Je 72 9/6:62
Slater's Plastic Rod: IM My 75 11/3:14
Sullivan Super Tank: airplane fuel tank: RC N 71 8/11:44
Trujust CL Handle: FM N 75 78/11:15-16
Vernon Palmer Wheels: WW-I style for flying scale: Sc Je 72 3/6:351-352
Wave Honeycomb Wing: RC Ag 71 8/8:86

PARODIES

Campbell Basic Kit: sugar pine block & razor blade: RMC D 75 44/7:96+
Fubar civil airline ground crew (striking): 1/72: RT Ag 73 6/8:85
P. R. E. model engine: AM Ap 74 78/4:42+
Penthouse Pets 1/1: MW F 74 2/6:331
Vonce A/3: free flight glider: AM Je 71 72/6:85-86